S0-ALK-322

LIFT TAKE YOUR STUDYING TO THE NEXT LEVEL.

This book comes with 1-year digital access to the
Examples & Explanations for this course.

Step 1: Go to **www.CasebookConnect.com/LIFT** and redeem your access code to get started.

Access Code:

Step 2: Go to your BOOKSHELF and select your online *Examples & Explanations* to start reading, highlighting, and taking notes in the margins of your e-book.

Step 3: Select the STUDY tab in your toolbar to access the questions from your book in interactive format, designed to give you extra practice and help you master the course material.

Is this a used casebook? Access code already scratched off?

You can purchase the online *Examples & Explanations* and still access all of the powerful tools listed above. Please visit CasebookConnect.com/Catalog to learn more about Connected Study Aids.

PLEASE NOTE: Each access code provides 12 month access and can only be used once. This code will also expire one year after the discontinuation of the corresponding print title and must be redeemed before then. CCH reserves the right to discontinue this program at any time for any business reason. For further details, please see the Casebook Connect End User Agreement.

PIN: 9111149629

12462

MODERN REAL ESTATE
FINANCE AND
LAND TRANSFER

ASPEN SELECT SERIES

MODERN REAL ESTATE FINANCE AND LAND TRANSFER

A Transactional Approach

Sixth Edition

Steven W. Bender
Professor of Law and Associate Dean for Planning and Strategic
Initiatives
Seattle University School of Law

Celeste M. Hammond
Professor of Law and Director of Center for Real Estate
The John Marshall Law School

Robert M. Zinman
Professor of Law (Ret.)
St. John's University

 Wolters Kluwer

Published by Wolters Kluwer in New York.

Wolters Kluwer Legal & Regulatory U.S. serves customers worldwide with CCH, Aspen Publishers, and Kluwer Law International products. (www.WKLegaledu.com)

To contact Customer Service, e-mail customer.service@wolterskluwer.com, call 1-800-234-1660, fax 1-800-901-9075, or mail correspondence to:

> Wolters Kluwer
> Attn: Order Department
> PO Box 990
> Frederick, MD 21705

Printed in the United States of America.

1 2 3 4 5 6 7 8 9 0

ISBN 978-1-4548-9811-5

About Wolters Kluwer Legal & Regulatory U.S.

Wolters Kluwer Legal & Regulatory U.S. delivers expert content and solutions in the areas of law, corporate compliance, health compliance, reimbursement, and legal education. Its practical solutions help customers successfully navigate the demands of a changing environment to drive their daily activities, enhance decision quality and inspire confident outcomes.

Serving customers worldwide, its legal and regulatory portfolio includes products under the Aspen Publishers, CCH Incorporated, Kluwer Law International, ftwilliam.com and MediRegs names. They are regarded as exceptional and trusted resources for general legal and practice-specific knowledge, compliance and risk management, dynamic workflow solutions, and expert commentary.

*To my mother, Irene, and to
my son Dominic*

— S.B.

*Love to my husband,
Michael Pensack,
my children,
Geoffrey and Elizabeth,
and my grandchildren,
Hazel & Lander Foubert and Gerard Francis Xavier Hammond*

— C.M.H.

*To Ruth and Arthur Zinman
and to Lillian and Noah Janel*

sine qua non

— R.Z.

Summary of Contents

Contents

PART II   101

FUNDAMENTALS OF REAL ESTATE FINANCE

Chapter 3   103

The Nature of a Mortgage and Mortgage Substitutes

PART IV 725
FUNDAMENTALS OF REAL ESTATE INVESTMENT

Chapter 12 727
Economics of Real Estate Investments

Preface

This sixth edition builds on the pedagogical vision of the first edition (then titled *Modern Real Estate Financing: A Transactional Approach*, by Michael Madison and Robert Zinman), the second edition (that added Steven Bender as coauthor), and the third edition (adding Celeste Hammond). We would like to thank Michael Madison, who has retired from teaching and from this sixth edition, for his contributions to prior editions and foresight on the need for practical skills-based legal education in complicated areas such as real estate transactions.

It has been our experience that most law students are more stimulated when they see some practical value in what they are learning in the classroom. The professor can stimulate students' intellectual curiosity to deal with complex issues in land transactions by simulating the real-world conditions of practice and avoiding pedantic discussions of peripheral issues (such as the doctrine of equitable mortgages, which rarely arises in a commercial real estate practice). For this reason, our casebook follows the transactional approach.

In our judgment, freedom of contract still remains the dominant theme in commercial real estate transactions despite the regulatory impact of public law on land investment and development. As long as the real estate project does not fail and the developer remains solvent, general rules of law will normally apply only in the absence of an agreement to the contrary. Perhaps this is because in most commercial real estate transactions the parties will be sophisticated—they will be represented by counsel and in a position to defend themselves at the bargaining table. For example, at common law the general rule (absent language to the contrary in the mortgage note) is that a lender does not have to accept voluntary prepayment of the mortgage indebtedness prior to maturity. We examine this rule in Chapter 5. But it is of equal if not greater importance for students to see what a typical prepayment privilege provision looks like and to understand the legal consequence of using one drafting approach as opposed to another. As counsel someday, students will be able to not only solve present problems but also avoid potential problems for their clients. This is what real estate planning that adds value to transactions is all about.

The practice of real estate transactions also requires an understanding of the steps within a transaction or lending cycle and how those steps relate to and flow from each other. For example, in Chapter 6 we examine why a borrower's ability to obtain construction financing will often depend on whether the borrower is able beforehand to secure a loan commitment for the postconstruction, or "permanent," loan.

Accordingly, our aim is to expose students to the legal issues they will confront in practice and to teach them to think as real estate lawyers do. To that end, the book follows the transactional approach and includes questions and planning problems designed to test the students' abilities to spot issues and arrive at logical conclusions based on cases, statutes, documents, articles, and other materials.

Organization

In addressing modern real estate financing, the book follows the actual lending cycle chronologically. We anticipate that when students begin to understand how one stage in the lending cycle follows from another, they will perceive a natural and cohesive flow in the classroom discussion. Chapters 3-6 deal with the fundamentals of real estate financing, and in doing so employ a master hypothetical involving a typical real estate developer ("Dan Developer") who plans to construct an office building in the fictional state of Fuller. Students follow Dan as he wades through the commercial real estate lending cycle from negotiating a loan commitment from a typical postconstruction lender to obtaining his construction financing from a typical construction lender. Foreclosure proceedings are covered in Chapter 8 and the Bankruptcy Code in Chapter 18. This is where the methodology of the book departs from an analytical-transactional to an analytical-doctrinal approach. Recently, borrower insolvency has become a litigation trigger for lawsuits against lenders. Accordingly, in Chapter 9 we examine lender liability.

This book also addresses advanced aspects of real estate investment and financing. For example, in Chapters 7 and 11 we discuss subordinated purchase money mortgages and leasehold mortgages. We also cover the sale and leaseback of underlying land to reduce initial cash outlay and possibly increase tax deductions by separately financing the cost of the land. In Chapter 15, we examine the phenomenon of securitization that swept commercial and residential mortgage financing, albeit cooling with the residential mortgage meltdown and global financial crisis in recent years. Then, as explained in Chapter 7, once a project has been completed and is successful, some of the accumulated equity in the project can be translated into tax-free cash through refinancings and secondary financings.

In addition to basic and advanced real estate financing, this book covers other important aspects of real estate transactions. These include issues in the acquisition and sale of developed or undeveloped realty (Chapter 2), an overview of commercial leasing (Chapter 10), advanced leasehold financing issues (Chapter 11), treatment of leases in bankruptcy (Chapter 18), and environmental liabilities in real estate financing, sale, and leasing (Chapter 19). Moreover, the book's third edition added new chapters addressing common interest community ownership (condominiums, cooperatives, and planned communities) (Chapter 16), and alternative dispute resolution (negotiation, mediation, arbitration) in real estate transactions (Chapter 17).

Because tax considerations play such an important role in real estate investment and financing decisions, this book attempts to integrate tax aspects of these decisions into the discussion. In addition, Chapter 13 provides an overview of issues relevant to the status of real estate as a limited tax shelter. Chapter 14 examines the taxation issues relevant in selecting the developer's ownership entity.

This book contains documentary excerpts because our aim is to make the relevant documentation the matrix for our discussion. We have also prepared a separate Documents Manual, which includes the major documents in their entirety. The Documents Manual is available on-line without cost to students at http://law.seattleu.edu/documents/faculty/ benders/docmanual.pdf.

Finally, in editing case materials and articles, we omitted many case, statutory, and other citations, as well as footnotes, without indication. Those footnotes that remain retain their original numbers.

Steven W. Bender
Celeste M. Hammond
Robert M. Zinman
December 2017

Acknowledgments

We would like to thank the many people who helped prepare this casebook. We are grateful for the patience and generous support of our administration and staff at our respective schools, including Claudette Parker, former Fordham deans, John Feerick and William Treanor, former John Marshall dean John Corkery, and current dean Darby Dickerson, Seattle dean Annette Clark, and St. John's dean, Michael A. Simons. We were fortunate to receive a high level of research support from former Seattle student Lauren Kominkiewicz, former Oregon students Mark Mengelberg and Aaron Wegner, Tony Longo, Patrick Schoolemmer and Scott Criss at John Marshall Law School, St. John's students Deirdre Burke, Grant Cartwright, Michael Drechsler, John Marck, Michael Sabella, Justin Tan and Ed Vopat, and other law students at Fordham, Seattle and Oregon. We give special thanks for the valuable suggestions and comments in connection with this book's first edition from Professors Roger Bernhardt, Karl Holtzschue, David Schmudde, and Aaron Schreiber. We also acknowledge the fine editorial assistance at Wolters Kluwer.

Finally, we thank the following authors and copyright holders for permission to reprint excerpts from their works:

American Land Title Association for permission to use the A.L.T.A. Owner's Policy (2006), Loan Policy (2006), and zoning endorsement.

Asbestos Litigation Reporter, para 17,037 (May 20, 1988). Reproduced with permission of Andrews Publications.

Bell, Negotiating the Purchase Money Mortgage, 7 Real Est. Rev. 51 (Spring 1977). Reprinted by permission of Warren, Gorham & Lamont, Inc.

Davis, The Permanent Lender's Role in the Construction Process, 3 Real Est. Rev. 70 (Spring 1973). Reprinted by permission of Warren, Gorham & Lamont, Inc.

Dickerson-Moore, Professor of Law, South Texas College of Law, affiliated with Texas A & M University, The Return of the Real Estate Investment Trust, 11 Prac. Real Est. Law. 49 (March 1995). Reprinted by permission of the author.

Ellwood, Appraisal for Mortgage Loan Purposes, Encyclopedia of Real Estate Appraising (3d ed. 1978). Reprinted by permission of the Appraisal Institute.

Forte, Environmental Liability Risk Management, 1989 Prob. & Prop. 57 (Jan./Feb.). Reprinted with permission. Copyright © 1989 by the American Bar Association. All rights reserved. No part of this publication may be reproduced without written permission.

Forte, CMBS Lending in the New Era of Credit Risk Retention (2017). Reprinted with permission.

Friedman, Contracts and Conveyances of Real Property 1146-1154. Reprinted with permission from Contracts and Conveyances of Real Property, 6th ed. (1998) by Milton Friedman, Published by Practising Law Institute 810 7th Ave., New York, NY 10019, Copyright 1998 by the Estate of Milton R. Friedman. Reprinted with permission of the publisher.

Fuller, Sale and Leasebacks and the *Frank Lyon* Case, 48 Geo. Wash. L. Rev. 60 (1979). Copyright 1979 by the George Washington Law Review. Reprinted with permission.

Garfinkel, The Negotiation of Construction and Permanent Loan Commitments II, 25 Prac. Law. 37 (April 15, 1979). Copyright 1979 by the American Law Institute. Reprinted with the permission of The Practical Lawyer.

Goldstein, When Does a Real Estate Broker Earn His Commission?, 27 Prac. Law. 43 (1981). Copyright 1981 by the American Law Institute. Reprinted with the permission of The Practical Lawyer.

Glasbergen, for permission to use his exotic mortgage cartoon.

Greenbaum, Hawkins, & Sklar for permission to use a hypothetical published in ADR Workshop course materials, presented by the American College of Real Estate Lawyers (ACREL) October 13, 2001. Copyright 2001 by ACREL. Reprinted by permission.

Halper, Introducing the Ground Lease, 15 Real Est. Rev. 24 (Fall 1985). Reprinted by permission of the author and Law Journal Seminars Press. Based on materials appearing in Ground Leases and Land Acquisitions by Emanuel B. Halper. Reproduced with the approval of the publisher. Published and copyrighted by Law Journal Seminars Press, 111 Eighth Avenue, New York, New York 10011. All rights reserved.

Halper, People and Property: The Role of a Real Estate Lawyer, 13 Real Est. Rev. 14 (Spring 1983). Copyright © by West Group (1-800-328-WEST). All rights reserved. Reprinted by permission of West Group.

Hammond, The (Pre)(As)sumed "Consent" of Commercial Binding Arbitration Contracts: An Empirical Study of Attitudes and Expectations of Transactional Lawyers, 36 J. Marshall L. Rev. 589 (2003). Copyright 2003 by the John Marshall Law Review. Reprinted by permission.

Harris, Legal Opinions: Real Estate Contracts, 14 Real Est. Rev. 12 (Spring 1972). Reprinted by permission.

Hawkes, Reaching the Bottom of the Barrel: How Securitization of Subprime Mortgages Ultimately Failed, Real Est. Fin. J. 55 (Spring 2008). Reprinted by permission of Thomson Reuters.

Hershman, Lease Pitfalls and Pratfalls, address presented at N.Y. Life Insurance Co. Reprinted by permission of the author.

Hudson-Wilson and Fabozzi, Why Real Estate?, J. Portfolio Mgmt. 12 (Sept. 2003). Reprinted by permission.

Hyatt, Common Interest Communities: Evolution and Reinvention, 31 J. Marshall L. Rev 303 (1998). Copyright 1998 by the John Marshall Law Review. Reprinted by permission.

Introductory Comment, Uniform Simplification of Land Transfer Act, 14 U.L.A. 271 (1977). Reprinted by permission of the National Conference of Commissioners on Uniform State Laws, Chicago, IL.

Joyce, Financing Real Estate Developments, 11 The Colo. Law. 2093 (Aug. 1982). Reprinted by permission of the Colorado Bar Association.

Kotlarsky, Capital Gains and Tax Policy, 41 Tax Notes 319 (1988). Reprinted by permission.

Lahny, Asset Securitization: A Discussion of the Traditional Bankruptcy Attacks and an Analysis of the Next Potential Attack, Substantive Consolidation, 9 Am. Bankr. Inst. L. Rev. 815 (2001), was the basis for the Lahny materials in Chapter 15C and is reproduced with permission.

Levy, Construction Loan Decision-Making Issues and Documents: Risks and Benefits. Chemical Bank, 1989. Reprinted by permission of the author.

Madison, The Real Properties of Contract Law, 82 Boston U. L. Rev. 405 (2002). Reprinted by permission of the author.

Madison, Dwyer, and Bender, The Law of Real Estate Financing, sections 1:6, 5:63-5:67, 5:128-131, 6:46-6:51, 8:20-8:24, 10:2. Copyright © by Thomson Reuters All rights reserved. Reprinted by permission of Thomson Reuters.

Mark, Leasehold Mortgages-Some Practical Considerations, 14 Bus. Law. 609 (1959). Reprinted by permission.

McKee, The Real Estate Tax Shelter: A Computerized Expose, 7 Va. L. Rev. 521, 556-567 (1971). Reprinted by permission.

Mehr and Kilgore, Enforcement of the Real Estate Loan Commitment: Improvement of the Borrower's Remedies, 24 Wayne L. Rev. 1011 (1978). Reprinted with permission from The Wayne Law Review.

Morrison and Senn, Carving Up the "Carve-outs" in Nonrecourse Loans, 9 Prob. and Prop. 8 (May/June 1995). Reprinted by permission of the authors.

Mortgage and Real Estate Executive's Report, Mar. 1, 1985, p. 5. May 15, 1987, p. 3-6. Reprinted by permission from the Mortgage and Real Estate Executive's Report. Copyright © by Warren, Gorham & Lamont, Inc. All rights reserved.

Nessen and Ragalevsky, The Changing Role of Lawyers in Real Estate Transactions, 5 Real Est. Fin. 32 (Spring 1988). Reprinted by permission from Federal Research Press.

Richards, "Gradable and Tradable": The Securitization of Commercial Real Estate Mortgages, 16 Real Est. L.J. 99 (1987). Reprinted by permission of Warren, Gorham & Lamont, Inc.

Roberts, Negotiating and Drafting Workout Agreements, 3 Mod. Real Est. Trans. 1393 (1987). Copyright 1987 by The American Law Institute-American Bar Association Committee on Continuing Professional Education. Reprinted by permission.

Schneider, The Elusive Definition of a Security, 14 Rev. Securities Regulation 981-991 (1981). Reprinted by permission of Standard & Poor's Corp.

Shenkman and Marshall, Commercial Real Estate and the 1993 Tax Act-Parts 1 and 2, 10 Real Estate Fin. J. 9-10 (Summer 1994), 15-16 and 13-16 (Fall 1994). Copyright 1999 by West Group (1-800-328-WEST). All rights reserved. Reprinted with permission from Real Estate Finance Journal.

Shurtz, A Decision Model for Lease Parties in Sale-Leasebacks of Real Estate, 23 Wm. & Mary L. Rev. 385, 435-438 (1982). Reprinted by permission of the author.

Schwartz, Real Estate and the Tax Reform Act of 1986, 16 Real Est. Rev. 28 (Winter 1987). Reprinted by permission of Warren, Gorham & Lamont, Inc.

Smith, Refinancing a Syndicated Property, 16 Real Est. Rev. 16 (Spring 1986). Reprinted by permission of Warren, Gorham & Lamont, Inc.

Smith and Lubell, The Permanent Mortgage Loan Commitment, 4 Real Est. Fin. 7 (Winter 1978). Reprinted by permission of Warren, Gorham & Lamont, Inc.

Smith and Lubell, Real Estate Financing: The High Credit Lease, 4 Real Est. Rev. 21 (Summer 1974). Reprinted by permission of Warren, Gorham & Lamont, Inc.

Smith and Lubell, Real Estate Financing: The Streamlined Mortgage, 4 Real Est. Rev. 21 (Summer 1974). Reprinted by permission of Warren, Gorham & Lamont, Inc.

Stewart, Note, Taxation of Sale and Leaseback Transactions, 32 Vand. L. Rev. 945 (1979). Reprinted by permission of Vanderbilt Law Review.

Urban Land Institute and PricewaterhouseCoopers LLP. Emerging Trends in Real Estate, 2012.

Uri, The Participating Mortgage: Spreading the Risks and Rewards of Ownership, 5 Real Est. Fin. 37 (Spring 1988). Reprinted by permission of Federal Research Press.

Washburn, The Judicial and Legislative Response to Price Inadequacy in Mortgage Foreclosure Sales, 53 S. Cal. L. Rev. 843 (1980). Reprinted with the permission of the Southern California Law Review.

MODERN REAL ESTATE
FINANCE AND
LAND TRANSFER

Chapter 1

The Nature of Modern Real Estate Transactions

A. THE EXPANDING ROLE OF THE REAL ESTATE LAWYER AS A PLANNER IN MODERN COMMERCIAL REAL ESTATE TRANSACTIONS

Real estate transactions, in practice, comprise an area of the law in which the transactional rights and responsibilities of the parties are usually governed by some fairly standardized form of agreement (for example, a "commitment" to lend money, a mortgage, or an occupancy lease) that the parties have negotiated and tailored to the particular transaction. Accordingly, the materials in this book follow a transactional approach, and, wherever possible, they examine the applicable legal, business, and tax issues in the context of the relevant documentation. To illustrate this approach, reference is made throughout these materials to a master hypothetical involving a typical real estate developer ("Dan Developer") who intends to construct an office building. As is usually the case, Dan plans to first obtain a commitment to extend postconstruction (or "permanent") financing from a typical institutional lender ("Ace Insurance Company") and then to obtain construction financing from a commercial bank ("Fuller National Bank") on the strength of that commitment.[1]

Despite the continuing importance of the negotiated agreement, the freedom of contract principle has been eroded somewhat by the regulatory impact of public law on real estate transactions and the emerging judicial trend toward striking down bargains that are either unconscionable or offensive to public policy. So if, for example, Dan Developer, in developing an office building, were to organize a limited partnership and without full disclosure solicit equity capital from a prospective limited partner, the ill-informed investor might be able to cancel the bargain with Dan and get its money back if Dan violated any of the laws governing the sale of securities to investors. Or if, in a jurisdiction such as New York, Dan were to demand an exculpatory provision in a lease with one of his occupancy tenants, that bargain may be deemed void (by statute or case law) as against public policy on the rationale that the clause purporting to exempt and indemnify Dan from any tort liability only encourages negligence on his part.

---

1. See Chapter 4 for discussion of the distinctions between construction and postconstruction financing.

If Dan should default or become insolvent during the mortgagor (borrower)-mortgagee (lender) relationship, the loan agreement between the parties may be superseded by either state or federal law. For example, state "antideficiency" law may preclude Ace's recovery of any shortfall that remains after Ace forecloses on the office building, and local "redemption" law may enable Dan to recover title to his project from the foreclosure purchaser by paying the foreclosure price within a statutory time period. Or, if Dan should file in bankruptcy, Ace's rights as a secured creditor could be affected under the federal Bankruptcy Code.

Nevertheless, subject to the public law and policy constraints discussed above, in most instances involving the financing (as well as the sale or leasing) of commercial real estate, general rules of law apply only in the absence of an agreement to the contrary. In other words, on the commercial side of real estate, freedom of contract may no longer reign supreme—but it still reigns! Perhaps this is because the interested parties (for example, the developer, postconstruction and construction lenders, and occupancy tenants) are usually sophisticated business professionals or entities that almost invariably are represented by legal and tax counsel and who, unlike the average consumer or investor, have the bargaining clout and business sophistication to protect themselves in their negotiations with one another. Therefore, their private bargains require less public scrutiny and paternalism. So, for example, if Dan Developer is foolhardy enough to bargain for a high-interest long-term postconstruction loan from Ace Insurance Company without demanding some right to prepay the mortgage loan before its maturity date (known as a "prepayment privilege"), the law will not rescue Dan from his folly if interest rates should later decline and Dan is precluded from "refinancing" (paying off the existing loan with a new one) at a lower interest rate.

Thus one can easily see that any student of real estate transactions when confronted with a particular transaction should know what general rules of law govern, should understand each rule's underlying rationale or policy purpose, and should know how (and if) each rule can be superseded by mutual consent of the parties. It is equally important to discern how the real estate planner can anticipate legal, business, and tax problems[2] that might befall his or her client in the future and devise means of avoiding them through the relevant documentation. The real estate lawyer who understands the increasingly complex legal, business, and tax issues surrounding modern commercial real estate transactions can transcend the role of a mere scrivener and actually add value to the client's transaction.

To help anticipate the client's needs, the modern real estate lawyer must also understand the chronology of the various transactions. For example, a developer of income property often proceeds as follows. First, primarily on the basis of tax

---

2. For instance, if Dan Developer were to organize a limited partnership, he may be forced to use a no personal liability mortgage ("nonrecourse financing") as opposed to a personal liability mortgage ("recourse financing") to fund his land acquisition and construction costs; otherwise, the investors in the limited partnership may be precluded from deducting tax losses in excess of their actual economic investment in the partnership. See Chapter 14A2.

shelter considerations, the developer will select the form of ownership entity (for example, a limited liability company) best suited for the dual purposes of raising venture capital and securing financing for the balance of the costs for the land and the building. See Chapters 13 and 14. In the case of new construction, once the entity is selected, the developer must make another important prefinancing decision: how to finance the cost of the underlying land. The developer may simply decide to obtain a fee mortgage loan to fund part of its land acquisition and construction costs. Alternatively, to reduce the initial cash outlay for the project and possibly increase the tax deductions, the developer may decide to finance the cost of the land separately from the improvements by means of a subordinated purchase money mortgage from the seller (see Chapter 7B3), sever the land from the improvements and finance each component separately (see Chapter 11B1), or lease rather than purchase the land and obtain a leasehold mortgage to help fund the cost of constructing the leasehold improvements. See Chapter 11A.

Customarily, the first stage in the commercial real estate lending cycle is for the developer to approach some institutional lender (frequently with the aid of an intermediary such as a mortgage broker) for a postconstruction loan commitment. If its application for the postconstruction loan is approved, then ordinarily the developer, on the strength of the postconstruction lender's commitment, obtains a short-term interest-only construction loan from some interim lender such as a commercial bank. This construction loan is "taken out" (in effect, purchased) by the postconstruction lender once the project is completed in accordance with the terms and conditions of the postconstruction loan commitment letter and is producing rental income. When each loan is funded, the lender will receive from the borrower a promissory note for the loan indebtedness and a mortgage (or deed of trust) as security for the borrower's performance of the loan obligation. In practical terms, the real function of the note, mortgage, and other loan documents given to the postconstruction lender is to implement the terms and conditions of the postconstruction commitment letter (for example, the rate of interest, amortization period, and prepayment privilege) that were negotiated by the parties at the beginning of the lending cycle. See Chapters 4 and 5. So, not only does the lending cycle for new income-producing property begin and end with the postconstruction loan commitment letter, but to a large extent this cardinal document also defines the business and legal parameters of the mortgagor-mortgagee relationship during the life of the mortgage loan.

After the project has been completed and it produces a positive cash flow through its occupancy leases, Dan Developer may wish to translate some of the equity into cash and assemble additional working capital by refinancing the existing loan for a larger amount and a longer term (possibly at a lower interest rate) with the same or another postconstruction lender. See Chapter 7A. Alternatively, if the prepayment penalty is steep, the interest rate on the existing loan low, or if Dan wants to attain "higher-ratio financing" (which would make the loan amount higher in relationship to the market value of the mortgaged property), he may seek a second mortgage from a secondary lender. See Chapter

7B. In addition, if the improvements are overdepreciated for tax purposes or the project is land-intensive, as an alternative to debt financing Dan might obtain the necessary capital by means of a sale-and-leaseback arrangement with an institutional investor. This might generate more working capital and tax deductions than would retaining the fee ownership and either refinancing or obtaining secondary financing. See Chapter 11B.

Leaving the worst for last, if the project should fail (or, in the parlance of the trade, "go belly-up"), foreclosure and related remedies are available to the mortgagee-lender, and "workouts" and bankruptcy complications are contingencies every real estate planner must know how to handle whether representing the developer or the lender. See Chapters 8 and 18.

Before we explore the above aspects of the various modern real estate transactions in subsequent chapters, consider the following materials that capture the broadening role of real estate lawyers in the current legal environment.

Halper, People and Property: The Role of a Real Estate Lawyer
13 Real Est. Rev. 14 (Spring 1983)

. . .What then are the roles that real estate lawyers play? Clients expect real estate lawyers to be business consultants, technical experts, and professional negotiators. To function properly, real estate lawyers must also be legislators, philosophers, and applied psychologists.

LEGISLATORS AND PHILOSOPHERS

In what respect are real estate lawyers really legislators or philosophers? They are concerned with legislation that affects only a few parties—the legislation of private contract. The law school graduate is trained to answer the question, what is the law? When [s]he becomes a real estate lawyer, [s]he must answer the question, what ought to be the law? . . .

The negotiating lawyer is called upon to think. Unless all of the other negotiators are stupid, they will ask [her] to justify clauses that [s]he drafts, and to demonstrate that they are reasonable, fair, or just. If [s]he cannot, the other negotiators may lose their trust in [her].

You say, who cares about trust, and that all that matters when a contract is negotiated is who has the most power? I tell you that you're wrong. Unless a lawyer is able to justify most of what [s]he drafts, the contracts and leases won't get signed.

BUSINESS CONSULTANTS

Real estate lawyers are business consultants. Consider this problem. Twenty years ago, a young lawyer's mother-in-law inherited 900 acres of land in Euphoria, Mississippi. The property was appraised at $26 for the estate tax audit, and it had not been a joy to its previous owners. Local garbage contractors made secret nocturnal visits to the site to dispose of their wares. The property's primary use was as a battlefield for delinquents and drug addicts.

But last year, [three] unexpected events occurred. Extensive uranium and oil deposits were discovered on the site. The state announced that a major interchange of a twelve-lane interstate highway would spill onto it. The largest manufacturer of electronic toys in Japan announced that, because of the modest economic expectations of the local population, it would move all of its manufacturing operations to the community. . . .

As you may imagine, these events aroused the interest of the real estate community. Delegations of brokers paid their respects to the mother-in-law. They courted her, wined and dined her, and then offered to lease her land for an annual net rent of $12 million. . . .[S]he calls upon her son-in-law to protect her interest (of course, for a reduced fee because of the loving family relationship). She wants him to tell her whether the rent is high enough. Can she get more? What would she do with the money?

The lawyer is suddenly visited by brokers, development executives, and developers' lawyers.

The developers may want the landowning mother-in-law to agree in advance to execute mortgages of her property to secure the developers' debts. They may want her to agree to execute nondisturbance agreements with subtenants. They may ask for exculpation clauses.

Most clients don't know what to do. They aren't always able to make business decisions in their own self-interest and ask their lawyer to put the decisions in writing for them. They want business advice too from a lawyer. So the real estate lawyer becomes a business consultant.

TECHNICAL EXPERTS

Real estate lawyers are also technical experts. There are hundreds of issues to understand for each contract that is negotiated, and specialized knowledge is needed to deal with each one of them. To discuss construction and repair clauses, a lawyer needs to know how a building is put together. To discuss insurance clauses, [s]he needs an understanding of tort and a knowledge of insurance industry practices. Condemnation is a problem for every lease and real estate contract, and a lawyer must appreciate how condemnation law impacts on leases and contracts. Most important of all, the lawyer must understand the American system of raising money to finance real estate projects and how lenders react to the clauses that are negotiated. There's a hidden party to almost every ground lease and occupancy lease—the mortgage lender, which bases its decision on whether or not to lend on the merits and deficiencies of those leases. A real estate lawyer must anticipate the problems that mortgagees usually raise. . . .

Nessen and Ragalevsky, The Changing Role of Lawyers in Real Estate Transactions
5 Real Est. Fin. 32 (Spring 1988)

[In the future], lawyers will be called upon to create something of additional value in the real estate transactions they handle. This "value-added lawyering" will require that firms go far beyond simply responding to technical problems posed by clients. Indeed, they will be asked to come up with innovative techniques and structures that will improve clients' positions and make their products more saleable in capital markets. They will also have to help clients gain access to the capital needed for their projects.

In order to meet these client demands, law firms will have to offer more than "traditional" legal services—something progressive firms are already beginning to recognize. This rather startling, albeit welcome, development is a culmination of over thirty years of growing complexity in the real estate industry.

THE CHANGING IMAGE OF THE REAL ESTATE LAWYER

Back in the 1940s and 1950s real estate lawyers were expected to know little more than how to complete a conveyancing or traditional mortgage financing. At least to most of us who were engaged in other areas of the profession, real estate practice was something of a sub-profession. In fact, many of the most prestigious law firms (especially the so-called Wall Street firms) either stayed away from real estate altogether or submerged it almost to the point of invisibility. Many senior members of the bar eschewed real estate as an insignificant and barely respectable backwater of legal practice. To the extent a firm engaged in real estate at all, it was done almost surreptitiously.

All of this has changed radically over the past thirty years. Even among the most "respectable" firms, real estate has become an integral part, if not the centerpiece, of their success. Real estate practitioners have been taken out of the shadows . . . and even permitted to meet with their firms' most valued clients.

AN EXPANDING AND COMPLICATED ENVIRONMENT

Why has this come about? Primarily because real estate has become far more complicated and conceptual than in the past. The development of a real estate project today involves an excruciatingly complex mix of elements. Just consider, for example, this short list of concerns a contemporary real estate lawyer must address:

- contracts for acquisition, design and construction;
- land use;
- zoning and subdivision control;
- condominium and cooperative forms of ownership;
- environmental impact;
- joint venture structures, partnerships, corporations and trusts;
- title and conveyancing matters;
- leasing, ground leases and sale-leasebacks;
- financing from conventional lenders, pension funds and foreign investors;
- federal and state tax issues; and
- federal and state securities laws.

Clearly, real estate law encompasses far more than ever before.

The need to deal with all of these diverse areas has increased the function and role of the real estate lawyer in the development process. Not so many years ago, the lawyer was often the last person brought into that process—the one who was required simply to reduce to writing the business arrangement struck by the principals. Now, the lawyer generally is one of the developer's most important advisers.

All real estate professionals have felt the pains of this growing complexity. To varying degrees, environmental, land use, tax and other considerations must be appreciated by the real estate broker, banker, architect and accountant. Clients, however, do not expect these professionals to have the same breadth of knowledge in so many areas as the real estate lawyer.

An accountant, for example, is not expected to have in-depth experience in environmental or land use issues; a broker is not expected to know very much about the impact of tax and securities laws; an architect is not ordinarily going to be an expert in mortgage and equity financing. But an experienced real estate developer or property owner would not hire a real estate lawyer or law firm that did not have a considerable base of knowledge in all facets of development. The need for this wide range of experience is one reason why the real estate lawyer must be brought into a transaction as close to its inception as possible.

There are other reasons as well. Real estate remains an area of the law where legalistic formality and the rule of caveat emptor still apply with vitality and vigor. The potential pitfalls in any transaction can be staggering. The developer must not only identify and anticipate all likely contingencies connected with a project, but also must estimate intelligently the amount of time it will take to satisfy those contingencies. Failure to do so may mean forfeited deposits and squandered up-front capital.

Further, the lawyer is likely to be the only professional who will be involved with and have access to all the other professionals on the development team (e.g., engineers, bankers, accountants and investors). This, combined with the highly transactional nature of the real estate business, positions the lawyer better than any other single advisor to spot potential problems and identify genuine opportunities.

BREAKING THE BONDS OF TRADITION

Thus, it has become imperative that lawyers be involved in the actual structuring of transactions—well before legal services have traditionally been required. Indeed, a client would be foolish not to get a lawyer involved at an early stage. After all, a successful real estate developer may do two or three deals a year; a successful real estate lawyer may participate in ten times that number, albeit on a more vicarious and less intense level. Thus, both lawyers and clients have begun to recognize that the lawyer's role has grown—from that of drafts[person], to advisor, to consultant.

All of this adds up to a fairly simple bottom line. The legal profession has to break the bonds of tradition. Indeed, the scope of services it is now being asked to provide would have been almost incomprehensible not more than a decade ago.

Accountants have gone through a similar experience. Long before law firms saw the need to expand their services, accountants were moving well beyond an auditing practice. Today, for example, management consulting contributes a significant, if not the most significant, portion of gross revenues for the largest accounting firms.

This trend has even extended to banks which were once deemed the bastion of conservatism. These institutions are now selling a full package of personal financial services—such as banking, insurance, tax and investment advice—to preferred clients through so-called private banker systems.

At long last, law firms are joining the club. They are beginning to understand the need to widen their scope if they are to meet the changing needs of their clients. There is no area in which those needs are clearer than real estate and real estate financing. In this context obviously, we are talking about matters that go far beyond routine legal work—matters such as networking, consulting, financing advising, structuring, and strategic planning. Each of these is examined briefly below.

EXTENDED SERVICES

First, a law firm usually has an impressive internal networking system which, too often, it does not make available to clients. In the case of a real estate transaction, a developer should be able to use the firm as a resource for contacts among accountants, mortgage brokers, and banking and other financial institutions.

Second, a law firm can offer general consulting services, such as developing conceptual products, that will help a client put together recurring transactions on an efficient basis. It can also help clients assess the legal and political environment surrounding issues that affect them. The truth is that lawyers already do a lot more in the way of general consulting than they think they do—generally because they give advice to clients on a broad range of issues at no charge through seminars and newsletters.

Third, a law firm can provide developers with a variety of financial services akin to those offered by investment bankers in the corporate setting. Many lawyers provide these kinds of services every day on an informal basis by introducing clients to sources of financing, including debt and equity investors. Real estate lawyers often have developed a list of contacts over the years that is the envy of most investment bankers and mortgage brokers.

Fourth, a law firm can be of inestimable value in helping clients structure basic business transactions. While some clients prefer to structure their own deals, the successful ones are smart enough to use all the costeffective resources available to them. If clients can be shown that they will save time and money by getting the lawyer involved in a project at the planning stage and by using the lawyer as a consultant rather than simply as a drafts[person], the client generally will do so. . . .

Finally, a law firm can do strategic planning for the client through specialized or "boutique" services that cannot be characterized as purely "legal" products. For example, a law firm with expertise in environmental matters can—in a consulting capacity—help the client design strategies that will eliminate, minimize or contain potential pollution liability problems.

LAW FIRM RESPONSE

The response of the legal profession to these new demands has run the gamut from refusal and reluctance to acceptance and enthusiasm. Our firm, for example, recently established a Corporate and Real Estate Finance Group consisting of lawyers specializing in taxation, health care, real estate, environmental law, securities law, banking and finance. It has become a team—a SWAT team, as someone has suggested—that can be mobilized quickly and efficiently to attack a client's problems in their broadest context.

Most clients do not cubbyhole problems as "legal problems," "accounting problems" or "banking problems." They want answers on a comprehensive level: Can we do the deal or not? Is there a better way to structure the transaction? How should the financing be put together so as to get the most money at the lowest cost? The Group's reason for being is to approach problems on this level, giving the firm an opportunity to address the clients' total needs.

Consider the following example. A corporate client needs capital. In order to raise it, the company has to make a series of decisions. First, it must decide whether to obtain the capital through the use of its general credit standing. If so, it could go to the public equity or bond markets for financing, or use its unsecured bank credit lines. Another alternative would be to finance off of its assets, such as its real estate and equipment.

If the company decides upon asset-based financing, it faces another series of decisions. It can borrow directly against its assets by obtaining mortgage debt, or it can take a more convoluted route and borrow indirectly, as would be the case with a sale and leaseback transaction. In deciding whether to take the direct or indirect approach in asset-based financing, the company is then faced with a set of considerations that will require highly sophisticated analysis. The company's law firm has an obligation to help the client make this analysis because its decision will affect the company in a number of very sensitive ways:

- It will affect the company's federal tax position.
- It will have significant impact on the company's financial statements, including the manner of reporting the transaction on its balance sheet.
- It will make a serious difference with regard to the company's cost of capital.
- It will affect the company's capacity to obtain capital in the future.

This may be territory where angels fear to tread, but lawyers must. . . .

Law firms should be at the forefront of finding new ways to structure transactions so that they will be saleable in the retail market. Investors are no longer looking to the tax benefits first and the quality of the real estate and developer second; old-fashioned economics now govern the success or failure of real estate [investment offerings] in the capital marketplace. Persuading retail investors to accept this "economic" analysis will require new methods of putting the transactions together, including developing appropriate credit facilities to stand behind them. When it comes to devising these new methods, lawyers cannot stand back as observers. They have to actively participate by bringing together several different disciplines within the law firm—from tax and securities to finance and real estate—to come up with a structure that will meet both client requirements and investor demands. . . .

SUMMARY

If a law firm is to grow and prosper over the next decade, it can no longer sit back and wait for the client to come up with the ideas—or the problems. Whether in real estate or other areas, lawyers can no longer be bystanders. They must be deeply immersed in the totality of a transaction from both a legal and business point of view. Most importantly, they must be prepared to add value to a client's product—a value far beyond simply putting together a set of papers based upon a term sheet originated by the client.

Such "value-added" lawyering . . . will require that lawyers be not only legal technicians, but also innovators and conceptualizers. The ability to be both is the key factor in a successful journey from drafts[person] to consultant.

NOTES AND QUESTIONS

1. Value-Added Lawyering. The concept of value-added lawyering discussed by Nessen and Ragalevsky was pioneered by Professor Gilson in his influential article Value Creation by Business Lawyers: Legal Skills and Asset Pricing, 94 Yale L.J. 239 (1984). See also Sargent, What Does It Take? Hallmarks of the Business Lawyer, 5 Bus. Law Today 11 (July/Aug. 1996). Professor Gilson acknowledged that clients often hold uncharitable views of the role that business lawyers play in their transactions:

> Business lawyers are seen at best as a transaction cost, part of a system of wealth redistribution from clients to lawyers; legal fees represent a tax on business transactions. . . . At worst, lawyers are seen as deal killers whose continual raising of obstacles, without commensurate effort at finding solutions, ultimately causes transactions to collapse under their own weight.

94 Yale L.J. at 241-242. Gilson, however, suggests a model by which skilled business lawyers acting as "transaction cost engineers" efficiently structure the transaction's form to reduce transaction costs and thereby generate transaction value. Although Gilson tests this hypothesis in the context of a corporate acquisition, his model applies equally to real estate transactions.

2. Lawyers as Business Consultants. Both the foregoing articles suggest that real estate lawyers must be prepared to help their clients make business decisions. Although lawyers have differing views on the appropriateness of their dispensing such business advice as whether the rent, purchase price, or interest rate of the real estate bargain is fair, or how the client should raise necessary capital, one nonlegal commentator advises flatly: "Never ask a lawyer or accountant for business advice. They are trained to find problems, not solutions." Brown, Life's Little Instruction Book (1991). Assuming that clients want advice about business matters, should real estate lawyers provide it? What are the dangers if they do so?"

B. THE DECLINING ROLE OF LAWYERS IN RESIDENTIAL REAL ESTATE TRANSACTIONS

The materials in this book emphasize commercial, as opposed to residential, real estate transactions. Primarily, this emphasis reflects the declining role of lawyers in the home buying process,[3] particularly in the western states. Increasingly, real estate brokers, mortgage brokers, title insurance companies, and others have assumed the lawyer's traditional role in negotiating the terms of the residential purchase and its "purchase money" financing, determining the status of the seller's title, and documenting the conveyance.

This shift can be explained in large part by the economics of residential transactions in relation to commercial ones as legal costs have risen. For example, the lawyer's time and fees in advising residential buyers on the most prudent means of acquiring and holding title (for example, as joint tenants or as tenants in common) may approximate those incurred in the commercial setting when the choice is among the various forms of business ownership associations. Simply, the lawyer is able to add greater value to the large dollar commercial transaction in relation to the lawyer's fees. This same economic reality explains why certain "due diligence" studies customarily undertaken in commercial sale and financing transactions, such as property surveys and environmental testing, are seen rarely in the residential setting.

While, as shown above, the commercial real estate lawyer is beginning to assume the transactional planning roles usually held by nonlegal professionals, in the residential market the lawyer's traditional role is giving way to brokers and other nonlawyers. As you might expect, there is tension in the residential market as to whether these nonlawyers are engaging in the unauthorized practice of law. Equally important is whether society is better off in allowing alternatives to lawyers in certain real estate transactions. These issues are among those explored in Chapter 2's discussion of the conveyancing process.

---

3. See generally Braunstein and Genn, Odd Man Out: Preliminary Findings Concerning the Diminishing Role of Lawyers in the Home-Buying Process, 52 Ohio St. L.J. 469 (1991) (compares the United Kingdom residential market where solicitors represent virtually all home buyers and sellers); see also Blair, The Vanishing Lawyer: Recapturing the Residential Real Estate Practice, 3 Prob. & Prop. 7 (Mar./Apr. 1989).

PRACTITIONER'S CORNER

Keeping Current

Any would-be practitioner of real estate law should be aware of the following comprehensive treatises and periodicals on real estate investment and financing. References to more specialized publications are included throughout this book.

Books

M. Madison, J. Dwyer, and S. Bender, The Law of Real Estate Financing (2016): a comprehensive treatise that follows a transactional approach and is tax-oriented.

Modern Real Estate Transactions, published by the American Law Institute (ALI): an annual publication that updates practitioners on recent developments and techniques with respect to all aspects of sophisticated real estate transactions using the relevant documentation as the referential point for discussion.

G. Nelson et al., Real Estate Finance Law (6th ed. 2015): a treatise with abundant citations.

Journals and Newsletters

Practical Real Estate Lawyer, published by ALI, which is practice-oriented and short on citations.

Probate and Property, published by the Real Property, Trust and Estate Law Section of the ABA.

Real Estate Finance Journal, published quarterly by Thomson Reuters.

Real Estate Law Journal, published by Thomson Reuters, which contains regular columns on real estate tax issues, digests of recent cases and statutes, and bibliographies of recent books and articles.

Real Estate Review, published by Thomson Reuters, which is business-oriented and short on citations.

Real Property, Trust and Estate Journal, published by the Real Property, Trust and Estate Law Section of the ABA.

Real Estate Law Report, published by Thomson Reuters.

Electronic Resources

The premier online discussion group among real estate lawyers is "DIRT," moderated by the University of Missouri-Kansas City School of Law.

Glossary of Terms

The Documents Manual accompanying this casebook includes a glossary of common terms used in real estate transactions.

Students using this casebook are authorized to access the Documents Manual at http://law.seattleu.edu/documents/faculty/benders/docmanual.pdf. Be aware that many of these documents are included for teaching purposes rather than as state-of-the-art forms for practitioners.

PART I

FUNDAMENTALS OF
LAND TRANSFER

Chapter 2

Overview of Contracts for Sale and the Conveyancing Process

In this chapter, assume that our typical real estate entrepreneur, Dan Developer, has decided to purchase an existing office building (perhaps with the aid of some intermediary such as a real estate broker). Dan has alerted you, his legal advisor, that negotiations have begun with the prospective seller (Sarah Seller). After negotiations, Dan and Sarah agree on a price of $40 million payable as follows: $5 million in earnest money to be delivered when the contract for sale is executed and an additional $35 million in cash at closing. Dan expects to obtain a mortgage loan from Ace Insurance Company or some other institutional lender in the amount of $30 million at the market rate of interest for first mortgage money to fund part of the purchase price, with the remaining funds to come from equity investors who have formed a business entity with Dan to acquire the property.

Dan now asks you to review a contract of sale drafted by Sarah's attorney. Your initial reaction should be one of relief—your client had the foresight to consult with you before executing the contract. In many instances (especially in single-family residential and small commercial transactions), the initial contract is drafted by the seller, broker, banker, or title company involved in the transaction and then submitted to one or both parties for acceptance even though the individual who prepares the contract may have neither sufficient information (other than price and payment details) nor an adequate legal background to prepare a complete contract that protects the interests of the parties. Moreover, some brokers entrusted with preparing the contract of sale may be more concerned about "making a deal" and collecting their commission than attending to the legal consequences of the transaction.

Before we examine your role as a real estate lawyer in the conveyancing process, consider the following overview of the theory and mechanics of land acquisition and transfer. Expressed in virtually every contract of sale is a promise by the seller to deliver title ("marketable title") that is free of all legal encumbrances except those that are agreeable to the reasonable purchaser. During the period between the date the contract is fully executed and the closing date,[1] the purchaser's attorney will examine the status of the seller's title based

---

1. In the case of an ordinary contract of sale, this interim period between the execution of the contract and the closing date is ordinarily about two months. By contrast, in the case of an installment land contract like the one in the *Crutchley* case, infra, the seller agrees to finance the purchase price and retains the legal title as security until all the installment payments are made; hence, in duration the contract period will resemble the term of a mortgage loan. See Chapter 3D.

on a title search conducted by a title insurance company, as well as inspect copies of relevant deeds and other documents that are recorded in either the Registry of Deeds or Registry of Probate office. For example, there may be recorded encumbrances (for example, easements, liens, restrictive covenants, leases) that adversely affect the value of the property. If there are no exceptions to marketable title or if they can be resolved to the satisfaction of the purchaser's attorney before the closing date, then the transaction will be closed on the stipulated date. At that time the seller will convey title by means of a deed to the purchaser, who must simultaneously deliver the balance of the agreed-on purchase price. Absent language to the contrary, once the purchaser accepts the deed, its rights under the contract of sale terminate and "merge" with the deed so that the purchaser's sole recourse against the seller (except for fraud) will depend on the covenants, if any, contained in the deed from the seller. However, even if the purchaser were to bargain for the highest degree of protection obtainable by a grantee—the standard covenants in a general warranty deed (for example, covenant of seisin, covenant against encumbrances, covenant of warranty)—the title protection afforded to the purchaser is limited because these covenants are nothing more than promises to indemnify, which can be worthless if the seller becomes insolvent. Consequently, a prudent purchaser will demand additional title protection in the form of title insurance, which is backed by the considerable net worth of the company that issues the policy. In some locations, purchasers may rely instead on an attorney's opinion as to the status of title, backed only by the attorney's professional liability insurance and personal assets.

Those students who haven't studied conveyancing in first-year property law, or those desiring a more comprehensive treatment than the overview presented in this chapter, might want to consult one of the standard conveyancing hornbooks such as M. Friedman, Contracts and Conveyances of Real Property (7th ed. 2005) or American Law of Property (Casner ed., 1952) as we proceed.

A. CONTRACTS FOR SALE OF REAL ESTATE

Since commercial sellers and purchasers are likely to be sophisticated, roughly equal in bargaining power, and represented by legal counsel, the disposition of commercial real estate is an area in which freedom of contract reigns virtually supreme. In commercial sale transactions, therefore, general rules of law usually apply only in the absence of an agreement to the contrary. Since the transactional rights and responsibilities of the seller and purchaser are invariably set forth in writing (as evidenced by the sample Sale Agreement in the Documents Manual), there is little need in this overview to dwell on those general property and contracts law rules that can be overridden by means of the written word. One example should suffice. Under the doctrine of equitable conversion,[2] the risk of any casualty loss (for example, fire) between the date on which the contract is executed and the closing date will be borne by the purchaser as the "equitable" owner.[3] By contrast, under a contract theory approach, a minority of jurisdictions hold that the seller should bear the risk of loss until the purchaser receives what it bargained for, namely, legal title in the form of a deed on the closing date.[4] Finally, under §1 of the Uniform Vendor and Purchaser Risk Act, which some states have adopted,[5] the risk of loss is on the party in possession. However, none of these rules apply when the contract of sale expressly provides otherwise, and (as illustrated by §9 of the sample Sale Agreement) the typical contract for the sale of commercial real estate will address this issue. Consequently, this overview focuses on drafting approaches to the contract of sale and on those legal theories that either are imposed by way of judicial gloss on the written words of the parties (for example, potential treatment of the earnest money deposit as an invalid penalty rather than as enforceable liquidated damages) or that relate to the essence of their legal relationship with one another (for example, the doctrine of marketable title).

1. The Real Estate Broker's Role in Sale Transactions

The following article addresses the pitfalls for sellers in their contracts with real estate brokers. Seller's counsel should ensure that the brokerage agreement is consistent with the seller's expectations as to when the commission is earned. Unfortunately, many sellers do not secure counsel until a purchaser is located and therefore are unrepresented in their dealings with brokers.

Goldstein, When Does a Real Estate Broker Earn His Commission?
27 Prac. Law. 43 (1981)

READY, ABLE, AND WILLING

For a broker to recover a fee in most jurisdictions, a writing for his hiring is not necessary, and the real estate transaction does not have to be consummated. See Note, 5 Mem. St. U. L. Rev. 59 (1975).

---

2. See generally M. Friedman, Contracts and Conveyances of Real Property §4.8 (7th ed. 2005); K. Holtzschue, Real Estate Transactions: Purchase and Sale of Real Property (1987); 3 American Law of Property §11.22 (Casner ed., 1952).

3. See, e.g., Ross v. Bumstead, 65 Ariz. 61, 173 P.2d 765 (1946).

4. See, e.g., Capital Sav. & Loan Ass'n v. Convey, 175 Wash. 224, 27 P.2d 136 (1933).

5. E.g., N.Y. Gen. Oblig. Law §5-1311.

The expression is often heard that the broker earns his commission when he produces a ready, able, and willing customer on the terms given to him by his principal. 12 C.J.S. Brokers §182 (1980). Let us examine this statement by considering it in the context of the following fact patterns.

Given the terms for a sale by the owner of a piece of land in New York City, the broker brings a proposal to the seller. The prospect, the seller, their counsel, and the broker arrange to meet for the purpose of signing a contract.

Seller's counsel employs a printed form of contract, distributed by the New York Board of Title Underwriters, which states that "the seller shall give and the purchaser shall accept such title as _____, a Member of the New York Board of Title Underwriters, will be willing to approve and insure." The clause can, of course, be deleted; but if it remains, then rather than name a particular company, the way the matter is usually handled is to insert in the blank space the words "any title company," i.e., any one that is a member of the New York Board of Title Underwriters. However, this seller's counsel inserts the name of "X Title Company."

Buyer's counsel does not like the provision about the X Title Company and he asks seller's counsel to correct the clause so that it applies to any title company that is a member of the New York Board of Title Underwriters. But [seller's] counsel resists any change, despite the arguments of buyer's counsel that the buyer should not be limited in his selection of a title company.

At this juncture, buyer's counsel tells his client:

> You know, there's something peculiar here. The insistence of seller's counsel upon the X Title Company makes me a little bit suspicious about his title. He may have had a defect—a little blemish that he is unable to remove—but somehow he has prevailed upon the X Title Company to omit it as an exception on the seller's title policy when he acquired the property. Furthermore, the insistence upon using the X Title Company may create an embarrassing situation if we try to procure financing and the proposed mortgagee uses the Y Title Company, not the X Company, for its title search.

As a consequence, the sale is never consummated.

The following day, the broker appears at the seller's office and hands him a bill for the brokerage commission. The seller says, "Evidently there is some misunderstanding. Don't you recall—you were there yesterday—that the deal broke up because of the title company problem?" "Oh," replies the broker, "so it did. But I had nothing to do with that. You said nothing in your offering that I handed to the prospect concerning the X Title Company." The broker is right. Freeman v. Creelman, 60 Cal. App. 14, 212 P. 56 (1922); Tanenbaum v. Boehm, 202 N.Y. 293, 95 N.E. 708 (1911).

Compare these facts with the following. The buyer makes an offer for a residence through the broker. The seller finds the offer acceptable and arrangements are made for the parties to meet to sign a contract. At that point, before any written contract is executed, the buyer calls the broker and says: "My [spouse] now has different feelings about the house, and we don't want it." In this case, the broker cannot recover his fee. Annot., 12 A.L.R.2d 1410, 1413 (1950).

In the first situation, the progress of the transaction to its ultimate consummation was interrupted by the interjection of an entirely new idea by seller's counsel. But in the second situation, while an understanding was reached orally, the prospect withdrew before signing a contract, so that the objective the seller sought in hiring the broker—to sell the property—was never achieved.

CONDITIONAL HIRING

The seller of the land in the first example, having had a bad experience with the broker, decides, when selling his residence, to engage a broker on the condition that a commission would be payable only if title actually closes. The broker procures a customer who makes an offer on the seller's terms. The contract is prepared by seller's counsel, based upon the seller's title papers. The contract is signed. A short while later, the buyer asks his counsel whether he could withdraw from the contract. Counsel responds, "It doesn't look as though you can. There might be objections to title, but seller's counsel showed me the seller's title policy issued when the seller acquired the property, and the contract followed that policy."

Fortunately for the buyer, the seller, when giving the title papers to his attorney to prepare the contract of sale, forgot to tell counsel that after acquiring title, he and his neighbors had made an arrangement for the construction of drainage ditches for their common use. Because the architect needed approval for the construction of the drainage ditches, he filed the necessary papers in the county clerk's office. Since the documents were recorded after the issuance of the title insurance policy to the seller on his acquisition of the property, they were not reflected in the title papers that were given to seller's counsel.

When buyer's counsel, in due course, received his title report from the title company, he discovered that the property was encumbered by a common drainage easement, for which there was no exception in the contract. The buyer refused to accept title and the closing never materialized.

Although title never closed, the broker still can recover his commission, because the seller's act made performance impossible. While a broker's commission can be contingent upon the consummation of the transaction, the seller cannot take advantage of conditions that he himself created to make performance impossible and thereby deprive the broker of his commission. Shear v. National Rifle Ass'n of America, 606 F.2d 1251 (D.C. Cir. 1979); Annot., 45 A.L.R.3d 1326 (1972).

On the other hand, had the brokerage agreement stated that no commission would be paid in case of a failure to close for any reason whatsoever, no commission would have been recoverable. Dixon v. Bernstein, 182 F.2d 104 (D.C. Cir. 1950). Even in that case, if the closing did not take place because of the bad faith or fraudulent action of the seller, the broker could recover. Langfan

v. Waltzer, 13 N.Y.2d 171, 194 N.E.2d 124, 244 N.Y.S.2d 305 (1963). But if the contract stated that commissions would not be paid if there was a failure to close for any reason whatsoever except willful default, if the seller released the buyer from the commitment prior to closing, there was no willful default. Warnecke v. Countrywide Realty, Inc., 29 App. Div. 2d 54, 285 N.Y.S.2d 428 (1967), aff'd without opinion, 22 N.Y.2d 823, 239 N.E.2d 656, 292 N.Y.S.2d 917 (1968).

THE PURCHASER'S LIABILITY

There is a minority view that the broker's engagement is not satisfied until title actually closes—unless failure to close is attributable to the principal—even without a specific provision to that effect in the brokerage agreement. Ellsworth Dobbs Inc. v. Johnson, 50 N.J. 528, 236 A.2d 843 (1967). See Tristram's Landing Inc. v. Wait, 367 Mass. 622, 327 N.E.2d 727 (1975). However, in order to protect the broker, if the purchaser rejects the deal capriciously and title does not close, Ellsworth suggests that the broker has an action against [the purchaser] for the loss of commission on the theory of an implied obligation by the purchaser to complete the transaction. For the nonapplicability of this purchaser liability in a noncommercial transaction like the purchase of a home, see Rothman Realty Corp. v. Bereck, 73 N.J. 590, 376 A.2d 902 (1977). . . .

EXCLUSIVE ARRANGEMENTS

Recently, many brokerage contracts have involved exclusive arrangements. There is a distinction between a complete exclusive arrangement, where the principal is foreclosed from competing with the broker, and an exclusive agency where such competition is not foreclosed. Annot., 88 A.L.R.2d 936 (1963). See Brown v. Miller, 45 Ill. App. 3d 970, 360 N.E.2d 585 (1977).

Real problems arise in connection with the so-called extension period [during which time the broker reserves the right to a commission in specified circumstances for a deal originating from the broker's efforts during the exclusive period but consummated after that period expires]. How are transactions concluded after the end of the exclusive period, the impetus for which originated during the [exclusive] period, to be treated? In Kaye v. Coughlin, 443 S.W.2d 612 (Tex. Civ. App. 1969), the owner sought to invoke the doctrine of unconscionability of section 2-302 of the Uniform Commercial Code as a defense to liability to the broker on a sale that was consummated directly with the purchaser during the extension period. The purchaser had learned of the offering during the exclusive period from the broker's advertisement. Although the broker had made no effort to bring owner and purchaser together the court found for the broker under the terms of the brokerage agreement, ruling that the exclusive contract was not unconscionable. See generally Annot., 51 A.L.R.3d 1149 (1973).

Thus, an exclusive arrangement should define both the duration of the extension period and the stage at which the negotiations must be at the end of the exclusive period for a transaction concluded during the extension period to be eligible for a commission. For example, only a transaction that is in active negotiation at the end of the exclusive period might entitle the broker to a commission if consummated during the extension period. . . .

Illustrating the pitfalls when parties elect to rely on brokers to document and explain their sale agreement, the following case involves an installment land contract with a nonrecourse clause. Installment land contracts are mortgage substitutes sometimes employed when sellers finance the buyer's real estate acquisition (see Chapter 3D). As used below, the nonrecourse clause (see Chapter 5A3) limited the lender-seller's recourse to recovering the property should the buyer default in making the installment purchase payments.

Crutchley v. First Trust & Savings Bank
450 N.W.2d 877 (Iowa 1990)

CARTER, Justice.

The estate of Don Fishel, a deceased real estate salesperson, appeals from a judgment awarding damages to plaintiffs, Harold E. Crutchley and Anita S. Crutchley. Plaintiffs' action sought to recover for the alleged negligence and breach of contract of Fishel and Jim Short, two licensed real estate agents who represented them in the sale of 600 acres of land in Linn County. Short, who is also a defendant against whom judgment was entered, has not appealed.

In 1980, the plaintiffs listed 600 acres of land for sale through the Mundel, Long & Luce real estate office in Cedar Rapids. Fishel and Short were salespersons associated with that firm. Plaintiffs were well acquainted with Fishel, who had previously represented them in selling other property. Short assisted Fishel on some of the prior sales as well as the transaction giving rise to the present controversy. After advertisement of the 600-acre tract in publications of general circulation in the Midwest, Carl Esker and two medical doctors participating with him agreed to pay a total consideration of $1,650,000 for the property pursuant to an installment contract. The contract called for a $300,000 down payment with the remaining balance to be paid over a twenty-year period.

The contract of sale came into being as a result of the plaintiffs' acceptance of an offer to purchase which contained the following language: ["]In the event of default on this contract, the sellers shall only be entitled to possession of the real estate as of the date of said default. Buyers will only lose their interest in said property and any payments made to date of default.["] The parties to this litigation have referred to this provision as a nonrecourse clause. Although the price and payment terms of the installment contract evolved from a series of offers and counteroffers, the nonrecourse clause had been included in the original offer and was not altered or amended in any way in the subsequent negotiations between buyers and sellers.

In 1985 the buyers defaulted on the contract. As a result, plaintiffs regained possession of the farmland by forfeiture proceedings pursuant to Iowa Code chapter 656. Plaintiffs retained the down payment and annual interest payments received on March 1 of 1982, 1983, and 1984. The parties to this action are in agreement that, as a result of the nonrecourse clause, plaintiffs were entitled to no further relief against the buyers.

Due to a plummeting decline in the value of farm real estate between 1980 and 1985, the value of the 600-acre tract plus the payments which plaintiffs received prior to default did not equal the contract price to be paid by the defaulting parties. Prior to bringing the present action, the plaintiffs sought federal bankruptcy protection. As a part of those proceedings, the 600-acre tract was liquidated in 1986 for $576,465.

On June 9, 1986, plaintiffs commenced the present action against Jim Short and the estate of Fishel, who by that time was deceased, seeking recovery of money damages on theories of negligence and breach of contract. They contended that Short and Fishel misadvised them concerning the legal significance of the nonrecourse clause and failed to observe the provisions of article 17 of the National Association of Realtors' Code of Ethics by not recommending that plaintiffs consult legal counsel on a matter in which their interests required it.

At the trial, plaintiff Harold Crutchley testified that, when the property was sold to Carl Esker and his associates, the sellers did not understand that the nonrecourse clause in the contract left them without any recourse other than to regain the property. Crutchley testified that Short had advised the sellers that this clause only protected certain of the buyers' assets from execution sale and protected the buyers' spouses from personal liability. Crutchley testified that he would not have accepted the offer to buy the land had he realized the legal import of the nonrecourse clause. He stated that neither Fishel nor Short recommended that plaintiffs seek legal counsel in culminating this transaction and that Short had affirmatively dissuaded them from so doing.

Fishel was deceased at the time of trial, but Short was called as a witness. Short conceded the applicability of article 17 of the National Association of Realtors' Code of Ethics for purposes of determining his and Fishel's responsibilities to their clients. He denied that either he or Fishel had dissuaded plaintiffs from seeking the advice of legal counsel on this transaction. He testified that plaintiffs were sophisticated in real estate transactions and that on other land sales in which Short had assisted them they had freely consulted attorneys concerning questions over legal matters. He testified that both he and Fishel had fully explained the legal significance of the nonrecourse clause to the plaintiffs and that he was satisfied they understood it and accepted it as a means of obtaining a favorable sale.

The case was submitted to the jury under the comparative fault provisions of Iowa Code chapter 668 (1987). . . . After a reduction of damages for plaintiffs' percentage [25 percent] of fault, judgment was entered against the two defendants jointly and severally for the sum of $536,250.

The issues raised by the Fishel estate on appeal concern (1) the sufficiency of the evidence to sustain a claim of realtor malpractice. . . .

We first consider the Fishel estate's contention that there was insufficient evidence presented to permit a finding of negligence or breach of contract by Fishel or Short and that the district court should have granted its motion for judgment notwithstanding the verdict. Throughout the course of the litigation, plaintiffs' breach-of-contract claims have been predicated on the same alleged acts or omissions as their negligence claims. Consequently, for purposes of the issues under discussion, the negligence and breach-of-contract claims are indistinguishable.

The district court permitted the jury to find that the defendants were negligent or had breached their duties under the listing agreement in the following particulars: (1) by giving an inadequate and incorrect explanation of the nonrecourse provision, (2) by not affirmatively recommending that plaintiffs obtain legal counsel in a matter in which their interests required it, and (3) in discouraging plaintiffs from seeking legal counsel. Although the Fishel estate strenuously argues that the evidence fails to support any of these theories of negligence or breach of contract, we believe that based on the evidence presented a jury might have found adversely to defendants as to any or all of the three specifications we have listed.

Plaintiffs offered evidence, including the testimony of Short himself, that both Short and Fishel were required to maintain the standards articulated in article 17 of the National Association of Realtors' Code of Ethics in representing their clients. That standard reads as follows: ["]The Realtor shall not engage in activities that constitute the unauthorized practice of law and shall recommend that legal counsel be obtained when the interest of any party to the transaction requires it.["] We recognized in Menzel v. Morse, 362 N.W.2d 465, 473 (Iowa 1985), that proof of a violation of this standard is evidence upon which a trier of fact may find negligence.

The evidence concerning that which was said or not said by the parties to the litigation concerning the legal effect of the nonrecourse clause or the desirability of plaintiffs seeking legal counsel was in sharp dispute. If, however, the evidence presented is viewed in the light most favorable to the plaintiffs, it will support a finding by the jury that defendants failed to exercise the standard of care required of persons engaged in their business or profession. . . .

NOTES AND QUESTIONS

1. Unauthorized Practice of Law. As you would expect, engaging in the practice of law without being licensed as an attorney may be subject to injunction or criminal penalties. The extent to which brokers may be involved in negotiating and drafting the sale transaction as a complement to or in replacement of real estate lawyers is the subject of local law that varies among the states. In many states, brokers may act as scriveners to complete "simple" standardized real estate forms (for example, the earnest money agreement and purchase contract), provided that these standard forms have been approved by lawyers (usually counsel to the local realtor's association) and that the broker does not charge separately for completing the forms. See, e.g., Pope County Bar Ass'n v. Suggs, 274 Ark. 250, 624 S.W.2d 828 (1981); Cultum v. Heritage House Realtors, 103 Wash. 2d 623, 694 P.2d 630 (1985). See also In re First Escrow, Inc., 840 S.W.2d 839 (Mo. 1992) (similar allowance to escrow companies). In Cook County, Illinois, and surrounding counties, an association of real estate lawyers has created, with the cooperation of real estate brokers, residential real estate contract forms that are intended to be initially completed without the assistance of lawyers. See Multi-Board Residential Real Estate Contract, Illinois Real Estate Lawyers Association, www.reallaw.org. Responding to a more restrictive decision by Arizona's Supreme Court that held brokers were engaged in the unauthorized practice of law in filling out printed conveyancing forms, brokers there secured a state constitutional amendment allowing them to "draft or fill out and complete, without charge . . . preliminary purchase agreements and earnest money receipts, deeds, mortgages, leases, assignments, releases, contracts for sale of realty, and bills of sale." Ariz. Const. art. 26, §1.

Recognizing the difficult balance between the cost savings of forgoing counsel and the risks presented by the broker's sometimes conflicting interest to close the deal and collect a commission, in 1995 New Jersey's Supreme Court ruled that with disclosure of these risks, brokers may order title insurance and may prepare conveyance deeds through their own counsel for unrepresented parties. In re Opinion No. 26 Comm. on the Unauthorized Practice of Law, 139 N.J. 323, 654 A.2d 1344 (1995) (prior decisions had established that brokers could draft sale contracts if they included three-day rights to cancel encouraging review by counsel but that only the parties' counsel could draft the deed). Why do you think that brokers might prefer to arrange for the drafting of the conveyance deed through their own counsel rather than rely on counsel obtained by one or both of the parties? As you explore the various steps in the conveyancing process in this chapter, consider which duties are appropriate for nonlawyers such as brokers and title companies and which duties should be the exclusive province of legal counsel. See generally Birnbaum, Illinois Real Estate Lawyers and the Battle to Control Residential Closings, 84 Ill. B.J. 132 (Mar. 1996); Stark, Navigating Residential Attorney Approvals: Finding a Better Judicial North Star, 39 J. Marshall L. Rev. 171 (2006).

2. The Broker's Duty of Care. In response to the *Crutchley* case, one commentator advised that brokers in similar situations might want to have their seller-clients sign a release acknowledging that they understand the buyer's proposal for nonrecourse financing. Lloyd, Brokers: Breach of Contract and

Negligence Established, 19 Real Est. L. Rep. 1 (May 1990). Would that release insulate the broker from liability if in fact the seller fails to appreciate the nature of a nonrecourse obligation? If the seller asks the broker to explain the legal meaning of the nonrecourse proposal, can the broker lawfully do so? Compare Chicago Bar Ass'n v. Quinlan & Tyson, Inc., 53 Ill. App. 2d 388, 203 N.E.2d 131, 145 (1964) (brokers cannot undertake to explain the legal effects of the conveyancing documents), modified on other grounds, 34 Ill. 2d 116, 214 N.E.2d 771 (1966), with Morley v. J. Pagel Realty & Ins., 27 Ariz. App. 62, 550 P.2d 1104, 1108 (1976) (having achieved the constitutional right to prepare conveyancing documents, real estate brokers "also bear the responsibility and duty of explaining to the persons involved the implications of these documents"). See generally, Goudey, Comment, Too Many Hands in the Cookie Jar: The Unauthorized Practice of Law by Real Estate Brokers, 75 Or. L. Rev. 889 (1996).

3. The Broker's Duty of Loyalty. As a complement to the duty of care, brokers also owe their clients a fiduciary duty of loyalty. In practice, this means that the broker cannot disclose to others information that prejudices the client. See Haymes v. Rogers, 70 Ariz. 257, 219 P.2d 339 (breach of duty of loyalty for seller's broker to inform prospective purchaser that seller probably would sell for less than listing price), rehearing, 70 Ariz. 408, 222 P.2d 789 (1950). At the same time, the seller's broker is obligated to disclose all material information to the seller, such as all offers made on the property, Moore & Co. v. T-A-L-L, Inc., 792 P.2d 794 (Colo. 1990), and adverse financial information concerning the purchaser, White v. Boucher, 322 N.W.2d 560 (Minn. 1982). Nor can the broker engage in self-dealing. Cf. Ross v. Perelli, 13 Wash. App. 944, 538 P.2d 834 (1975) (duty of loyalty compels broker to reveal to seller-principal any familial relationship between broker and prospective purchaser). However, the duty of loyalty does not prevent the seller's broker from showing a prospective purchaser the competing properties of its other clients. See Coldwell Banker Commercial Group v. Camelback Office Park, 156 Ariz. 226, 751 P.2d 542, 546 (1988) ("Unless a principal contracts for [his] exclusive time . . . a broker must be free to represent all his principals. He does not act adversely to any one of them so long as he presents each property in its best light and does not unfairly favor one principal over another.").

4. Earning a Commission. Does the listing price bind the seller to pay a broker commission, or can the seller hold out for more money? In RealPro, Inc. v. Smith Residual Co., LLC, 138 Cal. Rptr. 3d 255 (Ct. App. 4th Dist. 2012), the broker procured a ready, willing, and able buyer who made a cash offer for the full listing price of $17 million, but the seller countered at $19.5 million and the transaction fell through. The court held that the seller did not owe a commission to the broker, even though there was no indication that the broker's commission was conditioned on a successful closing. See generally Bernhardt and Whitman, When Is A Commission Due? Problems with Broker Listing Agreements, 27 Prob. & Prop. 30, 32 (Jan./Feb. 2013).

2.   The Real Estate Lawyer's Role in Sale Transactions

The materials below include a discussion of some of the important issues in documenting a real estate sale transaction, as reflected in the sample sale agreement in the Documents Manual. Be aware that the sample agreement's provisions generally are pro-seller. In reviewing the agreement, assume that you represent Dan Developer as buyer, and be alert to provisions that do not adequately protect his interests and expectations. The notes and questions in this section address some of these concerns.

THE ETHICAL REAL ESTATE LAWYER

Assuming Too Limited a Role in Real Estate Conveyancing Transactions

A 1994 Illinois State Bar Association advisory opinion on professional conduct cautions real estate lawyers who assume too limited a role in sale transactions. It details an impermissible scenario in which an attorney relies on the seller's broker to convey the deal-specific information necessary to prepare the closing documents (for example, the deed) and, after preparing those documents, allows the broker to explain them and to represent the seller in negotiating their provisions with the buyer. In addition to aiding the broker's unauthorized practice of law, the lawyer fails to fulfill her ethical duty to "explain a matter to the extent reasonably necessary to permit the client to make informed decisions regarding the representation." Illinois State Bar Ass'n Advisory Op. on Professional Conduct, 94-1, 83 Ill. B.J. 146 (1995). Cf. In re Opinion No. 26 Comm. on the Unauthorized Practice of Law, 139 N.J. 323, 654 A.2d 1344, 1362 (1995) (brokers may retain attorney to draft the conveyance deed only if the attorney personally consults with the seller).

Harris, Legal Opinion: Real Estate Contracts—Some Things to Think About
14 Real Est. Rev. 12 (Spring 1984)

It might seem that of all real estate transactions, the purchase and sale of real estate are the simplest. The buyer turns over the money and the seller gives a deed. What could be easier than that? Compared with financing, syndicating, or developing real estate, the purchase/sale transaction looks pretty fundamental.

However, it's not quite as simple as buying a bottle of milk at the grocery store, and most real estate transactions are accomplished pursuant to a written contract.[6]

WHY A CONTRACT?

Apart from strictly legal considerations, [due to] the intangible nature of interests in real estate, the fact that money is often borrowed to pay part of the purchase price and because defects in the nature of the seller's ownership are not apparent without review of public real estate (and other) records, the parties usually find it prudent and appropriate to negotiate the deal, reflect the terms in a written contract, and consummate or "close" the transaction at some future time which may be as short as a few days or very much longer.

The contract sets the purchase price, states the terms, establishes a time and place for closing, specifies situations that may allow one party or the other to withdraw from the deal (e.g., because financing cannot be obtained), describes just which title exceptions will be acceptable to the buyer and which won't, and describes the parties' rights if, prior to closing, surprises occur like the building burning down or part of the property being condemned. All this is pretty basic, but it does make the transaction a little more complicated than the purchase of milk.

It also makes the real estate contract begin to sound pretty important, and it is. It is also often the most casually, quickly, and poorly drafted legally binding document. Beleaguered real estate lawyers often discover that their clients have signed such a document before the attorney has had a chance to read it, revise it, or negotiate it. When this happens, there usually isn't much the lawyer can do but try to get the deal closed.

THE PREPRINTED CONTRACT FORM

Preprinted forms of real estate contracts abound. There may be no other legal document more commonly appearing in preprinted, fill-in-the-blank form. Title companies promulgate them, stationery stores sell them, legal printers prepare them, real estate brokers distribute them. Printed forms are designed to facilitate the quick completion and execution of real estate contracts without the help of lawyers. Often the forms are filled out by nonlawyers, real estate brokers, or the parties themselves. And, this does not just happen in house transactions.

There is nothing inherently wrong with printed forms. Most real estate deals include terms that are largely stereotypical and vary little from deal to deal. The forms can ensure that all these terms get included in an acceptable way. There is

---

6. The Statute of Frauds typically requires that a contract for the sale of real property be in writing and subscribed by the party to be charged. See, e.g., N.Y. Gen. Oblig. L. §5-703.—EDS.

no need to "reinvent the wheel" for every transaction. The intelligent use of printed forms can be a real time-saver, and the lawyer who drafts every contract from scratch probably is wasting time and, perforce, his client's money.

PITFALLS OF PRINTED FORMS

However, there are two pitfalls in the use of printed forms.

Forms can suppress thought. There is something seductive about the terms in a printed form. If they're in the form, they must be standard, must be boilerplate, must be right. Just because terms appear in print doesn't mean the parties to the deal and their lawyers shouldn't think about every term. Just because the form says that the seller pays for title insurance doesn't mean that the parties can't (in appropriate circumstances) shift this cost to the buyer.

Second, the forms inevitably allocate the risks and some of the economic obligations of a transaction in subtle ways. Let's face it, a real estate transaction is not a murder trial, but it is adversarial. In many respects, the parties' interests are inevitably and irrevocably in conflict. The problem with printed forms is that they resolve these conflicts in mysterious ways. In a state where real estate taxes are paid one year in arrears, it will usually be to the buyer's advantage to "reprorate" real estate tax when the actual bills are out in order to be protected from the almost inevitable tax increase. Yet, a form that says, "If the amount of the current general taxes is not then ascertainable, the adjustment thereof shall be on the basis of the amount of the most recent ascertainable taxes,". . . has shifted the economic risk of tax increases to the buyer.

SOME SUBTLE AND NOT SO SUBTLE PROBLEMS

Following are some of the problems that the parties to a contract should address, rather than relying on the terms in a form:

Who is the buyer? The phrase "x-company or assignee" is often inserted in the space for the buyer's name. The ostensible reason is to permit the buyer to designate at a later date a different entity to hold title to the purchased real estate. But if this is the intent, it can and should be expressed in just those words. For the seller, contracting with x-company or assignee may permit the named buyer to assign its rights and obligations to an unnamed substitute party. The seller can lose the credit of the buyer on the transaction and, worse yet, the named buyer's credit on a purchase money note and mortgage.

Who is the seller? Some care is also in order to have the titleholder of the property be the seller. If the seller doesn't own or can't convey title, the buyer will have an action for damages, for whatever that's worth. But will a suit for a specific performance against a nonowning seller encumber the real property? Probably not.

What is the property? Legal descriptions may not be in mind or at hand when the parties, anxious to get on with their deal, are ready to sign, but using a street address or permitting one or the other of the parties to fill in the legal description at a later date is illusory comfort. What if the address is wrong? Does it include the vacant lot next door? Does it include the driveway easement rights over adjoining land or will these terminate? . . .

"Covenants, conditions, and restrictions of record." When the parties are getting ready to sign the contract, no one may know the covenants, conditions, and restrictions affecting the property. The printed forms often resolve this dilemma easily (and horribly for the buyer) by saying that title will be conveyed subject to "all covenants, conditions and restrictions of record."

Resolving this can be a hard problem. If possible, the buyer should demand to know what "covenants, conditions and restrictions" he is expected to take subject to and examine these for acceptability. But even the purist will admit that this will not always be easy or possible within a short time frame. An acceptable solution for some deals and some property may be to obligate the buyer to take subject to restrictions "not violated by the present improvements and uses of the property or by purchaser's intended use of the property."

Damages I, title defects. It doesn't happen too often, but a deal can fail if unpermitted title exceptions crop up which the seller can't have waived. When this happens, it's usually an unpleasant surprise for everybody, like the building burning down prior to closing. Yet, most contract forms treat this "default" the same as if the seller did not appear at the closing with his deed. Does the seller want to be sued for damages or specific performance due to an unexpected title defect? If not, the parties should draft around it.

Damages II, earnest money. If the earnest money is substantial, the seller may be content to retain it as liquidated damages if the buyer defaults. With admirable symmetry, form contracts often provide that if the seller defaults, the earnest money is returned to the buyer. But getting his money back is cold comfort for the buyer. It is often necessary to modify the form to be sure the remedies of damages and specific performance are available to the buyer.

Damages III, broker's commission. Contracts often provide that if the buyer defaults, the earnest money goes first to pay the broker's commission then to the seller as damages. Interestingly, these form contracts are often promulgated by brokers. Yet, if sellers could vote, how many would agree that the broker should get a commission on a defaulted transaction?

Actually, arrangements with the broker including a statement of his commission don't belong in the real estate sale contract at all, but in the seller's agreement with the broker, the listing agreement. (This is another form the attorneys often don't see until after their client has signed.) Brokers don't usually sign the real estate sale contract, so anything said there about their rights or position may not bind them. A broker can be asked to sign the sale contract solely to evidence his agreement with the provisions about the broker's rights, and if one side or the other wants to repair the damage done by the listing agreement, this may be the way to do it.

When and where is the closing? Here is another vexing question the parties may be too fatigued to grapple with when the contract is signed so these unimportant details are left to be "mutually agreed to by the parties." Without delving too deeply into the metaphysics of contract law, the parties should be warned that generally "agreements to agree" are unenforceable and may taint the entire contract with unenforceability. Aside from this, without a definite time and place for closing, how will either party know when the other has defaulted? . . .

Before beginning the Notes and Questions, read the sample sale agreement in the Documents Manual.

NOTES AND QUESTIONS

1. Drafting Approaches to the Contract of Sale. Following their agreement on the terms of payment, assume that your client, Dan Developer, and Sarah Seller, along with her attorney, come to your law office to negotiate the other terms of the contract. Assume that the sample sale agreement will be the matrix for the negotiations that follow. You and Sarah's attorney agree that it represents a suitable standardized form of agreement that must be tailored to the unique facts and circumstances of this particular transaction.

Consider what your perspective should be as Dan's representative in the negotiations. First, you should assess Dan's bargaining clout with Sarah and identify the risks and rewards of the transaction before attempting to allocate them between the parties. Also, when assessing language that is proposed by the other party to the negotiations, try to think in terms of the worst-case scenario; in other words, if your client, Dan, should accept the proposed language, what rights (at common law, as modified by statute), if any, will Dan be forfeiting, and what additional responsibilities will he be assuming that someday might cause a serious legal, business, or tax problem for him? And, assuming there is relative parity in bargaining power, what alternative or compromise language might you suggest that should obviate or at least ameliorate the problem and yet be reasonably acceptable to the other side?

a. Financing Contingency. Most real estate developers and purchasers, like Dan, want to leverage their acquisition costs with mortgage financing; consequently, commercial real estate is rarely sold on a cash basis. Therefore, it is essential that the purchaser's attorney include a contingency clause for financing the purchase price; otherwise, the purchaser might lose the earnest money deposit (as discussed at Chapter 2A5, infra) if the necessary financing cannot be procured from the seller or a third-party lender.

If the real estate being sold is encumbered by a mortgage that secures the owner's promise to repay the mortgage note indebtedness and the owner is personally liable for performance of the underlying obligation, the existing mortgage might be *assumed* by the purchaser (in which event the purchaser would become personally liable on the mortgage note) or the purchaser might merely take title to the real estate *subject to* the mortgage (in which event the purchaser would not assume personal liability on the mortgage note). See D. Whitman et al., Real Estate Finance Law §§5.1-5.20 (6th ed. 2014). If, however, the existing mortgage note contains a due-on-sale clause (authorizing the lender to accelerate the mortgage indebtedness if the property is sold without its consent), the purchaser may be compelled to pay the market rate of interest on the existing mortgage or to substitute a new mortgage for the existing one by "refinancing" if the lender so demands. See Chapter 5A8. If the purchaser is allowed to assume the existing mortgage debt, the seller will remain secondarily liable unless it is able to obtain a release agreement from the lender (a form of "novation").

In most cases, however, the purchaser will arrange third-party financing from some institutional lender and the seller will use the sale proceeds to satisfy the existing clause that specifies the minimum financing requirements of the purchaser; for example, "a mortgage in the amount of no less than $ _____ at an interest rate of no more than _____%, with a fully amortized term of no less than _____ years." By contrast, the seller's attorney should resist any such open-ended contingency clause and might insist, for example, that the purchaser accept any mortgage loan from an institutional lender as long as the interest rate does not exceed the market rate and the loan amount covers the minimum financing needs of the purchaser. See generally Payne, Mortgage Contingency Clauses, 19 Real Est. L.J. 249 (1991) (explaining the risks to the seller of an open-ended contingency that requires a mortgage loan of "at least" or "not less than" a specified amount). The seller's attorney should also demand that the mortgage commitment be obtained within a reasonable period of time and ensure that the contract contains an exact mortgage contingency date. The purchaser's attorney should ensure the mortgage contingency date allows a reasonable amount of time to obtain a mortgage commitment and that the purchaser's mortgage contingency is deemed satisfied only upon obtaining a written *unconditional* mortgage commitment. If there is any doubt about the credit worthiness of the purchaser, the purchaser should be required to submit financials before the contract is executed; otherwise, valuable time might be wasted on a purchaser who is unable to obtain the necessary financing. In some jurisdictions, especially for residential sales, it is common for purchasers to submit a purchase offer along with a pre-approval letter from an institutional lender. Pre-approval letters provide attorneys with the details necessary to verify whether the mortgage contingency clause contains correct information, such as the amount of the loan, loan type, interest rate, etc.

Another option is seller financing. In seller financing, the seller funds the noncash portion of the purchase price by means of a purchase money mortgage. This technique is discussed at Chapter 7B3.

b. Development Approval Contingency. Developers purchasing raw land often demand a contingency clause that enables them to withdraw from the contract if they are unable to procure certain development approvals (for example, approval to subdivide into smaller parcels, zoning variances) from the relevant governmental authorities. Baldasarre v. Butler, infra, illustrates this contingency. As seller's counsel, how would you address the concern that the purchaser might manipulate a development contingency if it should have "buyer's remorse"?

Sometimes a contingency clause that appears innocuous on its face can cause problems for the parties. Suppose, for example, that a contract of sale is conditioned on a county's grant of a sewer allocation for the lots being sold, a contingency that is beyond the control of the parties. Can you think of any rule of law that you learned in first-year property that might render such a contract of sale unenforceable? See Dorado Ltd. Partnership v. Broadneck Dev. Corp., 317 Md. 148, 562 A.2d 757 (1989). Also, consider development contingency language that is so broad that it effectively allows the purchaser to unilaterally terminate the contract in its sole discretion. With language so broad, the right to terminate is not really a contingency to the contract but an option right afforded to the purchaser. See Steiner v. Thexton, 48 Cal.4th 411, 226 P.3d 359, 106 Cal.Rptr.3d 252 (2010). The peculiar facts of *Steiner* included a seller that sought to get out of a real estate deal to sell 12 acres to a developer by arguing that the broad language of the development contingency amounted to an option to purchase and the developer never paid for this option or provided any other consideration for the option right. Without consideration the deal must be deemed illusory. The trial court agreed; however, on appeal, the developer successfully argued that its part performance in pursuing the development, including spending $60,000 seeking county and municipal approvals of parcel splits of the land, represented valid consideration and made the recognized option irrevocable as to the developer.

c. Right of Inspection. Absent language to the contrary, the doctrine of caveat emptor applies. This means that unless the seller (or its agents) makes misrepresentations about the condition of the premises or fails to disclose latent defects known to the seller and not to the purchaser, the risk of any preexisting defect will be borne by the purchaser. See M. Friedman, Contracts and Conveyances of Real Property §2:12 (7th ed. 2005). Consequently, it is essential that the purchaser have the right to inspect the property and that the parties agree on what representations and warranties, if any, the seller will make with respect to the condition of the premises, whether the seller's promises will survive the closing of the transaction, and what remedies will be afforded to the purchaser in the event those promises are breached. Depending on the bargaining clout of the parties, the contract may provide for an "as is" sale, in which event the onus is on the purchaser to make a thorough inspection before it executes the contract. At the other end of the spectrum is a purchaser-oriented provision whereby the seller not only warrants in detail the condition of the premises but also agrees that the warranties shall survive the closing date. How does the language in §5 of the sample sale agreement in the Documents Manual strike a delicate balance between the foregoing approaches? The language in §5 presupposes, as is frequently the case, that the purchaser's inspection will not be completed until after the contract is executed. Doesn't this language provide the purchaser with a mere option to purchase the property and a handy pretext for "buyer's remorse"? If so, can you think of any drafting approach that protects the seller?

Typically, the purchaser's inspection will extend beyond the structural condition of the property to include such due diligence as (1) reviewing permits and licenses necessary for operation of the property, (2) confirming that the property and the buyer's intended use comply with zoning laws and building codes (often the seller will be asked to warrant such compliance), (3) inspecting the property for environmental contamination (see Chapter 19), and (4) reviewing financial information with respect to property income and expenses. For a comprehensive discussion of these studies and model language for seller representations and warranties with regard to these areas of concern, see Wayte, Purchase and Sale of Real Property, in Modern Real Estate Transactions (ALI-ABA 1990).

d. Risk of Loss. Closely related to the inspection clause is one that addresses which party should bear the risk of any casualty or condemnation loss before the closing date. As noted above, the majority rule places the onus on the purchaser by reason of the doctrine of equitable conversion unless the parties agree otherwise. See Friedman §4.8; Madison, The Real Properties of Contract Law, 82 B.U. L. Rev. 405, 435 (2002). By contrast, the approach taken by §1 of the Uniform Vendor and Purchaser Risk Act is that, absent language to the contrary, the party in possession bears the risk of loss because that party not only reaps the beneficial use of the property but normally is in a better position to protect the real estate against casualty loss and to keep the premises insured pending the closing date. The foregoing approach is sensible, and it explains why most contracts will shift the risk of loss to the seller, who in the case of an ordinary contract (as opposed to an installment land contract discussed infra at Chapter 3D) usually retains possession until the transaction closes.

As Dan's legal advisor, what do you think of the language in §9 of the sample sale agreement? Suppose that, in the case of a partial destruction or condemnation of the premises, Sarah's mortgage does not require that the insurance or condemnation award proceeds be used for restoration but instead allows the lender to reduce the loan balance with the proceeds. See Chapter 5A6. If this is the case, what alternative language might you suggest that should be reasonably acceptable to Sarah's attorney? In §9 an arbitrary loss amount is used to differentiate between a partial and a total casualty loss so that Sarah can extricate herself from the contract if the loss should exceed $10,000 (even though the restoration work might not substantially interfere with her use of the property). Can you think of a more flexible approach?

e. Time Is of the Essence. In most jurisdictions the times for performance of the seller's and purchaser's obligations will not be strictly enforced, and a court of equity will grant relief notwithstanding a delay in performance by either the purchaser or the seller—unless the parties stipulate that time is of the essence.

See American Law of Property §11.45. Moreover, there is case law allowing the seller a reasonable time beyond the closing date to remove an encumbrance or curable defect to render the title marketable, absent a time-is-of-the-essence clause in the contract. See Friedman § 4A:10.2.

Observe that §11.1 of the sample sale agreement stipulates that time is of the essence. Moreover, in most states, contracts for the sale of single-family residences usually stipulate that time is of the essence. What risks does this language pose for your purchaser client? What about Sarah? Can you envision any special circumstances that might prompt either Dan or Sarah to assume such a risk?

f. Assignment of the Contract. Absent language to the contrary, a contract for the sale of real estate is assignable by the buyer without the seller's consent. See Friedman §6.1. Can you think of any reasons why Sarah might require that any assignment be subject to her approval? See §11.8 of the sample sale agreement.

g. The Doctrine of Merger. As noted earlier, regardless of which kind of deed is stipulated in the contract of sale, under the doctrine of merger the purchaser's acceptance of the deed discharges most of the seller's obligations under the contract, including the duty to deliver marketable title (see infra Chapter 2A3). Thereafter, the purchaser's sole recourse against the seller must be based on the covenants (if any) contained in the deed. See Friedman §8:18; Madison at 428-435. However, this rule (like most others) applies absent language to the contrary. Accordingly, from the perspective of the purchaser, what contractual obligations and warranties should be made to survive the closing date?

h. Other Important Provisions and Documents. Drafting approaches to conveyance deeds, default provisions and exceptions to marketable title are discussed separately below. In addition, the sale agreement should include and address definitions; the legal description of the real estate and accompanying personalty; title examination and insurance; the date, place, and mechanics for closing the transaction; prorations of rents, ad valorem taxes, and insurance premiums; tenant security deposits; employees of the seller; transfer of existing insurance policies; bills of sale to convey personalty; brokerage liability; and notices to suppliers and creditors. See generally Hastie, Contracts for Disposition of Commercial Properties, in ALI-ABA, 1 Modern Real Estate Transactions 371 (7th ed. 1986); Taylor, Some Agreement of Sale Basics (with Forms), 4 Prac. Real Est. Law. 69 (May 1988).

2. Purchase Options. As an alternative to investigating the development potential of the property and seeking development approvals during the executory period of a purchase contract, Dan Developer might obtain the option to purchase the property at a fixed price at a future time when he is satisfied as to these matters. Options are useful in other circumstances, such as in connection with sale-and-leaseback transactions. See Chapter 11C. From the perspective of the optionee's (Dan's) counsel, the option contract must address such issues as the effect of the optionor's inability to convey good title because of a defect that originates after the option agreement is executed, and whether the option survives the death of any of the parties. Moreover, the option agreement must be structured to avoid any applicable rule against perpetuities. See Symphony Space v. Pergola Properties, 88 N.Y.2d 466, 669 N.E.2d 799, 646 N.Y.S.2d 641 (1996) (invalidating repurchase option in sale-and-leaseback agreement operative from 1978 until 2003). From the perspective of both parties, the well-drafted option agreement will resemble a purchase agreement (which may, in fact, be attached as an exhibit) because the parties will not want to leave the details of the purchase (for example, nature of the deed, warranties) to later negotiation.

3. Attorney Approval Provisions. In the last 20 years or so, the tension between real estate brokers and real estate attorneys over their respective roles in the representation of mutual clients has caused brokers to better accommodate the place of attorneys in real estate transactions. Today, residential real estate transactions in many regions of the country rely on broker's contract forms that include "attorney approval" or "attorney modification" provisions. Although brokers continue to be the driving force behind residential transactions, the forms used by brokers may allow input from the respective attorneys for the parties after an agreement is reached in principle. See Stark, Navigating Residential Attorney Approvals: Finding a Better Judicial North Star, 39 J. Marshall L. Rev. 171 (2006). The effect of these provisions, however, is not without controversy. Their intent may be to allow attorneys to "tweak" legal terms in the contract that may have been overlooked by the parties and the brokers at the outset of the negotiations, but is there any reason why an attorney could not attempt to materially change the agreement of the parties or, more significantly, assert the disapproval of the entire deal on behalf of one of the parties? A recent appellate case has confirmed this power by overruling a trial court to the dismay of a seller who thought he had been in a binding deal with a buyer and successfully brought suit for breach of contract to win over $200,000 in damages. Moran v. Erk, 11 N.Y.3d 452, 901 N.E.2d 187 (2008) (where a real estate contract contains an attorney approval contingency allowing a specific amount of time for an attorney approval without any further limitations, an attorney for either party may timely disapprove the contract for any reason or for no stated reason). If the attorney approval provision grants this power to the attorney, do the parties, in fact, have a deal when they sign the sales contract with these provisions? In the same way that other contract contingencies (e.g., inspection or financing) can become safety valves for a remorseful buyer, does the attorney approval provision represent the ultimate trump card that allows a party out of a deal for no reason at all? Typically these provisions allow only a short window (perhaps 3 or 5 business days) within which an attorney may act. Real estate brokers and parties to residential real estate transactions may simply now be accustomed to the fact that a deal is not really a deal until the attorney approval period has ended.

PRACTITIONER'S CORNER

Good Drafting

The sample sale agreement in the Documents Manual is relatively free of legalese. On the benefits of and techniques for removing legalese and other drafting flaws from real estate contracts, see:

Buckley, Good Writing for Real Estate Lawyers, 5 Prac. Real Est. Law. 39 (July 1989) (observing that the author had yet to see a contract invalidated or questioned because it did not contain the word *Witnesseth*; see the first page of the sample sale agreement).

Buckley, Improving Your Writing Is Worth the Effort, 5 Prac. Real Est. Law. 51 (Sept. 1989) (advising, among other things, that there is no need to specify zero cents in a contractual dollar figure, such as in §2.1 of the sample sale agreement ($50,000.00)).

H. Darmstadter, Hereof, Thereof, and Everywhereof: A Contrarian Guide to Legal Drafting (2002).

THE ETHICAL REAL ESTATE LAWYER

Dual Representation

Consider the following case that illustrates the disastrous ethical and tort consequences of a lawyer assuming representation of both seller and purchaser in the same transaction.

Baldasarre v. Butler

254 N.J. Super. 502, 604 A.2d 112 (Super. Ct. App. Div. 1992)

HAVEY, J. A. D.

... On appeal, plaintiffs contend that (1) their attorney, defendant William B. Butler, Esq., engaged in a conflict of interest by representing them and DiFrancesco in the subject real estate transaction. ...

Bernice M. Baldasarre and Margaret M. Neumann [plaintiffs] are surviving daughters of Arthur Santucci, who died in 1982. Butler and his law firm represented the Santucci estate and also represented plaintiffs and their respective spouses in various real estate transactions and third-party disputes. As beneficiaries of the Santucci estate, plaintiffs inherited a 40.55 acre tract in Warren Township, Somerset County, zoned for single-family residential use, and a contiguous parcel in Watchung Borough.

During the years 1986 and 1987, plaintiffs received offers to purchase the Warren Township tract, ranging from $60,000 to $117,000 per building lot, subject to subdivision approval. In most instances, plaintiffs discussed the offers with Butler, and for a variety of reasons each offer was rejected by plaintiffs. One of the offers was made by PML Associates, a partnership which included a local developer, Charles Messano.

According to Mrs. Neumann, at a meeting in early February 1987, Butler told plaintiffs that his client, DiFrancesco, a local real estate developer and brother of Butler's law partner, had offered to purchase the property at $100,000 per lot. Plaintiffs demanded $110,000 per lot, payable in cash with no mortgage contingency. According to Butler, plaintiffs had asked him to make an inquiry of his clients as to whether there was an interest in acquiring the tract. . . .

Butler thereafter discussed plaintiffs' proposal with DiFrancesco, who expressed an interest in purchasing the property at the $110,000 figure. He advised Butler he would pay a $50,000 deposit, and insisted upon the right to assign the agreement. He also asked Butler to represent him during the transaction and in obtaining subdivision approval.

Butler conveyed DiFrancesco's offer to plaintiffs, and explained to them the meaning of a buyer's right to assign the agreement. He also told plaintiffs that he had represented DiFrancesco in the past. According to Butler, he explained that if plaintiffs objected to him representing DiFrancesco, he would not do so. On February 6, 1987, DiFrancesco delivered the $50,000 deposit to Butler and signed the agreement as well as a "conflict of interest" letter prepared by Butler.

On February 9, 1987, Butler again met with plaintiffs and presented the proposed agreement to them. The agreement provided for a purchase price of $2,200,000 computed based on 20 subdivided lots. It was subject to DiFrancesco obtaining preliminary major subdivision approval of at least "15 sewered single family building lots" within six months, and provided that if DiFrancesco "has been moving . . . expeditiously," he was given 90 additional days to obtain approval. This subdivision contingency, however, was waivable by DiFrancesco. The agreement also provided the following: The Buyer may assign the within contract. In the event of assignment, the Buyer shall remain individually liable to satisfy all the obligations of the Buyer as set forth in this contract.

According to Butler, he explained to plaintiffs each paragraph of the agreement in detail as well as the potential conflicts of interest raised by various terms in the event he represented both plaintiffs and DiFrancesco. He also presented to plaintiffs a conflict of interest letter which disclosed his prior representation of DiFrancesco, his intent to represent DiFrancesco in the transaction and before the planning board, and that DiFrancesco was his law partner's brother. The letter also stated that plaintiffs had instructed Butler to find a purchaser for the property and acknowledged that the $110,000 per lot price was fair and reasonable. Butler testified that he suggested plaintiffs take the agreement and conflict of interest letter to another attorney "for independent advice and consultation" and plaintiffs rejected the suggestion. On February 12, 1987, plaintiffs signed the agreement and conflict of interest letter. It is undisputed that the purchase price was adjusted to $1,980,000 based on DiFrancesco's application to the planning board for an 18-lot, rather than 20-lot subdivision. It also is stipulated that the $1,980,000 price was "fair and reasonable" as of the date of the agreement.

On April 9, 1987, DiFrancesco entered into a written agreement with Messano Construction Co., Inc. (Messano), Charles Messano's company, to sell the subject property to Messano at a price of $3,600,000, based on $200,000 per subdivided lot. The agreement was contingent upon DiFrancesco closing with plaintiffs and his obtaining preliminary major subdivision approval within 18 months. It also included a "Confidentiality" clause, prohibiting Messano from entering the property and listing or advertising the property for sale during the term of the agreement. The agreement stated that the purpose of the clause was "among other things, not to jeopardize" the subdivision application process. However, according to Messano, the clause was inserted because Butler and DiFrancesco did not want plaintiffs to know that DiFrancesco had assigned the agreement. Messano also testified that Butler said "it would be [Butler's] problem when [plaintiffs] did find out about it." Butler denied he made these statements, and testified that the central purpose of the clause was to prevent the planning board from knowing that someone other than DiFrancesco owned the property.

On various occasions during the spring and summer of 1987, plaintiffs met with Butler to execute planning board documents and to discuss the status of DiFrancesco's subdivision application. The Messano agreement was never mentioned. Butler conceded he never told either plaintiff directly about the Messano agreement at any time because he had no confidence in it. According to Butler, on May 20, 1987, he met with Constant Baldasarre, plaintiff Baldasarre's husband, on an unrelated matter and advised him of the Messano agreement and asked him to "relay" the information to plaintiffs. He testified that he assumed Mr. Baldasarre had conveyed the information to plaintiffs. Mr. Baldasarre denied that Butler told him about the Messano agreement.

Upon the expiration of the six-month period within which subdivision approval was to be obtained under the plaintiffs/DiFrancesco agreement, the contingency was extended for 90 days, or until November 12, 1987. However, some time in October 1987, DiFrancesco indicated to Butler that subdivision approval could not be obtained within the agreed-upon time period because of difficulties encountered before the various boards. He therefore asked Butler to obtain from plaintiffs an additional six-month extension of the subdivision contingency with an additional 90-day extension, if necessary. In return, DiFrancesco offered to release to plaintiffs the $50,000 deposit held in escrow.

On October 7, 1987, Butler met with plaintiffs to discuss the extension requested by DiFrancesco. Mrs. Neumann testified that plaintiffs resisted the extension because the value of the property "was escalating so fast." Butler admitted he did not tell plaintiffs of the Messano agreement at this meeting because it "didn't occur" to him to tell them. Also, it is uncontradicted that at the meeting Butler did not give plaintiffs advice about whether or not to sign the extension, but did advise them that DiFrancesco could either void the deal or waive the subdivision contingency and close title if the extension was not granted. DiFrancesco testified that if plaintiffs had refused to extend, he was ready and able to close title immediately. Plaintiffs discussed the extension between themselves and agreed to it. The $50,000 was thereupon released to them in consideration for the extension.

In early January 1988, Mrs. Neumann heard a "rumor" that the property had been "resold" by DiFrancesco. She immediately called Butler who again made no disclosure of the Messano agreement but instead recommended that plaintiffs attend a board of health meeting on January 12, 1988 and discuss the matter with DiFrancesco. While Butler was present during a conversation between Mrs. Neumann and DiFrancesco at that meeting, the Messano agreement was not mentioned.

In the latter part of January 1988, plaintiffs learned that DiFrancesco had sold the property and that Butler represented DiFrancesco in that transaction. . . .

On March 17, 1988, plaintiffs filed the present action against Butler, his law firm and DiFrancesco, seeking a rescission of their agreement with DiFrancesco, and compensatory and punitive damages. The gravamen of the complaint is that Butler and DiFrancesco had committed legal and equitable fraud by wrongfully withholding the existence of the Messano agreement from plaintiffs, thereby inducing them to grant the October 7, 1987 extension. Plaintiffs also claimed that Butler had violated his professional responsibility to plaintiffs and that Butler's law firm was jointly and severally liable for his conduct. . . .

I

Plaintiffs first argue that the trial court erred in finding that Butler had not violated standards of professional ethics in representing both plaintiffs and DiFrancesco during the subject real estate transaction. The court found that an attorney may undertake a multiple representation of parties in such a transaction "so long as certain standards are met," and that Butler had met such standards. We agree with plaintiffs that Butler's dual representation, under the circumstances, constituted a conflict of interest. We also agree that plaintiffs' execution of the "conflict of interest" letter did not cure the conflict and that Butler's dual representation was the genesis of the underlying dispute between the parties.

IRPC 1.7 entitled "Conflict of Interest: General Rule," provides in part as follows: (a) A lawyer shall not represent a client if the representation of that client will be directly adverse to another client unless: (1) the lawyer reasonably believes that representation will not adversely affect the relationship with the other client; and (2) each client consents after a full disclosure of the circumstances and consultation with the client, except that a public entity cannot consent to any such representation. (b) A lawyer shall not represent a client if the representation of that client may be materially limited by the lawyer's responsibilities to another client or to a third person, or by the lawyer's own interests, unless: (1) the lawyer reasonably believes the representation will not be adversely affected; and (2) the client consents after a full disclosure of the circumstances and consultation with the client, except that a public entity cannot consent to any such representation. When representation of multiple clients in a single matter is undertaken, the consultation shall include explanation of the implications of the common representation and the advantages and risks involved. (c) This rule shall not alter the effect of case law or ethics opinions to the effect that: (1) in certain cases or categories of cases involving conflicts or apparent conflicts, consent to continued representation is immaterial. . . .

In In re Kamp, 40 N.J. 588, 594, 194 A.2d 236 (1963), our Supreme Court held that an attorney who represented a developer-seller and the buyer in a single-family residential transaction violated Canon 6 of the Canons of Professional Ethics when the attorney failed to disclose to the buyer his relationship with the seller and failed to "explain in detail the pitfalls that may arise in the course of the transaction which would make it desirable that the buyer have independent counsel." Id. at 596, 194 A.2d 236. See also In re Dolan, 76 N.J. 1, 9, 384 A.2d 1076 (1978) ("[i]n a real estate transaction, the positions of vendor and purchaser are inherently susceptible to conflict"). By implication the Court in In re Kamp found no conflict of interest in dual representation, at least in a simple real estate transfer, where full disclosure is made of potential conflicts, the limited scope of the attorney's intended representation of the buyer's interest is communicated, and the advantages of the buyer retaining independent counsel are revealed. 40 N.J. at 596, 194 A.2d 236. Indeed, in In re Dolan, 76 N.J. at 12-13, 384 A.2d 1076, the Court declined to adopt the per se ruling urged by Justice Pashman in In re Lanza, 65 N.J. 347, 353, 322 A.2d 445 (1974) (Pashman, J., concurring), which would be a complete bar of dual representation, because the consequences of such a per se rule would leave "many prospective purchasers in marginal financial circumstances . . . without representation." In re Dolan, 76 N.J. at 13, 384 A.2d 1076. However, we do not read *Lanza* or *Dolan* as endorsing dual representation in all real estate transactions where full disclosure is made by the attorney. To the contrary, in both decisions the Court underscored the inherent dangers that loom in dual representation and suggests that it will be the unusual case that no conflict of interest will exist.

In In re Lanza, the Court again underscored the "pitfalls that await an attorney representing both buyer and seller in a real estate transaction." Citing the Advisory Committee on Professional Ethics, Opinion 243, 95 N.J.L.J. 1145 (1972), the Court noted that "in all circumstances it is unethical for the same attorney to represent buyer and seller in *negotiating* the terms of a contract of sale." In re Lanza, 65 N.J. at 352, 322 A.2d 445. . . . Opinion 243 states that:

> Generally, it is at this stage of negotiations for the sale of property that a buyer and a seller have their greatest difficulties. Their interests are in conflict if for no other reason than the buyer wishes to obtain the property as cheaply as possible and the seller wishes to get the highest price. At this juncture, also, there can and frequently do arise disputes concerning fixtures to be left in the premises, assumption of

mortgages, mortgage contingencies, and other matters in which there can be serious disagreements, in all of which the interests of the buyer and seller will be diametrically opposed. . . .

We, therefore, conclude that . . . the representation of a buyer and a seller in connection with the preparation and execution of a contract of sale of real property is so fraught with obvious situations where a conflict may arise that one attorney shall not undertake to represent both parties in such a situation. . . .

We are satisfied that this is one of the "certain cases" contemplated by RPC 1.7 which made plaintiffs' execution of the "conflict of interest" letter "immaterial." Butler's dual representation of the parties during the negotiations of this complex transaction plainly ignored and violated the admonition in *Lanza* and Opinion 243 that "it is unethical for the same attorney to represent buyer and seller in negotiating the terms of a contract of sale." In re Lanza, 65 N.J. at 352, 322 A.2d 445. While it is true that the purchase price was not the subject of negotiation, other provisions of the agreement were fraught with potential conflicts. The $50,000 deposit, the figure offered by DiFrancesco, was agreed to by plaintiffs without any apparent effort on Butler's part to negotiate a higher figure. Although DiFrancesco demanded the right to assign the agreement without plaintiffs' consent, Butler could have demanded on plaintiffs' behalf that DiFrancesco at least give notice to plaintiffs of such assignment. Such notice would no doubt have prevented the present dispute. Also, during the pendency of the agreement, questions may have arisen as to whether DiFrancesco had pursued planning board approval "expeditiously," thereby giving him the right to the additional 90-day extension. A question may also have arisen as to the reasonableness of the number of lots DiFrancesco applied for, or whether title being conveyed by plaintiffs was marketable. In short, we cannot conclude that plaintiffs had shed their right to undivided loyalty during the negotiation of this complex agreement simply because they executed the conflict of interest letter and Butler had alerted them to the potential conflicts.

In any event, whatever may be said about Butler's initial representation of the parties, we are convinced that during the October 7, 1987, meeting with plaintiffs, when the extension of the subdivision contingency was discussed, Butler had an absolute duty to advise plaintiffs of the existence of the Messano agreement. At this point, Butler's representation of plaintiffs was "materially limited by [his] responsibilities to another client," DiFrancesco, and his failure to disclose plainly violated the letter and spirit of RPC 1.7. DiFrancesco needed more time to obtain subdivision approval in order to keep the Messano agreement alive and reap the approximate $1.6 million profit if that agreement was consummated. Thus, it was in DiFrancesco's best interest that Butler not disclose the Messano agreement to plaintiffs since such disclosure no doubt would have induced plaintiffs not to grant the extension.

On the other hand, it was in plaintiffs' best interest that Butler disclose the existence of the Messano agreement, since disclosure would have confirmed their belief that the value of the property had escalated and they were better off refusing the extension and seeking another buyer in the open market.

Alternatively, had plaintiffs known of the Messano agreement they may have insisted, with good reason, on a greater consideration for the extension than simply release of the $50,000 deposit. This option was never discussed, or even mentioned by Butler. Further, had DiFrancesco waived the subdivision contingency upon plaintiffs' refusal to extend, plaintiffs were at least entitled to an immediate closing of title and receipt of the entire $1,930,000 balance of the purchase price.

. . . In our view, Butler found himself in a position of conflicting loyalties during the October 7, 1987, meeting and his failure to disclose the Messano agreement constituted a conflict of interest which clearly compromised plaintiffs' rights.

II

Plaintiffs next argue that Butler's conduct constituted fraud. [T]he evidence is compelling that Butler intentionally withheld from plaintiffs the existence of the Messano agreement despite his duty as plaintiffs' attorney to disclose this material fact. . . .

We conclude that plaintiffs have clearly and convincingly established the elements of both legal and equitable fraud against Butler, and therefore he and his law firm are liable to plaintiffs for [compensatory and punitive] damages. . . .

Before the New Jersey Supreme Court heard Butler's appeal, Butler and his law firm settled with the sellers. In deciding issues remaining between the sellers and DiFrancesco, the New Jersey Supreme Court was prompted by Butler's conduct to establish a new standard of professional responsibility in commercial real estate transactions:

> This case graphically demonstrates the conflicts that arise when an attorney, even with both clients' consent, undertakes the representation of the buyer and the seller in a complex commercial real estate transaction. The disastrous consequences of Butler's dual representation convinces us that a new bright-line rule prohibiting dual representation is necessary in commercial real estate transactions where large sums of money are at stake, where contracts contain complex contingencies, or where options are numerous. The potential for conflict in that type of complex real estate transaction is too great to permit even consensual dual representation of buyer and seller. Therefore, we hold that an attorney may not represent both the buyer and the seller in a complex commercial real estate transaction even if both give their informed consent.

Baldasarre v. Butler, 132 N.J. 278, 625 A.2d 458, 467 (1993) (holding that DiFrancesco had no duty to inform the sellers about the Messano agreement nor was he vicariously liable for his attorney's fraud in this dual client/agency relationship).

NOTES AND QUESTIONS

1. Dual Representation of Sellers and Purchasers. Generally, rules of professional conduct permit lawyers to represent multiple parties if the lawyer believes that the representation will not adversely affect the exercise of professional judgment as to the interests of each client and the clients consent after full disclosure of the potential conflicts. See generally Sanford, Ethical, Statutory, and Regulatory Conflicts of Interest in Real Estate Transactions, 17 St. Mary's L.J. 79 (1985). The *Baldasarre* case illustrates that consent is not always effective to shield the lawyer from liability. Although the New Jersey Supreme Court limited its per se rule against dual representation to complex commercial real estate transactions, at least one commentator has urged that lawyers avoid any dual representation in residential sales. See Bolus, Comment, One for All Is Worth Two in the Bush: Mixing Metaphors Creates Lawyer Conflict of Interest Problems in Residential Real Estate Transactions, 56 U. Cin. L. Rev. 639 (1987). Because courts tend to be more paternalistic in the residential setting due to the lesser sophistication of the parties, can you justify the state Supreme Court's restriction of its holding in *Baldasarre* to complex commercial deals?

2. Business Advice Revisited. At one point the *Baldasarre* decision suggests that independent counsel for the seller might have negotiated for a higher earnest money deposit than $50,000 (approximately 2.5 percent of the purchase price). The earnest money deposit typically serves as the seller's liquidated damages on the purchaser's breach (see Chapter 2A5, infra). Should the seller's lawyer be responsible for advising on the adequacy or inadequacy of this deposit?

3. Attorneys as Brokers. In regulating real estate brokers, most states exclude licensed attorneys from their real estate licensing requirements. If the local custom is for the seller's broker to split its commission with any broker that locates a buyer, can a buyer claim that its lawyer is also its broker and thereby pocket half the commission? Although some courts have read these licensing exemptions expansively to allow attorneys to recover commissions without a broker's license, New Jersey's Supreme Court concluded that its statute did not contemplate the lawyer's recovery of any commission whether or not it was kicked back to the client. See In re Roth, 120 N.J. 665, 577 A.2d 490 (1990). See generally Sawyer, When Does an Attorney Need a Real Estate License?, 17 J. Legal Prof. 329 (1992). Is there any conflict of interest that arises if a lawyer can both charge for legal services and collect and keep a real estate commission? What if the lawyer obtains a broker's license? See generally Mortland, Attorneys as Real Estate Brokers: Ethical Considerations, 25 Real Prop., Prob. & Tr. J. 755 (1991).

4. Anti-Flip. Mortgage fraud was at epidemic levels during the housing boom in 2004 and 2005. One variety practiced on lenders—flipping schemes—required the cooperation or negligence of appraisers. In 2006, the FBI reported that 80 percent of all reported mortgage fraud losses involved some collaboration or collusion by industry insiders such as mortgage brokers and appraisers. A hypothetical flip scheme might involve one or more immediate resales of the property among conspiring parties at inflated prices financed by mortgage lenders who rely on inflated appraisals. Without the complicity of an insider loan appraiser, the flip scheme might rely on appraiser negligence by selecting for purchase (and flip) a property with structural, design, aesthetic, or other issues that will appraise on paper based on neighborhood comparable properties at an amount far exceeding the asking price. Although lenders can curtail this abuse by requiring the appraiser to physically visit the property, there are many other variations on the flip scam that leave the lender with undervalued properties and abandoning borrowers. With the involvement of dishonest appraisers, or by using a falsified appraisal and other loan qualification documents, more pernicious flipping schemes also operate with the same design to procure funding of a hugely inflated purchase price. The *Baldasarre* case involved a resale during the executory phase of the purchase contract, but it did not appear designed to generate the fraudulent appearance of value—rather, it reflected rapid appreciation of the property as its development potential unfolded. Many real estate investors, particularly in the condominium market, purchase property on speculation with the hope that, before the property is constructed, the property will appreciate to an extent that they can resell their ownership interest at a substantial profit. The entry fee for the speculation game is whatever down payment is required to hold the unit until its completion. Remember this background when you confront the *Uzan* ("Trump Tower") case later in this Chapter. Some condominium and home builders have tried to discourage flip transactions by inserting anti-flip clauses in the purchase contracts that prohibit resale for a specified period of time (e.g., one year). Can you think of any potential legal constraints on the enforceability of an anti-flip clause? Why would the developer care to discourage flip resale transactions?

5. Seller Concessions. Another variety of defrauding lenders and investors in securitization resale markets (see Chapter 15) involves so-called seller concessions. Take, for example, a seller who lists property at $500,000. A buyer offers $600,000, but with a side agreement that the seller will return $100,000 at close of escrow. The mortgage lender assumes the sale is for $600,000, and the loan is a likely candidate for foreclosure because the buyer may have no intention of ever making a payment; the buyer may take the $100,000 and disappear. In the housing market heyday of the mid-2000s, some lenders would even finance 100 percent of the purchase price, helping fuel these schemes. Consider the liability of the seller's or buyer's attorney to the mortgage lender left holding a mortgage on property worth less than the loan amount. Is there any responsibility to disclose the kickback at closing? What if the lawyer came into the transaction after the purchase contract and the side agreement were signed and merely acted as a closing attorney to facilitate the closing of the transaction? What if the kickback arises not from some predetermined scheme, but from a repair credit agreed to by the buyer following a home inspection that revealed structural problems with the property? Should the mortgage lender and the appraiser bear the responsibility for ensuring the value of the collateral to support the loan amount? See In re Labendz, 95 N.J. 273, 471 A.2d 21 (1984) (suspending lawyer for buyer who overstated sale price to lender so that buyer could obtain a larger loan); In re Opinion 710 of the Advisory Committee on Professional Ethics, 193 N.J. 419, 939 A.2d 794 (2008) (deeming it unethical for lawyer to assist in a seller's concession or kickback scheme except for "legal and legitimate" costs otherwise absorbed by the buyer, such as actual closing costs, but not addressing the lawyer's responsibility where the kickback is agreed to before the lawyer enters the transaction).

3. Marketable Title

In the absence of language to the contrary, the purchaser by implication is entitled to receive on or before the closing date a title that is free of record defects and encumbrances (such as leases, easements, mortgages and other liens, and restrictive covenants) that might adversely affect the full enjoyment and ownership of the property. The rationale for this doctrine of marketable title is that a purchaser should not be compelled to accept a title that may subject it to the hazard and expense of future litigation.[7] However, the requirement that title be marketable is governed by a standard of reasonableness: Title must be "free from reasonable doubt both as to matters of law and fact, a title which a reasonable purchaser, well informed as to the facts and their legal bearings and willing and ready to perform his contract, would, in the exercise of that prudence which business[people] ordinarily bring to bear upon such transactions, be willing to accept and ought to accept." American Law of Property §11.48; see generally Friedman §4.1. Thus, the marketability standard does not assure title free from any doubt. Rather, it assures against "defects in title that are more than simply possible or very remote."[8]

Like many definitional standards, the foregoing reasonable purchaser rule is abstract and leaves certain questions unresolved. For example, when confronted with a cloud on the title, how bleak must the worst-case scenario be before the purchaser can prudently abandon the bargain? If title is unmarketable, does the buyer have an action against the seller for loss of its bargain?[9] Does the buyer's willingness to accept a quitclaim deed (see Chapter 2A4, infra) waive its right to receive marketable title?[10] To what extent can a record defect in the seller's chain

---

7. See, e.g., Messer-Johnson Realty Co. v. Security Sav. & Loan Co., 208 Ala. 541, 94 So. 734 (1922).

8. In re Oyster Bar Cove, Ltd., 161 B.R. 338, 344 (Bankr. E.D.N.Y. 1993).

9. See generally J. Calamari & J. Perillo, Contracts §14-30 (4th ed. 1998) (noting the conflicting authorities).

10. Compare Wallach v. Riverside Bank, 206 N.Y. 434, 100 N.E. 50 (1912), with McManus v. Blackmarr, 47 Minn. 331, 50 N.W. 230 (1891).

of title be rendered obsolete because of adverse possession by the seller or one of its predecessors in title?[11] When must title be marketable in the case of an installment land contract, where the seller may not deliver the title for a number of years?[12] These are but some of the many questions that the doctrine of marketable title provokes.

The following case illustrates the fact-specific analysis of whether a particular defect renders title sufficiently imperfect (or in doubt) to enable a purchaser to reject the seller's title and refuse to perform under the sale agreement.

Van Vliet & Place, Inc. v. Gaines
249 N.Y. 106, 162 N.E. 600 (1928)

O'BRIEN, J.

[W]hen the time for closing arrived, a covenant embraced in a deed of the premises executed in the year 1834 and unknown both to the owner and to the broker . . . caused the prospective purchaser to refuse to take title. This covenant provides that if, at any time, the grantee, his heirs or assigns, should permit upon vitriol, turpentine, a tannery, blacksmith shop, forge, or furnace, or any other occupation usually deemed unwholesome, noxious, or offensive, "then said premises and every part thereof shall revert to said party of the first part and their heirs. . . . "

The possibility of reverter included in this covenant renders the title unmarketable. In view of the existence of statutes and ordinances which prohibit the maintenance of most of the objectionable structures enumerated in the deed, the ordinary covenant against nuisances has in recent years lost much of its force. Yet, even in populous cities, a blacksmith shop or a forge has not been wholly outlawed. The expression "any other occupation usually deemed . . . offensive" has been interpreted to include many which do not amount to a nuisance. The improbability that facts may some time arise to call the possibility of reverter into actual being will not create marketability in a title where it does not otherwise inhere. The contingencies are not so improbable that they can be totally disregarded. We cannot say as [a] matter of law that they are mere theoretical possibilities. . . . The record does not tell us whether these residential premises are located in a zone restricted to residential use. If they are so situated, changes may occur by which the district may be relegated to a business or mixed use. The

---

11. Compare Conklin v. Davi, 76 N.J. 468, 388 A.2d 598 (1978), with Messer-Johnson Realty Co. v. Security Sav. & Loan Co., 208 Ala. 541, 94 So. 734 (1922). See Friedman §4.5. What might the seller do of its own accord to render the title marketable? See N.Y. Real Prop. Acts. Law §1501.

12. See Luette v. Bank of Italy Natl. Trust & Sav. Ass'n, 42 F.2d 9 (9th Cir.), cert. denied, 282 U.S. 884 (1930) ("there can be no rescission by a vendee of an executory [installment land] contract of sale merely because of lack of title in the vendor prior to the date when performance is due," i.e., the date that the buyer has completed its installment payments of the purchase price and the seller is therefore required to convey title).

possibility of a change in the zoning ordinance cannot be said to be too remote for practical consideration. The penalty for a violation of this covenant goes beyond payment of money or subjection to an injunction: the title reverts to the heirs of the vendors of 1834. This is not the ordinary covenant against nuisances. It seems to be quite unusual. A prudent purchaser may not be labeled as unduly cautious when he refuses such a title. He would encounter difficulty in obtaining a loan or in conveying title. He would be under no obligation to assume risks of the drastic nature manifested by this covenant. A reasonable doubt as to the title is sufficient to authorize its rejection. . . .

In addition to their concern over liability for the cleanup of any preexisting hazardous waste contamination, purchasers (particularly those of undeveloped land) are wary of the presence of wetlands.[13] The presence of wetlands will trigger a complicated regime of federal and state law under which the property's development potential may be limited, made contingent on the developer's payment to wetland mitigation banks, or prohibited altogether. As addressed in Chapter 19B, the existence of hazardous waste contamination does not render title unmarketable. Similarly, the following case illustrates that the implied covenant of marketable title provides no comfort if the sale agreement fails to specifically address the subject of wetlands.

McMaster v. Strickland
305 S.C. 527, 409 S.E.2d 440 (1991)

SHAW, Judge.

Appellant-sellers, McMaster, Fishburne and Martin, brought this action against respondent-purchaser, Strickland, for breach of a contract to purchase certain property. From an order of the court in favor of the purchaser, the sellers appeal. We reverse and remand.

The purchaser entered into a contract of sale with the sellers on October 2, 1987 to purchase a .74 acre lot in North Myrtle Beach for $50,000. Prior to execution of the contract, the parties negotiated the terms of the contract. It was made clear during these negotiations that the purchaser intended to use the property for homesites, that the property was low and wet, and in order to fill the wet property, permits from regulatory agencies would be required. The purchaser, a realtor, first became involved with this property after a friend who was negotiating for the property decided to "back away" from it because of the wetlands situation. The purchaser believed he could obtain the permits and

---

13. See generally Sokolove and Thompson, The Future of Wetland Regulation Is Here, 23 Real Est. L.J. 78 (1994).

therefore went on with negotiations in place of his friend. Before he signed the contract, the purchaser's friend informed him that the Corps of Engineers had told the friend that the property in question was wetlands.

The contract at hand contains the following pertinent terms:

> 2. Conveyance. The conveyance of the aforesaid real property shall be subject to all easements, reservations, rights-of-way, restrictions, encroachments, and covenants of record which may affect the above described property, and all governmental statutes, ordinances, rules and regulations. . . .
>
> 5. Date of Conveyance. Sellers agree to convey the real property by marketable title and deliver a proper warranty deed . . . which transaction shall close on or before January 1, 1988. . . .
>
> 9. Title Condition. The Sellers represent as to the real property described above that their title is good and marketable and insurable by a title insurance company reasonably acceptable to Purchaser.
>
> 10. Representations by Purchaser. Purchaser represents and warrants that Purchaser has inspected Sellers' premises and knows it[s] physical condition. Purchaser represents and warrants that Purchaser has not relied upon any representations by Sellers as to the premises. Purchaser further agrees to accept the real property set forth herein in an "as is" condition. . . .
>
> 16. Disclaimer. It is expressly understood and agreed that Sellers make no representations, expressed or implied, about the fitness or condition of this property or any improvements thereon, that any such implied representations are hereby expressly disclaimed, and that the Purchaser takes the property, after full inspection, as it is.

On December 23, 1987, a biologist with the Army Corps of Engineers inspected the property in question and on January 19, 1988 sent a letter to the North Myrtle Beach Building Inspector stating the entire .74 acre lot would be classified as wetlands. On December 27, 1987, the purchaser notified the sellers that he did not intend to purchase the property. Sometime after the institution of this lawsuit, the purchaser applied for a permit to fill the lot. On January 25, 1988, the North Myrtle Beach Building Inspector wrote to advise him the property had been designated to be a wetlands area and therefore the grading and filling permit was denied.

After the hearing on this matter, the trial judge issued his order finding the purchaser's rejection of the contract was justified because the sellers could deliver neither marketable title nor insurable title. . . .

The sellers contend the trial judge erred in finding they could not deliver marketable title to the property based on the fact that the property was designated as wetlands rendering it useless and of no value. We agree. It is clear the trial judge confused the concepts of title and marketability with use and value. That is, there is no evidence that the sellers do not own the property, therefore they have title. Further, there is no evidence it was unlawful to sell the property, therefore it is legally, if not actually marketable.

While the purchaser may not be able to use the property for the purpose for which he sought, such does not mean the sellers cannot deliver marketable title.

This simply boils down to a case of the purchaser taking a calculated business risk. The fact that he is dissatisfied with the results will not excuse him from the contract without some condition stated in the contract allowing his refutation of the same. The record is clear that all parties, including the purchaser, were aware of the wetland nature of the property and the necessity of obtaining a permit to fill the property. Although the purchaser believed he would be successful on obtaining the necessary permits, no such contingency was placed in the contract. Neither was there any contingency that the purchaser be successful in borrowing funds on the property in question. In that there is no evidence the sellers were incapable of providing marketable title as required by the contract, we find the trial judge erred.

Further, there is no evidence whatsoever that the title to the property was not insurable. The record before us indicates title to the property is in fact insurable, albeit with exception taken to the fact the land has been designated as wetlands. The contract specifically provides that the property is subject to all governmental statutes, ordinances, rules and regulations. This would include wetlands laws and regulations. The fact that exception would have to be taken when insuring the title is irrelevant since such was contemplated by the contract. . . .

For the foregoing reasons, we find the purchaser was not entitled to rescission of the contract. The purchaser admitted he simply made a mistake by signing a contract without certain conditions to protect him in the event he could not obtain the necessary permits. The function of courts is to adjudge and enforce contracts as they are written and entered into by the parties. When such contracts are capable of clear interpretation, the court cannot exercise its discretion as to the wisdom of such contract. . . .

The ambiguities of "marketable title" can be overcome by the parties to a real estate transaction in the language of the contract where, once again, the rules of property law found in statutes and common law are trumped by the intent of the parties. A contract between a buyer and seller could remain silent on the nature of the title to be conveyed, in which event the purchaser would be entitled to receive marketable title according to applicable law of the jurisdiction. This is generally not the approach taken in sophisticated transactions and presupposes an expectation on the part of the seller's attorney that any title problems can be resolved before the closing date.

A second approach is to provide for delivery of marketable fee simple title free and clear of any exceptions (title defects) that are not specified (as "Approved Title Exceptions") in the sale agreement. For example, see §§3 and 4.3.1 of the sample sale agreement in the Documents Manual. Under this approach, the seller's attorney designates in the contract (if possible, by reference to a recorded instrument) as exceptions to marketable title (1) those exceptions that showed up in Schedule B of the seller's standard American Land Title

Association's (ALTA) owner's policy (see Chapter 2B, infra) when the seller acquired title, and (2) any new easements, restrictions, or other encumbrances that the seller created during its ownership. Presumably, the purchaser's attorney will have carefully reviewed each of the "Approved Title Exceptions," including any underlying documentation, before the purchaser agrees to their exclusion. Once the contract is executed, the seller's attorney would then order a preliminary title report from a title insurance company. (In some localities she might procure a title abstract from an abstract company. Alternatively, the purchaser's attorney might search the title and render an opinion.) If any defects show up that are not listed in the sale agreement as approved exceptions, and they are not waived by the purchaser or cured by the seller within a stipulated period of time, then the purchaser may rescind the contract and obtain a return of its earnest money deposit.

A third approach is for the seller's attorney to provide for the delivery of insurable title free of any exceptions that are not designated as approved title exceptions in the sale agreement. For example, paragraph 5 of N.Y.B.T.U. Form 8041, used in New York, provides that "SELLER shall give and PURCHASER shall accept such title as _____, a member of the New York Board of Title Underwriters will be willing to approve and insure in accordance with their standard form of title policy, subject only to the matters [the approved title exceptions] provided for in this contract." Under this approach, the insurer's willingness or unwillingness to insure over some unanticipated title defect substitutes for the marketability standard.

NOTES AND QUESTIONS

> **Problem 2-1**
> Of the three foregoing drafting approaches, which one would you favor as Dan's legal advisor? As Sarah Seller's attorney? What modifications to your preferred approach might you suggest? ◄

1. Reasonable Purchaser Standard. For additional cases on whether a particular defect renders title unmarketable under the standard of reasonableness, see Create 21 Chuo, Inc. v. Southwest Slopes, Inc., 81 Haw. 512, 918 P.2d 1168 (Ct. App. 1996) (unmarketable where presence of archaeological sites can lead to placement in state registry of historic places and attendant restrictions); Wilson Close, Ltd. v. Crane, 499 N.W.2d 732 (Iowa Ct. App. 1993) (8-inch encroachment of wall did not render title unmarketable); Rife v. Lybarger, 49 Ohio St. 422, 31 N.E. 768 (1892) (buyers were excessively particular in objecting to unreleased mortgage lien securing notes due over 19 years previously where seller offered to place on deposit any amount not barred by the statute of limitations).

2. Development Restrictions. How does the presence of wetlands operating to hinder development differ in practical effect from the deed covenant in *Van Vliet* supra that prohibited certain uses of the property? Does it make a difference that the penalty for violation of the covenant in *Van Vliet* was the reverter of title?

Assume that before taking title the purchaser discovers that the subject property is located in a flood plain. Does the perilous location of the collateral as reflected on federal flood zone maps breach the seller's covenant of marketable title? See Chicago Title Ins. Co. v. Investguard, Ltd., 215 Ga. App. 121, 449 S.E.2d 681 (1994).

> **Problem 2-2**
> Assume that you represent a developer planning to purchase 100 acres of farmland for development into a residential subdivision. What contractual provisions would you suggest to protect your client should it discover wetlands before or after the closing? Are there any other provisions necessary to protect your client's development expectations? Recall the *Baldasarre* case at Chapter 2A2, supra. See generally Lefcoe, How Buyers and Sellers of Development Land Deal with Regulatory Risk, 32 Real Prop., Prob. & Tr. J. 301 (Summer 1997). ◄

3. Malpractice. Real estate transactions generate a disproportionate number of legal malpractice claims, with the ABA Standing Committee on Lawyers' Professional Liability reporting in 2012 that real estate matters had eclipsed personal injury representation as the largest generator of malpractice claims. For a previous report with similarly alarming findings, see Gates, The Newest Data on Lawyer's Malpractice Claims, 70 A.B.A. J. 78 (Apr. 1984) (study concluded that lawyers faced greatest incidence of malpractice claims in real estate matters, with the majority of such realty claims relating to substantive mistakes rather than to client relations, intentional wrongs, or other failings). If you represented the purchaser in *McMaster*, how would you have protected your client? What if your client failed to mention the wetlands issue? Malpractice claims are often brought against lawyers by purchasers with dashed ownership and development expectations and who have no recourse against the seller. The case law results are fact dependent but reveal the wide range of risks that purchasers, and their lawyers, face in the marketplace. See, e.g., Schlindrer v. Manson, 2001 WL 1614633 (Conn. Super. Ct. 2001) (lawyer for purchaser hired to examine title to property was not responsible to discover that local zoning allowed only seasonal use of dwelling); Atkin v. Tittle & Tittle, 730 So. 2d 376 (Fla. Dist. Ct. App. 1999) (lawyer for purchaser liable when zoning prohibited the intended use of lot for construction of home); Farrauto, Berman, Fontana, & Selznick v. Keowongwan, 166 Misc.2d 804, 634 N.Y.S.2d 346 (City Ct. 1995) (purchaser's lawyer not liable where illegality of one of the units in the purchased apartment building was not readily discoverable).

4. *Deeds and Covenants for Title*

<u>Sample General Warranty Deed</u>

Standard N.Y.B.T.U. Form 8003

THIS INDENTURE, made the _____ day of _____

BETWEEN

party of the first part, and

party of the second part,

WITNESSETH, that the party of the first part, in consideration of ten dollars and other valuable consideration paid by the party of the second part, does hereby grant and release unto the party of the second part, the heirs or successors and assigns of the party of the second part forever,

ALL that certain plot, piece or parcel of land, with the buildings and improvements thereon erected, situate, lying and being in the [insert legal description and any encumbrances]

TOGETHER with all right, title and interest, if any, of the party of the first part in and to any streets and roads abutting the above described premises to the center lines thereof; TOGETHER with the appurtenances and all the estate and rights of the party of the first part in and to said premises; TO HAVE AND TO HOLD the premises herein granted unto the party of the second part, the heirs or successors and assigns of the party of the second part forever. . . .
AND the party of the first part covenants as follows: that said party of the first part is seized of the said premises in fee simple, and has good right to convey the same; that the party of the second part shall quietly enjoy the said premises; that the said premises are free from encumbrances, except as aforesaid; that the party of the first part will execute or procure any further necessary assurance of the title to said premises; and that said party of the first part will forever warrant the title to said premises.

The word "party" shall be construed as if it read "parties" whenever the sense of this indenture so requires.

IN WITNESS WHEREOF, the party of the first part has duly executed this deed the day and year first above written.

[Signature and acknowledgment clauses omitted.]

The deed is the formal instrument of conveyance and the legal evidence of title for the purchaser. The form of deed will depend on which deed is customarily used in the particular jurisdiction, whether the purchaser plans to obtain additional title protection and by what means (for example, through title insurance), and, finally, on the bargaining positions of the parties. At one end of the spectrum is the general warranty deed, which affords maximum protection to the grantee because it contains all of the standard "English" covenants for title, including a: (1) covenant of seisin; (2) covenant of the right to convey; (3) covenant against encumbrances; (4) covenant of quiet enjoyment; (5) covenant of warranty; and (6) covenant for further assurances. At the other end of the title protection spectrum are the special warranty deed, in which the grantor merely warrants that it has done or suffered nothing to encumber the property and does not warrant against acts of the grantor's predecessors, and the quitclaim deed (or "bargain and sale deed" in some jurisdictions), in which the grantor makes no covenants whatsoever and simply promises to convey to the grantee whatever interest, if any, the grantor might have in the property.

For all practical purposes, the covenant of quiet enjoyment and the covenant of warranty are identical. Likewise, for purposes of the discussion that follows, the covenant of seisin can be combined with the covenant of the right to convey because they both serve the same function.[14] The covenant for further assurances simply means what the phrase implies; namely, that the grantor promises to do whatever further acts are within its power to perfect the title of the grantee. Accordingly, in the discussion that follows, the focus will be on the three major covenants: the covenant of seisin, the covenant against encumbrances, and the covenant of warranty. With regard to each covenant, we will examine its definition and how it works, its nature either as a "present" or "future" covenant, whether it "runs with the land," the pertinent statutes of limitations that apply, and the measure of damages recoverable by the grantee against the grantor if the covenant is breached. The following diagram will be used to illustrate the rules that apply and their consequences to the seller (as grantor) and purchaser (as grantee).

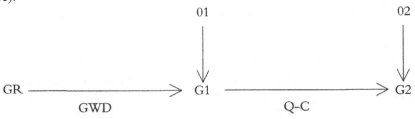

---

14. Although these covenants are essentially the same, in the situation where the grantor has the right to convey but does not own the property, as when the grantor is conveying the property pursuant to a power of appointment in a will, only the covenant of seisin is breached.

In the diagram above, *GR* refers to the grantor who originates the chain of title; *G1* and *G2* are subsequent grantees; *01* and *02* are potential adverse claimants who have better, or "paramount," title and are thus in a position to oust and evict *G1* and *G2*, respectively; *GWD* refers to a general warranty deed; and *Q-C* refers to a quitclaim deed.

   a. Covenant of Seisin. This covenant is created by the language in the sample general warranty deed that "the party of the first part covenants . . . that said party . . . is seized of the said premises in fee simple" or by similar phraseology. "Seisin" is the old common law code phraseology for possession based on ownership of a fee simple or other freehold estate, so the grantor is promising at the time of conveyance (usually the closing date) that the grantor has good title and ownership of a fee simple absolute and has the right to convey it. See American Law of Property §12.127 (Casner ed., 1952).

   At the time of conveyance the grantor (*GR*) either has good title or does not; hence the covenant is deemed to be a "present" covenant, since if it is breached it must be breached when made. See, e.g., Hilliker v. Rueger, 228 N.Y. 11, 126 N.E. 266 (1920). Like other present covenants, the covenant of seisin generally does not "run with the land." This means that while the immediate grantee *G1* can avail itself of the covenant if it should be ousted by someone with better title (*01*), remote grantees like *G2* who are evicted cannot. This is based on the formalistic rationale that a present covenant, once broken, leaves nothing left over that is assignable. However, a minority of jurisdictions adhere to the so-called English rule to the effect that a subsequent conveyance by the grantee (for example, from *G1* to *G2*) amounts to an assignment of a "chose in action" in favor of any remote grantee (like *G2*) who suffers damage by breach of the covenant (for example, by *GR*). See American Law of Property §12.127; Schofield v. Iowa Homestead Co., 32 Iowa 317 (1871).

   For the purpose of the statute of limitations, *G1*'s cause of action against *GR* generally does not accrue until *G1* has been evicted by *01*. See, e.g., N.Y. C.P.L.R. Law §206(c). However, it is not essential in an action to recover damages that *G1* be evicted. *G1* need only prove that there has been a total or partial failure of title. Hilliker v. Rueger, 228 N.Y. 11, 126 N.E. 266 (1920). Don't forget the doctrine of adverse possession—that there is a second statute of limitations involved in *01*'s right to eject *G1* in the event that *01* has the better record title. Finally, the measure of damages for breach of the covenant of seisin is actual loss sustained *not exceeding the purchase price plus interest.* In other words, if *G1* pays $100,000 for the real estate in 1985 and is ousted by *01* in 1995 when the property is worth $500,000, G1's maximum recovery against *GR* (assuming that *GR* is located and solvent) is $100,000 plus accrued interest. This is why title insurance is so important for grantees in the position of *G1*, as coverage may be increased (by periodic endorsements) to reflect the current market value of the insured property. Otherwise, owners may find themselves underinsured, especially in an inflationary economy. As explained at Chapter 2B infra, in commercial transactions the purchaser will almost invariably obtain title insurance from a title company.

b. Covenant against Encumbrances. This covenant is created by the language in the sample general warranty deed that "the party of the first part covenants . . . that the said premises are free from encumbrances, except as aforesaid." Like the covenant of seisin, it is a present covenant that does not run with the land except in a few jurisdictions (such as New York). Geiszler v. DeGraaf, 166 N.Y. 339 (1901). The covenant is breached when broken at the time of conveyance; however, for purposes of the statute of limitations, the cause of action accrues generally when there is an eviction. See, e.g., N.Y. C.P.L.R. Law §206(c). Also, the covenant is deemed to be a covenant of indemnity so that the measure of damages is the actual loss sustained by the grantee. Don't forget that if the encumbrance involved is a lien (for example, mortgage, tax, or judgment lien), the lienor is also subject to a statute of limitations on its claim. As noted earlier, in the case of a special warranty deed the grantor merely covenants that it has done nothing to encumber the property, so that a cause of action will not lie if the property were encumbered by the grantor's predecessor-in-title. See generally American Law of Property §12.128.

c. Covenant of Warranty. This covenant is created by the language in the sample general warranty deed that "said party of the first part will forever warrant the title to said premises." The distinction between the covenant of seisin and the covenant against encumbrances, on the one hand, and the covenant of warranty, on the other, is that the first two relate to the status of the title when the property is conveyed and are thus broken when the covenant is made, while the last deals with the quiet enjoyment of possession and is not broken until there has been a disturbance in the future, for example, if *G1* should be evicted by *01*, by the foreclosure of a tax lien, or by the enforcement of a restrictive covenant. Hence, the covenant of warranty granted by GR creates a right that can be asserted by *G2*. Again, the measure of damages generally is the actual loss sustained but not in excess of the purchase price plus interest.

The legal foundation of modern real estate transactions such as conveyancing is the law of property. Any serious student of real estate transactions should be aware of scholarly efforts at law reform that suggest a new paradigm that relies on a contracts law approach to conveyancing. We will confront this reformist theme again in the context of leasing transactions.

Madison, The Real Properties of Contract Law
82 Boston U. L. Rev. 405 (2002)

This article aims to prod the reader to see the law of real estate contracts and conveyancing in a new light. The contract/conveyance dichotomy in landlord-tenant law will be briefly revisited as the springboard for making the case that the revolution in landlord-tenant law based on a contract approach should be extended to the law of real property conveyancing. Such a move will jolt it out of its comatose state and make conveyancing law more responsive to the needs of a modern society and more sensitive to the intentions and common sense bargaining expectations of the parties. A close analogy to this contract approach model is the sale of personal property under Article 2 of the Uniform Commercial Code, where the passage of title is no longer a major problem-solving modality and freedom of contract principles predominate. The article then takes this hypothesis to the logical and policy-oriented conclusion that we should do away with the real estate deed and its obsolete legal appendages. In their place we should use instead an abbreviated version of the contract as the sole instrument for transferring and recording real estate titles under our recording statute/title insurance system. Professors who teach landlord-tenant law, real estate contracts, and conveyancing frequently identify the doctrinal confusion and uncertainty caused by the collision between modern contract principles and ancient property law as one of the unifying themes tying these materials together.

Flexible contract principles have achieved equitable results because they are based primarily on notions of fairness and bargaining expectations that shift over time in response to the changing needs of our society. Absent a substantial disparity in bargaining power, contract theory allows the parties the freedom to create their own bargains and have their intentions fulfilled without outside interference—so long as the terms of the bargain are not unconscionable and are not applied to produce unfair results. Such flexibility and freedom of contract allows for easier transferability of property interests, and this enhanced alienability makes for a more productive use of land. By contrast, most of the property theory that underlies landlord-tenant and conveyancing law has been quite rigid, because it is rooted in early common law history when England was an agrarian society and land uses remained static. As a result, commentators on the law of sales contracts and conveyancing complain that much of property theory has become obsolete and decry the lack of any internal consistency in the body of rules that still apply.

Indeed, much has been written about the need to modernize and simplify the law governing the contractual transfers of limited interests in real property such as leases, easements, and restrictive covenants. By contrast, little has been said or done about reforming the law governing the contractual sale of fee simple title and other freehold interests. Nor has much effort been directed at reforming the law of real estate deeds that governs the transfer of title to such interests. As explained in Part I and Part II, this effort at reform based primarily on a contract approach has been successful in landlord-tenant law but not in the law of real estate contracts and conveyancing, where old vestiges of property law continue to muddy the legal waters and cause problems for the parties to the transaction. Past reform efforts have failed, notwithstanding a valiant effort by the National Conference of Commissioners on Uniform State Laws to simplify and modernize the law of contracts and deed transfers. Nevertheless, a contract approach could eliminate or at least ameliorate the problems in conveyancing law caused by obsolete property principles.

Part III contends that contract theory, along with some form of redaction of the Restatement of Property, is the reformist engine that is needed to shock antiquated property law out of its comatose state. The use of contract theory will modernize the law of real estate contracts and conveyancing and make it less confusing, more equitable, and more in conformity with bargaining expectations. Furthermore, a contract approach to the law of conveyancing might resolve nettlesome and longstanding conflicts concerning the law of easements and restrictive covenants and leave the decision as to whether covenants of seisin or warranty should run with the land to the parties themselves. Accordingly, freedom of contract principles should be respected so that the parties themselves can create their own law by means of the written word, without outside interference, on the premise that both state legislation and equitable principles will protect each party from engaging in overreaching conduct towards one another. Part III also contends that judicial reform of property law is more likely to succeed than another attempt at statutory reform.

Part IV takes the contract versus property approach analysis one step further. If contract principles should govern and if, as contended, the real estate deed does not perform a function (other than a symbolic one), why not eliminate the real estate deed entirely and just use the contract? In a truncated form, the contract could also constitute the instrument of title and recordation. Why retain the deed as the conveyancing instrument if its legal appendages such as the doctrines of merger and equitable conversion have become obsolete? The contract can do whatever the deed has been doing and can do it better by spelling out in detail the cross-promises and intentions of the parties. As a matter of logic and symmetry, a contract approach to conveyancing should work better in tandem with a contract as opposed to a deed. Part IV also recommends that the current system of two transactions—execution of contract followed by a delivery of the deed on the closing date—should be collapsed into a single transaction where execution of the entire contract and recordation of an abbreviated version of the contract occur simultaneously. Doing so would clarify the intentions of the parties and reinforce the notion that the relevant law is the law of the contract and not the law of the deed. As is presently the case, subsequent purchasers and encumbrancers would be protected under our current recording statute/title insurance system. At the same time, the attendant formalities of recording a property interest would be simplified and the transactional costs would be reduced.

Part V of this article briefly raises certain practical considerations and issues such as what, if anything, would constitute legal evidence of ownership and how record notice would work in mechanical terms if the deed should be replaced by the contract as the instrument of recordation. . . .

II. CONTRACT VERSUS PROPERTY APPROACH TO THE LAW OF CONVEYANCING

The trend toward contract principles has clarified and modernized landlord-tenant law by exorcising obsolete property law doctrines. Accordingly, a contract approach could similarly reform the law of contracts and conveyancing. After all, if a lease, which is only part contract and part property, can be "contractized" to improve lease law, then a real estate contract, which is all contract, should be amenable to a contract approach. The same should apply to its obsolete and cumbersome appendage, the real estate deed. Yet this area of law, with a few notable exceptions, has been all but bypassed by the contract approach.

The following examples illustrate this proposition. Suppose Olin Owner agrees to sell land and a building he owns in fee simple (called Blackacre) to Pat Purchaser for $100,000 by means of an enforceable contract with a closing date set for three months after the contract is executed. Under traditional property law, the following results would occur:

(1) Suppose Olin promises in the contract to provide marketable title, to deliver a special warranty deed on the closing date, and to double the size of the barn within three months after the closing date. If once the title closes Pat discovers that someone else owns the land on which the barn is situated or, in the alternative, that Olin fails to make the barn larger, Pat would have no recourse against Olin under the contract because of the merger doctrine. To make matters worse, Pat would also have no remedy under the deed because a special warranty deed (like a quitclaim deed) contains no promises by the seller-grantor other than a limited covenant against encumbrances under which the grantor merely promises that it has done nothing to encumber the land.

(2) One month before the closing date, Olin is in possession and the house on Blackacre burns down through no fault of either Olin or Pat. Under property law, the risk of loss during the contract period must be borne by the purchaser, Pat, even though Olin is in possession, enjoys the benefits of the property, and is in a better position to protect it from a casualty loss. This result is based on the simplistic axiom "that equity regards as done what ought to be done," meaning that once the contract is executed the positions of the parties are reversed and Pat is regarded to be the "real" or beneficial owner and as such should bear the risk of loss.

(3) Suppose Pat obtains a warranty deed from Olin that contains a promise of good title in the form of a covenant of seisin and a promise of indemnity in the form of a covenant of warranty. Five years after the closing of title, Blackacre is worth $200,000, and Pat is evicted from Blackacre by someone with a better (paramount) title. If Pat sues Olin for damages for breach of the covenant of seisin, his recovery is limited to

the original purchase price of $100,000 plus accrued interest, and Pat is not entitled to any expectancy damages.

(4) Under traditional property theory, the so-called present covenants in a warranty deed that relate to the status of the title, such as a covenant of seisin and covenant against encumbrances, generally do not run with the land for the benefit of the promisee's successors in title whereas the so-called future covenants like the covenant of warranty do run with the land for the benefit of remote vendees. Suppose Olin delivers a deed that contains only a covenant of seisin to Pat and Pat subsequently delivers a deed without the covenant to Patricia Purchaser, who is ousted by someone with a better title to Blackacre. Because of the formalistic difference between present and future covenants, Pat, who received full payment for Blackacre, would be able to sue Olin and recover on the covenant of seisin (albeit nominal damages) but Patricia, the party who is really injured, cannot recover damages for breach of the covenant.

(5) Under traditional servitudes law, the parties are fettered by overlapping rules and obsolete property law doctrines such as the privity and the touch and concern requirements for enforcement of restrictive requirements that can lead to unjust results that defeat the bargaining expectations of the parties. Suppose Olin sells Blackacre but retains ownership of an adjacent property called Whiteacre, and to protect the value of Whiteacre, Olin insists that the deed to Pat contain a promise that neither Pat nor his successors and assigns will ever use Blackacre for nonresidential purposes. Further assume that Olin sells Whiteacre to Oliver and Pat leases Blackacre to Patricia and that, notwithstanding her notice of the restrictive covenant in her chain of title, three years later she commences a business activity on Blackacre when the character of the neighborhood is still residential. Under the property rule called "strict vertical privity," if Olin's successor, Oliver, who now owns Whiteacre, should sue Patricia for money damages based on the restrictive covenant, his suit would fail in those jurisdictions that still take privity seriously, because of the lack of strict vertical privity between Pat and Patricia. By contrast, under a contract approach, the right to sue on the covenant would be assignable and the burden transferable, and therefore Oliver would be allowed to recover.

(6) Suppose Pat purchases a residence from Olin and three months after the closing date a crack appears in a bearing wall that will cost $5000 to fix. The structural defect could have been discovered by an expert had Pat commissioned a diligent beforehand inspection. Pat chose not to arrange for such inspection because it would have been too expensive. Olin refuses to do anything about the problem. Even though the Uniform Commercial Code has rejected the antiquated and much-criticized property law doctrine of caveat emptor with respect to consumer goods, the doctrine is still tolerated with respect to the sale of a home that more directly impacts on the health, safety, and welfare of the consumer than

does a typical consumer good like a washing machine. Under a contract approach, a seller like Olin would be charged with an implied warranty of habitability on the rationale that the normal bargaining expectation of a typical purchaser is that he or she will receive premises that are fit for use.

A.   THE DOCTRINE OF MERGER

Under contract rules, all legal promises in the contract are presumed to have been bargained for by the parties, and absent impossibility of performance or other excuse, promises of an executory nature are enforceable against the promisor as soon as any conditions precedent are met. The buyer under a contract to purchase realty may, however, lose the power to enforce a promise in the contract upon closing of title because of the well-established rule that, once the deed is transferred on the closing date, the contract merges into the deed and the contractual rights of the purchaser disappear. Thereafter, the only remedy available to the purchaser-grantee is one based on the covenants, if any, contained in the deed. Historically, the merger rule is based on the property law concept that when the same owner winds up at the same time with two interests or estates that give him the same rights in the same property, then the two interests should collapse or "merge" into one. In a ground-lease, for example, if the ground-lessee has an option to purchase the fee title, a mortgagee who lends money on the security of a lien on the leasehold estate—called a "leasehold mortgage on an unencumbered fee"—will demand an anti-merger provision. Otherwise, the ground-lease as security for the leasehold could be extinguished once the mortgagor purchases the fee.

While the merger rule is said to be universally accepted, there is little agreement as to what its present rationale is, what exceptions exist, and when these exceptions apply. The rule is sometimes justified by the strained notion that a deed is a fully integrated secondary sales contract that supersedes prior agreements under the parol evidence rule and therefore bars contradictory terms in a prior contract. Under this rationale, the deed's status as a subsequent but totally integrated contract does not preclude collateral agreements that do not contradict the terms of the deed. Courts have used the strained reasoning and etiology of this "collateral agreement" exception to the merger doctrine to enforce all kinds of disparate promises beyond the closing date. They include the following covenants: (1) by the purchaser to assume the seller's mortgage; (2) by the seller to install utilities on the property; (3) by the purchaser to use an agent specified by the seller; and (4) by the seller to make repairs to the property.

Like the vague phraseology "touch and concern" in the law of restrictive covenants, the problem with the exception for collateral agreements is that there is little agreement on what the term "collateral" means. Some courts define a collateral agreement or collateral promise as an agreement that bears no relation to title, possession, quantity, or emblements of the property being transferred. For others it is an agreement that does not involve any matter that necessarily concerns a title agent. A third group defines it as one that deals with subject matter that differs from that which is addressed in the deed. Indeed, even courts within the same jurisdiction have articulated different definitions. Consequently, courts have used the collateral promise as a tool to enforce those promises that they feel should be enforced.

Other courts and commentators rationalize the merger doctrine by using contract principles such as the doctrines of substituted contract, substituted performance, accord and satisfaction, or some other principle dealing with the discharge of contracts. Williston argues that the merger doctrine is best explained by the rule of promissory estoppel. Other justifications of some anti-merger results rest on the mistake, accident and fraud rules. When language in the deed contradicts a provision in the contract, the merger result is often explained on the basis of contract modification, waiver or estoppel. To avoid forfeiture, and occasionally the merger doctrine, courts declare that the nature of a certain clause is such that it is not normally written into a deed, and thus it is presumed that the parties had intended it to survive the closing date. While the doctrine of merger affects virtually every real estate conveyancing transaction in the country, it is riddled with ambiguity and confusion, it is the subject of continuous litigation, and it does not provide the parties with the certainty they need to structure their affairs with a minimum degree of orderliness. For these reasons, commentators have universally condemned the rule.

In most cases the merger doctrine helps the seller. The vast majority of promises meant to survive the closing date are promises by the seller, and the typical seller wants to be released from as much liability as possible once the transaction has closed. Because application of this doctrine violates the purchaser's fair expectations, it has become common practice for the purchaser to demand a survival of liability clause or anti-merger provision in the contract. Such provisions extend the enforceability of the seller's promises beyond the closing date. Careful draftsmanship can resolve the question as to which promises should survive and which should be extinguished on the closing date. But reliance on express contract provisions, however, is an inadequate solution because the purchaser has to bargain twice: first to have the seller's promise contained in the contract and second to have the promise survive the closing date, by insisting upon anti-merger language in the contract (or to have the promise repeated in the deed). Moreover, in transactions involving residential real estate, purchasers, sellers, and even many attorneys are simply not cognizant of the merger doctrine. In the opinion of one experienced commentator, complete resolution of the issue by means of express contract provisions is "optimistic utopia but not a practical reality."

Without this anti-merger clause, the bargaining expectations of purchasers are often defeated and left vulnerable to unfair hardship. Under standard contract principles, absent fraud or mistake, the promises of the seller that deal with title (such as the implied promise to deliver marketable title) should nearly always terminate when title is transferred on the closing date. The purpose of the deed, after all, is to spell out the title promises of the seller-grantor and to specify any recorded exceptions to marketable title such as restrictive covenants and easements. Accordingly, the purchaser-grantee by accepting the deed usually is really accepting a substituted performance, an accord and satisfaction, or a substituted agreement.

The following example illustrates the function of the discharge rules and the related doctrine of estoppel. Under these discharge rules and the doctrine of estoppel, if the real property being sold (Blackacre) is subject to onerous restrictions such as a recorded easement right of a neighbor to drive through the middle of Blackacre or a restrictive covenant that prohibits certain types of residences, and if the purchaser nevertheless closes title and accepts a deed without any relevant covenants of title, then the overwhelming majority of courts has held that the promise to deliver marketable title merges into the deed and the purchaser, as grantee, would have no recourse against the grantor-seller for these exceptions to marketable title.

As to other promises in the contract, the guiding principle on survivability depends on the probable intentions and bargaining expectations of the parties as shaped by the customs and understandings in the industry as to what kinds of performances take place after title passes. In making such a determination, the trier of fact should also look at the transaction-specific circumstances and ask which promises or provisions would the parties, after thoughtful consideration, have chosen to extinguish or survive on the closing date. For example, express provisions or warranties concerning the quality of new construction or existing space, or provisions dealing with the repair of improvements, should survive because these undertakings have no relationship whatsoever with the title-conveying function of the deed and obviously do not come into play until after the purchaser has taken title and possession of the property. By contrast, the purchaser's acceptance of the deed is prima facie evidence that all the stipulations in the contract relating to title have been fulfilled.

In 1975, in response to the longstanding criticism of the merger doctrine, the National Conference of Commissioners on Uniform State Laws promulgated the Uniform Land Transactions Act, which would abolish the merger doctrine by providing that acceptance of a deed does not constitute a waiver of the rights of a buyer or secured party and does not relieve any party of the duty to perform all the obligations under the contract. Because the merger doctrine usually favors the seller, the courts have long battled to balance the equities by enforcing contracted-for provisions, upholding bargained-for expectations, and upholding express clauses that combat the merger doctrine. Such maneuvers should not be necessary. The merger doctrine does not belong in our modern system of conveyancing and should be abolished so that standard contract principles govern the question of which promises survive the closing date. . . .

C. PURCHASER'S RIGHT TO DAMAGES AFTER THE CLOSING DATE

Another dysfunctional result of property law's formalism occurs when a grantee seeks to recover damages against a grantor for breaching the covenant of seisin or the covenant of warranty in the deed transferred by the seller to the purchaser on the closing date. Standard contract principles dictate that if the seller commits a material breach of the contract before the closing date, the buyer can sue the seller for expectancy (general) damages, which may exceed the purchase price (especially in an inflationary economy). By contrast, if the breach occurs after the closing of title, the seller, as grantor-covenantor, can only be sued for damages equal to the purchase price plus accrued interest. This disparity in result is more pronounced in the case of an installment land contract as compared to the ordinary contract of sale because the installment period between the contract date and closing date can last for a number of years, depending on how long the seller is willing to finance the buyer's purchase of the property.

Returning to our hypothetical at the beginning of Part II, assume that Pat Purchaser and Olin Owner agree to a five-year installment land contract and that Olin defaults by not delivering marketable title on the closing date. Further assume that Pat has paid the full purchase price of $100,000 and that prices for comparable parcels have doubled over the five-year installment period. Under standard contract principles, if Olin is solvent, then Pat could make himself whole again by suing Olin for general damages based on the loss of bargain in the amount of $200,000. By contrast, had the vendor financed Pat's purchase of the land by means of a five-year purchase money mortgage, Pat would have immediately received the title, and if the deed were a warranty deed, Pat's only recourse against the vendor for failure of title would be based on the covenants of seisin and warranty in the deed. Assuming that Pat paid the entire purchase money indebtedness at the end of the five-year installment period, his maximum recovery would be limited to the consideration paid ($100,000) plus accrued interest. Assuming an average interest rate of five percent, compounded annually, the ceiling on damages for recovery by a covenantee under property law would be the $100,0000 plus accrued interest of $27,628 for a total of $127,628, as compared to the $200,000 damages recovery under standard contract principles.

The rule gained acceptance in an era when the frontier of this country was expanding and land values skyrocketed. During that era, one court described it as follows: "A rule that the damages should be the actual loss at the time of eviction, would work great injustice, and prevent the transfer of property in Pennsylvania. Our turnpikes, canals, and railroads have produced so many improvements, and such sudden changes in the value of property, that any other rule would produce incalculable mischief and ruin." Since this historic rationale no longer rings true, why not allow the grantee the same loss of bargain damages that a vendee would be entitled to under the same circumstances? Indeed, the reliance factor is probably stronger for a grantee who has lived on, worked on, or improved the land, believing that he or she has full ownership, than it is for a vendee who has yet to obtain the full legal title.

Some might contend that the ceiling on damages discussed above is not a problem for the individual grantees. Such grantees can protect themselves by obtaining a so-called market value endorsement to the standard American Land Title Association ("ALTA") Owner's Policy, which guarantees a payment equal to the market value of the property at the time the claim is made. This endorsement is only available in some jurisdictions such as New York. In some states, buyers rely not on title insurance but instead on title opinions of attorneys and abstract companies for their title protection.

D. THE DEFINITIONAL DISTINCTION BETWEEN PRESENT AND FUTURE COVENANTS CAN CAUSE ABSURD RESULTS

The formalistic distinction under property theory between present and future covenants in a warranty deed can lead to haphazard results for grantees in the same chain of title. Under this legal appendage to the deed, a grantor who promises that he has good title may provide protection to a grantee who does not need it. At the same time, another grantee who needs protection will not receive it even though both grantees represent links in the same chain of title. Except for title insurance, the highest degree of title protection for a buyer under our recording statute/title insurance system is the general warranty deed. This deed provides that the grantor, who previously was the seller prior to the closing of title, covenants to the grantee, who previously was the buyer, that (1) the grantor owns the interest that he or she is purporting to convey on the closing date (covenant of seisin, or right to convey), (2) there are no pre-existing liens, use restrictions, or other encumbrances reducing the value of the land on the closing date (covenant against encumbrances), (3) after the closing date, the grantee will not be evicted by someone with a superior or so-called paramount claim, and (4) the grantor will indemnify the grantee in the event that such an eviction should occur (covenant of warranty or covenant of quiet enjoyment).

Under common law dogma, covenants triggered by future events such as eviction of the grantee are called future (in futuro) covenants that run with the land and thereby benefit remote purchaser-vendees. By contrast, certain covenants, such as the covenant of seisin and the covenant against encumbrances, are called present (in praesenti) covenants because they can only be breached when the deed is presently delivered on the closing date. In other words, on the closing date, the grantor either has good title that is unencumbered or she does not. In most jurisdictions, such covenants do not run with the land. Moreover, in the past, contract claims of this nature characterized as choses in action were non-assignable. Hence the benefit of the covenant has been deemed to be personal in nature to the immediate grantee and cannot be transferred by implication to a subsequent party. The formalistic rationale behind the property theory rule, which is termed "the American rule," is that once the covenant is breached there is nothing of the covenant left over to pass to a subsequent purchaser-grantee.

By contrast, common law courts in England and in a minority of states apply a contract approach, the "English rule," to allow the benefit of the present covenant to pass down the chain of title. The contract rationale is that the rule prohibiting the assignment of choses in action was lost in history and the benefit of the covenant is in the nature of a chose in action that by implication is assigned to the next grantee when the title passes down the chain of title. Furthermore, the bargained-for purpose of the covenant is to provide protection for a grantee who needs it, regardless of whether the grantee is remote or immediate.

So under the American rule, we end up with the absurd result that an uninjured immediate grantee can use the covenant to sue the grantor (albeit for only nominal damages) while an injured remote vendee has no recourse under the covenant. In the words of Chancellor Kent, however, "[The subsequent vendee] is the most interested, and the most fit person to claim the indemnity secured by [the covenants], for the compensation belongs to him as the last purchaser and the first sufferer." In fact, the net result under property law (American rule) might be that no one gets the benefit of the covenant. An analogous argument can be made to support the notion that the contract approach justifies the running of restrictive covenants without having to resort to the strained concept called privity.

The Uniform Land Transactions Act Section 2-312 provides that, absent language to the contrary, all warranties of title, including present covenants such as the covenant of seisin and the covenant against encumbrances, run with the land. It might be contended that most buyers obtain title insurance or some other title protection so a remote grantee would still be protected if it does not get the benefit of the covenant. The premium costs of title insurance are reduced, however, by the fact that title companies—under stipulations in the standard ALTA owner's policy—have a right of subrogation once they pay a claim. Therefore, if under the American rule an injured party has title insurance protection but has no right to sue the grantor who gave the covenant, the title company, which steps into the shoes of the insured, gets no benefit from its right of subrogation, and premium costs for all policy-holders would increase. . . .

NOTES AND QUESTIONS

1. Covenant of Seisin. In the Schofield v. Iowa Homestead Co., 32 Iowa 317 (1871) case cited at (a) supra, a court of first impression had to decide whether the covenant of seisin should run with the land. In deciding in favor of the English rule (under which the covenant does run with the land), the court rejected the majority rule ("American rule") because "[w]hen the grantee [*G1*], under the deed, has sold and received pay for the land, it would be gross injustice to permit him to recover, for he would not in that case sustain damages. But under the rule to which we are now objecting [American rule], the grantee may recover on the covenant of seisin and, if there be covenant of warranty in the deed, the subsequent grantee [*G2*] may also recover upon that contract against the first grantor [*GR*]." In your opinion, is this double-damages argument against the American rule a cogent one?

> ➤ *Problem 2-3*
> Consult the diagram on page 55 in answering the following questions. In a jurisdiction that adheres to the American rule, if *G2* should be ousted by *02* because *02* had received an earlier conveyance from *G1* and under the local recording statute *02*'s title is better than *G2*'s title, what remedy, if any, would *G2* have against *G1*? Would *G2* have a remedy against *GR*?
> In the diagram, *GR* conveyed title to *G1* by means of a general warranty deed that included a covenant of warranty, and *G2* received a mere quitclaim deed from *G1*. Since the covenant of warranty in the deed to *G1* runs with the land, it protects *G2* as well as *G1*, so why would someone in the position of *G2* ever demand (and presumably pay extra compensation for) a general warranty deed from the grantor (*G1*)? In many commercial transactions, the seller (especially an institutional lender) will refuse to deliver a general warranty deed to the purchaser. Can you think of any reason why this is so? See Friedman, Contracts and Conveyances of Real Property §8:14 (7th ed. 2005).
> Suppose that in a jurisdiction following the American rule, *GR* sells the real estate to *G1* for $100,000 and *G1* resells the property to *G2* for $80,000. If *G2* were to be ousted by someone claiming under paramount title (*02*), should *G1* be able to recover from *GR*? If so, how much? ◄

2. Malpractice. The Tennessee Supreme Court held that an attorney hired by the seller to prepare a warranty deed conveying property to the purchasers was liable for damages to those non-clients when the deed proved defective for want of the language "with whom I am personally acquainted" in the deed's acknowledgment clause as required by Tennessee statute. Collins v. Binkley, 750 S.W.2d 737 (Tenn. 1988) (attorney knew purchasers would rely on him to prepare effective deed and thus assumed duty to non-clients). The statute of limitations can be a problem for deed malpractice claims. E.g., Snyder v. Heidelberger, 953 N.E.2d 415 (Ill. 2011) (six-year limitation barred claim by client's widow for negligently failing to effectuate client intent of joint tenancy deed, as client died more than six years after lawyer prepared the deed—the lawyer allegedly failed to ascertain the property title was in the name of a land trust rather than the husband who signed the joint tenancy deed in his personal capacity).

5. *Default Remedies*

In the hypothetical sale transaction, Dan Developer delivered $5 million in "earnest money" on executing the contract for sale. Should Dan default under the contract, Sarah Seller may wish to retain that deposit to compensate for her losses. Often, the parties' agreement will provide that the seller can retain the earnest money as liquidated damages. See §10 of the sample sale agreement in the Documents Manual. The following case explores whether courts should impose any judicial limits on these contractual understandings to govern remedies upon breach. The other materials in this section consider the relationship of retaining the earnest money deposit to the other traditional remedies for the purchaser's breach of contract—recovery of actual damages or a decree of specific performance that compels the purchaser to perform under the contract.

Uzan v. 845 UN Limited Partnership
10 A.D.3d 230, 778 N.Y.S.2d 171 (2004)

MAZZARELLI, J.

This appeal presents the issue of whether plaintiffs, who defaulted on the purchase of four luxury condominium units, have forfeited their 25% down payments as a matter of law. Because the governing purchase agreements were a product of lengthy negotiation between parties of equal bargaining power, all represented by counsel, there was no evidence of overreaching, and upon consideration of the fact that a 25% down payment is common usage in the new construction luxury condominium market in New York City, we hold that upon their default and failure to cure, plaintiffs forfeited all rights to their deposits pursuant to the rule set forth in Maxton Builders, Inc. v. Lo Galbo, 68 N.Y.2d 373, 509 N.Y.S.2d 507, 502 N.E.2d 184.

FACTS

In October 1998, Defendant 845 UN Limited Partnership (sponsor or 845 UN) began to sell apartments at The Trump World Tower (Trump World), a luxury condominium building to be constructed at 845 United Nations Plaza. Donald Trump is the managing general partner of the sponsor. Plaintiffs Cem Uzan and Hakan Uzan, two brothers, are Turkish billionaires who sought to purchase multiple units in the building. In April 1999, plaintiffs and an associate executed . . . purchase agreements for apartments in Trump World. . . . As relevant, Cem Uzan defaulted on contracts to buy two penthouse units on the 90th floor of the building, and Hakan defaulted on contracts to purchase two other penthouse units on the 89th floor.

The building had not been constructed when plaintiffs executed their purchase agreements. In paragraph 17.4 of those contracts, the sponsor projected that the first closing in the building would occur on or about April 1, 2001, nearly two years after the signing of the agreements. . . .

Plaintiffs were represented by experienced local counsel during the two-month-long negotiation for the purchase of the apartments. There were numerous telephone conversations between counsel, and at least four extensively marked-up copies of draft purchase agreements were exchanged. In consideration for plaintiffs' purchase of multiple units, the sponsor reduced the aggregate purchase price of the penthouse units by more than $7 million from the list price in the offering plan for a total cost of approximately $32 million. Plaintiffs also negotiated a number of revisions to the standard purchase agreement, including extensions of time for payment of the down payment. As amended, each purchase agreement obligated plaintiffs to make a 25% down payment: 10% at contract, an additional 7.5% down payment twelve months later, and a final 7.5% down payment 18 months after the execution of the contract. At no time did plaintiffs object to the total amount required as a non-refundable down payment.

There were other significant amendments to the standard purchase agreement which benefited plaintiffs. These included: (1) rights to terminate the contracts if the closing had not occurred by December 31, 2003; (2) rights to advertise the units for resale prior to closing; (3) conditional rights to assign the purchase agreements to a third party; and (4) the right of each brother to terminate his contracts if the sponsor terminated the purchase agreements for the other brother's units. It is noted that according to counsel for the sponsor, the right to assign the purchase contracts prior to closing had not been granted to any other purchaser of a unit at Trump World. Also, at plaintiffs' urging, the sponsor added language to the purchase agreements agreeing not to install machinery on the roof that would cause noise or vibration in the apartments.

The executed purchase agreements provide, at paragraph 12(b), that:

> [u]pon the occurrence of an Event of Default . . . [i]f Sponsor elects to cancel . . .
> [and i]f the default is not cured within . . . thirty (30) days, then this Agreement shall
> be deemed canceled, and Sponsor shall have the right to retain, as and for liquidated
> damages, the Down payment and any interest earned on the Down payment.

Plaintiffs paid the first 10% down payment installment for the penthouse units on April 26, 1999, when they signed the purchase agreements. They paid the second 7.5% installment in April 2000, and the third 7.5% installment in October 2000. The total 25% down payment of approximately $8 million was placed in an escrow account. . . .

On September 11, 2001, terrorists attacked New York City by flying two planes into the World Trade Center, the city's two tallest buildings, murdering thousands of people. Plaintiffs, asserting concerns of future terrorist attacks, failed to appear at the October 19, 2001, closing, resulting in their default. By letter dated October 19, 2001, plaintiffs' counsel stated:

> [W]e believe that our clients are entitled to rescind their Purchase Agreements in view of the terrorist attack which occurred on September 11 and has not abated. In particular, our clients are concerned that the top floors in a "trophy" building, described as the tallest residential building in the world, will be an attractive terrorist target. The situation is further aggravated by the fact that the building bears the name of Donald Trump, perhaps the most widely known symbol of American capitalism. Finally, the United Nations complex brings even more attention to this location.

That day, 845 UN sent plaintiffs default letters, notifying them that they had 30 days to cure. On November 19, 2001, upon expiration of the cure period, the sponsor terminated the four purchase agreements.

Plaintiffs then brought this action. They alleged that Donald Trump had prior special knowledge that certain tall buildings, such as Trump World, were potential targets for terrorists. Plaintiffs also alleged that Trump World did not have adequate protection for the residents of the upper floors of the building. In their first cause of action, plaintiffs averred that the sponsor's failure to advise prospective purchasers of the specific risks of a terrorist attack on Trump World, and to amend the offering plan to describe these risks, constituted common-law fraud and deceptive sales practices pursuant to General Business Law §352. Plaintiffs' second claim is that the same acts constituted violations of General Business Law §§349 and 350. The third cause of action sought a declaratory judgment that the down payment was an "unconscionable, illegal and unenforceable penalty." The IAS [New York's "individual assignment system" where a case is assigned to the same trial judge for its duration] court dismissed plaintiffs' first two claims in a March 2000 order not on appeal. . . .

After exchanging discovery and conducting various depositions, plaintiffs moved for summary judgment on their third cause of action, arguing that forfeiture of the down payments was an unenforceable penalty. . . .

In his affidavit in support of the cross motion, Donald Trump stated that he sought 25% down payments from pre-construction purchasers at the Trump World Tower because of the substantial length of time between contract signing and closing, during which period the sponsor had to keep the units off the market, and because of the obvious associated risks. Trump also affirmed that down payments in the range of 20% to 25% are standard practice in the new construction luxury condominium submarket in New York City. He cited three projects where he was the developer, The Trump Palace, 610 Park Avenue, and Trump International Hotel and Tower, all of which had similar down payment provisions. Trump also noted that,

> [i]n new construction condominium projects, purchasers often speculate on the market by putting down initial down payments of 10% and 15% and watching how the market moves. If the market value increases, they will then make the second down payment. If the market prices drop, they may then walk away from their down payment.

Weitzman's [president of a nationwide real estate consulting firm] affirmation echoed Trump's opinion that 20% to 25% down payments are customary in New York City for new construction condominium apartments, because of the volatility of the market. Weitzman also discussed other risk factors specific to developers of newly constructed luxury condominium projects. She concluded that from the sponsor's perspective, future competition is largely unknown, requiring an educated guess by the developer of the appropriate level of services and amenities to be provided at the building. Weitzman also noted that the demographic profile for potential purchasers in the luxury condominium submarket includes many foreign nationals, who are inherently high-risk purchasers because their incomes and assets are often difficult to measure, and to reach. Both Weitzman and Martin [a Trump consultant] stated, based upon research detailed in their affidavits, that the volatility of individual real estate transactions increases with the size of the unit involved, and that price swings for three- and four-bedroom units, such as the penthouse units plaintiffs sought to purchase here, were greater than for smaller apartments.

Defendant also presented a compilation of sixteen recent condominium offering plans, all of which required down payments of either 20% or 25 of the purchase price for the unit. Fourteen of the sixteen offering plans required 25% down payments. Further, defendant provided proof that in July 2001, plaintiff Cem Uzan closed on the purchase of an apartment on the 80th floor of Trump World after making a 25% down payment, and that he had previously purchased another apartment at 515 Park Avenue, also with a 25% down payment provision. . . .

After hearing oral argument on the motion, the IAS court granted defendant partial summary judgment, finding that plaintiffs forfeited the portion of their down payment amounting to 10% of the purchase price, pursuant to Maxton Builders, Inc. v. Lo Galbo, 68 N.Y.2d 373, 509 N.Y.S.2d 507, 502 N.E.2d 184, supra. The court held that the remainder of the down payment was subject to a liquidated damages analysis to determine whether it bore a reasonable relation to the sponsor's actual or probable loss. Defendant appeals from that portion of the order which denied it full relief.

DISCUSSION

More than a century ago, the Court of Appeals, in Lawrence v. Miller, 86 N.Y. 131 [(1881)], held that a vendee who defaults on a real estate contract without lawful excuse cannot recover his or her down payment. It reaffirmed this holding in *Maxton*, supra, again in 1986. The facts of *Lawrence* are common to real estate transactions, and parallel those presented here. In that case, plaintiff made a $2000 down payment on the purchase of certain real estate and then defaulted. The seller refused to extend plaintiff's time to perform the contract, retained the down payment, and ultimately sold the property to another purchaser. In plaintiff's subsequent action for a refund of the down payment, the Court of Appeals affirmed a judgment dismissing the complaint, stating:

> To allow a recovery of this money would be to sustain an action by a party on his own breach of his own contract, which the law does not allow. When we once declare in this case that the vendor has done all that the law asks of him, we also declare that the vendee has not so done on his part. And then to maintain this action would be to declare that a party may violate his agreement, and make an infraction of it by himself a cause of action. That would be ill doctrine.

(Lawrence, 86 N.Y. 131, 140.)

For over a century, courts have consistently upheld what was called the *Lawrence* rule and recognized a distinction between real estate deposits and general liquidated damages clauses. Liquidated damages clauses have traditionally been subject to judicial oversight to confirm that the stipulated damages bear a reasonable proportion to the probable loss caused by the breach. By contrast, real estate down payments have been subject to limited supervision. They have only been refunded upon a showing of disparity of bargaining power between the parties, duress, fraud, illegality, or mutual mistake.

In *Maxton*, plaintiff had contracted to sell defendants a house, and accepted a check for a 10% down payment. When defendants canceled the contract and placed a stop payment on the check, plaintiff sued for the down payment, citing the *Lawrence* rule. Defendants argued that plaintiff's recovery should be limited to its actual damages. In ruling for the vendor, the Court of Appeals identified two legal principles as flowing from *Lawrence*. First, that the vendor was entitled to retain the down payment in a real estate contract, without reference to his actual damages. Second, the "parent" rule, upon which the first rule was based, that one who breaches a contract may not recover the value of his part performance.

The Court noted that the parent rule had been substantially undermined in the 100 years since *Lawrence*. Many courts had rejected the parent rule because of criticism that it produced a forfeiture "and the amount of the forfeiture increases as performance proceeds, so that the penalty grows larger as the breach grows smaller."

The Court also noted that since *Lawrence*, the rule of allowing recovery of down payments of not more than 10% in real estate contracts continues to be followed by a "majority of jurisdictions," including in New York (Maxton, 68 N.Y.2d at 380, 509 N.Y.S.2d 507, 502 N.E.2d 184). Thereafter, the court noted the long and widespread reliance on the *Lawrence* rule in real estate transactions, and it concluded that, based upon notions of efficiency and avoiding unnecessary litigation, the rule should remain in effect.

After acknowledging that "[R]eal estate contracts are probably the best examples of arm's length transactions," the Court broadly concluded:

Except in cases where there is a real risk of overreaching, there should be no need for the courts to relieve the parties of the consequences of their contract. If the parties are dissatisfied with the rule of [Lawrence], the time to say so is at the bargaining table.

(Maxton, 68 N.Y.2d 373, 382, 509 N.Y.S.2d 507, 502 N.E.2d 184.)

The *Maxton/Lawrence* rule has since been followed by this Court as well as the other departments to deny a refund of a down payment when a default has occurred.

Further, other departments have specifically applied the *Maxton/Lawrence* rule, where, as here, a real estate down payment of greater than 10% of the purchase price is at issue (see Collar City Partnership v. Redemption Church, 235 A.D.2d 665, 651 N.Y.S.2d 729 [3rd Dept. 1997] [50% down payment]; Vitolo v. O'Connor, 223 A.D.2d 762, 636 N.Y.S.2d 163 [3rd Dept. 1996] [23% down payment]; Badame v. Bock Enters., Inc., 190 A.D.2d 1066, 593 N.Y.S.2d 384, [4th Dept. 1993] [more than 10% down payment]). . . .

Earlier, in the *Vitolo* case, the Third Department had also applied the *Lawrence/Maxton* rule and refused to return a 23% down payment made for the purchase of a single-family home. The court noted there that while application of the *Maxton/Lawrence* rule might seem severe, "the parties to [the] transaction were dealing at arm's length. Plaintiffs were aware that they were making a sizeable down payment; any negotiating over the amount . . . should have been done at the time of the agreement." (*Vitolo*, supra at 764-765, 636 N.Y.S.2d 163.)

. . .

Applying the reasoning of these cases to the facts of the instant matter, it is clear that plaintiffs are not entitled to a return of any portion of their down payment. Here the 25% down payment was a specifically negotiated element of the contracts. There is no question that this was an arm's length transaction. The parties were sophisticated business people, represented by counsel, who spent two months at the bargaining table before executing the amended purchase agreements.

Further, the record evidences that it is customary in the pre-construction luxury condominium industry for parties to price the risk of default at 25% of the purchase price. The purchase agreements included a detailed non-refundable down payment clause to which plaintiffs' counsel had negotiated a specific amendment. That amendment allowed for the payment of 25% of the purchase price in three installments: 10% at contract, an additional 7.5% twelve months later, and a final 7.5% eighteen months later. Clearly, plaintiffs were fully aware of and accepted the requirement of a non-refundable 25% down payment for these luxury pre-construction condominiums. In fact, Cem Uzan has purchased two other condominiums, one in the same building, with similar down payment provisions.

Plaintiffs negotiated the payment of the 25% down payments in installments to spread their risk over time. In the event of a severe economic downturn, plaintiffs were free to cancel the deal, capping their losses at the amount paid as of the date of their default. For the sponsor, the 25% deposit served to cover its risk for keeping the apartments off the market should the purchaser default.

Finally, there was no evidence of a disparity of bargaining power, or of duress, fraud, illegality, or mutual mistake by the parties in drafting the down payment clause of the purchase agreements. The detailed provision concerning the non-refundable deposit was integral to the transaction. If plaintiffs were dissatisfied with the 25% non-refundable down payment provision in the purchase agreements, the time to have voiced objection was at the bargaining table. Because they chose to accept it, they are committed to its terms. Thus, upon plaintiffs' default and failure to cure, defendant was entitled to retain the full 25% down payments. . . .

The interrelationship of the seller's potential remedies for the purchaser's breach (liquidated damages, actual damages,[15] specific performance) presents some interesting issues. In most states, notwithstanding a liquidated damages clause, the seller can elect to seek specific performance of the purchaser's obligation to pay the agreed-on purchase price, unless the parties' liquidated damages agreement specifically waives this remedy[16] or the seller has already resold the property so that specific performance is impossible. Under this authority, on the purchaser's breach the seller may elect between its liquidated damages and specific performance. Suppose, however, that the seller has reserved the right to elect between recovering actual damages and retaining the earnest money as liquidated damages. The following case considers whether this contractual election is inconsistent with the rationale behind the enforcement of liquidated damages clauses.

Lefemine v. Baron
573 So. 2d 326 (Fla. 1991)

GRIMES, Justice.

. . . Daniel and Catherine Lefemine entered into [and later breached] a real estate contract to purchase a residence from Judith W. Baron for $385,000. . . .

The issue before this Court is whether the default provision in the real estate contract was enforceable as a liquidated damages clause or was an unenforceable penalty clause. The default provision reads as follows:

15. For discussion of the appropriate measure of the seller's actual damages, see Korngold, Seller's Damages from a Defaulting Buyer of Realty: The Influence of the Uniform Land Transactions Act on the Courts, 20 Nova L. Rev. 1069 (1996).

16. Compare Miller v. U.S. Naval Institute, 47 Md. App. 426, 423 A.2d 283 (1980) (majority rule), with Uniform Land Transactions Act §2-516(b) (specific performance is unavailable unless expressly reserved in the liquidated damages clause).

1. DEFAULT BY BUYER: If Buyer fails to perform the Contract within the time specified, the deposit(s) made or agreed to be made by Buyer [in the amount of $38,500] may be retained or recovered by or for the account of Seller as liquidated damages, consideration for the execution of the Contract and in full settlement of any claims; whereupon all parties shall be relieved of all obligations under the Contract; or Seller, at his option, may proceed at law or in equity to enforce his rights under the Contract.

It is well settled that in Florida the parties to a contract may stipulate in advance to an amount to be paid or retained as liquidated damages in the event of a breach. In Hyman v. Cohen, 73 So. 2d 393 (Fla. 1954), this Court established the test as to when a liquidated damages provision will be upheld and not stricken as a penalty clause. First, the damages consequent upon a breach must not be readily ascertainable. Second, the sum stipulated to be forfeited must not be so grossly disproportionate to any damages that might reasonably be expected to follow from a breach as to show that the parties could have intended only to induce full performance, rather than to liquidate their damages.

We agree with the court below that the forfeiture of the $38,500 deposit was not unconscionable. The deposit represented only ten percent of the purchase price and half of this had to be paid to the broker [pursuant to the seller's listing agreement]. The $38,500 was not so grossly disproportionate to any damages that might reasonably be expected to follow from a breach of the contract so as to show that the parties intended only to induce full performance. The controversy in this case arises from the existence of the option granted to the seller either to retain the security deposit as liquidated damages or to bring an action at law for actual damages. . . .

The reason why the forfeiture clause must fail in this case is that the option granted to Baron either to choose liquidated damages or to sue for actual damages indicates an intent to penalize the defaulting buyer and negates the intent to liquidate damages in the event of a breach. The buyer under a liquidated damages provision with such an option is always at risk for damages greater than the liquidated sum. On the other hand, if the actual damages are less than the liquidated sum, the buyer is nevertheless obligated by the liquidated damages clause because the seller will take the deposit under that clause. Because neither party intends the stipulated sum to be the agreed-upon measure of damages, the provision cannot be a valid liquidated damages clause.

The decision we reach today is in harmony with authorities from other jurisdictions. Real Estate World, Inc. v. Southeastern Land Fund, Inc., 137 Ga. App. 771, 224 S.E.2d 747 (Ct. App. 1976), overruled on other grounds, Mock v. Canterbury Realty Co., 152 Ga. App. 872, 264 S.E.2d 489 (Ct. App. 1980); Jarro Bldg. Indus. Corp. v. Schwartz, 54 Misc. 2d 13, 281 N.Y.S.2d 420 (App. Term 1967); Dalston Constr. Corp. v. Wallace, 26 Misc. 2d 698, 214 N.Y.S.2d 191 (Dist. Ct. 1960). In J. Calamari & J. Perillo, The Law of Contracts §14-32, at 645 (3d ed. 1987), the authors state:

§14-32. Two Pitfalls of Draftsmanship: The Shotgun Clause and the Have Cake and Eat It Clause

. . . Another pitfall into which contract draftsmen have plunged involves an attempt to fix damages in the event of a breach with an option on the part of the aggrieved party to sue for such additional actual damages as he may establish. These have been struck down as they do not involve a reasonable attempt definitively to estimate the loss.

We hold that the default provision in the subject contract was not enforceable as a liquidated damages clause. The provision constituted a penalty as a matter of law because the existence of the option negated the intent to liquidate damages. We quash the decision below with directions to remand the case for a trial on the actual damages incurred by Baron as a result of the breach of contract. . . .

NOTES AND QUESTIONS

1. Default Remedies. The *Uzan* case discusses the decision in Maxton Builders v. LoGalbo, 68 N.Y.2d 373, 502 N.E.2d 184, 509 N.Y.S.2d 507 (1986) that enforced the rule of *Lawrence v. Miller* (a breaching buyer cannot recover any down payment) even when the sale contract failed to authorize the seller to retain the 10 percent down payment as its liquidated damages. Most prudent sellers and their counsel, however, will specify the disposition of the down payment or "earnest money deposit" explicitly as liquidated damages should the buyer fail to perform. The question then becomes, as confronted in *Uzan*, whether the courts should intervene and impose legal limits on the parties' contractual agreement.

Prices for the New York condo market have risen over the years during and after the *Uzan* litigation. The Trump World Tower project website, www.trump worldtower.com/index.shtml, offered units on the 89th and 90th floors at prices in 2007 of $12, $13, and near $16 million, thereby suggesting that despite the time value of money, Trump may have profited from the buyers' breach, especially upon retaining their 25 percent deposits. Later, in 2012, baseball great Derek Jeter sold his 88th floor unit for $15.5 million.

Suppose under the master hypothetical that immediately following Dan Developer's default, Sarah Seller is able to resell the property for $41 million ($1 million more than Dan agreed to pay), yet seeks to retain Dan's $5 million deposit delineated as "liquidated damages" in the purchase agreement. As this area of the law is fraught with uncertainty, any automatic reliance on the written agreement is misplaced. For example, as observed in *Lefemine*, liquidated damages clauses in purchase agreements have been struck down as unenforceable penalties where the seller's actual damages were readily ascertainable or the stipulated amount was unreasonable. See, e.g., Colonial at Lynnfield, Inc. v. Sloan, 870 F.2d 761 (1st Cir. 1989) (liquidated damages of $200,000 in contract for sale of fractional ownership interest in hotel for $3,375,000 held invalid where seller resold the interest three months later for $251,000 more than the contract price); Reid v. Auxier, 690 P.2d 1057 (Okla. Ct. App. 1984) (holding that liquidated damages provisions in realty sale contracts are void because it is neither impracticable nor extremely difficult to fix the seller's actual damages); 22 Am. Jur. 2d Damages §546. But see San Francisco Distrib. Ctr., LLC v. Stonemason Partners, LP, 183 So. 3d 391 (Fla. 3d Dist. App. 2014) (liquidated damages of $400,000 upheld where the contract price of commercial property was $5,250,000 and the property was subsequently sold for $200,000 more). In response to decisions such as these that imperil reliance on liquidated damages clauses, some states enacted laws that validate these provisions in real estate sale contracts provided that the amount stipulated does not exceed a specified percentage of the purchase price. See, e.g., Okla. Stat. Ann. tit. 15, §215 (liquidated damages provision in real estate sale contract not exceeding 5 percent of the purchase price "shall be held valid and not a penalty"; enacted following the *Reid* case, supra); Wash. Rev. Code Ann. §64.04.005 (validates 5 percent or less as liquidated damages). Under *Uzan*, what result if Sarah seeks to retain the $5 million earnest money as liquidated damages?

2. Excusing Performance for Force Majeure or Impossibility. The plaintiffs in *Uzan* notified the seller at the time of close of the transaction that they would not follow through on the bargain due to the terrorist attacks on the World Trade Center that occurred less than two months earlier. Many commercial contracts have provisions that explicitly excuse contract performance for "force majeure," which is translated to mean "greater force." These provisions typically apply when events outside the control of the contracting parties prevent one or both of the parties from performing under the contract terms. See Encina, Clause Majeure?: Can a Borrower Use an Economic Downturn or Economic Downturn-Related Events to Invoke the Force Majeure Clause in Its Commercial Real Estate Loan Documents?, 45 Real Prop. Tr. & Est. L.J. 731 (Winter 2011). The *Uzan* court did not explicitly consider a force majeure contract provision on appeal: the plaintiffs based their legal argument on the seller concealing knowledge of the risk of a potential terrorist attack on the building. Indeed, a force majeure provision may have not even been part of the contract to buy the trophy residences high above Manhattan. However, what if a force majeure provision was applicable to the transaction? Would the *Uzan* plaintiffs be excused from performance of the contract due to apparently new risks associated with living at the top of a high-rise building? As an aside, the plaintiffs, Cem Uzan and Hakan Uzan are members of the notorious Uzan family of Turkey that have since been implicated in numerous crimes, including fraud, racketeering and a scheme to siphon funds from banks in which they were principal investors. In a matter separate to the case cited in this text, a U.S. District Court Judge in New York previously asserted that "the Uzans are business imperialists of the worst kind, in that they would go to any lengths, including fraud and racketeering, to preserve their business empire." Would this reputation of unscrupulous, if not criminal, business practices influence a decision of a court of the same city to let them out of a bargain without remedy to the seller?

Similar to force majeure is the legal argument based on impossibility of performance which, if successfully raised, allows a party to rescind the contract. In the wake of the 2008 financial crisis, developers who were unable to complete deals because they failed to obtain adequate financing or were delinquent on their construction loans obtained prior to the crisis, have attempted to invoke the argument of impossibility of performance to abandon deals or to excuse or delay the repayment of their loans. One court has explicitly refused to acknowledge the impossibility of performance argument arising from the financial crisis, stating that the party asserting the doctrine must show the event creating the impossibility was not reasonably foreseeable at the time of contracting. YPI 180 N. LaSalle Owner, LLC v. 180 N. LaSalle II, LLC, 403 Ill. App. 3d 1, 933 N.E.2d 860, 342 Ill. Dec. 879 (2010). The plaintiff in *YPI* entered into a contract to purchase a commercial building prior to the financial crisis and subsequently fell victim to lenders pulling their financing to the deal after the 2008 credit freeze. The court reasoned that there were any number of reasons the developer might have not been able to obtain financing to complete the purchase and the burden was on the developer to account for this risk. For further reading on the applicability of force majeure and impossibility of performance, see Encina, Clause Majeure?, supra.

3. Electing an Actual Damages Remedy. In contrast to the court in *Lefemine*, the Colorado Supreme Court let a developer of condominiums have its cake and eat it too—enforcing the seller's election to keep the buyers' deposited earnest money pursuant to a contract provision that alternatively allowed the seller at its option to recover its actual damages. Ravenstar, LLC v. One Ski Hill Place, LLC, 401 P.3d 552 (Colo. 2017). The Colorado court rejected the reasoning of *Lefemine* and similar decisions as unpersuasive:

> These courts have assumed that the non-breaching party would choose the remedy of liquidated damages only when actual damages are lower than the stipulated sum and thereby inferred "an intent to penalize the defaulting buyer." See Lefemine, 573 So. 2d at 329. However, a non-breaching party might instead reasonably choose to retain liquidated damages even though actual damages may be higher for two primary reasons.

> First, whereas actual damages must be proved, liquidated damages offer certainty. Here, for example, at the time [seller] had to elect between remedies, the ultimate actual damages were difficult to ascertain because the real estate being sold was a condominium unit in a yet-to-be-constructed building. Thus, electing liquidated damages provided certainty of relief that may not have otherwise been available. Second, the non-breaching party may prefer to forgo the possibility of lengthy and costly litigation involved in seeking actual damages. This is particularly true where, as here, the liquidated damages consist of money already paid to the seller. Because, at the time of breach, the non-breaching party may not know its actual damages

without engaging in time-consuming and expensive fact and expert discovery, electing liquidated damages avoids this time and cost expenditure.

Which approach do you think is more persuasive—the Florida or the Colorado Supreme Court?

Presumably, the *Lefemine* case involved the situation where the seller's actual damages were less than the agreed-on liquidated damages. Invalidating the liquidated damages as a penalty would force the seller to prove and recover its lesser actual damages. Consider the situation, however, where the seller's actual damages would exceed its liquidated damages. In these circumstances, at the seller's urging, several courts have construed the parties' contract to permit the seller to forgo its liquidated damages and recover its greater actual damages. See, e.g., Margaret H. Wayne Trust v. Lipsky, 123 Idaho 253, 846 P.2d 904 (1993) (seller can recover actual damages under contract providing that earnest money was not a "waiver of other remedies available," as parties in residential deals seldom negotiate the amount of earnest money with any thought as to whether it is a reasonable preestimate of damages); Noble v. Ogborn, 43 Wash. App. 387, 717 P.2d 285 (1986) (seller can seek actual damages under contract providing that "[s]eller shall have the election to retain the earnest money as liquidated damages, or to institute suit to enforce any right Seller has"). What would be the effect in these circumstances of invalidating the liquidated damages clause under the reasoning in *Lefemine*? Do you agree with the Idaho court's observation in *Lipsky* on the parties' expectations in residential deals? Do you think that parties in commercial deals have different expectations concerning the role of the earnest money deposit?

Is it consistent with the reasoning in *Lefemine* to allow sellers either by implication or by express agreement to elect to forgo their liquidated damages and seek specific performance of the breaching purchaser's obligation to buy the property? Wouldn't the seller only be inclined to seek this remedy if its liquidated damages were in fact inadequate to fully compensate it for the purchaser's breach? Among the cases following *Lefemine* are Catholic Charities of Archdiocese of Chicago v. Thorpe, 318 Ill. App. 3d 304, 741 N.E.2d 651 (2000).

Providing further layers of ambiguity to this area of law is the language found in the Interstate Land Sales Full Disclosure Act (discussed more fully at Ch. 16C5) which can be applicable to the sale of condominium units in a new development. 15 U.S.C. §§1700 et. seq. Intended to protect prospective buyers of new condominiums, the language of 1703(d) requires inclusion of the following language in the sales contract:

> (3) that, if the purchaser or lessee loses rights and interest in the lot as a result of a default or breach of the contract or agreement which occurs after the purchaser or lessee has paid 15 per centum of the purchase price of the lot, excluding any interest owed under the contract or agreement, the seller or lessor (or successor thereof) shall refund to such purchaser or lessee any amount which remains after subtracting

(A) 15 per centum of the purchase price of the lot, excluding any interest owed under the contract agreement, or the amount of damages incurred by the seller or lessor (or successor thereof) as a result of such breach, whichever is greater, from

(B) the amount paid by the purchaser or lessee with respect to the purchase price of the lot, excluding any interest paid under the contract or agreement.

If developers of new condominiums are required to include this language in their sales contracts, are they creating damages alternatives that are prohibited by *Lefemine*? The court in Karimi v. 401 North Wabash Venture, LLC, 2011 IL App (1st) 102670, 952 N.E. 2d 1278, 352 Ill. Dec. 52 (2011), decided this language found in the sales contract did not undermine the seller's right to seek liquidated damages. The Illinois Appellate Court reasoned that despite the reference to actual damages as part of the calculation of damages due defendant, defendants did not really have the option to seek an actual damages remedy.

> ➤ *Problem 2-4*
> If you were Sarah Seller's attorney, what would you think of §10 of the sample sale agreement in the Documents Manual? Suppose that, when the contract is executed, the local real estate market is soft or volatile. Do you see any pitfall for Sarah if she accepts this language without modification? In light of the relatively large earnest money deposit ($5 million, or $12^{1/2}$ percent of the purchase price), what protective language might you, as Dan's legal advisor, want to insert in §10 of the sale agreement? In a jurisdiction where liquidated damages clauses are vulnerable to attack as penalties, what do you as the seller's attorney think about recharacterizing the earnest money deposit as something else (such as a rental payment or consideration for an option to purchase)? See N.Y. Real Est. Law Rep., Mar. 1987, at 6. ◄

4. Buyer's Remedies for Seller's Default. The foregoing discussions have considered seller's remedies in the event of the purchaser's default. However, in the event of a seller's refusal to sell to buyer or other breach of their agreement, to what rights of remedy should the buyer be entitled? Buyers are generally not protected by contract language granting liquidated damages. In the event buyers are foreclosed from pursuing the remedy of specific performance against the seller due to the seller's deficient title to the property or the sale of the property to a bona fide prospective purchaser, the buyer is left with trying to show damages caused by the loss of the deal. In a market of appreciating real estate, perhaps the buyer can establish evidence of lost value due to generally rising prices. Without an appreciating market, however, does the buyer have other arguments of loss due to seller's breach? The court in St. Lawrence Factory Stores v. Ogdensburg Bridge and Port Authority, 13 N.Y.3d 204, 918 N.E.2d 124, 889 N.Y.2d 534 (2009) explicitly denied a theory of lost profits of a future shopping center claimed by a buyer as too speculative, but the court did allow claims by the buyer for damages related to buyer's reliance on the deal. These expenditures included the title search, survey, and attorney's fees that were required to fulfill the transaction.

5. Malpractice. In *Maxton Builders* (supra note 1), the sale contract allowed the buyer to withdraw without penalty if the real estate taxes on a newly constructed home exceeded a specified amount. The buyer's lawyer determined the taxes were excessive but gave only oral notice of cancellation by telephone, rather than the timely written notice the contract demanded. The appellate court required strict compliance with the contractual right to cancel and allowed the seller to retain the buyer's 10 percent "down payment" check as discussed above. Do you think the buyer's lawyer was guilty of malpractice?

B. TITLE INSURANCE

Returning to the master hypothetical, assume that shortly after the sale contract is executed the parties arrange for a preliminary title examination (report) to determine whether Sarah Seller can convey marketable title, that is, title as described in the contract to Dan Developer, without any additional defects, liens, or encumbrances that might adversely affect the value of the property. Schedule A of the preliminary title report will indicate whether Sarah is vested with fee simple title in the property, and Schedule B will indicate whether the property is encumbered by any mortgage, tax lien, judgment lien, easement, restrictive covenant, or other interest that might interfere with Dan's beneficial use of the property.

Some of the encumbrances listed in Schedule B will be anticipated inasmuch as they represent an integral part of the bargain; for example, the sale agreement may contemplate that Dan will assume an existing mortgage or take subject to it as part of the agreed-on purchase price. Others will not be objectionable to you as Dan's attorney because they will maintain or enhance the value of the property (for example, utility easements and leases with prime tenants). Of course, you will want to review the language of the easements or leases (and any other encumbrances) to which Dan's title will be subject to determine if they contain any objectionable provisions such as rights of the utility to block access to the property or options of tenants to purchase the property. Just before title closes, the title examiner will make a final "rundown" check to make sure that no intervening conveyances or encumbrances were recorded after the preliminary title report was issued.

Finally, on the date of closing or shortly thereafter, Dan will receive his title insurance policy, insuring him of fee simple title as of the closing date subject to certain general exclusions from coverage, various conditions, and the approved property-specific title exceptions in Schedule B, all enumerated in the policy. Keep in mind that in contrast to other forms of insurance, such as life or hazard insurance, title insurance is predicated more on risk-prevention (based on prior events) than risk-assumption (based on future events). Following a careful examination of the public records,[17] the title company purports to do nothing more than assure the owner or mortgagee (lender), as the case may be, that the title is marketable and not subject to any defects, liens, or encumbrances (other than those designated as exceptions) as of the date the policy is issued. This is the date on which the title examination ceases, normally when the deed to the purchaser is recorded or, in the case of a loan policy issued to a mortgagee, the date on which the mortgage is recorded. Therefore, the policy will not cover encumbrances that do not accrue against the property until after the policy is issued. This makes sense; how could the title examiner be expected to discover defects or liens that don't come into existence until after the title examination is completed?

Without question, title insurance represents the principal source of protection for purchasers and mortgagees in today's commercial real estate transactions,[18] especially in light of the limited protection afforded to grantees under covenants for title in deeds. Remember that deed warranties amount to nothing more than promises to indemnify that depend on the future solvency of the grantor, while title insurance is backed by the often more substantial net worth of the company that underwrites the policy. Moreover, if the seller is a bank, insurance company, executor/trustee, or other institutional lender, it will most likely refuse to make such warranties to the purchaser (see Chapter 2A4, supra). Furthermore, the alternative of obtaining an attorney's opinion of title has virtually disappeared in commercial real estate transactions because attorneys are ill-equipped to undertake the search such an opinion requires (the cost of which in most cases would be prohibitive) and because attorneys are generally unwilling to do so unless their opinion assumes the accuracy of a title report prepared by a title company (thus affording little protection to the client). Moreover, while the attorney's liability must be predicated on negligence, the title company assumes strict liability for its assurance of title (subject to the various policy exceptions). For example, the title company will assure against such off-the-record risks as a prior grantor's adjudicated mental incompetence and the invalidity of deed signatures—matters that a reasonable searcher may not discover.

The national trade association for the title insurance industry, the American Land Title Association (ALTA), issues standard policy forms including: (1) the owner's policy (insuring the purchaser or other policyholder of fee simple title); (2) the loan policy (insuring the mortgagee that title is valid and the insured mortgage has lien priority);[19] (3) the construction loan policy (insuring the

---

17. See generally Fiflis, Land Transfer Improvement: The Basic Facts and Two Hypotheses for Reform, 38 U. Colo. L. Rev. 431 (1966) (describing the approaches used by title insurance companies to examine the public records and noting that some title companies have their own title plants in which their employees copy entries from the public records to create a duplicate set of the public records that they can search).

18. Private title insurance is available in every state except Iowa, which prohibits title insurance except through the state-run Iowa Title Guaranty Fund.

19. See discussion at Chapter 4D9.

construction lender);[20] and (4) endorsements to policies for leasehold owners and leasehold lenders.[21] At this juncture, let us examine the 2006 ALTA owner's policy in the Documents Manual. First, we examine the insuring provisions of the owner's policy, which tell the insured what coverage is provided. Then we analyze what these insuring provisions, now known as Covered Risks in the 2006 policy, are "subject to," namely, the standard exclusions from coverage, the property-specific exceptions from coverage contained in Schedule B, and the standard conditions. For the most part, the owner's and loan policies contain the same Covered Risks, exclusions, and conditions except that extra language is included in the latter policy.[22] Depending on local law variations and the proclivities of a particular title company, it may be possible on payment of an additional premium to expand the coverage of the insuring provisions by obtaining a so-called special endorsement to nullify one or more of the exclusions, exceptions, or conditions. For example, as discussed at Chapter 4D7, note 3, in some states it is possible to obtain a zoning endorsement to insure against the adverse effects of local land use regulations notwithstanding the language in Exclusion 1(a) of the 2006 policy.

Finally, because the standard title industry forms are revised periodically by the ALTA, lawyers dealing with title insurance issues must examine the specific policy in question. For example, the ALTA owner's policy in the Documents Manual was revised previously in 1992, 1990, 1987 (a major revision), and 1984 following its introduction in 1970. Moreover, in some states, notably California, New York, and Texas, title companies may be issuing policies based on forms supplied from other sources such as the California Land Title Association, the New York Board of Title Underwriters, and the Texas State Board of Insurance.

Before beginning the Notes and Questions, read the ALTA owner's policy of title insurance in the Documents Manual.

NOTES AND QUESTIONS

1. Insuring Provisions of Title Policy. The Covered Risk provisions of the 2006 ALTA owner's policy ("owner's policy") and the 2006 ALTA loan policy ("mortgagee's policy") protect the owner or mortgagee, as the case may be, against loss or damage by reason of: "1) Title to the estate . . . being vested other than as stated therein [in Schedule A]"; 2) any defect in or lien or encumbrance on the title; 3) unmarketability of the title; 4) lack of a right of access to and from the land; 5) violation or enforcement of any law, ordinance, permit, or governmental regulation (including those relating to building and zoning) if a notice describing the land is recorded in the public records but only to the extent of the violation referred to therein; 6) an enforcement action based on exercise of a governmental police power not covered in #5 if a notice of the enforcement

---

20. See discussion at Chapter 6B3d.
21. See discussion at Chapter 11A1.
22. See discussion at Chapter 4D9.

action is covered in the public records but only to the extent of enforcement referred to therein; 7) the exercise of eminent domain if a notice of the exercise is recorded in the public records; 8) any taking by a governmental body that has occurred and is binding on the rights of a purchaser for value without knowledge; 9) title being vested other than as stated in Schedule A or being defective (a) as a result of the avoidance in whole, or in part or from a court order providing an alternate remedy, of a transfer of the title or any interest in the land occurring prior to the transaction vesting title as shown in Schedule A because that prior transfer constituted a fraudulent or preferential transfer under federal bankruptcy, state insolvency, or similar creditors' rights laws, or (b) because the instrument of transfer vesting title as shown in Schedule A constitutes a preferential transfer by reason of the failure of its recording in the public records being timely or imparting notice of its existence to a purchaser for value or judgment or lien creditor; and 10) any defect in or lien or encumbrance on the title or other matter included in Covered Risks 1 through 9 created or attached or has been filed or recorded in the public records subsequent to the date of the policy and prior to the recording of the deed or other instrument of transfer in the public records that vests title as shown in Schedule A.

Covered Risk 1 assures the owner or mortgagee that title to the property is vested in the individual or entity described in Schedule A so that, for example, the title company is liable if the property purchased by Dan Developer were vested in Danielle Developer or if Dan's interest turned out to be a mere life estate when designated as a fee simple interest in Schedule A.

Covered Risk 2 is a vital provision because it protects the insured against any loss or damage sustained as a consequence of any defect, lien, or encumbrance that is not excepted under Schedule B or excluded from coverage by means of a boilerplate exclusion, condition, or stipulation.

Covered Risk 3 assures the owner that if it should enter into a contract of sale with a purchaser, the title to the insured property (as described in Schedule A) will be "marketable" (subject to the exceptions enumerated in Schedule B), as that term is indirectly defined in §1(k) of the Conditions. In some states, the ALTA form of policy does not insure against unmarketability unless the insured pays an extra premium. If title is "unmarketable" because of a defect that existed as of the date of the title policy, doesn't this mean that the title must be vested otherwise than as described in Schedule A (Covered Risk 1)? Alternatively, doesn't this mean that there is a defect in or lien or encumbrance on such title (Covered Risk 2)? Therefore, does Covered Risk 3 provide any additional coverage that justifies the extra premium charged in some states for its inclusion? Consider the following hypothetical.

> ➤ *Problem 2-5*

Dan Developer obtains a title insurance policy that does not contain Covered Risk 3 (a so-called Form A policy) from Worthier Title Company. Five years later he contracts to sell the property to Irma Investor. Shortly before the closing, an adjoining owner claims the rear 10 feet of Dan's property based on a 12-year-old deed recorded by the previous owner that was not mentioned in Dan's title policy. Dan's contract of sale with Irma purports to convey the entire property, including the rear 10 feet in question. The title company defends on the ground that Dan acquired title by adverse possession (that is, that Dan had occupied the 10 feet openly, continuously, notoriously, and adversely for the period of the applicable statute of limitations for actions by way of ejectment); hence, the neighbor is barred from contesting Dan's title. The neighbor disputes this defense, claiming that Dan had never occupied the rear 10 feet, and the matter goes to litigation. Meanwhile, Irma, searching for a way to extricate herself from the contract, successfully maintains that the neighbor's claim constitutes a cloud on the title, rendering it unmarketable, and Irma is released from the contract under the doctrine of marketable title discussed at Chapter 2A3, supra. One year later the neighbor's claim is ruled invalid by the courts. Would Worthier Title be liable for Dan's loss of his bargain with Irma? See Hilliker v. Rueger, 228 N.Y. 11, 126 N.E. 266 (1920). Suppose Dan's policy included Covered Risk 3 (a so-called Form B policy) and Dan is not able to find another buyer who is willing to pay what Irma had offered. Would Worthier Title be liable for Dan's loss of the bargain? See Montemarano v. Home Title Ins. Co., 258 N.Y. 478, 180 N.E. 241 (1932). If so, is §9 of the Conditions in conflict with Covered Risk 3? ◄

Covered Risk 4 provides coverage against "lack of right of access to and from the land." What does this mean? Is this provision implicated if the only access is by helicopter? By footpath? By a road that leads to a dead end? Observe that this provision only relates to "legal" access and does not ensure the physical nature and extent of the access. See Krause v. Title & Trust Co., 390 So. 2d 805 (Fla. Dist. Ct. App. 1980) (title insureds had legal access even though without road improvements the route was not passable by passenger vehicles). The limitations of this insuring clause point out the importance of a current survey and the need for the buyer's attorney to review the survey carefully to ensure the buyer's expectations of access. Surveys are discussed at Chapter 4D8.

2. Exclusions from Coverage. The Covered Risks are made subject to the exclusions from coverage, the property-specific exceptions, and the conditions in the policy. The first three exclusions and exclusions 4 and 5 in the Owner's Policy and exclusions 6 and 7 in the Loan Policy are essentially the same for both the owner's and mortgagee's policies; the mortgagee's policy adds additional exclusions discussed at Chapter 4D8. Exclusions 1 and 2 generally eliminate from coverage the effect of laws, ordinances, governmental regulations, and exercise of police power or the power of eminent domain, except to the extent that notice of a defect, lien, or encumbrance related to these restrictions or notice of the exercise of police power or eminent domain is recorded in the public records at the date of the policy. Under Exclusion 1, would the title company be liable if it is determined that Dan Developer's use of the property is unlawful under zoning laws?

Exclusion 3 covers five different situations. Exclusions 3(a) and (e) are fairly obvious. Do you understand why the title company is justified in imposing these limitations on coverage? Based on your understanding of the recording statute system, can you think of the probable rationale for Exclusion 3(e)?

Exclusion 3(c) eliminates any liability for the insurer where the defect, lien, or encumbrance does not result in any loss or damage to the insured claimant. Moreover, Condition 8(a)(ii) of the owner's policy stipulates that the liability of the title company may not exceed the lesser of the policy amount or the diminution in value of the insured property caused by the defect or encumbrance. But how is loss or damage to the insured measured? Assume, for example, that Dan Developer purchases three acres of raw land at a price of $4,000 per acre and that Dan obtains an owner's policy with coverage in a face amount of $12,000. In the case of an owner's policy, the amount of insurance coverage obtained is usually the purchase price paid for the land plus the cost of any improvements. Further assume that 10 years later, when the land is worth $6,000 per acre, an adverse claimant establishes superior title to one of the three acres (by means of an action to quiet title) based on a record defect in Dan's chain of title. Using the phraseology of the owner's policy, what is the amount of the "loss or damages" not exceeding the amount of insurance ($12,000) "sustained or incurred" by Dan? The title company might contend that title insurance operates to protect a purchaser or a mortgagee against defects or encumbrances on the title *as of the date of the policy* and that therefore the policy is retroactive rather than prospective in its operation. If this is the case, then how did Dan sustain a loss when the value of the untainted portion of his property (two acres at $6,000 per acre) has not been reduced below the original purchase price for the entire parcel? Even if Dan sustained a loss, since the policy necessarily looks to the past and not the future, the diminution in value caused by the defect arguably should be measured as of the date of the policy (at $4,000) rather than the time of its discovery (at $6,000). As counsel to Dan, what is your counterargument in favor of the $6,000 damage amount? Compare Beaullieu v. Atlanta Title & Trust Co., 60 Ga. App. 400, 4 S.E.2d 78 (1939), with Overholtzer v. Northern Counties Title Ins. Co., 116 Cal. App. 2d 113, 253 P.2d 116 (1953). See Stone, Note, The Insured's Rights Against the Title Insurer, 6 Case W. Res. L. Rev. 49, 59-61 (1954).

Exclusion 3(d) exculpates the title company for defects created or attaching after the date of the policy. As discussed above, title insurance doesn't cover encumbrances that accrue against the property after the date the policy is issued—usually when the purchaser's deed is recorded (for owner's policies) or the mortgage is recorded (for mortgagee's policies). While the operation of this exclusion would appear to be straightforward, its application is less clear when the particular defect is inchoate at the time the policy is issued; that is, when the encumbrance is based on prior events that do not come into fruition until after the policy is issued.

> ➤ *Problem 2-6*
>
> Suppose that a year before Dan Developer purchases waterfront industrial property, the local municipality adopts a resolution to fund the cost of a canal bulkheading project with a special assessment on all canal-front properties. The city council resolution provides that on completion of construction the city "shall levy a special assessment for such cost payable in 20 equal annual installments secured by a lien on the abutting properties." Assume that the improvements are completed sometime after Dan's title policy is issued (which is silent as to the assessment) and that on completion the city passes another resolution fixing a special assessment against Dan's property in the amount of $100,000 and notes the assessment on the city's assessment rolls. Does Dan have a claim under his title policy for this encumbrance that was set in motion before his title policy was issued? Compare Strass v. District-Realty Title Ins. Corp., 31 Md. App. 690, 358 A.2d 251 (1976); Cummins v. U.S. Life Title Ins. Co., 40 N.Y.2d 639, 357 N.E.2d 975, 389 N.Y.S.2d 319 (1976); Metropolitan Life Ins. Co. v. Union Trust Co., 283 N.Y. 33, 27 N.E.2d 225 (1940), with Bel-Air Motel Corp. v. Title Ins. Co. of Pa., 183 N.J. Super. 551, 444 A.2d 1119 (1981). See generally Annot., What Constitutes a Charge, Encumbrance or Lien Within Contemplation of Title Insurance Policy?, 87 A.L.R.3d 764 (1978). ◄

In response to recurring litigation of this nature, title companies will usually specify a Variable Exception in Schedule B of the policy (discussed below) for "[t]axes or special assessments which are not shown as existing liens by the public records [on the policy date]." See Rainier Natl. Bank v. Wells, 65 Wash. App. 893, 829 P.2d 1168 (1992) (this "clear" exception excluded an improvement district assessment created by an ordinance before the policy was issued but not entered onto the final assessment rolls until after the policy issuance). However, for an extra premium in most states, the insured can purchase a special endorsement covering assessments for street improvements under construction or completed when the policy is issued. In the new 2006 ALTA policies, Exclusions from Coverage include tax liens or other governmental assessments that attach to the land between the policy date and the date of recording in the public records.

Finally, Exclusion 4 of the Owner's Policy and Exclusion 6 of the Loan Policy address certain risks in bankruptcy proceedings that are discussed at Chapter 18C.

3. Schedules A and B. Schedule A tells you what is being insured. It contains the policy date and the face amount of insurance. This is important information because, as we observed earlier, the date of the policy is the operative date for insuring the title and the amount of insurance establishes the maximum amount of the title company's liability. Schedule A also furnishes the name of the insured and indicates the nature and extent of the estate covered by the policy and in whom the estate is vested as of the policy date.

Schedule B contains exceptions to the coverage of the policy. There are two types of exceptions: general exceptions applicable to all policies and "special exceptions" relating only to the specific property. In the 1970 form of the ALTA policy, the general exceptions were expressly enumerated in Schedule B, whereas in the current policy forms they have been omitted so that they can be adapted for local use. Nevertheless, most of these earlier general exceptions still appear in present policies; therefore, you should become familiar with them. They read as follows:

General Exceptions:

(1) Rights or claims of parties in possession not shown by the public records.
(2) Encroachments, overlaps, boundary line disputes, and any other matters which would be disclosed by an accurate survey and inspection of the premises.
(3) Easements or claims of easements not shown by the public records.
(4) Any lien, or right to a lien, for services, labor, or material heretofore or hereafter furnished, imposed by law and not shown by the public records.
(5) Taxes or special assessments which are not shown as existing liens by the public records.

In most instances, at least some of these general exceptions will require reasonable modification at the urging of the insured's attorney. For example, the first exception for rights of parties in possession is apparently aimed at tenants in possession. Under the doctrine of "inquiry notice" recognized in many jurisdictions, a purchaser may be charged with inquiry notice of the rights of parties in possession even if these rights have not yet been recorded. Thus, a tenant with a life estate or an option to purchase the property may be excepted from coverage by this clause. How might the title company modify this clause to provide reasonable protection for a purchaser client while retaining its purpose?

The second exception addresses matters that would be disclosed by an accurate survey or inspection of the premises. This is normally not acceptable to the insured's attorney. For example, even if the purchaser has obtained a recent survey that shows no defects, this exception would exclude liability if the survey happens to be inaccurate. Often title companies will agree to substitute a specific exception for matters disclosed by the purchaser's survey. This is sometimes known as "reading in" the survey.

The third exception relieves the title company of liability for easements or claims of easements not disclosed by the public records. Sometimes the title company will delete this exception. As counsel to the title company, what precaution should you take before agreeing to the deletion? As counsel to the insured, what precaution should you take if the title company refuses to delete the exception?

The fourth exception, dealing with coverage against mechanics' liens, is discussed at Chapter 6B3d.

The fifth exception covers liability for unpaid taxes or special assessments not yet elevated to the status of an existing lien in the public records. See the discussion supra following Problem 2-6.

In addition to these general exceptions, Schedule B contains exceptions applicable to the unique facts and circumstances of each particular piece of property. Each exception must be reviewed carefully by the attorney for the insured. Every recorded document referred to in Schedule B must be read thoroughly. All easements should be traced on the survey. Even a simple utility easement could pose a problem if, for example, it blocks access to the property or causes parking areas to be below the size mandated by local law.

> ➢ *Problem 2-7*

Assume that as counsel to Dan Developer you receive a preliminary title report listing the following property-specific exceptions in Schedule B:

1. Ad valorem taxes for 201_ and subsequent years;
2. Utility easements of record;
3. Encroachments of existing improvements onto utility easements;
4. Covenants, conditions, and restrictions recorded in the Office of the Clerk of the County of Feerick, State of Fuller on November 15, 2003 in Liber 325, page 20.
5. Mortgage dated August 5, 2016, in the principal amount of $25,000,000 made by Law Drive Associates in favor of Ace Insurance Company, recorded in the Office of the Clerk of the County of Feerick, State of Fuller, in Liber 596, page 120, on August 6, 2016.
6. Assignment of Lessor's Interest in Leases dated August 5, 2016, made by Law Drive Associates in favor of Ace Insurance Company and recorded in the Office of the Clerk of the County of Feerick, State of Fuller, in Liber 683, page 23, on August 6, 2016.
7. Mineral interests previously recorded or conveyed of record and all rights incident thereto.

What affirmative insurance might you ask for in the form of special endorsements (additions) to coverage, and what documents would you want to review, before approving or rejecting the foregoing exceptions? What information or explanation, if any, would you provide to Dan concerning the status of title to the property he plans to purchase? Should the title company be responsible to explain to the unrepresented purchaser the legal effect of the various property-specific exceptions in the title

> report? Would that assistance constitute the unauthorized practice of law? Cf. N.J. Stat. Ann. §17:46B-9 (requires title companies to disclose to insured the desirability of obtaining counsel to review the title report); see generally Brossman and Rosenberg, Title Companies and the Unauthorized Practice Rules: The Exclusive Domain Reexamined, 83 Dick. L. Rev. 437 (1978). ◄

Title companies often react to large-scale title claims that affect a particular region by taking specific exception to such claims in Schedule B of subsequently issued policies. For example, Hawaiian title companies may include a local exception for "claims arising out of rights customarily and traditionally exercised for subsistence, cultural, religious, access or gathering purposes as provided for in the Hawaii Constitution or the Hawaii Revised Statutes." This exception derives from decisions such as that of the Hawai'i Supreme Court that held these traditional rights of native Hawaiians must be protected to the extent possible in the issuance of property development permits. See Public Access Shoreline Hawaii v. Hawai'i County Planning Comm'n, 79 Haw. 425, 903 P.2d 1246 (1995), cert. denied, 517 U.S. 1163 (1996). Might any of the exclusions from coverage (discussed supra in note 2) or any of the general exceptions listed above encompass these rights?

4. Conditions. The following questions and comments highlight some of the more important sections of the conditions. While frequently ignored by practitioners, these boilerplate provisions may determine whether or under what circumstances the insured can recover against the title company.

a. Definitions (§1 of the Conditions). Observe that "knowledge" (§1(f)) is defined as "actual knowledge" as opposed to "constructive knowledge." This is important in applying such provisions as Exclusion 3(b). Suppose, for example, that the insured party, Dan Developer, decides to purchase real estate that is apparently in the possession of someone other than the seller. In a jurisdiction that recognizes "inquiry notice," would Dan have a claim against the title company if the party in possession, who paid value for the land but failed to record, should prevail against Dan in an action to quiet title?

Look at the definition of "land" in §1(g). Schedule A of the title policy describes the "land" covered by the policy. Would a description in Schedule A of the "land" that Dan owns in fee simple include an appurtenant easement over a neighbor's land? If not, what should Dan's counsel do before the policy is issued?

In the 2006 policy a new definition of "entity" in §1(c) as including "[a] corporation, partnership, trust, limited liability company, or other legal entity" clarifies the successors to the named insureds under the definition of "insured" in §1(d)(i)(C) to include "successors to the insured by its conversion to another kind of entity." This definition of insured clearly includes wholly-owned affiliates of the entity that is the named insured. These provisions should eliminate litigation over whether the title insurance covers deeding real estate to a wholly owned affiliate.

The definition of "insured" also includes a grantee of an insured under a deed delivered without payment of actual valuable consideration (§1(d)(i)(D)). Assume three family members own an apartment building, which they hold to meet income and appreciation goals. To avoid individual liability, they transfer to an LLC of which only they own the stock. Is the new LLC insured under the original owner's policy?

b. Continuation of Insurance (§2 of the Conditions). Coverage continues under a title policy only as long as the insured retains an interest in the property. Suppose Dan conveys his property by means of a general warranty deed, and a defect is later discovered that predates Dan's purchase of the property and that had not been excepted in the deed description or in Schedule B of Dan's title policy. The purchaser then makes a claim against Dan under some covenant or warranty contained in the deed from Dan. Would Dan's title policy protect him? Suppose Dan sells the property and takes back a purchase money mortgage. Would his original owner's policy protect him as a mortgagee? If so, as of what date? Suppose that instead of selling the property to a third party, Dan transfers the title as a gift to his children, without warranties. If a defect should be asserted subsequently, would Dan's policy protect his children?

c. Notices (§§3 and 4 of the Conditions). Under the 1992 version of the policy conditions, an insured seeking recovery must provide two notices to the title company. The first is prompt notice of any claim that is adverse to the insured title. The second notice in the 1992 Conditions is a proof of loss statement that must be submitted within 90 days after the insured shall "ascertain the facts giving rise to the loss or damage" (§5). By contrast, the 2006 ALTA form of policy requires that such proof of loss be submitted only after the title insurer makes a request (§4). In revising the form, the ALTA responded in part to the requests of the American College of Real Estate Lawyer's (ACREL) Title Insurance Committee that the conditions require the title insurer to give: "(1) notice of a breach of the insured's obligation either to give prompt notice of a claim or a proof of loss with an opportunity to cure prior to reduction of the title insurer's liability under the policy, and (2) receipts for notices and proofs received."[23] Nevertheless, the subtle shift in phraseology to a less objective standard might precipitate substantial litigation in the future. Why? Moreover, the 2006 policies only responded in part to the requests of ACREL. Condition §4 now requires proof of loss only after the title insurer makes the request for it and the 1992 form's consequence of terminating the insurer's liability under the policy if an inadequate proof of loss "prejudices the insurer" is eliminated.

d. Defense (§§5-9 of the Conditions). Suppose Dan Developer purchases real estate worth $1 million and obtains title insurance coverage in the same amount. Ten years later, when the property is worth $3 million, a defect is discovered

---

23. See Palomar, The 2006 ALTA Title Insurance Policies: What New Protections Do They Give?, 42 Real Prop., Prob. & Tr. J. 1, 27 (2007).

that, if substantiated, would result in a total loss for Dan. The title company agrees to defend and assigns the case to a law firm in which Dan does not have much confidence. With $2 million over the insurance amount at stake, can Dan demand that the title company employ another firm? What, if anything, could Dan do if the title company rejected his demand? Observe that in the event of a dispute over litigation strategy, the title company will most likely prevail over the insured based on the language in §5(a). Suppose, for example, that Dan discovers the possibility of an adverse claim but would prefer to do nothing until his adverse possession ripens into title, whereas the title company insists on bringing an action to quiet title. Can the title company sue the adverse claimant on behalf of Dan notwithstanding Dan's objections to the lawsuit? The answer is yes, and if the title company were to lose, Dan could wind up with a right to some money but be ejected from the land worth more than the policy coverage. Suppose that, in the worst case, the title company loses the cause of action and the adverse claimant ejects Dan. The title company, however, decides to appeal the decision to the highest court in the state if necessary, which may take five years or more. Must Dan wait until there is a final adjudication against him before obtaining his money from the title company? Look at Conditions §§8(b)(i) and (ii) for ALTA's response to this possibility in the 2006 owner's policy.

An important point to keep in mind is that the title company is not liable for more than the policy amount (except for the cost of attorneys' fees and litigation expenses in defending the insured's title). Thus, if the insured property appreciates significantly in value, the insured should consider obtaining an increase in the coverage amount for an additional premium in those areas where the title companies are willing to do so.

e. Rights of Recovery Upon Payment or Settlement (§13 of the Conditions). Subrogation is the substitution of one person in the place of another with respect to a claim. When a title company pays a claim, it is subrogated to the rights and remedies of the insured claimant as against third parties resulting from the title defect. Based on this right of subrogation in favor of the title company, most sellers in a commercial transaction (especially banks and other institutional lenders) will refuse to provide the purchaser with a general warranty deed. Can you think of the reason why? See discussion at Chapter 2A4, supra.

Suppose Dan Developer buys property and obtains mortgage financing from Ace Insurance Company. Pursuant to Ace's commitment, Dan pays for a title policy insuring Ace's mortgage. To save money, Dan decides not to get his own title insurance coverage. Later, a defect turns up. Ace makes a claim under its policy, which the title company pays. As most mortgages do, Ace's contains covenants of title under which the borrower assures the lender that the title is as described in the mortgage. Is the title company subrogated to Ace's rights against Dan under these covenants for the amount of its payment to Ace? Would your answer be different if the mortgage were nonrecourse under which Ace and Dan agreed Dan's liability would be limited to the property? See Berks Title Ins. Co. v. Haendiges, 772 F.2d 278 (6th Cir. 1985) (non-recourse clause in mortgage precluded title insurer's suit as subrogee against borrower to recover for mechanics' liens it had satisfied). How might Dan protect himself from subrogation liability?

f. Payment of Loss and the Extent of Liability (§§7 and 8 of the Conditions). These are important provisions that should be reviewed thoroughly. For example, the prefatory language to §8 provides that the contract is nothing more than a contract of indemnity against monetary loss. Added to policies in 1987, this is an attempt by the ALTA to counteract case law holding title companies liable for damages beyond what had been previously contemplated. This burgeoning of insurer liability based on tort theories, along with the doctrine of "reasonable expectancy of the insured," has made title companies more cautious about rejecting claims. See, e.g., Jarchow v. Transamerica Title Ins. Co., 48 Cal. App. 3d 917, 122 Cal. Rptr. 470 (1975) (title company held liable for inflicting emotional distress); Moe v. Transamerica Title Ins. Co., 21 Cal. App. 3d 289, 98 Cal. Rptr. 547 (1971) (company held liable for punitive damages); Tess v. Lawyers Title Ins. Corp., 557 N.W.2d 696 (Neb. 1997) (title company potentially liable in tort for misrepresentation); MacBean v. St. Paul Title Ins. Corp., 169 N.J. Super. 502, 405 A.2d 405 (1979) (company held liable based on reasonable expectations of the insured). But see Citibank v. Chicago Title Ins. Co., 214 A.D.2d 212, 632 N.Y.S.2d 779 (1995) (refuses to recognize an independent cause of action against a title insurer in tort for a negligent title search, limiting recovery to the terms of the insurance contract). See generally Davis, More Than They Bargained For: Are Title Companies Liable in Tort for Undisclosed Title Defects?, 45 Cath. U. L. Rev. 71 (1995).

5. Further Reading. For a general discussion of title insurance, see D. Burke, Law of Title Insurance (1993); Christie, The Title Insurance Industry: A Reexamination Revisited, 18 Real Est. L.J. 354 (Spring 1990); Rooney, Title Insurance: A Primer for Attorneys, 14 Real Prop., Prob. & Tr. J. 608 (Fall 1979); Taub, Rights and Remedies Under a Title Policy, 15 Real Prop., Prob. & Tr. J. 422 (Summer 1980). On the importance of title insurance, see Malloy and Klapow, Attorney Malpractice for Failure to Require Fee Owner's Title Insurance in a Residential Real Estate Transaction, 74 St. John's L. Rev. 407 (2000); Murray, Attorney Malpractice in Real Estate Transactions: Is Title Insurance the Answer?, 42 Real Prop., Prob. & Tr. J. 222 (2007). On the importance of legal representation in the title review process, see Shaffer, The Role of the Lender's Lawyer in Spotting and Fixing Title Problems, 30 Prob. & Prop. 50 (July/Aug. 2016). On the 2006 ALTA title insurance forms changes, see Palomar, The 2006 ALTA Title Insurance Policies: What New Protections Do They Give?, 42, Real Prop., Prob. & Tr. J. 1 (2007); Gurren, 2006 ALTA Title Insurance Policies: The Significant Changes, 24 Prac. Real Est. Law. 17 (2008).

C. CLOSING THE SALE TRANSACTION

The closing date has finally arrived and, pursuant to §4 of the sample sale agreement in the Documents Manual, you and Sarah Seller's attorney will be supervising the execution and exchange of the closing documents whereby Sarah will transfer ownership to Dan in exchange for Dan's payment of the balance of the purchase price. The following excerpt discusses the roles of the seller's and purchaser's attorneys at closing.

M. Friedman, Contracts and Conveyances of Real Property
1146-1154 (6th ed. 1998)

SECTION 11.13 PREPARATION FOR THE CLOSING

. . . The instruments to be delivered at the closing, such as the deed and purchase money mortgage papers, should be prepared in advance by seller's attorney. Unless these are routine, it is good practice to give copies to buyer's attorney, for checking, prior to the closing and before they are executed. For the most part, printed forms for these instruments are available and, if previously tested, they offer assurance against formal omissions or errors which may creep into typewritten papers. In a printed form of deed, for instance, there is less likelihood of error or omission in the granting and habendum clauses, the acknowledgement, or some statutory provision, such as the New York "lien clause," than if the deed is entirely typewritten. When a deed is hurriedly dictated, typewritten and checked at the closing, the lawyers, distracted by other matters, may see in the instrument what they expect to see and if a line, such as the granting clause, should be left out, the omission may easily be missed by all concerned. But the use of accepted printed forms does not dispense with the necessity of checking. The deed and purchase money mortgage will have a typewritten metes and bounds description of the premises. The mortgage papers will recite the amount of principal and time of payment of principal and interest. All these instruments must be dated. It is desirable that these and other instruments be checked by both attorneys when this can be done leisurely, without the distractions of a closing, and when errors can be corrected and differences resolved without embarrassment to anybody. Disposition of these matters in advance reduces the work necessary at the closing and makes for a smoother, more satisfactory and generally friendlier closing.

Usually, the closing instruments are executed at the closing by the principals and it is preferable that it be so done. It is certain, then, that the grantor is alive when the deed is delivered; and questions of identification and competency are thereby reduced. It may not be feasible to do this if a principal cannot be at the closing, and if the absentee is a grantor, the buyer should obtain an explanation of the absence. If the grantor's execution is more than a day or two before the closing, it is important to have proof that the grantor is alive. If execution is by an attorney-in-fact, proof should be obtained that the principal is alive and the power-of-attorney unrevoked.

The closing adjustments are necessarily detailed, though the amounts involved in many of the items may be very small in comparison with the total consideration for the conveyance. They are prepared by the seller's side from data taken from the seller's records. The computations may be made by the seller, his accountant or bookkeeper or attorney. In any event, they must be checked by his attorney in the light of the contract of sale and any relevant law. Thereafter, a statement of the figures should be sent to buyer's attorney for checking in advance of the closing. The adjustments may present an issue of fact, as the amount of fuel at the premises. And there may be a question of law with respect to the inclusion of some items. Mostly, however, the adjustments involve simple mathematics. Their preparation and checking are a chore that can be time-consuming at the closing and are more apt to be so than any other matter. Until they are agreed on, the buyer cannot obtain the cash payable to the seller in the proper amount and medium. It is a matter, then, that should be cleared in advance. The statement of adjustments should be reasonably detailed. If not, the items cannot be checked and are not much use as part of the permanent record of the closing. If the statement charges buyer with, for instance, $57.12 for insurance, this item cannot be verified. It is necessary to state the amount of insurance, the rate, the beginning and expiration of the term of policy and the length of the unexpired term as of the closing date. If the policy has been changed during the term, as by additional coverage or change in rate, this should appear. It is preferable to include the name of the insurance company and number of the policy. Rent adjustments should show the amount of rent and period covered by the adjustment, e.g., one month's rent at $1000 per month, and the number of days and amount chargeable to seller or buyer. . . . Some figures may not be available until the day of closing. If buyer is to pay for fuel on the premises on that date, a reliable estimate will not be available much in advance. If the closing is on the sixth day of the month, and rents are to be adjusted accordingly, the amount of current rents in the seller's hands will not be known before that day. Nevertheless, most computations can be determined well in advance of the closing and it is good practice to get tentative figures, i.e., those complete, in the buyer's hands and checked in advance.

Seller's attorney should prepare a check list of things to be done at the closing. These will include papers he is to deliver and receive, papers which he should inspect, and others that he must exhibit. . . .

The list might read:
Deliver:

    1. Deed, with $ _____ in stamps affixed and canceled.
    2. Leases.
        a. Leases and rental agreements listed in contract of sale.

        b. Instruments necessary to establish validity of rents under emergency rent laws, if any.

3. Check for tenants' security deposits.
4. Insurance.
        a. Original rent insurance policy.
        b. Certificates of fire policies (originals held by mortgagee).
5. Statement of first mortgagee (showing unpaid principal and interest and rate of interest).
6. Building certificates.
        a. Certificate of occupancy.
        b. Certificate of electrical inspection.
        c. Certificate of fire underwriters.
        d. Certificate of plumbing inspection.
7. Keys to premises.
8. Bill of sale to personal property included in sale.
9. Fuel estimate (letter of reliable fuel merchant) (retain counterpart copy).

Exhibit:

    Receipted bills for—
    Real estate taxes.[3]
    Water.
    Franchise taxes; (of corporate seller) or deposit with buyer or title company to insure payment; or letter of seller undertaking to pay amount ultimately fixed.[4]

Inspect:

    Certificate of incorporation of buyer.[5]

Obtain:

1. Balance of purchase price, as per closing computations.

---

3. If real estate taxes are payable in installments, it will be convenient for the buyer in paying future installments accruing during the current fiscal year if in possession of the tax bill. A meticulous seller may prefer to keep the receipt for his records. Delivery of a photocopy may be the solution.

4. The only satisfactory disposition of franchise taxes is evidence of final payment. This may be impossible if, as often occurs, the tax has not been finally fixed at the time of the closing. The insurance of a responsible title company against collection of this tax (and the same goes for estate and transfer taxes) is a common practical solution but leaves title technically unmarketable until actual payment and may not be acceptable to a subsequent purchaser or mortgagee, particularly if a rival title company is used in the later transaction. If the seller fails to carry out an undertaking to pay franchise taxes, the removal of their lien may be a nuisance to the buyer.

5. Seller is interested in the certificate of incorporation of a corporate buyer only if the latter is to execute and deliver a purchase money mortgage to the former.

2.   Purchase money mortgage papers.
     Mortgage note.
     Mortgage.
3.   Expenses re purchase money mortgage. Cost of recording mortgage.
     Mortgage tax.
     Legal charge for preparing mortgage papers.
4.   Receipts for instruments, etc., delivered to buyer.

This list will, of course, vary with the circumstances. . . .

The buyer's attorney should prepare his own checklist. This should recite virtually the same closing instruments as those on the list of the seller's attorney. If not, there may be some misunderstanding at the closing unless the difference is resolved in advance. The preparations of the buyer's attorney are not limited to closing papers. There is other preliminary work for him to do or have done. He must inform his client of the sums necessary and see that these are brought to the closing in cash or proper checks. The insurance to be transferred at the closing should be reviewed by the buyer's insurance representatives, who may recommend changes to improve the coverage or reduce the rate. It might be advisable to obtain types of insurance that the seller does not maintain. If any seller's policies are nontransferable—his public liability insurance may not be transferable—additional policies in replacement will be necessary. In any event, as soon as the deed and keys to the premises belong to the buyer—and not a day or a week later—the buyer should be covered by binder, endorsement or new policies with all the insurance he intends to have. In view of the rule that insurance is not transferable without the consent of the insurer, the best way of handling this is by having policies or endorsements, showing the new interest, at the closing. A telephone call made at the closing to an insurance broker is a poor substitute.

When the buyer leaves the closing he should be in a position to take over administration of the property with no breach of continuity. Gas, electricity, and other services must be continued. Building employees who are to be retained will expect their pay at the customary time. Tenants must be notified of the change and directed where and to whom rent will be payable. New contracts for services and utilities may be necessary. Some service contracts may be taken over from the seller. Tenants' rights, respecting services, maintenance, decorating, credit for security or advance rent, etc., must be observed. Some of this may be indicated in the leases. Others may be based on the custom at the premises. Whoever is to manage the property must be ready with all these things. If the property is large enough for the seller to employ a managing agent, there are obvious advantages in the buyer's continuing this agent. If the buyer supersedes the seller's agent with his own, it would be well for new and old agents to meet, at the closing or before, to turn over data to the new agent. If this should not be practical, because of resentment on the part of the superseded agent, it would be well for the buyer to continue the old agent temporarily and take over management of the property gradually.

Seller's attorney should have any necessary deed stamps[24] on hand at the time of closing. A seller's practice of delivering the deed without stamps, and paying the buyer or title company closer for his cost is not recommended. There is no occasion to affix the stamps until the end of the closing. If anything should go awry, it will be a nuisance to obtain a refund for canceled but unused stamps. In this connection, it should be noted that if a formal tender of the deed should be necessary, in order to lay the basis for some claim, the deed will be in proper form for this purpose without stamps affixed and canceled.

A last-minute inspection of the property should be made by the buyer or on his behalf to make sure that all personal property and fixtures included in the sale are on the premises, that no parties are in occupation other than those contemplated by the contract of sale, and that the premises have sustained no damage warranting rescission or an abatement in the purchase price.[25]

NOTES

Further reading. For general guidance in reviewing real estate documents, see Brat and Carey, A Guide to Underlying Document Review for A Major Commercial Real Estate Investment (with Forms), 31 Prac. Real Est. Law. 5 (2015).

24. Deed stamps represent a tax imposed by some states or localities on the transfer of real estate, usually based on the amount of the purchase price. See, e.g., Fla. Stat. Ann. §201.02 (imposing a deed stamp tax on land conveyances of 70¢ for each $100 of consideration for the transfer).—EDS.

25. See generally Lane and Clack, Preparing for a Real Estate Closing, 4 Prac. Real Est. Law. 61 (Sept. 1988).—EDS.

PART II

FUNDAMENTALS OF
REAL ESTATE FINANCE

Chapter 3

The Nature of a Mortgage and Mortgage Substitutes

MASTER HYPOTHETICAL

In analyzing commercial real estate transactions, we will refer frequently to this book's master hypothetical in which Dan Developer is a real estate entrepreneur with an excellent track record for developing office buildings and shopping centers. Dan acquired from Francine Farmer the fee simple title to some land in a growing city of McNiece in the County of Feerick, State of Fuller, on which he intends to construct an office building. Dan paid Francine $8 million for the land, and he anticipates spending approximately $25 million on the so-called soft costs (for example, architectural and legal fees, engineer's report) and hard ("brick and mortar") costs of constructing the office building. He has already talked to several prospective tenants that have expressed interest in leasing one or more floors in the building, and he expects to execute leases with a few credit ("prime") tenants (including the Widget Corporation of America) in the next month or so. Based on the estimated net rental income, he expects to receive from the prime and secondary (short-term) tenants, Dan is assuming that the fair market value of the project will equal its cost of $33 million. (This assumption that future market value equals cost is being made for simplicity's sake. In reality, a developer probably would not undertake the project unless the anticipated market value exceeds the projected cost.)

Dan has decided to finance the cost of the project by means of a mortgage loan from some institutional lender that specializes in postconstruction financing of commercial real estate, such as a life insurance company. He anticipates that the lender will require a first mortgage lien on the land and the completed improvements. He also expects to receive a maximum loan-to-value ratio on the loan of about 75 percent. Therefore, since the estimated market value of the project is about $33 million, he anticipates receiving a loan amount of approximately $25 million, which means that he will have to fund the balance of the development costs ($8 million) either by using his own funds or (if he is as leverage-minded as most developers) by raising the equity capital from outside investors.

On January 1 of this year, Dan applies to the Ace Insurance Company for a postconstruction loan of $25 million at a fixed interest rate of 5 percent per annum for a term of 15 years, with a closing date scheduled for December 15 of next year following completion of construction. He expects that construction will commence on June 15 of this year and be completed on or before the closing date, December 15 of next year. Dan has determined that construction financing will be available from the Fuller National Bank (FNB) in the same amount of $25 million on the strength of a "takeout commitment" whereby Ace agrees to buy the FNB construction loan once the project is completed should Dan comply with all the commitment conditions.

In the discussion that follows, we may vary some of the foregoing hypothetical facts for illustrative purposes as we address the many questions and considerations that relate to commercial real estate transactions.

This chapter examines some basic theories with respect to the nature of a mortgage and mortgage substitutes as a prelude to the more practice-oriented discussion of modern real estate financing in subsequent chapters. While the mortgagee's (lender's) remedy of foreclosure is examined closely in Chapter 8, reference is made to it in the intervening chapters; accordingly, a brief overview of foreclosure is presented herein, preceded by a historical overview of mortgage law. We then discuss some threshold questions about the function of a mortgage and the nature of its underlying obligation, such as (1) can a mortgage secure the performance of an act by the mortgagor (borrower) other than a promise to repay some indebtedness; (2) must the underlying obligation of the mortgagor be supported by valid consideration and enforceable, and when must the obligation be enforceable; and (3) must the mortgagor be personally liable for the performance of the underlying obligation? Next, we examine the nature of the two most common mortgage substitutes: the deed of trust and the installment land contract. Finally, we examine how a mortgage competes with other liens and interests in the same real estate held by parties other than the mortgagee.

A. A HISTORICAL OVERVIEW OF MORTGAGE LAW

The theory of mortgage law in American jurisprudence has largely been forged by developments in the early English common law. At common law, the first property security device was the pledge. You probably know the term better by its modern-day corollary, the pawn. In a pledge transaction, the lender would lend money to the borrower and the borrower would transfer possession of property to the lender as security for the indebtedness. When the loan was repaid, the lender would return the property. If the loan was not paid, the lender could keep the property.[1]

---

1. The forerunners of the modern mortgage were variants of the pledge device and included the Glanvillian gage, the Jewish gage, and the Bractonian mortgage. See 1 G. Glenn, Mortgages

The pledge device eased the virtual paranoia of early judges about "secret liens." Since possession was transferred to the lender, prospective creditors could not be misled into believing that the borrower owned the property free and clear of liens.[2] With real estate, it is impractical to transfer possession of the property to the lender except in rare situations. The borrower needs the property to run a business or as shelter for the borrower's family. How, then, could a person use real estate as security for a loan? The answer was the common law mortgage. While it may have been impractical to transfer possession of real estate, it was nevertheless feasible to transfer fee title. Accordingly, beginning around the fourteenth century, the mortgage took the form of a deed from the borrower (the "mortgagor") to the lender (the "mortgagee").[3] The differences between this common law mortgage and the ordinary deed of fee simple absolute were that the mortgagor was ordinarily allowed to remain in possession of the real estate during the term of the mortgage and that the mortgage conveyance was subject to a condition subsequent. If the borrower paid interest in a timely manner and otherwise performed the obligations under the promissory note and the mortgage, including paying the balance of the principal indebtedness on the due date, called the "law day," the deed would become void and title would automatically revert to the mortgagor. If, however, the mortgagor defaulted in its obligations, title would vest indefeasibly in the mortgagee. What happened to all the judicial concern about ostensible ownership? This was eventually resolved by recording statutes that substituted public notice—the recording of the mortgage document—for the change in physical possession.

The results of all this could be very severe for the borrower. What if on the date the mortgage became due the mortgagor's horse suffered an accident and it was impossible to get into town to make the payment until the next day? Too late. Time was regarded as of the essence. While this may have been unfair, there was no remedy for the mortgagor at law. As you may remember, when there was a wrong, and no remedy was available at law, the person wronged could appeal to the King's chancellor (later the courts of equity) to redress the injustice. To mitigate the harsh result to the defaulting borrower, the King's chancellor would frequently permit the mortgagor to "redeem," or buy back, the mortgaged property from the mortgagee subsequent to the law day on a special showing of

---

(1943); G. Osborne, Handbook on the Law of Mortgages 2-8 (2d ed. 1970) (hereinafter Osborne); Rabinowitz, The Story of the Mortgage Retold, 94 U. Pa. L. Rev. 94 (1945).

2. Before the advent of recording statutes, courts would strike down security interests, including mortgages, as fraudulent conveyances where the borrower retained possession of the property. Should they have been equally concerned about the lender who took possession of the collateral and therefore might appear to the lender's creditors as owning the collateral? If not, why not?

3. "Mortgage" literally means "dead pledge." As Littleton once said, "[T]he cause why it is called mortgage is, for that it is doubtful whether the feoffer will pay at the day limited . . .; and if he doth not pay, then the land . . . is taken from him forever, and so dead (to him. . . . And if he doth pay the money, then pledge is dead) as to the tenant, etc." Sir Thomas Littleton, Tenures bk. 111, ch. v, §332 (Wambaugh 1903). See Osborne §1.

fraud, accident, or some other equitable ground. By the seventeenth century, this "equity of redemption" was routinely recognized by equity courts.[4] Eventually the mortgagor's equity of redemption became recognized as an "equitable estate," and, like other full-fledged interests in land, could be transferred, subdivided into lesser estates, devised, and even mortgaged again by the same mortgagor.

On the other side of the coin, the mortgagor's equity of redemption, if unlimited, would have produced severe consequences for any mortgagee facing the specter of a redemption by a borrower at some uncertain time in the future. The mortgagee would be inhibited from improving the real estate and would encounter significant difficulty in selling the property to recoup its loan investment. Consequently, mortgagees, without any remedy for this wrong at law, turned to the same chancellor or equity court for relief, asking the court to cut off, or "foreclose," the borrower's equity of redemption. Born of this plea by mortgagees there developed what we now call foreclosure proceedings. On proper petition by a mortgagee, the early courts of equity responded by ordering the mortgagor to repay the outstanding indebtedness and accrued interest within a stipulated period of time. If the mortgagor failed to do so, the mortgage would stand foreclosed and the mortgagee would retain absolute fee title to the mortgaged real estate.

This common law mortgage has essentially remained the basis of mortgage financing until the present time. There have been some important changes, however. First, in a majority of jurisdictions, the mortgagee is regarded as merely obtaining a lien on the real estate to secure repayment of the indebtedness. These states are called "lien theory" states. In other jurisdictions, the "title theory" states, the original common law view is followed, so that the mortgagee is regarded as obtaining both legal title and the right to possession of the mortgaged premises.[5] However, in title theory states, the mortgagee's rights, as transferee of the legal title, generally have been ignored by both mortgagees and the courts except for the mortgagee's right to possession and rents to protect its security interest prior to a foreclosure sale of the property. Indeed, in the opinion of commentators, these rights to possession and rents are the only important practical differences between the title and lien theory points of view.[6]

---

4. See R. Turner, The Equity of Redemption 22 (1937); Osborne at 15-17.

5. See Restatement (Third) of Property (Mortgages) §4.1 (1997) (state-by-state classification of mortgage theory as "lien" (counting at least 32 states), "title," or "intermediate," the latter theory involving a passage of legal title to the mortgagee on the mortgagor's default rather than on execution of the mortgage).

6. See Sturges and Clark, Legal Theory and Real Property Mortgages, 37 Yale L.J. 691 (1928). Professor Sturges observes that, unlike their counterparts in lien theory states, mortgagees in title theory states retain the legal right to possession and rents prior to foreclosure. However, in practice few mortgagees exercise the right to possession prior to default. To do so would deprive the mortgagor of the meaningful use of the property either as residential shelter or as a source of rental or business income. Even after default, most mortgagees prefer to avoid entry into possession as a preforeclosure remedy because of the strict quasi-fiduciary responsibilities and potential tort-

Second, the format of the mortgage device has given way in some jurisdictions, especially in the western states, in favor of the so-called deed of trust format. California is a notable example. Under a deed of trust, real property owned by the borrower ("grantor" or "trustor") is conveyed to a third-party "trustee" who holds the property in trust as security for the repayment of indebtedness owed to the lender ("beneficiary"). Since the real function of a deed of trust is to operate as a security device, courts have generally accorded the trustee and beneficiary of the deed of trust only those incidents of ownership to which a mortgagee would be entitled in the jurisdiction. For example, in a lien theory state, the trustee may be said to have acquired legal title for the benefit of the lender, as beneficiary, but the borrower-trustor will ordinarily have the legal right to possession.[7]

Third, the methodology of foreclosure has changed. For example, "strict foreclosure," under which the lender keeps the mortgaged property on cutting off the borrower's equity of redemption, is still used in a few American jurisdictions.[8] However, because of the unfairness that can result to the borrower if the value of the property exceeds the amount of the outstanding mortgage

contract liabilities associated with being a mortgagee in possession. See Chapter 8B2. However, if in the event of a default a mortgagee should desire to obtain control over rents and profits (generally by virtue of phraseology in the mortgage or in a separate assignment of rents instrument), the mortgagee generally will encounter less difficulty in a title theory jurisdiction. See Chapter 8B2, note 1 and Chapter 8B4, note 1.

According to Professor Sturges, in other significant respects, courts in title theory states generally have regarded the mortgagee as but taking title for security purposes, and, except as between the mortgagor and the mortgagee, the mortgagor is deemed to be the real owner for both theoretical and practical purposes. Consider the following test of the validity of the theory propounded by Professor Sturges that, despite theoretical distinctions, in actual decisions of courts, it makes little difference whether a particular jurisdiction adheres to the lien theory or the title theory:

(1) Suppose that A, the owner of Blackacre, mortgages it to B to secure a loan. Thereafter, X procures a judgment against A and seeks to docket its judgment against Blackacre. Will X succeed in a title state even though title to Blackacre has, in theory, already passed to B?

(2) Suppose, instead, that X is a judgment creditor of B, the mortgagee in a title state. Can X docket its judgment against Blackacre, since B, theoretically, has title to Blackacre?

After painstakingly examining court decisions in numerous title and lien theory states, Professor Sturges concludes that, regardless of theoretical adherence to title or lien theories, the court decisions in these cases were uniform. In example (a), A's judgment creditor could have execution against the property mortgaged by A, while in example (b), the mortgagee's judgment creditor could not get execution against the property.

7. See Osborne at 663; see generally Price, Note, Comparison of California Mortgages, Trust Deeds and Land Sale Contracts, 7 UCLA L. Rev. 83 (1960); Comment, Mortgages and Trust Deeds, 5 S. Cal. L. Rev. 227 (1931-1932). Deeds of trust are examined in more detail at Chapter 3C, infra.

8. See, e.g., Conn. Gen. Stat. Ann. §49-24; Vt. Stat. Ann. tit. 12, §§4528, 4531 (requires finding of no substantial value of property in excess of mortgage debt).

indebtedness,[9] almost all jurisdictions have supplanted strict foreclosure with foreclosure by public sale.

There are generally two types of public sales. One is judicial foreclosure, whereby the property is sold pursuant to court order, and the other, where authorized, is foreclosure without a judicial proceeding under a power of sale contained in the mortgage or deed of trust instrument. See Chapter 8C2. In contrast to strict foreclosure, both of these methods envision a sale of the encumbered property. The foreclosure sale proceeds are first used to defray the expenses of the proceedings, then to satisfy the lien foreclosed and any junior liens. The balance, if any, is remitted to the defaulting mortgagor. If the net proceeds are insufficient to satisfy the debt claim, in most jurisdictions the foreclosing mortgagee has the right to obtain a deficiency judgment against the mortgagor. See Chapter 8C3a.

Judicial foreclosure has traditionally been the more popular of the two methods (especially in states east of the Mississippi), perhaps because a judicially supervised sale tends to be the best method for resolving the conflicting claims of the interested parties and for producing the firmest and most defensible title.[10] However, judicial foreclosure is complicated, time-consuming, and expensive. Consequently, in many states the second method of foreclosure, whereby the foreclosure is conducted pursuant to a provision in the mortgage or deed of trust empowering the mortgagee or trustee to sell the property without direct judicial involvement, is more common. State statutes authorizing such sales by a mortgagee or trustee require fewer and less complicated procedural steps than for judicial foreclosure; for example, neither actual receipt of notice of the sale nor a hearing is generally required for the benefit of the mortgagor and other affected parties.

Finally, the economic depression of the 1820s spawned in many jurisdictions redemption statutes affording the mortgagor (and junior lienors) the right to buy back (redeem) the property after foreclosure by paying the foreclosure sale price to the purchaser at the sale. This statutory protection following foreclosure is known as "statutory redemption," distinguished from the judicially created "equity of redemption" (as noted above) existing prior to foreclosure whereby the delinquent mortgagor can prevent foreclosure by paying the mortgage indebtedness. The purpose of this additional statutory right of redemption is to protect those parties whose interests could be extinguished at foreclosure from an unreasonably low foreclosure sale price. See Chapter 8C3d.[11] As with the Great

---

9. Typically, lenders will advance less than the appraised value of the property to protect themselves against possible diminution in the value of the property and because of loan-to-value constraints in statutes regulating their investment portfolios. See Chapter 4D1.

10. See Osborne at 663.

11. Because this brief review of the history of mortgages paints with a very broad brush, you may wish to consult the following materials for more background. See Chaplin, The Story of Mortgage Law, 4 Harv. L. Rev. 1 (1890); Rabinowitz, The Story of Mortgage Law Retold, 94 U. Pa. L. Rev. 94 (1945); American Law of Property §§16.1-16.7 (Casner ed., 1952).

Depression that gave rise in many states to statutory protections against deficiency judgments for the debt remaining after foreclosure, the mortgage crisis that began in 2007 sparked new statutory protections and judicial challenges to foreclosure, all addressed in Chapter 8.

THE REAL ESTATE LAWYER AND
THE UCC

Real estate finance law is marked by a lack of uniformity among states in recognition of mortgage substitutes and in procedures for enforcing the mortgage or mortgage substitute on default. By contrast, secured transactions involving personal property collateral are governed by Article 9 of the Uniform Commercial Code (UCC), which has been adopted universally. Article 9 specifies uniform rules governing the creation, perfection, and enforcement of security interests in personal property regardless of their form—whether the lien is styled as a conditional sale agreement reserving title in the seller, or as a chattel mortgage or other pre-UCC device.

In pursuit of the same degree of uniformity, in 1985 the National Conference of Commissioners on Uniform State Laws (NCCUSL) offered to the states the Uniform Land Security Interest Act (borrowing from Article 9 and based on the earlier effort, the 1974 Uniform Land Transactions Act). Capturing frustration over the lack of acceptance of this 1985 Act is Benfield, Wasted Days and Wasted Nights: Why the Land Acts Failed, 20 Nova L. Rev. 1037 (1996). More recently, NCCUSL narrowed its goal of uniformity in real estate financing and offered states the Uniform Nonjudicial Foreclosure Act (2002) addressing only nonjudicial foreclosures, which are unpermitted in some states and governed by nonuniform standards in the rest. Can you suggest reasons for the overwhelming acceptance of the UCC Article 9 for personalty security interests and, at the same time, the indifference of states to the Uniform Land Acts governing realty security interests? See Benfield, supra. Which of the parties to the security transaction, the lender or the borrower, has the greater interest in uniformity? How might uniformity be achieved in real estate finance transactions if not by state laws?

B. THE NATURE OF A MORTGAGE

1. *The Mortgage as Security for the Mortgagor's Performance of an Obligation*

Can a mortgage (or deed of trust) secure performance of an act by the mortgagor other than the promise to repay a money indebtedness owed to the mortgagee? Consider the following materials.

Application of Jeffrey Towers, Inc.
57 Misc. 2d 46, 291 N.Y.S.2d 41 (1968)

GAGLIARDI, Justice.

This is a petition to compel satisfaction of a mortgage dated October 29, 1965, in return for payment of the sum of $225,000, with interest in the sum of $3,712.50, on premises consisting of approximately five acres off Central Park Avenue in Yonkers, New York. The mortgagees do not contest that this is the amount due on the bond secured by this purchase-money mortgage which was part of the price of the sale of the land to petitioner's predecessor in title, but they do insist that they are entitled to keep the mortgage open of record to secure other promises made by the mortgagor in the mortgage agreement to benefit eight adjacent acres of land which the seller mortgagees have retained. Those promises are (1) to install a twelve-inch sewer main from Central Park Avenue across the petitioner's property to service the mortgagees' property before October 29, 1967, with provisions permitting the mortgagees to construct the sewer at the mortgagor's expense upon default and for a $20,000 surety bond to secure completion . . .; (2) to construct a 561.18 foot "alternative driveway" from Young Avenue across petitioner's property to service the mortgagees' property by October 29, 1968, with similar right to complete the driveway at mortgagor's expense; [and] (3) to consent to any applications for variances, changes of zone or special exception uses affecting the mortgagees' retained parcel. . . .

The initial question is whether a mortgage can secure the performance of unliquidated engagements, such as the promise to build a road and sewer. A mortgage has been defined as "any conveyance of land intended by the parties at the time of making it to be security for the payment of money *or the doing of some prescribed act*" (Burnett v. Wright, 135 N.Y. 543, 547) (emphasis added). This definition which can be found in modern treatises . . . admits the possibility of such an unusual purpose although it does not obviate the problems which would be caused by it.

There are recorded cases of mortgages securing promises to provide support in slated installments for the mortgagee's lifetime. . . . So, too, a mortgage was employed to secure a promise to purchase all of the gasoline sold at a garage premises from the mortgagee in *Blakeley v. Agency of Canadian Car & Foundry Co.* (73 N.Y.S.2d 571 [Sup. Ct., N.Y. County, 1947]). There, the court refused to compel satisfaction of the mortgage even when the principal amount was paid because of the open promise to purchase gasoline for an unexpired term. In addition section 1921 of the Real Property Actions and Proceedings Law which authorizes this proceeding to compel discharge of the mortgage, states that the satisfaction piece must certify "that the mortgage has been paid or *otherwise satisfied and discharged*" (emphasis added). The court concludes that in the absence of defects such as illegality, unliquidated promises in the nature of those presented in this case may be secured by a mortgage. It follows, therefore, that such promises must be fulfilled to entitle petitioner to a discharge of the mortgage. . . .

[T]he court doubts that the promise to consent to zoning applications is enforceable by the mortgage or may hinder its satisfaction. The reason is that the promises to do work are readily translatable into money, albeit without precision. But the value of a consent to a zoning application (which might not even influence the zoning authority) is of such speculative monetary value that it cannot be enforced as a mortgage lien. It would be impossible for the court in the event of foreclosure to fix the amount of the lien and direct the disposition of proceeds of a foreclosure sale. . . .

[T]he petition is granted to the extent that upon payment of $225,000, with interest in the sum of $3,712.50, the mortgagees must deliver an instrument in recordable form certifying that the principal and interest stated in the mortgage have been paid. . . .[12]

NOTES AND QUESTIONS

1.   Restatement Rule. The Restatement (Third) of Property (Mortgages) §1.4 (1997) states the rule as "[a] mortgage is enforceable only if the obligation whose performance it secures is measurable in terms of money or is readily reducible to a monetary value at the time of enforcement of the mortgage." As noted by the court in *Jeffrey Towers,* the problem with a mortgage purporting to secure a promise that is not measurable in monetary terms is that "[i]t would be impossible for the court in the event of foreclosure to fix the amount of the lien and direct the disposition of proceeds of a foreclosure sale. . . ." Can you foresee any other problems that might arise if such a mortgage were enforceable? Some are suggested in note 2 below.

---

12. The judgment of the court was modified on appeal to reflect that the mortgagor was not entitled to an absolute satisfaction and discharge of the mortgage on the record until the mortgagor performed the covenant to construct a driveway and sewer main. Jeffrey Towers, Inc. v. Straus, 31 A.D.2d 319, 297 N.Y.S.2d 450 (1969), aff'd, 26 N.Y.2d 812, 257 N.E.2d 897, 309 N.Y.S.2d 350 (1970).—EDS.

> ➤ *Problem 3-1*

Martha, a law student who owns unencumbered real estate worth $20,000, wishes to borrow $10,000 from her uncle for one year and agrees to give him a mortgage on the property to secure her promise. The uncle, a grocer, heads the antismoking drive being sponsored by the local cancer prevention society. Which, if any, of the following promises can be secured by the mortgage?

(a) Martha's promise to stop smoking immediately in addition to her promise to repay the loan
(b) The uncle's promise to cancel $5,000 of the loan indebtedness if Martha stops smoking within one year
(c) Martha's promise to purchase all her groceries from her uncle during the school year in addition to her promise to repay the loan ◄

2. Performance Obligations. Suppose Dan Developer purchases property from Francine Farmer, who owns a much larger tract and intends to continue to use the remainder of the property to grow corn. Dan determines that to build his building he will need a zoning variance, and Francine agrees to consent to and support Dan's zoning application. Because the variance is so important to Dan, he insists on obtaining security for Francine's promise in the form of a mortgage on Francine's remaining land. Can a mortgage secure such a promise? Do you agree with the court's apparent conclusion in *Jeffrey Towers* that a promise to consent to a zoning change is not sufficiently translatable into money to be enforced as a mortgage lien? Why did the court not simply subtract the value of the property without the zoning change from the value of the property with the zoning change to determine the value of the obligation?

If you were the official in the local mortgage recording office charged with recording a mortgage that does not set forth a specific indebtedness, how would you calculate any mortgage tax under applicable law (which is normally based on a percentage of the indebtedness)? What effect would such a mortgage have on Dan's ability to obtain secondary financing or refinancing or to sell the property? How might you draft the note to avoid these problems?

2. *The Mortgage Note as the Underlying Obligation*

As you might surmise, the obligation that the mortgage secures will almost invariably be a note in which the mortgagor promises to repay some indebtedness to the mortgagee. It is this note, and not the mortgage, that is the legal evidence of indebtedness. Accordingly, the note must delineate the terms of repayment, such as the loan amount, rate of interest, amortization period, and any prepayment privilege. Ordinarily, the mortgagee will insist that the note contain an "acceleration clause," which reserves to the mortgagee the right to declare the entire balance of the indebtedness to be immediately due and payable in the event of a default by the mortgagor. We will analyze these and other terms and conditions of postconstruction and construction financing in Chapters 4, 5, 6, and 8.

At this juncture, we confine our attention to the relationship between the mortgage and the mortgage note that it secures. We start with the often stated legal principle that to be valid and enforceable the mortgage must be supported by a valid consideration.[13] What is meant by this principle? As you know by now, a mortgage is the transfer of an interest in land as security for the repayment of money or for the performance of some other obligation that is measurable by money. Returning to the example at Chapter 3B1, supra, suppose Martha does not borrow $10,000 from her uncle but gratuitously promises to purchase all her groceries from him during the school year, giving him a mortgage on her property to secure the promise. Would such a promise support a valid mortgage?

Based on the foregoing definition of a mortgage, couldn't it be argued that the legal mortgage itself is an executed conveyance of an interest in land and no more requires consideration than does a gift or any other executed conveyance of an interest in land?[14] Moreover, the notion that a mortgage is enforceable without consideration is supported by the general rule that a valid mortgage may be given to secure a preexisting debt that is no longer enforceable under a local statute of limitations.[15] Nevertheless, numerous case law decisions take the position that while the mortgage itself is an executed conveyance, the obligation that the mortgage secures must be supported by adequate consideration and be enforceable.[16]

---

13. See, e.g., Tyler v. Wright, 122 Me. 558, 119 A. 583 (1923). Stated differently, because "the mortgage is a mere security for the debt . . . it logically follows that there must be some obligation for the lien to secure. When that obligation is discharged the mortgage becomes functus officio and legally dead." Egbert v. Egbert, 235 Ind. 405, 132 N.E.2d 910, 918 (1956).

14. See Restatement (Third) of Property (Mortgages) §1.2(b) (1997) ("A mortgage securing an obligation undertaken as a gift is enforceable . . . notwithstanding the unenforceability of the obligation standing alone.").

15. In the opinion of most courts, a mortgage is enforceable even though the underlying indebtedness is barred by a statute of limitations. The rationale generally provided reflects a "positivist" mode of thinking: The statute of limitations extinguishes the remedy of suing on the debt but not the debt itself. Accordingly, the mortgagee can still maintain an action to foreclose its lien on the property. And in the so-called title theory states, where the mortgagee retains both title and the legal right to possession, the mortgagee may also take possession or maintain an action of ejectment against a defaulting mortgagor even though the statute of limitations on the underlying indebtedness has expired. See, e.g., Phinney v. Levine, 116 N.H. 379, 359 A.2d 636 (1976); Taylor v. Quinn, 68 Ohio App. 164, 39 N.E.2d 627 (1941); Danielson, Note, The Statute of Limitations as a Defense to Foreclosure in Illinois, 1957 U. Ill. L.F. 469. However, in a minority of lien theory states, the barring of any remedy on the debt also precludes foreclosure or any other remedy on the mortgage. See, e.g., Allen v. Shepherd, 162 Ky. 756, 173 S.W. 135 (1915); 161 A.L.R. 882, 890 (1946).

16. See generally G. Nelson et al., Real Estate Finance Law §2.3 (6th ed. 2015) (hereinafter Nelson et al.).

Other issues that concern the relationship between the mortgage and the mortgage note include (1) whether the mortgage can secure loan advances under the mortgage note to be made at some future date, (2) which subsequent notes that the mortgagor may give the mortgagee are secured by the mortgage, and (3) whether present indebtedness can be secured by a mortgage lien on after-acquired property. The following materials explore these issues.

As to the first issue, the Restatement (Third) of Property (Mortgages) §2.1 (1997) states the general rule that advances made after the mortgage becomes effective are secured by the mortgage if the mortgage provides that future advances are secured or if the mortgage states a money amount to be secured and the future advances are within that maximum amount. This rule governs only the threshold issue of the enforceability of an open-end mortgage to secure future advances; Chapter 6B3a infra addresses the separate but related issue of whether future advances enjoy lien priority over the claims of other creditors (such as mechanic's liens) that attach after recordation of the mortgage but before future advances are made by the mortgagee. Several jurisdictions have enacted statutes to address the validity of mortgages to secure future advances; some require both a reference in the mortgage to future advances as security and a statement of the maximum amount of future advances secured.

The following decision addresses the related question of which subsequent notes that the mortgagor may give the mortgagee are secured by the mortgage.

Emporia State Bank & Trust Co. v. Mounkes
214 Kan. 178, 519 P.2d 618 (1974)

FONTRON, Justice.

The Emporia State Bank and Trust Company brings this action to foreclose a real estate mortgage. The defendants, Mr. and Mrs. Mounkes, filed an answer and cross petition. The court rendered personal judgment against the defendants for $1651.51 and a judgment in rem for $5911.53. The mortgage was foreclosed as to both sums. Judgment was also entered in favor of the bank on the defendants' cross petition. Mr. and Mrs. Mounkes have appealed.

No dispute exists concerning the facts. On February 13, 1963, Mr. and Mrs. Mounkes executed their promissory note to the bank in the amount of $12,500, and secured the same by a mortgage on an Emporia property which was their homestead. The face of the note indicates that monthly payments were started April 1, 1963. When the present proceedings were commenced the indebtedness had been reduced to $1573.57.

On February 27, 1971, some eight years after the mortgage was given, Mr. Mounkes executed his personal note to the bank for $5100. We were advised on oral argument that this loan was procured by Mr. Mounkes to assist a son in starting a restaurant business. . . .

. . . In its petition the bank prayed for the foreclosure of its mortgage not only as to the balance due on the original note executed by Mr. and Mrs. Mounkes in 1963, but also as to the amounts alleged to be unpaid on the [subsequent note] signed by Mr. Mounkes in 1971. The bank's contention in such regard was and is predicated on a so-called dragnet provision contained in the mortgage. It reads as follows:

> This mortgage is given to secure payment of the sum of Twelve Thousand Five Hundred & no/100 Dollars ($12,500.00) and interest thereon, according to the terms of promissory note/s this day executed and subsequently to be executed by the mortgagors to the mortgagee, and all other sums which may hereafter be owing to the mortgagee by the mortgagors or any of them, however evidenced; it being understood and agreed that the mortgagee may from time to time make loans and advances to the mortgagors or any of them and that all such loans and advances and the interest thereon will be secured by this mortgage: provided that the aggregate principal amount of the loans and advances hereunder shall at no time exceed the amount hereinbefore stated.

The trial court agreed with the bank's position so far as the $5100 note was concerned and decreed that the balance due thereon as well as the balance due on the original note be made a lien on the mortgaged property. The court further ordered the mortgage foreclosed as to both amounts, which then totaled $7563.10. In so doing, the court . . . granted judgment in rem against the real estate for the face amount thereof, plus interest. . . .

[D]efendants concede that the unpaid balance of the original note is secured by their mortgage of February 13, 1963. However, they take a quite different position with respect to the subsequent note signed by Mr. Mounkes on February 27, 1971. . . .

The dragnet syndrome is not a stranger in banking circles. [W]e apprehend that a future advances clause in a mortgage may provide an extremely useful and practical tool in facilitating many business and commercial type operations which involve frequent or continuing advancement of funds and extension of credits. One example, among others which come readily to mind, is found in the construction or building trade where the open end or dollar mortgage serves as a convenient device in facilitating the flow of funds at minimal expense. (See Potwin State Bank v. Ward, 183 Kan. 475, 327 P.2d 1091.) . . .

In the great majority of cases where the question has arisen, the courts have held that future advancements made pursuant to a dragnet or open end type of mortgage came within the contemplation of the parties and were thus secured thereby. . . .

Despite recognition by both judicial and legislative bodies that the dragnet mortgage fills a contemporary need in the complex world of business, it is not a favorite of the law and is subject to interpretation and construction. As the Iowa Supreme Court so aptly observed in First v. Byrne, 238 Iowa 712, 28 N.W.2d 509, 172 A.L.R. 1072, "'Dragnet' clauses are not highly regarded in equity. They should be 'carefully scrutinized and strictly construed.'" (Pp. 715, 716, 28

N.W.2d p. 511.) This view was mirrored in Berger v. Fuller, 180 Ark. 372, 377, 21 S.W.2d 419, 421, where the Supreme Court of Arkansas, in speaking of a mortgage having a future advancements clause, said:

> . . .Mortgages of this character have been denominated "anaconda mortgages" and are well named thus, as by their broad and general terms they enwrap the unsuspecting debtor in the folds of indebtedness embraced and secured in the mortgage which he did not contemplate, and to extend them further than has already been done would, in our opinion, be dangerous and unwise. . . .

Where the construction of a mortgage is brought in issue the primary question for determination is what was the intention of the parties. In arriving at a decision of the matter, all the circumstances attending the execution of the mortgage and the nature of the transaction are to be considered as well as the language of the instrument itself. . . .

It occurs to us that a number of circumstances bear on the intention of the parties to the mortgage now before us. It was executed in 1963 to secure an indebtedness contemporarily incurred. The record shows no additional funds advanced to the Mounkes or further financial dealings had between them and the bank for more than eight years, when Mr. Mounkes "by his lonesome" signed a note for $5100. This latter note contains no reference of any sort to the real estate mortgage jointly executed eight years before. We believe the omission is significant, especially in view of the fact that a space was provided in the note for recording the description of collateral security. In the space thus provided there was typed, presumably by the bank, the word "Sig." The record reveals from statements made by plaintiff's counsel that this means "signature" and that "Normally, you think of a signature loan as being a loan on which there was no security whatsoever." Furthermore, the record bares no evidence of any relationship between the 1963 loan to Mr. and Mrs. Mounkes and the subsequent loan to Mr. Mounkes. There is not the slightest intimation that any part of the loan to Mr. Mounkes was to be used in the repair or improvement of the Mounkes' residence—indeed, such a suggestion is negated by the statement that it was to help a son get into the restaurant business.

An opinion we find persuasive hails from our sister state in the far reaches of the Pacific Ocean. In Akamine & Sons v. Am. Sec. Bank, 50 Haw. 304, 440 P.2d 262, questions of priority arose between two creditors, it being contended on the part of one bank that its dragnet mortgage gave it priority as to property which had been mortgaged to a second bank at a later date. The Supreme Court of Hawaii did not look kindly on the contention thus advanced, nor did it view dragnet mortgages in general with unjaundiced eye. In the opinion it was said:

> We are prevented from holding a mortgage to secure future advances contrary to public policy by its statutory authorization and the undeniable benefits which it may engender. As a court of equity, however, we will construe such mortgages very strictly against the mortgagee. . . . Completely unrestricted enforcement of such mortgages would tend to reduce the borrower to the status of economic serf. . . .

Under the ejusdem generis rule, the statute does not require us to enforce a dragnet, or anaconda, clause in a mortgage as to debts or obligations not of the same kind as the specific principal debt or obligation for which the mortgage is given. Unless the prior or subsequent advance relates to the same transaction or series of transactions, the mortgage must specifically refer to it for the advance to be secured. This court will not assist a lending institution in an attempt to captivate a borrower by inclusion in a mortgage of a broad all inclusive dragnet clause. . . . To attempt to foreclose, for example, on the mortgagor's home for debts incurred in operating a business and which debts are not specifically covered by the mortgage would be unconscionable and contrary to public policy. (Pp. 312, 313, 440 P.2d p. 267)

We are aware that the trial court, in entering judgment in rem in favor of the bank, found it was the parties' intention at the time of the execution of the mortgage that it would secure payment of any sums of money which the mortgagee might loan the mortgagors or either of them. The difficulty with that conclusion is that the record contains no supporting evidence except for the dragnet clause itself. That clause we deem to be insufficient in the face of this record. As we have heretofore said, it is necessary, when determining the intention of the parties to a mortgage, that the attending circumstances and the nature of the transaction be considered. Here there is nothing from which it may be inferred that by mortgaging their homestead the defendants contemplated it would stand as security for a loan obtained by Mr. Mounkes to start his son in business eight years later. There is a total lack of evidence to sustain a presumption the two loans were related in any sense. The evidence is, indeed, quite to the contrary and we are constrained to hold the finding of the trial court is not sustained by the record.

In summary, we hold that in the absence of clear, supportive evidence of a contrary intention a mortgage containing a dragnet type clause will not be extended to cover future advances unless the advances are of the same kind and quality or relate to the same transaction or series of transactions as the principal obligation secured or unless the document evidencing the subsequent advance refers to the mortgage as providing security therefor. The loan extended to Mr. Mounkes in 1971 does not meet these criteria. . . .

NOTES AND QUESTIONS

1. Open-End Mortgages. Mortgages to secure future advances are commonly used with respect to construction financing and where the borrower and lender plan to transact business with one another on a continuous basis (for example, a home equity line of credit loan). The advantages to such an arrangement (whereby loan funds are advanced in increments rather than in one lump sum at the beginning) are that (a) in continuous dealings the parties to a multiple loan transaction are spared the expense and inconvenience of refinancing the original loan or executing a series of junior mortgages on each new transaction; (b) in the case of construction financing, the lender is assured prior to each loan advance that the work to date has been completed on schedule in accordance with approved plans and specifications and that the loan funds are being used properly to pay off the claims of subcontractors furnishing either labor (mechanics) or materials (materialmen); (c) both parties to the loan transaction may not be able to anticipate the nature or extent of the funds needed at the time the mortgage is executed; and (d) the borrower is spared the cost of paying interest on the future advances until it is ready to use the funds.

In the case of construction financing, a well-drafted construction or building loan agreement will specify the amount of the initial advance and the terms and conditions under which specified amounts of future advances will be made. In some transactions it may be impossible for the parties to stipulate either the amount or the terms of the future indebtedness, in which event phraseology (known as a dollar-mortgage) is frequently employed as follows: "the mortgage is intended to secure the payment of any sum or sums of money which may be loaned or advanced by the mortgagee from time to time, as the parties may now or hereafter agree." Do you see any problems with enforcing this type of broad-based language? What about the possibility of misleading third-party creditors? See Restatement (Third) of Property (Mortgages) §2.1 cmt. c (1997) (stating that if the mortgage merely mentions that future advances are secured, a subsequent creditor has no idea from the mortgage what the secured amount might be, but is on notice to inquire the amount from the mortgagee).

2. Dragnet Clauses. A broad variant of the open-end mortgage is the so-called dragnet or anaconda clause whereby the mortgaged real estate purports to secure automatically all other present or future indebtedness owed to the mortgagee regardless of when it is incurred and whether or not it relates to the instant transaction. While traditionally valid under mortgage law, these clauses have increasingly become the object of judicial scrutiny. As reflected by the holding in *Emporia State Bank*, the recently emerging trend is to construe such clauses narrowly against the mortgagee and to limit their reach to additional indebtedness only if it relates to the current business transaction. In light of this, what precautionary measures should a prudent mortgagee take to secure additional indebtedness not related to the original mortgage transaction? See Restatement (Third) of Property (Mortgages) §2.4(b) (1997).

3. Further Reading. For additional discussion of mortgages for future advances and dragnet clauses, see Nelson et al. §§12.7, 12.8; Blackburn, Mortgages to Secure Future Advances, 21 Mo. L. Rev. 209 (1956); Meek, Mortgage Provisions Extending the Lien to Future Advances and Antecedent Indebtedness, 26 Ark. L. Rev. 423 (1973). See also discussion at Chapter 6B3.

4. After-Acquired Property Clauses. If a mortgage can secure future indebtedness, does it logically follow that present indebtedness can be secured by a mortgage lien on after-acquired property? The answer is a qualified yes. To the extent that the after-acquired property consists of subsequent improvements on the land originally mortgaged, or additional personal property classified as a fixture under state law and becomes part of the real estate, the mortgagee can enjoy the benefit of this after-acquired property—even without an after-acquired property clause—because by their very nature the improvements and fixtures automatically become part of the mortgaged real estate under property law. 3 G. Glenn on Mortgages §14.50 (1943); Nelson et al. §9.3.

As to additional personal property that does not qualify as a fixture, an after-acquired property clause in a mortgage, properly identifying the collateral, creates only an unperfected security interest in such personal property when the property is subsequently acquired by the mortgagor. To perfect this security interest it would be necessary to file a financing statement under the applicable state's version of the Uniform Commercial Code. See In re Gray, 77 B.R. 970 (Bankr. S.D. Fla. 1987) (freestanding appliances removable by unplugging an electrical cord were not encumbered by the mortgage as fixtures).

A difficult problem exists when a mortgage purports to cover separate real property that the borrower may acquire in the future. In such a situation, the majority rule appears to be that the after-acquired property clause will be considered, in substance, a promise by the mortgagor to subject the after-acquired property to the lien of the mortgage and that such promise creates only an equitable lien warranting specific performance when the property is later acquired. 3 G. Glenn on Mortgages §412 (1943); Cunningham and Tischler, Equitable Real Estate Mortgages, 17 Rutgers L. Rev. 679, 719 (1963) (hereinafter Cunningham and Tischler); Jones, Comment, Mortgages—After-Acquired Property Clause in Mortgage Is Valid, 28 Rocky Mtn. L. Rev. 432 (1956). However, in some states such as New Jersey, the clause is effective only if the subsequently acquired property bears a functional relationship to the property originally mortgaged. See, e.g., Williamson v. New Jersey S.R.R., 29 N.J. Eq. 311, 337 (1878). See Cunningham and Tischler, at 718; 3 G. Glenn on Mortgages §414 (1943); Nelson et al. §9.3.

However, even in those states where the clause is effective, the mortgagee may be confronted with certain lien priority problems. Suppose, for example, that Dan Developer obtains a postconstruction mortgage loan from the Ace Insurance Company and that the mortgage contains an after-acquired property clause. Further assume that Dan's land subject to the lien of Ace's mortgage ("Greenacre") is surrounded by adjacent farmland ("Whiteacre") that Dan would like to acquire as a future building site. While the equitable lien created by the after-acquired property clause is binding between the parties Dan and Ace, it generally will be subordinate to any liens placed on it prior to Dan's acquisition of Whiteacre, including any purchase money mortgage given by Dan to acquire the additional property. See, e.g., Associates Discount Corp. v. Gomes, 338 So. 2d 552 (Fla. Dist. Ct. App. 1976); Chase Natl. Bank v. Sweezy, 281 N.Y.S. 487 (1931), aff'd, 261 N.Y. 710, 185 N.E. 803 (1933). It also may pose serious lien priority problems for Ace under the local recording statutes, as suggested by the following hypothetical facts, as diagrammed below.

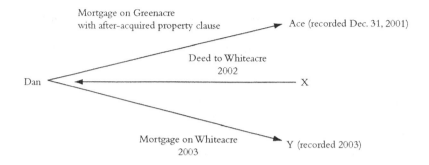

Consider the following dilemma confronting Ace: Since the after-acquired property clause in the original Ace mortgage (securing the postconstruction loan that was closed on December 31, 2001) did not contain a legal description of the after-acquired property, Whiteacre, and the Ace mortgage was recorded *before* Dan acquired title to Whiteacre, the rule in the overwhelming majority of jurisdictions (based on a title-search burden rationale) is that any subsequent mortgagee or purchaser in the position of *Y* would not have record notice of Ace's security interest in Whiteacre. Therefore, *Y* would obtain a superior mortgage lien or take title to Whiteacre as a purchaser free of Ace's interest. See Restatement (Third) of Property (Mortgages) §7.5(b) (1997). Otherwise, a title examiner who is searching Dan's chain of title on behalf of *Y* would have the onerous burden of checking in the grantor's index not only for conveyances and mortgages from each grantor (Dan's predecessors-in-title) after the grantor had acquired title, but also prior to the time that the grantor had acquired title (and conceivably as far back as the grantor's birth date). See Wheeler v. Young, 76 Conn. 44, 55 A. 670 (1903). Ayer v. Philadelphia & Boston Face Brick Co., 159 Mass. 84, 34 N.E. 177 (1893), is one of the few reported cases that holds to the contrary based on the so-called doctrine of estoppel by deed. The majority view would probably hold true even in a jurisdiction with a tract index, since the after-acquired property clause in Ace's mortgage makes no specific reference to Whiteacre; however, it is possible that the general reference to after-acquired property might constitute inquiry notice to subsequent takers in some jurisdictions. See, e.g., Guerin v. Sunburst Oil & Gas Co., 68 Mont. 365, 218 P. 949 (1923).

As counsel to Ace, can you think of any protective language or procedure that might assure Ace of lien priority over Whiteacre as against any adverse or subsequent claimant in the position of *Y*? See Cunningham and Tischler, at 719 n.188. Suppose Ace and Dan know on December 31, 2001, the date on which the postconstruction loan on Greenacre is scheduled to close, that Dan plans to acquire Whiteacre, and Ace insists that the legal description in its Greenacre mortgage make reference to Whiteacre even though at the time Dan has no legal or equitable title to Whiteacre. Assuming that Ace could somehow record its lien on Whiteacre in a way that would show up in the present owner's (*X*'s) chain of title and thus constitute record notice to *Y*, how might the present owner, *X*, be injured by such an unauthorized recordation? What, if any, recourse would *X* have against Ace or Dan? See Cawrse v. Signal Oil Co., 164 Or. 666, 103 P.2d 729 (1940) (describing requisites of action for slander of title).

3. *Personal Liability of the Mortgagor*

The following materials address whether the mortgagor must be personally liable for the performance of the obligation that the mortgage secures.

Bedian v. Cohn
10 Ill. App. 2d 116, 134 N.E.2d 532 (1956)

SCHEINEMAN, Justice.

In this suit the plaintiffs seek to hold defendant personally liable for the balance due on the purchase price of real estate, notwithstanding express provisions in the mortgage and note that defendants should not be liable for any deficiency.

The undisputed facts are that defendant Arnold Cohn contracted orally to purchase the property from plaintiffs, Asadour and Elizabeth Bedian, at a fixed price, to make a down payment, to pay the balance in installments, the defendant not to be liable for a deficiency in the event of foreclosure.

It is undisputed that the property is inadequate to cover the balance, but the chancellor decreed that though the plaintiffs were entitled to the property there was no personal liability on defendant.

On this appeal, it appears to be undisputed that pursuant to the oral contract, the parties met in a law office, the down payment was made, plaintiffs executed a deed to defendant, and the latter gave a mortgage and note for the balance, both of which expressly limited collection of the balance to the property pledged, and stated that the maker should not be personally liable for any deficiency. . . .

Plaintiff contends these provisions are inconsistent, and ambiguous, and the court should hold the restriction on personal liability void. Defendant cites cases from other states that it is valid. While there is no reported decision in this state of precisely similar facts, the principle has been stated in accord with the weight of authority. Thus, in City of Joliet v. Alexander, 194 Ill. 457, 62 N.E. 861, 863, the opinion states:

> The provision for a mortgage implies a debt, since a mortgage cannot exist without a debt. The mortgage is a mere incident to a debt or obligation secured by it, and which is an essential element in a mortgage. . . . It is not essential to a debt or to a mortgage that there should be any promise of the mortgagor to pay the debt. The mortgage may be merely to secure payment, and a debt exists in many cases where there is no personal liability, and where there could be no suit at law, and no personal decree could be rendered for a deficiency. One who pawns or pledges his property,

and who will lose the property if he does not pay, is indebted, although the creditor has nothing but the security of the property; and so, also, is a mortgagor who is liable to lose his property if he does not pay the money secured by the mortgage.

. . . Accordingly, we hold that a mortgage and note are evidence of a debt, but an agreement therein that the collection of the debt is limited to the property pledged, without personal liability on the maker, is valid and will be enforced according to the expressed terms. . . .

NOTES AND QUESTIONS

Recourse versus Nonrecourse Financing. In contrast to construction financing, it is the rental income stream from the mortgaged property, not the evanescent solvency of the developer-borrower, that secures the postconstruction loan. See Chapter 4 introduction. Indeed, in appraising the value of the property to be mortgaged, the lender will look primarily at the projected net rental income and make certain that the loan amount is low enough that the property will "pay for itself" by generating sufficient net income to cover the annual debt service payments on the mortgage. In addition, most postconstruction lenders will insist on receiving, as additional collateral, an assignment of the high-credit leases and rents from the mortgaged real estate in the event of the borrower's default. See Chapters 10B and 8B4.

In addition, if the borrowing-ownership entity is a limited partnership, the investor partners may not be able to deduct their distributive share of tax losses in excess of their equity investments if the partnership engages in recourse as opposed to "qualified" nonrecourse financing to fund its cost of acquiring or constructing the mortgaged income-producing real estate. I.R.C. §§704(d), 465(b)(6); Treas. Reg. §§1.752-2(a), 1.752-3(a). See discussion at Chapter 14A2.

Accordingly, in many cases the lender will agree to accept nonrecourse financing, which means that in the event of a default and foreclosure the lender can only seek recourse against the property and not sue the borrower on the debt or seek a deficiency judgment against the borrower. To accomplish this objective, simple nonrecourse language such as "the borrower shall not be personally liable hereunder," or "in the event of default, mortgagee will not seek a deficiency judgment against the borrower and recourse may only be had against the property," or alternative phraseology of similar import should be inserted in the mortgage note. See generally Restatement (Third) of Property (Mortgages) §1.1 cmt. (1997). See Chapter 5A3 for discussion of "carve-outs" from this exculpation that lender's counsel might require. Would nonrecourse language be necessary in a jurisdiction that bars deficiency judgments by statute? Such antideficiency judgment legislation is discussed at Chapter 8C3a.

4. *Equitable Mortgages*

Because a mortgage involves the transfer of an interest in land to the mortgagee, a mortgage must be in writing to comply with the Statute of Frauds.[17] However, equitable principles may dictate that a mortgage is created and enforceable at equity even though it is neither written nor subscribed to by the mortgagor or a lawful agent. Simply put, the equitable mortgage doctrine holds that equity will interpret what is a defective security agreement (such as a mortgage instrument that fails under the Statute of Frauds or the recording statutes) or what purports to be a nonsecurity transaction (such as a deed absolute) according to the intentions of the parties, and, as between the parties, such arrangement will be given effect as a lien or other security interest even though it does not meet the technical requirements for a legal mortgage. In addition, an equity court will sometimes impose a lien purely as a remedial device to protect someone who would otherwise be treated unfairly.[18]

The doctrine of equitable mortgages, which is broad-based and complicated, seldom surfaces in commercial real estate financing because the parties to the transaction are apt to be sophisticated and are almost invariably represented by legal counsel who will formalize the intentions of the parties using forms of mortgages or established mortgage substitutes. However, as examined at Chapter 11B2, commercial sale-and-leaseback transactions are sometimes recharacterized by courts as disguised mortgage loans.

NOTES AND QUESTIONS

1. Absolute Deed as Disguised Mortgage. There have been a few cases involving unsophisticated borrowers in which, at the lender's behest, a borrower delivered an absolute deed of conveyance on the oral understanding that the property would be reconveyed to the borrower once the indebtedness was repaid. Historically, the common law mortgage was also in the form of an ordinary deed of conveyance, but with an express defeasance clause providing that the conveyance would be void on the payment of a sum of money or the performance of some other act. It is when this condition of defeasance is not appended in writing to the deed, but is claimed orally, that the problem arises. If the borrower can prove through parol or extrinsic evidence that the conveyance was merely intended as a security device, most courts will treat the deed as an "equitable mortgage" even though its real nature is not reflected by the terms of the instrument. See Havana Natl. Bank v. Wiemer, 32 Ill. App. 3d 578, 335 N.E.2d 506 (1975). In a few states, the party seeking reformation of the deed must prove that the defeasance clause was inadvertently or fraudulently omitted. Newton v.

---

17. See, e.g., N.Y. Gen. Oblig. Law §5-703.
18. See generally Cunningham and Tischler, at 683.

Clark, 174 N.C. 393, 93 S.E. 951 (1917). And a few states place statutory restrictions on the equitable mortgage doctrine. See, e.g., Ga. Code Ann. §44-14-32; N.H. Rev. Stat. Ann. §479:2; Pa. Stat. Ann. tit. 21, §951. See R. Kratovil and B. Werner, Modern Mortgage Law and Practice §3.05(a)(1) (1981).

> ➤ *Problem 3-2*
>
> To discourage fraud by unscrupulous grantors who wish to rescind their bargains, clear and convincing evidence is generally required to establish that a deed absolute on its face is in reality a mortgage. As counsel to a borrower who claims that a deed it gave to a lender is really a mortgage, what evidence would help prove your client's allegation? See Cunningham and Tischler, Disguised Real Estate Security Transactions as Mortgages in Substance, 26 Rutgers L. Rev. 1 (1972); Restatement (Third) of Property (Mortgages) §3.2(b) (1997) (listing factors in proving absolute deed as a mortgage). ◄

Sometimes a deed may be given to a third party to hold in escrow to secure payment of the debt. If the debt is not paid, the deed is to be released to the lender. In such a case, even if the deed is released, it does not give the lender good title to the property. The instrument is deemed to be a mortgage. See Pollak v. Millsap, 219 Ala. 273, 122 So. 16 (1929); Hamud v. Hawthorne, 52 Cal. 2d 78, 338 P.2d 387 (1959); Plummer v. Ilse, 41 Wash. 5, 82 P. 1009 (1905).

A grantor who gives a deed absolute on its face instead of a mortgage runs a risk that the grantee may sell the land to a bona fide purchaser (BFP) for value without notice of the security arrangement. This BFP would then obtain an interest in the land superior to that of the borrower-grantor. If the grantor, however, remains physically in possession of the land, this may constitute inquiry notice, preventing the ultimate purchaser from acquiring BFP status. See R. Kratovil and B. Werner, Real Estate Law §223 (9th ed. 1988). Also, where the grantor delays in asserting its rights, the grantor may be barred by the doctrine of laches. See Clontz v. Fortner, 88 Idaho 355, 399 P.2d 949 (1965); R. Kratovil and B. Werner, Modern Mortgage Law and Practice §3.05(c) (1981). See generally Fogelman, The Deed Absolute as a Mortgage in New York, 32 Fordham L. Rev. 299 (1963).

2. Negative Lien. Another type of "equitable mortgage" may arise where a borrower covenants not to transfer or encumber its land as long as certain indebtedness owed to the lender-covenantee remains unpaid. Because this negative covenant evinces an intention to create a security interest in the debtor's land, a few courts have held that this arrangement constitutes an equitable mortgage. Compare Coast Bank v. Minderhout, 61 Cal. 2d 311, 392 P.2d 265, 38 Cal. Rptr. 505 (1964), rev'd on other grounds, 148 Cal. Rptr. 379 (1978), with Tahoe Natl. Bank v. Phillips, 4 Cal. 3d 11, 480 P.2d 320, 92 Cal. Rptr. 704 (1971), and Restatement (Third) of Property (Mortgages) §3.5 (1997) ("In the absence of other evidence of intent to create a mortgage, a promise by a debtor to a creditor not to encumber or transfer an interest in real estate does not create a mortgage, equitable lien, or other security interest in that real estate."). As opposed to a traditional mortgage, the negative lien, or negative pledge, arrangement can be advantageous where (1) a traditional security interest is disallowed; (2) a lender is prohibited by its regulatory statute from lending against a junior lien; and (3) it would be bothersome and expensive for a lender to use foreclosure to enforce a junior lien, especially where the debtor has other assets that could satisfy a small debt. For an excellent discussion of this financing device, see Reichman, The Anti-Lien: Another Security Interest in Land, 41 U. Chi. L. Rev. 685 (1974). The negative pledge is also used extensively in corporate debenture financing. Such financing is unsecured, but the lender is protected by covenants made by the obligor that are designed to ensure that its assets will be available to satisfy the unsecured indebtedness.

3. Equitable Liens for Vendors and Vendees. A purchaser (vendee) of real property who has paid the purchase price to the seller (vendor) but has not received title may have a lien thereon, especially if the vendee has taken possession of the property in addition to payment. See Elterman v. Hyman, 192 N.Y. 113, 84 N.E. 937 (1908); N.Y. C.P.L.R. Law §3002(f); Chappel, Comment, The Vendee's Lien in New York: Its Development, Applications and Status, 37 Alb. L. Rev. 470 (1973). Similarly, a vendor of real property who has conveyed title may have an equitable lien on the property conveyed for the unpaid balance of the purchase price even though there is no express reservation of a security interest in the deed or elsewhere. See Boyer and Evans, The Vendor's Lien in Florida, 20 U. Miami L. Rev. 767 (1966). For the value of having an equitable mortgage declared where the debtor is insolvent, see Application of Ross Dev. Co., 102 F. Supp. 753 (E.D.N.Y. 1952). Where the vendor inserts into the deed a reservation of a lien on the land, this is sometimes viewed as a legal, rather than an equitable, mortgage. See Norvell, The Vendor's Lien and Reservation of the Paramount Legal Title—The Rights of Vendors, Vendees and Subvendees, 44 Tex. L. Rev. 22, 24 (1965). Some states have enacted legislation recognizing vendor liens. See G. Osborne, Handbook on the Law of Mortgages 29 (2d ed. 1970). While such liens are binding as between the vendor and the vendee, they are subordinate to a federal tax lien, the claim of a trustee in bankruptcy, and junior encumbrances that are recorded.

C. THE DEED OF TRUST AS A MORTGAGE SUBSTITUTE

As noted previously, several jurisdictions authorize the deed of trust as a mortgage substitute. Trust deeds have become the preferred device for real estate financing in more than a dozen states, including Arizona, California, Texas, and

Virginia.[19] In a mortgage jurisdiction that does not authorize an out-of-court sale by the mortgagee (known as a power of sale), the foreclosure action must be supervised by a court, hence the term judicial foreclosure. By contrast, under a deed of trust, the sale is conducted by a trustee without the supervision of the court. This is why a deed of trust sale tends to be quicker and less costly for the lender; however, the title received by the purchaser is less firm than one received by a purchaser at a judicial foreclosure sale. Although there is little practical difference between a deed of trust and a mortgage, particularly in states that authorize mortgages with a power of sale, important differences may be contained in the statutory authorization of the deed of trust and in certain statutory protections of borrowers. For example, the deed of trust statutes may eliminate postforeclosure (statutory) redemption rights, while at the same time extending greater protection to borrowers from deficiency judgments than exists following a mortgage foreclosure. See Chapter 8C3.

Moreover, several unique issues arise from the three-party nature of the deed of trust with its trustor (borrower), trustee and beneficiary (lender). For example, what is the effect of failing to designate a trustee in the deed of trust, what is the nature of title that the trustee holds, what are the trustee's responsibilities to the other parties, and can the lender's lawyer serve as trustee? The following materials explore these issues.

In re Bisbee (Bisbee v. Security National Bank)
157 Ariz. 31, 754 P.2d 1135 (1988)

MOELLER, Justice.

. . . On December 7, 1982, Charles Martin Bisbee, acting as a married man dealing with his sole and separate property, executed and had recorded in Maricopa County, Arizona a deed of trust and assignment of rents to secure a debt in the original amount of $600,000, listing as beneficiary the Security National Bank and Trust Company of Norman, Oklahoma. The trust deed purports to encumber approximately 100 acres of undeveloped Maricopa County land but fails to designate a trustee. On March 28, 1983, Bisbee executed and recorded a similar trust deed and assignment to secure the Bank's additional loan of $218,000. That instrument also lacked a designation for a trustee and purported to cover the same realty. Charles and Wanta Rhea Bisbee, his wife, filed a voluntary business reorganization case under Chapter 11 of the Bankruptcy Reform Act of 1978 on April 11, 1983. Pursuant to Court order, the 100 acres were sold for $2,250,000.00 and nondisputed lienholders paid. Currently, the sum of not less than $834,076.23 is escrowed at interest pending

---

19. See B. Dunaway, The Law of Distressed Real Estate Appendix 9A (1992) (specifying the customary security agreement in each state).

resolution of the validity of the trust deeds. On February 10, 1986, Mr. and Mrs. Bisbee, as debtors in possession, filed an adversary complaint against Security National Bank seeking to invalidate the Bank's security interests. Under federal bankruptcy law, a Chapter 11 debtor in possession has the same rights to avoid security interests as those possessed by a hypothetical lien creditor or bona fide purchaser of real property. 11 U.S.C. §§544, 1107(a). Accordingly, debtors take the position that failure of the instruments to designate a trustee results in invalidity of the security instruments under Arizona law. On May 1, 1987, defendant's successor, the Federal Deposit Insurance Corporation, moved for summary judgment of dismissal, arguing inter alia the liens are enforceable as a deed of trust or, in the alternative, as an Arizona mortgage. At oral argument on June 25, 1987, the Bankruptcy Court reserved ruling on the merits of defendant's motion until the issue of apparent first impression could be considered by the Arizona Supreme Court. This certification procedure followed. . . .

[T]he determinative issue is whether the failure to designate a trustee in the two security instruments would preclude the Federal Deposit Insurance Corporation (FDIC), as successor in interest to the lending bank, from enforcing the two instruments against bona fide purchasers and/or lien creditors deemed to come into existence as of the date the debtors filed bankruptcy.

Under A.R.S. §33-801(5), a deed of trust is defined as: [A] deed executed in conformity with this chapter and conveying trust property to a trustee or trustees qualified under §33-803 to secure the performance of a contract or contracts. . . .

The debtors' argument is based on a theory of strict statutory construction. They correctly note that every definitional statute in the Arizona Deeds of Trust Act, A.R.S. §§33-801 et seq., (the Act) refers to a conveyance of trust property from a trustor to a trustee through a conveyance document. They maintain that because no trustee was designated, there was no one to receive a transfer of the property, and, therefore, no lien was created.

The Act is a comprehensive set of statutes governing the execution and operation of deeds of trust. Taken as a whole, we do not believe the Act supports the debtors' arguments. A.R.S. §33-804(D) expressly provides that if a trustee "fails to qualify or is unwilling or unable to serve or resigns, it does not invalidate the deed of trust." Under that subsection, the only effect of the absence of a valid trustee is that no action required to be taken by the trustee may be taken until a successor trustee is appointed. We perceive no logical distinction between a failure to designate a trustee and a failure to designate a legally qualified trustee. Nor do we perceive any valid policy reason to treat the two situations differently. In either event, there is no trustee. The Act clearly contemplates that the absence of a trustee does not invalidate the underlying lien.

. . .

Essentially, the debtors' argument is that it is an absolute requirement that conveyance of title be simultaneous with the creation of a deed of trust for the deed of trust to create a lien under the Act. That argument, however, ignores both the nature and purpose of a trustee in a deed of trust and the legal import of the conveyance of "title" transferred to a trustee upon execution of a deed of trust:

> The Arizona Act defines a trust deed as a deed conveying legal title to real property to a trustee to secure the performance of a contract. This definition suggests that the trust deed, unlike the Arizona mortgage, will convey title rather than create a lien. Nonetheless, the trustee is generally held to have bare legal title—sufficient only to permit him to convey the property at the out of court sale. All other incidents of title remain in the trustor. *Thus, in legal effect, there would seem to be no substantial difference between the trustee's "title" and the mortgagee's "lien."*

Brant v. Hargrove, 129 Ariz. 475, 480 n.6, 632 P.2d 978, 983 n.6 (App. 1981) (footnotes omitted; emphasis added), quoting Note, The Deed of Trust: Arizona's Alternative to the Real Property Mortgage, 15 Ariz. L. Rev. 194, 196 (1973).

In practical effect, a deed of trust is little more than a mortgage with a power to convey upon default. . . . Notwithstanding the conveyance of "title" in a deed of trust, the trustor remains free to transfer the property and continues to enjoy all other incidents of ownership. See A.R.S. §33-806.01(A). As stated in *Brant*: ["T]he bare legal title held by the trustee is very tenuous, and may at any time prior to sale be terminated by unilateral action of the beneficiary.["] A.R.S. §33-804(B). 129 Ariz. at 481, 632 P.2d at 984.

A trustee under a deed of trust has neither the legal powers nor the obligations of a trustee under traditional trust law. Instead he serves as a type of common agent for both parties. *Kerivan v. Title Insurance and Trust Co.*, 147 Cal. App. 3d 225, 229, 195 Cal. Rptr. 53, 56 (1983). The primary duty of a trustee arises upon default. . . .

We therefore hold that the mere failure to designate trustees does not render the deeds of trust invalid as between the parties to the trust deed instruments. Those instruments created liens on the property in favor of the FDIC's predecessor, the lending bank. This does not quite end our inquiry, however, since, for purposes of the certified question, the trustor Bisbee stands in the shoes of a subsequent bona fide purchaser and/or lien creditor. Thus, it is necessary to determine whether the recordation of the instruments in question constituted constructive notice to subsequent purchasers or encumbrancers.

The failure to name a trustee does not affect the manner in which a trust deed is indexed by the county recorder. A.R.S. §33-815 provides that trust deeds are indexed in the same way as mortgages, with the trustor indexed as the mortgagor and the beneficiary indexed as the mortgagee. It is undisputed that the instruments in this case were properly indexed. It is also undisputed that the property was correctly described and the instruments were properly acknowledged. They were recorded prior to the filing of the bankruptcy proceedings. Thus, under the express provisions of A.R.S. §33-818, the recordation constituted constructive notice to subsequent purchasers and encumbrancers unless it can be successfully argued that the failure to name a trustee renders the recording inoperative.

We believe *Watson Constr. Co. v. Amfac Mortgage Corp.*, 124 Ariz. 570, 606 P.2d 421 (1979), is dispositive on the issue of the validity of the constructive notice. In *Watson*, the court held that neither the failure to caption a deed of trust, nor the failure to include two pages of it, destroyed the constructive notice imparted by the recordation of the instrument. . . .[A]n instrument is constructive notice of the rights claimed thereunder if it is of a character which the recording statutes permit to be recorded and if it sufficiently apprises third parties of the rights claimed by it. Although the *Watson* deed of trust was not complete, it was of a character entitled to be recorded pursuant to A.R.S. §33-411, and, because it set forth the essential elements of the lien, it apprised readers of the nature of the transaction. . . .

We have held that the instruments validly created liens in favor of the lending bank. Because they were properly recorded, any subsequent purchaser or lien creditor, in whose place the debtors now stand, had constructive notice of the liens even if they could not identify the trustee from the recorded documents. . . .

THE ETHICAL REAL ESTATE LAWYER

Lender's Counsel as Trustee

Jurisdictions that authorize the deed of trust format normally specify eligible trustees by statute. Often included among those eligible are attorneys licensed in the state where the realty is located. But can the lender designate its own legal counsel as trustee? Consider that some courts have invalidated foreclosure sales held by trustees affiliated with the lender, whether as its counsel, as employees, or as related companies. See, e.g., In re Smith (United States v. Smith), 99 B.R. 724 (Bankr. W. Va. 1989) (foreclosure sale conducted by lender's employee as trustee was voidable). Other courts have concluded that so long as a commercially reasonable sale is conducted, the debtor has little interest served by insisting on an independent trustee. See, e.g., Wansley v. First Natl. Bank of Vicksburg, 566 So. 2d 1218 (Miss. 1990) (looking to U.C.C., which authorizes nonjudicial sales of personalty collateral by the secured party's agents and employees subject to an overriding rule of commercial reasonableness). Responding to the uncertainty created by this division of authority, some states have authorized interested trustees by statute. E.g., Miss. Code Ann. §89-1-63; Utah Code Ann. §57-1-21; Va. Code Ann. §64.2-1423 (counsel to or employee of corporate beneficiary may serve as trustee but cannot participate in setting the foreclosure bid amount). Do you agree with Virginia's exclusion of bidding strategy from its authorization of lender's counsel as trustees?

Despite these statutory authorizations, ethical dilemmas may arise for lender's counsel serving as trustee. For example, some jurisdictions treat the trustee as a fiduciary who owes duties of fairness and loyalty to the trustor. See, e.g., Blodgett v. Martsch, 590 P.2d 298, 302 (Utah 1978) (trustee has "duty to treat the trustor fairly and in accordance with a high punctilio of honor"); Cox v. Helenius, 103 Wash. 2d 383, 693 P.2d 683, 686-687 (1985). Contra Or. Rev. Stat. §86.713(7) (trustee owes no fiduciary duty to the borrower). What standard does the *Bisbee* case adopt? As a fiduciary to both the lender-beneficiary (as its counsel) and the borrower-trustor (as the trustee), the lawyer-trustee, at minimum, should consider whether it must obtain the informed consent of both parties to serve in this capacity. Cf. North Carolina State Bar Eth. Op. No. 82 (Jan. 12, 1990) (former trustee-lawyer not disqualified from representing lender in deficiency action following foreclosure, but current trustee cannot represent lender in bankruptcy proceeding to lift the automatic stay to permit foreclosure because fiduciary relationship demands that trustee be impartial to both trustor and beneficiary); North Carolina State Bar Eth. Op. No. 90 (Oct. 17, 1990) (trustee cannot negotiate loan modification or workout as attorney for lender). Moreover, several jurisdictions have not fully articulated the interrelationship of the ethical conflict of interest rules of dual representation explored at Chapter 2A2 and any statutory authorization allowing lender's counsel to serve as trustees. Cautious lender's counsel in these jurisdictions might substitute a disinterested trustee in the event of the trustor's default, limiting their own role to uncontested duties (for example, executing partial releases of the trust property pursuant to agreement). Does the standard for trustees articulated in *Bisbee* eliminate your concerns in serving as both lender's counsel and as trustee?

D.   THE INSTALLMENT LAND CONTRACT AS A MORTGAGE SUBSTITUTE

The installment land contract is commonly employed as an alternative to the mortgage to effect seller financing of real estate. Under this type of conveyancing, also known as the "contract for deed," "agreement for sale," "bond for deed," "long-term land contract," or "land sale contract," the purchaser typically takes possession of the property on execution of the contract, while the seller retains legal title in the property. Title is conveyed by deed only after the purchaser has completed a schedule of payments specified by the sales contract. The series of installment payments may take any number of forms, including interest-only followed by a balloon payment or mixed interest and principal payments amortized over a long or short period of time. Frequently employed by vendors of moderately priced tract housing or undeveloped lots in subdivisions, the installment land contract is also used in sales of small commercial businesses and agricultural property.

The absence of a third-party lender in installment land contract transactions makes this device attractive to both buyers and sellers for several reasons. It enables vendors to finance sales that, on account of either the purchaser's credit rating or the unacceptability of the property as security, would not qualify for third-party financing. Vendors also are able to reap the benefits of the finance charges they receive on the purchase price. They may also derive tax benefits from reporting their profits under the installment method of reporting income, as discussed at Chapter 7B3, note 5. Without the necessity (and protection to the parties) of appraisals, engineering inspections and credit reports, installment contract sales can be closed quickly and inexpensively on execution of the contract and receipt of a much smaller down payment than is usually required by institutional mortgagees.

It should be obvious that each of these advantages of the installment land contract is equally available when the sale is structured as a purchase money mortgage (or as a deed of trust). Differences between the two devices, however, do lead many vendors to favor the installment land contract. For example, because legal title is not conveyed until the end of the contract term, the installment land contract makes possible the sale of residential building lots held in a "subdivision trust" under which the vendor cannot convey title to individual lots until the trustee receives payment for them. The principal feature of installment land contracts that distinguishes them from their first cousin, the purchase money mortgage, is, however, their provision, in the event of the purchaser's default, for forfeiture of the property to the vendor and the vendor's retention of all payments made as liquidated damages. By including in their contracts forfeiture clauses of this kind, vendors seek to circumvent the often cumbersome, protracted, and costly foreclosure procedures that apply to, and protect, defaulting mortgagors. If vendors can invoke the forfeiture remedy, their willingness (despite the minimal cushion of a small down payment) to sell to purchasers whom other lenders would never consider assisting on any terms perhaps becomes more understandable. Yet, the chances of vendors being able to enforce forfeiture clauses as written have diminished substantially in recent years. In fact, the new Restatement (Third) of Property (Mortgages) takes the position that courts should treat installment land contracts (what it calls "contracts for deed") as mortgages and refuse to enforce the contractual remedy of forfeiture. See §3.4 (1997). These challenges to the enforceability of forfeiture clauses are discussed in detail at Chapter 8C6.

NOTES AND QUESTIONS

Further Reading. For a state-by-state survey of the legal treatment of installment land contracts, see B. Dunaway, The Law of Distressed Real Estate, Appendix 10A (1992). Detailed discussions of this topic may be found in G. Nelson et al., Real Estate Finance Law §§3.26-3.38 (6th ed. 2015); 7 Powell, Law of Real Property, ch. 84D (1996).

> ➤ *Problem 3-3*
> The following hypothetical transaction illustrates the use of the installment land contract method of financing. Francine Farmer, owner of Orangeacre, a

large farm near Miami, decides to sell her property and retire to Key West. Orangeacre's value would appreciate astronomically if it could be parceled out into quarter-acre homesites sold individually. Francine, however, doesn't have the experience to do the retail selling herself. Sam Subdivider does, but he hasn't got the cash to commit to buying Orangeacre outright. Francine, therefore, gives Sam 90 percent financing on Orangeacre under a purchase money mortgage and gets a good price with profits she can prorate for tax purposes over the life of the loan. To make the payments on his note with Francine, Sam needs to move his homesites quickly. He sets up a promotional operation in a rental hotel conference room on Miami Beach. There, dazzled by Sam's brilliant presentation of the development-community-to-be El Flamingo (Orangeacre redivivus), Harry Homeowner writes Sam a check and signs the installment land contract in the Documents Manual.

Regulations (12 C.F.R. §1011.2) promulgated by the Bureau of Consumer Financial Protection under the Interstate Land Sales Full Disclosure Act, 15 U.S.C. §§1701-1720 (ILSFDA), give homesite buyers like Harry a seven-day option to revoke their purchase agreement (perhaps to sober up from the complimentary cocktails served by the Sams of the real estate world). Suppose that Harry wants you, his lawyer, to shed the clear light of day on the contract he signed the night before. What reservations do you have? Consider the following. But first, read the installment land contract in the Documents Manual.

a. When may Harry get free and clear title to his parcel? Read Conditions 3(a) and 4 together. If he prepays the full contract price, does he get title then? Does he get anything then? Would Francine Farmer be likely to permit prepayment and a release-of-lien arrangement in her mortgage with Sam? See discussion at Chapter 7B3, note 2. Observe that Harry is not entitled to the use and possession of the land even if he prepays the balance of the purchase price. Under Condition 4, prepayment does not accelerate Sam's obligation to deliver a deed, and under Condition 3(d), Sam retains use and possession of the parcel until he delivers a deed to Harry. This looks like a disguised penalty for prepayment. Why would Sam want to discourage a prepayment by Harry?

b. Harry assumes responsibility to pay the real estate taxes if he records the contract. (The "Acknowledgment," when signed by Sam's agent before a notary, makes the contract recordable under Florida law.) This looks like a penalty for recording. Why would Sam do this to Harry? Would keeping Harry's interest off the record make it easier for Sam to resell the property if Harry defaults and forfeits? Is this the purpose of the second sentence of Condition 9? Not being in possession of the homesite, Harry does not give constructive notice of his interest in the property. Under most state recording statutes, this would mean another purchaser from Sam would take free of Harry's unrecorded interest. Similarly, a subsequent mortgagee would have lien priority over Harry. Some jurisdictions have mitigated these perils by legislation. In Maryland, for example, installment land contracts must be recorded, and the vendor is not permitted to mortgage the property in an amount exceeding the unpaid balance of the purchase price. Md. Code Ann., Real Prop. §§10-103(d), 10-104.

c. Under the installment land contract device, title may not pass until principal and interest payments have been made for a number of years. What safeguards might you devise to protect Harry in this regard while maintaining the essential financial structure of the contract? What do you think of the rather open-ended qualifications to "marketable title" found in the contract? See the discussion of marketable title in Chapter 2A3.

d. If Sam breaches his obligation to deliver title in accordance with the contract, what remedies are available to Harry under Condition 7? Would the refund of all payments made under the contract make Harry whole? If he had been making payments for several years, would a time value issue affect your answer, particularly in view of the fact that during this period Harry has not enjoyed the use of the property? What might cause Sam to default? What might entice him to default?

e. Explain to Harry the meaning of Conditions 8 and 9. Why, do you suppose, is there a graduated grace period? Arizona law mandates a comparable scheme for installment land contracts. See Ariz. Rev. Stat. Ann. §33-742.

Many of the questions you would have as Harry's attorney would be answered in the ILSFDA "statement of record" required to be filed with the Bureau of Consumer Financial Protection and provided to purchasers. In general, the ILSFDA covers only retail sales of undeveloped lots in large subdivisions and is similar to the full disclosure provisions and philosophy of the Securities Act of 1933. A reading of the regulations issued under ILSFDA will give you an idea of some of the perceived abuses in the subdivision industry that the Act was designed to curb. See 12 C.F.R. part 1010, app. A. ◄

E.   THE MORTGAGE IN COMPETITION WITH OTHER REAL ESTATE INTERESTS

Let us briefly examine the nature of a mortgage (and mortgage substitutes) in relation to other competing claims and interests in the same property. As you know, a mortgage is the transfer of an interest in land as security for the mortgagor's performance of an obligation to the mortgagee. Among the more typical claims and interests that may also encumber the mortgaged real estate are: (1) the lien of another mortgage on the same property; (2) a lease between the landlord-owner and tenant; (3) the lien of a judgment creditor docketed in the county where the debtor's real estate is situated;[20] (4) the lien of a bankruptcy trustee (or debtor in possession) where the owner of the real estate becomes a debtor under the Bankruptcy Code (see Chapter 18);[21] (5) the lien of the federal government against the owner's property (including real estate) for unpaid income taxes;[22] (6) the lien of the local government for unpaid real property taxes;[23] (7) the liens of a general contractor or subcontractors who are not paid after furnishing labor (mechanics' liens) or supplying materials (materialmen's liens) in connection with the construction of improvements on the land (see Chapter 6B3); (8) the equitable interest (under the doctrine of equitable conversion) of a purchaser of the mortgaged real estate; and (9) the interest of a holder of an easement on the land.

The very purpose of foreclosure is to enable the mortgagee to be made whole again from the security as it existed at the time the mortgage was created, free and clear of any junior interests. Accordingly, when the mortgaged property is sold at foreclosure following the mortgagor's default, the mortgagor and the holders of junior interests, including liens and encumbrances ("junior parties"), must face the specter of having their interests extinguished and of sharing whatever surplus remains after the foreclosure sale (in order of their lien priority) after payment of the expenses of the foreclosure sale and the mortgage indebtedness. See Chapter 8C2. By contrast, the position of senior interestholders ("senior parties") is not vulnerable to foreclosure.

1.   *Principles Governing Priority of Interests*

How are priorities established for conflicting liens and interests in mortgaged real estate? Specific priority problems are discussed throughout this book. For example, special rules apply to after-acquired property clauses (see Chapter 3B2, note 4, supra); to mechanics' and materialmen's liens and the doctrine of obligatory versus optional advances (see Chapter 6B3a); to leasehold mortgages (see Chapter 11A); to purchase money mortgages (see Chapter 7B3); and to the doctrine of marshaling assets (see Chapter 7B1, note 3) and other miscellaneous subject areas. In this brief overview, we confine our attention to general principles.

Prioritization of conflicting liens and interests in the mortgaged real estate generally follows the common law rule "first in time, first in right," as modified by the recording statute in the jurisdiction where the mortgaged property is situated. The policy purpose of the recording statute system is to facilitate land

---

20. See, e.g., Pa. Stat. Ann. tit. 21, §351.
21. Bankruptcy Code, 11 U.S.C. §544(a).
22. See I.R.C. §6321.
23. See, e.g., N.Y. Real Prop. Tax Law §902.

transfers by enabling a subsequent purchaser or encumbrancer to rely on what was recorded in the Registry of Deeds office as a source of information on the status of title and existence of any prior claims. Some recording statutes, called "race statutes," emphasize the race to the Registry of Deeds office; thus "first in time" means the time that the subsequent interest is "perfected" by recordation. The emphasis of these statutes is to penalize the interestholder that fails to record its interest promptly. At the other end of the policy spectrum are "notice statutes," which emphasize protecting the subsequent purchaser or encumbrancer who takes without notice of any prior claim even if the subsequent taker is slow in recording its interest. Under these statutes "first in time" means the time that the subsequent interest is taken without notice. In the middle of the penalty-protection spectrum are "race-notice" statutes, under which a subsequent purchaser or encumbrancer is protected against a prior claim only if the subsequent interest is recorded first and is taken without notice of the prior interest. Accordingly, "first in time" in this context means the time that the subsequent interest is taken without notice and recorded.[24]

As applied to foreclosure this means, for example, that if Dan Developer executes and delivers a mortgage to Ace Insurance Company and Ace immediately records, then, subject to certain exceptions, Ace occupies the position of a senior party and is accorded lien priority over any interest that is created after Ace records its mortgage. In general, Ace's mortgage will take priority over subsequently recorded tenants, mortgagees, buyers, judgment creditors, holders of easements, and other subsequent interests in the property.

Notable exceptions to the general rule include that: (1) a lien for unpaid local property taxes is generally prior to all other interests in the mortgaged real estate, regardless of when recorded;[25] (2) in some jurisdictions, a mechanic's lien may take precedence over a previously recorded mortgage;[26] and (3) an unrecorded purchase money mortgage may prevail over any prior judgment lien creditor (see discussion at Chapter 7B3, note 3).

While a junior party is afforded some protection by virtue of its right of redemption and its ability to bid at the foreclosure sale (as discussed at Chapter 7B1, note 3), the general rule is that the mortgagee that forecloses its mortgage can terminate all interests that are junior in lien priority to the mortgage that is being foreclosed. Returning to our hypothetical, assume that Dan Developer has fee simple title to some rental real estate (Greenacre) that is security for a mortgage loan made to Dan by the Ace Insurance Company. Dan then executes a long-term lease with the Widget Corporation of America (WCA), which is recorded after Ace records its mortgage. Finally, Dan obtains a second mortgage

---

24. For a discussion of recording statutes, see generally American Law of Property §17 (Casner ed., 1952).

25. See, e.g., N.Y. Real Prop. Tax Law §§912, 914. Local property taxes are discussed at Chapter 5A5.

26. See R. Powell and P. Rohan, Real Property ¶¶483-490 (1981); see generally discussion at Chapter 6B3.

loan from Fuller National Bank (FNB), the lien of which also covers Greenacre, as diagrammed below.

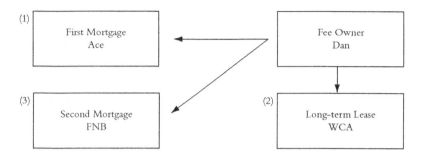

The numbers indicate the chronological order of recordation.

Suppose that the first mortgage (held by Ace) had a loan-to-value ratio of 75 percent and was in the amount of $25 million, and the second mortgage (held by FNB) amounted to $8 million. Because of Ace's lien priority over FNB, the foreclosure of Ace's mortgage would cut off FNB's mortgage. FNB could protect itself by attending the foreclosure sale and bidding an amount at least equal to the balance of Ace's mortgage, thus, in effect, paying off Ace's mortgage and obtaining the property free and clear of the first mortgage lien.

Are the consequences of the "first in time" rule fair? Suppose, for example, that Greenacre had a value of $33 million at the time Ace and FNB made their mortgage loans. Ace's loan would then have been secured by a mortgage lien on 75 percent of the original value of the property, which would still have provided FNB with an equity cushion of $8 million as security for its loan. Further assume that when Ace forecloses its mortgage the balance of the loan has been scaled down to $22 million, which amount exactly equals the current market value of the property. Could FNB reasonably contend that Ace's lien priority should be limited to 75 percent of the $22 million loan balance, or $16.5 million, to preserve the relative lien priorities that existed at the time the mortgages were consummated? Such an approach would compel both the senior and junior interestholder to share the burden of any loss caused by the reduced value of the property, thus enabling FNB to protect itself at the foreclosure sale by bidding only $16.5 million instead of $22 million for the property.

Although clearly not the law, this concept of "relative priority" (as opposed to what amounts to "absolute priority" under established law) raises some interesting questions. For example, why would Ace limit its loan to 75 percent of the value of the property in the first place? When FNB made its loan, did it assume the risk that any future erosion of Dan's equity cushion might impair its security interest?

Under the circumstances diagrammed above, a foreclosure of the Ace mortgage might also cut off the long-term lease because Ace (or some other purchaser at the foreclosure sale) would have the right to obtain the same state of title that existed when the mortgage lien was perfected, that is, when Ace's mortgage on the property was recorded. On the other hand, since WCA's long-term lease had been executed and recorded prior to the recordation of the second mortgage, the foreclosure of FNB's mortgage would have no effect on the lease. FNB (or some other purchaser at the foreclosure sale under the FNB mortgage) would acquire title subject to the interests of both senior parties—Ace's mortgage and WCA's leasehold estate.

THE REAL ESTATE LAWYER AND THE UCC

Although the Uniform Commercial Code follows the "first in time" rule for personal property security interests, UCC §9-322, this rule is riddled with more exceptions than under most mortgage laws. The raft of UCC exceptions to such priority include those for certain later-in-time purchase money lenders, UCC §9-324, and those for certain buyers of the collateral. UCC §9-320. By contrast to the UCC, which includes among its "first in time" exceptions one protecting buyers of inventory from a dealer, realty law generally will preserve the lender's recorded mortgage against a later purchaser from the developer/borrower. (See Chapter 7B3, note 2, for discussion of mortgage release provisions to facilitate subdivision sales.) The UCC's protection of certain later-in-time purchase money lenders is not as radical a departure from realty law as may first appear. Because the later-in-time purchase money lender is favored only in the newly acquired purchase-money collateral, the UCC's protection is akin to the limited rights of a prior recorded realty lender asserting an interest against after-acquired real estate. See Chapter 3B2, note 4, supra.

---

2. *Altering Priorities by Agreement: Subordination and Nondisturbance Agreements*

Lien priorities (or their consequences at foreclosure) can be altered by means of an agreement between the parties such as a subordination or a nondisturbance agreement.[27] Such agreements are used for various kinds of real estate financing situations. For example, a seller of land who takes back a purchase money

---

27. See G. Osborne, Handbook on the Law of Mortgages 381-387 (2d ed. 1970); cf. U.C.C. §9-339 (priority rules for personalty secured loans subject to any subordination agreement). Much of the recent litigation pertaining to subordination agreements deals with whether such contracts are sufficiently definite and reasonable on their face to be enforceable, hence the need for careful drafting by the party who is seeking enforcement. See generally Lambe, Enforceability of Subordination Clauses, 19 Real Prop., Prob. & Tr. J. 631 (1984).

mortgage from a buyer-developer might be required by the latter to subordinate the lien of its purchase money mortgage to any subsequent mortgage lien held by an institutional lender. Otherwise, the developer might be required to pay off the purchase money indebtedness before it could finance the improvement of the real estate because most institutional lenders will require a first mortgage lien on the improved property. See Chapter 7B3.

In the context of foreclosure, subordination frequently becomes important with respect to mortgage loans where the security for the loan is the value attributable by the lender's appraiser to the rental obligations of specified credit, or so-called prime tenants. Examples include loan transactions involving shopping centers, office buildings with long-term tenants, and urban renewal projects that are master-leased to a local housing authority. As discussed at Chapter 8C2a, when judicial foreclosure is employed, a junior interest cannot be terminated in most jurisdictions unless the junior party is joined as a party defendant in the foreclosure proceedings.[28] Consequently, with respect to the diagram in Chapter 3E1, WCA's leasehold estate would not be terminated unless Ace joins WCA as a party-defendant. However, in some deed of trust jurisdictions such as California, and in a few states where the mortgage form is employed, any lease that is subsequently recorded or otherwise junior to a mortgage will be automatically extinguished at foreclosure, whether or not the lessee is joined as a defendant.[29] In such a jurisdiction, Ace might execute and record a subordination agreement whereby Ace would agree to subordinate its mortgage to the WCA lease. Otherwise, this valuable lease (that feeds Ace's mortgage) could be inadvertently terminated at foreclosure, and Ace or some other purchaser at the foreclosure sale could no longer rely on the rental income stream from the WCA lease to defray the expenses associated with the ownership and operation of the property.

As an alternative to subordination, a junior lease will survive foreclosure, even in a jurisdiction where such a lease is ordinarily extinguished at foreclosure, if a tenant such as WCA agrees to execute a so-called attornment agreement, whereby the lessee agrees beforehand to "attorn to," or recognize, the mortgagee or other purchaser at the foreclosure sale as the new landlord. As quid pro quo for the attornment agreement a well-advised tenant would require the mortgagee to execute a nondisturbance agreement, whereby Ace agrees that if its senior mortgage is foreclosed, it will, depending on state foreclosure procedure, not cut off the lease with WCA; or, if the lease is nevertheless terminated, Ace agrees to recognize WCA as tenant under a lease containing the same terms and conditions as the previous lease. One benefit to Ace of this procedure over subordination is that Ace's contractual rights under the mortgage (for example, those regarding

28. See Metropolitan Life Ins. Co. v. Childs Co., 230 N.Y. 285, 130 N.E. 295, reh'g denied, 231 N.Y. 551, 132 N.E. 885 (1921); Davis v. Boyajian, 11 Ohio Misc. 97, 40 Ohio Op. 2d 344, 229 N.E.2d 116 (1967).

29. See, e.g., Dover Mobile Estates v. Fiber Form Prods., 220 Cal. App. 3d 1494, 270 Cal. Rptr. 183 (1990).

disposition of insurance proceeds) would remain superior to those of the tenant under the lease.[30]

The foregoing discussion has assumed that, absent subordination or attornment, the lease would be junior to the mortgage. Alternatively, if the lease is executed before recording of the mortgage and is superior to the mortgage, the mortgagee may require that the tenant subordinate its lease to the mortgage. Otherwise, the tenant's rights under the lease would override contrary provisions in the mortgage. Moreover, the senior lease might violate legal requirements that the mortgagee obtain a first lien on the mortgaged premises. As a condition to the voluntary subordination of its lease, the tenant would typically require a nondisturbance agreement providing the following language or language of similar import: "The mortgagee covenants that, in the event of a foreclosure, the tenant will remain on the leased premises so long as the tenant continues to comply with the terms of the lease and the lease is not in default." See Fisher and Goldman, The Ritual Dance Between Lessee and Lender—Subordination, Nondisturbance, and Attornment, 30 Real Prop., Prob. & Tr. J. 355 (Fall 1995); Stein, Needless Disturbances? Do Nondisturbance Agreements Justify All the Time and Trouble? 37 Real Prop., Prob. & Tr. J. 701 (Winter 2003). See the subordination agreement in the Documents Manual. Completing the arrangement, the lender will require the tenant's agreement to "attorn to," or recognize, the mortgagee or other purchaser at the foreclosure sale as the new landlord and thereby establish privity between them. To facilitate these "ritual" arrangements, Dan Developer should have anticipated the expectations of Ace in drafting the WCA lease. See Chapter 10B.

3.   *Direct versus Indirect Encumbrances*

An indirect encumbrance is an interest (such as a leasehold mortgage) that does not directly encumber the fee but merely encumbers an interest that does (such as a leasehold estate that constitutes the security for the leasehold mortgage). See the diagram below. As you read the materials dealing with leasehold mortgage financing at Chapter 11A, keep in mind the special priority rule that in the event of a foreclosure the rights of indirect interestholders, like those of a leasehold mortgagee, will depend not on their own lien priority but on the lien priority of the direct encumbrancers. The following diagram illustrates this rule.

---

30. As attorney for WCA, you would want to caution your client that a nondisturbance agreement does not afford the same protection as a subordination agreement. The nondisturbance agreement is a contract that might be disaffirmed by any trustee in bankruptcy or any conservator appointed in the event of Ace's insolvency, while a subordination agreement, once executed and recorded, is an accomplished act that is not subject to disaffirmance under §365(a) of the Bankruptcy Code.

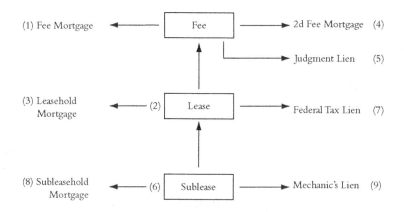

Once again the parenthetical numbers indicate the chronology of recordation and perfection of the various interests. First, the fee owner obtains a mortgage loan (1) secured by a first mortgage lien on the fee owner's title to the land. Next, the fee owner "ground leases" (essentially a long-term lease) (2) the fee to the ground lessee, who in turn borrows money to construct a building on the land by obtaining a leasehold mortgage (3), the lien of which covers the leasehold estate (including the building and other leasehold improvements situated on the land). Then, the fee owner obtains a second mortgage loan (4); thereafter a judgment (5) is docketed by a judgment creditor, thus creating a lien on the fee title to the land. Next, the ground lessee subleases (6) the building to an occupancy tenant. Then the ground lessee fails to pay a tax liability that is owed to the federal government and a tax lien (7) is filed on the leasehold estate. Finally, the subtenant obtains a subleasehold mortgage (8) to fund the cost of renovating the building, and a subcontractor files a mechanic's lien (9) on the subleased building.

NOTES AND QUESTIONS

Indirect Encumbrances. Based on the foregoing scenario, what would happen to the federal tax lien (7) if the second mortgagee (4) were to foreclose its mortgage? The answer is nothing. Even though the federal tax lien was filed after the recordation of the second mortgage, there is no direct legal relationship between these encumbrances because the federal tax lien encumbers the leasehold estate, while the second mortgage lien encumbers the fee. As for the *direct* encumbrances that encumber the fee, the ground lease (2) is senior in lien priority to the second mortgage (4) because it was recorded earlier; hence, the federal tax lien (7) will survive because its viability depends on the lien priority of the interest to which it attaches rather than on its own lien priority as an indirect encumbrance. Conversely, if the second mortgage had been recorded ahead of the ground lease, foreclosure of the former could terminate the latter and indirectly terminate the federal tax lien, which depends on the ground lease for its survival.

Likewise, there is no direct legal relationship between the fee mortgage (1) and the leasehold mortgage (3) because the former encumbers the fee while the latter is an indirect encumbrance that merely encumbers the leasehold estate. Nevertheless, foreclosure of the fee mortgage could indirectly terminate the leasehold mortgage. Why is this so? Indeed, as observed at Chapter 11A2, this is why regulatory statutes frequently prohibit lenders from making a leasehold mortgage loan where the fee title to the underlying land is subject to a prior lien or possibility of reverter. After reviewing the discussion at Chapter 3E2, supra, can you explain why a leasehold mortgagee would be protected against a prior first mortgage lien on the fee if the first mortgagee agrees to subordinate its lien to the ground lease? Would such a subordination mean that foreclosure of the leasehold mortgage could extinguish the fee mortgage, or would its sole effect be to prevent the foreclosure of the fee mortgage from affecting the ground lease and the leasehold mortgage?

> ➤ *Problem 3-4*
> Based on the hypothetical facts in the above diagram, what would happen to the sublease (6) if the ground lease (2) were terminated because of a default under the lease by the ground lessee or because the fee mortgagee forecloses its mortgage (1)? Do you see why the consequences for the sublessee (6) are the same as they would be for the leasehold mortgagee (3)? Would a nondisturbance agreement from the fee mortgagee (1) in favor of the sublessee (6) protect the subleasehold mortgagee (8) in the event that the fee mortgagee were to foreclose its mortgage (1)? Similarly, could a foreclosure of the judgment lien (5) threaten the viability of the subleasehold mortgage (8)? ◄

Chapter 4

Preclosing Terms and Conditions of the Mortgage Loan Commitment

According to conventional wisdom, mortgage financing is the foundation of real estate development. As such, Dan Developer undoubtedly will seek a mortgage loan to finance part of the cost of the office building project in the master hypothetical that begins Chapter 3. While it is possible for some developers to fund the acquisition and improvement of real estate with their own money, few are able to do so. Even if able, still fewer would forgo the tax and business advantages of financial leverage that result from using the mortgage loan and other forms of real estate financing.[1] In the case of debt financing, not many real estate borrowers have the wherewithal to borrow on an unsecured basis, that is, without furnishing collateral on which the lender can rely for satisfaction of its loan indebtedness on default. Woe to the lender who is relegated to the status of an unsecured creditor, for if the defaulting borrower becomes insolvent, without security the lender's sole remedy would be to compete with the borrower's other general creditors for recourse against the unsecured, and no doubt depleted, assets of the borrower. Therefore, the lender will insist on mortgage financing whereby the borrower's loan indebtedness is evidenced by a promissory note, and the borrower, as mortgagor, transfers a security interest in the real estate to the lender, as mortgagee, to secure the mortgagor's promise in the note to repay the borrowed funds. Thus, the mortgage becomes a lien on the real estate until the indebtedness is satisfied.

As we shall see, in the case of new improvements, while the postconstruction lender (such as Ace Insurance Company) normally commits to make the loan before construction commences, it does not actually "close" (fund) the loan until the building is constructed; therefore the security for the postconstruction loan is the lender's mortgage lien on a fully completed project. However, what really secures (or "feeds") the postconstruction mortgage, even more than the land and the intrinsic ("brick and mortar") value of the building, is the rental income stream from the project tenants. This is a major reason why nonrecourse financing (whereby the borrower-developer is exculpated from personal liability) is sometimes available in the postconstruction financing of income-producing real estate.

The improvements are usually constructed with funds provided by a construction lender (such as Fuller National Bank), whose security is merely a partially completed project consisting of the underlying land and the materials

---

1. See Chapter 12A1 for discussion of the concept of leverage.

supplied and services rendered by the general contractor and subcontractors at the building site. Even though the developer-borrower is personally liable for repayment of the construction loan, there is no rental income to feed the construction mortgage, and therefore the real security for the construction loan is frequently the agreement of the postconstruction lender to supply funding on completion of construction that will be used to "take out" (satisfy) the construction loan. In most cases, both the postconstruction lender and the construction lender will obtain a first mortgage on the improved real estate so that, in the event of a default by the mortgagor, the mortgagee need not compete with other encumbrancers who might be holding a lien or other competing interest in the same real estate. In fact, as explained below, the postconstruction lender, in paying off the construction lender, often will purchase the construction lender's mortgage and lien priority pursuant to a so-called buy-sell agreement.

A. PREFINANCING CONSIDERATIONS

It has been said that back in the 1950s, a developer could invest virtually anywhere and probably become wealthy. If this was true, it is no longer so. Today, with periodic inflation, tight mortgage money, and an oversupply in certain types of building stock, a developer must be willing to endure a tremendous amount of study before deciding whether a proposed project is feasible and, if so, how to obtain the necessary financing and venture capital to fund the land acquisition and construction costs. The following is a summary of certain important prefinancing considerations.[2]

1. Selection of the Real Estate

Before selecting the real estate to be developed, a developer will need to commission a marketing survey reflecting consumer demand, tax rate trends, and

___

2. Some salient prefinancing considerations that are examined elsewhere include deciding: (1) which ownership entity should be used (see Chapter 14); (2) whether the underlying land should be purchased or leased and, if leased, determining if leasehold financing will be available (see Chapter 11A); (3) how to obtain fee title and title protection for the purchaser (see Chapter 2); (4) whether the cost of the land should be separately financed by means of a subordinated purchase money mortgage (see Chapter 7B3), an installment land contract (see Chapter 3D), sale and leaseback of the land (see Chapter 11B), or some variant of component financing (see Chapter 11B1); (5) whether the project should be financed by means of a mortgage loan, joint venture, or some combination of debt and equity financing (see Chapter 5A1); and (6) whether the cost of developing or acquiring the real estate can be superleveraged by means of some high-ratio financing technique such as high-credit lease financing, a tax-free exchange, or tax-exempt bond financing (see Chapters 7C and 13A2d). For an in-depth discussion of prefinancing considerations, see Hastie, Real Estate Acquisition and Development—The Developer's Perspective, in 1 Modern Real Estate Transactions 503, 503-563 (7th ed. 1986).

rent and vacancy levels for comparable properties and, based on such information (along with efforts to prelease the building), the developer will make an educated guess as to whether there will be sufficient rental income from the project to both cover the anticipated operating expenses (primarily interest payments on the mortgage) and yield an after-tax rate of return that will be acceptable to the investors in light of the probable degree of risk involved. The developer must also conduct engineering studies at the construction site to determine if soil conditions and other topographical features are suitable and whether sufficient utilities exist to service the proposed site. If the developer plans to acquire real estate with existing improvements, it must also examine the physical condition of the improvements, prior rent schedules and operating expenses, the quality of the tenants, and the lease terms, and must determine what rate of return it can expect based on an estimate of future rental income and expenses (including financing costs). For discussion on rates of return, see Chapter 12A2.

2.   *The Function of Postconstruction Financing*

Historically, the postconstruction loan was known as a "permanent loan" because it had been used to replace (pay off) the temporary construction financing. Also, postconstruction financing frequently lasted as long as 25 to 30 years. Recently, with commercial real estate lenders reducing the term of postconstruction loans as a hedge against inflation, the phrase "permanent loan" has become a misnomer. For this reason, we use the phrase "postconstruction loan" to describe the type of financing that replaces and still remains distinct from construction financing.

a.   The Commercial Lending Cycle

The traditional commercial lending cycle begins when the developer solicits a postconstruction loan commitment and ends with the closing of that loan. See Figure 4-1. The postconstruction commitment is the all-important first step because the construction loan commitment frequently will be issued only after there is a firm commitment from a postconstruction lender.

Once the developer has the postconstruction commitment in hand, the next step is obtaining the construction loan commitment. Often the construction loan commitment will be accompanied by the execution of a "buy-sell" agreement among the construction lender, the postconstruction lender, and the borrower under which the construction lender agrees to sell and the postconstruction lender agrees to buy the construction loan.

After the construction mortgage is recorded, the next stage occurs, in which the improvements are constructed with the construction loan funds that are periodically advanced by the construction lender ("progress payments") in accordance with the construction loan agreement. Finally, the construction loan is assigned to (or "taken out" by) the postconstruction lender pursuant to the buy-sell agreement, and the postconstruction loan is closed, when the project is completed in accordance with the terms and conditions of the postconstruction loan commitment letter. Hence, the commercial lending cycle, as diagrammed in Figure 4-1, begins and ends with the commitment from the postconstruction lender.[3]

Figure 4-1

The Commercial Lending Cycle

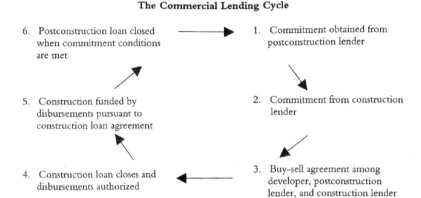

6. Postconstruction loan closed when commitment conditions are met

1. Commitment obtained from postconstruction lender

5. Construction funded by disbursements pursuant to construction loan agreement

2. Commitment from construction lender

4. Construction loan closes and disbursements authorized

3. Buy-sell agreement among developer, postconstruction lender, and construction lender

This traditional model is beginning to give way to other development approaches. Some construction loans have included a short-duration "mini-perm" phase following completion of construction to enable the developer to lease-up the completed improvements and obtain a stable cash flow before procuring longer-term postconstruction financing, but the traditional model has prevailed. However, increasingly, construction loans are applied for and obtained without any postconstruction financing in place. The general availability of credit in the marketplace lessened the impetus for a postconstruction loan commitment at the construction phase. Query whether this deviation from the traditional commercial lending and development cycle will survive the credit crunch that accompanied the subprime mortgage crisis and the larger global economic crisis that impacted development of commercial real estate.

b.   Selection of the Postconstruction Lender

3. The closing of the postconstruction loan does not represent the end of the story for the developer. After the project has been constructed and in operation for some time ("on stream," as developers call it), the developer may seek to "mortgage out" tax-free equity to the investors or raise additional working capital by refinancing the existing loan for a longer term and possibly at a lower rate of interest. See Chapter 7A. Alternatively, if the prepayment fee is steep or the interest rate on the existing loan is low, the developer may seek an ordinary secondary mortgage. See Chapter 7B. If the value of the land component is relatively high or the depreciation of the improvements is relatively low, the developer might obtain more working capital and tax deductions by means of a sale-and-leaseback arrangement (see Chapter 11B). In the alternative, the developer may increase its financial leverage by means of a tax-free exchange, component or split financing, or some other high-ratio financing technique. See Chapters 7C and 13A2d.

In selecting the postconstruction lender, the developer will have to consider which type of lending institution specializes in the kind of financing it seeks. The loan preferences of the various types of postconstruction lenders are the product of each lender's historical habits, external regulation of its investment portfolio, the source and stability of its funding sources, market competition, and a host of other variables. For example, most life insurance companies have tended to prefer large projects such as office buildings, shopping centers, and apartment houses to reduce their overhead-per-loan costs. Savings banks traditionally have made commercial loans involving small-to-medium-size apartment buildings. In their heyday, the less regulated and more audacious real estate investment trusts were generally more likely to be interested in land development loans and high-risk loans to develop hotels, motels, mobile home parks, and other specialty properties. These traditional distinctions, however, have become blurred in recent years, and within each group of lenders, individual institutional preferences may vary dramatically.

Life insurance companies have been a significant source of commercial postconstruction loans because the main source of their lending funds, insurance premiums, is not as subject to interest rate influence as are the savings deposits and federal reserve borrowings that fund the lending of banks. Because commercial banks are more immediately affected by monetary policy and inflationary pressures, they "tend to lend only on a short-term basis, and usually only when the real estate involved is secondary security to a permanent loan commitment." See Joyce, Financing Real Estate Developments, Colo. Law. 2093, 2101 (Aug. 1982). Commercial banks, therefore, are the primary source of construction loan funds.

An experienced developer will probably have little difficulty in choosing the right lender to approach. Developers with less of a track record may choose to act through an intermediary who will place the loan with the most appropriate lender. Such a developer may use a mortgage broker, who will undertake to find a postconstruction lender and, if successful, earn a fee geared to a percentage of the loan amount. Alternatively, the developer may look to a mortgage banker or, in the parlance of postconstruction lending institutions, a mortgage loan correspondent, who will commit to make the postconstruction loan based on an agreement from the ultimate postconstruction lender to purchase the closed loan from the correspondent. Generally, this process is used for smaller loans because the assets of the correspondents are limited. If the correspondent handles a larger loan, it will normally wish to use the institution's money to fund the loan. The loan is then closed in the name of the institution or simultaneously assigned to the institution if closed in the name of the correspondent.

B. NEGOTIATING THE MORTGAGE LOAN COMMITMENT

In large commercial transactions, the proposed borrower will apply for the loan on the lender's form of loan application, and, following approval and the negotiation of the major loan terms, both parties will execute an individually prepared, lengthy contract called a "commitment letter" that constitutes the lender's agreement to make the loan on the terms specified. The more complicated and the larger the transaction, the less the developer and the lender will make use of preprinted standard forms, and the more the documents (starting with the commitment letter) will be tailored to the particular facts and circumstances of the transaction.

The borrower's attorney should carefully examine the terms of the lender's form of commitment so that the developer can determine in advance whether the essential terms are acceptable. This certainly should be done when the form of loan application incorporates by reference the lender's commitment terms. In that event, a commitment issued by the lender tracking the application might constitute a binding contract (in first-year contracts terms, the commitment in these circumstances might serve as the lender's acceptance of the borrower's offer in the loan application). Moreover, a developer who feels uncomfortable with a loan provision in the application should not count on the lender's real estate or finance committee to agree to modify or delete the objectionable term in the commitment agreement. Any objections the developer may have should be resolved during the application stage. To simplify matters, some lenders, especially in small transactions, use a single integrated document that incorporates all the terms and conditions of both the application and commitment letter.

Contrary to popular belief, the single most important document in real estate financing is the commitment for the postconstruction loan, not the mortgage, because, with few exceptions, it is the commitment letter (or application-commitment) that establishes the legal and business parameters for the postconstruction financing. The following materials explore the content of the typical loan commitment and the duties of the parties in carrying out its terms and conditions. Because a commitment is, at bottom, a contract between the lender and borrower, the notes and questions will require that you consider commitments from the vantage point of traditional contract law, which calls for an offer and acceptance and imposes various implied duties on the parties.

Smith and Lubell, Real Estate Financing: The Permanent Mortgage Loan Commitment
4 Real Est. Rev. 7 (Winter 1975)

Mortgage loan commitments are as essential to the financing of real estate as contracts of sale are to the selling of real estate. However, while one can purchase a standard form of contract of sale at most neighborhood stationery stores, there are no standard forms of loan commitments. [O]ne will find in law reviews and journals few articles or commentaries on the legal aspects of commitments. Since we cannot today conceive of a mortgage loan which has not been initiated by a commitment, it is strange that we lack the same standardization for this important document that exists for mortgages, deeds of trust, promissory notes, deeds, and a considerable number of other instruments routinely encountered in real estate transactions.

WHAT IS A COMMITMENT

A mortgage loan commitment is a contract between a prospective creditor and debtor under which the debtor agrees to borrow a sum of money from the creditor and the creditor agrees to lend such sum to the debtor. It customarily arises as a consequence of an application for mortgage loan financing by an owner, purchaser, or developer. The application is an offer by the prospective debtor to borrow a specified amount of money upon stated terms and conditions, and the commitment is the lender's acceptance of the offer. Both application and commitment should set forth the amount, rate of interest, maturity, and other basic terms and conditions of the proposed loan. If the terms and conditions set forth in the commitment vary materially from those set forth in the application, the commitment constitutes a counteroffer which must be accepted by the borrower before a contract arises.

THE ESSENTIAL CONDITIONS OF A COMMITMENT

Commitments are issued by savings banks for loans on single-family residences, by commercial banks and real estate investment trusts for construction loans of all kinds, and by life insurance companies for permanent financing on office, apartment, retail, and other income producing properties. While the substance of a commitment varies considerably with the purpose and type of property, the following common elements should be contained in all commitments:

- Agreement by the lender to lend a specific amount.
- Designation of the party to whom the loan will be made (name of mortgagor or identity of borrowing entity).

- Terms of the loan including rate of interest and maturity.
- Method of repayment (e.g., constant monthly installments, interest only, etc.).
- Prepayment privilege, if any.
- Description of the security. (A legally satisfactory description, such as metes and bounds, is not essential; the description need only adequately identify the mortgaged property. If the lender requires a lien on personal property, it should be included in the description of the security.)

The above elements of the commitment reflect the essential business considerations of both lender and borrower—the heart of the loan transaction.

OTHER USUAL COMMITMENT CONDITIONS

Let us assume that a developer has applied to the ABC Life Insurance Company for a loan of $4,275,000, with interest at 8.5 percent per year and a term of twenty-seven years, to be repaid in equal monthly payments of $33,700 each, such payments to be applied first in payment of interest and the balance in reduction of principal. The security is a proposed garden apartment project containing 422 units and recreational facilities, to be constructed by the developer on a 22-acre site. The developer and ABC have negotiated a prepayment privilege effective after ten loan years with a declining penalty for prepayment. The commitment issued by ABC should incorporate all of the foregoing basic elements of the loan and should also contain the following customary conditions or requirements:

- *Documents.* All documents which evidence or secure the loan must be in form and substance satisfactory to the lender's attorney. This includes the note, the mortgage, or deed of trust, the assignment of rents and any other instruments which may be unique to the particular loan transaction. The lender cannot be arbitrary and capricious in its legal requirements. Otherwise the commitment would be a hollow instrument devoid of the substance of a contract.
- *Title insurance.* All prudent lenders insist upon title insurance in a form approved by their attorneys.
- *Survey.* Most lenders require a survey dated within a reasonable time prior to the date of closing the mortgage loan (usually thirty days). The survey should not only show the dimensions of the exterior lot lines but should also include the dimensions and location of improvements and easements, if any.
- *Hazard insurance.* Policies in amount, form, and substance satisfactory to the lender are required. Such policies must name the lender as beneficiary, as its interest may appear.

- *Fees and expenses.* Lenders invariably impose upon the borrower the cost of title insurance, survey, recording and filing fees, mortgage taxes, and attorneys' fees, if any.

VARIATIONS ON A THEME

The insertion of further conditions in the commitment is largely determined by the amount of the loan, the nature of the security, and the complexity of the transaction. In a commitment for a large and complicated loan transaction, the lender is much more likely to include additional provisions for the greater protection of its interests. In the foregoing example of a $4,275,000 loan on a garden apartment complex, there are a number of conditions that may be contained in the commitment, depending upon the lending policies of the institution making the loan. For example, a lender concerned with the ability of the mortgagor to obtain anticipated rents may require certain leasing criteria to be met as a condition precedent to the loan closing. The condition might read as follows:

> It is a condition of this loan that the annual rental from not more than 77.5% of the rooms in the development on an unfurnished basis shall be not less than $625,000 and the space rented shall be rented on a basis so that if the building were 100% rented, the annual rental would be at least $807,480. Such rooms shall be occupied by tenants on a current rent-paying basis under written leases or rental agreements having terms of not less than one year.

Where the commitment has such a *rental achievement requirement*, the lender naturally will require evidence that the leasing requirement has been accomplished before it funds the loan. The result is the additional condition "that the borrower shall deliver to the lender a rent roll certified to be correct, indicating the apartments of which said rooms comprise the total rooms relied upon to satisfy the condition."

If the loan is to be made on the security of a shopping center or office building, the credit-oriented lender will look carefully at the source of the leases and evaluate the credit of the tenants. In these transactions, the lender wants to pass upon the acceptability of the tenants, and a condition reflecting this will be inserted in the commitment.

In almost all cases where the commitment requires occupancy leases with specific tenants, the lender will insist upon being given in the commitment the right to approve or disapprove of the leases. The lender looks to the leases for the income which will repay the mortgage indebtedness. The prudent lender further reluctantly visualizes itself as a potential owner of the property in the event of the mortgagor's default. For these reasons there are many caveats which the developer, as a prospective borrower, must keep in mind when negotiating shopping center or office leases. . . .

THE COMMITMENT FOR NEW CONSTRUCTION

If our hypothetical $4,275,000 loan commitment on the garden apartment complex contemplated the construction of the development by the borrower, there would ordinarily be two commitments involved in the financing—a commitment for a construction loan and a commitment for a permanent loan. These two are usually obtained from different institutions. Life insurance companies are a common source of permanent mortgage loan financing and commercial banks are often a source of construction financing. Legal and regulatory restrictions imposed on each of these lenders limits their respective construction and permanent lending activities.

The permanent loan commitment is usually obtained first and forms the basis for the construction loan commitment. The construction lender, relying upon the permanent "takeout" supported by a buy-sell agreement among itself, the borrower and the permanent lender, patterns its construction loan commitment after that of the permanent lender.

Conditions which are unique to new construction and are found in most permanent loan commitments are often incorporated verbatim into construction loan commitments. They include the following:

- *Dates of commencement and completion of construction.* In the absence of these dates, the borrower is afforded an opportunity to "shop" for the most favorable mortgage loan.
- *Requirement for approval of plans and specifications.* Obviously, the lender desires to determine, in advance, the value of the security for its loan and will prohibit material changes in the plans and specifications without its consent for the same reason.
- *Completion of construction in accordance with plans and specifications.* The lender wants to be assured that it is receiving, as security for its loan, exactly what it bargained for.
- *Compliance with law.* Evidence must be submitted that the improvements comply with applicable building and zoning laws. In addition, some lenders now insist in their commitments upon evidence of compliance with all applicable environmental protection and equal opportunity employment laws.
- *Street dedication.* Streets necessary for access to the security must be completed, dedicated, and accepted for public use by the appropriate governmental authorities, and evidence of this must be submitted to the lender.

COMMITMENT FEES

Before seriously entertaining an application for a mortgage loan, an institutional lender must appraise the property, evaluate the borrower's integrity and financial responsibility, and also determine the economic feasibility of the real estate as security for the proposed loan. These tasks involve expenses which call for payment of an application fee by the borrower. Such fee is usually expressed as a fractional percentage of the loan and is paid simultaneously with the submission of the application. In some cases, the application fee is also regarded as the consideration paid by the borrower for the issuance of the commitment. An application fee should be distinguished from a commitment fee, which is in the nature of a security deposit to protect the lender against the uncertainties of the money market since a borrower may go elsewhere for his loan if interest rates soften. The amount of the security deposit or commitment fee constitutes a designation of the monetary damages which the lender will sustain in the event of the borrower's breach of the commitment.

In the ordinary mortgage loan transaction, actual damages are uncertain and difficult to ascertain because of the vagaries of the money market and the complexities of attributing a precise cost to the lender for holding funds available for the loan and for the postcommitment processing of the loan. Therefore, an arbitrary commitment fee expressed in the form of a percentage of the loan is usually employed. Although arbitrarily fixed, such fee should represent a reasonable estimate of the loss to the lender in the event of the borrower's failure to honor the commitment. Commitment fees of at least 2 percent of the face amount of the loan are most common.

Sometimes, in an effort to hedge his bet, a prospective borrower anticipating more favorable rates or terms in the future secures a "standby" commitment from a lender. Such a commitment obligates the lender to make the loan but does not obligate the borrower to take down the loan. Fees for this commitment are frequently geared to the period of time during which the commitment remains outstanding. This form of commitment usually constitutes a developer's last resort in the event he is unable to secure more favorable financing elsewhere and is generally obtained by him solely because his construction lender requires some type of firm takeout.

A BINDING CONTRACT

The commitment is the initial contract between the borrower and the lender. It defines the terms and conditions of the loan. The subsequent loan documents are to a commitment what the deed is to a contract of sale.. . . Therefore, commitments should be treated with the same regard accorded any other binding contract.

Teachers Insurance & Annuity Association of America v. Butler

626 F. Supp. 1229 (S.D.N.Y. 1986)

WEINFELD, District Judge.

Plaintiff, Teachers Insurance and Annuity Association of America ("Teachers"), is a New York nonprofit corporation which provides annuities and insurance programs to colleges, independent schools and other educational institutions, and derives income for such programs from various investments, including long-term loans on commercial real estate.

The defendant, One City Centre Associates ("OCCA"), is a California limited partnership which undertook the development and construction of a high rise office building, One City Centre, in Sacramento, California. It has three general partners, David L. Butler, James E. Kassis, and James L. Grauer, also named as defendants (collectively "defendants" or "the Butler group").

In connection with the development of the building, OCCA needed temporary or construction financing for the period during which the building was under construction and upon completion "permanent financing," which would be applied to the repayment of the construction financing. Bank of America made the construction loan.

Teachers, after extended negotiations with representatives of Sonnenblick-Goldman Corp., mortgage bankers and realtors who acted as the defendants' agents, and with Butler and Kassis on behalf of OCCA, issued on September 9, 1982 a Commitment Letter which was accepted by the individual defendants on behalf of OCCA. Under the Commitment Letter, which the parties acknowledge constituted a binding agreement between them, Teachers agreed to lend and OCCA agreed to borrow $20,000,000 for a thirty-five year term at a fixed interest rate of 14.25% per annum, to be secured by a first deed of trust on the building. The Commitment Letter, among other matters, granted Teachers a contingent interest in the rental returns over the life of the loan, referred to as a "kicker." One provision precluded the defendants from prepayment of the mortgage during the first seventeen years (the "Lock-in Period") and another permitted prepayment during the remainder of the loan upon payment of a premium ("Prepayment Premium") at 6% in the eighteenth year and in reduced amounts thereafter until the expiration date of the loan. These provisions, to be discussed hereafter, are at the heart of this litigation.

In October 1982, Teachers, OCCA and Bank of America, the construction lender, executed a related agreement called a Take-Out Agreement. It provided that Teachers would "take out" (i.e., purchase) Bank of America's construction loan or repay it the sums it advanced for construction of the building and succeed to its rights.

In July 1983, Teachers' counsel sent to OCCA for review and comment the closing documents which Teachers proposed be executed by OCCA at the closing of the loan, including a California Deed of Trust and California Deed of Trust Notes, which in relevant part provided:

> In the event Holder exercises its right to accelerate the maturity date following default by Maker, any tender of payment of the amount necessary to satisfy the entire indebtedness secured hereby made thereafter at any time prior to a foreclosure sale, either by Maker, its successors or assigns or by anyone in behalf of Maker, shall be deemed to constitute evasion of the prepayment privilege and shall be deemed to be voluntary prepayment herein and such prepayment, to the extent permitted by law, shall include the premium required to be paid under the prepayment privilege set forth herein. If such occurrence takes place prior to the eighteenth loan year then the agreed premium due and owing one [sic] the unpaid indebtedness shall be the product of the premium otherwise due under the formula herein for prepayment during the eighteenth loan year multiplied by three.

The parties refer to this provision as the "Default Prepayment Fee Language" and to the second sentence thereof as the "Lock-In Period Default Prepayment Fee Language."

Prior to the time set for the closing on April 30, 1984, Teachers and OCCA, through their respective counsel, had resolved all disagreements with respect to the language of the closing documents except the Default Prepayment Fee Language. On April 30, 1984, Kassis and Grauer (with a power of attorney authorizing them to act for Butler) appeared at the office of the escrow agent the parties had mutually agreed upon and made certain changes in provisions unrelated to the Default Prepayment Fee Language which had been agreed upon by their respective attorneys. However, they also struck the Default Prepayment Fee Language in each Deed of Trust Note and the Deed of Trust before signing the documents. Later that day, OCCA's attorney informed plaintiff's attorney that OCCA was unwilling to accept the Teachers loan as long as the documents contained the Default Prepayment Fee Language. Teachers then drew the full amount of a $200,000 letter of credit which previously had been provided by OCCA under the Commitment Letter. Soon thereafter, Teachers commenced this diversity action.

Plaintiff seeks to recover damages upon a claim of breach of contract—that defendant failed to negotiate in good faith the dispute with respect to the Default Prepayment Fee Language and that OCCA's claimed objection thereto was no more than a pretext for its unwillingness to proceed with the transaction as a result of a dramatic decline in interest rates from the date the Commitment Letter was signed to the date of the closing; that OCCA adamantly refused to negotiate the amount of the Default Prepayment Fee and insisted upon its deletion in its entirety—in sum that its position was wholly arbitrary and in bad faith. Plaintiff seeks to recover as damages the sum of $3,991,408, the difference between 14.25%, the rate of interest set forth in the Commitment Letter and 11.89%, the prevailing rate of interest on Teachers' loans during the month after the closing, over the thirty-five year period of the loan, discounted to present value.. . .

The defendants reject plaintiff's claim, essentially upon the ground that the Commitment Letter makes no provision for a Default Prepayment Fee payable after Teachers' exercise of a right to accelerate for default during the first seventeen years of the loan. The essence of their position is that although the Commitment Letter contains a detailed provision entitled "prepayment," that provision does not mention anything about Teachers' right to an 18% default prepayment fee. Therefore, according to the defendants, it was plaintiff that breached the contract by insisting on the inclusion of a provision in the closing documents that was not in the Commitment Letter. Defendants counterclaim to recover the . . . commitment fee retained by plaintiff and the $25,000 appraisal and engineering inspection fee paid to plaintiff. . . .

Under New York law, a duty of fair dealing and good faith is implied in every contract. As this Court has said: "Where the parties are under a duty to perform that is definite and certain the courts will enforce a duty of good faith, including good faith negotiation, in order that a party not escape from the obligation he has contracted to perform." Here, defendants signed the Commitment Letter, an agreement they concede was binding on both parties, obligating them to borrow and plaintiff to lend $20,000,000. Obviously the Commitment Letter did not contain, and the parties understood that it did not contain, all the final and definitive terms that were to be incorporated in the closing documents. Both parties were required to negotiate in good faith with respect to the closing documents needed to consummate the transaction. Defendants breached that duty to negotiate in good faith and therefore breached the contract with Teachers.

. . . The evidence supports a finding . . . that the Butler group, almost from the time the parties obligated themselves under the Commitment Letter, communicated with various lenders and brokers to avoid taking the Teachers loan. Beginning shortly after the Commitment Letter, with its interest rate of 14.25%, was signed, interest rates started to decline and as construction went forward, continued to decline so that when the loan was ready to be closed, financing was available at approximately 12% and without a kicker. Having obtained the permanent loan commitment necessary for construction to begin, defendants took advantage of the nineteen-month period before the scheduled closing to seek a more favorable loan package from other lenders.

Defendants do not deny communicating with other lenders in an attempt to arrange for permanent financing, but they contend that their purpose was to protect themselves against their inability to meet a requirement of the Commitment Letter that the building be 50% pre-leased at the time of closing. Defendants point to the financial difficulties of Attorneys Office Management Inc. ("AOMI"), a tenant to whom the defendants were required to lease a fixed percentage of building space. The evidence establishes that this claim was spurious. The pre-leasing requirement clearly was for the benefit of Teachers alone; a condition which Teachers could, and ultimately did, waive. . . .

Defendants' actions during the last few months prior to the scheduled closing date conclusively establish that, as the closing drew near, the defendants deliberately intended not to proceed with this loan—at least not on the terms contained in the Commitment Letter. . . .

Defendants said nothing about any of the provisions of the closing documents until it became apparent that their attempts to convince Teachers not to go forward with the loan or alternatively, to lower the interest rate, would not succeed. Although Butler admitted knowing sometime in February that the closing documents contained the Default Prepayment Fee Language, neither he nor Kassis ever mentioned defendants' objections to the inclusion of this provision in the closing documents in any of their conversations or communications with Teachers. In fact, the Butler group's objections to the Default Prepayment Fee Language were not raised until April 26, 1984—only four days before the closing—in a letter sent to Teachers' counsel.

Defendants insisted that the Default Prepayment Fee Language be deleted in its entirety. They made no counteroffers with respect to the amount of any default prepayment fee nor were they willing to negotiate its terms. . . .

Here, defendants not only had an implied duty of good faith negotiation, but they expressly agreed in the Commitment Letter to abide by all matters pertaining to the due execution of documents that Teachers' attorneys found "reasonably necessary for the transaction." The Default Prepayment Fee Language included by Teachers in the closing documents was not only "reasonably necessary," it was essential to protect Teachers from a voluntary default by OCCA.

The purpose of such language is to protect a lender against a drop in market interest rates which induces the borrower to default in the early years of the loan, forcing the lender to accelerate the balance, and enabling the borrower to prepay the loan with a second loan obtained at the lower interest rate. There can be no doubt that the loan, if consummated, would have been a highly desirable one to plaintiff, with its prospect of a stream of income over a thirty-five year period at a high interest rate and additional income by way of a kicker. The Default Prepayment Fee Language was intended to implement the Lock-in provision of the loan; without it, the borrowers could circumvent the Lock-in without consequence, depriving Teachers of the benefit of its bargain. Financial lenders in the California market, to protect themselves against such practices, included in their closing documents Default Prepayment Fee clauses at fixed amounts which were not immutable but subject to negotiation. The evidence fully establishes that the inclusion of such clauses was the custom and practice in the California real estate financing market. Indeed, defendants' own expert acknowledged this was so, although he testified some loans were closed without its inclusion. . . . Teachers' inclusion of such language in the closing documents for the OCCA loan is consistent with both Teachers' practice and industry practice.

Even Teachers probably would agree that it would have been more prudent for it to have included the Default Prepayment Fee Language in the September 1982 Commitment Letter. Some lenders include it in their commitment letters and the industry trend during the past few years appears to be towards greater specificity in commitment letters, in part due to a desire to avoid litigation such as this over provisions not contained in commitment letters. But this does not undermine the Court's conclusion that the Butler group breached its duty to negotiate in good faith to close the loan. As discussed above, defendants had the closing documents in their possession for nine months and, despite repeated reminders from Teachers to review the documents, they waited until four days before the closing to object to the Default Prepayment Fee Language. Then, instead of making a counteroffer or engaging in good faith negotiations with respect to the amount of the fee or its terms, defendants arbitrarily refused to negotiate and insisted that it be deleted in its entirety. Nine months after insisting that Teachers delete the Default Prepayment Fee Language from the closing documents, defendants signed the closing documents from Aetna Life Insurance Company which provided defendants with more money at a lower interest rate and without a kicker, but which contained a Default Prepayment Fee based on a formula which potentially could result in the imposition of a fee much greater than the 18% fee in Teachers' documents.

In sum, the inescapable conclusion the Court draws from the totality of the evidence is that defendants' refusal to negotiate with respect to the Default Prepayment Fee Language was simply a last-ditch attempt to scuttle the loan agreement they had entered into nineteen months earlier. The defendants signed the permanent financing agreement with Teachers to enable themselves to obtain construction financing from Bank of America. Almost immediately thereafter, as interest rates declined, defendants sought alternative financing from other lenders. When they were unable to persuade Teachers to lower the interest rate agreed to in September 1982 and when they realized that Teachers was serious about living up to its commitments, defendants engaged in an eleventh hour comparison of the closing documents to the Commitment Letter to come up with an ostensible reason for not going forward with the loan. Defendants breached the Commitment Letter and are obligated to Teachers for its damages. . . .

Before beginning the Notes and Questions, read the form of postconstruction loan commitment in the Documents Manual.

NOTES AND QUESTIONS

1. Vague Language. From the lender's perspective, the application form, the commitment letter, and any form of combined application-commitment should contain precise language and should include all the essential terms and conditions of the financing (for example, agreement to lend a specified amount; identity of the borrower; loan terms; prepayment privilege, if any; and a description of the security). Otherwise, any vague language will be construed against the lender, or the agreement may be unenforceable for want of certainty in its terms. For example, in Willowood Condominium Ass'n v. HNC Realty Co., 531 F.2d 1249

(5th Cir. 1976), the alleged commitment agreement for a $4.7 million loan to develop a condominium project failed to specify how and when the "floating rate" of interest would be paid, failed to fix a closing date, and was ambiguous as to the method of disbursement and repayment of principal. The court held that there was no binding contract. See also Peterson Dev. Co. v. Torrey Pines Bank, 233 Cal. App. 3d 103, 284 Cal. Rptr. 367, 374-375 (1991) (commitment with vague and missing terms did not create an enforceable contract); Leben v. Nassau Sav. & Loan Ass'n, 40 A.D.2d 830, 337 N.Y.S.2d 310 (1972), aff'd, 34 N.Y.2d 671, 312 N.E.2d 180, 356 N.Y.S.2d 46 (1974) (vague language construed against mortgagee).

The standard form of commitment letter is usually hedged with numerous conditions to protect the lender's interests. One such condition normally provides that the "form and substance of each and every document evidencing the loan and the security therefor or incident thereto, and the title and evidence thereof must be satisfactory to Lender and its counsel." What legal problems, if any, do you see with this boilerplate language? See Draper, Tight Money and Possible Substantive Defenses to Enforcement of Future Mortgage Commitments, 50 Notre Dame L. Rev. 603, 606-611 (1975). See also Mehr and Kilgore, Enforcement of the Real Estate Loan Commitment: Improvement of the Borrower's Remedies, 24 Wayne L. Rev. 1011, 1038-1042 (1978). By contrast, what are the drawbacks of the lender's lawyer simply attaching the lender's form of loan documents to the commitment letter as an exhibit?

2. Offer and Acceptance. As observed in the excerpt by Smith and Lubell, if the lender's commitment letter tracks the application without significant change, the commitment letter would normally be construed as the lender's acceptance of the borrower's offer contained in the application and would constitute a binding contract for a loan. Would the inclusion of language requiring the borrower's "acceptance" or "confirmation" of the commitment letter change that result? See Consolidated Am. Life Ins. Co. v. Covington, 297 So. 2d 894 (Miss. 1974), and 1 A. Corbin, Corbin on Contracts §61, at 252 (1963).

Suppose that the borrower accepts the commitment but its acceptance is conditioned on the approval of its board of directors. Will this condition prevent the commitment from binding the borrower where the negotiations reflect an intention by both parties to reach a final agreement? See Teachers Ins. & Annuity Ass'n v. Tribune Co., 670 F. Supp. 491 (S.D.N.Y. 1987).

3. Malpractice. The Louisiana Court of Appeal once confronted a legal malpractice action brought by a developer of an apartment complex who failed to meet a permanent loan commitment condition requiring delivery of certain documentation forty-five days before the closing date. See Meyers v. Imperial Casualty Indemnity Co., 451 So. 2d 649 (La. Ct. App. 1984). Apparently the developer's attorney, hired to prepare a loan opinion (see Chapter 4E2) and to handle the loan closing, had not examined the mortgage loan commitment to determine its conditions. Based on testimony of another real estate attorney that counsel handling a loan closing owes a duty to read the loan commitment and ascertain its conditions, the court held the lawyer breached a duty to his developer client.

4. Oral Commitments. Borrowers often assert claims that a lender committed orally to lend funds for a particular project. To reduce litigation based on alleged oral commitments, beginning in 1985, a majority of states have enacted new, or amended their existing, statutes of fraud to require that agreements to lend money be in writing. See generally Culhane and Gramlich, Lender Liability Limitation Amendments to State Statutes of Frauds, 45 Bus. Law. 1779 (1990).

5. Duty to Negotiate in Good Faith. At common law, each party to a contract is obligated to exercise good faith and fair dealing in the performance and enforcement of the contract. Restatement (Second) of Contracts §205 (1981). Lender liability based on this duty of good faith is discussed at Chapter 9A. The precise content of the duty varies according to the particular circumstances but will typically reflect the justified expectations of the parties and community standards of decency and fairness.

Under this standard of good faith and fair dealing that originates in the parties' commitment letter agreement, real estate borrowers and lenders will be held accountable to one another for their conduct while negotiating and closing mortgage loans. In Teachers Ins. & Annuity Ass'n of Am. v. Tribune Co., 670 F. Supp. 491 (S.D.N.Y. 1987), the court stated that the principal duty imposed by a commitment is good faith negotiation of the details left open by the commitment letter. Making negotiations depend on the other party's acceptance of new terms unexpressed in the commitment or on terms inconsistent with the commitment agreement may violate the duty of good faith. See also Penthouse Intl. v. Dominion Fed. Sav. & Loan Ass'n, 855 F.2d 963 (2d Cir. 1988), cert. denied, 490 U.S. 1005 (1989), rev'g in part and aff'g in part 665 F. Supp. 301 (S.D.N.Y. 1987), wherein the lender's bad faith was held to have constituted an anticipatory breach of a loan commitment to finance a casino in Atlantic City. The Second Circuit overturned a $128.7 million award for the borrower on the ground that it was not ready, willing, and able to perform at the time of the lender's alleged breach.

In the *Butler* case, the court assumed that the contested provision in the draft promissory note, the so-called default prepayment provision, was a customary (boilerplate) provision in the California real estate financing market as opposed to an unusual term that might precipitate serious negotiations between the borrower and lender during the application-commitment stage. Examples of boilerplate provisions in the mortgage loan documents that are within the borrower's reasonable expectations include the standard affirmative covenants (for example, the duty to make repairs, the duty to pay insurance premiums and property taxes) and negative covenants (for example, not to cancel a credit lease or to alter the mortgaged premises without the mortgagee's consent) by a mortgagor that are designed to protect and preserve the mortgagee's security interest during the term of the loan. By contrast, examples of terms in the loan documents that are deal-specific include the financial terms of the loan (for example, fixed and contingent interest, amortization period, prepayment privilege). Had the prepayment provision in the *Butler* case not been viewed as a customary provision, do you think the result might have been different? In *Butler*, the borrower had waited until four days prior to the closing date before objecting to the default prepayment provision. Meanwhile, during the 19-month commitment period, interest rates had declined dramatically. Obviously, this fact must have influenced the court, and common sense would dictate (as a planning suggestion for both borrowers and lenders) that any objectionable language in the loan closing documents should be brought to the attention of the other party as soon as possible to render the dissatisfied party less vulnerable to a charge of bad faith. Moreover, to obviate or minimize the possibility of an impasse in negotiations and possible accusations of bad faith, the parties should seriously consider "preclosing" the postconstruction loan transaction by using a preclosed form of buy-sell agreement, discussed at Chapter 4D6, infra.

> ➢ *Problem 4-1*

Suppose that, sometime near the end of a lengthy commitment period, a prospective purchaser of a postconstruction loan on the secondary market expresses concern over the dollar amount of the lender's loan commitment. In response, the postconstruction lender insists that the borrower agree to modify the loan commitment to reduce the amount to be lent and thereby increase the borrower's equity contribution to the project. Instead of pursuing its remedies for breach of the commitment examined in Chapter 4C2, infra, the borrower accedes to the lender's demand because it needs to close on schedule. Can you think of any theories by which the borrower can recover damages for the less favorable loan terms that it felt compelled to accept? See McCallum Highlands, Ltd. v. Washington Capital Dus, Inc., 66 F.3d 89 (5th Cir. 1995) (involving similar facts). ◄

C.   REMEDIES FOR BREACH OF MORTGAGE LOAN COMMITMENTS

The commercial real estate financing industry is a relatively small and close-knit community where reputations of borrowers and lenders depend on their willingness to respect and honor their commitments to one another; in the opinion of one commentator: ". . . a financing commitment continues to be an extremely important contractual agreement that is an integral part of the development process and, therefore, a matter worthy of the highest honor among industry participants."[4] Nevertheless, commitment letters are breached from time to time by both borrowers and lenders. But why do these breaches occur? A large part of the answer has to do with the volatility of interest rates for first mortgage money during fluctuations in the business cycle. In contrast to construction financing, which is usually based on a floating (variable) rate of interest,[5] postconstruction financing is ordinarily based on a fixed rate structure, which is agreed on when the loan commitment is made by the postconstruction lender, even though the loan funds are not actually disbursed until two years (or more) thereafter when the improvements are completed. Accordingly, if during this hiatus interest rates should increase, some postconstruction lenders may be tempted to find ways to extricate themselves from their previous loan commitments so that they can lend the otherwise committed funds at a higher rate to some other borrower. Conversely, if interest rates should decline, a borrower such as Dan Developer would be tempted to avoid his existing commitment with Ace Insurance Company so that he could obtain cheaper financing from some other lender.

For example, suppose Dan pays Ace both a 1 percent nonrefundable application or commitment fee and a 2 percent refundable commitment fee (sometimes referred to as a "security" or "good faith" deposit, which might be in the nature of a liquidated damages provision), which total 3 percent of the $25 million loan amount, or $750,000. Assume for simplicity's sake that the loan calls for 15-year interest-only payments without any amortization requirement.[6] By way of analogy to the predicament of the borrower in the *Butler* case (excerpted at Chapter 4B, supra) and to illustrate the worst-case interest-rate scenario for Dan, assume further that the commitment had been executed in the second quarter of 1982, when the average interest rate on commercial real estate loans made by life insurance companies was 15.23 percent and that only one year later, when the loan was about to close, the rate had dropped almost 300 "basis points" to a rate of 12.25 percent. What this means to Dan is that the loss of the 3 percent commitment-related fee amount of $750,000 may not be a sufficient sanction to induce him to honor the commitment to Ace when the annual difference in payments on a $25 million interest-only loan at 15.23 percent and 12.25 percent would be $745,000, and the difference in total interest payments over the 15-year life of the loan would be a whopping $11,175,000! Of equal significance to Dan would be the possibility for him to increase the loan amount. Based on a debt-coverage ratio of 120 percent, a decrease of $745,000 in annual interest charges, or $62,083 in monthly debt service payments, means that, at

---

4. Somers, A Forward Loan Should Be Equally Binding on All Parties, 1 Real Est. Fin. J. 91, 92 (Spring 1986).

5. See Chapter 5A1 for discussion of variable interest rate mortgage loans. As observed earlier, the principal source of loan funds for commercial construction loans is commercial banks. Because their sources of loan funds are more susceptible to influence by federal credit and monetary policy, these banks tend to charge variable rates that float over the prime rate. See Joyce, Financing Real Estate Developments, Colo. Law. 2093, 2101 (Aug. 1982).

6. See Chapter 5A2 for discussion of loan amortization.

12.25 percent interest, the same monthly payments would justify a loan amount of $31,081,633, compared to a loan amount of $25 million at the higher rate of 15.23 percent. Moreover, in a mortgage market where interest rates are declining and demand is weakening relative to supply, some other postconstruction lender may be willing to reduce its front-end charges for the sake of making a "spot loan" to Dan so that it can immediately invest its loanable funds and avoid the risks of making a forward commitment to lend money in the future (as Ace is doing). Therefore, an institutional postconstruction lender such as Ace would be exposed to a significant risk of loss if the retention of the 1 percent application fee and the 2 percent security deposit were its only remedy if the borrower should willfully default on its commitment to borrow the loan funds.

In this section we examine the remedies available to both parties in the event of a breach under the commitment letter, including the right to damages and the right to specific performance. Once again, this is an area in which freedom of contract principles predominate. Therefore, we will closely scrutinize the pertinent language in the commitment that addresses the issue of breach.

1. Breach of Commitment by Borrower

Commitment-related fees serve a variety of functions. For example, the commitment will occasionally contain language providing that the borrower will deposit a sum of money as a "security deposit" or "good faith deposit" for the performance of the borrower's obligations. The fee is refundable on the closing of the loan. The following is a commitment provision requiring such a deposit.

Amount and Nature of Deposit

Simultaneously with the delivery to Lender of a counterpart of this Commitment with the acceptance of Borrower endorsed thereon, Borrower shall deposit with Lender the sum of $ _____ which shall be in the form of $ _____ in cash and the balance in the form of an irrevocable letter of credit in the form and substance acceptable to Lender and its attorneys (herein collectively referred to as the "Deposit"). The Deposit will be held by Lender as security for the collection of damages Lender suffers by reason of Borrower's failure to perform its obligations under this Commitment, but the amount of damages that Lender shall be entitled to collect shall not be limited to the amount of the Deposit. As used herein, the term "damages" shall include, without limitation, loss of interest by reason of changing interest rates or otherwise, and expenses incurred by Lender including salaried time of Lender's employees in connection with or attributable to the issuance and administration of this Commitment.

Return of Deposit

Within five business days after the date Lender disburses or acquires the Loan, Lender shall return the Deposit, without interest, to Borrower.

Retention of Deposit by Lender

In the event that any or all of the terms, provisions and conditions of this Commitment are not fulfilled within the time limitations prescribed herein for any reason, other than the willful default of Lender, and as a result thereof Lender does not disburse or acquire the Loan, Lender may retain the Deposit to compensate Lender for time spent, labor and services performed, loss of interest and for any other loss which might be incurred by Lender in connection with this transaction. It is understood that the foregoing provision for retention of the Deposit shall not constitute an option on Borrower's part not to complete the loan transaction herein contemplated, and that Lender reserves any and all rights which it may have at law or in equity, including but not limited to, specific performance.

Additional Nature of Obligations

Borrower's obligations under this Article with respect to the deposit referred to in this Article are in addition to all obligations provided elsewhere in this Commitment with respect to payment of fees to Lender or to payment to any other entity, of fees, charges or expenses.

The deposit mentioned in the commitment above is refundable if the borrower lives up to the terms of the commitment. It should not be confused with a nonrefundable fee charged by the lender at the time the commitment is executed. Both the refundable and the nonrefundable fees are referred to as "commitment fees," but their objectives are quite different. The refundable deposit is designed to keep the borrower honest or serve as liquidated damages. In contrast, the nonrefundable fee is usually regarded by the lender as the consideration paid by the borrower to compensate the lender for keeping sufficient loan funds on hand to disburse the loan. If the borrower has deposited fees with the lender that the commitment designates as nonrefundable, courts have uniformly allowed the lender to retain them.[7] Both the refundable and nonrefundable payments are usually geared to a percentage of the loan amount, often a 1 percent nonrefundable application fee for each year the commitment will be outstanding and a 2 percent or greater refundable fee. The amount often will depend on the

---

7. See, e.g., Lowe v. Massachusetts Mut. Life Ins. Co., 54 Cal. App. 3d 718, 127 Cal. Rptr. 23 (1976); Goldman v. Connecticut Gen. Life Ins. Co., 251 Md. 575, 248 A.2d 154 (1968).

volatility of interest rates, applicable usury laws,[8] and the bargaining power of the parties.[9]

The following cases illustrate the difficulties lenders face when they fail to require a deposit or, if they do, when they fail to make clear the purpose for which the deposit is made.

Lincoln National Life Insurance Co. v. NCR Corp.
772 F.2d 315 (7th Cir. 1985)

BAUER, Circuit Judge.

This case involves an alleged failure by Defendant NCR to honor a mortgage loan commitment issued by plaintiffs-lenders. NCR Corporation intended to build a world headquarters on the banks of the Greater Miami River in Dayton, Ohio. To that end, in 1975 NCR secured the services of the United California Mortgage Company (UCM) [as mortgage broker] to obtain financing for its new project. UCM promptly lined up the plaintiffs in this case as lenders: The Lincoln National Life Insurance Co. (Lincoln); Provident Mutual Life Insurance Co. (Provident Mutual); Provident Life & Accident Insurance Co. (Provident Life); and Life & Casualty Insurance Co. of Tennessee (Life & Casualty). After a good deal of negotiations and exchanges of papers and signatures, all of which are now a matter of dispute, plaintiffs thought they had a contract to finance the construction of NCR's headquarters. We do not know what NCR thought it had, but we do know that in January 1976 in Dayton, Ohio, D.W. Russler, the Treasurer of NCR, made that always delightful discovery of an extra $200,000,000 cash on hand. Russler immediately formed an Excess Cash Committee, which loyally voted to spend the excess cash on construction of the world headquarters. NCR then notified plaintiff that because of Mr. Russler's happy discovery, NCR would not need outside financing. The plaintiffs, angry at having to erase the NCR loans from all of their flow charts, filed suit in the Northern District of Indiana, alleging that NCR had failed to consummate the mortgage loan commitment, and seeking damages or specific performance. After a two day bench trial, the District Court for the Northern District of Indiana held that the mortgage loan commitment was a contract which NCR had breached. The court looked carefully for some damage to plaintiffs, but finding none, suggested instead that plaintiffs ought to have been happy to have lucked out of what now looks in retrospect to have been a bad investment. Undeterred by the court's optimistic wisdom, the lenders appeal, arguing that the district court erred in holding that they had failed to prove damages. NCR on appeal applauds the

---

8. See Chapter 5A1 for discussion of usury laws.

9. See generally Smith and Lubell, Real Estate Financing: The Permanent Mortgage Loan Commitment, 4 Real Est. Rev. 10 (Winter 1975).

district court's reasoning on damages but suggests on a cross-appeal that the court erred in even finding a contract. We affirm.

I

In 1975 NCR sought a loan of $14,000,000 to finance the construction of their world headquarters. NCR agreed to pay UCM a fee of one-half of 1 percent of the principal amount of the loan for UCM's services in securing lenders for the financing of the NCR headquarters. Thereafter UCM operated as an intermediary between the parties and arranged the participation amounts per party, the loan terms, and interest rates. Plaintiff Lincoln requested and received a good faith deposit of $50,000 from NCR in order to insure that UCM would act for NCR. The plaintiffs then secured approval for their loans from their respective loan committees, and, receiving such approval, placed the NCR loan on their cash flow charts.

On November 5, Lincoln, on behalf of all the plaintiffs, issued a Mortgage Loan Commitment to NCR which set forth various terms and conditions of the loan. The commitment provided for a loan of up to $14,000,000 at an interest rate of $9^{7/8}$ for a term of 25 years. A specified portion of the loan was to be provided for by each plaintiff. The Mortgage Loan Commitment began by stating that the plaintiffs "have approved your application for a mortgage loan subject to fulfillment of and compliance with the terms and conditions of this letter." The paragraph concerning the "funding and commitment expiration date" provides that "NCR agrees to take the loan funds down no later than the fourth quarter of 1976," and that if the loans were not taken by December 31, 1976, the "commitment and Lenders' obligation under it shall terminate by that date unless the expiration date is extended in writing by Lenders."

The commitment also made reference to NCR's good faith deposit in the following language: "Lenders hereby acknowledge receipt of the sum of $50,000 submitted by NCR as a good faith deposit. It is understood and agreed that this deposit will be refunded immediately upon NCR's acceptance and return of this commitment." Above NCR's Vice-President's signature was the sentence: "The undersigned has read, approved, and accepted the foregoing mortgage loan commitment, including the general conditions," noting in addition that this acceptance was conditioned on the enclosed amendments. The commitment was signed by Charles Marcus of Lincoln on behalf of the plaintiffs. NCR's Vice-President executed its acceptance of the commitment on November 17, 1975, subject to amendments which it had attached regarding prepayment premiums and other conditions of the agreement. Acceptance of the commitment was made expressly subject to the approval of the Board of Directors of NCR. On November 19, 1975, the Board of Directors authorized and directed the officers of NCR to execute the [commitment]. On December 30, 1975, NCR wired the $70,000 [broker's] fee to UCM and on the same day NCR sent clarifications of NCR's proposed amendments.

On January 20, 1976, the plaintiffs executed the clarifications, sent the executed clarification document to NCR and returned the $50,000 good faith deposit to NCR. Plaintiffs then drafted and executed a loan participation agreement amongst themselves as required, and planned for funding the loan.

During January and February, when NCR recognized its unexpected cash surplus, the interest rates had also declined, so that NCR began to reconsider the terms of the plaintiffs' loan. On April 23, 1976, NCR sent two letters of authorization to UCM. The first letter, not to be disclosed to the plaintiffs, authorized UCM to renegotiate the NCR loan with plaintiffs at a rate not to exceed $9^{3/8}$ in return for a sliding scale fee which depended on the size of the reduction in the interest rate. Alternatively, UCM could earn a fee by negotiating a penalty for NCR's cancellation of the commitment. The second letter, also dated April 23, 1976, which could be disclosed to the plaintiffs, authorized the renegotiation of a mortgage loan in the amount of $13,000,000 at a rate not exceeding 9 7/8 annually and also specified that "NCR should have the opportunity to consider a reasonable penalty fee to cancel the loan."

On May 14, 1976, UCM sent a letter to Lincoln stating that a letter from NCR was enclosed "with a real sense of regret." The letter from NCR to UCM was dated May 10, 1976, and stated that NCR did not need the money and that NCR could not "justify consummating a loan at a rate significantly above the market when the fund[s] will not even be required for some time." In its letter, NCR specifically pointed out that $9^{7/8}$ was "extremely high by today's standards" and that NCR should not consummate a loan at that interest rate when "the same deal could be done today for less than 9%, and even that figure is improving almost daily." The letter suggested cancellation of the arrangement with a reasonable damage payment to the lenders or "a new arrangement with an interest payment in tune with the current market."

These letters were the first notice that plaintiffs received with respect to NCR's desire to avoid consummating the loan agreement as written and to renegotiate its terms. On May 26, 1976, plaintiffs responded with a letter directly to NCR. That letter stated that there was an enforceable contract and insisted that the loan be consummated.

In July 1976, the plaintiffs removed the NCR loan from their cash flow charts. Since the plaintiffs expected to fund the loan to NCR from cash flow, no funds were ever set aside specifically to be loaned to NCR. After NCR decided not to borrow the funds, the cash flow which would have funded the loan became available as part of the total investment activity of the plaintiffs. The record indicates that the plaintiffs made a variety of investments after the NCR loan was removed, some of which returned a higher yield than the NCR loan would have returned, whereas others returned a lower yield. Testimony at trial indicated that because of subsequent increases in interest rates, the loan to NCR, if it had been made, would have been a bad investment. . . .

II. ENFORCEABILITY OF COMMITMENT

The district court held that the mortgage loan commitment was a contract obligating the lenders to lend and the borrower to borrow. The court looked to parol evidence to reach this result, finding that the contract on its face was ambiguous. The court relied specifically on several pieces of evidence to establish the contractual nature of the commitment. First, the court noted that the plaintiffs, in conferring amongst themselves over the draft of the original commitment letter, had considered and rejected a "1% refundable fee to anchor the deal" on the grounds that "NCR is regarding the commitment as a contract." Second, the court recognized testimony that indicated that NCR knew that the lenders would be "unhappy" if NCR did not go through with the deal. Third, the fact that Board approval had been required by NCR suggested the importance of the contract to NCR. Finally, the payment of and plaintiffs' refunding of the "good faith deposit" revealed "the binding nature" of the commitment.

The defendant proposed two arguments in support of the proposition that no binding contract existed, but the court rejected both of them. The court found that the absence of a commitment fee was not determinative of the nature of the contract because its only purpose would have been to serve as liquidated damages had NCR breached the agreement. The court found further that the absence from the contract of the words "NCR agreed to borrow" does not mean that there cannot be a contract on the basis of the language used and the conduct considered.

On its cross-appeal, NCR argues that the court erred in considering extrinsic evidence because the mortgage loan commitment is plain on its face and not ambiguous. NCR argues that the plain meaning of the commitment gave NCR an option to borrow money, but did not obligate it to borrow. NCR argues that a contract must be strictly construed against the drafting party, in this case the plaintiffs, and that therefore the absence of specific language requiring NCR to borrow is critical. The plaintiffs argue further that the language of the funding provision, "NCR agrees to take the loan funds down no later than the fourth quarter," is not ambiguous. When read in the context of the agreement the phrase merely states one of the numerous conditions NCR would have to perform if NCR decided to borrow funds from the plaintiffs. NCR argues that the commitment offered an option to borrow, and that while no commitment fee was required by the plaintiffs to keep the deal open, nonetheless the performance of the conditions enumerated in the agreement by NCR would have been sufficient consideration to keep the contract open. NCR concludes therefore that it cannot be held liable for refusing to exercise this option.

We find much that is appealing in NCR's argument. . . . We need not, however, decide the issue raised by NCR in its cross-appeal here. Because we hold that the district court was correct in holding that the plaintiffs proved no damages from NCR's conduct, it is not necessary to decide whether the commitment in this case was a mutually binding contract or a promise of the plaintiffs to lend if NCR opted to borrow. We assume for purposes of discussion of the damages issue that the mortgage loan commitment was a contract.

III

. . . Under Indiana law, the burden of pleading and proving damages rests with the plaintiff. A mere showing of a breach of contract does not necessarily entitle a plaintiff to damages. It is an elemental rule of law that, while a plaintiff will not be denied a recovery merely because of uncertainty as to amount or valuation, in dollars, of the injury suffered, he is limited, ultimately, only to such relief as the evidence will support. . . .

Indiana law also provides that plaintiffs have the burden of mitigating damages. Where an agreement to lend money is breached, obtaining a substitute loan constitutes mitigation. Indiana courts have held that the measure of damages for the breach of such an agreement is generally the difference between interest on the contract note and interest the non-breaching party incurred or earned in a substitute loan.

The plaintiffs in this case sought damages in the amount of $1,200,000 in their original complaint, framing the damages suffered as "lost profits and lost interest." The plaintiffs also originally sought specific performance as an alternative remedy to damages, but on January 18, 1979, plaintiffs moved to amend their complaint by dropping Count II for specific performance. The plaintiffs gave no explanation for their request and presiding District Judge Jesse Eschbach granted the motion without comment.

After trial, the district court found that plaintiffs had made a claim for "expectation" interest, that is, for damages to put plaintiffs in the position that they would have been in had the loan been taken down. The court found that the plaintiffs had made no claim for damages for detrimental reliance on the defendants to the extent that their employees expended effort on the loan commitment. . . . They ask instead that we reverse and remand the lower court's order denying damages, instructing the court on remand "to enter a money judgment in favor of plaintiffs in an amount based on the present value of the difference between the interest which would have been earned on the NCR loan and the interest which would have been earned on a comparable loan as of December 1976 plus prejudgment interest."

The district court found that the plaintiffs in this case failed "to prove that they have, *in fact*, been damaged." To reach this finding, the court reviewed the plaintiffs' lending procedures and their testimony as to the use of these procedures in this case. The court found that when plaintiffs obtain a loan, they place proposed loans on a cash flow chart, which projects estimated future lending dates, so that they will be sure to have funding at the appropriate time. The court found that plaintiffs in this case placed the NCR loan on the charts before committee approval and removed it from the chart within two months after NCR's notification that it did not intend to take down the funds. The court concluded that, based on this evidence, the "proposed funding for NCR was nothing more than a paper transaction." No investments were changed at its inclusion, and any money which would have gone to NCR was invested elsewhere. The court concluded, however, that based on the testimony, it "is impossible to determine" the nature, terms and yield of the substitute investments. The plaintiffs concede as much in their briefs to this court: "Since cash is fungible . . . it is impossible to trace the funds which would have been loaned to NCR into some other substitute investment." The court concluded therefore that because the plaintiffs had not proven that "the NCR breach had any effect on their investment opportunities, they have not shown entitlement to damages for their expectation interest." . . .

We cannot find any error with the district court's finding of no damages, or with its reasoning on reaching that result. The plaintiffs failed to show that they were in any way damaged by NCR's failure to honor the mortgage loan commitment. . . .

Woodbridge Place Apartments v. Washington Square Capital
965 F.2d 1429 (7th Cir. 1992)

WOOD, JR., Circuit Judge.

. . . . In 1984 Woodbridge Place Apartments Limited Partnership ("Woodbridge Partnership") developed Woodbridge Place Apartments ("Woodbridge Apartments"), a 192-unit apartment complex in Evansville, Indiana. Woodbridge Partnership's sole general partner is Robert Jarrett. Late in 1986, Woodbridge Partnership decided to replace the financing on Woodbridge Apartments. For this purpose, Jarrett was introduced to Jerry Karem, a mortgage broker. . . . Karem put Jarrett in contact with Washington Square Capital ("Washington Square"). In the negotiations with Jarrett, Washington Square acted on behalf of two lenders, Northern Life Insurance Company ("Northern Life") and Ministers Life Insurance Company ("Ministers Life"). All of Jarrett's dealings were with Karem; he had no direct contact with Northern Life, Ministers Life, or Washington Square.

With Karem's assistance, Jarrett executed a mortgage application on behalf of Woodbridge Partnership. . . . This loan application set forth the basic format for the mortgage loan and it set forth the conditions necessary for the funding of the loan. [W]ith Karem's assistance, Jarrett filled in the requested loan amount of $4,665,000 for a term of 10 years at an interest rate of 9 1/4% based on a 30-year amortization schedule with Woodbridge Apartments serving as the mortgage security for this loan.

Paragraph 11(i) of this form application provides for a 3% standby deposit. A dispute over the nature of the standby deposit provided for in this paragraph is what brings the parties to this court. This paragraph reads as follows:

> Refundable Standby Deposit and Inspection Fee: A Refundable Standby Deposit ("Standby Deposit") of 1% of the Loan amount is submitted with this Application, and an additional 2% of the Loan shall be paid within 5 days of our receipt of the Commitment to increase the Standby Deposit to $139,950. It will be transferred to the Lender and be refunded at a reasonable time after funding and receipt by Lender of the original Note and title policy. In the event we do not consummate the Loan in accordance with the Commitment, we [borrower] shall pay the fees and expenses of your Special Counsel, and further, we shall have no right to any refund of the Standby Deposit, and the same shall become the sole property of the Lender. . . . If the Premises are not as described in the accepted submission, appraisal report or plans and specifications, this Commitment shall become null and void and the standby fee shall not be returned. However, should the Lender wrongfully refuse to fund the Loan, the Standby Deposit . . . shall be refunded.

In filling out the loan application, Jarrett, acting on behalf of Woodbridge Partnership, typed in a modification to paragraph 11(i) which stated that, "In lieu of the 2% additional points, the Borrower will furnish the Lender with an irrevocable Letter of Credit in a form acceptable to the Lender." The lenders accepted this modification. Woodbridge Partnership deposited $46,650.00 with Washington Square on January 22, 1987. . . .

After agreement was reached, Jarrett deposited a Letter of Credit secured by a certificate of deposit in the amount of $93,000.00. . . .

According to the loan commitment, the loan was to fund by the close of July 1987. The loan agreement provided for numerous conditions which had to be satisfied in order for the loan to fund. The loan never funded because a few of these conditions were not satisfied, including an apparently significant condition—the minimum occupancy requirement. That is, Woodbridge Apartments did not meet the 93% minimum occupancy requirement at the time in which the loan was to close. The district court concluded that the lenders benefitted from the loan's failure to fund because interest rates increased between the time in which the agreement was entered and the closing date.

What is at issue is whether or not Woodbridge Partnership is entitled to a return of the 3% standby deposit. Woodbridge Partnership brought suit requesting the return of $139,500.00 of this deposit, as well as prejudgment interest on the theory that this deposit constitutes an unenforceable penalty. The district court agreed that the deposit constitutes an unenforceable penalty and entered judgment for $139,500.00 in favor of Woodbridge Partnership. . . . Washington Square filed a timely notice of appeal with this court arguing that the agreement between the parties precludes return of the deposit and that this provision is enforceable because the standby deposit constitutes either an option, a [nonrefundable] commitment fee, or enforceable liquidated damages. . . .

. . . The parties seem to agree that the language of the loan commitment contemplates a refund in one situation: if the lenders wrongfully refuse to fund the loan. The plaintiffs-appellees, Woodbridge Partnership and Jarrett, (hereinafter collectively referred to as "Woodbridge Partnership") do not assert that the lenders wrongfully refused to fund this loan. Rather, Woodbridge Partnership argues it is entitled to a refund because this provision is a penalty provision—an unenforceable attempt to provide for damages. Washington Square, however, argues that this is not a penalty provision. Indeed, Washington Square argues that this provision is not a damage provision at all. Instead, Washington Square argues that the standby deposit constitutes consideration.

Washington Square sets forth two theories in support of its argument that the deposit fee constitutes consideration. One theory is that the deposit constitutes consideration for Washington Square's irrevocable offer to carry through with the loan if the conditions are satisfied. The second theory is that the deposit constitutes a [nonrefundable] "commitment fee" which serves as consideration for the risk that lenders incur in committing to fund a loan in the future at a specified interest rate. Alternatively, Washington Square argues that even if this is a damage provision, it is a reasonable and valid liquidated damage provision, not an unenforceable penalty provision. . . .

. . . The problem is that the disputed provision fails to characterize the standby deposit as either consideration for an option, consideration for a commitment ("commitment fee"), or as a damage provision. Indeed, the standby deposit provision fails to use any one of numerous operative terms which might help to resolve this ambiguity. For example, this provision does not even mention such terms as consideration, commitment, fee, damage, or option.

Washington Square's failure to use any operative language indicating the nature of the standby deposit distinguishes this case from . . . other cases in which similar provisions were enforced as option contracts or commitment fees. That is, many of the cases which have upheld similar deposits under an option or commitment fee theory involved contracts which either labeled the deposit as a fee, or at least stated that the deposit constituted consideration. . . .

Assuming arguendo that this is an option contract in which only Washington Square is obligated to carry through with the loan, Washington Square's argument that the standby deposit constitutes consideration for such an option is persuasive. This is especially true when we consider that under traditional contract theory some consideration is necessary to make an option contract enforceable. Moreover, a damage provision has no place in this loan commitment if it truly constitutes an option contract because, as Washington Square has pointed out, damages are appropriate only when there is a breach of contract. Failure to exercise an option does not constitute breach.

The problem, however, is that it is far from clear whether or not this loan commitment constitutes an option contract or a conditional bilateral contract. The agreement's language fails to resolve this issue because the drafters of this agreement not only failed to specify the nature of the standby deposit, but the drafters also failed to specify whether or not the agreement between the parties constitutes an option contract or a bilateral conditional contract.

In order for the loan commitment to constitute an option agreement, the loan commitment must be one . . . which binds the lenders and not the borrowers. In other words, if both the borrower and lenders are bound to carry through with the loan upon satisfaction of the specified conditions, then the loan commitment could only be a bilateral conditional agreement. Under such a reading the option theory fails. Recognizing this fact, Washington Square asserts that the agreement between the parties did not obligate the borrower to carry through with the loan. However, the agreement's language offers no definitive support for this proposition because the loan application and the accompanying letters fail to indicate whether the borrower is bound to accept the loan if the conditions are met. Indeed, one reasonable reading of this loan commitment leads to the conclusion that the borrower has covenanted to make a good faith effort to satisfy the conditions and that the borrower is obligated to carry through with the loan if the conditions are satisfied.

[W]hen a loan commitment's language fails to resolve the ambiguity some jurisdictions tend to presume that loan commitments are bilateral conditional contracts. . . . See, for example, Murphy v. Empire of America, FSA, 746 F.2d 931, 934 (2d Cir. 1984) [applying New York law]. Other jurisdictions seem to presume that ambiguously worded mortgage loan commitments constitute option contracts in which only the [lender] is obligated. Moreover, a third interpretation of ambiguously worded loan commitments is that neither side is bound. . . .

If this standby deposit was intended as consideration, it would have been easy for the lenders to state this in the loan application. And, if such an intent had been stated, or even hinted at, this would be an entirely different case. But, as it stands, the lenders never indicated in the contractual language or in the negotiations what purpose the standby deposit was intended to serve. Nor did the lenders indicate whether the agreement constituted an option contract or a conditional bilateral agreement. . . .

. . . The drafter should suffer the consequences of poor draftsmanship, and we therefore interpret the standby deposit provision as a damage provision.

F. UNAVAILABILITY OF LIQUIDATED DAMAGES

Now that we have determined that this is a damage provision, the next question is whether this can be enforced against Woodbridge Partnership as a liquidated damage provision in the context of this case. The district court held that this provision constitutes an unenforceable penalty provision. The district court reached this decision after concluding that this "provision does not attempt to secure an amount for the non-breaching party which is reasonably proportionate to the amount of actual damages likely to occur by failure of the loan to fund." We, however, need not address whether this provision is a valid liquidated damage provision because liquidated damages are not available on the facts before this court.

Washington Square, in support of its earlier argument that the standby deposit served as consideration, emphasized that damages are only appropriate upon breach. We agree.

In its decision the district court stated that, "For reasons not pertinent to this action, the plaintiff failed to satisfy the *conditions* of funding the loan." (Emphasis added.) The fact that the district court used the label "conditions" indicates that the district court viewed the failure to fund as a failure of a condition precedent, not as a breach of some covenant. The defendants-appellants have not challenged this characterization on appeal. . . .

Not only does it appear that Washington Square has effectively conceded that the contract failed because of a failure of a condition rather than breach, the language of the contract also supports this conclusion. Both parties agree that at least one primary reason for the loan's failure to fund was that Woodbridge Apartments, the proposed security for the mortgage loan, dipped below the required 93% minimum occupancy rate. The provisions which outline this minimum occupancy requirement are contained in Schedule I of the loan commitment. Paragraph 2 of this schedule refers to these occupancy requirements as "conditions." We see no reason not to hold the drafters to this chosen label. Granted, courts sometimes, in order to avoid forfeiture, interpret provisions labeled as conditions as covenants. However, in this case no forfeiture will result if we construe this provision expressly labeled as a condition as such. Indeed, something akin to a forfeiture will result if we construe it otherwise. We, therefore, construe the minimum occupancy requirement as a condition, not a covenant.

[B]reach sometimes results from the failure of a condition precedent under the theory of implied covenants. For example, Indiana courts often imply a covenant of good faith when the satisfaction of a condition is within the control of one of the parties. In such situations, if the party in control fails to make a good faith effort to satisfy the condition, this party has breached the implied covenant. Nonetheless, the district court made no finding of bad faith. . . . We must assume, therefore, that the contract failed because of a failure of a condition precedent, and not because of a breach of contract. Liquidated damages are therefore inappropriate. As such, the district court correctly ordered Washington Square to return the standby deposit.

G. RESPONSE TO AMICUS CURIAE BRIEF

The American Council of Life Insurance filed a brief as amicus curiae. In that brief, amicus pointed out that the insurance industry is a large provider of real estate mortgage loans and standby deposits are an integral aspect of these loans. Amicus argues that in today's market of fluctuating interest rates such deposits protect the lender from losses incurred when interest rates drop and the borrower walks away from the agreement: "borrowers would place the lending industry in a precarious situation if they could walk away from loan commitments whenever interest rates drop without forfeiting the standby deposit, but retain the benefit of financial commitments when interest rates rise." Brief of Amicus Curiae at 6. Amicus, therefore, predicts doom and gloom for the insurance industry if we refuse to enforce the standby deposit provision before us today.

However, we are not convinced that our narrow holding today will result in such dreary consequences. First, much of amicus's rationale assumes that borrowers are completely free to walk away from mortgage loan commitments. We have already indicated that this is not necessarily an accurate statement of the law, especially in Indiana where the courts are likely to hold that the borrower is bound to make a good faith effort to satisfy the conditions in the loan commitment and to follow through with the commitment once these conditions are satisfied. Moreover, this decision in no way prohibits insurance companies from requiring standby deposits as either consideration for an option, consideration to commit money to the future at a locked-in interest rate, or for reasonable liquidated damages for the breach of an agreement. Today, we simply conclude under Indiana law that the drafter of a loan commitment must provide some hint as to the purpose of the deposit, and if we can find no hint of such a purpose in the provision at issue, the agreement as a whole, or in the extrinsic evidence, the document will be construed against the drafter. It is also important to note that, in construing against the drafter, this court did not hold that the attempt at providing for liquidated damages was invalid. Rather, we simply held that if a standby deposit is to serve as liquidated damages, the lender must somehow demonstrate that the borrower breached an implied or express covenant rather than conceding on appeal that the borrower merely failed to satisfy a condition precedent. We are sympathetic to the insurance industry's plight. Nonetheless, we do not see how our narrow holding today will result in doom and gloom for the insurance industry. . . .

NOTES AND QUESTIONS

1. Bilateral versus Unilateral Commitments. The *Lincoln* and *Woodbridge* decisions illustrate some of the difficulties confronting an aggrieved lender that relies on a poorly drafted commitment letter for remedial relief against a borrower who fails to close the loan. For example, if the lender wishes to seek remedies against a borrower that fails to close the loan, the commitment should expressly provide that the borrower agrees to borrow the agreed-on loan amount and to accept the loan. Other courts have struggled with this same issue because of lenders' failures to clearly specify whether the loan commitment was intended to be bilateral (binding on both parties) or unilateral (binding on the lender alone; an "option" contract). See, e.g., Lowe v. Massachusetts Mutual Life Ins. Co., 54 Cal. App. 3d 718, 127 Cal. Rptr. 23 (1976); B.F. Saul Real Estate Inv. Trust v. McGovern, 683 S.W.2d 531 (Tex. Ct. App. 1984). If the commitment is bilateral, the lender can recover damages if the borrower refuses to close the loan and if, as the court suggests in *Lincoln*, the lender can prove that it has suffered damages as a consequence of the borrower's default. By contrast, if the lender agrees to lend but the borrower does not agree to borrow, the commitment would be unilateral and in the nature of an option agreement. In the real world of real estate financing, commitments that are intended to be unilateral are almost invariably standby commitments. As observed at Chapter 6A, the risks inherent in construction lending are such that many construction lenders view the takeout commitment from the postconstruction lender as the principal source of repayment at the end of the construction period. If a developer is unable to obtain an ordinary postconstruction takeout commitment, it may be necessary for the developer to pay an exorbitant fee to obtain a standby commitment to qualify for a construction loan. Therefore, in contrast to a refundable commitment fee designed to prevent the developer from walking away from a bilateral commitment when interest rates decline, the purpose of the standby (option) commitment fee is to compensate the standby lender for committing to a postconstruction loan that no other lender is willing to make. In other words, the ordinary *refundable* commitment fee compensates the lender for damages if the borrower should default whereas the standby commitment fee is *non-refundable* compensation paid to the lender for an option to borrow if the borrower should fail to obtain a less onerous takeout loan from some other lender.

  2.   The Refundable Commitment Fee as Liquidated Damages in Bilateral Commitments. Where actual damages may be difficult to ascertain, the courts will allow the parties to establish beforehand in their contract what the damages will be on default, provided, as the *Woodbridge* case suggests, that the predetermined amount is not plainly disproportionate to the potential loss that may be sustained by the injured party. This, as you know from contract law, is called "liquidated damages." However, if the actual damages can be ascertained with reasonable certainty or the predetermined amount is excessive, the liquidated damages clause might be struck down as an unenforceable "penalty." See J. Calamari and J. Perillo, Contracts §14.31 (6th ed. 2009). Often the refundable commitment deposit in mortgage loan commitments is intended to serve as liquidated damages in the event of a breach by the prospective borrower. The *Woodbridge* decision indicates that some courts will construe a deposit as liquidated damages when the commitment does not clearly specify the parties' intent. In what circumstances might the lender urge that the court interpret the deposit as something other than liquidated damages? Why did the lender in *Woodbridge* so claim? Based on the outcome in *Woodbridge*, do you see another situation in which the lender might urge that the deposit was intended as something other than damages?

  As the *Lincoln* court suggests, in the event of a breach by the borrower the lender's damages would generally equal the difference (in present value) between the contract rate of interest under the breached commitment and the interest the lender could earn from an alternative investment at the time of the borrower's breach. However, in most loan transactions it is extremely difficult to measure the lender's actual loss of interest income and the preparatory expenses incurred for a particular loan. Unless all of the lender's remaining loanable funds are fully committed, it would be expensive, time-consuming, and administratively burdensome for the lender to trace the funds earmarked for the use of the defaulting borrower. Moreover, how would you measure in monetary terms the expenses the lender would have incurred unnecessarily if the loan transaction were never consummated, such as reviewing and verifying the data in the loan application, reviewing the occupancy leases, and compensating the lender for a prospective loss of investment income while alternative investments are being sought? Consequently, courts have generally enforced liquidated damages clauses in commitment letters when the amount of damages stipulated is reasonable. See, e.g., White Lakes Shopping Center v. Jefferson Standard Life Ins. Co., 208 Kan. 121, 490 P.2d 609, 615 (1971); Boston Road Shopping Center v. Teachers Ins. & Annuity Ass'n of Am., 13 A.D.2d 106, 213 N.Y.S.2d 522, 528 (1961), aff'd, 11 N.Y.2d 83, 182 N.E.2d 116, 227 N.Y.S.2d 444 (1962).

But suppose interest rates rise and the aggrieved lender is immediately able to commit and reinvest all of its loanable funds at the higher rate. Do you think the defaulting borrower could argue here that the lender cannot receive the liquidated damages? In other words, should the validity of the liquidated damages clause be tested in light of the circumstances existing when the breach of contract occurs, or those when the agreement is entered into? See Seidlitz v. Auerbach, 230 N.Y. 167, 129 N.E. 461 (Ct. App. 1920) (involving liquidated damages clause in commercial lease).

3.   *Lender's Dilemma: Liquidated Damages versus Actual Damages.* The *Woodbridge* case makes clear that if the lender intends a deposit to serve as something other than damages, it should clearly specify its intent in the commitment. If it intends the deposit to serve as a damages remedy, the lender should specify further in the commitment's default provision whether the refundable commitment fee constitutes liquidated damages or simply a security deposit (akin to the ordinary security deposit in a lease agreement) against which the lender can seek recourse for actual damages in the event of a default by the borrower that prevents the loan from closing. If interest rates were to decline precipitously after the commitment is executed (which may be the very reason for the borrower's default), the predetermined amount of liquidated damages may be insufficient to compensate the lender for its actual loss. As suggested by the hypothetical at the beginning of this section, any significant decline in rates may cause the lender's actual damages to exceed the liquidated damages deposit, which is customarily between 1 and 3 percent of the loan amount, especially where a proposed loan has a relatively long term. Conversely, if the lender intends to recover its actual damages, it may encounter the kinds of evidentiary and burden-of-proof problems that prevented recovery by the lender in the *Lincoln* case. Moreover, the lender that relies on actual damages (with the deposit serving as a security deposit) may find there are no damages recoverable if interest rates increase during the period between the commitment date and the time of the borrower's breach. Of course, any prospective borrower capable of doing elementary arithmetic would understand why it would be imprudent to

default in a rising interest rate market. The default, however, may be unintentional.

Do the sample default provisions excerpted above provide for actual damages (with the commitment fee serving as a security deposit) or liquidated damages? Certainly what the lender would really like is a provision that specifies that the lender may, at its option, keep the deposit as liquidated damages, or sue for any greater actual damages while keeping the deposit as partial payment. As borrower's counsel to Dan Developer, how would you respond to such a provision? Should the courts enforce a provision that clearly provides for such an election? See Chapter 2A5 discussing challenges to similar provisions in contracts of sale. See generally Zinman, Mortgage Loan and Joint Venture Commitments: The Institutional Investor's Remedies, 18 Real Prop., Prob. & Tr. J. 750, 754-757 (1983).

Can you think of any reason relating to these commitment letter breach materials that explains why a lender might want to impose a relatively long lock-in period during which any prepayment of the loan would be prohibited? Prepayment clauses are discussed at Chapter 5A4.

With respect to the sample commitment provisions, can you think of any business reason why the borrower (as did the borrower in *Woodbridge*) might insist that the damages deposit be in the form of a letter of credit, as opposed to cash?

4. Force Majeure. Returning to our master hypothetical, suppose that just before the plumbing fixtures are installed in Dan's office building the local union calls a citywide plumbers' strike. As a result, Dan is not able to complete construction by the scheduled closing date. As discussed at Chapter 4D4, infra, most postconstruction loan commitments will require completion of construction by a specified date as a condition to the lender's obligation to fund the loan. On the basis of these facts, could Ace refuse to fund the loan? Could Dan claim "impossibility of performance" as a defense? See Hawkins v. First Fed. Sav. & Loan Ass'n, 291 Ala. 257, 280 So. 2d 93 (1973) (rejecting this theory in case where developer was unable to obtain building permit because of pending condemnation). If not, under *Woodbridge*, could Ace keep Dan's refundable deposit? What commitment language might Dan desire to protect against the lender's refusal to fund the loan because of these circumstances that are beyond his control?

5. Lender's Right to Specific Performance. Absent relevant language in the loan documents, do you think that courts should grant specific performance against either a borrower or lender who intentionally defaults under its loan commitment? In theory, a contract to lend money is not specifically enforceable by either party because there is an adequate remedy at law, namely money damages. 5 A. Corbin, Contracts §1152 (1964). And yet, as observed at Chapter 4C2, note 2, infra, this remedy has been generally available to an aggrieved borrower against a defaulting lender, especially where alternative financing was not available.

Conversely, there is a conspicuous lack of case law supporting specific performance against a defaulting borrower, presumably on the rationale that the aggrieved lender's money damages are readily computable. Do you agree with this underlying assumption? It has been suggested that a lender might argue for specific performance on the rationale that the security for a specific loan is unique (for example, a lien on a particular parcel of real estate; the reputation, creditworthiness, and construction-management skills of a particular borrower). By way of analogy to a contract of sale, the right of specific performance has been extended to aggrieved purchasers on the premise that every parcel of real estate is unique. See Draper, The Broken Commitment: A Modern View of the Mortgage Lender's Remedy, 59 Cornell L. Rev. 418, 434 (1974). In your opinion, is the analogy of a loan commitment to a contract of sale of real estate for this purpose a sound one? See G. Nelson et al., Real Estate Finance Law §12.3, at 1056-1057 (6th ed. 2015).

Another argument in support of specific performance is that no comparable investment alternatives may be available to the lender at the time of the borrower's breach. See Draper at 432-433; Groot, Specific Performance of Contracts to Provide Permanent Financing, 60 Cornell L. Rev. 718 (1975) (responding to Draper's article).

Should a lender who commits to a participating loan (one that shares in the property income or in the property's appreciation in value as additional interest)[10] receive specific performance on either of the above grounds? See City Centre One Assocs. v. Teachers Ins. & Annuity Ass'n of Am., 656 F. Supp. 658 (D. Utah 1987) (refusing specific performance notwithstanding that breached commitment provided for "contingent interest" based on gross receipts from the office building collateral in addition to a 12 percent fixed interest rate).

Do you think the aggrieved lender might have a stronger case if, instead of specific performance, it asks the court to enjoin the defaulting borrower from seeking a loan from any other lender? See Chicago Coliseum Club v. Dempsey, 265 Ill. App. 542 (1932). See also Zinman, Mortgage Loan and Joint Venture Commitments: The Institutional Investor's Remedies, 18 Real Prop., Prob. & Tr. J. 750 (1983).

Why would specific performance be unfeasible if the defaulting borrower has already gone out and procured a first mortgage loan from another lender? Would equitable relief be sensible if the project is no longer a viable one?

In the *Lincoln* case, the lenders initially pleaded in the alternative for specific performance. Three years after the breach, in 1979, the lenders amended their complaint to drop this request. Given the ultimate holding denying any damages recovery, was this a prudent decision? Why do you think the lenders dropped their request for specific performance?

---

10. See Chapter 5A1 for discussion of participating loans.

2. Breach of Commitment by Lender

Many of the remedial considerations that we just examined also apply to the enforcement rights of a borrower against a defaulting lender. However, the borrower's measure of damages is different, as the following case explains.

Pipkin v. Thomas & Hill, Inc.
298 N.C. 278, 258 S.E.2d 778 (1979)

SHARP, Chief Justice.

Plaintiffs, as individuals and general partners doing business under the name of P.W.D. & W., brought this action for damages against defendant, a West Virginia corporation engaged in the mortgage banking business, to recover damages for its breach of an alleged contract to make plaintiffs a long-term loan to repay a construction loan from Central Carolina Bank (CCB). . . .

In August 1972 plaintiffs acquired property on U.S. Highway 70 and 401 just south of Raleigh for the purpose of constructing and operating a motel and restaurant. At that time they were experienced business men but inexperienced real estate developers. After extended negotiations with Ward [defendant's officer], on 19 April 1973 plaintiffs jointly and severally filed with him, on a form furnished by defendant, an application for a "long-term permanent loan commitment from the defendant" in the amount of $1,162,500, repayable over 25 years at an interest rate of nine and one-half percent (9 1/2%) per annum, with monthly payments of $10,156.76 for amortization of principal and interest. . . .

. . . Ward and plaintiffs agreed that defendant would receive a fee of $11,625 for the loan commitment and a fee of $11,625 for closing the loan, a total of $23,250. . . .

Specifically, the question for our determination is the following:

What is the measure of damages for breach of a contract to make a loan of $1,162,500 at 9 1/2% interest per annum, the loan to be amortized over 300 monthly installments and to be used to take out a short-term construction loan, when a substitute loan was unobtainable upon any terms at the time of the breach and, in order to forestall foreclosure, the borrowers had to refinance the construction loan by a demand note at a fluctuating rate of interest for a period of 18 months?

At trial plaintiffs sought to recover—and the judge purported to assess—their past, present, and prospective damages. The case was tried upon the fiction that at the time of trial plaintiffs had obtained a permanent loan at 10 1/2% interest, which the court found was the lowest prevailing rate of interest for a comparable long-term commercial loan as of 1 October 1974, the date of the breach. In attempting to fashion a rule which would appropriately measure plaintiffs' damages the trial judge analogized this case to those in which the borrower actually obtained another loan. On this theory, the trial court awarded plaintiffs general damages in the amount of $120,000, this amount being the difference between the interest on a 25-year loan of $1,162,500 at 10 1/2% per annum and a similar loan at 9 1/2%, reduced to present value *and* "discounted for the likelihood of early payment." As special damage, Judge McKinnon awarded plaintiffs $5,888.12, the total of amounts which plaintiffs reasonably expended in refinancing their construction loan with CCB to prevent foreclosure, and in their unsuccessful attempts over 18 months to secure a replacement long-term loan. The judge, however, refused to allow any recovery of the $184,619.49 in interest which plaintiffs paid CCB on the demand note during that 18-month interim.

The Court of Appeals affirmed the trial judge's award of $5,888.12 in special damages. This ruling was clearly correct, and we affirm it. As the Court of Appeals pointed out, additional title insurance and brokerage, accounting and appraisal fees "were foreseeable expenses which, but for the breach, plaintiffs would not have incurred." . . .

The Court of Appeals also ruled that the trial judge was correct in using the lowest prevailing rate of interest for a long-term commercial loan (10 1/2) to determine "the basic measure" of plaintiffs' damages, i.e., the difference between the interest on the loan at the contract rate during the agreed period of credit and the rate (not exceeding that permitted by law) which plaintiffs would have had to pay for the money in the market on the date of breach. Defendant argues that the use of a hypothetical loan at the lowest prevailing rate of interest for comparable long-term loans, at least in cases where an alternative lender cannot be found, is too speculative and uncertain a technique for approximating the borrower's prospective losses. However, a party seeking recovery for losses occasioned by another's breach of contract need not prove the amount of his prospective damages with absolute certainty; a reasonable showing will suffice. . . .

In our view, plaintiffs have reasonably demonstrated that as a consequence of defendant's breach of its loan commitment they will suffer prospective losses; and we agree with the Court of Appeals that the trial court's use of the lowest prevailing rate for comparable long-term loans as a figure to be compared with the contract interest rate represents effort to provide relief from these prospective damages. We also agree that the trial judge erred in reducing the present worth of plaintiff's prospective damages ($143,282.03) to the amount of $120,000 "for the likelihood of early payment."

Although a witness for defendant opined that the average life of a commercial loan such as the one defendant was committed to make for plaintiffs was "approximately seven years," no witness attempted to fix the value of such a probability. Further, there was no evidence that plaintiffs contemplated early payment of the loan. The Court of Appeals, therefore, properly ordered this reduction stricken, and we affirm.

Finally, the Court of Appeals concluded that the trial judge erred in refusing to allow plaintiffs to recover the $184,61[9].49 in interest which they paid CCB on the demand notes during the 18 months elapsing between the date of defendant's breach of its contract and the date of the trial. This interest, that court said, was recoverable as special damages which defendant should have foreseen as the probable consequence of its failure to provide plaintiffs the promised long-term financing. Thus, the question remaining is whether, in order to avoid foreclosure, a disappointed borrower to whom a defaulting lender had committed long-term financing to pay off a temporary construction loan, is entitled to obtain temporary refinancing at a higher rate of interest and to recover the cost of this refinancing as special damages.

On the ground that such refinancing was an unforeseeable consequence of the breach defendant argues that the trial court properly denied plaintiffs any recovery of the interest they paid on the demand note which refinanced the temporary construction loan. In our view, this contention by a defaulting lender, fully aware of the purpose for which plaintiffs had secured its commitment, is entirely unrealistic. In 11 Williston on Contracts §1411 (3d ed. Jaeger 1968) it is stated:

> It will frequently happen that the borrower is unable to get money elsewhere, and, if the defendant had notice of the purpose for which the money was desired, he will be liable for damages caused by the plaintiff's inability to carry out his purpose, if the performance of the promise would have enabled him to do so. . . .

Whether the loan commitment be for $4,800,000 or $1,162,500, we harbor no doubt that a committed permanent lender on a substantial building project certainly must foresee that a breach of his commitment a relatively short time before the date he has contracted to provide the money to pay off the interim construction loan will result in substantial harm to the borrower.

Defendant, in this case, being unable to find a lender willing to make the permanent loan it had committed itself to provide plaintiffs formally notified them on 6 August 1974—less than two months before the scheduled closing date—that it would not make the loan. At that time the same conditions which had thwarted defendant's efforts to obtain the loan also thwarted plaintiffs. In a reasonable effort to minimize their losses, while they continued their search for another permanent loan plaintiffs refinanced the construction loan to prevent foreclosure of property in which they had acquired equity of approximately $627,500. That their search during the subsequent 18 months proved futile is no reason to deny them compensation for the resulting damages they sustained during that period.

However, our conclusion that plaintiffs should recover as foreseeable damages their losses arising from the interest payments on the demand notes does not necessarily entail an award for the full amount of interest actually paid to CCB. On the contrary, we hold that the Court of Appeals erred insofar as it awarded plaintiffs both the full amount of interest actually paid CCB from the date of the breach until the date of trial *and* the present value of the difference between the interest on $1,162,500 amortized over 25 years from the date of the trial at the hypothetical rate of 10 1/2% per year and the contract rate of 9 1/2%.

In Bridgkort Racquet Club v. University Bank, 85 Wis. 2d 706, 271 N.W.2d 165 (1978), [t]he Wisconsin court recognized the [borrower's] damages as the difference between the cost of obtaining substitute money at an increased rate of interest and the interest rate specified in the contract. In the case at bar, plaintiffs contracted with defendant to have the use of $1,162,500 from 1 October 1974 until 1 October 1999. To award plaintiffs the entire amount of interest paid to CCB from the time of the breach until the time of the trial ($184,619.49), with no deduction for interest at the contract rate of 9 1/2, would give plaintiffs the use of $1,162,500 interest-free for that 18-month period. When defendant failed to make the agreed loan on 1 October 1974 it became liable to plaintiffs *at that time* for the increased cost of obtaining the use of the money "during the agreed period of credit," that is, 25 years from 1 October 1974.

We are of the opinion that the Wisconsin Court in *Bridgkort Racquet Club*, supra, was correct in determining the plaintiffs' damages to be the differential between the cost of obtaining new financing and the interest payments specified in the contract. Based on this principle, plaintiffs' recovery of interest payments made to CCB during this 18-month period must be reduced by the amount of interest which would have been payable to defendant at the contract rate of 9 1/2.

. . .

This cause is returned to the Court of Appeals for remand to the Superior Court of Wake County with instructions that, after hearing such additional evidence as may be necessary to make the calculations required to determine the amounts defined in subsections (b) and (c) below, that court shall enter judgment that plaintiff recover of defendant as damages the sum of the amounts specified in subsections (a), (b), and (c) as follows:

(a) $5,888.12 expended for additional title insurance, brokerage, accounting, and appraisal fees necessitated by defendant's breach;

(b) $184,619.49, less the amount of interest plaintiffs contracted to pay defendant from 1 October 1974 until 31 March 1976; [and]

(c) the present value of the amount determined by subtracting the interest payments which were to have been made by plaintiffs pursuant to the contract from 1 April 1976 until 1 October 1999, from the interest payable during the same period on a loan of $1,162,500, amortized over 300 months from 1 October 1974 bearing an interest rate of 10 1/2 per annum. . . .

The *Pipkin* case involved a postconstruction lender's breach of the loan commitment. What damages result if the project never gets built in the first place because the construction lender defaults?

Great Western Bank v. LJC Development, LLC

238 Ariz. 470, 362 P.3d 1037 (Ct. App. 2015)

JONES, J.

Great Western Bank (Great Western) appeals a judgment entered in favor of Appellees on its claim and counterclaim following a bench trial. For the following reasons, we affirm.

FACTS AND PROCEDURAL HISTORY

This appeal arises from two construction loan agreements between Great Western's predecessor [a failed bank] and Cedar Ridge Investments, L.L.C. (Borrower). Appellees are the guarantors of Borrower.

In early 2007, Borrower sought funding to develop a fifty-home subdivision in Flagstaff to be known as Cedar Ridge. Borrower first obtained a loan from Great Western to acquire and develop infrastructure (the A & D Loan) in May 2007. Appellees agreed to guarantee the A & D Loan in an amount up to but not exceeding Borrower's total principal indebtedness to Great Western. In January 2008, Borrower entered into a second agreement with Great Western to fund the actual construction of homes (the Agreement). The Agreement required Appellees to execute a guaranty separate from that securing the A & D Loan and was signed by eight bank officials. By its terms, the Agreement expired on December 1, 2008.

In July 2008, as acquisition and development of the infrastructure was nearing completion and Borrower was preparing to obtain permits for the construction of model homes, Great Western made an internal decision to cease construction financing in Arizona and advised Borrower it was withdrawing from the Agreement. When notified of this decision, Borrower immediately expressed to Great Western its concern regarding the continued viability of the project without the financing agreement in place, slowed construction in an effort to save money, and attempted to secure alternate financing. Borrower's efforts were ultimately unsuccessful, and without financing to build model homes, Borrower could not sell homes in Cedar Ridge and was therefore unable to generate revenue through which to service the A & D Loan.

Great Western then foreclosed on the A & D Loan, sold the property to another developer, and sued Appellees for the balance of approximately $2.6 million. Appellees conceded they, as guarantors, failed to repay the A & D Loan but sought offset and affirmative relief for profits Borrower lost as a result of Great Western's termination of the Agreement, which they contend constituted anticipatory repudiation and breach of the implied covenant of good faith and fair dealing. The case proceeded to trial for determination of the merit and value, if any, of Appellees' claims and counterclaims which might offset the deficiency owed to Great Western. Great Western submitted a timely request for findings of fact and conclusions of law.

At trial, Great Western argued it was not required under the Agreement to actually finance construction within Cedar Ridge, asserting the Agreement was merely a "guidance line" or an outline of proposed future loans, and Great Western retained complete discretion to decline funding. The trial court disagreed, noting the Agreement was titled "Loan Agreement," contained express language obligating Great Western to "make the Loans to Borrower," and required Borrower to "accept such Loans," subject to various terms and conditions. And, according to the Agreement's terms, the only basis upon which Great Western was entitled to withdraw its participation was Borrower's default—an event never alleged by Great Western.

The trial court concluded Great Western breached the Agreement by unilaterally terminating its obligation to extend financing without conducting case-by-case review of individual loan requests. The court determined Great Western's breach had prevented Borrower from receiving the benefit of the contract—namely, financing it required to build and market homes within Cedar Ridge, which would have, in turn, provided Borrower revenues through which it would be able to repay the A & D Loan. The court found Great Western had no valid excuse for doing so because Borrower had the ability to begin construction and was not in default of the Agreement. Finally, the court determined Borrower had proven with reasonable certainty it would have profited between $2,808,000 and $3,500,000 had Great Western not terminated the Agreement. Because the lost profits exceeded the outstanding balance on the A & D Loan, the court found Appellees' liability under the guaranty was reduced to zero. The trial court determined Appellees were the prevailing parties, having "effectively recovered $3.1 million, absolving them of their liability" to Great Western, and awarded Appellees their attorneys' fees and double their taxable costs. . . .

I. INTERPRETATION OF THE AGREEMENT

In its opening brief, Great Western characterizes the Agreement as "an agreement between Borrower and [Great Western] under which Borrower could request loans after satisfying certain terms and conditions, and subject to an individual case-by-case review by [Great Western]." Upon this premise, Great Western argues the trial court erred in concluding that "[b]y entering into the [Agreement], [Great Western] agreed to make loans, on a case-by-case basis, provided Borrower complied with the terms and conditions set forth [there] in," re-advancing its theory that the documents were simply an "outline" for future financing. The interpretation of a contract is a question of law which we review *de novo*. In doing so, our primary purpose is to discover and enforce the parties' intent at the time the contract was made, looking first to "the plain meaning of the words as viewed in the context of the contract as a whole."

Setting aside that Great Western's own description of the purpose of the Agreement is nearly identical to the trial court's finding, we find no error. Although Great Western refers to the Agreement as a "guidance line," these words have no legal significance and appear nowhere within the provisions of the Agreement. The contract itself is specifically titled "Loan Agreement."

Great Western's internal communications and writings to Borrower refer to the Agreement inconsistently as a "commitment," a "line of credit," a "guidance line of credit," and a "loan agreement." However, in correspondence to Borrower dated the day prior to the execution of the Agreement, Great Western explained the term "guidance line," stating: "The line of credit that has been approved is a 'guidance line,' which is an indication of the maximum allowable amount of loans outstanding that you may have with [Great Western] during the term of the guidance line. Even though this is a commitment, each individual housing start and lot purchase is subject to [Great Western]'s individual case-by-case approval. . .. The guidance line amount is $3,600,000.00." Marlin Hupka, a vice president of both Great Western and its predecessor, provided the same explanation at trial.

Great Western's explanation is inconsistent with the actual terms of the Agreement, which identifies Great Western as "Lender" and begins with an "Agreement to Make and Take Loan," stating: "Subject to the terms and conditions set forth in this Agreement, *Lender agrees to make the Loans to Borrower*, each such Loan to be used by Borrower for the acquisition of a Lot and for subsequent construction by Borrower of Improvements thereon, and *Borrower agrees to accept such Loans from Lender* as hereinafter described." (Emphasis added). The Agreement continues: "Lender will, from time to time, make Lot Specific Advances to Borrower *under the Loan* for the purchase of the Related Lot and construction of Improvements thereon." (Emphasis added). It was only after Great Western withdrew from the Agreement that it informed Borrower it considered the Agreement an "uncommitted credit facility" or described the Agreement as "not a commitment" but "a set of terms" by which to make future loans. To accept this explanation would render the language within the "Agreement to Make and Take Loan" meaningless. We decline to adopt such a construction.

Great Western relies upon language within the Agreement that "[t]he Loans are not a line of credit" and each lot-specific loan "is subject to Lender's individual, case-by-case approval and Borrower's satisfaction of all terms and conditions contained in this Agreement with respect thereto." These statements are not, however, dispositive of the issue before us because, within the Agreement, "Loans" is defined as "one or more of the Loans *which Lender agrees to make to Borrower pursuant to this Agreement.*" (Emphasis added). The Agreement thus states only that the lot-specific loans were not a line of credit; it is silent as to whether the financing structure contemplated by the Agreement as a whole operated as a line of credit. The existence of a defined maximum amount which the Borrower could request certainly suggests otherwise.

By requiring Borrower to follow a specified procedure and furnish additional information to obtain each lot-specific loan, the lending arrangement is distinguished from a traditional line of credit where a certain sum is available to the borrower as he deems appropriate without any further explanation to the lender or qualification by the borrower. But the fact that individual loans were "subject to the terms and conditions" set forth within the Agreement does not change Great Western's express agreement to "make loans" to Borrower upon its compliance with those terms, particularly in light of the agreed upon purpose of the arrangement "to insure that a lender will be available for construction financing." Additionally, that approval of individual lot-specific loans could be given without further input from the full lending committee, who had already signed off on the Agreement, suggests the process to obtain a lot-specific loan was more ministerial than substantive. Effectively, the Agreement was as much a loan agreement, i.e., a contract binding its signatories to the lending and borrowing of money, as any loan agreement ever written, notwithstanding Borrower's obligation to provide certain information to Great Western before it could make a draw.

Great Western argues that, as a matter of public policy, affirming the trial court's ruling "would discourage lenders from offering uncommitted loan facilities such as the Guidance Line, for fear that exercising their discretion to withdraw the same will result in a judgment against them." We are not persuaded that a sophisticated financial institution capable of lending monies on a scale allowing for the construction of residential subdivisions would be incapable of drafting a document evidencing an uncommitted loan facility in a manner that clearly and accurately describes the rights and obligations of the parties involved if it so intended. And if, as here, the financial institution introduces the term "guidance line" into the transaction, defines the term as a "line of credit" and "a commitment," and subsequently executes a "loan agreement" to memorialize the parties' rights and obligations, we find no offense in holding the financial institution to the terms of those instruments.

Further, to accept Great Western's position would place the court's imprimatur upon what has commonly been deemed an illusory contract. "[T]o agree to do something and to reserve the right to terminate the agreement at will is no agreement at all"—executory or otherwise. *Shattuck v. Precision–Toyota, Inc.*, 115 Ariz. 586, 588, 566 P.2d 1332 (1977) ("[A]n illusory contract is unenforceable for lack of mutuality. . . . [A] contract must have mutuality of obligation, and an agreement which permits one party to withdraw at his pleasure is void.").

Here, both the language of the Agreement and its context reflect the parties' intent that it would operate, effectively, as a line of credit, subject to certain limitations and preconditions. We agree with Great Western that it was not committed to grant any particular request for a lot-specific loan; however, Great Western agreed to be available and was required under the terms of the Agreement to at least consider Borrower's requests on a case-by-case basis. As discussed below, the trial court acted well within its discretion in finding Great Western breached the Agreement by refusing to honor these terms.

II. VIABILITY OF CLAIM FOR BREACH OF THE IMPLIED COVENANT OF GOOD FAITH AND FAIR DEALING

. . . The covenant of good faith and fair dealing is implied in every contract, including the Agreement at issue here, and can be breached even where the express terms are not violated. Here, Appellees properly alleged Great Western acted in a manner that denied Borrower the reasonably anticipated benefit of the Agreement, when it unilaterally withdrew from that agreement, and Appellees were properly permitted to proceed upon that theory. . . .

A. TERMINATION OF THE AGREEMENT

Great Western argues the trial court abused its discretion in finding Great Western breached the Agreement by unilaterally terminating its obligation to extend financing. Great Western does not dispute it withdrew from the Agreement, but argues instead it was within its discretion to do so. Whether a party has breached a contract is a question of fact.

The language of the Agreement authorizes termination only upon Borrower's default. It does not grant Great Western authority to unilaterally withdraw from the Agreement. Great Western did not assert Borrower had defaulted, and its termination of the Agreement was a direct violation of its written terms. By definition, Great Western's actions constitute a breach of contract, and we find no error.

B. BORROWER'S ABILITY TO PERFORM

Great Western next argues the trial court erred in finding Borrower was capable of performing under the Agreement, a necessary precursor to its conclusion that Great Western committed anticipatory breach. Specifically, Great Western contends that because Borrower had yet to obtain permits for any vertical construction or to construct an access road required by the City of Flagstaff, it "was never in a position to build" and was therefore unable to perform.

The trial court's finding that Borrower had the ability to perform its obligations when Great Western breached the Agreement is supported by the record. Great Western withdrew from the Agreement in early July 2008. It is uncontested that Borrower was current on its payments for the A & D Loan at least through October 2008. The court was advised that Great Western's own construction inspection, undertaken in August 2008, rated Borrower's progress as "acceptable." In fact, prior to being notified of Great Western's repudiation of the contract, Borrower had planned to start obtaining building permits toward vertical construction that same month.

Great Western points to evidence that the preconditions to financing were not actually completed until after the Agreement would have expired. That the project was ultimately delayed when Borrower purposefully slowed construction in an effort to conserve funds while it searched for alternate financing does not conclusively establish Borrower was unable to perform at the time of Great Western's breach; "the law does not require the nonbreaching party to do a futile or useless act." And, Borrower still had six months before the Agreement expired to complete any infrastructure required prior to requesting lot-specific loans. Additionally, any purported concern over Borrower's ability to perform is belied by the testimony of Great Western's vice president, Hupka, who, within the purview of his task "to manage the risk" for Great Western in its Arizona market, recommended reinstating the Agreement and extending additional loans to Borrower immediately post-repudiation and through mid–2009, believing "[l]ong term, . . . [Borrower] has a good product and location for the project and should be able to sell enough homes to settle the debt."

In light of the conflicting evidence, the trial court acted within its discretion in concluding Borrower was able to perform at the time of Great Western's breach. . . .

D. Breach of Implied Covenant of Good Faith and Fair Dealing

Great Western argues the trial court abused its discretion in finding it breached the implied covenant of good faith and fair dealing by withdrawing from the Agreement because Borrower could not have had a reasonable expectation it would receive funding from Great Western in the absence of a binding obligation to make loans. . . .

To accept this argument requires us to accept Great Western's overarching premise that when it wrote the Agreement, it did not do so for the purpose of memorializing an agreement to loan money—a position belied by the specific language of the Agreement and one which we have rejected. Contrary to Great Western's assertions otherwise, that Borrower was unable to obtain alternate financing does not illustrate Great Western's decision to terminate the agreement to provide financing was made in good faith. Indeed, by unilaterally terminating the Agreement six months before it was to expire and depriving Borrower of the ability to construct homes within the development, Great Western stripped Borrower of the precise benefit for which it contracted and violated the covenant of good faith and fair dealing.

We likewise reject Great Western's suggestions that: (1) it acted in a commercially reasonable manner and with Borrower's best interest in mind when it terminated the Agreement given the declining economic conditions and its general concerns regarding the success of then-existing real estate development projects, and (2) it was authorized to terminate the Agreement at its pleasure so long as it had a good faith intention, at the time of execution, to make loans to Borrower. Beyond being both an incorrect statement of the law, see Wells Fargo [v. Arizona Laborers], 201 Ariz. at 490, ¶59, 38 P.3d 12 [2002] (stating the "implied covenant of good faith and fair dealing prohibits a party from doing *anything* to prevent other parties to the contract from receiving the benefits and entitlements of the agreement," without limiting the obligation to execution of the contract) (emphasis added), and contrary to the specific language of the agreement, these claims were raised in this Court for the first time at oral argument and were thus waived.

Alternatively, Great Western argued at oral argument that since it had decided not to loan Borrower the contracted-for monies, it was more efficient to repudiate the entire contract at once rather than process, and reject, applications for funding as they were received. In doing so, Great Western conflates the issue of whether it would have approved a lot-specific loan request with that actually presented here—its obligation to consider requests for funding on a case-by-case basis. The Agreement specified it was effective until December 2008, and the only basis for termination was an event of default by Borrower. Hupka agreed it would be reasonable for Borrower to expect the Agreement to continue until at least the stated expiration date. That Borrower had not yet requested a loan under the Agreement is irrelevant; it had an additional six months, according to the express terms of the contract, to do so. Great Western's arguments that Borrower would not have satisfied the preconditions to approval are rejected for the same reasons set forth in [the discussion above under Borrower's Ability to Perform]. And, it can reasonably be inferred, based upon Hupka's personal and repeated requests to Great Western to either reinstate the Agreement or issue new loans to Borrower, that, had Borrower submitted one or more loan requests, they would have been approved by Great Western had it dealt with Borrower in good faith.

In sum, substantial evidence supports the trial court's implicit finding that Borrower reasonably expected Great Western to provide construction financing and its conclusion that Great Western's failure to do so violated the implied covenant of good faith and fair dealing.

E. LOST PROFITS

Finally, Great Western contends Appellees failed to establish with reasonable certainty that Borrower lost profits of $2.8 to $3.5 million as a result of Great Western's breach of the Agreement. Generally, the non-breaching party to a loan agreement is entitled to recover an amount that will reasonably and fairly compensate him for losses resulting from the breach—the amount that would place him in the same position in which he would have been had the contract been performed. Both the existence and amount of lost profits present questions of fact which must be proven with reasonable certainty.

Regarding lost profits, the trial court concluded:

Had [Great Western] not breached, after payment of the A & D loan, Borrower would have realized an estimated net profit in the range of $2,808,000 to $3,500,000. The Court concludes that the 50 homes would have sold eventually. At a minimum, Borrower would have been able to sell approximately half of the homes based on the original projection of $70,000 net profit per home and the remainder for at least the revised projection of $42,320 net profit per home. More likely, with Borrower's ability to reduce construction costs to lower price, profits would have been on the higher end of that range.

Great Western first argues the award of lost profits was inappropriate because, it contends, the loss was more likely caused by a declining economy rather than breach of the Agreement. Although this is a possible explanation, it is one which the trial court rejected in favor of evidence from Great Western's own appraiser that home sales in Flagstaff remained largely consistent through 2009. The record also reflects that demand for housing in Flagstaff was significant given the limited availability of land in the area and the lower-cost housing proposed for Cedar Ridge would fill an underserved niche in the community even in the down economy. Great Western's appraiser also concluded Borrower would have been able to sell at least one home per month in 2009 which would have been sufficient to service the loans with Great Western. And, even if Great Western had decided not to extend the Agreement beyond its expiration in December 2008, Borrower would have been able to build several model homes in the meantime and enhance its chances of obtaining alternate financing, thereby mitigating its damages.

We will not second-guess the trial court's resolution of disputed questions of fact where its findings are supported by the record. We will certainly not do so where the findings of the court were based upon the testimony of the objecting party's own witnesses. . . .

Mehr and Kilgore, Enforcement of the Real Estate Loan Commitment: Improvement of the Borrower's Remedies
24 Wayne L. Rev. 1011, 1025-1030 (1978)

. . . The traditional rule in equity has been that a contract to loan money will not be specifically enforced. Because equity requires an inadequate remedy at law as a prerequisite to relief, specific performance will be refused unless the borrower can demonstrate that the subject matter of the contract is unique, or that exceptional circumstances justify equitable relief. Since money is considered as a commodity, there is a strong presumption against the uniqueness of the loan commitment, and the availability of substitute performance ordinarily is assumed. Further, reliance alone is insufficient to support a claim for equitable relief, and the scope of the "exceptional circumstances" doctrine is too unclear for consistent application by the courts. Consequently, the borrower's recovery for the interest rate differential and the reasonably foreseeable costs and expenses of obtaining substitute performance has been presumed to constitute an adequate remedy at law.

This inadequacy doctrine is largely derived from the historical English division of law and chancery. Since the chancery courts were established primarily to mitigate the harsh application of common law in the law courts, the applicant in chancery had to first demonstrate that his remedy at law was "inadequate." Because the politically powerful law courts were jealous of their authority, the inadequacy requirement became solidly entrenched as a jurisdictional limitation on the power of the chancellors. Thus, the policy considerations behind the inadequacy rule are largely jurisdictional, based upon the function of the equity courts in English jurisprudence. Although the merger of law and equity has rendered these considerations anachronistic, American courts continue to apply the rule without fully evaluating the continuing validity of its underlying policy considerations.

American courts, however, do not consistently apply the inadequacy rule. Several courts have found an inadequate remedy at law when the borrower was unable to obtain alternate financing, although these courts have not clearly explained what constitutes an inadequate remedy at law. However, at least four rationales may be advanced in support of the borrower's claim that the legal claim is inadequate when refinancing is unavailable: (1) the loan commitment is unique, because it is the only one available, (2) the loan commitment is unique, because the borrower will forfeit his interest in the land upon the construction lender's foreclosure, and the law presumes all land to be unique, (3) the lack of alternative financing is an "exceptional circumstance," since the law cannot fully compensate the borrower for his consequential losses following the construction lender's foreclosure, and (4) justifiable detrimental reliance is an "exceptional circumstance" when refinancing is unavailable. Although a number of borrowers have argued these theories successfully when alternate financing was unavailable, (1), (2) and (4) have not yet been established as independent and sufficient reasons for granting specific enforcement absent actual injury not compensable at law. Thus, the primary thrust of these decisions falls under (3) in that the borrower has an actual injury which is not compensable through damages.

These theories, however, are fundamentally at odds with the traditional inadequacy rule. Under the traditional rule, the availability of damages was ipso facto an adequate remedy at law. Under this theory of "legal" adequacy, the court's inquiry was directed primarily at the availability of damages, rather than the sufficiency of such damages. Therefore, equitable relief would be granted only if the injury was not measurable in damages. On the other hand, if the term "adequate" is used as it is commonly understood, the court must determine whether damages would as fully and completely compensate the borrower for all his injury as would specific enforcement. This is essentially the inquiry under (3). Although it could be argued that this construction would obviate the need for the adequacy rule since the court would then have the discretionary power to choose the more appropriate remedy, the developer has continued to bear the burden of proving an inadequate remedy at law. However, the courts have shifted their focus from that of availability to the sufficiency of damages as the test of adequacy in cases where the borrower has not been able to refinance.

When, however, it is demonstrated that the borrower can refinance, specific performance is conceptually difficult because the most expedient means of obtaining relief appears to be substantially within the borrower's control. Consequently, the availability of damages to compensate for the increased cost of alternate financing will preclude a claim for specific performance when the borrower is able to refinance even though the borrower's remaining noncompensable injuries such as lost profits and detrimental effect on credit standing may be substantial. Although these injuries are significant, the courts continue to apply the traditional rule rigorously in cases where the borrower can refinance, and will not compare the actual sufficiency of the damage remedy with that of specific performance.

NOTES AND QUESTIONS

1.   Foreseeable Damages. Illustrating the familiar contracts rule in Hadley v. Baxendale, the court in *Pipkin* held that the injured borrower could recover all of the foreseeable damages proximately caused by the lender's breach of the loan commitment, including not only the discounted present cash value of the difference in interest rates and other costs of obtaining alternative financing but also the borrower's consequential damages if they are established with reasonable certainty and are not merely speculative. If after the postconstruction lender's breach the injured borrower is unable to obtain alternative financing, can the borrower recover, by way of consequential damages, the value of the loss of business (as measured by lost profits) caused by the lender's default and resulting foreclosure by the construction lender? Compare W-V Enterprises v. Federal Sav. & Loan Ins. Corp., 234 Kan. 354, 673 P.2d 1112 (1983) (future profits were not speculative), with Coastland Corp. v. Third Natl. Mortgage Co., 611 F.2d 969 (4th Cir. 1979) (trial court erred in allowing recovery of projected profits). See also First Miss. Bank v. Latch, 433 So. 2d 946 (Miss. 1983); Mehr and Kilgore, Enforcement of the Real Estate Loan Commitment: Improvement of the Borrower's Remedies, 24 Wayne L. Rev. 1011, 1032-1033 (1978). What about recovery of lost profits when a project never gets built due to the construction lender's default and the developer's inability to obtain replacement funding— what did the court in *Great Western Bank* allow? What about more remote damages, such as mental distress? See Westesen v. Olathe State Bank, 78 Colo. 217, 240 P. 689 (1925) (breach of agreement to lend money for California vacation).

Observe that in *Pipkin* the borrower was allowed to recover consequential damages of $5,888.12 expended for the additional expenses it had incurred (such as brokerage and appraisal fees) in its search for alternative takeout financing. Had the borrower paid the defendant the agreed-on commitment fees in the amount of $23,250, do you think the court would have allowed the borrower to recover the $23,250 amount as additional damages? If not, why not? See Rubin v. Pioneer Fed. Sav. & Loan, 214 Neb. 364, 334 N.W.2d 424 (1983).

Is the borrower the only possible plaintiff where a lender has breached the commitment? See Silverdale Hotel Assocs. v. Lomas & Nettleton Co., 36 Wash.

App. 762, 677 P.2d 773 (1984), where a general contractor recovered damages from a defaulting construction lender.

    2. Borrower's Right to Specific Performance. While there does not appear to be any case law supporting specific performance as a remedy for an aggrieved lender, there is ample case authority supporting this remedy for the borrower (as cited in the foregoing excerpt by Mehr and Kilgore). As explained by one leading commentator, many of these decisions can be explained by the fact that the defaulting lender had already closed the loan and recorded its mortgage when it stopped making disbursements on a construction loan. Therefore, since the project had not been completed, the borrower was precluded from refinancing its construction loan with a takeout loan from a postconstruction lender. Moreover, alternative financing from another construction lender would be impractical because the existing mortgage would prevent a substitute lender from obtaining a first mortgage lien until the prior construction loan indebtedness was discharged. See G. Nelson et al., Real Estate Finance Law §12.3, at 1060 (6th ed. 2015); Destiny USA Holdings, LLC v. Citigroup Global Markets Realty Corp., 69 A.D.3d 212, 889 N.Y.S.2d 793 (App. Div. 2009) (granting specific performance of loan to construct energy-saving shopping center/tourist destination given uniqueness of project and prevailing economic recession imperiling sources of substitute financing).

    But suppose the project is already completed and the borrower is unable to refinance its construction loan because the postconstruction lender, without justification, refuses to honor its takeout commitment, and the borrower searches for but cannot find alternative financing. Under these circumstances, should a borrower receive specific performance, or should the court confine the borrower's remedy to consequential damages based on an estimate of what the borrower might have paid for reasonable alternative financing? In the above excerpt, Mehr and Kilgore point out reasons why a loan commitment is unique. Is there another reason when the breaching lender is an established and reputable one? See M. Madison, J. Dwyer, and S. Bender, The Law of Real Estate Financing ¶5:79 (2016). Why are courts more apt to grant specific performance to a borrower who has not obtained alternative financing than to one who has? See, e.g., Selective Builders v. Hudson City Sav. Bank, 137 N.J. Super. 500, 349 A.2d 564 (1975). Mehr and Kilgore believe that such a distinction is "questionable." They assert that "the difference between a borrower who refinances and a borrower who does not is merely one of degree. The fact that the consequences are more severe in the one case does not justify a denial of relief where the consequences are less severe, if the injuries in either case merit relief and are not fully compensable in damages." Mehr and Kilgore at 1034. What "consequences" are Mehr and Kilgore talking about? By contrast, other commentators argue that specific performance should not be granted where the borrower has refinanced its construction loan with another postconstruction lender. See Groot, Specific Performance of Contracts to Provide Permanent Financing, 60 Cornell L. Rev. 718, 736-739 (1975). Which position is more persuasive? If you think that specific performance should generally be available, would your opinion change with respect to a borrower who has insisted on a liquidated damages clause in the commitment letter to protect itself? Can you think of any reason why a poorly drafted commitment that is lacking in detail could jeopardize the borrower's right, if any, to specific performance?

For additional discussion of specific performance of loan commitments, see Brannon, Enforceability of Mortgage Loan Commitments, 18 Real Prop., Prob. & Tr. J. 724, 738-749 (Winter 1983); Draper, The Broken Commitment: A Modern View of the Mortgage Lender's Remedy, 59 Cornell L. Rev. 418, 421-439 (1974); Linzer, On the Amorality of Contract Remedies—Efficiency, Equity and the Second Restatement, 81 Colum. L. Rev. 111, 126 (1981).

3.   *Back to the Drawing Board.* As with many cases in this casebook, in *Great Western Bank* the court was called on to interpret the parties' agreement. Here, the court rejected the proffered interpretation of the party that likely prepared the first draft of the agreement and, held somewhat in check by custom among lenders and marketplace realities, the party that could insist on its desired deal terms or reject the deal. Consistent with the court's invitation to the lender, how might you draft the loan commitment in future transactions to be more consistent with the lender's interpretation? As counsel for the developer/borrower, would you advise your client to accept such language? The lender's withdrawal from construction lending in Arizona coincided with the outset of the subprime foreclosure and global financial crisis. Can you suggest language of more limited operation that would allow the construction lender to withdraw its commitment to lend without liability when the housing market begins to crash?

D. PRECLOSING COMMITMENT TERMS AND CONDITIONS

The materials that follow address some of the more substantial conditions usually found in the commitment agreement, such as the lender's requirement that the collateral be free of objectionable encumbrances, and conditions requiring the borrower's compliance with land use regulations and environmental laws, and, in the case of postconstruction financing, completion of construction in accordance with the approved plans and specifications. Also discussed are certain important covenants of the commitment, such as restrictions on its assignment by the prospective borrower. Deferred until Chapter 5 is discussion of various covenants that, while normally specified in the commitment due to their importance, are ultimately included in the loan documents signed at closing because they govern the postclosing (administration) stage of the loan. Examples include due-on-sale clauses, prepayment penalties, and nonrecourse provisions.

1. The Loan Amount as a Percentage of Appraised Value

The mortgage loan portfolios of lenders such as life insurance companies, thrift organizations, and state-chartered commercial banks are frequently subject to both qualitative and quantitative constraints imposed by state regulatory statutes and federal agencies. For example, in most states a life insurance company is required by statute to limit the amount of any mortgage loan to a percentage of the appraised value of the mortgaged property that secures the loan. While the maximum loan-to-value ratios for multifamily and commercial real estate loans vary from state to state, they are generally in the range of 75 to 80 percent.[11] Federally regulated institutions such as thrifts and national banks are required by regulation to establish their own loan-to-value ratios consistent with those specified in federal "Interagency Guidelines for Real Estate Lending Policies."[12] These guidelines specify generally applicable limits of 65 percent for raw land loans, 80 percent for commercial construction loans, and 85 percent for commercial postconstruction loans.[13] In the absence of such external restrictions, prudent underwriting practices nonetheless dictate some form of self-imposed limitation on loan-to-value ratios, and therefore every mortgage lender will require an appraisal of the mortgaged property as a condition precedent to the issuance of or funding under a commitment letter.

In the following excerpt, Leon W. Ellwood (a former chief appraiser of the New York Life Insurance Company and widely regarded as the forerunner of modern mortgage loan appraisal theory) explains how the "income method" of appraisal operates and why it has become the primary method for valuing income-producing real estate. While the excerpt is somewhat outdated as to capitalization rates, the principles that Ellwood expounds are still widely accepted by mortgage loan appraisers in their valuation of real estate for purposes of determining maximum loan amounts.

Ellwood, Appraisal for Mortgage Loan Purposes
Encyclopedia of Real Estate Appraising 1095 (E. J. Friedman, 3d ed. 1978)

NATURE OF VALUE FOR MORTGAGE LOAN PURPOSES

There is no validity to an appraisal made from the viewpoint of a prospective seller. The seller's interest in property ceases upon receipt of his price. Success of any mortgage investment depends upon the future performance of the

---

11. See, e.g., Mass. Ann. Laws ch. 175, §63(7) (limited to 75 percent appraised value of the real estate in most cases).

12. See, e.g., 12 C.F.R. §560.101.

13. See 57 Fed. Reg. 62890, 62897 (1992); see generally Frachioni, Leveraging the Land: The Changing Loan to Value Ratio for Real Estate Lending by National Banks, 112 Banking L.J. 41 (1995) (detailing the history of loan restrictions on national banks and criticizing the adoption of these new restrictions as guidelines rather than as regulations).

property. In this respect, both the mortgage lender and buyer have common interests. They both depend upon future benefits of ownership. For this reason, any appraisal for mortgage loan purposes must be based on anticipated benefits of ownership, and must be made from the standpoint of a well-informed and prudent buyer.

Thus, the value of real property as security for mortgage investment may be defined broadly as follows:

> The maximum amount in dollars that a prudent purchaser, well-informed as to the potential benefits of ownership, and buying subject property for the right to enjoy such benefits, would be justified in paying for it as of the effective date of appraisal on the following terms: cash down to the maximum available ratio of mortgage loan to purchase price, with such loan at the prevailing rate of interest, and with provision for sufficient periodic amortization to protect the margin of security against future decline in value from all causes.

INCOME APPROACH TO VALUE

The economic or Income Approach to value is generally the primary method used in appraising income-producing real estate for mortgage loan purposes. This is the only process that employs future benefits of ownership as the basis of valuation, and the only approach to value from a prudent buyer's point of view. Moreover, it is the only method in which value is geared to the ability of the property to produce income and pay all expenses, including debt service. Every mortgage investor knows that he will encounter difficulty in collection of interest and [principal] whenever the security for a loan fails to earn them.

. . . The Income Approach to value usually consists of dividing net income by a selected rate of capitalization. The resulting quotient is the estimate of value. Net income (the numerator) and rate (the denominator) are judgment factors. The reliability of the result will depend on the quality of judgment exercised in selecting these critical factors. The estimate of income must be acceptable to prudent buyers, and the capitalization rate must be a composite of yields with provisions for recovery of capital that will attract mortgage and equity money to produce a price acceptable to the market place. . . .

ESTIMATING NET INCOME

Net income derived from property is a benefit of ownership; gross income, in itself, is not. For this reason, in using the Income Approach to value, the appraiser must compile a careful estimate of average annual net income and apply to such net income a proper capitalization rate in order to estimate value. Net income is arrived at by deducting expenses and allowances from gross income. The appraiser must itemize the costs of management, fuel, utilities, payroll, repairs, painting, taxes, insurance, vacancies, and other expenses and allowances.

SELECTION OF A CAPITALIZATION RATE

The capitalization rate in mortgage loan appraisals is made up of the following components:

1. Available ratio of mortgage money to appraised value.
2. Interest rate that will attract mortgage money at the time of appraisal.
3. Maximum full mortgage amortization term [see Chapter 5A2] available at the time of appraisal.
4. Income projection term in years.
5. Prospective yield that will attract prudent equity money at time of appraisal.
6. Allowances for decline or increase in market value during the income projection period.

The first three components of the capitalization rate listed above are known at the time of appraisal, and there is little or no conjecture concerning them. The limit of loan in relation to appraised value is fixed by law. The prevailing interest rates with regard to various property types in the locality are readily ascertainable. The required provision for repayment is known. For example:

Assume that:

1. The legal loan limit is 75% of appraised value.
2. The prevailing interest rate is 8 1/2 % per annum.
3. The available term for full amortization by level monthly installments is 25 years.

The required monthly installment in this case would be $8.06[1] per $1,000 of borrowed purchase capital. Multiplying $8.06 by 12 to get the annual requirement, dividing by 1,000, and taking three-fourths of the quotient, gives a capitalization factor that takes care of both yield and capital recovery with regard to three-fourths of the appraised value, to wit:

$$\frac{8.06 \times 12 \times 3}{1,000 \times 4} = 0.07254$$

In other words, the factor .07254, combined with a factor based on the yield and provision for recovery that will attract prudent equity capital, comprises the correct capitalization rate. Equity capital, in this case, would represent one-fourth of appraised value. . . .

---

1. The periodic installment of interest and principal required to amortize a loan fully by the end of its term is taken from standard compound interest and annuity tables. The installment is rounded out to eliminate the complication of fractions and the final installment is decreased to balance out.

PROSPECTIVE YIELD TO ATTRACT EQUITY MONEY

The prospective yield that will attract equity money to real estate is measured by substitution (opportunity cost) or yields obtainable from alternate properties or forms of investment. The yield is never known until the investment is liquidated. It can then be computed on the basis of annual earnings and the proceeds of sale. If this results in a net yield greater than could have been realized by placing the same money in a non-speculative type of investment, the equity investment may be considered successful.

Potential benefits to the equity owner are usually two-fold: (1) net income in excess of mortgage payments during the term of ownership, and (2) proceeds of sale in excess of any unamortized mortgage balance at the end of the term of ownership. . . .

Since an investor is concerned not only with the rate of return but also with the risk involved, it is necessary to make a comparison with the alternate non-real estate forms of investment subject to less risk competing for the investment funds. Assume that the following yields are obtainable:

Prime commercial loans	7.75%
Municipal tax exempt bonds	5.05%
U.S. Bonds—taxable	6.78%
Commercial mortgages	8.50%

The highest yield obtainable above is the first mortgage rate. Since the characteristics of an equity investment include risk and non-liquidity, together with the added burden of management, an increment above that obtainable from a first mortgage must be necessary to attract the buyer to the equity position. The quality of judgment in estimating the equity yield and equity value is one of the most important phases of the appraisal. The mortgage balance can never be in jeopardy so long as there is a substantial and marketable equity above it. . . .

TESTING INCOME BY OTHER APPROACHES TO VALUE

A prudent buyer will not pay more for property than the cost of its duplication, as indicated by a Cost Approach and a comparative sale or Market Approach to value. Accordingly, in addition to employing the economic or Income Approach to value, the mortgage loan appraiser should further test the result of income analysis and capitalization by comparison with the estimate of value found by physical cost summation and comparable sales data.

If these tests indicate that an equally desirable property could be acquired for less money, the capitalization rate is too low. It should be adjusted to bring the estimates into line, despite the fact that an analysis of the rate appears to promise attractive profits. Such adjustments are rarely necessary when care and good judgment have been exercised in the Income Approach. Nevertheless, the appraisal will not be complete or convincing without cost and market comparisons to back it up.

NOTES AND QUESTIONS

1. *Real Estate Appraisal.* It may be a gross understatement to say that appraisal of real estate is an inexact science. Indeed, one often hears the joke of the attorney who saw "M.A.I." (Member, Appraisal Institute) after an appraiser's name and thought the letters stood for "Made As Instructed." In reality, appraisers may be getting a bad press. It is fairly easy to determine with reasonable accuracy the value of a three-bedroom home in a development with comparable sales occurring all the time. It is far more difficult to determine the value of the land underlying an office building, for example, especially when it is being valued as if the land were vacant and unimproved. Likewise, in the master hypothetical, difficulties would be encountered in appraising the value of Dan Developer's office building as of the date of the loan commitment two or three years before the building is constructed and fully leased. Yet these are some of the issues confronting appraisers when appraising income-producing real estate. See Miller and Kates, How to Value Real Estate Subject to an Equity Participation, 2 Real Est. Rev. 89 (Spring 1972).

2. *Appraiser Regulation.* Inaccurate and even fraudulent real estate appraisals have been cited as one of the major contributing factors to the infamous savings and loan crisis of the late 1980s as well as the subsequent subprime mortgage crisis. See Vickory, Regulating Real Estate Appraisers: The Role of Fraudulent and Incompetent Real Estate Appraisals in the S&L Crisis and the FIRREA Solution, 19 Real Est. L.J. 3 (1990). Responding to concerns about lack of government regulation of the appraisal industry, in 1989 Congress enacted the Financial Institutions Reform, Recovery, and Enforcement Act (FIRREA). Among other requirements in FIRREA, appraisals used in loans by federally regulated lenders must be prepared by state licensed or certified appraisers. See generally Wooley, Comment, Regulation of Real Estate Appraisers and Appraisals: The Effects of FIRREA, 43 Emory L.J. 357 (1994). As part of the Dodd-Frank Wall Street Reform and Consumer Protection Act of 2010, Congress established new requirements of appraiser independence in order to prevent coercion in the property valuation.

3. *The Income Method.* As Ellwood points out, the economic, or income, approach is the primary method used to appraise commercial property for postconstruction loan purposes. Under the income method, the net income from the property is divided by a capitalization rate to determine the value of the property. Observe that in the example provided by Ellwood, the capitalization

(cap) rate consists of two major components: an equity yield and a mortgage yield on the debt-financed three-fourths portion of the property based on assumptions as to the loan-to-value ratio, amortization, and level of interest rates. The cap rate, then, is essentially a composite of two rates: the market, or prevailing, rate for first mortgage money combined with the rate of return on an equity investment that would attract a prudent person to purchase the property. The initial rate is then adjusted to take into account certain purchase risk factors (for example, depreciation, decline, or increase in future market value) to arrive at a final capitalization rate. Expressed as a formula, fair market value would equal the estimated annual net income divided by the final capitalization rate. Therefore, the appraised value will decrease to the extent that the cap rate increases because of any increase in the anticipated rate of interest and risk factors (noted above) or because of any decrease in the anticipated stream of net operating income, and vice versa. For example, by using a cap rate of 10 percent, a building that produces annual net rental income of $100,000 would be valued at $1 million, or "ten times earnings." By contrast, a building that produces the same net rental income but happens to be a riskier investment (for example, a motel situated on a secondary road that has been superseded by a new highway) might be assigned a cap rate of 20 percent and be valued at only $500,000, or "five times earnings." It is not unusual for appraisers to differ both as to the anticipated stream of income that is to be capitalized and the appropriate cap rate to be applied, especially in the case of new construction where the appraisal is made before the improvements are completed. Moreover, even slight changes in these variables can dramatically change the estimated value. However, the objective of any mortgage loan appraisal based on the income approach is to apply a cap rate that is high enough to produce a correspondingly low enough appraised value and loan amount so that the projected net rental income stream from the mortgaged property will be sufficient to cover the borrower's debt service payments and other operating expenses.

Under the income method of appraisal, if property is expected to produce an annual net income of $1 million, and this stream of income is capitalized at 15 percent, the present value of the property would be the amount that would be needed at a 15 percent return to produce $1 million per year, or $6,666,666 (.15X =$1 million). What would the present value be if a 10, 20, or 25 percent cap rate were applied to the $1 million stream of income, and what would those values be if the income stream were estimated at $750,000 or $1,250,000?

4. Ellwood Today. Outlined in the excerpt by Ellwood is what is known as the classical appraisal theory, that is, the income method, as corroborated by the "cost" and "market" approaches to value. During the 1979-1982 period of stagflation (high inflation with stagnant economic growth), many real estate professionals discovered that the classical theory did not always work with large rental projects; the real estate failures of that era tended to expose the inaccuracy of appraisers' estimates of anticipated income and capitalization rates. The traditional cap rate theory may be too static a method of valuation for a cyclical economy that becomes volatile unless the theory is modified to take into account the time value of money and expected rates of inflation during the property's holding period. In 1981, G. Gordon Blackadar, then vice president of Metropolitan Life Insurance Company, propounded a theory of "dynamic capitalization," a corollary to Ellwood's classical theories, under which appraisal is accomplished using what he calls "real rates of interest" that are designed to take into account the time value of money. In a vast oversimplification, the theory might be explained as modifying capitalization rates based on projected inflationary and deflationary pressures during a forward period of approximately 10 years. See discussion on measuring the profitability of a real estate investment based on the net present value and internal rate of return methods at Chapter 12A2; see also Beckhart, Note, No Intrinsic Value: The Failure of Traditional Real Estate Appraisal Methods to Value Income-Producing Property, 66 S. Cal. L. Rev. 2251 (1993).

   5. Fluctuations in Appraised Value. Assume in the master hypothetical that Ace Insurance Company is limited by regulatory statute or by its internal underwriting standards to a maximum loan amount of 75 percent of the appraised value of the mortgaged property and that Ace's appraiser anticipates that Dan Developer's net operating income from the completed office building will be $4 million per year, thus producing a free and clear rate of return of 12 percent (estimated net income of $4 million ÷ estimated cost to construct of $33 million). There is a common misconception that cost equals value. Why are these two measurements not necessarily equivalent? Based on the difference between the two, how could a leverage-minded borrower such as Dan achieve 100 percent financing with a mortgage from Ace that has a loan-to-value ratio of only 75 percent? What capitalization rate would produce the requisite value to justify the $25 million loan amount?

2. The Gap Financing Problem

In the master hypothetical, the construction loan from Fuller National Bank to Dan Developer in all likelihood will be limited to the $25 million amount specified in Ace Insurance Company's postconstruction loan commitment. Therefore, if construction costs exceed $25 million, Dan will have to find alternative sources of financing to fund the gap caused by the cost overruns; or, in the alternative, he may have to do something developers normally like to avoid, namely, contributing more of their own funds to the project.

   A gap financing problem frequently arises in an inflationary economy in which the costs of labor and materials are escalating and the borrower-developer is unable to obtain a firm commitment from a general contractor (or from subcontractors, if the developer is acting as its own general contractor) whereby the contractor agrees or "guarantees" that the overall hard costs of construction will not exceed a specified maximum amount. However, even with firm commitments from contractors, it is virtually inevitable that the building design and specifications will be changed (by means of "change orders") on numerous occasions during the construction period. Because such changes are frequently "upgrades" that are beyond the guaranteed maximum amount, an excessive number of these changes can create a gap financing problem unless the developer's contingency fund is large enough to cover these self-imposed cost overruns. To obviate this problem, the developer should solicit firm bids that are as detailed as possible, and most of the prefinancing requirements (for example, construction surveys, an architectural rendering of plans and specifications, organization of the ownership entity) should be completed before construction commences to avoid unnecessary and costly delays in the completion of construction. In addition, developers should avoid the so-called fast track method of construction whereby construction is commenced before the plans and specifications are completed. Although this method is designed to save construction time (and interest on the construction loan), it prevents the developer from obtaining bids of the "guaranteed max" variety and invites the possibility of cost overruns.

Another real concern for the developer and the construction lender is the possibility that notwithstanding a fixed price contract, the general contractor might become insolvent or simply abandon the project because of cost overruns. While this contingency can be addressed by a bonding requirement, performance bonds tend to be expensive and are so fraught with exculpatory provisions that, in the opinion of some commentators and practitioners, they constitute little more than a license to sue.[14]

The gap financing problem for Dan may be exacerbated if Ace, the postconstruction lender, imposes a rent roll requirement, as is frequently done in the case of office buildings and shopping centers that are not preleased and in virtually all apartment project loans (recall the *Woodbridge* case at Chapter 4C1, supra). This requirement may be in the form of what is known as a "platform," "floor-ceiling," or "floor-top" loan, under which part of the loan (the "floor" amount) will be funded on the closing date if Dan has obtained executed leases providing him with a rent roll equal to a specified minimum amount, with the remainder "ceiling" or "top" amount to be disbursed if and when the aggregate rent roll requirement is achieved within a stipulated period of time following the closing date. Ace may also insist on an escrow arrangement, or a "hold back" provision, under which Ace can withhold a portion of the loan amount pending completion of all standard tenant work or other construction items.

The following excerpt briefly explains the gap financing problem; it is followed by a sample commitment letter provision for a floor-ceiling loan, under which the loan amount depends on whether a certain rent roll requirement is achieved.

---

14. See generally G. Nelson et al., Real Estate Finance Law §12.2 (6th ed. 2015); Hart and Kane, What Every Real Estate Lawyer Should Know About Payment and Performance Bonds, 17 Real Prop., Prob. & Tr. J. 674 (1982). See generally discussion at Chapter 6B4b.

Garfinkel, The Negotiation of Construction and Permanent Loan Commitments (Part 2)

25 Prac. Law. 37, 41-43 (Apr. 15, 1979)

GAP STANDBY COMMITMENTS

Standby commitments might be characterized either as gap standby commitments or full-value standby commitments. A gap standby commitment is often intended to cover the contingent portion of the permanent commitment—that amount by which the maximum sum to be advanced by the permanent lender in the event of maximum rental achievement exceeds the sum to be advanced without regard to rental achievement. The minimum sum to be paid under the most disadvantageous rental experience is referred to as "the floor" of a permanent commitment, while the spread between the minimum and maximum amount of the commitment is referred to as the "gap."

The conventional practice is for the gap to be covered by the developer's cash deposit with the construction lender. An exceptionally credit-worthy developer might be permitted to cover the gap with a personal guarantee. Other developers may supply a letter of credit from a bank or deposit securities or other collateral with the construction lender. A marginal developer with neither cash, credit, or securities to cover the gap may resort to a commitment from a standby lender to provide a second mortgage for the amount of the differential.

Dependence upon a gap standby commitment is, at best, a dangerous approach for the developer, for it may face a catastrophic exposure in the event projected rental or sales are not achieved. A knowledgeable construction lender will be leery of any standby commitment so onerous as to indicate that the standby lender does not contemplate funding the commitment or that the developer will seek to prevent the construction lender from assigning the loan to a standby lender who may immediately call the loan.

HOLDBACKS

Commitments for investment type projects often involve holdbacks of all or a portion of the loan proceeds pending satisfaction of completion, occupancy, or rental achievement requirements. On occasion, holdback requirements are absolute in nature, as when the full funding of the permanent commitment is conditioned upon meeting specific conditions. More often, a period of time after the delivery of the loan will be allowed for the satisfaction of the holdback requirements. For instance, a $5 million permanent commitment for an apartment house may call for delivery of the loan within 2 years, with the full $5 million being paid by the permanent lender only if a rent roll of $960,000 is achieved. The same commitment may provide that if at closing the rent roll is less than $960,000, only four and a half million dollars is to be disbursed, with the remaining $500,000 to be paid only if the $960,000 rent roll is achieved within one year thereafter.

Typically, a rent achievement clause is not based only upon gross rentals. The lender has to protect itself against a reduction in scheduled unit rents by a developer pressed to meet a rent achievement clause. The usual requirement, therefore, interrelates the gross rent to a specified level of rent. Often a rental achievement clause is articulated in terms both of a minimum occupancy and a minimum rent roll for actual occupancy. Permanent lenders are leery of the possibility of a rental achievement condition being satisfied with a limited number of high rent leases that provide for rents in excess of those anticipated at the time the permanent commitment was issued, since those leases may not reflect the long-term rental potential of the project.

In the case of a shopping center or a special-purpose building such as a movie theater or hotel, the disbursement by the permanent lender of the entire amount of the loan will usually depend upon the existence at settlement [closing] of fully executed leases, in form and substance acceptable to the permanent lender, with major tenants either specified by name or who satisfy specified conditions. Since the construction lender is looking to the permanent commitment as its principal payment source, it will generally not disburse funds equal in amount to the contingent portion of the permanent commitment until it is satisfied that all "accomplished rental" provisions have been met.

As with all commitment conditions, a construction lender feels most secure when the permanent lender acknowledges prior to the commencement of construction that a commitment condition has either been satisfied or waived. Thus, a construction lender will seek at the time of the construction loan closing to have the permanent lender waive a condition based on a lease that is already in existence. There is, of course, the possibility that circumstances occurring after the construction loan settlement and prior to permanent loan closing may invalidate or terminate the lease. At issue is whether the construction lender or the permanent lender should bear the risk of changed circumstances, such as the bankruptcy of a major tenant prior to the permanent loan closing or the failure of the developer to satisfy all of the conditions of a major lease. Usually it is the construction lender who assumes substantially all the risks of events prior to the permanent loan closing.

Sample Floor-Ceiling Loan Leasing Requirement

Rent Roll. The annual rental from the Real Property shall not be less than $_____ and the space rented shall be rented on a basis so that if the building were 100% rented, the annual rental would be at least $_____. Such rental shall be payable by tenants in possession of their demised premises on a current, rent-paying basis, under leases for terms of not less than five years. The Borrower shall have furnished Lender with a rent roll certified to be correct, indicating the tenants, space and annual rentals relied upon to satisfy this condition.

Floor Loan. Upon completion of construction and compliance with all the terms and conditions of this Commitment except the rent roll requirements set forth in paragraph _____, Lender shall disburse or acquire a reduced loan of $ _____ (herein referred to as the "Floor Loan") with the same terms as the [full] Loan except that the monthly interest and principal payments shall be $ _____ each, beginning on _____. Lender's obligation to disburse or acquire the Floor Loan shall expire on _____, unless prior thereto, Lender, having the sole option to do so, extends such time in writing.

Top Loan. If only the Floor Loan has been disbursed, Lender, upon receipt of evidence on or before _____, that the rent roll requirements of the foregoing paragraph have been achieved, will, provided the loan is not in default, increase the Floor Loan by $ _____ to $ _____ and the Loan documents shall be amended to increase the total monthly payments of principal and interest to $ _____ each beginning on the first day of the month following disbursement, with interest from the day of disbursement.

NOTES AND QUESTIONS

1. *The Gap Problem Caused by Construction Cost Overruns.*   Returning to the master hypothetical, why would a prudent construction lender (in the position of FNB) limit its loan amount to the $25 million amount specified in Ace's commitment letter? If the total cost of construction were to exceed this amount and if Dan were unable to raise extra venture capital to fund the cost overruns, he might request additional loan funds from FNB or, as a last resort, be compelled to borrow the shortfall from a so-called gap lender. In either case, the gap financing would be secured by a second, not a first, mortgage lien, and would be quite expensive for Dan. Why is this so? See Cheatham, Gap Financing: An Opportunity for Venturesome Thrift Organizations, 15 Real Est. Rev. 49 (Summer 1985).

2. *The Gap Problem Caused by the Lender's Leasing Requirements.* Observe the postconstruction lender's leasing requirement for a floor-ceiling loan in the foregoing commitment letter excerpt. Can you think of the reason why the annual rental requirement is geared to the percentage of space actually rented as of the closing date? Since the real security for the loan is the anticipated rental income stream, the lender requires that the building be completed and ready for occupancy before it disburses the postconstruction loan. In the case of an apartment building loan, where the leases are virtually the same (and "fungible commodities" from the lender's perspective), as opposed to a shopping center or office building loan, where tenant-specific leases secure the loan, a postconstruction lender will frequently impose a leasing requirement whereby the loan amount is two-tiered and the borrower's entitlement to the maximum or "top" loan amount depends on the borrower's achievement of a minimum aggregate rent roll amount when the project is completed and the

postconstruction loan is closed. If the leasing requirement is not met on or before the closing date, the loan is funded for the "floor" amount and the borrower is given a few months beyond the closing date to meet the leasing requirement and obtain the additional funds.

> ➤ *Problem 4-2*
> Suppose the security for the master hypothetical loan is an apartment building (instead of a preleased office building). Ace commits to a floor-ceiling loan with a floor amount of $22 million and a ceiling amount of $25 million on the condition that if the rent roll requirement is not achieved by the closing date, Dan will only receive the floor amount; but Dan has three months beyond the closing date within which to achieve the rent roll requirement and thereby obtain the extra $3 million. Why might postconstruction lenders such as Ace insist on the floor-ceiling loan format? What is the worst-case scenario for the construction lender, FNB, if in its construction loan commitment it agrees to lend Dan the full $25 million rather than the floor amount of $22 million? Can you think of any precautionary measures that Dan might take to avoid the gap financing problem? Suppose that on the closing date Dan is only entitled to the floor amount of $22 million because of a leasing gap. Is there any interim solution that should satisfy Ace and allow Dan to obtain the extra $3 million in loan funds while the project is being "leased up"?
> Suppose that Ace's commitment to make the 15-year postconstruction loan of $25 million requires that Dan execute a 15-year occupancy lease with a major ("prime") tenant, Widget Corporation of America (WCA), whereunder WCA agrees to rent 10 percent of the leasable space in the office building at a minimum rental of $20 per square foot. Otherwise, the loan amount will be reduced to $24 million. Observe that the term of WCA's lease coincides with the term of Ace's proposed mortgage loan. Why is this desirable? Suppose that WCA has executed a letter of intent to lease the requisite space at the requisite rental but WCA refuses to execute a lease until construction of its office space is completed in accordance with WCA's plans and specifications. As the attorney for FNB, the construction lender, what maximum construction loan commitment amount would you recommend to your client, and why? ◀

> ➤ *Problem 4-3*
> In addition to negotiating alternative means of satisfying the rent roll requirement, Dan must also pay close attention to the language of the rent roll provision itself. See the sample provision, supra. For Dan to comply with this requirement, not only must the leases be executed, but the tenants must also be in possession and currently paying their rents. If you were negotiating this provision on behalf of Dan, what changes might you request from Ace? ◀

3. *Assignment of the Commitment*

In deciding whether to commit their loanable funds, lenders rely heavily on the reputation and expertise, or track record, of the borrower. This is why a lender is normally unwilling to permit the prospective borrower to assign the commitment to anyone else without the lender's consent. Lenders are so steadfast on this point that they may not even accept, by way of compromise, the qualification that such consent shall not be "withheld unreasonably."

A typical commitment provision prohibiting assignment might read as follows:

> Neither this commitment nor the Loan proceeds shall be assignable without the prior written consent of Lender, and without such consent there shall be no right to designate a payee of such Loan proceeds. Any attempt at assignment without such consent shall be void. It is understood, however, that consent will not be withheld to assignment of the commitment to a bank or other financial institution for the purpose of obtaining interim financing.

Garfinkel, The Negotiation of Construction and Permanent Loan Commitments (Part 2)
25 Prac. Law. 37, 43-44 (Apr. 15, 1979)

TRANSFER OF PERMANENT COMMITMENT

A permanent commitment normally will be issued on the basis not only of the facility being built but also the developer who is responsible. On occasion, a permanent commitment will even stipulate that the developer must manage the project for a specified period of time, often for 5 years after the permanent loan closing. Thus, the assignment of the permanent commitment is usually prohibited and often a specified entity is required to own the project at the time of settlement on the permanent commitment.

A construction lender will be extremely circumspect as to any limitations in the permanent commitment upon the transferability of the commitment, the underlying real estate, or the owning entities, since it seeks to fund the commitment with the permanent loan even if it or its nominee takes over the project following a default by the developer. The construction lender will therefore require that the commitment be assignable to it. It will also generally require that in the event of a default, it be permitted to reassign the commitment to any party to whom the real estate is transferable. The permanent lender will generally resist any such right and, in fact, will seek to include "no adverse change" clauses and condition its obligation to close on the permanent loan upon the absence of default on the construction loan.

If the assignment clause permits an assignment to the construction lender but not a reassignment by the construction lender, then in the event the developer fails to complete construction, the construction lender will be forced to complete the project itself so as to be able to transfer its loan to the permanent lender. Its decision may be academic since, in the event of a developer default, the time required for the construction lender to exercise its remedies and complete the project will usually exceed the period within which the permanent commitment must be delivered. In most construction-phase project workouts, the developer remains involved in some manner, while the construction lender controls all expenditures and advances the funds to complete the project. As a practical matter, in default situations the construction lender often has to renegotiate the permanent commitment—if it is fortunate enough to have a prospective permanent lender who continues to be interested in the project.

NOTES AND QUESTIONS

Assignment to the Construction Lender. Observe that in the sample commitment provision excerpt, supra, the postconstruction lender agrees to permit an assignment of its commitment to an interim lender such as a construction lender. Such assignments are often permitted. Under the master hypothetical, if Dan should default under the terms of the construction loan and the construction lender, FNB, faces the specter of having to foreclose its mortgage before construction is completed, why might FNB want to take an assignment of Ace's postconstruction loan commitment to Dan? While not agreeing to such an assignment, some postconstruction lenders will agree to make a loan to the construction lender on terms similar to the postconstruction loan terms if the construction lender should become the new owner of the mortgaged property through foreclosure of the construction loan.

4. Timely Completion of Improvements in Accordance with Approved Plans and Specifications

Obviously, the postconstruction lender will require that the improvements serving as security for the loan be of sound construction. If the building is poorly designed or if the materials and workmanship are shoddy, the real security for the loan, namely, the future rental income stream, may be impaired, the landlord's covenants in the leases to make repairs are more likely to be breached, tenants are more likely to leave (without liability if there has been a "constructive eviction"), and the mortgaged property would be less marketable in the event of a foreclosure sale.

Since commitments for postconstruction loans are usually executed 18 to 36 months before the loans are funded, the lender must employ sound money management techniques to ensure that the requisite loanable funds will be available on the closing date. Therefore, the postconstruction lender will insist that construction commence promptly and that the building be completed within a designated period of time before the scheduled closing date for the loan. For example, in the master hypothetical, Ace Insurance Company, as a condition to funding the postconstruction loan, might require that (i) the plans and specifications be submitted to and approved by Ace and its architect; (ii) construction be commenced in accordance with the approved plans and specifications on or before a specified date; (iii) the building be fully completed at least 6 weeks prior to the scheduled closing date and, except where written approval is given by Ace, be built in accordance with the previously approved plans and specifications; and (iv) the transaction be closed, once the conditions of the commitment are met, on or before the scheduled closing date.

The following is typical language from a postconstruction loan commitment letter that purports to impose these requirements.

Plans and Specifications:

Detailed plans and specifications for all Improvements must be submitted to Lender's architect (hereinafter referred to as "the Architect") and must meet with the Architect's written approval. Such plans and specifications shall include, but shall not be limited to, architectural, structural, mechanical, electrical, site, landscaping and sprinkler and other fire and safety control plans and specifications. In addition, complete curtain [exterior] wall drawings and specifications must be submitted for review and approval by a curtain wall consultant to be retained by the Architect at the expense of the Borrower and such drawings and specifications must meet with such consultant's written approval. Whenever the Architect's requirements exceed the requirements of local codes, the Architect's requirements shall govern. Upon completion of the Improvements, Lender shall be furnished with a complete set of "as built" plans and specifications.

Construction and Inspections:

The construction of the Improvements (including any grading, landscaping and any other on-site or off-site work) shall be in accordance with the plans and specifications as approved in writing by the Architect. The Architect and representatives of the Architect shall have the right to inspect all such Improvements periodically during and after construction.

Completion of Construction:

The construction shall be completed within a reasonable period of time prior to the scheduled closing date, in accordance with the plans and specifications approved by the Architect, and the final construction must be approved in writing by the Architect as being in conformity with such plans and specifications. No review, approval, disapproval or acquiescence by Lender or the Architect during the course of construction or otherwise, shall constitute a waiver of any term, provision or condition of this Commitment, including, but not limited to, the requirements concerning completion of construction, nor give rise to any liability on Lender's part with respect to the matter reviewed, approved, disapproved or acquiesced in.

Time of Disbursement of the Loan:

If the Loan does not close on or before the scheduled closing date, for any reason other than Lender's willful default, Lender's obligation hereunder shall cease, and Lender shall have all the rights and remedies provided for in this Commitment, unless prior thereto, Lender, having the sole option to do so, extends the Commitment by notice to Borrower in writing.

Commencement of Construction:

At Lender's option, this Commitment may be terminated unless actual construction is started within one hundred twenty days after the date of acceptance by Borrower of this commitment and is continuously and diligently pursued thereafter.

Purchase or Disbursement Date:

Notwithstanding anything to the contrary contained in this Commitment, Lender shall be under no obligation to disburse or acquire the Loan prior to the scheduled closing date of this loan. However, if at any time during the term of this Commitment and in the sole judgment of Lender, the Property has been sufficiently completed and otherwise complies with the terms of this Commitment, Lender may, in its sole discretion, by notice to Borrower, disburse or acquire the Loan within sixty days after such notice. Notwithstanding anything in this Commitment to the contrary, Lender shall have no obligation to disburse or acquire the Loan before sixty days after the completion of the Improvements, unless Lender, in its sole discretion, elects otherwise.

The following case illustrates the disagreements that might arise over the meaning of "completion" of construction in accordance with the plans and specifications as employed in the sample commitment letter provisions.

Whalen v. Ford Motor Credit Co.
475 F. Supp. 537 (D. Md. 1979)

BLAIR, District Judge.

This is an action arising out of the issuance of a loan commitment for a condominium project in Towson, Maryland. The plaintiffs are the owners, Towson Associates Limited Partnership and its general partner, Cornelius Whalen, and the general contractor for the project, Robert Whalen Co., Inc. The defendant is Ford Motor Credit Company (Ford Credit). In substance, the plaintiffs allege that Ford Credit breached its contractual obligations under the loan commitment by refusing to provide without justification the required funding when due. . . . Ford Credit has moved for summary judgment, contending that . . . the financing commitment expired by its terms when the condition precedent that the building be completed was not satisfied. . . .

Towson Associates developed a condominium project in Towson, Maryland known as the "Towson Center." The project is a 28-story building containing approximately 240 units. Ford Credit issued a commitment in February 1973 to Towson Associates to lend it $9,750,000 for a period of two years after completion of the project. During this two-year period, Towson Associates planned on completing the sale of condominium units to the public. In exchange for the commitment, Towson Associates paid Ford Credit $195,000 and also obligated itself to pay a release fee of 1% upon the sale of each unit. Under the terms of the commitment, Ford Credit was required to advance the funds as long as the building was completed by the expiration date, March 1, 1975. Pursuant to an amendment to the commitment, the expiration date was extended to September 1, 1975 in consideration of an additional fee of $48,750 which was paid by Towson Associates to Ford Credit.

In May 1973, Equibank, a national banking association, issued a construction commitment to Towson Associates, also in the amount of $9,750,000, to provide funds for the construction of the project. On August 28, 1973, the construction loan closing was held. At that time, Towson Associates, with Ford Credit's approval, assigned to Equibank the Ford Credit commitment; this was done to provide Equibank with additional security for the construction loan it had made to Towson Associates. Also on August 28, 1973, Ford Credit issued a letter which has been referred to by the parties as a buy-sell agreement. Under the terms of this agreement, Ford Credit agreed to purchase from Equibank the loan in the maximum amount of $9,750,000 provided that the construction loan documents were assigned to Ford Credit and that Towson Associates complied with all the terms of the Ford Credit commitment, including completion of construction by September 1, 1975. In short, Equibank financed the construction of the project, and Ford Credit agreed to provide the financing thereafter by purchasing the loan from Equibank if certain conditions were met.

On September 2, 1975, when the parties intended to close the purchase by Ford Credit of Equibank's loan to Towson Associates, Equibank tendered to Ford Credit the documents required under the buy-sell agreement and asked Ford Credit to provide the funding in accordance with its commitment and the buy-sell agreement. Ford Credit, however, inspected the building and determined that it was incomplete. It therefore took the position that the condition precedent to funding, completion of the building, was not satisfied, and it did not advance the $9,750,000. . . .

One of the conditions of the Ford Credit commitment was that the building "shall be completed in accordance with plans and specifications." The expiration date of the commitment, as extended by amendment, was September 1, 1975.

While the extent to which the building was completed has been hotly contested, the parties do agree that the building was not fully completed by that date. Ford Credit argues that the commitment required that construction of the building be 100% complete by the expiration date, and that substantial performance could not satisfy the condition precedent of completion, citing Della Ratta, Inc. v. American Better Community Developers, Inc., 38 Md. App. 119, 380 A.2d 627, 638 (1977). The court disagrees and holds that substantial completion of the building by the expiration date was sufficient to trigger the obligation to fund.

Ford Credit submits that *Della Ratta* holds that a condition precedent must be exactly fulfilled and that the doctrine of substantial performance does not apply to express conditions precedent. The Court of Special Appeals in *Della Ratta* stated:

> The substantial performance doctrine, therefore, applies to constructive conditions precedent and not to express conditions. Under certain circumstances, however, where there is such a substantial performance of a promissory duty, an express condition qualifying that obligation which has not fully been complied with may sometimes be excused. To prevent a serious forfeiture of labor and materials, the party who has thus substantially performed his obligation may still recover the contract price, less whatever amount may be necessary to compensate the defendant for failure to comply with the condition. See 6 Williston on Contracts (Third Edition), §805. As a general rule, however, an express condition must be fully performed.
>
> Under no circumstances would the substantial performance doctrine apply here. Since the contract was wholly executory, no forfeiture was involved. Full compliance, therefore, with the express condition precedent was necessary.

380 A.2d at 638. Thus, the court in this portion of its opinion makes it clear that under certain circumstances the doctrine of substantial performance does apply to conditions precedent. Even if it is assumed that completion of the building was an express condition precedent to Ford Credit's duty of performance under the commitment, the court concludes that substantial performance, not full performance, is all that is required to satisfy that condition under the circumstances of this case. Towson Associates has incurred substantial expense in its efforts to develop the project, and Ford Credit has received in exchange for its commitment over $200,000 in fees from Towson Associates. This is a quite different factual situation from that involved in *Della Ratta*. It would be quite inequitable to allow Ford Credit to retain the fees it has received and avoid its obligations under the commitment simply because the building was not 100% complete.

The court's conclusion that substantial completion is sufficient to satisfy the condition of completion of the building is firmly supported by the cases of St. Paul at Chase Corp. v. Manufacturers Life Insurance Co., 262 Md. 192, 278 A.2d 12, 29-32, cert. denied, 404 U.S. 857 (1971); Selective Builders, Inc. v. Hudson City Savings Bank, 137 N.J. Super. 500, 349 A.2d 564, 566-67 (1975); and First National State Bank v. Commonwealth Federal Savings and Loan Association,

455 F. Supp. 464, 468-69 (D.N.J. 1978). . . . In *First National State Bank*, the loan commitment included a provision that "[t]he entire project shall be constructed according to the plans and specifications." 455 F. Supp. at 467. In rejecting the lender's argument that it was not bound by the commitment since the building was not completed, the court stated:

> it is clear that a mortgage lender is bound to perform once the building contractor has "substantially completed" construction. When the contractor has fairly met this requirement, the mortgage lender may no longer avoid its commitment, although he may be entitled to a set-off for minor defects or omissions. All that is required of the building contractor is a good faith compliance with all the important particulars of the plans and specifications. One hundred per cent completion, unless called for, is not necessary.

Id. at 468-69.

Ford Credit has attempted to distinguish these cases on the basis that the loan commitment involved in each of them contained language different from that present in the Ford Credit commitment. The court recognizes that such differences do exist. However, the import of all three cases is the same; the lender may not avoid his commitment once the building has been substantially completed, unless 100% completion is expressly required by the commitment, which it was not in the Ford Credit commitment. Ford Credit's position that full and exact completion of a large construction project such as this one is required as a condition precedent to its obligations under the commitment is somewhat unreasonable. If that were the case, no borrower in circumstances such as these could rely on the commitment because of the immense difficulties present in bringing, by a specific date, a complex project to the state of 100% completion without a single item being left unfinished. It is not surprising that Ford Credit has been unable to cite any case in which a court has found that a loan commitment contained such a requirement. For these reasons, Ford Credit's motion for summary judgment will be denied. . . .

NOTES AND QUESTIONS

1. Commencement of Construction. Because the sample commitment letter provides that the lender has no obligation to fund if the loan does not close by a certain date and that the lender is not required to close until the improvements are completed, what is the probable purpose of the language in the section entitled "Commencement of Construction" which provides the lender with the right to terminate if construction does not *commence* within 120 days of the acceptance of the commitment by the borrower?

2. Timely Disbursement. Observe that in the section of the sample commitment letter entitled "Time of Disbursement of the Loan" the lender is relieved of its obligation to fund the loan if the loan does not close by a certain date (unless the failure to close is caused by lender's willful default). This means that construction must be completed by that date. On what protective language do you think a borrower such as Dan Developer might reasonably insist?

3. Disbursement Date. Can you think of the probable reason for the language in the sample commitment letter stating that the lender has no obligation to close the loan before the specified closing date?

4. Completion in Accordance with Plans. Because postconstruction commitments will normally prohibit changes in the plans and specifications without the lender's written approval, one would think that a sophisticated developer or construction lender would not risk making any changes without such approval. As the following problem illustrates, this does not always happen.

> ➤ **Problem 4-4**
> The following hypothetical typifies the kinds of real-world conflicts that occur between postconstruction lenders and cost-conscious developers during the construction period. Returning to the master hypothetical, assume that the office building is under construction when certain fire and safety problems associated with use of aluminum wiring are suddenly publicized. Ace's architect believes that copper wire is superior to aluminum and accordingly had required that the plans and specifications provide for copper wiring. Dan ascertains that aluminum wiring is far less expensive. He discounts the adverse publicity and, without informing the construction lender or Ace, substitutes aluminum wire for copper wire. Meanwhile, interest rates have been rising, and the interest rate stipulated in Ace's commitment is now about 3 percent below the market rate. Ace's demand that Dan replace the aluminum wiring with copper wiring is ignored by both Dan and the construction lender, FNB, which has continued to make its construction loan disbursements notwithstanding the dispute over Dan's use of aluminum wiring. Ace's experts confirm that copper wire is superior to the aluminum wire Dan is using but at this time are unwilling to state without equivocation that the aluminum wiring is defective or constitutes a significant safety hazard. After reviewing the analogous fact pattern in the *Whalen* decision, can you think of anything that Ace can do, or might have done, to prevent the possible impairment of its security interest? ◄

5. Substantial Performance. While there is some case law holding that the doctrine of substantial performance is inapplicable to loan commitments (see, for example, Johnson v. American Natl. Ins. Co., 126 Ariz. 219, 613 P.2d 1275 (Ct. App. 1980) (borrower unable to obtain refund of commitment fee after failing to complete construction of office building in timely manner), the opinion in *Whalen* appears to represent the majority view, namely, that because of their abhorrence of forfeitures, courts may construe the "completion of construction" language as requiring only substantial compliance. If you were counsel to Ace Insurance Company, what drafting techniques might you employ to mitigate the effects of decisions like *Whalen*?

5. *Approval of the Security Documents*

From the postconstruction (and construction) lender's standpoint, the mortgage (or deed of trust), promissory note, assignment of leases, and other documents creating the security interest in the real estate, together with the collateral documents such as the hazard insurance policy (discussed at Chapter 5A6), preliminary title report (Chapter 4D9), and certificate of occupancy (Chapter 4D7), are of utmost importance. It is through these documents that the lender receives assurance that its loan is a safe and legal investment and that it can realize on the security in the event of the borrower's default. The lender, therefore, will condition its obligation to fund the loan on approval by its in-house or outside legal counsel of the form and substance of all security and collateral documents. The following is typical commitment language to that effect:

> The form and substance of each and every document evidencing the Loan and the security therefore or incident thereto, and any proceedings incident thereto, and the title and evidence thereof, must be satisfactory to our Law Department.

In the master hypothetical, the best way for Dan Developer to avoid "closing shock," that is, discovering at the last moment that the documents are not satisfactory to Ace Insurance Company, is to obtain approval of the documents well in advance of the scheduled closing date. There is a tendency among busy people, and accomplished real estate lawyers certainly fit within this category, to put out the most immediate fire first and to put everything else on the back burner. In this hectic atmosphere, the bulk of documentary problems tend to be resolved close to the projected closing date. Sometimes the problem is caused by the business decisionmakers, who may not have fully negotiated the terms of the loan transaction until shortly before the closing date. However, if the closing is to run smoothly and be consummated on schedule, the attorneys representing Dan and Ace must make every effort to resolve any title problems and to draft, negotiate, and approve the loan documentation before matters become in extremis. If Dan and Ace have previously transacted business with one another, Dan's attorney should already be familiar with Ace's requirements and loan closing procedures. If this is Dan's first transaction with Ace, Dan's attorney should try to become familiar with these requirements long before the closing date.

Where there is a buy-sell agreement with the construction lender of the "pre-closed" variety (discussed below in Chapter 4D6), then some of these problems can be obviated inasmuch as it requires early approval by the postconstruction lender of the note and mortgage or deed of trust, as well as most of the collateral documents, such as the hazard insurance policy and the preliminary title report.

NOTES AND QUESTIONS

1. Reasonableness of Approval. The commitment language excerpted above is very open-ended. Under the master hypothetical, suppose that the market rate of interest for first mortgage money escalates to 7 percent shortly before the date on which the loan is scheduled to close, and Ace would like to extricate itself from its loan commitment to Dan. If Ace were to employ the language in the approval clause to impose arbitrary and unreasonable closing requirements on Dan, as Dan's counsel, what argument could you make, based on general contract principles, that Ace's right to approve all loan documents should be governed by a standard of reasonableness?

2. Closing Costs. The commitment will normally require that the borrower reimburse the lender for all out-of-pocket costs and expenses incurred by the lender to close the loan and to satisfy the terms and conditions of its commitment letter. Included among these closing costs are attorney's fees of lender's counsel in preparing the security documents and other tasks in closing the loan, title insurance charges, mortgage taxes, and recording fees. Consider the following sample provision:

> Exclusive of the Non-Refundable Application Fee required herein and whether or not the Loan is made by Lender, Borrower will pay all costs and expenses in connection with the transactions contemplated herein, including, but not limited to: (a) the legal fees, charges and disbursements of special counsel of Lender, if any; (b) survey costs; (c) title company charges; (d) documentary stamp taxes or mortgage taxes, if any; (e) recording and filing fees for all documents which Lender's Law Department requires be recorded or filed; (f) inspection fees; (g) printing costs; (h) fees, charges and expenses of architects, engineers, soil consultant, vertical transportation consultant and curtain wall consultant for Lender; and (i) reasonable out-of-pocket traveling expenses of Lender's personnel.

The borrower's responsibility to pay closing costs is generally nonnegotiable. Sometimes the borrower can get the lender's approval to negotiate some fees and charges directly with the supplier of the services. Borrowers are especially concerned about escalating fees of lender's counsel. What problems do you see in allowing Dan Developer to negotiate fees with Ace's legal counsel?

6. The Buy-Sell Agreement

The postconstruction loan commitment frequently will require that the borrower obtain a construction loan commitment by a specified date and that the construction lender enter into a "buy-sell" agreement with the postconstruction lender and the borrower before the construction loan is closed. The buy-sell is an agreement among the construction lender, the developer, and the postconstruction lender under which the construction lender agrees to assign (sell) its loan to the postconstruction lender; the postconstruction lender agrees to buy the loan from the construction lender provided the terms and conditions of its commitment are satisfied; and the borrower agrees to be bound by the arrangement. This tripartite agreement binds all the parties to one another by privity of contract and expressly provides for the remedy of specific performance in the event of a default. It also assures the postconstruction lender, especially when interest rates are declining, that the borrower will not "shop around" during the construction period for better terms and, in the vernacular of the trade, "walk" from the commitment to the postconstruction lender. The construction lender is assured that its loan will be "taken out" by the postconstruction lender when construction is completed in conformity with the postconstruction commitment.

The buy-sell agreement can be "preclosed," which means that the postconstruction lender approves the form of the construction loan note and mortgage (along with most of the collateral documentation such as the preliminary title report and leases) before the construction loan is closed and the buy-sell agreement is executed. Consequently, the form of the note and mortgage will either combine the terms and conditions of the construction and postconstruction loans or be amended to conform to the latter, so that the postconstruction lender can take an assignment of these instruments when the postconstruction loan is closed. By contrast, in a transaction that is not preclosed, each lender will close "on its own paper" and the construction loan will, in effect, be refinanced when at the closing of the postconstruction loan the borrower executes a new note and mortgage in favor of the postconstruction lender. The advantages of preclosing are (1) the lien priority of the construction loan mortgage automatically inures to the benefit of the postconstruction lender, as assignee, who is thereby protected against intervening lienors who record their claims before the date on which the postconstruction loan closes; (2) as observed in Chapter 4D5, supra, the use of integrated loan documents permits the postconstruction lender to approve much of the documentation early in the lending cycle, while the parties still have time to resolve their differences; and (3) by collapsing the two loan closing transactions into one, the borrower can avoid extra mortgage taxes, recording fees, and other closing expenses.

Typical commitment language requiring a preclosed buy-sell agreement with integrated loan instruments might read as follows:

> Within 120 days after your acceptance of this commitment, you shall have obtained a construction loan commitment from an interim lender approved in writing by this

Company, and you and the interim lender shall have executed loan documents incorporating the terms of the postconstruction loan to be made by this Company, which documents shall be in form and substance satisfactory to this Company as evidenced by our written approval. On or before such date, you and the interim lender shall have also entered into a written agreement with, and in form and substance satisfactory to, this Company assuring us of the right to purchase such loan documents.

NOTES AND QUESTIONS

1. Buy-Sell Agreements. Why do postconstruction lenders insist on a provision requiring the borrower to obtain a construction loan by a certain date? Absent a buy-sell agreement, would the construction lender have recourse against a postconstruction lender that refuses to purchase ("take out") the loan from the construction lender even though the borrower has satisfied the terms of the postconstruction commitment? See Golbar Properties v. North Am. Mortgage Investors, 51 N.Y.L.J. 1 (N.Y. Sup. Ct. 1979), affirmed, 78 A.D.2d 504, 431 N.Y.S.2d 820 (1980); Republic Natl. Bank v. National Bankers Life Ins. Co., 427 S.W.2d 76 (Tex. Civ. App. 1968).

2. Preclosed Buy-Sell Agreements. Notwithstanding the advantages of the "pre-closed" buy-sell procedure, circumstances may exist in which this procedure may pose a problem for one of its three parties. Suppose in the master hypothetical that the State of Fagan has a usury limit (these legal limits on interest are discussed at Chapter 5A1) of 12 percent, which is higher than the amount of interest provided for under Ace's postconstruction loan, and that the construction loan provides for interest at a floating rate not to exceed 12 percent. If Ace suspects that FNB, the construction lender, has extracted certain fees from Dan that might be considered additional interest by the local courts, it would be foolhardy for Ace to take an assignment of the construction loan and thereby expose itself to a potential problem under the local usury law. Can you think of any other circumstances in which it might be advisable for one of the parties to avoid the preclosed loan format?

3. Holder-in-Due-Course Doctrine. If the construction note is negotiable, and the note is ultimately assigned to the postconstruction lender, that lender can qualify for "holder-in-due-course" status under the Uniform Commercial Code if it meets the holder, value, good faith, and notice requirements of the Code. U.C.C. §3-302. In such event, the postconstruction lender would take the construction note free from all "personal defenses," such as lack or failure of consideration (for example, when the borrower claims that the construction lender failed to make the loan or that the loan has been paid). Also, if a construction note is assigned to a postconstruction lender or some other assignee, the construction lender customarily will absolve itself from any secondary liability in contract by endorsing the note "without recourse." See generally G. Nelson et al., Real Estate Finance Law §§5.27-5.35 (6th ed. 2015).

4. Pitfalls of Inconsistent Conditions. Suppose Dan were to obtain a "floor-ceiling" loan (examined at Chapter 4D2, supra) whereby Ace agrees to fund the $25 million ceiling amount if certain leasing requirements are met when the postconstruction loan is closed. Assume that Ace had executed a buy-sell agreement with FNB, the construction lender, and that FNB did not include the floor-ceiling condition in its own loan commitment. If the leasing requirement is not met and Ace refuses to fund more than the floor amount of $22 million on the closing date, would FNB be able to compel Ace to take out the construction loan for the full loan amount of $25 million?

> ➤ **Problem 4-5**
> Read the buy-sell agreement in the Documents Manual.
> Assuming that you represent the postconstruction lender (Ace) in its negotiations with the construction lender (FNB), what problems, if any, do you see in these provisions for your client? What would you propose to overcome these problems? ◄

7. Compliance with Land Use Regulations and Environmental Law

In the master hypothetical, when Ace Insurance Company enters into a loan commitment with Dan Developer, it is relying on the fact that if Dan defaults on the loan, it can look to the land and building as security for Dan's obligation. However, if the building is constructed or used in contravention of local zoning ordinances, or if environmental statutes and other legal requirements applicable to the project are not met, the security could be substantially reduced in value, if not rendered worthless. For this reason, a postconstruction lender normally will condition its commitment to fund the loan on receiving satisfactory evidence that all building codes, zoning restrictions, and other regulatory requirements have been satisfied.

Asking for assurance of compliance is the easy part. The difficult task for the lender and its counsel is to determine what laws are applicable and what evidence is sufficient to give the lender reasonable assurance that the various legal requirements have been met. In this section, we explore some of these difficulties.

The following is a typical postconstruction commitment provision requiring proof of compliance with law:

> For the purpose of this commitment, the construction of the Improvements shall be deemed to have been completed when ready for occupancy and fully equipped for proper operation of the facility as approved by Lender's Architect and when Certificates of Occupancy permitting space which is to be occupied to be legally

occupied and all other proper certificates by federal, state or local agencies or departments or any other governmental authorities having or claiming to have jurisdiction over the construction or occupancy, have been validly issued and delivered to Lender.

In addition, the loan commitment will often require that, before closing, the lender receive an opinion from borrower's counsel (or occasionally from lender's counsel or a specialist in environmental protection or zoning) that applicable laws and regulations have been satisfied. See the discussion of opinion letters at Chapter 4E2, infra. Also, if available, title insurance against zoning violations may be required. As the notes that follow illustrate, these assurances are not always sufficiently comprehensive to allay the concerns of lender's counsel.

Environmental constraints may present even greater problems than zoning. Most real estate lawyers are ill-equipped to render opinions on this specialized area of the law, and title companies, exhibiting their traditional reluctance to enter new problem areas, maintain that it is not a proper subject for title insurance protection except for hazardous waste cleanup liens that exist in the public records at the policy date. As with zoning and building codes, the design architect should be responsible for preparing plans and specifications that conform to environmental law requirements. Where there is enough money involved, it might be advisable for the developer or the lender to engage an environmental "expert" as a consultant.

In response to the burgeoning number of environmental law restrictions on real estate development, many postconstruction lenders now incorporate specific language in their commitment letters to the effect that "the borrower must furnish copies of permits and other satisfactory evidence that the Land and the Improvements, and their use comply with all applicable environmental restrictions imposed by federal, state, and local law." More specifically, the commitment will often require the borrower to engage an environmental engineer suitable to the lender to perform a site investigation. See Chapter 19A (discussing so-called Phase 1 assessments). A comprehensive examination of environmental law is beyond the scope of this book; however, the following examples illustrate the degree to which this body of regulatory law impacts real estate development:

a. The National Environmental Policy Act of 1969, 42 U.S.C. §§4321 et seq., mandates the preparation of an environmental impact statement (EIS) by the appropriate federal governmental agency with respect to any "major federal action" that would significantly affect the quality of the human environment. An example of such action was the funding of a federally subsidized $3.5 million loan for the construction of a small high-rise apartment building in an area containing no such projects. San Francisco Tomorrow v. Romney, 472 F.2d 1021 (9th Cir. 1973). In most instances, a time-consuming and expensive backup study will be required of the private land developer before the governmental agency will issue its own EIS.

b. Under the federal Clean Air Act, 42 U.S.C. §§7401 et seq., all new "major sources" of air pollution require state-administered preconstruction permits, and, as a consequence, shopping center and office building projects can be disapproved under the notion that parking facilities attract automobiles and thus a large parking lot may be indirectly responsible for causing air pollution. See, e.g., New York City Air Pollution Control Code, N.Y.C. Admin. Code tit. 24, §§24-101 et seq. By contrast, such projects can be disapproved under local zoning ordinances because of inadequate parking facilities.

c. Water pollution control permits are generally required under the federal Clean Water Act, 33 U.S.C. §§1251 et seq., with respect to the discharge of any pollutants into navigable waters, which may even include run-off from rainstorms. Under the Act, permits may be denied to industrial and commercial-use facilities based on certain chemical and ecological standards.

d. Responding to concerns over hazardous waste contamination and dumping, Congress enacted the Comprehensive Environmental Response, Compensation, and Liability Act of 1980 (CERCLA), which, along with similar legislation in many states, authorizes governmental authorities to clean up hazardous wastes and to impose a lien on the real property for the cleanup cost. Lender liability under CERCLA is discussed at Chapter 19A.

e. In a number of states, notably California and New York, coastal zone management statutes give state agencies far more land use control over real estate development in designated coastal areas than is exercised by local zoning authorities.

NOTES AND QUESTIONS

1. The Certificate of Occupancy. The "certificate of occupancy" (C.O.) referred to in the above commitment provision is a statement by the local governing authorities that both the construction and intended use of the premises conform with local zoning laws and building codes. In some jurisdictions, however, a C.O. means only that the certificate holder can occupy the premises at the time it is issued, subject to cancellation or revocation if zoning regulations or building codes are changed. A C.O. may also be revoked if invalidly issued. For example, in S. B. Garage v. Murdock, 185 Misc. 55, 55 N.Y.S.2d 456 (Sup. Ct. 1945), the court upheld the revocation of a C.O. when it was discovered 20 years after its issuance that the improvements (a commercial garage) had been constructed in violation of a zoning resolution prohibiting such garages on streets with an existing public school entrance. Neither the mortgage lender's good faith nor the passage of time estopped the City of New York from revoking the C.O. In some jurisdictions, however, ameliorative statutes protect good faith purchasers of certain properties. See, e.g., N.Y. Mult. Dwell. Law §§301-305 and N.Y. Mult. Resid. Law §§302-305 (C.O. not revocable against a good faith purchaser or mortgagee of a multiple dwelling even if issued invalidly). Notwithstanding their limited value, C.O.s are universally requested by lenders in those jurisdictions that issue them. In light of the foregoing, what is the purpose of a lender's requiring the delivery of a C.O. at closing?

In Parkview Assocs. v. City of New York, 71 N.Y.2d 274, 519 N.E.2d 1372, 525 N.Y.S.2d 176, cert. denied, 488 U.S. 801 (1988), the New York Court of Appeals held that New York City was not estopped from requiring a developer to remove 12 stories of an almost completed building because of a violation of height restrictions, notwithstanding that the building was constructed pursuant to a building permit issued by the city and that the zoning map prepared by the city was at best ambiguous as to whether the building met the height restrictions. The court held that the developer was charged with the language of the zoning ordinance and could not rely on the building permit or the zoning map. The tone of the opinion, however, may indicate that the court did not consider the developer wholly innocent; if so, this may have influenced the holding.

Any lawyers involved tend to be pursued in this situation, as was the case in 2011 when both the lender and developer sued their lawyers claiming inaccurate zoning advice after the New York City Department of Building shut down construction of a condominium tower (the site of a fatal crane collapse in 2008) it decided had been erroneously approved.

2. Zoning and Police Power. A comprehensive examination of zoning law is beyond the scope of this book. The following brief overview is intended to illustrate the state of flux of the law and to sensitize you to the problems and concerns of lenders and developers as the law evolves.

State and local government have the duty to protect the health and safety of the public. The exercise of this "police power" includes the right to control the use, height, bulk, aesthetics, and location of real estate by means of zoning and subdivision regulations. In Village of Euclid v. Ambler Realty Co., 272 U.S. 365 (1926), Justice Sutherland observed that in zoning "the line which . . . separates the legitimate from the illegitimate assumption of power is not capable of precise delimitation" and that a "zoning ordinance, which would be clearly valid as applied to the great cities, might be clearly invalid as applied to rural communities." Nevertheless, he held that a comprehensive zoning plan, even one that excludes businesses and retail stores from residential districts, is not unconstitutional unless clearly arbitrary and unreasonable with no substantial relation to the public health, safety, morals, or general welfare. Of course, not all zoning ordinances pass such constitutional scrutiny. The courts will often weigh the extent of the invasion of property rights and economic harm caused by the regulation against the benefit that the land use restriction provides to the community as a whole.

Given the legality of most comprehensive "Euclidian" zoning ordinances, what would happen if, after Dan Developer constructs his office building and Ace Insurance Company makes its loan, the town of McNiece should enact a comprehensive zoning ordinance restricting the area in which Dan's building is located to single-family residences? In most cases, a response that Dan's use may continue as a "nonconforming" use would be correct. However, zoning is not the only means by which governmental officials may block what they deem to be "undesirable" uses. For example, in Hempstead, New York, when a zoning ordinance imposed against the defendant to prevent excavation failed because of the defendant's prior nonconforming use, the local government successfully enacted an ordinance, upheld by the Supreme Court, imposing conditions on dredging and pit excavation, and thus completely prohibited the beneficial use to which the property had been primarily put. See Goldblatt v. Town of Hempstead, 369 U.S. 590 (1962) (upholding ordinance requiring mining permit and prohibiting mining within two feet of water table; defendant had already mined below the water table).

Developers often argue that a particular zoning ordinance, as applied to them, is so devastating that it constitutes a regulatory "taking" for which the Fifth Amendment requires payment of just compensation. Although the standard for compensation remains in great flux, decisions of the Supreme Court give hope to developers that they can challenge zoning ordinances that impose too severe a financial hardship or where the municipality fails to demonstrate a sufficient nexus between the public interest at stake and the particular restriction imposed on the property. In Lucas v. South Carolina Coastal Council, 505 U.S. 1003 (1992), the Court held that landowners are entitled to compensation when regulations deprive them of all economically beneficial or productive use of their land, regardless of the public interest advanced by the regulatory restraint. Also, in Dolan v. City of Tigard, 512 U.S. 374 (1994), the Court required the municipality to demonstrate some "rough proportionality" between the conditions it imposed on a developer (the dedication of a public flood-plain easement and bike path) and the impact of the proposed development (a building expansion).

3. Zoning Endorsements. The lender normally will obtain a title policy insuring that the mortgage or deed of trust is a first lien on the borrower's premises subject only to the exceptions specified therein. See discussion at Chapter 2B2 and Chapter 4D9, infra. Standard provisions in title policies exclude from their coverage violations of zoning laws except where notice of the violation is recorded in the public records. However, a title policy endorsement covering zoning is available in many states for a substantially increased premium. The approved form of zoning endorsement of the American Land Title Association (the title industry trade association) for a completed structure provides:

ALTA Endorsement Form 3.1-06

(Zoning-Completed Structure) (6/17/06)

ENDORSEMENT

Attached to Policy No. _____

Issued By

TITLE INSURANCE COMPANY

1. The Company insures against loss or damage sustained by the Insured in the event that, at Date of Policy,
    a. according to applicable zoning ordinances and amendments, the Land is not classified Zone FILL IN;
    b. the following use or uses are not allowed under that classification: FILL IN
    c. There shall be no liability under this paragraph 1.b. if the use or uses are not allowed as the result of any lack of compliance with any conditions, restrictions, or requirements contained in the zoning ordinances and amendments, including but not limited to the failure to secure necessary consents or authorizations as a prerequisite to the use or uses. This paragraph 1.c. does not modify or limit the coverage provided in Covered Risk 5.
2. The Company further insures against loss or damage sustained by the Insured by reason of a final decree of a court of competent jurisdiction
    a. prohibiting the use of the Land, with any existing structure, as insured in paragraph 1.b.; or
    b. requiring the removal or alteration of the structure on the basis that, at Date of Policy, the zoning ordinances and amendments have been violated with respect to any of the following matters:
        i.   Area, width, or depth of the Land as a building site for the structure
        ii. Floor space area of the structure
        iii. Setback of the structure from the property lines of the Land
        iv. Height of the structure, or
        v.   Number of parking spaces.
3. There shall be no liability under this endorsement based on
    a. the invalidity of the zoning ordinances and amendments until after a final decree of a court of competent jurisdiction adjudicating the invalidity, the effect of which is to prohibit the use or uses;
    b. the refusal of any person to purchase, lease or lend money on the estate or interest covered by this policy.

This endorsement is issued as part of the policy. Except as it expressly states, it does not (i) modify any of the terms and provisions of the policy, (ii) modify any prior endorsements, (iii) extend the Date of Policy, or (iv) increase the Amount of Insurance. To the extent a provision of the policy or a previous endorsement is inconsistent with an express provision of this endorsement, this endorsement controls.

Otherwise, this endorsement is subject to all of the terms and provisions of the policy and of any prior endorsements.

> ➢ *Problem 4-6*
> Based on the facts in the master hypothetical, decide whether the title company would be liable under this zoning endorsement in the following circumstances:
>
> a. Unbeknownst to Ace, Dan Developer obtained his C.O. by bribing a local official. The certificate is revoked after the postconstruction loan is closed.
>
> b. The applicable zoning ordinance permits office buildings not in excess of 17 stories. Dan's building is 20 stories.
>
> c. Some years after the postconstruction loan is closed, Ace forecloses its mortgage and, as the foreclosure sale purchaser, later contracts to sell the building for $40 million. The mortgage balance was $22 million at the time of foreclosure. Ace's sale falls through when a zoning defect is discovered.
>
> d. Ace committed to make the mortgage loan at 5 percent interest. At the closing date, the market rate had risen to 7 percent. Ace refuses to close the loan because it has discovered a zoning defect. Dan then files a claim with the title company based on the same zoning endorsement in his fee (owner's) title policy.
>
> e. A zoning defect is discovered, and Dan, as owner of the property, makes a claim under the zoning endorsement in his fee title policy. The title company does not agree with the adverse determination of the zoning board. It tells Dan that he, not the title company, must challenge the determination and that the title company will not make any payment until there is a final adjudication by the highest appellate court in the state where the property is located. ◄

4. The Architect's Certificate. Whether or not a C.O. is obtained, lenders normally will look to the architects for assurance that the construction is completed and complies with law. The design architect is considered responsible for such compliance, and plans and specifications should be accompanied by the design architect's certificate to that effect. Architects are not anxious to subject themselves to personal liability if they can avoid it. This means that the developer must be careful in negotiating the terms of construction contracts and architectural agreements to provide for such certifications.

Even if the design architect is willing to certify that the plans and specifications met legal requirements when drawn, the lender will need further assurance that the improvements were built in accordance with such plans and that there have been no changes in building codes or zoning ordinances (or no such changes pending) that would affect the legality of the improvements. This is

easier to request than to receive. The design architect actually may not know if the building was in fact constructed in accordance with the plans or whether the law has changed since the plans were drawn. Consider the following form of architect's certificate that Ace Insurance Company might receive from the borrower's design architect.

Certificate of Architect

Reference is made to that certain proposed $25,000,000 loan from Ace Insurance Company ("Lender") to Dan Developer ("Borrower") concerning the real property described on Exhibit A attached hereto (the "Property") and improvements constructed thereon (the "Improvements").

To induce Lender to advance the aforesaid proposed loan, I, Anne Architect, hereby certify to Lender that:

1. I am the design architect in connection with the construction of the Improvements.
2. The plans and specifications described on Exhibit B attached hereto were prepared by me and are in compliance with all applicable laws, building codes, ordinances, rules, regulations, and governmental authorities including, without limitation, environmental and zoning requirements.
3. To the best of my knowledge, after due inquiry, the Improvements constructed on the Property have been completed and are in full compliance with the plans and specifications described on Exhibit B and such Improvements as completed and their use as an office building and parking garage are in full compliance with all applicable laws, building codes, ordinances, rules, regulations, and restrictions of local, state and national governmental authorities including, without limitation, environmental and zoning requirements. No zoning or subdivision approvals relating to the Property or the Improvements cover any real property or rights appurtenant thereto other than the Property.

Anne Architect

Dated _____

Observe that the architect certifies that the construction complies with plans and specifications "to the best of my knowledge, after due inquiry." If you represented Ace, would you accept this compromise language? If you represented Anne Architect, what steps would you advise her to take to protect herself under the certificate? What is the purpose of its last sentence?

5. Americans with Disabilities Act. Enacted by Congress in 1990, the Americans with Disabilities Act (42 U.S.C. §§12101-12213) requires that owners and operators of "public accommodations" and "commercial facilities" construct their facilities in compliance with specified standards to provide access to disabled persons. Among other things, the developer's noncompliance with the ADA can affect the value of the mortgaged property. Lenders often ensure compliance through consultants with ADA expertise before closing postconstruction loans on covered facilities. See generally Jones, Real Estate Impact of the Americans with Disabilities Act, 21 Real Est. L.J. 3 (Summer 1992); Shore, The Impact of the Americans with Disabilities Act of 1990 on Lenders, 47 Consumer Fin. Q. Rep. 259 (1993).

8. Survey

The postconstruction lender's obligation to fund the loan is normally conditioned on receiving an "as built" survey (showing completed buildings). A survey is a map of the property that is prepared, signed, and certified by a licensed surveyor. The survey shows such items as the boundary lines (which form the matrix for the legal description in all the legal documents, including the mortgage and title insurance policy), the location of the improvements, streets, any easements or encroachments, setback lines, and other required details (as standardized by the American Congress on Surveying and Mapping). Consider the following sample commitment provision.

Survey:

Lender is to be furnished with a currently dated metes and bounds survey of the Land, which must be satisfactory to its Law Department, showing: (a) the courses and measured distances of the exterior property lines of the Land; (b) the total square foot area of the Land; (c) the location of the improvements, the dimensions thereof at ground surface level and the distance therefrom to the facing exterior property lines of the Land; (d) the location of adjoining streets; (e) the location of easements, building setback lines and rights of way; (f) encroachments, if any, upon adjoining property by the Improvements upon the Land; and (g) the location and number of parking spaces.

Under the master hypothetical, assume that Dan Developer has completed the building and that Figure 4-2 is the "as built" survey submitted to Ace Insurance Company pursuant to the postconstruction loan commitment. The accompanying description contains the legal description of the property that tracks the survey.

NOTES AND QUESTIONS

1. Legal Description. The legal description of Dan Developer's property accompanying Figure 4-2 is a "metes and bounds" description, so-called because the boundaries of the property are determined by following certain "courses and distances" from a point of beginning along the length and direction of each lot line until the description "closes," or returns to the beginning point. While there are other methods of describing property, such as by "lot and block" or by reference to the Federal Survey of Public Lands, a description by metes and bounds is by far the most common in commercial transactions.

As you know, a circle is divided into 360 degrees. If a circle is split into four equal parts, or quadrants, each will have 90 degrees. North is 0°, East is 90°, South is 180°, and West is 270°. In a description by courses and distances, the first letter will indicate a direction, North, South, East, or West, toward which the line is pointing. This will be followed by the number of degrees and fractions of degrees away from that direction and facing the other direction toward which the line is pointing. Fractions of degrees are minutes (') and seconds ("). Sixty minutes equals a degree and, as you might suspect, 60 seconds equals a minute.

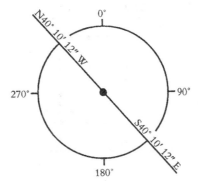

The figure above illustrates the foregoing. The course shown is N40° 10' 12" W. Is this course the same as S40° 10' 12" E? Go to the description of Dan Developer's property accompanying Figure 4-2 and see if you can trace it on the survey. Notice that the description contains three descriptions of Dan's property. The first is by metes and bounds, the second is by lot and block, and the third is by street address. If the lot and block description or the street address were the only description provided to you as Ace's attorney, would you accept it?

2. Survey. Surveys are expensive, especially in large commercial transactions; therefore, where possible an existing survey should be updated rather than superseded by a new one. Because Dan Developer is obligated to pay the cost of the survey as well as Ace's title insurance, he may contend that a survey or an update of an existing one is not necessary, especially when the title insurance policy will insure that Ace has a first lien. How would you respond as Ace's counsel?

Figure 4 – 2

– Property of –

DAN E. DEVELOPER

COUNTY OF FEERICK, STATE OF FAGAN

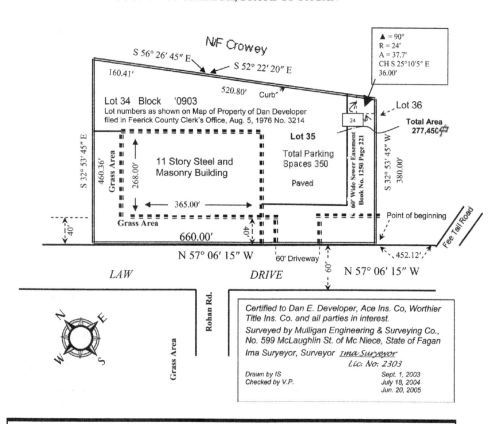

DESCRIPTION

All that certain tract, lot, piece or parcel of land being, lying and situated in the City of McNiece, County of Feerick, State of Fagan, more particularly described as follows:

BEGINNING at a point on the northerly side of Law Drive, 60 feet wide, a distance of 452.12 feet from the intersection of the northerly sideline of Law Drive, with the westerly sideline of Feetail Road, running thence the following six (6) courses and distances:

1. North 57° 06′ 15″ West along Law Drive, 60 feet wide, 660 feet to a point; thence
2. North 32° 53′ 45″ East, 460.36 feet to lands now or formerly

> of Joseph Crowley; thence
> 3. South 56° 26' 45" East, 160.41 feet to an angle point in said lands; thence
> 4. still along said Crowley lands, South 52° 22' 20" East 520.80 feet to a point on a curve; thence
> 5. to the right in a southerly direction along the arc of said curve with a radius of 24 feet, a single angle of 90° 00' 00", a chord bearing of South 25° 10' 5" East, a chord distance of 36 feet and an arc distance of 37.70 feet; thence
> 6. South 32° 53' 45" West 380 feet to the northerly line of Law Drive, 60 feet wide, the point and place of BEGINNING.
>
> BEING Lots 34 and 35 in Block 0903 as shown on "Map of Property of Dan E. Developer in the County of Feerick, State of Fagan, surveyed by Mulligan Engineering & Surveying Company, July 1986" and filed in the Feerick County Clerk's Office on August 6, 1986, as No. 3314.

> ➤ *Problem 4-7*
> What problems does the survey in Figure 4-2 reveal to you as attorney for Dan? For Ace? Specifically, what additional document would you demand? Assuming that the survey is correct, are there any inaccuracies in the legal description that need to be corrected? Does anything in the survey cause you to be concerned about zoning? Access? See generally M. Williams, Land Surveys: A Guide for Lawyers and Other Professionals (2nd ed. 1999); Kanner, What You Should Know About Surveys, 5 Prac. Real Est. Law. 9 (May 1989); Sutin, A Survey Requirements Checklist, 4 Prac. Real Est. Law. 45 (Nov. 1988); Williams and Onsrud, What Every Lawyer Should Know About Land Surveys, 2 Prob. & Prop. 13 (1988). ◀

9. *Title Insurance*

The postconstruction loan commitment will condition the obligation to fund the loan on the lender's receipt of title insurance satisfactory to it. The title insurance policy insures the lender that, as of the closing date, it has lien priority over any other interests in the mortgaged property, except for those liens and encumbrances specifically itemized in a schedule (usually Schedule B) to the policy. Therefore, if the loan commitment requires that the mortgage (or deed of trust) be a first lien, the lender will condition its obligation to fund on its receipt of a title policy insuring that no interests are superior in lien priority to the mortgage other than those set forth in the loan commitment or not objected to by the lender's attorney. Consider the following sample commitment provision:

Borrower at its sole cost and expense shall furnish to Lender an ALTA 2006 policy or policies of mortgage title insurance (or its equivalent in form, scope and substance satisfactory to Lender's Law Department), with such co-insurance and reinsurance as Lender may require, in the full amount of the Loan, insuring, inter alia, that Lender has a first lien on the Property, free of encumbrances or other exceptions to title, other than those which are approved and accepted in writing by Lender. The issuing company or companies and the amount of title insurance issued by any company and any reinsurance and co-insurance shall be approved by Lender.

Most lenders will require title insurance rather than an attorney's title opinion, and they generally prefer the form of lender's policy issued by the American Land Title Association (ALTA) where available. Why would lenders prefer a title policy to an attorney's opinion? See Chapter 2B.

Lenders normally will permit the borrower to select the title company from a preapproved list, subject to limitations on the amount of coverage the lender will accept from any one insurer. The title industry has limited assets, and lenders carefully review annual reports from each company in establishing limits on acceptable coverage. When the assets of one insurer are considered insufficient to cover the risk, the lender will require coinsurance or reinsurance with another company or companies.

You should realize that title insurance in many respects is like a guaranty of the accuracy of a search of the title records. The important thing is to determine what title defects the search has revealed. Many weeks before the loan closing, the title company should prepare a preliminary "title report," sometimes called a "title binder" or "title certificate." This is the title company's agreement to insure the property subject to the listed exceptions revealed by the title search. Therefore, it is the task of both lender's and borrower's counsel to scrutinize the report very thoroughly and resolve any marketability or lien-priority problems with the title company as quickly as possible.

At Chapter 2B we reviewed the terms of the standard title insurance policy including insuring provisions, exclusions from coverage, conditions and stipulations, and property-specific exemptions from coverage. In addition to the covered risks in the ALTA owner's policy (such as title vested other than as stated; defects, liens, or encumbrances on title; unmarketability of title; lack of access), the ALTA mortgagee's policy insures the lender, whether postconstruction or construction, against the following contingencies:

> 9. The invalidity or unenforceability of the lien of the insured mortgage upon the title. . . .
>
> 10. The lack of priority of the lien of the insured mortgage upon the title over any other lien or encumbrance [see Chapter 3E for discussion of general lien priority principles].
>
> 11. The lack of priority of the lien of the insured mortgage upon the title
>
> (a) as security for each and every advance of proceeds of the loan secured by the insured mortgage over any statutory lien for services, labor, or material arising from construction of an improvement or work related to the land when the improvement or work is either (i) contracted for or commenced on or before Date of Policy; or (ii)

contracted for, commenced, or continued after Date of Policy if the construction is financed, in whole or in part, by proceeds of the loan secured by the insured mortgage that the insured has advanced or is obligated on Date of Policy to advance [see Chapter 6B3d, discussing special construction loan title policies and issues]; and

(b) over the lien of any assessments for street improvements under construction or completed at Date of Policy.

12. The invalidity or unenforceability of any assignment of the insured mortgage, provided the assignment is shown in Schedule A, or the failure of the assignment shown in Schedule A to vest title to the insured mortgage in the named insured assignee free and clear of all liens.

The standard exclusions from coverage (as well as the boilerplate conditions) in mortgagee policies are the same as those in the ALTA owner's policy in the Documents Manual discussed at Chapter 2B, except the ALTA loan policy contains the following additional exclusions:

4. Unenforceability of the lien of the insured mortgage because of the inability or failure of the insured to comply with applicable doing-business laws of the state where the land is situated.

5. Invalidity or unenforceability in whole or in part of the lien of the insured mortgage that arises out of the transaction evidenced by the insured mortgage and is based upon usury or any consumer credit protection or truth-in-lending law.

> **Problem 4-8**

Returning to the master hypothetical, suppose that Dan, Ace, and FNB execute a preclosed form of buy-sell agreement on June 1 of this year, the same day that FNB records its construction mortgage, and that construction commences two weeks later, on June 15. Three weeks prior to the closing of the postconstruction loan (which is scheduled to close on December 31 of this year), you, as Ace's attorney, receive a copy of the preliminary title report that reveals the following encumbrances and exceptions to title in Schedule B:

a. telephone and other utility easements recorded on May 15 of this year;

b. mortgage to secure a gap loan of $5 million to Dan (to fund construction cost overruns) that was recorded by the gap lender on September 1 of this year;

c. a long-term lease (pursuant to a minimum leasing requirement in Ace's commitment letter) recorded on December 31 of last year;

d. a lien for past due local property taxes filed on November 1 of this year; and

e. a judgment lien filed against Dan on October 1 of this year arising from a tort claim unrelated to the office building development.

Which interests, if any, should be extinguished or subordinated before the closing date to assure Ace's commitment expectations? You may wish to review the discussion at Chapter 3E on how a mortgage competes for lien priority with other adverse interests in the same real property.

Note that by statute, local real estate taxes often become a lien on the property as of the beginning of the tax year or at some other time in advance of the date on which the taxes become due and payable. Because of the time value of money, most taxpayers refuse to pay their taxes until they actually become due even if the taxes are a lien on their property.

As attorney for Dan Developer, would you recommend that he obtain an owner's title policy in addition to paying for the mortgagee's policy? Your answer would ordinarily be yes, for several reasons. First, without an owner's policy, Dan's equity in the property will not be insured. Second, the standard mortgage or deed of trust contains the borrower's covenant that it has good title to the mortgaged property, subject only to the exceptions set forth therein. If a title defect is discovered and the title company pays the lender, under standard title policy language the title company becomes "subrogated" (steps into the shoes of) the lender and has all the lender's rights against the borrower under the covenant of title. Do you understand why Dan will not be liable to the title company if he has his own policy? Third, and the reason most likely to convince Dan, is that the cost of combining fee (owner's) insurance with mortgage insurance is usually quite modest and, in some states, nominal. ◄

10.   *No Material Adverse Change Allowed between Commitment and Closing*

During the interval of perhaps 18 to 36 months between the commitment date and the scheduled closing date, the postconstruction lender needs to be assured that it may terminate the commitment if there are adverse changes in the financial condition of the borrower or in certain other aspects of the transaction on which the lender relied when it decided to make the loan. The following is a typical "no material change" clause from a postconstruction loan commitment:

> At the time Lender makes the Loan, except as may otherwise be provided specifically by this commitment, the financial condition and credit of Borrower and its major tenants, and all other features of the transaction shall be as represented to Lender without material, adverse change. No part of the Property shall have been damaged and not repaired to Lender's satisfaction nor taken in condemnation or other like proceeding, nor shall any such proceeding be pending. In the event that there has been a condemnation or other taking, Lender shall have the option to cancel this commitment or reduce the amount of the Loan by the amount of the award received in connection with the condemnation or other taking. Neither the Borrower nor any space tenant under any assigned space lease, nor any guarantor of the Loan

or any such space lease, shall be involved in any bankruptcy, reorganization or insolvency proceeding.

NOTES AND QUESTIONS

1. No Adverse Change. As you might expect, construction lenders who rely on takeout commitments from postconstruction lenders for repayment of their construction loans look askance at "no adverse change" provisions in postconstruction commitment letters. Indeed, some construction lenders will regard the commitment as "unbankable" unless the clause is deleted. Can you think of any alternative language that should be reasonably acceptable as a compromise? How might a construction lender otherwise protect itself against the pitfalls of such a clause?

The "no adverse change" clause is worrisome from the borrower's perspective as well, especially if interest rates have risen since the commitment date, an event that may tempt the postconstruction lender to view this provision as an escape clause. The borrower can protect itself by making conservative estimates in the loan application as to its financial status and the financial affairs of its prime credit tenants. Can you think of any protective language that the borrower might want to include to avoid any attempt by the postconstruction lender to extricate itself from the commitment because of an adverse change in the creditworthiness of any prime tenant?

2. Effect of Bankruptcy. The Bankruptcy Code (11 U.S.C. §365(e)) recognizes the lender's need for protection by excepting loan commitments (defined as any "contract to make a loan" or to extend financial accommodations) from its general rule against termination of contracts because of the insolvency or financial condition of the debtor. A similar exception to the trustee's right to assume or assign executory contracts is found in §365(c). When the Bankruptcy Code was being drafted and attorneys representing lenders requested the exception for loan commitments under §365(e), congressional staff members queried them as to why such an exception was necessary inasmuch as real estate lenders sometimes exculpate the borrower from personal liability and rely solely on the real estate for repayment of their loans. As a lender's attorney, how would you respond to the question?

E.   THE LAWYER'S ROLE IN CLOSING
THE MORTGAGE LOAN

1.   *The Ethical Real Estate Lawyer: Professional Responsibility Issues in Closing the Mortgage Loan*

Typically, each party in a large commercial transaction is represented by separate counsel rather than the parties sharing counsel or going without representation. An attorney ordinarily cannot represent both the lender and the borrower in the same transaction without obtaining the informed consent of each in accordance with the applicable rules of professional conduct for dual representation.[15] Some jurisdictions impose more restrictive rules on dual representation of lenders and borrowers, either restricting the dual lawyer's role to that of a scrivener[16] or prohibiting such dual representation altogether.[17] If, on the other hand, the borrower is unrepresented, the lender's lawyer should urge the borrower, in writing, to obtain counsel to review the draft loan documents and otherwise to represent it.

Even where both parties have competent, independent counsel, thorny issues can arise in mortgage loan closings when the duty to zealously represent one's client collides with and, in some instances, gives way to standards of honest and fair dealing. For example, does lender's counsel owe any duty to the borrower or to borrower's counsel to point out unexpected provisions in the loan documents prepared by lender's counsel? Similarly, might alert borrower's counsel have any duty to point out a drafting error by lender's counsel that may affect the validity of the documents or otherwise frustrate the lender's contractual expectations? The following materials explore this tension.

Wright v. Pennamped
657 N.E.2d 1223 (1995), reh'g denied, 664 N.E.2d 394
(Ind. Ct. App. 1996)

SHARPNACK, Chief Judge.
. . . Wright is a self-employed general contractor and real estate developer who lives in Beech Grove, Indiana. He owns and operates a sixty-unit apartment complex in Beech Grove called the Diplomat Apartments. In early 1991, Wright

---

15. See Chapter 2A2 for discussion of dual representation in conveyancing transactions.

16. See, e.g., Association of the Bar of the City of New York, Comm. on Professional Ethics Op. 81-4 (1981). See generally Sanford, Ethical, Statutory, and Regulatory Conflicts of Interest in Real Estate Transactions, 17 St. Mary's L.J. 79, 88-90 (1985).

17. See, e.g., Maryland State Bar Ass'n Comm. on Ethics Op. 82-42 (1982); N.J. Stat. Ann. §46:10A-6 (West 2003) (prohibiting a mortgage lender from requiring that its counsel represent the borrower). Cf. Baldasarre v. Butler, 132 N.J. 278, 625 A.2d 458, 467 (1993) (prohibiting the dual representation of sellers and purchasers in complex conveyancing transactions).

began looking to refinance the Diplomat Apartments in the amount of $500,000.00.

On May 29, 1991, Ray Krebs, the vice president of mortgage banking at SCI Financial Corporation ("SCI"), submitted a proposal of financing to Wright. In pertinent part, the proposal provided:

> . . . PREPAYMENT: Not available during the first 12 months. Thereafter, at an amount consistent with the Federal Home Loan Bank of Indianapolis prepayment formula. . . .

After signing the proposal, Wright provided Brown's [Wright's real estate attorney] name, address, and telephone number to Krebs. Krebs then relayed this information to Pennamped. Pennamped, a partner in the law firm of Lowe Gray Steele & Hoffman, became involved in the loan transaction on July 2, 1991, when he had a luncheon meeting with Krebs. SCI retained Pennamped and the firm to represent its interests and to prepare the necessary loan documents. At the direction of Krebs, Pennamped began drafting the loan documents on or about July 15th. Pennamped drafted the loan documents on July 31, 1991, and forwarded copies marked "DRAFT DATED 7-31-91" to Krebs and Brown.

A draft mortgage note was among the many draft loan documents hand delivered to Brown. The prepayment provision of the draft note read:

> Borrower may not prepay the principal balance of the Loan, or any part thereof, at any time during the first (1st) Loan Year of the Loan. Borrower shall have the right to prepay the Loan, in whole but not in part, upon ten (10) days written notice first given Lender, after the first (1st) Loan Year. The Borrower, in the event of prepayment, shall pay Lender a fee equal to one percent (1%) of the then outstanding principal balance together with accrued interest until payment is received by Lender.
> . . .

On Friday, August 2, 1991, Brown reviewed the draft documents and discussed them with Wright. Brown and Wright discussed the prepayment provision as well as additional terms in the draft documents. Wright did not indicate to Brown that the prepayment provision in the draft note was any different than the one in the proposal for financing. Based on their discussion, both Wright and Brown accepted and approved the form and substance of the draft documents.

On August 1, 1991, Krebs mailed a copy of the draft documents to Don Wilson, Senior Vice President of Kentland Bank which was the funding bank. Wilson received and reviewed the documents on August 2nd. Wilson marked various provisions of the loan documents, including the prepayment penalty provision. At his deposition, Wilson testified the prepayment penalty provision was to be consistent with the Federal Home Loan Bank prepayment penalty, rather than a flat one percent. Upon completion of Wilson's initial review, Wilson and Krebs discussed a number of changes to be made to the draft loan documents, including those necessary to the prepayment penalty provision.

[O]n the morning of Monday, August 5th[,] Krebs sent a facsimile transmission of the changes, including a new prepayment penalty clause, to Pennamped with a cover transmittal sheet that stated "Don Wright Loan Document changes per our discussion."

Also on Monday, Brown and Pennamped discussed the transaction and the draft loan documents. Pennamped asked Brown if he had any problems with the proposed loan documents, and Brown responded that he did not. Brown informed Pennamped he had two cases set for the following morning and he would be unable to attend the closing set for 9:00 A.M. on August 6, 1991. Brown also spoke with Krebs on August 5th. Neither Pennamped nor Krebs informed Brown that they anticipated making any changes to the loan documents. Brown prepared his opinion letter for the closing with specific reference to the draft loan documents dated July 31, 1991.

After Pennamped received the facsimile of the changes, he spoke with Krebs and indicated that somebody needed to speak with the borrower, Wright, to explain the changes in the prepayment penalty clause. Krebs informed him that he would take care of it. Pennamped neither attempted to reach Brown to inform him of the changes nor followed up to see if Krebs had contacted Wright with the changes. Pennamped completed the changes to the loan documents on the afternoon of August 5, 1991. Krebs did not inform Wright of the changes.

The loan closing occurred on Tuesday, August 6, 1991. Because Brown was in court, Wright attended the closing alone. Pennamped, Krebs, Wilson, and a representative of the title insurance company who acted as the closing agent were also at the closing. . . . Wright did not review the documents prior to signing them because he believed them to be the same documents that his attorney, Brown, had reviewed. Wright was never informed of the revisions that had been made to the draft loan documents. . . .

In September of 1992, Wright obtained a favorable refinancing commitment from another lender. Brown contacted Kentland Bank to obtain a payoff statement. The prepayment penalty quoted by Kentland Bank was far greater than the one percent Brown had anticipated. . . . The final note contained the following prepayment provision:

> Borrower may not prepay the principal balance of the Loan, or any part thereof, at any time during the first (1st) Loan Year of the Loan. Borrower shall have the right to prepay the Loan, in whole but not in part, upon ten (10) days written notice first given Lender, after the first (1st) Loan Year. The Borrower, in the event of prepayment, shall pay Lender a fee equal to the greater of: i) the sum of (a) the present value of the scheduled monthly payments on the Loan from the date of prepayment to the maturity date and (b) the present value of the amount of principal and interest due on the maturity date of the Loan (assuming all scheduled monthly payments due prior to maturity were made when due) minus (c) the outstanding principal Loan balance as of the date of prepayment. The present values described in (a) and (b) are computed on a monthly basis as of the date of prepayment discounted at the rate of the U.S. Treasury Note or Bond closest in mautrity [sic] to the remaining term of this Loan (as reported in the Wall Street Journal on the fifth

business day preceding the date of prepayment) plus 250 basis points; [or] ii) one percent of the then outstanding principal balance. . . .

On July 1, 1993, Wright paid $595,799.09 to Kentland Bank, under protest, representing payment in full of the loan, including all outstanding principal and interest, as well as the prepayment penalty of $97,504.38 calculated under the terms of the final note.

As of the July 1, 1993, payoff date, the principal balance of the note was $493,148.71. Under the terms of the draft note, a one percent prepayment penalty would have been $4,931.49. This amount is approximately $92,500.00 less than that amount required under the terms of the final, revised note. In addition, the prepayment penalty charged by Kentland Bank was approximately $60,000.00 greater than the amount charged under the Federal Home Loan Bank formula. On July 18, 1993, Wright filed a complaint for damages against Kentland Bank, Krebs, SCI, Pennamped, and Lowe Gray Steele & Hoffman. Wright sought recovery from the defendants based on fraud, constructive fraud and breach of fiduciary relationship, obtaining money and property by false pretenses, deception, criminal mischief, conversion and theft, and forgery. . . .

Wright argues he has designated sufficient evidence to survive summary judgment on his actual fraud claim. Wright contends that we should reverse the granting of summary judgment [in favor of Pennamped] because he has shown (1) that Pennamped made a representation of past or existing fact to Wright or Brown, (2) that Wright relied on representations by Pennamped, or (3) that Pennamped acted with actual knowledge of the falsity of any representations made or in reckless disregard of their falsity. We agree.

First, Wright claims Pennamped's failure to inform Brown of the changes in advance of the closing and Pennamped's presentation of the documents for Wright's signature, "while continuing to remain silent, constituted a representation by Pennamped that the documents so presented were in form and substance identical to the documents that had been submitted to Brown." Appellant's brief, p. 32. Construing the facts in the light most favorable to Wright, we agree that Pennamped, by remaining silent and not informing Brown or Wright of the changes to the loan documents, impliedly represented that the final loan documents conformed to the draft loan documents which had been reviewed and approved by Brown.

The Appellees contend, however, that Pennamped's "silence" cannot be construed as a representation in the present case because Pennamped had no duty to speak. We disagree.

The Appellees are correct that silence will not support a claim for actionable fraud absent a duty to speak or to disclose facts. In addition, the party alleging fraudulent concealment has the burden of demonstrating the existence of a duty to speak. We conclude, however, that Wright has satisfied this requirement.

By undertaking the tasks of a drafting attorney, including the distribution of draft loan documents and the solicitation of review and approval of the documents, Pennamped assumed a duty to disclose any changes in the documents prior to execution to the other parties or their respective counsel. The existence of such a duty is supported by common sense and notions of fair dealing. Thus, Pennamped, as the drafting attorney, had a duty to inform Brown or, in his absence, Wright, of any changes occurring after Brown's review and approval of the loan documents. Were the rule otherwise, pre-closing review of loan documentation would become a futile act, and counsel would be required to scrutinize every term of each document at the moment of execution.

Wright's second contention is that he had a right to rely on representations made by Pennamped. However, the Appellees contend Wright did not have a right to rely because he "was an experienced business man who had full access to all relevant facts at all times."

A person relying upon the representations of another is bound to exercise ordinary care and diligence to guard against fraud. . . . Where the evidence is conflicting, the issue of whether a particular person has exercised reasonable prudence and whether the reliance was justified is for a jury's determination. . . .

As has been noted recently by our supreme court, a demanding standard is applied with regard to the representations made by attorneys. Fire Insurance Exchange v. Bell (1994), Ind., 643 N.E.2d 310, 312. "A lawyer's representations have long been accorded a particular expectation of honesty and trustworthiness." Id. "The law should promote lawyers' care in making statements that are accurate and trustworthy and should foster the reliance upon such statements by others." Id. at 313.

Undoubtedly, Wright exercised ordinary care and diligence by having his attorney review the loan documents prior to closing. . . . Contrary to the Appellees' position, Wright was under no obligation to review documents at the closing once they had been reviewed and approved by his attorney, absent some indication from Pennamped that changes had been made. As a matter of law, Wright established a reasonable right of reliance on Pennamped's alleged misrepresentations.

Wright's third contention is that Pennamped acted with actual knowledge of the falsity of any representations made or in reckless disregard of their falsity. Wright claims the trial court erred because the presence of fraudulent intent is a factual issue for the jury and the evidence supports a reasonable inference of intent to deceive when viewed in the light most favorable to Wright. We agree. . . .

In issuing its ruling on the motion for summary judgment, the trial court held: "Here, it is uncontroverted that attorney Pennamped, upon learning of his client's intention to make last minute changes in the loan documents, instructed his client to notify the Plaintiff immediately of such changes and stressed the importance of such notification. In the face of such uncontroverted evidence, it is incumbent upon the Plaintiff to come forward with some evidence supporting an inference of fraud. The Plaintiff has failed to do so." Record, p. 247. Although we would agree that the evidence supports finding an absence of fraudulent intent, we do not agree that the evidence on this issue is uncontroverted.

Viewing the evidence in the light most favorable to Wright, Pennamped first learned that changes would be made to the loan documents on Friday, August 2,

1991. Pennamped received the changes via facsimile during the morning hours of Monday, August 5, 1991, the day prior to closing. Although speaking with Brown by telephone on August 5th, and although aware that Brown would be unable to attend the closing, Pennamped did not tell Brown the documents had been or would be changed. Pennamped neither informed Wright that changes had been or would be made after Brown's review and approval nor made any attempt to confirm that Krebs had informed Wright of the changes.

Wright has designated evidence showing that Pennamped knew there were last-minute changes made to the loan documents and that Pennamped failed to inform Wright and his counsel of these changes. This is evidence from which a jury might infer an intent to deceive on the part of Pennamped and the law firm. . . .

We conclude, therefore, that the trial court erred in granting summary judgment on Wright's claim for actual fraud. . . .

NOTES AND QUESTIONS

1. Lessons in Lawyering. What advice would you suggest to ensure that lender's counsel avoids litigation of the sort in *Wright*? In reversing the trial court's entry of summary judgment for the lender's attorney on the related claim of constructive fraud (an action that does not require proof of intent to deceive), the court in *Wright* quoted the expert testimony of a real estate lawyer on the relevant custom in commercial financing transactions:

> (a) At any time changes or revisions are made to draft or proposed loan documents by the attorney charged with the responsibility of drafting such documents—no matter how trivial or seemingly insignificant such changes or revisions may be—it is expected and understood by all other attorneys involved in the transaction that the drafting attorney will take whatever steps are necessary and/or appropriate to fully disclose and identify all such document changes and revisions to other attorneys involved in the transaction. (b) Typically, when any changes or revisions are made to proposed or draft loan documents, the drafting attorney will circulate, in writing, a "red-lined" copy or some other written materials which will highlight and/or more particularly identify and/or describe the changes and revisions that have been or are contemplated to be made. . . .

657 N.E.2d at 1235.

In the Penthouse casino litigation discussed at Chapter 4B, note 4, supra, the district court ruled that the lender's lawyer was liable to the borrower for $128.7 million in fraud damages because he failed to disclose his role as the lender's "hatchet man" to "scuttle" the closing of the loan transaction. On appeal, the Second Circuit reversed because it concluded that the lender had no intention to avoid its loan commitment obligations at the time of its lawyer's dilatory tactics. See Penthouse Intl. v. Dominion Fed. Sav. & Loan Ass'n, 855 F.2d 963 (2d Cir. 1988), cert. denied, 490 U.S. 1005 (1989), rev'g in part and aff'g in part 665 F. Supp. 301 (S.D.N.Y. 1987). Nevertheless, the district court's depiction of the conduct it viewed as fraudulent lawyering is instructive to avoid such litigation in the first instance. Among the ill-advised tactics of the lender's lawyer, who was brought into the deal once underway as replacement counsel, were (1) his reference to the existing draft loan documents as "idiotic"; (2) his insistence on redrafting the loan documents yet failing to do so within a reasonable period of time; (3) his insistence that the borrower supply extensive information that was not essential to close the deal nor required by the commitment; and (4) his insistence, apparently without authorization from the lender, that the borrower pay him a $150,000 bonus for his trouble in giving the closing "priority status," which the trial judge labeled "extortion."

2. Fairness in Drafting. Does an attorney owe a duty to the other party, when unrepresented, to protect against unfair contract terms? Consider the facts of The Florida Bar v. Belleville, 591 So. 2d 170 (Fla. 1991), in which the Florida Supreme Court suspended the buyer's attorney for 30 days for drafting a sale agreement signed by the elderly, unrepresented seller that overwhelmingly favored the buyer. The purchase agreement for the seller's apartment complex included the seller's personal residence across the street, which the seller did not intend. As well, the purchase money loan was unsecured, was interest and payment-free the first four months, required the seller to pay closing costs including buyer's counsel fees, and was deemed forgiven if the seller died (he was 83). The court concluded that when faced with such a one-sided transaction, the lawyer ethically must "explain to the unrepresented opposing party the fact that the attorney is representing an adverse interest. Second, the attorney must explain the material terms of the documents that the attorney has drafted for the client so that the opposing party fully understands their actual effect." 591 So. 2d at 172. Compare Restatement (Third) of Law Governing Lawyers §103 (2000):

> In the course of representing a client and dealing with a nonclient who is not represented by a lawyer:
>
> (1) the lawyer may not mislead the nonclient, to the prejudice of the nonclient, concerning the identity and interests of the person the lawyer represents; and
>
> (2) when the lawyer knows or reasonably should know that the unrepresented nonclient misunderstands the lawyer's role in the matter, the lawyer must make reasonable efforts to correct the misunderstanding when failure to do so would materially prejudice the nonclient.

3. The Case of the Three Missing Zeros. In the well-known litigation of Prudential Ins. Co. v. Dewey, Ballantine, Bushby, Palmer & Wood, 80 N.Y.2d 377, 605 N.E.2d 318, 590 N.Y.S.2d 831 (1992), the lender's mortgage had erroneously specified the loan balance it secured as $92,885 rather than as $92,885,000. As a result, the lender incurred substantial losses in settling priority battles in the mortgagor's bankruptcy proceedings. Despite having issued an opinion letter assuring the lender of the enforceability of its loan documents, borrower's counsel escaped liability because it rendered no assurance that the lien effectively secured any specific dollar amount. Opinion letters are discussed at Chapter 4E2, infra. Suppose, however, that borrower's counsel was aware of this error or of some other mistake that affects the validity of the mortgage or other loan documents. In light of the *Wright* case, do you think that borrower's counsel has a duty to disclose the error to the lender or to lender's counsel? If borrower's counsel wants to disclose the mistake, must it get its client's consent before doing so? See ABA Model Rule of Professional Conduct 1.6(b) (as amended in 2003 to read "A lawyer may reveal information relating to the representation of a client to the extent the lawyer reasonably believes necessary . . . to prevent the client from committing a crime or fraud that is reasonably certain to result in substantial injury to the financial interests or property of another. . . ."); ABA Informal Op. 86-1518 (if lawyer inadvertently omits an agreed-on provision, the other lawyer has implied authority to correct this obvious drafting error without client consultation notwithstanding Rule 1.6); and Wright v. Pennamped, 664 N.E.2d 394, 395 (Ind. Ct. App. 1996) (in denying a rehearing of the decision excerpted above, the court remarked that informing opposing counsel that changes were made in the proposed contract "is clearly not privileged and our opinion does nothing to disturb the attorney's obligation of confidentiality and fidelity to the client"). See generally Geronemus, Lies, Damn Lies, and Unethical Lies, 6 Bus. L. Today 11, 14 (May/June 1997).

2. *Loan Opinion Letters*

As the following provision illustrates, the commercial mortgage loan commitment typically will require that opinion letters of counsel be issued to the lender on various aspects of the loan transaction:

> At the time of disbursement of the Loan, the Lender shall receive from its special counsel and from the Borrower's counsel, opinions addressed to the Lender in form, scope and substance satisfactory to the Lender and its Law Department concerning the legality, validity and binding effect of all documents required in connection with the disbursement of the Loan. . . .

The following excerpt provides an overview of the issuance of opinion letters while focusing on the core opinion in mortgage loan transactions—the enforceability opinion. As will be seen, as yet there is no universal approach to the phrasing of this enforceability assurance.

M. Madison, J. Dwyer, and S. Bender,
The Law of Real Estate Financing
§§5.63-5.66 (2016)

OPINION LETTERS IN REAL ESTATE FINANCING TRANSACTIONS

Opinion letters are often required in commercial mortgage loan commitments. Until recently, law firms had little authoritative guidance in setting opinion letter practices ranging from the scope of opinions the firm was willing to render (e.g., whether the opinion extends to the real property's compliance with applicable land use laws) to the wording of the opinions (e.g., whether the opinion is clean or "reasoned") to the breadth of exceptions taken (e.g., whether the enforceability opinion itemizes provisions of dubious enforceability or states some general exception). Protracted negotiations between counsel over the various firm specific opinion practices sometimes eclipsed debate over the provisions of the loan documents themselves. This negotiation not only added significant transaction costs to loans, it sometimes detracted from the fundamental purpose of opinion letters: to facilitate counsel's due diligence in ensuring the lender's basic expectations from the loan transaction (usually an enforceable repayment obligation effectively secured by collateral). Responding to similar concerns surrounding opinions in business transactions generally, in the 1980s several state bar associations undertook to prepare guidelines for a more uniform opinion letter practice. California, Colorado, Connecticut, Hawaii, Maryland, New York, Oregon, Texas, and Washington are among the states that did so specifically for mortgage loan opinions. At the national level, in 1991 the ABA Section of Business Law issued its *Third-Party Legal Opinion Report*[2] that grew out of the pathbreaking 1989 conference on legal opinions at Silverado, California (hence the common reference to this report as the "Silverado Report" or the "Silverado Accord"). Although it was designed for opinions in business transactions generally, the Accord provided significant national guidelines for opinion letters and opinion letter practice that were useful for mortgage loan transactions. However, the Accord's comprehensive design fell short of adequately dealing with certain issues in mortgage loan opinions. In 1994, a joint drafting committee from the ABA Section of Real Property, Probate and Trust Law and from the American College of Real Estate Lawyers (ACREL) issued a report (the "Real Estate Report")[4] discussed subsequently that adapted the Accord for use in mortgage loan transactions but specifically recommended against using the Accord without the modifications that it proposed.. . .

---

2. Third-Party Legal Opinion Report Including the Legal Opinion Accord of the Section of Business Law, American Bar Association, 47 Bus. Law. 167 (1991)....

4. Report on Adaptation of the Legal Opinion Accord, 29 Real Prop., Prob. & Tr. J. 569 (1994)....

To concretize the modifications to the Accord in the Real Estate Report, the joint drafting committee in 1999 issued a form of opinion letter—the "Inclusive Real Estate Secured Transaction Opinion" (the "Inclusive Opinion"). . . .

Later, the ABA Real Property Section and ACREL issued Real Estate Opinion Letter Guidelines that address such issues as the appropriateness of certain opinions and the process for issuing an opinion. Finally, in 2012, the ABA section, ACREL, and the American College of Mortgage Attorneys updated and expanded the Inclusive Opinion with additional guidance on opinion letter custom and language in real estate finance transactions—the Real Estate Finance Opinion Report of 2012 (the "2012 Opinion Report"). . . .

FORM OF OPINION LETTERS

Whether adopted from the Inclusive Opinion, the 2012 Opinion Report, state bar reports, or law firm specific custom, most forms of mortgage loan opinions follow a similar format: they identify the attorney's role in the transaction (e.g., as local or lead counsel) and specify the documents reviewed, they state certain assumptions and a practice limitation,[1] they render certain opinions that are preceded or followed by exceptions, limitations, and qualifications, they state the scope of the parties entitled to rely on the opinion and, finally, are signed on behalf of the issuing law firm. Mortgage loan opinions often encompass both borrower entity status (e.g., opinions assuring that the borrower is validly existing and in good standing, has the power to execute and perform under the documents, and has authorized the transaction) and enforceability issues (e.g., the loan documents are valid, binding, and enforceable against the borrower). In fact, these opinions are inextricably related: presumably the loan documents cannot be valid and binding obligations of a borrower if the party signing lacked authority to bind the borrower or if the borrower is improperly constituted.

The enforceability opinion is the core opinion in mortgage loan transactions. As stated in the New York bar form of mortgage loan opinion letter . . . (herein the New York Report), this opinion assures that "[t]he Loan Documents are the valid and binding obligations of Borrower, enforceable against Borrower in accordance with their respective terms. . . ." This statement of enforceability is usually followed by a so-called bankruptcy or insolvency exception (the New York Report version excepts "bankruptcy, insolvency or similar laws affecting the rights and remedies of creditors generally") and a so-called equitable principles exception (reading in the New York Report as "general principles of equity"). . . .

Opinion issuers tend to further address the various unenforceable or dubious provisions in the loan documents with a generic qualification (e.g., in the New York Report, "In addition, we advise you that certain provisions of the Loan

---

1. The New York State Bar form of mortgage opinion ... provides the following practice limitation: "The law covered by the opinion is limited to the federal law of the United States and the law of the State of New York. We express no opinion with respect to the law of any other jurisdiction...."

Documents may be further limited or rendered unenforceable by applicable law. . . .”), followed by an “assurance” to restore some meaning to the enforceability opinion (in the New York Report, but “such law does not render the Loan Documents invalid as a whole or substantially interfere with [the] realization of the principal benefits and/or security provided thereby”). Commentators fault this generic approach for its ambiguity. For example, the parties may have differing expectations of the “principal benefits” of the loan documents, as well as what constitutes a “substantial” interference with those benefits. Despite this shortcoming, the Real Estate Report strongly recommends that counsel use the generic qualification. While it does not articulate an assurance to accompany the generic qualification, the Real Estate Report examines several possible formulations of the assurance. Among those formulations is the “traditional” phrasing, as in: “but such laws and judicial decisions [that make certain provisions of the documents unenforceable] do not make the Security Documents legally inadequate for the practical realization of the principal benefits and/or security intended to be provided thereby.” The 2012 Opinion Report specifically discourages use of this traditional practical realization/principal benefits language because of its vagueness and subjectivity. Instead, it supplies a more pointed assurance to the generic enforceability qualification (“Certain provisions of the Transaction Documents may not be enforceable”), reading:

> [S]uch unenforceability will not render the Transaction Documents invalid as a whole or preclude (i) the judicial enforcement in accordance with applicable Law of the obligation of the Borrower to repay as provided in the Note the principal, together with interest thereon (to the extent not deemed a penalty) . . . ; (ii) the acceleration of the obligation of the Borrower to repay such principal, together with such interest, upon a material default by Borrower in the payment of such principal or interest [or upon a material default by the Borrower in any other material provision of the Transaction Documents]; and (iii) the foreclosure in accordance with Applicable Law of the lien on and the security interest in the Collateral created by the Security Documents upon maturity or upon acceleration pursuant to clause (ii) above.

Despite the customary inclusion of the so-called bankruptcy exception, an equitable principles exception, and the generic enforceability qualification with an assurance, most opinion letters in mortgage financing transactions add additional exceptions for provisions in the loan documents that are either always unenforceable, unenforceable in some circumstances, or otherwise of dubious or unsettled enforceability. Several approaches are employed to articulate this additional exception, including the so-called laundry list exception. An opinion using the laundry list approach will specifically reference each of the questionable provisions in the loan documents unless they clearly fall within the bankruptcy or equitable principles exceptions. For example, items specified in a laundry list might include:

- Limitations on stated default remedies such as any statutory right to reinstate the loan and any statutory restrictions on the recovery of deficiency judgments;
- Prepayment charges;
- Waivers of jury trials;
- Arbitration clauses; and
- Forum selection provisions.

This laundry list approach is criticized because, among other things, it is a costly exercise for both issuing and reviewing parties that turns opinion letters into secured land treatises.

One commentator, Robert Thompson,[13] identifies another common approach (which he calls the "hybrid generic approach") that employs both a generic enforceability qualification (with an assurance) combined with a specific listing of unusual provisions under local law (e.g., California's antideficiency scheme) and in the loan documents that warrant specific mention. Presumably that list is less detailed than that under the laundry list approach, reserving reference only for certain transaction and local law-specific issues. This approach seems particularly suited for opinions to an out-of-state lender whose expectations of enforcement may differ from those of local lenders familiar with a particular state's limitations.

The 2012 Opinion Report, in its Illustrative Language of a Real Estate Finance Opinion Letter, adopts the generic enforceability qualification (with an assurance), followed by both a listing of so-called "other transaction-related qualifications," and a more general listing of "other general qualifications." In the transaction-related discussion, the opinion giver presumably would detail and address provisions specific to the particular transaction and loan documents, such as usury, choice of law, jury trial waivers, assignment of rents enforcement, prepayment clauses, and environmental and other indemnities. Augmenting this transaction-specific list would be a more general listing of "generally applicable rules of law" that affect enforceability and which tend to relate to the pursuit of remedies. For example, the 2012 Opinion Report includes among a long list of laws those that "limit the availability of a remedy under certain circumstances where another remedy has been elected," and those that "govern and afford judicial discretion regarding the determination of damages and entitlement to attorneys' fees and other costs." At the same time, the 2012 Opinion Report recognizes that "many practitioners are more selective in adding limitations, and do not use an exhaustive 'laundry list' of qualifications or other limitations because the bankruptcy exception, the equitable principles exception, and the generic enforceability qualification, if written properly, perhaps along with a selective list, may be sufficient." . . .

---

13. See Thompson[, Real Estate Opinion Letter Practice 157 (1993)].

EXCLUDING OPINIONS ON TITLE

Lawyers rendering mortgage loan opinions are often asked to opine that the real estate security document is sufficient to create a lien. The 2012 Opinion Report suggests the following language:

> the Mortgage is in a form sufficient to create a lien on all right, title, and interest of Borrower in and to the Real Property. Further, the [Security Agreement] is in a form sufficient to create a security interest in those items of the personal property stated as constituting part of the Collateral in which a security interest can be created under Article 9 of the Uniform Commercial Code.

Regardless of whether this sufficiency opinion is given, counsel will normally want to exclude any opinion on the actual creation, perfection, or priority of the lien; the lender can rely on its policy of title insurance for these assurances. In this regard, the 2012 Opinion Report provides as exclusions from the above sufficiency opinion that the following opinions are not rendered unless explicitly addressed in the opinion letter:

> (i) the creation, attachment, perfection, or priority of a lien, or security interest in, or to, Collateral, or enforcement of a security interest in Collateral comprising personal property; . . .
> (u) title to any property, the characterization of any property as real property, personal property, or fixtures, or the accuracy or sufficiency of any description of collateral or other property

Relatedly, the 2012 Opinion Report specifies a number of assumptions in its illustrative language that relate to the creation of an effective lien, such as "The Security Documents have been or will be duly and properly recorded or filed and duly and properly indexed in all places necessary," and "The description of the Collateral is accurate and reasonably identifies the Collateral.'"

OPINION LETTER PREPARATION

Despite the focus of the above materials on the wording of the opinion letter, the crucial task of the opinion issuer is to perform the due diligence involved in the lawyer's analysis of the transaction, the documents, and the borrower's organizational status.[1] To facilitate due diligence, Robert Thompson suggests that

---

1. See [Real Estate Report] at 577 ("The giving of an opinion should always involve independent inquiry and analysis; undue reliance upon model opinions or upon broadly stated assumptions and qualifications may mask important legal issues and thereby mislead both the Opinion Giver and the Opinion Recipient.").

counsel prepare a due diligence checklist but warns that each transaction must still be approached separately.[2] Some law firms have established comprehensive opinion letter procedures that may include mandates for second partner review, the creation of opinion committees to give overall direction or to perform the review, and the preparation of procedure manuals containing due diligence checklists and firm specific forms of opinion letters for mortgage loans and other business transactions in which the firm is asked regularly to issue opinions. These endeavors grew out of the experience of thrift counsel in the [late 1980s savings and loan] crisis and its aftermath. For example, following its representation of the failed thrift Lincoln Savings, the Kaye, Scholer firm was required in an OTS settlement order to prepare legal opinions regarding compliance with statutes or regulations under the supervision of a partner "with at least 10 years of banking law experience" and to seek review and approval of each opinion by a second partner. This prompted commentators to call on firms to establish opinion letter committees to review opinions, or at least that a senior lawyer approve them. . . .

NOTES AND QUESTIONS

1. Role of Borrower's and Lender's Counsel. Debate is ongoing on whether borrower's or lender's counsel is better suited to issue the various opinions that lenders demand in commercial loan transactions. One commentator suggests that borrower's counsel should be responsible for borrower entity opinions (for example, that the borrower is authorized to execute the loan documents) but that lender's counsel may be in a better position to issue enforceability opinions. R. Thompson, Real Estate Opinion Letter Practice 12 (1993). Thompson concedes, however, that lenders customarily will insist on an enforceability opinion from borrower's counsel. Id. at 136. By contrast, Rhode Island law prohibits lenders from obtaining opinions from borrower's counsel on the "validity, binding effect, or enforceability of any of the loan documents or the availability of remedies thereunder." R.I. Gen. Laws. §19-9-7 (allowing borrower's counsel to render opinions on the authority and status of the borrower and on "matters relating to collateral"). What considerations justify this prohibition? For background, see In re Ethics Advisory Panel Opinion, 554 A.2d 1033 (R.I. 1989); see also Holtzschue, Opinions on Real Estate Secured Transactions in a Post-Accord World: The Opinion Giver's Perspective, 29 Real Prop., Prob. & Tr. J. 655, 675-679 (Fall 1994). Do you think those considerations should be left for the parties to negotiate without the legislature's intervention?

2. Enforceability Opinions. As Dan's counsel, which approach would you favor in qualifying your opinion as to the enforceability of Ace's loan documents?

---

2. See Thompson, [supra note 13, at 61].

3. Title Opinions. Consider carefully the Real Estate Report's treatment of opinions concerning the mortgage lien. On the one hand, the Report's form of opinion assures that the security documents are "sufficient to create a lien." At the same time, the Report excludes any opinion on the "creation of a lien" on the collateral. Are these inconsistent? See Report on the Adoption of the Legal Opinion Accord, 29 Real Prop., Prob. & Tr. J. 569, 604 (1994). Note further that the Real Estate Report anticipates that lawyers will opine as to whether the documents are sufficient to create a security interest in collateral governed by Article 9 of the Uniform Commercial Code. This reflects the commercial mortgage lender's typical insistence that its lien extend to personalty used in connection with the realty, such as furnishings and other equipment. Moreover, it reflects the assumption that the real estate lawyer is also an expert in obtaining a security interest under the UCC.

4. Multistate Opinions. Assume that you are a California lawyer who is representing Dan Developer in his acquisition and development of California property through the ownership vehicle of a Delaware limited liability company. Do you see any problems with your rendering an opinion to FNB, the construction lender, that Dan's ownership entity is validly organized and existing under the laws of Delaware? See M. Madison, J. Dwyer, and S. Bender, The Law of Real Estate Financing §§16:9-16:13 (2016); Thompson at 174-175, 223-224. See generally Needham, The Multijurisdictional Practice of Law and the Corporate Lawyer: New Rules for a New Generation of Legal Practice, 36 S. Tex. L. Rev. 1075 (1995); Needham, Negotiating Multi-State Transactions: Reflections on Prohibiting the Unauthorized Practice of Law, 12 St. Louis U. Pub. L. Rev. 113 (1993); Wolfram, Sneaking Around in the Legal Profession: Interjurisdictional Unauthorized Practice by Transactional Lawyers, 36 S. Tex. L. Rev. 665 (1995).

5. Compliance with Laws. Borrower's counsel is sometimes asked to render an opinion that the borrower's use or anticipated use of the property complies with all applicable laws (for example, zoning ordinances, environmental laws) affecting the property. As Dan's counsel, what objections might you have to this request? See Thompson at 213-215.

6. Further Reading. The ABA Section of Business Law Third Party Legal Opinion Report, the ABA-ACREL report on the adaptation of that Business Law Section opinion report for use in real estate secured transactions, and a number of excellent articles on mortgage loan opinions are compiled at 29 Real Prop., Prob. & Tr. J. 461-733 (Fall 1994).

3. The Mechanics of Closing the Mortgage Loan

Closings of major loan transactions tend to be problematic no matter how much foresight is exercised by the attorneys for the borrower, the postconstruction lender, and the construction lender. Therefore, it is advisable to obtain early approval of the survey, preliminary title report, and loan documentation so that the parties will be free to deal with the closing problems that will inevitably arise.

The following excerpt describes the parties at the closing and their respective duties and gives a checklist of the documentation required at the closing.

M. Madison, J. Dwyer, and S. Bender,
The Law of Real Estate Financing
§§5:129-5:131 (2016)

CLOSING THE PERMANENT LOAN . . .

PARTIES AT CLOSING

The primary concern of the attorney representing the developer is to orchestrate a permanent loan closing as smoothly and efficiently as possible. In many cases, the developer is paying a higher rate of interest on the construction loan and can save a substantial amount of funds by closing quickly on the permanent loan. From the outset, upon issuance of the permanent commitment, the attorney should be aware of the various parties involved in the permanent loan closing and develop a working relationship with them. Many times, worthwhile assistance will be given by the title company, which often acts as escrow agent for the permanent lender, by counsel for the construction lender (who is interested in seeing that the loan funds supplied by the construction lender are repaid as quickly as possible), and last but not least, by counsel for the permanent lender.

Many permanent lenders will use their in-house staff of attorneys to close the loan. Some will rely completely on special and local counsel, and others will use both. There are advantages and disadvantages to each of the three methods. When the permanent lender is using its in-house staff of attorneys only, the borrower does not have to pay the out-of-pocket legal fees incurred by the permanent lender. Just as important, the in-house attorney is usually experienced with the loan closing procedures, requiring special counsel only when an unusual question or problem arises with regard to local law. (Of course, outside counsel who have long represented the interests of the permanent lender will be just as familiar with the closing requirements and procedures involved with the closing as would be an in-house attorney.) The obvious disadvantage in using special counsel is that the legal fees must be paid for by the developer. More importantly, because there is one more person who must be satisfied that the closing requirements have been met and the funding is in proper order, there is the possibility of a loan closing being unduly dragged out, creating expense and ill will on the part of all. One adage that should faithfully be kept is that the developer's attorney should not wait until the last minute and hope that the permanent loan will close itself. Even when started well in advance, permanent loan closings tend to be postponed and extended.

In most permanent loan closings, there is a division of responsibility required by the permanent lender's counsel. Usually, it is the responsibility of the permanent lender's counsel to prepare the loan documents (although in some cases the permanent lender will require that the title company prepare the documents); accordingly, the developer's attorney should be persistent in making certain that the permanent loan documents are prepared several months in advance. This will give the attorney and the borrower an opportunity to review the documents and request changes where necessary and appropriate.

DOCUMENTATION AT CLOSING

The next division of work encompasses loan closing documents, such as the certified inventory statement, tenants' acceptance letters, architect's certificate, and estoppel certificates prepared by the permanent lender's counsel. These documents, together with the assignment of leases and notices of assignment, must be executed at or near the time of closing by third parties unrelated to the developer. Many times, a tenant will take weeks before executing an acceptance letter. It would be embarrassing for the attorney representing the developer to tell his client that the closing cannot take place until the architect, who drafted the plans and specifications, returns from a three-month vacation in the Amazon and executes the architect's certificate. Before the occupancy leases (and in the case of a leasehold mortgage, the ground lease) are executed, the developer's attorney should obtain early approval from the permanent lender so that the lender, prime tenants, and ground lessor will be able to work out their differences and avoid any delay in the closing of the permanent loan.

Another area that must be carefully coordinated are closing documents to be prepared by third parties: the hazard insurance policy, the title policy, and the survey. It is appropriate and desirable for the developer's attorney to send a copy of the permanent commitment pertaining to the requirements for title insurance, hazard insurance, and survey to the respective parties so that they can become familiar with the requirements of the permanent lender. With regard to the title company, the developer's attorney should make certain that months in advance a title binder is sent to the permanent lender for review and to request necessary endorsements so that there will be no surprises or problems with the final title insurance policy to be issued at the closing. By using a preclosed form of buy-sell agreement, the developer's attorney will be able to obtain early approval of the note and mortgage (or deed of trust) and most of the collateral documentation, such as the hazard insurance policy and the preliminary title report.

Sometimes there may be a breakdown in communications between the real estate department and the office of the general counsel of the permanent lender because many permanent lenders require the real estate department to review and make a final inspection of the property within two weeks before closing. Other permanent lenders require their in-house appraiser to inspect the property. The developer's attorney should make certain that these arrangements have been made by the permanent lender so as not to hold up the closing.

The final category of documents are those to be prepared by the attorney for the developer—for example, the attorney's opinion letter. He should make certain that drafts of these closing requirements are prepared and submitted to the permanent lender's counsel for its review well in advance of the closing date.

Where the permanent lender is purchasing the construction lender's documents by assignment, the permanent lender will require, in addition to the foregoing documents and the assignment of the loan documents, an acknowledgment from the construction lender that the loan is current and not in default, as well as an estoppel certificate from the borrower.

Finally, three or four days before the settlement date, counsel for the permanent lender will frequently submit a closing disbursement instruction letter to the title company or some other outside closing agent.

CHECKLIST FOR CLOSING PERMANENT LOAN

- The mortgagor should review the note, security instrument, lease assignments, and guaranty (all prepared by the lender) prior to closing. Do this early, because review of these documents may require some time.
- Obtain the title insurance binder and boundary survey, making sure the title company supplies photocopies of any easements, covenants, or restrictions of record. The lender will need these to prepare the security instrument and to assess the effects of any encumbrance or exceptions.
- Request, at least forty-five days before closing, the building location survey, which also should depict the location of all easements. The lender also may want a certification that the engineer is covered by errors and omissions (E&O) insurance.
- Gather the fully executed leases for review by the lender early. Use and occupancy clauses, renewal options, percentage rents, common areas contributions, etc. may require modifications which take time to discuss, negotiate, and put into effect. Check to see if any corporate parent guarantees are required and that appropriate corporate resolutions are appended to each lease.
- The lender will require forms from the tenants indicating their legal acceptance of the premises and establishing the lease and rent

commencement dates. These must be obtained when construction is completed.

- A final inspection of the property must be made and a certificate of completion furnished to the lender. A letter must be obtained from the appraiser indicating that the project meets the conditions of his original appraisal. The appraiser may also need leasing data if he conditioned the value estimate on anticipated rents.
- If some portion of construction is delayed, an escrow agreement may need to be executed so that funds may be held in escrow until all work is completed.
- A satisfactory hazard insurance policy, with the first annual premium paid, must be obtained and delivered to the permanent lender. The loan commitment must be checked to determine the minimum insurance company rating acceptable to the lender.
- Copies of occupancy permits issued by the local authority when construction is completed must be obtained. Also, it is advisable to obtain letters from the utility companies confirming that service is available and acknowledging payment by the mortgagor of applicable initial charges.
- Prepare and execute any joint-use documents that may be required if the project was built in stages, with an earlier phase financed by a different lender.
- Take steps to dedicate roads or other land to the state, if such action is required. This type of situation is time-consuming and delays may occur.
- Obtain the required evidence from the appropriate state commission that the mortgagor is authorized to do business in the state and that its charter is current.
- Obtain results of environmental audit if one is required. Find out if pertinent environmental law obligations required of the developer have been met.
- Check to see if other miscellaneous documents are required for your specific closing. Examples might include a common-wall agreement, key[person] insurance, off-site easements, or, if the lender wants [its] security instrument subordinated to certain leases, a subordination agreement.

PRACTITIONER'S CORNER

Drafting the Typical Real Estate Loan Transaction

The following background materials may prove useful in documenting the typical real estate loan transaction. Forms in the Documents Manual might also serve as appropriate starting points.

Books
M. Madison, J. Dwyer, and S. Bender, The Law of Real Estate Financing ch. 5 (2016) (also contains various commercial mortgage loan forms).
J. Stein, A Practical Guide to Real Estate Practice (2001).

ALI-ABA Modern Real Estate Transactions series (especially Wayte, Selected Issues in the Preparation and Negotiation of Mortgage Loan Documents, C532 ALI-ABA 289 (1990)).

Articles

Bergman, How to Protect Mortgage Value with Astute Mortgage Drafting, 2 Prac. Real Est. Law. 55 (May 1986).

Fisher, How to Draft Loan Commitments, 3 Prac. Real Est. Law. 9 (Sept. 1987).

Keyles, How to Draft Mortgage Loan Commitments from the Lender's Perspective, 8 Prac. Real Est. Law. 41 (Jan. 1992).

Rockwell, Basic Considerations in Reviewing Commercial Loan Documents, 6 Prac. Real Est. Law. 13 (Sept. 1990) (examines the drafting-negotiating process from the perspective of borrower's counsel).

Chapter 5

Postclosing Terms of the Mortgage Loan Commitment

Real estate financing is an area of the law in which freedom of contract has traditionally reigned supreme. However, in recent years, federal law, state and local regulation, and case law have intruded somewhat on the ability of the parties to write the law that will govern their relationship. Nevertheless, subject to these intrusions, the transactional rights and responsibilities of the interested parties (for example, Dan Developer and Ace, the postconstruction lender) are usually governed by some fairly standardized and well-tested written agreements that are tailored by legal counsel representing each party to the particular transaction.

With few exceptions, the postconstruction loan commitment will establish the legal and business terms and parameters for the postconstruction financing and, to some extent, for the construction loan also, because the postconstruction lender (Ace) may refuse to "take out" (pay off) the construction loan (by FNB) unless the terms and conditions of the postconstruction loan commitment have been met. Moreover, prior to foreclosure, the mortgage or deed of trust merely implements, or "tracks," the terms of the commitment, because the language of the mortgage, unless otherwise agreed, must be consistent with the commitment. Except for standard provisions that are customary in a particular geographical area, no essential conditions or provisions omitted from the commitment letter can be foisted on the borrower by means of language in the mortgage or deed of trust. See Chapter 4B.

The discussion that follows analyzes some of the essential terms of a postconstruction loan commitment letter that will govern the parties' relationship during the period of repayment of the loan. These terms, therefore, will be included in the note and in some cases the mortgage or deed of trust.

At this point, you should scan the provisions of the sample mortgage note and the fee mortgage and deed of trust in the Documents Manual to get a feel for the terms of these basic loan documents.

A. POSTCLOSING TERMS OF MORTGAGE FINANCING

1. *The Rate of Interest*

In today's creative real estate financing environment, the straight fixed interest rate mortgage is but one of many techniques used to finance income-producing real estate. Real estate financing has changed dramatically since the 1960s, the decade that marked the beginning of substantial inflation in the United States. The rampant inflation and volatility of interest rates from 1979 to 1981 made life insurance companies, thrift organizations, pension funds, and other traditional long-term postconstruction lenders increasingly disenchanted with long-term fixed rate mortgages and deeds of trust. See Strum, Current Trends in Institutional Financing of Real Estate in the United States, 17 Real Prop., Prob. & Tr. J. 486 (1982). Today's multitude of possible financing approaches makes the task of the real estate lawyer far more interesting—and far more complex.

Most real estate financing techniques fit somewhere within a debt-equity spectrum that ranges from the traditional long-term fixed rate mortgage to pure equity financing. See Table 5-1. As illustrated in Table 5-1, postconstruction lenders may not be content with fixed rates of return on their mortgage loan investments and may instead (or in addition, as a hedge against inflation) require a contingent rate of interest or even an ownership (equity) interest in the property. During the inflationary period of 1979-1981, some lenders would only make a mortgage loan if they acquired an equity interest in the mortgaged property. Such equity-sharing arrangements usually consist of a "joint venture," whereby the lender purchases an interest in the property and creates a general or limited partnership, or other ownership entity, between itself and the developer, or a convertible mortgage, whereby the lender reserves the right to convert some or all of the mortgage indebtedness into a partnership or other equity interest or, alternatively, obtains an option to purchase all or part of the mortgaged property during the term of the loan.

Lenders might alternatively insist on the so-called participating mortgage whereby the lender's investment return is contingent on the income and/or appreciation in the value of the mortgaged property. While situated on the debt side of the debt-equity spectrum, the participating mortgage represents a kind of "debt joint venture" because the lender is allowed to share in the profits from the venture but the borrower nevertheless retains most of the incidents of ownership including the tax benefits, control over management decisions, and most if not all of the appreciation.

Table 5 – 1

The Debt-Equity Spectrum

PURE DEBT→ FINANCING	PARTICIPATING→ MORTGAGES	POTENTIAL→ EQUITY	PURE EQUITY FINANCING
	(borrower shares income with lender but retains ownership, tax benefits, and management control)		(lender shares ownership, and tax benefits, and management control)
1) Fixed Rate Mortgage	1) Contingent Interest Mortgage	1) Convertible Mortgages	1) Joint Venture
2) Variable Rate Mortgage	2) Shared Appreciation Mortgage		

The following is a typical interest payment provision from a mortgage note pursuant to a postconstruction loan commitment that contemplates a fixed rate mortgage loan with no participation in income or appreciation:

> Commencing on the date of this Note, interest shall accrue at the rate of _____ per annum on the unpaid principal balance of this Note.
> Commencing on the first day of _____ and continuing on the first day of each calendar month thereafter, to and including the first day of _____, principal and interest shall be paid in equal monthly installments in the amount of _____ each.
> The entire unpaid principal balance of this Note, together with all accrued and unpaid interest thereon, shall, if not sooner paid, be due and payable on the first day of _____. Each monthly installment when paid, shall be applied first to interest and the balance of each monthly installment shall be applied in reduction of the unpaid principal balance of this Note.

If a postconstruction lender is dissatisfied with a straight fixed rate return, a plethora of contingent return approaches can make interest rates more responsive to changing market conditions. For example, in addition to a fixed rate of interest, a lender might require a so-called kicker whereby it would receive, as contingent interest, a percentage of the gross income (receipts) or net income (cash flow) from the property or a percentage of the gain based on appreciation in the value of the mortgaged property when it is sold or refinanced. The following is a sample contingent interest clause (excerpted from a commitment letter) that is geared to the gross income from the property, along with a typical audit provision, which entitles the lender to monitor the financial operation of the property to assure itself that the borrower is complying with its obligation to pay the agreed-on amount of contingent interest.

Additional Interest. In addition to payments of the fixed monthly installments as herein-above provided, Borrower shall pay Lender annually, as additional interest, within thirty days after the expiration of each fiscal year of Borrower, a sum equal to 25% of the amount, if any, by which the gross income from the Property in such fiscal year shall exceed $ _____. Additional interest for any partial fiscal year shall be pro rated. The term "gross income" as used herein shall mean the total revenue derived from the Property by Borrower as owner, from rents for the use and occupancy of space in the building, fees from parking facilities, and charges, if any, for heating, air conditioning, and utilities, without any deductions whatsoever except that (1) tax increases after the first full year in which the property shall be assessed as a completed building and (2) insurance premium increases after the first year in which the Property shall be occupied as a completed building shall be deducted from gross income before computing the additional interest.

Audit. The mortgage documents shall contain a covenant requiring the mortgagor, without expense to us [lender], to deliver to us (a) within 30 days after the expiration of each fiscal year of the mortgagor, a written statement signed by the mortgagor setting forth in reasonable detail the gross income for such fiscal year, (b) within 90 days after the close of such fiscal year, an annual audit of the operation of the Real Property, showing in complete detail total income received and total expenses, together with annual balance sheets and profit and loss statements, prepared and certified by a certified public accountant, and (c) such rent rolls and interim balance sheets and profit and loss statements as may be required by us. The mortgage documents shall contain further covenants by the mortgagor (i) permitting us at any time to examine the books, records and accounts of the mortgagor in so far as they relate to the Real Property, and to make copies thereof, (ii) requiring the mortgagor to exhibit such books, accounts and records to us or to any person designated by us for that purpose, and (iii) if any such audit by us or any person designated by us discloses that the actual gross income for any fiscal year exceeded that reported to us by more than _____%, that the mortgagor shall pay the cost of such audit.

Uri, The Participating Mortgage: Spreading the Risks and Rewards of Ownership
5 Real Est. Fin. 37 (Spring 1988)

GENERAL CHARACTERISTICS

In its generic form, a participating mortgage is a real estate loan with a normal coupon interest rate, and additional or contingent interest in the form of a percentage of the cash flow, refinancing proceeds, sales proceeds and, if applicable, casualty and condemnation proceeds related to a particular property. The additional or contingent interest is also known as the participation or profits interest.

A participating mortgage is a debt instrument: the loan investor is the lender, and the real estate investor is the owner/borrower. Generally, both the loan amount and the loan-to-value ratio are higher than those achievable with a conventional mortgage loan. The coupon interest rate is usually lower. The higher loan amount and lower coupon rate compensate the owner for relinquishing a percentage of its ownership rewards to the lender, and for the lender's priority of payment. Because the loan is secured debt, not equity, the lender is entitled to its return (i.e., currently due principal, coupon interest and participation interest) prior to the receipt of any proceeds by the borrower. Conversely, the lender's additional contingent interest is its compensation for providing full financing at below-market rates and thereby assuming a higher degree of risk.

The participating mortgage loan appears to be a fairly simple transaction. In practice, however, it is an inherently complex financing tool that should be pursued only by sophisticated real estate players.

The participation interest is usually calculated pursuant to an agreed-upon formula included in the loan documents. There are normally several different transactions, events, or time periods that may trigger calculation and payment of the participation. For example, it may be due and paid:

- monthly based upon project cash flow;
- upon repayment of the loan;
- upon refinancing with a new and subordinate loan;
- upon sale of the property;
- upon receipt of condemnation awards or casualty insurance proceeds; and/or
- upon maturity of the loan.

The negotiations that establish the basic structure of a participating mortgage are often arduous.

A CONDUCIVE ENVIRONMENT

Participating mortgages usually gain in popularity during periods of high market interest rates, such as between 1981 and 1985 in the U.S. In such an environment, the flow of investment capital generally and real estate investment capital in particular is severely curtailed. Many lending institutions, including commercial banks, thrifts and life insurance companies, suffer disintermediation and are forced, through actions of the Federal Reserve, to tighten credit policies and thereby restrict the amount of funds available for real estate and other investments. These institutions also shift a higher proportion of their investment portfolios to higher yielding, safer, fixed income investments such as high-grade government and corporate bonds.

More [important], it is difficult to justify the economics of a real estate project during periods of high interest rates, when the real estate developer or investor normally is faced with negative leverage. This occurs when the cost of debt expressed as a percent is greater than the ratio of the project's net operating income (i.e., gross income less vacancy and operating expenses) to its cost. In addition, interest expense, included as part of the "soft costs" of development, typically comprise 10 percent to 20 percent of the total development budget. As interest rates rise, costs can mushroom, making the project uneconomical.

Thus, a developer or investor may have difficulty finding a conventional mortgage loan without a large infusion of equity. Yet, at the same time, high financing rates reduce the return available to equity investors, thereby making equity investment more difficult to attract.

In a high interest rate environment, the lender and borrower may structure a participating loan with the coupon rate lowered to achieve a 1:1 debt coverage ratio, i.e., the project's net operating income is equal to current debt service. (As noted above, negative leverage occurs when the ratio is less than one with 100 percent financing.) Although the coupon rate on such a loan is lower than the market rate, the lender derives additional yield from its future profits interest. Furthermore, the lower rate permits a development cost budget that is both reasonable and financable. . . .

[The participating mortgage device enables real estate investors] to obtain high leverage with little or no equity investment—something few lenders are generally willing to permit. By using the participating mortgage structure, however, the lender is able to create a potentially more profitable and safer transaction. In lieu of cash equity, the lender may negotiate recourse provisions and other guarantees, and/or direct any excess cash flow to principal amortization or to a sinking fund. The participating mortgage also permits institutional mortgage investors, many of whom lack the market prowess, management capabilities and entrepreneurial insight to locate and enhance the value of real estate projects on their own, to share in some of the rewards of ownership.

THE LENDER'S PERSPECTIVE

From the lender's perspective, the participating loan provides the opportunity to achieve a higher overall rate of return (generally 20-30 percent) over a five- to ten-year holding period. The participation interest also gives the lender an inflation hedge since the return from the participation interest will increase as rents and net cash flow increase.

The potential for higher returns also entails a higher degree of risk—a result of the higher loan-to-value ratio and the contingent nature of the participation interest. Usually, the lender will fund 100 percent of acquisition costs, or 80 percent to 90 percent of appraisal value for a development project. The higher the level of debt, the greater the risk of nonpayment and monetary loss to the lender. The risks are mitigated by the lender's due diligence on the project, the market and the borrower. The due diligence process requires a thorough review and an in-depth understanding of the project economics, the market, the lease structure and the physical condition of the property, and the experience of the owner/borrower.

The participating loan as discussed here provides the lender with additional security because it is a debt obligation secured by a recorded mortgage or deed of trust. This structure is in contrast to a joint venture investment that is considered as equity, not debt. Normally, however, the borrower will not be required to invest cash equity. While this does not by itself make the transaction precarious, it does reduce the borrower's incentive to maintain and enhance the value of the real estate. . . .

THE BORROWER'S PERSPECTIVE

From the borrower's perspective, a well-structured [participating] loan may be the most useful real estate financing tool available. The owner can obtain 100 percent financing with little or no equity investment, and can achieve an infinite rate of return.

The disadvantage of putting in no equity is that most likely the lender will require the owner to guarantee all or a portion of the loan. This recourse is necessary to give the owner some incentive to maintain and enhance the value of the property. The guarantee also provides a degree of protection to the lender, which advances 100 percent of the funds but must wait to receive the majority of its return from the property's future profits.

Another disadvantage is that a participating mortgage generally subjects the owner to numerous loan requirements that severely limit the owner's flexibility. For example, the loan documents usually place restrictions on prepayment rights [see Chapter 5A4 infra], sale of the project, execution of new leases, and the use of casualty or condemnation proceeds [see Chapter 5A6]. It may also require the lender's approval for major repairs. . . .

CURRENT CASH FLOW

In addition to the stated interest rate on the mortgage, the participating lender usually receives a portion of the project's net cash flow (see Table 1). The amount of this interest and the frequency of payment (monthly, quarterly, annually) are subject to negotiation, and there is an infinite variety of ways to calculate the amount to be paid.

Federal tax regulations restrict the ability of many institutions, particularly pension plans and REITs [real estate investment trusts], to receive income from an interest in a property's net cash flow. Under certain circumstances, these institutions may be subject to tax on income received from non-passive sources, for example, from residual cash flow or profits that accrue to owners. To comply with these regulations, such institutions generally seek to structure their cash flow participation interest as either a percentage of the property's gross income (which is considered passive), or as a percentage of gross income in excess of a specified floor amount.[1] . . .

FUTURE PROPERTY PROFITS

In addition to an interest in the property's current cash flow, [sometimes] the [participating] lender also receives an interest in the future profits generated by a capital transaction—primarily sale or refinancing of the property or maturity of the loan. In all of these events, the most critical factor for both lender and borrower is the determination of the value of the participation interest.

Upon refinancing (or the addition of a new loan subordinate to the existing participating mortgage), the lender will receive the negotiated percentage of the proceeds of the new financing. In a typical refinancing, this will be calculated as the gross amount of the new loan, less reasonable and necessary closing costs and the balance of the participating mortgage. The loan base for future calculations of any remaining participation interest becomes the new loan amount. Most participating loans restrict the borrower's prepayment rights to prevent refinancing without payment of the participating interest. In the event of any addition of new debt, the lender usually will retain a profit interest subordinate to that of the new mortgagee. The subordinate interest will then be held and paid upon maturity of the original participating mortgage.

Table 1

Typical Calculation of Lender's Participation Interest in Property Cash Flow

Net operating income before debt service	$5,000,000.00
Debt service (based on coupon rate)	4,000,000.00
Net distributable cash flow	$1,000,000.00
Lender's participation interest (50%)	× .50
Additional interest payable to lender	$ 500,000.00

---

1. REITs are discussed at Chapter 15A.—EDS.

Table 2

Typical Calculation of Lender's Participation
Interest upon Property Sale

Gross sales price	$20,000,000.00
Closing costs	250,000.00
Participating mortgage principal balance	$16,000,000.00
Net distributable sales proceeds	$ 3,750,000.00
Lender's participation interest (50%)	× .50
Sales proceeds payable to lender	$ 1,875,000.00

Upon a sale of the property, the lender is paid the remaining principal balance of the mortgage loan, plus its future profits interest. In negotiating the original loan documents, the lender must take care to protect its position by establishing strict guidelines to police any sales transaction. For example, the loan documents should:

- give the lender the right to approve the sale;
- preclude any sale to a buyer affiliated with the borrower;
- require that the sales price be determined pursuant to arm's-length negotiations as evidenced by a purchase contract;
- require that the entire arrangement be a bona fide sales transaction.

These provisions will protect the lender from a bogus or dummy sale engineered by the borrower to escape payment of the participation interest.

Once the property has been sold, the lender will receive as its participation interest the negotiated percentage of the net value of the property, i.e., the contract sales price, less reasonable closing costs and the principal balance of the participating mortgage (see Table 2) . . . .

NOTES AND QUESTIONS

1. The Participating Mortgage: Risks and Rewards. As a rule, participating arrangements between borrowers and lenders become more popular during periods of high interest rates, when the supply of mortgage money declines. This is what happened during the credit crunch of 1980-1982. During such tight-money periods, high fixed rate mortgage loans may require debt-service payments that exceed the free and clear rate of return from the property. When confronted with the specter of negative leverage, or worse, a negative cash flow, developers may be willing to sacrifice a share of the future increases in cash flow (or a share of refinancing or sale proceeds) by means of a participating mortgage, for the sake of obtaining an initial below-market fixed rate of interest and a correspondingly sufficient amount of cash flow at the beginning of the project. Otherwise, the project may have to be abandoned as unfeasible if there is not enough cash flow to attract outside equity investors and pay the operating expenses of the venture. Don't forget that when interest rates increase, so do capitalization rates (see Chapter 4D1), which means lower valuations and loan amounts. Borrowers accordingly become more dependent on outside equity capital as a funding source unless the rental income from (and value of) the project increases because of some inflation hedge such as a percentage rental (see Chapter 10A1).

Moreover, just like a commercial tenant that agrees to pay a fixed rent plus a percentage rental (in lieu of a higher fixed rent), a developer-borrower may not mind sharing its profits and gains with the lender if gross receipts were to escalate because of inflation or if its profits should increase because the project is doing well, because the developer knows that the converse is also true—the total (fixed plus contingent) interest will decline if gross receipts or profits shrink because of a recession or lack of business success. In other words, such profit-sharing arrangements may constitute a hedge against inflation for the lender, but they also act as a hedge against recession for the developer.

On the other hand, when interest rates are declining or are already relatively low (in comparison to the free and clear rate of return from the mortgaged property), developers generally prefer to pay the fixed market rate of interest rather than enter into a participation arrangement that will dilute their profits and gains from the property.

As suggested in the excerpt by Uri, any prudent postconstruction lender that makes a participating loan will attempt to prohibit the sale of the property during the term of the loan. By way of analogy, a landlord who receives a percentage rental would likewise fetter the right of the tenant to assign or sublet without the landlord's consent. See Chapter 10A4. Why are these restrictions necessary to protect the interest of a lender or landlord who is receiving a contingent return based on the income property? From the borrower's perspective, can you think of any compromise language (less stringent than a flat prohibition against the sale of the property) that would address the legitimate concerns of the lender and not render the property unmarketable during the loan term?

2. Contingent Interest Based on Gross Income. Real estate borrowers such as Dan Developer are apt to object strenuously to any contingent interest clause that is geared to gross (as opposed to net) income, while postconstruction lenders such as Ace may insist on the former type of kicker in a participating mortgage. Why? In the master hypothetical, Dan might insist that the occupancy leases provide for escalations of rentals based on any increase in local property taxes, insurance premiums, operational expenses, or some cost of living index such as the Consumer Price Index. However, each such rent escalation payment will itself increase Dan's gross income and could increase the amount of the contingent interest payment to Ace. Observe that the gross income clause excerpted supra (captioned Additional Interest) provides that rent escalations for tax and insurance premium increases are excluded from the definition of gross income. Should Dan insist that the definition of gross income for contingent interest purposes also exclude any other of these increases (resulting from an escalation clause) in his gross income? See Richman, Negotiating Operating Expense Provisions in Office Leases, 18 Real Est. Rev. 44 (Fall 1988).

The gross income clause excerpted above provides for contingent interest equal to 25 percent of the gross income in excess of a yet-to-be negotiated floor amount. If Ace were to propose such an onerous provision, Dan would undoubtedly make every effort to negotiate as high a floor amount as possible. At a minimum, he would insist that the floor amount be sufficient to cover his estimated operating expenses and debt service payments and that it provide a cushion for unanticipated contingencies. In addition to a floor amount, what additional limitation on contingent interest might Dan try to obtain in his negotiations with Ace?

3. Contingent Interest Based on Net Income. From the borrower's perspective, a contingent interest clause based on net income is both fairer and safer than one based on gross income, because the borrower will have to share with the lender only that portion of its income that exceeds its debt service payments and other operating expenses. From a lender's point of view, however, the net income approach has serious drawbacks that, taken together, make it the less desirable alternative. Drafting the definition of net income is itself a major undertaking. Merely providing that contingent interest equals a percentage of net income is an open invitation to litigation since the parties most probably will disagree on what items should be deducted from gross income to arrive at net income. See, for example, Mileage Realty Co. v. Miami Parking Garage, 146 So. 2d 403 (1962), cert. denied, 153 So. 2d 307 (Fla. 1963) (involving, by way of analogy, a contingent rental based on profits in a percentage lease). A prudent lender will demand a comprehensive definitional clause that starts with a broad definition of gross income and then specifies with particularity the various deductions that should be subtracted to arrive at the net income amount.

Even with an adequate definition, the lender will be concerned about how to enforce the clause and will undoubtedly insist on annual audited financial statements from an independent certified public accountant approved by it. See the sample audit provision on page 260. Any participating lender should be cautioned against undue reliance on such a statement to ensure compliance, because the financial statements will not reveal, for example, whether Dan is paying a market rate for cleaning services or is paying a premium to the cleaning company in exchange for obtaining such services at a discount in other buildings Dan owns that are not covered by the participating mortgage. In addition, the borrower's financial statements may not reveal whether the borrower is paying for services that are not being performed, packing the office staff with relatives in no-show jobs, or including a personal automobile on the building's insurance policy. What can a prudent lender do to protect against such potential abuses by the borrower?

In addition, a participating mortgage based on profits rather than on gross income would render the debt financing arrangement more vulnerable to a recharacterization as equity by the Internal Revenue Service as well as to litigation against the lender by third-party creditors and tort plaintiffs on the theory that the profit-sharing arrangement is in substance a partnership between the lender and the borrower, especially if the lender participated in the control of the venture to protect its profit share. See generally Kelley, Advantages of Participating Mortgages, 17 Real Est. Rev. 54 (Spring 1987).

4. Convertible Mortgages. In its simplest form, the convertible mortgage is a hybrid financing device that combines a debt feature (in the form of a traditional postconstruction loan to the borrower at a below-market rate) with an equity feature (in the form of a lender's option to purchase all or a portion of the mortgaged property at some future time). An example of a convertible mortgage is the long-term loan in the amount of $815 million obtained by Sears, Roebuck & Company in 1989 that was secured by a first mortgage lien on its 110-story headquarters tower in Chicago. According to Wall Street analysts, the annual interest rate was fixed at about 6 percent (as compared to the then-prevailing rate of about 9 percent for large blue-chip corporate borrowers). In exchange for the below-market rate, the lending group (headed by a subsidiary of Prudential Insurance Company of America) received an option to purchase the Sears Tower at the end of the 15-year loan term. Sears was to receive a share in any appreciation in the value of the building, and because of interest deductions it expected to reduce its annual after-tax cost of borrowing the money to less than 5 percent during the term of the loan. N.Y. Times, Nov. 16, 1989, at D1, col. 4. Dreams for substantial appreciation apparently went unrealized. The Tower sold in 1997 for a reported $804 million. After the September 11th attacks devalued trophy properties, that buyer transferred ownership to its mortgage lender, MetLife, which sold the Tower in 2004 for a reported $835 million. In 2007, the new owners refinanced their variable-rate purchase money loan with a 10-year, $780 million loan from a Swiss bank at the fixed rate of 6.26 percent. The Tower appraised at $1.2 billion.

One of the pitfalls of the convertible mortgage is the common law restriction against "clogging the mortgagor's equity of redemption." Under this public policy doctrine, the courts protect against agreements by which the mortgagor, at the time of the original loan transaction, surrenders the right to redeem (pay off) the loan following default to avoid loss of the mortgaged property. Rather, the mortgagee must exercise its foreclosure rights to extinguish the mortgagor's right to redeem. See generally Restatement (Third) of Property (Mortgages) §3.1 (1997).

Some courts have applied this doctrine to invalidate a mortgagee's option to purchase the mortgaged property when that option is granted concurrently with a mortgage on the same property. See, for example, Star Enters. v. Thomas, 783 F.

Supp. 1564 (D.R.I. 1992); Humble Oil & Refining Co. v. Doerr, 123 N.J. Super. 530, 303 A.2d 898 (1973). However, some state statutes exempt certain convertible mortgages from the anticlogging rule and permit them to be governed by freedom of contract principles. See, for example, Cal. Civ. Code §2906 (validating option to purchase in favor of mortgagee where exercise of option is not conditioned on occurrence of default by borrower and the real property is nonresidential); N.Y. Gen. Oblig. L. §5-334 (validates convertible mortgages in which the loan amount is over $2.5 million and the option is not dependent upon the occurrence of a default).

For additional background on the clogging issue, see Licht, The Clog on the Equity of Redemption and Its Effect on Modern Real Estate Finance, 60 St. John's L. Rev. 452 (1986); Mailer, Financing Ideas, Unclogging the Equity of Redemption, 14 Real Est. L.J. 161 (1985); Preble and Cartwright, Convertible and Shared Appreciation Loans: Unclogging the Equity of Redemption, 20 Real Prop., Prob. & Tr. J. 821 (1985); and Siegman and Linquanti, The Convertible Participating Mortgage: Planning Opportunities and Legal Pitfalls in Structuring the Transaction, 54 U. Colo. L. Rev. 295 (1983).

For additional pitfalls of the convertible mortgage device, see Welborn, Convertible Mortgages: Legal and Drafting Issues, ALI-ABA 2 Modern Real Estate Transactions 1191 (7th ed. 1986).

5. Joint Ventures. In our master hypothetical, Dan Developer may find it difficult in times of tight money or adverse economic conditions to obtain sufficient long-term postconstruction financing. In addition, Dan may not be able to raise the necessary equity capital to cover the shortfall between the amount of the postconstruction loan and the cost of the project. To meet this problem, Dan may propose to Ace Insurance Company that Ace purchase an interest in the equity as a partner in a joint venture owning the property and make a postconstruction loan to the proposed joint venture.

The real estate joint venture actually antedated the convertible mortgage by almost 15 years, having emerged in the late 1960s from what, at the time, were turbulent market conditions. Although both convertible mortgages and participating mortgages have become permanent fixtures on the real estate financing scene, equity participations structured as joint ventures have waned since the early 1980s, primarily because of a conflict in investment philosophy between lenders (who, at the risk of overgeneralizing, want to share in the rewards of ownership but are conservative about risk taking) and developers (who are aggressive risk takers but abhor loss of management control).

The overwhelming majority of equity participations structured as joint ventures between developers and institutional lenders have been organized as either limited or general partnerships. With the advent of real estate joint ventures, the lender found itself in the position not only of a mortgagee but also of a partner in the borrowing entity. Because the interests of the borrower and lender often are not consistent, the joint venture scenario contains some inherent conflicts that could result in lender liability suits. In the famous case of Meinhard

v. Salmon, 249 N.Y. 458, 164 N.E. 545 (1928), Judge Cardozo eloquently articulated the fiduciary duty of loyalty owed to a coventurer: "A [coventurer] is held to something stricter than the morals of the marketplace. Not honesty alone, but the punctilio of an honor the most sensitive, is then the standard of behavior."

While it is easy to agree that partners owe a duty of loyalty to each other, it is more difficult to determine the line between the legitimate right of a partner to protect her own interest and the partner's obligation of loyalty to the copartner. This difficulty worsens in the context of the modern financing joint venture. The following are two examples of problems that can arise.

a. Assume in the master hypothetical that the office building being constructed will be owned by a joint venture ("Law Drive Associates") composed of Dan Developer and Ace Insurance Company as general partners. Assume there is a substantial amount of vacant or undeveloped land near the venture property. If the venture is a success, the adjacent land probably will increase in value and become the site for developments less risky than this one. If Dan were to acquire this adjacent land without informing Ace, hoping to make a killing after the present building became successful, would he be violating his fiduciary obligation to Ace? Would it help Dan if he had owned the adjacent land at the time the venture was formed? How could Ace protect itself in the documentation of the joint venture?

b. Assume the Law Drive joint venture is formed before construction commences. The venture executed a commitment with Ace for a postconstruction loan at 14 percent, slightly below the market rate at the time of commitment. By the time construction is completed, market interest rates have dropped to 11 percent. Assume further that if the borrower does not take down the loan, it forfeits its commitment fee and that the loss of the commitment fee is much less than the present value of the interest differential. Does Ace have a duty as a partner to vote to "walk" from the commitment and forfeit the fee? If Ace management voted to reject the loan, would they then be in breach of their obligations to Ace's own stockholders or policyholders? Assume the commitment provided for remedies in addition to liquidated damages (see discussion at Chapter 4C1). Is Ace under any obligation not to enforce its rights against the partnership as mortgage lender under the commitment? Would Ace be in a better position if the joint venture agreement expressly provided for taking down the Ace loan?

For further discussion of joint ventures, see Barach, A Practical Guide to Equity Participation Loans: Legal Principles and Drafting Considerations, 20 Real Est. L.J. 115 (1991); Behrens, Joint Venturing in Real Estate, 20 Real Est. Rev. 64 (Spring 1990); Casey and Norcross, Structuring Real Estate Joint Ventures, 6 Prac. Real Est. Law. 41 (Nov. 1990); Roegge, Talbot, and Zinman, Real Estate Equity Investments and the Institutional Lender: Nothing Ventured, Nothing Gained, 39 Fordham L. Rev. 579 (1971).

6. The Usury Constraint on the Rate of Interest. In biblical times, before the "time value of money" concept was appreciated, the word "usury" meant the taking of interest—any interest—for the use of borrowed funds. With few exceptions, usury in this broad sense was forbidden. Psalm 15 seems to convey the spirit of this biblical proscription: "Lord who shall abide in thy tabernacle? Who shall dwell on thy holy hill?. . . He that putteth not out his money to usury. . . ." It was not until the late Middle Ages that a distinction arose between the taking of interest, which was deemed lawful, and the exaction of excessive interest, which was unlawful usury.

The early revulsion concerning the receipt of interest was probably due to the fact that most borrowers were hard-pressed or poverty-stricken individuals funding their personal, family, or household needs. Accordingly, the underlying rationale against the taking of interest was undoubtedly protection of the necessitous borrower. Much of our modern usury legislation is still based on this rationale.

As businesses began to borrow for the purpose of making money, however, it became apparent that using or borrowing someone's money to be able to manufacture, say, widgets for sale was not much different than using or leasing someone's factory for making the widgets, or using or leasing someone's horses or trucks for transporting the widgets. It began to be understood that there was no moral or ethical reason to prohibit a charge for the use of money in this context.

While the price for factory space or transportation equipment was generally determined by the law of supply and demand, the price of money, with the early biblical injunctions in mind, was regulated by statutes known as usury laws. Many of these statutes imposed artificial limits on the price of money, a requirement that has often produced counterproductive results. From the standpoint of real estate entrepreneurs, artificial limits on interest have contributed to the tightening of available credit, forcing them either to adopt cumbersome financing structures to avoid the application of the usury laws or to abandon otherwise sound development projects.

As explained by Mendes Hershman in Usury and the Tight Mortgage Market, 22 Bus. Law. 333, 336-338 (1967), the common definitional elements of usury, all of which must be present to establish usury, consist of (1) an agreement to lend money or its equivalent or to forbear to require repayment for a period of time; (2) the borrower's obligation to repay absolutely and not contingently; (3) the exaction of a greater compensation for making the loan or agreeing to forbear than is allowed by the applicable state constitution or usury statute; and (4) an intention to violate the usury statute. As suggested by the first element, usury laws generally apply only to transactions that are structured as loans. Therefore, one advantage of this "form over substance" approach for borrowers and lenders is that nondebt financing techniques such as the installment land contract, sale and leaseback, and tax-free exchange are generally outside the scope of the usury laws. The second element means that the borrower must have an absolute obligation to repay the debt and the interest payable on the debt. Can you think of the rationale for this requirement? As pointed out by Hershman, the last definitional requirement (intent) should not be construed too literally inasmuch as the lender need not actually intend to commit usury. Under case law, the lender's intent to collect the money is usually enough. Id. at 336.

In an attempt to address the problems of usury laws as artificial limits on commercial credit, states traditionally exempted loans to corporate borrowers from usury law restrictions. In recent years, we have seen a further retrenchment of usury limitations, with states enacting exemptions for business loans generally and for loans over a specified dollar amount. The Uniform Land Security Interest Act would remove usury restrictions entirely for commercial loans and, if the state so elects, for certain consumer loans as well. Unif. Land Sec. Int. Act §403 (1985). In addition, by federal exemption, many state usury statutes no longer apply to first mortgage loans on residential real estate made by federally regulated institutions, which is important from our standpoint because residential real estate loans for purposes of this statute include apartment building loans. Depository Institutions Deregulation & Monetary Control Act of 1980, 12 U.S.C. §1735f-7. For a discussion of statutory exemptions and circumvention devices (such as incorporation of the borrower and invoking choice of law principles), see generally M. Madison, J. Dwyer, and S. Bender, The Law of Real Estate Financing §§5:23-5:24 (2016). The result of this deregulation has been to make usury a less serious problem in commercial lending. However, the penalties for committing usury can be onerous. For example, in Texas the borrower has the right to recover three times the amount of all interest "contracted for" in violation of the usury statutes, even if the interest has not been paid. Texas Fin. Code Ann. §305.001. Consequently, it is essential for lenders' attorneys to recognize what circumstances may render a loan usurious under applicable law. Likewise, to enable their clients to obtain mortgage financing, attorneys for borrowers must understand the usury laws so that they can participate in the process of structuring financing that will meet the requirements of the usury laws.

Apart from constraints imposed by usury laws, courts may regulate the reasonableness of interest rates under the equitable doctrine of unconscionability. See generally M. Madison, J. Dwyer, and S. Bender, The Law of Real Estate Financing §5:25 (2016); First Mut. Corp. v. Grammercy & Maine, Inc., 423 A.2d 680, 687 (N.J. Super. Ct. Law Div. 1980) (noting that courts have applied this doctrine even to corporate borrowers not entitled to the usury defense).

7. Wraparound Financing and Usury. So-called wraparound mortgages raise usury issues when they provide additional funds to the borrower. Under this arrangement, the "wraparound" mortgage is structured as a second mortgage whereby the wraparound lender makes a cash advance to the borrower (for example, of $50,000) and also agrees to make debt-service payments on the underlying first mortgage note balance (for example, $150,000) that otherwise would be made by the borrower. The face amount of the wraparound indebtedness is overstated (here as $200,000) so that the lien of the wraparound mortgage not only covers the new funds actually disbursed ($50,000) but also "wraps around" the unpaid balance ($150,000) on the existing first mortgage loan. As the wraparound mortgage interest rate (for example, 9 percent) is always higher than the rate on the first mortgage (for example, 6 percent), the wraparound lender is able to take advantage of the interest rate spread as to the unpaid balance on the first mortgage and thereby increase the effective rate of interest it earns on the additional funds that are actually disbursed. The usury question is which rate of interest is scrutinized: the face amount (9 percent) that the borrower pays on the entire wraparound indebtedness ($200,000) or the effective yield that the wrap lender receives on the funds ($50,000) that are actually advanced to the borrower. In deciding which argument makes more sense, don't forget that if a lender receives something of value (such as an equity kicker) in addition to the stated rate of interest, the additional compensation for the use of borrowed funds is generally treated as interest for usury purposes regardless of whether the additional compensation is arranged by means of a separate legal transaction. Compare Hool v. Rydholm, 467 So. 2d 1038 (Fla. Dist. Ct. App. 1985), with Mindlin v. Davis, 74 So. 2d 789 (Fla. 1954). See generally Galowitz, How to Use Wraparound Financing, 5 Real Est. L.J. 107, 124-125 (Fall 1976); Hershman, Usury and the "New Look" in Real Estate Financing, 4 Real Prop., Prob. & Tr. J. 315 (1969); Tanner, Usury Implications of Alternative Mortgage Instruments: The Uncertainty in Calculating Permissible Returns, 1986 B.Y.U. L. Rev. 1105, 1114-1116.

8. Late Payment Charges and Default Interest. Mortgage notes often encourage timely payment and compensate for costs incurred when borrowers pay late by imposing late payment charges and default interest. Often expressed as a percentage of the unpaid installment, the late fee is meant to compensate the lender for its internal costs in administering the delinquent borrower. By contrast, the default interest provision tends to increase the contract rate by a specified percentage (for example, 5 percent) after default in order to compensate the lender for its increased risk in dealing with a borrower that has defaulted, as well as for its potential lost opportunity costs in reinvesting the installment payment and its internal costs in administering a defaulted loan once accelerated (thereby ending the application of further late fees).

The mortgagee faces a variety of challenges to the validity of these provisions both outside of and in bankruptcy. In scrutinizing the fairness of late payment charges under state law, courts tend to apply the liquidated damages standard of reasonableness rather than the more lax unconscionability standard of exorbitance. Even under this more rigorous reasonableness review, oftentimes late payment charges withstand scrutiny if they are within industry custom. Compare Travelers Insurance Co. v. Corporex Properties, Inc., 798 F. Supp. 423 (E.D. Ky. 1992) (enforcing four percent late fee) and MetLife Capital Financial Corp. v. Washington Ave. Assocs. L.P., 159 N.J. 484, 732 A.2d 493 (1999) (upholding five percent late charge) with Ridgley v. Topa Thrift and Loan Association, 17 Cal. 4th 970, 953 P.2d 484, 73 Cal. Rptr. 2d 378 (1998) (striking down clause imposing charge of six months' interest if the borrower prepaid the loan and had made a prior late payment or otherwise defaulted under the loan). The allowance of late charges for residential loans may also be governed by more restrictive federal and state statutory and administrative requirements. E.g., 15 U.S.C. §1639 (prohibiting in high-cost residential mortgage loans any late fees exceeding 4 percent and also any default rate exceeding the contract rate); Cal. Civ. Code §2954.4 (limiting late fee to greater of $5 or 6 percent of late installment); N.Y. Real Prop. Law §254-b (imposing maximum fee of 2 percent of late installment).

In the case of default interest rates, courts more often apply the unconscionability standard of exorbitance than the liquidated damages standard of reasonableness. E.g., Citibank, N.A. v. Nyland (CF8) Ltd., 878 F.2d 620 (2d Cir. 1989); Chemical Bank v. American National Bank and Trust Co., 180 Ill. App. 3d 219, 535 N.E.2d 940 (1989) (seeing no reason to relieve the sophisticated borrower from default interest it agreed to); Emery v. Fishmarket Inn of Granite Springs, Inc., 173 A.D.2d 765, 570 N.Y.S.2d 821 (1991) (upholding rate increase on default from 8 to 18 percent). But see MetLife Capital Financial Corp. v. Washington Ave. Assocs. L.P., 159 N.J. 484, 732 A.2d 493 (1999) (subjecting default interest to reasonableness standard but upholding 3 percent increase as reasonable estimate of potential damages, as within the range of customary charges, and as the subject of negotiation between sophisticated commercial entities); Art Country Squire, L.L.C. v. Inland Mortgage Corporation, 745 N.E.2d 885 (Ind. Ct. App. 2001) (refusing to abandon a reasonableness test for default interest rates). Which standard seems most appropriate for default interest? For late fees? See generally Bender and Madison, The Enforceability of Default Interest in Real Estate Mortgages, 43 Real Prop. Tr. & Est. L.J. 199 (2008).

In bankruptcy, the mortgagee's rights to late fees and default interest are constrained by Section 506(b) of the Bankruptcy Code, which allows the lender "interest on [its mortgage loan balance] claim, and any *reasonable* fees, costs, or charges provided for under the agreement" (emphasis added). See Mack Financial Corp. v. Ireson, 789 F.2d 1083 (4th Cir. 1986) (in bankruptcy, late payment charges are enforceable under Section 506(b) if reasonable). Although default interest could be regarded as "interest" rather than as "fees, costs, or charges," most bankruptcy courts tend to invoke equitable considerations in subjecting default interest to scrutiny beyond the exorbitance standard. The outcomes under this bankruptcy review of the equities are case-specific and depend on such factors as prejudice to other parties and the prevailing industry standard. Compare In re Terry Limited Partnership, 27 F.3d 241 (7th Cir. 1994) (upholding default rate given testimony of demonstrated need and prevailing industry standard) with In re DWS Investments, Inc., 121 B.R. 845 (Bankr. C.D. Cal. 1990) (no evidence to show 25 percent default rate was industry standard or was related to actual or projected loss).

9. Alternative Mortgage Instruments and Inflation-Related Commercial Mortgage Devices. As a hedge against inflation and to make loans more affordable for borrowers, depository institutions that make home mortgage loans, such as thrift organizations, commercial banks, and credit unions, have originated and popularized a variety of innovative "alternative" residential mortgage devices. These devices employ formulas that require periodic adjustments of the interest rate and principal balance and may also allow some participation by the lender in the appreciation of the mortgaged real estate. While the adjustable interest rate format is commonly employed in construction financing, as of this writing alternative mortgage instruments are rarely used in postconstruction financing of commercial real estate, with the possible exception of the so-called variable rate mortgage (VRM). VRMs include different varieties of variable interest rates that are geared to some objective reference point, either domestic (for example, U.S. Treasury bill rates) or foreign (for example, Eurobond and the London Interbank Offered Rate rates), or simply renegotiated at regular intervals.

Alternative mortgage instruments such as the variable rate mortgage have become increasingly popular with residential borrowers as the affordability index for homeowners has decreased (because the average price of new and existing homes in the United States has been rising at a faster rate than household income). By contrast, most developers are reluctant to commit themselves to mortgages with floating rates (like the variable rate mortgage) during the postconstruction period after the mortgaged property becomes operational. How do you account for this difference in attitude? In commercial transactions, inflation-related mortgage devices sometimes used by institutional lenders as alternatives to the long-term fixed mortgage include the following.

a. Bullet Loans. These are relatively short-term loans (with 3- to 10-year terms) with provisions for periodic interest rate adjustments (for example, every 5 years) and with interest-only payments or with partial amortization based on long-term (for example, 25- to 35-year) amortization schedules. Sometimes bullet loans are structured as long-term loans (for example, 25-year term) with a so-called call provision permitting the lender to call in the loan after a stipulated period of time (for example, 10 years), at which time the borrower must satisfy the outstanding loan balance by refinancing or by selling the property. Originally, these loans were designed for developers without takeout commitments whose construction loans had expired and who could not immediately obtain adequate postconstruction financing. At present, these loans are being made primarily by life insurance companies to developers who are purchasing or refinancing existing properties with strong rental schedules.

b. Mini-perms and Bowtie Loans. The mini-permanent loan, or mini-perm, is a combined construction-permanent loan that is relatively short-term (for example, 7 to 10 years) and converts from an interest-only construction loan to a (prenegotiated) fixed rate permanent loan once construction is completed. The principal advantage to the developer-borrower is that it has a number of years after construction is completed to negotiate a satisfactory postconstruction loan without paying a prepayment fee; moreover, based on the accumulating equity in the project, the borrower can refinance for a larger loan amount when interest rates decline and thereby pay off the mini-perm loan amount and cash out some tax-free equity.

The "bowtie loan" is attractive to developers because, while it features a floating rate (like the variable rate mortgage), it contains a cap on interest payments, so that any interest above a stipulated ceiling amount is deferred as a balloon payment that is not payable until the loan matures. Conversely, if rates should decline, the lower interest expenses may help offset declining revenues during a recession. These loans are made primarily by commercial banks, thrift organizations, and finance companies. They are usually short-term (for example, loan terms of 5 to 10 years), permit prepayment without a penalty, and are secured by second as well as first mortgage liens. They derive their name from the fact that their rates move up and down in irregular patterns.

c. Rollover Mortgages. Ordinarily, the rollover mortgage has a long-term amortization schedule (for example, 25 to 35 years), and because the term of the loan is so short (for example, 3 to 5 years) it is customary for the lender to extend, or "roll over," the loan for another short-term period at the prevailing market rate of interest for short-term loans if the borrower has not refinanced elsewhere.

10. Exotic and Subprime Loans. During the housing boom in 2004 and 2005, loan originations exploded, particularly among so-called subprime borrowers— those with poor credit histories and typically carrying a credit score below 620. In 2006, for example, subprime loans accounted for 20 percent of mortgage loans. In order to match borrowers with marginal incomes to inflated home prices, lenders and mortgage brokers developed many innovative ("exotic") but potentially disastrous loan products. Replacing the traditional down payment requirements were combination or piggyback financing plans that combined a traditional 80 percent of value loan with a 20 percent loan akin to a home equity loan product and carrying a higher interest rate. Adjustable rate loans shifted to the credit card model of teaser below-market fixed interest rates that float (become variable) after the teaser period expires. See generally Carrillo, Dangerous Loans: Consumer Challenges to Adjustable Rate Mortgages, 5 Berkeley Bus. L.J. 1 (2008) (describing exotic loans in California). Also mirroring the trend for credit card payments, some mortgage lenders implemented "flex" loans that allowed borrowers to choose their payment option each month—full amortization (see the discussion in the next section below), interest-only payments, or even a lesser payment with the unpaid interest added to the principal balance (known as negative amortization loans), or an entirely skipped payment with the same result. So-called no documentation, stated income, or, more cynically, liar loans, allowed the self-employed borrower aiming to increase his borrowing potential to specify his income without traditional documentation of tax returns and verification. Loans with variable or onerous fixed interest rates tended to carry prepayment penalties to effectively preclude a refinancing to a more favorable rate structure (see Chapter 5A4). In 2007, these subprime and exotic loans began failing at an alarming rate (see Chapter 15C), triggering highly publicized bankruptcies of loan originators and the tightening of loan underwriting standards to eliminate much of this easy mortgage money as investors on the mortgage securitization front stopped purchasing fractional interests in these loans. As with usury legislation, the disastrous subprime lending experience prompts the question of whether the law should disallow certain borrowers, many of them racial minorities, to borrow under oppressive terms and conditions the market is otherwise willing to extend. If you were a federal or state legislator looking to pick up the pieces of this mortgage meltdown, what approach might you take? Who is to blame for the subprime loan boom and bust? Lenders that dispensed with traditional loan underwriting safeguards? Mortgage brokers? Investors in the loan securitization markets? Credit rating agencies that facilitated securitization with favorable investment ratings? Appraisers whose appraisals fueled housing speculation? The borrowers themselves? Through the Dodd-Frank Wall Street Reform & Consumer Protection Act of 2010, Congress opted to discourage many popular varieties of exotic loans. For example, lenders must now obtain verifiable income documentation (in contrast to "stated income" loans) evidencing the borrower's ability to repay the mortgage loan.

Copyright © by Randy Glasbergen.
www.glasbergen.com

"As an alternative to the traditional 30-year mortgage, we also offer an interest-only mortgage, balloon mortgage, reverse mortgage, upside down mortgage, inside out mortgage, loop-de-loop mortgage, and the spinning double axel mortgage with a triple lutz."

2. The Amortization Period

Repayment of principal during the life of a loan is known as "amortization." Not many years ago, commercial real estate loans were for terms of 30 or more years and were "self-amortizing" in that the regular debt-service payments were sufficient to pay interest and repay the entire amount of the principal indebtedness by the maturity date. Such regular payments of principal and interest are called "constant" payments because the amount of each periodic debt-service payment remains the same during the life of a loan. As you can see from the amortization schedule in Table 5-2, the portion of the constant payment allocable to interest will decline and the remainder allocable to principal will increase over the life of the loan.

Under the master hypothetical, Dan Developer might have preferred a long-term self-amortizing loan of 30 years instead of the 15-year term he appears to be settling for because by prolonging the repayment period and reducing amortization Dan would lessen the amount of each debt-service payment. Also, if Dan expects interest rates to increase, he would want to "lock in" at the lower rate for the longest possible term. However lending institutions are no longer very tolerant of long-term fixed rate mortgages. In the late 1960s, most lending institutions began to foresee the inflationary period that lay ahead and began to shorten the terms of their loans. See ABA Sec. of Real Prop., Prob. & Tr. L., Financing Real Estate During the Inflationary 80s, at 23 (B. Strum ed., 1981). Thus, the average term to maturity for commercial loans declined from 21 years, 5 months in 1979 to 11 years, 2 months for retail projects, and a low of 7 years, 2 months for hotel/motel loans, in 2006.[2] Therefore, at the current time it may be unrealistic for Dan to request a loan term in excess of 15 years.

However, since the debt-service payments required to fully amortize a constant-payment loan in 15 years might be prohibitively expensive for Dan, he might request that the amortization schedule be recast over a period longer than the actual 15-year term of the loan, such as a 25-year period. This partially amortizing loan results in what is referred to as a "balloon" payment at the end of the 15-year term, that is, the unamortized portion of the principal balance that must be paid in a lump sum at the end of the loan term. Partially amortized loans have become increasingly popular with developers as loan terms have become shorter. While these loans reduce the developer's debt-service payments and increase the cash flow and equity yield to the developer and investors, the developer must either refinance the property at current rates or sell the property to satisfy the balloon indebtedness when the loan matures.

Table 5 – 2

15-Year Loan with 25-Year Amortization Schedule
Amortization Periods: 300 Loan Amount: $25 million
Rate: 5% Payment: $146,147.51

	First Year		
Payment	*Principal*	*Interest*	*Balance*
1	41,980.84	104,166.84	24,958,019.16
2	42,155.76	103,991.75	24,915,863.39
3	42,331.41	103,816.10	24,873,531.98
4	42,507.79	103,639.72	24,831,024.19

---

2. Figures based on data from American Council of Life Insurers.

5	42,684.91	103,462.60	24,788,339.28
6	42,862.76	103,284.75	24,745,476.51
7	43,041.36	103,106.15	24,702,435.15
8	43,220.70	102,926.81	24,659,214.46
9	43,400.78	102,746.73	24,615,813.67
10	43,581.62	102,565.89	24,572,232.05
11	43,763.21	102,384.30	24,528,468.84
12	43,945.56	102,201.95	24,484,523.29

Table 5-2 contains excerpts from the 25-year amortization schedule for Dan's 15-year loan from Ace Insurance Company. As you can see, an amortization schedule shows the loan amount, the interest rate, the amount that is due on each payment date, how that amount is allocated between payments of interest and payments of principal, and the principal balance after each payment. In this schedule, the constant payment is a monthly payment of $146,147.51. It is applied first to the payment of interest, and the remainder is then applied to the reduction of principal. Observe how the amounts applied to interest and principal vary over the months.

Tenth Year

Payment	Principal	Interest	Balance
109	65,777.54	80,369.97	19,223,014.31
110	66,051.62	80,095.89	19,156,962.70
111	66,326.83	79,820.68	19,090,635.86
112	66,603.19	79,544.32	19,024,032.67
113	66,880.71	79,266.80	18,957,151.96
114	67,159.38	78,988.13	18,889,992.58
115	67,439.21	78,708.30	18,822,553.38
116	67,720.20	78,427.31	18,754,833.17
117	68,002.37	78,145.14	18,686,830.80
118	68,285.72	77,861.79	18,618,545.08
119	68,570.24	77,577.27	18,549,974.84
120	68,855.95	77,291.56	18,481,118.90

Fifteenth Year

Payment	Principal	Interest	Balance
169	84,416.18	61,731.33	14,731,102.55
170	84,767.92	61,379.59	14,646,334.63
171	85,121.12	61,026.39	14,561,213.51
172	85,475.79	60,671.72	14,475,737.73
173	85,831.94	60,315.57	14,389,905.79
174	86,189.57	59,957.94	14,303,716.22
175	86,548.69	59,598.82	14,217,167.53
176	86,909.31	59,238.20	14,130,258.22
177	87,271.43	58,876.08	14,042,986.78
178	87,635.07	58,512.44	13,955,351.72
179	88,000.21	58,147.30	13,867,351.50
180	88,366.68	57,780.63	13,778,984.63

Had Dan been successful in convincing Ace to make the loan self-amortizing (with a loan term of 25 years instead of 15), the payments in the 25th year would have been as follows.

Twenty-Fifth Year

Payment	Principal	Interest	Balance
289	139,034.25	7,113.26	1,568,147.26
290	139,613.56	6,533.95	1,428,533.70
291	140,195.29	5,952.22	1,288,338.41
292	140,779.43	5,368.08	1,147,558.98
293	141,366.01	4,781.50	1,006,192.96
294	141,955.04	4,192.47	864,237.92
295	142,546.52	3,600.99	721,691.40
296	143,140.46	3,007.05	578,550.94
297	143,736.88	2,410.63	434,814.06
298	144,335.78	1,811.73	290,478.27
299	144,937.18	1,210.33	145,541.09
300	145,541.09	606.42	

NOTES AND QUESTIONS

1. Balloon Payments. Dan should be concerned about how he will make the balloon payment of $13,778,984 that will be due at the end of the 15-year loan term. Such a large payment might be too much of a drain on the cash reserves of Dan and his investors. Consequently, Dan probably will want to refinance the loan at maturity, that is, obtain a replacement loan from Ace or some other lender. Refinancing is discussed at Chapter 7A. However, if the supply of mortgage money is tight at the time, these funds might not be readily available. Moreover, even if the substitute loan funds are available, the terms of the refinanced loan could adversely affect the profitability of the property and even put the enterprise at risk if interest rates should be significantly higher. As observed at Chapter 4D1, if future interest rates were higher, this could mean higher capitalization rates. If the rental income stream remained relatively stable—under long-term leases, rental income does not always keep pace with capitalization rates—the application of higher capitalization rates might reduce the appraised value of the mortgaged property, perhaps to a point where the balloon payment exceeds the maximum amount allowable for the new loan under local law loan-to-value ratios. If this is the case, it might be incumbent on Dan to fund the shortfall with his own cash reserves (or with additional capital contributions from his investors). Alternatively, prior to maturity Dan might prefer to sell the property at a net sale price at least equal to the balloon payment amount.

Conversely, as Dan hopes and anticipates, his "equity" in the office building project (its appraised value less the amount of the Ace indebtedness) may start to accumulate because of (1) an increase in the value of the underlying land caused by inflation and (2) an increase in the value of the building caused by higher net operating income if rent should rise because of a greater demand for rental space, management efficiency, or simply because of inflation. If market rentals increase, Dan plans to renegotiate higher rentals with his short-term "secondary" tenants as their leases expire; he also hopes to negotiate for periodic increases in rent (geared to such indices as the Consumer Price Index, the Producers Price Index, or the rental component of the All Urban Consumers Index) with his long-term "prime" tenants that will take into account any increase in the rate of inflation. Based on such accumulation of equity, Dan might be able to refinance for a larger loan amount that will enable him to make not only the requisite balloon payment to Ace but also to "mortgage out" the excess refinancing proceeds in the form of tax-free cash to himself and his investors.

2. Call Provisions and Partial Amortization. In addition to shortening the term of the loan, some postconstruction lenders offer fixed rate loans with relatively long terms but reserve the right to "call in" the loan prior to the original maturity date as a hedge against inflation and loss of interest income due to an increase in prevailing interest rates. For example, many partially amortized loans are structured as long-term fixed rate loans (with 25- to 30-year amortization schedules) with perhaps a 10- to 15-year call provision. While the long-term amortization schedule makes the loan affordable to the borrower, the call provision ameliorates the lender's inflation and interest rate risk. See generally Ling and Peiser, Choosing Among Alternative Financing Structures: The Developer's Dilemma, 17 Real Est. Rev. 39, 40 (Summer 1987).

As a general rule, developer-borrowers are resistant to call provisions because, among other things, the financial uncertainty as to whether the mortgage will reach its full term could discourage a prospective purchaser who wants to assume the existing mortgage (and is willing to pay the current rate, as required by a due-on-sale clause, discussed at Chapter 5A8, infra). At a minimum, the developer-borrower should insist that any call provision provide adequate notice that the lender intends to exercise its privilege so that the borrower has a reasonable opportunity to refinance the loan elsewhere.

> ➢ *Problem 5-1*
> Returning to the master hypothetical, suppose Ace were to offer Dan either a 10-year interest-only loan at a fixed rate of interest (but with a call option at the end of the fifth year of the loan) or a 10-year loan at the same fixed rate, without a call option but with a requirement that Dan repay the principal based on a 20-year amortization schedule. As Dan's attorney, how would you assess (in nonmathematical terms) the relative risks and rewards of these financing alternatives for Dan as a prospective owner-borrower? ◄

3. Nonrecourse Loans and Carve-outs

As discussed at Chapter 3B3, some postconstruction lenders may be willing to extend mortgage financing on a nonrecourse basis by which the borrower does not assume personal liability for repayment and the lender agrees to look solely to its collateral if a default occurs. Don't get the false impression that the nonrecourse loan is a charitable gesture to the borrower—the nonrecourse lender will factor any additional risk into the interest rate and other loan terms that it offers the borrower. The nonrecourse lender nonetheless may be unwilling to assume certain risks and may insist that the borrower accept personal liability in specific circumstances. The following article examines the give-and-take process of negotiating "carve-outs" of such risks from the nonrecourse provision in the postconstruction loan commitment.

Morrison and Senn, Carving Up the "Carve-outs" in Nonrecourse Loans
9 Prob. & Prop. 8 (May/June 1995)

For decades, commercial real estate lenders made a common practice of extending nonrecourse mortgage loans that exculpated borrowers from personal liability for repayment. If the borrower defaulted, the lender's only recourse was a foreclosure sale of the mortgaged property. In contrast to a traditional loan, in which the lender could seek to enforce a deficiency judgment against the borrower's personal assets if the loan was not fully repaid from proceeds of the foreclosure sale, the borrower was exculpated from personal liability for defaults such as nonpayment of principal and interest, breach of its representations, or violation of its covenants.

Lenders soon found that exculpation enabled a borrower to neglect or even abandon an unprofitable property and to impose on the lender the risk that the property might be worth less than the unpaid loan. As a result, lenders identified defaults that posed special risks and carved them out of the general nonrecourse provision. For those defaults, lenders reserved the right to sue the borrower personally.

Despite their risks to lenders, nonrecourse loans are well established; what has changed in recent years is the growing number of exceptions to the nonrecourse concept. Not only do these exceptions arise in new nonrecourse loans, but lenders are also renegotiating the nonrecourse carve-outs as a condition to restructuring older loans. Consequently, lawyers must focus renewed attention on the boundaries of the borrower's liability and the lender's risk.

COMPLETE LOSS OF EXCULPATION

Many lenders are now providing that their loans are fully recourse . . . if certain defaults occur. Usually those defaults relate to conduct that is blameworthy or at least within the borrower's control. The prospect of full recourse is meant to ensure the borrower's compliance with provisions that the lender deems essential to its bargain. . . .

• *Sale or subsequent encumbrance.* Believing that the borrower's identity and capability are material inducements for the loan, lenders often reserve recourse liability in the event of an unpermitted sale of the property. Recourse liability also deters attempts to avoid the consequences of violating due-on-sale provisions [see Chapter 5A8, infra], such as [the imposition of] prepayment premiums [see Chapter 5A4, infra]. The borrower resists this liability, arguing that a transfer of title does not necessarily mean any loss in value of the collateral. The borrower may fall back to a request that the lender allow one sale during the term of the loan on payment of a transfer fee. In any event, the borrower will try to exclude immaterial sales such as grants of utility easements and conveyances among beneficial owners. Lenders perceive risk in subsequent encumbrances of the real estate because secondary loans are typically recourse loans, which create incentive for the borrower to service the second at the expense of the nonrecourse first mortgage. Furthermore, even though the borrower may intend only to capture its equity, secondary financing can be a step toward a change in control of the property. The borrower counters that it should lose exculpation on the first mortgage only in an amount equal to its personal exposure on the secondary financing. The borrower may also attempt to exclude secondary financing used to make improvements to the property that should enhance the first lender's collateral.

• *Bankruptcy and contested enforcement proceedings.* Because lenders rarely foreclose for reasons other than "objective" defaults, such as failure to pay principal, interest, taxes or insurance, they doubt the borrower's ability to raise good faith defenses to foreclosure. To discourage use of frivolous defenses as a delaying tactic, some lenders provide that their loans become fully recourse if the borrower resists foreclosure or other enforcement proceedings. . . . Some lenders go further and eliminate exculpation if the borrower asserts a "lender liability" claim or counterclaim [see Chapter 9]. Borrowers resist accepting those high stakes consequences of asserting a defense or a claim, being loath, in effect, to release unknown claims. They argue that they should be personally liable at most for attorneys' fees if the lender prevails.

Some lenders provide that their loans become recourse if the borrower files bankruptcy. Lenders have become skeptical of bankruptcies commenced when the loan far exceeds the value of the property and there is no realistic hope of reorganization. They have found that borrowers file bankruptcy to preserve their cash flows or tax positions rather than to facilitate payment of their loans. Borrowers raise many of the same objections to this controversial carve-out as to the carve-out for contest of enforcement proceedings, and they certainly resist loss of exculpation when the lender itself commences an involuntary bankruptcy.

If a court construes a "no-contest" carve-out as a waiver of a right that is not waivable under local law (for example, the defense of usury in some jurisdictions), the provision might not be enforceable. Justifiable doubts also may arise about the enforceability of a carve-out based on the commencement of bankruptcy proceedings. The Bankruptcy Code prohibits a direct waiver of the borrower's right to file for bankruptcy protection; however, this problem may be avoided if the loan imposes liability on a partner or other guarantor in the event of the borrower's bankruptcy. . . .

• *Environmental risks.* The impossibility of predicting the magnitude of the risk of environmental contamination compels lenders to allocate all environmental risks to their borrowers. Lenders often feel that they are better off recovering their loans by recourse to the borrower than by recourse to the property because they do not want to be in the chain of title to the property or involved in management of the remediation. Lenders shift the risk to the borrower either by a provision eliminating the nonrecourse features of the loan if the property is contaminated or by a separate environmental indemnity agreement that can be assigned to a purchaser after foreclosure.

Quite rightly, the lender believes that the borrower bears environmental risks before the loan is made and should bear them after the loan is made. The borrower can hardly expect its lender to have any responsibility for contamination unless the loan was underwritten with knowledge of the contamination. The borrower, however, resists complete loss of exculpation if the contamination is small and fully remediated. . . .

Lenders often insist that the borrower represent, on a recourse basis, that the property is not contaminated. Of course, the borrower wants to make that representation only in reliance on an expert's report and not on the basis of its own knowledge. . . .

• *Fraud.* Many lenders provide that their loans become fully recourse if procured by fraud. This is probably no more than a restatement of the right of rescission for fraud in the inducement, which could well override a full exculpation in the loan. However, when lenders move from culpability for willful and deliberate acts to inclusion of "misrepresentations" as the basis for the loss of nonrecourse provisions, borrowers become more concerned. Misrepresentations can be innocent or negligent, and they can be immaterial. Borrowers argue that the carve-out for misrepresentation should be limited to willful, deliberate and intentional acts that go to the basis of underwriting the loan.

EVENTS LEADING TO BORROWER LIABILITY FOR DAMAGES

Many carve-outs lead to the borrower's liability for damages rather than the loss of exculpation altogether. As a rule, these carve-outs are the lender's efforts to protect itself from the loss or erosion of value of the property or diversion of its proceeds. Unlike the carve-outs that lead to loss of exculpation, these defaults are quantifiable. Generally, they also consist of acts or omissions that no prudent property owner would allow, even without the lender's constraints. Nevertheless, the borrower often wants to "fine tune" these broad carve-outs.

• *Failure to apply insurance or condemnation proceeds properly.* The lender wants to assure that proceeds of casualty insurance or an award in condemnation are applied as required by the loan documents. Because casualty policies usually pay the borrower and the lender as their interests appear, and because condemnation awards are made jointly to owners and encumbrancers, there may appear to be little realistic risk of misapplication. Nevertheless, many lenders permit the borrower to use proceeds (especially in small amounts) without supervision.

• *Diversion of security deposits and prepaid rents.* The lender is concerned about tenant security deposits or advance rentals held by the landlord/borrower. If the lender forecloses, it believes that tenants may assert claims or take offsets for these amounts. The sparse case law has tended to relieve lenders of responsibility for security deposits paid to their erstwhile borrowers and not received by the lender on foreclosure, but the law regarding prepaid rent is less clear. Ultimately, the borrower will have a difficult time justifying diversion of either security deposits or prepaid rents without risk of liability.

The lender is also concerned about the borrower's failure to perform its obligations to tenants; in the event of a foreclosure, the lender may find itself with tenants that contest their leases or assert rental offset rights. The borrower argues that the lender should be content with recourse liability for the borrower's failure (1) to perform duties under leases for which the borrower needed—but did not obtain—the lender's approval; (2) to pay amounts for initial tenant improvements or monetary lease inducements; and (3) to perform duties giving rise to monetary obligations that accrue before the foreclosure sale or appointment of a receiver. If a subordination, nondisturbance and attornment agreement exists among the tenant, the landlord/borrower and the lender, it may provide a clear understanding of the parties' respective rights and liabilities in these matters.

• *Misuse of revenue after default.* Lenders want personal recourse against the borrower for revenue from the property received after a default to the extent the revenue is not used to pay the loan or expenses of the property. They may also extend recourse liability to revenue received in the month before the default or cash on hand at the time of the default on the theory that those funds should have been used to make the defaulted payment. Lenders may also seek recourse for payments to the borrowers' affiliates—such as a management company—after default. The lenders' motivation is some borrowers' practice of amassing cash for distribution to partners or for a litigation "war chest" in anticipation of a loan default. . . .

At the very least, the borrower wants to condition this carve-out on its receipt of a notice of default, as opposed to the occurrence of an event that could be a default with notice or the passage of time. The borrower also is likely to oppose liability to the extent that property cash flow is used for legitimate expenses of ownership, maintenance and management (even if the manager is affiliated but doing acceptable work at prevailing cost). The borrower cannot, however, advance a convincing reason why it should not be liable if it distributes or holds cash proceeds while the loan goes unpaid.

WASTE

The term "waste" encompasses a great many acts or omissions that affect the property. Traditionally waste has even included making improvements that enhanced the property. In several recent cases, waste has included failure to pay taxes. . . . Courts seem increasingly willing to amplify the concept to include economic waste. As a result, borrowers prefer to substitute specific acts for waste as the basis for recourse liability. Some examples of carve-outs that may be subsumed under waste are discussed below.

• *Failure to discharge mechanics' liens.* In some states, mechanics' liens "prime" a first mortgage and compel the lender to pay the claim to assure its lien priority. Thus the mechanic's lien results in a dollar-for-dollar reduction in the value of the lender's collateral. Although the borrower cannot escape responsibility for mechanic's liens, it may ask for notice and an opportunity to defend lien claims so long as the property is not jeopardized.

• *Failure to insure.* The adequacy of the security to satisfy the loan is threatened by the risk of an uninsured or underinsured casualty loss, so the lender seeks recourse liability if the borrower fails to maintain insurance. Most lenders will bear the risk of underinsurance, limiting the borrower's liability to loss resulting from failure to carry coverage that complies with the insurance covenants set forth in the loan documents.

• *Failure to comply with laws.* The lender wants recourse against its borrower for any loss the lender sustains as a result of the borrower's failure to comply with laws. In the case of ERISA, RICO and state forfeiture statutes, violation of which may result in loss of or inability to reach the security, the lender may want to lift the exculpatory clause altogether. The borrower asks for notice and an opportunity to defend alleged violations before a complete loss of exculpation becomes effective.

• *Failure to maintain the property.* This carve-out elicits the borrower's fear that subjective judgments will become a pretext for declaring a default. Even if the lender and borrower are comfortable with a standard such as "first class," they may not agree, for example, whether "first class" requires patchwork repair or complete replacement of a cracked parking lot. Realistically, in these days of large lender liability verdicts, no prudent lender is likely to begin a foreclosure for anything less than an egregious and unmistakable failure to maintain the property despite repeated notices and opportunities to cure. . . .

• *Removal of personal property.* The lender wants recourse against the borrower if it "strips" the property before a foreclosure. The borrower usually does not object so long as the documents permit disposal of obsolete personal property or useful personal property that is replaced.

• *Failure to pay real estate taxes and insurance premiums.* Real estate taxes and assessments "prime" mortgages. The lender wants recourse to the extent that failure to pay taxes reduces the value of the lender's security. Conversely, the borrower wants to exclude liability to the extent of funded escrows for taxes and insurance. The borrower also resists liability for amounts due from tenants approved by the lender. The borrower and lender often disagree about the period for which the borrower is liable. In descending order of preference, the borrower believes that period should end when a receiver is appointed, when a foreclosure sale occurs or when the lender sells the property after foreclosure. In fairness, after the borrower and lender agree on the end date for the borrower's liability, they should prorate taxes to that date and the borrower should be liable for taxes and assessments to that date on the same basis as in a typical sale transaction in the jurisdiction.

FURTHER CONSIDERATIONS

In addition to reserving the right to sue the borrower and any other guarantor for the "carve-outs," the lender must take care that the exculpation clause permits it to name the borrower in foreclosure proceedings and to assert equitable claims, such as claims for specific performance or injunction, that do not involve the recovery of money.

Lenders must give careful thought to the question of who will be responsible for the carve-outs. The most exhaustive carve-outs are useless if the borrower is a single-purpose entity [for example, its only asset is the mortgaged property] such as a limited partnership with a thinly capitalized corporate general partner. . . .

Lawyers for many borrowers insist that, in addition to the promissory note, all other loan documents recapitulate the nonrecourse provision to avoid any implication that the borrower has recourse liability for the covenants in those documents. This cumbersome process is probably no more effective than a single thorough statement of the carve-outs in the promissory note.

CONCLUSION

Because the carve-outs constitute the borrower's only risk under a nonrecourse loan, other than loss of equity, they are a focal point in negotiation of loan terms. In view of their importance, they are best raised in full at the application or commitment stage so that irresolvable differences are identified in the early stages of the loan process.

Lenders are driven by two fair motives: to preserve the value of the loan security and to avoid having greater exposure to liability at the foreclosure sale than at the loan closing. Although the borrower often resists personal exposure when the property's economic performance—not the borrower's "bad acts"—cause a loss, the lender is less focused on culpability than on risk allocation. A nonrecourse loan is the borrower's option to "sell" the property to the lender in total satisfaction of its liability under the loan. The borrower believes it should have the right to turn over the keys to the lender with impunity if the property does not succeed. For example, if the revenue is not sufficient to pay real estate taxes or maintenance costs, the borrower believes it should have no obligation to make the lender whole.

At bottom lurks a fundamental disagreement between borrowers and lenders about the nature of nonrecourse financing. The lender's best case is repayment of the loan with interest, generally without sharing in the property's success. Although nonrecourse financing assumes that the lender will bear the risk of the loss of collateral value from general market forces, the carve-outs are the lender's attempt to shift most of the other elements of risk of loss to the borrower. The point at which the borrower cuts its losses is the point at which the lender's losses begin to accrue. The negotiation of the nonrecourse carve-outs identifies that point.

CSFB 2001-CP-4 Princeton Park Corporate Center, LLC v. SB Rental I, LLC

410 N.J. Super. 114, 980 A.2d 1 (2009)

PARRILLO, J.A.D.

At issue is whether a non-recourse carve-out clause in a mortgage note, providing that borrowers are personally liable to lender for damages resulting from violation of a particular loan obligation, is a liquidated damages provision, and if so, whether it constitutes an unenforceable penalty. Defendant SB Rental I, LLC (SB Rental) and its principals (collectively, defendants) appeal from a summary judgment in favor of plaintiff CSFB 2001-CP-4 Princeton Park Corporate Center, LLC (CSFB or plaintiff), adjudicating defendants personally liable in the amount of $5,195,932.72. We affirm, concluding, as a matter of first impression in this State, that the disputed clause fixes liability rather than damages and is therefore fully enforceable.

The facts are undisputed. On May 2, 2001, plaintiff's predecessor in interest, Credit Suisse First Boston Mortgage Capital, LLC, gave a mortgage loan to SB Rental in the amount of $13,300,000. The loan was memorialized by a note and secured by a first mortgage encumbering commercial property located on Cornwall Road in South Brunswick. The loan was also secured by a guaranty of payment executed by SB Rental's principals, defendants Philip Seltzer, Eric Seltzer, and David Seltzer (now deceased) (collectively, guarantors).

The loan was a non-recourse obligation, which precluded the lender from seeking recovery against either SB Rental or its principals in the event of a default. The mortgage note, however, contained a carve-out clause, providing that the debt would be fully recourse if the borrower failed to obtain the lender's prior written consent to any subordinate financing encumbering the property. Specifically, Paragraph 13 of the note provides as follows:

> Notwithstanding anything to the contrary in this Note or any of the Loan Documents . . . (B) the Debt shall be fully recourse to Maker in the event that . . . (iii) Maker fails to obtain Payee's prior written consent to any subordinate financing or other voluntary lien encumbering the Mortgaged Property. . . .

The guaranty held the guarantors liable to the same extent as provided in the loan documents:

> Notwithstanding anything to the contrary in any of the Loan Documents . . . (ii) Guarantor shall be liable for the full amount of the Debt in the event that . . . (C) Borrower fails to obtain Lender's prior written consent to any subordinate financing or other voluntary lien encumbering the Mortgaged Property. . . .

During the term of the loan, on May 10, 2004, SB Rental procured $400,000 in subordinate financing and pledged a $400,000 second mortgage on the property in favor of L.G. Financial Consultants, Inc. (L.G.) without first obtaining plaintiff's written consent. In so doing, defendants triggered the non-recourse carve-out provision of the loan documents, rendering the loan fully recourse as to SB Rental and the guarantors. However, the L.G. mortgage was fully satisfied seven months later, in December 2004, and was therefore terminated, although L.G. neglected to timely discharge the obligation. In any event, eighteen months later, in May 2006, SB Rental failed to make its monthly mortgage payment to CSFB, presumably because of the loss of its sole tenant and rental income stream, and has not made any principal or interest payments since then.

Shortly thereafter, plaintiff instituted a foreclosure action, which SB Rental did not contest. Accordingly, summary judgment was entered in plaintiff's favor on March 28, 2007, and the property eventually sold at sheriff's sale. Consequently, plaintiff instituted the present action against defendants in the Law Division, seeking recovery of the deficiency on the balance of the May 2, 2001, mortgage note, reduced by the proceeds of the sheriff's sale. Following defendants' answer, plaintiff moved for summary judgment, seeking full recourse liability against both SB Rental and its principals based on their subordinate financing default. Defendants opposed such relief, arguing that since plaintiff was not harmed by the added encumbrance on the property, the breach was unrelated to any damages suffered by plaintiff and therefore the non-recourse carve-out clause extracted an unenforceable penalty in this instance.

The motion judge disagreed, finding that the damages sought by plaintiff were neither speculative nor estimated, but actual, ("equal to the outstanding loan balance and nothing more") and fair, ("[t]he defendants hav[ing] received the benefit of their bargain by receiving and retaining the loan proceeds"). Concluding that the disputed provision addresses liability rather than damages, the judge emphasized the business sophistication of defendants, who acted with full knowledge and understanding of the carve-out position:

> These are sophisticated defendants that were dealing at arms length when they signed the absolute and unconditional guarantee to govern the instances in which recourse liability would be triggered. The parties understood the provisions, and how they would operate, when they entered into the agreement, as they bargained for the opportunity to avoid recourse liability in certain instances, yet engaged in conduct that they knew would implicate personal liability if discovered.

On appeal, defendants mainly argue, as they did below, that the non-recourse carve-out clause is unenforceable as a liquidated damages provision because the penalty extracted from the borrower's breach of a covenant not to further encumber the mortgaged property bears no reasonable relationship to any harm suffered by the lender. This argument fails. . . .

[T]he decision whether a stipulated damages clause is enforceable is a question of law for the court. Equally well-settled is that when the terms of a contract are clear, "it is the function of a court to enforce it as written and not to make a better contract for either of the parties." Kampf v. Franklin Life Ins. Co.,

33 N.J. 36, 43, 161 A.2d 717 (1960). Absent ambiguity, the intention of the parties is to be ascertained by the language of the contract. . . .

Here, there is no dispute that the loan made by plaintiff to SB Rental is a non-recourse loan, excluding the borrower and guarantors from personal liability for the remaining debt upon default and leaving the creditor's recourse solely to repossession of the property given as security for the loan. The loan documents, however, expressly carve out from this exemption certain breaches that implicate personal liability, including the failure to obtain the lender's consent to any subordinate financing or other lien encumbering the mortgaged property. This is unambiguous language. Further, this was a commercial transaction negotiated between business entities with comparable bargaining power. The parties knew and agreed to the carve-out of the non-recourse loan, which, because it affects the value of the collateral, was a material term in acquiring the $13 million loan. Where, as here, sophisticated parties agree to carefully crafted terms, they should be held to the plain and clear language they chose.

Contrary to defendants' argument, the carve-out clause is not a liquidated damages provision, much less an unenforceable penalty. A clause is a liquidated damages provision if the actual damages from a breach are difficult to measure and the stipulated amount of damages is "a reasonable forecast of the provable injury resulting from [the] breach." Wasserman's Inc. v. Twp. of Middletown, 137 N.J. 238, 645 A.2d 100 (1994). Such clauses are deemed "presumptively reasonable" and therefore enforceable, and "the party challenging [a stipulated damages provision] should bear the burden of proving its unreasonableness." Id. at 252, 645 A.2d 100. Because the harm is necessarily incapable of accurate estimate, "'reasonableness' emerges as the standard for deciding the validity of stipulated damages clauses." Wasserman's, supra, 137 N.J. at 249, 645 A.2d 100. The amount fixed is unreasonable if it serves not as a pre-estimate of probable actual damages, but rather as "punishment," grossly disproportionate to the actual harm sustained.

Non-recourse carve-out clauses like the one here are not considered liquidated damages provisions because they operate principally to define the terms and conditions of personal liability, and not to affix probable damages. Generally speaking, because non-recourse loans may create issues of a borrower's motivation to act in the best interest of the lender and the lender's collateral, "lenders identified defaults that posed special risks and carved them out of the general nonrecourse provision." Portia Owen Morrison and Mark A. Senn, Carving Up the "Carve-Outs" in Nonrecourse Loans, 9 Prob. & Prop. 8 (1995). These carve-outs, which are perceived to affect the value of the collateral that secures the loan, afford the lender the protection required by causing the debtor and any guarantors to be personally liable, thus enabling the creditor to look beyond simply the mortgaged property for repayment of the loan. In other words, whereas the non-recourse nature of the loan operates as an exemption, the carve-outs exist to implicate personal liability.

The carve-out clause is not a liquidated damages provision for yet another reason: it provides for only actual damages. Unlike the typical stipulated damages provision, which reasonably estimates an amount otherwise difficult to compute, the carve-out clause permits the lender to recover only damages actually sustained, namely the amount remaining on the loan at the time of breach. Such an amount is fixed by the terms of the loan and is therefore neither speculative nor incalculable. As noted, this action involves a loan made by plaintiff to SB Rental, who, along with the guarantors, agreed to its repayment, having received the full benefit of the contract. Plaintiff, in turn, made the loan with the assurance of full repayment. In filing this lawsuit, plaintiff simply seeks the amount left on the loan at the time of ultimate default. This amount is the actual damage to plaintiff based on defendants' failure to make mortgage payments. Since the carve-out clause imposes personal liability for plaintiff's actual damages, it is not a liquidated damages provision, much less an unconscionable penalty.

Nonetheless, defendants contend that since the breach that triggered personal liability was eventually cured, resulting in no harm to plaintiff, enforcement of the carve-out here is unfair and unjust. We disagree.

Although the issue has not previously been decided in this State, other courts have uniformly held that non-recourse carve-out provisions are valid and enforceable. See, e.g., Blue Hills Office Park LLC v. J.P. Morgan Chase Bank, 477 F. Supp. 2d 366, 377-383 (D. Mass. 2007) (transfer of mortgaged property without the lender's consent and various other conduct rendered the borrower and guarantors fully liable for a loan deficiency); First Nationwide Bank v. Brookhaven Realty Assocs., 223 A.D.2d 618, 637 N.Y.S.2d 418 (N.Y. App. Div.), appeal dismissed, 88 N.Y.2d 963, 647 N.Y.S.2d 715, 670 N.E.2d 1347 (1996) (bankruptcy filing triggered recourse liability under a loan carve-out provision); FDIC v. Prince George Corp., 58 F.3d 1041 (4th Cir. 1995) (recourse liability affirmed where the borrower filed a bankruptcy petition in violation of a carve-out provision).

In *Blue Hills Office Park*, the lender made a $33 million loan evidenced by a promissory note and secured by a mortgage and a guaranty. 477 F. Supp. 2d at 370. The promissory note and guaranty both contained a non-recourse carve-out provision that made the loan fully recourse in the event mortgaged property was transferred without the lender's consent. When the borrower settled a zoning board appeal in exchange for payment of $2 million that was diverted by the borrower to a hidden account of an affiliate, the lender argued that mortgaged property had been transferred without its consent, rendering the loan fully recourse. The court agreed, finding the borrower and the guarantors jointly and severally liable for the $17.5 million balance of the mortgage loan.

In *Prince George Corp.*, supra, the lender brought an action for a deficiency judgment following a borrower's bankruptcy filing in violation of a non-recourse carve-out provision in the mortgage note. The Fourth Circuit rejected the borrower's argument that it possessed a statutory right to avail itself of bankruptcy protection, holding that the carve-out provision did not waive, or even compromise, the borrower's right to file bankruptcy, but merely imposed a consequence in the event the borrower exercised that right. Having not contravened South Carolina's statutory foreclosure scheme, the carve-out provision was not void as against public policy, and thus, under the clear and unambiguous terms of the note, the borrower was not entitled to escape liability for a deficiency judgment if it voluntarily became part of a proceeding that impaired the lender's right of recourse to the collateral.

It matters not, as defendants argue, that they eventually cured the very breach that triggered their personal liability and that no harm accrued to plaintiff as a result thereof. In *First Nationwide Bank*, supra, a lender made a non-recourse loan to a real estate partnership that provided for full recourse liability upon the commencement of a voluntary bankruptcy proceeding that was not dismissed within 90 days. Nevertheless, the partnership filed a voluntary bankruptcy petition that was dismissed *after* the 90-day period had expired. The court held that even though the default was "cured" in the sense that the bankruptcy was ultimately dismissed, the subsequent dismissal was ineffective to avoid recourse liability for the partnership and its partners.

Similarly, here, the fact that the subordinate financing was paid off well before defendants' ultimate default on payment of the principal loan does not alter the fact that defendants breached the very obligation identified by both parties as posing a special risk to plaintiff, and therefore requiring the covenant's special protection. By further encumbering the property, even if only temporarily, defendants' action had the potential to affect the viability and value of the collateral that secured the original loan. Indeed, it cannot be said with any certainty that the subordinate financing in this case was entirely unrelated to defendants' ultimate default on their mortgage payments. In any event, the fact that such potential may not have actualized does not diminish the breach of obligation nor vitiate its contracted-for consequences. Having freely and knowingly negotiated for the benefit of avoiding recourse liability generally, and agreeing to the burden of full recourse liability in certain specified circumstances, defendants may not now escape the consequences of their bargain. . . .

Although the previous case dealt with a challenge to the fairness and enforceability of the nonrecourse carve-out as written, the courts are also called on to interpret what the parties meant by the carve-out language, as in the following case.

GECCMC 2005–C1 Plummer Street Office Limited Partnership v. NRFC NNN Holdings, LLC

204 Cal. App. 4th 998, 140 Cal. Rptr. 3d 251 (2012)

ROTHSCHILD, J.

NRFC NNN Holdings, LLC (Northstar) appeals from a judgment holding it liable as a guarantor on a loan in favor of GECCMC 2005–C1

PLUMMER STREET OFFICE LIMITED PARTNERSHIP (Plummer) and a post-judgment order awarding Plummer attorney fees and costs. We conclude that as a matter of law the guaranty was not triggered. Therefore we reverse the judgment and the post-judgment order.

FACTS AND PROCEEDINGS BELOW

Plummer lent $44 million to a borrower. Borrower used the money to purchase two commercial properties in Chatsworth. Borrower leased these properties under two leases to Washington Mutual Savings and Loan as the sole tenant. The loan was a non-recourse loan, secured by the properties and certain other enumerated items but not by the assets of Borrower in general, subject to exceptions for certain forms of borrower misconduct. In addition, Northstar, an affiliate of Borrower, executed a guaranty that would be triggered by the same forms of borrower misconduct that triggered the exceptions to the non-recourse character of the loan. The guaranty provided in relevant part that "[t]he Loan shall be fully recourse to Guarantor, and Guarantor hereby unconditionally and irrevocably guarantees payment of the entire Loan, if any of the following occurs after the date hereof: . . . (iv) without the prior written consent of [Plummer] [either lease] is terminated or canceled."

Washington Mutual went out of business[3] and it and its successors ceased paying rent to Borrower and abandoned the property. In February 2009, Borrower ceased making loan payments to Plummer. In May 2009, Plummer took title to the properties through a non-judicial foreclosure sale in which it bid approximately $11 million. Plummer then brought this suit against Northstar as guarantor for the balance due on the loan—approximately $42 million plus attorney fees and costs.

Plummer and Northstar filed cross-motions for summary judgment. The principal issue was whether Washington Mutual's ceasing to pay rent and abandoning the property terminated the leases triggering Northstar's duty to pay the amount owing on the loan if the leases were "terminated" "without the prior written consent of Lender." The trial court concluded that the leases were terminated without Plummer's consent and, therefore, Northstar was liable on the guaranty. The court awarded Plummer damages of $42,220,349.35 plus prejudgment interest. In a separate order the court awarded Plummer attorney fees and costs in the amount of $760,797.50. Northstar filed timely appeals from the judgment and the post-judgment attorney fees award.

---

3. For background on the catastrophic failure of Washington Mutual at the outset of the mortgage meltdown, see K. Grind, The Lost Bank: The Story of Washington Mutual—The Biggest Bank Failure in American History (2012)—EDS.

DISCUSSION

The guaranty states in relevant part: "The Loan shall be fully recourse to Guarantor, and Guarantor hereby unconditionally and irrevocably guarantees payment of the entire loan, *if* any of the following occurs after the date hereof: . . . (iv) *without the prior written consent of [Plummer]* . . . (2) *either [lease] is terminated or canceled* . . . or the term of either [lease] is surrendered. . . ." (Italics added.)

It is undisputed that Washington Mutual breached the leases by ceasing to pay rent and abandoning the premises. The lease agreements between Washington Mutual and the Borrower provided: "13.1 *Defaults.* The occurrence of any one or more of the following events shall constitute a material default and breach of this Lease by Lessee: [¶] (a) The abandonment or surrender of the Premises by Lessee. [¶] (b) The failure by Lessee to make any equal monthly payments pursuant to paragraph 5.1 or any other rental payment required to be made by Lessee hereunder, as and when due. . . ."

Plummer argues Washington Mutual's breaches terminated the leases. It quotes the following language from Civil Code section 1951.2, subdivision (a): 2 "if a lessee of real property breaches the lease and abandons the property before the end of the term . . . the lease terminates." But section 1951.2, subdivision (a) does not apply to this case, as we explain below.

Plummer ignores paragraph 5.3 of the lease which states in relevant part: "It is the intention of the parties hereto that this Lease shall not be terminable for any reason by Lessee[.] . . . Any present or future law to the contrary shall not alter this agreement of the parties." Thus, under the plain language of the lease, neither the lessee's failure to pay rent nor its abandonment of the property terminates the lease. Furthermore, this lease provision states that it overrides any "law to the contrary."

Plummer also omits the beginning words of section 1951.2, subdivision (a). The first sentence of subdivision (a) states in relevant part: "*Except as otherwise provided in Section 1951.4,* if a lessee of real property breaches the lease and abandons the property before the end of the term . . . the lease terminates." (Italics added.) Section 1951.4, subdivision (b) states in relevant part: "Even though a lessee of real property has breached the lease and abandoned the property, the lease continues in effect for so long as the lessor does not terminate the lessee's right of possession." In this case the leases state: "No act by Lessor other than giving notice of termination to Lessee shall terminate Lessee's right to possession." It is undisputed that Borrower never gave notice of termination to Washington Mutual.

For section 1951.4 to apply, however, there must be a provision in the lease in substantially the following form: "'The lessor has the remedy described in California Civil Code Section 1951.4 (lessor may continue lease in effect after lessee's breach and abandonment and recover rent as it becomes due, if lessee has right to sublet or assign, subject only to reasonable limitations).'" (§1951.4, subd. (a).) The leases in this case satisfy this requirement. Paragraph 13.2 states in relevant part that in the event of a material breach by the lessee, the lessor may: "(b) Continue this Lease in full force and effect, and this Lease will continue in effect as long as Lessor does not terminate Lessee's right of possession, and Lessor shall have the right to collect rent when due. . . . [I]f Lessee obtains Lessor's consent, Lessee shall have the right to assign or sublet its interest in this Lease. . . . Lessor's consent to a proposed assignment or subletting shall not be unreasonably withheld."

Based on the lease provisions and the undisputed facts, we conclude the leases did not terminate and, therefore, the guaranty was never triggered.

As Northstar points out, this interpretation of the guaranty is consistent with the parties' intent, expressed in the deed of trust and other loan documents, to carve out exceptions to the loan's non-recourse provision only in the event that Borrower commits certain "bad boy acts" that pose particular risks to Plummer's interests and collateral. Those same acts trigger the liability of the guarantor. In the deed of trust, for example, Borrower covenants not to terminate either of the leases without Plummer's prior written consent. In the guaranty, Northstar agrees to be liable for the entire loan if either of the leases is "terminated" "without the prior written consent of [Plummer]." Thus, both the borrower and the guarantor are liable only if the borrower engages in the specified bad acts. In the absence of such misconduct by the borrower, the sole security for the loans is the property.

Plummer argues that although the lease termination provision in the guaranty "superficially resembles a 'bad boy' guaranty" in reality it operates like an absolute guaranty because full recourse is triggered regardless of whether the lease is terminated by the tenant or the landlord (i.e., Borrower). (Cf. Wells Fargo Bank, NA v. Cherryland Mall Limited Partnership (2011) 295 Mich. App. 99, 812 N.W.2d 799, 815 [borrower's insolvency triggered the guaranty even though insolvency was not the result of the borrower's "bad boy act" because the guaranty "does not require insolvency to occur in any specific manner"].) The argument fails even assuming that we would follow the *Cherryland* opinion because it is based on a faulty premise—that the leases were terminated. Only *Borrower* had the right to terminate the leases and it is undisputed that Borrower never did so.

For the reasons set forth above, we conclude that the trial court erred in granting Plummer's motion for summary judgment and its motion for attorney fees. The court should have granted Northstar's motion instead. . . .

NOTES AND QUESTIONS

1. Nonrecourse Loans. If the parties' nonrecourse agreement states simply that the lender's recourse is limited to the mortgaged property and that the borrower shall have no personal liability, should the court imply any of the carve-outs discussed in the Morrison and Senn article? See Homecorp v. Secor Bank, 659 So. 2d 15 (Ala. 1994) (nonrecourse mortgagee entitled to security deposits held by borrower-landlord after foreclosure). For example, what if the nonrecourse borrower fails to pay the real property taxes and the undersecured lender suffers loss to the extent its mortgage is "primed" by the superpriority tax lien? Compare Travelers Ins. Co. v. 633 Third Assocs., 14 F.3d 114 (2d Cir. 1994) (borrower's intentional failure to pay property taxes or to maintain the property in good condition is waste that is unprotected by nonrecourse agreement), with Chetek State Bank v. Barberg, 170 Wis. 2d 516, 489 N.W.2d 385 (Ct. App. 1992) (failure to pay taxes does not entitle nonrecourse lender to sue on theory of tortious waste); see generally Saft, Recourse Liability Arising from a Nonrecourse Mortgage, 12 Real Est. Fin. J. 13 (Summer 1996); St. Claire, Nonrecourse Debt Transactions: Limitations on Limitations of Liability, 19 Real Est. L.J. 19 (Summer 1990).

As observed by Morrison and Senn, the trend in commercial nonrecourse financing is for the mortgage loan documents to specify a growing list of exceptions to the nonrecourse agreement. But are these carve-outs enforceable, particularly those that lead to a complete loss of exculpation? Suppose you represent a borrower who agreed to nonrecourse financing conditioned on its agreement not to contest any foreclosure procedures. Can you argue against the enforcement of this provision on any grounds? What if the lender's damages (for example, its attorneys' fees) from the borrower's groundless resistance of foreclosure are far less than the extent of the borrower's personal liability that has "sprung" from the carve-out clause? The court in *SB Rental* suggests the lender under a similar carve-out receives no more than its actual damages—the amount owed on the loan. Do you agree with this reasoning?

Violations of so-called due-on-encumbrance clauses are customarily carved out of nonrecourse clauses. As addressed infra at Chapter 5A7, clauses in commercial loan transactions requiring the mortgagee's consent to junior encumbrances are both customary and enforceable in accordance with their terms. Ironically, the neglect of the junior lender in *SB Rental* to release its recorded mortgage on full payment probably led to its discovery by the foreclosing senior lender and, ultimately, the imposition of a $5 million deficiency judgment on the defendants pursuant to the nonrecourse carve-out.

The spiraling occasions on which courts are called on to interpret carveouts suggest that lenders must draft with experiential foresight. E.g., Aozora Bank, Ltd. v. 1333 North California Blvd., 119 Cal. App. 4th 1291, 15 Cal. Rptr. 3d 340 (2004) (nonrecourse carve-out "if and to the extent that" the borrower commits waste construed to encompass unpaid real estate taxes, but not $1.4 million in attorney's fees incurred by lender in litigating scope of the carve-out). Having read the *GECCMC* case, how would you redraft the carveout at issue in that case to ensure the lender's interpretation, rejected by the California appeals court, would govern a subsequent loan transaction?

2. Exploding Guarantees. Morrison and Senn observe that the most exhaustive carve-outs can be useless when the borrower is a single-purpose entity with no assets beyond the mortgaged property. For these occasions, lenders have begun to demand so-called exploding or springing guarantees whereby individuals or entities in control of the borrower agree to assume personal liability upon the occurrence of some undesirable event such as the filing of bankruptcy or the assertion of defenses to the foreclosure action. Given the close relationship of these agreements to the liability of the borrower entity that arises under a carve-out to a nonrecourse agreement, lenders can expect challenges to their validity similar to those discussed in the preceding note. The *SB Rental* case, involving what was no doubt an exploding guarantee, illustrates that courts may be reluctant to rescue sophisticated guarantors from their agreements. The most dramatic example comes from Michigan: Wells Fargo Bank, NA v. Cherryland Mall Limited Partnership, 295 Mich. App. 99, 812 N.W.2d 799 (2011) (enforcing guaranty imposing recourse in event borrower failed to remain solvent and pay debts as they came due, despite the incongruency with the concept of nonrecourse debt, as "[i]t is not the job of this Court to save litigants from their bad bargains or their failure to read and understand the terms of a contract"). Is the guarantor's lawyer liable for malpractice by failing to catch and explain this provision to the client at the time of the loan closing? Responding to the *Cherryland* case, the Michigan legislature outlawed nonrecourse carveouts and exploding guarantees based on borrower solvency. Mich. Comp. Laws §445.1593. See generally M. Madison, J. Dwyer, and S. Bender, The Law of Real Estate Financing §15:6 (2016); Murray and Scott, Enforceability of Carveouts to Nonrecourse Loans: An Evolution, 48 Real Prop. Tr. & Est. L.J. 217 (2013).

> **Problem 5-2**
Read the nonrecourse provision and the agreed-on carve-outs therefrom in Section 2.05 of the sample postconstruction loan commitment in the Documents Manual.
Based on the foregoing materials and particularly the article by Morrison and Senn, what modifications would you request on behalf of Dan Developer? ◄

4. The Prepayment Privilege

When interest rates decline, there is a tendency among borrowers to replace existing debt with new debt—to "refinance" at the lower rate. For example, if interest rates in the master hypothetical for first mortgage money should decrease from 5 percent to 3 percent by the tenth year of the loan, refinancing with a new 15-year term loan (with a 25-year amortization) at the lower rate could save Dan as much as $376,000 in interest expenses during the first year of the new loan. In addition, a borrower such as Dan may want to refinance an existing loan with a new larger one from Ace or some other lender to cash out some tax-free equity in the project for the purpose of expanding or renovating the office building. Or perhaps Dan might want to use the net refinancing proceeds for another investment opportunity (assuming that he obtains an after-tax rate of return that is higher than the after-tax cost of borrowing the extra money). Finally, a purchaser from Dan may want to obtain a new mortgage so that it can finance the portion of the purchase price attributable to Dan's equity in the property being sold.[4]

The chief obstacles to refinancing are a prohibition on repayment of the existing loan or the imposition of prepayment charges by the existing lender for the privilege of prepaying the existing indebtedness before the agreed-on maturity date. Under basic property law, in the absence of language to the contrary in the loan documents, a lender does not have to accept a prepayment because a lender is entitled to receive the anticipated rate of return and recapture the cost of making the loan during the agreed-on term of the loan.[5] Moreover, prepayment charges are used by lenders in conjunction with "due-on-sale" clauses (discussed infra at Chapter 5A8) to protect themselves against fluctuations in market rates of interest. When interest rates climb above the rate on the existing mortgage, the due-on-sale clause may compel refinancing by the purchaser and prepayment by the borrower when the property is sold, thereby enabling the lender to relend the recaptured funds at the higher market rate. Conversely, when interest rates decline, the prepayment penalty discourages borrowers from refinancing at the lower market rate.[6]

This conflict in the interests of the parties usually results in a compromise. The mortgage note may provide for a "lock in" period so that no prepayment is permitted for a certain number of years after the inception of the loan. Thereafter, there is usually a prepayment charge that the borrower will have to pay, traditionally equal to a specified percentage of the loan amount that is being prepaid. This percentage is higher during the early years of the prepayment period and usually declines as the loan approaches maturity. This prepayment charge is designed to be sufficiently onerous to make it unlikely that the loan will be prepaid unless interest rates decline substantially or unless expansion, sale, or tax considerations warrant the payment of the prepayment charge.

The following prepayment provision that might appear in Ace's commitment letter illustrates this traditional approach:

> The Note shall provide that the Borrower will have the privilege of prepaying the entire principal balance of the Loan (but not a part thereof) on the first day of any month commencing with the first day of the first month of the _____ Loan Year upon _____ days' prior written notice to Lender of Borrower's intention to so prepay and upon payment by Borrower to Lender of the principal balance due on the Note together with the accrued interest thereon and all other sums due and payable under the Note and a prepayment fee equal to _____ percent of the unpaid principal balance if prepayment is made during the

---

4. Refinancing is discussed in greater detail at Chapter 7A.

5. See, e.g., Metropolitan Life Ins. Co. v. Strnad, 876 P.2d 1362 (Kan. 1994); Young v. Sodaro, 456 S.E.2d 31 (W. Va. 1995). But see Restatement (Third) of Property (Mortgages) §6.1 (1997) (abandons the common law rule as inconsistent with the borrower's expectations when the documents are silent).

6. See M. Madison, J. Dwyer, and S. Bender, The Law of Real Estate Financing §5:34 (2016); G. Nelson et al., Real Estate Finance Law §6.1 (6th ed. 2015).

_____ Loan Year, said prepayment fee declining _____ percent each succeeding Loan Year thereafter and with no prepayment fee if the Loan is paid at its normal maturity; and that if the Borrower gives notice of its intention to prepay as hereinabove provided, the entire principal balance of the Loan shall, at the option of Lender become due and payable on the date specified in the notice indicating an intention to prepay by Borrower.

Under this traditional approach, the prepayment charge is due regardless of whether the prepayment has caused the lender any economic loss—such as where market interest rates have risen since the loan origination. The recent trend among lenders is to replace this traditional sliding percentage formula with a "yield equivalent" or "yield maintenance" formula to compensate them for the actual loss of their investment as a consequence of a prepayment. The following is a typical yield equivalent provision that is keyed to the market rate of interest at the time of prepayment:

The prepayment charge shall equal the amount of the excess, if any, which would be required over and above the principal balance of the Loan outstanding at the time of such prepayment for the mortgagee to purchase on the date of such prepayment, a United States Treasury Bond with a maturity date closest to that of the Loan providing the same investment yield the mortgagee would have received had all payments been made on the Note as therein provided.

The following case considers the enforceability of a variant of the yield maintenance approach. The lower court it reversed had garnered national attention for its lack of deference to the dickered terms of the deal in this commercial development loan.

River East Plaza, L.L.C. v. Variable Annuity Life Insurance Co.
498 F.3d 718 (7th Cir. 2007)

KANNE, Circuit Judge.

This diversity case involves a loan used to finance a significant commercial real estate development. When the borrower sold the property and pre-paid the loan, it balked at paying a "prepayment fee" according to the terms of the note. The borrower eventually paid the fee, subject to a reservation of rights, and sued the lender. After a bench trial, the district court entered judgment in favor of the borrower and the lender now appeals. For the reasons set forth below, we reverse the judgment of the district court. . . .

I.   HISTORY

River East Plaza, L.L.C. (River East) is a real estate developer. Third-party defendant Daniel E. McLean is the president of River East. River East had worked with another party to develop a large retail store on the north side of Chicago. In 1999, the other developer offered to sell its share of the project to River East for roughly $12 million. River East, through a mortgage broker, shopped around for a loan to allow it to buy out the other developer's share. Variable Annuity Life Insurance Company (VALIC) offered to meet River East's demand for a closing date before the end of the year and agreed to an interest rate that River East wanted. Among the other terms of VALIC's offer was a "yield maintenance" prepayment clause. A yield maintenance prepayment clause is an attempt to ensure that prepayment does not deprive the lender of the yield that they bargained for over the life of the loan.

The final version of the note contained a yield maintenance calculation which the parties describe as "Treasury-flat." To arrive at the amount of the yield maintenance fee in the event that River East decided to prepay, the parties would need to know the outstanding principal as of the date of prepayment and the scheduled loan payments from that date to maturity. They would also need to determine the prevailing interest rate on United States Treasury bonds or notes maturing closest to the loan's maturity date of January 2020 ("Treasuries"). With those three amounts in hand, the clause calculates the difference between the scheduled payments and potential interest if the prepaid principal were invested in Treasuries. That amount is compared to an amount equal to one percent of the outstanding principal. The larger of these two numbers is then compared with the highest rate allowed by law, and the lesser of those two numbers is the yield maintenance fee. In short, the remaining interest due under the note is discounted by the current interest rate on Treasuries. The provision is described as Treasury-flat because parties can (and apparently occasionally do) negotiate a discount rate that is different from the Treasury yield.

Some examples are in order. If River East decided to exercise the privilege of prepayment and interest rates had fallen since the time that the loan was funded, River East would be on the hook to pay VALIC the difference between what VALIC would have received in interest over the life of the loan and what VALIC could receive by investing the prepaid principal into Treasuries. Assuming that VALIC placed the unexpected principal into Treasuries and received the prepayment fee from River East, the expected yield that VALIC bargained for would be "maintained" by River East supplementing the interest on the reinvested funds with the prepayment fee. If, however, River East prepaid the loan and interest rates had risen substantially in the interim, the interest on the Treasuries would presumably exceed the interest rate called for in the loan and the prepayment fee would equal the minimum fee of one percent of the outstanding principal. But in no case would the fee exceed the maximum interest rate allowed by law.

The parties dickered over several of the terms in the note. River East sought to have the yield maintenance fee removed, but VALIC refused. Prior to closing, River East's counsel offered to both parties a seven-page opinion letter that, among many other opinions, "express[ed] no opinion as to the enforceability of any provision . . . providing for a prepayment premium in the event . . . such premium is held to be a penalty." Appellant's App. at 183F. Nevertheless, the parties went forward with the closing.

Several years later, River East sought to sell the property. The tenant had a right of first refusal, and offered to purchase the property. But the tenant would not assume the loan. River East eventually sold the property to the tenant and prepaid the loan.

The parties then began to dispute the size and enforceability of the prepayment penalty. River East eventually paid the penalty under protest, and brought suit in the state courts of Illinois. VALIC removed the case to the federal district court and counter-claimed against River East and McLean for costs and fees. . . . The district court conducted a bench trial, and entered judgment in favor of River East on the question of whether the prepayment fee was enforceable under Illinois law. . . .

II. ANALYSIS

VALIC appeals the judgment entered after a bench trial. We review the district court's findings of fact for clear error and review legal conclusions de novo. A federal court sitting in diversity applies the substantive law of the state in which the district resides. Erie R.R. Co. v. Tompkins, 304 U.S. 64, 78 (1938).
. . .

A. ENFORCEABILITY OF THE PREPAYMENT FEE

Yield maintenance prepayment clauses are nothing new. See Dale A. Whitman, Mortgage Prepayment Clauses: A Legal and Economic Analysis, 40 UCLA L. Rev. 851, 871 (1993). The idea behind a yield maintenance clause is to protect a lender during times when interest rates are falling. "Yield maintenance formulas are calculated to cover the lender's reinvestment loss when prepaid loans bear above-market rates." George Lefcoe, Yield Maintenance and Defeasance: Two Distinct Paths to Commercial Mortgage Prepayment, 28 Real Est. L.J. 202, 202 (2000). A lender who makes a long-term loan expecting a particular rate of interest runs the risk that prepayment during a period of lower interest rates will reduce its income. VALIC argues that some lenders, itself included, need to be able to rely on predictable payments in order to live up to their other financial and regulatory obligations. When the loans in question are measured in eight digit figures, as in this case, the lost interest income can be substantial.

One method that lenders might use to guard against this risk is to refuse to allow borrowers to prepay the loan. See Restatement (Third) Prop. (Mortgages) §6.2 (1997) ("an agreement that prohibits payment of the mortgage obligation prior to maturity is enforceable"). Or lenders might charge a fixed fee, a percentage of the loan balance, or a declining percentage of the loan balance. Whitman, 40 UCLA L. Rev. at 871. However, assuming that the borrower would like the privilege of prepaying the loan instead of being locked in for its entire term, fees based on fixed numbers or the loan balance do not take into account long-term fluctuations in interest rates. Hence the development of yield maintenance clauses: formulas that attempt to account for the expected interest, the outstanding principal, and fluctuations in prevailing interest rates.

We should note at the outset that the parties are unable to agree on the legal standard that Illinois courts would apply to this question. River East maintains that Illinois would analyze the prepayment fee under a liquidated damages analysis. VALIC argues that Illinois would consider the clause to be a bargained-for form of alternative performance. The district court applied Illinois's liquidated damages analysis but did not cite any Illinois cases to support that decision.

The parties can point us to no case from the Illinois Supreme Court that establishes a rule of law for the enforceability of prepayment fees in commercial real estate loans, and we are unable to find one. Illinois has placed statutory limitations on the ability of lenders to charge prepayment fees, but those provisions apply only to certain residential mortgages. See 815 Ill. Comp. Stat. 205/4. River East argues that "the Illinois Supreme Court has adopted the Restatement of Contract's prohibition against penalty clauses." Appellee's Br. at 19 (citing Bauer v. Sawyer, 134 N.E.2d 329, 333 (1956)). VALIC appears not to take issue with this statement of the law. But we should note that *Bauer* was not a case concerning mortgage prepayment, and it specifically cited to Section 356(1) of the Restatement, which stands more precisely for the proposition that some liquidated damages clauses are void as against public policy because they are penalties. Restatement (Second) of Contracts §356(1). . . . The comments to the Restatement clarify: "Punishment of a promisor for having broken his promise has no justification on either economic or other grounds and a term providing such a penalty is unenforceable on grounds of public policy." Rest.2d Contr. §356(1) cmt. a.

If we start from the position that Illinois will not enforce penalty clauses, and that Illinois recognizes that some liquidated damages clauses cross the line and become penalty clauses in disguise, the underlying question is whether this clause is punitive in nature. "[W]hen the sole purpose of the clause is to secure performance of the contract, the provision is an unenforceable penalty." Checkers Eight Ltd. P'ship v. Hawkins, 241 F.3d 558, 562 (7th Cir.2001). Penalties, or liquidated damages clauses in general, are distinct from alternative forms of performing the obligations under the contract. See John D. Calamari & Joseph M. Perillo, Contracts §14-34 (3d ed.1997). In order to distinguish between the two, "a court will look to the substance of the agreement to determine whether. . .

the parties have attempted to disguise a provision for a penalty that is unenforceable. . . . In determining whether a contract is one for alternative performances, the relative value of the alternatives may be decisive." Restatement Second of Contracts §356 cmt c.

Using the Restatement as a guide, we will first consider the "relative value of the alternatives" to see if they are decisive. All of the figures that follow (although rounded for ease of reading) come from the stipulated facts dated February 14, 2005 that the parties agreed on, and which the district court adopted. River East borrowed $12.7 million from VALIC at 8.02% interest. If River East had paid as scheduled over the course of twenty years, it would have paid roughly $16.4 million in interest to VALIC before the note matured in 2020. By July 2003, when River East prepaid the loan subject to reservation of rights, the outstanding principal remained over $12 million, and River East had already paid roughly $3.45 million in interest. On July 1, 2003, River East paid slightly more than $4.7 million in prepayment fees, but that sum was reduced to approximately $3.9 million while this litigation was pending when VALIC reimbursed [an] overcharge.

Looking at the relative value of the alternatives, we are not convinced that the parties used this clause to disguise a penalty that is unenforceable. By electing an option to pay early, River East avoided paying the $13 million in remaining interest payments that would have been due between 2003 and 2020, and instead paid only $3.9 million. Even assuming, due to the time value of money, that the $3.9 million was worth more in 2003 than it would have been worth over the course of the loan, River East seems to have benefited from this bargain. This hardly seems to be a clause whose "sole purpose is to secure performance of the contract." Checkers Eight, 241 F.3d at 562. Note, for example, that this prepaid interest is automatically reduced by the operation of the discount rate in the prepayment clause: River East was not obligated to pay any of the forgone interest that VALIC could have earned back by investing the returned principal in Treasuries.

But what of the "relative value of the alternatives" to VALIC? River East makes much of the fact that VALIC was "overcompensated" by the prepayment clause. Of course, a value-laden term such as "overcompensated" only begs the question of "compared to what?" It certainly cannot be the case that VALIC was overcompensated by receiving more from River East than it contracted for. It contracted to receive $16.4 million over twenty years. Loan amortization being what it is, that income from interest would have been front-loaded into the first half of the loan term. Instead, VALIC received $3.45 million over three years and an additional $3.9 million in year four. River East also does not make the argument that the prepayment overcompensated VALIC compared to what the prepayment clause required. . . .

Instead, River East relies on a clever argument that VALIC is overcompensated because VALIC can now, if it so chooses, reinvest the returned principal and eventually get an even greater income stream from somebody else than it would have received from River East. This argument is worth considering in more detail. The prepayment provision is termed "Treasury-flat." This means that VALIC's 8.02% interest rate was discounted by the prevailing rate on Treasuries as of the date that River East elected to prepay. As we noted above, the unwritten assumption in such a formula is that VALIC can take the returned principal, invest it in Treasuries, and by taking the income from the Treasuries and adding it to the prepayment fee, VALIC gets the exact return it expected from the loan. Reality, we might suspect, will be different. One might believe, and expert testimony at trial supported this belief, that interest rates on commercial real estate loans will almost always exceed the interest rates on Treasuries. This spread in interest rates gives VALIC a chance to profit from the prepayment. The argument goes that sophisticated lenders like VALIC will not invest the returned principal in Treasuries, but will simply line up a new commercial real estate loan. But there is an irony to this argument. In trying to argue that the prepayment clause is a penalty, which by definition is a clause whose sole purpose is to secure the performance of the contract, River East argues that VALIC would have been effectively worse off if the contract had been repaid over the term of the loan instead of prepaid.

In short, viewing the contract in light of Illinois's reliance on the Restatement, we find nothing to suggest that the clause is an unenforceable penalty. Under Illinois law, the loan could have explicitly prohibited any prepayment whatsoever. River East desired the option to prepay. VALIC accommodated that desire and included a Treasury-flat yield maintenance prepayment fee. River East voluntarily prepaid, and by doing so River East escaped paying $13 million in interest over seventeen years by prepaying $3.8 million in 2003. VALIC received its principal, and was free to either reinvest it in Treasuries (in which case it would be no worse off), hold it as cash (in which case its income would be less than bargained for from River East), or invest it in additional real estate mortgages with their attendant higher risks of default. The relative value of the alternatives for both parties leads us to believe that the clause is not punitive in nature.

River East and the district court believe that Illinois courts would apply the rubric of liquidated damages to determine if the prepayment clause is unreasonable. As River East notes in its brief, Illinois follows the Restatement in holding that "[d]amages for breach by either party may be liquidated in the agreement but only at an amount that is reasonable in the light of the anticipated or actual loss caused by the breach and the difficulties of proof of loss." Restatement Second of Contracts §356. Certainly under any ordinary view of the contract's unambiguous terms, the prepayment is not a breach: the parties explicitly provided that River East would be allowed to prepay. The fee for prepaying seems a long stretch from damages for a breach if both parties entered the contract believing that the contract allowed River East to prepay.

Nevertheless, it is conceivable that a state might use the law of liquidated damages as some sort of analogy to determine whether the prepayment clause is a penalty as opposed to alternative performance. As we noted above, we find nothing in decisions of Illinois courts to indicate that this is the case in Illinois.

The Illinois cases that the parties have drawn to our attention are silent on the question. The only case that uses the term is clearly off-topic. . . . Even the law review article that River East cites to support its argument contradicts River East's position. Appellee's Br. at 20 (citing 40 UCLA L. Rev. 851, 889-90). In surveying the legal landscape of how state courts confront prepayment clauses, Professor Whitman observes that "state courts have ignored the law of liquidated damages (perhaps appropriately) when faced with the issue of the validity of prepayment fee clauses." 40 UCLA L. Rev. at 889. Professor Whitman continues: "a freely-bargained prepayment fee clause ought to be enforced against the borrower who makes a voluntary prepayment, irrespective of the amount of money that the lender's clause demands." Id. at 890. After concluding that such clauses likely are, in a theoretical sense, liquidation of damages, Professor Whitman concludes that the "confusing pastiche" of liquidated damages laws should be ignored by courts, a result that is "consistent with nearly all of the nonbankruptcy cases involving voluntary prepayments." Id. . . .

River East considers the clause unreasonable because the lender will almost always be able to re-lend the principal at a rate higher than the Treasury rate, because commercial real estate loans frequently carry a rate higher than the treasury rate. River East notes that many players in the industry have adjusted their prepayment clauses to account for some of that cushion between the Treasury rate and the loan's rate by adding twenty-five [a quarter percent interest] or more basis points to the discount rate. But this only shows that lenders and borrowers are involved in a market where the relative risk of "breach" (if we were to make an analogy to damages) is weighed against the potential fluctuations of interest rates, regulatory pressures faced by insurers like VALIC, long-term risk of depressed real estate markets, availability of suitable replacement property owners, and any of a myriad other factors. But even the lenders who are most generous, by adding twenty-five or fifty basis points to the Treasuries, would have made an "unreasonable" fee according to River East's argument because the fee would allow them to recover more from their future investments than they would have from the original borrower.

River East includes a make-weight argument that the parties never intended to agree to the clause. This claim should never have been allowed to proceed to trial. "The intention of the parties to contract must be determined from the instrument itself, and construction of the instrument where no ambiguity exists is a matter of law." Farm Credit Bank of St. Louis v. Whitlock, 581 N.E.2d 664, 667 (Ill. 1991). Even if the parol evidence were allowed and credited, it falls far short of establishing that the parties did not intend to be bound by the prepayment clause. An opinion letter from a party's lawyer, which itself "expresses no opinion" on the enforceability of a term, is a poor excuse for evidence that the party did not intend to be bound. This is particularly true in light of the fact that the parties went forward with the closing despite the opinion letter. The fact that a party would have preferred a different term does not make a clause in the contract unilaterally voidable at a later date.

In short, we hold that VALIC is entitled to judgment as a matter of law on River East's first count of the complaint. We are convinced that a contrary result would have broad implications for both lenders and borrowers of mortgage-secured loans in Illinois, and might inadvertently effect a wide-ranging alteration of the law of real estate financing in Illinois. . . . Accordingly, we must reverse the judgment of the district court with respect to count one of River East's complaint. . . .

Another development in mortgage custom is that mortgagees now include language in the note that requires payment of the prepayment charge upon any prepayment prompted by the borrower's default. The following language is typical:

> Maker agrees that if an Event of Default (as defined in the Mortgage, such definition being incorporated herein by reference and made part hereof) shall occur and the maturity hereof shall be accelerated, then a tender of payment by Maker or by anyone on behalf of the Maker of the amount necessary to satisfy all sums due hereunder made at any time prior to judicial or public sale of the real and/or other property mortgaged under the Mortgage shall constitute an evasion of the payment terms hereof and shall be deemed to be a voluntary prepayment hereunder, and any such payment, to the extent permitted by law, therefore must include the fee required under the prepayment privilege, or if at that time there be no such privilege of prepayment, then such payment, to the extent permitted by law, must include a fee [of _____ % of the then unpaid principal balance of this Note][calculated in accordance with the yield equivalent formula specified in Section _____ of this Note].

Lenders require this default language in response to decisions holding that prepayment charges were not payable when the loan was repaid following the lender's acceleration of the debt in response to the borrower's default. Courts reasoned either that the parties did not contemplate payment of the charge for such an "involuntary" prepayment, or that the lender's acceleration advanced the maturity date so that payment was, in fact, made after maturity rather than as a "pre" payment.[7] By including language that expressly invokes the prepayment charge in these circumstances, lenders have forced courts to consider whether some public policy principle overrides the parties' freedom to protect the lender's expectation interest by contract. Thus far, most courts have enforced these explicit default prepayment provisions.[8]

---

7. See, e.g., In re LHD Realty Corp., 726 F.2d 327 (7th Cir. 1984).

8. See, e.g., Parker Plaza W. Partners v. Unum Pension & Ins. Co., 941 F.2d 349 (5th Cir. 1991); Travelers Ins. Co. v. Corporex Properties, 798 F. Supp. 423 (E.D. Ky. 1992); Financial Ctr. Assocs. v. TNE Funding Corp. (In re Financial Ctr. Assocs.), 140 B.R. 829, 835 (Bankr. E.D.N.Y. 1992); Biancalana v. Fleming, 45 Cal. App. 4th 698, 53 Cal. Rptr. 2d 47 (1996).

NOTES AND QUESTIONS

1. Terms of Prepayment. Loan payment terms, including prepayment terms, are found in the promissory note. Some lenders repeat these payment terms in the mortgage or deed of trust, while others refuse to do so. Might their reluctance be attributable to the fact that the note is not recorded? Observe that the sample traditional clause above requires the borrower to provide notice of its intention to prepay on a specified date and that failure to prepay in accordance with such notice constitutes a default under the mortgage note. Why will a prudent lender impose such a notice requirement (regardless of the method for calculating the prepayment charge)? Can you think of the business reason why lenders increasingly use the yield maintenance variety of prepayment clause?

2. The Prepayment Charge as a "Penalty." The law abhors a penalty and where a predetermined payment for breach of a contract does not bear a reasonable relationship to the anticipated loss, the courts may strike down the parties' determination as a "penalty." See generally 5 S. Williston, Contracts §775A (3d ed. 1961 & Supp. 1995). In a leading case from California, Lazzareschi Investment Co. v. San Francisco Federal Savings & Loan Assoc., 22 Cal. App. 3d 303, 99 Cal. Rptr. 417 (1971), the court ruled that the litmus test for enforceability of a prepayment charge in a nondefault situation was whether the charge was "palpably exorbitant" and not whether the charge was an unreasonable "penalty" under a liquidated damages analysis. Do you agree that prepayment is not a breach and therefore prepayment charges should not be scrutinized as liquidated damages clauses? See Whitman, Mortgage Prepayment Clauses: An Economic and Legal Analysis, 40 UCLA L. Rev. 851, 898-890 (1993); Carlyle Apts. Joint Venture v. AIG Life Ins. Co., 333 Md. 265, 635 A.2d 366 (Ct. App. 1994) (following *Lazzareschi*). Under the generous standard of exorbitance applied in *Lazzareschi*, prepayment charges tend to survive judicial scrutiny. For example, against the backdrop of a rising interest market, *Lazzareschi* upheld a somewhat arbitrary fee of six months of interest on amounts prepaid in excess of 20 percent of the original loan balance. See also Williams v. Fassler, 110 Cal. App. 3d 7, 167 Cal. Rptr. 545 (1980) (a 50 percent prepayment charge was neither exorbitant nor unconscionable). The Seventh Circuit in *River East* applied the more rigorous liquidated damages analysis somewhat reluctantly, it seems, but in the end upheld the charge. Assuming the court used the right standard, do you agree with the result? In light of the *River East* litigation and the national attention it garnered, do you think lenders or borrowers might seek to modify the prepayment clause at issue? How so?

In addition to potential judicial scrutiny, the lender's prepayment clause may be governed by laws in many states that disallow or restrict the amount of prepayment charges, especially for residential mortgage loans. See Restatement (Third) of Property (Mortgages) §6.2 Statutory Note (1997) (compiling these laws). But see 12 C.F.R. §560.34 (preempting state regulation of prepayment charges by thrifts); 12 C.F.R. §34.23 (national bank adjustable rate loans may impose fees for prepayments notwithstanding any state law limitation). At the same time, the federal Dodd-Frank Wall Street Reform and Consumer Protection Act of 2010, enacted in response to the subprime mortgage crisis, restricts or prohibits prepayment charges in residential mortgage loans.

   3. Enforceability in Bankruptcy. Bankruptcy courts have subjected prepayment charges to a more exacting standard of reasonableness, either by use of the liquidated damages analysis, or under §506(b) of the Bankruptcy Code that includes only reasonable fees and charges in the lender's secured claim in bankruptcy against its collateral. See In re Duralite Truck Body & Container Corp., 153 B.R. 708 (Bankr. D. Md. 1993); In re Outdoor Sports Headquarters, Inc., 161 B.R. 414 (Bankr. S.D. Ohio 1993); In re AJ Lane & Co., 113 B.R. 821 (Bankr. D. Mass. 1990). Under this analysis, traditional prepayment clauses that require payment of a fixed percentage of the loan regardless of the prevailing market rate may not withstand scrutiny. Even yield maintenance clauses have been struck down in bankruptcy when they ignore the time value of money and fail to discount the yield payment to its present value, or when they choose a market reinvestment rate index that is systematically lower than mortgage loan yields. Compare In re Skyler Ridge, 80 B.R. 505 (Bankr. C.D. Cal. 1987) (Treasury Bond yield formula would overcompensate the mortgage lender); In re Kroh Bros. Dev. Co., 88 B.R. 997 (W.D. Mo. 1988), with In re Financial Ctr. Assocs., 140 B.R. 829 (Bankr. E.D.N.Y. 1992). See generally Blum, The Oversecured Creditor's Right to Enforce a Prepayment Charge as Part of its Secured Claim Under 11 USC Section 506(b), 98 Com. L.J. 78 (Spring 1993); Stark, Enforcing Prepayment Charges: Case Law and Drafting Suggestions, 22 Real Prop., Prob. & Tr. J. 549, 550-552 (Fall 1987); Stark, Prepayment Charges in Jeopardy: The Unhappy and Uncertain Legacy of *In re Skyler Ridge*, 24 Real Prop., Prob. & Tr. J. 191 (Summer 1989).

   4. Involuntary Prepayments. In the case of debt acceleration following a total condemnation or casualty destruction of the mortgaged premises, a lender frequently will insist on the right to apply the condemnation award proceeds or hazard insurance proceeds against the outstanding balance on the mortgage loan. See Chapter 5A6, notes 4 and 5, infra. If so, can the lender enforce a prepayment charge if this contingency is not dealt with in the prepayment clause? As borrower's counsel, what would be your argument against enforcement when the prepayment, as here, is involuntary? See DeKalb County v. United Family Life Ins. Co., 235 Ga. 417, 219 S.E.2d 707 (1975) (condemnation); Chestnut Corp. v. Bankers Bond & Mortgage Co., 395 Pa. 153, 149 A.2d 48 (1959) (fire destruction). See also Landohio Corp. v. Northwestern Mutual Life Mortgage & Realty Investors, 431 F. Supp. 475 (N.D. Ohio 1976); Jala Corp. v. Berkeley Sav. & Loan Ass'n, 104 N.J. Super. 394, 250 A.2d 150 (1969); Silverman v. New York, 48 A.D.2d 413, 370 N.Y.S.2d 234 (1975).
   Suppose the lender anticipates this issue and the loan documents specify that a fee is payable in these circumstances regardless of whether the prepayment is

voluntary. Would enforcement of a prepayment charge following a total or partial condemnation or destruction be held unconscionable? In other words, which of the two innocent parties, the borrower or the lender, should bear the risk of fluctuations in the market rate of interest if the loan is repaid before maturity because of circumstances beyond the control of either party? See generally Whitman, Mortgage Prepayment Clauses: An Economic and Legal Analysis, 40 UCLA L. Rev. 851, 911-921 (1993). How relevant is it that the borrower might have fully restored the premises with the insurance proceeds had the lender been willing to transfer the funds to the borrower for that purpose? See Restatement (Third) of Property (Mortgages) §6.3 (1997) (prepayment charge should not be enforced in these circumstances). Certainly this issue becomes more troublesome in the case of a *partial* destruction or condemnation, when a restoration of the premises is usually feasible. These matters are negotiable, and the borrower should strenuously resist any attempt by a lender to reserve the right to collect a fee while denying the borrower the right to restore the premises (and stay in business). At a minimum, borrower's counsel should insist that the prepayment fee be waived in the event of any involuntary partial prepayment. Also, in the case of a partial prepayment where the loan balance is reduced by either insurance or condemnation award proceeds, borrower's counsel should insist that the future debt-service payments be proportionately reduced over the original term of the loan. See M. Madison, J. Dwyer, and S. Bender, The Law of Real Estate Financing §5:36 (2016).

Prompted by the devastation of Hurricane Katrina, Louisiana by statute prohibited collection of prepayment charges for any payment made with insurance proceeds resulting from a gubernatorially declared disaster. La. Rev. Stat. Ann. §9:3532.1.

5. Intentional Default as a Stratagem for Circumventing the Prepayment Charge. Returning to the master hypothetical, suppose Dan Developer walks into your law office during the tenth year of the loan with Ace Insurance Company when the outstanding balance on the loan is approximately $22 million and the market rate of interest for first mortgage money has suddenly dropped from 5 percent to 3 percent. Assume that the loan documents provide that Dan must pay a prepayment fee amounting to 2 percent of the outstanding principal balance if the loan is discharged after the third year and before the twelfth year of the loan term. Dan wants to refinance the loan immediately, but he doesn't want to pay the prepayment fee, which would amount to $440,000. He tells you he intends to purposely default on the loan and, when Ace accelerates the unpaid mortgage indebtedness because of the default, he plans to redeem the property prior to foreclosure or have his relative purchase the property at the foreclosure sale. Dan plans to use the net refinancing proceeds to fund the redemption (or the purchase, as the case may be) and hopes to avoid paying the prepayment fee. In your opinion, will Dan's ploy work? Can you think of any preforeclosure counterstrategy that Ace could employ to protect itself? See Stark, Enforcing Prepayment Charges: Case Law and Drafting Suggestions, 22 Real Prop., Prob.

& Tr. J. 549, 557, 559-560 (Fall 1987). Alternatively, Ace may have contemplated these circumstances in the contract. As discussed above, most courts will enforce the parties' agreement to impose a prepayment charge on repayment in connection with the debtor's default.

6. *Participating Mortgages.* As suggested in the excerpt by Uri (at Chapter 5A1, supra), any prudent postconstruction lender that makes a participating loan (whereby it is entitled to contingent interest based on the borrower's gross or net income) will probably insist on a stringent "lock-in period" or prepayment charge. Why?

7. *Defeasance Provisions.* Issuers of commercial mortgage-backed securities (CMBS) (see Chapter 15C) tend to employ a defeasance approach to address pre-default prepayment instead of a yield maintenance formula. Under defeasance, the borrower must purchase (presumably with the proceeds from selling the mortgaged property) Treasury or other government obligations as substitute collateral for the mortgaged property, which is released from the mortgage lien. These substitute obligations must precisely match the dates and amounts for scheduled principal and interest payments on the loan. Securities are used instead of a replacement mortgage on substitute property to avoid negative tax consequences for real estate mortgage investment conduits typically used in these CMBS transactions. See generally Lefcoe, Prepayment Disincentives in Securitized Commercial Loans, 12 Prob. & Prop. 6 (Sept./Oct. 1999); Schonberger, Defeasance: A Prepayment Substitute, 15 Real Est. Fin. J. 37 (1999). The defeasance approach is not yet tested in the appellate courts. Among the risks faced as to its enforceability is the potential for challenge in bankruptcy as a preference (for substitution within the preference period) based on the substitution of safe government securities in place of real estate.

5. *Payment of Taxes and Insurance: Escrows*

Assume in the master hypothetical that Dan Developer's office building is assessed for tax purposes at $18 million and that the real property tax rate is $1.50 per $1,000 of assessed value, or $270,000 annually. Assume further that the insurance premiums for casualty coverage equal $25,000 per year. Because unpaid real estate taxes will normally result in a lien superior to a first mortgage or deed of trust, and because unpaid insurance premiums could result in no coverage when a casualty occurs, Ace Insurance Company is naturally very concerned that taxes and insurance be paid when due. As a consequence, Ace insists that Dan pay one-twelfth of the estimated annual taxes and premiums along with each monthly payment of debt service. Ace or its loan servicing agent will keep the funds in an escrow account and make the payments directly to the taxing authorities and the insurance company when due. Ace does not intend to pay interest to Dan on the escrowed funds, whether or not Ace receives interest or other compensation (such as using the escrow as compensating balances for loans) from the bank in which the funds are deposited. In large postconstruction loans in which the borrower has significant bargaining clout, however, lenders may waive the requirement for escrow payments; or, in the alternative, the lender may agree to remit the interest on the escrow to the borrower. Below is a typical commitment escrow provision:

> The Mortgage shall provide that the Borrower will deposit on the first day of each month such amount as in the discretion of Lender will enable Lender or a depositary satisfactory to Lender to pay at least thirty (30) days before due, all taxes, assessments, insurance premiums, and similar charges affecting the Property and further provide that no interest on such deposits shall be paid to the Borrower by Lender or the depositary.

The following provision from a mortgage implements this commitment language:

> 5. TAXES AND OTHER CHARGES. Mortgagor shall pay all real estate taxes, water and sewer rents, fines, impositions, and other similar claims and liens assessed, or which may be assessed, against the Premises or any part thereof, without any deduction, defalcation or abatement, not later than ten (10) days before the dates on which such taxes, water and sewer rents, fines, impositions, claims and liens commence to bear interest or penalties, and not later than such dates shall produce to Mortgagee receipts for the payment thereof in full and shall pay every other tax, assessment, claim, fine, imposition, lien or encumbrance which may at any time be or become a lien upon the Premises prior to, or on a parity with, the lien of this Mortgage; provided, however, that if Mortgagor shall in good faith, and by proper legal action, contest any such taxes, assessments, fines, impositions, claims, liens, encumbrances, or other charges, or the validity thereof, and shall have established on its books or by deposit of cash with Mortgagee (as Mortgagee may elect) a reserve for the payment thereof in such amount as Mortgagee may require, then Mortgagor shall not be required to pay the same, or to produce such receipts, during the maintenance of said reserve and as long as such contest operates to prevent collections, and is maintained and prosecuted with diligence, and shall not have been terminated or discontinued adversely to Mortgagor. In addition to the foregoing, Mortgagor will pay when due and will not suffer to remain outstanding, any charges for utilities, whether public or private, with respect to the Premises.
>
> 6. ESCROW FUNDS. Without limiting the effect of Paragraph 5 hereof, at the request of Mortgagee, the Mortgagor shall pay to Mortgagee monthly at the time when the monthly installment of principal, interest or principal and interest is payable, an amount equal to 1/12th of the annual premium for such fire and extended coverage insurance, other hazard insurance and such annual real estate taxes, water rents, sewer rents, special assessments, and any other tax, assessment, claim, lien or encumbrance which may at any time be or become a lien upon the Premises prior to, or on a parity with, the lien of this Mortgage to enable Mortgagee to pay same at least thirty (30) days before they become due, and on demand from time to time shall pay to Mortgagee additional sums necessary to pay such premiums and other payments, all as estimated by Mortgagee, the amounts so paid to be security for such premiums and other payments and to be used in payment thereof. No amounts so

paid shall be deemed to be trust funds but may be commingled with general funds of Mortgagee, and no interest shall be payable thereon. If, pursuant to any provision of this Mortgage, the whole amount of said principal debt remaining or any installment of interest, principal or principal and interest becomes due and payable, Mortgagee shall have the right, at its election, to apply any amounts so held against all or any part of the indebtedness secured hereby, any interest thereon or in payment of the premiums or payments for which the amounts were deposited.

NOTES AND QUESTIONS

Escrow Interest Litigation. In recent years borrowers have initiated class-action litigation to compel lenders to pay interest on escrow accounts, basing their claims on theories ranging from breach of contract and unjust enrichment to fraud and breach of trust. The clear majority view rejects any duty of the mortgagee to pay interest on escrowed funds when the loan documents are silent on the payment of interest. See, for example, Carpenter v. Suffolk Franklin Sav. Bank, 370 Mass. 314, 346 N.E.2d 892 (1976) (absent a manifestation of intent to create a trust, an escrow arrangement created a mere contractual relationship and the bank was not obligated to pay interest on the escrowed funds). What can a lender do at the drafting stage to strengthen its position against attack? Especially in the case of residential loans, legislation in several states now requires the payment of interest on escrowed funds. See, for example, N.Y. Banking Law §14-b.

6. Satisfactory Hazard Insurance

A fire or other unanticipated casualty could destroy the very improvements and rental income stream that secure the postconstruction loan; therefore, lenders commonly regard the insurance requirement as one of the most important provisions in the commitment letter and mortgage, as reflected by the companion provision just discussed that mandates the periodic collection of escrows for insurance premiums as each debt-service payment is made to ensure continuous coverage of the mortgaged property. In this section we scrutinize both the form and content of the hazard insurance coverage that mortgage lenders require in their loan documents. We also explore the issue of control over the hazard insurance and condemnation award proceeds in the event of a full or partial destruction or condemnation of the mortgaged premises.

Consider the following sample language in a commitment letter (which will also be included in the mortgage or deed of trust):

1. Borrower shall keep the Premises continuously insured against loss by fire, with extended coverage and against such other hazards, and in such amounts, as Lender may from time to time reasonably require but such amount on the buildings and improvements on the Land shall in no event be less than the greater of (i) 100%

of the full replacement cost of the buildings and improvements on the Land without deduction for depreciation; (ii) an amount sufficient to prevent the Lender or Borrower from becoming a coinsurer within the terms of the applicable policies; or (iii) the principal amount of the Loan. Borrower shall also maintain rent insurance on the Premises in an amount equal to no less than one year's gross rent from the buildings and improvements on the Land. The policy or policies for all such insurance shall contain replacement cost endorsements and shall be maintained in full force and effect until such time as the indebtedness hereby secured is fully repaid. All policies and any renewals thereof, including but not limited to policies for any amounts carried in excess of the aforesaid minimum and policies not specifically required by the Lender, shall be with an insurance company or companies, and in form and substance satisfactory to Lender, and shall be deposited, premiums paid, with Lender.

2. The loss, if any, shall be payable to Lender according to the terms of a standard mortgagee clause, not subject to contribution, or such other form of mortgagee or loss payment clause as shall be satisfactory to Lender. Lender shall have the right, at its election, to adjust or compromise any loss claims under such insurance and to collect and receive the proceeds thereof and to apply such proceeds, at its election, either to reduce the indebtedness secured hereby or to restore the Premises. All renewal policies shall be delivered, by Borrower, premiums paid, to Lender, at least ten days before the expiration of the expiring policies. The insurance company shall agree in the policy to provide Lender with twenty days prior written notice before any termination or cancellation becomes effective as to Lender. If Lender becomes the owner of the Premises or any part thereof by foreclosure or otherwise, such policies shall become the absolute property of Lender. In the event of damage by fire, other casualty or catastrophe, Borrower agrees forthwith thereafter to restore the Premises to their prior condition, without regard to the adequacy or availability of insurance proceeds.

3. All proceeds in the event of a condemnation or other taking shall be paid to the Mortgagee and applied towards the reduction of the principal balance of the loan indebtedness.

Savarese v. Ohio Farmers Insurance Co.
260 N.Y. 45, 182 N.E. 665 (1932)

CRANE, J.

Does the repair of the premises by the owner after a fire prevent the mortgagee from recovering the insurance payable to [the mortgagee]?

On the 6th day of June, 1927, the defendant Ohio Farmers' Insurance Company of Le Roy, Ohio, issued its policy of insurance whereby it insured Loretta Realty & Finance Corporation for the term of three years from the 26th day of May, 1927, to the 26th day of May, 1930, against all direct loss or damage by fire to the extent of $7,500 on the brick building No. 16 West 119th Street, New York City. The property was thereafter conveyed to Leopold Kirven, the defendant, and the change of ownership duly noted on the policy. Within the period covered by the insurance, and on the 28th day of June, 1929, a fire occurred, causing damage to the extent of $4,230.

At the time of the issuance of said policy and at the time of the fire, the plaintiffs, Pasquale Savarese and Giacomo Savarese, were the owners of a bond secured by a mortgage upon said premises for $7,500, upon which there was due at the time of the loss $6,500, with interest from April 1, 1929. The mortgage provided that the mortgagor should keep the premises insured against loss by fire for the benefit of the mortgagee. The policy referred to contained the usual standard mortgagee clause, reading as follows: "Loss or damage, if any, under this policy, shall be payable to Pasquale Savarese & Giacomo Savarese as mortgagee, as interest may appear, and this insurance, as to the interest of the mortgagee only therein, shall not be invalidated by any act or neglect of the mortgagor or owner of the within described property," etc.

The defendants Markowitz and Grey, as contractors with the owner, repaired the premises, so that by the 6th day of September, 1929, the property was restored to the condition in which it existed before the fire. As compensation for their work, the owner transferred to Markowitz and Grey his interest in the fire insurance policy, and the defendant insurance company stands ready to pay them the sum of $1,178.64, by applying, in calculation, the pro rata provisions of the policy. Judgment for this amount has been awarded to these contractor-defendants, and they have not appealed from the amount adjudged to be due. The plaintiffs, mortgagees, have appealed, claiming the full benefit of the policy of insurance and the recovery of the full amount of the loss, $4,230, unimpaired by any act of the owner in making repairs and restoring the property to its previous good condition.

The Appellate Division has taken the position, with some force of reasoning, and with some authority to support it, that the mortgagees sustained no damage, because when this action was commenced the security for their mortgage was the same building in the same state of repair as at the time the mortgage was taken. At first blush this conclusion seems quite plausible, but upon further analysis must yield to other considerations.

Under the mortgagee clause the policy issued by the defendant insured the mortgagees' interest as fully and to the same extent as if they had taken out a policy directly with the insurance company. In Eddy v. London Assurance Corp., 143 N.Y. 311, 322, 38 N.E. 307, 309, 25 L.R.A. 686, this court said: "The effect of the mortgage clause hereinbefore set forth is to make an entirely separate insurance of the mortgagee's interest, and he takes the same benefit from his insurance as if he had received a separate policy from the company, free from the conditions imposed upon the owners.". . .

Thus it has been held that recovery may be had by the mortgagee on his insurance policy, although his security under the mortgage is perfectly good and valid. Kernochan v. New York Bowery Fire Ins. Co., 17 N.Y. 428, 435. The court there said: ". . . Whether the loss by diminishing the mortgage security, endangers the collection of the debt, or the security remains ample, is not by the contract made of any importance; in either case it is insured against and the amount of it is to be paid.". . .

From these authorities we must conclude that whether the mortgagee takes out his own insurance, or whether he is insured by the mortgagor, under the usual mortgagee clause in the insurance policy, his right to recover in case of a fire is not dependent upon the sufficiency or insufficiency of the mortgage security after the fire. . . .

When we further analyze the terms of the policy and the situation of the mortgagee, reason also points to the conclusion that when a fire occurs the insurance company must pay the loss to the mortgagee in accordance with its contract with him. The mortgagor benefits by such payment as the insurance money reduces the amount of the mortgage debt. . . . The value taken out of the property by the fire is taken off the mortgage by the payment of the insurance money, and the parties remain in the same relative position after as before the fire.

If it be that the mortgagor can wipe out the benefits to the mortgagee under a policy by repairing the premises without the knowledge or against the consent of the mortgagee, how long can the owner take in deciding to make repairs? . . . Under the ruling below, no [time] limit is placed upon the owner, for if he restores the property to its previous condition any time before action brought or tried, the mortgagee has sustained no loss. In the meantime the property may remain in its destroyed condition, with loss of income to the owner with which he might pay taxes and interest on prior incumbrances. Must the mortgagee litigate the extent and sufficiency of the repairs, or, if partially repaired, is his insurance to be reduced in proportion? We do not think that the insurance contract can thus be modified by the act of a third party to the material disadvantage of the mortgagee. Section 254 of the Real Property Law (Consol. Laws, ch. 50), subdivision 4, says that the mortgagee at his option may apply the insurance toward the payment of the mortgage or (at his election) "the same may be paid over either wholly or in part to the mortgagor . . . for the repair of said buildings . . . and if the mortgagee receive and retain insurance money for damage by fire to said premises, the lien of the mortgage shall be affected only by a reduction of the amount of said lien by the amount of such insurance money received and retained by said mortgagee." This choice given to the mortgagee to apply the insurance money either to his mortgage or to the repairs excludes a like choice in the owner-mortgagor without the mortgagee's consent. Such a right is single by nature; it cannot exist in both the mortgagor and the mortgagee, otherwise the former might decide for repairs and the other for payment, and nothing would result. No; the choice is with the mortgagee alone and in this case he asks for payment of the insurance money and does not consent that it be applied to repairs. . . .

The defendant, therefore, being liable to the mortgagee on the policy, how much is it obliged to pay? The plaintiffs claim the full amount of the fire damage, $4,230, but the policy does not obligate the insurance company to pay the full amount of the loss. The contract by the New York standard average clause provides: "This Company shall not be liable for a greater proportion of any loss or damage to the property described herein than the sum hereby insured bears to eighty per cent (80%) of the actual cash value of said property at the time such loss shall happen." . . .

The value of the property at the time of the loss was $22,500, of which 80 percent is $18,000. The proportion of $7,500, the sum insured, to $18,000, is as 5 to 12. The loss being $4,230, five-twelfths of this amount is $1,762.50, which the insurance company must pay the plaintiffs. . . .

NOTES AND QUESTIONS

1. Selection of Carrier. Many states have laws that prohibit lenders from selecting the borrower's insurance carrier or broker. See, for example, N.Y. Ins. Law §2502(a) (violations punishable as a misdemeanor). Is there any conflict between such statutes and commitment language giving the lender the right to approve the carrier?

2. Coinsurance. As illustrated by the judgment in *Savarese*, a coinsurance provision relieves the insurer of the obligation to pay a portion of the loss if the property is underinsured. Insurance companies use these clauses to equalize the distribution of premium costs among all policyholders by penalizing those who are underinsured. While the percentage of the value of the property that must be insured to avoid application of the coinsurance provision varies, it is typically 80 percent or more of the actual cash value of the property insured at the time of loss. "Actual cash value" usually refers to replacement cost less depreciation. A typical 80 percent coinsurance clause reads, in part, "This company shall not be liable for a greater proportion of any loss or damage to the insured property than the sum hereby insured bears to 80% of the actual cash value of said property at the time such loss shall happen."

Returning to the master hypothetical, assume that at the time of loss the actual cash value of Dan Developer's property was $34 million ($30 million for the building and $4 million in land value) and that Dan (without Ace's knowledge or consent) carried only $20 million in insurance under a policy with an 80 percent coinsurance clause. How much would Dan receive from the insurance company if he suffered a $4 million loss? If Dan carried $12 million in insurance, how much would he receive in the event of a $4 million loss? If Dan's mortgage contained a clause such as the sample clause excerpted above, and Ace did a proper monitoring job, would Dan ever be carrying these amounts of insurance?

3. Loss Payable Clauses. Essentially, there are two types of loss payable clauses: the old "open mortgage" clause and the more recent and widely prevalent "New York standard," "standard," or "union mortgage" clause. Under an open mortgage clause, the mortgagee is deemed to be a mere "appointee" of the mortgagor, who stands in the shoes of the latter and is therefore subject to any defenses the insurer might have against the mortgagor. See, for example, Fred v. Pacific Indemnity Co., 53 Haw. 384, 494 P.2d 783 (1972). By contrast, under the standard loss payable clause, the mortgagee may recover even if the loss is caused by the insured mortgagor (for example, by arson) and (as held in *Savarese*) even where the mortgagee's security interest was not impaired by the loss. But the mortgagee would not be protected if the mortgagor neglects to pay the insurance premiums in a timely manner. To review: What commitment and mortgage provision makes the latter occurrence unlikely?

Under a standard mortgage clause as supplied in the *Savarese* case (where it was called the standard mortgagee clause), would an insurer be able to deny coverage to the mortgagee if the policy had been issued in reliance on misrepresentations by the mortgagor? What would be the mortgagee's likely counterargument to such a defense pleaded by an insurer?

Under the standard mortgage clause, the mortgagee must notify the insurer of any change in ownership so that the insurer can reassess its risk and protect itself by canceling the policy on notice or by increasing the premium. Suppose, in the hypothetical, that Dan defaults under the postconstruction mortgage and Ace, as the successful bidder, purchases the property for the full amount of the debt at the foreclosure sale but fails to notify the insurer about the change in ownership. In the event of a subsequent casualty loss, can the insurer deny a claim made by Ace? See Shores v. Rabon, 251 N.C. 790, 112 S.E.2d 556 (1960), aff'd per curiam, 253 N.C. 428, 117 S.E.2d 1 (1960); see also Consolidated Mortgage Corp. v. American Security Ins. Co., 69 Mich. App. 251, 244 N.W.2d 434, 437 (1976) (disagreed with by Citizens Mortgage Corp. v. Michigan Basic Property Ins. Ass'n, 111 Mich. App. 393, 314 N.W.2d 635 (1981)). What if the casualty loss occurs after Ace accelerates the debt, but before the foreclosure sale in which Ace bids in the full amount of the outstanding mortgage indebtedness? Can Ace still recover the insurance proceeds? See Smith v. General Mortgage Corp., 73 Mich. App. 720, 252 N.W.2d 551 (1977), mod., 402 Mich. 125, 261 N.W.2d 710 (1978); Northwestern Natl. Ins. Co. v. Mildenberger, 359 S.W.2d 380 (Mo. Ct. App. 1962); see generally Comment, Foreclosure, Loss, and the Proper Distribution of Insurance Proceeds Under Open and Standard Mortgage Clauses: Some Observations, 7 Val. U. L. Rev. 485 (1973).

4. Control over Insurance Proceeds. From the borrower's viewpoint, one of the most onerous provisions in a typical loan commitment is the language providing the postconstruction lender with the option to apply the insurance proceeds to reduce the indebtedness or to restore the premises (see the second paragraph in the sample commitment letter excerpted supra). Because the mortgagee can effectively deny to the mortgagor the use of the proceeds to rebuild the premises, even in the case of a partial destruction, this provision has been criticized as being inherently unfair to the mortgagor unless the mortgagee can demonstrate that its security interest will be impaired if the proceeds are not applied to the debt. Do you agree? A mortgagor such as Dan Developer would argue that it had bargained for maintaining the loan for a stated period of time and that the lender, Ace, should not have the right to deprive him unilaterally of being able to continue to operate the office building by withholding the insurance proceeds. Can you think of any arguments that Ace can make as to why it should have control over the application of the funds? Would Ace's argument be any stronger if the loss occurred after Dan had defaulted on the mortgage or the mortgage note had already matured? See G. Nelson et al., Real Estate Finance Law §4.15, at 168 (6th ed. 2015). If under this language Ace decides to use the insurance proceeds to reduce the mortgage indebtedness rather than for restoration, could Ace also insist that Dan restore the premises with his own funds?

Notwithstanding the predicament in which this clause places Dan, such clauses are usually held enforceable. Indeed, even in the absence of specific language in the mortgage, most courts have held that the mortgagee, under a standard mortgage clause in the insurance policy, may apply the proceeds to reduce the debt even where the value of the uninjured portion of the premises exceeds the balance of the indebtedness (see, for example, English v. Fischer, 660 S.W.2d 521 (Tex. 1983)), or, as in *Savarese*, where the mortgagor has restored the premises with its own funds. But see Schoolcraft v. Ross, 81 Cal. App. 3d 75, 146 Cal. Rptr. 57 (1978), and a New York statute that gives the mortgagor a qualified right to the insurance proceeds. N.Y. Real Prop. Law §254(4) (as amended after *Savarese*). See also Restatement (Third) of Property (Mortgages) §4.7(b) (1997) (on mortgagor's request, insurance proceeds must be used for restoration where sufficient in amount and where property value once restored will equal or exceed that at the time the mortgage was made; mortgagee's inclusion of contrary provision in the mortgage may be enforced unless under the particular circumstances it is unconscionable or bad faith).

> ➤ *Problem 5-3*
> In light of the concerns expressed by Justice Crane in the *Savarese* decision (for example, relinquishing control over the funds may force the mortgagee to "litigate the extent and sufficiency of the repairs") and the lender's anxiety with respect to mechanic's liens filed against the property if workers are not paid, what compromise commitment language would you, as attorney for Dan Developer, suggest to Ace that should be reasonably acceptable to both parties? Another concern of Dan's is that under Ace's proposed language Ace would not be obligated to reduce or postpone subsequent amortization payments if Ace were to use the proceeds to reduce the mortgage indebtedness in the event of a partial destruction. As attorney for Dan, what language should you insist on in the prepayment provision to protect Dan? ◄

5. Control over Condemnation Proceeds. The economic predicament and negotiating demands of a mortgagor who wants to continue its business notwithstanding a partial fire destruction are analogous to those of a mortgagor confronted with a partial taking of the mortgaged premises.

> ➤ *Problem 5-4*

After reviewing the sample mortgage in the Documents Manual, what modifications in the condemnation clause in Paragraph 6 of the sample mortgage would you request (as counsel for the borrower) to protect your client in the event of a partial taking? If the mortgagee's counsel agrees to your proposed changes with respect to the consequences of a partial taking, what additional protective provisions will it most likely require for its client by way of a compromise? See generally Branch, Negotiating Casualty Insurance Proceeds and Condemnation Awards Clauses (with Forms), 13 Prac. Real Est. Law. 33 (Jan. 1997). ◄

While it would appear that their interests should coincide in any condemnation proceeding, the mortgagor and mortgagee will sometimes be in conflict. For example, if the proposed condemnation award settlement amount is way below the balance of the mortgage indebtedness, the borrower may lose interest in the proceedings. If the settlement amount is sufficient to discharge the indebtedness, the mortgagee may not be willing to assume the risk of receiving a lesser amount at litigation, while the borrower may want to litigate because it has nothing to lose. Can you suggest any additional language in the sample mortgage provision that might help to ameliorate such potential conflicts of interest?

Observe that the sample provision requires the mortgagor to reimburse the mortgagee for all of its costs and expenses incurred in connection with collecting the condemnation award, even though it is possible that the mortgagor may receive nothing. Can you think of some alternative language that would be more balanced and yet be reasonably acceptable to both parties? See generally Teague, Condemnation of Mortgaged Property, 44 Tex. L. Rev. 1535 (1966).

To review: In the event of a total condemnation or destruction of the premises where the mortgagee uses the condemnation award or insurance proceeds, respectively, to pay off the outstanding indebtedness, could the mortgagee demand that the mortgagor pay a prepayment charge? See Chapter 5A4, supra.

6. Drafting Pitfalls. Occasionally lenders have failed to control insurance or analogous compensatory proceeds due to unfavorable interpretations of the reach of their loan documents. For example, mortgagees have encountered problems reaching earthquake insurance proceeds where their loan documents did not require such coverage, but the mortgagor nonetheless obtained it. In Ziello v. Superior Court, 36 Cal. App. 4th 321, 42 Cal. Rptr. 2d 251 (1995), the deed of trust required the borrower to insure the property against loss by fire, hazards within the term "extended coverage," and other hazards for which the lender required insurance, with loss payable to the lender. Although the lender did not require earthquake insurance, the borrower purchased coverage on her own. Following California's Northridge quake, the mortgagee asserted an interest in the insurance proceeds. The appellate court rejected the lender's argument that the deed of trust anti-waste provisions entitled it to the insurance proceeds. A different result was reached where the deed of trust specified that if the borrower obtained coverage not required by the lender, the borrower would name the lender as loss payee and the lender could determine whether such insurance proceeds were applied to repairs or to the loan balance. Martin v. World Savings and Loan Assoc., 92 Cal. App. 4th 803, 112 Cal. Rptr. 2d 225 (2001) (earthquake coverage); see also JEM Enterprises v. Washington Mutual Bank, F.A., 99 Cal. App. 4th 638, 121 Cal. Rptr. 2d 458 (2002) (although its deed of trust did not require the earthquake insurance obtained by the borrower, the mortgagee prevailed under a clause assigning to the lender "all sums due or payable . . . for injury or damage to such property").

In an analogous case, the Ninth Circuit rejected a mortgage lender's conversion claim against the lawyers who represented the borrowers in their recovery from the project builders for construction defects. In re Emery, 317 F.3d 1064 (9th Cir. 2003). The deed of trust assigned to the lender all sums "for injury or damages to the Property" to be applied to "any amount that I may owe the Lender." Because the borrowers were not in default at the time, the court construed the amount "owe[d]" as zero and held the lender had no interest in the construction defect proceeds.

7. Terrorism Insurance. Following the September 11th attacks, many insurers excluded terrorism coverage from renewal policies; when available, premiums for such coverage soared. At the same time, mortgage lenders demanded terrorism coverage in commitments for loans on trophy properties, as well as under existing loan provisions requiring such insurance as the lender may request from time to time. In litigation in New York, the mortgage borrowers disputed the lender's insistence that they purchase terrorism coverage on the mortgaged property—the 47-story Condé Nast building—pursuant to a mortgage provision requiring the borrowers to purchase generally available insurance coverage on the building at commercially reasonable premiums. See Four Times Square Assocs., LLC v. Cigna Investments Inc., 306 A.D.2d 4, 764 N.Y.S.2d 1 (2003) (issuing preliminary injunction barring lender's declaration of default based on borrower refusal to purchase terrorism coverage). But see BFP 245 Park Co., LLC v. GMAC Commercial Mortgage Corp., 12 A.D.3d 330, 786 N.Y.S.2d 425 (2004) (construing loan documents to authorize lender to require terrorism coverage for building near Grand Central Terminal); Omni Berkshire Corp. v. Wells Fargo Bank, 307 F. Supp. 2d 534 (S.D.N.Y. 2004) (terrorism insurance properly demanded under "other reasonable insurance" clause).

7. *The Prohibition of Junior Financing*

Returning to the master hypothetical, suppose that 12 years after the project is completed it is now worth $40 million and that loan payments have reduced the principal balance on the Ace mortgage from $25 million to approximately $20 million, so the present market value of the ownership interest, or "equity," in the project is about $20 million. Dan would like to translate some of this accumulated equity into tax-free cash so that he can expand or renovate the office building; alternatively, Dan (and his investors) simply want these funds for their own personal use. One option would be for Dan to refinance the Ace mortgage with a larger substitute first mortgage loan in the amount of $30 million (at the same 75 percent loan-to-value ratio). After paying the balance on Ace's loan, Dan would have net refinancing proceeds of about $10 million. Alternatively, Dan could obtain a second mortgage loan from a secondary lender in the amount of $10 million that would be junior in lien priority to the Ace mortgage. However, the first mortgage note (held by Ace) may contain a provision prohibiting such junior financing and providing Ace with the right to call in ("accelerate") the first mortgage indebtedness if the provision is violated. Such a provision is referred to as a "due-on-encumbrance" clause, and is closely related to the "due-on-sale" clause discussed in Chapter 5A8, infra. The following is a typical due-on-encumbrance clause from a postconstruction commitment letter:

> The Mortgage shall contain a provision prohibiting any financing by the Borrower in addition to the Loan without the prior written consent of Lender, which financing is secured by either a mortgage lien or other encumbrance on the Improvements or Property (or any part thereof).

Alternatively, as a compromise, the due-on-encumbrance clause might permit junior liens that meet certain specified requirements:

> SUBORDINATE FINANCING. Mortgagor covenants and agrees that it will not further encumber or mortgage the Premises, or any part thereof, or any interest therein and will not execute, deliver or take back any mortgage or mortgages, unless such mortgage or mortgages (hereinafter referred to as "Subordinate Mortgage") shall contain provisions to the effect that upon foreclosure of such Subordinate Mortgage: (i) no tenants under leases of space in the Premises will be made parties defendant nor will any other action be taken with respect to such tenants which would result in the termination of their leases or tenancies without the prior written consent of Mortgagee; and (ii) the rents, income, receipts, revenues, issues and profits issuing from the Premises, or from any lease of space therein, shall not be collected, except through a Receiver appointed by a court after notice of application for such appointment has been given to Mortgagee; the money collected by the Receiver shall be first applied and used for the payment of interest and principal due and owing under this Mortgage and the indebtedness secured hereby, real estate taxes, water rates, sewer rents, assessments or other governmental charges affecting the Premises and all other maintenance and operation charges and disbursements incurred in connection with the operation and maintenance of the Premises, and if during the pendency of any such mortgage foreclosure proceeding, action is instituted for the foreclosure of this Mortgage, and an application is made by Mortgagee for an extension of such Receivership for the benefit of Mortgagee, any and all funds collected by the Receiver prior to the date of such application shall be held by such Receiver and applied solely for the benefit of the Mortgagee hereunder and the holder of such Subordinate Mortgage shall not be entitled to any part thereof,

unless and until there is a surplus remaining after all of the aforesaid payments and any other necessary payments; and (iii) immediate notice of the institution of such foreclosure proceeding shall be given to Mortgagee and true copies of all papers served or entered in such foreclosure proceeding shall be served upon Mortgagee.

An executed counterpart of each Subordinate Mortgage shall be delivered to Mortgagee by Mortgagor within ten (10) days after the execution and delivery thereof by Mortgagor.

Such Subordinate Mortgage shall contain an express covenant to the effect that it is in all respects subject and subordinate to this Mortgage and that the Mortgagee thereunder will upon demand further subordinate said Mortgage to the lien and terms, covenants and conditions of this Mortgage as hereinafter extended, renewed, modified or consolidated.

A "wraparound" mortgage is a form of junior financing whereby the face amount of the secondary financing includes the outstanding balance of the first mortgage debt and the junior lender pays the debt service on the senior indebtedness directly to the first mortgagee. The following adjunct to the due-on-encumbrance clause in a mortgage might be called a "due-on-wrap" clause:

WRAPAROUND FINANCING. Mortgagor agrees that should the Premises at any time be or become subject to the lien of any mortgage or deed of trust in connection with which payments on account of the indebtedness secured hereby are to be made directly or indirectly by or through the mortgagee or beneficiary thereunder, regardless of such mortgagee or beneficiary, the whole of the principal and interest and other sums hereby secured, at the option of Mortgagee, shall immediately become due and payable.

The following case illustrates the type of judicial challenge that borrowers have mounted against the due-on-encumbrance clause.

La Sala v. American Savings & Loan Association
5 Cal. 3d 864, 489 P.2d 1113, 97 Cal. Rptr. 849 (1971)

TOBRINER, Justice.

Plaintiffs Frank La Sala, Grace La Sala, and Dorothy Iford brought a class action against American Savings & Loan Association, (hereinafter "American") alleging that a provision in American's form of trust deed, which permits American to accelerate if the borrower executes a junior encumbrance on the secured property, constituted an invalid restraint upon alienation. . . .[W]e hold that, although the clause in American's trust deed is not per se an illegal restraint upon alienation, the enforcement of that clause unlawfully restrains alienation whenever the borrower's execution of a junior encumbrance does not endanger the lender's security. . . .

American utilizes a form deed of trust which contains, on the reverse side in fine print, a clause stating: "Should Trustor sell, convey, transfer, dispose of or further encumber said property, or any part thereof, or of any interest therein, or agree to do so without the written consent of Beneficiary being first obtained, then Beneficiary shall have the right, at its option, to declare all sums secured hereby forthwith due and payable." We shall refer to this clause as a "due-on-encumbrance" provision; we thereby distinguish it from clauses which provide for acceleration only upon the sale, but not upon the encumbering, of secured property.

On August 13, 1958, plaintiff Dorothy Iford and her late husband borrowed $9,500, at 6.6 percent interest, from American, and executed a promissory note and a trust deed which included the due-on-encumbrance provision. On November 20, 1963, Frank and Grace La Sala, the other named plaintiffs, borrowed $20,700 from American at 6 percent interest; they also executed a note and a trust deed with the due-on-encumbrance clause.

On June 9, 1969, the La Salas borrowed $3,800 from Fred D. Hudkins, and executed a note and second deed of trust; Statewide Home Mortgage Co. acted as loan broker. On June 11, 1969, Iford borrowed $2,500 from Edward and June Ulrich, and also gave a note and second trust deed; Lanco Mortgage Co. acted as broker. About July 7 of 1969 both Iford and La Salas received a form letter from American notifying them of American's right to accelerate. The letter to La Salas offered to waive American's right to accelerate in return for a payment of $150 and an increase in the rate of interest on the first deed of trust from 6 to 9 percent. The letter to Iford was identical in form, but asked a waiver fee of $50 and an increase in interest to 8.75 percent.

Plaintiffs then filed the present action for declaratory relief "for themselves and all other persons similarly situated." . . .

We conclude . . . that whether the enforcement of the due-on-encumbrance clause unlawfully restrains alienation turns upon whether such enforcement is reasonably necessary to protect the lender's security—an issue which cannot be resolved merely by examination of the pleadings and declarations now before us. . . .

Defendants [lender and the trustee] argue that whenever a borrower takes out a second lien, his very conduct demonstrates that he has become financially irresponsible or at least a poor credit risk. Such an assertion, however, is an overgeneralization, a proposition true of some borrowers but not of others. Moreover, American does not claim a right to accelerate merely upon learning that the borrower has encountered economic adversity. In light of these considerations we find no justification in American's arbitrary seizure of the making of a second lien, a fact not necessarily indicative of declining credit ability, as a basis for acceleration.

We recognize, however, as defendants point out, that instances may occur when the institution of a second lien does endanger the security of the first lien. In some cases the giving of a possessory security interest, for example, a conveyance to a mortgagee in possession, would pose the same dangers of waste and depreciation as would an outright sale. In other cases, a second lien may be employed as a guise to effect a sale of the property. In still others a bona fide second loan may still leave the borrower with little or no equity in the property.

We conclude, then, in instances in which the borrower's subsequent conduct endangers the lender's security, the enforcement of the due-on-encumbrance clause may be reasonably necessary to protect the lender's interests. In many other instances, however, the clause serves no such purpose. In fact, American itself recognizes that enforcement of such a provision cannot invariably be sustained as reasonably necessary to protect the primary security. When a borrower takes out a secondary loan American itself maintains that it does not elect automatically to accelerate, but examines the circumstances of the transaction. If its security is safe, American states that it then waives its right to accelerate. . . .

Yet defendants claim, in essence, that the lender should retain an *absolute* discretion to determine whether the transaction calls for enforcement of the due-on-encumbrance clause. Such an uncontrolled power, however, creates too serious a potential of abuse. Even when the lender's security has not been exposed to danger, the lender, by threatening to accelerate, could compel the borrower to pay a fee or give other valuable consideration for the waiver. The Attorney General, as amicus curiae, charges that as a matter of practice American requires waiver fees whenever a borrower makes a junior encumbrance. Defendants deny this charge yet seek from us a declaration that a lender enjoys an unconditional right to enforce the due-on-encumbrance clause and, as a necessary corollary the unconditional right to obtain from a borrower whatever consideration it can exact for the waiver, however inequitable such exaction may be. . . .

The judgment of the superior court dismissing the action on behalf of the class is reversed, and the cause remanded to that court for further proceedings in accord with the views expressed in this opinion.

NOTES AND QUESTIONS

1. The Borrower's Perspective. Why is the right to obtain junior financing on the property so important to a borrower such as Dan Developer, who is locked into a long-term postconstruction loan?

2. The Lender's Perspective. In the past, most postconstruction lenders were not concerned about subsequent junior financing and some even welcomed such subordinate financing. Because foreclosure of the first mortgage could extinguish any junior lien, the junior lender was likely to cure any defaults of the borrower under the first mortgage and treat such outlays on behalf of the borrower as additional indebtedness under the second mortgage. The junior lender will normally require a "cross default" clause in its mortgage, under which a default by the borrower on the first mortgage is automatically deemed to be a default under the second, thus enabling the junior lender, as a last resort, to seek recoupment of these additional expenditures by foreclosing its own mortgage. Thus, the postconstruction lender viewed subordinate financing as added assurance that its senior indebtedness would be paid.

In recent years, however, many lenders have begun to limit or prohibit junior financing, for a wide variety of reasons. For example, some lenders are concerned about the borrower's overburdening the property with financing that could cause the economic collapse of a project that would otherwise remain viable. If the borrower were to use all the income from the property for debt service, unexpected expenses could result in deferred maintenance and tenant dissatisfaction, eventually converting a good loan in the senior lender's portfolio into a problem one. Other senior lenders might be concerned that the borrower would not receive sufficient income from the property to keep it interested in the project. Most large borrower-developers have numerous concurrent projects that are bound to impose competing demands on their time and expertise. Senior lenders want to make sure that the borrower will feel it is worthwhile to devote the necessary attention to the project to make it a success.

Some lenders like the fact that the equity cushion is increasing behind their secured first position. Because in an economic downturn a borrower would be more reluctant to abandon the project if there is equity in the property, the equity tends to serve as additional security that the loan will be repaid. Others are wary of allowing junior financing because the junior mortgagee represents an additional party who might complicate any foreclosure or bankruptcy proceeding. For example, in most states a junior lender must be joined as a party defendant in a foreclosure action by the senior mortgagee. Also, the presence of a junior lender may prevent the senior lender from avoiding foreclosure by convincing the borrower to transfer the property voluntarily to the senior lender by means of a "deed in lieu of foreclosure." See Chapter 8A. Also, a junior lender may interfere with the senior lender's control over any fire insurance or condemnation award proceeds or prevent changes in the first mortgage (for example, the loan amount) without its consent. In addition, if the junior lender is in bankruptcy, the senior lender may be prevented ("stayed") from foreclosing its own mortgage. See Chapters 18C1.

Finally, some nonrecourse lenders fear that if the property becomes subject to junior liens securing recourse loans, and the property becomes financially troubled, the developer might first seek to satisfy these junior creditors, who can sue it personally, rather than keep the first mortgage current.

> ➤ *Problem 5-5*
> If you were Ace's lending officer, what position would you take if Dan Developer wanted to delete the due-on-encumbrance clause? If you would insist on retaining the clause, which of the foregoing reasons would be most significant in your determination? Are there any compromise solutions you can suggest that might be reasonably acceptable to both Dan and Ace, the senior lender? ◄

The *La Sala* case held that a senior mortgagee can enforce a due-on-encumbrance clause only when such enforcement is reasonably necessary to protect the senior lender's security interest. What examples does the court cite? Can you think of any others?

An oft-cited danger to lenders' security is that a foreclosing junior mortgagee could terminate subordinate occupancy leases and thereby threaten the rental income stream on which the lender relies as primary security for its loan. See the discussion at Chapter 3E. How do lenders address this problem in the sample compromise due-on-encumbrance provision set forth above? Do you think this approach will work?

3. Wraparound Financing. Wraparound financing is a form of junior financing whereby the wraparound (junior) lender agrees to advance funds in excess of first mortgage indebtedness and to repay the first mortgage indebtedness pursuant to its terms. The face amount of the wraparound loan includes or "wraps around" the existing indebtedness. Therefore, because of leverage provided by the low interest rate on the existing first mortgage, the wraparound lender can achieve an above-market yield on the funds it actually disburses and can afford to charge the borrower a below-market rate on the net amount of such loan advances. Why might a first mortgagee insist that its mortgage include a "due-on-wrap" clause?

4. Federal Legislation. The Garn-St. Germain Depository Institutions Act is examined at Chapter 5A8, infra. Under this Act, subject to certain exceptions, "due-on-sale" clauses are freely enforceable in accordance with their terms notwithstanding contrary state law, including any court decisions that would limit enforcement to transfers that jeopardize the lender's security. The Act expressly invalidates due-on-encumbrance clauses in residential real estate loans (with fewer than five dwelling units). See 12 U.S.C. §1701j-3(d)(1). With regard to commercial properties, however, there is some uncertainty whether the Act encompasses due-on-encumbrance clauses and thereby preempts state law, such as the *La Sala* case, that might prohibit or limit their enforcement. Consider the Act's definition of "due-on-sale" clauses found infra. Do you think it encompasses due-on-encumbrance clauses?

8. The Right to Sell Mortgaged Property

Most lenders will insist on a clause in the promissory note and the mortgage or deed of trust providing them with the right to accelerate the mortgage indebtedness if the mortgagor should sell the mortgaged property without first obtaining their consent. In lieu of acceleration, the lender may be willing to accept a provision that would permit a sale but require the purchaser to assume the existing mortgage at the current rate of interest or require that the seller-mortgagor make a substantial prepayment or "pay down" of principal when the property is sold.

Developers are, of course, opposed to such a constraint, which could make it more difficult to sell the property if interest rates should rise and the purchaser is precluded from assuming the existing mortgage at the lower interest rate. Nevertheless, these provisions, referred to as "due-on-sale" clauses, have traditionally been required by lenders when the developer's management expertise and credit reputation have been relied on in the decision to make the loan.

Today, due-on-sale clauses are also being used by postconstruction lenders as a hedge against inflation on their fixed rate loans. In the case of relatively long-term loans, most developer-owners will sell their properties before their loans mature; therefore due-on-sale clauses enable lenders to adjust their loans to current higher interest rates when these properties are sold during inflationary periods.

Like its companion, the due-on-encumbrance clause, the due-on-sale clause has been the subject of a protracted struggle in the courts between borrowers, who contend that these clauses constitute illegal restraints on alienation, and lenders, who regard these clauses as vital protection against impairment of their security interests and their major source of economic protection against inflation and volatility in interest rates. Finally, in 1982, Congress stepped in to enact the Garn-St. Germain Depository Institutions Act, that was designed to validate due-on-sale clauses. The Act contains the following provision:[9]

> (a) For the purpose of this section—
>
> (1) the term "due-on-sale clause" means a contract provision which authorizes a lender, at its option, to declare due and payable sums secured by the lender's security instrument if all or any part of the property, or an interest therein, securing the real property loan is sold or transferred without the lender's prior written consent;
>
> (2) the term "lender" means a person or government agency making a real property loan or any assignee or transferee, in whole or in part, of such a person or agency;
>
> (3) the term "real property loan" means a loan, mortgage, advance, or credit sale secured by a lien on real property, [or] the stock allocated to a dwelling unit in a cooperative housing corporation. . . .
>
> (b)(1) Notwithstanding any provision of the constitution or laws (including the judicial decisions) of any State to the contrary, a lender may . . . enter into or enforce contract containing a due-on-sale clause with respect to a real property loan.
>
> (2) Except as otherwise provided in subsection (d) [certain exceptions for residential loans] of this section, the exercise by the lender of its option pursuant to such a clause shall be exclusively governed by the terms of the loan contract, and all rights and remedies of the lender and the borrower shall be fixed and governed by the contract.

---

9. 12 U.S.C. §1701j-3(a)-(b).

Following the enactment of Garn-St. Germain, the struggle has shifted from the courts to the bargaining table as courts must, with very few exceptions, enforce the parties' due-on-sale agreement in accordance with its terms, whether onerous or not. The following is an example of a commitment provision requiring a due-on-sale clause in the loan documents:

> The Note and Mortgage shall contain clauses providing that in the event the Borrower conveys, transfers or assigns the property, or any part thereof, or any interest therein, without the lender's prior written consent, such transfer shall be deemed an "Event of Default" under which the whole of the principal sum remaining unpaid, together with all accrued interest thereon, may at the option of the mortgagee become immediately due and payable and may be recovered at once by foreclosure or otherwise.

The pay-down approach is illustrated by the following commitment provision:

> The Note and Mortgage shall contain clauses in form, scope and substance satisfactory to Lender's law department, providing that in the event that without Lender's prior written consent (i) Borrower conveys, transfers, assigns or sells the Property, or any part thereof, or interest therein, or (ii) any partner of Borrower transfers, sells or otherwise disposes of his or her interest, or any part thereof in the Partnership, then in any or all such events, Lender shall have the right, at its option, to declare an amount equal to 25% of the outstanding principal balance of the Loan to be immediately due and payable, whereupon it shall be so due and payable. Such prepayment shall be without prepayment fee and shall be applied to the reduction of the Loan in the inverse order of maturity of the required payments of principal. The Note and Mortgage shall contain such other provisions as Lender's law department deems necessary to monitor and enforce the provisions of this Article.

Sometimes the borrower anticipates a conveyance that would otherwise trigger the due-on-sale clause and succeeds in gaining the lender's advance consent to the transfer at the commitment stage. Assume that the following language was added to the commitment in the master hypothetical at the behest of Dan Developer:

> A transfer by Dan Developer of 100% of the outstanding common stock in Borrower to a trust or other entity acceptable to Lender for the benefit of the immediate family of Dan Developer shall not constitute a transfer for the purposes of this section so long as Lender is furnished with evidence, satisfactory to Lender, that said trust or other entity is solely for the benefit of the immediate family of Dan Developer and that there are no other beneficiaries of said trust or other entity, and that Dan Developer shall continue to manage or control the management and operation of the Premises after such transfer. For purposes of this section, the term "immediate family" is defined solely as the spouse and/or children of Dan Developer. A transfer by will or intestacy of the ownership interest of Dan Developer shall not constitute a transfer for the purposes of this section.

NOTES AND QUESTIONS

1. Assumption v. "Subject to" Sales. In the event that real property is sold while encumbered by mortgage financing that is not satisfied in connection with the sale, the purchaser will either acquire the property "subject to" the mortgage or will "assume" the mortgage loan. A purchase "subject to" the mortgage means that, upon default on the obligation secured by the mortgage, the mortgagee will have recourse against the property and the original mortgagor (except for nonrecourse loans or applicable antideficiency laws discussed at Chapter 8C3a), but will have no personal recourse against the "subject to" purchaser. In contrast, the purchaser that promises the seller or lender to personally repay the mortgage obligation "assumes" the mortgage loan and is thereby personally liable to the mortgagee (either on direct or derivative theories) for its repayment. See generally G. Nelson et al., Real Estate Finance Law §§5.1-5.20 (6th ed. 2015). The mortgagee ordinarily will prefer that the purchaser assume its mortgage; the presence of an appropriately worded due-on-sale clause will enable the mortgagee that consents to a transferee to insist, among other things, that the transferee assume personal liability for the loan. Cf. 12 C.F.R. §591.5(b)(4) (regulation under Garn-St. Germain for residential loans providing that upon agreement of assumption between lender and prospective purchaser, the lender shall release the original borrower from personal liability under the mortgage loan).

2. The Debate between Borrowers and Lenders. Prior to the enactment of the Garn-St. Germain Act, the majority and traditional view had been that due-on-sale clauses constituted neither direct nor unreasonable restraints on alienation. For example, after reviewing the Restatement of Property §404 (1944), the Nebraska Supreme Court, in Occidental Sav. & Loan Ass'n v. Venco Partnership, 206 Neb. 469, 293 N.W.2d 843 (1980), concluded that a due-on-sale clause does not itself constrain the conveyance of title but merely causes debt acceleration; accordingly, the restraint, if any, attaches to the mortgage rather than to the conveyance. In other words, the predicament confronting a borrower wishing to sell is not caused by the due-on-sale clause. Rather, it is caused by the borrower's inability to prepay the mortgage. See also Baker v. Loves Park Sav. & Loan Ass'n, 61 Ill. 2d 119, 333 N.E.2d 1 (1975) (although they constitute restraints on alienation, due-on-sale clauses will be enforced without necessity of case-by-case inquiry for reasonableness because they are necessary to protect the lender's interests); Mutual Real Estate Investment Trust v. Buffalo Sav. Bank, 90 Misc. 2d 675, 395 N.Y.S.2d 583 (1977) (lender's refusal to consent to a sale involving a financially responsible purchaser was not, per se, an unconscionable or inequitable exercise of the lender's contractual right to accelerate the loan indebtedness); Volkmer, The Application of the Restraints on Alienation Doctrine to Real Property Security Interests, 59 Iowa L. Rev. 747, 774 (1973). By contrast, prior to Garn-St. Germain other courts followed the approach enunciated in the *La Sala* case (excerpted at Chapter 5A7, supra) by striking down due-on-sale clauses unless the sale endangered the security of the lender. For example, in Clark v. Lachenmeier, 237 So. 2d 583 (Fla. Dist. Ct. App. 1970), a Florida appellate court refused to allow a mortgagee to foreclose based on a sale that, in the opinion of the court, caused the mortgagee no harm. In Baltimore Life Ins. Co. v. Harn, 15 Ariz. App. 78, 486 P.2d 190 (1971), petition denied, 108 Ariz. 192, 494 P.2d 1322 (1972), an Arizona court likewise held that the lender must show that the sale would impair its security. See also Dawn Investment Co. v. Superior Court, 30 Cal. 3d 695, 639 P.2d 974, 180 Cal. Rptr. 332 (1982).

In addition, before Garn-St. Germain, although most courts sanctioned the use of these clauses by lenders to maintain their mortgage loan portfolios at current interest levels during periods of inflation and increasing interest rates (see, for example, Century Fed. Sav. & Loan Ass'n v. Van Glahn, 144 N.J. Super. 48, 364 A.2d 558 (Ch. Div. 1976)), other courts had taken the position that lenders could not use these clauses merely to protect their economic position. For example, in Wellenkamp v. Bank of Am., 21 Cal. 3d 943, 582 P.2d 970, 976 (1978), the court observed that lenders take into account their projections of future economic conditions in setting interest rates for long-term loans, and that it would be unfair to place the burden of mistaken projections on property owners exercising their right to freely alienate property. See also Patton v. First Fed. Sav. & Loan Ass'n, 118 Ariz. 473, 578 P.2d 152 (1978). See generally Annot., 61 A.L.R.4th 1070 (1988); Dunn and Nowinski, Enforcement of Due-on-Transfer Clauses, An Update, 16 Real Prop., Prob. & Tr. J. 291 (1981).

The principal rationale adopted by the minority approach in striking down due-on-sale clauses is that they represent an unreasonable restraint on alienation. Lenders argue that due-on-sale clauses do not constrain the borrower's right to sell the property. Rather, they claim that such clauses merely prevent the borrower from increasing profit at the lender's expense. Consider the argument that when interest rates and land values are inflated, the sale of real property may produce a profit for the owner for two principal reasons. First, the owner may realize a benefit from appreciation in the value of the real estate. Varying our master hypothetical somewhat, assume that Dan Developer purchases land with a completed building on it for $10 million, free and clear of any mortgage, and because of inflation in land values Dan is later able to sell the property for $15 million. He obviously has realized a profit of $5 million, or a 50 percent return on his equity investment (exclusive of transactional costs and income tax consequences). Second, Dan may benefit from the reduced value of a mortgage or deed of trust on the property caused by rising interest rates. Suppose Dan had obtained a $7.5 million mortgage loan from Ace at the current market rate of interest when he purchased the property. The purchase price, then, would have been funded by only $2.5 million of Dan's own money and $7.5 million from Ace. Under the mortgage, Ace would receive a steady stream of income. In an inflationary market characterized by rising interest rates the mortgage will be repaid with less valuable dollars. Increased interest rates will also produce higher capitalization rates (see Chapter 4D1), which, when applied to the steady stream of income Ace receives, will reduce the value of Ace's mortgage even as Ace's capital and overhead costs are increasing. Stated differently, no one would be willing to buy Ace's mortgage for the amount of the remaining principal balance if the interest rate on the mortgage were below the market rate. Ace could sell the mortgage only at a discount.

Conversely, Dan Developer could sell his property at a higher price because it would be subject to a mortgage at below-market rates. Assume that Dan could sell the property for $18 million (subject to the favorable mortgage) instead of $15 million if the mortgage were paid off. Assuming the mortgage balance is still $7.5 million, Dan's profit or equity would now be $8 million instead of $5 million, or 80 percent on the original purchase price (which represents a 320 percent return on Dan's original cash investment). From Ace's point of view, that extra $3 million profit comes out of its own pocket and the pockets of its other borrowers.

If the due-on-sale clause were enforceable, the property would sell for $15 million rather than $18 million. Of the $15 million purchase price, $7.5 million would go to Ace to pay off the mortgage, leaving Dan with $7.5 million, which would still allow him to realize a profit of $5 million, or a 200 percent rate of return on his original cash investment. Consequently, the purpose of the due-on-sale clause from Ace's standpoint is not to prevent Dan from alienating his property or realizing on the appreciation in its value but rather to prevent Dan from realizing on the depreciated value of Ace's property, namely, its mortgage loan to Dan. Can you think of the counterargument on behalf of borrowers such as Dan Developer? Is there a compromise drafting approach that would address the economic concerns of both parties? See Western Life Ins. Co. v. McPherson, 702 F. Supp. 836 (D. Kan. 1988).

In addition, lenders such as Ace have contended that a due-on-sale clause is necessary to prevent a purchaser from assuming (without Ace's consent) an existing loan that was made partially in reliance on Dan's credit reputation and management expertise. In this regard, is there a limited version of a due-on-sale clause that should be reasonably acceptable to both Dan and Ace? Suppose Ace agrees to nonrecourse financing, perhaps because the borrower is a limited partnership (see tax discussion at Chapter 14A3b). How would this change the negotiating positions of the parties with respect to the need for a due-on-sale clause?

3. Garn-St. Germain. This statute was not the first federal preemption in this area. Under the Homeowner's Loan Act of 1933, the Federal Home Loan Bank Board was empowered to issue regulations with respect to federal savings and loan associations. In 1976, the board authorized these lenders to employ due-on-sale clauses in their mortgage loan document. In Fidelity Fed. Sav. & Loan Ass'n v. De La Cuesta, 458 U.S. 141 (1982), the Supreme Court held that this regulation barred the application of contrary state laws or judicial decisions. Can you explain the federal government's position in support of due-on-sale clauses?

See S. Rep. 97-536, 97th Cong., 2d Sess., 1982 U.S. Code Cong. & Admin. News 3056.

Because Garn-St. Germain defines "due-on-sale" clauses as those authorizing the lender to accelerate if the property is sold without the lender's prior consent, most lenders will specify some mechanism of consent in order to assure that their clause is eligible for the federal preemption of restrictive state laws. Some of the issues raised by consent provisions are: (1) what constitutes unreasonableness where the clause specifies that consent to a proposed sale cannot be withheld unreasonably, and (2) if the clause requires advance consent but does not mention reasonableness, should reasonableness be implied or can the lender act in its absolute discretion. Thus far, most courts have interpreted these clauses in favor of lenders. See, for example, Western Life Ins. Co. v. McPherson K.M.P., 702 F. Supp. 836 (D. Kan. 1988) (lender can condition its consent to sale on reasonable increase in interest rate under provision that its consent not be withheld unreasonably); Destin Sav. Bank v. Summerhouse of FWB, Inc., 579 So. 2d 232 (Fla. Dist. Ct. App. 1991) (construing Garn-St. Germain to prohibit courts from imposing standard of reasonableness when due-on-sale clause is silent on appropriate standard for withholding of consent). What drafting suggestions for lenders might help assure these outcomes? Why might lenders hesitate to provide explicitly that they can withhold consent to a sale in their sole and absolute discretion?

4. The Pay-Down Approach. Would Garn-St. Germain validate a clause requiring a pay-down of the note on sale as in the sample commitment provision excepted above?

5. The "Double Whammy" Question: Can a Lender Enforce Both a Prepayment Charge and a Due-on-Sale Clause? When the mortgage instruments contain both a prepayment clause and a due-on-sale clause, a question arises as to whether the lender can enforce both provisions simultaneously. Specifically, absent relevant language in the prepayment clause, if a lender elects to accelerate the indebtedness in the event of an unauthorized sale, could the borrower contend that the lender is not entitled to a prepayment fee because the acceleration payment should not be treated as a prepayment? See In re LHD Realty Corp., 726 F.2d 327 (7th Cir. 1984); Slevin Container Corp. v. Provident Fed. Sav. & Loan Ass'n, 98 Ill. App. 3d 646, 424 N.E.2d 939 (1981); America Fed. Sav. & Loan Ass'n v. Mid-Am. Service Corp., 329 N.W.2d 124 (S.D. 1983); McCausland v. Bankers Life Ins. Co., 110 Wash. 2d 716, 757 P.2d 941, 946-947 (1988). If so, would express language in the prepayment clause authorizing the fee be enforceable or vulnerable to challenge as an illegal restraint on alienation? Compare Tan v. California Fed. Sav. & Loan Ass'n, 140 Cal. App. 3d 800, 189 Cal. Rptr. 775, 782 (1983) (dictum), with Metropolitan Sav. & Loan Ass'n v. Nabours, 652 S.W.2d 820, 822 (Tex. Civ. App. 1983). Would such a clause be vulnerable as an unenforceable penalty? See the *Lazzareschi* decision excerpted supra at Chapter 5A4. See generally Stark, Enforcing Prepayment Charges: Case

Law and Drafting Suggestions, 22 Real Prop., Prob. & Tr. J. 549, 555-559 (Fall 1987). For loans secured by homes occupied or to be occupied by the borrower, a regulation issued under the Garn-St. Germain Act prohibits the collection of a prepayment charge when the lender accelerates the loan under its due-on-sale clause. See 12 C.F.R. §591.5(b)(2).

6. *Eluding the Due-on-Sale Clause.* As a general proposition, should a lender be able to invoke a due-on-sale clause where the borrower is a corporation or partnership that sells a majority share of ownership to an outsider without the lender's consent? See Fidelity Trust Co. v. BVD Assocs., 492 A.2d 180 (Conn. 1985); Standard Operations v. Montague, 758 S.W.2d 442 (Mo. 1988). Can you think of some compromise language that would allow a restructuring of the borrowing entity without unduly threatening the lender's collateral and prospects for repayment?

THE ETHICAL REAL ESTATE LAWYER

Circumventing Due-on-Sale Clauses

Suppose that a seller-client asks you to document a conveyance of real estate that is encumbered by a mortgage loan with an interest rate substantially below the current market rate. The mortgage contains a due-on-sale provision that the lender could use to adjust its loan to the market rate as a condition to approving the sale. Your client, however, has heard of a so-called silent sale technique whereby the conveyance is accomplished through an installment land contract (described at Chapter 3D) with no recording of the buyer's interest until several years later when the buyer has made all the purchase payments including those necessary to satisfy the existing mortgage. During the contract period, the seller will collect the purchaser's payments and remit them to the mortgagee in the seller's name. Finally, pending the transfer of title, the property tax records and insurance policies will be maintained in the seller's name. This structure is designed to keep the mortgagee from discovering the sale and invoking its rights under the due-on-sale clause.

Suppose that the lender discovers the "silent sale." How might that happen? Can you think of any theories under which the seller would be liable to the lender for engaging in a silent sale? What might the lender claim as its damages (in other words, is the lender limited to accelerating its debt for the due-on-sale clause breach)? Assuming that state law allows borrowers to undo a lender's acceleration by curing the default before foreclosure (see discussion of such rights at Chapter 8B1), how would you cure a default based on a silent sale? As the seller's attorney who documented the silent sale, is there any theory under which you could be liable to the lender for its damages? See Roszkowski, Drafting

Around Mortgage Due-on-Sale Clauses: The Dangers of Playing Hide-and-Seek, 21 Real Prop., Prob. & Tr. J. 23 (1986) (discussing various theories against the seller and those who participated in the silent sale). Consider further whether the seller's lawyer has an ethical obligation to inform the lender that a silent sale has occurred or, if no such duty exists, whether the seller's lawyer must nonetheless refrain from assisting in documenting the transfer. G. Nelson et al., Real Estate Finance Law §5.25 (6th ed. 2015) (discussing these ethical implications for attorneys counseling the seller in a silent sale transaction).

Suppose, instead, that the existing mortgage contains a due-on-sale clause that covers conveyances of the realty but does not appear to encompass a sale of a controlling interest in the corporate borrower's stock. Does the seller's lawyer face the same risks in structuring a stock purchase that eludes the due-on-sale clause as written?

Chapter 6

Construction Financing

A. THE ROLE OF CONSTRUCTION FINANCING IN THE COMMERCIAL LENDING CYCLE

The traditional dichotomy between postconstruction and construction financing can be explained by the fact that commercial banks, which do most of the construction lending, obtain their loanable funds chiefly from short-term demand and time deposits that are vulnerable to the vagaries of seasonal fluctuations and swings in the business cycle. These banks prefer to engage in short-term construction financing because of their need to maintain liquidity to meet sudden drains on their cash reserves. Also, some commercial banks and mortgage companies prefer to maintain a brisk turnover in their real estate loan portfolios so that, as "loan correspondents" for postconstruction lenders, they can earn origination fees and annual servicing charges on the construction loans they sell and assign to the postconstruction lender. Moreover, because the short-term interest rates charged by banks and other construction lenders are usually geared to a daily floating (variable) prime or dealer commercial paper rate, commercial banks find that as construction lenders they are in a better position than postconstruction lenders (such as life insurance companies) to protect themselves against inflation and shifting market conditions.

The distinctions between construction and postconstruction lending affect the way these two groups of lenders view a real estate financing transaction. The basic objective of the construction lender is to make sure that the improvements are completed for the amount of the construction loan, plus the borrower's equity investment, in accordance with the terms and conditions specified in the postconstruction lender's takeout commitment. The construction lender does not have to deal with the long-term, "down the road" problems facing the postconstruction lender and will not normally concern itself with them.

Conversely, while the postconstruction lender is relieved of dealing with risks that arise during the construction period, it commits to make its loan some 18 to 36 months before funding and must anticipate any contingencies that might render the loan investment unsound during this time and during the life of the loan (such as market downturns that make a completed project unrentable). The postconstruction lender will insert in its commitment certain conditions that the property must meet at the time of funding. For example, the lender will require that the improvements be completed within the prescribed time limits in a "good, substantial and workmanlike manner," fully equipped with "first class" equipment[1] and built in accordance with the approved plans and specifications; that the property be free of mechanics' liens; that title to the property be good, marketable, and unencumbered by liens senior to the mortgage or deed of trust other than those specifically authorized; and that the property and improvements be in full compliance with all applicable laws and regulations for which all required governmental permits have been properly issued.

These requirements will not ensure that the project will be an economic success. This is a risk that the postconstruction lender assumes, based on its evaluation of the economic realities of the transaction. To mitigate that risk, postconstruction lenders often ask for commitment provisions that require, inter alia, the achievement of certain leasing conditions by closing and the absence of any material adverse change in the financial condition of the borrower or certain key tenants.

The following excerpt examines the influence that the postconstruction (or "permanent") lender has on the construction lender and the construction loan.

Davis, The Permanent Lender's Role in the Construction Process
3 Real Est. Rev. 70 (Spring 1973)

Lurking in the background in any discussion of construction lending is the specter of the permanent lender. Writing as one who represents a permanent lender, my own inclination is to state that the permanent lender is the key [entity] in any new real estate venture. At the very least, certainly, the permanent lender is a vital factor in a new real estate venture. It is [its] money that is relied upon to finance the project even though it will not be disbursed until after completion of construction. Without a permanent commitment most construction lenders will not make a construction loan.

Nevertheless, once the permanent commitment is issued, the other parties feel free to criticize the permanent lender for seeking various rights to approve, for refusing to waive commitment requirements, and for declining to take a back seat during construction. . . .

Why should the permanent lender be interested in construction matters? [It] concerns [itself] with construction primarily because [it] wishes to be sure that the building to be constructed is the one on which [it] has committed [itself] to make a loan. It too often occurs that the final structure is not the one envisioned by the permanent lender at the time of making the commitment.

---

1. You will find terms such as "first class" in many real estate documents. What does "first class" mean? What if the lender thinks the equipment is second class and the borrower thinks it is first class? Compare Bettancourt v. Gilroy Theatre Co., 120 Cal. App. 2d 364, 261 P.2d 351 (1953) (contract to build a "first class" theater held sufficiently definite), with Hart v. Georgia R.R., 101 Ga. 188, 28 S.E. 637 (1897) (contract to build a "first class hotel" held too indefinite). The drafting lesson is to avoid the use of vague terms and wherever possible employ definitional language that is geared to some objective standard.

Second, [it] is concerned with construction because [it] will have a security interest in the building for as long as [it] holds the mortgage. . . . If the building is improperly constructed, the permanent lender's security can be severely impaired since in most instances, [it] looks first to the improvements and to the income therefrom for security, and only to a lesser extent, to the borrower. Needless to say, a potential owner is interested in the building [it] may someday own. . . .

Having discussed the relevance of construction matters to the permanent lender, let us now consider the relationship between the construction lender and the permanent lender. Basically, their interests are substantially similar:

- To have the building completed as provided for in their commitments and in accordance with the approved plans and specifications. (It is a good idea to have the two lenders use the same engineer or architect; this will reduce the likelihood of disputes over the adequacy of the plans.)
- To have their funds invested pursuant to their commitments.
- To have the construction loan paid upon completion of construction.
- To have the permanent lender then hold the loan with the long-term security [it] contemplated when making [its] commitment.

. . . During the early stages of discussion, before [it] closes [its] construction loan, the construction lender will want approvals from the permanent lender on as many closing conditions of the permanent commitment as possible. [It] will ask for approval of title, survey, leases, appraisal, plans and specifications, and the operating agreement.

The permanent lender can review the state of title at this early date and set forth those exceptions or areas which disturb [it]. At the time of the construction loan closing, however, [it] can neither know nor approve the state of title for purposes of the permanent closing. Any approvals [it] gives, therefore, must reserve [its] right to reexamine title for the permanent closing.

The permanent lender can also approve the survey at this stage, okaying the location of the premises and its relation to roads, intersections, and so forth. But [it] must reserve the right to see a final survey showing the improvements as built to determine if they accord with the commitment [it] contemplated. To avoid confusion, any approvals the permanent lender gives to plans and specifications should be by detailed plan number, date, and revision number.

The permanent lender may approve leases and any operating agreements if they are in existence at the time of the construction loan closing, but this is unlikely.

The items which the permanent lender cannot approve in advance can cause great concern to a construction lender. But by the nature of things, certain matters are not in existence at the time of the construction loan closing; and so the risk of the permanent lender not giving final approval to them must remain with the construction lender. Such items include the final survey, an independent engineer's report, any estoppel certificates that the permanent lender may want from tenants and from adjoining department stores (in the case of a shopping center), the final title search, and executed leases. . . .

GAP MORTGAGES

Further problems can develop in the relationship between the construction lender and the permanent lender when "floor loans" are made. This is particularly true of office buildings. Very often in an office building loan, the permanent lender agrees to buy the loan from the construction lender when the building shell is complete; but [it] will advance no additional loan funds to the borrower at that time. This is the floor loan. "Completion" is defined in such a situation as not including installation of the tenant partitions or similar work. When the tenants' work is fully complete and the premises occupied, the balance of the loan is funded. For the borrower, this means that additional money must be raised after the first disbursement of permanent loan funds in order to fully complete the structure, and since borrowers are loath to invest their own funds, they will seek to finance this gap. Usually, this financing is sought from the construction lender who must, with respect to the gap financing, resort to a second mortgage for security. Since some permanent lenders do not want junior financing on their projects, a gap loan might require the permanent lender to waive any prohibitions against second mortgaging. If the construction lender has advanced more money on its construction loan than the floor amount for which the permanent lender committed, that excess would have to be deemed the advance made under the gap second mortgage. Because of technical difficulties with respect to this, most permanent lenders will restrict the construction lender in the buy-sell agreement from advancing more than the floor loan. . . .

The following excerpt by Gerald M. Levy, the managing director of Chemical Bank, one of the nation's leading construction lenders, discusses the factors and considerations that the construction lender must evaluate and review before committing itself to making a construction loan.

Levy, Construction Loan Decision-Making: Issues and Documents; Risks and Benefits
In-house Memorandum for Chemical Bank, New York, New York, 1989

. . . Accounting and financial skills are important in determining the financial condition of a real estate customer. Yet, a banker may be a virtuoso in analyzing business enterprises which are more in the mainstream of credit granting activities and still prove to be woefully inadequate in gauging a real estate borrower's current financial condition and prospects. The analysis of a real estate client cannot provide meaningful conclusions without an informed and experienced approach to the investigation and analysis of the cash flows derived from individual real estate assets; the economic results of specific properties are only summarized in possibly oblique or confusing fashion in the balance sheet, income statement, and other financial reports.

By the nature of the risks inherent in the construction process the account officer and the credit committee must be satisfied that the construction loan under consideration is to be made to an experienced and financially responsible borrower who is likely to comply with the terms of loan documents. At almost all stages of a construction loan, the collateral is not a completed and occupied property but an asset which is in the process of being created. If work on the project stops for any one or more of an almost endless number of reasons, a bank is in the unenviable position of deciding whether or not to "work with" the present developer. If the financial institution decides to undertake the foreclosure of the ownership position it must endure all the inherent delays and defenses built into the legal process; meanwhile, an incomplete project is exposed to possible weather damage, structural deterioration, vandalism and the escalation of construction costs. In addition, the construction of competitive developments may be continuing; consequently, market demand which the now troubled project was relying on could be preempted. All these adverse effects remind us of the need to deal with a strong, responsible and credit-worthy borrower.

In prior years some construction lenders considered an extensive real estate analysis of a proposed project to be redundant; instead they placed great reliance on and "found value" in the "takeout" commitment of a permanent lender who would be expected to fund upon completion of the project with the proceeds utilized to repay the construction lender. Numerous real estate disasters illustrate that permanent loan commitments are not iron clad; some issuers may resort to narrow technical grounds, real or imagined, to avoid funding. Consequently, most experienced construction lenders have concluded that they should not finance the development of a project unless property and market fundamentals are persuasive; then, if a permanent commitment is not funded or another loan is not available in timely fashion, the construction lender will still have productive collateral. Due diligence concerning the economics of a project is even more important at the present time because many construction loans are funded "open ended," i.e., with no permanent loan takeout commitment in place.

Either a "pure credit" or a "pure real estate" approach to a construction lending decision is without significant meaning because credit and real estate factors are so entwined. Generally, it is not wise to lend construction funds to a customer of marginal credit-worthiness even though he has a feasible real estate project proposal; similarly, it is not prudent to provide funds to a "strong" borrower for the construction of a poorly conceived and economically questionable project. Both the borrower and the real estate concept should be sound.

NOTES AND QUESTIONS

The Risks and Returns of Construction and Postconstruction Lending Compared. As observed above and Chapter 4D, the postconstruction lender typically includes the following conditions among those in its commitment: (a) completion of the improvements in accordance with plans and specifications it approved; (b) compliance with applicable laws and regulations and obtaining of necessary permits; (c) title unencumbered by liens superior to the postconstruction mortgage or deed of trust; (d) leases in effect with certain major ("prime") tenants (for shopping center or office building projects); and (e) no material, adverse change in the financial condition of the borrower. Might any of these clauses trouble a prospective construction lender and render a takeout commitment from a postconstruction lender "unbankable"? (A "bankable" commitment from a postconstruction lender refers to one that also meets the normal requirements of a construction lender.)

In what respects do the goals of a construction lender and postconstruction lender resemble one another? In what respects are they different? Based on what you have learned about postconstruction financing, what planning suggestions would you offer to a construction lender who wishes to minimize the risks that: (1) notwithstanding a buy-sell agreement, the postconstruction lender might refuse to take out the construction loan because it does not approve the form and content of a lease with a major "prime" tenant; or (2) a gap financing problem might arise because of construction cost overruns or because of the borrower's failure to comply with a rent roll requirement contained in the postconstruction commitment letter, in which event the construction lender might find itself relegated to the status of an unpaid junior lienor with respect to a portion of its loan indebtedness? See Chapter 4D2 and 4D6.

Investment returns differ qualitatively and quantitatively for construction and postconstruction lenders. For example, the lender's rate of return is usually higher on construction loans and, in contrast to a typical fixed rate postconstruction loan with monthly debt service payments, the typical construction loan requires no amortization (see Chapter 5A2) and the interest rate is generally a "floating" (variable) rate geared to a certain number of percentage points over a particular bank's prime rate. Incidentally, while floating rates became commonplace for construction financing long before the variable rate mortgage was introduced into residential financing, the variable rate format is still not popular in commercial postconstruction financing transactions. In addition, unlike many postconstruction loans in which the borrower is exculpated from personal liability for the repayment of the debt and the lender only has recourse against the real estate, personal liability on the note is almost always required in construction financing. Why do these distinctions exist?

> ## Problem 6-1
> In summary, how would you assess the relative risks involved in both kinds of lending-in what respects is a construction loan riskier than a postconstruction loan? In what respects is it safer? ◄

B. TERMS AND CONDITIONS OF CONSTRUCTION FINANCING

Consider the following overview of the terms and conditions of construction financing as reflected in the construction lender's commitment letter.

Joyce, Financing Real Estate Developments
Colo. Law. 2093 (Aug. 1982)

[A] central focus of the construction lender is to insure the availability of a permanent loan commitment prior to making the construction loan. In order to insure that the permanent loan commitment is fulfilled, the construction lender requires the developer, in the loan agreement and associated security documents, to comply with all requirements of the permanent loan commitment. The "pre-closed" form of the buy-sell agreement normally enables the construction lender to obtain the permanent lender's concurrence to the security documents and the note prior to disbursal of the construction loan proceeds. The permanent lender should also agree in advance to the form of ancillary documents, such as insurance binders, title commitments, lease forms, plans and specifications and any other matters upon which the permanent loan is conditioned.

In addition to rate, date of maturity and fees, the developer must use great care in determining the actual amount of the loan. From the construction lender's perspective, the face amount of the loan is limited by the permanent commitment, which is predicated on a preconstruction cost and income projection. The developer must have contingency funds available in the construction loan to deal with construction overruns and unexpected conditions encountered during construction, such as bad soil or construction strikes. . . .

The construction loan application, when separate from the permanent loan application, becomes the basis of the contract between the construction lender and the developer. In addition to the items noted above as requirements for a permanent loan application, the developer will be asked to provide a variety of specific information, including the following:

1. The nature and exact identification of the ownership group;
2. The specific location of the project;

3. The site plan and plans and specifications for construction;
4. Pro forma operating statements for the project; and
5. The proposed tenants or marketing studies which support the projected income stream. . . .

The construction lender often requires that construction financing be in the form of a recourse loan or that the construction loan be guaranteed by the developer. The developer will resist this requirement, but without clearly identifiable collateral other than the proposed project, the lender is unlikely to change it. Lenders make such requirements because of the possibility that if a default occurs prior to completion, its foreclosure of the deed of trust may not be sufficient to secure the entire amount of the loan. . . .

The amortization of the entire debt, including interest and principal of a development project is anticipated to come from income related to operation of the project. Because the project has little if any income prior to project completion, there is normally no reduction in principal [that is, amortization] during the construction loan period. Rather, the construction loan includes an amount sufficient to pay interest on a monthly basis and the permanent loan will ultimately include payoff of both the principal and accrued interest charges on the construction loan. If for no other reason, this feature of development loans makes it important to the construction lender that [it] rigorously underwrite the loan and seek additional collateral. The inclusion of the soft costs in the construction loan make it a virtual certainty that a foreclosure, in the event of a default during the construction period, will yield the lender less than the amount of the loan outstanding at the time.

In this matter, the developer may believe that, since the construction loan contains amounts sufficient for debt amortization and the developer has obtained a permanent loan commitment, the lender has no risk of default. This viewpoint, of course, seeks to minimize the possibility of strikes, cost overruns, the death of the developer or other unplanned catastrophic events. A creative developer can use third-party guarantees, such as performance bonds and life insurance policies, in an effort to avoid providing security in additional collateral or personal guarantees. However, except with FHA-insured projects in which the entire amount of the disbursed construction loan is insured, the developer's ability to avoid personal guarantees is limited.

After the construction lender reviews the developer's application, [it] responds in the form of a commitment letter. The commitment letter represents a counteroffer to the developer and, upon acceptance by the developer, constitutes a binding contract between the two. That commitment includes provisions related to the following matters:

1. The principal amount and form of the promissory note to be executed; and the interest to be paid, along with terms of repayment, prepayment and any provisions for early call.

2. The specific provisions made for disbursements, along with the exact documentation which must be presented to the lender prior to authorization of disbursements.
3. Identification of the specific forms of collateral, including guarantees, promissory notes, assignment of rents and leases, letters of credit and cash escrows.
4. The specific nature of the first deed of trust [or mortgage]. . . .
5. The specific personal guaranty if it is contemplated by the lender.
6. The specific construction schedule, including commencement and completion dates, as well as a projected progress schedule.
7. Any required pre-leasing arrangements and minimum terms and sample forms of such leases, along with the form of collateral assignment of the lease to the lender.
8. Identification of the general contractor, along with major subcontractors, and any performance or payment bonds which must be provided to bond the various contractors' work. Bonds are not always required but should be anticipated in larger projects.
9. The specific requirements for insurance, including type and amount of coverage, terms of payment, terms of cancellation and beneficiaries. Insurance coverage normally includes builder's risk, public liability and property damage and workers' compensation insurance.
10. Specified deadlines for the delivery and approval of the plans and specifications for the project, along with appropriate engineering reports.
11. Requirements for surveys, including an initial survey, a construction survey indicating the limits of the construction contract and a post-construction survey showing improvements as built.
12. Identification of all expenses, including fees to be paid to the lender, title insurance, attorneys' fees and closing costs. Also, an allocation of those expenses between the lender and developer, along with some limits on the actual amounts to be expended, although some will not be exactly determinable at this stage. . . .
13. General conditions related to legal opinions, resolutions of corporations authorizing borrowing and any other organizational authorities required by the lender.
14. Provisions for cost certification of all expenditures, along with an audit by an identified certified public accountant.
15. Variety of certifications required related to zoning and other government approval processes, including a determination of the availability of waste water, utility and water services, water, compliance with traffic and zoning regulations and the issuance of building permits.
16. Mechanic's lien protection and specific provisions with respect to the lender's individual protection against such liens. . . .

Since the construction loan commitment forms the basis of the contractual arrangement between the developer and the lender, it is absolutely crucial that details of this arrangement be explored in great depth prior to payment of the commitment fee and acceptance of the commitment. . . .

1. Loan Amount, Interest Rate, and Other Payment Terms

In the master hypothetical, an assumption was made that the fair market value of the project will equal its land and building cost of $33 million and thus Dan would finance the project with the $25 million postconstruction loan from Ace and with equity funds (through investor contributions) in the amount of $8 million. In reality, most developers will not engage in such an undertaking unless they believe that the value of the project will exceed its costs. So assume that the projected cost of the building is only $23 million so that Dan would obtain more than 100 percent financing of his construction costs by means of the $25 million loan from Ace. Further assume that the "hard costs" of constructing the building will amount to $20 million and that the "soft costs" will amount to $3 million. In the parlance of real estate the hard costs are the actual or physical costs of labor and materials, including fees paid to the construction manager and the profit return to the general contractor, and the soft costs are the intangible costs of construction, including the fees paid by Dan to attorneys, architects, appraisers, engineers, brokers, and consultants; the costs of advertising, builder's risk insurance, and bond premiums; mortgage recording taxes and other construction loan closing expenses; and possibly construction loan interest payments as well.

FNB may retain the services of outside consultants and take other precautionary measures to make certain that Dan's cost estimates are realistic and not exaggerated. Specifically, FNB will be watchful about any attempt by Dan to keep his loan funds ahead of his actual costs by overestimating costs (called "front-end loading") during the early phases of construction. Conversely, FNB wants to ensure that Dan has not underestimated the costs of construction to convince FNB that the project is feasible.

As observed above, while postconstruction loans ordinarily bear a fixed rate of interest, most construction loans have a floating (variable) rate geared to a percentage above the bank's prime rate. The margin above prime usually depends on several factors including market conditions, the front-end fees charged to the borrower, and the depository relationship between the bank and the borrower. In rare situations a construction lender might countenance a fixed rate, for example, where it also provides postconstruction financing for the project or engages in an equity-sharing arrangement with the borrower.

NOTES AND QUESTIONS

1. Loan Amount. Assuming that Dan's net worth and outside income are minimal and that the construction lender's (FNB's) management team is dominated by experts who emphasize "property fundamentals" (the income potential and value of the collateral) rather than "credit predominance" (the borrower's creditworthiness and financial strength), what is the maximum construction loan amount that Dan might expect from FNB on the above facts? Would it be the full $23 million cost of construction, or merely the $20 million of hard costs? How would Dan argue for a $25 million loan, which would allow Dan to make a $2 million profit (or "mortgage out") on the construction loan?

Assume that the postconstruction commitment from Ace provides for a floor-ceiling loan and, in the opinion of FNB, prudence dictates that it should limit its loan commitment to the floor amount. Would this protective measure necessarily be in FNB's best interest if Dan should need the ceiling amount to complete the construction? How might FNB and Dan protect themselves against this contingency? See discussion at Chapter 4D2.

2. Amortization of Construction Loans. While the interest payments might be drawn from the proceeds of the loan during the construction period, the principal amount ordinarily is not amortized but is repayable in full from the postconstruction takeout proceeds. Why is this approach necessary?

3. Hedging Interest Rates with Match Funding and Swap Agreements. Construction loan interest rates are normally floating rates that fluctuate at some level above the "prime" rate. The prime rate is the rate that banks charge from time to time to their more favored customers. Floating rates are favored by commercial banks because they can be adjusted to take into account what the banks will be paying to their demand depositors during the periods of their construction loans. With the advent of open-ended construction financing (funding without a postconstruction takeout commitment in place), new approaches have been devised by banks and other construction lenders who are willing to make relatively long-term fixed rate construction loans and yet because of their short-term liability structure must protect themselves against sudden increases in the fluctuating rates that they pay to their depositors.

One hedging strategy for construction lenders making fixed rate loans is a technique called "match funding." Simply stated, the bank "buys" or "borrows" funds at a rate slightly less than the rate it will receive under the open-ended "long-term" construction loan and for the same period of time. In this way the bank receives and has the use of money equal to the construction loan at a cost that is less than the interest rate the developer is paying. Otherwise, if the short-term interest rates payable to the bank's depositors were to exceed the long-term fixed rate on the open-ended construction loan, the resultant mismatch between expenses and revenues could deteriorate the bank's earnings and profits position.

Conversely, to convert a floating-rate construction loan into a fixed rate obligation, the developer might enter into a so-called swap agreement with a third party. In the typical swap agreement, the developer agrees to pay the third party a fixed rate of interest on the construction loan amount for the construction loan term. In exchange, the third party agrees to pay the variable construction loan rate on the same amount for the same loan period. For the complexities in negotiating and drafting these agreements, see Stark, Negotiating Interest Rate Exchange Agreements, 4 Real Est. Fin. L.J. 493 (1987); Stark, Interest Rate Swaps: A Reassessment, 11 Prob. & Prop. 36 (May/June 1997); see also Malhotra and McLeod, Using Interest Rate Swaps and Swaptions in Hedging Interest Rate Risk, 10 Real Est. Fin. L.J. 60 (1995).

2. Conformity with the Postconstruction Commitment

As suggested in the foregoing excerpts by Davis and Joyce, in most cases the construction lender's real security for the repayment of its loan is the takeout commitment from some postconstruction lender rather than the lien of the construction loan mortgage on the partially completed improvements or the ephemeral net worth of the borrower. Therefore, a prudent construction lender will insist that the terms and conditions of its commitment letter closely track the requirements of the postconstruction commitment. Accordingly, most construction loan commitments will contain language such as the following:

> *Section 5.08. Compliance with Postconstruction Loan Commitment*
> Borrower will observe and comply with all of the terms, provisions, conditions, covenants and agreements on its part to be performed, observed and complied with to obtain the loan under the Postconstruction Loan commitment, and Borrower will not amend the Postconstruction Loan commitment or suffer or permit any conditions to exist which would permit a termination of the obligations to provide the loan pursuant to the Postconstruction Loan commitment.

Returning to the master hypothetical, consider whether this clause affords FNB any protection if Dan Developer were to breach its provisions and violate the terms of the postconstruction commitment with Ace Insurance Company. Suppose Dan's default leads to an abrogation of the postconstruction loan commitment. Dan would clearly be in default under the construction loan agreement, and FNB would not be required to fund. However, if FNB has already disbursed a substantial portion of the construction loan, neither foreclosure on half-completed buildings nor an action against Dan for damages would provide FNB with a viable remedy. Indeed, the real importance of this clause is its delineation of conditions in Ace's commitment letter that should be fulfilled by Dan prior to any loan advances made by FNB.

Rather than rely on hollow legal remedies for Dan's possible breach of the compliance clause, FNB must determine in advance that it is feasible for Dan to comply with the terms of the postconstruction commitment and also monitor the loan transaction during the construction period to ensure such compliance. For example, the terms of the postconstruction commitment may impose certain leasing requirements. See Chapter 10B. Failure to execute the required leases may release Ace from its commitment entirely. Or, Dan's failure to attain a rent roll requirement might allow Ace to provide only a floor loan amount rather than the full ceiling loan amount. See Chapter 4D2. In either instance, sufficient funds may not be available to take out the entire amount of FNB's loan. The construction loan agreement should therefore require that these conditions be met before FNB closes its loan and becomes obliged to make disbursements. Likewise, there may be other terms and conditions in Ace's commitment letter that could be satisfied before the construction loan closing, such as Ace's approval of the preliminary plans and specifications and the status of Dan's fee simple title to the underlying land. To review: Can you think of any others? See Chapter 4D.

NOTES AND QUESTIONS

Buy-Sell Agreements. Suppose FNB executes a buy-sell agreement with Ace. Would this cure the compliance problem and assure FNB that its loan will be taken out by Ace once the construction period is over? If not, what form of buy-sell agreement could be used to at least ameliorate the concerns of FNB? See Chapter 4D6.

3. Priority against Mechanics' Liens

The construction lender normally requires a first lien on the land and improvements to secure the construction advances. Often the developer has acquired the land with borrowed funds and may have received a development loan to finance the installation of sewers, the laying out of streets, and other site development costs. Typically, these loans are secured by mortgage liens that must either be satisfied or subordinated prior to construction. In most cases, land and development costs are considered to be part of the cost of the improvements and, therefore, these mortgages can be satisfied out of the first construction loan draw (advance). However, when the competing lien is that of a mechanic or materialman, more complex problems arise that are not as easily resolved.

In recognition of the principle that mechanics and materialmen add value to the property and in furtherance of the public policy of encouraging rehabilitation and new construction, states have enacted mechanics' lien statutes providing mechanics and materialmen with liens that often are accorded special lien priority over existing mortgages on the property. These statutes vary widely from state to state. In some states a mortgage will take priority over subsequently filed mechanics' liens.[2] In others, the lien priority accorded to a mortgage is confined to disbursements made prior to the filing of any mechanics' liens.[3] In still others, mechanics' liens will relate back to the commencement of construction.[4] And in

---

2. E.g., N.J. Stat. Ann. §2A:44-22.
3. E.g., N.Y. Lien Law §13.
4. E.g., Cal. Civ. Code §§3134, 3137; Ill. Comp. Stat. ch. 82, §16.

some states, mechanics' liens have priority as to the improvements but not as to the land.[5]

One of the greatest challenges facing the construction lender, as distinguished from the postconstruction lender, is to protect the priority of its disbursements against the rights of mechanics and materialmen during the course of construction. Language from a typical construction loan agreement dealing with these rights might read as follows.

Section 5.09 Liens

The Project shall be kept free and clear of liens and encumbrances (unless the same are bonded or insured over by the title insurance company in a manner satisfactory to Lender) of every nature or description (whether for taxes or assessments, for charges of labor, materials, supplies or service, or any other thing) other than Permitted Exceptions. . . .

Section 5.12 Mechanics and Materialmen

Borrower will furnish to Lender upon request, at any time and from time to time, affidavits listing all materialmen, laborers, subcontractors and any other party who might or could claim statutory or common law liens and are furnishing or have furnished materials or labor to the Project or any portion thereof, together with affidavits, or other evidence satisfactory to Lender showing that such parties have been paid all amounts then due for labor and materials furnished to the project. In addition, Borrower will notify Lender immediately and in writing, if Borrower receives any notice, written or oral, from any laborer, subcontractor or materialman to the effect that said laborer, subcontractor or materialman has not been paid when due for any labor or materials furnished in connection with the construction of the Improvements. Borrower will also furnish to Lender, at any time and from time to time upon demand by Lender, lien waivers bearing a then current date, on Lender's standard form, from Contractor and such subcontractors or materialmen as Lender may designate.

NOTES AND QUESTIONS

Commencement of Construction. Many if not most states (called "priority states") provide that mechanics' liens relate back to the date of the commencement of construction. See G. Nelson et al., Real Estate Finance Law §12.4 (6th ed. 2015). But when does the construction commence? Would the date relate back to the completion of the first engineering study or the drafting of the architect's plans and specifications? Probably not. How about delivery of materials to the site? The arrival of the bulldozers? The fencing of the property? The digging of the first ceremonial shovelful of dirt? The general rule is that construction commences when the work begun is conspicuous and substantial enough to make it reasonably apparent that improvements are intended to be constructed at the site. See Annot., 1 A.L.R.3d 822 (1965). As counsel to a

---

5. E.g., Va. Code Ann. §43-21.

construction lender, what precautionary measures might you suggest to establish that construction has not commenced before the recordation of your client's mortgage?

a. The Optional-Obligatory Doctrine

The following cases illustrate the "optional-obligatory" doctrine created by courts to subordinate an otherwise prior mortgage lien to a mechanic's or materialman lien to the extent that the mortgage loan advances are merely "optional." In reading the cases and accompanying notes, consider whether this much-criticized doctrine provides adequate certainty to construction lenders in forecasting whether their advances are sufficiently "obligatory" to avoid this judicial subordination.

National Bank of Washington v. Equity Investors
81 Wash. 2d 886, 506 P.2d 20 (1973)

HALE, Chief Justice.

. . . Columbia Wood Products, Inc., furnished lumber for the apartment house project, commencing deliveries to the site May 26, 1969, and continuing to about August 5, 1969. [I]t received partial payment, but when construction came to a halt there was still due and unpaid the sum of $119,672 for material sold, delivered and utilized in the nearly completed buildings. The trial court awarded Columbia Wood Products, Inc., a judgment of $119,672.26 on this unpaid bill, with 12 percent accrued interest from September 5, 1969, in the amount of $28,721.34, and statutory costs. The court decreed, however, that Columbia Wood Products' judgment lien be subordinate and junior to the lien of National Bank of Washington's deed of trust to the extent of all advances made by that bank on its loan for the construction of the apartment house complex. Columbia Wood Products appeals that part of the judgment and decree which rendered its materialman's lien inferior and junior to the bank's total secured loan advanced for the construction.

Columbia Wood Products' lien was declared inferior to the entire amount of the bank's advances on a theory that the National Bank of Washington possessed a prior and superior deed of trust lien in effect before and continuing during the delivery of the lumber. According to the bank's theory, its priority was established as of about May 9, 1969, when [the lender's agent] filed the trust deed of Equity Investors, a limited partnership, naming the National Bank of Washington as beneficiary, securing a promissory note in the amount of $1,850,000—all in accordance with a construction loan agreement of May 7, 1969, between the National Bank of Washington as lender and Equity Investors as borrower. As work on the project progressed, the bank advanced the funds. . . .

Columbia Wood Products began deliveries of lumber to the project on May 26, 1969, and continued supplying material until August 5, 1969, but with the last delivery there was, as earlier noted, still due and unpaid on the lumber bill some $119,672. Its claim of a lien superior in part to that of the National Bank of Washington is based on the contention that the advances made by the bank under the construction loan agreement as the work progressed were optional advances and could not have been legally enforced against the bank. . . .

We think that Columbia Wood Products' contention is sound and that for the purpose of determining lien priorities the advances were in law optional. In the construction loan agreement, the bank made such explicit reservations for the disbursement of the loan as, in our judgment, render the advances of $1,750,000 optional and not obligatory at law. Although such reservation of discretionary authority appears to be a sound banking practice and designed to protect the financial interests of the party to the project which would wind up with the greater sum of money in it, these protective reservations operated, in law, we think, to subordinate the bank's lien for undelivered advances to those of the materialmen and workmen whose work, services and materials went into the project to enhance the bank's security. It has, we realize, long been the rule in this jurisdiction that a mortgage to secure future advances takes priority over mechanics' and materialmen's liens accruing after recordation of the mortgage . . ., but there is a well-established corollary to the rule that, if under the contract the advances are optional and not obligatory, then the lien priority for the advances is determined as of the time the advances are actually made.

What made the advances optional in law rather than obligatory? The very terms of the construction loan agreement gave the bank discretion as to which of the subcontractor materialmen would be paid from the advances. The construction loan agreement contained a promise to lend Equity Investors the $1,750,000 "upon the terms and conditions set forth below." This agreement provided that, after deducting all fees, charges and expenses agreed to by the borrower, the remaining proceeds of the loan would be credited to the borrower's construction loan account in the lending bank. Thus, the advances were not to be delivered over to the borrower but would remain on deposit in the lending bank as the contract stated to "finance the construction of apartment buildings on property described in the Deed of Trust."

The construction loan agreement specified that, prior to the first advance of construction funds, the bank was to be supplied with a current appraisal satisfactory to it; that all loan funds must be used for payment of material and labor; and that the loan proceeds were to be assigned by the borrower to the bank for that purpose. The borrower, according to this agreement, had to retain an architect satisfactory to the bank, and this approved architect had to supply the bank with periodic progress of construction reports, and before each advance of loaned money certify that satisfactory progress had been made and in the future would be made in keeping with the remainder of the unexpended loan.

The construction loan agreement left the loan moneys largely under the control and dominion of the bank, "to be advanced at such times and in such amounts as the Lender shall determine." It provided, too, that "no advance shall be due unless, in the judgment of the Lender" all work for which the advance had been made had been done in a good and workmanlike manner, and unless the construction be approved by the architect. The lender, at his option, could advance and pay the loan installments before they became due, if he deemed it advisable to do so—but all such advances were to be treated as a performance of the agreement and not a modification of it. Also, according to the construction loan agreement, the lender was not obligated to disburse more than 90 percent of the loan until the construction was completed and the property free of liens and claims of all kinds except the lender's lien.

There were other provisions in the construction loan agreement, giving control over the funds to the bank, including:

> If the construction of said building be at any time discontinued or not carried on with sufficient dispatch in the judgment of the Lender to protect the building from depredation or the weather, said Lender may purchase materials and employ workmen to protect the building so that the same will not suffer from depredation or the weather, or to complete said building, so that it may be used for the purposes for which it was designed under the said plans and specifications.

Accordingly, the disbursements of funds by the bank under an agreement placing discretionary controls in the lender over the disbursement of the loan funds with an additional reservation that the loan is "to be advanced at such times and in such amounts as the Lender shall determine," we think left so wide an area of discretion in the bank as to render the amounts to be advanced and the intervals of their advancing optional rather than compulsory as a matter of law. Had the borrowers sought a decree to overcome these reservations and to compel the advances, or to override the bank's discretionary power to advance or withhold the loan funds, they would have met with nearly insuperable obstacles at law. So broad and yet so specific were the bank's discretionary powers under the contract as to the times and amounts of the advances, a court could not properly override such discretion without abrogating the contract.

Although in a given case there may be difficulty in ascertaining from the circumstances and the language of the mortgage and loan papers covering the whole agreement whether the advances are to be regarded as optional or mandatory, we think that the contractual reservations giving the lender the broad discretion of deciding when and in what amounts, or if at all, he must advance the money render the advances optional rather than obligatory where the purpose is to decide construction lien priorities arising after the initial filing for record of the lender's security documents. As a means of protecting its security, the lender retained broad discretionary powers to determine under what circumstances it would advance the money, to withhold the advances any time that it believed its security in jeopardy or doubted the sufficiency or quality of the construction work or felt that an impending insolvency on the borrower's part would threaten the completion of the project or repayment of the loan. There was no hard and fast commitment to deliver the loan money over to the borrower at a given and stated time, nor to advance the money at more or less fixed intervals and in stated amounts. The lender, in reserving such broad protective discretion, thereby rendered the advances optional rather than obligatory for the purpose of determining the priority of liens.

Thus, we are adhering to what we perceive to be the weight of authority embodied in the rule that, where the advances of promised loan moneys are, under an agreement to lend money, largely optional, that is, where the time and the amount of the moneys to be advanced are largely discretionary in the lender, the legal effect of such provisions is to bring the transaction under the rule for optional advances rather than the rule governing mandatory advances for the purpose of determining lien priorities. Optional advances under a construction loan agreement attach when the advances are actually made. Any liens attaching prior to an optional advance would thus be superior to it, and attaching afterwards, junior to it. . . .

A contrary rule on that point would allow a lender, having power to allocate the loan moneys in such a way as to insure that . . . work, materials and efforts serve to enhance the value of the security, to sit idly by and watch his security grow, while at the same time potentially leaving the materialmen, subcontractors and workmen in the position of doing their work and supplying materials for little or nothing. The rule here contended for by lender would lead to an inevitable unjust enrichment, enabling the lender to withhold or apply the loan money as he saw fit; all the while knowing that putative lien claimants were furnishing valuable materials and doing valuable work to the enhancement of his security. The bank here had the option of withholding its advances on the loan from the borrower, and the right to apply the money to the account of Columbia Wood Products in payment of the lumber that company was delivering to the construction project.

Accordingly, the judgment and decree of the trial court on the claim of Columbia Wood Products, Inc. is reversed.

Irwin Concrete v. Sun Coast Properties
33 Wash. App. 190, 653 P.2d 1331 (1982)

WORSWICK, Judge.

. . . Chaves [the subcontractor] contends that his lien was not foreclosed by the trustee sale because it was senior to that of Continental [the construction lender]. He argues that the loan agreement between Continental and Olympic [the developer] made advances optional with Continental; thus, he claims, to the extent of monies advanced after he started work, his lien claim was senior, citing National Bank of Washington v. Equity Investors, 81 Wash. 2d 886, 506 P.2d 20 (1973). We disagree. . . .

Unlike *Equity Investors*, the contract between Continental and Olympic did not allow Continental to disburse funds based on its own criteria. Subsection (2)(c) of the contract stated:

> The remaining $80,000 shall be disbursed after said lease to a national retail grocery chain has been secured and approved by Continental, for the purpose of site developments, plans for which shall be approved by Continental, and disbursements for which shall be made monthly against actual development costs, based on cost verification as site preparation progresses. Disbursements hereunder shall be subject to approval of Continental.

Disbursements were subject to Continental's approval. However, Continental was not free to advance or retain the money as it saw fit. The quoted language specifies the conditions under which Continental could approve or disapprove of disbursements: "disbursements for which shall be made monthly against actual development costs, based on cost verification as site preparation progresses." Continental's control over disbursements was limited to verifying each advance requested for the cost of work completed on the land. If the amount requested of Continental was verified, Continental had no option, but was required to disburse the money. Continental was obligated to loan $350,000 to Olympic. The only control Continental had over future advances was the ability to see that Olympic spent the loan money for improvements to the land. That control did not render the future advances optional.

Because Continental's advances were mandatory, its deed of trust securing the future advances was perfected on June 9, 1972, the date of filing. Chaves' mechanic's lien arose on June 16, 1972, the date he commenced work, and consequently was junior to the deed of trust. . . .

Responding to the problems faced by the construction lender in attempting to establish that its construction advances are "obligatory," several states (including Washington) have enacted laws that abolish the optional-obligatory doctrine and thereby protect the lender's "optional" future advances. Many of these statutes protect the lender for future advances only when the advances are used to improve the real estate. Others, such as the Florida statute excerpted below, are much broader in scope and encompass advances under revolving lines of credit.

Fla. Stat. Ann. §697.04

§697.04. Future Advances May Be Secured

(1)(a) Any mortgage or other instrument given for the purpose of creating a lien on real property, or on any interest in a leasehold upon real property, may, and when so expressed therein shall, secure not only existing indebtedness, but also such future advances, whether such advances are obligatory or to be made at the option of the lender, or otherwise, as are made within 20 years from the date thereof, to the same extent as if such future advances were made on the date of the execution of such mortgage or other instrument, although there may be no advance made at the time of the execution of such mortgage or other instrument and although there may be no indebtedness outstanding at the time any advance is made. Such lien, as to third persons without actual notice thereof, shall be valid as to all such indebtedness and future advances from the time the mortgage or other instrument is filed for record as provided by law.

(b) The total amount of indebtedness that may be so secured may decrease or increase from time to time, but the total unpaid balance so secured at any one time shall not exceed a maximum principal amount which must be specified in such mortgage or other instrument, plus interest thereon; except that the mortgagor or his successor in title is authorized to file for record a notice limiting the maximum principal amount that may be so secured to an amount not less than the amount actually advanced at the time of such filing, provided a copy of such filing is also sent by certified mail to the mortgagee and in the case of an open-end or revolving credit agreement, the mortgagor surrenders to the mortgagee all credit cards, checks, or other devices used to obtain further advances at the time of filing the notice which notice shall be recorded and shall be effective from the date of filing. Notwithstanding the foregoing, any increase in the principal balance as a result of negative amortization or deferred interest shall be secured by the mortgage; and any disbursements made for the payment of taxes, levies, or insurance on the property covered by the lien, and any advances or disbursements made under a construction loan agreement referred to in a mortgage to enable completion of the contemplated improvement, with interest on such advances or disbursements, are secured by the mortgage or other instrument even though the mortgage or other instrument does not provide for future advances, or the advances or disbursements cause the total indebtedness to exceed the face amount stated in the instrument. . . .

NOTES AND QUESTIONS

1. "Obligatory" versus "Optional" Advances. As observed above, states accord various special priorities to holders of mechanics' liens over mortgagees and other holders of prior-in-time interests in the real estate. In most states the special lien priority accorded to mechanics' liens does not change the general priority rule under the recording statutes of first in time, first in right. See Chapter 3E1. Instead, priority is established by moving the date of the mechanic's lien back to a date before the actual filing of the lien, such as the date of the commencement of construction. Once the date of the mechanic's lien is determined, it will then take priority over interests in the real estate that are recorded subsequent to that date. Now consider the other side of the coin—when does the construction mortgage create a security interest in the real estate against which the mechanic's lien will be tested? Is it when the mortgage is recorded? For all advances made in the future? Or is a separate interest in the real estate created with each new advance?

As explained in Chapter 4, except for a floor-ceiling loan, a typical postconstruction loan is closed and funded in its entirety if and when the project is completed in accordance with the terms and conditions of the postconstruction commitment letter. By contrast, as explained in greater detail at Chapter 6B5, infra, a prudent construction lender will insist on a progress payment procedure detailed in the construction loan agreement whereby loan advances are periodically made to the borrower (or directly to the general contractor) prior to each stage of the project so that the lender will be continuously assured that the improvements are being constructed in accordance with the plans and specifications, that the bills for labor and materials are being paid as they become due so that neither mechanics' nor materialmens' liens are pending, and that the loan is "in balance," meaning that there are sufficient undisbursed loan and equity funds on hand to fund the balance of the projected construction costs.

The foregoing overview explains why construction loan mortgages are structured as mortgages to secure future loan advances rather than as mortgages to secure present advances. Such mortgages (or deeds of trust) can either designate beforehand a specified maximum loan amount (frequently the amount of the postconstruction loan) that will be disbursed incrementally as the project advances, or the mortgage may merely identify the amount of the initial advance and specify that the mortgage will secure future advances as well. The construction loan agreements at issue in both *Equity Investors* and *Irwin Concrete* expressly stated the maximum loan amounts to be advanced.

Can you explain why the courts in these cases either ruled or assumed that the mortgages to secure future advances were enforceable notwithstanding the general rule that a valid mortgage requires an underlying obligation that is presently enforceable? See discussion at Chapter 3B2. Of the construction loan mortgage that identifies a specified maximum loan amount and one that merely designates the amount of the initial advance, the former approach is far more prevalent in the case of income-producing real estate. Why?

Assume that FNB agrees in its loan commitment to advance to Dan a maximum loan amount of $25 million subject to the terms and conditions of its construction loan agreement. Further assume the facts as diagrammed in Figure 6-1 and that the State of Fuller has a statute under which all mechanics' liens (when filed) automatically date back to the date on which construction commences. Under these facts, who will have lien priority as to Advances 1 and 2 made by FNB—FNB or the mechanic (M1)? As suggested in the cases excerpted above, in many jurisdictions the answer turns on whether the loan advances were obligatory or optional. Based on the equitable doctrine of relation back and the operation of the recording statutes, the lien priority of an obligatory advance dates back to the time at which the original mortgage was created and recorded. See G. Nelson et al., Real Estate Finance Law §12.7 (6th ed. 2015). Therefore, in the hypothetical, if FNB had been obliged to make both advances (as reflected by the language in its mortgage and construction loan agreement), then both advances would date back to January and be superior in lien priority to the mechanic's lien filed by M1 that under the priority rule would date back to March.

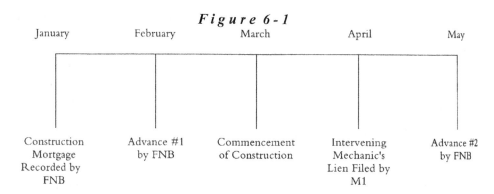

Figure 6-1

| January | February | March | April | May |

Construction Mortgage Recorded by FNB

Advance #1 by FNB

Commencement of Construction

Intervening Mechanic's Lien Filed by M1

Advance #2 by FNB

By contrast, under the common law of several jurisdictions, if a loan advance under a mortgage to secure future advances is optional and the mortgagee has notice of a subsequent lienor when the advance is made, then the optional advance is not predated and included within the original mortgage lien. Therefore, in the hypothetical, FNB's lien priority as to Advance 2 would be defeated if the advance had been optional and if FNB had notice of the intervening lien at the time it made the advance.

2. Notice of Optional Advances. As noted, the optional-obligatory doctrine includes a notice element. What kind of notice is required? In most jurisdictions the mortgagee must obtain actual notice of a subsequent security interest before its subsequent optional advance loses priority—constructive notice will not suffice. See Nelson et al. §12.7, at 1102-1103. This means that, absent actual notice by FNB, FNB's lien priority as to Advance 2 under Figure 6-1 will not be defeated even though the advance was optional and FNB had record notice of M1's lien before the advance was made. Can you think of the probable rationale for this result?

3. Rationale and Criticism of the Optional-Obligatory Doctrine. The optional-obligatory doctrine has been questioned by some commentators. Why should obligatory advances be included within the prior lien of the original mortgage when optional advances are not? What does notice to the mortgagee have to do with the issue of whether advances should relate back to the original mortgage? See Nelson et al. §12.7, at 1096-1098. Perhaps the notion is based on policy considerations. For example, if a mortgagee such as FNB should obligate itself to make future advances and puts itself on record as doing so (by recording its construction mortgage), then contractors and other potential third-party creditors (who might also have access to a copy of the construction loan agreement) are put on notice of the mortgagee's intentions and prior claim. By contrast, it would be inequitable to apply the equitable doctrine of relation back to impair the rights of intervening lienors when a mortgagee such as FNB can quit making optional advances at any time.

One problem with the doctrine of obligatory versus optional advances is the dilemma confronting a construction lender. As Chief Justice Hale conceded in the *Equity Investors* case, sound banking practice dictates that a cautious construction lender retain a considerable measure of control over its loan advances to protect its financial interests, which is the very purpose of the construction loan agreement. Evidence suggests that sloppy lending practices and poor supervision of loans in the deregulatory climate of the 1980s were significant contributory factors to the savings and loan crisis in the late 1980s. And yet, if a cautious lender were to overstep the ill-defined threshold limit on what is reasonable control, it might lose its lien priority as to future advances (in addition to other consequences, such as the potential for third-party tort liability discussed at Chapter 9B).

Can you think of any additional reasons in favor of or against the doctrine of optional versus obligatory advances? See generally Hughes, Future Advance Mortgages: Preserving the Benefits and Burdens of the Bargain, 29 Wake Forest L. Rev. 1101 (1994); Kratovil and Werner, Mortgage for Construction and the Lien Priorities Problem—The "Unobligatory" Advance, 41 Tenn. L. Rev. 311 (1974); Skipworth, Should Construction Lenders Lose Out on Voluntary Advances If a Loan Turns Sour?, 5 Real Est. L.J. 221 (1977); Tindall, The Obligatory Advance in the Construction Lending Context, 12 Const. Law. 13 (Jan. 1992).

In the *Equity Investors* case, Chief Justice Hale found that the language of the construction loan agreement made such explicit reservations for the disbursement of the loan as to render the advances optional. What provisions did Chief Justice Hale rely on in reaching his conclusion? Do you agree with him? If so, which of those provisions were determinative? If construction lenders eliminated the offending provisions, would that affect the viability of construction financing? Does the language of the contract in *Irwin Concrete* suggest how construction lenders can protect themselves without falling into the optional advance trap?

> ➤ *Problem 6-2*
> After reviewing the language of the sample construction loan agreement in the Documents Manual, can you identify any provisions that might render the loan advances optional? ◄

4. Effect of Waiver of Defaults. An especially thorny dilemma may confront the construction lender who waives defaults and works with the developer to avoid foreclosure. For example, assume the construction loan agreement provides that the building must be built according to the plans and specifications as approved by Ace and that FNB need not fund if Dan Developer is in default. The plans and specifications call for the marble slabs that form the "curtain wall" (the outside, nonsupporting wall of the building) to be attached with stainless steel clips. With costs rising, Dan uses clips made of a less expensive alloy. Ace's architects spot the change, and Ace notifies both Dan and FNB that it considers the substitution dangerous and a violation of the postconstruction commitment. By virtue of a "cross-default" provision in the construction loan agreement, a breach of the postconstruction commitment is a breach under the construction loan agreement. FNB, Ace, and Dan consult experts, who state that if the substitute clips are anodized to reduce the possibility of corrosion the slabs will be safe but still less desirable than stainless steel clips. Dan agrees to anodize the offending clips. Ace and FNB agree to go along with this and waive Dan's default (the failure to comply with the plans and specifications). Might FNB's waiver of the default render its advances merely optional? Compare J.I. Kislak Mortgage Corp. v. William Matthews, Builder, 287 A.2d 686 (Sup. Ct. 1972), aff'd, 303 A.2d 648 (Del. 1973) (lender's waiver of disbursement requirement of receipts from subcontractors made advances optional), with Home Lumber Co. v. Kopfmann Homes, 535 N.W.2d 302 (Minn. 1995) (question of whether advances were optional or obligatory is answered solely by reference to provisions of the loan documents without regard to whether the lender in fact waived certain disbursement conditions).

5. Statutory Protection for the Construction Lender. Those jurisdictions that have abolished the judicial optional-obligatory doctrine by statute include Washington. See Wash. Rev. Code Ann. §60.04.226 (any mortgage or deed of trust shall be prior to subsequently recorded liens to the extent of all sums secured thereby regardless of whether the disbursements are obligatory). Several of these statutes employ a so-called cutoff notice exception to the relation-back priority enjoyed by future advances. For example, the Florida statute on future advances excerpted above provides that the owner-mortgagor may file a notice limiting the maximum amount of advances that may take priority as of the date of the original mortgage recording to those advances already made at the time of the filing. What is the probable purpose of this provision, and when would it be used? Can it be used to the detriment of a construction lender on a half-completed project? The Restatement (Third) of Property (Mortgages) §2.3 (1997) abolishes the optional-obligatory distinction and adopts this cutoff notice approach; see generally Nelson and Whitman, Rethinking Future Advance Mortgages: A Brief for the Restatement Approach, 44 Duke L.J. 657 (1995).

b. The Uniform Construction Lien Act Approach

The Uniform Construction Lien Act (UCLA)[6] represents what its drafter, the National Conference of Commissioners on Uniform State Laws, considered the best of the emerging state legislation on mechanics' lien priority and related issues. In the following excerpt from the introductory comment to the predecessor to that Act, the commissioners discuss the thrust of state legislation and the major issues dealt with in the UCLA.

Introductory Comment to Article 5 of the Uniform Simplification of Land Transfer Act
14 U.L.A. 271 (1977)

All states presently have mechanics' lien laws. Those laws present an extraordinarily varied approach, in substance, and in language, to the issues involved in mechanics' lien legislation. In fact, variation among the states may be greater in this area than in any other statutory area. In an era of national lenders and suppliers and of many multistate builders, the variation among the states as to mechanics' lien matters may be as great a hindrance to an efficient real estate market as are variations in state real estate security interest (mortgage) law. Furthermore, the present priority, and owner liability rules present difficult problems for contractors, owners, lenders, and courts and add substantial expense and risk to many real estate transactions. Therefore, it is appropriate . . . that a uniform mechanics' act be proposed. . . .

While there is great diversity in mechanics' lien laws, they deal with common issues, and tend to fall into a limited number of patterns on each of the major issues involved. . . .

WHO MAY SECURE A LIEN?

Mechanics' lien statutes give liens against the real estate being improved to persons who supply services (including labor) and materials for the improvement. In about half the states, any person who supplies services or materials is allowed a lien, no matter how far removed he is from the owner. Other states limit those who can secure a lien to two tiers (prime contractor, subcontractor), three tiers (prime contractor, subcontractor, sub-subcontractor) or

---

6. 7 U.L.A. 366 (2002). See generally Benfield, The Uniform Construction Lien Act: What, Whither, and Why, 27 Wake Forest L. Rev. 527 (1992). The UCLA was adopted in 1987 along with other uniform acts designed to carve up the comprehensive provisions of the 1976 Uniform Simplification of Land Transfers Act (USLTA) (as amended in 1977) into smaller units more attractive for state adoption. The UCLA provisions are modeled on those in Article 5 of the USLTA excerpted below.

four tiers. A few others allow a lien to two tiers plus all materialmen and laborers, and one gives a lien to all who contract with licensed contractors. . . .

PRIORITY OVER THIRD PARTIES

Most mechanics' lien laws date the lien claimant's priority over third parties from the time of "commencement" or "visible commencement" (hereafter both statements of the rule are referred to by the use of the word "commencement") of the improvement, provided that the claimant records his lien within a limited period of time after he completes his work on the project. A commencement priority rule makes it difficult for persons who deal with real estate to determine whether it may be subject to subsequently asserted lien claims since a record title examination will not provide the necessary information. That priority rule, in effect, gives the lien claimant a secret lien. The secret lien is of limited duration since all statutes require the claimant to record a notice of lien within a fairly short period of time (2 to 18 or so months after completion) if he is to realize on the lien. Nevertheless, the title difficulties created are substantial. A commencement priority rule also creates particular difficulties for construction lenders. Such lenders usually record their mortgage at about the time the work is beginning, and, with some regularity, a construction lender discovers that work had commenced prior to the time he recorded so that he is junior to the construction lien claimant. . . .

A number of states, in response to the problems created by the commencement priority rule, have fixed other mechanics' lien priority dates. A few states date mechanics' lien priority from the time of recording the individual claimant's lien. This system protects the integrity of the real estate records, but prevents a contractor or materialman who furnishes services or materials late in the construction from getting priority equal with that of those who furnish services or materials early.

Illinois makes the time the owner and a prime contractor enter into the improvement contract the priority date for that prime and claimants who claim through him. A few states date all claimants' priority from the time the prime contract or a notice thereof is recorded in the real estate records. That system, also, protects the integrity of the public records, but gives claimants under different primes different priorities in cases in which the owner uses more than one prime contractor on an improvement project.

This Act adopts a notice recording device, first developed in Florida, under which the owner, prior to the beginning of work on an improvement, records a "notice of commencement" which puts third parties on notice that construction liens may be claimed against the real estate. If a lien claimant records his lien during the effective period of a notice of commencement, his priority date is the date the notice of commencement was recorded. . . .

The following excerpts from the UCLA indicate how the commissioners felt the mechanics' lien priority question should be answered.

Section 5-209 of Uniform Simplification of Land Transfer Act
[later adopted as Section 210 of the UCLA]

(a) Except as provided in this section, a construction lien has priority over adverse claims against the real estate as if the construction lien claimant were a purchaser for value without knowledge who had recorded at the time his lien attached.

(b) Except as provided in subsection (c), a construction lien has priority over subsequent advances made under a prior recorded security interest if the subsequent advances are made with knowledge that the lien has attached.

(c) Notwithstanding knowledge that the construction lien has attached, or the advance exceeds the maximum amount stated in the recorded security agreement and whether or not the advance is made pursuant to a commitment, a subsequent advance made under a security agreement recorded before the construction lien attached has priority over the lien if:

(1) the subsequent advance is made under a construction security agreement[7] and is made in payment of the price of the agreed improvements,

(2) the subsequent advance is made or incurred for the reasonable protection of the security interest in the real estate, such as payment for real property taxes, hazard insurance premiums, or maintenance charges imposed under a condominium declaration or other covenant, or

(3) the subsequent advance was applied to the payment of any lien or encumbrance which was prior to the construction lien.

(d) To the extent that a subsequent security interest is given to secure funds used to pay a debt secured by a security interest having priority over a construction lien under this section, the subsequent security interest is also prior to the construction lien.

(e) Even though notice of commencement has been recorded, a buyer who is a protected party [a consumer] takes free of all construction liens that are not of record at the time [the] title document is recorded. . .

---

7. A "construction security agreement" is one that identifies itself as such and "that secures an obligation which the debtor incurred for the purpose of making an improvement of the real estate in which the security interest is given."—EDS.

Section 5-301 of Uniform Simplification of Land Transfer Act
[later adopted as Section 301 of the UCLA]

(a) [A] notice of commencement must be signed by the contracting owner, be denominated "notice of commencement," and state:

(1) the real estate being or intended to be improved or directly benefitted, with a description thereof sufficient for identification;

(2) the name and address of the contracting owner, [the owner's] interest in the real estate, and the name and address of the fee simple titleholder, if other than the contracting owner; and

(3) that if, after the notice of commencement is recorded, a [construction] lien is recorded as to an improvement covered by the notice of commencement, the lien has priority from the time the notice of commencement is recorded.

(b) The notice of commencement may state its duration, but if a duration is stated of less than six months from the time of recording, the duration of the notice is six months. If no duration is stated, the duration of the notice is one year after the recording. . . .

(d) A contracting owner may extend the duration of a notice of commencement by recording before the lapse thereof a continuation statement signed by [the owner] which refers to the record location and date of recording of the notice of commencement and states the date to which the notice of commencement's duration is extended. . . .

Section 5-207 of Uniform Simplification of Land Transfer Act
[later adopted as Section 208 of the UCLA]

(a) A claimant's lien does not attach and may not be enforced unless, after entering into the contract under which the lien arises, and not later than 90 days after [the] final furnishing of services or materials, [the claimant] has recorded a lien.

(b) If a lien is recorded while a notice of commencement is effective as to the improvement in connection with which the lien arises, the lien attaches as of the time the notice is recorded, *even though visible commencement occurred before the notice is recorded* [emphasis supplied]. A notice of commencement is not effective until recording and, after recording, is effective until its lapse. A notice of commencement lapses at the earlier of its expiration (Section 5-301(b)) or the date it is terminated by a notice of termination (Section 5-302).

(c) If a lien is recorded while there is no recorded notice of commencement covering the improvement in connection with which the lien arises, the lien attaches at the earlier of visible commencement of the improvement or the recording of the lien. But, if visible commencement has occurred before or within 30 days after the lapse of the last notice of commencement covering the improvement:

> (1) the lien attaches at the time the lien is recorded if the lien is recorded within 30 days after lapse of the last effective notice of commencement; or

> (2) the lien relates back to and attaches 31 days after the termination date if the lien is recorded more than 30 days after lapse of the last effective notice of commencement.

(d) If new construction is the principal improvement involved and the materials, excavation, preparation of an existing structure, or other preparation are readily visible on a reasonable inspection of the real estate, "visible commencement" occurs when:

> (1) materials are delivered to the real estate to which the lien attaches prepatory to construction;

> (2) excavation on the real estate to which the lien attaches is begun; or

> (3) preparation of an existing structure to receive the new construction, or other preparation of the real estate to which the lien attaches, is begun.

(e) In all cases not covered by subsection (d) the time visible commencement occurs is to be determined by the circumstances of the case.

NOTES AND QUESTIONS

Uniform Construction Lien Act. Consider the following broad-brush formulation of the construction lien priority rules under the UCLA. A mechanic's or material-man's lien ("construction lien") is perfected by a recordation of the lien, which becomes effective as of the time a valid "notice of commencement" is filed by the owner or a lien claimant (for example, a subcontractor), even though the visible commencement of construction occurred before the notice is recorded. UCLA §§208, 301. If such notice was not filed, the mechanic's lien attaches when the commencement of construction became visible or when the lien was filed, whichever came first. UCLA §208(c). The mechanic's lien will be junior in lien priority to a future advance made under a previously recorded construction mortgage ("construction security agreement") regardless of whether the advance was obligatory or optional (thereby rejecting the optional-obligatory doctrine), even where the mortgagee had notice of the intervening mechanic's lien before the advance was made and even where the advance happened to exceed the maximum loan amount stipulated in the recorded mortgage, provided that:

1. the advance was made "in payment of the price of the [agreed-on] improvements";

2. the advance was made to preserve the mortgagee's security interest in the property; or

3. the advance was used toward the payment of any lien or encumbrance that was senior in lien priority to the mechanic's lien. UCLA §210(c).

> ➢ *Problem 6-3*
>
> Returning to the facts in the hypothetical as diagrammed in Figure 6-1, assume that the State of Fuller has not adopted the UCLA and follows the traditional priority rule to the effect that all mechanics' liens relate back to the date on which the construction becomes visible. Unbeknownst to FNB, excavation of the land by M1 and other visible preliminary site work began in December of the previous year, even though the actual "brick and mortar" construction of the improvements did not actually begin until March. FNB recorded its mortgage in January and made its first loan advance in February, and M1 recorded its mechanic's lien in April. In May, FNB made its second loan advance even though it had actual notice of M1's lien at that time. Finally, in August, FNB discovers that Dan used the second loan advance to pay his gambling debts. The project collapses; FNB commences a foreclosure action and attempts to extinguish M1's lien on the assumption that both its loan advances are superior in lien priority to the mechanic's lien filed by M1.
>
> Who has lien priority as to Advance 1—FNB or M1? As to Advance 2? Would these lien priority results change with respect to either Advance 1 or Advance 2 if Fuller had adopted the UCLA and FNB had insisted that the owner, Dan Developer, record a notice of commencement in January when it recorded its construction loan mortgage? See UCLA §301, comment 1. ◄

A notice of commencement, if filed by Dan, not only protects FNB against contractors but also serves to put the contractor on notice that it will be subordinate to the construction financing. Also, the notice of commencement can be filed by a contractor or other lien claimant. Thus, if no notice of commencement had been filed and no mortgage recorded at the time of its contract with Dan Developer, the contractor could file a notice of commencement at that time, thereby ensuring that any mechanic's lien it later records will date from the time of its notice and be prior to any subsequent mortgage. See UCLA §301, comment 1.

In your opinion, do the priority concepts adopted by the UCLA provide a rational way to balance the interests of the construction lender and mechanics' lien claimants?

c. Protection for the Construction Lender: Title Insurance

The risk of construction lending posed by mechanics' lien claimants can be ameliorated by title insurance from title companies with sufficient assets. However, as suggested by the excerpts that follow and the general discussion of title insurance at Chapter 2B, the scope of the coverage is somewhat limited.

The following sample construction loan agreement provision illustrates the lender's typical requirements for title insurance coverage:

> Section 4.04. Prior to the first Advance under this Agreement, Borrower shall deliver or cause to be delivered to Lender a 2006 ALTA loan policy or policies of title insurance issued by a company or companies approved in writing by Lender and Post-Construction Lender, issued to Lender (and a commitment or commitments to issue a substantially similar policy or policies to the Post-Construction Lender upon substantial completion of the Project in form and content approved by Lender and Post-Construction Lender) in the face amount of the Note, as of the date of the first Advance hereunder, insuring that the Mortgage is a first lien on the Land and the Improvements as constructed (including, without limitation, specific insurance against filed and unfiled mechanic's and materialmen's liens), subject to no encumbrances or any other matters except those set forth in the Permitted Encumbrances or approved in writing by Lender and Post-Construction Lender. As a condition to each advance hereunder, such insurance shall be extended by endorsement to cover such advance. The title policy or policies shall contain such endorsements and shall be issued with such coinsurance and re-insurance as Lender may request.

Observe that this clause requires use of the 2006 loan policy form of the American Land Title Association (ALTA), the industry's trade organization. First introduced in 1970, and revised periodically, the ALTA loan policy form was designed primarily for the benefit of postconstruction lenders but has been issued to construction lenders as well. Starting in the mid-1970s, in response to heavy mechanics' lien claim losses incurred by title companies, the ALTA introduced a specialized title policy form for construction loans. The 1975 construction loan title policy greatly pared down the risk assumption by title companies for mechanics' lien claims and allowed construction lenders to carve out specific protection from mechanics' lien risk with one of four specific endorsements. The construction loan industry had never placed high value in the ALTA construction loan policy, and it never became well accepted. Recently, the ALTA abandoned the construction loan policy by decertifying the policy form and its accompanying endorsements, although title companies in some states still offer the protection afforded from the decertified form.

As is illustrated by the language of the construction loan agreement excerpt above, construction lenders have typically relied on title insurance in the form of the standard 2006 ALTA loan policy. The 2006 ALTA loan policy (which, unlike the 1975 ALTA construction loan policy, has maintained its accreditation) generally insures at and after the policy date against loss or damage as a result of Covered Risk 11, with the following language:

> The lack of priority of the lien of the Insured Mortgage upon the Title (a) as security for each and every advance of proceeds of the loan secured by the Insured Mortgage over any statutory lien for services, labor, or material arising from construction of an improvement or work related to the Land when the improvement or work is either (i) Contracted for or commenced on or before Date of Policy; or (ii) Contracted for, commenced, or continued after Date of Policy if the construction is financed, in whole or in part, by proceeds of the loan secured by the Insured Mortgage that the Insured has advanced or is obligated on Date of Policy to advance . . .

When a construction loan is insured under the ALTA 2006 policy, Covered Risk 11 is deleted and replaced with either: (1) ALTA Endorsement 32-06 (Construction Loan—Loss of Priority), insuring against loss or damage "by reason of . . . the lack of priority of the lien of the Insured Mortgage, as security for each Construction Loan Advance made on or before the Date of Coverage over any Mechanic's Lien, if notice of the Mechanic's Lien is not filed or recorded in the Public Records, but only to the extent that the charges for the services, labor, materials or equipment for which the Mechanic's Lien is claimed were designated for payment in the documents supporting a Construction Loan Advance disbursed by or on behalf of the Insured on or before Date of Coverage" (ALTA Endorsement 32-06 does not cover possible mechanics' lien claimants which were omitted or understated in the documents presented to support a loan payout, and expressly excludes coverage for mechanics' liens arising from services, labor, material or equipment furnished after date of coverage, or not designated for payment in the documents supporting a construction loan advance disbursed by or on behalf of the Insured on or before date of coverage.) or (2) ALTA Endorsement 32.1-06 (Construction Loan—Loss of Priority—Direct Payment), insuring against loss or damage "by reason of . . . the lack of priority of the lien of the insured Mortgage as security for each Construction Loan Advance made on or before the Date of Coverage over any Mechanic's Lien if notice of the Mechanic's Lien is not filed or recorded in the Public Records, but only to the extent that direct payment to the Mechanic's Lien claimant has been made by the Company or by the Insured with the Company's written approval." (ALTA Endorsement 32.1-06 covers only possible mechanics' lien claimants which were paid directly by the title company as escrowee or by the insured lender with written approval by the title company, and expressly excludes coverage over mechanics' liens arising from services, labor, material, or equipment furnished after the date of coverage, or not directly paid by the title company or by the insured with the company's written approval.)

 Both ALTA Endorsement 32-06 and 32.1-06, in reducing the scope of coverage previously given under the 1975 ALTA Construction Loan Policy, constitute a response to perceived heightened risk in the marketplace. This coverage is subject to exclusion 3 in the loan policy, which excludes the following from coverage:

3. Defects, liens, encumbrances, adverse claims or other matters:

    (a) created, suffered, assumed or agreed to by the insured claimant;

    (b) not known to the Company, not recorded in the public records at Date of Policy, but known to the insured claimant and not disclosed in writing to the Company by the insured claimant prior to the date the insured claimant became an insured under this policy;

    (c) resulting in no loss or damage to the insured claimant; [or]

    (d) attaching or created subsequent to Date of Policy [except to the extent the policy insures priority of the insured mortgage's lien over any statutory lien for services, labor or material]; . . .

Interpreting the most-litigated provision of the construction loan policy, courts are often faced with deciding whom between the construction lender and the title company should pick up the pieces of a troubled project. In Bankers Trust Co. v. Transamerica Title Ins. Co., 594 F.2d 231 (10th Cir. 1979), the construction lender obtained a title insurance policy insuring against, inter alia, mechanics' liens. The loan policy contained the standard exclusion 3(a) (excerpted above), excluding from coverage "defects, liens, encumbrances, adverse claims or other matters" that are "created, suffered, assumed or agreed to by the insured claimant." Construction was halted after 13 disbursements when the lender declared the loan out of balance and in default. Note that a loan is deemed to be "in balance" when the amount is sufficient to complete the project (whether from the loan itself or together with cash equity paid in by the developer). Mechanics' liens were filed against the property, and the lender made a claim on its title policy. The Tenth Circuit affirmed the dismissal of the lender's complaint against the title company based on the 3(a) exclusion—the mechanics' liens were created or permitted by the lender because the lender had knowingly made a loan that was below the lender's estimated actual cost to complete the construction.

On similar facts, in Brown v. St. Paul Title Ins. Corp., 634 F.2d 1103 (8th Cir. 1980), the Eighth Circuit held the lender had "created" or "suffered" mechanics' liens within the 3(a) exclusion by failing to provide adequate funds to pay for work completed prior to the developer's default on the loan. "While [the insured lender] admittedly was under no obligation to continue the project after default, it seems clear that the parties contemplated the insured would provide adequate funds to pay for work completed prior to the default." In a subsequent case, the Eighth Circuit refused to interpret its decision in Brown to exclude coverage under 3(a) whenever the lender fails to advance sufficient funds to complete the project. Rather, it limited the holding in Brown to when the construction lender withholds committed loan funds earmarked for already completed work, thereby assuring that mechanics' liens will arise. See Chicago Title Ins. Co. v. RTC, 53 F.3d 899 (8th Cir. 1995); see also BB Syndication Services, Inc. v. First American Title Ins. Co., 780 F.3d 825 (7th Cir. 2015); American Sav. & Loan Ass'n v. Lawyers' Title Ins. Corp., 793 F.2d 780 (6th Cir. 1986) (distinguishing Bankers Trust and Brown in holding the construction lender had not suffered or assumed the risk of mechanics' liens in financing less than the entire cost of construction).

NOTES AND QUESTIONS

Title Insurance Coverage. If it is understood that title insurance is considered a "risk prevention" type of insurance rather than a "risk assumption" type of insurance, explain the general difficulty to title insurance companies of providing effective title insurance to construction lenders for mechanics' lien claims.

d. Protection for the Construction Lender: Payment Bonds and Lien Waivers

Two additional protective devices for the construction lender are labor and materials payment bonds from a surety company and lien waivers from the contractors and subcontractors. A labor and materials payment bond will bind the bonding company, as surety, to pay the charges of subcontractors and suppliers if the general contractor fails to make these payments. The purpose is to prevent mechanics' or materialmen's liens from being filed against the property. See Chapter 6B4b, infra, for additional discussion of payment bonds and the related performance bond. As you might imagine, the more the bond is needed, the less available and the more expensive it will be, and the prospective borrower will almost certainly resist a requirement for such bonding in a lender's proposed commitment. Perhaps because of this, the bonding approach has not been widely used in the real estate construction industry.

Waivers of liens by contractors and subcontractors are used extensively with dramatic differences in effect, depending on which jurisdiction's law applies. Generally, a predisbursement waiver by a contractor, subcontractor, or materialman of a lien for work already performed will be enforceable. See G. Nelson et al., Real Estate Finance Law §12.4, at 1072-1073 (6th ed. 2015). The logistics of this can be complicated. The general contractor will provide a sworn list of subcontractors and materialmen prior to each disbursement. The contractor, subcontractors, and materialmen will then execute waivers indicating that they have been fully paid for work thus far performed. Armed with the waivers, the construction lender will then make the disbursement.

It would be much easier if the waiver would cover not only work performed or materials supplied up to the date of the waiver but also all work or materials to be performed or furnished in the future. Then only one waiver would need to be obtained from the contractor and each subcontractor or materialman. However, prospective waivers are void as against public policy in many jurisdictions, and some courts in jurisdictions where such waivers are valid construe them rather strictly. See, for example, Boise Cascade Corp. v. Stephens, 572 P.2d 1380 (Utah 1977).

In some states a provision in a construction contract (or in a separate agreement between the contractor and the developer) that waives any rights to liens on the property is valid against subcontractors or materialmen if the contract is executed and recorded before performance by any subcontractor or materialman. In other states, it may be valid only against the contractor and those subcontractors or materialmen who have specifically agreed to be bound thereby. See Nelson et al. §12.4, at 1072. Obviously, lien waivers can be a very cumbersome form of protection in many jurisdictions, but they are, in many cases, the best protection available to the lender.

e.   Equitable Lien Theory

The following case discusses the application of the equitable lien theory, a judicial doctrine to protect contractors.

Swinerton & Walberg Co. v. Union Bank
25 Cal. App. 3d 259, 101 Cal. Rptr. 665 (1972)

FLEMING, Associate Justice.

Union Bank (Bank) appeals a portion of a judgment imposing an equitable lien in favor of Swinerton & Walberg Co. (Swinerton) on funds held by Bank in a construction loan disbursement account.

FACTS

In February 1964 James and Audrey Casey (Casey) contracted with Swinerton, a building contractor, for the construction of a 78-unit apartment building on Casey's property in Redondo Beach at a price of $785,000. To finance construction and related expenses Casey in March 1964 borrowed $892,000 from Bank, signing a promissory note secured in part by a trust deed on the property.

Casey and Bank entered into a building loan agreement pursuant to which the $892,000 loan was deposited with Bank in a construction loan disbursement account. At Bank's request Casey deposited an additional $37,700 in the account to make a total of $929,700. $186,000 was to be disbursed for purposes other than construction, and $3,700 was to be held in the account for unforeseen expenses. The balance of $740,000 was to be disbursed as construction progressed to Swinerton (who was named in the agreement as the contractor) but $74,000 of that amount would be withheld until a title insurance company on completion of construction guaranteed that no mechanics' liens were outstanding against the property. The building loan agreement provided that if Casey should default on any obligation to Bank, the latter could apply funds in the construction loan disbursement account against Casey's obligation, and it recited "that nothing contained in this agreement shall be construed to vest in any contractor . . . any interest in or claim upon the funds so set aside in this agreement." As contractor, Swinerton signed a declaration in the building loan agreement that it accepted the agreements, conditions, and provisions of the loan agreement, and that these would control inconsistent provisions in its building contract with Casey.

Construction began in March 1964 and was completed in January 1965. Casey ordered extras amounting to $5,000, thereby raising the contract price to $790,000. During the construction period Bank disbursed $666,000 to Swinerton.

In March 1965 Casey defaulted on obligations to both Swinerton and Bank, and Swinerton recorded a mechanics' lien for $150,932.93 against Casey's property. On 16 September 1965 Swinerton offered to release its mechanics' lien, the only lien outstanding, if Bank would disburse the withheld amount of $74,000 on deposit in the construction loan account. Bank refused. In November 1966 Bank foreclosed its trust deed on the Casey property, buying in the property on the foreclosure sale for $810,000 and thereby wiping out Swinerton's mechanics' lien, a result Swinerton did not challenge.

Bank never sought to press its claim under the building loan agreement to apply undisbursed construction funds to Casey's defaulted obligation to Bank, and $104,472.68 remains undisbursed in the construction loan account. Swinerton instituted the present action against Casey and Bank for breach of contract and for imposition of an equitable lien against funds on deposit in the construction loan account.

TRIAL COURT'S DETERMINATION

The trial court found: Swinerton was induced to construct the apartment building by Casey and Bank; Swinerton was induced to rely on, and did rely on, the construction loan disbursement fund for payment; Swinerton, in signing the building loan agreement, did not intend to give up its rights to an equitable lien against undisbursed construction funds; Swinerton completed the construction called for by its contract in a workmanlike manner, and the reasonable value of construction exceeded $740,000; Bank had no reason to refuse to disburse $74,000 to Swinerton after Swinerton offered to release its mechanics' lien on 16 September 1965.

The trial court concluded that Casey was indebted to Swinerton for $124,000 [$790,000 contract price, less $666,000 construction loan disbursement]; Swinerton had no contractual rights against Bank; Swinerton was entitled to $74,000 plus interest from 16 September 1965 from Bank; and Swinerton's recovery against Bank was to be credited against Casey's debt to Swinerton. . . .

EQUITABLE LIEN

Bank argues that a general contractor may not assert an equitable lien, and it insists that this conclusion is compelled by Gordon Building Corp v. Gibraltar Savings & Loan Assoc., 247 Cal. App. 2nd 1, 4, 10, 55 Cal. Rptr. 884. We disagree. In *Gordon* a general contractor, sued by a subcontractor for money due for labor and materials, cross-complained against a lender, in part to impose an equitable lien on construction loan proceeds held by the lender on the construction project on which the contractor had worked. The lender's demurrer was sustained without leave to amend, and judgment of dismissal was affirmed on appeal, because two allegations essential to the imposition of an equitable lien were missing from the general contractor's cross complaint against the lender: an allegation that the general contractor directly supplied labor or materials to the construction project, and an allegation that the general contractor justifiably relied on the construction loan proceeds. . . .

Gordon does state: "It would be a novel theory that the general contractor should accede to the benefit of loan proceeds heretofore considered to constitute a trust for the payment of liens and claims established by subcontractors and materialmen. Indeed, the demonstrated attitude of the law has been to implement the existing statutory scheme protecting subcontractors by methods calculated to forestall the misapplication or diversion of construction funds by the entrepreneurs of the project, including owner, builder, and the general contractor. . . ." That language, however, was used to support the court's conclusion that under the circumstances of the case the general contractor's complaint did not state a cause of action based on a third-party beneficiary theory, i.e., a contract theory of recovery. Since recovery in the present case is not grounded on contract but rather on equitable considerations arising out of estoppel and unjust enrichment, its disposition is not controlled by the foregoing language from *Gordon*. Significantly, the latter case did not declare that a general contractor, entirely unrelated to the owner and builder, could never assert an equitable lien against construction loan proceeds.

Bank next argues that all cases in which equitable liens have been upheld involve subcontractors and not general contractors, and from this it concludes that a general contractor can never become entitled to an equitable lien against construction loan funds. Yet the fact that all other cases recognizing equitable liens have involved subcontractors, even if true, does not by itself preclude imposition of an equitable lien against construction loan funds on behalf of a general contractor. The lender of construction funds stands in the same approximate relationship to a subcontractor as it does to a general contractor who is wholly independent from the borrower. In both instances the position of the lender is that summarized in the following language: "Where the lender has received the benefit of the claimant's performance, and therefore a more valuable security for its note, it is not justified in withholding or appropriating to any other use money originally intended to be used to pay for such performance and relied upon by the claimant in rendering its performance." (Miller v. Mountain View

Sav. & Loan Assoc., 238 Cal. App. 2nd 644, 661, 48 Cal. Rptr. 278, 290. . . .)
Here, Swinerton performed its work and completed the construction of the
apartment building (work whose reasonable value exceeded $740,000) but
received only $666,000. Bank obtained the benefit of that performance by
foreclosing on its trust deed and selling the apartment building for $810,000. It is
equally clear that Swinerton was induced by the creation of the building
construction loan fund to supply work, labor, and materials for the project and
that in rendering its performance it relied on the fund for payment. Indeed, since
Bank had acquired a first lien on the property to protect its construction loan,
Swinerton could look to little else for security. The only contractual obstacle to
Swinerton's right to the undisbursed construction loan fund was the existence of
its own mechanics' lien against the property, a lien which on 16 September 1965
it offered to release if Bank would disburse $74,000 from the remaining
construction loan funds. Bank refused the offer. Under these circumstances—full
performance by the contractor and reliance by the contractor on the fund for
payment—we think Swinerton became entitled to the $74,000 withheld in the
construction loan disbursement account for payment of construction costs.

There are no statutory impediments to this conclusion, for the events with
which we are concerned took place in 1964 and 1965. A 1967 addition to former
Code of Civil Procedure section 1190.1, subdivision (n) (now Civil Code section
3264) provides:

> The rights of all persons furnishing labor, services, equipment, or materials for any
> work of improvement, with respect to any fund for payment of construction costs,
> are governed exclusively by this article, and no such person may assert any legal or
> equitable right with respect to such fund, other than a right created by direct written
> contract between such person and the person holding the fund, except pursuant to the
> provisions of this article.

Bank argues that this provision shows legislative opposition to the imposition
of equitable liens against construction funds. We do not read such a broad
meaning into that section . . . but in any event that section does not apply
retrospectively. The legislature specifically provided that the addition . . . "shall
not apply to any work of improvement commenced prior to [8 November 1967]."
. . .

Finally, Bank argues that the equitable lien was designed to aid only those
who are entitled to a stop notice but fail to properly perfect it, that general
contractors are not entitled to stop notices (Civ. Code, §3159), and that because a
general contractor's equitable rights should not exceed his legal rights, a general
contractor is not entitled to an equitable lien. Bank's major premise is incorrect:
The equitable lien is wholly independent of the statutory mechanics' lien and
stop notice remedies, and therefore does not depend on the availability to the
claimant of the statutory stop notice remedy.

We conclude that in 1965 a general contractor could claim an equitable lien
on construction loan proceeds, and that in this case the general contractor became
entitled to such a lien. . . .

NOTES AND QUESTIONS

1. Stop Notice. Enacted in a handful of jurisdictions, stop notice statutes generally give the mechanic the right to enforce its claim against any undisbursed construction loan proceeds. See, for example, Alaska Stat. §34.35.062; see generally Annot., 4 A.L.R.5th 772 (1993). The unpaid mechanic accomplishes this by filing a notice under the statute, which has the effect of stopping future construction and bringing the entire project to a halt pending what may turn out to be extensive litigation to determine the validity and amount of the claim.

Do you see any constitutional problem in the mechanic's exercising its rights under the stop notice statute and bringing the construction to a halt without a hearing? See the discussion at Chapter 8C5 on due process as it relates to power-of-sale foreclosures of mortgages or deeds of trust and Comment, California's Private Stop Notice Law: Due Process Requirements, 25 Hastings L.J. 1043 (1974). Compare Connolly Dev. v. Superior Court, 17 Cal. 3d 803, 132 Cal. Rptr. 477, 553 P.2d 637 (1976) (upholding California law) with Noatex Corp. v. King Construction of Houston, L.L.C., 732 F.3d 479 (5th Cir. 2013) (invalidating Mississippi stop notice law as facially unconstitutional). See generally Ilyin, Stop Notice—Construction Loan Officer's Nightmare, 16 Hastings L.J. 187 (1964); Comment, Mechanics' Liens: The "Stop Notice" Comes to Washington, 49 Wash. L. Rev. 685 (1974).

2. Equitable Liens. In *Swinerton*, the court applied the equitable lien doctrine notwithstanding the fact that there was a stop notice statute in California. If the passage of a mechanic's lien law doesn't prevent the application of the equitable lien, should not the passage of a stop notice statute do so? How did the court deal with this in *Swinerton*? See generally Lefcoe and Schaffer, Construction Lending and the Equitable Lien, 40 S. Cal. L. Rev. 439 (1967); Annot., 5 A.L.R.3d 848 (1990).

4. *Assurance of Completion*

To review: The construction lender's real security for its loan is usually the commitment issued by a postconstruction lender, which will "take out" (pay off) the construction loan. One condition to the postconstruction lender's obligation to fund its loan common to all postconstruction loan commitments is that the building must be completed in accordance with the approved plans and specifications.

Thus, assurance of completion in accordance with the approved plans and specifications is key to the construction lender's hope for a take out of its loan. Returning to our hypothetical situation, what steps would be necessary or appropriate for FNB to take to help assure itself that Ace will have no excuse for extricating itself from the postconstruction loan commitment? See Chapter 6B2, supra. In this section we consider the major protective devices to assure completion.

a. Lender's Approval of Contractor's Building Contract and Architect's Contract

The construction lender will require its approval of the construction contract between the owner-borrower and the general contractor (if the owner does not act as its own contractor). Such an agreement may be structured as (1) a "fixed price" contract whereby, after competitive bidding, the contractor chosen by the owner agrees to construct the improvements for a firm price; (2) a "cost-plus" contract whereby the contractor is paid for actual costs plus a fee based on a percentage of the costs; (3) a "fast-track construction" contract whereby construction commences before the plans and specifications are finalized; or (4) a "design-build" contract whereby the contractor both designs and constructs the improvements. If the construction lender requires approval of the construction contract (and, with it, the contractor) prior to the execution of the construction loan agreement, the construction loan agreement would then contain a clause similar to the following:

> Both Borrower and Contractor are in full compliance with their respective obligations under the Construction Contract [defined in the loan agreement to mean the contract identified by date that had been reviewed by the construction lender]. The work to be performed by Contractor [defined to indicate a specific contractor by name and address] under the Construction Contract is the work called for by the Plans and Specifications [meaning the specific plans and specifications approved by the construction lender]. All work on the Project shall conform to the Plans and Specifications and shall be free of all defects. The Construction Contract shall not be amended without the prior written consent of Lender.

Similarly, the construction lender may require its review and approval of the architect's contract before the construction loan agreement is executed. If so, the construction loan agreement would provide as follows:

> Both Borrower and Borrower's Architect [meaning a specific architect identified by name and address] are in full compliance with their respective obligations under the Architect's Contract [meaning a specific contract entered into on a specific date between the borrower and the borrower's architect]. Borrower shall from time to time upon request by Lender cause Borrower's Architect to provide Lender with reports relative to the status of construction of the Improvements. The Architect's Contract shall not be amended without the prior written consent of Lender.

NOTES AND QUESTIONS

Construction Contracts. By way of review, why would a cautious construction lender discourage use of the fast-track format? See Chapter 4D2. Can you think of any protective strategies that a contractor might employ to protect itself against cost overruns in the case of a fixed price contract? Can you think of any protective language that a prudent owner should insist on in the case of a cost-plus contract? Which sort of contract is the construction lender most likely to favor? See Goldenhersh, Essentials of Building Contracts, 13 Colo. Law. 1 (Jan. 1984); Symposium, Construction Management and Design-Build/Fast Track Construction, 46 Law & Contemp. Probs. 1 (1983).

b. Performance Bonds; Guarantees; Letters of Credit; Insurance; Disbursement Programs

In this section we discuss some miscellaneous devices designed to assure that the project will be completed. Perhaps the most widely known is the surety bond, under which, for a fee, the surety company purports to guarantee against unpaid claims of mechanics and materialmen and to guarantee that the project will be completed on time for the contract price. A "payment bond" is one that guarantees payment of the bills of suppliers of labor and materials and is designed to reduce significantly the risk of mechanics' liens. A "performance bond" guarantees that the contractor will perform the terms and conditions of the construction contract, including completing the project for the amount set forth in the contract. In the past, surety companies issued a combined form of payment and performance bond. Today, it is more likely that separate bonds will be issued, but for a single combined premium. A typical construction loan agreement provision requiring bonding follows:

> Borrower shall obtain payment and performance bonds, in form and substance satisfactory to Lender, naming Lender as an obligee covering the construction contract and such contractors and subcontractors as Lender shall have requested, true and complete copies of which, together with all amendments, supplements and modifications thereto, will have been delivered to Lender, and shall be in full force and effect, free from default, unmodified and enforceable strictly in accordance with their respective terms. Borrower will obtain such additional payment and performance bonds with respect to contracts and subcontracts for work for the Project as Lender may, from time to time, request, and will timely deliver true and complete copies thereof to Lender, in form and substance satisfactory to Lender. All such bonds shall be recorded if the recording of such bonds serves to preclude the filing of any liens.

At first glance the concept of bonding would appear to be an ideal completion assurance device. However, bonds are costly and often not available to contractors who do not have substantial financial strength. Second, where available, the bonds are usually subject to numerous defenses to payment, for example: (1) the liability of the surety may be limited to the construction described in the original construction contract for an amount of coverage geared to the original contract price, so that the surety would not be liable for design or construction changes (which are virtually inevitable); (2) losses are generally not covered if caused by matters outside the construction contract (for example, the contract provides for a 15 percent holdback, but the loan agreement provides for only a 10 percent holdback and the developer has squandered the extra 5 percent of the construction funds) or if occasioned by violations of the construction contract (for example, the developer makes payments in advance of dates specified in the construction contract); (3) where the bond covers a subcontractor, rather than the general contractor, the surety may argue that the failure to perform arose from the failure of the other subcontractors, not the bonded subcontractor; and (4) based on the so-called Los Angeles clause in some surety bonds, the surety may claim that its liability is conditional on the performance by other parties to the agreement. For example, where the project cost is $1 million, $800,000 to be supplied by the construction loan and $200,000 by the developer, the surety may claim its performance under the bond is conditioned on the developer, or, on default by the developer, the construction lender supplying the $200,000. Or, where parts of the project are being constructed by others not covered by the surety bond, the surety company may claim that the performance of the contractor was hampered or frustrated by the breach of other contractors. Or, the surety may claim that the contractor was prevented from performing because the developer delayed in approving change orders or making payments to subcontractors.

Indeed, because these bonds tend to be expensive and riddled with exculpatory provisions, it has been suggested that their real importance to lenders such as FNB is the knowledge that the contractor was solvent enough to obtain the bond. See generally Hart and Kane, What Every Real Estate Lawyer Should Know About Payment and Performance Bonds, 17 Real Prop., Prob. & Tr. J. 674 (1982).

Another means of completion assurance is a guarantee of performance from the general contractor directly to the construction lender. The lender agrees to disburse construction advances by means of a check made payable jointly to the contractor and the borrower, thus insuring the contractor against diversion of the funds, and the contractor agrees that on default by the borrower and on demand by the lender the contractor will complete construction for the then-remaining undisbursed portion of the construction funds without personal liability by the lender under the contract.

In some cases, it is possible for the borrower to obtain a letter of credit from a bank covering part or all of the construction obligation. To serve its purpose, the letter of credit must be irrevocable and unconditional, with the bank obligated to pay on tender of the sight draft. Obviously, one would have to be (or be willing to become) an important customer of the bank to obtain such a letter, especially if the sums involved are large, and even then it will be issued only on depositing collateral with the bank (often in the form of a certificate of deposit) equal to a substantial percentage of the letter of credit.

In the early 1970s several title companies initiated what became known as construction disbursement programs, under which the title company or its subsidiary would issue insurance guaranteeing completion of the project in accordance with the construction contract. The theory was that the title company would then supervise the disbursements and monitor construction, thus minimizing the risks normally faced by issuers of performance bonds.[8] Many title companies have since discontinued the program, and thus it is of only limited availability today.

The final protective device to assure completion of the project we discuss is the so-called holdback requirement to "keep the loan in balance" (of the sort described in the *Equity Investors* case, excerpted at Chapter 6B3a, supra). This requirement is examined in the excerpt from *The Law of Real Estate Financing* in the next section of this chapter.

Be aware that the various devices we have discussed for assuring completion are only as effective as the corporation, surety, bank, or other entity providing the assurance. Obviously, a contractor's guarantee is not very helpful if the contractor is virtually insolvent. Not so obvious, but just as troublesome, is the fact that some surety companies, title companies, and even banks, while completely solvent, may not be in a position to assume the significant risks associated with major real estate development construction contracts. For example, one expert suggests that the surety be checked for a minimum "A" rating by A. M. Best's Key Rating Guide and that bonds not be accepted in an amount in excess of 10 percent of the surety's capital and surplus.

Even when all parties are doing their best to comply with the terms of the construction contract, casualties may occur that are beyond the control of the parties, for example, fire, windstorm, or explosion. These risks can be covered by a standard builder's "all risk" insurance policy protecting the developer, the contractor, and the lender. The "all" in "all risk" may be somewhat misleading, however. Most policies will exclude coverage for riots attending a strike, earthquake, flood, design and workmanship errors, and the like.

NOTES AND QUESTIONS

Bonds. If you represented FNB in its construction loan on Dan Developer's property, and it was decided to require both a payment and a performance bond, what would you ask for to ensure that FNB would have rights under these bonds on default by Dan Developer? For a general discussion of the rights of the developer and lender vis-à-vis the bonding company, see Comment, Mechanics' Liens and Surety Bonds in the Building Trades, 68 Yale L.J. 138 (1958); see also

---

8. See Dwyer, New Protection for Construction Lenders, 3 Real Est. Rev. 76 (1973).

Roberts, Counseling the Client in Payment and Performance Bonds, 10 Prac. Real Est. Law. 37 (July 1994).

Note the last sentence of the sample bonding provision from a construction loan commitment letter. What is the probable purpose of this language? How would you revise the language to better achieve this purpose?

5. Closing the Construction Loan and Disbursing Funds under the Construction Loan Agreement

The construction loan agreement is the operative document in construction financing, setting forth the rights of the parties and how and when the funds will be disbursed. Generally, before each disbursement the lender will require proof that construction has commenced to the point contemplated by the agreement and that all other conditions precedent to the disbursement have been complied with.

The sample construction ("building") loan agreement in the Documents Manual also deals with items that arise during the course of construction: inspections, defects, accounting, change orders, payment of bills, application of the loan proceeds, and the like. It also covers definitions, rights of the lender on default by the borrower, insurance, and other (largely boilerplate) provisions. Change orders (discussed below) are particularly sensitive, because they can lead to cost overruns. The lender will normally require its approval for most change orders. The following excerpt explains how properly drafted construction loan agreements (or "building loan agreements") can guide the construction lender's loan servicing department or loan administrator, in collaboration with the developer's architect and the title company, from the time the construction loan is closed to the day when the construction loan is taken out by the postconstruction ("permanent") lender.

M. Madison, J. Dwyer, and S. Bender, The Law of Real Estate Financing
§§6:46-6:51 (2016)

FUNCTION OF BUILDING LOAN AGREEMENT

The building loan agreement, unique to construction financing, identifies all of the collateral and supportive documents such as construction contracts, cost breakdowns, and payment and performance bonds. It stipulates the conditions for when and how construction is to commence, continue, and be completed. While the basic mortgage instrument secures the construction loan indebtedness and sets forth the terms and conditions of default, the building loan agreement is concerned with the day-to-day turmoil and activity encountered during the construction period. It attempts the formidable task of giving the lender control over construction, without unduly impeding its progress.

During construction and prior to any default, the building loan agreement is the operative document. Hence, counsel for lenders and developers should spend as much time reviewing and drafting this important document as they do the mortgage and note. The building loan agreement should be drafted so that it conforms to the method of construction disbursements employed by the lender, as modified by changes requested by the developer based on the characteristics of the particular project. Unfortunately, some lenders use methods of disbursements that, while satisfactory, are nonetheless incompatible with their standard form of building loan agreement, which may have been copied from another lender's form, notwithstanding differences in their methods of disbursement.

BORROWER'S INITIAL REPRESENTATIONS AND WARRANTIES

Most building loan agreements contain a warranty by the borrower-developer to the lender that the latter's loan advances will at all times be accorded lien priority over any intervening liens. However, such lien priority may depend on circumstances beyond the developer's control. For example, if under the building loan agreement the lender's discretionary authority to make loan advances is not geared to some objective criteria, such optional advances may, in some states, be junior in lien priority to any intervening mechanics' liens [see Chapter 6B3a, supra]. Accordingly, reliance on this warranty by the construction lender is misplaced if it fails to use title insurance or some other protective device against mechanics' liens. Also, under this warranty, the lender is not obligated to continue making disbursements if it cannot be assured of a first and prior lien for its loan advances, and, in the so-called priority states, the lender will require the developer to warrant that no work has commenced on the land prior to the recording of the construction loan mortgage.

In addition, the developer will be required to warrant that it will commence, continue, and complete construction within stipulated time limits and in a first-class workmanlike manner, in accordance with the approved plans and specifications and in conformity with private and local law restrictions. Most lenders apply general criteria in deciding when a project should be completed (e.g., garden apartments: twelve to fourteen months); failure to complete construction within the stipulated period is a material default. Accordingly, in negotiations with the construction and permanent lenders, the developer's attorney should demand realistic time limits and attempt to procure the so-called Act of God clause, a clause that allows for extensions in the event of strikes or other causes of delay beyond the control of the developer. However, the construction lender should resist any attempt to have this protective language inserted in its building loan agreement unless the permanent lender agrees to incorporate the same in its takeout commitment.

PREDISBURSEMENT REQUIREMENTS

As each phase of construction is completed, the lender's loan administrator advances loan funds to pay for the finished work. [The administrator] must make certain that the work conforms to the plans and specifications, that it is being done on schedule and free of mechanics' liens, and that sufficient undisbursed loan proceeds remain to fund the remaining costs of construction. If these objectives are not met, the basic conditions of the takeout commitment will not be satisfied, and the construction lender will not be able to assign its loan to the permanent lender once the construction is completed. Although the methods employed by lenders for making disbursements vary, the following are typical of predisbursement requirements that must be met prior to each new loan advance in cases where the developer is not acting as the general contractor.

First, upon notification that construction has progressed to the next planned stage, the developer, after receiving the contractor's requisition for payment, will submit its formal request for payment to the construction lender. As an alternative to the "stage of completion" method of payment, the developer will request his "draws" on a monthly basis, after finishing a designated percentage of the total work to be completed under the contract. The lender will require that the request for payment be accompanied by an affidavit of the contractor that identifies all the subcontractors, indicates the nature and dollar amounts of labor and materials furnished by them to the date of the affidavit, and contains recitals by the contractor and subcontractors (partial lien waivers) to the effect that they waive their lien rights for work and materials for which they have received payments. The loan administrator or his draw inspector will then examine the dollar amounts recited in both the affidavit and lien waivers along with copies of receipted work and purchase orders. Any discrepancies are investigated to make certain that loan funds have not been improperly diverted from the subcontractors by the developer or general contractor, and the loan administrator will check the billings and lien waivers to make certain that the payments are up-to-date and in conformity with the payment schedules in the building loan agreement.

Second, prior to each loan advance, the developer's architect will inspect the work progress on the site and will match the payment request with the work completed to make certain that neither the general contractor nor the subcontractors receive payment for work that has not been done. [The architect] will also certify that the work was performed in a timely first-class manner in accordance with the previously approved plans and specifications. Many, if not most, lenders will also employ, at the developer's expense, their own draw inspectors (licensed engineers or architects specializing in this area), to further certify these matters if the lender believes that such corroboration is necessary.

Third, after receiving the partial lien waivers, the title company will continue its search to the date of the proposed advance and will issue an endorsement to the title policy or "bring to date a letter" certifying that no liens or encumbrances have been filed against the project since the previous advance. In compliance with the lender's commitment, the building loan agreement may also require the developer to furnish a "date-down" survey to ensure that the improvements are being constructed within the lot or easement lines. The title company then certifies that there are no encroachments or violations of "set back" line restrictions.

As a general rule, lenders will require between a 5 and 15 percent holdback or retainage of construction loan funds, which amount is released along with the final loan advance upon completion of the project. Thus, for example, a 10 percent hold-back means that for each 90 cents of construction loan proceeds, the lender expects to receive performance of at least one dollar of value. However, some lenders are willing to decrease the retainage by one-half upon completion of 50 percent of the project. Many developers are also successful in having the retainage released upon completion of construction within a specific construction code instead of having to wait for completion of the entire project. In the event the developer is unable to impose holdbacks of like amounts on the contractor and subcontractors, it will be forced to fund the difference out of its own funds. In addition, prior to each loan advance, the construction lender may require that the reserves available for the completion of the improvements, whether in the form of undisbursed loan funds or the developer's equity, be sufficient to complete construction. The developer's architect is sometimes required to certify that this requirement has been met. Frequently, this predisbursement requirement will be waived by lenders, especially when the project being financed is relatively small, since such cost audits tend to be expensive and time-consuming. However, if at any time, the lender discovers that these reserves have been depleted because of cost overruns, it will require the developer to deposit sufficient equity funds, which, when added to the remaining balance of undisbursed loan funds, will cover the remaining cost of construction. However, in the event the lender concludes that there are [in]sufficient funds to complete the project, and the developer objects to such a conclusion, a possible compromise would be for the parties to agree to a binding cost audit to be performed by an independent party, during which time disbursements and construction would continue. To protect the lender, the developer would be required to deposit by means of a letter of credit, cash, or a CD, a sum sufficient to cover any deficiency amount revealed by such audit. This objective approach could also benefit the lender in the event there is a default based on a cost overrun; the existence and amount of said cost overrun would for purposes of litigation be predicated on the opinion of an independent third party.

Most lenders resist making any disbursements for stored materials in light of the dangers posed by possible thefts or damage caused by the elements. However, there are several avenues open for compromise, depending on the strength and the experience of the developer. For example, the lender and the developer may fix a maximum monthly dollar amount for stored materials, or may arrange a time schedule for incorporating stored materials into the project. In the event the lender does agree to fund stored on-site materials, a special endorsement to the builder's risk insurance policy for fire, damage, and theft of the stored material should be procured from the casualty company because some policies exclude such materials from coverage. Where the materials will not be stored at the project site and the lender is still willing to pay for such materials, it should insist that the materials be stored in a bonded warehouse and should carefully perfect its lien on the materials under the UCC.

In addition, the building loan agreement frequently will contain a statement specifying that any request for an advance by the developer constitutes an affirmation that all of the representations and warranties made at the time the agreement was executed remain true and correct, unless the developer says otherwise. The developer must therefore be very careful to review these representations at the time of each advance.

Finally, some developers, after having executed the building loan agreement, fail to take down construction advances and instead shop around for short-term credit that may be extended to them on more favorable terms on the security of the building loan agreement. To avoid this practice, construction lenders sometimes insert a clause in the loan agreement requiring the developer to pay interest on the amount of loan proceeds to which he would have been entitled on the basis of the completed construction, whether or not the loan advance is actually made, or else provide that such a failure to take down loan funds constitutes a default.

PAYMENT OF LOAN ADVANCES

When the construction loan administrator has received the report of the developer's architect, and perhaps its own inspector's affidavit as well as the updated file report, it will make the next loan advance and credit the funds to the account of either the developer (to whom the funds belong) or the general contractor, as the developer directs. In some states, loan advances can be made to the title company that acts as the disbursing agent of the lender.

Frequently, the construction lender will reserve the right to make disbursement checks jointly payable to the developer and the contractor, or to the contractor and the subcontractors, or even the right to make payments directly to each subcontractor. The lender's purpose in obtaining control over the payment of disbursements is to protect itself against forged lien waivers and to forestall the improper diversion of construction loan funds from the subcontractors by either the developer or the general contractor. However, if the construction lender makes payments directly to the subcontractors, it may unwittingly become liable to the Internal Revenue Service and to the subcontractors for any unpaid or unwithheld FICA [payroll] taxes.

In addition, there is case law suggesting that when a lender steps into the shoes of another party in the project, the lender must assume all of the responsibilities of that party to others and, protect the interests of the party whose prerogatives it has preempted. For example, in MSM Corp. v. Knutson Co. the construction lender, bypassing the developer, made loan advances directly to the contractor and was held liable, as a fiduciary, to the developer for loan funds diverted by the lender to satisfy an unrelated debt owed to it by the contractor, even though the developer owed the contractor an amount far in excess of the diverted amounts. In so holding, the Minnesota court stated that:

> When a mortgagee undertakes to disburse funds for a mortgagor under a construction contract, a fiduciary relationship arises. Under such circumstances, the mortgagee has the duty not only to apply all of the proceeds to the use of the mortgagor without diverting them for unrelated obligations incurred by contractors or subcontractors, but also to account for all of the sums, expended on behalf of the mortgagor and to furnish adequate proof of the sums paid and the purpose of the disbursement.[4] . . .

Likewise, in Fulmer Building Supplies, Inc. v. Martin[5] a construction lender, to protect its loan funds, bypassed the developer and made loan payments directly to the contractor even though the subcontractors, as holders of mechanics' liens, were first entitled to payment. After the contractor failed to pay the subcontractors, the subcontractors sued the lender for the amount of the diverted funds and the lender defended on the ground that the South Carolina statute automatically confers lien priority for all construction loan advances. The court, holding in favor of the subcontractors, stated:

> When the mortgagee assumed absolute control of the disbursement of the proceeds of the construction loan, it occupied the same position as the owner with respect to the duties and obligations imposed by statute as to the payment of the remaining funds after the perfection of the mechanic's lien.

COST OVERRUNS AND OTHER CHANGES DURING CONSTRUCTION PERIOD

Both the construction and permanent lenders' determination of the loan amount and value of the security is based in part on a careful examination of the plans and specifications submitted by the developer's architect. Therefore, the construction lender will require its approval of any change order that provides for extra work or materials, or alters the plans and specifications in a manner that could result in additional costs or in a significant change in the improvements. Ordinarily, these change orders must be approved by the architect and the lender's draw inspector or supervising engineer, and then examined for adherence to proper construction standards and existing building codes. A prudent construction lender should also require the consent of the bonding company. Any significant changes should also be approved by the permanent lender inasmuch as such approval is required under the terms of its takeout

---

4. [283 Minn. 527, 529, 167 N.W.2d 66, 68 (1969) (per curiam).] Implicit in the court's decision is the analogy to a mortgagee in possession [see Chapter 8B2] who must account to the mortgagor for the rentals and other income earned from the property.

5. [251 S.C. 353, 162 S.E.2d 541 (1968).]

commitment. In addition, if the lender consents to any such change order, it may require the developer to deposit additional equity funds to cover any extras or cost overruns. If construction lenders carefully monitor their disbursements under this language in the building loan agreement, many of the cost overruns by defaulting developers may be prevented.

If, however, a change order produces a cost overrun on a particular item, the developer may be able to avoid an additional cash outlay if the construction lender is willing to reallocate funds from other items listed in the cost breakdown or, if the developer is not the contractor, in the construction contract so that the net change will not result in additional dollar requirements beyond those committed by the construction lender. The building loan agreement will list by code categories loan funds earmarked to pay both hard construction costs ("construction funds") and soft nonconstruction costs, such as construction period interest, hazard insurance premiums, and architect's fees ("nonconstruction funds"). Most construction lenders treat construction loan interest as a fundable soft cost during the construction period and will disburse loan funds to the developer so that it can remit these amounts back to the lender as interest payments. However, a prudent construction lender should demand the right to discontinue such disbursements for soft costs and should reserve the right to reallocate such funds toward the payment of hard construction cost overruns. Otherwise, if the developer is not required to fund the interest payments with nonloan sources, a loan headed for default could be artificially kept alive and further jeopardize the lender's ability to recoup its loan investment. Moreover, unless the building loan agreement specifies that the obligation of the developer to make interest payments is not predicated on the disbursement of these funds by the lender, the developer could argue that such failure to fund under the interest [provisions] would force it into default and will thus constitute a breach of contract by the lender.

Throughout construction of the project, tempers occasionally flare, disputes arise, and developers in their off moments sometimes want to fire their once-favorite architect or contractor, or even give up on the project and convey it to a third party. However, during construction, lenders usually take a dim view of any proposed changes other than those that relate to the actual completion of construction. The lender naturally prefers that the architect who drafted the plans and specifications supervise the construction on behalf of the developer, since someone who has a first-hand familiarity with the plans and specifications is always in a better position to have them implemented. Moreover, any contractor who is thrown off the job-site during a dispute may hold up construction by filing a lien on the project or by not relinquishing the building permits. Consequently, the lender will insist upon a high degree of control if any of the foregoing types of changes are proposed by the developer.

THE FINAL LOAN ADVANCE

Prior to the final loan advance, the construction loan administrator will require the following:

- A final lien waiver from the contractor and subcontractors covering all labor and materials furnished or to be furnished so that no liens may be claimed for follow-up repairs or for the replacement of defective materials that may become necessary in the future
- A certificate of substantial completion executed by the developer's architect and, in some cases, by the lender's draw inspector or supervising engineer as well, along with certificates of occupancy indicating that the construction and use of the improvements comply with all zoning and other local law regulations [see Chapter 4D7]
- All the approvals required by state and federal regulatory agencies
- Where there is a permanent takeout, a letter from the permanent lender stating that the improvements have been properly constructed and that its takeout commitment is still in force and effect

Where the project is a shopping center, the lender should also condition its final advance on acceptance of the premises by the major tenants.

NOTES AND QUESTIONS

> ➢ *Problem 6-4*
> Examine the sample construction ("building") loan agreement in the Documents Manual. As counsel to the construction lender Fuller National Bank, advise your client as to whether the provisions therein provide adequate protection against the possibility of mechanics' liens, a failure on Dan Developer's part to complete construction, and the other major risks associated with construction financing. ◄

Chapter 7

Refinancing, Secondary Financing, and High-Ratio Financing

Long before the mortgage meltdown that began in 2007, the slump in real estate in the early 1990s along with the shakeout periods of 1974-1975 and 1979-1981 made institutional lenders wiser and warier about underwriting commercial real estate loans. Gone are the days when real estate developers could rely on self-serving appraisals and maximum loan-to-value ratios on demand.[1] In addition, the Tax Reform Act of 1986, as modified primarily by the Revenue Reconciliation Act of 1993 and the Taxpayer Relief Act of 1997, reduced the utility of real estate as a tax shelter, and so investors have become more cash flow-oriented and increasingly concerned about cash-on-cash rates of return and the ability to translate some of their equity into cash before the project is sold or liquidated. As a consequence, in today's real estate market, many projects could not be developed, marketed to investors, or even sold without the extra funds and higher yields available by means of certain high-ratio leasehold and debt-financing techniques. Chapter 11 shows how real estate developers are able to leverage their acquisition costs and thereby increase the rates of return to their investors by means of leasehold mortgage financing and split financing techniques such as the sale and leaseback of land plus a leasehold mortgage on the improvements.

The aim of this chapter is to analyze debt-financing techniques (such as refinancing and secondary financing) used to cash out the accumulated equity in a real estate project. In addition, we will examine certain high-ratio financing techniques that enable developers and purchasers to leverage their cost of acquiring and constructing income-producing real estate. These techniques run the gamut from well-established ones such as the subordinated purchase money mortgage (used in new construction to leverage the cost of the underlying land) to more exotic financing devices such as synthetic leasing and mezzanine financing. Some involve junior, or "secondary," financing techniques such as the

---

1. The average loan-to-value ratio on commercial mortgage loan commitments made by life insurance companies declined from 74.1 percent in 1979 to 68 percent in 2002 (among the lowest periods was 1982's average of 66.5 percent). American Council of Life Insurers, Investment Bull. No. IB03-003 (Apr. 7, 2003). Through 2010 life insurance companies continued their stringent underwriting—at year-end only 4 percent of their outstanding loan value was held in mortgages with a loan-to-value ratio above 95 percent, compared with $228 billion (72%) in mortgages with a ratio below 71 percent; similarly, almost all life insurer loans by 2014 had a ratio below 71 percent. Consequently, 99.3 percent of their mortgage loans were in good standing in 2010, and 99.4 percent in 2014. Mortgage loan appraisals and loan-to-value ratios are discussed at Chapter 4D1.

ordinary second mortgage and the subordinated purchase money mortgage, while others, such as refinancing, involve only first mortgage financing. Some are tax-oriented, such as tax-exempt bond financing, while others, such as high-credit lease financing, are not. All of these devices, however, have one thing in common: They are designed to make extra funds or financing available when needed, and some of these techniques theoretically can be used to achieve 100 percent or more financing.

A. REFINANCING

Under the master hypothetical, assume that Dan Developer was able to obtain a first mortgage loan from Ace Insurance Company in the amount of $25 million and that Dan raised the additional venture capital needed to fund both the construction of the office building and the cost of the underlying land. Further assume that the land and building, which together cost $33 million, are now worth $40 million and that amortization payments have scaled down the principal balance on the Ace mortgage from $25 million to $20 million, and thus the current market value of the ownership interest, or "equity,"[2] in the project is $20 million. At this juncture, Dan Developer wants to translate some of the accumulated equity into tax-free cash for use as extra working capital to expand or renovate the office building or for another investment opportunity.

Equity in a real estate project can accumulate as the result of debt-service payments on the mortgage, inasmuch as the portion of the payments allocable to amortization reduces the principal balance of the mortgage indebtedness. For example, in the master hypothetical, the loan amount at the end of the tenth year would be paid down to $18,481,119 (because of amortization payments as reflected in Table 5-2 at Chapter 5A2) and, correspondingly, the amount of equity would increase by $6,518,881. Equity can also accumulate through inflation, which increases the value of the underlying land, or by means of an increase in the value of the building caused by higher net operating income[3]

2. "Equity" simply means net assets (assets minus liabilities) and, as such, is a way to measure, in accounting terms, either the book value of an ownership interest (if the assets are reflected at cost or, in the case of an income-producing asset such as a building, at cost less accumulated depreciation) or the cash value of an ownership interest (if the assets are valued at market value, for example, the value of a building based on a capitalization of current earnings). See Chapter 4D1, wherein the income approach to appraisal is briefly examined. If the ownership entity is a partnership or corporation, the net worth of the entity is reflected by the proprietary accounts of the partners, called "capital accounts," or shareholders (capital stock plus retained earnings), respectively. Another way to define the concept would be to regard "equity" in mortgage terms as the value of the mortgagor's equity of redemption.

3. Determination of value under the so-called income method of appraisal is based on applying a capitalization rate (as determined by interest rates and by the degree of risk associated with the project) to a projected stream of net operating income; for example, a cap rate of 10 percent applied to annual income of $100,000 ($100,000 ÷ 10 percent) would produce a market value of $1 million

when rents rise because of management efficiency (especially in the case of active real estate such as hotels and parking garages), greater demand for rental space, or simply because of inflation.

Chapter 11 discusses how the accumulated equity in a project can be cashed out by means of a sale and leaseback, which ordinarily is a taxable event. In this chapter, we examine two debt-financing techniques that owners can use to translate their equity into cash without taxation: refinancing and secondary financing. "Refinancing" simply means the substitution of a new loan for an existing one, for example, obtaining a new first mortgage loan to discharge an existing one that is more expensive. Returning to our hypothetical and assuming the same 75 percent loan-to-value ratio, Dan could refinance by obtaining a new first mortgage loan of $30 million, using the funds to satisfy the existing mortgage balance (assume $20 million) and cashing out the $10 million leftover as net refinancing proceeds. Generally, real estate owners prefer refinancing to secondary financing when interest rates decline or remain the same because secondary financing is usually more expensive. Moreover, secondary financing may be prohibited without the consent of the first mortgagee if the first mortgage note contains a due-on-encumbrance clause.[4]

However, the converse may be true if first mortgage interest rates escalate. Moreover, pending a future or further decline in interest rates, Dan may want to use a short-term interest-only second mortgage loan as a temporary expedient until he can refinance at a lower first mortgage rate. Moreover, secondary financing may be more feasible than refinancing where the existing first mortgage contains an onerous prepayment charge.[5] Indeed, during any lock-in period, when no prepayment is allowed, the refinancing option might be precluded altogether.

In addition to translating equity into working capital, a refinancing may be undertaken for other reasons such as increasing the project's cash flow and net operating income (by reducing interest expenses with a new, cheaper mortgage or by reducing debt-service payments with an extended loan term) and resuscitating the real property as a tax shelter[6] by using a new mortgage cycle to reduce amortization payments.

based on ten times earnings. The higher the risk factor the higher the cap rate. This means that if the rate were increased from 10 percent to 20 percent, a prudent purchaser or lender would respectively purchase or loan money based on a return of capital within 5 years as opposed to 10 years. See discussion at Chapter 4D1.

4. See Chapter 5A7.

5. See Chapter 5A4.

6. It is the excess of depreciation over mortgage amortization that produces tax shelter. See Chapter 13A2b.

Smith, Refinancing a Syndicated Property
16 Real Est. Rev. 16 (Spring 1986)

Refinancing—the substitution of one mortgage for another—is one of real estate's most neglected topics, perhaps because people assume that analyzing a refinancing is simple. Actually, it is anything but. Many factors affect the attractiveness of a proposed refinancing. Without a clear understanding of why the partnership [or other ownership entity] is refinancing, the partnership might decide unwisely.

Refinancing proceeds must first be divided into two elements: net proceeds and the cost of obtaining capital. The transaction costs or costs of obtaining capital may include (1) application fees and legal costs to prepare and review new documents and (2) up-front points to the new lender.

REASONS TO REFINANCE

Conceptually, there are four basic uses of net proceeds:

1. To lower the cost of existing debt;
2. To provide necessary or desirable operating capital;
3. To take out cash flow and equity buildup; and
4. To reschedule obligations and thus improve the health of the entity.

A refinancing should be analyzed by allocating the net proceeds among these four uses and weighing the benefits of each use against the cost.

LOWERING THE COST OF EXISTING DEBT

Lowering the cost of the current debt is the refinancing reason most readers probably think of first. If the existing mortgage carries a rate higher than borrowing rates now available in the marketplace, a refinancing is indicated. Can it ever be wrong to refinance for this purpose?

Yes it can. Although it may carry a lower rate, the new mortgage amount will be higher than the old mortgage—if only by the amount of transaction costs. These costs vary but are always significant. Usually (but not always), the new mortgage will have a lower constant debt service payment, so there will be some annual savings resulting from the lower interest rate. In exchange, the partnership will have increased the principal amount of its debt, and thus it will have reduced the property's net residual value.

The soundness of a refinancing to reduce existing debt cost depends on holding the new mortgage long enough to make the cumulative debt service saving during that holding period exceed the decreased residual value. Any refinancing, therefore, involves the concept of a *payback period.* The partnership must be certain that it will not sell or refinance the property before the payback period expires. When the new mortgage has a rate that is subject to future adjustment, the payback period should be shorter than the period for which the rate is fixed.

Mortgages are usually held for surprisingly short periods. The median home mortgage, for instance, is prepaid after about seven years. The typical income-producing rental property changes ownership (and, therefore, its financing) roughly every ten years.

The partnership must satisfy itself that not only is the refinancing better than the current mortgage, but that the refinancing is as good as or better than mortgages that might otherwise become available during the payback period.

As a rule. . ., a refinancing that requires a payback period of more than five years is unwise. Too many things can happen in five years.

PROVIDING NECESSARY OR DESIRABLE CAPITAL TO THE PROPERTY

Developers forced to operate properties with too little operating capital inevitably make decisions that help short-run cash flow but hurt long-run value. Time and again, such shortsightedness proves painfully costly.

A property that needs capital for physical improvements can raise it from only two sources: (1) additional contributions from the partners or (2) refinancing to liquidate equity buildup and make it available for reinvestment in the property.

In order to examine the implications of using the proceeds of a refinancing for physical improvements, the partnership must consider both benefits and costs.

Financial impact of improvements. Most well-designed capital improvement programs generate more net operating income (NOI) than the increased debt service required to pay for them. Recarpet vacant apartments, for example, and they are much more easily rented. Repaint and replace appliances, and the apartment's rent may be raised. An analyst must be careful, however, to count only that portion of anticipated increase in NOI that results from the improvements and to exclude NOI increases attributable to external factors (inflation or improved local economy) . . . .

CASH DISTRIBUTIONS TO THE PARTNERS

If the refinancing will produce excess distributable cash, the partners must compare the refinancing costs to the after-tax benefits. Because the proceeds are matched by an increase in partnership indebtedness, a distribution of refinancing proceeds is tax-free. Partners should compare the after-tax rate at which they can reinvest the distribution to the after-tax borrowing cost of the money. . . .

RESCHEDULING CURRENT INDEBTEDNESS

The last reason to refinance is the simplest. If the current mortgage is in default, or if it will shortly balloon, the partnership *must* refinance or face the loss of its property and all the associated equity buildup. Here, the question is not *whether* to refinance, but *how*. . . .

NOTES AND QUESTIONS

1. Refinancing at a Lower Interest Rate Increases the Value of the Real Estate. One of the truisms of real estate investing is that, assuming everything else remains the same, a decline in interest rates will increase the value of real estate. Real estate investors are leverage-minded; therefore, mortgage debt-service payments typically represent a large percentage of a project's annual operating expenses and cash flow requirements. Therefore, even a modest decline in the mortgage rate of interest can cause a significant increase in net operating income and thereby enhance the market value of the project (as measured by a capitalization of the increased earnings). See discussion at Chapter 4D1, note 3. Under the master hypothetical, assume that the office building project costing $33 million yields an annual free and clear return of 15 percent (instead of 12 percent), or $5 million net rent (instead of $4 million) (after all expenses other than income taxes and mortgage payments), and that Dan obtains the same loan terms from Ace except that the interest rate on the $25 million mortgage (amortized over 25 years) is 3 percent rather than 5 percent. His constant monthly payment of principal and interest would be $118,552.83 instead of $146,147.51, and therefore, as a consequence of the 2 percent rate reduction, his annual pretax net income would increase from $3,246,230 to $3,577,366. After applying a capitalization rate of 7 percent, the market value of the project would increase from $46,374,714 ($3,246,230 ÷ 7%) to $51,105,229 ($3,577,366 ÷ 7%), an increase in market value of $4,730,515.

2. Circumventing Prepayment Charges on Refinancing. If a borrower were to default on the mortgage loan, the lender most probably would accelerate the loan indebtedness. In such event, would the lender be able to collect a prepayment fee out of the net foreclosure sale proceeds or add the charge to the amount needed to redeem the mortgage in advance of foreclosure when such prepayment was caused by the borrower's inability to make debt-service payments on the mortgage, notwithstanding the borrower's good faith attempt to do so? There is case authority holding that, absent language to the contrary, when the lender accelerates because of default, no prepayment fee is payable because "acceleration, by definition, advances the maturity date of the debt so that payment thereafter is not prepayment but instead is payment made after maturity." In re LHD Realty Corp., 726 F.2d 327 (7th Cir. 1984). Other courts have likewise ruled that the prepayment charge should not apply following the lender's decision to accelerate the mortgage indebtedness after default because the borrower's prepayment is precipitated by the election of the lender and not by the voluntary act of the borrower. See Kilpatrick v. Germania Life Ins. Co., 183 N.Y. 163, 75 N.E. 1124 (1905) (improper for mortgagee to include prepayment fee in amount needed by borrower to redeem); George H. Nutman, Inc. v. Aetna Business Credit, 115 Misc. 2d 168, 453 N.Y.S.2d 586 (Sup. Ct. 1982). However, if the agreed-on prepayment clause in the existing mortgage is broadly phrased so that the charge applies to any and all prepayments including those triggered by debt acceleration and regardless of whether the prepayment is voluntary or not, the prevailing view among commentators and courts is that freedom-of-contract principles should prevail; thus the prepayment charge amount should be included as part of the unpaid mortgage indebtedness. See G. Nelson et al., Real Estate Finance Law §6.3 (6th ed. 2015); Parker Plaza W. Partners v. Unum Pension & Ins. Co., 941 F.2d 349 (5th Cir. 1991); Travelers Ins. Co. v. Corporex Properties, 798 F. Supp. 423 (E.D. Ky. 1992); Financial Ctr. Assocs. v. TNE Funding Corp. (In re Financial Ctr. Assocs.), 140 B.R. 829, 835 (Bankr. E.D.N.Y. 1992).

Suppose that a borrower who wishes to refinance is discouraged by a steep prepayment charge or barred from refinancing during an initial lock-in period, when no prepayments are allowed. See Chapter 5A4. It might be possible for the borrower to circumvent the prepayment charge and lock-in restriction by intentionally defaulting on the loan, thereby compelling the lender to accelerate. Having arranged more favorable financing, the borrower could then redeem the property prior to foreclosure by paying the accelerated mortgage indebtedness (which would not include the prepayment charge), or the borrower or its affiliate could purchase the property at the foreclosure sale. The court in In re LHD Realty Corp. suggested by way of dictum that such a ploy was implausible because it would adversely affect the borrower's credit rating and because the lender might avoid acceleration by electing to sue merely for the overdue payments as they mature. 726 F.2d at 331. Suppose, however, that the prepayment fee is substantial and that the loan is nonrecourse, so the borrower could not be sued for each installment as it becomes due. In your opinion, should this stratagem work for a borrower who intentionally defaults? If not, why not? Compare G. Nelson et al. §6.3 with Sanders, Commercial Prepayment Fees: A New Legal Frontier, 60 Fla. B.J. 69 (June 1986). To protect themselves, lenders have been including phraseology in their prepayment clauses to the effect that on any default that results in debt acceleration, a tender of payment prior to a foreclosure sale shall constitute a willful evasion of the prepayment terms and be deemed a voluntary prepayment with regard to which the charge shall apply (recall the *Butler* case, Chapter 4B). As noted above, most courts will enforce these provisions.

3. Tax Aspects of Refinancing. A fundamental principle of our system of taxation is that although income is taxable, cash flow is not; hence, the act of borrowing money is not a taxable event. Although the borrower receives money, it has a reciprocal obligation to repay the same; therefore the borrower receives no economic benefit and its net assets remain the same. Thus, net refinancing proceeds are not subject to taxation even if the owner of real estate "mortgages out," that is, obtains loan proceeds in excess of its tax basis in the mortgaged property. See Woodsam Assocs. v. Commissioner, 16 T.C. 649 (1951), aff'd, 198 F.2d 357 (2d Cir. 1952); see generally Glynn, Federal Taxes Affecting Real Estate §2.02[2][b][v] (2012). However, while a prepayment charge is deductible as a current expense (Rev. Rul. 57-198, 1957-1 C.B. 94), loan origination fees, or "points," and commitment fees generally must be amortized and deducted, even by a cash-basis taxpayer, over the life of the loan. See I.R.C. §461(g)(1). However, in the case of a home mortgage, points can be currently deducted to the extent that the loan proceeds are used to finance home improvements. I.R.C. §461(g)(2). See Rev. Rul. 87-22, 1987-1 C.B. 146. See generally Banoff, Tax Aspects of Real Estate Refinancing and Debt Restructuring: The Best and Worst of Times, 64 Taxes 926 (Dec. 1986).

B. SECONDARY FINANCING

Like refinancing, secondary financing is used both to translate equity into tax-free cash and to leverage the cost of acquiring real estate. However, in contrast to refinancing, a second mortgage supplements rather than replaces a first mortgage; hence, the former is (or becomes) junior in lien priority to the latter. In real estate jargon, secondary, or junior, debt financing—consisting of ordinary second mortgages (or those of lesser priority), wrap around mortgages, gap loans, subordinated purchase money mortgages, and other types of junior mortgages—is the "grease" that makes a project operate or sell more easily because it provides the extra funds that may be needed by a real estate owner or purchaser.

When interest rates are rising, borrowers can use secondary financing to reduce their overall interest expenses. This can be cheaper than refinancing the existing first mortgage. Under our hypothetical, suppose that the office building project is now worth $40 million and that interest rates are escalating. Dan Developer decides to cash out some of the equity in the amount of $10 million by means of a five-year conventional second mortgage loan from the Fuller Finance Company ("FFC"). Assume that it will be less expensive, on the whole, for Dan to pay the required 10 percent rate on the new second mortgage money and continue paying 5 percent on the $20 million balance of the Ace mortgage (for a cumulative interest-only payment of $2.2 million each year) than for Dan to refinance the Ace mortgage with a new long-term first mortgage in the amount of $30 million at the higher prevailing market rate of 8 percent, which would require an annual interest-only payment of $2.4 million.

In addition, secondary financing can be used to reduce the portion of the borrower's debt-service payments allocable to amortization and thereby increase the cash flow and the borrower's yield on its equity investment. For simplicity's sake, the above hypothetical presupposes interest-only financing; in reality, first mortgage loans by institutional lenders are usually fully or partially amortized. For example, in 2002, about 83 percent of the mortgage commitments on multifamily and commercial properties by life insurance companies required some form of amortization. American Council of Life Insurers, Invest. Bull. No. IB03-003 (Apr. 7, 2003). By contrast, most second mortgage loans are short-term (for example, 5 years or less) and interest-only (or with amortization based on a long-term schedule of perhaps 25 to 30 years), with a balloon payment required at the end of the term. Therefore, total debt-service payments on the existing first mortgage and new second mortgage may be less than for a refinanced first mortgage because the interest rate on the existing mortgage is relatively low or because of deferred amortization (or even negative amortization, whereby interest is accrued but not paid) during the term of the second mortgage.

By way of review, can you think of any other reasons why a borrower would prefer secondary financing to refinancing? See Chapter 5A4 and Chapter 7A, supra.

In addition, secondary financing tends to be more creative than first mortgage financing, as reflected by its higher loan-to-value ratios, lower debt-coverage ratios, and more liberal prepayment clauses. As a consequence of this flexibility in loan terms, developers occasionally will use a second mortgage as interim financing on the expectation that the existing first mortgage can be refinanced at a lower rate in the future when first mortgage rates decline. The extra interest expended on the second mortgage during the interim can be more than offset by the interest saved on a refinanced long-term mortgage. Likewise, junior mortgages are sometimes used to resolve a gap financing problem. For example, suppose a permanent loan is insufficient in amount to take out a construction loan because the construction lender decides to fund some unanticipated cost overruns or because it elects to fund the ceiling (maximum) amount of a platform loan even though the borrower has failed to comply with a rent roll requirement that is specified in the permanent lender's takeout commitment. If the developer is unable to finance the shortfall with its own equity capital and the construction lender is unwilling to relegate itself to the status of a junior lienor with respect to the gap amount, to forestall a default the developer might be compelled to repay the extra construction loan indebtedness with a second mortgage ("bridge") loan from a gap lender. The bridge loan would be satisfied when the property is sold or refinanced for a larger loan amount. See Chapter 4D2.

1. Conventional Second Mortgage Financing

Under our master hypothetical, suppose that Dan Developer's completed office building project now worth $40 million is encumbered by Ace's first mortgage loan that has been scaled down to a $20 million balance. Suppose further that Dan wants to translate one-half of the accumulated equity ($10 million) into cash for the purpose of renovating the property. As observed at Chapter 7A, supra, secondary financing is often unattractive when interest rates decline below the first mortgage rate because a developer could simply refinance the existing mortgage at the lower market rate and pay any necessary prepayment charges. However, if first mortgage interest rates were to escalate and the first mortgage note held by Ace does not contain a due-on-encumbrance clause, it might be less expensive, on the whole, for Dan to pay a higher rate of interest on a small amount of new second mortgage money than to refinance the existing first mortgage at the increased rate for first mortgage money.

NOTES AND QUESTIONS

1. Risks of Secondary Financing. According to conventional wisdom, a second mortgage tends to be a riskier loan investment; it justifies a higher rate of interest than a first mortgage because the second mortgagee's security interest extends only to the value of the secured property that exceeds the first mortgage lien. Can you think of any reason why a second mortgage may be a safer investment than a first mortgage loan? By deferring amortization or even interest payments, creative secondary financing can reduce debt-service payments and sharply increase the cash flow rate of return to an equity investor. However, to increase the yield, what additional risk must the owner-borrower assume?

2. Special Protections Demanded by Junior Mortgagees. Returning to the hypothetical, if Dan Developer were to obtain a second mortgage loan in the amount of $10 million, on the advice of counsel, the secondary lender, Fuller Finance Company (FFC), would require the same protective provisions that are customarily contained in a first mortgage and the same closing documentation as the first mortgagee (including a title policy ensuring the validity of the second mortgage lien, final survey, copies of leases, and estoppel certificates from tenants). Counsel for FFC will also review the existing first mortgage loan documentation to make certain that Ace has not proscribed any secondary financing by means of a due-on-encumbrance clause. See Chapter 5A7.

In addition, because its status as a junior lienor makes it vulnerable to a foreclosure of the senior mortgage, FFC will attempt to have the following covenants included in the loan documents:

1. The second mortgagee will be notified of any default under the senior mortgage and be given a reasonable opportunity to cure such default; and any payment made by the second mortgagee on behalf of the mortgagor will be added to the second mortgage indebtedness.
2. Any default under the first mortgage shall automatically be deemed a default under the second mortgage.
3. There shall be no material change in the terms and conditions (nor any extension or renewal) of the first mortgage or of any leases without the prior written consent of the second mortgagee.

Can you think of the reasons for the foregoing covenants? In what respects are they designed to protect the second mortgagee against any impairment of its security interest?

As a prerequisite to permitting junior financing, a postconstruction lender such as Ace will sometimes require that any subsequent mortgage be junior in lien priority (or become so by means of a subordination agreement) to any and all leases on the property. Why would a senior mortgagee impose such a requirement? Can you think of any other precautionary measures that Ace might require? See M. Madison, J. Dwyer, and S. Bender, The Law of Real Estate Financing §8:18 (2016).

3. Statutory and Common Law Protections Afforded to Junior Mortgagees.

a. *Appointment of a Receiver and the Right to Possession Prior to Foreclosure.* If a borrower defaults under a first mortgage, it is likely to be in default under the second mortgage as well, either because it is insolvent or because of a cross-default provision in the second mortgage. When a borrower is in default under both mortgages, a conflict may develop between the senior and junior mortgagees over the priorities of their respective claims to the rents and profits from the mortgaged property. While the rules are not clear as to claims based on mortgage clauses that purport to assign or pledge the rents and profits, the law is settled that a junior mortgagee who first obtains a court-appointed receiver or takes over possession will prevail over a senior mortgagee as to rents and profits collected prior to the intervention of the senior mortgagee. Otherwise, a junior mortgagee who acts promptly to prevent the property from being "milked" by the mortgagor-landlord would not be rewarded for its diligence. See Restatement (Third) of Property-Security (Mortgages) §4.5(b) (1997); see also Tefft, Receivers and Leases Subordinate to the Mortgage, 2 U. Chi. L. Rev. 33 (1934). See discussion of preforeclosure remedies at Chapter 8B.

b. *Rights of a Junior Mortgagee at Foreclosure.* The principal objective of an action to foreclose is to enable the foreclosing mortgagee to become whole again by realizing on its security to the maximum extent possible. To that end the mortgagee is allowed to join in as a defendant not only the mortgagor but also any junior party whose interest might adversely affect the value of the property. As a consequence of such joinder (or notice, in the case of foreclosure by power of sale), the mortgagee is able to extinguish the defendant's interest so that the purchaser at the foreclosure sale can receive the same title that existed when the mortgagor executed the mortgage. See Chapter 3E and Chapter 8C2; see generally Osborne, Mortgages §§321, 323 (2d ed. 1970) (hereinafter Osborne).

Returning to the hypothetical, suppose Dan Developer defaults under the first mortgage (with Ace) when the outstanding balance on the first mortgage is $15 million and the balance on the second mortgage (with FFC) is $5 million. In the event that Ace accelerates the unpaid indebtedness and goes to foreclosure, the risk to the junior mortgagee, FFC, is that it will be joined in as a party defendant by Ace and that a forced sale of the property will attract few if any bidders besides the mortgagees themselves and that the net foreclosure sale proceeds may not be sufficient to satisfy both the junior and the senior indebtedness. Thus a net sale price at foreclosure of, say, $18 million would produce an economic loss of $2 million for FFC unless it is able to recoup some or all of the deficiency by exercising any of the following rights accorded to a junior mortgagee at foreclosure.

i. *The Right to a Deficiency Judgment.* If Dan defaults under both mortgages and both mortgagees foreclose against Dan, FFC theoretically could recoup its mortgage investment by obtaining a personal judgment against Dan for the deficiency amount, provided that the second mortgage note does not exculpate Dan from personal liability and that the applicable jurisdiction does not have an antideficiency statute. The distinction between recourse and nonrecourse financing is discussed at Chapter 5A3, and deficiency judgments are examined at Chapter 8C3a including discussion at note 3 of the sold-out junior mortgagee. Obviously, however, defaulting borrowers tend to be insolvent, and, in reality, only a nominal dollar-amount percentage of deficiency judgments are ever realized by lenders against defaulting borrowers. See Prather, A Realistic Approach to Foreclosure, 14 Bus. Law. 132 (1958).

ii. *The Right to Redeem the Mortgage of Any Senior Mortgagee.* If FFC anticipates that the current action to foreclose by the senior mortgagee, Ace, will produce net sale proceeds of less than $20 million because of adverse market conditions, FFC can prevent an untimely foreclosure sale by exercising its equitable right of redemption—that is, by paying to Ace the $15 million amount of its outstanding indebtedness. By doing so, FFC would become subrogated to the rights of Ace against Dan and, in effect, become the holder of both the first and the second mortgage so that it could delay the foreclosure sale until market conditions improve.

iii. *The Right to Purchase at the Foreclosure Sale.* Alternatively, FFC might believe that a purchase will be necessary to obtain the requisite control to salvage the situation. For example, if the property is beset by chronic management and leasing problems, or if the foreclosure sale attracts few if any outside bidders, FFC might want to bid up to the second mortgage amount ($20 million) and become the new owner on the expectation that with proper management and marketing efforts it might become whole again by reselling the property for at least $20 million. See Chapter 8C2; see generally Osborne §328.

iv. *The Rights of Omitted Junior Parties.* It is a well-known axiom with respect to judicial foreclosure that when a junior lienor (such as a junior mortgagee) is not named in the foreclosure lawsuit as a party defendant, its lien will survive and the purchaser will take subject to it. Otherwise, the junior lienor would be deprived unfairly of the opportunity to bid for the property itself or to maximize the sale price (and its ability to recoup its investment) by drumming up other bidders. Therefore, the omitted junior lienor may either foreclose its lien or redeem any senior mortgage, and the purchaser at the foreclosure sale in turn may eliminate the junior lien by paying it off, by reforeclosing the senior mortgage, or, in some states, by using the strict foreclosure method against the junior lienor. See generally G. Nelson et al., Real Estate Finance Law §7.16 (6th ed. 2015).

v. *The Right of Statutory Redemption.* After a foreclosure by the senior mortgagee and subsequent extinction of the junior mortgagee's lien, the rule in some states is that the rights of the junior mortgagee will reattach if the mortgagor subsequently redeems the property pursuant to its statutory right of redemption discussed at Chapter 8C3d. See, for example, Martin v. Raleigh State Bank, 146 Miss. 1, 111 So. 448 (1927). Compare Cal. Civ. Proc. Code §729.080(e) (liens extinguished by foreclosure do not reattach after redemption). To protect junior parties from an artificially low sale price when a senior mortgage is foreclosed, some states provide junior interestholders (such as junior mortgagees) with their own statutory right of redemption. For a specified period of time after the mortgagor's redemption period has elapsed, the junior lienors have the right (in order of their respective lien priorities) to redeem the title to the property from the purchaser at the foreclosure sale by paying the foreclosure sale price plus the lien of any lienor who has previously redeemed the property. See Nelson et al. at §8.7.

c. *The Doctrine of Marshaling of Assets.* Simply put, where a senior mortgage is secured by more than one parcel of land and a junior mortgage is secured by only one, under the equitable doctrine of marshaling of assets, a court may require the senior mortgagee to satisfy its claim in a manner that affords the junior claimant maximum protection. For example, assume that mortgagor owns land parcel 1 (worth $20,000) and land parcel 2 (worth $10,000) and that mortgagor obtains a mortgage from the senior mortgagee for $20,000 that is secured by both land parcels. Later, the mortgagor borrows $10,000 from a junior mortgagee, which is secured only by land parcel 1. Both mortgages are properly recorded, and both the senior and junior mortgagee have actual notice of one another. If the mortgagor defaults on both loans, the senior mortgagee can be compelled at equity to first satisfy its indebtedness out of land parcel 2 before resorting to land parcel 1. See generally Osborne at §286; Restatement (Third) of Property (Mortgages) §8.6 (1997).

2. Mezzanine Financing

As an alternative to second mortgage financing that senior lenders may prohibit under their due-on-encumbrance clause (see Chapter 5A7), Dan Developer might obtain secondary financing based on his ownership interest in the entity that owns the mortgaged property. Rather than obtaining a junior mortgage in the realty, as described below, the so-called mezzanine lender takes a security interest in Dan's ownership interest in the development entity—for example, in the corporate shares owned by Dan where the development entity is a corporation. Consider to what extent mezzanine financing holds the potential to replace mortgage financing with financing secured by such equity interests that is accomplished under the UCC.

M. Madison, J. Dwyer, and S. Bender,
The Law of Real Estate Financing
§§8:20-8:24 (2016)

MEZZANINE FINANCING

As a result of the shakeout in the real estate industry in the early 1990s, many first mortgage lenders became increasingly hostile to secondary financing involving a junior mortgage. Senior mortgage lenders addressed what they viewed as obstructionist tactics by borrowers and their principals by using so-called exploding guarantees, nonrecourse carveouts, and arbitration provisions to chill lender liability actions, as well as bankruptcy filings and other tactics to delay foreclosure. Junior mortgage lenders possess a similar ability to frustrate the expectations of senior mortgagees by, among other things, their potential to involve the mortgagor in involuntary bankruptcy proceedings and their role in cramdown and other bankruptcy issues. In reliance on due-on-encumbrance provisions in the mortgage loan documents, senior mortgage lenders began to object to secondary mortgage financing. At the same time, rating agencies crucial for their role in the securitization of senior mortgage financing, viewed secondary mortgage financing as detrimental to the senior lien.

In this climate, alternatives to secondary mortgage financing, often referred to as mezzanine financing, emerged to address the needs of borrowers to obtain leverage and to boost equity yields while reducing equity capital needs. Mezzanine financing is sometimes used to refer to a range of innovative secondary financing, such as A-B note structures, the taking of preferred equity, and even second mortgages. However, as used in this discussion, mezzanine financing refers to non-mortgage financing secured by equity pledges in an entity or entities in the property ownership structure.

MEZZANINE FINANCING SECURED BY EQUITY INTERESTS

In the typical mezzanine financing arrangement, the borrower is not the owner of the mortgaged property. This separation avoids the potential for conflict between the mezzanine and mortgage lenders, with the consequence that the mezzanine lender will not have a mortgage lien. Instead, it will lend to the entity or entities that own 100% of the equity interests in the mortgage borrower and take a security interest in that equity interest. Typically, the borrowing entity will be a singlepurpose, bankruptcy remote entity and thus cannot be the general partner of a limited partnership or the managing member of a limited liability company. In a structure where the mortgage borrower is a limited partnership, for example, the mezzanine lender typically would lend to the holder(s) of the limited partnership interests and obtain a pledge of those interests. In order to allow the mezzanine lender to assume control of the mortgage borrower in this arrangement, the limited partnership agreement should permit the mezzanine lender upon default to remove the general partner of the mortgage borrower and to convert that entity to the status of a limited partner.

Thus, the mezzanine lender ordinarily obtains its collateral interest in an ownership interest, which is personal property under the Uniform Commercial Code. Yet, the mezzanine loan is based in part on the presence of equity owned by the mortgage borrower in the mortgaged property. Because it has no direct lien interest in the real estate, the mezzanine lender is in a precarious position with regard to actions of the mortgage lender to foreclose the property and actions of the borrower or creditors to further encumber the realty thereby appropriating the equity in the mortgaged property. The mezzanine lender, then, must protect itself with covenants flowing from the mortgage lender with regard to the mortgaged property, as well as with covenants from the mezzanine borrower with regard to the borrower's ability to control decisions affecting the mortgaged property.

The potential for indirect control by the mezzanine lender over the mortgage borrower and mezzanine borrower, as well as the potential for direct ownership and control in the event of foreclosure of the equity interest by the mezzanine lender raises the specter of various control risks ranging from lender liability (e.g., duress), and responsibility for environmental clean-up as an operating party, to the potential for invalidation of the mezzanine loan structure as an impermissible clog. For example, the mezzanine lender's ability to foreclose on the equity interest or otherwise to assume control in the event of the mortgage borrower's default under the mortgage loan might be viewed as impairing the mortgage borrower's ability to redeem.

Because of the various risks assumed by the mezzanine lender, interest rates on mezzanine financing tend to be substantially higher than those charged by senior mortgage lenders. Loan terms tend to range from one to five years, in contrast to those for mortgage loans. Variable rather than fixed interest rates are often employed.

INTERCREDITOR AGREEMENT

Mortgage lenders undoubtedly will include a due-on-encumbrance provision in their mortgage loan documents that will prohibit junior encumbrances without the mortgagee's consent. Even though the mezzanine lender does not obtain a direct lien interest in the mortgaged property, the mezzanine transaction may implicate the closely related due-on-sale clause in the mortgage loan documents, especially if that clause extends beyond transfers of the property to reach transfers of control, either at the inception of the mezzanine loan or at least at the time of any action by the mezzanine lender to enforce its collateral interest in the equity. Thus, the mezzanine lender must approach the mortgage lender to the entity that owns the underlying realty and obtain consent to the mezzanine arrangement. Even if the mortgage lender does not have the contractual right to approve the mezzanine transaction under its loan documents, the mezzanine lender must obtain certain protections from the mortgage lender. Therefore, the typical mezzanine financing arrangement will require an intercreditor agreement under which the mezzanine lender obtains various covenants and protections from the mortgage lender, while at the same time giving covenants in favor of the mortgage lender.

The mezzanine lender will want covenants from the mortgage lender that protect the mortgage borrower's equity stake in the property. As would a secondary mortgagee, the mezzanine lender will desire notice and the opportunity to cure defaults under the mortgage loan. The mezzanine lender will also desire provisions that the secondary mortgagee would not need. For example, the mezzanine lender will desire the senior mortgagee's agreement that it will not accept a deed in lieu of foreclosure, enter into a friendly foreclosure agreement with the borrower, or approve a sale transaction under its due-on-sale provision that does not provide for full payment of the mezzanine loan. Secondary mortgagees do not require these protections, as their mortgage liens would survive a deed in lieu or other consensual transfer.

In the event that the mezzanine transaction could implicate a due-on-encumbrance provision, or more likely a due-on-sale or transfer of control clause in the mortgage loan documents, the mezzanine lender will require the approval of the senior lender of the mezzanine loan transaction and the potential under the mezzanine loan documents for a transfer of control over the mortgage borrower. The mezzanine lender may also desire the option to purchase the senior lien in the event of default thereunder.

The senior mortgagee may desire some of the same subordination and standstill provisions it would demand in approving a junior mortgage. Such subordination provisions ordinarily include the junior lender's agreement that the junior debt is subordinate in lien and right of payment to the senior lender. Standstill provisions include the junior's agreement to forebear from instituting foreclosure or related proceedings against the mortgage borrower until the first lien is paid. Although these protections may not be necessary where the lender is providing mezzanine financing without taking a lien interest in the mortgaged property, the senior lender may nonetheless desire standstill provisions in the form of a waiver of the right to file an involuntary bankruptcy against the mortgage borrower. The senior lender may also desire an assignment from the mezzanine lender of its voting rights in bankruptcy proceedings, as well as the agreement of the mezzanine lender not to seek adequate protection payments. Moreover, the senior lender may desire standstill provisions with regard to recourse against any common guarantor, as well as an agreement to prevent leapfrogging of priority through the acquisition of any lien interest by the mezzanine lender senior to that of the mortgagee (e.g., real property tax liens, or superiority liens in bankruptcy).

MEZZANINE LOAN DOCUMENTS

Among the documents required by the mezzanine lender will be a security agreement pursuant to the Uniform Commercial Code in which the mezzanine borrower grants a security interest in its ownership interest in the mortgage borrower, including rights to distributions of income from the mortgage borrower.

The mezzanine loan terms are reflected in a promissory note and often in a separate mezzanine loan agreement. Among the other provisions, the mezzanine loan agreement will require the mezzanine borrower to perform or cause the mortgage borrower to comply with covenants similar to those given mortgage lenders with regard to property maintenance and preservation of equity.

In order to help ensure (or to replace) the preservation of equity in the mortgaged property, mezzanine financing may require recourse in certain circumstances against the mezzanine borrower (structured as carveouts to otherwise nonrecourse protection) or against a guarantor (structured as an exploding or springing guaranty) who is oftentimes the parent entity of the mezzanine borrower. Occurrences that could threaten the mortgage borrower's (and indirectly the mezzanine lender's) equity interest in the mortgaged property, and which form the basis for such carveouts and springing recourse, include (a) the placement of voluntary or involuntary junior liens or mechanics' liens on the property; (b) nonpayment of real property taxes; (c) default under property leases by the mortgage borrower; (d) the granting of a deed in lieu of foreclosure under the senior lien or a friendly foreclosure agreement; (e) the unapproved sale of the property; and (f) the filing of bankruptcy proceedings by the mortgage borrower, the mezzanine borrower, or the guarantor.

PERFECTION . . . OF EQUITY INTERESTS

The mezzanine lender typically obtains a security interest in the mezzanine borrower's equity interest in another entity, such as the mortgaged property owner. Typically, this security interest would be governed by the Uniform Commercial Code. The proper means of perfecting such a security interest is quite complex and turns on the nature of the equity interest taken. For example, for purposes of the UCC, a share or similar equity interest issued by a corporation is a "security" and thus is "investment property" for purposes of Article 9. Security interests in such investment property, whether or not the securities are certificated, can be perfected by the filing of a financing statement. (Under Article 9's 2001 revision, filing is accomplished in the jurisdiction where the corporation is registered.) However, a security interest in investment property that is perfected by filing will be subordinate to a competing security interest in the investment property that is perfected by means of control or, in the case of a certificated security, by the secured party taking delivery of the security.

If the equity interest taken as collateral is an interest in a partnership or limited liability company, generally it is not a security (and thus not Article 9 investment property) unless "it is dealt in or traded on securities exchanges or in securities markets, its terms expressly provide that it is a security governed by this Article [8 of the UCC], or it is an investment company security." The partnership or LLC interest may also fall within the scope of Article 9 investment property if it is held in a securities account. When the partnership or LLC interest does not fall within the scope of investment property under Article 9, it likely is classified as a general intangible that is perfected only by the filing of a financing statement (in the case of a registered organization such as most limited partnerships and LLCs, in the state where the entity is registered).

The securitization rating services view mortgage liens as superior to UCC equity interests. Among other things, title insurance is not available for UCC interests as it would be for mortgage interests [although recently some companies introduced UCC insurance]. As well, in the case of investment property (securities), the security interest perfected by filing may be primed by one perfected by control or possession. Despite this lesser quality in relation to mortgage liens, the adverse impact of mortgage liens on senior mortgage debt makes mezzanine financing an attractive compromise for secondary financing.

3. *Subordinated Purchase Money Mortgages*

In addition to converting equity into tax-free capital during ownership, developers and purchasers use junior mortgages to leverage their costs of improving and acquiring real estate. For example, under the master hypothetical, Dan plans to construct an office building (at a cost of $25 million) and to purchase the underlying fee from Francine Farmer, an investor in raw land (for a price of $8 million) and to finance these costs by means of an ordinary first mortgage loan on the fee from Ace Insurance Company in the amount of $25 million. This presupposes that when the project is completed the land and improvements will be worth $33 million and that the fee mortgage loan is being made at a loan-to-value ratio of 75 percent. Because the total cost of the land and improvements is $33 million, Dan must raise equity capital in the amount of $8 million to fund the balance of the venture costs. As explained at Chapter 11A, it may be possible for Dan to leverage his cost of developing the land by obtaining an ordinary leasehold mortgage loan that does not encumber the fee. For example, if Dan were to ground lease the underlying land from Francine Farmer (instead of purchasing it) and obtain a leasehold mortgage loan at the same loan-to-value ratio of 75 percent, he would have to raise venture capital of only $6,250,000 to fund the remaining cost of constructing the improvements. Alternatively, however, Dan may be able to use a form of secondary financing called the subordinated purchase money mortgage to separately finance the cost of acquiring the land. As illustrated below, by this method Dan would be able to reduce his cash outlay to only $800,000, and, in contrast to leasehold mortgage financing, he would not have to forgo acquiring fee simple title to the underlying land. A purchase money mortgage is a mortgage taken back by a seller to secure the purchaser's promise to pay the remainder of the purchase price or a mortgage obtained by a third-party lender to secure purchase funds advanced to the purchaser. Like the installment land contract, which is examined at Chapter 3D, the purchase money mortgage has traditionally been associated with high-ratio seller financing, wherein the purchaser of some real estate such as raw land is only able to borrow or raise part of the purchase price from outside sources and the seller agrees to accept a small down payment and allow the purchaser to pay the balance of the purchase price in installments over a designated period of time. In contrast to an installment land contract, however, the installment indebtedness is immediately secured by a purchase money mortgage lien on the land so that the purchaser obtains the legal title to the property without waiting until the indebtedness is fully repaid.

To illustrate, suppose the fee owner, Francine Farmer, agrees to separately finance Dan's purchase of the underlying land by taking back a purchase money mortgage at a high loan-to-value ratio—say, 90 percent. For Dan to later obtain his development financing, Francine must also agree to subordinate her purchase money mortgage to the liens of any subsequently recorded construction or postconstruction mortgages to be held by institutional lenders such as Fuller National Bank and Ace Insurance Company. In that event, Dan could reduce his net cash outlay to only $800,000 because, as the new fee owner, he could include the underlying land once as security for Ace's first mortgage loan on the land and the completed improvements and again as collateral for Francine's second mortgage loan on the fee. Hence, the total $33 million cost of the project would be supported by cumulative financing in the amount of $32.2 million ($25 million from Ace plus $7.2 million from Francine).[7]

Bell, Negotiating the Purchase-Money Mortgage
7 Real Est. Rev. 51 (Spring 1977)

. . . The purchase-money mortgage must establish a delicate balance. It must restrict the purchaser-mortgagor sufficiently to protect the mortgagee against the deterioration of security or loss of investment. However, it must not be so restrictive as to interfere with the mortgagor's intended use of the property or with his ability to deal adequately with changes in the economic or physical

---

7. This presupposes sufficient rental income to cover the debt-service payments on both mortgages. Second mortgagees such as Francine frequently tolerate low (for example, 100 percent) debt-coverage ratios and sometimes are willing to defer some or all of the interest or amortization to decrease the amount of debt service on the second mortgage. Such deferral produces an increasing principal balance over time, which must be repaid in the form of a balloon payment when the property is sold or refinanced.

conditions of the property. However, too often neither the buyer nor the seller anticipates his future needs adequately, nor does he fully appreciate the economic or legal effects of the arrangement he is negotiating.

The discussion which follows examines some of the aspects of purchase-money financing (particularly subordinated purchase-money debt) and explores the options by means of which the purchaser-mortgagor and seller-mortgagee can expect to improve their respective positions.

PURCHASE-MONEY MORTGAGE AS A SUBORDINATE LIEN

The purchase-money mortgagee is free to waive his priority over subsequent interests in any manner or subject to any conditions he deems appropriate. Once established, however, the conditions of any subordination will generally be strictly construed against the mortgagee. In practice, purchase-money mortgages frequently are subordinated to future debt because the purchase mortgage is intended to fill a "gap" between the buyer's desired financing and that which he anticipates he will be able to obtain from an institutional lender. Just as often, purchase-money mortgages come into existence as subordinated debt (i.e., second mortgages) because the existing financing on the property which the buyer wants to retain is not sufficient, together with his maximum cash equity, to equal the purchase price.

In analyzing the potential risks inherent in assuming a subordinated position, the seller-mortgagee should consider his own financial position after the sale is consummated since his ability to avail himself of certain key rights in the mortgage (most notably, the right to cure monetary defaults under the senior debt so as to keep the junior mortgage alive) may become a function of his own financial capabilities.

From the point of view of the buyer, the seller often is a ready and willing source of financing. However, the buyer should bear in mind that when the purchase-money mortgage is intended to become subordinated to a new mortgage to be obtained subsequently by the buyer (either for development of the property or merely the refinancing of existing senior debt), the buyer is negotiating the terms of the seller's subordination not only for the buyer himself, but also for the benefit of any future senior lender against the property. Therefore, when the seller asks for conditions or restrictions on the subordination of the seller's debt, the buyer must take care that any such restrictions or conditions do not impose burdensome affirmative obligations on the senior mortgagee or increase its basic risk.

THE SELLER'S CONDITIONS TO SUBORDINATION
OF THE PURCHASE-MONEY MORTGAGE

The seller's conditions to the subordination of the purchase-money mortgage fall into *two* general categories. First are those that may be referred to as *economic conditions;* second are those conditions which tend to be more *technical or legal* in nature. Economic conditions reflect the seller's business judgments as to the economic viability of an investment in a subordinated mortgage position. Technical or legal conditions are procedural in nature and are expected to keep the economic risk within intended limits.

ECONOMIC CONDITIONS TO SUBORDINATION

Among those conditions which might be deemed to be economic in nature are the following:

Institutional lender. An agreement by the seller to subordinate to senior debt to be arranged at some time in the future should be conditioned upon the senior lender being "a bank, insurance company or other similar institutional lender." Generally, an institutional lender will be more sympathetic to the position of the subordinated mortgagee than the private lender; the institutional lender not only is better able to temporarily withstand the financial effects of a default on its mortgage, but often has less of a desire to become the owner of the property.

Debt service. A major element entering into the valuation of real property is the amount of the annual "free and clear" cash flow generated. "Free and clear" generally means the balance after deducting both interest and amortization payments on all mortgages. Therefore, the higher the debt service on the mortgages or (from the point of view of the subordinated mortgagee) on the senior debt, the less the coverage or "cushion" which will be available to the subordinated mortgagee in terms of the owner's remaining equity in the property.

The buyer-mortgagor would be ill advised to accept an absolute limit on the interest rate which he may pay on the senior debt (particularly if it is to be a construction loan which generally has a floating rate and also in view of the possibility that the senior debt will have a variable rate clause). It may be more practical for the seller-mortgagee, in his effort to limit the total debt service payable on the senior debt, to focus on the amortization rate and leave the matter of interest rate to the protection afforded by a requirement that the lender be a financial institution. Further limitations on interest such as "market interest rate" or "prevailing rate" can cause difficulties if bank counsel is unwilling to accept the risk that the rate being charged meets such criteria.

Moratoriums. As the mortgagor makes payments of principal on the senior debt, he is increasing his equity in the property and the security of the subordinated lender. Many times, a senior lender which is comfortable with its security is willing to grant a moratorium (or reduction) in payments of principal. At the other extreme, when a property becomes distressed, a moratorium (or reduction) may be granted as an incentive to the owner to continue to operate the property. The seller-mortgagee, to protect *his* position, should seek a covenant in the purchase mortgage that all amortization payments be made according to the original terms of the senior mortgagee. This will give the subordinated mortgagee the option to decide whether such a moratorium or reduction is in his own best interest.

Proceeds of refinancing. When the seller-mortgagee is taking a position subordinate to *existing* financing, a major issue becomes the disposition of the proceeds of any future refinancing that generates cash in excess of the mortgage debt. A corollary issue is the division of proceeds if the buyer-mortgagor resells the property. In essence, the question becomes one of whether buyer or purchase-money mortgagee should have the right to withdraw his equity first, or whether such withdrawal should be in some agreed-to ratio. If there is to be a division of the excess proceeds, the buyer-mortgagor is likely to ask that he be given a credit for any capital improvements made by him prior to the sale or refinancing. As a matter of drafting the refinancing clause, it should be made clear whether the "excess" in question is over the outstanding senior debt at the time of the purchase, or at the time of the refinancing.

Release clauses. When the property is to be developed in stages and the entire parcel is subject to the seller's mortgage, the buyer generally will need to obtain the release of completed sections in order to effect a sale or permanent financing. The design of such release clauses will depend upon the nature of the project. However, certain general suggestions may be made:

- The buyer should at the appropriate time be given the right, independent of his right to obtain the release of specific parcels, to obtain a release for the installation of public utilities and the dedication of roads.
- Releases should be described in terms of an existing survey or subdivision map.
- Release prices should be related to the value of the property being released and to the effect of such release upon the value of the remaining property.
- Released parcels should be contiguous and should be located in a manner which will not destroy the marketability of the remaining acreage.
- The granting of the release should be conditioned upon the buyer not being in default under the terms of the purchase-money financing *or* under the terms of any other financing or agreements affecting the property.

Subordination to construction loan. The matter of designating the terms and conditions for subordination of the purchase-money financing to a construction loan depends upon the nature of the project to be built and the general facts and circumstances. Although an in-depth analysis of this subject is beyond the general scope of this article, certain observations may be made:

First, the seller-mortgagee should require that certain minimum rights be given to him to review and approve plans for project development and leasing of the completed facility. All agreements with architects, engineers, prospective tenants, or other agreements, permits, documents, and drawings affecting the development or use of the premises should be made assignable by their terms and be assigned (subject to the right of a prior institutional lender to such assignments) to the seller-mortgagee as additional security for his mortgage. This will put the seller-mortgagee in a position where he can either complete development or offer a more salable package in the event of the buyer-mortgagor's default.

Second, although it may not be practical to limit the senior lender as to interest rate or absolute amount of loan, consideration should be given to restricting the use of the proceeds of the senior mortgage to the physical development of the property and related costs such as interest, real estate taxes, and the like. However, any such provision must be broad enough so that the senior lender does not feel that his position will be jeopardized if an advance is made on account of an item not specifically enumerated.

Third, from the buyer-mortgagor's viewpoint, it is generally advisable to insert a requirement in the purchase-money mortgage to require the mortgagee to execute such further documents as may be necessary or appropriate to carry out the terms and intentions of the parties.

LEGAL AND TECHNICAL CONDITIONS TO SUBORDINATION

Conditions which are more procedural in nature include the following:

Notice of default. One of the most important protections to be obtained by the seller-mortgagee is the covenant to give him notice of any default under the terms of the senior debt *and* the opportunity to cure such default. Such notice (at least as to matters relating to a monetary default such as nonpayment of interest on senior debt, real estate taxes, insurance premiums, etc.) can take the form of a notice either from the mortgagor or (preferably) from the senior mortgagee in sufficient time to permit the subordinate mortgagee to cure the default. Alternatively, the mortgage can impose an affirmative obligation on the mortgagor to deliver to the subordinate mortgagee proof of payment of all monetary obligations prior to the expiration of any applicable grace period. . . .

It is extremely difficult to impose any affirmative obligation on an institutional lender which becomes a condition precedent to a right to foreclose—for example, the obligation to give notice of default and an opportunity to cure to the junior mortgagee. But it is not unreasonable for the mortgagee to require the mortgagor to provide proof of payment (as described above) and to use his best efforts to require the senior lender to give notice of default and opportunity to cure at least those defaults which the senior lender intends to use as a basis for immediate foreclosure.

Of course, any provisions in the junior mortgage permitting payments to be made by the seller-mortgagee should provide that the mortgage will be increased by the amount of such payments. . . .

Prepayment. The mortgagor generally has no right to prepay a mortgage unless the right is specifically set out in the instrument. To maintain flexibility for the future, the buyer-mortgagor should seek the right to prepay the purchase-money mortgage "in whole or in part at any time, and from time to time." However, from the seller's viewpoint, requiring a penalty upon prepayment is not unreasonable since he has invested an "overhead" in the form of legal and other front-end fees which he normally would recoup only after the entire life of the mortgage.

Right to financial information. It has become almost standard operating procedure of institutional mortgagees to require the submission by the mortgagor of periodic operating information. This is particularly important to the subordinate mortgagee whose anticipation of repayment may depend almost entirely on the economic growth of the property and the potential for refinancing senior debt in an amount sufficient to pay off or significantly amortize the purchase money debt. The seller-mortgagee should require that such operating statements be personally guaranteed as to accuracy by the purchaser of the property and any successor in interest to the purchaser.

If the junior mortgagee anticipates that payment of the purchase-money debt will depend upon refinancing the senior debt, he should reserve the right to negotiate for such financing on behalf of the mortgagor and to use the financial data in such negotiations. The right of the seller to seek refinancing and the obligation of the mortgagor to accept the same should be carefully spelled out in order to prevent the seller from interfering with the legitimate efforts of the mortgagor himself to obtain refinancing and to permit the mortgagor to reject what he deems to be unfavorable financing arranged by the seller. Absent such a provision, it is arguable that the seller would be liable for interfering with the mortgagor's ownership rights in the property.

INTEGRATING THE TERMS OF SENIOR AND SUBORDINATE DEBT

In the process of negotiating the terms of subordinated purchase-money debt, the parties must keep in mind the provisions of existing senior debt and try to anticipate the requirements of any senior debt which may be created in the future so that the separate mortgage instruments do not conflict or contradict each other.

Real estate tax escrows. Unpaid real estate taxes generally have a priority over all mortgages, whether created before or after the tax liability arises. In order to prevent a significant liability (e.g., a quarter-or half-year of unpaid taxes) from accruing before it becomes actionable, a mortgage will generally require a monthly escrow of real estate taxes. If the senior financing has not been arranged at the time of the sale, the escrowing of real estate tax payments with the seller-mortgagee should be subordinated to the right of the senior mortgage to require such escrows.

Defaults and grace periods. Events of default under both the junior and senior mortgages generally will parallel one another. However, the junior mortgagee should seek to have the grace periods (during which no default can be declared) be shorter in his mortgage than in the senior lien. In this way, the junior lender is in a position to declare a default—and immediately take steps to remedy it— before a default occurs under the senior mortgage. When the senior mortgage is to be arranged in the future, the seller-mortgagee can dictate the allowable grace periods by conditioning his subordination upon the senior mortgage containing specified grace periods prior to the existence of a default.

Insurance. The use of proceeds that may be paid in the future under casualty insurance policies should be treated similarly in all mortgages and in a manner compatible with leases which may affect the premises. The key issue is whether the insurance proceeds are to reduce the mortgage balance or may be used to reconstruct the premises. Whatever the decision, the treatment should be the same in all mortgages. (A distinction in this connection frequently is made between a total destruction and a partial destruction.) Similarly, the landlord's obligation to rebuild under a lease should be tied into the disposition of insurance proceeds under the terms of the mortgage.

Events of default. Any event which is an event of default under any senior mortgage should be an automatic event of default under the purchase-money mortgage permitting acceleration of the unpaid balance of the purchase-money mortgage. . . .

Sample Subordination Agreement

SUBORDINATION AGREEMENT

THIS AGREEMENT is made this _____ day of _____, 20 _____, by _____ (the "Seller"), in favor of INTERIM BANK, N.A., a national banking association ("Bank").

WITNESSETH:

WHEREAS, the Seller has recorded at Book _____, Page _____, of the records of Oklahoma County, Oklahoma, a certain Mortgage (the "Seller Mortgage") securing payment of the sum of $ _____ executed by Homestead Development Corporation, an Oklahoma corporation ("Homestead"), as mortgagor, and covering the real property described at Schedule "1" attached as a part hereof (the "Land");

WHEREAS, Homestead has mortgaged the Land to Bank pursuant to a certain Mortgage and Security Agreement (the "Bank Mortgage") securing payment of the sum of $ _____ recorded in Book _____ at Page _____, of the records of Oklahoma County, Oklahoma; and

WHEREAS, Bank has requested that the Seller subordinate the lien of the Seller Mortgage to the lien of the Bank Mortgage by means of this Agreement.

NOW, THEREFORE, in consideration of Ten Dollars ($10.00) and other good and valuable consideration, the receipt of which is hereby acknowledged, it is agreed as follows:

1. The Seller hereby agrees and covenants with Bank and Bank's successors and assigns that the lien granted by the Seller Mortgage will be in all respects subordinate, junior and inferior to the Bank Mortgage.
2. Except for the agreements herein contained, the Seller Mortgage will continue in full force and effect.
3.

IN WITNESS WHEREOF, the undersigned has executed this instrument as of the date first above written.

_____

SELLER

NOTES AND QUESTIONS

1. Separate Land Financing by Means of a Subordinated Purchase Money Mortgage. As observed above, developers frequently use purchase money mortgage financing to leverage their cost of developing a new income-producing project. By separately financing the cost of the underlying land using a high-ratio subordinated purchase money mortgage from the seller of the land, a developer can reduce its need for venture capital and, in most cases, increase the cash-on-cash rate of return to its equity investors. The hypothetical described at the beginning of this section presupposes that Francine Farmer is willing to subordinate the lien of her purchase money mortgage to the liens of future mortgages that Dan anticipates he will obtain from a construction lender such as Fuller National Bank and a postconstruction lender such as Ace Insurance Company, both of whom will demand a first mortgage lien on the property. But why would Francine be willing to assume the risk of a secondary lien position, especially on a purchase money mortgage with such a high loan-to-value ratio? Francine might be persuaded by the fact that her security interest will be enhanced by the value of the proposed improvements. After all, as Dan would explain to Francine, a second mortgage on an office building project worth $33 million is better security than a first mortgage on land worth only $8 million. Moreover, Dan might not be willing or able to improve the land without the additional financing. Also, in exchange for the subordination agreement Dan might be willing to pay Francine a purchase price that exceeds the market value of the land (subject to the tax constraints on nonrecourse seller financing imposed by the Crane doctrine discussed at Chapter 13A2a, note 1).

> ➤ *Problem 7-1*
> Assume that Francine agrees to subordinate. After reviewing the excerpt by Bell, do you think that the sample subordination agreement is adequate and enforceable by the parties? As Francine's attorney, what additional language might you require in the subordination agreement to protect the interests of your client? What additional language might Ace's attorney require? See Korngold, Construction Loan Advances and the Subordinated Purchase Money Mortgagee: An Appraisal, A Suggested Approach, and the ULTA Perspective, 50 Fordham L. Rev. 313 (1981); McNamara, Subordination Agreements as Viewed by Sellers, Purchasers, Construction Lenders, and Title Companies, 12 Real Est. L.J. 347 (Spring 1984); Miller, Starr, and Regalia, Subordination Agreements in California, 13 UCLA L. Rev. 1298 (1966). ◄

Real estate malpractice actions are common and subordinations are just one of the flashpoint sources of claims against lawyers brought by disgruntled clients who did not fully comprehend the risks they had assumed. For example, the New Jersey Supreme Court in Conklin v. Hannoch Weisman, P.C., 145 N.J. 395, 678 A.2d 1060 (1996) issued rulings on a case where a jury had found a law firm negligent for failing to explain to the seller/lender the risks associated with subordinating a purchase money loan to a construction mortgage to develop low income housing on rezoned agricultural land. Among other things, the litigants disagreed on whether the client fully understood the meaning and consequences of subordination. The law firm unsuccessfully pointed to the higher sales price of the farmland based on its potential for rezoning and redevelopment as demonstrating the seller client understood the need for a development loan with first priority; the jury rejected that understanding. Mindful of the potential for litigation and liability should the development project collapse and the junior lien seller be faced with bidding an amount beyond its reach in the senior construction loan foreclosure sale to protect its interests, how would you ensure your client understood the risks of subordination and that you could demonstrate that understanding in any later dispute?

    2. Subdivision Financing. So far the focal point of our discussion has been the financing of income-producing real estate. By contrast, land development financing includes land acquisition and development loans made to developers of subdivisions who acquire raw land at wholesale prices primarily for the purpose of building roads, installing utilities, and otherwise developing the land into finished lots for resale at retail prices to home builders (both professionals and individuals) and land speculators. In addition, the term "land development financing" encompasses loans made to developers of multiunit residential developments such as condominiums and town-house projects where the community facilities, called common areas, are owned or managed by some form of unit owners' association.

    What distinguishes land development financing from the financing of income-producing real estate is the disparate natures of the security for each type of loan and the differing regulatory environment for both kinds of developments. In contrast to an ordinary construction lender, who relies beforehand on a single takeout commitment to become whole again once the construction period is over, the ultimate source for repayment of the land development loan is the borrower's legal ability to fractionalize the collateral into separate ownership interests and to sell these interests (in the form of lots or residential units) at a predetermined minimum price. This means that during the development phase of the project the market demand for the real estate might slacken or the process of development could be curtailed or even halted.

    Because of the frequently speculative nature of land development, institutional lenders normally will lend only at low loan-to-value ratios, typically 50 to 75 percent. Therefore, loans to acquire raw land are usually financed by means of high-ratio seller financing. A land development loan usually will be secured by a first mortgage on the property. This means that if a land developer has acquired the raw land by means of a high-ratio purchase money mortgage (or installment land contract), the purchase money mortgage must be subordinated to the development loan before the institutional lender will permit the developer to make its first draw on the land development loan.

In the case of a development loan, additional collateral such as cash or securities or the personal guarantee of the borrowers may be sought as well. Further security may be given by assigning to the lender the promissory notes of lot purchasers or their installment land contracts in accordance with Article 9 of the U.C.C. See M. Madison, J. Dwyer, and S. Bender, The Law of Real Estate Financing §5:123 (2016). As additional protection, in the event of the borrower's default the lender should receive an assignment of the contracts of the various parties in the development work and have a security interest in their work products; this would enable the lender to step in and complete the project if necessary. In this regard, the lender may require that it be designated as an obligee in the case of a performance bond.

To facilitate the sale and conveyance of individual lots, it is often desirable in the case of both land acquisition and land development loans that a mechanism be established for the release of individual lots from the lender's blanket mortgage covering the entire tract. For example, suppose an investor buys some raw land that she plans to subdivide into lots for resale to lot buyers. If the purchase is financed by means of a purchase money mortgage from the seller, the purchaser should insist on a partial-release-of-lien clause in the mortgage so that clear and unencumbered title to specific portions of the land may be acquired as the land acquisition loan is repaid. Otherwise, the purchaser would not be able to convey marketable title to any of the lots until the entire purchase money indebtedness is repaid. If the purchase price were, say, $200,000, the purchaser might arrange with the seller (1) to acquire clear title to 20 percent of the land when the principal balance on the mortgage note is scaled down (by 25 percent) to $150,000; (2) to acquire clear title to an additional 20 percent of the land when the balance is reduced (by 50 percent) to $100,000; and (3) to obtain clear title on all the land when the final payment is made. Under such an arrangement, the purchaser would be able to resell the land and deliver clear title to buyers of individual lots and yet the seller-mortgagee would be protected because if at any time the purchaser-mortgagor defaulted, the value of the unreleased land probably would be higher than the outstanding loan balance at the time of default as a consequence of the five-percentage-point spread between the scale-down and the release-of-lien percentage rates.

The following language from a partial release clause was the subject of litigation in Lambert v. Jones, 540 S.W.2d 256, 257 (Tenn. Ct. App. 1976):

> [T]he privilege is reserved and given so that the parties of the first part, their heirs, or assigns, may at any time subsequent to January 1, 1973, and from time to time, obtain a release or releases from the lien of this deed of trust of part or parts of the aforedescribed real property upon payment to the owner and holder of the indebtedness secured hereby, either by way of obligatory payments or by way of prepayments, of the sum of $1,500.00 per acre to be released; provided further, however, that each released tract subsequent to the first tract released shall be contiguous to a tract previously released; provided further, however, that all accrued interest upon any principal sum paid pursuant to this release clause shall be paid at

the time of such payment; and provided further, however, that the release payments shall apply upon the next maturing note or notes secured hereby.

Can you identify potential problems with this clause? If the tract is nonhomogenous, which portion would the developer seek to have released first? Would this put the lender at an unconscionable disadvantage? As an adjunct to seeing that the loan-to-value ratio is maintained, the lender will want to be sure that the unreleased lots are not cut off from access to roads and utilities and that the size and shape of the remaining mortgaged portions are saleable. Generally, courts view release clauses as covenants running with the land so that, absent language to the contrary, they may be enforced by purchasers from the mortgagor, even where the mortgagor is in default under its obligations to the mortgagee. This comports with the primary purpose of the release clause. See generally Annot., Mortgage—Partial Release Provisions, 41 A.L.R.3d 7 (1972).

In contrast to the development of commercial real estate, the sale of residential lots and units to consumers raises important public policy concerns that have prompted protective legislation such as the Interstate Land Sales Full Disclosure Act, 15 U.S.C. §§1701 et seq. (ILSFDA). Enacted in 1968 with the intention of curbing perceived abuses and providing remedies to consumers in the retail sale and leasing of building lots, the ILSFDA is in essence a disclosure and antifraud statute analogous to those regulating the sale of securities. The federal statute regulates all covered transactions except when substantially equivalent state laws have been certified by the Bureau of Consumer Financial Protection. It generally targets high-volume sales of residential lots in large subdivisions to out-of-state purchasers; thus, for example, sales of lots with contracts for building construction to be completed within two years, sales of commercial or industrial lots, and sales to building contractors are exempt from its application. For additional background on land acquisition financing, see Martin, Land Investments in Today's Market: An Overview of Factors That Influence the Success of Raw Land Investments, 4 Real Est. Fin. 49, 53-54 (Winter 1988). An excellent discussion of all aspects of land development financing can be found in R. Harris, Construction and Development Financing 1-2 to 2-31 (1982).

3. Special Lien Priority for Purchase Money Mortgages. A purchase money mortgagee generally has lien priority over any claim against the purchaser attaching to the property (for example, a judgment lien). This priority is not limited to the seller but may extend to a third person who advances the buyer the money for the purchase as long as the money is lent solely for this purpose. See, for example, Sarmiento v. Stockton, Whatley, Davin & Co., 399 So. 2d 1057 (Fla. Dist. Ct. App. 1981); Hand Trading Co. v. Daniels, 126 Ga. App. 342, 190 S.E.2d 560 (1972); Commerce Sav., Lincoln v. Robinson, 213 Neb. 596, 331 N.W.2d 495 (1983). The purchase money mortgage will also prevail over claims for dower, community property, or homestead. See, for example, Associates Discount Corp. v. Gomes, 338 So. 2d 552 (Fla. Dist. Ct. App. 1976); Kneen v.

Halin, 6 Idaho 621, 59 P. 14 (1899); Stow v. Tift, 15 Johns. 458, 8 Am. Dec. 266 (N.Y. 1818). In some jurisdictions the lien priority is based on a statute. See, for example, Cal. Civ. Code §2898.

The legal rationale for the special lien priority accorded to purchase money mortgages (absent a subordination agreement) is based on the notion that the title, once conveyed to the grantee, automatically shoots out of the grantee and into the purchase money mortgagee so fleetingly that no other interest has time to fasten itself to it; hence, the grantor-mortgagor is deemed to be nothing more than a conduit for the mortgagee. G. Nelson et al., Real Estate Finance Law §9.1 (6th ed. 2015). Does this theory of transitory seisin make sense in a jurisdiction such as New York, which subscribes to the lien (as opposed to the title) theory with respect to the nature of a mortgage? If not, what *policy* rationale best explains why such favoritism is bestowed on purchase money mortgages? See Nelson et al. at §9.1.

On a precautionary note, observe that the lien priority accorded to a purchase money mortgage can be defeated if the mortgagee does not comply with the requirements of the recording statute in the jurisdiction where the property is located. For example, while a purchase money mortgagee who does not record the mortgage will nevertheless prevail over any prior judgment lien creditor under the special priority rules applicable to purchase money mortgages, a subsequent purchaser or mortgagee who takes or encumbers the property without record or actual notice of the purchase money mortgage will prevail in a notice jurisdiction and in a race-notice jurisdiction. In a pure race jurisdiction (where notice is irrelevant) all that is required is that the subsequent purchaser or mortgagee record before the purchase money mortgagee records. See Nelson et al. at §9.2.

4. No Right to Deficiency Judgment. As explained elsewhere (Chapter 8C3a), in the event that the net foreclosure sale proceeds are insufficient to satisfy the underlying debt, if recourse financing was used the mortgagee may obtain a deficiency judgment against the mortgagor. However, several states, such as Arizona (Ariz. Rev. Stat. Ann. §33-729(A), California (Cal. Civ. Proc. Code §580b), Montana (Mont. Code Ann. §71-1-232), North Carolina (N.C. Gen. Stat. §45-21.38), Oregon (Or. Rev. Stat. §88.070), and South Dakota (S.D. Codified Laws §44-8-20) do not permit deficiency judgments for purchase money mortgagees. Can you think of any legal or policy rationales for this rule? See G. Nelson et al. §8.3.

5. The Availability of the Installment Method for Reporting Gain from the Sale of Seller-Financed Real Estate. One tax advantage associated with the use of purchase money mortgage (and installment land contract) financing where the seller is scheduled to receive at least one payment in a taxable year subsequent to the year of sale is that the seller is allowed to use the "installment method" for reporting income under I.R.C. §453 (unless it elects otherwise) by reporting as gain, each year, only that portion of each installment "payment" that corresponds to the ratio of "gross profit" on the sale to the "contract price." The balance of the payment is treated as a nontaxable return of capital (basis). "Payment" means the cash or other property actually received in the year of payment; it includes the amount of the existing mortgage ("qualified indebtedness") assumed or taken subject to by the purchaser *only* to the extent that it exceeds the seller's adjusted basis in the property being sold. Temp. Reg. §15A.453-1(b)(3)(i). "Gross profit" means the total gain to be realized on the sale, or the selling price (as reduced by commissions and other selling expenses) less the seller's adjusted basis in the real estate being sold. I.R.C. §453(c); Temp. Reg. §15A.453-1(b)(2)(v). The "contract price" is the selling price as reduced by that portion of the qualified indebtedness that, after an adjustment to reflect commissions and other selling expenses, does not exceed the seller's adjusted basis in the property. Temp. Reg. §15A.453-1(b)(2)(iii).

The following illustration appears in M. Madison, J. Dwyer, and S. Bender, The Law of Real Estate Financing at §8.48:

Example. Seller transfers title to Blackacre worth $100,000, which is encumbered with a $40,000 mortgage and has an adjusted basis in the seller's hands of $80,000, to the purchaser on January 1, 2003 in exchange for $10,000 in cash at the closing and a $50,000 purchase-money mortgage from the purchaser. The mortgage is payable in annual installments of $5,000, bears an annual interest rate of 10 percent, and provides that the first installment will become due and payable on June 1, 2003. Commissions and selling expenses amount to $2,000. The results are as follows:

Gross profit on sale:		
Selling price		$100,000
Less:		
Adjusted basis	$80,000	
Selling expenses	2,000	82,000
		$18,000
Contract price:		
Selling price		$100,000
Less existing mortgage		40,000
		$60,000
Payments received in year of sale:		
Cash at closing		$10,000
Installment received 6/1/03		5,000
		$15,000

Gain reportable in year of sale:

$$\frac{\$18,000 \text{ (gross profit)}}{\$60,000 \text{ (contract price)}} \times \$15,000 \text{ (payments in year of sale)} = \$4,500$$

Accordingly, $4,500 is reported as taxable gain in the year of sale (2003) and 18/60, or 30 percent, of each of the $5,000 installments received in 2004 through 2012 ($1,500) will be reported as gain, and the balance ($3,500) will be treated as a nontaxable return of the seller's basis in the property. Over the remaining nine-year installment period, the sum of the gain to be reported (9 ×$1500 =$13,500) plus the gain reported in 2003 ($4,500) will equal the total gross profit or gain to be realized on the sale ($18,000).

The Revenue Act of 1987 introduced a new rule (based on a time value rationale) that requires an interest charge on the deferred gain if deferred payments from all dispositions during the taxable year exceed $5 million. I.R.C. §453A(c). Also, special restrictions apply with respect to the use of escrow arrangements and third-party guarantees, the pledging of installment obligations as security for a loan, sales to related parties, and the sale or other disposition of installment obligations. See Madison, Dwyer, and Bender at §8:48. Further, any egregious inflation of the sale price and debt amount in exchange for a below-market rate of interest is vulnerable to challenge under I.R.C. §1274; however, the limitations imposed by the *Crane* doctrine (discussed at Chapter 13A2a), the reduction of preferential treatment for capital gains, and the reduction of depreciation benefits under the 1986 Act, as amended, have discouraged sellers from engaging in such tax abuse. See Holthouse and Ritchie, Installment Sales Update, 15 J. Real Est. Tax'n 341, 349-352 (Summer 1988); see also Aronsohn, The Tax Reform Act of 1986—Some Selected Real Estate Problems and Possibilities, 14 J. Real Est. Tax'n 203, 213-215 (Spring 1987).

6. Deducting Interest on Seller-Financed Sales. Special rules have evolved for federal taxation purposes to regulate interest deductions and interest income in seller-financed sales because these loan transactions are more vulnerable to tax-avoidance abuses than are transactions involving third-party lenders that tend to be more arm's length in nature. Prior to the Tax Reform Act of 1986, sellers were tempted to reduce the interest rate on the installment payments to a below-market rate in exchange for an inflated sale price as a way of trading less ordinary income for extra capital gains. I.R.C. §483 was enacted to curb this tax-avoidance technique by imputing additional interest to installment payments where the stated interest is unreasonably low. Under Treas. Reg. §1.483-1, interest will be imputed on payments due more than one year after the date of sale (under a contract that provides for a selling price of more than $3,000 and where some or all of the payments are due more than one year after the sale) if the interest rate stipulated in the contract is less than the "safe harbor" rate. See Treas. Reg. §1.483-3. Excluded from the ambit of I.R.C. §483 are transactions to which the original-issue discount rates (discussed below) apply. Also, limitations imposed by the *Crane* doctrine, discussed at Chapter 13A2a, may permit the I.R.S. to disallow interest and depreciation deductions where the purchaser's cost basis in the property is so inflated by nonrecourse indebtedness that it exceeds the fair market value of the property. See Estate of Franklin v. Commissioner, 64 T.C. 752 (1975), aff'd, 544 F.2d 1045 (9th Cir. 1976).

The Tax Reform Act of 1984 imposed the so-called original-issue discount (OID) rules, a highly complex and convoluted scheme based on a time-value-of-money approach, that are designed to constrain certain tax-avoidance techniques commonly perceived by the I.R.S. to be associated with seller-financed sales. I.R.C. §§1271-1275. Specifically, the rules discourage any contrived mismatching of interest deductions and interest income by purchasers and sellers; for example, a purchase money mortgage featuring negative amortization whereby an accrual basis purchaser deducts interest and a cash basis seller defers interest income by deferring the actual payment of the interest until the installment loan matures. In addition, the OID rules codify the judicial limitations on the *Crane* doctrine in an effort to prevent the improper manipulation of the purchase price and amount of purchase money indebtedness to suit the tax interests of the parties. I.R.C. §1274(b)(3)(A). See generally G. Robinson, Federal Taxation of Real Estate ¶7.12[1] (1995); Lipsey and Friedman, Transitional Rules for Original Issue Discount, 12 J. Real Est. Tax'n 361 (Summer 1985); McGuire, Tax Shelters: Time Value of Money Anomalies in Section 483 and Section 1232, 11 J. Real Est. Tax'n 281 (Spring 1984); Moore, Analyzing the Complex New Proposed Regs on Imputed Interest and Original Issue Discount, 65 J. Tax'n 14 (July 1986); Wiesner and Smith, Equity Participation Loans: Uncertainty Increases under the New OID Rules, 62 J. Tax'n 330 (June 1985).

C. SPECIAL TYPES OF HIGH-RATIO FINANCING

Certain high-ratio financing techniques based primarily on tax inducements have evolved as alternatives to ordinary mortgage-debt financing. They include: (1) certain types of industrial development bond (IDB) financing whereby some municipality or municipal agency acts as a conduit to qualify interest received by a mortgage lender for tax-free treatment under I.R.C. §103(a) so that the developer-borrower can reduce its interest costs on new construction; (2) sale-and-leaseback financing and component financing (discussed at Chapter 11B), whereby the landowner can sell the real estate without losing possession and depreciate the cost of land in the guise of a rental deduction; and (3) so-called high-credit lease financing and off-balance sheet financing through synthetic leases.

1. High-Credit and Synthetic Lease Financing

Smith and Lubell, Real Estate Financing: The High-Credit Lease
4 Real Est. Rev. 19 (Fall 1974)

THE HIGH-CREDIT LEASE

There are very few forms of financing which offer the developer an opportunity for 100 percent mortgage financing. But in the limited area of high-credit lease financing, optimum leverage is the rule, rather than the exception. As consideration for maximum financing, the developer must frequently be prepared to accept a modest return on investment and perhaps sacrifice an inflationary hedge.

Life insurance companies are the major source of high-credit lease financing. Restrictions imposed by regulatory authorities on the investments these lenders may make determine which leases are acceptable for high-credit financing. The developer of an office, industrial, or retail property may be able to obtain 100 percent long-term mortgage financing for his project if three conditions apply:

- The entire property is leased to a single corporate tenant, or the single tenant's obligations under the lease are guaranteed by a corporation.
- The corporate tenant or corporate guarantor has a good balance sheet and a proven track record of earnings.
- The lease, in form and substance, is what is generally called a "financing" lease.

WHAT IS 100 PERCENT FINANCING?

With 100 percent financing, the lender looks primarily at the credit of the corporate tenant and only secondarily at the real estate for repayment of the loan. If the credit of the corporate tenant is acceptable and the lease meets the requirements of the lender, the loan may be in an amount equal to either the appraised value of the property or the hard-cash costs of the property to the developer, whichever is less.

Hard-cash costs are basically the costs of land acquisition and construction of the improvements. The so-called soft-cash costs attributable to the developer's time and expertise will not be recognized in determining the amount of the loan.

WHY A SINGLE TENANT?

Before a lender will furnish 100 percent financing, [it] must be satisfied that the net rental income from the property will be sufficient to pay interest on the loan and to amortize it in full by maturity. This requirement can most readily be fulfilled by a single net lease of the entire property, provided the tenant's credit standing is such that the lender will regard it as absolutely reliable for payment of rent and for all expenses relating to the property over the entire term of the loan. Some lenders . . . are subject to a statutory requirement that the tenant have a minimum record of earnings over a designated period of time.

In rare instances, the developer may be able to obtain approximately 90 percent financing where the property is leased to a number of tenants on either a net or a gross lease basis. However, in these times [1974] of galloping inflation, lenders are reluctant to rely on gross leases. Even where gross leases contain escalation clauses providing for additional rent to cover increases in real estate taxes and operating expenses, they may not be adequate security against skyrocketing costs. Moreover, developers frequently experience substantial difficulties in negotiating adequate "financing" leases in a multiple-occupancy situation.

WHY A CORPORATE TENANT?

The lender's greatest concern with high-credit lease financing is assurance of net rental payments throughout the life of the loan in an amount sufficient to cover debt service. With a high financial rating and permanent corporate existence, a corporation as tenant affords greater assurance of such payment than does an individual or partnership. The latter two are subject to the vagaries of death or incompetency. They are also more prone to make improvident personal investments which may result in bankruptcy or insolvency. . . .

RENTAL OBLIGATIONS

A financing lease is a net lease pursuant to which the tenant is obligated to pay a fixed basic rent, as well as all real estate taxes and all other expenses of any nature whatsoever arising out of the ownership and operation of the premises. The basic rent must be at least sufficient to pay interest and principal on the loan to the developer, and the tenant's obligation to pay such rent must be absolute and unconditional. In many cases, the amount of each monthly payment of rent is the same as the amount of the monthly payment on account of interest and principal required by the loan documents. For this reason, many financing leases are negotiated with the term, amount, and interest rate of a particular loan in mind.

In the instances where all of the rental is used to cover principal and interest on the mortgage, the developer receives no cash flow from the property. The landlord-developer's only inducements to obtain high-credit lease financing in these cases are the tax benefits derived from ownership. The tenant, of course, pays all real estate taxes and operating expenses. Obviously, the risks to the developer would then be minimal if the tenant is a Fortune-500 corporation or its equivalent.

The lender, who is relying upon the credit of the tenant in making the loan, must have absolute assurances that the tenant's obligation to pay rent is unconditional. If for any reason whatsoever the rent obligation is not met, the lender must be assured that the loan will be repaid in full. Consequently, the lease cannot permit the tenant any rent abatement or offset, even under any of the following conditions:

- The landlord defaults or violates a term or condition of the lease.
- There is a constructive eviction of the tenant.
- There is a violation of a zoning ordinance.
- Building violations are imposed against the property.
- The landlord's title to the property is jeopardized or even fails.
- There is a temporary taking for governmental use (i.e., temporary rerouting of highway) or occupancy.

CASUALTY LOSS

The provisions of the lease relating to damage by fire or other casualty merit special consideration. In the event the premises are damaged or destroyed by fire or other casualty, the tenant must be obligated to repair or restore, irrespective of the availability or sufficiency of insurance proceeds. There can be no abatement or reduction of rent for the period during which the premises cannot be occupied. Otherwise, the lender would be deprived of the source of repayment of its loan. The tenant can protect itself against this exposure with rent or occupancy insurance. . . .

CONDEMNATION CLAUSE

The negotiation of a condemnation clause which will be acceptable to the lender is often difficult. As a general proposition, the tenant's obligation to pay rent may be reduced only to the extent of the condemnation award received by the lender. Even though the entire premises are taken by eminent domain (or taken to such an extent as to render them unsuitable for the tenant's use), the tenant must remain obligated for the rental or a reduced rental, unless the condemnation award is sufficient to pay the debt in full.

The lease may provide, however, that the tenant can terminate by paying the lender an amount sufficient to make up the difference between the condemnation award and the outstanding mortgage debt. And in a partial taking, since the tenant is unconditionally obligated to pay rent, it is only fair to provide that the tenant may apply the entire award against the costs of restoring the untaken portion of the property.

ASSIGNMENT OF THE LEASE

To avoid any problems that might arise if the landlord became bankrupt or insolvent, the lender will require that the financing lease be assigned to [it] as collateral security for the loan. [It] will usually also require that the tenant pay the rent directly to the lender. However, since direct rental payments to the lender impose the burden of accounting to the landlord whenever a payment exceeds the periodic installments of interest and principal on the loan, a lender may occasionally permit the landlord to collect the rents.

CONCLUSION

In order to structure acceptable documents for high-credit lease financing, all parties to the arrangement (lender, tenant, and landlord-borrower) should understand the lease's basic underlying concepts. Since the lender looks to the tenant's unconditional obligation to pay rent for repayment of the loan, the lease and its assignment to the lender constitute the real security behind the loan. The property itself and the borrower's obligations under the note and the mortgage become of somewhat lesser importance. High-credit lease financing is possible only if the tenant recognizes and accepts the proposition that the [lease] is a credit transaction. It is up to the developer to bring the tenant to such recognition and acceptance.

NOTES AND QUESTIONS

1. Off-Balance Sheet Financing and the Enron Scandal. A once popular means of obtaining near 100 percent financing, as well as certain tax and accounting benefits, was through off-balance financing using so-called synthetic leases. See Murray, Off-Balance Sheet Financing: Synthetic Leases, 32 Real Prop., Prob. & Tr. J. 194 (Summer 1997). In the typical arrangement, the developer, such as Dan Developer, will lease the property from an investor in a lease structure designed to enable Dan to claim the tax status of an owner as the party with the benefit of asset appreciation and the risk of a decline in value. The "lessor"-investor holds legal title to the property and finances near 100 percent of its cost. The lease transaction must comply with Financial Accounting Standards Board (FASB) requirements to assure the desired off-balance sheet accounting treatment whereby the developer need not show the asset (building) or the liability (lease) on its balance sheet. To meet these accounting and tax requirements, the synthetic lease was often structured as a short-term arrangement under which the developer was obligated at expiration either to purchase the property for a predetermined price (usually the investor's costs) or to sell the property to a third party for its fair value while partially guaranteeing any loss the investor has suffered. See generally M. Madison, J. Dwyer, and S. Bender, The Law of Real Estate Financing §8:59 (2018).

Following the spectacular collapse of energy giant Enron in 2001, the commercial world began to steer clear of off-balance sheet financing arrangements such as synthetic leasing. See M. Madison, et al., §8:59. Further, in response to the Enron scandal and the Sarbanes-Oxley Act of 2002 it prompted, the SEC requested the FASB to curb off-balance sheet reporting. The FASB responded in 2016 with an expansive new accounting approach that will treat every lease (except short-term leases of 12 months or less) as requiring disclosure on the lessee's balance sheet, effective in 2019 for public companies and 2020 for nonpublic companies. The new approach effectively eliminates off-balance sheet financing for these leases, abandoning the previous accounting distinction between capital (balance sheet treatment) and operating leases (off-balance sheet) by requiring both capital and operating leases to be shown on the lessee's balance sheet as representing both an asset and a liability.

2. Recharacterization. One of the perils of the synthetic lease is the possibility that the lease will be recharacterized as a financing transaction (mortgage). What are some of the risks to the "lessor" in the event of such a recharacterization? See Murray, Off-Balance-Sheet Financing: Synthetic Leases, 32 Real Prop., Prob. & Tr. J. 193, 217-224 (Summer 1997).

2. Bond Financing

The tax-exempt mortgage is essentially an industrial development bond (IDB) structured as a tripartite mortgage loan. An IDB is a debt obligation issued in the name of a state or local government to finance the acquisition, construction, or rehabilitation of property to be leased or sold to a private developer. Generally, the mortgage loan is made to a state or municipal issuer that places its bond with the lender and simultaneously engages in either a net lease (with an option to purchase) or an installment sale of the mortgaged real estate with the developer. The payments required under the lease or sale contract (as the case may be) are usually an amount sufficient to cover interest and amortization of the bonds. In reality, as diagrammed below, the developer is the real obligor on the loan; when the transaction is finalized, the mortgage lender has a first lien on the property and receives its debt-service payments directly from the developer under the lease or contract that is assigned to the lender as additional collateral for the loan.

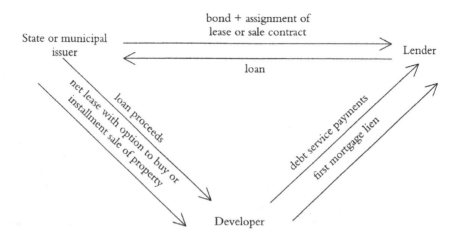

The purpose of the governmental issuer's role as a conduit is to qualify the mortgage interest for tax-free treatment. Generally, interest paid on state and local obligations is exempt from federal income taxes pursuant to I.R.C. §103(a). In a 1988 decision, the Supreme Court ruled that the federal government does have the constitutional right to tax interest on state and municipal bonds.[8] However, to date there has been no impact on the marketing of tax-free bonds, and Congress has not evinced any intent to repeal I.R.C. §103. When interest is tax-exempt, the lender frequently will reduce the interest rate below the market rate for conventional loans.[9] The resultant reduction in debt-service requirements is passed on to the developer in the guise of lower rental or installment payments, hence lower financing costs. Moreover, external constraints on the loan-to-value ratios of mortgage loans made by federally chartered commercial banks, a major source of tax-exempt financing, were removed by the Garn-St. Germain Depository Institutions Act of 1982. 12 U.S.C. §371(c), as amended by Pub. L. No. 97-320, §403 (1982). In addition, internal constraints on loan-to-value ratios may be less stringent. Postconstruction lenders traditionally use the "income approach" in valuating real estate for the purpose of complying with self-imposed constraints on their maximum loan-to-value ratios. The income approach involves capitalizing the projected earnings from the secured real estate. See discussion at Chapter 4D1, note 3. Since the capitalization rate is theoretically related in part to the interest rate on the loan, the lower rate of interest enables the lender to use a lower capitalization rate. Consequently, the loan amount for a tax-exempt mortgage is frequently larger than it is for an ordinary mortgage loan.

8. The benchmark ruling upheld denial of the federal tax exemption for interest on coupon bonds with maturities of one year or more under the Tax Equity and Fiscal Responsibility Act of 1982. In so ruling, the Court rejected arguments that states and municipalities have the constitutional right to issue tax-free bonds under the Tenth Amendment and the so-called doctrine of intergovernmental tax immunity. South Carolina v. Baker, 485 U.S. 505 (1988).

9. Throughout their 60-year history IDBs have averaged 3.5 percent lower interest rates than conventional bank loans. In 2011 the average IDB blended rate was 2.75 percent as compared to an average rate of 5.50 percent for bank financing. See www.IDBFinancing.com.

In addition to reduced financing costs and greater leverage, the tax-exempt bond offers other significant economic advantages for the developer. First, for tax and accounting purposes, under either the net lease or installment sale arrangement the developer's expenditure of capital to acquire or construct the property entitles it to a reasonable allowance for depreciation under I.R.C. §167. Second, tax-exempt IDBs are generally exempt from registration under the Securities Act of 1933 (described at Chapter 15B), while corporate bonds generally are not. Therefore, if the developer were to finance the project by issuing its own bonds, it would have to go through the expensive and time-consuming registration process. Finally, the developer may be relieved of paying state and local property taxes inasmuch as legal title to the property is held by the tax-exempt governmental issuer until the installment sale is consummated or the option to purchase is exercised. Many states, however, require the developer to make additional property tax payments in an amount equal to what the tax liability would be if the project were taxable.[10]

The types of projects that qualify for tax-exempt bond financing vary from state to state depending on how broadly the definition of "industrial development facility" is construed in a particular state's enabling statute. While some states permit financing of commercial facilities such as shopping centers (see, for example, N.Y. Gen. Mun. Law §§854(4), 858, 864), others confine tax-exempt financing to manufacturing and industrial facilities. To comply with state constitutional requirements, these enabling statutes explicitly or impliedly require that the project serve some (albeit remote) public purpose, and some states (such as Virginia) provide for a litigation mechanism (called a validation suit) to determine whether an intended bond issuance will comply with the statute.[11]

In response to a spate of adverse publicity caused by the abusive use of tax-exempt bond financing to fund projects that were either economically unviable or, as in the case of fast-food franchises and discount stores, beyond the congressional intent for the program, since 1982 Congress has progressively curtailed the use of such financing for private development so that, under current law, tax-exempt financing remains a viable financing alternative only for private developers of low- and moderate-income multifamily housing and certain quasi-public facilities such as airports, docks and wharves, and waste treatment and disposal facilities. Briefly, the Tax Equity and Fiscal Responsibility Act of 1982[12] imposed more stringent rules with respect to "private-purpose" IDBs, such as the reduction of depreciation benefits and the imposition of additional reporting and local law approval requirements; it also tightened the definitional and duration requirements for IDBs used to finance projects for low- and moderate-income families. Next, the Tax Reform Act of 1984 imposed additional restrictions including a prohibition against the use of tax-exempt financing to fund the acquisition of raw land, certain luxury items, or existing facilities; and

10. See Mumford, The Past, Present and Future of Industrial Development Bonds, 2 Urb. Law. 147 (1969).

11. Va. Code Ann. §§15.2-2650-2658.

12. Pub. L. No. 97-34, 96 Stat. 324.

an annual ceiling on the amount of "private activity" bonds that each state could issue.

To make IDB financing even more restrictive, the Tax Reform Act of 1986 repealed the use of such financing for "private activities" unless (1) the amount of the issue fits within new state volume limitations (I.R.C. §146); (2) with few exceptions, the average maturity of the private activity bond does not exceed 120 percent of the average reasonably anticipated economic life of the financed facilities (I.R.C. §147(b)); and (3) the IDB qualifies as an exempt facility bond, or as a qualified mortgage bond. Other qualified private activity bonds include a qualified veteran's mortgage bond, a qualified small issue bond to fund manufacturing facilities, a qualified student loan bond, a qualified redevelopment bond, and a qualified bond issued on behalf of a tax-exempt organization such as a private university or nonprofit hospital (I.R.C. §141(e). The amount of a private issue bond must not exceed the lesser of 5 percent of the bond proceeds or $5 million, whichever is less (I.R.C. §141 (c)). However, in the opinion of experts such as IDB Financing, the feasible size of stand-alone projects should be least $3 million or $1 million in the case of issues that are combined with larger offerings.

Of the foregoing categories, the exempt facility bond is the most significant for private real estate developers, who may still be eligible for tax-exempt financing provided that at least 95 percent of the net bond proceeds are used for the development of the quasi-public facilities described in Table 7-1. I.R.C. §142. However, in the case of multifamily residential projects for low- and moderate-income families, any private developer must satisfy one of the following occupancy requirements (on a continuous annual basis): (1) 20 percent of the residential units must be occupied by tenants having incomes of 50 percent or less of the median income for the area (low-income tenants); or (2) 40 percent of the residential units must be occupied by tenants having incomes of 60 percent or less of the median income for the area (moderate-income tenants). I.R.C. §142(d).

Table 7-1

Privately Developed Facilities That Qualify for Tax-Exempt Bond Financing

Hazardous waste-treatment facilities

High-speed intercity rail facilities

Airports, docks and wharves

Mass commuting facilities

Qualified multifamily residential rental property

Sewage and solid waste disposal facilities

Qualified public educational facilities

Facilities for the furnishing of water (including irrigation)

Facilities for the local furnishing of electric energy or gas

Local district heating and cooling facilities

Environmental enhancements of hydroelectric generating facilities

Qualified green building and sustainable design projects

Qualified highway or surface freight transfer facilities

Another type of tax-exempt bond financing that qualifies as a private activity bond is the mortgage bond, or so-called mortgage revenue bond, issued by a state or municipality, the proceeds of which are used to make below-market loans to middle- and low-income first-time home buyers (including co-op purchasers). (I.R.C. §141(e)(1)(B)). To qualify for such below market interest rate loans the mortgaged property must be a 1-3 family home which is the principal residence of the taxpayer-mortgagor. The purchase price of the property may not exceed 90 percent of the average purchase price of sales of comparable properties in the area during the previous 12 months (or 110 percent in blighted ("targeted") neighborhoods), and the family income may not exceed 115 percent of the median family for the area. (I.R.C. §§141(e), 143(f)).

Notwithstanding the low and middle income requirements for qualified multifamily property and mortgage revenue bonds, the curtailment of other tax benefits for low-income housing by the Tax Reform Act of 1986 makes it unlikely that the low-income housing market will rebound from its current slump in the near future unless direct governmental subsidies are increased to compensate developers for their loss of rental and tax benefits. Unfortunately, low-income housing is the one sector of the real estate market most in need of venture capital and yet it was more adversely affected by the Tax Reform Act of 1986 than any other.

NOTES AND QUESTIONS

Additional Reading. Bailkin and Merlino, Private Initiatives on Industrial Revenue Bonds, 3 Real Est. Fin. J. 9 (Fall 1987); Bates, Changes Made in Tax-Exempt Bond Area by 1986 Act Usher in New Era in Public Finance, 66 J. Tax'n. 72 (Feb. 1987); Joslin, Haynes, and Diskin, Multifamily Housing Bonds: A Primer, 18 Real Est. Rev. 57 (Summer 1988); Sullivan, Financing Multi-Family Housing with Tax-Exempt Revenue Bonds: The New Rules, 4 Real Est. Fin. J. 30 (Spring 1987).

> ➤ *Problem 7-2*
> Assume under the master hypothetical that Dan Developer wants to construct an office building and expects to have a few major leases with prime tenants executed in the next month or so. The construction cost of the building will be approximately $25 million and, based on a capitalization of estimated rents, the market value of the building should

equal its cost. The underlying land is owned by Francine Farmer, who is willing to sell her fee interest for $8 million in cash, or for $8,600,000 if Dan wants to separately finance the land by means of a high-ratio (90 percent) subordinated purchase money mortgage. Dan has learned that Ace Insurance Company is willing to make a fee postconstruction loan at a 75 percent loan-to-value ratio for a self-amortizing term of 15 years. Dan also has determined that construction financing will be available from Fuller National Bank, provided that Dan is able to obtain a takeout commitment from Ace.

Dan comes to your law office and tells you that he is having trouble raising venture capital. He wants to know which of the following financing techniques is best suited to provide the most financial leverage and thus reduce his initial cash outlay as much as possible. Briefly explain, and make assumptions where necessary.

a. a fee mortgage from Ace covering the land and building;
b. high-credit lease or synthetic lease financing;
c. tax-exempt bond financing; or
d. a subordinated purchase money mortgage on the land from Francine followed by a fee mortgage from Ace covering the land and building. ◄

Chapter 8

Defaults, Workouts, and Foreclosure

As long as the real estate project remains economically viable and the borrower remains solvent, the transactional rights and responsibilities of the borrower and lender are governed primarily by the negotiated terms and conditions of the postconstruction loan commitment as implemented by the language in the note and mortgage (or deed of trust). While the regulatory impact of public law has eroded the freedom of contract principle somewhat, the law of the written word remains a dominant theme in commercial real estate financing. Perhaps the notion is that extrinsic judge-made and statutory law should not be paternalistic because, in most cases, the parties will be sophisticated, ably represented by counsel, and in a position to defend themselves at the bargaining table.

However, if Dan Developer becomes insolvent or if the project goes "belly up," then the focal point of the documentation and the attitude of legal authorities are likely to change. While the principal grounds for borrower default are negotiated beforehand in the postconstruction loan commitment letter, it is the note, mortgage, and assignment-of-lease instruments that become the operative documents in the event of a default by the borrower inasmuch as they identify the grounds for default and spell out both the consequences of default to the borrower and the remedies available to the aggrieved lender as mortgagee. At this juncture, if the lender were to institute a foreclosure action or the borrower were to invoke the protection of bankruptcy law, public law may intervene and supersede the language in the mortgage and other loan documents if necessary to protect the financially distressed borrower (as mortgagor) and resolve the competing claims against the real estate and the other depleted assets of the borrower. The impact of bankruptcy on real estate transactions is examined in Chapter 18. In these distressed circumstances, the private bargain between the borrower and lender becomes less relevant and the postdefault rights and responsibilities of the parties are likely to be governed by extrinsic law based on public policy considerations.

A. WORKING OUT DEFAULTS BY AGREEMENT

As one observer explained, a real estate project usually becomes distressed because "[i]t is a bad piece of property, it has a bad developer, or it is simply a victim of current market forces."[1] In the master hypothetical, if Dan Developer should default because of one or more of these circumstances, the worst-case scenario for the construction lender, Fuller National Bank (FNB), or the postconstruction lender, Ace Insurance Company, would be having to institute foreclosure proceedings. Even though Dan agreed to be personally liable for repayment of the construction loan, chances are he is insolvent and his assets have been depleted. In the real world, deficiency judgments against distressed borrowers are virtually worthless. Indeed, according to a comprehensive (albeit dated) study, lenders recover only a small dollar-amount of deficiency judgments against defaulting borrowers.[2] The foreclosure proceeding holds its own perils— legal expenses, time-consuming delays, and attendant publicity. In the overwhelming majority of foreclosure sales, the only bidder is the foreclosing mortgagee. Moreover, even if outside bidders are present at Dan's foreclosure sale, the construction lender, FNB, knows that a half-completed office building or other project will not bring much at foreclosure, and unless FNB is able to complete the project itself and assign its loan to Ace pursuant to a buy-sell agreement,[3] FNB will probably not recoup its loan.

Likewise, if Dan should default after the project is completed and the post-construction loan is closed, the postconstruction lender, Ace, would be reluctant to foreclose for these same reasons. In addition, because Ace's loan is nonrecourse (which is often the case for postconstruction financing),[4] Ace can seek recovery only against the property.

Therefore, in most cases, the lender and the borrower will strive to improve the economic viability of the project and to restructure the loan transaction by means of a workout agreement between the parties that might include (1) short-term loan forbearances or renewals, (2) modification of interest rates, (3) recasting of amortization payments, or (4) infusion of outside venture capital or financing.

Timing is critical in workout arrangements. If the developer-borrower is willing to admit to cash flow or management problems soon after they develop, a workout agreement can often be arranged. However, as the following excerpt points out, not every project can be saved. Still, if the parties are willing to cooperate, the lender can avoid the unappealing foreclosure scenario described above through a negotiated "deed in lieu of foreclosure." See the sample Workout Agreement and the Deed in Lieu of Foreclosure in the Documents Manual.

---

1. McDermott, Workout Specialist Looming Large in '90s, Crain's New York Business, Oct. 22, 1990 (quoting a real estate brokerage executive).
2. See Prather, A Realistic Approach to Foreclosure, 14 Bus. Law. 132 (1958).
3. Buy-sell agreements are discussed at Chapter 4D6.
4. Nonrecourse loans are discussed at Chapters 3B3 and 5A3.

Roberts, Negotiating and Drafting the Workout Agreement
3 Modern Real Estate Transactions 1393 (ALI-ABA 1987)

1. QUESTIONS RAISED BY DEFAULT

Before determining which course to pursue, a lender and its counsel must make appropriate inquiries. What are the net worth and liquidity of the borrower and any guarantors? Can they be expected to economically sustain the project if they retain ownership? Is the value of the mortgaged property sufficient to justify an increased loan or, if a deed in lieu of foreclosure is considered, a reduction or release of liability? Is the property one the lender willingly would own and can easily resell? Are leasing, income, and operating expense information available? What is the physical condition of the building? Is it a conforming use, and was a certificate of occupancy validly issued?

A construction lender must determine the percentage of completion of work, what contractors and suppliers remain unpaid, the quality of work to date and its conformance with plans and specifications and with the requirements of the long-term or end [postconstruction] loan lender. Most important, it must determine the need for remedial work and the estimated cost to complete the project.

Further questions must be asked. Can the borrower do a better job than the lender in completing, marketing, or managing the property? Does the borrower have any special benefits, such as a franchise agreement, spot zoning, development rights, or permits that are not readily transferable to the lender? Is the borrower uniquely equipped to deal with a sensitive local problem? What might be the impact of a foreclosure on a marketing program for a property such as a condominium or a land sales project? What federal or state regulatory problems might foreclosure of the property entail? In the event of a litigated foreclosure, what defenses, colorable or otherwise, might the borrower raise? How long might resolution of such issues take? How expensive might foreclosure be in terms of project deterioration, legal costs, and lost opportunity cost for invested funds?

What rights of third parties need be considered? Are there subordinate liens which eventually must be foreclosed? Will necessary consents to a negotiated workout be forthcoming from guarantors, bonding companies, or franchisors? How substantial are the borrower's debts to others? How hard are such creditors pressing? Is an insolvency proceeding imminent?

If the lender plans to take title and invest additional funds, will those funds be at risk if creditors attack the transfer as voidable under state or federal insolvency laws? Would the lender be safer waiting to negotiate a private sale with the court after the borrower has filed in bankruptcy? Does the lender have other investments with the borrower? Will the commencement of a foreclosure on this property trigger a bankruptcy?

Defaults can take various forms. The most frequent is failure to pay debt service when due. Whatever the nature of a default, and however communicated or ascertained, counsel should advise against sending any notice of default until the situation has been properly evaluated. In order to enhance the prospects for a successful workout, it is desirable to preserve the trust of the borrower. . . .

2.   A RESTRUCTURING WORKOUT

Where a default is to be worked out by restructuring, it is probable that the lender is satisfied with the borrower's honesty and competence as well as the economic bona fides of the project and that other creditors have agreed to cooperate. Also, possibly, the lender may not wish to own or operate the type of property involved, or the borrower may have some colorable or better defense to enforcement of the loan.

For a lender, the objectives in documenting a restructured loan depend upon the seriousness of the default, whether lender or borrower is providing additional funds, whether the borrower is remaining fully liable, whether additional security will be provided, and whether there is a reasonable expectation of consummating a successful workout.

It is a cardinal rule that any loan modification agreement, even a letter agreement effecting a minor change to a loan which is in good standing, contain an estoppel clause, to the effect that the borrower has no claim, offset or defense against the lender or with respect to the collateral. Such a provision should be included in all workout agreements. It is desirable for a workout agreement to contain an acknowledgment by the borrower that a default has occurred, and that in consideration of entering into the new agreement such default is being waived. This will provide an appropriate perspective from which a court later may determine the rights and obligations of the parties under the restructured loan arrangement. . . .

Where, based upon receiving additional collateral, a loan will be increased to provide operating capital for a period which the parties deem sufficient to market or otherwise successfully deal with the property, such collateral will be contemporaneously received only for the increased loan amount and will be subject to attack [in bankruptcy proceedings under §547 of the Bankruptcy Code] as a preference insofar as it may provide additional security for the original loan amount. It is desirable, therefore, for the operating capital to be sufficient to assure continued operations for at least the ninety-day preference period (assuming the lender is not an insider), after which the new collateral should effectively secure the entire loan. A non-bankruptcy pitfall to avoid when making operating capital available to a distressed borrower is to be sure either that such funds will not be used for payroll, or, if they are, that federal withholding taxes are paid. In most situations, the only safe way to assure this is to have the lender make the tax payments. Failure to withhold payroll taxes may subject the lender to liability to the IRS, irrespective of any claim which the lender may have against the borrower.[12] . . .

In situations where the lender recognizes that the default is a product of the economy, the market, or other factors which the borrower cannot control, a loan workout may be negotiated providing for debt service to be paid only with available cash flow from operation of the property. Such "cash flow" workouts involve negotiation of a number of issues and terms which can materially affect the manner in which the property is operated and net operating funds calculated.

Forbearance agreements normally waive defaults with respect to past events, and they permit acceleration of maturity only if additional, defined defaults arise. Where appropriate, the lender may request that the waiver of prior defaults be conditioned upon no further default occurring, upon which the rights of the parties again may be governed by the original documents. When a new partner is investing with the initial borrower based upon an expectation of a minimum guaranteed period in which to operate the property and receive tax benefits, the new partner will negotiate to eliminate any future uncontrolled event of default which might shorten the agreed forbearance period. If the new partner is providing funds which will make the project viable, such investor will bargain more effectively than the borrower, and the lender will be more receptive to minimizing possible future events of default. Negotiations to obtain additional investment by a new party should be conducted by the borrower, rather than the lender, and the documents should state that the lender has made no representation or commitment with respect to the project not expressly set forth in the agreement.

Where debt is totally or partially nonrecourse, and the borrower will continue to operate the property and handle funds, the definition of nonrecourse in the original loan documents may be modified to permit the lender to sue the borrower . . . for a personal judgment in the event funds are misappropriated or certain other covenants of the loan agreement are not performed. If the original documents did not so provide, the workout agreement or collateral documents should subordinate repayment by the borrower of debt to any project-related party.

Where the lender is accepting a cash-flow debt service or below market rate of interest to accommodate a workout, it may bargain for the right to share in future benefits from the operation, refinancing or sale of the property. The manner in which such interest is to be received, and decisions with respect to operation, refinancing or sale of the property require careful consideration. Among other things, the lender must protect against any right to prepay the loan after the project has been turned around but before such benefits have been realized. Rights to participate in profits erode a pure borrower-lender relationship and may complicate enforcement of the workout agreement, should this later become necessary.

12. 26 U.S.C.A. §3505 (1982); Fidelity Bank, N.A. v. United States, 616 F.2d 1181 (10th Cir. 1980).

Projects which are benefitted by state or federal housing programs or by nonassignable tax benefits entail additional workout problems. It could be highly detrimental to a project were a rent or mortgage supplement to be lost because of a foreclosure or other change in ownership. Certain federal and state agencies are sympathetic to these problems, but it is necessary to reach agreement with them before the workout can be structured.

In situations where there are other participating lenders, there may be need to review and modify the participation agreement in areas such as control of the investment after default, waiver of claims by participants, sharing of setoffs, sharing of costs of enforcement, selection of counsel, and possibly perfection of participants' interests in the loan or the underlying mortgage investment.

The workout agreement will contain provisions with respect to conditions to closing, representations and warranties, title insurance, perhaps cross-default or cross-collateralization with other outstanding credits, covenants respecting management, sales, financial statements, leasing, payment of expenses, and waiver of any alleged defenses. Representations with respect to the net worth, liquidity, and ultimate solvency of non-lending parties to a workout, coupled with accountants' financial statements and legal opinions, where available, add important layers of protection. Appraisals substantiating values of assets are desirable. Closing of the restructuring workout agreement should include title insurance for any new security instrument, or at least a continuation search, including tax lien, bankruptcy, and judgment dockets; opinion of borrower's counsel; and estoppel statements from available third parties.

3.   A DEED-IN-LIEU WORKOUT

When the holder of a defaulted mortgage is not comfortable with prospects for repayment if the property is left under continued ownership by the borrower, the relevant issue becomes whether an adversarial foreclosure proceeding must ensue or whether a friendly course can be followed.

A.   BENEFITS

Several benefits may be realized through utilization of a negotiated deed in lieu of foreclosure. Perhaps the most attractive one for a lender is speed in gaining control and use of the property. If necessary, a deed could be prepared and recorded in a day, while a litigated foreclosure may take more than a year and possibly face outstanding redemption rights thereafter. Foreclosure of a mortgage has adverse connotations for the property and the borrower, but a deed in lieu is merely a conveyance, and the property transfer can be characterized positively. Title may be taken in a designee of the lender, so that the public may assume the borrower merely sold the property. After the transfer, the borrower may continue in a management or consulting capacity for a period of time. The problem of creating an adverse image for the project and the borrower can thus be minimized. The borrower should prefer a private relinquishment of its interest in the property.

Of equal importance, the borrower and staff will cooperate and assist the new owner in taking over. They will aid in the delivery of leases, elevator wiring diagrams, utility deposits, payroll and employee benefit information, and data necessary to pursue real estate tax reduction proceedings based on prior years' operating expenses and tax payments.

There are advantages to a deed in lieu of foreclosure should the borrower subsequently file in bankruptcy. Once title and possession have passed to the lender, the property no longer is subject to automatic bankruptcy court jurisdiction or to a stay of foreclosure. Although a deed in lieu of foreclosure conveys title subject to mechanics' liens and other encumbrances, in many jurisdictions the deed may provide for non-merger, and the mortgage thus may be preserved as a means of dealing with subordinate interests.

B. NEGOTIATIONS

Once it makes the decision to take title through a deed in lieu of foreclosure, the lender must negotiate the terms of the transfer with the borrower, who may wish to bargain for certain benefits. A borrower usually seeks a reduction of or release from liability. In order to preserve reputation in the industry, the borrower may ask the lender to assume all or a portion of the trade payables [for example, past due utilities and property maintenance services]. In seeking personal consideration, the borrower may bargain for a residual interest in the property or a right of first refusal to purchase the property at a later date. Not infrequently, a borrower will disagree with a lender's conclusion that a change in ownership and management is necessary. Although acknowledging default under the loan, the borrower may be seeking time in which to sell or refinance the property or to bring in a new money partner. Consequently, the borrower may offer a deed to be held in escrow for a period of time in order to induce the lender to forebear.

Apart from the usual give and take of negotiations, a number of potentially serious legal problems are inherent in such requests. These problems lie in the areas of title and insolvency.

C. TITLE PROBLEMS

The borrower's offer of a deed held in escrow for a period of time while working things out may confer no benefit on the lender, at least in jurisdictions where the doctrine of clogging the equity of redemption holds sway. The procedural and substantive protections of foreclosure proceedings which evolved during the Year-book era in England's Court of Chancery to protect a borrower's equity may not easily be contracted away. The deed offered to the lender in escrow may be deemed no more than an equitable mortgage, which the lender already holds, and the period in which such deed may be challenged as an avoidable preference will not commence until it is recorded.

Granting the borrower a residual interest in the property, in whatever form, may in time subject the lender to claims by the borrower that the property was not properly managed, leased, or sold, or that construction was performed improperly or too expensively, and such an interest may adversely affect the lender's title. One company refused to insure title on resale by the lender of property on which the original borrower (which had given the lender a deed in lieu) had been granted an option to repurchase which long since had lapsed. The title company considered the option to be a mortgage and required that a quitclaim deed be obtained from the original borrower. This was done, but at a price.

Release of the borrower from liability on the original note may constitute a satisfaction of the mortgage debt and thus an extinguishment of the mortgage. A lender wishing to keep the mortgage alive in order to maintain priority over subordinate encumbrances should not permit that to happen. A covenant not to sue the borrower for a deficiency judgment is a substitute that preserves the mortgage. Mere release of liability or satisfaction of antecedent debt may not, in certain jurisdictions, constitute "valuable consideration." Consequently, a lender which records its deed in lieu may not receive the benefits of recording acts, and the deed to the lender may be subordinate to prior unrecorded interests.

D. INSOLVENCY PROBLEMS

Significant obstacles to a lender accepting a deed in lieu of foreclosure may arise under federal and state insolvency laws. Although granting the borrower a residual interest in the property may facilitate negotiations for a deed in lieu of foreclosure, such interest may, in the event of an ensuing bankruptcy, subject the property to bankruptcy court jurisdiction. If a deed in lieu can be successfully attacked as preferential or as a fraudulent conveyance, and voided, the benefits for which the lender has bargained may be lost. Meanwhile, if the lender has released the borrower from liability for a deficiency judgment, it has relinquished a consideration that it might have been able to use at a later date to persuade the bankruptcy court to grant leave to foreclose. . . .

Depending upon the circumstances and upon whether a deed in lieu of foreclosure is attacked as a preference or as a fraudulent conveyance, a lender may be reduced to a claim as an unsecured creditor when it attempts to recover any new consideration given for the deed. It may even lose its original secured interest in the property, particularly if it is found not to have acted in good faith. The problems that may arise if the transfer effected by a deed in lieu is subsequently voided are particularly troublesome if the property is in the course of construction, which the lender must complete. . . .

E. THE "FRIENDLY FORECLOSURE"

A far less desirable alternative that is used with some frequency is the so-called friendly foreclosure. In return for the same types of consideration that may be given to induce a borrower to grant a deed in lieu, cooperation is obtained in not resisting foreclosure. This technique has advantages when mechanics' liens exist and foreclosure is necessary to extinguish them. However, while there is no case that has so ruled, the risk exists that a negotiated and compensated agreement not to resist a foreclosure, together with the transfer of title resulting therefrom, may be deemed a voidable transfer under the Bankruptcy Code or state law. . . .

F. RECOMMENDED STRUCTURE

[In structuring a deed in lieu of foreclosure,] [t]here are several advantages to having the borrower convey title to the lender's subsidiary rather than directly to the lender. Lenders may be able to originate or hold mortgage loans outside their home states without being required to qualify to do business locally, but an entity which owns property, particularly one that may have to undertake active development, may find it necessary to qualify and be subject to taxation, service of process, and other local burdens. Use of a subsidiary or designee entity that is locally qualified relieves the lender of these requirements. The use of a separate corporation also can insulate the lender from the liabilities of ownership. An owner whose name does not contain the word "bank" is better able to avoid the deep pocket problems of effectively negotiating terms with contractors.

The requirement of fairness of consideration given for a deed in lieu of foreclosure presents the transferee with several problems. The contract or memorandum of sale should recite, as appropriate, that the mortgage loan is in default, that the borrower has been unable to sell or refinance the property, and, accordingly, does not consider the value of the property to exceed the amount of the mortgage. It is desirable to have a current appraisal of the property showing the consideration given to be adequate. The contract also may recite the fact that taxes are unpaid and trade payables are due. In the case of a construction mortgage loan, the contract may include recitals about the uncertain cost of completion. However, while the contract description of the distress nature of the property should support the adequacy of the consideration given, it must stop short of an admission of insolvency, which could facilitate a subsequent bankruptcy avoidance attack on the transfer.

If it is the case, the memorandum or contract should contain a representation that the borrower is solvent, and the lender should attempt to obtain a recent confirming financial statement.

In any deed in lieu of foreclosure, it is prudent to pay some cash consideration to the borrower, at least the amount of title, recording, and transfer charges that the lender may in any event be required to fund. This not only strengthens the lender's position if a subsequent insolvency proceeding is instituted, but also assures valuable consideration for the purpose of qualifying for the benefits of various recording statutes. If the lender contemplates further improvement of the property, such as the completion of construction, the lender should consider assuming all or certain of the obligations of the borrower to pay for such work, so that funds expended by the lender may be deemed part of the consideration paid to the borrower for the transfer. In the event of a subsequent attack on the transfer under insolvency laws, the lender can then argue that the cost of such improvements was fresh consideration.

The lender has several approaches available to protect itself against the possibility of having to claim as an unsecured creditor for the consideration it gives to obtain a deed in lieu of foreclosure, in the event the transaction is voided.

It may have all or part of the consideration held in escrow for at least a year, to be made available to the borrower if title is not challenged. The agreement not to sue the borrower on the debt may be conditioned upon no party successfully challenging the title received by the deed in lieu. The lender may give as partial consideration a purchase-money note to be paid on a deferred and subordinate basis out of the profits of the property, after the lender has received repayment of its investment, capital improvements, interest, and fees. This note also may be held in escrow. An agreement may specify that upon disposition of the property by the lender, any proceeds in excess of the lender's investment are to be used first to pay any then remaining unpaid creditors of the borrower. Such a note should contain strong language that it is solely an unsecured debt obligation; gives the lender or its subsidiary no obligation to develop or market the property; and expires under stated conditions, such as disposition of the property at a loss. Although it may create other problems, such a note may be an effective deterrent to an attack upon the transfer by creditors, and it should be considered in sensitive situations. . . .

NOTES AND QUESTIONS

1. *Risk of Default.* According to conventional wisdom, construction loans are riskier than postconstruction loans and defaults are more likely to occur during the construction period. Many unique risks and problems may occur during the construction period, such as cost overruns, work stoppages, abandonment of the job, insolvency on the part of the general contractor or a major subcontractor, and mechanics' and materialmen's liens (as explained at Chapter 6B). These factors make defaults more probable for construction loans and, because of the number of parties involved in the event of a default, these multifarious problems are difficult to resolve by voluntary agreement. However, notwithstanding these risks, construction loan defaults frequently result from the lender's failure to monitor properly the periodic loan disbursement or the amount of equity capital on hand to keep the loan amount "in balance" with the projected costs of the

project in accordance with the protective terms and conditions of the building loan agreement. What safeguards can the construction lender employ to ameliorate the above-mentioned risks? See Chapter 6B. Does a buy-sell agreement with the postconstruction lender protect the construction lender in the event of a default during the construction period? See Chapter 4D6. In what respect does the "assignment" provision in the postconstruction commitment provide protection for the construction lender in the event of a default by the borrower? See Chapter 4D3. See generally Roberts, Workouts of Construction Mortgage Loans, in 3 Modern Real Estate Transactions 1373 (ALI-ABA 1987).

The conventional wisdom regarding the lesser risk of default under postconstruction loans must be reconsidered in light of practices that helped induce the late 1980s shakeout in the real estate industry. For example, in the 1980s, preleasing requirements in postconstruction commitment letters were not as rigorous as they once had been; to accommodate developers "building on spec," lenders frequently agreed to take out (pay off) the construction loan once the building was completed even in the absence of a rental income stream sufficient to cover the projected debt service payments. In addition to imposing a stringent preleasing requirement, can you think of any other protective devices a postconstruction lender might employ to ameliorate the risk of a default during the postconstruction period?

2. Personal Dynamics and the Impetus for Workouts. Assume that Charles Credulous, a young "fast track" business school graduate, was Ace's loan officer on its loan to Dan Developer. Dan was the first major developer Charles had negotiated with one-on-one, and this was Charles's first big deal. He wanted the negotiations to be successful, and they were. When he presented the transaction to Ace's Real Estate Investment Committee, Charles had some doubts about whether the tenants Dan said were interested would actually sign leases, yet he assured the committee of the economic soundness of the project. (Many institutions appoint a group of experienced real estate investment officers to a committee formed to review and approve or disapprove all proposed investments, each such officer acting as a devil's advocate, poking holes in and making the loan officer defend the transaction.)

Now Dan is in default and comes to see Charles, bringing with him a real estate lawyer and, for emphasis, a bankruptcy lawyer. Thinking that Dan must be right that this is a temporary difficulty that will turn around if Dan has more time, Charles approves a forbearance agreement on behalf of Ace. Charles begins to consult with Dan on how the project should be run. He even gets Ace to pay for some project repairs and improvements. What problems do you see developing for Ace? What arguments do you think Dan might make if Ace finally decides the situation is hopeless and commences foreclosure? More generally, would you recommend any restructuring of Ace's handling of troubled properties?

3. Modification of Senior Lien. Workout agreements typically modify such terms of the mortgage loan as the interest rate, maturity date, and other provisions. Suppose that the mortgaged property also is encumbered by a junior lien, such as a junior mortgage. Does the senior lender's modification jeopardize its senior lien priority status? Is any loss of priority partial or complete? The Restatement (Third) of Property (Mortgages) §7.3 (1997) adopts the rule that, notwithstanding a modification, the senior mortgagee will retain its priority against junior interests except to the extent that the modification is "materially prejudicial" to the junior lien. Which varieties of loan modifications cause material prejudice? Extensions of time for repayment of the loan? Reductions in the maturity date? Increases in the interest rate? Increases in the principal balance through forbearance on collecting overdue amounts? Additional loan advances to enhance or protect the property's value? See generally M. Madison, J. Dwyer, and S. Bender, The Law of Real Estate Financing §§12:26-12:31 (2016). Suppose the senior mortgage contains the following provision: "This mortgage shall also secure all extensions, amendments, modifications, or alterations of the secured obligation including amendments, modifications, or alterations that increase the amount of the secured obligation or the interest rate on the secured obligation." Should courts enforce this provision when they would otherwise judicially subordinate all or part of the senior's priority?

4. Deeds in Lieu of Foreclosure. Where a negotiated loan restructuring is not feasible, in the excerpt above, Roberts appears on balance to advocate a negotiated deed in lieu of foreclosure rather than an adversarial foreclosure. See also Roberts, Deeds in Lieu of Foreclosure, 8 Real Est. Rev. 4 (1979). A deed in lieu of foreclosure is a consensual conveyance and therefore subject to the risks inherent in any conveyance, especially one by a grantor in financial difficulties. Assume in the master hypothetical that one year after the Ace mortgage (or deed of trust) is recorded Dan Developer has a cash flow problem. He borrows money from Friendly Bank and gives Friendly a second mortgage on the property. Dan also enters into a lease with Widget Corporation of America at a below-market rental in exchange for up-front payments. Later Dan defaults under the Ace mortgage and offers Ace a deed in lieu of foreclosure. If Ace were to agree, how would Ace's title to the property differ from what Ace would receive as the successful bidder at a foreclosure sale? See Chapter 3E. As attorney for Ace, why would you require a title report before agreeing to a deed in lieu of foreclosure, and title insurance as a condition to accepting the deed?

Roberts points out that deeds in lieu of foreclosure expose the lender to the risk of allegations of fraudulent transfer and unlawful preference. Fraudulent transfers are discussed at Chapter 18D. Fraudulent transfer laws regard as a constructive fraud any transfers, made while the transferor is insolvent, within a specified period before bankruptcy, for a consideration not reasonably equivalent to what the property being transferred is worth. In the case of foreclosure, the price obtained at a noncollusive, regularly conducted foreclosure sale will be deemed to be reasonably equivalent value. See Chapter 18D. In a deed in lieu situation, do you see why this argument might not be available? See Chapter 18D, note 3.

5. *Duty to Negotiate.* In the absence of a statute or express contractual obligation, the courts hold consistently that the mortgagee has no duty sourced in the implied covenant of good faith to undertake workout negotiations with the mortgagor. E.g., Travelers Ins. Co. v. Corporex Properties, Inc., 798 F. Supp. 423 (E.D. Ky. 1992). Many agricultural states, such as Iowa, have laws that authorize or require mediation before foreclosure of farm property. Iowa Code Ann. §654A.6. Prompted by the subprime foreclosure crisis and the rise of dispute resolution alternatives in U.S. law, many states enacted mandatory mediation programs as a condition to residential foreclosure. E.g., N.Y. Civ. Prac. Law Rule 3408 (mandates judicial settlement conference in residential foreclosure actions in which the mortgagor and mortgagee must negotiate in good faith toward "a mutually agreeable resolution, including a loan modification, if possible"); IndyMac Bank, F.S.B. v. Yano-Horoski, 26 Misc. 3d 717, 890 N.Y.S.2d 313 (Sup. Ct. 2009) (cancelling entire principal balance owed by borrower as sanction for mortgagee failing to negotiate in good faith), reversed, 78 A.D.3d 895, 912 N.Y.S.2d 239 (Sup. Ct. App. Div. 2010) (holding severe sanction of cancelling mortgage note not authorized by statute or consistent with equitable powers of court in foreclosure proceedings).

6. *Forgiveness of Debt: Tax Consequences.* Depending on the nature of the workout, significant tax consequences may be implicated. For example, if the parties agree to a workout under which any principal loan indebtedness is forgiven, the debt forgiven is taxable as debt cancellation income. Its recognition, however, might be deferred under the Revenue Reconciliation Act of 1993 to a specified extent in the case of certain debtors with qualified real estate business indebtedness. See generally Hirschfeld, Antacid for the Real Estate Industry: Newly Enacted Debt Discharge Relief, 79 J. Tax'n 268 (1993). In contrast, deeds in lieu of foreclosure (and foreclosure sales) are treated for federal income tax purposes as sales of the property. In a nonrecourse loan, the excess of the debt over the taxpayer's basis in the property is treated as taxable gain, as if the debtor sold the property for the amount of the discharged loan. In recourse loans, the taxpayer realizes gain to the extent of the difference between the fair market value of the property conveyed by deed in lieu and the debtor's lesser basis in that property. The difference, if any, between the amount of the debt discharged and the lesser value of the property is treated as cancellation of indebtedness income. See generally Frankel, Real Estate Workouts—A Step-by-Step Analysis, CA04 ALI-ABA 709, 754-760 (ALI-ABA 1995). Against the backdrop of the subprime mortgage crisis, Congress enacted temporary relief (effective through 2016) from taxation for home owners able to negotiate a reduction of the mortgage indebtedness on their principal residence.

Known as short sales, many lenders during this crisis agreed to release their mortgage liens to allow sales by the borrower of an "underwater" residence for less than the mortgage loan balance. Protecting the expectations of borrowers who may fail to realize that a short sale agreement does not necessarily erase their personal liability under the mortgage note for the shortfall, the California legislature outlawed such deficiency liability following a residential short sale. Cal. Civ. Proc. Code §580(e).

7. Additional Reading. The ACREL Papers: Real Estate Loan Workouts (1991); A. Kuklin and P. Roberts, eds., Real Estate Bankruptcies and Workouts, ABA Sec. of Real Prop., Prob. & Tr. L. (1983); Zinman, Chairman, Boom, Bust and Bankruptcy: Financing, Unfinancing and Refinancing of Troubled Real Estate, ABA Sec. of Real Prop., Prob. & Tr. L. (1987). Articles include Black, Working on Loan Workouts, 6 Prac. Real Est. Law. 55 (July 1990); Boneparth, Taking a Deed in Lieu of Foreclosure: Pitfalls for the Lender, 19 Real Est. L.J. 338 (1991); Jacobson, Drafting a Deed in Lieu of Foreclosure Agreement, 10 Prac. Real Est. Law. 37 (Sept. 1994); Madison, Use of Deeds in Lieu of Foreclosure in Defaults and Workouts, 20 Real Est. L.J. 247 (1992); Murray, Deeds in Lieu of Foreclosure: Practical and Legal Considerations, 26 Real Prop., Prob. & Tr. J. 459 (1991); Paris and Williams, What Lender's Counsel Should Know About Deeds in Lieu of Foreclosure, 6 Prac. Real Est. Law. 57 (Sept. 1990); Stark, Avoiding the Recharacterization of Certain Deed-in-Lieu-of-Foreclosure Transactions: Ensuring That What You Draft Is What You Get, 110 Banking L.J. 330 (1993).

THE ETHICAL REAL ESTATE LAWYER

Dual Representation in Loan Workouts

Dual representation of two clients with opposing interests has been considered previously in the case of buyers and sellers in conveyancing transactions (see Chapter 2A2) and lenders and borrowers in the initial loan transaction (see Chapter 4E1). In a case involving a law firm that represented both the lender and the borrower in a commercial loan restructuring, a Maryland court, after warning in dictum about the ethical and legal pitfalls of joint representation, observed:

We recognize that counsel may have been motivated by the possibility of assuming the role of mediator as much as the maximizing of fees. At no time, however, did counsel act as a mediator, nor could such function be performed by a law firm retained by two adverse parties to a workout arrangement where legal advice was to be rendered to both sides.

See Winmark Limited Partnership v. Miles & Stockbridge, 109 Md. App. 149, 674 A.2d 73 (1996), vacated and remanded on other grounds, 693 A.2d 824 (1997).

B.   RIGHTS AND DUTIES OF THE PARTIES PRIOR TO FORECLOSURE

1.   *The Mortgagee's Right to Accelerate the Indebtedness*

Just about every promissory note will contain a debt-acceleration clause such as the following: "Upon any default the holder of this note, if it so elects, notice of election being expressly waived, may declare that the remaining unpaid indebtedness with accrued interest shall at once become due and payable." Almost invariably, the mortgagee will exercise its right to accelerate the indebtedness as a prelude to foreclosure. What is a commonsense reason for doing so? As the following case illustrates, however, there are equitable limits on the mortgagee's right to accelerate and initiate foreclosure.

Vonk v. Dunn

161 Ariz. 24, 775 P.2d 1088 (1989)

FELDMAN, Vice Chief Justice.

The Vonks brought this action to foreclose a mortgage that the Dunns had given to secure the purchase of land. . . . We granted the Dunns' petition for review to determine whether equitable considerations apply to acceleration clauses and, if so, whether a factual issue concerning unconscionability precluded summary judgment foreclosing the mortgage. . . .

The Dunns bought 160 acres in Cochise County from the Vonks in 1982 for $28,000. The Dunns paid $4,000 down and signed a promissory note for the $24,000 balance, securing the note with a mortgage on the property. The note ran at eight percent per annum and was payable in regular monthly installments on the first of each month. The note contained a ten-day grace period, which ran without notice from the first day of the month. The mortgage also required the Dunns to pay property taxes. The sanction for delinquent mortgage or property tax payments was acceleration and foreclosure at the Vonks' election. Finally, the mortgage required payment of the mortgagee's attorney's fees and costs in any collection proceeding.

For about three years, the Dunns made timely mortgage payments. For the first six months of 1986, however, the Dunns were late. The Vonks wrote the Dunns, putting them on notice that they must make their payments on time. The notice also called on the Dunns to pay delinquent property taxes. The Dunns acknowledged the reinstatement notice, paid the property taxes, and made timely payments for the rest of 1986.

However, the Dunns' bank mistakenly returned the February 1987 payment check marked "Insufficient Funds." The Vonks notified their attorney, who prepared to foreclose. The attorney learned that the Dunns had not paid their November 1986 property taxes. Without contacting the Dunns, the Vonks began foreclosure on February 27, 1987. The complaint alleged default for failure to make the February mortgage payment and the delinquent property taxes. At this point, the Dunns had paid nearly thirty-five percent of the purchase price.

After the Vonks' filed their complaint on February 27, 1987, the Dunns obtained and sent to the Vonks a letter from their bank stating that it had mistakenly dishonored their check. Subsequently, the Vonks offered to dismiss the action if the Dunns brought the payments current and paid attorney's fees and costs incurred to that time: $932.65.

The Dunns rejected this offer, arguing that the Vonks could have avoided the entire matter by contacting the Dunns during the note's ten-day grace period. The Dunns, however, paid the delinquent taxes in March 1987. In addition, during the intervening months the Dunns continued to make regular installment payments on the note, totalling $2,338, which the Vonks accepted. The record does not reveal the Vonks' reason for accepting these payments, but they nevertheless continued with the foreclosure proceeding. The parties did not raise the issue of waiver. Two months later, the trial court granted summary judgment to the Vonks. At the sheriff's sale, the Vonks purchased the property for the amount of their judgment.

On appeal, the Dunns argued the foreclosure was oppressive and unconscionable, relying on Arizona Coffee Shops, Inc. v. Phoenix Downtown Parking Association, 95 Ariz. 98, 387 P.2d 801 (1963) . . . .

A.   THE DUNNS' DELINQUENCY IN TAX PAYMENTS

The note and mortgage allowed the Vonks to accelerate and foreclose for tax delinquency. However, a mortgage foreclosure is an equitable proceeding. If a mortgagee has acted in an "oppressive or unconscionable" manner, the court may relieve the mortgagor of his default. Indeed, as the Dunns argue, equitable considerations specifically apply to acceleration clauses.

Because foreclosure is an equitable proceeding, the plaintiff must do more than merely establish that the defendant has violated the strict terms of the mortgage or note. The plaintiff must additionally show that some "purpose of the [acceleration] clause is . . . being circumvented or that the mortgagee's security is jeopardized." [Baltimore Life Ins. Co. v.] Harn, 15 Ariz. App. [78] at 81, 486 P.2d [190] at 193. . . .

The Dunns owed no more than $66 in property taxes and the arrearage was not of long duration. The county treasurer had not yet issued the "notice of delinquent taxes" required by A.R.S. §42-385, nor did he commence proceedings for sale by issuing a "notice of proposed sale" as A.R.S. §42-387 requires. Thus, the property was not in danger of being lost for tax delinquency. We believe that with equitable considerations in mind, a factfinder could find that the Vonks' invocation of the acceleration clause was unnecessary to protect their security.

Further, the factfinder could have considered whether the breach of the tax obligation was trivial. Considering that the Dunns had already made forty-nine of the sixty note payments, paying nearly 35 percent of the purchase price, the $66 tax delinquency appears insignificant. The factfinder could conclude that given the Dunns' investment, including the $4,000 down payment and their improvements on the property, it was oppressive and unconscionable to accelerate and foreclose for a $66 tax arrearage without giving notice and an opportunity to cure. . . .

We further noted in Arizona Coffee Shops that

> [t]here can be no doubt of the right of a chancellor to deny foreclosure based upon an acceleration where there are substantial equities in the case which render the acceleration unconscionable.

95 Ariz. at 101, 387 P.2d at 803.

We believe a reasonable factfinder could conclude that acceleration and foreclosure for the $66 tax delinquency was both oppressive and unconscionable. Because there was an issue of fact, the court of appeals improperly affirmed the grant of summary judgment on the ground that the taxes were delinquent.

B. LATE PAYMENT AND THE BANK'S WRONGFUL DISHONOR OF THE DUNNS' CHECK

The Vonks do not dispute that the bank wrongfully dishonored the Dunns' check for the February 1987 payment. They argue, however, that under the terms of the note and mortgage, they had no duty to notify the Dunns of the dishonored check. The Vonks contend that it was the Dunns' responsibility to pay on time and assert that the bank's wrongful dishonor of the Dunns' check was not their concern.

The Dunns argue that it was inequitable for the Vonks to initiate foreclosure proceedings without notice. A telephone call or letter could have prevented this litigation. Consequently, foreclosure was oppressive and unconscionable.

A check constitutes only conditional payment of the underlying obligation unless the parties agree otherwise. Thus, if the mortgagor's bank dishonors his check, the mortgagee still has a right to receive payment. Under this analysis, the Vonks argue, actual payment alone satisfies the creditor/mortgagee and a bank's wrongful dishonor is not the mortgagee's concern. The remedy for wrongful dishonor, the Vonks contend, is to allow the debtor/mortgagor to maintain an action against the bank for damages resulting from foreclosure.

So rigid an analysis, however, is inconsistent with modern conditions, good legal policy, and existing law. Modern-day commerce involves the transfer and exchange of a huge volume of paper. Mortgage payments are expected to be made through the mail to the mortgagee's or collecting agent's place of business. Mortgagors in Arizona no longer saddle their horses and call on their mortgagees to tender gold coin in payment of their monthly obligations. Given the volume of computerized transactions, we must expect that banks will occasionally wrongfully dishonor checks. It would be bad law to hold that every time a bank wrongfully dishonors a check tendered for a mortgage payment, the mortgagee may accelerate and foreclose, the mortgagor lose his property, and the bank left to pay the damages. . . . Such a rule would effectively mean that one bank will pay another bank, and lawyers will get a share both going and coming. In our view, neither existing law nor common sense requires such a result. . . .

The tender of a "good" check in accordance with commercial practice and the wrongful dishonor of that check are matters a court must consider in determining whether equity will allow acceleration of the note and foreclosure of the mortgage. See *Arizona Coffee Shops*, 95 Ariz. at 100, 102, 387 P.2d at 802, 803 (illness of bookkeeper resulting in late tender of check for mortgage payment was circumstance court must consider on the issue of unconscionability). The Vonks incorrectly assert that our court of appeals has held that equity will not relieve a mortgagor from late payments resulting from "mistake." Actually, our court of appeals held that it will not relieve a mortgagor from a default "caused *by his* negligence, mistake or by accident" when the mortgagee has not acted in bad faith or fraudulently. Ciavarelli v. Zimmerman, 122 Ariz. 143, 144-45, 593 P.2d 697, 698-99 (Ct. App. 1979) (emphasis added). As *Ciavarelli* recognized, the court may protect a mortgagor from a default that results from accident, a good faith mistake, or some unusual circumstance beyond his control. Id. at 145, 593 P.2d at 699.

Here, the undisputed fact remains that the bank wrongfully dishonored the Dunns' check to the Vonks. Thus, the Dunns were technically in default not because of their own mistake or accident but because of the bank's. This certainly was a circumstance beyond the Dunns' control.

We hold, therefore, that the factfinder could decide it was oppressive and unconscionable to permit the Vonks to accelerate the note and foreclose the mortgage because the bank wrongfully dishonored the Dunns' check for the monthly payment. . . .

We conclude that the trial judge erred by granting summary judgment. The following are all matters the factfinder should consider in determining whether acceleration and foreclosure were unconscionable: the mortgagors' timely tender of a valid check, the bank's wrongful dishonor of that check, the trivial nature of the mortgagors' breach of the covenant to pay taxes, the amount the Dunns had already paid on the property, the making and acceptance of payments after the purported acceleration, the danger to the Vonks' security, and the Vonks' offer to withdraw the foreclosure action on payment of attorney's fees. . . .

NOTES AND QUESTIONS

1. Enforceability of Debt Acceleration Clauses. As you may recall from first-year property, a rent-acceleration clause whereby the landlord has the right to terminate and reenter the leased premises on the tenant's default while accelerating the entire rental obligation for the balance of the original lease term is regarded by some courts as an unenforceable penalty. Compare Ricker v. Rombough, 120 Cal. App. 2d Supp. 912, 261 P.2d 328 (1953) (penalty), with Aurora Business Park Assocs. v. Michael Albert, Inc., 548 N.W.2d 153 (Iowa 1996) (valid). How do you reconcile this proposition with the universal view that a debt acceleration clause is enforceable because it simply reflects the contractual determination by the parties as to when the debt is payable? Saunders v. Stradley, 25 Md. App. 85, 333 A.2d 604 (1975); Verna v. O'Brien, 78 Misc. 2d 288, 356 N.Y.S.2d 929 (Sup. Ct. 1974).

In light of the security-impairment rationale for the decision in *Vonk*, can you think of any non-debt-service-related defaults that would justify acceleration by the mortgagee? See United States v. Angel, 362 F. Supp. 445 (E.D. Pa. 1973); Strong v. Merchants Mutual Ins. Co., 2 Mass. App. 142, 309 N.E.2d 510 (1974); Kaminski v. London Pub., 123 N.J. Super. 112, 301 A.2d 769 (1973). See also Cal. Fin. Code §1487 (enforcing any loan provision authorizing a state or national bank to accelerate and foreclose based on a failure to pay taxes, rents, assessments, or insurance premiums). Consider the effect on mortgagees of the holding in *Vonk* that the tax delinquency of $66 might be too insubstantial (at least before the tax lien is enforced) to justify acceleration of the loan and foreclosure. Assume that, after several years of payments reducing the principal balance, a borrower tenders a $9800 loan payment that is $200 short of the $10,000 monthly installment payment required by the mortgage note. Can the lender accelerate and initiate foreclosure or is this default too insubstantial? If the latter, what can the lender do in these circumstances? What does the lender risk by accelerating and initiating foreclosure on a default that is ultimately held too "trivial" or under other circumstances that are held unconscionable? Do you have any drafting suggestions to discourage "trivial" defaults?

2. When the Courts Will Protect the Mortgagor. In discussing the wrongful dishonor of the borrower's check, the court in *Vonk* states the harsh common law view that no relief is afforded to a mortgagor against debt acceleration where a default occurs by reason of the mortgagor's negligence, mistake, or accident and the mortgagee has not acted in bad faith or fraudulently. However, some equity courts have refused to enforce acceleration clauses, despite the mortgagor's mistake and without regard to the mortgagee's conduct, where enforcement would be unjust or unconscionable. See Bisno v. Sax, 175 Cal. App. 2d 714, 346 P.2d 814 (1959) (one-day delay in making a debt-service payment); Middlemist v. Mosier, 151 Colo. 113, 377 P.2d 110 (1962) (denying acceleration for inadvertent failure to correctly endorse check for single monthly payment). See generally Rosenthal, The Role of Courts of Equity in Preventing Acceleration

Predicated upon a Mortgagor's Inadvertent Default, 22 Syracuse L. Rev. 897 (1971); Restatement (Third) of Property (Mortgages) §8.1 (1997) (adopting the strict common law approach because it avoids "difficult and time-consuming judicial inquiries" into the vagaries of the mortgagor's financial and personal situation and enhances predictability in mortgage remedies). What approach does the court adopt in *Vonk*? Was the dishonor of the check a result of the borrower's own negligence, mistake, or accident? What about the borrower's failure to pay the $66 real property tax payment?

In addition to the potential for relief in equity, an increasing number of states have enacted arrearages legislation that allows the mortgagor to deaccelerate ("reinstate") the loan and terminate the foreclosure by curing the default. See G. Nelson et al., Real Estate Finance Law §7.7 (6th ed. 2015).

Debt-acceleration clauses are almost invariably "optional" because the mortgagee may wish to pursue a less drastic remedial course of action. Absent language to the contrary, no formal notice is required of the mortgagee to exercise a debt-acceleration clause. However, the mortgagee must perform some act evidencing its intention to invoke the clause. This may be done by taking steps to institute foreclosure, as, in the case of a power-of-sale foreclosure, the advertisement of property for sale pursuant to the terms of the mortgage or deed of trust. 2 L. Jones, Jones on Mortgages (1928). Otherwise, if the mortgagee fails to take such action before the defaulting mortgagor tenders what is past due, the mortgagee will lose its right to accelerate for that particular default and must accept the tendered cure. See, for example, Comer v. Hargrave, 93 N.M. 170, 598 P.2d 213 (1979); Ogden v. Gibralter Sav. Ass'n, 640 S.W.2d 232 (Tex. 1982). In light of the foregoing discussion, what planning suggestions would you make to a mortgagee-client? To a mortgagor-client?

3. Waiver of Time-of-the-Essence. Ordinarily, the mortgage loan documents will demand the mortgagor's strict compliance with the repayment terms and declare time to be of the essence in the borrower's payment and performance obligations. In some jurisdictions, by case law, the mortgagee that accepts late payments consistently will be said to have waived time-of-the-essence; alternatively, the court may declare the mortgagee estopped from declaring default based on subsequent untimely payments or performance. See Restatement (Third) of Property (Mortgages) §8.1, cmt. e (1997) (authorizing a finding of waiver following a consistent pattern of acceptance of late payments). Despite having accepted late payments, mortgagees can avoid these waiver/estoppel arguments by sending notice to the borrower reinstating time-of-the-essence that provides a reasonable time for cure and reestablishment of the contract deadlines. Mortgagees often attempt to overcome such waiver/estoppel arguments by including nonwaiver provisions in their loan documents that purport to authorize acceptance of late payments while retaining the right to immediately accelerate and initiate foreclosure upon any subsequent late payments. Should courts enforce these nonwaiver provisions? Compare Federal Nat. Mortgage Ass'n v. Cobb, 738 F. Supp. 1220 (N.D. Ind. 1990) (nonwaiver clause effective) with

Miller v. Uhrick, 146 Ariz. 413, 706 P.2d 739 (Ct. App.), approved, 707 P.2d 309 (1985) (refusing to enforce agreement that acceptance of late payments would not waive time-of-the-essence provision).

2. The Mortgagee's Right to Possession

During the often time-consuming foreclosure process, the mortgagee is anxious to obtain control of the property to stop deterioration and possible vandalism when the borrower is unable or unwilling under the circumstances to maintain the property. To this end the mortgage (or deed of trust) document normally gives the mortgagee the right to take possession of the property as a "mortgagee in possession" prior to completion of foreclosure. However, as the following case illustrates, mortgagees in possession assume duties and responsibilities to the borrower and junior lien creditors that make lenders hesitant to exercise this right.

New York & Suburban Federal Savings & Loan Association v. Sanderman
162 N.J. Super. 216, 392 A.2d 635 (Ch. 1978)

DWYER, J. S. C.

New York and Suburban Federal Savings and Loan Association (Association) commenced an action to foreclose a first mortgage it held against the lands and buildings which were formerly the Convalescent Hospital of the City of Newark. . . .

On September 22, 1975 a partnership consisting of Philip Tatz, Bernard Bergman et al., conveyed the subject premises to Richard Sanderman and Louis Cesarano for $901,479.10. The deed recited that it was subject to a $301,479.10 mortgage in favor of Association and that a $600,000 purchase money second mortgage in favor of the grantors was the balance of the consideration. . . .

Thereafter, Bernard Bergman assigned his interest in the second mortgage to the Franklin National Bank as part of the collateral for a loan. In connection with the liquidation of that bank the Federal Deposit Insurance Corporation (FDIC) succeeded to the bank's interest in the second mortgage. It initially contested the validity of the first mortgage and a number of items for which Association claimed a right to be reimbursed for preserving the property as a mortgagee in possession. After a hearing all issues but one were resolved—that is, Association's claim to be reimbursed the sum of $45,360 for the cost of maintaining a guard on the premises 24 hours a day at a cost of $120 a day from February 5, 1977 to February 17, 1978. . . .

In connection with the foreclosure of mortgages on real property in certain of the central cities, there have been requests for reimbursement of expenses, such as boarding up the windows and doors to protect the property against vandalism between the date of entry of the judgment of foreclosure and the time of sale. . . .

FDIC urges that the expense was unnecessary because the license to operate the nursing home had been revoked, the structures could not be economically used, and to salvage the land value the structures will have to be torn down; hence there was no need for guard service. Its counsel points out that the officers of the Association who testified at the hearing admitted that when the Association received an appraisal report from an outside appraiser pointing these facts out, the Association immediately suspended the guard service. To allow this sum as part of the amount to be raised will shift the cost to the junior lienholders in this case and in others to a mortgagor seeking to redeem; therefore, the FDIC urges that the sum be disallowed.

Association urges that under the decisions in Zanzonico v. Zanzonico, 2 N.J. 309, 66 A.2d 530 (1949), cert. den. 338 U.S. 868 (1949), a mortgagee in possession has a duty to protect against vandalism or be held liable for loss or destruction of the property. It points to the following statement in *Zanzonico*:

> A mortgagee who goes into possession of the mortgaged lands assumes a grave responsibility for the management and preservation of the property. It is notorious that in Newark untenanted property is apt to be wrecked by vandals. When the tenants in the six-family house vacated the premises on the order of the public authorities [Tenement House Commission], complainant [mortgagee]. . . allowed the house to remain empty and took inadequate means to protect it. He is liable for the resulting damage. . . .

[66 A.2d at 533.]

A mortgagee who goes into possession is under a duty to maintain and preserve the property. The standard by which the discharge of that duty should be judged is that of a provident owner. . . . However, until the mortgagee has foreclosed he is not the owner and must act with due regard to the interests of the junior encumbrancers and the holder of the equity of redemption. . . .

FDIC employed its appraiser before June 1, 1977, the date of his rather extensive report. FDIC made a copy of it available to Association at least by October 1977. . . . Association received a letter report from its own appraiser dated February 10, 1978. It reached the same conclusions as the FDIC report. All concur that the building will have to be demolished. . . .

There is no evidence that [Association] inquired of the State Department of Health as to the circumstances, if any, under which the premises could be operated as a nursing home, or as to what could be done with the premises. It basically inquired whether the structure was weather tight and structurally sound.

Although tax assessment practices in Newark have been the subject of litigation in recent years, there is no evidence that [the Association] considered that the land was assessed at almost three times the value of the structure and for an aggregate amount $50,000 below the amount of its first mortgage. The court finds that this is not a situation where Association acted in good faith on a temporary basis in order to secure time to find out what a provident owner should do. The court concludes that a provident owner would have rather promptly gathered the data on tax assessments, licensing condition, structural condition, zoning, neighborhood conditions and the probability of generating any income from the property while in possession, as well as various means to appropriately preserve the property. Based on the record the court concludes all this data could have been available within a week or ten days if the effort had been made to get it. The court finds that this was not done.

The court also finds that a mortgagee in possession, acting as a provident owner, would give notice at least to a holder of a junior encumbrance in the amount held by FDIC before incurring a per diem [day] expense of $120 for which it would seek reimbursement.

The court concludes that Association did not act as a provident owner and denies the application for reimbursement for guard service. . . .

NOTES AND QUESTIONS

1. The Title Theory versus the Lien Theory. As you will recall, some states still adhere to the early common law theory of mortgage law, the title theory, under which the mortgagee is regarded as holding the legal title and legal right to possession until the mortgage is discharged through payment or foreclosed. By contrast, lien theory states (numbering at least 32) view the mortgage as a mere security interest that does not deprive the owner of the legal incidents of ownership. See discussion at Chapter 3A. This disparity in theory can produce different legal consequences where the mortgagee has the right to possession and rents, as preforeclosure remedies, in the event of a default by the mortgagor under the loan documents.

In the absence of an agreement to the contrary, in a title theory jurisdiction the mortgagee has the legal right to possession before or after a default by the mortgagor. However, as suggested by the *Sanderman* decision, any mortgagee in possession has a quasi-fiduciary duty to manage the property in a prudent and productive manner. In addition, because all net rents and profits must be applied toward the mortgage indebtedness, the mortgagee is strictly accountable to the mortgagor for such income when the mortgage indebtedness is finally paid or otherwise satisfied. See G. Osborne, Mortgages §165 (1970). By contrast, absent language to the contrary, in lien theory states the borrower-mortgagor is entitled as a matter of legal right to possession and rents even after a default. In the opinion of commentators, this distinction is the most important (if not the singular) practical difference between the title and the lien theories. See R. Kratovil and R. Werner, Modern Mortgage Law and Practice §20.02 (2d ed. 1981); see also Jordan v. Nationstar Mortgage, LLC, 185 Wn.2d 876, 374 P.3d 1195 (2016) (lien theory jurisdiction invalidates loan document provision allowing lender a post-default right to enter and secure an abandoned residence by changing locks, winterizing, and removing dangerous conditions). How might the lender protect its interests in jurisdictions that disallow these provisions?

In your opinion, which doctrine makes more *practical* sense in a postdefault situation? In the absence of any applicable provision in the relevant documentation, what are some policy arguments and counterarguments for allowing the mortgagee to have possession and the right to rents after a default by the mortgagor? See generally American Law of Property §16.95 (Casner ed., 1952).

After reviewing the discussion at Chapter 3A, consider the following: If a mortgagee were to enter into possession of the collateral in a lien theory jurisdiction with the consent of a defaulting mortgagor (which consent is usually expressed in the mortgage), any existing leases that are not in default could not be affected regardless of whether they were junior or senior to the mortgage, except that the mortgagee could collect the rents thereunder. In a title theory state, a mortgagee in possession could not terminate a senior lease, notwithstanding the mortgagor's default, because the interest of the mortgagee extends only to the interest of the mortgagor at the time the mortgage was created, namely, title in the property that was subject to the prior lease. However, if the lease were junior to the mortgage, the mortgagee in possession who has not entered into a nondisturbance agreement with the tenant could terminate the lease on taking possession in at least some title theory jurisdictions.

The Uniform Land Security Interest Act (ULSIA) would change this result by providing that without court approval, the creditor in possession may not disturb existing leases until foreclosure, even if they are subordinate. ULSIA §505(f). The drafters comment that "this is existing law in lien theory states but may change the rule in many title or intermediate theory states." (Under the so-called intermediate theory, the mortgagee has title but does not have a right to possession until the borrower defaults.) The ULSIA approach is based on the theory that if the mortgagee could terminate leases prior to foreclosure, it could negatively affect the mortgagor's equity of redemption (redemption is discussed at Chapter 8C3d, infra).

2. Liability of a Mortgagee in Possession. Although most mortgages provide that the mortgagee may enter into possession on default by the borrower, most mortgagees are hesitant to take that step. For example, the *Sanderman* case illustrates that each expenditure the mortgagee makes with respect to the property is subject to review by the court. In that case the mortgagee was unable to recover the expense of 24-hour guard service. Suppose the mortgagee had decided against guard service. Might claims then be made against the mortgagee for failure to exercise due diligence to protect the property and third parties? For example, if vandals started a fire that burned a neighboring house or injured pedestrians or firefighters, might there be an action against the mortgagee for failure to protect against these casualties? There may be other liabilities under other statutes; for example, the mortgagee in possession may be liable as an operator under the Comprehensive Environmental Response, Compensation, and

Liability Act of 1980 (CERCLA) for hazardous wastes spilled by the borrower. See Chapter 19A.

Recognizing these problems, the ULSIA provides that a mortgagee in possession must manage the property as would a prudent person, but that if the mortgagee "by contract delegates the managerial functions to a person in the business of managing real estate of the kind involved who is financially responsible, not related to the creditor, and prudently selected, the creditor satisfies the creditor's obligation to act prudently, and is not responsible to the debtor or other persons for the omissions and commissions of the management agent." ULSIA §505(c). Would this language have validated the mortgagee's claim for the cost of guard service in *Sanderman?* Would the mortgagee have been able to recover the cost of a managing agent under the reasoning of that case? Does the ULSIA protect the mortgagee against liability under federal statutes (such as obligations under CERCLA for hazardous waste cleanup)?

3. Trash-Outs. During the subprime foreclosure crisis, many borrowers abandoned their homes, leaving personal property behind. Aiming to protect their business interests pending the foreclosure sale without the expensive proposition of obtaining a court-appointed receiver (discussed in the next section below), mortgage lenders hired companies to enter the residences, remove the "trash" left behind, and winterize the plumbing. In addition to concerns over ousting the borrower by changing the locks to secure the dwelling, these "lock/trash-outs" are problematic if the borrower contends the items left behind weren't garbage at all. See Wells Fargo v. Tyson, 27 Misc. 3d 684, 897 N.Y.S.2d 610 (Sup. Ct. 2010) (although mortgage authorized lender to enter to secure property and change locks on abandonment of property, locked-out borrower established he visited the property weekly while residing elsewhere and left valuable items behind such as a portable generator and ladders that were removed or stolen; borrower held entitled to recover from mortgagee for value of lost personalty and $150,000 in punitive damages for the trespass), reversed, 82 A.D.3d 757, 917 N.Y.S.2d 914 (Sup. Ct. App. Div. 2011) (reversed on procedural grounds). See generally Odinet, Banks, Break-Ins, and Bad Actors in Mortgage Foreclosure, 83 U. Cinn. L. Rev. 1155 (2015) (discussing inadequacies of existing laws to protect homeowners from such abuses).

During the mortgage foreclosure crisis, some states and localities such as Chicago and Las Vegas addressed the decay of neighborhoods with high rates of residential foreclosures by imposing affirmative obligations on mortgagees to maintain vacant mortgaged property or abandoned (but tenanted and therefore occupied) property during the pendency of the foreclosure or even before initiating foreclosure. See N.Y. Real Prop. Acts. Law §1307 (operative upon mortgagee obtaining judgment of foreclosure in this judicial foreclosure jurisdiction). See generally Boyack and Berger, Bankruptcy Weapons to Terminate a Zombie Mortgage, 54 Washburn L.J. 451 (2015) (addressing the consequences on the borrower and the surrounding community of lenders delaying foreclosure of vacated houses). Do you think it is fair for the mortgagee to have to incur expenses to maintain the property before the foreclosure sale? Why might the lender be reluctant to incur such expenses, which presumably would be in its own interest to preserve the value of the property? The new Uniform Home Foreclosure Procedures Act, offered to the states for adoption in the spirit of the Uniform Commercial Code, addresses the decay of abandoned homes by providing an expedited foreclosure procedure and requiring lenders to maintain abandoned properties during the pendency of that accelerated procedure. At the same time, the Act would preempt local laws that impose broader maintenance obligations.

3. The Mortgagee's Right to Appointment of a Receiver

Given the potential liabilities of a mortgagee in possession, many lenders prefer to have the court appoint a third-party "receiver" to take possession of and manage the mortgaged property following default. Thus the mortgagee hopes to prevent the defaulting borrower from "milking" the property of potential rental income and otherwise to preserve the security interest pending completion of the foreclosure proceedings. Use of a third-party receiver, in contrast to the mortgagee assuming possession, will place responsibility for imprudent management decisions on the receiver, as well as insulate the mortgagee from tort liabilities associated with operating the property.

In title theory jurisdictions the principal impediment to the appointment of a receiver has been the notion among equity courts that, in contrast to lien theory states, the mortgagee already has an adequate remedy at law, namely, title and the right to possession. In both title theory and lien theory states, however, the mortgagee seeking a receiver generally will be successful if it can demonstrate that the mortgaged property is, or will be, inadequate security without the rents and profits relative to the amount of the outstanding mortgage indebtedness.[5] In practice, institutional lenders almost invariably include in their mortgages a "receivership" clause under which the mortgagee, on the mortgagor's default, is entitled, without notice, to the appointment of a receiver without proving the security is inadequate. While these clauses are not controlling (especially where the security is clearly adequate)[6] they tend to influence courts, and in some jurisdictions these clauses are automatically enforceable.[7]

Once appointed, a receiver in a title theory jurisdiction may have the right to terminate leases that are junior to the mortgage being foreclosed and that are not protected by a nondisturbance agreement. So, for example, if the contract rental is less than market, the receiver would have the option of disavowing the existing lease and charging the junior tenant who remains in possession with the higher

---

5. 2 G. Glenn, Glenn on Mortgages §173 (1943).

6. E.g., Aetna Life Ins. Co. v. Broecker, 166 Ind. 576, 77 N.E. 1092 (1906); 2 G. Glenn, Glenn on Mortgages §175.1 (1943); G. Nelson et al., Real Estate Finance Law §4.35(6th ed. 2015).

7. E.g., N.Y. Real Prop. Law §254(10); see also Restatement (Third) of Property (Mortgages) §4.3(b) (1997) (court shall appoint receiver on default if mortgage authorizes such appointment).

market rental. But suppose, in contrast, that a junior tenant who is paying an above-market rental desires to extricate itself from the lease agreement. The better and prevailing view is that the junior tenant, at the option of the receiver, is bound to the lease because the receiver's action is that of the court, not the mortgagee, and thus the title of the mortgagor and its privity of estate with the junior tenant is not extinguished until the foreclosure sale.[8]

4. *Assignment of Leases and Rents*

The prime leases with the high-credit tenants form the foundation of any major commercial real estate enterprise. As you will recall, the amount of the postconstruction loan depends on the appraised value of the property based on a capitalization of the anticipated net rental income from the subject property. See Chapter 4D1. Moreover, the primary security for the loan is the projected rental income stream from the tenants, not the land and improvements or the net assets of the borrower (as reflected by the tolerant attitude of many postconstruction lenders toward nonrecourse financing). This is why mortgages and deeds of trust almost invariably contain language (usually in the so-called granting clause) that their lien shall cover the mortgaged property "together with all the rents, issues, and profits thereof." In addition, the postconstruction lender will normally include a more detailed assignment-of-rents clause in the mortgage instrument. A popular form of such assignment language contained in the New York Board of Title Underwriters mortgage form (which figured prominently in the *Ganbaum* case, excerpted below) reads in part as follows:

> 13.[T]he mortgagor hereby assigns to the mortgagee the rents, issues and profits of the premises as further security for the payment of said indebtedness, and the mortgagor grants to the mortgagee the right to enter upon and take possession of the premises for the purpose of collecting the same and to let [rent] the premises or any part thereof, and to apply the rents, issues and profits, after payment of all necessary charges and expenses, on account of said indebtedness. . . . The mortgagee hereby waives the right to enter upon and to take possession of said premises for the purpose of collecting said rents, issues and profits, and the mortgagor shall be entitled to collect and receive said rents, issues and profits, until default under any of the covenants, conditions or agreements contained in this mortgage, and agrees to use such rents, issues and profits in payment of principal and interest becoming due on this mortgage and in payment of taxes, assessments, sewer rents, water rents and carrying charges becoming due against said premises.. . . Mortgagor will not, without the written consent of Mortgagee, receive or collect rent from any tenant of said premises or any part thereof for a period of more than one month in advance. . . .

---

8. See G. Nelson et al., Real Estate Finance Law §4.42 (6th ed. 2015). The impact of foreclosure sales on leases is examined infra at Chapter 8C2.

Although some assignments of rents are conditional on the default by the borrower under the mortgage and are generally considered assignments for security only, some, such as the mortgage language quoted above, are unconditional, with the lender waiving only the right to collect the rents until default. The effect of language providing for an unconditional (or "absolute") assignment is discussed in the following case.

Ganbaum v. Rockwood Realty Corp.
62 Misc. 2d 391, 308 N.Y.S.2d 436 (Sup. Ct. 1970)

SPIEGEL, Justice.

The . . . cause of action is . . . for damages in the amount of $31,180.64, allegedly sustained by plaintiffs-mortgagees due to the failure of defendant Levine, for the period of approximately two years prior to the commencement of this action, to apply the rents upon the subject real property to the payment of real estate taxes, sewer and water rents, other charges, and interest and principal on the first mortgage and plaintiff's second mortgage, and for rent which Levine collected from the tenants thereof for more than a period of one month in advance.

The second mortgage, subject to which defendant Levine acquired title to the subject real property, contains the following clause [here the court quotes the language of the assignment-of-rents clause 13 excerpted above].

Defendant Levine contends that the . . . cause of action cannot be maintained as the "assignment of rents" clause in the mortgage does not become effective until foreclosure or until the appointment of a receiver.

The courts of this State and the Federal courts, applying the law of this State, have held that "an assignment of rents" clause in a mortgage is not self-executing, but becomes effective only upon foreclosure or upon the appointment of a receiver of the rents of the mortgaged property. . . . Plaintiffs contend, however, that the law of these cited cases is inapplicable to the case at bar, as in each of the cited cases the "assignment of rents" clause was conditional upon default of the conditions of the mortgage, whereas in the case at bar, in paragraph 13 of the mortgage there is stated an unconditional assignment in praesenti. Accordingly, plaintiffs allege defendant Levine, who became owner of record of the subject realty subject to plaintiffs' second mortgage, is bound by the assignment of rents clause therein and is personally liable for her failure, prior to foreclosure, to apply the rents for the purposes stated in that clause. To this extent plaintiffs . . . contend they were damaged thereby, and further [that] by her collection of rents for more than a period of one month in advance she violated that clause of the mortgage. . . .

The Federal court [in Empire State Collateral Co. v. Bay Realty Corp., 232 F. Supp. 330 (E.D.N.Y. 1964)], applying the law of New York, held that the "assignment of rents" clauses in the mortgages therein sued upon were by their terms conditional upon default of the mortgagor and were not operative until the mortgagees took affirmative action to enforce them. However, the court declared (at p. 335): "It is only when a clause in a mortgage constitutes an absolute and unqualified assignment of rents, to operate in praesenti, and is clearly intended as such by the parties, that an assignment of rents clause operates as such, without more. . . ."

However, we do not herein agree with the foregoing reasoning of the learned United States District Court. . . . It is the law of New York that a mortgage gives the mortgagee only a lien upon the mortgaged premises. The common law doctrine that the mortgagee held title thereto or any incidents thereof has long ago been abolished. . . . Defendant Levine during the period relevant to the . . . cause of action, held title to the mortgaged realty. . . . Certainly the title of defendant Levine included, for the period in issue, the rights to the rents upon the realty and the right to apply the rents as she saw fit. As a mortgage cannot convey title to the mortgagee, the assignment of rents clause in paragraph 13 in the mortgage herein sued upon cannot convey ipso facto to the mortgagee the right to the rents, which is an incident of title. Therefore, though defendant Levine is bound by the terms of plaintiffs' second mortgage, subject to which she acquired title to the subject premises, she is not liable to plaintiffs for the rents collected by her prior to foreclosure nor for the use made of them.

In the case of a commercial real estate project (such as an office building or shopping center) where the lender's appraisal-underwriting process (and thus the security for its loan) is based on the long-term rental obligations of certain high-credit tenants, the postconstruction lender will frequently require a separate assignment instrument to cover these specified leases. This document is referred to as an "Assignment of Lessor's Interest in Leases" to avoid the implication that the mortgagee is assuming the lessor's duties under the lease. Nevertheless, some assignment instruments include the following exculpatory language:

> The Mortgagee shall not be obligated to perform or discharge, nor does it hereby undertake to perform or discharge, any obligation, duty or liability under the Lease, by reason of this assignment, and Mortgagor shall and does hereby agree to indemnify the Mortgagee against and hold it harmless from any and all liability, loss or damage which it may or might incur under the Lease or under or by reason of this assignment and of and from any and all claims and demands whatsoever which may be asserted against it by reason of any alleged obligation or undertaking on its part to perform or discharge any of the terms, covenants or agreements contained in the Lease. . . .

In addition, most assignments include estoppel and "antimilking" language similar to the following:

Owner represents that Owner now is the absolute owner of said Lease, with full right and title to assign the same and the rents, income, and profits due or to become due thereunder; that said Lease is valid, in full force and effect, and has not been modified or amended except as stated herein; that there is no outstanding assignment or pledge thereof or of the rents, income, and profits due or to become due thereunder; that there are no existing defaults under the provisions thereof on the part of either party; that the lessee has no defense, set-off or counterclaim against Owner; that the lessee is in possession and paying rent and other charges under the Lease and as provided therein; and that no rents, income or profits payable thereunder have been or will hereafter be anticipated, discounted, released, waived, compromised, or otherwise discharged except as may be expressly permitted by said Lease. Owner covenants not to cancel, abridge, surrender, or terminate said Lease or change, alter, or modify the same, either to reduce the amount of said rents, income, and profits payable thereunder, or otherwise change, alter, abridge or modify said Lease, or make any subsequent assignment of said Lease, or consent to subordination of the interest of the lessee in said Lease without the prior written consent of Mortgagee. Any attempt at cancellation, surrender, termination, change, alteration, modification, assignment, or subordination of the Lease without the written consent of Mortgagee shall be null and void (excerpted from the Assignment of Lease Agreement in the Documents Manual).

Normally, when the postconstruction loan is closed any separate assignment instrument is recorded along with the mortgage, and notice of the assignment is sent (by certified mail) to the tenant mentioned in the assignment instrument. If any of the credit leases are junior in lien priority to the mortgage, the lender may also require as a condition to closing that the tenants execute attornment agreements (whereby each tenant agrees that in the event of any default and foreclosure it will recognize (or "attorn to") the mortgagee as its new landlord), especially in jurisdictions such as California where junior leases are automatically extinguished at foreclosure. See Chapter 3E.

NOTES AND QUESTIONS

1. Enforceability of Assignment of Rents Clauses. The enforceability of these clauses depends on their format and on local law considerations. There are three major formats.

a. The least desirable for the mortgagee is a mere pledge of rents and profits. According to one court in a leading decision, "There is a marked difference between a pledge and an assignment. Ordinarily, a pledge is considered as a bailment, and delivery of possession, actual or constructive, is essential, but transfer of title is not. On the other hand, by assignment, title is transferred, although possession need not be." Accordingly, it was held that rents pledged to a mortgagee were not accessible because the mortgagee had not entered into possession. Nor had a receiver been appointed. Paramount Building & Loan Ass'n v. Sacks, 107 N.J. Eq. 328, 152 A. 457, 458 (1930).

b. The second format is an absolute and unconditional in praesenti assignment of the rents and profits providing that, in the absence of any default, the mortgagee will remit to the mortgagor any surplus rental remaining after the debt-service payment is made. While this approach obviates the taking of affirmative action by the mortgagee to activate the rent assignment and prevents the cancellation or modification of the leases without its consent, this form of assignment is seldom used because of the mortgagor's objection to loss of control over the rental income prior to default. Such absolute assignments are mainly associated with high-credit lease financing (examined at Chapter 7C1) where, in exchange for 100 percent or more financing, the lender will demand complete control over a high-credit noncancellable lease that constitutes the real security for the loan. See Note, The Mortgagee's Right to Rents after Default, 50 Yale L.J. 1424, 1425 (1941).

c. The third and most prevalent approach is one in which the mortgagor makes an in praesenti assignment of its right, title, and interest in the leases to the mortgagee as additional security for the mortgage loan. This assignment may purport to be absolute and unconditional as well, but is distinguishable from the second format by its deference to the mortgagor to collect the rents—the mortgagor retains a present license to collect the rents and enforce the lease provisions as the lessor so long as there is no default under the note, mortgage, or separate assignment instrument. The treatment of such a provision by courts will depend to some extent on whether the local jurisdiction subscribes to a lien or a title theory of mortgage law. In many title theory and a few lien theory states, it has been held that an assignment of rents for additional security of this third variety is self-activating on default, pursuant to the terms of the assignment, as soon as the mortgagee serves notice on the tenants (e.g., Randel v. Jersey Mortgage Investment Co., 306 Pa. 1, 158 A. 865, 866 (1932); Bevins v. Peoples Bank & Trust Co., 671 P.2d 875 (Alaska 1983)), while other courts, mainly in lien theory jurisdictions such as New York (where *Ganbaum* was decided), hold that such assignments only create security interests and therefore further affirmative action is required of the mortgagee (such as commencing foreclosure, taking possession as a mortgagee in possession, or having a receiver appointed) before it can collect the rents. See, for example, Bornstein v. Somerson, 341 So. 2d 1043 (Fla. Dist. Ct. App.), cert. denied, 348 So. 2d 944 (Fla. 1977) (lien theory); Taylor v. Brennan, 621 S.W.2d 592 (Tex. 1981) (lien theory); Levin v. Carney, 161 Ohio St. 513, 120 N.E.2d 92 (1954) (title theory). But see In re Ventura Louise Properties, 490 F.2d 1141 (9th Cir. 1974) (deciding in lien theory jurisdiction that assignment of third variety is absolute and not a mere security interest). See generally Kratovil, Mortgages—Problems in Possession, Rents, and Mortgagee Liability, 11 DePaul L. Rev. 1, 11 (1961).

Perhaps the court in *Ganbaum* is correct in concluding that even an unconditional, absolute assignment of rents and leases of this third variety is nothing more than an assignment for security purposes (that is, a pledge) in a lien theory jurisdiction such as New York and therefore it cannot convey ipso facto the right to rents, which is an incident of title. Does it necessarily follow (as a matter of contract theory) that a mortgagor should not be liable in damages for breach of the promise contained in the assignment clause to apply the rents to debt service and property expenses? Why wouldn't the plaintiff-mortgagee in *Ganbaum* be able to recoup its damages through a deficiency action against the defendant?

Made available to the states for adoption in 2005, and thus far enacted in Nevada, New Mexico, North Dakota, Texas, and Utah, the Uniform Assignment of Rents Act modernizes and conforms the law of rents to the expectations of mortgagees. Section 4 of that Act borrows the approach of Article 9 of the Uniform Commercial Code with regard to personal property security interests, however styled or named, and provides that an assignment of rents creates a "presently effective security interest" in rents regardless of whether the assignment documentation purports to create an absolute assignment, an assignment as additional security, or any other form. This will help end the highly dubious legal distinctions among these different drafting techniques. Further, adoption of the Act should change the result in the *Ganbaum* case— under the Act the assignor (defined to include a successor owner of the real estate subject to an assignment of rents) is obligated to turn over rents it collects that the assignee (mortgagee) was entitled to collect. Uniform Act, §14 (authorizing a civil action to recover such rental proceeds).

2. Enforceability of Assignment-of-Rents Clauses in Bankruptcy. The enforceability of assignment-of-rents clauses under state law has been of particular consequence in the mortgagor's bankruptcy proceedings. If the mortgagee had not taken the affirmative action required under applicable state law to enforce its assignment of rents before the bankruptcy filing, the bankruptcy trustee could use the rental monies without the lender's consent or the court's approval. Before the bankruptcy court would recognize the mortgagee's interest in the rents the lender often would have to attempt to lift the automatic stay (discussed at Chapter 18C1) and then take the requisite enforcement action. Responding to lenders' concern over the delay in this procedure and the lack of uniformity in the treatment of assignments of rent under state law, in 1994 Congress amended the Bankruptcy Code to establish, in the opinion of some commentators, that the lender's assignment of rents is perfected for bankruptcy purposes, without regard to local law, solely by its recordation in the public records. (11 U.S.C. §552(b)). But see Freyermuth, The Circus Continues— Security Interests in Rents, Congress, the Bankruptcy Courts, and the "Rents Are Subsumed in the Land," Hypothesis, 6 J. Bankr. Law & Prac. 115, 117-121 (1997) (suggesting how this amendment may fall short of overriding state law). Subsequent to this amendment, courts could conclude that rents subject to a recorded assignment of rents (as a separate instrument or a clause in the mortgage) constitute the lender's "cash collateral" in bankruptcy and cannot be used without the mortgagee's consent unless authorized by the bankruptcy court after notice and a hearing. 11 U.S.C. §363(c)(2). The Uniform Act bolsters this result as a matter of local law by providing in section 5 that, upon its recording, the assignment of rents is fully perfected. See additional discussion of assignment-of-rents clauses in bankruptcy at Chapter 18C1, note 6.

3. The "Antimilking" Function of Assignment Clauses. The "antimilking" language of the sample assignment-of-lease clause excerpted above originated in the Depression era, when owners facing the specter of insolvency and foreclosure would sometimes out of desperation accept large lump-sum prepayments of rent in exchange for terminating or reducing the future rental obligations of the tenants and then abscond with the money. Review the restrictions in the assignment clause and observe how they are designed to prevent this. Observe also that immediately before the closing of the postconstruction loan, the lender will require that each prime tenant (whose lease has been assigned to the mortgagee) receive a copy and notice of the recorded assignment by certified mail so that the tenant will be apprised in advance that the owner-landlord may not terminate or modify the lease without the lender's consent and that in the event of a default by the landlord-mortgagor the tenant will be required to pay the rent to the mortgagee.

4. What Is the Lessor's Interest? When a tenant assigns its leasehold estate, it is clear that what is being assigned is the tenant's right to possession for the duration of the lease term subject to the terms and provisions of the lease. However, when an owner assigns its interest as lessor under a lease, the consequences are not quite so clear. For example, is the owner's reversionary interest being temporarily assigned to the mortgagee? If so, are the burdens as well as the benefits of being a landlord transferred? Consider the following example.

> ➤ **Problem 8-1**
> Returning to the master hypothetical, if Ace Insurance Company takes an assignment of Dan's interest in the lease with the Widget Corporation of America, would Ace be responsible for performing all of the landlord's covenants in the lease agreement (for example, Dan's promise to construct additional space and make alterations to suit WCA)? Is there any language in the assignment clauses quoted above that addresses this issue? ◄

C. RIGHTS AND DUTIES OF THE PARTIES AT FORECLOSURE

1. Balancing the Interests of Borrower and Lender

As discussed at Chapter 3A, a mortgage represents an interest in (title theory) or lien on (lien theory) real estate that secures payment or performance of an obligation. Originally, the mortgage took the form of a deed from the borrower to the lender, subject to a condition subsequent that if the borrower paid the amount owed on the note when due, the title would revest in the borrower. Until the due date, the borrower was often allowed to remain in possession of the property. If the borrower failed to pay the debt when due, regardless of excuse, the condition subsequent failed and title vested indefeasibly in the lender in fee simple absolute.

Because of the hardships that resulted from this procedure, the equity courts stepped in and permitted the defaulting borrower to "redeem" (buy back) the property from the lender by paying the balance of the mortgage notwithstanding that the documents vested title indefeasibly in the lender. But this "equity of redemption" resulted in hardship for the lender by impeding its ability to dispose of or renovate the property. Accordingly, lenders were allowed to petition equity courts to "foreclose," or cut off, a borrower's equity of redemption. This is how the process called foreclosure originated. These historical developments are discussed in greater detail at Chapter 3A.

This early clash between the rights of the borrower and those of the lender continued throughout the history of foreclosure law. Under the original method of foreclosure, called "strict foreclosure," the court simply issued a decree foreclosing, or cutting off, the mortgagor's equity of redemption if the debtor did not pay the debt within the grace period specified by the court. Returning to the master hypothetical, suppose Dan Developer defaults on his loan with Ace Insurance Company when the principal balance on the loan is approximately $15 million and the property value is $20 million. Under this procedure, Ace, on foreclosure of its mortgage, would effectively acquire Dan Developer's property for the $15 million balance of the mortgage. Strict foreclosure would mean a $5 million windfall for Ace at the expense of Dan and Dan's other creditors.

As a practical matter, it is unlikely in this type of commercial situation that Dan would let the property go to foreclosure if he had substantial equity in it; he would sell the property and keep the equity. Nevertheless, because of the possibility of such an inequitable outcome, most jurisdictions abandoned strict foreclosure in favor of a public sale of the property. In some states, however, a form of strict foreclosure is still possible, or even customary, with protections for the borrower built in by the courts and the legislatures.[9]

Despite the safeguard of a public foreclosure sale, there was usually a dearth of competitive bidding at such sales, and lenders could bid nominal amounts and obtain large deficiency judgments—judgments for the difference between the

---

9. See, e.g., Conn. Gen. Stat. Ann. §§49-14 to 49-31; Vt. Stat. Ann. tit. 12, §4941. On the constitutionality of strict foreclosure, see Dieffenbach v. Attorney Gen. of Vt., 604 F.2d 187 (2d Cir. 1979). With respect to the limited application of strict foreclosure in Illinois, see Prather, Foreclosure of the Security Interest, 1957 U. Ill. L.F. 420, and Brodkey, Current Changes in Illinois Real Property Law, 10 DePaul L. Rev. 567 (1961). Some courts in states not providing for strict foreclosure have been known to grant it on petition of the mortgagee in special circumstances, such as to correct a good faith failure to join certain necessary parties in a judicial foreclosure. See G. Nelson et al., Real Estate Finance Law §7.11 (6th ed. 2015); Note, 88 U. Pa. L. Rev. 994 (1940); Note, 25 Va. L. Rev. 947 (1939).

foreclosure purchase price and the amount of the debt. To counter this, other protections were built into the process: restrictions on deficiency judgments (for example, judgment available only to the extent the lender proves the value of the collateral, as distinct from the foreclosure price, was less than the debt); confirmation of the foreclosure sale by the court; the setting of upset prices below which the property will not be sold; and statutory "rights of redemption" under which the borrower can repurchase the property for the foreclosure sale price during a specified period of time following the sale.

Notwithstanding the evolution of the foreclosure process, the effort to balance the rights of borrowers and lenders is not over. Today there are new challenges to foreclosure arising under such diverse sources as the Constitution, fraudulent conveyance law, and the Bankruptcy Code. Additionally, the most common foreclosure defenses today arise from the changed nature of residential mortgage financing—from the traditional Main Street model where the lender retained the mortgage loan for its full repayment life, to the current securitization model that contemplates multiple transfers and fractionalization of ownership that often conflicts with formalistic foreclosure rules. Below we discuss modern foreclosure practices in the United States, the protections built into law to effect rough justice between the borrower and lender, and some of the current attacks on the foreclosure process. Chapter 18 examines attacks on the mortgagee's ability to realize on the collateral in reorganizations under the Bankruptcy Code and efforts in bankruptcy to overturn a previously conducted foreclosure sale.

2. *Methods of Foreclosure*

a. **Foreclosure Procedures**

The most prevalent method of foreclosure in the United States is foreclosure by judicial sale. It is the only procedure permitted in some states and the method most generally used in about half of the states.[10] Significantly, it appears to be permitted in all states, so that even in a power-of-sale jurisdiction, when there is a dispute as to priorities or validity of liens, the mortgagee may choose a judicial foreclosure to produce a result similar to a "quiet title" action and feel somewhat more comfortable that the title obtained at foreclosure will not be subject to attack. Judicial foreclosure, however, is complex, expensive, and time-consuming. In some jurisdictions, it is not unusual for the process to go on for years, during which time litigation and other costs (which are added to the debt for foreclosure purposes) eat away at whatever equity the borrower may have in the property.

The following are some of the usual steps when foreclosing judicially:

---

10. See B. Dunaway, The Law of Distressed Real Estate Appendix 9A (1992) (specifying the customary security agreement and method of foreclosure in each state).

1. The lender must obtain a title search to determine who has an interest in the property. Junior interests must be joined as parties defendant or they will not be cut off by the foreclosure.
2. The lender must file a lis pendens notice to prevent bona fide purchasers and others from acquiring an interest in the property during the foreclosure proceedings that will not be extinguished by the sale.
3. The lender must file its foreclosure complaint and serve the summons and complaint on the necessary parties to the action—those whose interests are to be affected by the foreclosure.
4. A hearing will be held, perhaps before a master in chancery who will prepare and submit a report to the judge regarding the status of the debt, the debtors, and the security, following which there will be a court judgment that a sale will be held and setting forth its terms.
5. The sale is advertised to the general public pursuant to statutory requirements.
6. A court official conducts a sale. The lender will attend and must be prepared to bid to protect its interest. As discussed in note 6 below, determining how much to bid is a complex process.
7. After the sale, a report of sale is made to the court (in many states, confirmation of the sale by the court is also required) and a determination is made as to the borrower's and the borrower's other creditors' rights to any surplus.
8. The lender may petition for a deficiency judgment decree if the borrower (or anyone else) is personally liable on the note and if such a judgment is permitted in the applicable jurisdiction.
9. In states that have enacted legislation giving the borrower a right of redemption after foreclosure, the foreclosure purchaser cannot possess the property until that period has expired.

The purchaser at the foreclosure sale receives the title the borrower had when the mortgage was recorded, that is, title free of all junior liens and interests in the property (provided the holders of the junior liens or interests have been joined in the foreclosure action) and subject to all senior liens and interests. Normally, in a power-of-sale foreclosure junior interests are automatically cut off; in a judicial foreclosure only those interestsholders that are made a party defendant can be affected by the proceeding. This gives the mortgagee foreclosing judicially the option of keeping junior interests that are beneficial (for example, leases to good tenants with rents at market or above). The judicial foreclosure does not normally affect senior interests, so they are not usually joined in the action.

A majority of states authorize the other principal mode of foreclosure—the power-of-sale foreclosure.[11] Under this method, there is usually a public sale of the property preceded by advertising and other forms of notice that are prescribed

---

11. New York joined the list, except for certain residential collateral, in 1998, but repealed its nonjudicial foreclosure procedure in 2009.

in the statute authorizing the power of sale. In contrast to the judicially supervised foreclosure proceeding, this nonjudicial method of sale is typically supervised by a trustee under a deed of trust or by the mortgagee under a power-of-sale provision contained in a mortgage. As discussed at Chapter 3C, several jurisdictions (for example, California) authorize the deed of trust as a mortgage substitute under which the borrower ("trustor") conveys the real property to a third-party "trustee" in trust, with power-of-sale, for the benefit of the lender ("beneficiary").

A power-of-sale foreclosure is usually less expensive, speedier, and less complicated than a judicial foreclosure. The borrower, however, is afforded less protection, and the purchaser at the foreclosure sale is apt to receive a title that is not as firm as would be produced at a judicial foreclosure sale. This is because the proceedings are nonadversarial and lack the finality of a judicial foreclosure decree.

The following are excerpts from California's statutory notice requirements for certain power-of-sale foreclosures. (These excerpts are the subject of Problem 8-3 below.)

Cal. Civ. Code §2924f

§2924F. SALE OR RESALE OF PROPERTY; NOTICE; CONTENTS; POSTING AND PUBLICATION

. . . (b)(1) Except as provided in subdivision (c), before any sale of property can be made under the power of sale contained in any deed of trust or mortgage . . . notice of the sale thereof shall be given by posting a written notice of the time of sale and of the street address and the specific place at the street address where the sale will be held, and describing the property to be sold, at least 20 days before the date of sale in one public place in the city where the property is to be sold, if the property is to be sold in a city, or, if not, then in one public place in the judicial district in which the property is to be sold, and publishing a copy once a week for three consecutive calendar weeks.

(2) The first publication to be at least 20 days before the date of the sale, in a newspaper of general circulation published in the city in which the property or some part thereof is situated, if any part thereof is situated in a city, if not, then in a newspaper of general circulation published in the judicial district in which the property or some part thereof is situated, or in case no newspaper of general circulation is published in the city or judicial district, as the case may be, in a newspaper of general circulation published in the county in which the property or some part thereof is situated.. . .

(3) A copy of the notice of sale shall also be posted in a conspicuous place on the property to be sold at least 20 days before the date of sale, where possible and where not restricted for any reason. If the property is a single-family residence the posting shall be on a door of the residence, but, if not possible or restricted, then the notice shall be posted in a conspicuous place on the property; however,

if access is denied because a common entrance to the property is restricted by a guard gate or similar impediment, the property may be posted at that guard gate or similar impediment to any development community.

(4) The notice of sale shall. . . be recorded with the county recorder of the county in which the property or some part thereof is situated at least 20 days prior to the date of sale. . . .

(c)(1) This subdivision applies only to deeds of trust or mortgages which contain a power of sale and which are secured by real property containing a single-family, owner-occupied residence, where the obligation secured by the deed of trust or mortgage is contained in a contract for [consumer] goods or services. . . .

(2) Except as otherwise expressly set forth in this subdivision, all other provisions of law relating to the exercise of a power of sale shall govern the exercise of a power of sale contained in a deed of trust or mortgage described in paragraph (1).

(3) If any default of the obligation secured by a deed of trust or mortgage described in paragraph (1) has not been cured within 30 days after the recordation of the notice of default,[12] the trustee or mortgagee shall mail to the trustor or mortgagor, at his or her last known address, a copy of the following statement:

YOU ARE IN DEFAULT UNDER A

(Deed of trust or mortgage)

DATED _____. UNLESS YOU TAKE ACTION TO PROTECT YOUR PROPERTY, IT MAY BE SOLD AT A PUBLIC SALE. IF YOU NEED AN EXPLANATION OF THE NATURE OF THE PROCEEDING AGAINST YOU, YOU SHOULD CONTACT A LAWYER.

Consider the following case on whether the lender foreclosing by power-of-sale owes a duty to a third-party bidder-purchaser to disclose defects in the real property being sold.

---

12. In addition to the notice specified in §2924f(c)(3), California law requires that the beneficiary or trustee record a notice of default and mail it by registered or certified mail to the trustor and certain other persons. See Cal. Civ. Code §§2924, 2924b, 2924c.—Eds.

Karoutas v. HomeFed Bank

232 Cal. App. 3d 767, 283 Cal. Rptr. 809 (1991)

CHIN, Associate Justice.

This appeal involves the right to sell property under a deed of trust after the borrower's default. We must determine whether a beneficiary with actual knowledge of facts materially affecting the value of property has a duty to disclose those facts to prospective bidders at a trustee's sale. George A. and Anastasios A. Karoutas (the Karoutases) were successful bidders at a trustee's foreclosure sale. They later filed a complaint seeking rescission or damages in connection with their purchase. The trial court sustained, without leave to amend, the general demurrer of HomeFed Bank (HomeFed) to the Karoutases' complaint. On appeal, the Karoutases argue that the complaint stated facts sufficient to constitute a cause of action in alleging that HomeFed failed to comply with its duty to disclose to the Karoutases information within its possession that materially affected the value of the property. We agree. Therefore, we reverse.

FACTUAL AND PROCEDURAL BACKGROUND

HomeFed was the successor in interest to Columbus Savings and Cal America Savings and Loan Association (Cal America). It was the beneficiary under a deed of trust on real property, including a residence, owned by Michael and Sandra Lawrence. The deed of trust secured a $100,000 loan to the Lawrences. The Lawrences defaulted. Pursuant to the power of sale in the deed of trust, Cal America declared a default and instructed the trustee to record a notice of default and election to sell.

On December 5, 1989, the trustee recorded a notice of trustee's sale. On January 3, 1990, the Karoutases opened the bidding at $130,000, the minimum opening bid the trustee set and the amount of the unpaid balance on the Lawrences' obligation, plus fees and costs. HomeFed, through the trustee, raised the bid by $5,000. The Karoutases then bid $1 more. The parties repeated this pattern three times. The Karoutases were the high bidders at $155,001. . . .

After the sale, the Karoutases discovered that soil conditions and other defects in the residence would cost in excess of $250,000 to repair. Before the sale, the Karoutases did not and could not inspect the property or residence. The Karoutases allege that the Lawrences disclosed these defects to HomeFed before the sale. Home-Fed also obtained reports that repairs would cost in excess of $350,000 and would not be economically feasible. The reports recommended that the residence be demolished. The Karoutases demanded rescission. HomeFed refused.

On January 24, 1990, the Karoutases filed a complaint for rescission, declaratory relief, fraud, and negligent nondisclosure. HomeFed demurred on the ground that the complaint failed to state facts sufficient to constitute a cause of action because the absence of a disclosure duty defeated all four claims. . . .

The principal issue on appeal is whether HomeFed, given its alleged knowledge of defects in the property and residence, had a duty to disclose the defects to the Karoutases.[3] In the absence of a fiduciary or confidential relationship, a duty to disclose arises at common law if material facts are known only to the defendant and the defendant knows that the plaintiff does not know or cannot reasonably discover the undisclosed facts. Undisclosed facts are material if they have a significant and measurable effect on market value. . . .

In their complaint, the Karoutases allege that (1) the property they purchased has been and is subject to substantial, permanent, and progressive soil movement; (2) this condition subjects the residence on the property to severe forces and stresses; (3) HomeFed knew, through the Lawrences and expert reports, of these conditions but suppressed and failed to disclose them; (4) the Karoutases, at the time they purchased the property, did not know of these conditions and would not have purchased the property had they known; and (5) the Karoutases could not and did not inspect the property prior to purchase. . . .

HomeFed does not contend that the Karoutases' allegations fail to establish a common law duty to disclose. Rather, it argues that the comprehensive nature of the nonjudicial foreclosure statutes (Civ. Code, §2924 et seq.), which do not contain a duty to disclose, precludes us from imposing such a duty on a beneficiary. . . .

. . . HomeFed argues that in I. E. Associates v. Safeco Title Ins. Co. (1985) 39 Cal. 3d 281, 216 Cal. Rptr. 438, 702 P.2d 596 (hereafter *Safeco*), "[t]he California Supreme Court . . . specifically held that the statutory scheme regulating nonjudicial foreclosure of deeds of trust . . . supplanted the common law with respect to the rights and duties of the parties to a deed of trust." HomeFed's contention overstates *Safeco*'s holding. In *Safeco*, the Supreme Court held that, in light of the detailed statutory notice provisions governing nonjudicial foreclosures, a trustee has no additional common law duty to make reasonable efforts to provide a defaulting trustor with actual notice of sale. It expressly limited its holding to notice considerations, stating that "[t]his case deals only with the question of notice that must be given before a foreclosure sale." . . .

In limiting its *Safeco* holding, the Supreme Court expressly preserved a long line of cases imposing duties on a trustee in addition to those statutorily established. *Safeco* also cites Baron v. Colonial Mortgage Service Co. (1980) 111 Cal. App. 3d 316, 168 Cal. Rptr. 450. In *Baron*, this District imposed on the trustee a "duty to exercise reasonable discretion in qualifying bidders," and held that a breach of that duty may warrant rescission. It premised this holding in part on the fact that courts have imposed on trustees a duty to conduct sales "'. . . fairly, openly, reasonably, and with due diligence and sound discretion to protect the rights of the mortgagor and others, using all reasonable efforts to secure the

---

3. Thus, this appeal does not raise the issue of whether a beneficiary under a deed of trust has a duty to investigate for defects.

best possible or reasonable price.' *That duty may thus fairly be said to extend to all participants in the sale, including prospective bidders.*" (Id., at pp. 323-324, 168 Cal. Rptr. 450, emphasis added.) Thus, *Safeco* expressly does not hold that the nonjudicial foreclosure statutes eliminate common law duties owed to prospective bidders over and above those the statutes provide.[7] . . .

Finally, we reject HomeFed's contention that the imposition of a duty to disclose under the facts of this case runs afoul of the public interest in speedy disposition of property under deeds of trust. There is also a public interest in the prevention of fraud. Moreover, the doctrine of caveat emptor does not apply to nonjudicial foreclosure sales. Thus, "[i]t is the general rule that courts have power to vacate a foreclosure sale where there has been fraud in the procurement of the foreclosure decree or where the sale has been improperly, unfairly or unlawfully conducted, or is tainted by fraud, or where there has been such a mistake that to allow it to stand would be inequitable to purchaser and parties." (Bank of America, etc., Ass'n v. Reidy (1940) 15 Cal. 2d 243, 248, 101 P.2d 77.) We cannot believe that the Legislature, in enacting section 2924 et seq., intended to immunize beneficiaries from liability for deceit, or to expand the risks borne by purchasers to include the assumption of damages resulting from a beneficiary's fraud.

In sum, we find that neither the statutes nor public policy prohibits us from finding that a beneficiary under a deed of trust selling property pursuant to a power of sale may owe a common law duty to prospective bidders to disclose known facts materially affecting the value of the property. . . .

NOTES AND QUESTIONS

1. Judicial Foreclosure: Junior Interests. In judicial foreclosures a junior interest-holder must be joined as a party defendant to be cut off by a foreclosure of a senior interest. You may have heard the terms "necessary party" and "proper party" used in the consideration of who must be joined as a party defendant in a foreclosure proceeding. The meaning of these terms is somewhat obscure. Generally, a "necessary party" is one that must be joined in order to give the purchaser at the foreclosure sale essentially the same title as the borrower had on recording of the mortgage. Don't be confused by the word "necessary." While failure to join a necessary party will give the mortgagee or other purchaser title

---

7. In Sumitomo Bank v. Taurus Developers, Inc. (1986) 185 Cal. App. 3d 211, 221, 229 Cal. Rptr. 719, the court refused to impose on the trustor [borrower] a duty to disclose known defects in the property being sold at a trustee's sale. It relied, not on the comprehensive nature of the nonjudicial foreclosure statutes ... but on the unique role of the defaulting trustor, who "was not setting the price at the sale, and in general was not representing the value of the property at the sale." Accordingly, the court concluded, the trustor could not be fairly characterized as a "'seller'" subject to the traditional duties imposed on sellers. By contrast, "[i]t was the beneficiary ... and the trustee who controlled the sale." This distinction justifies imposition on the beneficiary of a duty to disclose under appropriate circumstances.

subject to the rights of the nonjoined junior party, it will not invalidate the foreclosure.

A "proper party," on the other hand, is one whose interest need not be cut off to give the mortgagee or purchaser at the foreclosure sale the borrower's state of title at mortgage recording. The term refers to a party that might conveniently be joined for specific purposes and will be bound by the proceedings but not subject to being cut off by them. For example, it might be appropriate for a prior interestholder to be joined for the purpose of definitively establishing the amount of the senior lien to which the purchaser at the foreclosure sale will take subject.

From the mortgagee's point of view, the key issue is not whether a party is labeled necessary or proper but whether the mortgagee intends that the foreclosure affect or impair the party's rights. If the foreclosure is so intended, the party must be joined for that purpose. Failure to do so leaves the party unaffected by the foreclosure. If you were attorney for a foreclosing mortgagee, what steps would you take to avoid missing a junior interest?

> ➤ *Problem 8-2*
> Assume that you represent Ace Insurance Company as foreclosing mortgagee in our master hypothetical. To facilitate your identification of junior interestholders, you order a title search. The title search reveals (i) a mortgage held by Fuller National Bank, executed and recorded after recordation of Ace's mortgage; (ii) a mechanic's lien recorded subsequent to the mortgage but that purports to relate back to the commencement of work two days before the recording of Ace's mortgage; (iii) a lease to Widget Corporation of America executed after recordation of the mortgage, together with an agreement between WCA and Ace of nondisturbance and attornment; (iv) a lease to Sans Argent, Inc., executed subsequent to the recording of Ace's mortgage; (v) a lease to American Telephone and Telegraph Company, executed after recordation of Ace's mortgage, the term of which will end in eleven years, covering three full floors, at a below-market rental rate; (vi) a deed executed and recorded after Ace's mortgage was recorded, conveying to Sam Speculator an undivided one-half interest in the property; and (vii) a judgment in favor of Paula Plaintiff obtained prior to the recording of Ace's mortgage and docketed in the county where the property is located after the recording of Ace's mortgage. Which of these interestholders would you join as a party defendant? What considerations should you weigh in making the decision? Before answering, review the lien priority rules discussed in Chapter 3E. ◄

It should be noted that, notwithstanding the problems it can create, the joinder requirement provides the lender with a unique opportunity. Because failure to join a party means that the party is unaffected by the foreclosure, the mortgagee can pick and choose which of the junior interests it wishes to cut off and which it wishes to leave unaffected. You can readily see why many tenants will insist, as a condition to signing the lease, that a prior mortgagee subordinate or agree that it will not disturb the tenant on any foreclosure of the mortgage. If this is unfamiliar to you, review Chapter 3E2.

2. The Omitted Junior Interest. Assume in the master hypothetical that Ace holds a first mortgage and Fuller National Bank holds a second. In its foreclosure, Ace fails to join Fuller as a party defendant. As a result of this omission, the foreclosure would be ineffective as to Fuller, and the purchaser at the foreclosure sale would take title subject to Fuller's mortgage. If you represented Ace, and Ace was the successful bidder at the foreclosure sale, after overcoming your initial embarrassment at not joining Fuller (and thoroughly reviewing your professional liability policy), you would think of the steps you would recommend to Ace.

For obvious reasons, you probably would not want to recommend that Ace pay off the second mortgage, either in whole (if it had been accelerated or if prepayment were possible) or periodically as it became due. How about reforeclosure? Are there any disadvantages? Would you have to go through a full judicial foreclosure or could you use one of the other methods we have been discussing? Courts often recognize that a first mortgage can be revived for the purpose of foreclosing against the omitted junior mortgage. The concept is that since the original foreclosure did not affect the junior interest, as to that interest it is as though the first foreclosure hadn't taken place. See Vanderkemp v. Shelton, 11 Paige 28 (N.Y. 1844); Platt, The Dracula Mortgage: Creature of the Omitted Lienholder, 67 Or. L. Rev. 287 (1988).

3. When Is the Junior Interest Cut Off? In Metropolitan Life Ins. Co. v. Childs Co., 230 N.Y. 285, 130 N.E. 295 (1921), the mortgagee joined a junior lessee as a party defendant. A foreclosure judgment was obtained and served on the lessee providing for a sale that would forever bar all interest of the lessee in the premises. The lessee vacated the premises and moved elsewhere. Thereafter (but before the sale) the mortgagee changed its mind and successfully moved to discontinue the action against the lessee and to vacate the judgment against it. This meant that the foreclosure would not cut off the lease and the lessee would remain liable for rent. The lessee argued that the mortgagee either elected its remedy against the lessee or was estopped from holding the lessee liable under the lease. Holding for the mortgagee, the New York Court of Appeals reasoned that the lender's decision to join a junior interest is not an election of remedies, nor could the lessee reasonably assume that its lease was terminated before the foreclosure sale was held. If the holding were otherwise, then consider how the court would deal with the lessee's rights if the court vacated the foreclosure judgment, not because the foreclosing lender changed its mind but because the borrower sold the property and paid off the mortgage, or cured the defaults and reinstated the mortgage before the foreclosure sale as an arrearages law would allow (see Chapter 8B1, note 2, supra).

If a junior party such as a junior lessee or junior mortgagee is joined in as a defendant by the foreclosing mortgagee, the junior party can obtain some protection by exercising, where applicable, its right of equitable and statutory redemption, its right as a mortgagee to maintain an action for a deficiency judgment (or as a lessee to sue the lessor for breach of its lease), and its ability to bid in as a purchaser at the foreclosure sale. See discussion at Chapter 7B1, note 3b.

4. Tenant Protections. The unfairness for subordinate tenants inherent in examples such as the one discussed in note 3 led Congress and the states during the subprime mortgage crisis to protect residential tenants. Before it expired at the end of 2014, the federal Protecting Tenants at Foreclosure Act of 2009 entitled the residential tenant to remain until the lease term ended, unless the property was sold to someone who intended to occupy it as a primary residence. In any event, and for month-to-month tenancies otherwise subject to termination, the tenant was entitled to 90 days notice of the termination. Several states enacted similar protections for residential tenants that remain in place. Open questions under some of these laws include the ability to evict a tenant who is delinquent in paying the contractual rent, as well as whether these statutes apply to the increasingly common practice of financially strapped homeowners renting a room in their residence.

5. Power-of-Sale Legislation. Apply California's power-of-sale statute excerpted above to the following problem.

> ➢ *Problem 8-3*
> Assume that Goria Swansong, an aging screen actress, owns a house on Sunset Strip in Beverly Hills, California, and 30 acres of undeveloped land in the hills overlooking Malibu. There is a deed of trust on her home securing a loan from Star Savings Bank and one on the 30 acres securing a loan from Pepperdine National Bank. Ms. Swansong has not had a starring role for 25 years, and in fact has not acted in any role for the last 10 years, but she has not changed her lifestyle. Now she has just about run out of cash and is in default on both her deeds of trust. Star and Pepperdine begin foreclosure under power-of-sale provisions in their deeds of trust. Notices meeting the statutory requirements are posted at the courthouses in Beverly Hills and Malibu, recorded in the appropriate offices, and published among the legal advertisements in the *Beverly Hills Bugle* and the *Malibu Gazette* for the times required by statute. In addition, Pepperdine posts a notice on a tree on the 30 acres along Gulch River Trail, a small country road that abuts the property. Star does not post a notice on the door of Ms. Swansong's home, or any other place on her property, but does mail the statement to her as provided by subsection (c) of the California statute.
> Ms. Swansong does not visit her 30 acres in the 20 days prior to the sale, during which time the notice was posted. She reads the *Los Angeles Times* and *Variety* but not the *Beverly Hills Bugle* or the *Malibu Gazette*. She has never been in the recording office and has not been in the courthouse since

her last divorce 15 years ago. Unaware of the sales, she does not attend either of them. At the sale of her home, Barry Broker, who does read legal notices, bids $800,000 (the mortgage balance) to become the successful bidder. In better times the house was worth $1.5 million, but there has been somewhat of a downturn in the real estate market, and Star, concerned that values would continue to fall and fearful of a large portfolio of foreclosed properties, was happy to get its money back. It ceased bidding when the price equaled the mortgage balance. At the sale of the 30 acres, there was no competitive bidding, and Pepperdine acquired the property for the mortgage balance of $250,000.

On learning of the sales, Ms. Swansong engages you as her counsel. Based on those portions of the California power-of-sale legislation excerpted above, are there any arguments to overturn the sales? Will your arguments succeed? (We will come back to the issue of foreclosure sale bids of less than the property value when we examine borrower protections later in this chapter and, in Chapter 18, fraudulent transfer issues.) ◄

6. Bidding. The following problem explores some of the complexities the lender faces in determining its foreclosure bid amount.

> ➤ **Problem 8-4**

Under the master hypothetical, assume that Ace Insurance Company is foreclosing on its mortgage on Dan Developer's building. The mortgage balance is $15 million, and Ace's in-house appraisers value the property at $18 million. Prior to foreclosure, a title search reveals a second mortgage held by Fuller National Bank (FNB) for $10 million and a real estate tax lien for $1 million filed after both mortgages were recorded that, by state statute, takes priority over prior mortgages. Having known that the property was in trouble for some time, Dan has been trying to sell it but has been unsuccessful in finding any purchasers willing to pay more than the mortgage balances. He has decided to let the property go to foreclosure.

If there is competitive bidding at the sale, how much must Ace bid to protect its investment? What should its maximum bid be? How much will FNB have to bid to protect its interest? If its appraisers feel the property is worth $16 million, should FNB bid at all? See discussion at Chapter 7B1, note 3b. Assuming that the property is worth $18 million, Dan is in the unenviable position of trying to unload the property while it is encumbered by $26 million of total debt. In these circumstances, how might Dan avoid a foreclosure and the damage it may cause to his credit and his reputation in the development community? ◄

7. Circular Priorities. Assume in the situation discussed in Problem 8-4 that the title search reveals a federal income tax lien of $2 million instead of the FNB mortgage. Notice of the federal tax lien was filed after the Ace mortgage was recorded but before the $1 million real estate tax lien was filed. Under I.R.C. §6323, a federal tax lien will be effective against mortgages (as well as purchasers, other holders of security interests, mechanic's lienors, and judgment lienors) when filed. Normally, a federal tax lien will prime any subsequent interest. Thus the federal tax lien would be inferior to the mortgage and superior to the real estate tax lien. The real estate tax lien would, however, be superior to the mortgage. At the foreclosure sale, the property is purchased by a third-party bidder for $16 million. In absence of a statutory solution, how do you think the proceeds would be distributed if the real estate tax lien primes the mortgage, the mortgage is prior to the federal tax lien, and the federal tax lien trumps the real estate tax lien? This raises the "circular" priority situation that arises when two different priority statutes are involved in the same distribution. To see how Congress dealt with the real estate tax lien priority problem check out I.R.C. §6323(b)(6).

8. *Disclosure Duties in Foreclosure.* As stated in footnote 3 of *Karoutas*, because the purchaser alleged that the lender knew of the property defect, the case did not raise the issue of whether a foreclosing lender without such knowledge has an affirmative duty to investigate the collateral for defects. The outcome in *Karoutas* nonetheless may have troubling implications for lenders. For example, if the lender investigates the property and meticulously lists actual and suspected defects in the sale notice, might the borrower argue that the lender has improperly chilled potential bids? Do you think the court in *Karoutas* would hold the trustee to the same standard of disclosure? What if the trustee is the lender's legal counsel? Should the lender have the same duty to disclose when the property is sold pursuant to a judicial foreclosure? What was the lender in *Karoutas* doing bidding in excess of its loan balance if, in fact, it knew of the defect? Finally, notwithstanding the decision noted in footnote 7 of the *Karoutas* case, do you think that the borrower in *Karoutas* should be liable to the foreclosure sale purchaser on a theory of unjust enrichment?

THE REAL ESTATE LAWYER AND THE UCC

In authorizing nonjudicial sales of personal property collateral on default, the UCC acknowledges the variety of personalty collateral and avoids articulating definite standards for conducting post-default disposition. Rather, every aspect of the sale or other disposition, including its method, time, and place, must be "commercially reasonable." UCC §9-610(b). By contrast, realty power of sale legislation tends to mandate specifically the method of sale publicity and the other terms of the sale. As a real estate lender, which statutory approach do you favor?

9. Additional Reading. Geis, Escape from the 15th Century: The Uniform Land Security Interest Act, 30 Real Prop., Prob. & Tr. J. 289 (1995); Johnson, Critiquing the Foreclosure Process: An Economic Approach Based on the Paradigmatic Norms of Bankruptcy, 79 Va. L. Rev. 959 (1993); Mattingly, The Shift From Power to Process: A Functional Approach to Foreclosure Law, 80 Marq. L. Rev. 77 (1996); Stark, Facing the Facts: An Empirical Study of the Fairness and Efficiency of Foreclosures and a Proposal for Reform, 30 Mich. J.L. Ref. 639 (1997); Tefft, The Myth of Strict Foreclosure, 4 U. Chi. L. Rev. 575 (1937); Turner, The English Mortgage of Land as a Security, 20 Va. L. Rev. 729 (1934); Wechsler, Through the Looking Glass: Foreclosure by Sale as De Facto Strict Foreclosure—An Empirical Study of Mortgage Foreclosure and Subsequent Resale, 70 Cornell L. Rev. 850 (1985); and Kocian, Note, Mortgage Foreclosures: The Lingering Effect of the Common Law of Separation of Legal and Equitable Remedies, 52 Chi.-Kent L. Rev. 121 (1975).

b. Residential Securitization

As evident in Chapter 15, securitization of residential loans on the debt side has become the norm. The materials below address the uneasy relationship of securitized lending with often traditional, formalistic state foreclosure law. In reading the materials, form your own opinion on the legitimacy of borrowers admittedly in default relying on what might be considered technical defenses to stave off foreclosure.

U.S. Bank National Assoc. v. Ibanez
458 Mass. 637, 941 N.E.2d 40 (2011)

GANTS, J.

After foreclosing on two properties and purchasing the properties back at the foreclosure sales, U.S. Bank National Association (U.S. Bank), as trustee for the Structured Asset Securities Corporation Mortgage Pass-Through Certificates, Series 2006-Z; and Wells Fargo Bank, N.A. (Wells Fargo), as trustee for ABFC 2005-OPT 1 Trust, ABFC Asset Backed Certificates, Series 2005-OPT 1 (plaintiffs), filed separate complaints in the Land Court asking a judge to declare that they held clear title to the properties in fee simple. We agree with the judge that the plaintiffs, who were not the original mortgagees, failed to make the required showing that they were the holders of the mortgages at the time of foreclosure. As a result, they did not demonstrate that the foreclosure sales were valid to convey title to the subject properties, and their requests for a declaration of clear title were properly denied.

Procedural history. On July 5, 2007, U.S. Bank, as trustee, foreclosed on the mortgage of Antonio Ibanez and purchased the Ibanez property at the foreclosure sale. On the same day, Wells Fargo, as trustee, foreclosed on the mortgage of Mark and Tammy LaRace and purchased the LaRace property at that foreclosure sale.

In September and October of 2008, U.S. Bank and Wells Fargo brought separate actions in the Land Court under G.L. c. 240, §6, which authorizes actions "to quiet or establish the title to land situated in the commonwealth or to remove a cloud from the title thereto." The two complaints sought identical relief: (1) a judgment that the right, title, and interest of the mortgagor (Ibanez or the LaRaces) in the property was extinguished by the foreclosure . . .[and] a declaration that title was vested in the plaintiff trustee in fee simple. U.S. Bank and Wells Fargo each asserted in its complaint that it had become the holder of the respective mortgage through an assignment made *after* the foreclosure sale.

In both cases, the mortgagors—Ibanez and the LaRaces—did not initially answer the complaints, and the plaintiffs moved for entry of default judgment. In their motions for entry of default judgment, the plaintiffs addressed . . . whether the plaintiffs were legally entitled to foreclose on the properties where the assignments of the mortgages to the plaintiffs were neither executed nor recorded in the registry of deeds until after the foreclosure sales. The two cases were heard together by the Land Court, along with a third case that raised the same issues.

On March 26, 2009, judgment was entered against the plaintiffs. The judge ruled that the foreclosure sales were invalid because, in violation of G.L. c. 244, §14, the notices of the foreclosure sales named U.S. Bank (in the Ibanez foreclosure) and Wells Fargo (in the LaRace foreclosure) as the mortgage holders where they had not yet been assigned the mortgages. The judge found, based on each plaintiff's assertions in its complaint, that the plaintiffs acquired the mortgages by assignment only after the foreclosure sales and thus had no interest in the mortgages being foreclosed at the time of the publication of the notices of sale or at the time of the foreclosure sales.

The plaintiffs then moved to vacate the judgments. At a hearing on the motions on April 17, 2009, the plaintiffs conceded that each complaint alleged a postnotice, postforeclosure sale assignment of the mortgage at issue, but they now represented to the judge that documents might exist that could show a prenotice, preforeclosure sale assignment of the mortgages. The judge granted the plaintiffs leave to produce such documents, provided they were produced in the form they existed in at the time the foreclosure sale was noticed and conducted. In response, the plaintiffs submitted hundreds of pages of documents to the judge, which they claimed established that the mortgages had been assigned to them before the foreclosures. Many of these documents related to the creation of the securitized mortgage pools in which the Ibanez and LaRace mortgages were purportedly included.

The judge denied the plaintiffs' motions to vacate judgment on October 14, 2009, concluding that the newly submitted documents did not alter the conclusion that the plaintiffs were not the holders of the respective mortgages at the time of foreclosure. We granted the parties' applications for direct appellate review. . . .

The Ibanez mortgage. On December 1, 2005, Antonio Ibanez took out a $103,500 loan for the purchase of property at 20 Crosby Street in Springfield, secured by a mortgage to the lender, Rose Mortgage, Inc. (Rose Mortgage). The mortgage was recorded the following day. Several days later, Rose Mortgage executed an assignment of this mortgage in blank, that is, an assignment that did not specify the name of the assignee.[11] The blank space in the assignment was at some point stamped with the name of Option One Mortgage Corporation (Option One) as the assignee, and that assignment was recorded on June 7, 2006. Before the recording, on January 23, 2006, Option One executed an assignment of the Ibanez mortgage in blank.

According to U.S. Bank, Option One assigned the Ibanez mortgage to Lehman Brothers Bank, FSB, which assigned it to Lehman Brothers Holdings Inc., which then assigned it to the Structured Asset Securities Corporation,[12] which then assigned the mortgage, pooled with approximately 1,220 other mortgage loans, to U.S. Bank, as trustee for the Structured Asset Securities Corporation Mortgage Pass-Through Certificates, Series 2006-Z. With this last assignment, the Ibanez and other loans were pooled into a trust and converted into mortgage-backed securities that can be bought and sold by investors—a process known as securitization.

For ease of reference, the chain of entities through which the Ibanez mortgage allegedly passed before the foreclosure sale is:

Rose Mortgage, Inc. (originator)
↓
Option One Mortgage Corporation (record holder)
↓
Lehman Brothers Bank, FSB
↓
Lehman Brothers Holdings Inc. (seller)
↓
Structured Asset Securities Corporation (depositor)
↓
U.S. Bank National Association, as trustee for the Structured Asset Securities Corporation Mortgage Pass-Through Certificates, Series 2006-Z

11. This signed and notarized document states: "FOR VALUE RECEIVED, the undersigned hereby grants, assigns and transfers to _____ all beneficial interest under that certain Mortgage dated December 1, 2005 executed by Antonio Ibanez...."

12. The Structured Asset Securities Corporation is a wholly owned direct subsidiary of Lehman Commercial Paper Inc., which is in turn a wholly owned, direct subsidiary of Lehman Brothers Holdings Inc.

According to U.S. Bank, the assignment of the Ibanez mortgage to U.S. Bank occurred pursuant to a December 1, 2006, trust agreement, which is not in the record. What is in the record is the private placement memorandum (PPM), dated December 26, 2006, a 273-page, unsigned offer of mortgage-backed securities to potential investors. The PPM describes the mortgage pools and the entities involved and summarizes the provisions of the trust agreement, including the representation that mortgages "will be" assigned into the trust. According to the PPM, "[e]ach transfer of a Mortgage Loan from the Seller [Lehman Brothers Holdings Inc.] to the Depositor [Structured Asset Securities Corporation] and from the Depositor to the Trustee [U.S. Bank] will be intended to be a sale of that Mortgage Loan and will be reflected as such in the Sale and Assignment Agreement and the Trust Agreement, respectively." The PPM also specifies that "[e]ach Mortgage Loan will be identified in a schedule appearing as an exhibit to the Trust Agreement." However, U.S. Bank did not provide the judge with any mortgage schedule identifying the Ibanez loan as among the mortgages that were assigned in the trust agreement.

On April 17, 2007, U.S. Bank filed a complaint to foreclose on the Ibanez mortgage in the Land Court under the Servicemembers Civil Relief Act (Servicemembers Act), which restricts foreclosures against active duty members of the uniformed services. See 50 U.S.C. Appendix §§501, 511, 533 (2006 & Supp. II 2008). In the complaint, U.S. Bank represented that it was the "owner (or assignee) and holder" of the mortgage given by Ibanez for the property. A judgment [was] issued on behalf of U.S. Bank on June 26, 2007, declaring that the mortgagor was not entitled to protection from foreclosure under the Servicemembers Act. In June 2007, U.S. Bank also caused to be published in the *Boston Globe* the notice of the foreclosure sale required by G.L. c. 244, §14. The notice identified U.S. Bank as the "present holder" of the mortgage.

At the foreclosure sale on July 5, 2007, the Ibanez property was purchased by U.S. Bank, as trustee for the securitization trust, for $94,350, a value significantly less than the outstanding debt and the estimated market value of the property. The foreclosure deed (from U.S. Bank, trustee, as the purported holder of the mortgage, to U.S. Bank, trustee, as the purchaser) and the statutory foreclosure affidavit were recorded on May 23, 2008. On September 2, 2008, more than one year after the sale, and more than five months after recording of the sale, American Home Mortgage Servicing, Inc., "as successor-in-interest" to Option One, which was until then the record holder of the Ibanez mortgage, executed a written assignment of that mortgage to U.S. Bank, as trustee for the securitization trust. This assignment was recorded on September 11, 2008.

The LaRace mortgage. On May 19, 2005, Mark and Tammy LaRace gave a mortgage for the property at 6 Brookburn Street in Springfield to Option One as security for a $103,200 loan; the mortgage was recorded that same day. On May 26, 2005, Option One executed an assignment of this mortgage in blank.

According to Wells Fargo, Option One later assigned the LaRace mortgage to Bank of America in a July 28, 2005, flow sale and servicing agreement. Bank of

America then assigned it to Asset Backed Funding Corporation (ABFC) in an October 1, 2005, mortgage loan purchase agreement. Finally, ABFC pooled the mortgage with others and assigned it to Wells Fargo, as trustee for the ABFC 2005-OPT 1 Trust, ABFC Asset-Backed Certificates, Series 2005-OPT 1, pursuant to a pooling and servicing agreement (PSA).

Wells Fargo did not provide the judge with a copy of the flow sale and servicing agreement, so there is no document in the record reflecting an assignment of the LaRace mortgage by Option One to Bank of America. The plaintiff did produce an unexecuted copy of the mortgage loan purchase agreement, which was an exhibit to the PSA. The mortgage loan purchase agreement provides that Bank of America, as seller, "does hereby agree to and does hereby sell, assign, set over, and otherwise convey to the Purchaser [ABFC], without recourse, on the Closing Date . . . all of its right, title and interest in and to each Mortgage Loan." The agreement makes reference to a schedule listing the assigned mortgage loans, but this schedule is not in the record, so there was no document before the judge showing that the LaRace mortgage was among the mortgage loans assigned to the ABFC. . . .

Wells Fargo did provide the judge with a copy of the PSA, which is an agreement between the ABFC (as depositor), Option One (as servicer), and Wells Fargo (as trustee), but this copy was downloaded from the Securities and Exchange Commission Web site and was not signed. The PSA provides that the depositor "does hereby transfer, assign, set over and otherwise convey to the Trustee, on behalf of the Trust . . . all the right, title and interest of the Depositor . . . in and to . . . each Mortgage Loan identified on the Mortgage Loan Schedules," and "does hereby deliver" to the trustee the original mortgage note, an original mortgage assignment "in form and substance acceptable for recording," and other documents pertaining to each mortgage.

The copy of the PSA provided to the judge did not contain the loan schedules referenced in the agreement. Instead, Wells Fargo submitted a schedule that it represented identified the loans assigned in the PSA, which did not include property addresses, names of mortgagors, or any number that corresponds to the loan number or servicing number on the LaRace mortgage. Wells Fargo contends that a loan with the LaRace property's zip code and city is the LaRace mortgage loan because the payment history and loan amount matches the LaRace loan. . . .

At the foreclosure sale on July 5, 2007, Wells Fargo, as trustee, purchased the LaRace property for $120,397.03, a value significantly below its estimated market value. Wells Fargo did not execute a statutory foreclosure affidavit or foreclosure deed until May 7, 2008. That same day, Option One, which was still the record holder of the LaRace mortgage, executed an assignment of the mortgage to Wells Fargo as trustee; the assignment was recorded on May 12, 2008. Although executed ten months after the foreclosure sale, the assignment declared an effective date of April 18, 2007, a date that preceded the publication of the notice of sale and the foreclosure sale.

Discussion. The plaintiffs brought actions under G.L. c. 240, §6, seeking declarations that the defendant mortgagors' titles had been extinguished and that the plaintiffs were the fee simple owners of the foreclosed properties. . . . There is no question that the relief the plaintiffs sought required them to establish the validity of the foreclosure sales on which their claim to clear title rested.

Massachusetts does not require a mortgage holder to obtain judicial authorization to foreclose on a mortgaged property. See G.L. c. 183, §21; G.L. c. 244, §14. With the exception of the limited judicial procedure aimed at certifying that the mortgagor is not a beneficiary of the Servicemembers Act, a mortgage holder can foreclose on a property, as the plaintiffs did here, by exercise of the statutory power of sale, if such a power is granted by the mortgage itself.

Where a mortgage grants a mortgage holder the power of sale, as did both the Ibanez and LaRace mortgages, it includes by reference the power of sale set out in G.L. c. 183, §21, and further regulated by G.L. c. 244, §§11-17C. Under G.L. c. 183, §21, after a mortgagor defaults in the performance of the underlying note, the mortgage holder may sell the property at a public auction and convey the property to the purchaser in fee simple, "and such sale shall forever bar the mortgagor and all persons claiming under him from all right and interest in the mortgaged premises, whether at law or in equity." Even where there is a dispute as to whether the mortgagor was in default or whether the party claiming to be the mortgage holder is the true mortgage holder, the foreclosure goes forward unless the mortgagor files an action and obtains a court order enjoining the foreclosure.

Recognizing the substantial power that the statutory scheme affords to a mortgage holder to foreclose without immediate judicial oversight, we adhere to the familiar rule that "one who sells under a power [of sale] must follow strictly its terms. If he fails to do so there is no valid execution of the power, and the sale is wholly void." Moore v. Dick, 187 Mass. 207, 211, 72 N.E. 967 (1905).

One of the terms of the power of sale that must be strictly adhered to is the restriction on who is entitled to foreclose. The "statutory power of sale" can be exercised by "the mortgagee or his executors, administrators, successors or assigns." G.L. c. 183, §21. Under G.L. c. 244, §14, "[t]he mortgagee or person having his estate in the land mortgaged, or a person authorized by the power of sale, or the attorney duly authorized by a writing under seal, or the legal guardian or conservator of such mortgagee or person acting in the name of such mortgagee or person" is empowered to exercise the statutory power of sale. Any effort to foreclose by a party lacking "jurisdiction and authority" to carry out a foreclosure under these statutes is void.

A related statutory requirement that must be strictly adhered to in a foreclosure by power of sale is the notice requirement articulated in G.L. c. 244, §14. That statute provides that "no sale under such power shall be effectual to foreclose a mortgage, unless, previous to such sale," advance notice of the foreclosure sale has been provided to the mortgagor, to other interested parties, and by publication in a newspaper published in the town where the mortgaged land lies or of general circulation in that town. Id. . . . Because only a present holder of the mortgage is authorized to foreclose on the mortgaged property, and because the mortgagor is entitled to know who is foreclosing and selling the property, the failure to identify the holder of the mortgage in the notice of sale may render the notice defective and the foreclosure sale void.

For the plaintiffs to obtain the judicial declaration of clear title that they seek, they had to prove their authority to foreclose under the power of sale and show their compliance with the requirements on which this authority rests. Here, the plaintiffs were not the original mortgagees to whom the power of sale was granted; rather, they claimed the authority to foreclose as the eventual assignees of the original mortgagees. Under the plain language of G.L. c. 183, §21, and G.L. c. 244, §14, the plaintiffs had the authority to exercise the power of sale contained in the Ibanez and LaRace mortgages only if they were the assignees of the mortgages at the time of the notice of sale and the subsequent foreclosure sale.

The plaintiffs claim that the securitization documents they submitted establish valid assignments that made them the holders of the Ibanez and LaRace mortgages before the notice of sale and the foreclosure sale. We turn, then, to the documentation submitted by the plaintiffs to determine whether it met the requirements of a valid assignment.

Like a sale of land itself, the assignment of a mortgage is a conveyance of an interest in land that requires a writing signed by the grantor. See G.L. c. 183, §3. In a "title theory state" like Massachusetts, a mortgage is a transfer of legal title in a property to secure a debt. Therefore, when a person borrows money to purchase a home and gives the lender a mortgage, the homeowner-mortgagor retains only equitable title in the home; the legal title is held by the mortgagee. Where, as here, mortgage loans are pooled together in a trust and converted into mortgage-backed securities, the underlying promissory notes serve as financial instruments generating a potential income stream for investors, but the mortgages securing these notes are still legal title to someone's home or farm and must be treated as such.

Focusing first on the Ibanez mortgage, U.S. Bank argues that it was assigned the mortgage under the trust agreement described in the PPM, but it did not submit a copy of this trust agreement to the judge. The PPM, however, described the trust agreement as an agreement to be executed in the future, so it only furnished evidence of an intent to assign mortgages to U.S. Bank, not proof of their actual assignment. Even if there were an executed trust agreement with language of present assignment, U.S. Bank did not produce the schedule of loans and mortgages that was an exhibit to that agreement, so it failed to show that the Ibanez mortgage was among the mortgages to be assigned by that agreement. Finally, even if there were an executed trust agreement with the required schedule, U.S. Bank failed to furnish any evidence that the entity assigning the mortgage—Structured Asset Securities Corporation—ever held the mortgage to be assigned. The last assignment of the mortgage on record was from Rose Mortgage to Option One; nothing was submitted to the judge indicating that Option One ever assigned the mortgage to anyone before the foreclosure sale.

Thus, based on the documents submitted to the judge, Option One, not U.S. Bank, was the mortgage holder at the time of the foreclosure, and U.S. Bank did not have the authority to foreclose the mortgage.

Turning to the LaRace mortgage, Wells Fargo claims that, before it issued the foreclosure notice, it was assigned the LaRace mortgage under the PSA. The PSA, in contrast with U.S. Bank's PPM, uses the language of a present assignment ("does hereby . . . assign" and "does hereby deliver") rather than an intent to assign in the future. But the mortgage loan schedule Wells Fargo submitted failed to identify with adequate specificity the LaRace mortgage as one of the mortgages assigned in the PSA. Moreover, Wells Fargo provided the judge with no document that reflected that the ABFC (depositor) held the LaRace mortgage that it was purportedly assigning in the PSA. As with the Ibanez loan, the record holder of the LaRace loan was Option One, and nothing was submitted to the judge which demonstrated that the LaRace loan was ever assigned by Option One to another entity before the publication of the notice and the sale.

Where a plaintiff files a complaint asking for a declaration of clear title after a mortgage foreclosure, a judge is entitled to ask for proof that the foreclosing entity was the mortgage holder at the time of the notice of sale and foreclosure, or was one of the parties authorized to foreclose under G.L. c. 183, §21, and G.L. c. 244, §14. A plaintiff that cannot make this modest showing cannot justly proclaim that it was unfairly denied a declaration of clear title.

We do not suggest that an assignment must be in recordable form at the time of the notice of sale or the subsequent foreclosure sale, although recording is likely the better practice. Where a pool of mortgages is assigned to a securitized trust, the executed agreement that assigns the pool of mortgages, with a schedule of the pooled mortgage loans that clearly and specifically identifies the mortgage at issue as among those assigned, may suffice to establish the trustee as the mortgage holder. However, there must be proof that the assignment was made by a party that itself held the mortgage. A foreclosing entity may provide a complete chain of assignments linking it to the record holder of the mortgage, or a single assignment from the record holder of the mortgage. The key in either case is that the foreclosing entity must hold the mortgage at the time of the notice and sale in order accurately to identify itself as the present holder in the notice and in order to have the authority to foreclose under the power of sale (or the foreclosing entity must be one of the parties authorized to foreclose under G.L. c. 183, §21, and G.L. c. 244, §14).

The judge did not err in concluding that the securitization documents submitted by the plaintiffs failed to demonstrate that they were the holders of the Ibanez and LaRace mortgages, respectively, at the time of the publication of the notices and the sales. . . .

We now turn briefly to three other arguments raised by the plaintiffs on appeal. First, the plaintiffs initially contended that the assignments in blank executed by Option One, identifying the assignor but not the assignee, not only "evidence[] and confirm[] the assignments that occurred by virtue of the securitization agreements," but "are effective assignments in their own right."

But in their reply briefs they conceded that the assignments in blank did not constitute a lawful assignment of the mortgages. Their concession is appropriate. We have long held that a conveyance of real property, such as a mortgage, that does not name the assignee conveys nothing and is void; we do not regard an assignment of land in blank as giving legal title in land to the bearer of the assignment.

Second, the plaintiffs contend that, because they held the mortgage note, they had a sufficient financial interest in the mortgage to allow them to foreclose. In Massachusetts, where a note has been assigned but there is no written assignment of the mortgage underlying the note, the assignment of the note does not carry with it the assignment of the mortgage. Barnes v. Boardman, 149 Mass. 106, 114, 21 N.E. 308 (1889). Rather, the holder of the mortgage holds the mortgage in trust for the purchaser of the note, who has an equitable right to obtain an assignment of the mortgage, which may be accomplished by filing an action in court and obtaining an equitable order of assignment. Id. ("In some jurisdictions it is held that the mere transfer of the debt, without any assignment or even mention of the mortgage, carries the mortgage with it, so as to enable the assignee to assert his title in an action at law. . . . This doctrine has not prevailed in Massachusetts, and the tendency of the decisions here has been, that in such cases the mortgagee would hold the legal title in trust for the purchaser of the debt, and that the latter might obtain a conveyance by a bill in equity"). In the absence of a valid written assignment of a mortgage or a court order of assignment, the mortgage holder remains unchanged. This common-law principle was later incorporated in the statute enacted in 1912 establishing the statutory power of sale, which grants such a power to "the mortgagee or his executors, administrators, successors or assigns," but not to a party that is the equitable beneficiary of a mortgage held by another. G.L. c. 183, §21, inserted by St.1912, c. 502, §6.

Third, the plaintiffs initially argued that postsale assignments were sufficient to establish their authority to foreclose, and now argue that these assignments are sufficient when taken in conjunction with the evidence of a presale assignment. They argue that the use of postsale assignments was customary in the industry, and point to Title Standard No. 58(3) issued by the Real Estate Bar Association for Massachusetts, which declares: "A title is not defective by reason of . . .[t]he recording of an Assignment of Mortgage executed either prior, or subsequent, to foreclosure where said Mortgage has been foreclosed, of record, by the Assignee." To the extent that the plaintiffs rely on this title standard for the proposition that an entity that does not hold a mortgage may foreclose on a property, and then cure the cloud on title by a later assignment of a mortgage, their reliance is misplaced, because this proposition is contrary to G.L. c. 183, §21, and G.L. c. 244, §14. If the plaintiffs did not have their assignments to the Ibanez and LaRace mortgages at the time of the publication of the notices and the sales, they lacked authority to foreclose under G.L. c. 183, §21, and G.L. c. 244, §14, and their published claims to be the present holders of the mortgages were false. Nor may a postforeclosure assignment be treated as a preforeclosure assignment simply by declaring an "effective date" that precedes the notice of sale and foreclosure, as did Option One's assignment of the LaRace mortgage to Wells Fargo. Because an assignment of a mortgage is a transfer of legal title, it becomes effective with respect to the power of sale only on the transfer; it cannot become effective before the transfer. . . .

Finally, we reject the plaintiffs' request that our ruling be prospective in its application. A prospective ruling is only appropriate, in limited circumstances, when we make a significant change in the common law. We have not done so here. The legal principles and requirements we set forth are well established in our case law and our statutes. All that has changed is the plaintiffs' apparent failure to abide by those principles and requirements in the rush to sell mortgage-backed securities.

Conclusion. For the reasons stated, we agree with the judge that the plaintiffs did not demonstrate that they were the holders of the Ibanez and LaRace mortgages at the time that they foreclosed these properties, and therefore failed to demonstrate that they acquired fee simple title to these properties by purchasing them at the foreclosure sale.

CORDY, J. (concurring, with whom Botsford, J., joins).

I concur fully in the opinion of the court, and write separately only to underscore that what is surprising about these cases is not the statement of principles articulated by the court regarding title law and the law of foreclosure in Massachusetts, but rather the utter carelessness with which the plaintiff banks documented the titles to their assets. There is no dispute that the mortgagors of the properties in question had defaulted on their obligations, and that the mortgaged properties were subject to foreclosure. Before commencing such an action, however, the holder of an assigned mortgage needs to take care to ensure that his legal paperwork is in order. Although there was no apparent actual unfairness here to the mortgagors, that is not the point. Foreclosure is a powerful act with significant consequences, and Massachusetts law has always required that it proceed strictly in accord with the statutes that govern it. As the opinion of the court notes, such strict compliance is necessary because Massachusetts both is a title theory State and allows for extrajudicial [nonjudicial] foreclosure.

The type of sophisticated transactions leading up to the accumulation of the notes and mortgages in question in these cases and their securitization, and, ultimately the sale of mortgage-backed securities, are not barred nor even burdened by the requirements of Massachusetts law. The plaintiff banks, who brought these cases to clear the titles that they acquired at their own foreclosure sales, have simply failed to prove that the underlying assignments of the mortgages that they allege (and would have) entitled them to foreclose ever existed in any legally cognizable form before they exercised the power of sale that accompanies those assignments. The court's opinion clearly states that such assignments do not need to be in recordable form or recorded before the foreclosure, but they do have to have been effectuated. . . .

NOTES AND QUESTIONS

1. MERS and the Mortgage Note. Established to facilitate the residential loan securitization markets, Mortgage Electronic Registration Systems, Inc. (MERS) symbolizes the uneasy transition in foreclosure law and procedure from the Main Street model of lending, where the original lender retained its home loans, to the Wall Street model of multiple transfers and securitizations of the loan payment stream. Under the MERS system, rather than record each transfer of the mortgage in the local real estate records and incur multiple recording fees, the loan documents designate MERS as the mortgagee's nominee and MERS documents subsequent loan transfers on its private electronic database that carries cheaper fees.

The MERS model and the securitization protocol it supports collide with traditional judicial and statutory foreclosure requirements. In the former Main Street approach of mortgage lending in which the same bank held long-term possession of the loan it funded, a requirement that the lender initiating foreclosure possess the signed promissory note would pose little problem. For securitized loans, however, keeping track of possession of the note through multiple transfers proved difficult. Particularly in the context of judicial foreclosure actions, some courts require the mortgagee initiating the action to establish its possession of the original signed mortgage note. Also problematic is when loan servicing companies, who do not hold any beneficial interest in the promissory note and act as a designee or nominee for the real party in interest lender, initiate foreclosure in their own name rather than those of the lender/investors actually receiving the loan payment stream. Relatedly, servicing agents face standing issues in seeking to lift the automatic stay in bankruptcy proceedings in order to pursue a state foreclosure action. See Chapter 18C1 for discussion of the automatic stay. Further, the eligibility of MERS, as the lender of record, to receive foreclosure notices sent by senior lenders is suspect in some jurisdictions. But see Kan. Stat. Ann. §60-219(e) (requiring joinder in foreclosure of nominees of record, thereby rejecting a state Supreme Court decision denying standing of MERS to receive such critical notice and service in the senior lien's foreclosure action, Landmark Nat. Bank v. Kesler, 289 Kan. 528, 216 P.3d 158 (2009)).

The *Ibanez* decision captures similar tensions between the Main Street and Wall Street models of mortgage lending, as well as that court's reluctance to relax longstanding requirements, in suggesting: "The legal principles and requirements we set forth are well established in our case law and our statutes. All that has changed is the plaintiffs' apparent failure to abide by those principles and requirements in the rush to sell mortgage-backed securities."

2. Assignments of the Mortgage. Distinct from transferring possession of the mortgage note (typically endorsed with the signature of the transferor), is the potential need (especially in nonjudicial foreclosure jurisdictions with statutorily-prescribed powers of sale) to ensure transfers of the mortgage document (or the beneficial interest under a deed of trust). The *Ibanez* decision involved neither MERS nor, miraculously, an absence of possession of the mortgage note. Rather, it confronted the failure to prove the mortgage had been assigned to the current lender (as trustee for the securitization investors) before that lender initiated foreclosure proceedings. Rejecting the notion that the mortgage follows the note so that formal assignments of the mortgage are unnecessary, the *Ibanez* decision sent bank stocks briefly downward and attracted national media attention. A later decision of the Supreme Judicial Court of Massachusetts confirmed lenders' worst fears in holding that post-foreclosure sale purchasers of foreclosed homes acquired no title from sales suffering the *Ibanez* defect. Bevilacqua v. Rodriguez, 460 Mass. 762, 955 N.E.2d 884 (2011). Still, lenders can readily surmount the requisites of *Ibanez* with the foresight of obtaining an assignment of the mortgage document from each lender in the ownership chain before foreclosing, or even, as sanctioned by *Ibanez*, simply obtaining a single assignment from the original named mortgagee. Other courts, construing state statutory requirements, are more rigid, some insisting that assignments of the mortgage be recorded in the land records before foreclosure, as well as insisting on a complete chain of recorded assignments from each successor to the current lender initiating foreclosure. Compare In re McCoy, 446 B.R. 453 (Bankr. D. Or. 2011) (rejecting sufficiency of MERS as nominee of record assigning beneficial interest under deed of trust to successor lender before foreclosure, as crucial recorded assignments in the chain of ownership were missing) with Calvo v. HSBC Bank USA, N.A., 199 Cal. App. 4th 118, 130 Cal. Rptr. 3d 815 (2011) (California statute requiring recorded assignment construed to apply only to mortgages with powers of sale, not to deeds of trust, thereby allowing nonjudicial foreclosure initiated by MERS without recorded assignment to current lender). Presumably, in the future, lenders will change their protocols to ensure compliance with these Main Street requisites, such as by obtaining possession of the mortgage note as well as procuring an assignment of the mortgage or deed of trust for later recording as needed in advance of initiating foreclosure. Given the relative ease of overcoming these decisions, and the state statutes they construe, that are hostile to the Wall Street securitization model, do you agree with the *Ibanez* decision that "[a]lthough there was no apparent actual unfairness here to the mortgagors, that is not the point[?]" Should the borrower, admittedly in default, be able to rely on what might be viewed as procedural technicalities, here presumably forcing a re-foreclosure and gaining the borrower additional time to remain in possession without tendering payment?

3. Targets of Subprime Lending. As one might surmise from the borrower names from some of the principal foreclosure cases above that likely involved subprime or exotic loan terms, such as Antonio Ibanez and Pablo Rodriguez (Bevilacqua v. Rodriguez), subprime loan originators targeted Latino/a (and Black) borrowers previously excluded from institutional credit markets. Language barriers accentuated the unfairness and fraud inherent in some of these home loan programs, leading to mass litigation against loan originators and others in the securitization chain by individual borrowers (e.g., Vasquez-Lopez v. Beneficial Oregon, Inc., 210 Or. App. 553, 152 P.3d 940 (2007)) as well as by state attorney generals. How should legislators balance the credit and home ownership desires of those with low incomes or marginal credit with the interest of protecting these necessitous borrowers from improvident credit? See S. Bender, Tierra y Libertad: Land, Liberty, and Latino Housing (2010).

3. Protection of the Borrower

As discussed earlier, the history of mortgages has seen the courts and legislatures working constantly to balance the rights of borrowers and lenders to keep the procedure as fair as possible to both sides. In modern times the changes have been largely designed to protect the borrower as perceptions of unfairness have developed and economic conditions have warranted. These developing rules, generally in the form of limitations on freedom of contract—the ability of the lender to implement the terms of its agreement with the borrower—are studied in great detail in an article by Professor Washburn, The Judicial and Legislative Response to Price Inadequacy in Mortgage Foreclosure Sales,[13] excerpted in part below.

a. Antideficiency Judgment Legislation

If real property subject to a mortgage or deed of trust is sold in foreclosure and brings less than the amount of the debt, the borrower is liable under the note for the deficiency. The lender's action to recover the deficiency results in what is known as a deficiency judgment.

Imagine the onerous consequences that might arise from a deficiency judgment. Under the master hypothetical, assume that Ace's mortgage has a balance of $15 million and is in default. Assume further that the value of the property is only $12 million, so Dan, having no equity, lets the property go to foreclosure. At the sale there are no bidders other than Ace. (This is because Ace would match any competitive bid at least up to the value of the property and probably up to the mortgage balance, which means that any third-party bidder would have to bid in excess of the value of the property to be successful.) Ace bids $100 and acquires the property. If Dan were liable on the note, Ace could theoretically obtain a personal judgment against Dan in the amount of $14,999,900. Fortunately, this scenario is unlikely, at least in a commercial setting, because deficiency judgments are extremely rare as a consequence of workout agreements between the parties, nonrecourse financing, practical considerations, and legislative restrictions.

---

13. 53 S. Cal. L. Rev. 843 (1980).

Recall that postconstruction financing of commercial real estate is often nonrecourse. This means that in the event of default the lender agrees to seek recourse only against the property and not against the personal assets of the borrower, whether through a deficiency judgment following foreclosure or by suit on the note without foreclosure.[14] In the field of home mortgage financing, where nonrecourse financing is unusual, institutional lenders seldom seek deficiency judgments because of severe limitations on deficiency judgments imposed by statute and the fact that institutions do not relish the publicity they would receive if they took away their borrowers' homes and then attached their salaries to recover a deficiency.

In the following excerpt from his 1980 article, Professor Washburn discusses the types of antideficiency legislation existing at that time. Similar restrictions exist today.

Washburn, The Judicial and Legislative Response to Price Inadequacy in Mortgage Foreclosure Sales
53 S. Cal. L. Rev. 843, 916-919 (1980)

C. STATUTES PROHIBITING DEFICIENCY JUDGMENTS

A number of state statutory schemes prohibit deficiency judgments instead of controlling them through appraisal or fair market value procedures. These laws do not prohibit all deficiencies, but apply to specific types of transactions, including purchase money mortgages, mortgages on homesteads, private sales, abandoned property, and sales with short redemption periods. Most of these statutes originated during the Depression, at which time their purpose was to shift the loss from the debtor to the creditor as a means of avoiding an acceleration of the downturn. The statutes reflect a legislative intent that public policy requires continued debtor protection in the specified transactions.

1. PURCHASE MONEY MORTGAGES

Seven states prohibit deficiency judgments when the defaulted obligation is a purchase money mortgage. While purchase money mortgages include mortgages given to secure money lent to purchase any type of property, these statutes are intended to protect purchasers of single-family homes. Several of these statutes

---

14. A principal reason why lenders permit nonrecourse financing is that in most loan transactions, especially large ones, it is the rental income stream and not the solvency of the borrower that really protects the lender and feeds the mortgage. See discussion at Chapter 3B3. In addition, if the borrower is a limited partnership, the limited partners may be precluded from maximizing their tax shelter benefits unless the borrower obtains qualified nonrecourse financing. See discussion at Chapter 14A2.

are expressly limited to mortgages on single- or two-family houses or homesteads.

These enactments apply to funds borrowed to purchase property; mortgages securing money borrowed for other purposes, such as refinancing or second loans against accumulated equity, are not covered. The Montana, North Carolina, and South Dakota statutes apply only to mortgages given by the purchaser to the vendor to secure payment of the balance of the purchase price. The statutes in North Dakota and Arizona apply to both vendor lenders and institutional lenders, while those in California and Oregon distinguish between these two types of lenders. In general, deficiency judgments are prohibited on any mortgage given by the purchaser to the vendor, regardless of the type of property. Institutional purchase money financing is subject to the prohibition in California only if the property is a one- to four-family dwelling, and in Oregon if it is a primary or secondary single-family residence. This special allowance for family dwellings is based on a policy that attempts to balance the protection of residential borrowers with the encouragement of institutional mortgage financing by not unduly restricting lenders' recovery.

The Arizona statute allows a deficiency judgment in the amount of any voluntary waste committed or permitted by the debtor while in possession of the property. Since waste reduces the foreclosure sale price, the mortgagee is permitted to recover this loss, as determined by the court, in the form of a deficiency judgment.

2. PRIVATE SALES

To avoid potential unfair advantage in the nonjudicial sale, several states prohibit deficiencies when the mortgagee sells property under a trust deed or mortgage power of sale. Since the mortgagee can purchase at its own sale or at the trustee's sale, the private sale format resembles strict foreclosure. A creditor could not obtain a deficiency judgment after strict foreclosure. The statutes prohibiting deficiencies following nonjudicial sales thus render the process a modern equivalent of strict foreclosure.

In most states, private sales need not be followed by judicial confirmation. The Georgia statute modifies this rule by allowing a deficiency judgment in power of sale foreclosures only if the mortgagee petitions the court to confirm the sale and the court cooperates. . . .

3. SHORT TERM REDEMPTION PERIOD

Several states prohibit deficiency judgments when the mortgagee, by complying with the statutory scheme, has effected a shortening of the redemption period. Although these statutes deprive the debtor of part of his statutory redemption protection, they also free him from deficiency liability. Under the North Dakota Short Term Mortgage Redemption Act, a mortgage of property of less than [40] acres may provide that the redemption period will be six rather than twelve months if the judgment is greater than two-thirds of the original secured indebtedness. No deficiency judgment is permitted if this procedure is followed. The Wisconsin statute, which applies to property of less than twenty acres, shortens the redemption period from twelve to six months if the mortgagee waives a deficiency judgment. If the property is abandoned, the Wisconsin statute shortens the redemption period further to two months. The Washington statute applies to nonagricultural property that has been abandoned for six months or more; no deficiency judgment is allowed and the purchaser takes free of all statutory redemption rights.

Illustrating the purchase money approach, the Uniform Land Security Interest Act (ULSIA)[15] shields certain "protected" parties from deficiencies in any purchase money loan, defined in Section 111 to encompass loans from both sellers and third parties to enable the acquisition of the real estate collateral. Under Section 113 of the ULSIA, a protected party includes "an individual who gives a security interest in residential real estate all or part of which the individual occupies or intends to occupy as a residence" as well as certain guarantors of the loan. For this purpose, "residential real estate" means "real estate, improved or to be improved, containing not more than [three] acres, not more than four dwelling units, and no nonresidential uses for which the protected party is a lessor."

In addition to the foregoing approaches to restrict deficiencies, some states have enacted so-called fair market value laws to prevent windfalls. The following is an excerpt from New York's statute, which is typical of those that substitute the value of the property for the lesser foreclosure sale price in determining a deficiency.

N.Y. Real Prop. Acts. Law §1371

. . . 2. Simultaneously with the making of a motion for an order confirming the sale, provided such motion is made within ninety days after the date of the consummation of the sale by the delivery of the proper deed of conveyance to the purchaser, the party to whom such residue shall be owing may make a motion in the action for leave to enter a deficiency judgment upon notice to the party against whom such judgment is sought or the attorney who shall have appeared for such party in such action. Such notice shall be served personally or in such other manner as the court may direct. Upon such motion the court, whether or not the respondent appears, shall determine, upon affidavit or otherwise as it shall

---

15. The ULSIA was approved by the National Conference of Commissioners on Uniform State Laws in 1985 and is found at 7A U.L.A. 403 (1999).

direct, the fair and reasonable market value of the mortgaged premises as of the date such premises were bid in at auction or such nearest earlier date as there shall have been any market value thereof and shall make an order directing the entry of a deficiency judgment. Such deficiency judgment shall be for an amount equal to the sum of the amount owing by the party liable as determined by the judgment with interest, plus the amount owing on all prior liens and encumbrances with interest, plus costs and disbursements of the action including the referee's fee and disbursements, less the market value as determined by the court or the sale price of the property whichever shall be the higher.

The following decision reflects the potential for courts to apply a fair market value standard as judge-made law in a deficiency proceeding in those states without fair market value laws.

Trustees of the Washington-Idaho-Montana Carpenters-Employers Retirement Trust Fund v. Galleria Partnership
239 Mont. 250, 780 P.2d 608 (1989)

SHEEHY, Justice.
. . . On March 17, 1982, in Great Falls, Montana, 16 individuals made, executed and delivered a promissory note for $1,200,000.00 payable to the Trustees on terms set out in the written note. The note was signed by the individuals not as partners of the Galleria Partnership, but in their individual capacity, except that three of the individuals also signed as partners in Great Falls Investors [a partner of the Galleria Partnership]. Under the terms of the promissory note, the individuals undertook jointly and severally to pay the principal sum of the note and the interest accruing thereon.

At or about the same time . . . Galleria Partnership, composed of 10 of the individuals who signed the promissory note, and three additional persons comprising the Great Falls Investors made, executed and delivered to Safeco Title Insurance Company as trustee, a [deed of] trust indenture and security agreement, wherein the Trustees were named as beneficiaries, to secure the . . . promissory note above referred to.

The real property which was the subject of the trust indenture was the location of a warehouse which had been remodeled for the purpose of leasing to various business tenants. The building had been purchased and remodeled beginning in 1982 by a prior partnership, Galleria Associates, managed by one Dan Cook.

Cook had obtained a $1,950,000.00 appraisal of the building in its remodeled state so he could get a long-term loan to pay off Galleria Associate's interim construction loan. For this purpose Cook approached third party defendant, Compass, which specializes in handling loans of union pension trust funds and then servicing those loans. . . . Cook was advised by Compass that Galleria Associates could not borrow from the Trustees because Cook was disqualified under the provisions of the Federal Employee Retirement Income Security Act (ERISA) statutes. 29 U.S.C., sections 1001 et seq. Thereupon, Cook set about the formation of Galleria Partnership, to which Galleria Associates would eventually sell the building, and the Galleria Partnership would qualify as a borrower under ERISA. Cook developed a prospectus on the project, and lined up the 13 individuals and Great Falls Investors that eventually signed the trust agreement. The individuals who became partners in the Galleria Partnership held varying fractions of interest in the partnership. Compass knew that Cook was procuring such interest; the agents of Compass had no idea what representations Cook was making to the prospective investors in Galleria Partnership, and did not ask.

It seems clear that Cook, himself, or through others that were acting on his information, represented to each of the persons who ultimately signed the loan documents that the loan was to be nonrecourse. At least three lawyers were among the investors, each of whom was of the view that a deficiency judgment could not be recovered on the foreclosure of a trust indenture.

Cook hand-carried the loan documents, including a commitment from Compass as to the terms of the loan, which stated that security for repayment was to be a first lien on the building and thus he secured the signatures of the borrowers. Each of the borrowers was told that the loan was nonrecourse. Only one attorney read the note or trust indenture, and he found nothing in them that was contrary to his view that the loan was nonrecourse.

In capsule, then, after the loan was closed, it turned out that the bulk of the tenants in the Galleria building were businesses Cook had an interest in, which had been known to Compass when the loan commitment was made. Cook's economic situation deteriorated, which ultimately resulted in the failure of various tenants to pay their rents in a timely basis. The Galleria Partners were using those rents to cover operating expenses and to make the monthly loan payments which were $14,916.00 each. As the tenants' rents fell into arrears, the monthly payments on the loan were made progressively later. . . .

[O]n December 11, 1984, Compass sent a default notice . . . accelerating the entire loan balance of $1,225,668.81 and demanding its payment in nine days. . . .

Thereafter there were proposals for settlement which never reached fruition. In that period of time, Compass had the building appraised in the summer of 1985 and the appraisal came in at $1,100,000.00. The Trustees were unwilling to accept that sum as an appraisal and no settlement for deficiency was arrived at by the parties.

On April 12, 1985, the Trustees filed an action in the District Court for the purpose of foreclosing on the trust indenture. After lengthy discovery and complex proceedings, the District Court on October 29, 1987, determined in a summary judgment that the trust indenture constituted a first lien upon the real property of Galleria Partnership, and issued its order for decree of foreclosure.

The order directed the Sheriff of Cascade County, Montana, to sell the real estate in one parcel at public auction under the laws governing the sale of real estate under execution upon proper notice being given; and to deliver a deed to the purchaser. . . . It is reflected in the order of the District Court, dated October 7, 1988, when the deficiency judgment was rendered against the Galleria Partnership, that the Sheriff's sale took place on December 8, 1987, and that the bid price [by the Trustees was $565,000]. . . .

4. IS DEFICIENCY JUDGMENT BARRED BECAUSE THIS IS A PURCHASE MONEY MORTGAGE?

Under the mortgage foreclosure laws of this State, a deficiency judgment is not allowed on the foreclosure of a purchase price mortgage. Section 71-1-232, MCA. Galleria Partnership contends in this case that because the Trustees lent the money, knowing that the proceeds of the loan would be used by the Partnership to pay off Galleria Associates, the prior partnership, for the purchase of the real property, that the arrangement in effect was that of a purchase price mortgage and so a deficiency judgment was barred under the statute.

The language of the statute itself defeats the contention. It provides:

> Upon the foreclosure of any mortgage, executed to any vendor [of] real property or to his heirs, executors, administrators, or assigns for the balance of the purchase price of such real property, the mortgagee shall not be entitled to a deficiency judgment on account of such mortgage or note or obligation secured by the same.

Plainly, the Trustees are not the vendor in this case, nor are they the assignee of any vendor. The language simply does not fit the Trustees so as to prevent their obtaining a deficiency judgment. . . .

6. DID THE [MISREPRESENTATION BY COOK] BAR A DEFICIENCY JUDGMENT?

. . . The Partners contend[] that . . . the alleged representations by Cook, that there would be no personal liability for the Partnership, created a reasonable belief in the minds of the potential partners that they would not be liable personally for deficiency judgment. The District Court disposed of the issue on the theory of misrepresentation, saying that if a misrepresentation was made, the other party nevertheless has a duty to use diligence with respect to any such representation made, and here, the borrowers, for the most part, did not read the loan documents; and if they had read the note they would have seen that the payments required by them were phrased in terms of personal liability.

The Partnership appears to concede the duty of diligence on the part of the borrowers, but contends that the District Court missed the issue of lack of consideration. The Partnership contends that no deficiency judgment was bargained for, and because in the minds of the borrowers a deed of trust secured a nonrecourse loan, there is no consideration to which the court could point for a deficiency judgment. . . .

Of course, all representations made by Cook were superseded by the written instruments, the promissory note, and the deed of trust. The validity of neither the promissory note nor the trust indenture is in dispute, and there is no claim here of a mistake in those instruments or an imperfection in their writings, so extrinsic evidence may not be considered to vary the terms of those written instruments. Section 28-2-905, MCA. . . .

7. DID THE REPRESENTATION BY COOK THAT THE LOAN WOULD BE NONRECOURSE BAR A DEFICIENCY JUDGMENT?

On this issue, the Partnership seeks to impute to the Trustees on agency grounds responsibility for the alleged misrepresentations made by Cook in securing the signatures of the borrowers to the promissory note and the trust indenture.

The Partnership cites numerous cases involving principals and agents to the effect that the principals are bound by the acts or representations of the agents. None of those cases is applicable here. The District Court rejected this contention saying there was no evidence of any kind that would make Cook either an actual or an ostensible agent of Compass or the Trustees in procuring the signatures. Since any evidence that Cook was representing either Compass or the Trustees in procuring the signatures is totally lacking, no imputations can be made by any court that either Compass or the Trustees were responsible for the alleged misrepresentations made by Cook. A deficiency judgment cannot be barred on this contention.

8. DISPOSITION

As the foregoing discussion shows, there is no question that the Partnership members are jointly and severally liable on the promissory note which they signed individually, and that, after foreclosure of the real property given to the security obligation, the individual Partners are also liable for deficiency judgment. The size of the deficiency judgment in relation to the original note is however a matter of concern.

It is uncontroverted in the evidence here that in 1981, when Dan Cook was first arranging for a loan, he obtained an appraisal of the property as remodeled at $1,950,000.00. In 1982, that appraisal had sufficient validity to justify the Trustees in extending a loan of $1,200,000.00 to the Galleria Partnership.

In 1985, after the default notice had been served by the Trustees, they obtained an appraisal of the property which they did not accept, but which apparently valued the remodeled property at $1,100,000.00.

At the sheriff's sale, in 1987, the Trustees, as beneficiary under the trust indenture, submitted a bid on the real property as remodeled for $565,000.00. The District Court found that the principal amount of the obligation due on November 1, 1984, was $1,185,655.49. Accrued interest, attorneys fees and recoverable costs brought the eventual deficiency judgment to $1,500,368.35. The fact that the real property was bid in at the sheriff's sale for a sum at approximately 30% of its original appraised value is the basis for what must be a catastrophic deficiency judgment for the Partners.

Montana's statutes have no direct provisions under the mortgage foreclosure procedures to determine the fair market value at the time of the forced sale of the property subject to foreclosure. [S]everal of the states surrounding us have statutory provisions which serve to protect judgment debtors when foreclosure of their property is made to satisfy the judgments. Our examination of the statutes of surrounding states, and of the interpretations of their respective courts concerning those statutes show that predominantely [sic], a deficiency judgment is limited to the difference between the fair market value of the secured property at the time of the foreclosure sale, regardless of a lesser amount realized at the sale, and the outstanding debt for which the property was secured. . . . California, Washington, Arizona, Utah, Idaho, and Oregon, are states with such protective provisions, with Alaska being the sole exception. . . .

Some states surrounding us also have other provisions relating to the protection of the judgment debtor. Thus in Wyoming, the mortgagee or party to whom the debt is owed may bid in at the sheriff's sale, but his bid must be made "fairly and in good faith." Wyo. Stat. §34-4-108 (1989).

As we said, the Montana statutes are silent . . . as to the duty of a court to determine if the sheriff's sale reflects the fair market value of the property. A mortgage foreclosure proceeding[], however, is in the equity jurisdiction of the courts.. . . Courts sitting in equity are empowered to determine all the questions involved in the case and to do complete justice; this includes the power to fashion an equitable result. . . . An equity court whose jurisdiction has been invoked for an equitable purpose, will proceed to determine any other equities existing between the parties connected with the main subject of the suit, and grant all relief necessary to the entire adjustment of the subject.

Had the sole bid at the sheriff's sale for the property here been for $100 or $1,000, undoubtedly we would be moved by equity to inquire as to its fairness. The actual bid of $565,000.00 is only a matter of degree. In the exercise of our equity jurisdiction therefore, we deem it proper to remand to the District Court to determine the fair market value of the property at the time of the sheriff's sale. The "fair market" is the intrinsic value of the real property with its improvements at the time of sale under judicial foreclosure, without consideration of the impact of the foreclosure proceedings on the fair market value.

The method of determining fair market value we will leave to the District Court, though it seems appropriate that each opposing party should be allowed to present the opinion of appraisers selected by them respectively.

When the fair market value of the property is determined by the District Court, that figure would be the basis for the determination of a deficiency judgment if any.

MCDONOUGH, Justice, dissents.

. . . Section 71-1-222, MCA (1987), governs as to [deficiency] proceedings in foreclosure suits. The section is as follows: . . .

(2) If it appears from the sheriff's return that the proceeds are insufficient and a balance still remains due, judgment can then be docketed for such balance against the defendant or defendants personally liable for the debt, and it becomes a lien upon the real estate of such judgment debtor, as in other cases on which execution may be issued.

[S]ubsection (2) . . . does not provide for the calculation of a deficiency judgment by applying a fair market value, as determined by the court, to the amount due. Rather, it directs that a deficiency judgment should be calculated by applying the proceeds of the sale to the amount due. This statute clearly sets forth how a deficiency is to be calculated. The statute prevails over any common law. . . .

Although antideficiency laws such as those in New York and under the ULSIA may appear relatively straightforward, the courts have had to address a wide variety of questions arising under them, such as: (1) Does the statute apply to a junior lienor that is "sold out" (extinguished) by the senior's sale? (2) If the statute prohibits a deficiency, can the mortgagee avoid its application by waiving its collateral and suing on the debt? (3) Is the mortgagor's predefault waiver enforceable? (4) If the statute governs residential real estate loans, does it look to the borrower's actual use or to the physical nature of the real estate? (5) How is value determined under fair market value laws? (6) Does a law barring any deficiency insulate a mortgagor who has defrauded the mortgagee or committed waste on the property? As reflected by the conflicting authorities in the notes that follow, the answers to many of these questions depend on the wording of the specific antideficiency law.

NOTES AND QUESTIONS

1. ULSIA Provisions. ULSIA prohibits deficiency judgments when the borrower is a "protected party" and the mortgage is a "purchase money security interest." Does this effectively protect the people in need of protection? Suppose Hortense Homeowner purchased her home from Dan Developer. Hortense financed her purchase with a mortgage from Friendly Bank. Is the mortgage a purchase money security interest under the ULSIA? Among the questions courts have needed to confront under these purchase money antideficiency statutes are whether they protect a borrower who refinances the original purchase money loan. E.g., Union Bank v. Wendland, 54 Cal. App. 3d 393, 126 Cal. Rptr. 549 (1976) (residential loan refinanced with different lender lost its purchase money character; but in 2012 California's legislature explicitly protected borrowers who refinance their purchase money loans, except for excess "cash out" funds received by the borrower).

> ➤ *Problem 8-5*
> Assume that Dan Developer builds the new Danley Hotel on approximately one acre of land in the center of downtown McNiece, obtaining construction financing from Fuller National Bank. When completed, the hotel will be run pursuant to the terms of an operating contract with Danley Hotel Corporation, a national chain controlled by Dan. The hotel will be 30 stories tall and will have a penthouse devoted to a lavish apartment for Dan—the only unit in the hotel built exclusively for apartment use. There are, however, five other large suites that Dan hopes will be leased by major corporations for use by their executives. Dan is personally liable on the construction loan. If that loan goes into default and FNB forecloses, acquiring the almost completed building at less than the mortgage balance, will FNB be able to obtain a deficiency judgment against Dan under the ULSIA? Is this "residential real estate" within ULSIA's definition? Would it be "residential" if there were no large suites (other than Dan's) that could be leased? Is Dan a "protected party"? ◀

For one state's experience with the uncertain scope of residential real estate protected under its antideficiency laws, compare Northern Ariz. Properties v. Pinetop Properties Group, 151 Ariz. 9, 725 P.2d 501 (Ct. App. 1986) (antideficiency law governing mortgaged property used as a dwelling protects a limited partnership borrower that rented out the condominium collateral as an investment) and Independent Mortgage Co. v. Alaburda, 230 Ariz. 181, 281 P.3d 1049 (Ct. App. 2012) (one-month fractional interest in vacation condo mortgaged by owner with intent to occupy it is protected residential real estate) with Mid Kans. Fed. Sav. & Loan Ass'n v. Dynamic Dev. Corp., 167 Ariz. 122, 804 P.2d 1310 (1991) (same antideficiency law inapplicable when collateral consisted of substantially finished but unsold residences in subdivision).

2. Fair Market Value. The beginning of this section referenced a scenario in which Dan Developer became subject to a deficiency judgment of $14,999,900. Under the New York statute, what would the limit be on the deficiency in that scenario? The Restatement (Third) of Property (Mortgages) adopts a fair market value approach (as judge-made law) under which the mortgagor, at its option, can request the court to value the property at the date of the foreclosure sale and use that value (if greater than the foreclosure price) in calculating the deficiency. §8.4 (1997); see Sostaric v. Marshall, 766 S.E.2d 396 (W.Va. 2014) (overruling a decision just 15 years earlier and adopting the Restatement approach). Does the *Galleria* court establish a right to valuation that, like the Restatement approach, applies in all circumstances, or is the right to valuation under *Galleria* contingent on a showing of inequitable circumstances in the particular deficiency action? For decisions that refuse to adopt a judicial fair market value standard in states without statutory fair value protection, see Illini Fed. Sav. & Loan Ass'n v. Doering, 162 Ill. App. 3d 768, 516 N.E.2d 609 (1987); First Bank v. Fischer & Frichtel, Inc., 364 S.W.3d 216 (Mo. 2012); Rhode Island Depositors' Economic Protection Corp. v. Macomber, 658 A.2d 511 (R.I. 1995). Do you find the Restatement position persuasive, or should the courts leave borrower protection to the legislature? For discussion of the related (and more settled) doctrine under which courts may exercise their equitable discretion to invalidate a foreclosure sale bid that is so low that it shocks the court's conscience, see Chapter 8C3c, infra.

How is value determined under these fair market value laws or court decisions? Many statutes, or decisions that construe them, look to the property value in normal market conditions rather than the distressed circumstances of foreclosure. Some may consider the post-foreclosure resale price of the property. See PlainsCapital Bank v. Martin, 459 S.W.3d 550 (Tex. 2015). There is substantial disagreement, however, on whether the court should subtract the mortgagee-purchaser's holding costs and costs of resale. See Restatement (Third) of Property (Mortgages) §8.4, cmt. c (1997) (deducting from market value the mortgagee-purchaser's anticipated reasonable costs of resale, such as a broker's commission, but not deducting anticipated holding costs such as taxes and maintenance even if they would exceed property income).

The *Galleria* litigation illustrates the guesswork involved in adjudging property value for deficiency purposes. On remand to determine the value "without consideration of the impact of the foreclosure proceedings," the district judge entertained appraisals that ranged from less than the lender's bid to more than the loan balance. On appeal, the Montana Supreme Court affirmed that judge's discretion to average the expert values in determining the value to be $1,100,000. See Trustees of the Washington-Idaho-Montana Carpenters-Employers Retirement Trust Fund v. Galleria Partnership, 250 Mont. 175, 819 P.2d 158, 163 (1991).

3. Sold-Out Juniors. Whether antideficiency laws apply to a junior lien that is extinguished at the foreclosure sale of a senior lien often depends on the wording of the specific statute, as well as its rationale. The fair market value laws applied in the problem that follows aim to protect against the windfall if a lender could underbid in a depressed market, acquire the collateral, and then sue for a large deficiency.

> ➤ *Problem 8-6*

Assume in the scenario at the beginning of this section that a junior lienor, FNB, holding a $1 million second mortgage, is extinguished in Ace's foreclosure sale. Further assume that Ace purchased the collateral at its sale for $15 million and that FNB chose not to bid. FNB now wishes to pursue other more liquid assets held by Dan to satisfy the $1 million loan balance. Finally, assume that the property "value" is $16 million, sufficient to have paid both the Ace $15 million and the FNB $1 million mortgage loans in full. Under the language and rationale of the New York statute excerpted above, what arguments can you make that the property value should limit (and in this case prohibit) FNB's action for a deficiency? What arguments can you make that the statute should be inapplicable to FNB as a "sold-out" junior? What if FNB had purchased the property at Ace's sale for a bid of $15,000,001? See Walter E. Heller Western, Inc. v. Bloxham, 176 Cal. App. 3d 266, 221 Cal. Rptr. 425 (1985) (rationale of fair market value laws compels their application when junior purchases at senior's sale). ◄

4. Waivers. Although courts typically will not enforce waivers of the anti-deficiency laws contained in the loan documents, some enforce waivers executed subsequent to the mortgage loan, such as those in connection with a loan workout agreement. Compare Brunsoman v. Scarlett, 465 N.W.2d 162, 168 (N.D. 1991) with DeBerard Properties, Ltd. v. Lim, 20 Cal. 4th 659, 85 Cal. Rptr. 2d 292, 976 P.2d 843 (1999) (contractual waivers of purchase money antideficiency law invalid even when given in loan renegotiation). For discussion of waivers by guarantors of anti-deficiency laws, see infra Chapter 8C4. Why might a court distinguish between pre- and postloan waivers for purposes of their enforceability? Can the mortgage lender elude the protection of a law barring deficiencies by waiving its (inadequate) collateral and suing the borrower on the mortgage note obligation? Compare Ross Realty Co. v. First Citizens Bank & Trust Co., 296 N.C. 366, 250 S.E.2d 271, 275 (1979) (to allow waiver would circumvent the "spirit and purpose" of antideficiency laws), with In re Daraee, 279 B.R. 853 (Bankr. D. Or. 2002) (lender may avoid Oregon deficiency laws by waiving mortgage remedies and suing on note subject to protection of residential debtor homestead laws).

5. Borrower Fraud or Waste. Suppose that Dan Developer had fraudulently induced Ace to make the loan by supplying false income and expense documents that inflated the value of the collateral. In these circumstances, the antideficiency laws typically will give way to permit the mortgagee's action for its fraud damages. See, for example, Alliance Mortgage Co. v. Rothwell, 10 Cal. 4th 1226, 900 P.2d 601, 44 Cal. Rptr. 2d 352, 358 (1995). During the heyday of subprime financing in the early 2000s, many homeowners obtained stated income loans (sometimes referred to condescendingly as "liar loans") that did not require documentation of their actual (and typically lower) earnings. Should antideficiency protections give way if borrower income has been inflated?

Suppose that Dan Developer forgoes necessary property maintenance and repairs and, as a result, the mortgaged property is sold at foreclosure for less than the loan balance. In these circumstances, the California Supreme Court adopted a distinction between what it termed "bad faith" waste by a malicious despoiler of property (which overrides the antideficiency laws) and waste resulting from the economic pressures of a market depression. See Cornelison v. Kornbluth, 15 Cal. 3d 590, 542 P.2d 981, 125 Cal. Rptr. 557 (1975). This distinction has proved difficult to apply. Compare Mills v. Sdrawde Titleholders, Inc. (In re Mills), 841 F.2d 902 (9th Cir. 1988) (lender failed to demonstrate that disrepair and infestation of low-rent hotel resulted from borrower's malicious acts) with Fait v. New Faze Development, Inc., 207 Cal. App. 4th 284, 143 Cal. Rptr. 3d 382 (2012) (court refused to protect a good-intentioned developer who demolished a building as part of a redevelopment plan for a new mixed-use building that the economic recession cut short). Widespread instances during the recent foreclosure crisis of disgruntled or opportunistic homeowners stripping their foreclosed homes of fixtures such as carpeting, cabinets, countertops, doors, and the like fall more clearly into the category of bad faith waste. Cf. Bell v. First Columbus Nat. Bank, 493 So. 2d 964 (Miss. 1986) (affirming punitive damage award against borrower who stripped residence five days before foreclosure sale).

Because waste is customarily carved out of nonrecourse provisions, what constitutes waste of the mortgaged property also matters for nonrecourse commercial loans. See discussion at Chapter 5A3.

THE REAL ESTATE LAWYER AND THE UCC

In contrast to the number of states that prohibit deficiencies following realty foreclosures, the UCC generally permits deficiency actions against the obligor in personal property secured loans. UCC §9-615(d). The UCC does contain a unique provision, akin to the realty fair market value standard, regulating deficiencies following a UCC foreclosure sale or other disposition in which the secured party is the transferee. See UCC §9-615(f). Deficiencies may also be barred or limited under the UCC if the secured party fails to comply with the UCC enforcement rules. See UCC §9-626. Consider the appropriateness of state statutes that bar or limit deficiency judgments following realty foreclosures. Is the UCC standard for personalty financing that generally allows deficiencies the better approach?

---

6. Morality of Default. In the throes of the mortgage meltdown from 2007 to 2012, many homeowners found themselves "underwater," owing more on their mortgage loans than their deflated homes were worth. Particularly in antideficiency jurisdictions, many borrowers chose to strategically default— meaning they had the means to continue making their scheduled mortgage loan payments but chose to default and walk away from their homes in order to escape the ominous loan balances owed. A law professor sparked national controversy by suggesting these homeowners abandon their loans without moral guilt. White, Underwater and Not Walking Away: Shame, Fear and the Social Management of the Housing Crisis, 45 Wake Forest L. Rev. 971 (2010). Predictably, lender representatives weighed in, suggesting among other things that morality figures into the neighborhood destabilization that such strategic foreclosures hasten. Harney, Professor Advises Underwater Homeowners to Walk Away from Mortgages, L.A. Times, Nov. 29, 2009. Do borrowers, having signed a repayment contract, owe some moral obligation to fulfill their loan agreements? Consider the morality of involuntary default when a borrower loses her job and has no savings. What about a wealthy owner of a vacation home protected by state antideficiency law who opts to strategically default? Are commercial borrowers opting to walk away from a nonrecourse loan on any higher moral ground?

7. *Profiteering in Debt Collection.* Lenders who foreclosed during the subprime mortgage crisis tended to fall short of satisfying their loan balance. Oftentimes they sold the shortfall to collection agencies for pennies on the dollar. Although the borrower might successfully discharge the now unsecured deficiency debt in bankruptcy, the chance of a partial or full collection led some companies to profit by buying the deficiency claim from the foreclosing party at a steep discount and successfully dogging the debtor for the balance. In the midst of outcry over abusive collection practices and accusations of windfall profiteering, the Nevada legislature enacted a unique approach, restricting the purchaser of the debt to the amount of consideration paid to acquire the debt. For example, legislative history suggested that when the foreclosure shortfall is $100,000 but the bank sells the judgment to a collection agency for $20,000, all the agency may collect is the $20,000 it paid to acquire the debt. See Nev. Rev. Stat. §40.459 (later amended to only govern purchase of debt secured by a principal residence). Do you think this approach is a prudent and fair solution to concerns over profiteering?

8. *Additional Reading.* M. Madison, J. Dwyer, and S. Bender, The Law of Real Estate Financing §§12:69-12:83 (2016); Accomazzo, Avoiding Sister State Antideficiency Laws, 14 Colo. Law. 775 (1985); Brabner-Smith, Economic Aspects of the Deficiency Judgment, 20 Va. L. Rev. 719 (1934); Hughes, Taking Personal Responsibility: A Different View of Mortgage Anti-deficiency and Redemption Statutes, 39 Ariz. L. Rev. 117 (1997); Leipziger, Deficiency Judgments in California: The Supreme Court Tries Again, 22 UCLA L. Rev. 753 (1975); Perlman, Mortgage Deficiency Judgments During an Economic Depression, 20 Va. L. Rev. 771 (1934).

b.   The One-Form-of-Action Rule

Somewhat akin to the antideficiency judgment legislation is the "one-form-of-action" requirement of some states, designed primarily to protect the borrower from a suit on the note prior to foreclosure. Most notably, California law embodies this "security first" principle by requiring that the lender exhaust its real property security before seeking a money judgment for any deficiency permitted by law:

> There can be but one form of action for the recovery of any debt or the enforcement of any right secured by mortgage [or deed of trust] upon real property or an estate for years therein, which action shall be in accordance with the provisions of this chapter. In the action the court may, by its judgment, direct the sale of the encumbered property. . . .[16]

The effect of this rule is to prevent the lender's resort to the borrower's general assets (when not otherwise restricted by antideficiency laws) in advance of foreclosure. Thus, the one-action rule has been applied to prevent such recourse as the banker mortgagee's setoff of the debtor's bank account (a debt of the bank to the depositor) in advance of foreclosure.

California's one-action law does not specify the appropriate sanction for non-compliance. Although this rule may not appear too threatening, it was held in Bank of America v. Daily that the lender bank's setoff of the borrower's checking account against the mortgage debt was an election of remedies under the one-action rule that prohibited the bank from later commencing a judicial foreclosure or apparently making claim for the unpaid balance of the debt.[17] Certainly decisions such as *Daily* do not inspire lender confidence in reasonable treatment by the courts in interpreting the one-action rule.

NOTES AND QUESTIONS

> ➢ *Problem 8-7*
> Assume that Dan Developer's property in the master hypothetical is located in California. Ace committed to make a $25 million mortgage loan on completion of construction in accordance with the approved plans and specifications. When the time for disbursement was at hand, a significant amount of tenant finish work had not been completed. Nevertheless, a note and a deed of trust for $25 million were executed in favor of Ace, and the

---

16. Cal. Civ. Proc. Code §726(a).

17. 152 Cal. App. 3d 767, 199 Cal. Rptr. 557 (1984). But see Security Pac. Natl. Bank v. Wozab, 51 Cal. 3d 991, 800 P.2d 557, 275. Cal. Rptr. 201 (1990), wherein the court established judicial rules to govern the appropriate sanction for a preforeclosure setoff; these rules limit loss of collateral and waiver of the unpaid balance of the debt to when the bank refuses to promptly restore the setoff funds on the mortgagor's demand.

deed of trust was recorded; Ace, however, held $2 million of the loan proceeds in escrow to be disbursed as the tenant finish work was completed. If the work were not completed by a specified date, the agreement authorized Ace to apply the escrow to reduce the indebtedness. Without completing the tenant finish work, Dan goes into default in the payment of principal and interest. Ace applies the $2 million to reduce the indebtedness and then commences foreclosure. Under *Daily*, does Ace risk losing $23 million? If so, can you think of any way Ace could have modified the arrangement to avoid such a result? ◄

Letters of Credit. Assume Ace accepted a letter of credit to cover certain of Dan's obligations. If Dan defaults and Ace draws on the letter of credit, does Ace risk violating the one-action rule? Uncertain as to the extent of the rule, some lenders in California opted to create two separate obligations: one note secured by the real estate and another backed by a letter of credit or escrow account. One law firm, in a letter to clients, points out some nasty side effects of this dual-note approach, including "potential compliance problems with respect to investment statutes" affecting "the availability of certain usury and shared appreciation exemptions under California law," and "potential defenses of marshalling of assets, application of proceeds and certain bankruptcy issues." Further, a draw on a letter of credit or escrow account might be deemed to cure the default and reinstate the debt under California arrearage law. Finally responding to lender concerns over the one-action rule, in 1994 California's legislature amended that rule to allow preforeclosure recourse to letters of credit except in certain residential loans. See Cal. Civ. Proc. Code §§580.5, 580.7.

c. Sale Confirmation, Upset Prices, and Unconscionable Prices

State statutes provide a variety of safeguards designed to produce a foreclosure sale price as close as reasonably possible to market value, given the forced nature of the sale. The protections are not uniform throughout the country; some states have so encumbered the process with borrower protections as to make foreclosure a very time-consuming and expensive proposition. With foreclosure costs added to the debt, this tilt toward borrower protection may be equally disadvantageous to borrower and lender. Many borrower protective provisions were designed originally to protect unsophisticated borrowers dealing with sophisticated institutional lenders, but they also apply where the parties are dealing at arm's length and their degree of sophistication is more or less equal.[18]

On the other hand, some states have so streamlined power-of-sale procedures that there is a sense of unfairness to the borrower. For example, in the case of

---

18. See recommendations for law reform in Lifton, Real Estate in Trouble: Lender's Remedies Need an Overhaul, 31 Bus. Law. 1927, 1930, 1942-1945 (1976).

Turner v. Blackburn,[19] the borrower first learned of the power-of-sale foreclosure one month after the sale was held, when the purchaser visited the property to inspect his purchase.

Arguably, such patently unfair situations are infrequent. Especially in a commercial setting, the borrower usually knows that trouble is brewing long before it defaults. This affords the borrower the opportunity to go to the marketplace and obtain the current market value for the property. After default, most state statutes provide a substantial additional period before the foreclosure sale can be held,[20] during which time a borrower can sell the property at private sale at a price closer to its market value than can be obtained at a forced foreclosure sale.

State statutes provide additional safeguards should the property go to foreclosure. Some states will not allow the property to be sold for less than a minimum sum at the foreclosure sale. For example, some statutes provide that a sale will not be confirmed, or will be overturned by the court, if the price paid for the property is less than two-thirds of the appraised value or if the sale price is less than some other "upset price" established by the court.[21] In addition to these statutory requirements, courts, using their inherent equity power, have invalidated sales at unfair (unconscionable) prices.

In re Krohn
203 Ariz. 205, 52 P.3d 774 (2002) (en banc)

FELDMAN, Justice.

Linda Lorraine Krohn (Krohn) filed a . . . bankruptcy petition seeking to have the sale of her home vacated for gross inadequacy of price. Bankruptcy Judge Redfield T. Baum certified a question of Arizona law to this court: "May a trustee's sale of real property [under a deed of trust] be set aside solely on the basis that the bid price was grossly inadequate?". . .

[T]he trustee's sale was held on September 27, 2000. The amount paid at that sale was $10,304.00 by Sweetheart Properties, LTD, an Arizona corporation ("Sweetheart"). . . .

The debtor states that her residence is worth at least $57,500.00 and no other evidence of value has been presented to the court by the parties. The foregoing facts are compounded by the fact that debtor is disabled and resides in the residence with her two daughters.

In the present case the winning (and only) bid was slightly more than $10,000 for a property worth $57,000. Judge Baum found "the price paid is not merely

---

19. 389 F. Supp. 1250 (W.D.N.C. 1975). See Chapter 8C5 infra for discussion of constitutional due process challenges to the nonjudicial foreclosure process.

20. See, e.g., Cal. Civ. Code §2924(c), (f), and (g); Okla. Stat. Ann. tit. 46, §4.

21. See, e.g., W. Va. Code §38-4-23. These protective devices and their effectiveness are discussed in Washburn, The Judicial and Legislative Response to Price Inadequacy in Mortgage Foreclosure Sales, 53 S. Cal. L. Rev. 843 (1980).

inadequate but under applicable case law 'grossly' inadequate because the price was less than 20% of fair market value"....

A.   JUDICIAL FORECLOSURE

Sales in actions to foreclose mortgages are subject to judicial review for substantive fairness as well as for procedural compliance.

. . . The general rule is simply that judicial foreclosure sales are set aside when "the inadequacy [of price is] so great as to shock the conscience. . . ." Graffam v. Burgess, 117 U.S. 180, 192, 6 S.Ct. 686, 692, 29 L.Ed. 839 (1886). While the rationale of setting aside judicial foreclosure sales for gross inadequacy is well understood, it is not the only basis for upsetting such sales. Judicial foreclosure sales have been set aside even in the absence of gross inadequacy when there has been some irregularity. "[W]here there is an inadequacy of price which in itself might not be grounds for setting aside the sale, slight additional circumstances or matters of equity may so justify." Mason v. Wilson, 116 Ariz. 255, 257, 568 P.2d 1153, 1155 (App. 1977) (citing Johnson v. Jefferson Standard Life Ins., 5 Ariz. App. 587, 429 P.2d 474 (1967)). The question is whether the same rules are applicable to trustee's sales.

B.   DEED OF TRUST AND BORROWER'S PROTECTION FROM INEQUITY

Unlike their judicial foreclosure cousins that involve the court, deed of trust sales are conducted on a contract theory under the power of sale authority of the trustee. They are therefore held without the prior judicial authorization ordered in a mortgage foreclosure. . . .

The deed of trust scheme is a creature of statutes that do not contain explicit provisions for courts to set aside non-judicial sales based on the price realized at the sale, and no policy for such action has yet evolved with these sales as there has in judicial foreclosure sales.

A mortgage generally may be foreclosed only by filing a civil action while, under a Deed of Trust, the trustee holds a power of sale permitting him to sell the property out of court with no necessity of judicial action. The Deed of Trust statutes thus strip borrowers of many of the protections available under a mortgage. Therefore, lenders must strictly comply with the Deed of Trust statutes, and the statutes and Deeds of Trust must be strictly construed in favor of the borrower.

Aside from the issue in this case, the primary loss in protection for deed of trust borrowers lies in the absence of redemptive right because purchasers at a deed of trust sale no longer take title subject to a mortgagor's six-month right of redemption. Most observers could regard that loss of right as quite disadvantageous to the mortgagor. However, an offsetting theory holds that because there is less uncertainty as a consequence of the elimination of redemptive rights and because there is no judicial oversight, bidders can afford to offer higher prices at a deed of trust sale. . . .

The present case is one of first impression as neither we nor our court of appeals has ever considered the particular issue of setting aside a deed of trust sale for gross inadequacy of price. We also note that the statutes dealing with deeds of trust are silent on that question. Moreover, as we have already discussed, we have always followed the rule that courts of equity have the power to vacate a judicial sale for gross inadequacy of price compared to fair market value even though there is no express statutory authorization to do so. . . .

. . . The mortgage banking and lending industry is of great importance to our economy, but lenders are primarily and vitally concerned with getting their money back with the agreed upon interest payments. The health of their industry depends on repayment, not on foreclosure. Borrowers are justifiably concerned with legitimate protection against inequitable loss of their property if there is a foreclosure. To the extent that judicial oversight to prevent gross inadequacy of bidding at trustee's sales may actually increase prices realized, both lenders and borrowers would benefit. . . . There are, of course, those waiting for opportunities based on individual misfortune, and we believe this makes it even more important that courts of equity are open to assure debtors receive not only procedural but fundamental fairness. Windfall profits, like those reaped by bidders paying grossly inadequate prices at foreclosure sales, do not serve the public interest and do no more than legally enrich speculators. . . .

D. RESOLUTION

. . .[Sweetheart argues] that judicial oversight will chill the market and discourage bidders, that the status of bona fide purchasers will be undermined, and that it will be difficult to determine the appropriate fair market value against which evaluations of gross inadequacy will be made. We will discuss those in turn.

1. CHILLED MARKET

We are presented with no evidence or data indicating that prices paid at sales made under a power of sale bring an appreciably higher percentage of fair market value than prices bid at judicial foreclosure sales. . . . Moreover, we have been presented with no data indicating that the traditional judicial foreclosure market has been disrupted by existing judicial oversight to prevent grossly inadequate prices, and such a result is not self-evident. In fact, without apparent adverse effect on the market, even sales under deeds of trust have been set aside when prices have been grossly inadequate and there was also absence of strict statutory compliance. . . .

2. BONA FIDE PURCHASER

. . .[T]he price paid is completely within the purchaser's control. Knowledgeable purchasers can reasonably evaluate the fair market value of a property to make an appropriate bid that is not grossly inadequate. Thus, [Sweetheart]. . . is chargeable with knowledge as to the sale price.

3. FAIR MARKET VALUE

The United States Supreme Court has stated that fair market value cannot be expected in foreclosure sales. "In short, 'fair market value' presumes market conditions that, by definition, simply do not obtain in the context of a forced sale." BFP v. Resolution Trust Corp., 511 U.S. 531, 538, 114 S.Ct. 1757, 1761, 128 L.Ed.2d 556 (1994). We agree and do not expect that prices in forced sales would reflect the same market value "as would be fixed by negotiation and mutual agreement, after ample time to find a purchaser, as between a vendor who is willing (but not compelled) to sell and a purchaser who desires to buy but is not compelled to take the particular . . . piece of property." Id. (quoting Black's Law Dictionary 971 (6th ed. 1990)). It is to be expected, therefore, that courts will occasionally experience difficulty when attempting to determine fair market value in the context of a forced sale. But again, we must note that the debtor will have the burden of showing gross inadequacy as compared to fair market value, and the need to make these judgments has not disrupted the system of judicial foreclosure.

Simply because a determination of fair market value is or may be difficult does not mean the courts should or could avoid the problem. For example, there is statutory protection in Arizona when a deficiency judgment is sought following a deed of trust sale and the debt owed is more than the amount bid at sale. In such cases, the debt(s) owed will be credited with "the *fair market value* of the trust property on the date of the sale as *determined by the court* or the sale price at the trustee's sale, whichever is higher." A.R.S. §33-814(A) (emphasis added). It is clear, therefore, that our legislature contemplated that courts might have to consider the fair market value of property sold through a deed of trust. By adopting the statutory procedure described above, it is also clear that the legislature determined the risk of a below-market sale price belonged with the mortgagee and not the mortgagor.

4. DETERMINING GROSS INADEQUACY

There is an additional problem, of course, in determining just when a price is grossly inadequate. However, guidance can be found in the comment to [Restatement (Third) of Property (Mortgages)] Section 8.3:

"Gross inadequacy" cannot be precisely defined in terms of a specific percentage of fair market value. *Generally*, however, a court is warranted in invalidating a sale where the price is less than 20 percent of fair market value and, absent other foreclosure defects, is usually not warranted in invalidating a sale that yields in excess of that amount.

Restatement §8.3 cmt. b (emphasis added). In [Security Sav. & Loan v. Fenton, 167 Ariz. 268, 806 P.2d 362, 364 (Ct. App. 1990)], our court of appeals noted, "even assuming that the price was inadequate, that fact standing alone would not justify setting aside the trustee's sale . . .'there must be in addition proof of some element of fraud, unfairness, or oppression as accounts for and brings about the inadequacy of price.'" We believe gross inadequacy is proof of unfairness, and as we have seen, gross inadequacy, as defined in comment b to Restatement §8.3, is more than inadequacy. Thus, a rule allowing limited judicial oversight does not conflict with Fenton—it is still the law in Arizona that trustee's sales will not be set aside for inadequacy of price without more. . . .

E. THE DISSENT

The dissent is concerned that no statute permits a court to use its equity powers to intervene in a trustee's sale. That is true, but as we have noted, it is also quite true that there is no statute prohibiting it. There is also no statute permitting or prohibiting intervention in a trustee's sale in which there has been some procedural irregularity. But as the dissent acknowledges, case law establishes that courts may do so. Moreover, though there is no Arizona statute permitting a court of equity to intervene in a judicial sale because of gross inadequacy of the bid price, this court did not hesitate to hold that it had equitable power to do so.

Why should the equitable rule regarding gross inadequacy be different with respect to trustee's sales? The dissent says that in overseeing judicial sales, the court is simply supervising its own process—the writ of execution. But equitable powers are not limited to supervision of the court's process. Our court long ago faced the issue presented by the present case: In the absence of statutory authority, can a court use its equitable powers to intervene and set aside a foreclosure sale made for a grossly inadequate price? The argument against doing so was the argument recognized in the cases, that the sale can be set aside only if the inadequate price was accompanied by some other irregularity. We rejected that argument for judicial sales in 1905 and do so today with regard to non-judicial sales for the same reasons. . . .

Nor do the cases that recite that the court may use its equitable power to intervene if the inadequacy of price is combined with some procedural irregularity explain why the combination is required and why, to borrow a phrase, we cannot have one without the other. . . .

[D]eeds of trust are creatures of statute, and if the legislature believes that the doors of the courthouse should be closed and the courts forbidden to grant relief to those who are unjustly and inequitably deprived of their homes by speculators or others seeking windfall profits, it may say so.

The dissent is also concerned for boundaries for today's holding. There is, of course, no statute of limitations as to when the question of gross inadequacy must be raised, though the legislature could certainly enact such a statute. Of course, the doctrine of laches applies, and we seem to have survived despite there being no statute limiting the time when gross inadequacy may be raised as a ground for setting aside a judicial sale. Moreover, the balance of equities would be considerably different if the person who acquired the property for a grossly inadequate price sold it to a bona fide purchaser. As to the guidance provided by this opinion in defining grossly inadequate price, we can only point out that the Restatement indicates that twenty percent of market value is generally considered a grossly inadequate price. The parties, of course, are free to argue under the facts of a particular sale that a different percentage is or is not grossly inadequate. See Restatement §8.3 cmt. b and illus. 6.

Finally, the dissent asserts that there is no question of unjust enrichment in the present case because the purchaser at the trustee's sale "was not the lender, but a third party." We are unable to understand the distinction. It makes little difference whether a lender or a speculator was unjustly enriched. The important considerations are the questions of inequity on the one hand and unjust enrichment on the other. When these are present, the court may use its equitable powers.

CONCLUSION

As we said earlier, if one result of our adoption of Restatement §8.3 is that slightly higher prices prevail for sales conducted at the margin of the 20 percent yardstick, then we believe public policy is served. Accepting Sweetheart's argument and approving the sale in question would yield an inequitable and illogical result. It would protect the financial interests of defaulting mortgagors with high debt who receive credit for fair market value when creditors pursue a deficiency judgment and would neglect the financial interests of defaulting mortgagors with low debt . . . who lose all or nearly all their equity to a grossly inadequate bid price.

The rule we adopt today is consistent with our legislature's concern for debtors and its desire to respond to needs of the mortgage and home lending industry. The interests of debtors in need are protected without changing the obligations of debtors or the rights of lenders or trustees conducting valid sales, without throwing into disorder the well-established procedures for making purchases at those sales, and without creating risk for purchasers seeking bargains, albeit fair ones.

For the foregoing reasons we answer the question in the affirmative. We adopt Restatement (Third) of Property: Mortgages §8.3: a sale of real property under power of sale in a deed of trust may be set aside solely on the basis that the bid price was grossly inadequate.

McGREGOR, Vice Chief Justice.

I respectfully dissent. . . . Today's opinion . . . writes a new statutory section that defines and requires a minimum bid, if the bidder wishes to avoid a challenge to the trustee's sale at some undefined future time. It may well be wise policy for the legislature to add a minimum bid requirement to the Act, but the legislature, not this court, should make that decision. The answer to the question why the rule for a trustee's sale should be different than that for judicial foreclosures, thus is simply that the trustee's sale proceeds under statutory authority, which we lack authority to amend. . . .

In addition to the dearth of legal authority supporting the Restatement rule for non-judicial sales, the policies underlying Restatement section 8.3 do not apply in this case. The comments to section 8.3 describe two intertwined policy considerations that support the rule: protecting debtors from large deficiency judgments and preventing lenders from being unjustly enriched. Restatement §8.3 cmt. a. We further neither of these considerations by applying the Restatement rule here. Our deficiency statute addresses the first concern, by limiting deficiencies to the difference between the amount owed and the fair market value of the property. A.R.S. §33-814.A. While the second consideration may apply generally, it does not apply to this case because the purchaser was not the lender, but a third party. . . .

NOTES AND QUESTIONS

Unconscionable Foreclosure Prices. Can you think of a situation in which the fair market value laws discussed supra at Chapter 8C3a would not supplant the need for the equitable protection against unconscionably low foreclosure prices supplied in *In re Krohn*? That equitable standard, however, has proven of little comfort to borrowers because of the large disparity between the lesser foreclosure price and the collateral's market value that courts generally insist on before invoking their discretion to overturn a foreclosure sale that was conducted according to applicable state procedures. See generally Washburn, The Judicial and Legislative Response to Price Inadequacy in Mortgage Foreclosure Sales, 53 S. Cal. L. Rev. 843 (1980). Borrowers' short-lived success (through debtors in possession and the trustee in bankruptcy) in overturning otherwise properly conducted foreclosure sales as fraudulent transfers under the federal Bankruptcy Code when the collateral sold for less than 70 percent of the property's value is discussed with the bankruptcy materials at Chapter 18D.

The dissent in *Krohn* suggests that the majority essentially has written new legislation in allowing challenge of grossly inadequate sale prices in trustee's sales. Do you recall another instance in which we encountered the same objection of judicial activism?

d. Rights of Redemption

One important device for borrower protection is a legislatively mandated right of redemption. You already know about the equity of redemption, that is, the right of the borrower to redeem (buy back) the property *before* foreclosure by paying the lender the balance of the mortgage loan. The right of redemption is also made available by statute in many states for a period *after* foreclosure (particularly a judicial foreclosure), during which time the borrower or other parties affected by the foreclosure may redeem the property, generally for the amount bid at the foreclosure sale plus interest and costs.[22] Its purpose is to encourage bidders at foreclosure sales to bid the real value of the property as well as to give (primarily) consumer borrowers, who may have been too distracted by family problems to protect themselves in the foreclosure, a second opportunity to do so. The *Stadium Apartments* case below illustrates the reaction of the federal government when it was in the position of a mortgagee subject to a borrower's right of redemption. It also shows that some courts feel that statutory redemption does not always achieve its desired objectives.[23]

United States v. Stadium Apartments
425 F.2d 358 (9th Cir.), cert. denied, 400 U.S. 926 (1970)

DUNIWAY, Circuit Judge.

This case presents the question whether state redemption statutes should apply when the Federal Housing Authority (FHA) forecloses a mortgage which it has guaranteed. We hold that such statutes do not apply.

The federal statute here involved is Title VI of the National Housing Act, 12 U.S.C. §§1736-1746a. The stated objective of Title VI is "to assist in relieving the acute shortage of housing . . . available to veterans of World War II at prices within their reasonable ability to pay . . ." 12 U.S.C. §1738(a). . . .

. . . In 1949, appellee Stadium Apartments, Inc., desired to construct, under Title VI, an apartment house in Caldwell, Idaho. It applied to Prudential Insurance Company for a loan. Such a loan was eligible for insurance under 12 U.S.C. §1743(a). The conditions for eligibility are set out in 12 U.S.C. §1743(b). The mortgagor must be approved by the Secretary, who can impose certain regulations upon both the mortgagor and the property mortgaged. . . . The

22. See Washburn, id. at 930-932.

23. Because of the federal-state issues involved, the Ninth Circuit invited the attorneys general of the states within the circuit to submit amicus briefs. References to the argument of California are undoubtedly to the brief, amicus curiae, of the California attorney general.

mortgage was executed upon a form prescribed by FHA, and accepted for insurance. The amount of the insured loan was $130,000. The mortgage contained this provision:

> The Mortgagor, to the extent permitted by law, hereby waives the benefit of any and all homestead and exemption laws and of any right to a stay or redemption and the benefit of any moratorium law or laws.

Stadium Apartments defaulted in 1966, and Prudential assigned the mortgage to the Secretary of Housing and Urban Development, pursuant to 12 U.S.C. §1743(c). The Secretary paid Prudential the amount then due, as required by 12 U.S.C. §1743(c). The United States then obtained a default judgment foreclosing the mortgage. The district judge, in spite of the foregoing provision, framed the foreclosure decree to allow for a one-year period of redemption, as provided by 2 Idaho Code §11-402. The question is whether this was error. . . .

[S]hould the federal courts adopt the local law granting a post-foreclosure sale right of redemption in those states where it exists? Here, both authority and policy convince us that they should not.

Every federal appellate case dealing with the government's foreclosure remedy under insured mortgages applies federal law to assure the protection of the federal program against loss, state law to the contrary notwithstanding. . . .

Through all of these cases there runs a dominant rationale[:]. . . "Now [after default] the federal policy to protect the treasury and to promote the security of federal investment which in turn promotes the prime purpose of the Act—to facilitate the building of homes by the use of federal credit—becomes predominant. *Local rules limiting the effectiveness of the remedies available to the United States for breach of a federal duty can not be adopted.*" . . .

Reasons of policy dictate the same result. In the first place, only 26 of the states provide for post-foreclosure redemption. The periods of redemption vary widely. So do other conditions to redemption and the rules governing right to possession, right to rents, making repairs, and other matters arising during the redemption period. . . . There is a split of authority as to whether the right of redemption can be waived. Similarly, there is a split of authority as to the right of the mortgagee to recover the value of improvements made during the redemption period. It would be contrary to the teaching of every case that we have cited to hold that there is a different federal policy in each state, thus making FHA "subject to the vagaries of the laws of the several states." Clearfield Trust Co. v. United States, 1943, 318 U.S. 363, 367. . . .

In response to our request, the government has informed us of the views of federal agencies involved in the lending or insuring of funds for private housing purposes. . . . We quote the government's response:

> The Farmers Home Administration, the Federal Housing Administration, and the Veterans Administration have informed us that their experience has indicated that the imposition of post-foreclosure-sale redemption periods makes the foreclosure

remedy more costly and administratively time-consuming in those states whose local law so provides. Generally, the reasons given in support of this conclusion are . . . that existence of a post-sale period for redemption chills bidding at the foreclosure sale, forcing the United States to buy the property at the sale and to hold it (paying meanwhile the costs of maintenance) until the expiration of the period, when it finally can give good title to a purchaser.

Additional reasons stated by the government are quoted in the margin.[7] We do not find the policy arguments presented by California convincing. First, it is argued that the purpose of the redemption statutes is to force the mortgagee and others to bid the full market price at the sale. We assume that this is the purpose; we are not convinced that the statutes accomplish it. What third party would bid and pay the full market value, knowing that he cannot have the property to do with as he wishes until a set period has gone by, and that at the end of the period he may not get it, but instead may be forced to accept a payment which may or may not fully reimburse him for his outlays? . . .

Our doubts as to whether the statutes accomplish the purpose is reinforced by the fact that in many states, partly because of these statutes, real estate financing is almost exclusively secured by trust deeds with power of sale. This is certainly true in California, and the statutory right of redemption does not apply to such sales. . . . One is tempted to inquire why, if public policy so strongly favors a post-sale period of redemption, the legislature has not applied it to sales under trust deeds? Perhaps it is because the redemption statute has, in some states, made the use of mortgages almost a dead letter.

Moreover, the policy of FHA is to bid the fair market value at the foreclosure sale. For this purpose, it has the property carefully appraised before bidding. . . .

It is also suggested that a purpose of the redemption statutes is to protect junior lienors. Perhaps. But if the objective of the statutes is to obtain bids equal to market value, and if as is argued, the bidding would be lower in the absence of the statutes, then junior lienors could more easily protect themselves in the latter

---

7. The Farmers Home Administration has stated that where post-sale redemption periods have been imposed, the mortgaged property may after sale and before expiration of the redemption period, "stand unoccupied and unattended for considerable periods of time and consequently [may] deteriorate substantially in value, to the detriment of the financial interest of the United States and without concomitant benefit to any other party." Similarly, the Veterans Administration reported to us that where a post-sale redemption period is imposed[,] unless the former owner redeems timely, the mortgagee or his assignee are obligated to pay holding costs during the redemption period, i.e., taxes, public improvements, if any, the cost of repairs to preserve the security, and the cost of hazard insurance premium when necessary. There is also for consideration the interest normally accruing on the outstanding investment.... The Federal Housing Administration reported to us: ... ["]with the notable exception of Alabama, redemption statutes permit a foreclosure purchaser to receive from a redemptioner little more than the price bid at the foreclosure sale, so that a purchaser is well advised to keep rehabilitation expenses to an absolute minimum until the redemption period expires. As a practical matter, this delays the day when FHA, as such purchaser can safely embark on a program involving capital expenditures, thereby delaying the day when the property may be placed in condition for its best use and for advantageous sale which will reimburse the insurance fund for a portion of the loss incurred as a result of the mortgagor's default."

situation. They could buy the property at the sale for less. It is always open to the junior lienors to protect themselves by bidding. . . .

That portion of the judgment providing for a right and period of redemption is reversed. . . .

ELY, Circuit Judge (dissenting):

. . . The harshness of strict foreclosure led to the concept of foreclosure by sale. Theoretically, the property was to be sold to the highest bidder with the mortgagee having first claim to the proceeds. . . . Unfortunately, this expectation was frustrated by reason of the immense advantages favoring the mortgagee at the sale. First, it was unnecessary for the mortgagee to raise and expend any cash up to the amount of the unpaid debt. Secondly, there would not often be an interested outside buyer, or junior lienholder with cash, at the precise time of the sale. Thus, the senior mortgagee was assured of being almost always the only bidder at the sale. The junior lienors, in particular, suffered under this method since their interests were cut off by the judicial sale. Since they had no weapons with which to force the sale price above the amount of the senior's claim, they often realized nothing on their claims.

The response of many jurisdictions to the unsatisfactory results of the foreclosure-by-sale procedure was the adoption of a statutory redemption period. . . .

The key to understanding the statutory redemption right lies in the proposition that the statute's operation is in the nature of a threat. When redemption is exercised, it is thereby evidenced that the mortgagee has not bid adequately at the sale and the statute has not had its intended effect. On the other hand, if the threat functions successfully and the mortgagee does bid adequately, then the mortgagor and junior lienors, if any, will have been satisfied to the full value of the property and there will be no reason for exercising the redemption right. If he bids the full market value of the property, then the mortgagee may rest secure in the knowledge that it will not be redeemed. . . .

It seems no less clear to me that, disregarding the question of protection of the individual mortgagor, the goals of *any* federal housing program could not be served by the majority's decision. From the viewpoint of a mortgagor in a state with redemption provisions, and in the light of the majority's decision, it would be more desirable to finance privately than to finance through an FHA guaranteed mortgage. Even more important, potential junior lienors, such as contractors and suppliers, will be less willing to extend credit under these circumstances. Nor can junior lienors protect themselves, as the majority suggests, by bidding at the foreclosure sale. I have already explained that one reason for the existence of the redemption statutes is that the enormous leverage of the foreclosing mortgagee is not matched by junior lienors, who typically have very small cash reserves. . . .

Thus one effect of the majority's decision will be to lower the attractiveness of FHA financing in states that have enacted redemption statutes.

The Government, and also the majority, make several arguments designed to show that redemption statutes are neither important nor necessary. The first is that the statutes do not work because no third party will bid at the sale, knowing that he will be subject to redemption. The statutes, as I have tried to explain, are not the least bit concerned with the actions of third parties since they were necessitated by the observation that third parties do not ordinarily bid at foreclosure sales in any event. Instead of trying to stimulate bidding at the sale, they set up the more realistic possibility that the property will be redeemed if the mortgagee's bid is inadequate. . . . The Government argues at one point that the policies of the redemption right are satisfied by the alleged practice of the FHA carefully to appraise the fair market value of the property and to make its bid accordingly at the foreclosure sale. . . .

[S]uch unilateral action of the FHA could not satisfy the premise of the redemption statutes. That premise is that the fair market value is realizable only through the interplay of competing economic forces. This premise is not satisfied by judicial sale because of the demonstrated falsity of the assumption, made by the majority, that a third party will come in to force the price up to market value at the sale. . . .

NOTES AND QUESTIONS

1. The Effectiveness of Statutory Redemption Rights. The *Stadium Apartments* majority raises some disturbing questions about the effectiveness of statutes granting the borrower and others a right to redeem property after the foreclosure sale. In discussing the effect of rights of redemption in protecting junior interests cut off in foreclosure, Judge Ely states in dissent that since the junior interestholders "had no weapons with which to force the sale price above the amount of the senior's claim, they often realized nothing on their claims." The proceeds of a sale will go to pay off the first mortgagee before a junior encumbrancer is paid and, unless the bid exceeds the senior interest, the junior interestholder will realize nothing. Is Judge Ely correct in stating that the junior interestholder has no way to protect itself?

> ➤ *Problem 8-8*
> Assume your client holds a second mortgage of $5 million on Dan Developer's property. Ace's first mortgage, with an unpaid balance of $15 million, is in default, and Ace has commenced foreclosure. Your client's appraisers conclude that Dan's property is worth $19 million. What "weapon" would you have at the foreclosure sale, and how would you use it? If your appraisers had concluded that Dan's property was worth only $14 million, what would you do? Is Judge Ely's concern based on his presumption that junior lienors have limited funds and may be unable to bid enough to satisfy the prior lien? Even if the presumption were correct, isn't this problem inherent in the subordinate position the junior lienor bargained

for? ◄

2. *Federal Loan Programs.* The issue of the application of state foreclosure protections to federal loan programs arises as well in the case of antideficiency laws and is resolved by reference to the purposes and provisions of the particular loan program. Compare Carter v. Derwinski, 987 F.2d 611 (9th Cir. 1992) (en banc) (no state antideficiency law imposes any constraint on the ability of the Veterans Administration to recover on the veteran's contractual obligation to reimburse the VA for any amount the VA has paid to the lender on the veteran's default), cert. denied, 510 U.S. 821 (1993) and Munoz v. Branch Banking and Tr. Co., Inc., 348 P.3d 689 (Nev. 2015) (Nevada law limiting deficiency recovery of successor lender would impede market for resale of loans by failed banks and is therefore preempted by federal Financial Institutions Reform, Recovery and Enforcement Act of 1989) with United States v. Levine, 902 F. Supp. 367 (S.D.N.Y. 1995) (New York deficiency requirements apply to Small Business Administration loans). See generally Alexander, Federal Intervention in Real Estate Finance: Preemption and Federal Common Law, 71 N.C. L. Rev. 293 (1993). Notwithstanding the *Stadium Apartments* decision, the application of state redemption laws also turns on the purposes and provisions of the federal loan program at issue, as well as the nature of the state redemption requirement. For example, the Ninth Circuit later upheld the application of Montana redemption law in an SBA loan foreclosure. See United States v. Pastos, 781 F.2d 747 (9th Cir. 1986). Given the government's position and the outcome in the *Stadium Apartments* litigation, it is somewhat ironic that under federal law the government ordinarily has a one-year right to redeem when a foreclosure sale extinguishes its junior lien position. See 28 U.S.C. §2410.

In some instances, federal loan programs by statute override contrary state law to provide a federal power-of-sale foreclosure procedure aimed at making available the quicker, cheaper process of nonjudicial foreclosure. See 12 U.S.C. §§3751-3768 (allows foreclosure of HUD single-family mortgages by HUD-appointed commissioners using a nonjudicial power-of-sale). See generally Randolph, The New Federal Foreclosure Laws, 49 Okla. L. Rev. 123 (1996) (discussing drawbacks of bill to extend the HUD procedure to other federal-owned agency loans).

3. *The Sufficiency of Borrower Protection Provisions.* Notwithstanding the litany of protections afforded by statute or by the courts for the protection of the borrower, unfair prices are sometimes still obtained at foreclosure sales. In many such situations, the inequity may have resulted from the relative lack of sophistication of the borrower with a resulting underutilization of the marketplace and of the statutory protections available. Does this suggest that different foreclosure rules should apply to single-family residential properties, as distinguished from commercial properties? In the wake of the subprime loan crisis, what protections should ensue under state (or federal) law? Do you think these protections should sunset once the crisis eases, or be made permanent?

> ➤ *Problem 8-9*
>
> If you were asked to draft a model foreclosure statute designed to protect the consumer borrower without making mortgage financing unattractive to lenders, what protective provisions would you incorporate? ◄

4. Protection of the Guarantor

Having seen the various statutory and equitable protections accorded to borrowers before, during, and after foreclosure, we consider here the more limited protection of guarantors. In this era of commercial loans obtained by limited liability entity borrowers such as limited liability companies and limited partnerships, lenders often have no recourse beyond foreclosing the real estate collateral. Aware of that risk, commercial mortgage lenders typically require as a condition of making the loan that the individuals[24] behind the single-asset borrower entity guaranty payment of the loan. Guarantors tend to have meaningful assets distinct from the real estate collateral, both ensuring the mortgage lender will look to them for any shortfall, and giving the guarantors incentive to challenge the mortgage lender's recourse against them when the loan goes sour.

Enforcement of the mortgage guaranty often follows a foreclosure that falls short of satisfying the loan balance. Although most guarantees (except for so-called collection guarantees and some state laws)[25] permit recourse against the guarantor before the foreclosure sale, as a practical matter many lenders complete the foreclosure sale before seeking recourse against the guarantor for the leftover loan balance. Guarantors faced with a post-foreclosure collection might invoke the protection of state antideficiency laws (discussed at Chapter 8C3a), many of which once failed to specify whether their protection encompassed the guarantor as well as the "mortgagor" or "debtor" ownership entity. By now, most state deficiency laws explicitly answer whether or not they protect guarantors, and courts have construed the silent statutes. The battleground between commercial lenders and guarantors has thus shifted in states protecting guarantors to whether the guarantor could effectively waive that protection. Court decisions have confronted both the question of the enforceability of a guaranty waiver on public policy grounds (be aware that some state statutes explicitly outlaw or authorize any such waivers and keep the issue from the courts) and, assuming waiver is possible, whether the particular waiver language in the guaranty agreement was specific enough and sufficient to accomplish that purpose.

---

24. Sometimes the guarantors are entities themselves, so long as they have demonstrable assets separate from the real estate collateral. For example, the guarantor in GECCMC 2005–C1 Plummer Street Office Limited Partnership v. NRFC NNN Holdings, LLC, 204 Cal. App. 4th 998, 140 Cal. Rptr. 3d 251 (2012), excerpted at Chapter 5A3, was an affiliate entity to the borrower.

25. See generally M. Madison, J. Dwyer, and S. Bender, The Law of Real Estate Financing §§15:9-15:13 (discussing exceptions to pre-foreclosure pursuit of the guarantor sourced in the language of the guaranty itself and in statutes such as one-action rules, discussed supra at Chapter 8C3b, and so-called *Pain v. Packard* laws in a few states).

CSA 13-101 Loop, LLC v. Loop 101, LLC
236 Ariz. 410, 341 P.3d 452 (2014)

Chief Justice BALES

When a deed of trust secures a promissory note and the trust property is sold at a trustee's sale, A.R.S. §33-814(A) entitles judgment debtors, including guarantors, to have the fair market value of the property credited against the amount owed on the note. We hold that parties may not prospectively waive this provision.

I

Loop 101, LLC ("Loop") borrowed $15.6 million from MidFirst Bank in February 2007 to construct an office building. The promissory note was secured by a deed of trust and payment was guaranteed by four individuals. The promissory note, deed of trust, and guarantee all expressly waived the fair market value provision of A.R.S. §33-814(A).

Loop defaulted on the loan in June 2009, and MidFirst began a non-judicial foreclosure under the deed of trust. At the time, nearly $11.2 million remained outstanding on the loan. MidFirst assigned its rights under the loan and deed of trust to CSA 13-101 Loop, LLC ("CSA"), which bought the property at a trustee's sale for a credit bid of $6.15 million. CSA then sued Loop and the guarantors for a deficiency judgment of approximately $5 million plus interest. Loop and the guarantors counterclaimed against CSA and filed a third-party claim against MidFirst for breach of the implied covenant of good faith and fair dealing.

CSA and MidFirst moved to dismiss the claims on the ground that Loop and the guarantors had waived their right under A.R.S. §33-814 to a fair market value determination. The superior court denied the motion, ruling that the parties could not waive this statutory right. After holding an evidentiary hearing, the court found the fair market value of the property to be $12.5 million. On cross-motions for summary judgment, the court ruled that no deficiency existed because the property's fair market value exceeded the amount owed on the note.

The court of appeals affirmed. We granted review because whether A.R.S. §33-814(A)'s fair market value provision may be waived is a recurring issue of statewide importance. . . .

II

Contract provisions are enforceable unless prohibited by law or otherwise contrary to identifiable public policy. Our law values the private ordering of commercial relationships and seeks to protect parties' bargained-for expectations.

Accordingly, if a contractual term is not specifically prohibited by legislation, courts will uphold the term unless an otherwise identifiable public policy clearly outweighs the interest in the term's enforcement . . . Restatement (Second) of Contracts §178.

Consistent with these principles, we have sometimes observed that waivers of statutory rights may "impliedly" be prohibited. Our past decisions have also stated that parties may waive statutory rights granted solely for the benefit of individuals, but rights enacted for the benefit of the public may not be waived. The key inquiry, however, is whether an identifiable public policy clearly outweighs the interest in enforcing prospective waivers of particular statutory provisions.

We discern public policy from our constitution, statutes, and judicial decisions. Statutory provisions are examined in light of the overall legislative scheme, including its history and purpose. Restatement (Second) of Contracts §179 cmt. b. Even when not expressly prohibited, contract terms may be invalidated "if the legislature makes an adequate declaration of public policy which is inconsistent with [them]." Shadis v. Beal, 685 F.2d 824, 833-34 (3d Cir.1982). We therefore turn to the public policy concerns reflected in §33-814(A) and the deed of trust scheme more generally.

A

In 1971, the Arizona Legislature enacted the deed of trust scheme, A.R.S. §§33-801 to -821, as an alternative to the often cumbersome mortgage and judicial foreclosure system. A deed of trust allows for the sale of the property at a trustee's sale (often referred to as a non-judicial foreclosure) rather than exclusively through judicial process. Once the trust property is sold pursuant to the trustee's power of sale, the statute limits the lender's right to seek a deficiency judgment against the debtor. Deficiency judgments are barred altogether for most residential properties. A.R.S. §33-814(G). For other properties, the debtor may credit the fair market value of the trust property against the amount owed on the debt. A.R.S. §33-814(A). Similar limits on deficiency judgments exist for debts secured by mortgages.

A.R.S. §33-814(A) governs deficiency recovery actions against parties liable on debts secured by deeds of trust. The statute provides, in relevant part: In any such action against such a person, the deficiency judgment shall be for an amount equal to the sum of the total amount owed the beneficiary as of the date of the sale, as determined by the court less the fair market value of the trust property on the date of the sale as determined by the court or the sale price at the trustee's sale, whichever is higher.

The fair market value provision applies equally to guarantors and borrowers. Id. Moreover, the statute does not draw distinctions based on the resources or sophistication of the parties, nor does it distinguish between commercial and residential transactions. "[S]o long as the subject properties fit within the statutory definition, the identity of the mortgagor as either a homeowner or developer is irrelevant." Mid Kan. Fed. Sav. & Loan Ass'n of Wichita v. Dynamic Dev. Corp., 167 Ariz. 122, 128, 804 P.2d 1310, 1316 (1991).

The fair market value provision, as well as the deed of trust framework generally, accords with Arizona's long-recognized public policy of protecting debtors. In line with this public policy, Arizona's deed of trust framework streamlines the foreclosure process but maintains protections for borrowers and the public. It does this by protecting against artificially increased deficiency judgments.

The fair market value provision, unlike the anti-deficiency statutes, does not bar deficiency judgments altogether. Compare A.R.S. §33-814(A) (reducing deficiency by property's fair market value), with A.R.S. §§33-729(A), 33-814(G) (prohibiting deficiency judgments). But the statutes share a common purpose of protecting borrowers. Section 33-814(A) protects against artificially inflated deficiencies by preventing windfalls resulting from below-market credit bids. The anti-deficiency statutes prevent artificial deficiencies resulting from forced sales and further protect certain borrowers from exposing other assets to the risk of default. Thus, both the fair market value provision and anti-deficiency protections serve to alleviate the harmful effects of economic recession on borrowers.

B

We must next decide whether the public policy of preventing artificial deficiencies outweighs the interest in enforcing the waiver provisions here. Routine waiver of A.R.S. §33-814(A) would seriously disrupt the statute's public purpose of preventing artificial deficiencies and protecting borrowers. Consistent with the statute's purpose and the overall statutory scheme, we hold that A.R.S. §33-814(A)'s fair market value provision cannot be prospectively waived.

When Loop defaulted on its debt, CSA (or its predecessor in interest, MidFirst Bank) could have obtained a judgment for the entirety of the outstanding debt by suing on the note alone. A.R.S. §33-722 (mortgagee may elect between action on the debt or foreclosure of the mortgage given to secure it). But CSA chose to foreclose and seek recovery under the deed of trust scheme. Because this scheme "is a creature of statutes," CSA is limited to the recovery the statutes provide. See Register v. Coleman, 130 Ariz. 9, 14, 633 P.2d 418, 423 (1981) ("When a statute creates a right and also creates a remedy for the right created, the remedy thereby given is exclusive."). And because the deed of trust scheme strips borrowers of many of the protections afforded under the mortgage laws, we strictly construe the statutes in favor of borrowers.

Unlike some real property statutes, A.R.S. §33-814(A) is silent as to advance waiver. Cf. A.R.S. §33-729(A) (providing for anti-deficiency protection "notwithstanding any agreement to the contrary"). CSA argues we should read this omission as the legislature's implied endorsement of waiver. Cf. Ballesteros

v. Am. Standard Ins. Co. of Wis., 226 Ariz. 345, 349 ¶ 15, 248 P.3d 193, 197 (2011) (declining to construe an insurance statute to require a Spanish language form where other statutes explicitly require it). But here the omission cuts both ways, as the legislature also has expressly allowed waiver in other statutes. See, e.g., A.R.S. §33-819 (allowing parties to waive deed of trust provisions when deed is not given to secure a contract). Because the legislature has sometimes allowed and sometimes prohibited waiver in the deed of trust statutes, the omission of a term addressing waiver in §33-814(A) is not conclusive as to the legislature's intent.

As discussed above, . . . the fair market value protection of A.R.S. §33-814(A) furthers the public interest of preventing artificial deficiencies and protecting borrowers generally. Such deficiencies harm not only individual debtors but also the regional economy. Cf. DeBerard Props., Ltd. v. Lim, 20 Cal .4th 659, 85 Cal. Rptr. 2d 292, 976 P.2d 843, 849 (1999) (explaining that a "key purpose" of California's anti-deficiency law "is to stabilize the state's economy, to the benefit of all"). This identifiable public policy weighs heavily against the interest in enforcing the waiver provisions of the contracts here.

The Restatement (Third) of Property further counsels against allowing waiver. Section 8.4 provides fair market value protection similar to that in A.R.S. §33-814(A). . . . Absent controlling authority to the contrary, we generally follow the Restatement when it sets forth sound legal policy.

Like Arizona's statute, Restatement §8.4 is silent as to advance waiver of its provisions. But the comment explains that "[a]ny agreement in or created contemporaneously with the mortgage documents by which any person against whom a deficiency may be sought purports to waive the protection of this section is ineffective." Restatement (Third) of Property: Mortgages §8.4 cmt. b. If advance waiver were permitted, "most mortgage forms would routinely incorporate waiver language and the impact of this section would be significantly weakened." Id. Reporters' Note. And by barring waivers by both guarantors and borrowers, the Restatement "seeks to ensure that its primary goal of preventing unjust enrichment of the mortgagee is not subverted by the routine exaction of waivers from guarantors and sureties." Id.

CSA argues that the Restatement's prohibition of waiver is inapposite because §8.4 is modeled after statutes expressly prohibiting waiver. The Reporters' Note does state that the section is "consistent with" California and Pennsylvania statutes that expressly prohibit waiver. Id. (citing Cal. Civ. Code §2953 and 42 Pa. Cons. Stat. §8103(e)). We note that Reporters' Notes are not endorsed by the American Law Institute, but instead reflect the views of the Reporter. See, e.g., American Law Institute, Capturing the Voice of the American Law Institute: A Handbook for ALI Reporters and Those Who Review Their Work 45 (2005) ("Unlike the Introduction, Introductory Notes, black letter, and Comment (including Illustrations), the Reporter's (or Reporters') Notes are regarded as the work of the Reporter (or Reporters)."). But more importantly, the Reporters' observation that §8.4 is "consistent with" these statutes does not make the provision rise or fall with the language of those statutes. Rather, the text of

§8.4, like that of A.R.S. §33-814(A), is silent as to waiver. The comment therefore indicates that §8.4 bars waiver even without express language to that effect.

Like the Arizona deed of trust scheme, Restatement §8.4 seeks to protect against artificially increased deficiencies. And consistent with Arizona law, the Reporters' Note recognizes that allowing waiver would result in lenders routinely exacting this term as a matter of course. See Forbach [v. Steinfeld], 34 Ariz. [519] at 526, 273 P. [6] at 9 [1928] ("If the [lender] has the right to demand a waiver of statutory rights, he will almost certainly do it, and the [debtor] generally is in no position to protect himself."); see also Brunsoman v. Scarlett, 465 N.W.2d 162, 167 (N.D.1991) ("The rights and defenses granted debtors by the anti-deficiency judgment law would be largely illusory if a prospective creditor could compel a prospective debtor to waive them at the time the mortgage is executed."). Thus, allowing waiver would seriously disrupt the public purpose of A.R.S. §33-814(A)'s fair market value protection.

C

CSA urges us to follow other jurisdictions that have interpreted their fair market value statutes to allow waiver. Most directly on point is LaSalle Bank Nat'l Ass'n v. Sleutel, 289 F.3d 837 (5th Cir.2002), recently endorsed by the Texas Supreme Court in Moayedi v. Interstate 35/Chisam Rd., L.P., 438 S.W.3d 1, 6 (Tex.2014). In *LaSalle Bank*, the Fifth Circuit interpreted a Texas statute that, like Arizona's, provides for a fair market value credit but is silent as to advance waiver. 289 F.3d at 839–40 (discussing Tex. Prop. Code Ann. §51.003). Although the borrower argued that allowing waiver would violate the public policy of protecting borrowers from unfair lending practices, the court held that this concern did not apply to transactions between lenders and guarantors. The court also found dispositive the fact that the Texas Legislature had addressed waiver in other statutes. In agreeing with *LaSalle Bank*, the Texas Supreme Court added that it would prohibit waiver of a statutory right only when its legislature clearly proscribes such waivers. Moayedi, 438 S.W.3d at 6.

LaSalle Bank and *Moayedi* are distinguishable from this case in material respects. First, unlike the Texas statute, A.R.S. §33-814(A) applies both to borrowers and guarantors. The public policy of protecting borrowers thus applies with equal force to guarantors and is relevant to our analysis. Second, although our legislature has expressly prohibited waiver in other statutes, it also has expressly allowed it. Neither *LaSalle Bank* nor *Moayedi* addressed whether other Texas statutes expressly allow waiver, but the fact that Arizona statutes do means we cannot draw a determinative inference from the omission in A.R.S. §33-814(A). Finally, unlike the Texas Supreme Court, we do not require that the legislature "speak clearly" to prohibit waiver, but can instead find that a statute impliedly prohibits it as a matter of public policy.

Because the identifiable public policy served by A.R.S. §33-814(A) clearly outweighs the interest in enforcing prospective waiver terms, we hold that such terms are unenforceable. . . .

III

We . . . affirm the superior court's judgment, and award attorney fees to Loop and the guarantors pursuant to A.R.S. §12–341.01.

Moayedi v. Interstate 35/Chisam Road, L.P.
438 S.W.3d 1 (Tex. 2014)

Justice WILLETT

This dispute asks whether a party waives the statutory right of offset under section 51.003(c) of the [Texas] Property Code by agreeing to a general waiver of defenses in a guaranty agreement. The court of appeals answered yes, holding that section 51.003 creates an affirmative defense and that the guaranty agreement waives all possible defenses against liability, including the offset provision at issue here. We affirm.

I.   Factual and Procedural Background

Villages of Sanger, Ltd. borrowed $696,000 from lenders I–35/Chisam Road, L.P. and Malachi Development Corporation. The three-year note was secured by a deed of trust covering real property in Denton County. Merhdad Moayedi, as president of Villages' general partner, Pars Investment, Inc., guaranteed the loan. The guaranty agreement provides that Moayedi's liability is limited to $196,000 plus accrued interest and collection costs. The agreement also includes the general waiver of defenses at issue here:

> 7. Guarantor further agrees that this Guaranty shall not be discharged, impaired or affected by (a) the transfer by the Borrower of all or any portion of the real estate or improvements thereon, or of any security or collateral described in the Deed of Trust or in any other security document, or (b) any defense (other than the full payment of the indebtedness hereby guaranteed in accordance with the terms hereof) that the Guarantor may or might have as to Guarantor's respective undertakings, liabilities and obligations hereunder, each and every such defense being hereby waived by the undersigned Guarantor.

After Villages defaulted on the loan, I–35 purchased the secured property in a nonjudicial foreclosure sale at which I–35 was the sole bidder. The parties agree that the fair market value of the property at the time of the foreclosure sale was $840,000. The purchase price at foreclosure, however, was $487,200. After applying all credits and the proceeds from the sale, I-35 sued Moayedi to recover the $266,748.84 balance remaining on the note.

Moayedi included in his answer that under Property Code section 51.003, any deficiency owed should be offset by the difference between the fair market value and the foreclosure price. Later he moved for summary judgment based on that same section, asking the trial court to apply the offset. Moayedi argued that because the . . . the fair market value . . . exceeded the amount owed, his liability should be extinguished. I-35 did not contest the fair market value of the property, and argued instead that paragraphs 7 and 13 of the guaranty agreement waived section 51.003. Moayedi eventually filed two motions for summary judgment, and I-35 also moved for summary judgment. The trial court granted summary judgment for Moayedi.

The court of appeals reversed, holding that in paragraph 7, Moayedi waived his right to apply section 51.003. The court of appeals held that the offset is an affirmative defense. It concluded that the use of "any," "each," and "every" in the agreement encompassed all possible defenses and conveyed an intent that the guaranty would not be subject to any defense other than payment. It further concluded that at least three other provisions in the agreement indicated the same intent, including Moayedi's agreement that I-35 could enforce the guaranty without first resorting to or exhausting any security or collateral. According to the court, then, because Moayedi waived all defenses, he waived the right to avail himself of section 51.003's offset provision. . . .

Before this Court, Moayedi argues that section 51.003 should not be characterized as a defense and that the waiver in paragraph 7 is so lacking in specificity that Moayedi could not be said to have knowingly and intentionally waived his right to apply section 51.003. We disagree.

II. Discussion

We review a trial court's grant of summary judgment de novo. When both parties move for summary judgment, each party bears the burden of establishing its entitlement to judgment as a matter of law.

A. Deficiency Judgments

. . . B. Property Code Section 51.003

. . . Section 51.003 was added to the Property Code in 1991. No doubt it is intended to protect borrowers and guarantors. When lenders are the sole bidders at a foreclosure sale, they can control the foreclosure sale price and by implication the deficiency judgment. There is little incentive for them to bid high when a low bid preserves the amount they might get in a judgment against the borrower. Thus, the nonjudicial foreclosure sale often does not directly represent what a buyer might pay in the market.

Under the new law, a deficiency judgment is still the amount by which the debt and foreclosure costs exceed the foreclosure sale price. But, that amount may be reduced if the borrower or guarantor files a motion under section 51.003. Section 51.003 provides that if the fact-finder determines that the fair market value is greater than the foreclosure sale price, the party obligated on the debt may ask the court to offset the deficiency owed by the difference between the fair market value and the foreclosure sale price. . . .

As an example, imagine a debtor owes $100,000 secured by a piece of property. At the foreclosure sale the property is sold for $60,000. The resulting debt is the amount owed minus the proceeds from the foreclosure sale. That amount is affected by the costs associated with foreclosure, but for simplicity's sake, we will ignore those variables. Here, the resulting deficiency would be $100,000 minus $60,000, or $40,000.

If section 51.003 applies, the court can hear evidence regarding what the fair market value of the property was at the time of the foreclosure sale. If the fair market value exceeded the foreclosure sale price, the court shall offset the deficiency by that difference. Using our example, let us assume that the fair market value of the property at the time of foreclosure is $75,000. Because the fair market value, $75,000, exceeds the foreclosure sale price, $60,000, the deficiency judgment can be reduced by the difference between those amounts, that is, by $15,000. The resulting amount owed is $40,000 (the deficiency) minus $15,000, or $25,000.

1

. . . Section 51.003 is designed to ensure that debtors receive credit when their foreclosed property is sold at an unreasonably low price. But, like many statutory provisions designed to protect one contracting party or another, the benefit offered may be refused.

C. Whether Moayedi Waived Section 51.003

Texans have long embraced the principle of freedom of contract. And this Court's decisions respect the strong public policy of respecting parties' freedom to design agreements according to their wishes. Whether Moayedi can waive section 51.003 is not disputed by the parties. . . . In general, parties may waive statutory and even constitutional rights. Occasionally, the Legislature decides that some benefits are too important—and thus may not allow them—to be waived. But, when it does decide to prohibit waiver, we ask that the Legislature speak clearly. And indeed, other provisions in the Property Code do include anti-waiver language. This anti-deficiency law, however, nowhere prohibits waiver.

So, Moayedi could waive section 51.003. The question is whether he did. We agree with the court of appeals that the general waiver in paragraph 7 of the guaranty agreement waives the application of section 51.003. To be effective, a waiver must be clear and specific. The United States Supreme Court has defined waiver as an "intentional relinquishment or abandonment of a known right or privilege." This Court has defined waiver as the "intentional relinquishment of a known right or intentional conduct inconsistent with claiming that right." Determining whether there has been an "intelligent waiver" depends on the circumstances of the case. Waiver is a matter of intent as "[t]here can be no waiver unless so intended by one party and so understood by the other."

Courts construe unambiguous guaranty agreements as any other contract. If the meaning of a guaranty agreement is uncertain, "its terms should be given a construction which is most favorable to the guarantor." The interpretation of an unambiguous contract, however, is a question of law for the court. "In construing a written contract, the primary concern of the court is to ascertain the true intentions of the parties as expressed in the instrument." . . . When parties disagree over the meaning of an unambiguous contract, we determine the parties' intent by examining the entire agreement. Moreover, unless the agreement shows the parties used a term in a technical or different sense, the terms are given their plain, ordinary, and generally accepted meaning.

Until now, this Court has not addressed the level of specificity required to waive section 51.003. Most cases in which courts have concluded section 51.003 was waived involved language with more specificity than the language at issue here. Moayedi argues that our decision in *Shumway v. Horizon Credit Corp.* [801 S.W.2d 890 (Tex. 1991)] should apply here. *Shumway* addresses the necessary specificity of a debtor's waiver of rights to presentment, notice of the note holder's intent to accelerate, and notice of acceleration of the balance due upon default. In *Shumway*, we noted that a lender can neither create nor exercise its right to accelerate a debt unless the provisions creating that right are clear and unequivocal. Having held that a lender has no right to accelerate a debt without saying so in clear and unequivocal language, it necessarily followed that a debtor could waive notice of acceleration only by meeting the same exacting standard of clarity and precision.

Thus, the specificity required to waive notice of acceleration in *Shumway* was premised on the rule that the right itself was not created unless the lender initially met the high standard of specificity and precision. "To meet this standard," we held, "a waiver provision must state specifically and separately the rights surrendered." Moayedi relies on *Shumway* to argue that just as "all notice" or "any notice whatsoever" is ineffective to waive notice of acceleration and notice of intent to accelerate, here, the general waiver language in his guaranty contract is similarly ineffective.

Moayedi argues that he cannot be said to have knowingly and intentionally waived section 51.003, but we must ask, if that's the case, then what did Moayedi think he was waiving when he waived "any," "each," and "every" defense? We have no doubt that the waiver would include the UCC defenses under the Business and Commerce Code, and Moayedi conceded in oral argument that it does operate to waive ordinary, common-law defenses. Thus, the waiver is not meaningless. Nor is there any indication that Moayedi was not a sophisticated businessman. After all, he was the president of Villages' general partner. But, we can see no principled way to distinguish common-law defenses from that created by section 51.003. It is true that unlike the ordinary common-law defenses, section 51.003 is a legislative creature. But that distinction gets us nowhere.

As the court of appeals concluded, the plain meaning of "any," "each," and "every" used in paragraph 7 results in a broad waiver of all possible defenses. Just because the waiver is all encompassing does not mean that it is unclear or vague. To waive all possible defenses seems to very clearly indicate what defenses are included: all of them. Indeed, a waiver provision such as this one may be more descriptive to a layperson than a waiver referencing Property Code section numbers.

The parties disagree about the effect of other waivers and statements of liability in the agreement. We agree with Moayedi that the meaning of the waiver in paragraph 7 depends on the rest of the agreement, but we agree with the court of appeals that these provisions indicate an intent that the guaranty would not be subject to any defense other than full payment. In particular, Moayedi agreed that I–35 could enforce the guaranty without first resorting to or exhausting any security or collateral and waived diligence on I–35's part in the collection of payment from Villages. Read as a whole, then, we think the waiver in paragraph 7, though broad, is not without meaning and is intended to include all defenses....

III. Conclusion

The guaranty agreement yields but one conclusion: Moayedi waived his statutory right to an offset [for fair market value]. We affirm the court of appeals' judgment.

NOTES AND QUESTIONS

1. *Limited Guarantees.* Some mortgage loan guarantees, as in *Moayedi*, are limited by agreement to not exceed a specified dollar amount or percentage of the loan, thus placing some of the potential risk of declining property value on the

lender. Drafting the limited guaranty can be tricky. When a fair market value statute applies and is not effectively waived by the guarantor, at least one court has interpreted that valuation law to frustrate the lender holding a limited guaranty. See Federal Home Loan Mortg. Corp. v. Arrott Associates, Ltd., 60 F.3d 1037 (3rd Cir. 1995) (prompting a subsequent amendment of Pennsylvania's fair market value law to reject this ruling). In *Arrott*, the guarantors agreed to be liable for up to $223,000 of the $2.5 million debt. Setting the fair market value at $1 million, the court relieved the guarantors of liability since the market value exceeded the amount guaranteed. Yet, no doubt, the lender expected the limited guaranty would survive so long as any amount of the loan exceeding the fair market value was unpaid. Lenders can bolster this result by specifying in the limited guaranty that the fair market value as mandated under state law, or any foreclosure sale proceeds, are applied first to the unguaranteed part of the indebtedness. In other words, that the limited guaranty is meant to be a "last out" guaranty. See M. Madison, J. Dwyer, S. Bender, §15:4.

2. *Application of Antideficiency Laws to Guarantors.* Although the two excerpted cases involve fair market value laws, other deficiency protections might explicitly, or by judicial interpretation, protect guarantors. California courts have developed a unique estoppel approach to protect guarantors in limited circumstances. California law bars a deficiency after a nonjudicial foreclosure, but will allow a deficiency (except for some purchase money loans) if the lender opted for a judicial foreclosure. If the lender of a guaranteed debt elects to foreclosure nonjudicially and then pursue the guarantor of the non-purchase money loan, the guarantor might justifiably feel prejudiced by the lender's strategy—the debtor is insulated from any later action by the guarantor for reimbursement simply because the creditor opted for nonjudicial foreclosure. Thus, the California courts, while not directly protecting guarantors under the deficiency laws, recognize an estoppel to protect the guarantor from a post-foreclosure lawsuit following the lender's nonjudicial foreclosure. Union Bank v. Gradsky, 265 Cal. App. 2d 40, 71 Cal. Rptr. 64 (1968). Still, the courts allow prospective waivers of this estoppel protection, known as *Gradsky*-waivers, and California eventually codified model language for an effective waiver. See Cal. Civ. Code §2856(d). How can the guarantor who signed a waiver protect against the above scenario?

3. *Waivers.* Guaranty agreements tend to include several waiver provisions encompassing everything from antideficiency laws to one-action rules (see Cal. Civ. Code §2856(a) (validating guarantor waiver of state's one-action rule explained at Chapter 8C3b) and advance notice of the foreclosure sale to defenses based on the lender impairing the collateral such as by failing to properly record its mortgage in the land records. Most guaranty agreements supply a laundry list of statutory and common law rights and obligations waived by the guarantor, often describing statutory rights by citing to the specific statute otherwise protecting (or possibly being read to protect) the guarantor. Given the

waiver language found effective in *Moayedi* of "each and every" defense, do you agree this language is sufficient to put the guarantor on notice as to the broad scope of rights waived? Should the courts require more specificity? E.g., D. W. Jaquays & Co. v. First Sec. Bank, 101 Ariz. 301, 419 P.2d 85, 89 (1966) (only the "most unequivocal language" will effectively waive the guarantor's subrogation rights). Or should courts encourage and expect guarantors to hire competent legal counsel at the bargaining table to advise them of their rights?

Assuming the guarantor is unprotected by fair market value laws either by the absence of law in the jurisdiction, their inapplicability to guarantors, or an effective waiver, how can the guarantor protect itself from an inadequate sale price?

THE ETHICAL REAL ESTATE LAWYER

Joint Representation of Borrower and Guarantor

Suppose you represent Dan Developer who established a limited liability company to own and develop a piece of property. The construction lender issued a loan commitment to that entity, as the borrower, requiring the personal guaranty of Dan, who is a member of the limited liability company. Assume you were hired to represent the borrower entity in the loan transaction. Are you comfortable in representing Dan in his individual capacity as a guarantor? As discussed in Chapter 2A2, generally the rules of professional responsibility permit lawyers to represent multiple parties if the lawyer believes that representation will not adversely affect the interests of the other client, and each client consents. Here, Dan tells you he has authority to sign the consent for the entity and himself, and tells you the lender will only make the loan with his signature as guarantor, and that the company needs the loan to fulfill its goals. Are you convinced? What is the alternative if you are uncomfortable with joint representation?

---

5. *Constitutional Attacks on Power-of-Sale Foreclosures*

Under the Fifth and Fourteenth Amendments to the U.S. Constitution, neither Congress nor the states may deprive a person of life, liberty, or property without due process of law. "Due process" includes notice and an opportunity for a hearing. In a foreclosure, property of the debtor is transferred to the purchaser at the sale. Where the sale is conducted under a power-of-sale and not by virtue of a judicial proceeding, the question has been raised whether the procedure provides notice and opportunity for a hearing sufficient to pass constitutional muster.

In Mullane v. Central Hanover Bank & Trust Co.[26] and Mennonite Bd. of Missions v. Adams,[27] the Supreme Court was called on to determine what kind of notice the Fifth and Fourteenth Amendments require and concluded that the form of notice must be reasonably calculated to apprise affected parties. Thus, under *Mullane*, notice by publication and posting was insufficient "[w]here the names and post office addresses of those affected by a proceeding are at hand.. . ."[28] In *Mennonite*, the Supreme Court struck down a tax sale against a mortgagee identified in a publicly recorded mortgage where the only notice given to the junior mortgagee was constructive notice by publication, stating that "unless the mortgagee is not reasonably identifiable, constructive notice alone does not satisfy the mandate of *Mullane*."[29] In Sniadach v. Family Finance Corp.,[30] the Supreme Court held that a garnishment law violated the due process clause of the Fourteenth Amendment because it failed to provide for a judicial hearing prior to the garnishment. In Fuentes v. Shevin,[31] a state replevin statute was found to be unconstitutional for the same reasons, even though the property had been seized only temporarily.

While power-of-sale foreclosure procedures vary from state to state, some seem to fail either the notice requirements of *Mullane* and *Mennonite* or the hearing requirements of *Sniadach* and *Fuentes*. One of the defenses raised to the unconstitutionality of power-of-sale foreclosure in those states, however, is that the Fifth Amendment limits federal action and the Fourteenth Amendment limits state action, and neither is involved in a power-of-sale foreclosure.

In an analogous decision involving a nonjudicial sale of goods to satisfy a warehouse lien as authorized under the Uniform Commercial Code (UCC), the Supreme Court in Flagg Bros., Inc. v. Brooks[32] found no state action. Three unsuccessful arguments were presented in *Flagg Bros.* to contend that state action was involved. The first involved direct state action, such as that found in *Fuentes*, where state agents seized the property under a state replevin statute. The Court rejected this argument because UCC §7-210 provides for a private sale of goods to enforce a warehouse lien, and, unlike *Fuentes*, there were no public

---

26. 339 U.S. 306 (1950).

27. 462 U.S. 791 (1983).

28. 339 U.S. at 318.

29. 462 U.S. at 798.

30. 395 U.S. 337 (1969).

31. 407 U.S. 67, reh'g denied, 409 U.S. 902 (1972). The effect of the *Sniadach* and *Fuentes* holdings was limited somewhat by the Supreme Court in Mitchell v. W.T. Grant Co., 416 U.S. 600 (1974), where it upheld the constitutionality of a Louisiana sequestration statute that did not provide an opportunity for a *prior* hearing. However, in later striking down a Georgia prejudgment garnishment statute that did not provide for a prior hearing, the Supreme Court, in North Georgia Finishing, Inc. v. Di-Chem, Inc., 419 U.S. 601 (1975), distinguished *Mitchell* on the ground that the Louisiana statute provided that only a judge could issue the writ based on a verified complaint setting forth the specific facts supporting the petition and in addition provided for an immediate right to a hearing after sequestration. Under the Georgia statute, the writ was issued by a clerk on an affidavit stating only conclusory and nonspecific supporting grounds for its issuance, and there was no provision for an immediate hearing after the writ was issued.

32. 436 U.S. 149 (1978).

officials involved in the sale. This is normally true in a power-of-sale foreclosure as well.[33] The second argument was that the state shared in the deprivation of property because the state encouraged the private activity through its enactment of the UCC authorizing the nonjudicial sale. The Court, however, concluded that the state had not compelled the sale but had merely announced the circumstances under which its courts would not interfere with the sale. This "mere acquiescence" was not state action. The third argument was that it is state action when a private person performs a governmental function. The Court rejected this argument on the ground that foreclosure of liens has not traditionally been an exclusively governmental function.

NOTES AND QUESTIONS

1. State Action. There are other theories invoked in an effort to supply state action in analogous challenges. One is that state action is involved where a state judicially enforces private parties' rights. This harkens back to Shelley v. Kraemer, 334 U.S. 1 (1948), where state action was found when the state specifically enforced a racially restrictive covenant. See also Moose Lodge v. Irvis, 407 U.S. 163 (1972). Consider the effect this argument could have. What if, after a completely private power-of-sale foreclosure, the borrower refuses to leave the premises? Would the consequent ejectment procedure constitute state action?

Another theory is that where the state pervasively regulates the activity of the private individual, the action may be treated as that of the state itself. In connection with power-of-sale foreclosures, state statutes specify the form of the sale and the protection that must be afforded parties with interests in the property. This theory was rejected with respect to a Texas power-of-sale statute in Barrera v. Security Building & Inv. Corp., 519 F.2d 1166 (5th Cir. 1975).

2. The Irony of "State Action." Earlier we examined the origins of mortgage law as a conveyance from the borrower to the lender with title vesting indefeasibly in the lender on the borrower's default, without notice or a hearing. We saw that mortgage foreclosure law developed to limit the ability of the lender to take property in this manner. The sale itself was substituted for strict foreclosure to protect the borrower. Should a statute designed to limit private

---

33. Prior to the *Flagg Bros.* decision, a federal district court (Turner v. Blackburn, 389 F. Supp. 1250 (W.D.N.C. 1975)) had struck down a North Carolina power-of-sale foreclosure for inadequate notice procedures, finding direct state action because the North Carolina statute interposed the clerk of the court in the proceeding, requiring a report to be filed with and approved or disapproved by the clerk as a precondition to the power to convey the property pursuant to the sale. The role of the trial court in confirming Georgia nonjudicial foreclosure sales, however, does not supply the state action necessary for a constitutional challenge. See Alliance Partners v. Harris Trust & Sav. Bank, 266 Ga. 514, 467 S.E.2d 531 (1996) (treating the confirmation proceeding as separate from the foreclosure process because judicial review to confirm the sale is only necessary when the lender seeks a deficiency).

action to protect the party affected by that action be the basis for finding state action that would make the otherwise constitutional private action unconstitutional? Is it reasonable to look to the purposes of the state involvement to determine whether it constitutes state action?

> ➢ *Problem 8-10*
> What amendments would you suggest to California's power-of-sale statute (excerpted at Chapter 8C2, supra) to help ensure against constitutional challenges should the requisite state action be supplied under one of the above theories or some other theory? See generally G. Nelson et al., Real Estate Finance Law §§7.24-7.31 (6th ed. 2015). ◄

3. Federal Action. Where a foreclosing lender is an instrumentality of the federal government, the requirement of due process in the Fifth Amendment clearly applies, and state action is not an issue. See, for example, Johnson v. United States Dept. of Agriculture, 734 F.2d 774 (11th Cir. 1984); Ricker v. United States, 417 F. Supp. 133 and 434 F. Supp. 1251 (D. Me. 1976). Can you make an argument that this reasoning should not apply to mortgages made by others and assigned to a governmental agency such as the FHA, acquired in the takeover of a banking institution by the federal regulatory authority, or acquired by the Government National Mortgage Association (GNMA), a corporation wholly owned by the federal government that acquires mortgages on the secondary market? See Warren v. Government Natl. Mortgage Ass'n, 611 F.2d 1229 (8th Cir.), cert. denied, 449 U.S. 847 (1980). If GNMA foreclosure is federal action, what about actions of a quasi-governmental organization such as the Federal National Mortgage Association?

4. Additional Reading. Barklage, Extra-Judicial Mortgage Foreclosure Not State Action, 41 Mo. L. Rev. 278 (1976); Leen, Galbraith, and Grant, Due Process and Deeds of Trust—Strange Bedfellows, 48 Wash. L. Rev. 763 (1973); Nelson, Deed of Trust Foreclosures Under Power of Sale—Constitutional Problems—Legislative Alternatives, 28 J. Mo. B. 428 (1972); Pedowitz, Current Developments in Summary Foreclosure, 98 Real Prop., Prob. & Tr. J. 421 (1974); Krock, Comment, The Constitutionality of Texas Nonjudicial Foreclosure: Protecting Subordinate Property Interests from Deprivation without Notice, 32 Hous. L. Rev. 815 (1995).

6. *Enforceability of Forfeiture Provisions in Installment Land Contracts*

Introduced in Chapter 3D as a mortgage substitute in purchase money financing transactions, the installment land contract is distinguished by its contractual remedy of forfeiture. The following hypothetical illustrates this remedy and its sometimes deleterious consequences to the borrower-vendee. Assume that Sam Subdivider sells Harry Homeowner a tract house in 1973 under an installment land contract for a purchase price of $15,000, payable at 5 percent over 15 years with interest and principal payments of $118.62 per month, and that there is a fixed grace period of 30 days. For eight years Harry punctually makes his payments. He has also landscaped his lot and built a garage on it. Property values in his neighborhood are beginning to skyrocket; the fair market value of Harry's house has grown to $44,000. In year nine, Harry, alas, takes ill and is out of work and misses a monthly payment. Thirty-one days after his last payment, Sam tells Harry he is exercising his contractual right to terminate the installment land contract (see Articles 8 and 9 of the sample installment land contract in the Documents Manual), which, as Sam points out, Harry had agreed to and signed. Forfeiture under Harry's uncured default gives Sam the house, worth $44,000, and retention of about $12,000 in payments ($7,000 principal and $5,000 interest) Harry has made over the past eight and one-half years. Had Harry fully performed under the contract, Sam would have received about $21,000 in principal and interest payments. Harry's misfortune enriches Sam by $35,000 (a total of $56,000 received and retained on default less $21,000 expected from full performance under the contract). If you feel Sam's enrichment is unjust, note that on just these facts a New York trial court granted summary judgment in favor of the seller in an ejectment action against the defaulting purchaser. A deal is, after all, a deal.[34]

In practice, however, most courts are unwilling to strictly follow the letter of such "deals." In refusing to enforce the forfeiture provision, the court in Looney v. Farmers Home Administration (excerpted infra) treats the installment land contract as, in effect, a mortgage by invoking equitable principles that courts have used to alleviate the harsh consequences of forfeiture to defaulting purchasers. The equities among the parties in that case, however, were arguably less compelling than those in the New York litigation, and in reaching its decision the court engaged in some rather result-oriented legal and financial maneuvering. Another case, Heikkila v. Carver (excerpted infra), while deciding against the purchasers, presents a number of arguments grounded on contract law

---

34. The ruling was overturned on appeal. Bean v. Walker, 95 A.D.2d 70, 464 N.Y.S.2d 895 (1983). A notorious illustration of a vendor's insistence on strict compliance with contact terms to precipitate a forfeiture can be seen in the "hog house" case. There, the purchaser in possession allegedly breached the sales contract requirement of maintaining the property by having failed to replace half a dozen small window panes in an abandoned hog house. Forfeiture for this default was claimed by the vendor after $284,000 had been paid on the $300,000 contract. The court held for the purchaser. Lett v. Grummer, 300 N.W.2d 147 (Iowa 1981).

that are typically summoned to avoid or mitigate forfeiture. The rationales set forth by the courts have been far from consistent or predictable and, together with the results of adjudication, vary widely among jurisdictions. Installment land contracts represent an area of law that is still very much unsettled and that has been beset by conflicting policy and financial considerations.

Looney v. Farmers Home Administration
794 F.2d 310 (7th Cir. 1986)

CUDAHY, Circuit Judge.

Lowry and Helen McCord ("the McCords" or the "buyers") arranged to purchase the property of John and Esther Looney ("the Looneys" or the "appellees") in Rush County, Indiana. When the McCords fell into financial troubles, they secured an emergency loan through the Farmers Home Administration (the "FmHA" or the "government"). In exchange, the FmHA received a second mortgage on the property. Later, after paying $123,280 to the Looneys, the McCords defaulted. The Looneys filed suit in the District Court for the Southern District of Indiana seeking forfeiture under the forfeiture clause in the buyers' contract. The FmHA filed a counterclaim asking instead for foreclosure, the usual remedy in cases of default. The court granted forfeiture, concluding that the buyers had paid too small an amount toward the contract principal to justify foreclosure. In light of the totality of circumstances surrounding the transactions at issue, we believe that foreclosure was the more appropriate remedy and therefore reverse.

On October 7, 1976, the Looneys and the McCords entered into a conditional land sales contract to convey 260 acres of property to the McCords for $250,000. The contract specified that this sum was to be amortized over a 20-year period at an annual interest rate of 7 percent. The McCords were to make annual payments of $23,280 on November 15 of each year until the purchase price and all accrued interest was paid. They also agreed to pay real estate taxes, insurance and maintenance costs for the property.

Four years after agreeing to these terms, the McCords received an economic emergency loan for $183,800 from the FmHA under the 1978 version of the Emergency Agricultural Credit Adjustment Act, 7 U.S.C. note prec. §1961. In return for the loan, the McCords executed a promissory note for the amount of the loan plus 11 percent annual interest. As security for the note, the McCords granted the FmHA a mortgage on the land subject to the land sales contract. The Looneys were aware of and consented to this mortgage.

The McCords subsequently defaulted on their payment obligations to the Looneys. At the time of their default, the McCords had paid $123,280 to the Looneys but still owed $249,360.12 on the contract price. In 1983, the Looneys brought suit against the McCords and the FmHA seeking ejectment and forfeiture of the contract. Both the Looneys and the McCords moved for summary judgment and the court granted the Looneys' motion. On June 5, 1984, the government sought leave to file a counter-claim seeking foreclosure of its mortgage. The court allowed the government to file. The government then moved for summary judgment. Together with its motion, the government included two affidavits stating that the property had appreciated in value to $455,000.

The district court denied the government's motion for foreclosure. It held that the traditional presumption under Indiana law in favor of foreclosure did not apply because the McCords had made only minimal payments on the contract and had not paid their fall taxes or insurance installments. Because $249,360.12 was still owed on an initial base price of $250,000, the court found the McCords' equity in the property to be $639.88, only .26% of the principal. The court therefore found forfeiture appropriate, awarded the FmHA $639.88 and extinguished the FmHA's mortgage.

The FmHA appeals. It contends that foreclosure was the appropriate remedy because it would have protected all parties' interests. In receiving forfeiture, the government argues, the Looneys got a windfall. They kept the $123,280 that the buyers had paid over 7-1/2 years and got back property which the government's two uncontested affidavits stated had appreciated substantially. Moreover, the government states, the court miscalculated the McCords' payments on the contract and equity in the property and thus greatly undervalued what the government could justly recover. . . .

In response, the Looneys note that the government had the opportunity to cure the buyers' default but did not. If the government really believed the property to have appreciated, appellees argue, it would have protected its interest by paying up the full amount of the annual installments and expenses. Since the government did not do this, it accepted the consequences. . . .

Under Indiana law a conditional land sales contract is considered in the nature of a secured transaction, "the provisions of which are subject to all proper and just remedies at law and in equity." Skendzel v. Marshall, 261 Ind. 226, 241, 301 N.E.2d 641, 650 (1973) (italics omitted), cert. denied, 415 U.S. 921, 94 S. Ct. 1421, 39 L. Ed. 2d 476 (1974). Recognizing the common maxim that "equity abhors forfeitures," the *Skendzel* court concluded that "judicial foreclosure of a land sales contract is in consonance with the notions of equity developed in American jurisprudence." 301 N.E.2d at 650. Foreclosure generally protects the rights of all parties to a contract. Upon judicial sale the proceeds are first applied to the balance of the contract principal and interest owed the seller. Then, any junior lienholders take their share. Any surplus goes to the buyer.

Skendzel recognized, however, two instances where forfeiture was the appropriate remedy:

> In the case of an abandoning, absconding vendee, forfeiture is a logical and equitable remedy. Forfeiture would also be appropriate where the vendee has paid a minimal amount on the contract at the time of default and seeks to retain possession while the

vendor is paying taxes, insurance, and other upkeep in order to preserve the premises.

301 N.E.2d at 650.

While the Looneys' counsel contended at oral argument that the McCords were abandoning and absconding vendees, the district court did not rely on this first *Skendzel* exception in finding forfeiture appropriate. The court in McLendon v. Safe Realty Corp., 401 N.E.2d 80, 83 (1980) described the circumstances under which this exception applied:

> [F]or there to be an abandonment of a conditional land sales contract one must actually and intentionally relinquish possession of the land and act in a manner which is unequivocally inconsistent with the existence of a contract. . . .
>
> Furthermore *Skendzel* spoke of an "abandoning, *absconding* vendee." The word "abscond" means to hide, conceal, or absent oneself clandestinely with the intent to avoid legal process.

No evidence in the record demonstrates that the McCords intended to relinquish all title to the property or avoid legal process.

If forfeiture is justified, then, it is only because the second *Skendzel* exception is met. This requires that the vendee have paid only a minimum amount on the contract at the time of default. In this case, the district court concluded that "this is patently a situation contemplated by the court in *Skendzel* in which forfeiture is the logical and equitable remedy." However, the buyers in *Skendzel* had in fact paid more than a minimum amount on the contract and the court cited no examples of what would "patently" constitute a "minimum amount." Rather, later Indiana cases have interpreted *Skendzel* as requiring a case by case analysis that examines the "totality of circumstances surrounding the contract and its performance." Johnson v. Rutoskey, 472 N.E.2d 620, 626 (Ind. App. 1984).

Here, while $123,280 was paid to the Looneys, the court considered all but $639.88 to be interest rather than a part of the contract price. The court equated contract price with what was paid to reduce principal and implicitly determined that all the interest owed had to be paid before principal would in any degree be reduced.

But nothing in Indiana law compels the district court's construction of payment on the contract. On the contrary, several Indiana courts have considered and given weight to both payments to reduce principal and those to reduce interest in determining whether buyer falls within the second *Skendzel* exception. . . . Here, the contract contemplates the payment of interest. If interest payments are included in the calculus, the McCords paid almost 33 percent toward the contract price rather than .26 percent as the court determined.

It is true that certain cases have looked solely at the reduction of principal to determine payment on the contract. But many of these cases have not had to include interest payments in their calculi because the [principal] paid was enough to justify foreclosure rather than forfeiture. See Bartlett v. Wise, 169 Ind. App.

125, 348 N.E.2d 652, 654 (1976) ("she had paid one-third of the principal amount due on the contract—certainly more than a 'minimal amount'") . . . .

Even when no principal is paid, a buyer's stake in the property may be sufficient to justify foreclosure. As the court stated in McLendon v. Safe Realty Corp., 401 N.E.2d at 83:

> We cannot say McLendon had paid a "minimal amount" on the contract at the time of default, giving him little if any equity in the property. The trial court found McLendon had no equity in the real estate as the principal owed under the contract and the accumulated real estate taxes exceeded the original contract price. However, "equity" in this context is the amount or value of the property above the liens and charges against it.

Here, two uncontested affidavits indicate the property to be worth over $200,000 more than the McCords owe the Looneys. With the evidence of appreciation, the court was incorrect to conclusively value the McCords' equity at only $639.88.

When the second *Skendzel* exception has been invoked it has frequently been because the vendee is contributing to a decline in the value of the security. As the court said in Johnson v. Rutoskey, 472 N.E.2d 620, 626, "the second *Skendzel* exception will be met only where the purchaser has paid a minimum amount *and* the vendor's security interest in the property has been endangered" (emphasis in original). Thus in Goff v. Graham, 159 Ind. App. 324, 337, 306 N.E.2d 758, 766 (1974), forfeiture was proper because not only had the vendees only made a down payment on the property but "[e]vidence indicated that the purchaser had committed waste and deliberately neglected the properties." There is no allegation or evidence of waste in this case.

. . . The Looneys received $123,280 and the McCords paid the necessary real estate taxes, insurance premiums and upkeep expenses for over six years. The Looneys make no showing that foreclosure would not satisfy their interest and the court below made no such determination. While foreclosure would appear to satisfy all parties' needs, forfeiture leaves the FmHA with a $639.88 recovery on a $183,800 loan. In view of the "totality of circumstances" this result seems inequitable and unnecessary. . . .

Heikkila v. Carver
378 N.W.2d 214 (S.D. 1985)

FOSHEIM, Chief Justice.

This is an appeal by Russell and Norma Carver from a judgment decreeing the Carvers in default on a contract for deed. We affirm.

On January 2, 1979, Howard and Reino Heikkila sold their 5,920 acre Harding County ranch to Carvers on contract for deed. The contract fixed the purchase price at $592,000.00 allocating in part $394,900.00 for real estate, $75,000.00 for the house located on the property, and $50,000.00 for 10 percent of the Heikkilas' mineral interests. The contract reserved to the Heikkilas an undivided 90 percent interest, including future interests, in "all minerals of whatsoever nature," including the right to "prospect for, mine and/or drill for said minerals."

Under the terms of the contract, payment was to be made by the assumption of a $12,908.70 debt on a state land contract, a downpayment of $159,091.31 and annual installments of principal and interest in the amount of $41,202.00 beginning on January 3, 1980, and thereafter on the third day of January each year for nineteen years. The rate of interest stipulated in the contract was 7-1/2 percent; however, upon default in making any payment, interest would accrue at a rate of 11 percent until the default was cured.

The contract also contained a default clause, which reads:

> . . . If the Buyers fail to timely pay or breach any of the covenants or conditions or obligations imposed upon them then the Sellers shall give the Buyers sixty (60) days notice of such default during which time the Buyers may make such payment or correct the breach of any term, covenant, or conditions or obligations imposed upon them, making the contract current, but if such action is not taken by the Buyers during this sixty (60) day term, then the Sellers shall have the right to retake possession of the property. . . .
>
> In such event, the Sellers and the Buyers may, and do, agree that it would be impractical or extremely difficult to fix actual damages in case of Buyers' default, and that all payments which have been made on and under the terms and conditions of this agreement by Buyers, or on their behalf by any other person shall be deemed liquidated damages and is a reasonable estimate of damages and that Sellers shall retain said sum or sums as their sole right to damages for Buyers' default. . . .

Carvers were delinquent in making their 1982 and 1983 payments. On each occasion, however, they tendered payment within the sixty-day grace period provided for in the contract.

In 1984, Carvers again failed to make their January 3 installment payment. On January 18, 1984, Heikkilas notified Carvers by mail of their intention to foreclose if payment was not made within the sixty-day grace period. Carvers, however, did not tender payment, and on March 23, 1984, Heikkilas brought suit for strict foreclosure of the contract.

At the time of default, Carvers had made payments on the contract to Heikkilas totaling $195,002.32 in principal and $124,343.15 in interest.

Following a trial, judgment was entered in favor of Heikkilas, granting them strict foreclosure of the contract. The trial court further ordered that Carvers could redeem the ranch property upon payment to Heikkilas within ninety days following entry of judgment of the total balance due and owing on the contract, including interest, in the amount of $448,901.52. . . .

I. LIQUIDATED DAMAGES

Carvers first contend that the default clause in the contract for deed is an unenforceable penalty.

. . . We have held that ordinarily such a provision will be upheld if (1) at the time the contract was made the damages in the event of breach were incapable or very difficult of accurate estimation, (2) there was a reasonable endeavor by the parties to fix compensation, and (3) the amount stipulated bears a reasonable relation to probable damages and is not disproportionate to any damages reasonably to be anticipated. . . .

The burden of establishing that the liquidated damage provision is an unlawful penalty rests with the party against whom enforcement is sought. . . .

Here, the trial court found that both Carvers and Heikkilas had retained competent legal counsel experienced in farm and ranch real estate sales; that at the time the contract was executed, damages in the event of default by Carvers were incapable or very difficult of accurate estimation, including the length of redemption period a court might set, the risk of overgrazing or other waste before or during the redemption period, other possible damage to the property, unknown future market value of the property, projected rental value of the ranch, and the potential loss of royalty income should the buyer interfere with mineral development. The court also found that the parties had used reasonable efforts in trying to estimate damages but were unable to do so, and that the default provision itself was the best evidence of the parties' efforts and intentions at the time of sale.

In addition, the record discloses that Russell Carver, who was experienced in real estate transactions of this nature, reviewed the contract for deed with his attorney prior to signing it. Indeed, Carvers' attorney testified that it was his practice to review real estate agreements with his clients on a "paragraph by paragraph" basis. Carvers also negotiated several changes in the contract, including an extension of the grace period in the default clause from thirty to sixty days. There is no evidence in the record of overreaching or unfairness on the part of Heikkilas or their attorney. In short, the record supports the finding that the parties bargained at arms-length over the contract for deed, including the default clause.

Based upon these considerations, we cannot say that the trial court clearly erred in finding that the parties were unable at the time the contract was made to determine prospectively what damages might arise in the event of breach by the vendee.

Nevertheless, a court may decline to enforce a forfeiture clause if the defaulting vendee establishes by clear evidence that a substantial disparity exists between the payments made on the contract, together with the improvements made to the property, and the loss of rents and other detriment suffered by the vendors due to the loss of use and possession of the property. . . .

The trial court found that at the time of default, Carvers had paid approximately one-third of the contract price and "had received and continued to receive the benefits of the use of the land together with 10% of the mineral royalties." In contrast, the trial court determined that Heikkilas had sustained damages in excess of $500,000.00 as a result of Carvers' breach as well as Heikkilas' lost use and possession of the land. . . .

We conclude . . . that several of Heikkilas' damage claims should have been disregarded by the trial court on the ground that they were either too speculative or simply unfounded, including [lost natural gas royalties, lost timber sales, lost gravel sales, lost payment for surface damages, travel expenses, lost wages and mental anguish and inconvenience]. Notwithstanding that the aforementioned items should have been disallowed by the trial court, there is still no clear evidence in the record of a substantial disparity between the relative detriment sustained by the parties.

Accordingly, we conclude that the trial court did not err in holding as a matter of law that the default clause in the contract for deed was not a penalty pursuant to SDCL 53-9-5.

II. Reinstatement of the Contract

Carvers next contend that the trial court should have reinstated the contract under its equitable powers.

Carvers first tendered their 1984 installment payment to Heikkilas on March 29, 1984, six days after Heikkilas commenced this action to foreclose on the contract. The sixty-day grace period had expired on March 18, 1984. . . .

The parties had expressly agreed that time was of the essence in the performance of this contract. Moreover, Carvers were on notice of Heikkilas' intention to insist upon strict compliance with the terms of the contract. When Carvers were delinquent in making their 1982 and 1983 payments, Heikkilas, as in 1984, gave notice of default with intention to foreclose if payment was not made within the sixty-day grace period.

> Most courts agree that time may be expressly made of the essence of the contract, and where this is done it is binding on the parties not only at law but in equity as well. A court of equity is not at liberty to disregard the contract of the parties in this respect where deliberately made and clearly expressed, for equity follows the law and will neither make a new contract for the parties nor violate that into which they have freely and advisedly entered. . . .

Jesz v. Geigle, 319 N.W.2d 481, 483 (N.D. 1982) (quoting 77 Am. Jur. 2d, Vendor and Purchaser §73 (1975)).

III. RESTITUTION

Carvers maintain that even if foreclosure is warranted, the trial court erred in not allowing restitution to the extent that improvements and payments made exceed the damages suffered by Heikkilas.

Carvers, however, did not present this claim to the trial court. Where the trial court has determined that enforcement of the liquidated damage provision would not be unconscionable, the defaulting vendee bears the burden of proving that the vendor would be unjustly enriched by retention of all payments made on the contract. In Vines [v. Orchard Hills, Inc., 181 Conn. 501, 510-512, 435 A.2d 1022, 1028 (1980),] the Connecticut Supreme Court stated:

> The purchaser's right to recover in restitution requires the purchaser to establish that the seller has been unjustly enriched. The purchaser must show more than that the contract has come to an end and that the seller retains moneys paid pursuant to the contract. To prove unjust enrichment, in the ordinary case, the purchaser, because he is the party in breach, must prove that the damages suffered by his seller are less than the moneys received from the purchaser. It may not be easy for the purchaser to prove the extent of the seller's damages, it may even be strategically advantageous for the seller to come forward with relevant evidence of the losses he has incurred and may expect to incur on account of the buyer's breach. Nonetheless, only if the breaching party satisfies his burden of proof that the innocent party has sustained a net gain may a claim for unjust enrichment be sustained.

The trial court may order restitution to the defaulting vendee by virtue of its powers to equitably adjust the rights of the party in a foreclosure action. This does not, however, relieve the vendee of his burden of proving that he is so entitled. It is only on appeal that the Carvers raise the claim that they are entitled to restitution. We have repeatedly said that an issue may not be raised for the first time on appeal.

. . . We note that Carvers did present evidence to the trial court of improvements made to the property totaling approximately $79,000.00 of which approximately $16,000.00 was insurance proceeds which was left over after Carvers had built a home on the ranch property to replace the one that had burned down shortly after they had taken possession of the property. This evidence, however, was not offered by Carvers pursuant to a claim for restitution. Rather, this evidence was received by the trial court in considering the relative equities of the party so as to determine whether the enforcement of the default clause would be unconscionable under the circumstances.

Thus, we cannot hold that the trial court erred in not awarding restitution inasmuch as restitution was not requested at trial nor was sufficient evidence presented to the court from which it could, upon its own accord, award restitution. . . .

HENDERSON, Justice (dissenting).

I respectfully dissent as the equities do not justify enforcement of a forfeiture provision. An old maxim of equity proclaims "Equity abhors a forfeiture." I dare say this case, precedentially, so far as contracts for deed and agriculture are concerned, is one of the most important cases in this Court's history.

In addition to the $319,345.47 buyers paid sellers, buyers improved the ranch property by at least $80,000 consisting of improving cropland, improving the timber stand, constructing four new wells, improving outbuildings and corrals, and furnishing the included item of extensive labor. These improvements are not essentially in dispute. Therefore, in five years the buyers poured and contributed approximately $400,000 into this ranch. Buyers tendered delayed installment, including principal and interest in full, just 11 days late! Under the decision of the trial court, now affirmed by this Court, the buyers lose everything, the sellers keep the $400,000, and sellers are reinvested with the entire ranch—much improved. This is too hardball for me to swallow in an equitable action. It is an unconscionable foreclosure. . . .

There are different colors and hues in flowers; there are different degrees of sin; there are different degrees of breach of contract. Some breaches of contract are indeed most serious and substantial and some are not. There are often subtle gradations. However, the 11-day full, but late, tender is not such a serious and substantial breach that it deserves a total elimination of all equity in this ranch of the buyers. I perceive this forfeiture as being unconscionable. If the same penalty applies to all breaches, that is, total forfeiture, it is inversely proportional to the degree of breach. . . .

NOTES AND QUESTIONS

1. Recharacterization as a Mortgage. Skendzel v. Marshall, 261 Ind. 226, 301 N.E.2d 641 (1973), cert. denied, 415 U.S. 921 (1974), is the seminal modern case characterizing the installment land contract as a mortgage. For similar decisions in other jurisdictions, see, for example, Woods v. Monticello Dev. Co., 656 P.2d 1324 (Colo. Ct. App. 1982); Hoffman v. Semet, 316 So. 2d 649 (Fla. Dist. Ct. App. 1975); Sebastian v. Floyd, 585 S.W.2d 381 (Ky. 1979). The Restatement (Third) of Property (Mortgages) adopts and extends this judicial trend to treat an installment land contract (referred to as a "contract for deed") as a mortgage by refusing to recognize the remedy of forfeiture regardless of the particular circumstances of the case. §3.4 (1997). Although there are legal and functional similarities between a mortgage and an installment land contract, do you agree that courts should rewrite the installment land contract as a mortgage and thus deprive the vendor of the forfeiture remedy that it bargained for in the contract?

It has been said under Florida recharacterization decisions that "the only remedy available for vendors holding agreements for deed [installment land contracts] is foreclosure pursuant to Florida law. Cancellation of the agreement for deed is only a form drafter's dream." D. Simmons, The Agreement for Deed as a Creative Financing Technique, 55 Fla. B.J. 395, 396 (1981). That an intimidated or unsophisticated purchaser may simply accept the terms of the contract as dictated by the vendor and not seek protection available under the law may not, however, be so dreamlike and may in part explain the continued popularity of such contracts containing forfeiture clauses. The forfeiture clause continues to remain a stock feature of installment land contracts published in real estate form books.

Installment land contracts were back in the news after the subprime mortgage crisis as the preferred financing vehicle for some companies that purchased foreclosed homes in bulk and resold them to new buyers using installment land contracts with high (often 10 percent) interest rates. See Goldstein and Stevenson, High-Risk Deals on Shabby Homes Ensnare Buyers, N.Y. Times, Feb. 21, 2016, A1 (describing resale of broken-down homes in U.S. Rust Belt at prices several times more than the investors paid).

2. *Convertibility.* Ohio law provides that the vendor must foreclose the installment land contract if the default occurs after the fifth year or after the vendee has paid 20 percent of the purchase price. Ohio Rev. Code Ann. §5313.07. Whether required by law or the contract, the approach that triggers foreclosure protections when the purchaser's interest, as measured by time or money, reaches a certain level has been termed the "convertibility" approach. Does this approach create a reasonable balance between the interests of vendees in protecting their equity in the property and those of vendors in having a quick and inexpensive means of recovering their property from defaulting vendees? See Danielson, Note, Installment Land Contracts: The Illinois Experience and the Difficulties of Incremental Judicial Reform, 1986 U. Ill. L. Rev. 91. What is the rationale for including the time over which payments are made as a factor to be considered when invoking foreclosure protection? Consider the sensitivities voiced by the court in Potter v. Oster, 426 N.W.2d 148 (Iowa 1988):

> Most importantly, the fair market value of the homestead at the time of forfeiture is an incorrect measure of the benefit Potters lost. It fails to account for the special value Potters placed on the property's location and residential features that uniquely suited their family. For precisely this reason, remedies at law are presumed inadequate for breach of a real estate contract.
>
> From Oster's perspective, Potters actually benefitted from the forfeiture because their purchase, in light of subsequent events, proved to be unprofitable. But the record convinces us that profit measured by Wall Street standards was of little consequence to Potters. This was the Potters' home, the place their first son was born, the place Charles Potter testified "was worth everything we ever gave for it, because we planned on living there the rest of our lives."

3. *Measuring the Vendee's Equity.* In *Looney,* the Seventh Circuit's determination of whether forfeiture or foreclosure was the appropriate remedy for the purchasers' default hinged on what constituted payment of a "minimal amount on the contract": if the purchasers had made more than "minimal"

payments, foreclosure would be required; if not, the court would enforce forfeiture. The sellers wanted to construe the phrase to mean the purchaser's "net equity," that is, principal paid less current and accrued interest. The FmHA, on the other hand, held a position as second mortgagee. Forfeiture under an installment land contract will extinguish the claims of junior mortgagees, although prior to forfeiture the juniors in most jurisdictions have the right to notice and to cure defaults on the contract (an option, however, not pursued by the FmHA). The FmHA argued, therefore, that payments made on the contract should be considered in the aggregate without regard to whether they satisfied principal or interest.

Although the Court of Appeals does not provide details of the calculations behind the District Court's conclusion that the buyer's "equity" in the property was $640, we may assume that the lower court must have regarded the equity represented by that part of payments in prior years apportioned to principal to have been "wiped out" by accrued unpaid interest. Thus, if the McCords had made the first 5 years' $23,280 annual payments, totaling $116,400, assuming simple interest, $33,241 of this amount would have been credited toward reduction of principal. If they failed to make payments in years 6 and 7, accrued interest due, compounded annually, would have amounted to $32,505 at the end of year 7, leaving them with "net equity" of about $735, arguably a de minimis forfeiture. On the other hand, if their equity "vested," as it were, at the end of year 5, when their paid-up principal was over $33,000, one could argue their right to foreclosure (through judicial recharacterization as a mortgage) should have been unaffected by any subsequent accrual of unpaid interest. If *Skendzel* (excerpted in *Looney*) stands for the proposition that purchasers with substantial "equity" should be able to avoid forfeiture and receive the benefits of foreclosure, is it more consistent with that decision to equate equity with "net equity" or with principal in fact paid?

4. Contract Law Challenges to Forfeiture Provisions. By characterizing the installment sale transaction as a mortgage, the *Looney* court provided defaulting purchasers the protections afforded under foreclosure procedures. In *Heikkila*, the purchaser-appellants invoked, albeit unsuccessfully, a number of arguments based on contract law that are frequently raised to defeat the harsh consequences of forfeiture to purchasers. Note that these arguments accomplish the same ends of purchaser protection as does foreclosure, namely, the opportunity for redemption, or payment to the purchaser of excess sale proceeds above the amount due the seller and junior lenders. Legislation in various jurisdictions that similarly affects the parties' contractual rights is also mentioned in the following discussion.

a. Forfeiture as an Unenforceable Liquidated Damages Penalty. The forfeiture provision in installment land contracts is very commonly contained in a liquidated damages clause that recites that in the event of the purchaser's uncured default the seller shall have the right to repossess the property and retain all payments made as liquidated damages compensating for the purchaser's use, rental, and occupancy of the property. The use of such clauses in the context of earnest money deposits under a contract of sale is discussed at Chapter 2A5.

Liquidated damages clauses must frequently run a judicial gamut flanked by the maxims "equity abhors a forfeiture" and "equity will not enforce a penalty." Where actual damages cannot be measured with certainty, courts will enforce the parties' estimate of damages provided that it meets basic standards of reasonableness and fairness. Since the standard liquidated damages clause in an installment land contract calls for complete forfeiture by the purchaser regardless of whether its default is on the first payment or on the last, isn't such a clause unreasonable on its face? Would a clause be more reasonable if it were drafted to restrict forfeiture as liquidated damages to when an amount less than a certain percentage of the purchase price had been paid? See Hertz, Note, Default Clauses in the Contract for Deed: An Invitation to Litigation?, 28 S.D. L. Rev. 467 (1983).

b. Reinstatement of the Contract. Occasionally, in exercise of their equitable powers, courts will refuse to enforce forfeiture clauses in installment land contracts and order that the contract be reinstated, provided the purchaser tenders delinquent payments due plus interest. See, for example, Barkis v. Scott, 34 Cal. 2d 116, 208 P.2d 367 (1949); Wu v. Good, 720 P.2d 1005 (Colo. Ct. App. 1986); Call v. Timber Lakes Corp., 567 P.2d 1108 (Utah 1977). Absent arrearages statutes, defaulting mortgagors are not afforded this kind of protection but rather must tender the entire balance due on the debt following acceleration if they are to retain their property. Thus, through this equitable intervention, contract purchasers may receive more favorable treatment than mortgagors.

The right to reinstate the installment land contract may also be provided for by statute. For example, Ariz. Rev. Stat. Ann. §33-742(D) allows for different time periods in which the purchaser may cure default, depending on how much of the purchase price has been paid (for example, 30 days when less than 20 percent of the purchase price has been paid, 60 days when between 20 and 30 percent of the purchase price has been paid, and so on). See also Iowa Code Ann. §656.2(1)(c) (30 days to cure); Minn. Stat. Ann. §559.21 (60 days); N.D. Cent. Code §32-18-04 (6 months if less than one-third purchase price paid, 12 months if more than one-third); Ohio Rev. Code Ann. §5313.05 (30 days from date of default). Grace periods may also be contained in the contract itself.

In jurisdictions where vendors cannot enforce forfeiture clauses but must foreclose, it may be advisable for them to include express acceleration provisions in their contracts that require the purchaser to tender on default the full balance of principal due. One court, for example, rejected a seller's argument that acceleration could be implied from the forfeiture-on-default provisions of the contract and held that the seller at most could receive a judgment of foreclosure in the amount of principal and interest past due plus costs. The balance would survive as a lien on the property sold at foreclosure and would be payable in installments pursuant to the contract. Adkinson v. Nyberg, 344 So. 2d 614 (Fla. Dist. Ct. App. 1977).

c. Restitution. Where forfeiture is ultimately enforced, courts have become increasingly willing to mitigate its effects by awarding purchasers restitution in the amount of the forfeited property and payments that exceeds the seller's losses. This is a marked departure from traditional contract law, which denied restitution to the party in breach. Among the equities commonly weighed by the courts in deciding whether to grant restitution to the defaulting vendee are the willfulness of the defaulting purchaser's breach and, as with the question of the enforceability of liquidated damages clauses, the degree to which the vendee's payments exceed the vendor's damages. The critical issue in determining restitution awards is, then, a matter of measuring what the purchaser has given up in forfeiture and what the seller has lost by the breach; this necessarily involves thorny problems defining the parties' property interests and the valuation of those interests.

Suppose Seller (*S*) and Purchaser (*P*) enter into an installment contract for property with a purchase price of $135,000 and terms of $25,000 down and $845 monthly until the balance is paid. After 10 months, *P* defaults. Assume by that time the fair market value of the property has declined to $90,000; its rental value has been $1,687.50 per month. If *P* forfeited the property and payments and *S*'s damages were calculated as the rental value of the property during *P*'s occupancy, *P* would be entitled to $16,575 in restitution—the amount *P*'s payments exceed rental value. Were this the exclusive measure of damages, wouldn't the contract, in effect, be a lease with an option to buy, since the purchaser could simply default when the property value dropped below the purchase price and thereafter be liable only for rental value? What result if *S*'s damages were based on a benefit-of-the-bargain theory? See Honey v. Henry's Franchise Leasing Corp., 64 Cal. 2d 801, 52 Cal. Rptr. 18, 415 P.2d 833 (1966). Should *S*'s damages include both the rental value of the property *and* the decline in its market value? In this hypothetical, which is taken from the fact pattern in *Honey*, not only is *S*'s property worth $45,000 less than the contract price, but *S* lost its use, worth $16,875, for 10 months as well. Consider the reasoning in the following decision that requires the vendor to choose between two remedies based on mutually exclusive legal theories. In Kudokas v. Balkus, 26 Cal. App. 3d 744, 103 Cal. Rptr. 318 (1972), an action brought by the vendor against defaulting vendees to recover and quiet title to a motel, the trial court sustained the vendor's claim and, on a benefit-of-the-bargain theory, awarded the vendees restitution in the amount by which their payments plus the depreciated value of the motel exceeded the sum of the contract price and the vendor's consequential damages. The vendors argued that the restitution award should be reduced by the rental value of the motel for the period the defendant purchasers were in possession. The trial court agreed and granted a limited new trial to recalculate the vendor's damages to include rental value. The vendees appealed.

In seeking to justify the limited new trial order, plaintiff [vendor] makes a number of unacceptable arguments. She compares herself to a rescinding vendor, who is entitled to recover the property's use value during the entire period of the vendee's possession. Plaintiff does not occupy that position. When the vendee breaches the contract, the vendor has an election to rescind or enforce the contract. Rescission would require plaintiff to restore or offer to restore all the money and credits she has received under the contract. She has not done so. . . .

In this action she sought forfeiture of the vendee's rights, a quiet title decree and retention of the vendee's payments. Such an action is one to enforce rather than rescind the contract. . . .

Contrary to plaintiff's contention, the benefit-of-bargain rule does not give defendants free occupancy during the two years they had possession under the contract. At this point plaintiff overlooks the fact that during these two years defendants took the risk—and relieved plaintiff of the risk—of a decline in capital value. In selecting a remedy for breach of the contract, the vendor has a choice between rescission and enforcement. Conceivably, rescission and restoration of the vendee's payments would put the vendor in a position to recover use value. Here the vendor chose not to rescind. Here the vendor seeks to quiet title "on condition that he refund the excess, if any, of the payments received over the amount necessary to give him the benefit of his bargain.". . .

This lawsuit manifests an election to treat the property as though it had been sold, not rented. In arguing for rental value in addition or as an alternative to "benefit of the bargain," plaintiff would treat the property as though it had not been sold. The trial court erred in ordering a new trial on the theory that the plaintiff-vendor was entitled to rental value during the period of the defendant-vendees' possession under the contract.

103 Cal. Rptr. at 323-324. Does the argument based on legal theory in *Kudokas* dispel the intuitive inclination to award the vendor in our hypothetical both rental value and declined market value measures of damages? Forfeiture may be viewed as a component of the vendor's remedy based on contract rescission or, alternatively, contract termination. See E. Freyfogle, Installment Land Contracts, in 7 Powell, Law of Real Property ¶938.22[2] (1996). The object of recission is to return the parties to their positions before the contract was made, so forfeiture represents the return of the property to the vendor, while the purchaser receives the return of its payments as restitution. The purchaser must also "return" to the vendor the use it had of the property; this is accomplished by offsetting from the amount of restitution the rental value of the property. On the other hand, where the vendor pursues a contract termination remedy, it is entitled to an award of the benefit of its bargain, namely, the contract price. In this case, the property and payments are forfeited as credits toward the contract price, and the purchaser receives as restitution the amount by which they exceed the contract price plus consequential damages. Rent is not includable in a benefit-of-the-bargain-based award, since the contract contemplates the purchaser's receiving ownership of the property. Does this mean that if the value of the property forfeited equals the purchase price the defaulting purchaser should receive all of its payments as restitution, thereby receiving use of the property at no cost? The answer to this question depends on the contract's provision for installment payments and interest. Compensation for use of the property will have been made to the extent the purchaser has lost and the vendor has gained the use of funds paid out in

installments. Similarly, when the contract calls for interest on the deferred principal, the vendor receives what in effect is a major incident of ownership of the purchase price at the same time the purchaser in possession receives incidents of ownership of the property. Thus, a simplistic formulation that calculates restitution as the amount by which the seller's payments exceed the difference between the contract price and market value of the returned property may be erroneous if the contract calls for interest payments. Such a formula credits the vendee with interest rather than including it as part of the bargain due the vendor. For a discussion of this issue in terms of the time value of money see Nelson and Whitman, Installment Land Contracts—The National Scene Revisited, 1985 BYU L. Rev. 1, 24 n.80.

If the vendor has not bargained for interest, then in effect it has agreed to the purchaser's "free" use of the property, and courts should not make up for this by assessing the purchaser rent when they calculate a benefit-of-the-bargain remedy. Under what theory would restitution to the purchaser include interest on the down payment and payments of principal? This question was addressed in Dow v. Noble, 380 N.W.2d 359 (S.D. 1986), where the purchaser had paid $125,000 down. The vendor was awarded rental value of the property, but the purchaser was not credited with interest on his payments of principal. *Dow* typifies the inconsistent manner in which the courts have applied the rescission and contract termination theories of forfeiture.

When the forfeited property has appreciated in value, on account of either market changes or improvements made by the purchaser, under a benefit-of-the-bargain theory it is clear that the purchaser is entitled to restitution of this increase. Conversely, when the property's value has declined and principal payments fall short of making up this loss, the vendor is entitled to a deficiency judgment, unless, of course, forfeiture is being enforced as liquidated damages. Where the contract is rescinded, purchaser-made improvements or waste would also result in restitution or deficiency adjustments. How should the risks (rewards) of market-induced declines (increases) in value be allocated in rescission? Is it inconsistent to charge the purchaser with both rent and depreciation? Would the vendor's decision to terminate rather than rescind obviate this problem?

The concept of restitution has been incorporated in many state statutes that regulate forfeiture under installment land contracts. Pennsylvania's installment land contract law, for example, provides that payments of up to 25 percent of the purchase price together with forfeiture of the property may comprise enforceable liquidated damages for default, but that the purchaser is entitled to restitution for any payments above the 25 percent mark that exceed the seller's actual damages. Pursuant to regulations under the federal Interstate Land Sales Full Disclosure Act, 12 C.F.R. §1011.4, similar rights vest in the purchaser who has paid at least 15 percent of the purchase price.

d. Redemption. The remedy granted the vendors in *Heikkila* was that of "strict foreclosure," a special kind of foreclosure action infrequently encountered except in installment land contract cases. See Chapter 8C1 supra. In strict foreclosure, the court gives the defaulting purchaser a certain time within which it may redeem its property by paying the balance of the purchase price plus accrued interest and costs. Absent such payment, title vests in the vendor free of any equitable interest in the purchaser. Unlike judicial foreclosure (or foreclosure by power-of-sale), which calls for a sale of the mortgaged property, this remedy does not mandate a sale and therefore does not afford the purchaser any right to the excess of property value over the debt owed or the opportunity to redeem during a statutory period following the sale. See Vanneman, Strict Foreclosure on Land Contracts, 14 Minn. L. Rev. 342 (1930). Courts on occasion will exercise their equitable powers to allow defaulting vendees a period in which they are permitted to redeem their property. The decision is discretionary, and courts will weigh a number of factors including the amount of the vendee's equity, the length of the default period, the willfulness of the default, improvements made on the property by the vendee, and the vendee's care in maintaining the property. See, for example, Grombone v. Krekel, 754 P.2d 777 (Colo. Ct. App. 1988).

5. Additional Reading. Freyfogle, Vagueness and the Rule of Law: Reconsidering Installment Land Contract Forfeitures, 1988 Duke L.J. 609; McKeirnan, Note, Preserving Real Estate Contract Financing in Washington: Resisting the Pressure to Eliminate Forfeiture, 70 Wash. L. Rev. 227 (1995).

Chapter 9

Lender Liability

A. THEORIES OF LENDER LIABILITY

The period from default to bankruptcy has become a catalyst for lender liability claims, requiring the lender to be sensitive to such risks throughout what might be referred to as the default process. In this chapter, we discuss these risks and steps lenders are taking to reduce them.

The burgeoning area of the law now commonly referred to as "lender liability" is, like "products liability," a constellation of traditional theories of liability coupled with evolving rules applicable to a certain family of defendants. In the past, lender liability was ordinarily limited to causes of action for straightforward breach of contract alleging a violation or nonperformance of the express terms of the loan agreement. Today, however, many plaintiffs level shotgun suits at lenders, firing off multiple claims such as those for negligence, tortious interference, duress, fraudulent misrepresentation, tortious breach of the implied covenant of good faith, and breach of fiduciary duty.[1]

This development has alarmed lenders for several reasons. Damages awarded, both punitive and consequential, have been enormous in some cases. The law in this area is unsettled, and outcomes are unpredictable. Liability is frequently alleged in areas (such as "good faith," "fiduciary duty," and "control") that by their nature elude being mapped out. Claims of lender liability often arise in default situations, where future good will and cordial business relations are not high priorities. This is especially true in bankruptcy, where the debtor's bankruptcy estate, rather than the debtor, is bringing the action. Indeed, the trustee or debtor in possession may feel duty-bound to raise every reasonable claim to gain as much as possible for the debtor's creditors.

Following initial successes by borrowers at the trial court level during the lender liability "revolution" in the 1980s, lender liability has suffered many blows. As evidenced by the *Garrett* case below, many appellate courts have ruled that the lender's breach of the implied covenant of good faith and fair dealing is

---

1. Other predicates for lender liability are covered elsewhere in this casebook. They include liability based on (1) defects in the borrower's construction (Chapter 9B); (2) federal regulations such as those under the Interstate Land Sales Full Disclosure Act (Chapter 3D); (3) a lender's status as a mortgagee in possession (Chapter 8B2); (4) a lender's breach of a loan commitment (Chapter 4C2); (5) claims by third-party creditors against a lender that is recharacterized as an equity partner in the case of certain participating mortgages (Chapter 5A1); and (6) fiduciary duties owed by lenders in joint ventures with their borrowers (Chapter 5A1).

not tortious, limiting the plaintiff to contract remedies that ordinarily do not include punitive damages. Moreover, as evidenced by the *Uptown* case below, several jurisdictions have construed this covenant narrowly to deny its operation in situations controlled by express contractual rights. Further, many lender liability cases have reached the appellate courts, providing lenders with more definite standards and guidance to avoid future claims.

Garrett v. BankWest, Inc.
459 N.W.2d 833 (S.D. 1990)

KEAN, Circuit Judge.

This appeal involves a dispute between an agricultural debtor and a creditor bank. It has its basis in the debtor's inability to satisfy a large debt load while faced with the rural economic crisis of the 1980's.

Glen and Elizabeth Garrett (Garrett) owned and operated a 5400 acre farm and cattle ranch (ranch) in Sully County, South Dakota for many years prior to 1980. The other plaintiffs who assisted in this endeavor are their sons. In 1980 a family decision was made to expand the crop growing capabilities of the ranch and an irrigation system was planned. . . .

The expansion decision would require a large infusion of new capital and a significant loan was required. Garrett went to BankWest, Inc. (BankWest) to discuss the plan. Garrett and BankWest (and its predecessor BankWest, N.A.) had a debtor-creditor relationship since 1978 although the operation loans Garrett received were much less in comparison to the scope of the irrigation project.

After a review of Garrett's plan, BankWest agreed to expand the limits of the operation financing to accommodate the partial irrigation of the ranch. However, the financing of the irrigation equipment was done through an agricultural subsidiary of John Hancock Life Insurance Company (Hancock). The loan from Hancock to Garrett was over one million dollars. The irrigation equipment was installed in 1981 at which time Hancock received a first mortgage on the Garrett ranch. BankWest, for its operation financing, had security in livestock, crops and machinery.

In 1982 the rural economy in the United States began to suffer. Farm prices for livestock and crops fell. Land values declined from record highs, inhibiting borrowing power. Garrett was not exempt from these financial deficiencies and began to experience significant cash problems. The immediate impact was his inability to meet the payment requirement on the Hancock loan.

The economic situation did not improve in 1983. In this year Garrett had problems, not only with the Hancock loan, but also with the operating loan at BankWest. On November 10, 1983, BankWest renewed Garrett's operating loan which had by then swollen to $1,085,000.00. BankWest took a second mortgage on the real estate as further security. This renewed loan was written as two separate "lines of credit," one for $300,000.00 and the other for $785,000.00. As part of this loan arrangement, Garrett signed a "Memorandum of Understanding and Loan Covenants" (memorandum) which required Garrett to adhere to a cash flow statement submitted and accepted by BankWest. Any deviation from the cash flow statement required BankWest's approval. The cash flow statement was prepared from anticipated revenue data that Garrett provided.

According to the memorandum, Garrett would repay the $300,000.00 line of credit by April 1, 1984 from a series of specified sales of grain and livestock. The other loan of $785,000.00 was to be reviewed on April 1, 1984. This loan was due November 1, 1984. The memorandum required BankWest's approval of any capital expenditures and instructed Garrett to pursue the sale of real estate to reduce the debt load.

The rural economy had not improved by early 1984 and the cash flow from the specified sales was significantly less than what had been projected in the memorandum. Further, other income was down and operation expenses were up. Garrett was unable to make the first [semiannual] 1984 loan payment to Hancock due May 1, 1984. When asked, BankWest refused to loan Garrett the money for the loan payment because it did not want to loan money to pay off a debt.

While the parties agree that BankWest refused to loan Garrett the money for the Hancock payment, there is a dispute whether [BankWest's employee] Jack Lynass (Lynass) offered to ask Hancock to delay the payment. Regardless of the dispute, Hancock accelerated the loan and began foreclosure proceedings against the Garrett ranch.

After the foreclosure began, BankWest and Garrett met several times and discussed options to stave off the foreclosure. Eventually BankWest offered to buy out Hancock's loan at a figure $200,000.00 less than the principal and interest due. Hancock rejected the offer. Garrett also claims, however, that BankWest, through Lynass, contracted with him to buy out Hancock and then lease the ranch back to Garrett with an option to buy. BankWest claims that this arrangement was only discussed as an option provided it could be done at a value which would allow BankWest to protect its interests.

Hancock proceeded with its foreclosure action after it rejected BankWest's offer. With no chance to save the ranch, Garrett and BankWest, after the redemption period, entered into a liquidation agreement under which Garrett turned over his remaining property to BankWest to settle his outstanding indebtedness.

Garrett and his family then brought this action asserting a very wide variety of legal theories. . . . BankWest and Lynass then moved for summary judgment on all counts directed against each of them individually and jointly. The trial court granted summary judgment and Garrett appealed.

FIDUCIARY DUTY

. . . Garrett asserts that BankWest and Garrett had a fiduciary relationship which BankWest breached in an effort to improve its economic position without consideration of the effect its actions might have on Garrett.

This court has not addressed the issue of when a bank owes a fiduciary duty to a borrower. Many other courts have addressed this issue, however, and can be looked to for guidance. The Supreme Court of Kansas, in Denison State Bank v. Madeira, 230 Kan. 684, 230 Kan. 815, 640 P.2d 1235, 1241 (1982), a case involving an experienced businessman who established a line of credit at the bank when he bought a car dealership, described a fiduciary relationship:

> A fiduciary relationship imparts a position of *peculiar confidence placed by one individual in another.* A fiduciary is a person with a duty to *act primarily for the benefit of another.* A fiduciary is in a position to have and exercise, and does *have and exercise influence over another.* A fiduciary relationship implies a condition of *superiority of one of the parties over the other.* Generally, in a fiduciary relationship, the property, interest or authority of the other is *placed in the charge of the fiduciary.*
> . . .

The Supreme Court of North Dakota recently addressed the issue of the fiduciary duty of a bank to its customers:

> In a commercial context, the mere rendering of advice by the lender to the borrower, even if given in a sincere effort to help the borrower prosper, does not transform a business relationship into a fiduciary relationship. . . . Rather, actual day-to-day involvement in management and operations of the borrower or the ability to compel the borrower to engage in unusual transactions is required for the purposes of showing that a lending institution had "control" over a borrower. (Citations omitted.)

Union State Bank v. Woell, 434 N.W.2d 712, 721 (N.D. 1989). Earlier in this decision, the North Dakota court held that the relationship between a bank and its customer is normally viewed as a debtor-creditor relationship which imposes no special or fiduciary duties upon the bank. Such a relationship can become a fiduciary relationship if the borrower reposes a faith, confidence and trust in the bank which results in dominion, control or influence over the borrower's affairs. Finally, the borrower who reposes the confidence must be in a position of "inequality, dependence, weakness or lack of knowledge." Id. at 721.

Garrett alleges that BankWest acted as friend, confidante, and financial advisor during 1980-1986. Garrett further alleges that BankWest's actions during this period resulted in BankWest taking over complete control of the financial operations of the Garrett ranch. More specifically, Garrett claims the farm and ranch operation was financially controlled by BankWest via the 1983 "Memorandum of Understanding and Loan Covenants."

The record from the depositions prior to mid-1983 indicates that Garrett was an experienced businessman-rancher-farmer who acquired a college degree in agriculture in 1958 from South Dakota State University with a minor in agricultural economics. Garrett stated that he was competent to run his own business; that BankWest never attempted to physically operate his ranch; that he understood he was in a debtor-creditor relationship with BankWest; and, that BankWest had no control over the day-to-day functioning of the farm-ranch. . . .

The claim of a fiduciary relationship hinges upon whether the 1983 memorandum and cash flow statement gave BankWest the type of control over Garrett that is sufficient to establish a fiduciary relationship.

The memorandum and the cash flow statement represent a negotiated agreement between BankWest and Garrett about how to repay the $1,085,000.00 loan. Garrett was involved in creating the cash flow projections with BankWest. Two cash flow statements were prepared based upon information supplied by Garrett and data from BankWest. Garrett was never required to agree to either, but accepted the second because it gave him more money for living expenses. Garrett agreed to the conditions BankWest required in order to obtain the loan renewal, but he understood he could have refused and declined BankWest's offer.

The post mid-1983 record indicates that BankWest had an interest in Garrett's ranch only as a secured lender. . . . BankWest had a right to expect payment on its loan and to require Garrett to maintain an adequate accounting of the ranch operations. See NCNB Nat. Bank of North Carolina v. Tiller, 814 F.2d 931, 936 (4th Cir. 1987) (monitoring and protection of collateral are "normal incidents of a borrower-lender relationship" and do not amount to control); In re W. T. Grant Co., 699 F.2d 599, 610-11 (2d Cir. 1983) (creditor's monitoring of operations and proffering management advice, without more, does not constitute control); Cooper v. Union Bank, 527 F.2d 762, 765 (9th Cir. 1975) (provisions in loan agreement giving bank right to accelerate debt if debtor fails to remit monthly activity reports is not control).

Garrett's property was not placed in the charge of BankWest. BankWest did not have an advantage over Garrett by way of business intelligence, knowledge of the facts involved, or mental strength. BankWest was not in charge of day-to-day management and operations of the Garrett ranch. Under the general principles of fiduciary relationships, supra, BankWest was not in a fiduciary relationship with Garrett and, therefore, owed no fiduciary duties to Garrett.

The existence of a duty and the scope of that duty are questions of law for a court to decide. This issue was therefore appropriate for decision on a summary judgment motion. The trial court is affirmed on its grant of summary judgment for BankWest and Lynass on the fiduciary duty claim.

BREACH OF CONTRACT TO REDEEM/LEASE BACK

Garrett claims that there was sufficient evidence in the record to show the existence of a contract between BankWest and Garrett to purchase and redeem the Garrett real estate from Hancock and lease it back to Garrett. We disagree. . . .

In his deposition Garrett admitted that some of the terms of the alleged lease agreement were never discussed. Garrett also admitted that the lease was intended to be put in writing and signed by both parties at a later time. In addition, Garrett's son (Brad) admitted that the terms of the purchase of the Garrett ranch by BankWest were never discussed. Specifically, Brad stated that the date of purchase and the purchase price were never stated. Therefore, the date the alleged lease was to begin was also an unsettled term.

The record clearly indicates that there was never a complete agreement between Garrett and BankWest concerning the purchase and lease-back. This fact warrants affirmance of the trial court's grant of summary judgment for BankWest on the "breach of contract to redeem" claim. . . .

BREACH OF DUTY TO ACT IN GOOD FAITH

Garrett claims that the trial court erred in granting a summary judgment for BankWest and Lynass on the issue of a breach of an implied duty to act in good faith "and to refrain from doing anything that will injure the rights of the other party to receive the benefits of their agreement." This claim is made under both a common law duty and an obligation imposed by statute. Garrett further alleges that BankWest and Lynass have, apart from the contract, an implied duty of good faith and fair dealing, and breach of this duty gives rise to an independent cause of action in tort.

Every contract contains an implied covenant of good faith and fair dealing which prohibits either contracting party from preventing or injuring the other party's right to receive the agreed benefits of the contract. Restatement (Second) of Contracts, §205 (1981). 3 A. Corbin, Contracts §541, at 97 (1960); 5 S. Williston, A Treatise on the Law of Contracts §670, at 159 (3rd ed. 1961). A majority of American jurisdictions recognize a duty to perform a contract in good faith. See Burton, Breach of Contract and the Common Law Duty to Perform in Good Faith, 94 Harvard L. Rev. 369 (1980). The concept is written into the Uniform Commercial Code (U.C.C.) §1-203 [now §1-304] which is set forth in SDCL 57A-1-203:

> Every contract or duty within this title imposes an obligation of good faith in its performance or enforcement. . . .

The application of this implied covenant allows an aggrieved party to sue for breach of contract when the other contracting party, by his lack of good faith, limited or completely prevented the aggrieved party from receiving the expected benefits of the bargain. A breach of contract claim is allowed even though the conduct failed to violate any of the express terms of the contract agreed to by the parties.

Good faith is derived from the transaction and conduct of the parties. Its meaning varies with the context and emphasizes faithfulness to an agreed common purpose and consistency with the justified expectations of the other party. Restatement (Second) of Contracts, supra, Comment a. But good faith is not a limitless duty or obligation. The implied obligation "must arise from the language used or it must be indispensable to effectuate the intention of the parties." Sessions, Inc. v. Morton, 491 F.2d 854, 857 (9th Cir. 1974). Before applying a duty to act in good faith in contractual matters to the facts of this case, we must first address Garrett's claim that a separate tort for breach of good faith should be recognized.

A. THE TORT OF BREACH OF GOOD FAITH

An implied covenant of good faith was initially strictly confined to the sphere of contract law. The strict contract approach was somewhat eroded over thirty years ago when, in Comunale v. Traders & General Insurance Company, 50 Cal. 2d 654, 328 P.2d 198 (1958), the California Supreme Court recognized that breach of an implied covenant of good faith and fair dealing in insurance contracts would constitute a separate and distinct tort. This tort concept, in the context of bad faith insurance settlement, has been recognized in most states . . .
. . . Garrett failed to present this court with reasons why such a tort should exist [in the context of a lender-borrower relationship]. The contractual and tort remedies which now exist in South Dakota, whether by statute or case law, are adequate to protect a person's right for proven damages. As an illustration, for the breach of an obligation arising from contract, the measure of damages is the amount which will compensate the injured party "for all the detriment proximately caused thereby, or which, in the ordinary course of things, would be likely to result therefrom." SDCL 21-2-1. Thus, if Garretts could establish a contract and its breach, they would be entitled to prove damages.
Further, causes of action exist in tort in South Dakota for fraud and misrepresentation, negligent misrepresentation, negligence and breach of duty of common law or by statute, intentional infliction of emotional distress, and, intentional torts. This listing of causes of action which exist based upon tort is not exhaustive. It does, however, give an indication of the breadth of remedies available to a litigant in this state which are not dependent upon contract or the proof of a fiduciary relationship. We are of the opinion that the existing remedies are adequate to protect a commercial debtor's rights.

B. BREACH OF CONTRACTUAL GOOD FAITH OR GOOD FAITH UNDER THE U.C.C.

We now consider whether there has been a breach of good faith either under contractual obligations or the U.C.C. . . .
Although Garrett's allegation of breach of good faith on the 1983 loans is somewhat vague, it appears centered upon BankWest's failure to continue the line of credit and refusal to loan additional funds to pay the semi-annual installment due Hancock. Garrett argues that this failure to loan the money caused the default which led Hancock to accelerate the note and commence foreclosure. Causally this is correct; but, this causation does not give rise to breach of good faith under the facts. . . .

Good faith means "honesty in fact in the conduct or transaction concerned." SDCL 57A-1-201(19). Although written in the context of general contract law and Article 2 of the U.C.C., a definition which adequately sets forth good faith so far as it should be defined is:

> [G]ood faith is an "excluder." It is a phrase without general meaning (or meanings) of its own and serves to exclude a wide range of heterogeneous forms of bad faith. In a particular context the phrase takes on specific meaning, but usually this is only by way of contrast with the specific form of bad faith actually or hypothetically ruled out.

Summers, Good Faith in General Contract Law and the Sales Provision of the Uniform Commercial Code, 54 Va. L. Rev. 195, 201 (1968). Professor Summers suggests some categories to identify bad faith in performance of a contract including: evasion of the spirit of the deal; abuse of power to determine compliance; and, interference with or failure to cooperate in the other party's performance. Id. And . . . the good faith must arise from the language used or be indispensable to effectuate the intention of the parties.

When Garrett and BankWest met in November 1983 to discuss the financial plight, Garrett owed BankWest in excess of one million dollars. The so-called line of credit was not for an additional one million dollars. The memorandum and other documents mutually agreed to by the parties attest to this conclusion and set forth a definitive method to liquidate the first $300,000.00 and the date by which the remaining balance was due. Garrett argues that the line of credit was ongoing and that once he paid down part of the loan, he was entitled to go back and request funds back up to the limit of $1,085,000.00. Such an agreement ignores the plain language of the memorandum. The agreement of the parties was to reduce the huge debt at BankWest, not to provide a continuous source of funds. . . .

We conclude that there was no breach of good faith on the part of BankWest or Lynass. The refusal to loan the May 1984 payment to Hancock was not a breach of the loan agreement. More importantly, the refusal did not violate the spirit of the contract or the justified expectations of the parties. Garrett received the loan when the renewal occurred. An anticipation of more funds for Hancock was not within either the expectations or contemplation of the parties. Nor did BankWest or Lynass abuse their power to determine compliance. In April 1984 Garretts were in technical default on the $300,000.00 payment. A demand of all sums due at that time could have been made but was delayed. During this time BankWest attempted to prevent foreclosure, but Hancock refused the offer. In early 1985 BankWest tried to redeem, but the offer was again refused.

The most telling aspect of the lack of bad faith by BankWest is simply stated: BankWest never sued Garrett on the consolidation loan. Nor did BankWest ever interfere with Garrett's operation of the ranch thereby preventing him from attempting to raise the needed funds by farming and ranching. Instead, Garrett and BankWest, both realizing that the situation was futile, eventually entered into a liquidation agreement in March, 1986 where Garrett transferred machinery and certain parcels of land (subject to existing claims and contracts) to BankWest. In return BankWest paid Garrett $5,000.00. The liquidation agreement noted two key items:

1. The Debtors (Garrett) are currently in default on their obligations under the notes and other debt instruments in favor of BankWest; and

2. The parties mutually desire to avoid further litigation and costs of foreclosure against the secured property.

BankWest itself absorbed a loss of $685,000.00 by entering into the liquidation agreement.

These facts demonstrate that neither BankWest nor Lynass abused their power to determine compliance nor did they fail to cooperate in Garrett's performance. The facts demonstrate that BankWest continued to work with Garrett even after default No lawsuit was brought. BankWest absorbed a large loss and did not seek personal liability from Garrett. Of such facts bad faith is not made.

Garrett cites K.M.C. Co., Inc. v. Irving Trust Co., 757 F.2d 752 (6th Cir. 1985) to support his claim that bad faith existed. In this case Irving Trust extended K.M.C $3.5 million in credit. All of K.M.C.'s receipts went into an account controlled by Irving Trust. K.M.C. relied upon the line of credit for its operation since it could not secure other financing on short notice. Without any notice Irving Trust refused to advance any money on the line of credit or to release the account funds. The court held that notice of cutting off the line of credit was a prerequisite to execution of the contract. The failure of Irving Trust to give notice left K.M.C. at its mercy and was a breach of good faith even though Irving Trust had not breached any specific provisions of the contract.

The *Irving Trust* case is distinguishable. At the time Garretts were asking for funds to pay Hancock, Garretts had used the maximum loan amount. The request was made after April 1, 1983, the due date of the $300,000.00, at a time Garrett was in default on the first major portion of the loan. Garrett knew the loan was in default Contrast these facts with the *Irving Trust* case where no breach existed when the line of credit was terminated, nor was the maximum credit used. This court should not require a bank to totally disregard its own interests and compel it to place itself in a worse position when neither the contract nor the requirement of good faith demand such action.

. . . The trial court is affirmed on its grant of summary judgment for BankWest and Lynass on breach of the implied duty of good faith. . . .

Uptown Heights Associates Limited Partnership v. Seafirst Corp.

320 Or. 638, 891 P.2d 639 (1995)

GRABER, Justice.

. . . The present controversy arose from a construction loan made . . . by defendant Seattle-First National Bank (Bank) [to plaintiff Uptown].

In 1988 or 1989, Bank learned of Uptown's plans to construct a "high-end" apartment complex in Portland. Bank aggressively solicited Uptown and, on June 20, 1989, Uptown entered into a construction loan agreement with Bank. Uptown borrowed $7,500,000, with interest at one-half of one percent over prime. The loan was secured by a deed of trust on the land and buildings that comprised the apartment complex.

Under the terms of the loan, Uptown was to pay monthly interest until the loan matured. The principal amount was due at maturity, January 1, 1991, with a provision for two six-month extensions until January 1992.

Soon after construction of the apartment complex was completed, the rental market dropped dramatically from Uptown's pre-construction forecasts. For that reason, Uptown encountered difficulty in meeting its obligation to make its monthly interest payments on the loan. In October 1990, Bank agreed to one six-month extension on the loan. Although rental rates improved in late 1990 and early 1991, Uptown was unable to make its full interest payment to Bank in April 1991. Bank had the apartment complex appraised by an independent appraiser; the appraised value was $8,850,000, slightly more than $1 million above the outstanding balance of Bank's loan to Uptown.

Uptown and Bank continued to negotiate concerning the loan. Bank personnel who handled the loan assured Uptown that Bank would work with Uptown to resolve any problems surrounding the loan. Despite those assurances, in June 1991, Bank elected not to grant the second six-month extension. Bank transferred the Uptown account to a department for problem loans known as "Special Credits." . . . Bank personnel began to threaten foreclosure on the apartment complex. That pressure forced Uptown to seek a quick sale to try to avoid the harm to its investment and business reputation that would flow from a foreclosure.

Uptown told Bank that it planned to sell the apartment complex and notified Bank that a foreclosure action would damage or destroy Uptown's chances of selling the complex and avoiding a foreclosure sale. Uptown told Bank that potential buyers would have no interest in buying the property from Uptown if they knew that it was threatened with foreclosure, because buyers typically wait to try to buy such a property at a bargain price after foreclosure.

On July 29, 1991, Uptown received an offer to purchase the apartment complex. . . . On July 31, 1991, Uptown notified Bank of that offer. On August 2, 1991, Bank initiated a foreclosure action, filed for appointment of a receiver, and scheduled a trustee's sale for December 20, 1991. Before the hearing on the appointment of a receiver, Uptown provided Bank with the purchase offer that it had received. Bank refused to postpone the hearing to permit further negotiations between Uptown and the offeror and, as a result, the offeror did not proceed further.

The receivership hearing was held on August 16, 1991. The court appointed a receiver chosen by Bank. Uptown continued to look for a buyer for the apartment complex to avoid the harm that would result to its business reputation from a foreclosure sale and to attempt to recover some of its investment. On October 22, 1991, Uptown notified Bank that it had received a second offer for the apartment complex, which would result in a price of between $8.1 and $8.6 million. Uptown also asked that the receiver be replaced immediately. Bank responded to the October 22 notice on November 7, 1991. At that time, Bank refused to extend the foreclosure sale to permit steps to be followed toward closing the sale proposed by Uptown.

Uptown continued to negotiate with the second potential buyer and provided Bank with a copy of a signed purchase agreement. Uptown again asked Bank to postpone the foreclosure sale, this time for the purpose of allowing the second potential buyer to arrange for financing. Bank refused. Uptown and the second potential buyer were unable to work out an agreement under which they could meet Bank's deadline for a full payoff before the foreclosure sale. The foreclosure sale took place on December 20, 1991. Bank bid $7.8 million (the outstanding balance of the loan) and took title to the apartment complex. In January 1992, Bank entered into a purchase and sale agreement with the same second potential buyer for $7.8 million. Uptown received nothing.

Uptown brought this action against Bank, raising one claim for "breach of contractual duty of good faith and fair dealing," . . . and three claims for intentional interference with economic relations. The circuit court dismissed the complaint . . . on the ground that Uptown failed to state facts sufficient to constitute a claim. The Court of Appeals, sitting in banc, affirmed as to the duty of good faith claims, but reversed as to the claims for intentional interference with economic relations. . . .

IMPLIED CONTRACTUAL DUTY OF GOOD FAITH
(FIRST CLAIM FOR RELIEF)

This court reiterated in Pacific First Bank [v. New Morgan Park Corp., 319 Or. 342, 876 P.2d 761 (1994)] that every contract contains an implied duty of good faith. That duty "is to be applied in a manner that will effectuate the reasonable contractual expectations of the parties." Id. at 353, 876 P.2d 761. . . . But, "it is only the objectively reasonable expectations of [the] parties that will be examined in determining whether the obligation of good faith has been met." Tolbert v. First National Bank, 312 Or. 485, 494, 823 P.2d 965 (1991). In *Pacific First Bank*, the court also restated the precept that the duty of good faith cannot serve to contradict an express contractual term: . . . "'[t]he obligation of good faith does not vary the substantive terms of the bargain . . ., nor does it provide a remedy for an unpleasantly motivated act that is expressly permitted by contract.'" *Pacific First Bank*, 319 Or. at 352-53, 876 P.2d 761.

Under the foregoing established principles, if a written contract between the parties expressly allows for a particular remedy by one of the parties, in the face of a specified breach, the parties' objectively "reasonable expectations" under the contract include the invocation of that remedy in the face of that breach. The party invoking its express, written contractual right does not, merely by so doing, violate its duty of good faith.

The agreement between Uptown and Bank, as pleaded by Uptown, gave Bank the right to foreclose should Uptown default on the loan. Uptown also pleaded that it defaulted on the loan. Uptown did not plead any additional facts that would support a claim for violation of the duty of good faith. For example, Uptown did not plead that Bank caused the default to occur, which in turn gave rise to the contractual right to foreclose. Neither did Uptown plead that Bank failed to follow the proper method of foreclosure.

Uptown argues that, when a contract gives one party discretion as to when to invoke a bargained-for remedy, the circumstances giving rise to that invocation may permit a claim for breach of the duty of good faith. Uptown argues that this duty was breached when Bank refused to grant the second loan extension and continued to seek foreclosure, because those acts would harm Uptown, while Bank would derive no benefit. In support of its argument, Uptown relies on statements made by this court in Best v. U.S. National Bank, 303 Or. 557, 739 P.2d 554 (1987). Reliance on *Best* is misplaced in this context.

In *Best*, the court considered whether a bank's fees for processing nonsufficient fund (NSF) checks were so high as to violate the bank's duty of good faith in the performance of its account agreements with its depositors. Under the bank's contracts with its customers, the bank "had the contractual discretion to set its . . . fees." Because the court concluded that there was a "genuine issue of material fact whether the Bank set its . . . fees in accordance with the reasonable expectations of the parties," the court held that the defendant's motion for summary judgment should not have been granted on that issue. In reaching that conclusion, the court stated:

> When one party to a contract is given discretion in the performance of some aspect of the contract, the parties ordinarily contemplate that that discretion will be exercised for particular purposes. If the discretion is exercised for purposes not contemplated by the parties, the party exercising discretion has performed in bad faith.

Id. at 563, 739 P.2d 554.

Relying on *Best*, Uptown argues that the underlying purpose of Bank's power to foreclose was to secure its loan. That was the reasonable expectation of the parties when they bargained for the foreclosure provision in the contract. Because the value of the property was in excess of the loan balance and because Uptown had located a prospective buyer who was willing to purchase the property for a price in excess of the balance, Uptown argues that "a jury may infer that [Bank] acted for some other purpose not consistent with the parties' expectations when they agreed that [Bank] would have this" contractual right to foreclose.

Best is inapposite, because in that summary judgment case that bank had the discretion to fill in an open price term, and no method of setting the NSF fee was spelled out in the depositors' contracts. . . .

By contrast, in this case, there was a specific agreement. The loan agreement as pleaded by Uptown authorizes foreclosure for any default, not merely for a default that jeopardizes security. . . .

Here, Uptown has pleaded that it defaulted on the interest payments that it was required to make under the loan and that the remedies pursued by Bank are expressly permitted by the parties' written contract in the event of such a default. Uptown's pleading does not suggest that the contract contained any other precondition on Bank's right to foreclose, except for such a default. The contractually described purpose of Bank's power to foreclose was, then, to remedy a default. Thus, "[i]n the present case, the reasonable contractual expectations of the parties are shown, by the unambiguous terms" of the contract as those terms are relayed in Uptown's pleadings. See *Pacific First Bank*, 319 Or. at 353, 876 P.2d 761 (stating principle). Under those terms, "the parties agreed to—that is, reasonably expected—a unilateral, unrestricted exercise of discretion" in Bank's choice of foreclosure as a remedy should Uptown breach the contract by failing to make its mortgage payments. See id. at 354, 876 P.2d 761 (stating principle).

Accordingly, the trial court did not err when it dismissed the first claim for relief. . . .

TORTIOUS INTERFERENCE WITH ECONOMIC RELATIONS

. . . In its third and fourth claims, Uptown contends that Bank interfered with contractual relations between Uptown and a prospective "buyer for the Uptown Heights Apartments." To state a claim for intentional interference with economic relations, a party must allege: (1) the existence of a valid business relationship or expectancy, (2) intentional interference with that relationship, (3) by a third party, (4) accomplished through improper means or for an improper purpose, (5) a causal effect between the interference and damage to economic relations, and (6) damages. Straube v. Larson, 287 Or. 357, 360-61, 600 P.2d 371 (1979); Wampler v. Palmerton, 250 Or. 65, 73-76, 439 P.2d 601 (1968). The dispositive issue here is the fourth element, the accomplishment of an interference through improper means or for an improper purpose.

[I]n order to prevail, a plaintiff must establish not only . . . that defendant intentionally interfered with his business relationship but also that defendant had a duty of noninterference; i.e., that he interfered for an improper purpose rather than for a legitimate one, or that defendant used improper means which resulted in injury to plaintiff. Therefore, a case is made out which entitles plaintiff to go to a jury only when interference resulting in injury to another is wrongful by some measure beyond the fact of the interference itself.

Straube, 287 Or. at 361, 600 P.2d 371. . . .

Uptown makes no allegation of improper means here. Uptown alleges only an improper purpose. The essence of Uptown's argument is that a party who invokes an express contractual remedy by proper means still may be liable for intentional interference with economic relations if that party simply has a malevolent reason for enforcing its written contract. We disagree. When a party invokes an express contractual remedy in circumstances specified in the written contract—conduct that reflects, by definition, the reasonable expectations of the parties—that party cannot be liable for intentional interference with economic relations based solely on that party's reason for invoking the express contractual remedy. That is because, if the defendant has interfered with the plaintiff's economic relations, the defendant has done so for a "legitimate" purpose— invocation of an express, written contractual remedy—in such circumstances.

A contrary ruling would contravene public policy and undermine the stability of contractual relations. As this court's decision in *Pacific First Bank* made clear, courts will not read implied terms into a contract if those terms would contradict the express terms of the contract. It would be anomalous to hold that a party to a contract nonetheless must defend a tort claim when a complaint shows that the party did precisely what the party was entitled to do under the contract. "Economic relations are controlled by contract[,] and the public [as well as the individual contracting party] has an interest in maintaining the security of such transactions." *Wampler*, 250 Or. at 73, 439 P.2d 601.

Uptown's third and fourth claims for relief were properly dismissed by the trial court. The Court of Appeals erred when it reversed that dismissal. . . .

NOTES AND QUESTIONS

1. Decline of the Bad Faith Tort. Those courts rejecting liability in tort for the commercial lender's breach of the implied covenant of good faith and fair dealing include Black Canyon Racquetball Club v. Idaho First Natl. Bank, 804 P.2d 900, 905 (Idaho 1991); Rodgers v. Tecumseh Bank, 756 P.2d 1223 (Okla. 1988); and Charles E. Brauer Co. v. Nationsbank of Va., 466 S.E.2d 382, 385 (Va. 1996). See generally Macintosh, Gilmore Spoke Too Soon: Contract Rises from the Ashes of the Bad Faith Tort, 27 Loy. L.A. L. Rev. 483 (1994). The same court that established the tort of bad faith in the insurance context and later in other settings has repudiated any tort recovery for bad faith outside of insurance contracts. See Freeman & Mills, Inc. v. Belcher Oil Co., 11 Cal. 4th 85, 900 P.2d 669, 44 Cal. Rptr. 2d 420 (1995). Among the factors the court identified in support of this result were "the need for stability and predictability in commercial affairs, the potential for excessive tort damages, and the preference for legislative rather than judicial action in this area." 44 Cal. Rptr. 2d at 431. Do you find these reasons and those identified in *Garrett* persuasive?

2. Good Faith. In the 2001 revision of Article I of the Uniform Commercial Code, the definition of good faith was expanded beyond "honesty in fact" to encompass "the observance of reasonable commercial standards of fair dealing." §1-201(20). Would this broader language, if adopted in South Dakota, have affected the outcome in the *Garrett* case? In *Garrett*, the South Dakota Supreme Court set forth categories of bad faith articulated by Professor Summers (of White and Summers fame) that include "evasion of the spirit of the deal, . . . abuse of power to determine compliance, and interference with or failure to cooperate in the other party's performance." Summers, Good Faith in General Contract Law and the Sales Provision of the Uniform Commercial Code, 54 Va. L. Rev. 195, 232-233 (1968). In *Uptown*, the Oregon Supreme Court characterized the lender's election to foreclose following the borrower's default as an exercise of discretion unrestricted by the dictates of the good faith doctrine. Is that result consistent with the standard that Professor Summers articulates? For example, might the lender's insistence on prosecuting its foreclosure have interfered with the borrower's efforts to perform by selling the distressed property to repay the indebtedness? Does the court in *Uptown* mean that the lender's decision to foreclose can never constitute bad faith? What if a borrower can establish that the lender tolerated late payments from other borrowers so long as the collateral value exceeded the loan balance, but that due to animosity the lender seized on the first default and initiated foreclosure without efforts to work with the borrower? Has this lender acted in bad faith? Given that foreclosure is an equitable proceeding, can you think of a strategy that the borrower in *Uptown* might have pursued during the pendency of the foreclosure proceeding? See Chapter 8B1. Would the outcome in *Uptown* have been different had the lender resold the foreclosed property for a profit? Cf. Greenwood Assocs. v. Crestar Bank, 248 Va. 265, 448 S.E.2d 399 (1994) (upholding dismissal of claim that lender breached contract to credit the borrower with profit from resale of foreclosed property).

Compare a decision by the Colorado Court of Appeals affirming the trial court's finding of bad faith when "the lender deliberately delayed the foreclosure process in order to increase the debt through the accrual of default interest and to realize its ultimate goal of taking all of the borrower's collateral." Wells Fargo Realty Advisors Funding v. Uioli, Inc., 872 P.2d 1359, 1364 (Colo. Ct. App. 1994). Do you think that the Oregon Supreme Court would recognize a bad faith claim here? If a court imposes liability for a precipitous foreclosure, and at the same time for an unreasonable delay in foreclosing, is the lender in a catch-22 dilemma?

Several courts appear to adopt the same restrictive standard for good faith as Oregon in their refusal to recognize bad faith claims when the lender exercises rights or privileges expressly reserved in the loan documents. See, for example,

Kham & Nate's Shoes No. 2 v. First Bank, 908 F.2d 1351, 1357 (7th Cir. 1990) (good faith operates only as a gap filler and is an "implied undertaking not to take opportunistic advantage in a way that could not have been contemplated at the time of the drafting, and which therefore was not resolved explicitly by the parties"; using good faith to add an "overlay of 'just cause'" to the exercise of contractual privileges reduces commercial certainty and breeds costly litigation); Gaul v. Olympia Fitness Center, 88 Ohio App. 3d 310, 623 N.E.2d 1281, 1288 (1993) (lender's acceleration of loan and foreclosure of mortgage following default are exercises of its contractual rights that cannot constitute "bad faith"). But see Duffield v. First Interstate Bank, 13 F.3d 1403 (10th Cir. 1993) (covenant of good faith applies to lender's decision to exercise default remedies because these provisions involve an exercise of discretion; rejecting lender's interpretation that under Colorado law good faith does not attach to any contract provisions that unambiguously define the duties of the parties). See generally Overby, Bondage, Domination, and the Art of the Deal: An Assessment of Judicial Strategies in Lender Liability Good Faith Litigation, 61 Fordham L. Rev. 963 (1993) (preferring the approach in *Kham & Nate's Shoes* and observing that it is becoming the dominant standard, perhaps due to judicial concern over the lender liability explosion).

As it did in the early 1980s, the farm economy suffered again in the wake of the September 11th attacks, prompting another rash of farm foreclosures and lawsuits against lenders. This time, the South Dakota Supreme Court, citing its landmark decision in *Garrett*, as well as the Oregon *Uptown* and federal *Kham & Nate's Shoes* decisions, rejected a farmer's claim that the lender refused in bad faith a requested 7-month extension of a late installment payment where the collateral value exceeded the debt. See Farm Credit Services of America v. Dougan, 704 N.W.2d 24 (S.D. 2005).

3. Fiduciary Duty. A substantial majority of courts agree with the approach taken in *Garrett* that treats the lender-borrower relationship as a nonfiduciary one absent special circumstances. See Hunt, The Price of Trust: An Examination of Fiduciary Duty and the Lender-Borrower Relationship, 29 Wake Forest L. Rev. 719 (1994); see also Cappello and Komoroske, Fiduciary Relationships between Lenders and Borrowers: Maintenance of the Status Quo, 15 W. St. U. L. Rev. 579 (1988). Professor Hunt, however, reports "massive confusion" in the case law over just what special circumstances convert the lending relationship into a fiduciary one. For example, is the borrower's repose of trust and confidence in the lender enough (as some decisions appear to support), or must the lender have acquired control and dominion over the borrower? Further, must the borrower also be in a position of weakness, dependence, or inequality? What standard does the *Garrett* court adopt? Professor Hunt discusses *Garrett* at 749-750.

What are the consequences of concluding that the lender owes fiduciary duties to its borrower? Ordinarily those duties include an obligation to disclose to the borrower all material facts, a duty to maintain confidentiality regarding borrower information, a duty not to appropriate the borrower's business opportunity (similar to the so-called corporate opportunity doctrine), and a duty to act in the borrower's best interests. See generally Lodge and Cunningham, The Banker as Inadvertent Fiduciary: Beware a Borrower's Special Trust and Confidence, 98 Com. L.J. 277 (1993) (noting the boundaries of the latter duty are still unclear); Schaumann, The Lender as Unconventional Fiduciary, 23 Seton Hall L. Rev. 21 (1992); see also Pardue v. Bankers First Fed. Sav. & Loan Ass'n, 175 Ga. App. 814, 334 S.E.2d 926 (1985) (absent a fiduciary relationship the lender had no duty to inform borrowers of income tax consequences of lender's acceptance of discounted loan balance in prepayment). For which of these purposes did the borrower in *Garrett* urge the court to impose fiduciary responsibilities on the lender? Does the implied covenant of good faith in the parties' loan contract impose the same obligation as a fiduciary owes to act in the borrower's best interests? See DeMott, Beyond Metaphor: An Analysis of Fiduciary Obligation, 1988 Duke L.J. 879.

4. Intentional Torts. Given most courts' refusal to recognize a remedy in tort for bad faith, savvy borrowers might plead their lender liability claims under established intentional torts such as fraud, tortious interference, or duress that may support punitive damages. Consider the outcome in State Natl. Bank v. Farah Mfg. Co., 678 S.W.2d 661 (Tex. Ct. App. 1984), dismissed by agreement. The Farah Manufacturing Company had a $22 million loan agreement that contained a clause enabling the four participating lenders to declare a default on any change in management which any two of the four lenders considered to be adverse to their interests "for any reason whatsoever." When a former CEO, William Farah, sought reinstatement, the lenders' representative informed the board of directors that the lenders would call a default in that event, and one lender's attorney threatened to padlock the doors and bankrupt the company if Farah returned. The board appointed different management that improperly managed the company. After Mr. Farah regained control through a proxy fight, the company recovered $19 million from the lenders using theories of fraud, duress, and interference with business relations. The lenders' conduct was deemed fraudulent because the court concluded that their threat to call a default was made at a time when the lenders had either decided not to declare a default or had reached no decision on the matter.

Duress is a little harder to classify. Duress was found mainly because the lenders' threats to declare a default were made in bad faith for the purpose of forcing the board not to reinstate Mr. Farah. The lenders had no reasonable, good faith belief that their security was about to become impaired, and, although they had a legal right to declare a default, the court found that given the serious consequences of default their threat constituted economic coercion, a form of duress. The court cited authority that although duress often arises in connection with a breach of contract, it is nevertheless a tort. See generally Ebke and Griffin, Lender Liability to Debtors: Toward a Conceptual Framework, 40 Sw. L.J. 775 (1986); Dickens, Note, Equitable Subordination and Analogous Theories of

Lender Liability: Toward a New Model of "Control," 65 Tex. L. Rev. 801 (1987).

The tort of interference with business relations with a third party was found because the court determined that the lenders interfered willfully, intentionally, and without justifiable cause in the debtor's business relations, its election of directors and officers, and its protected rights.

Each of these grounds for liability involves some form of bad faith. As a lender struggles to avoid liability under these grounds, however, does it find that "good faith" means different things depending on which basis of liability is involved? For example, in the *K.M.C.* case (discussed in *Garrett*), the lender was found to have breached its implied contractual duty of good faith when it failed to give notice of its decision not to fund discretionary future advances under the parties' line of credit agreement. In *Farah*, a threat *to take* an action in the future was held to constitute fraud and duress because it was made without present intent to carry it out. What if the lenders in *Farah* had not said anything and then decided to declare a default after Mr. Farah was reinstated? Would a court that follows *K.M.C.* say that under the management change clause in the contract the lender's duty of good faith required the lenders to give the board adequate warning of what action it would or might take? Is there a safe path for the lenders through this dilemma?

5. Negligence. Borrowers sometimes sue lenders on a common law negligence theory alleging that the lender had a duty to exercise reasonable care toward the borrower that it breached, resulting in damage to the borrower. As their first line of defense against such claims, lenders typically urge that they owe no duty to exercise care on the borrower's behalf. Compare Nymark v. Heart Fed. Sav. & Loan Ass'n, 231 Cal. App. 3d 1089, 283 Cal. Rptr. 53 (1991) (lender ordinarily owes no duty of care to borrower in appraising collateral for purposes of loan qualification); Yousef v. Trustbank Sav., 81 Md. App. 527, 568 A.2d 1134 (1990) (commercial lender had no duty to borrower to ensure that space leases in shopping center that borrower was purchasing were satisfactory), with Larsen v. United Fed. Sav. & Loan Ass'n, 300 N.W.2d 281 (Iowa 1981) (lender owed duty of care to borrower in preparing in-house appraisal). Cf. Connor v. Great Western Sav. & Loan Ass'n, 69 Cal. 2d 850, 447 P.2d 609, 73 Cal. Rptr. 369 (1968) (construction lender owed duty to protect those purchasing homes from its borrower against construction defects, excerpted below).

Courts ordinarily will conclude that the lender has no duty to protect the borrower from investing the loan proceeds in an imprudent manner. See Wagner v. Benson, 101 Cal. App. 3d 27, 161 Cal. Rptr. 516 (1980). Consider, however, the following circumstances. In 1981, the Meyer brothers purchased a 6,400-acre ranch near Douglas, Wyoming, for $1.5 million. Apparently they financed their acquisition with two mortgages that encumbered other property they owned, which they hoped to sell to satisfy the mortgages. Travelers Insurance Company was the mortgagee. When the brothers couldn't sell the other properties, debts mounted, and Travelers foreclosed. Alleging negligence, bad faith, and other claims, the Meyer brothers sued Travelers, apparently on the grounds that they had placed their trust in Travelers (they even signed blank forms for the Travelers people to fill in) and that Travelers knew or should have known the brothers could not make a success of the ranch (perhaps with the hope of obtaining the property through foreclosure?).

In discovery, a memo was found from a local Travelers agent to his superiors urging a workout. In part it said: "These boys are losing all they accumulated. In a way we are not entirely blameless. We made them a 17% loan in Colorado to put a down-payment on a deal that was too big for them. They were in danger of losing that down-payment unless we revamped the loan on the Wyoming place. We did this, at a rate higher than they had bargained for. . . . It was a bad deal all around and we helped make it so." The jury awarded the Meyer brothers damages of $3.2 million. The case was eventually settled out of court for an undisclosed sum. The trial decision was not reported; the above facts were obtained mainly from *The Economist*, Nov. 7, 1987, at 38. A related appellate decision was reported at 741 P.2d 607 (Wyo. 1987). Does the Travelers litigation tell us that lenders owe borrowers a duty to look into and correctly judge the economic viability of property on which they make loans?

Consider the lessons of the memo from the Travelers' agent. What do you think the purpose of the memo was? Why was the agent pushing so hard for a workout? Perhaps it was the result of a genuine feeling that Travelers was at fault. Perhaps it was motivated in part by a desire not to add to an already growing portfolio of foreclosed properties.

In the residential mortgage context, allegations of imprudent loans made to borrowers with insufficient income prompted Congress to impose ability-to-pay requirements in the Dodd-Frank Wall Street Reform & Consumer Protection Act of 2010. Under Dodd-Frank, lenders must obtain verifiable income documentation (in contrast to the infamous subprime stated income or "liar" loans) evidencing the borrower's ability to repay the mortgage loan.

6. Lender Liability in Loan Participations. A loan participation is a loan sharing arrangement whereby the lender who originates a loan—the so-called lead lender—sells portions of the loan to other participating lenders who receive undivided fractional interests in both the loan and the underlying collateral. Such an arrangement may be used by an institutional lender to satisfy the high-ratio financing needs of a valuable borrower that otherwise might not be met because of the lead lender's lack of loanable funds or because the loan amount exceeds some limitation on the loan amount to a single borrower that may be imposed by some regulatory statute.

Because the note, mortgage, and other loan documents are held by the lead lender (who is designated as the mortgagee of record) and the parties' participation agreement is not recorded, the participating lenders are vulnerable as unsecured creditors if an unscrupulous lead lender were to pledge, assign, or accept prepayment of the note without satisfying their claims. In most cases, the loan participants have no direct legal relationship with the borrower. The promissory note is payable exclusively to the lead lender, who holds it and the collateral for the participants' benefit and is empowered by them to collect and distribute the loan proceeds.

Participants faced with losses from loan defaults frequently blame the lead lender. Generally, their lender liability lawsuits are premised on the theories of breach of fiduciary duty or the implied covenant of good faith and fair dealing, or on negligence or fraud. Most courts have refused to impose a fiduciary obligation on the lead lender toward the loan participants. See, for example, First Citizens Fed. Sav. & Loan Ass'n v. Worthen Bank & Trust Co., 919 F.2d 510 (9th Cir. 1990) (fiduciary relationships should not be inferred in loan participation agreements among sophisticated lenders absent unequivocal contractual language). Common law claims based on fraud, good faith, and negligence are often overcome by the lead lender's reliance on contractual provisions in loan participation agreements providing that the lead lender makes no warranty as to the collectibility of the loan and that each participant warrants that it has independently evaluated the borrower's creditworthiness. See, for example, Continental Illinois Natl. Bank & Trust Co. of Chicago v. FDIC, 799 F.2d 622 (10th Cir. 1986) (terms of participation agreement defeat bad faith claim); Colorado State Bank of Walsh v. FDIC, 671 F. Supp. 706 (D. Colo. 1987) (terms of participation agreement defeat negligence claim). See generally M. Madison, J. Dwyer, and S. Bender, The Law of Real Estate Financing §§11:14-11:18 (2016); G. Nelson et al., Real Estate Finance Law §5.35 (6th ed. 2015); Leon, The Lead Lender's Liability to Its Participant, 109 Banking L.J. 532 (Nov./Dec. 1992).

7. Subprime Lender Liability. The rash of risky subprime residential mortgage loans (discussed at Chapter 5A1) in the mid-2000s launched a volley of lender liability claims on theories of predatory lending that encompass fraud, unconscionability, and other theories. E.g., Vasquez-Lopez v. Beneficial Oregon, Inc., 210 Or. App. 553, 152 P.3d 940 (2007) (fraudulent inducement of oppressive terms). However, most of these loans were securitized (see Chapter 15) and resold on the securitization market to investors. Under Article 3 of the Uniform Commercial Code enacted by the states, a purchaser of a loan in good faith without notice of such defenses would take free of most of these defenses as a "holder in due course." Although federal law effectively abolishes this holder in due course protection for purchasers of notes arising from the provision of consumer goods or services, purchasers of home loans are generally insulated. But some have begun to call for eliminating the holder in due course "super-plaintiff" protection for all non-commercial loans as a means of forcing the securities markets to police abuses among lenders originating loans. See Eggert, Held Up in Due Course: Predatory Lending, Securitization, and the Holder in Due Course Doctrine, 35 Creighton L. Rev. 503 (2002); Johnson, Preventing a Return Engagement: Eliminating the Mortgage Purchasers' Status as a Holder-in-Due-Course: Properly Aligning Incentives among the Parties, 37 Pepp. L. Rev. 529 (2010). The new Uniform Home Foreclosure Procedures Act, if adopted by a state, would supplant the UCC for home loans and enable the borrower to assert claims of fraud or material breach of contract arising out of the original loan transaction against the innocent subsequent loan purchaser, while limiting relief to the outstanding loan balance.

B. THE CONSTRUCTION LENDER'S LIABILITY TO THIRD PARTIES AND THE BORROWER

When things go wrong, parties who suffer financial loss are apt to look around for someone to sue. And when things go wrong in construction, it is normally the construction lender who has the deep pocket. It is not surprising, then, that numerous attempts have been made to seek compensation from the construction lender on a variety of legal theories. One of the most famous of these efforts is the *Connor* case below, which dealt with the potential liability of a lender who had the right to approve plans and specifications and inspect the construction. The irony is that the more the construction lender injects itself into the business of the construction to assure itself that the construction will be done properly in accordance with the postconstruction lender's takeout commitment, the greater the construction lender's exposure to potential liability when problems arise.

Connor v. Great Western Savings & Loan Association
69 Cal. 2d 850, 73 Cal. Rptr. 369, 447 P.2d 609 (1968)

TRAYNOR, Chief Justice.

These consolidated appeals are from a judgment of nonsuit in favor of defendant Great Western Savings and Loan Association in two actions consolidated for trial.

Plaintiffs in each action purchased single-family homes in a residential tract development known as Weathersfield, located on tracts 1158, 1159, and 1160 in Ventura County. Thereafter their homes suffered serious damage from cracking caused by ill-designed foundations that could not withstand the expansion and contraction of adobe soil. Plaintiffs accordingly sought rescission or damages from the various parties involved in the tract development. . . .

There was abundant evidence that defendant Conejo Valley Development Company, which built and sold the homes, negligently constructed them without regard to soil conditions prevalent at the site. . . .

In addition to seeking damages from Conejo, plaintiffs sought to hold Great Western liable, either on the ground that its participation in the tract development brought it into a joint venture or a joint enterprise with Conejo, which served to make it vicariously liable, or on the ground that it breached an independent duty of care to plaintiffs. . . .

Great Western agreed to make the necessary construction loans to Conejo only after assuring itself that the homes could be successfully built and sold. During the negotiations on the terms of the contemplated construction loans to Conejo and the long-term loans to be offered to the buyers of homes in the proposed development, Great Western investigated Goldberg's [one of two principals of Conejo] financial condition and learned that it was weak. Moreover, Great Western received, without comment or inquiry, an August 1959 financial statement from Conejo that set forth capital of $325,000, of which $320,000 was accounted for as estimated profits from the sales of homes when the sales transactions, then in escrow, were completed. Such an entry was far outside the bounds of generally accepted accounting principles. The estimated profits, representing 64/65 of the total purported capital, were not only hypothetical, but were hypothesized on the basis of houses that had not yet been constructed.

Great Western delved no deeper into the proposed foundations of the houses than into the conjectural bases of Conejo's capital. It did require Conejo to submit plans and specifications for the various models of homes to be built, cost breakdowns, a list of proposed subcontractors and the type of work each was to perform, and a schedule of proposed prices. Conejo, which at no time employed an architect, purchased plans and specifications from a Mr. L. C. Majors that he had prepared for other developments, and submitted them to Great Western.

Great Western departed from its normal procedure of reviewing and approving plans and specifications before making a commitment to provide construction funds. It did not examine the foundation plans and did not make any recommendations as to the design or construction of the houses. It was preoccupied with selling prices and sales. It suggested increases in Goldberg's proposed selling prices, which he accepted. It also refused any formal commitment of funds to Conejo until a specified number of houses were pre-sold, namely, sold before they were constructed. . . .

When Conejo sold the lots, its sales agents informed the buyers that Great Western was willing to make long-term [loans] secured by first trust deeds to approved persons, and obtained credit information for later submission to Great Western. This procedure was dictated by the right of first refusal that Conejo agreed to give Great Western to obtain the construction loans. If an approved buyer wished to obtain a long-term loan elsewhere, Great Western had 10 days to meet the terms of the proposed financing; if it met the terms and the loan was not placed with Great Western, Goldberg, Brown [the other principal of Conejo], and South Gate [predecessor entity to Conejo] were required to pay Great Western the fees and interest obtained by the other lender in connection with the loan. Most of the buyers of homes in the Weathersfield tract applied to Great Western for loans. They obtained approximately 80 percent of the purchase price in the form of 24-year loans from Great Western at 6.6 percent interest secured by first trust deeds. Great Western charged Conejo a 1 percent fee for loans made to qualified buyers, and a 1-1/2 percent fee for loans made to Conejo on behalf of buyers who, in Great Western's opinion, were poor risks.

By September, the specified number of houses had been reserved by buyers, and Great Western accordingly made approximately $3,000,000 in construction loans to Conejo. Conejo agreed to pay Great Western a 5 percent construction loan fee and 6.6 percent interest on the construction loans as disbursed for six months and thereafter on the entire amount. . . .

A subcontractor employed by Conejo began grading the property before Great Western made a final commitment to provide construction loan funds, and while Great Western still nominally owned the land. During the course of construction, Great Western's inspectors visited the property weekly to verify that the prepackaged plans were being followed and that money was disbursed only for work completed. Under the loan agreement, if construction work did not conform to plans and specifications, Great Western had the right to withhold disbursement of funds until the work was satisfactorily performed; failure to correct a nonconformity within 15 days constituted a default. Representatives of Great Western remained in constant communication with the developers of the Weathersfield tract until all the houses were completed and sold in mid-1960.

The evidence establishes without conflict that there was no express agreement either written or oral creating a joint venture or joint enterprise relationship between Great Western and Conejo or Goldberg. Without exception the testimony of the principal witnesses discloses specific disclaimers of all intention that any such relationship should exist, and the written documents provided only for typical option and purchase agreements and loan and security terms.

A joint venture exists when there is "an agreement between the parties under which they have a community of interest, that is, a joint interest, in a common business undertaking, and understanding as to the sharing of profits and losses, and a right of joint control." . . . Although the evidence establishes that Great Western and Conejo combined their property, skill, and knowledge to carry out the tract development, that each shared in the control of the development, that each anticipated receiving substantial profits therefrom, and that they cooperated with each other in the development, there is no evidence of a community or joint interest in the undertaking. Great Western participated as a buyer and seller of land and lender of funds, and Conejo participated as a builder and seller of homes. Although the profits of each were dependent on the overall success of the development, neither was to share in the profits or the losses that the other might realize or suffer. Although each received substantial payments as seller, lender, or borrower, neither had an interest in the payments received by the other. Under these circumstances, no joint venture existed. . . .

Even though Great Western is not vicariously liable as a joint venturer for the negligence of Conejo, there remains the question of its liability for its own negligence. Great Western voluntarily undertook business relationships with South Gate and Conejo to develop the Weathersfield tract and to develop a market for the tract houses in which prospective buyers would be directed to Great Western for their financing. In undertaking these relationships, Great

Western became much more than a lender content to lend money at interest on the security of real property. It became an active participant in a home construction enterprise. It had the right to exercise extensive control of the enterprise. Its financing, which made the enterprise possible, took on ramifications beyond the domain of the usual money lender. It received not only interest on its construction loans, but also substantial fees for making them, a 20 percent capital gain for "warehousing" the land,[2] and protection from loss of profits in the event individual home buyers sought permanent financing elsewhere.

Since the value of the security for the construction loans and thereafter the security for the permanent financing loans depended on the construction of sound homes, Great Western was clearly under a duty of care to its shareholders to exercise its powers of control over the enterprise to prevent the construction of defective homes. Judged by the standards governing non-suits, it negligently failed to discharge that duty. It knew or should have known that the developers were inexperienced, undercapitalized, and operating on a dangerously thin capitalization. It therefore knew or should have known that damage from attempts to cut corners in construction was a risk reasonably to be foreseen. (See Lefcoe & Dobson, Savings Associations as Land Developers (1966) 75 Yale L.J. 1271, 1293.) It knew or should have known of the expansive soil problems, and yet it failed to require soil tests, to examine foundation plans, to recommend changes in the prepackaged plans and specifications, or to recommend changes in the foundations during construction. It made no attempt to discover gross structural defects that it could have discovered by reasonable inspection and that it would have required Conejo to remedy. It relied for protection solely upon building inspectors with whom it had had no experience to enforce a building code with the provisions of which it was ignorant. The crucial question remains whether Great Western also owed a duty to the home buyers in the Weathersfield tract and was therefore also negligent toward them.

The fact that Great Western was not in privity of contract with any of the plaintiffs except as a lender does not absolve it of liability for its own negligence in creating an unreasonable risk of harm to them. . . . The basic tests for determining the existence of such a duty are clearly set forth in Biakanja v. Irving, [1959] 49 Cal. 2d 647, 650, 320 P.2d 16, 19, as follows: "The determination whether in a specific case the defendant will be held liable to a third person not in privity is a matter of policy and involves the balancing of various factors, among which are [1] the extent to which the transaction was intended to affect the plaintiff, [2] the foreseeability of harm to him, [3] the degree of certainty that the plaintiff suffered injury, [4] the closeness of the connection between the defendant's conduct and the injury suffered, [5] the

---

2. Land "warehousing" refers to an arrangement in which the lender holds fee simple title to the raw land until the developer, who holds a purchase option, is ready to use it. As explained in an omitted portion of the opinion, the arrangement was employed here to circumvent statutory restrictions on the maximum loan-to-value ratio of raw land loans.—EDS.

moral blame attached to the defendant's conduct, and [6] the policy of preventing future harm."

In the light of the foregoing tests Great Western was clearly under a duty to the buyers of the homes to exercise reasonable care to protect them from damages caused by major structural defects. . . .

Great Western contends that lending institutions have relied on an assumption of nonliability and hence that a rule imposing liability should operate prospectively only. In the past, judicial decisions have been limited to prospective operation when they overruled earlier decisions upon which parties had reasonably relied and when considerations of fairness and public policy precluded retroactive effect. . . . Conceivably such a limitation might also be justified when there appeared to be a general consensus that there would be no extension of liability. Such is not the case here. At least since MacPherson v. Buick Motor Co. (1916) 217 N.Y. 382, 111 N.E. 1050, there has been a steady expansion of liability for harm caused by the failure of defendants to exercise reasonable care to protect others from reasonably foreseeable risks. . . . Those in the business of financing tract builders could therefore reasonably foresee the possibility that they might be under a duty to exercise their power over tract developments to protect home buyers from seriously defective construction. Moreover, since the value of their own security depends on the construction of sound homes, they have always been under a duty to their shareholders to exercise reasonable care to prevent the construction of defective homes. Given that traditional duty of care, a lending institution should have been farsighted enough to make such provisions for potential liability as would enable it to withstand the effects of a decision of normal retrospective effect.

Great Western contends finally that the negligence of Conejo in constructing the homes and the negligence of the county building inspectors in approving the construction were superseding causes that insulate it from liability. Conejo's negligence could not be a superseding cause, for the risk that it might occur was the primary hazard that gave rise to Great Western's duty. . . . The negligence of the building inspectors, confined as it was to inspection, could not serve to diminish, let alone spirit away, the negligence of the lender. Great Western's duty to plaintiffs was to exercise reasonable care to protect them from seriously defective construction whether caused by defective plans, defective inspection, or both, and its argument that there was a superseding cause of the harm is answered by the settled rule that two separate acts of negligence may be the concurring proximate causes of an injury. . . .

[J]udgment is reversed.

PETERS, TOBRINER and SULLIVAN, JJ., concur.

MOSK, Justice (dissenting).

. . . At the threshold, it would be helpful to review some elementary economic factors and relationships that appear to be involved in this proceeding.

The function of the entrepreneur in a free market is to discern what goods or services are in apparent demand and to gather and arrange the factors of production in order to supply to the consumer, at a profit, the goods and services desired. In so doing, the entrepreneur undertakes a number of risks. The demand may be less than he calculated; the costs of production may be greater. He is not only in danger of losing his own capital investment but he incurs obligations to the suppliers of land, materials, labor and capital, and he stands liable under now-accepted principles of law for harm and loss caused by defects in his products to those persons injured thereby.

The entrepreneur undertakes these calculated risks in the hope of an ultimate substantial monetary reward resulting from the return over and above his costs, which include not only land, materials and labor but the charges incurred in obtaining capital. Indeed, "profit" has been commonly understood to be the return above expenses to innovators or entrepreneurs as the reward for their innovation and enterprise. The upper limit of the entrepreneur's profit is determined by his success in the market, and this results from his skill in assessing the demand for his product and his minimizing losses through skillful production.

CONEJO VALLEY DEVELOPMENT COMPANY AND ASSOCIATED PARTIES WERE ENTREPRENEURS

The role of the supplier of capital is entirely different. The lender, as a supplier of capital, is to receive by contract a fixed return or price for his investment. He owns no right to participate in the profits of the enterprise no matter how great they may be. On the other hand, he is insulated from the risk of loss of capital and interest in return for making his money available, other than the risk of nonpayment of the contract obligations. Indeed, it is elementary that the owner of money lends it to an entrepreneur and receives only a fixed return, rather than obtaining the gain from using the money himself as an entrepreneur, on the condition that he be relieved of risk. The basic, underlying risk in mortgage lending is that the lender might not get back what is owed to him in principal and interest.

It seems abundantly clear, both legally and logically, that if the lender has no opportunity to share in the profits or gains beyond the fixed return for his supplying of capital, i.e., if he has no chance of reaping the entrepreneur's reward and exercises no control over the entrepreneur's business, elementary fairness requires that he should not be subjected to the entrepreneur's risks.

GREAT WESTERN SAVINGS AND LOAN ASSOCIATION WAS A LENDER, A SUPPLIER OF CAPITAL

Great Western's position, as indicated above, was no different from that of any other lender: it had no contractual or statutory right to conduct the operations of the builder-borrower. Even if it were to be established that Great Western was negligent in its duty to its own shareholders by extending loans to a builder of dubious competence, this did not set in motion the subsequent relationship of the builder to the third parties, and the builder's superseding negligence insulates Great Western from liability for whatever negligence resulted from merely lending money. "If the accident would have happened anyway, whether the defendant was negligent or not, then his negligence was not a cause in fact, and of course cannot be the legal or responsible cause." (2 Witkin, Summary of Cal. Law (1960) Torts, §284, p. 1484.) . . .

NOTES AND QUESTIONS

1. Theories of Liability. Connor dealt with potential liability of the construction lender for negligence. Under what other legal theories could the action have been brought? See Ferguson, Lender's Liability for Construction Defects, 11 Real Est. L.J. 310 (1983). If it is determined that a lender is liable for construction defects under these theories, could not the same theories be applied to make the lender liable for other things as well? For example, if the construction lender carelessly misjudges the ability of the borrower to complete the project with the construction loan plus contemplated equity or postconstruction advances, has the lender, an expert in construction financing, breached some duty owed to the borrower, prospective tenants, or other third parties? In Kinner v. World Sav. & Loan Ass'n, 57 Cal. App. 3d 724, 129 Cal. Rptr. 400 (1976), the court rejected the borrower's claim that once the lender agreed to make a construction loan it was obligated to the borrower to lend funds sufficient to complete the proposed construction project.

It is fairly clear that the *Connor* case and extensions of its negligence doctrine to other areas have not received much support. See, for example, Baskin v. Mortgage & Trust, Inc., 837 S.W.2d 743 (Tex. Ct. App. 1992) (construction lender had no duty to inspect houses on behalf of ultimate homebuyers); DeBry v. Valley Mortgage Co., 835 P.2d 1000 (Utah Ct. App. 1992) (in absence of allegations of unusual circumstances that exceed normal lending practices, court affirms dismissal of complaint against construction lender by purchaser of building with defects and code violations because the normal construction loan relationship created no duty to purchaser), cert. denied, 853 P.2d 897 (Utah 1993). However, a future case involving substantial recklessness or covert complicity by a construction lender might arouse what is now a sleeping dog.

In *Connor*, Judge Mosk in his dissent seemed to rely heavily on the fact that Great Western did not participate in the profit from the enterprise. Why should this matter? Do you think Judge Mosk would have dissented if Great Western had been granted the right to participating interest based on gross income? Net income?

> *Problem 9-1*
Section 3434 of the California Civil Code purports to overrule *Connor.*
Does it? ◄

Cal. Civ. Code §3434

A lender who makes a loan of money, the proceeds of which are used or may be used by the borrower to finance the design, manufacture, construction, repair, modification or improvement of real or personal property for sale or lease to others, shall not be held liable to third persons for any loss or damage occasioned by any defect in the real or personal property so designed, manufactured, constructed, repaired, modified or improved or for any loss or damage resulting from the failure of the borrower to use due care in the design, manufacture, construction, repair, modification or improvement of such real or personal property, unless such loss or damage is a result of an act of the lender outside the scope of the activities of a lender of money or unless the lender has been a party to misrepresentations with respect to such real or personal property.

2. *Self-exculpation.* The sample construction loan agreement in the Documents Manual provides with respect to inspections by the construction lender that

[t]he right of inspection is solely for the benefit of Lender. Borrower acknowledges and confirms that neither Lender nor its representatives, employees or agents shall be deemed in any way responsible for any matters related to design or construction of the Project. This section shall not be deemed to impose upon Lender any obligation to undertake such inspections or any liability for failure to detect or failure to act with respect to any defect which was or might have been disclosed by such inspections.

How effective do you think such a clause is in avoiding *Connor*-type liability to third parties? If it is not effective, why is it used? Cf. Kim v. Sumitomo Bank of Cal., 17 Cal. App. 4th 974, 21 Cal. Rptr. 2d 834, 838-839 (1993) (similar provision effective against the borrower).

3. *"Drafting Around" Liability.* See the discussion of Fulmer Building Supplies v. Martin, 251 S.C. 353, 162 S.E.2d 541 (1968), in the excerpt by Madison, Dwyer, and Bender at Chapter 6B5, supra. In M.S.M. Corp. v. Knutson Co., 283 Minn. 527, 167 N.W.2d 66 (1969), the court went even further and found the construction lender accountable to the borrower for the proper disbursement of funds. In that case, the lender diverted some of the construction funds to pay a collateral debt owed by the contractor to the lender. In holding against the lender, the court stated that "when a mortgagee undertakes to disburse funds for a mortgagor under a construction contract, a fiduciary relationship arises." According to the court, the construction lender had a duty not only to refrain from diverting funds to "unrelated obligations" but also "to account for all

of the sums expended on behalf of the mortgagor and to furnish adequate proof of the sums paid and the purpose of the disbursement." Do you think the latter requirement may impose too heavy a burden on construction lenders? Suppose you represent the construction lender. Is there any language you can insert in the construction loan agreement that would mitigate the effects of the *M.S.M.* decision? Would that type of language help in the *Fulmer* situation? If not, what if anything could be done to reduce the lender's risk without sacrificing control?

4. Liability to the Developer. In addition to the theory of liability invoked in *M.S.M.*, construction lenders have been held accountable to their borrowers on other grounds. For example, in Davis v. Nevada Natl. Bank, 103 Nev. 220, 737 P.2d 503 (1987), the Nevada Supreme Court held a construction lender could be liable if it advanced funds to the contractor in disregard of the borrower's complaint that substantial construction deficiencies affected the structural integrity of the project. The court recognized, however, that a lender can continue to pay the contractor if, after a reasonable investigation, it concludes in good faith, but erroneously, that the borrower's request to withhold payment is unwarranted. Assume you represent Fuller National Bank in its construction loan to Dan Developer and that Dan demands that disbursements cease because of defects in construction. Under this qualification in *Davis*, would you advise the construction lender that it risks no liability in paying the contractor if the lender disagrees with Dan after investigating his complaint?

5. Liability of the Postconstruction Lender. Certainly the construction lender is the lender that plays the greater role in the construction process and therefore is more susceptible to liability when the roof (literally) falls in. Does this mean that if you represent Ace Insurance Company, the postconstruction lender in our hypothetical, you do not have to worry about liability to third parties for construction and other defects? Didn't you carefully condition Ace's obligations on prior approval by Ace and its architects of the plans and specifications? Didn't you provide for inspection by Ace's inspecting architect to see that the building is completed in accordance with the approved plans and specifications? Did Ace know, or should Ace have known, that the building would not withstand a small earthquake, that defective wiring was installed, or that the windows would fall out? What is Ace's duty, if any, to third parties? Are Ace's responsibilities any different than the construction lender's?

6. Additional Reading. Hiller, Mortgagee Liability for Defective Construction and Negligent Appraisals, 108 Banking L.J. 386 (1991); Pfeiler, Construction Lending and Products Liability, 25 Bus. Law. 1309 (1970); Franck, Note, Construction Lending: The Mortgagee's Right to Inspect the Construction Project and Duty to Ensure Proper Disbursement of Construction Loan Proceeds, 81 Ky. L.J. 511 (1992-1993); Comment, Lenders Who Voluntarily Assume a Right of Control over Developers May Be Liable to Home Buyers for Damages that Could Have Been Prevented by a Reasonable Exercise of Control, 6 Houston

L. Rev. 580 (1969); Comment, Torts—Lender Liability for Defects in Home Construction, 73 Dick. L. Rev. 730 (1969); and Comment, The Expanding Scope of Enterprise Liability, 69 Colum. L. Rev. 1084 (1969).

C. AVOIDANCE OF LENDER LIABILITY

Responding to the recent lender liability "revolution," many lenders now employ preventive measures to reduce the risk of lender liability claims. General suggestions to help prevent these claims include to (1) avoid displaying animosity toward the borrower; (2) avoid threats to initiate remedies or to take actions that the lender does not intend to follow through on (recall the *Farah* case supra at Chapter 9A, note 4); (3) refrain from controlling the borrower's business decisions, particularly designating which creditors should be paid or selecting the borrower's officers; (4) avoid sudden action following the borrower's default or unsuccessful workout negotiations; and (5) follow the lender's own policies and practices as reflected in any internal loan manuals.

Lenders also try to subdue lender liability claims through contractual devices to avoid juries. One borrower's counsel once suggested that "a lender would rather open its vault to the homeless than submit its claim to a jury."[3] Do you see any reason why lenders might fear juries? To avoid jury trials, lenders now provide routinely in their loan documents for either a waiver of trial by jury or for arbitration of certain loan disputes. Courts tend to enforce conspicuous jury waivers that are made by borrowers in equal bargaining positions. Some states have laws that outlaw or dictate the form of such waivers.[4]

In addition to substituting an arbitrator for a jury, arbitration clauses may allow for faster and cheaper resolution of commercial loan disputes. Drawbacks of arbitration, however, include the limited grounds for review of arbitration decisions on appeal, the fear that arbitrators compromise disputes that should have all-or-nothing outcomes, and the need to carefully carve out certain claims in realty loan disputes that require judicial resolution, such as judicial foreclosure and receivership proceedings. Arbitration clauses have been controversial in residential loans where the borrower lacks bargaining power, prompting Congress, as part of the Dodd-Frank Wall Street Reform & Consumer Protection Act, to abolish clauses requiring arbitration in residential mortgage loans and in open-end (home equity) loans secured by a primary residence. 15 U.S.C. §1639c(e)(1). Arbitration is discussed in more detail in Chapter 17.

Adding to the lender's arsenal, since 1985 a majority of states have enacted new or amended their existing statutes of fraud to reduce lender liability litigation based on certain oral agreements. Claims barred under these statutes may include

---

3. Phoenix Leasing v. Sure Broadcasting, 843 F. Supp. 1379, 1387 (D. Nev. 1994), aff'd, 89 F.3d 846 (9th Cir. 1996).

4. See, e.g., N.C. Gen. Stat. §22B-10 (outlaws prelitigation waivers).

those based on oral loan commitments or on oral promises to forbear on collection remedies or to restructure the loan.

NOTES AND QUESTIONS

1. Impact of Lender Liability Claims on Loan Transactions. Although most of the above suggestions to prevent lender liability claims appear to make good sense from society's perspective of efficient lender-borrower relations, consider whether this is true for the suggestion that lenders avoid too much involvement in the borrower's business operations. Do you see any potential value in such involvement that the fear of lender liability has inhibited? What other concerns of lenders serve to inhibit excessive involvement in a borrower's business operations?

> ➤ **Problem 9-2**
> Based on the *Garrett* case and the foregoing materials, how might you advise a lender to lessen the risk that its lender-borrower relationship will be recharacterized as a fiduciary one? Do you have any drafting suggestions to help avoid recharacterization? ◄

> ➤ **Problem 9-3**
> Assuming that the touchstone of enforceability of a jury trial waiver is its conspicuousness, do you have any drafting suggestions to ensure a conspicuous waiver? Would you refer to this provision in the loan commitment? See Chapter 4B. ◄

2. Additional Reading. M. Madison, J. Dwyer, and S. Bender, The Law of Real Estate Financing §§14:23-14:38 (2016); Culhane and Gramlich, Lender Liability Limitation Amendments to State Statutes of Frauds, 45 Bus. Law. 1779 (1990); Johnson and Gaffney, Lender Liability: Perspectives on Risk and Prevention, 105 Banking L.J. 325 (1988); Murphy, An Introduction to the Defense and Prevention of Lender Liability Claims, 4 Prac. Real Est. Law. 41 (May 1998).

PART III

FUNDAMENTALS OF
COMMERCIAL REAL ESTATE
LEASING

Chapter 10

Overview of Commercial Leasing Transactions

In developing income property, such as Dan Developer's construction of an office building in the master hypothetical, the developer and the developer's lawyer must understand the mechanics of modern commercial leasing transactions. Because the rental income stream from the property leases will "feed" the mortgage loan, the postconstruction lender, such as Ace Insurance Company, and its counsel, must understand which lease provisions are necessary to protect the mortgagee's interest. Accordingly, this chapter provides an overview of some of the significant issues of commercial leasing, as well as materials to aid your understanding of how post-construction lenders analyze occupancy leases. Chapter 11 introduces the ground lease and sale-leaseback devices. And Chapter 18 examines the impact of the landlord's or tenant's bankruptcy on the commercial lease agreement.

A. OVERVIEW OF COMMERCIAL LEASING

We begin our study of the role of leasing and lease-related financing in the development of income property by looking at some of the most litigated areas in commercial leasing transactions.

1. Percentage Rent

At Chapter 5A1 we examined the participating mortgage under which, in exchange for a lower rate of base interest, the borrower agrees to share its rental income stream or appreciation in property value with the mortgagee. In the context of commercial leases, the parties may utilize the similar device of percentage rent to provide the landlord with a hedge against inflation. Because percentage rentals are usually based on sales income that the tenant derives from the leased premises, this device is common in shopping center and retail store leases but is rarely required of the service-oriented tenants (for example, banks, law offices) in an office building project. The typical percentage rent clause will specify a formula for additional rent based on a percentage of the tenant's gross sales or income that exceeds some specified amount (for example, the base rent obligation).

NOTES AND QUESTIONS

1. Drafting the Percentage Rent Clause. Although the landlord and tenant will tend to handle the negotiation of the general nature of any percentage rent calculation themselves, as they would the other economic terms of the lease, they will look to their counsel for such details as the definition of gross sales and any exclusions therefrom. A gross sales formula is favored by the landlord because it is less easily manipulated by the tenant than a net income index. Do you see why? See Chapter 5A1, note 3. Nevertheless, the gross sales approach presents a formidable task for drafters. Landlord's counsel desires to express the definition of gross sales in the broadest possible terms, whereas the tenant often desires numerous exclusions from gross sales. For example, should the definition exclude state or local sales taxes on the merchandise sold? Should it exclude returned or exchanged merchandise? How should coupons be dealt with? What about off-premises sales? Cf. Scot Properties, Ltd. v. Wal-Mart Stores, Inc., 138 F.3d 571 (5th Cir. 1998) (rejecting landlord's assertion that gross sales provision encompassed sales made at replacement Wal-Mart location after leased location closed); Bombay Realty Corp. v. Magna Carta, Inc., 100 N.Y.2d 124, 790 N.E.2d 1163, 760 N.Y.S.2d 734 (2003) (construing gross sales clause to encompass only the commissions paid by telecommunications provider to tenant cellular retailer, not the full monthly amount paid to that provider by purchasers of phones from tenant). What about Internet sales by the tenant from its website? See Murray, Percentage Rent Provisions in Shopping Center Leases: A Changing World?, 35 Real Prop., Prob. & Tr. J. 731 (Winter 2001). If the tenant licenses its premises to concessionaires (for example, a sandwich cart at the store entrance), does the percentage rent formula encompass the concessionaire's gross sales or just the concession fee the tenant is earning? What about sales of store equipment or fixtures? Is revenue included from customer convenience items such as pay telephones and vending machines? Should credit cards be treated the same as cash sales; what if the merchant pays a fee to the card issuer? Does gross sales include state lottery tickets when lottery sales were not contemplated when the lease was drafted? See Circle K Corp. v. Collins (In re Circle K Corp.), 98 F.3d 484 (9th Cir. 1996) ("gross sales" construed to encompass only the commissions the merchant received from selling lottery tickets, not the total sales price). See generally Feinschreiber, The Practitioner's Corner: What Constitutes Gross Sales under a Percentage Lease, 19 Real Est. L.J. 165 (Fall 1990); Gross, Annotation, Calculation of Rental Under Commercial Percentage Lease, 58 A.L.R.3d 384. For a sample percentage rent clause that addresses some of these definitional issues, see the Documents Manual.

From a tenant's perspective, why would it prefer a percentage rent clause geared to net sales income? Can you think of a compromise between the gross and net sales approaches that would accommodate the tenant's concern under a gross sales formula? Regardless of whether the formula is based on gross or net sales income, how should the landlord protect against inaccurate reporting of sales income by the tenant? See Chapter 5A1, note 3.

Finally, consider the impact of the percentage rent clause on other provisions of the lease. For example, would the assignment or sublet of the leasehold estate concern the landlord? See Chapter 10A4, infra, for discussion of the landlord's right to restrict transfer of the tenancy. Also consider the following materials on the need for an express covenant of continuous operation.

2. Rental Escalation Formulas. An advantage of the percentage rent approach is that it avoids the need under long-term leases to adjust rent periodically for inflation. But what about a long-term office lease? A common approach is to base increases on changes in the Consumer Price Index (CPI) as published by the U.S. Bureau of Labor Statistics and which measures increases in prices for goods and services. Using this measure is challenging, however, as among other things the drafter must select between the CPI for all urban consumers and that for urban wage earners and clerical workers, and must also select an appropriate geographical area for the index. Alternatively, the parties might agree to future rent adjustment, particularly for lease renewal periods, based on the then-reasonable or fair market value of the premises. Assuming this approach is not struck down for lack of definiteness, the drafter faces a challenging task in articulating the method for determining such rental value. See H. Ominsky, Real Estate Lore: Modern Techniques and Everyday Tips for the Practitioner 317-325 (2006). For additional discussion in the context of long-term ground leases, see infra Chapter 11A3, note 2.

2. Covenant of Continuous Operation

Consider the scenario where a retail tenant decides to relocate to a more profitable location but is unable to find a suitable substitute tenant in accordance with the lease restrictions on assignment and subletting (or assume that the tenant does not want a rival business to open in its old location). Could the tenant simply shut down its operation at the unprofitable location (known as "going dark"), yet continue to fulfill its payment obligations under the lease? What impact would the tenant's scheme have on the landlord's collection of percentage rent? Although the tenant could not succeed if the lease contains an express covenant requiring the tenant's continuous operation, assume there is no such clause. Will the courts imply one? If so, in what circumstances? Should they do so whenever the lease provides for percentage rent? The following materials examine these issues.

Lagrew v. Hooks-SupeRx, Inc.
905 F. Supp. 401 (E.D. Ky. 1995)

WILHOIT, District Judge.

. . . Plaintiffs, David C. Lagrew and his wife Betty J. Lagrew, along with Lois S. Lagrew, d/b/a Lagrew Properties, are successors-in-interest to the Beaumont Plaza Shopping Center ("Beaumont Plaza") in Harrodsburg, Kentucky. Defendant Hooks-SupeRx, Inc., ("SupeRx") is the successor-in-interest to the lease of a 6,300 square foot space in Beaumont Plaza. In this matter, the Court is asked to interpret the long-term commercial lease that was executed on October 17, 1966.

The initial term of the lease was fifteen (15) years with three five-year renewal options for a potential maximum term of thirty years. The lease provided for a base rent of $1.79 per square foot or $940.50 per month. In addition to base rent, the lessee must pay 2 percent of sales exceeding $564,300.00, excluding the sale of cigarettes and other tobacco products. The history of payments made under the lease is as follows:

Year	Base Rent	Overages
1968	$ 11,286	$ 0
1969	11,286	0
1970	11,286	0
1971	11,286	0
1972	11,286	926
1973	11,286	2,547
1974	11,286	2,862
1975	11,286	3,648
1976	11,286	6,127
1977	11,286	7,160
1978	11,286	8,912
1979	11,286	11,025
1980	11,286	11,203
1981	11,286	12,297
1982	11,286	14,135
1983	11,286	17,075
1984	11,286	15,710
1985	11,286	11,874
1986	11,286	12,656

1987	11,286	12,019
1988	11,286	9,355
1989	11,286	4,592
1990	11,286	4,596
1991	11,286	0
1992	11,286	0

At the time the lease was executed, The Kroger Company, Inc., was operating a full-service grocery store that served as the anchor tenant at Beaumont Plaza.... SupeRx did have the right to sublet the space with several significant limitations. They could not offer to sublease to food stores, department stores, variety stores, skating rinks, liquor stores, beer taverns, or any other business that might interfere with the exclusive rights granted by the landlord in leases to other tenants. SupeRx also retained the property rights to its fixtures.

Due to declining profitability, SupeRx closed its doors in January, 1991. In all likelihood, this decision was related to the closing of Kroger, the anchor tenant, in January of 1988. SupeRx, while evaluating whether to discontinue operations, was notified by a leasing agent that negotiations had begun with Food Lion, another grocery store, however, they had not yet committed to signing a lease. While Food Lion did open at Beaumont Plaza on December 13, 1991, SupeRx chose not to reopen its doors at the Beaumont Plaza location having already opened a new drug store at Gateway Shopping Center located one mile from Beaumont Plaza. SupeRx's Beaumont Plaza site remains vacant.

When SupeRx closed its doors in January of 1991, nearly two years were remaining on the second of three five year renewal option[s]. On July 1, 1992, despite its move, SupeRx exercised its third renewal option on the lease at Beaumont Plaza. SupeRx attempted to sublet the Beaumont Plaza site to a discount store, Dollar General Store, but plaintiffs' representatives objected to the sublease in accord with the terms of the lease prohibiting the subleasing to a discount store.

SupeRx claims that three other enterprises expressed interest but decided against subletting, more than likely due to the ongoing litigation and the short time remaining on the lease. Plaintiffs, on the other hand, argue that they had begun preliminary negotiations with Rite-Aid Drug Company for the space at Beaumont Plaza. When they attempted to ascertain SupeRx's intentions in the spring of 1992, SupeRx refused to relinquish its rights to the final five year option. . . .

Plaintiffs' theory in this case is that the lease contains an implied covenant of continuous operation because such a provision is necessarily involved in the contractual relationship so that the parties must have intended it and only failed to express it because of shear inadvertence or because the provision was too obvious to need expression. Defendant, on the other hand, argues that no covenant of continuous operation existed in the lease and that the plain language of the lease precludes such a finding. . . .

. . . The courts will declare implied covenants to exist only when there is a satisfactory basis in the express contract of the parties which makes it necessary to imply certain duties and obligations in order to effect the purposes of the parties to the contract made. Such covenants can be justified only upon ground of legal necessity arising from the terms of the contract or the substance thereof. The implication from the words must be such as will clearly authorize the inference or an imputation in law of the creation of a covenant. It is not enough to say that it is necessary to make the contract fair, that it ought to have contained a stipulation which is not found in it, or that without such covenant it would be improvident, unwise, or operate unjustly. The covenants raised by law from the use of particular words in an instrument are only intended to be operative when the parties themselves have omitted to insert the covenants. But when a party clearly indicated to what extent he intends to warrant or obligate himself, that is the limit of his covenant, and the law will not hold him beyond it. . . .

To determine whether to imply a covenant of continuous operation, the courts look to the terms of the lease and the surrounding circumstances. Generally, the courts take several factors into account: (1) whether base rent is below market value, (2) whether percentage payments are substantial in relation to base rent, (3) whether the term of the lease is lengthy, (4) whether the tenant may sublet, (5) whether the tenant has rights to fixtures, and (6) whether the lease contains a noncompetitive provision.

[A]pplication of the relevant interpretive factors . . . to the lease in the case at hand mitigate towards a finding of an implied covenant of continuous operation.

First, shopping centers are designed for going concerns, not empty store fronts. Thus, when an entity in the business of operating a retail drug store negotiates a lease with a shopping center, absent a showing of unusual circumstances, it is implicit that the [lessee] intends to operate a store and that the lessor is leasing the space for that purpose. See Piggly Wiggly Southern, Inc. v. Heard, 197 Ga. App. 656, 399 S.E.2d 244, 247 (1991) (noting that a landlord of a shopping center would not want a vacant store in a shopping center even though the original tenant remained solvent and paid minimum monthly rent).

Second, the fixed base rent alone provides the lessor no hedge against inflation. No landlord using good sound business judgment would burden his 6,300 square foot space in a shopping center for thirty years at base rent level without some hope of a satisfactory return on his commercial venture. Courts have found that where there is a showing of disparity between the fixed rent in the lease and the market value of the property, a covenant of continuous operation can be implied. Defendant argues that a material issue of fact exists as to this point claiming that the determinative factor as to market value is whether the base rent was at market value at the time the lease was executed in 1967 and not whether the base rent was at market value in 1991.

Plaintiffs have tendered the affidavit of Edward Pease, who states that the $1.79 rate was below market in 1966. In contrast, Defendant's expert, Malcom

W. McKinnon, Jr., opines that the base rent was within market range for 1966. The Court does not see this dispute as a material issue of fact because it is not outcome determinative. Instead, it merely creates another factor to be weighed by the Court. Mr. Pease's affidavit supports a finding that the base rent was below market value at the time of execution. Moreover, both Pease and McKinnon agree that the base rent presently is well below market value.

The logical explanation is that percentage payments are intended as an integral part of the bargain to protect the lessor by creating a market driven guarantee of a fair return. Percentage payments are the lessor's only hedge against inflation, and such payments are only possible when the lessee is operating on the premises. Thus, the lease's base-plus-percentage rent term is strong evidence in favor of . . . finding an implied covenant [of] continuous operation. First American Bank & Trust Co. v. Safeway Stores, Inc., 151 Ariz. 584, 729 P.2d 938, 940 (App. 1986).

Third, once SupeRx began operating profitably, percentage payments quickly became *substantial* in relation to base rent. From 1976 until 1990 percentage payments exceeded 40% of base rent. In many years overages exceeded base rent, peaking at approximately 150% of base in 1983. While the lease expressly states that percentage payments are not "rent," such semantic distinctions do not cloud the fact that percentage payments are a substantial part of the lessor's overall return on the lease. It was rent.

Fourth, while the limited sublease provision theoretically supports SupeRx's contention that the lease does not contemplate continuous operation by the lessee, the sublease term is so narrowly tailored that it implies that some suitable replacement business would occupy the leased space if not SupeRx. Thus, a more precise statement of the implied covenant is that the lessee, *or some suitable sublessee*, will continuously operate on the premises.

Defendants attempt to persuade the Court that their right to sublease was not narrowly tailored and that the landlord's willingness to include this provision negates a finding of an implied covenant. SupeRx was prohibited from subleasing to a food store, department store, variety store, skating rink, beer tavern, liquor store, discount store, or any other business which would conflict with the exclusive rights granted by the landlord in leases to other tenants. "The presence of a right to assign or sublet is not necessarily inconsistent with an implied covenant of continuous operation. The two covenants can be harmonized to permit subletting or assignment to a business of the same character." First American Bank & Trust Co., 729 P.2d at 941. Obviously, the plaintiffs' predecessors intended for a SupeRx, or another fitting business, to occupy these premises.

The plaintiffs' predecessor had a logical justification for including the clause regarding their right to approve the proposed sublessee. The landlord should feel certain he has a tenant that can generate revenues in excess of $564,300. At this point, the overages would become an important avenue for the landlord to recoup an adequate return on the lease. Otherwise, the tenant could lease the space to a business, such as a discount store, where no substantial revenue could ever be generated. An even better example would be if the tenant subleased to an office where no revenue is generated.

Fifth, SupeRx argues that the lessee's right to retain fixtures negates any implication of a covenant of continuous operation. While a term requiring accession of fixtures would present stronger evidence that the parties intended the lessee to continuously operate on the premises, the absence of such a term does not necessarily prove the converse. In the present case, the lease's fixtures provision appears to address the parties' relative property rights in the event of a sublease or the lease's expiration rather than to the issue of continuous operation.

Sixth, the existence of a noncompetition provision is a factor to consider by this Court. SupeRx was given the exclusive right to operate from the shopping center a full service drug store and the landlord committed not to lease space to a competitor within a radius of one and one-half miles of the Beaumont Plaza. This inures a benefit to SupeRx and in consideration for plaintiffs' predecessor entering into this agreement, the tenant impliedly agreed to continue to operate a particular type of business.

Finally, SupeRx's opening of a new store nearby Beaumont Plaza while simultaneously holding the Beaumont Plaza premises vacant smacks of bad faith. Even at substantially below market rates, the Beaumont Plaza lease is no bargain if not productively used unless SupeRx's motive is to deprive competitors of an auspicious, neighboring location. Such a design would be a restraint on trade. The Court will not permit an overly literal reading of the lease to allow SupeRx to achieve such an illegitimate end. Fairness in business dealing is of great importance to this Court. See Piggly Wiggly Southern, Inc. v. Heard, 197 Ga. App. 656, 399 S.E.2d 244, 247 (1991) (holding that it would be intolerable for tenant to refuse to sublease to keep out competition for the benefit of its other store).

Defendant attempts to disclaim any implied covenant by referring to Paragraph 27 of the lease, "No obligation not stated herein shall be imposed by either party hereto." . . .

The defendant must recognize, when dealing with "implied" covenants, such provision will never be written into an agreement and a failure to specify a provision is not necessarily "evidence that there was no such understanding." The courts look to the terms and circumstances of the parties' agreement to see if the law must necessarily imply a provision to effectuate the true intent of the agreement. Under such circumstances, an oblique reference to the situation, like Paragraph 27, is not always given full force and effect. . . .

In sum, the implication of a covenant of continuous operation is necessary to a rational understanding of the lease in light of the surrounding circumstances. Without an implied covenant of continuous occupation by the lessee or a suitable sublessee the entire agreement is nonsensical. The implied covenant of continuous operation is necessary to effectuate the true intentions of these parties. Accordingly, the Court must imply such a covenant. Since SupeRx ceased operations at the Center without subleasing to a suitable business as defined by the lease, as a matter of law, SupeRx is in breach of the lease. If SupeRx was unable to make a profit at the Beaumont Plaza, felt that a different location would improve their economic well-being, and could not find a sublessee meeting with the landlord's approval, SupeRx should have offered to surrender up their lease to plaintiffs. To hold the premises in order to keep out competition for their other location is completely unacceptable.

SupeRx argues that it has made good faith efforts to sublet the premises, but good faith attempts to comply with a contract is no defense to breach. Additionally, SupeRx relies on dicta from a previous unpublished opinion of this Court for the proposition that unprofitability is an excuse for breach of an implied covenant of continuous operation. The Court recognizes the possibility that a lessee with a base-plus-percentage lease might efficiently breach an implied covenant of continuous occupation in the event of unprofitability.

In the present case, during the period that the Beaumont Plaza lacked an anchor grocery store, SupeRx's breach may very well have been without damages to Plaintiffs. On the other hand, from the time the new anchor store opened and SupeRx did not reopen, Plaintiffs may have a substantial damages claim. These questions are for a jury. In sum, in a base-plus-percentage lease with an implied covenant of continuous operation, in the event of unprofitability, lessee's breach may be a good business decision, but the lessor may nevertheless then seek other available remedies such as cancellation of the lease even if damages are not owing. . . .

On the declaratory judgment count, the Court will enter judgment declaring Plaintiffs have the right to cancel the lease agreement and reoccupy the premises. SupeRx has materially breached the lease, and by the lease's terms Plaintiffs are entitled to reoccupy the premises.

The issue of monetary damages is for the jury. The proper measure of damages is the fair rental value of the premises during the time of breach. . . .

NOTES AND QUESTIONS

1. Express Covenants of Continuous Operation. Aside from a landlord who is relying on percentage rentals from a tenant who might "go dark," can you think of any other situation in which the landlord would want to require the tenant's express covenant to continuously operate its business? In answering this question, consider the impact of the closure of the grocery store on the drug store tenant in the *SupeRx* case. Cf. Columbia East Assocs. v. Bi-Lo, Inc., 299 S.C. 515, 386 S.E.2d 259 (Ct. App. 1989) (implying the covenant in a supermarket lease without percentage rent).

> ➤ *Problem 10-1*
> Assume that a prospective retail tenant (a sporting goods store) has agreed to the concept of a continuous operation covenant. Dan Developer, the prospective landlord, asks you to incorporate this covenant in a draft lease agreement for the tenant's counsel to review.

(Note that certain chain stores or other tenants with significant bargaining leverage may supply their own form of lease agreement as a starting point.) Draft the continuous operation covenant. You will see that it is difficult to capture this slippery concept. For example, if you describe the tenant's obligation in general terms such as "The tenant shall continuously operate the business of a sporting goods store on the leased premises throughout the term of the lease," could a tenant inclined to "go dark" elude the covenant by opening one day a week? By closing at noon and on weekends? By reducing its stock of merchandise? ◄

2. Implying Covenants of Continuous Operation. As an alternative to "going dark," why can't the tenant simply procure a substitute tenant to operate the leased premises as an assignee or subtenant? What kept the tenant in *SupeRx* from doing so? Can you think of a situation where the vacating tenant would not want to locate a substitute tenant even if the lease permitted substitution?

Commercial leases often contain "use clauses" that provide, for example, that the leased premises can be used only for a drug store. One rationale for use clauses is that the shopping center landlord may have granted exclusive rights to certain tenants to conduct their particular line of business free from on-site competition. Placing use clauses in each lease thus ensures that the tenants' operations will not overlap. Landlords sometimes argue that the presence of a use clause obligates their tenant to conduct the designated "use" for the lease term either as an express covenant or as the basis for an implied covenant to operate. However, the majority of courts interpret use clauses as restricting the type of use allowed *if* the leased premises are used, but not as obligating the tenant to use the property. For example, Weil v. Ann Lewis Shops, 281 S.W.2d 651 (Tex. Ct. App. 1955).

3. Remedies. What was the remedy awarded the landlord in *SupeRx* for the tenant's breach of its implied covenant of continuous operation? Assume that the tenant "going dark" in violation of an implied (or express) covenant is an "anchor" tenant (for example, a major department store). In addition to any monetary loss under the anchor tenant lease, the landlord might suffer the loss of percentage rentals from smaller tenants in the complex whose sales decline due to decreased shopper traffic now that the big "draw" has left. Would the remedy in *SupeRx* compensate the landlord for such losses? The court in *SupeRx* recognized that under the remedy it awarded, the tenant might efficiently breach an implied covenant of continuous operation. Is it possible, however, for the landlord to obtain a decree of specific performance requiring the tenant to resume operations on the premises? Because of their unwillingness to supervise a tenant's business over the long term, courts generally refuse to award specific performance in these circumstances. But see Massachusetts Mut. Life Ins. Co. v. Associated Dry Goods Corp., 786 F. Supp. 1403 (N.D. Ind. 1992) (court issued preliminary injunction forcing anchor tenant to reopen).

4. Related Theories. Notwithstanding the outcome in *SupeRx*, in most reported cases the landlord has sought unsuccessfully to establish an implied covenant of continuous operation. See, for example, Worcester-Tatnuck Square CVS, Inc. v. Kaplan, 601 N.E.2d 485 (Mass. Ct. App. 1992); Plaza Assocs. v. Unified Dev., Inc., 524 N.W.2d 725 (Minn. Ct. App. 1994); Sampson Invs. v. Jondex Corp., 176 Wis. 2d 55, 499 N.W.2d 177 (1993). According to one commentator, these decisions reflect that the parties to commercial lease negotiations are sophisticated and able to express any intent to require continuous operation in formal language in the lease. Randolph, Going Dark Aggressively, 10 Prob. & Prop. 6, 9 (Nov.-Dec. 1996).

Because the landlord appears to face an uphill battle in seeking the implication of a continuous operation covenant, landlords have begun to rely on other legal theories that depend on the conduct of the tenant rather than on construction of the lease agreement. The opinion in *SupeRx* hints at two potential theories in remarking that the tenant's conduct in opening a nearby store while going dark in the old location "smacks of bad faith" and would be a restraint of trade if the tenant's motive in keeping the old lease alive was to deprive competitors of a neighboring location.

Thus far, antitrust and related business tort claims have not yielded much success for landlords in these circumstances. For example, the Seventh Circuit rejected the landlord's antitrust claim against an anchor tenant that moved its grocery store to a competing location and then exercised its renewal option at the vacant premises. Although competing grocery stores and customers would have standing to bring an antitrust claim, the court held the landlord did not. Serfecz v. Jewel Food Stores, 67 F.3d 591 (7th Cir. 1995), cert. denied, 516 U.S. 1159 (1996). In a related fact pattern, an anchor tenant grocery store renewed its lease, despite closing its doors, allegedly in a scheme to purchase the shopping center at a depressed price. The landlord sued under the tort of interference with prospective economic advantage (a hybrid of interference with contractual relations) to recover its loss in selling the anchorless project to a third party. The court rejected the landlord's expansive tort claim because, at the time of the tenant's alleged misconduct, the landlord had no existing relationship with an identifiable buyer. See Westside Center Assocs. v. Safeway Stores, 42 Cal. App. 4th 507, 49 Cal. Rptr. 2d 793 (1996). On the other hand, in dictum, the court recognized that tenants have a duty of good faith and fair dealing in lease renewals, leading one commentator to speculate that the implied covenant of good faith might be used against tenants who renew dead space knowing it will seriously injure the landlord's economic interests. Randolph, Going Dark Aggressively, 10 Prob. & Prop. 6, 11 (Nov.-Dec. 1996). For a general survey of state court treatment of implied covenants of continuous operation, see McKinney, Are You Trying to Imply Something?: Understanding the Various State Approaches to Implied Covenants of Continuous Operation in Commercial Leases, 31 U. Ark. Little Rock L. Rev. 427 (Spring 2009).

5. Additional Reading. Hammett, Percentage Leases: Is There a Need to Imply a Covenant of Continuous Operation?, 72 Marq. L. Rev. 559 (1989); Hood, Continuous Operation Clauses and Going Dark, 36 Real Prop., Prob. & Tr. J. 365 (2001); Mastroianni, Caveat Lessor: Courts' Unwillingness to Find Implied Covenants of Continuous Use in Commercial Real Estate Leases, 24 Real Est. L.J. 236 (Winter 1996); DeAngelo, Comment, Commercial Leasing: Implied Covenants of Operation in Shopping Center Leases, 95 Dick. L. Rev. 383 (1991).

3. *Restrictive Covenants*

The lease agreement in the *SupeRx* decision excerpted at Chapter 10A2, supra, contained three related restrictive covenants commonly found in shopping center leases. The tenant drug store had secured the exclusive right (known as an exclusive clause) to operate a "full service drug store" on the leased premises. Moreover, the landlord covenanted not to rent space to a competing drug store within a 1 1/2 mile radius (a radius clause).[1] Finally, because the landlord had been similarly obliging in granting exclusives to other tenants, it required a "use" clause restricting the drug store's ability to sublease to certain types of business operations and presumably restricting the original tenant's operations as well.

These restrictive covenants are fraught with peril for drafters because it is difficult to anticipate some of the future conflicts that might arise.[2] Aside from inevitable lease-specific disputes over the construction of these restrictive covenants, the clauses are generally upheld against attack on grounds that they serve the public interest by promoting the orderly use of commercial property.[3] Moreover, the clauses are generally upheld when challenged as illegal restraints

---

1. In addition, some landlords will employ a radius clause in their favor to protect their recovery of percentage rent by restricting the tenant from operating another store within a specified radius of the leased premises. Walmart sidestepped such a clause that prevented any store within seven miles similar "to that then being conducted" on the leased premises. When Walmart shut down its operations, as the lease permitted, the radius clause was no impediment to a new adjacent Walmart because there was no longer a store business "then being conducted" on the leased premises. Diamond Point Plaza LP v. Wells Fargo Bank, 400 Md. 718, 929 A.2d 932 (2007).

2. Cf. Hibbett Sporting Goods v. Biernbaum, 391 So. 2d 1027 (Ala. 1980) (landlord violated exclusive clause prohibiting lease to another "sporting goods store" by leasing to an "Athlete's Foot" shoe store); 72nd & Broadway Gourmet Restaurant Inc. v. Stahl Real Estate, 118 Misc. 2d 372, 460 N.Y.S.2d 408 (Sup. Ct. 1981) (lease clause limiting tenant's use to Mexican restaurant was violated by tenant's installation of three video game machines). For drafting tips, see Osborn, Restrictive Covenants in Retailing: Drafting Do's and Don'ts, 10 Prob. & Prop. 32 (Mar.-Apr. 1996); Silverman, Pitfalls in Shopping Center Lease Use and Exclusive Clauses, 20 Real Est. Rev. 60 (Summer 1990); Marsh, A Fresh Look at Restrictive Use Covenants in Retail Leasing (with Sample Provisions), 32 Prac. Real Est. Law. 35 (March 2016).

3. For example, Valley Properties v. King's Dept. Stores, 505 F. Supp. 92 (D. Mass. 1981) (radius clause).

on competition.[4] However, in the 1970s, the Federal Trade Commission actively challenged restrictive covenants in favor of major retailing tenants, obtaining consent decrees outlawing, for example, covenants granting the tenant the right to approve subsequent tenants in the shopping center.[5]

On occasion, a tenant contends that consistent with restrictions in the lease against the tenant's use of the property, the landlord impliedly assumed a reciprocal obligation to restrict its leasing of the project; for example, to preserve the character of a shopping mall by only leasing to retail tenants. The following case considers whether a lease agreement imposed an express restrictive leasing covenant on the landlord.

Herman Miller, Inc. v. Thom Rock Realty Co.
46 F.3d 183 (2nd Cir. 1995)

CARDAMONE, Circuit Judge.

This is a suit over the meaning of a lease provision. Neither the landlord, Thom Rock Realty Company, L.P., nor the tenant, Herman Miller, Inc., disputes that the expectations of the parties at the time the lease was entered into have been frustrated. What was to have been a world class showroom building exclusively devoted to the contract furniture trade has now become an ordinary commercial structure. Concomitantly with the dashing of the parties' bright prospects came the instant litigation in which the tenant seeks damages and asks to be relieved from its lease. The landlord insists that the thwarting of the parties' joint expectations was brought about by a general downturn in economic conditions—particularly severe in the contract furniture industry—and that its actions to mitigate the effects of such an economic downturn were in no way limited by its lease with the tenant.

. . . It devolves on us to decide whether, under the terms of this lease, it is the landlord or the tenant who must suffer pain, in the form of damages, after their leasing scheme goes awry.

---

4. For example, Child World v. South Towne Centre, 634 F. Supp. 1121 (S.D. Ohio 1986) (radius restriction); Optivision, Inc. v. Syracuse Shopping Center Assocs., 472 F. Supp. 665 (N.D.N.Y. 1979) (exclusive clause); Venture Holdings v. Carr, 673 A.2d 686 (D.C. 1996) (use clause); Pyramid Co. v. Mautner, 153 Misc. 2d 458, 581 N.Y.S.2d 562 (Sup. Ct. 1992) (radius clause).

5. For example, Sears, Roebuck & Co., 89 F.T.C. 240 (1977), modified, 112 F.T.C. 1 (1989) (on modification allowing Sears to exercise limited approval rights for neighboring tenants within 150 feet). See Pearson, Comment, The Texas and Federal Antitrust Implications of Restrictive Covenants Not to Compete in Shopping Center Leases, 20 Tex. Tech. L. Rev. 1189 (1989).

BACKGROUND

In 1983 defendant Thom Rock Realty Company (Thom Rock), a New York limited partnership, began to develop property it owned in Long Island City, Queens, New York, with the goal of making the property a world-renowned first-class interior design showroom center. It named the development the International Design Center of New York (Center). The construction plan, created by I.M. Pei & Partners, envisioned at least four buildings devoted to this purpose. The first phase of the Center's development comprised two buildings known as Center I and Center II that together totaled almost one million square feet of commercial space to be devoted exclusively to showroom tenants. By 1984 the plan had been refined so that Centers I and II would become showroom facilities for the contract furniture industry. Contract furniture manufacturers make and sell furniture products for commercial users such as offices and hotels.

The concept of a design center is to house tenants in the same or complementary businesses so that client traffic generated by one tenant provides potential customers to the other tenants. Because the success of such a center is dependent upon the synergy it creates for its tenants, the nature and character of the tenant base is critical. Therefore, the marketing strategy for the Center targeted as potential tenants only the largest and most important contract furniture manufacturers.

In its early years, a principal concern of the Center was whether or not it would successfully attract a critical mass of tenants to enable it to lease only to showroom tenants. As a result, the early leases included an "escape clause," giving the Center the right to lease to non-showroom tenants, and the tenant the right to terminate the lease if more than ten percent of the space on its floor was occupied by non-showroom tenants. Other than support or service companies—like restaurants and a photocopy center—all of the tenants in the Center at the time plaintiff entered into its lease and became a tenant of defendant Thom Rock were contract furniture companies which, by the terms of their leases, were required to use their space for showrooms and sales to the trade.

The plaintiff is Herman Miller, a Michigan corporation and a leading company in the contract furniture industry. At the time of the Center's development, Herman Miller had a New York presence located on Madison Avenue near 56th Street in mid-town Manhattan. On September 8, 1986, after a two-year solicitation, the Center succeeded in signing Herman Miller to a ten-year lease for premises located on the second floor of Center I. The lease did not include the escape clause included in earlier leases. As was the case for all tenants other than restaurants and the photocopy center, the lease provided that Herman Miller could use the premises only for showroom display and sale of contract furniture to the trade. Contained in the lease was the following standard provision: "Landlord covenants that the Project shall be constructed as a first class commercial building intended to be used for showrooms and other related uses." This clause is the subject of the instant litigation.

The growth of the contract furniture industry in the early and mid-1980s seemed to ensure the success of the Center. Neither party anticipated the general economic downturn of the late 1980s and early 1990s and the effects of that downturn on the contract furniture industry. Demand decreased significantly, resulting in the failure of numerous manufacturers and consolidation and mergers of the surviving companies. In addition, buyers of contract furniture began demanding services such as mock-ups and on-site testing of furniture, rather than visiting showrooms. As a result of these economic and industry trends—combined with the reluctance of the design community to travel to Long Island City and the failure of New York City to complete construction on improved access roads surrounding and leading to the Center—large numbers of tenants left the Center prior to the expiration of their leases. The Center incurred substantial cash losses, losing over $31 million in 1991 alone. Notwithstanding cash infusions from investors of over $50 million, its losses mounted so that its liabilities exceeded its assets, and it was forced to default on outstanding bank loans.

To mitigate these devastating losses, Thom Rock abandoned, or at least modified, its plan to rent only to showrooms. In January 1990 it leased space on the second floor of Center I, directly adjacent to Herman Miller, to Stars Production Services, Inc. (Stars), a video tape duplication and storage company. The following month approximately 157,000 square feet of space also in Center I was rented to the New York City School Construction Authority (NYCSCA). This space occupies three of the building's six floors, including the second floor where Herman Miller is located, and comprises about 28 percent of Center I. Neither of these tenants is in the contract furniture industry, nor do they use their space as showrooms. In order to accommodate NYCSCA, Thom Rock made numerous changes to the physical appearance of the building that effectively isolated tenants in Center I from Center II, and generally reduced the ability of clients to travel easily from showroom to showroom.

In late 1991 the Center proposed consolidating all the contract furniture showrooms into one building. It asked Herman Miller to move its showroom into a smaller space in Center II, extend its lease, covenant not to open any other showrooms in New York City and relinquish any claims it might have against the landlord. Plaintiff refused to accept these suggestions and in March 1992 brought the instant action against Thom Rock in the United States District Court for the Southern District of New York (Sweet, J.), seeking, as noted, to be relieved of its lease obligations and to recover damages.

After a bench trial, Judge Sweet ruled, in a written opinion dated April 22, 1994, that the lease between the parties contained a covenant restricting the landlord to lease premises only to contract furniture showrooms, and that this covenant was breached by Thom Rock when it leased premises to Stars and NYCSCA. 849 F. Supp. 911. The district court declined to grant the rescission requested by plaintiff. Determining that the proper measure of damages was the difference in value of the leasehold with and without the breach, the district court concluded that the value of Herman Miller's space had declined by a total of 60 percent, that 50 percent of the decline was caused by factors other than Thom Rock's breach, and therefore that 10 percent of the decline in value was attributable to the breach of the restrictive use covenant. Since damages were calculated to be a ten percent loss in value of the lease and since Herman Miller had, at the time of the breach, 7.5 years remaining under the lease, the trial court reduced the lease's remaining term by .75 years. That is, the lease was shortened from its ten-year term ending May 31, 1997 by a period of nine months to terminate on August 31, 1996. An order was entered accordingly on May 20, 1994.

Thom Rock appeals from this judgment, challenging the finding that the lease contained a restrictive use covenant. Herman Miller cross-appeals the damages remedy of reducing the lease term by nine months. We affirm with respect to the existence of a restrictive use covenant and reverse and remand with respect to damages.

DISCUSSION

Herman Miller insists the lease contains a restrictive use covenant. Thom Rock, in urging the contrary, argues primarily that the district court correctly ruled that the subject provision, standing alone, was not a restrictive use covenant. But, the landlord maintains, the trial court erred when it looked first to the entire lease and later to extrinsic evidence to ascertain the provision's meaning. This, Thom Rock asserts, was error because to constitute a restrictive use covenant, the language of the lease must expressly and explicitly state such an intent. Such a use may not be inferred. Thus, defendant concludes, if the provision is sufficiently ambiguous to call for extrinsic evidence to divine its meaning, it cannot at the same time be so clear and explicit as to constitute a use restriction.

. . . The lease itself provides that its construction is governed by the laws of New York. Under long established law, New York construes restrictive use covenants so as to carry out the intent of the parties, provided that such intent is found unmistakably expressed in the lease. Such intent may be discerned from an examination of the whole lease and need not, as Thom Rock urges, be drawn solely from the particular provision under scrutiny. Unless the language of the lease makes it clear that a restriction is intended, the language is viewed simply as descriptive of the use a party may make of the premises, and not as a limitation on that use. If, after examination of the whole lease, a court is persuaded that a restrictive use was intended by the parties, it should give effect to that intention.

Analyzing the lease in light of New York law, the already cited restriction on use found in paragraph 2B bears repeating: "Landlord covenants that the [Center] shall be constructed as a first class commercial building intended to be used for showrooms and other related uses." While this provision, standing alone, does not expressly and explicitly convey the intent to restrict the landlord's use of the property, an examination of other lease provisions in conjunction with paragraph 2B makes such intention clear. Paragraph 2A restricts tenant's use of the leased premises to "showroom display and sale to the trade, at wholesale only, of [contract furniture] and for no other use or purpose." This boilerplate restriction, contained in the lease of every Center tenant other than the restaurants and copy center, carries out the overall concept of the landlord's building as an exclusive showroom center for the contract furniture industry.

Under New York law restrictions on a tenant's use, without more, will not be extended by implication to create a reciprocal restriction on the landlord. In the instant lease, the intention to restrict the Center to a design showroom facility is evinced by other provisions of the lease. Paragraph 2D prohibits any Center tenant from using the premises in any manner which, in Thom Rock's reasonable judgment, would adversely affect "the appearance, character or reputation of the [Center] as a first class building with showrooms and other related uses." This concern over the Center's showroom character is further shown by Rule 15, appended to the lease as part of Schedule 1, which prohibits any tenant advertising that "tends to impair the reputation of the [Center] or its desirability as a building for showrooms." Also, in order to bolster the synergy that the Center sought by creating client traffic beneficial to all Center tenants, paragraph 2D includes a covenant by each tenant to "open its showroom for business and continuously be open for business at all times" during the Center's operating hours. Because disregard for such an obligation would be injurious to all other tenants seeking to capitalize on complementary client traffic, Article 32 provides that if a tenant fails to open for business such tenant shall pay liquidated damages in the amount of 150 percent of its rent for every day it remains closed.

Further, examination of Articles 28 and 29, entitled "Promotions and Trade Shows" and "Tenants Advisory Committee," respectively, is particularly instructive as to how the Center was viewed by the landlord as a property restricted to the use of showrooms. Paragraph 28A obligates the landlord to undertake "a program of advertising and promotional events in order to assist and promote the business of the tenants in the [Center]." Use of the singular "the business" to refer to all the tenants clearly envisions a homogenous tenant base. In undertaking its obligations to promote the Center and its wares, Article 29 established a tenants advisory committee to advise landlord regarding such advertising, promotional events and trade shows and obligates landlord to meet with this committee.

We are persuaded after reviewing all these lease provisions, as was the district court, that the intention of the parties was that the Center would be devoted exclusively to contract furniture showrooms. Because this intention is clearly found within the four corners of the lease, the covenant set forth in paragraph 2B cannot be read as merely descriptive. Consequently, we hold that paragraph 2B is a restrictive use covenant restricting Thom Rock from leasing Center space to any tenants outside the contract furniture showroom business. . . .

. . . [W]e [further] hold that because the measurement of the value of plaintiff's leasehold after defendant's breach was erroneously based on its value as office space and because certain testimony favorable to the tenant was ignored, the district court's remedy of a nine-month reduction in the term of the lease must be reversed and the matter remanded for a new determination of damages. . . .

NOTES AND QUESTIONS

1. Herman Miller. Rather than setting judicial limits on the enforceability of the parties' agreement, much of commercial real estate case law involves discernment of the parties' intent. Which category does the *Herman Miller* decision fall into? In retrospect, had you represented the tenant in *Herman Miller* at the outset of the lease, how might you have better expressed the tenant's intent? Conversely, in representing the landlord at the drafting stage, how might you have helped to avoid this litigation when the rental market soured?

2. Lease Restrictions on Cotenants. Even when parties to a lease are fully aware of a potential issue of contention regarding the type of co-tenant that is acceptable and their attorneys are conscious of drafting a lease provision to reflect their intent, ambiguity can still arise. In the recent case of Staples the Off. Superstore E., Inc. v. Flushing Town Ctr. III, L.P., 90 A.D.3d 638, 933 N.Y.S.2d 732 (2011), the tenant to a long-term commercial lease sought a declaratory judgment that it was within its right to cancel the lease because the landlord did not fill a vacancy with an anchor tenant having a reputation as a "national retailer" as required by the lease. The landlord had filled the vacant space with a business that had retail operations in 15 states, primarily on the east coast. The landlord naturally argued it upheld its obligation to lease to a "national retailer" and claimed the tenant therefore had no right to cancel the lease. The specific language of the lease stated that the anchor tenant must be a "national retailer having not less than 100 stores and occupying not less than 100,000 square feet," but the term "national retailer" was not further defined. The court found the new tenant did not meet the criteria of a "national retailer" and held the tenant was within its rights to cancel the lease. How do you think the parties wound up facing this ambiguous provision in their lease even after the term had clearly been negotiated? Do you think the attorneys for the parties could have or should have done more to reflect the intent of the parties or do you think ambiguities invariably arise despite the intent to reach a meeting of the minds?

In 2011, Winn-Dixie (Plaintiff) sued 97 Dollar General, Dollar Tree, and Big Lots stores (Defendants) with locations in Florida, Alabama, Georgia, Mississippi, and Louisiana on the grounds that Defendants violated the "grocery exclusive" provisions contained in Plaintiff's leases with shopping centers which prohibited the landlords from renting to other tenants who operate grocery stores in the same shopping center. Dixie Stores, Inc. v. Dolgencorp, LLC, 746 F.3d 1008 (2014). Plaintiff did not sue the landlords. Plaintiff alleged that it suffered $90 million in lost profits because Defendants violated the restrictive covenants by selling groceries in sales areas that were exclusive to Plaintiff. Defendants argued that items they sold did not fall within the definition of "staple or fancy groceries" and that such items were properly sold within the "sales area" designated in the leases. Defendants also argued that they were not parties to Plaintiff's shopping center leases, and therefore, Plaintiff could only proceed against the landlords and not the other tenants. The district court first analyzed whether Defendants violated the terms "staple or fancy groceries" and "sales area" as contained in the subject leases. For stores located in Florida, Alabama, and Georgia, the court applied general principles of Florida law and "construed [the] terms narrowly, reading groceries as only food items and measuring sales area only by shelving space." These narrow definitions defeated the majority of Plaintiff's claim. The appellate court reversed the district court's decision, finding that it applied the wrong analysis when construing such terms. It remanded the case for a new trial applying broader definitions such that "groceries" would include nonfood items such as household supplies, including soap, matches, and paper napkins, and "sales area" would not be limited to just shelving space. *Id.* at 1026.

The district court also considered whether cotenants can enforce restrictive covenants against one another when such cotenants are not parties to a contract. The district court held, and the appellate court agreed, that a grocery exclusive provision is a restrictive covenant running with the land that is valid and enforceable against cotenants under the laws of Florida, Georgia, and Alabama. *Id.* at 1019, 1027. With regards to the stores in Mississippi and Louisiana, the court could not enforce the grocery exclusive provision against them. In Louisiana, unless expressly stated otherwise, a lease contract conveys only a personal property right, not a real property right; therefore, lease covenants do not run with the land. In Mississippi, the law "requires that privity of estate must exist between the person claiming the right to enforce the covenant and the person upon whom the burden of covenant is to be imposed." *Id.* at 1031. For a detailed analysis of the case and the impact it may have on the retail leasing industry, see Marsh, Because of Winn-Dixie: The Common Law of Exclusive Use Covenants, 69 U. Miami L. Rev. 935 (2015).

3. *Implied Duties of Landlord.* Smaller tenants in a shopping center may depend on traffic generated by anchor tenants and other stores in the complex. Assume that vacancies in a shopping center increase to the point where they imperil a tenant's business. In addition, assume the landlord has leased some of the vacant retail space to office and other nonretail uses. If there is no express covenant in the tenant's lease requiring the landlord to operate the project as a shopping center (in effect, the mirror image of a tenant's covenant to operate), should the courts imply one? Are the standards for implying covenants of continuous operation (Chapter 10A2, supra) in favor of the landlord relevant here? See Michigan Sporting Goods Distribs. v. Lipton Kenrick Assocs., 927 S.W.2d 570, 573 (Mo. Ct. App. 1996) (refusing to imply a covenant ensuring the existence of a shopping center with a certain number of stores). How would the

court in *Herman Miller* address a tenant's attempt to imply a covenant restricting the landlord's ability to lease the project for nonretail uses?

4. Restatement 2d Contracts Section 205: Good Faith & Fair Dealing Applied (or Misapplied) to Restrictive Use Clauses. Professor Daniel Bogart is critical of application of the Restatement 2d Contracts §205 good faith and fair dealing doctrine to commercial leases.[6] Bogart, Good Faith and Fair Dealing in Commercial Leasing: The Right Doctrine in the Wrong Transaction, 41 J. Marshall L. Rev. 275 (2008). Using Illustration 2 of the Restatement where an owner of a shopping center leases part of it to a tenant, giving the tenant an exclusive right to conduct a supermarket in the space, Bogart comments on the landlord's subsequent acquisition of adjacent land and expansion of the original shopping center. The Restatement's position is apparently that the landlord's allowing a competing supermarket on the newly acquired land constitutes a breach of the lease because a reasonable party in the position of the original supermarket tenant would have thought that any addition to the shopping center property should be subject to the exclusive use restriction. Bogart argues that while §205 might apply reasonably to residential leases, in commercial leases between sophisticated parties and their lawyers, the doctrine rewards opportunistic behavior. How might the original supermarket tenant have protected itself without resort to §205?

5. Implications for Mortgagees. At Chapter 10B we consider lease agreements from the perspective of the landlord's mortgagee holding the leases as additional collateral and poised to assume the position of the landlord in the event of foreclosure. At this juncture, consider whether any of the types of restrictive covenants discussed in this section will be objectionable to the landlord's mortgagee, and why.

4. *Assignments and Sublets*

In negotiation of commercial leases the provisions for assignments and sublets by the tenant often become a major aspect of the discussions. In commercial tenancies, landlords have employed limitations on assignments and sublets to both protect against financially unstable or otherwise unsuitable tenants and also as a hedge against inflation to recapture some of the appreciated rental value of the premises over a long-term lease. The landlord may seek to recapture this value by withholding its consent to an otherwise suitable assignee or sublessee unless the tenant pays the consideration that the landlord demands. Is the landlord in these circumstances protecting a legitimate interest, or is it engaging in extortion? And, in a market where there is no appreciation for landlords to

---

6. See generally, Stein, Assignments and Subletting Restrictions in Leases and What They Mean in the Real World, 44 Real Prop. Tr. & Est. L.J. 1 (2009).

recapture, withholding consent may interfere with a tenant's change in rental requirements, including the need to terminate the business or to expand.

At common law, a tenant could assign or sublet freely unless the lease prohibited such transfers. If the lease prohibited transfers absolutely, or if the lease required the landlord's consent to a transfer without specifying standards for exercise of that consent (for example, that consent could not be withheld unreasonably), the common law permitted the landlord to act as arbitrarily and capriciously as it desired. As the following case illustrates, the common law approach has eroded somewhat as a substantial minority of courts now apply the contract principle of good faith and fair dealing when interpreting consent to transfer clauses in leases. Consider the impact of this authority on a landlord's effort to capture appreciation in the value of the leasehold estate by withholding consent to a transfer.

Newman v. Hinky Dinky Omaha-Lincoln, Inc.
229 Neb. 382, 427 N.W.2d 50 (1988)

SHANAHAN, Justice.

. . . In the absence of an express lease provision specifically permitting a lessor to [arbitrarily] withhold consent to an assignment of the lease or subletting, must a lessor have a commercially reasonable objection to the assignment or subletting, when the lease allows assignment or subletting only with the lessor's consent?

Newman is the owner of real estate located in Lincoln, Nebraska. On July 1, 1977, Newman entered into a written lease of the premises with American Community Stores Corporation (ACS), a Texas corporation. The lease refers to Newman as the "Landlord" and ACS as the "Tenant," and calls for payment of fixed rent, with additional rent based on the tenant's gross receipts. ACS operated a chain of Hinky Dinky supermarkets in Nebraska. Section 10.1 of the lease provides: "Tenant may not assign or transfer this Lease voluntarily or by operation of law or sublet the Leased Premises or any portion thereof without the written consent of Landlord first had and obtained."

ACS ceased all operations of its Hinky Dinky grocery store chain on February 16, 1985. Before that date, ACS asked Newman's consent for a proposed lease assignment to Nash Finch Company, and a subsequent sublease by Nash Finch to the appellant, Hinky Dinky. Although brief negotiations ensued concerning ACS' arrangement for the prospective lease assignment and sublease, Newman did not consent to the proposal. Later in February, ACS' lease assignment to Nash Finch and the sublease to Hinky Dinky were executed without Newman's consent.

On March 1, 1985, Newman notified ACS, Nash Finch, and Hinky Dinky, which then occupied the premises, that ACS was in default under the lease as the result of the assignment and subletting without Newman's consent, and . . . filed a petition for restitution of the premises on August 22, 1985. . . .

After a hearing on Newman's motion for summary judgment, the district court ruled that . . . "the landlord may withhold consent for whatever reason the landlord deems proper. . . . There is not a genuine issue of fact as to this point." . . .

Hinky Dinky does not contend that Newman's consent to an assignment or sublease was unnecessary, but suggests that a lessor cannot unreasonably withhold consent. On the other hand, Newman suggests that, according to the language of the lease, a lessor has an absolute right to withhold consent to a lease assignment or subletting, however unreasonable or arbitrary the lessor's refusal might be. . . .

Newman relies on B & R Oil Company v. Ray's Mobile Homes, 139 Vt. 122, 422 A.2d 1267 (1980), in which the Vermont Supreme Court, construing lease language identical to the consent requirement in Newman's lease, embraced a rule recognizing a lessor's right to arbitrarily withhold consent to an assignment of a lease. . . .

Another line of authority, however, recognizes that, where a lease contains an approval clause, such as a provision stating that the lease cannot be assigned without the lessor's prior consent, a lessor may withhold consent only when the lessor has a good faith reasonable objection to assignment of the lease, even in the absence of a lease provision stating that the lessor's consent will not be unreasonably withheld. See Kendall v. Ernest Pestana, Inc., 40 Cal. 3d 488, 709 P.2d 837, 220 Cal. Rptr. 818 (1985); Boss Barbara, Inc. v. Newbill, 97 N.M. 239, 638 P.2d 1084 (1982); Funk v. Funk, 102 Idaho 521, 633 P.2d 586 (1981); Hendrickson v. Freericks, 620 P.2d 205 (Alaska 1981); Warmack v. Merchants Nat'l Bk., Ft. Smith, 272 Ark. 166, 612 S.W.2d 733 (1981); Homa-Goff Interiors, Inc. v. Cowden, 350 So. 2d 1035 (Ala. 1977). Many courts which adhere to the foregoing rule of reasonableness have accepted the general principle recited in Restatement (Second) of Property §15.2(2) at 100 (1977):

> A restraint on alienation without the consent of the landlord of the tenant's interest in the leased property is valid, but the landlord's consent to an alienation by the tenant cannot be withheld unreasonably, unless a freely negotiated provision in the lease gives the landlord an absolute right to withhold consent.

. . . Factors to be considered in determining whether a lessor has acted with good faith and reasonably in withholding consent to an assignment of a commercial lease or subletting include: financial responsibility of the proposed assignee or sublessee; the assignee's or sublessee's suitability for the particular property; legality of the proposed use; need for alteration of the premises; and the nature of the occupancy. Pertinent to an assignee's or sublessee's financial responsibility under the lease may be past revenue received by the assignee or sublessee and, insofar as demonstrable or ascertainable, prospective receipts in relation to rent based on gross receipts from the business conducted or to be conducted on the leased premises. The foregoing factors are neither exhaustive nor components in an arithmetical formula for reasonableness. None of the factors is weighted so that more or less weight is attributable or assigned to any particular factor utilized in evaluating a lessor's good faith or reasonableness in withholding consent to a commercial lease assignment or subletting. Additional factors may be educed in future situations involving a lessor's withholding consent in cases similar to that now reviewed by this court.

The requirement of good faith and reasonableness in a commercial transaction is not totally foreign to Nebraska law. See Neb. U.C.C. §1-203 (Reissue 1980): "Every contract or duty within this act imposes an obligation of good faith in its performance or enforcement." We realize that the U.C.C. requirement of good faith is statutory, but a similar theme of requisite good faith and reasonableness appears in this court's decisions pertaining to aspects of a commercial lease other than the question of a lessor's good faith and reasonableness in withholding consent to an assignment or sublease. For instance, in Bernstein v. Seglin, 184 Neb. 673, 171 N.W.2d 247 (1969), this court held that a lessor cannot arbitrarily or unreasonably refuse to accept a new tenant in mitigation of damages which resulted from the lessee's default under the lease. . . .

We believe that the rule of reasonableness . . . is the correct rule and, therefore, hold that where a commercial lease does not expressly permit a lessor to withhold consent to an assignment or subletting and contains an approval clause, such as a provision that there can be no assignment of the lease or subletting without the lessor's prior consent, a lessor may withhold consent only when the lessor has a good faith and reasonable objection to assignment of the lease or subletting, even in the absence of a lease provision that the lessor's consent will not be unreasonably withheld. In the case before us, the lease does not expressly permit or authorize Newman to withhold consent to an assignment of the lease or subletting. In the absence of an express provision of such nature, that is, a lessor's right to withhold consent, the provisions of the lease in question require that the lessor act in good faith and reasonably in withholding consent to an assignment or subletting. Whether Newman acted in good faith and reasonably in withholding consent to the assignment and sublease is a question of material fact.

Although the . . . Restatement (Second) of Property §15.2(2) (1977) contain[s] expressions of a policy against a restraint on alienation, our decision today is limited to the issue raised by the parties, namely, the question of a lessor's good faith and reasonableness in withholding consent to an assignment of the lease or subletting, when the commercial lease in question does not contain an express provision specifically permitting a lessor's withholding consent. We leave for another day and another case the question whether an express lease provision permitting a lessor to withhold consent amounts to a restraint on alienation, in contravention of public policy in Nebraska. . . .

Although decisions like *Hinky Dinky* will permit the landlord to withhold consent to transfers to tenants that are unsuitable based on economic or other good faith reasons, these decisions imperil the landlord's use of a consent clause solely to capture the appreciated value of the leasehold estate. Commercial landlords responded by inserting so-called recapture or profit-sharing provisions into their leases. Recapture clauses allow the landlord to terminate the lease at its option on the tenant's request to assign or sublet and thereby to appropriate the leasehold value. By contrast, profit-sharing clauses require the tenant to share with the landlord some or all of the profit received from any substitute tenant. The following case considers a tenant's challenge to a profit-sharing clause as one-sided.

Ilkhchooyi v. Best
37 Cal. App. 4th 395, 45 Cal. Rptr. 2d 766 (1995)

WALLIN, Associate Justice.

In this case we decide that the doctrine of unconscionability applies to invalidate an express condition on transfer in a commercial lease, despite the Legislature's broad authorization of transfer restrictions and reaffirmation of the principle of freedom of contract in a commercial setting. Citing an express clause in the lease, the lessor of a shopping center refused to allow an assignment to the prospective buyer of a drycleaning establishment unless the transferring tenant paid it a portion of the purchase price. The tenant did not comply and the sale was never consummated. The tenant filed this action against the lessor for declaratory relief, breach of lease and the implied covenant of good faith and fair dealing, and for intentional interference with contractual relations. Following a nonjury trial, the trial court entered judgment in favor of the tenant on all causes of action and awarded $40,000 in damages and $30,000 in punitive damages. The lessor appeals, insisting the lease clause was valid and claiming there was no evidence of bad faith. It also challenges the punitive damages award because there was no evidence of malice or its financial condition. We affirm the award of general damages but reverse the punitive damages.

[I]n July 1984, Westar Management, Inc., leased space to the Rosenblatts for a drycleaning establishment in a Garden Grove shopping center. The lease was for a 10-year term, provided for an assignment or sublease with the consent of the landlord, and contained a profit-shifting clause: "[S]hould Tenant receive rent or other consideration either initially or over the term of the assignment or sublease, in excess of the minimum rent called for hereunder, or in case of the sublease of a portion of the Premises in excess of such rent fairly allocable to such portion, Tenant shall pay to Landlord as additional rent hereunder, one-half (1/2) of the excess of each such payment of rent or other consideration received by Tenant promptly after its receipt."

In July 1987, the Rosenblatts sold their business to Javad Ilkhchooyi and Mohammad Bahar, the plaintiffs below (sometimes collectively referred to as Ilkhchooyi), entering into a sublease of the premises approved by Westar. The sublease provided it would terminate if the Rosenblatts' interest under the 1984 lease terminated for any reason.

In June 1988, Ruben and Helen Rosenblatt filed a petition in bankruptcy. . . . The Rosenblatts were discharged from bankruptcy in February 1989. When Westar received notice of their discharge, it notified Ilkhchooyi that the bankruptcy had terminated the lease and thus he was operating with no possessory rights to the premises. . . .

In May 1989, Barbara Lamb, Westar's director of leasing, sent Ilkhchooyi a proposed lease requesting his signature and a check for the balance of the security deposit, which had been increased from one to two months minimum rent. Ilkhchooyi did not respond for a month, testifying he tried to compare the new lease with the old "as much as I could" during that time. Although he knew he should consult an attorney, he decided not to because "I wasn't making enough money to even feed myself."

On June 28, Lamb wrote again and stated the offer to lease would be withdrawn if the executed forms were not received by July 5. Ilkhchooyi called her and . . . demanded to know why the security deposit had been increased and why Bahar's wife was on the new lease when she had not been included on the sublease. Ilkhchooyi testified Lamb said, "[T]his is the way it is, take it or leave it." They got into a heated argument about the changes, and Ilkhchooyi told her he would not sign the new lease. She threatened to evict him if he did not, and assured him it was basically the same lease as the sublease. Ilkhchooyi ultimately did sign the new lease and sent it to Lamb, but he scratched out Bahar's wife's name and included a note indicating he did not accept it. In this note, he agreed to the increase in the deposit; noted that the new lease was not the same as the sublease as promised; and demanded that the effective document be the original lease of July 13, 1984, amended to reflect the deposit increase and to substitute him and Bahar for the Rosenblatts as lessees. Westar did not respond to Ilkhchooyi's comments, but decided to accept the new lease without Bahar's wife's signature and signed the document.

In May 1990, Ilkhchooyi and Bahar entered into an agreement to sell the dry cleaning business to Ramsin Zobalan for $120,000. The escrow instructions allocated $80,000 to fixtures and equipment and $40,000 to a covenant not to compete. Ilkhchooyi testified he and Zobalan determined his existing lease was higher than the current market, so the value of the lease added nothing to the sales price of the business.

When Ilkhchooyi sought Westar's consent to the assignment of the lease, Westar responded in a letter dated July 6, and pointed out paragraph 14c of the 1989 lease. This paragraph provided in part: "If in connection with the transaction involving the proposed assignment or sublease, tenant receives rent or other consideration, including without limitation any consideration for tenant's business, business opportunity, good will, a covenant not to compete and/or the like, either initially or over the term of the assignment or sublease, in excess of all sums then payable hereunder, whether as minimum rent, percentage rent, or otherwise, . . . tenant shall pay to landlord as additional rent hereunder three-quarters (3/4) of the excess of each such payment of rent or other consideration received by tenant promptly after its receipt." Westar demanded arrangements be made for the payment of three-quarters of the value of the covenant not to compete, or $30,000, to it through escrow before it would consent to the assignment.

Ilkhchooyi testified that before he received Westar's letter of July 6, he and Zobalan had modified the escrow instructions on the advice of his accountant to delete the covenant not to compete and reallocate the $40,000 to leasehold improvements. Ilkhchooyi informed Westar of this and stated his intention not to pay Westar $30,000. Westar responded by turning the matter over to its attorney, Douglas Alani, who wrote Ilkhchooyi's attorney on August 15 insisting on the payment of $30,000. "Be advised that Landlord does not consent to the Assignment of the Lease at this time. Mr. Ilkhchooyi is still obligated to pay Landlord Thirty Thousand Dollars ($30,000) in consideration for the covenant not to compete. Your client's surreptitious amendment to the Escrow Instructions, after receipt of notification of Landlord's demand for consideration pursuant to the Lease, will not relieve him of this obligation.". . . As a result . . . Zobalan reduced the price he was willing to pay for the business from $120,000 to $80,000. . . .

III.   THE PROFIT-SHIFTING CLAUSE IN THE 1989 LEASE IS NOT AUTHORIZED BY STATUTE AND HAS NOT BEEN SANCTIONED BY THE SUPREME COURT

Westar argues that the profit-shifting clause in the 1989 lease is specifically authorized by Civil Code section 1995.240, which provides, "A restriction on transfer of a tenant's interest in a lease may provide that the transfer is subject to any express standard or condition, including, but not limited to, a provision that the landlord is entitled to some or all of any consideration the tenant receives from a transferee in excess of the rent under the lease." Westar claims the term "any consideration" encompasses not just consideration attributable to the leasehold interest but consideration for the business itself, including a covenant not to compete. Our role when construing a statute is to ascertain the legislative intent; we turn to the legislative history of the section to effectuate that purpose.

Civil Code section 1995.240 . . . was intended to clarify rules regarding transfer restrictions in commercial leases in the wake of the Supreme Court's opinion in Kendall v. Ernest Pestana, Inc. (1985) 40 Cal. 3d 488 [709 P.2d 837, 220 Cal. Rptr. 818]. . . . In *Kendall*, the Supreme Court adopted the minority view that ". . . where a commercial lease provides for assignment only with the prior consent of the lessor, such consent may be withheld only where the lessor has a commercially reasonable objection to the assignee or the proposed use."

The provision of section 1995.240 regarding the shifting of profits on the transfer of a leasehold emanated from a footnote in the *Kendall* case: "[W]e make [it] clear that . . . 'nothing bars the parties to commercial lease transactions from making their own arrangements respecting the allocation of appreciated rentals if there is a transfer of the leasehold.'" In a law review article solicited by the Law Revision Commission as a background study for their recommendation, Professor William Coskran observed that the court had apparently approved a "profit shift" clause which allowed the lessor to profit from the assignment or sublease. (Coskran, Assignment and Sublease Restrictions: The Tribulations of Leasehold Transfers (1989) 22 Loyola L.A. L. Rev. 405, 447.) Professor Coskran explained the motive behind such a clause: "The tenant and lessor share the motive to profit from an appreciation in the rental value of the premises. When the rental value increases above the agreed rent in the lease, the difference creates a leasehold bonus value. So long as there is no transfer, the tenant indirectly enjoys the benefit by occupying property which is worth more rent than he is obligated to pay. However, when a transfer occurs, both the landlord and the tenant would like the profit generated from the third party who comes into the premises with a higher rental value. It is at that point that a dispute is likely to occur, and questions of express language and reasonableness become involved." (Id. at p. 422.)

Thus, section 1995.240 had its genesis in the concept of appreciated rental value. And the materials left in the path of the legislation indicate it was assumed the consideration in question related to the rental value of the premises. Among the comments solicited by the commission on its tentative recommendation was one by a senior real estate attorney for the Gap, Inc. Arguing against legitimizing the profit-shifting clause as a per se reasonable condition of the landlord's consent to transfer, he framed the problem as follows: "Many landlords resent the fact that a tenant may transfer the lease and retain the appreciation in rental value ('bonus value' or 'profit') that has occurred since the lease was first signed. They vehemently complain that the *landlord* is in the real estate business rather than the tenant. While this statement is true, it fails to take into account the magnitude of the risk assumed by the tenant in a commercial lease. . . . The landlord really wants to have it both ways—to receive the agreed-upon rent while at the same time be guaranteed fair rental value despite his failure at the time of lease execution to negotiate a more favorable rent scheme to protect him in the future. He seizes upon the opportunity of an assignment to realize the increase in rental value. It must be remembered that no one is taking money out of the landlord's pocket—at best, we are talking about a windfall caused by rising real estate values." (Cal. Law Revision Com. Study H-111, exhibit 5.) . . .

In light of the context and history of the legislation, it is clear the Legislature intended the term "consideration" in section 1995.240 to be limited by its connection to the value of the lease. . . .

Westar also insists its profit-shifting clause has been expressly approved by the Supreme Court in Carma Developers (Cal.), Inc. v. Marathon Development California, Inc. (1992) 2 Cal. 4th 342 [826 P.2d 710, 6 Cal. Rptr. 2d 467]. But the clause held valid in *Carma* gave the lessor, upon notice by the lessee of intent to sublet or assign, the option to terminate the lease and recapture the leasehold or reasonably consent to the transfer. Because the lessor exercised its termination option in order to realize the appreciated rental value of the leasehold, the court found the clause was authorized by the new legislation, pointing out that section 1995.240 allowed the lessor to recapture appreciated rental value. Here, there was no appreciated rental value to be recaptured. Westar was attempting to share in the consideration for the business itself.

IV.   THE TRIAL COURT CORRECTLY FOUND THE PROFIT-SHIFTING CLAUSE IN THE 1989 LEASE UNCONSCIONABLE AND REFUSED TO ENFORCE IT

A.   THE 1989 LEGISLATION BROADLY AUTHORIZES RESTRICTIONS ON TRANSFER

Westar argues even if its profit-shifting clause is not specifically authorized by section 1995.240, it is nonetheless valid as an express bargained-for condition of transfer. Westar claims the 1989 legislation was intended to reaffirm the principle of freedom of contract in a commercial lease and to authorize all transfer restrictions expressly stated. . . .

. . . The [legislation] confirms the validity of an express restriction on transfer in a commercial lease (§1995.210, subd. (a)), authorizes an absolute prohibition on transfer (§1995.230), and allows the restriction to be subject to "any express standard or condition" (§1995.240). The commission's final comments verify the breadth of the new law's intent: "Neither the law governing unreasonable restraints on alienation . . . nor the law governing the implied covenant of good faith and fair dealing . . . prevents the enforcement of a restriction on transfer in accordance with the express terms of the restriction." (Cal. Law Revision Com. com., 10 West's Ann. Civ. Code, §1995.210 (1995 pocket supp.) p.71.) The commission was careful to point out, however, that this broad authority "remains subject to general principles limiting freedom of contract."

B.   WESTAR'S CLAUSE IS UNCONSCIONABLE

A party to a commercial lease who is trapped in a bad bargain has only one escape route left: to invoke the doctrines of adhesion and unconscionability. In the face of the strong legislative policy in the 1989 legislation, the challenger to an express restriction on transfer has a formidable burden. Nevertheless, Westar's profit-shifting clause is unconscionable.

The established doctrine that a court may refuse to enforce an unconscionable provision in any contract was codified in 1979 in section 1670.5: "(a) If the court as a matter of law finds the contract or any clause of the contract to have been unconscionable at the time it was made the court may refuse to enforce the contract, or it may enforce the remainder of the contract without the unconscionable clause, or it may so limit the application of any unconscionable clause as to avoid any unconscionable result." Although the section's coverage includes noncommercial contracts as well as commercial ones, it is based on Uniform Commercial Code section 2-302; thus, the roots of the doctrine are in a commercial setting.

In A & M Produce Co. v. FMC Corp. (1982) 135 Cal. App. 3d 473 [186 Cal. Rptr. 114], the court delved into the definition of unconscionability and reported that the term "'has generally been recognized to include an absence of meaningful choice on the part of one of the parties together with contract terms which are unreasonably favorable to the other party.'" The court then analyzed unconscionability as having procedural and substantive elements, both of which must be present to invalidate a clause. The procedural element includes (1) oppression "aris[ing] from an inequality of bargaining power which results in no real negotiation and 'an absence of meaningful choice'"; and (2) surprise "involv[ing] the extent to which the supposedly agreed-upon terms of the bargain are hidden in a prolix printed form drafted by the party seeking to enforce the disputed terms." The substantive element includes terms that are one-sided, lacking in justification, and "reallocate[] the risks of the bargain in an objectively unreasonable or unexpected manner."

Here, both the procedural and substantive aspects of unconscionability are present. The profit-shifting clause was buried in diminutive print in the middle of one of five lengthy paragraphs under the heading "Assignment and Subletting." Ilkhchooyi noticed certain differences from the original lease, such as the addition of Bahar's wife and the increase in the security deposit, but these terms were clearly set out in large type on the first page of the lease. When he attempted to investigate the differences in the two leases, he was assured by Westar's agent that the new lease was basically the same as the original. But the profit-shifting clause in the new lease was very different, specifying Westar was entitled to 75 percent of any consideration for the business itself.

"'The burden should be on the party submitting [a standard contract] in printed form to show that the other party had knowledge of any unusual or unconscionable terms contained therein.'" (A & M Produce Co. v. FMC Corp., supra, 135 Cal. App. 3d at p.490.) The profit-shifting clause in the new lease must certainly be considered "unusual"; Ilkhchooyi had no reason to suspect, given Lamb's assurances, that it was included. Furthermore, Lamb's "take it or leave it" attitude, a hallmark of an adhesive contract, indicates there was no meaningful negotiation over the terms. Although Ilkhchooyi managed to prevail on the omission of his partner's wife's name, this was ultimately accepted by Westar as unimportant.

We concede, however, that the procedural infirmities of this case alone would not sustain a finding of unconscionability in the context of a commercial lease. But there is a "sliding scale relationship between the two concepts [of procedural and substantive unconscionability]: the greater the degree of substantive unconscionability, the less the degree of procedural unconscionability that is required to annul the contract or clause." (Carboni v. Arrospide (1991) 2 Cal.

App. 4th 76, 83 [2 Cal. Rptr. 2d 845].) And it is the substantive unconscionability of the clause in question that concerns us the most.

Westar's preprinted 1989 lease prohibits the transfer of the leasehold without Westar's prior written consent, "which shall not be unreasonably withheld." Additionally, it gives Westar the right to elect to terminate the lease upon a proposed assignment (as in *Carma*), or, if it consents, to increase the minimum rent to the market value. Thus, Westar's legitimate interest in the possible increase in rental value is amply protected. Westar's attempt to appropriate a portion of the sales price for the business was blatant overreaching. Although the Legislature has insulated express transfer restrictions in commercial leases from attack as unreasonable restraints on alienation or as breaches of good faith, it did not intend to allow commercial lessors to gouge their tenants in the name of freedom of contract.

Unconscionability is ultimately a question of law. . . . Substantial evidence supports the trial court's findings and the profit-shifting clause is unconscionable as a matter of law.

Under section 1670.5, the trial court had the power to strike that portion of paragraph 14(c) of the 1989 lease. Westar refused its consent to transfer the lease to Zobalan solely because Ilkhchooyi would not pay it $30,000 of the sum he was to receive for the covenant not to compete. In the absence of the offending clause, Westar's refusal to consent was wrongful and resulted in Zobalan reducing the price he was willing to pay for the business from $120,000 to $80,000. Ilkhchooyi was entitled to a judgment establishing that Westar's refusal of consent was wrongful and to damages for breach of the lease. "For the breach of an obligation arising from contract, the measure of damages . . . is the amount which will compensate the party aggrieved for all the detriment proximately caused thereby. . . ." The trial court's award of $40,000 is supported by Ilkhchooyi's cause of action for breach of lease.

V.   THE EVIDENCE DOES NOT SUPPORT RECOVERY IN TORT; THUS, THE PUNITIVE DAMAGES MUST BE STRICKEN

. . . Ilkhchooyi's claim regarding the profit-shifting clause is grounded in contract: the dispute is over an express term in the lease, and the doctrine of unconscionability is a contract principle. . . .

Tort damages are designed to vindicate social policy and to compensate the victim for injury suffered, including mental suffering and emotional distress; punitive damages, available only for the "breach of an obligation not arising from contract," (§3294, subd. (a)), are designed to punish and deter wrongful conduct. By contrast, contract damages seek to approximate the agreed-upon performance by allowing the injured party to recover what he would have received had the contract been performed. The motive of the party breaching a contract has no bearing on the scope of damages recoverable. Ilkhchooyi is made whole by the recovery of contract damages; recovery in tort would be superfluous.

The award of $30,000 in punitive damages is stricken. As so modified, the judgment is affirmed. . . .

NOTES AND QUESTIONS

1. Sole Discretion Clauses. Assume that landlords with sufficient bargaining power respond to decisions such as *Hinky Dinky* by specifying in the lease transfer provision that the landlord can withhold consent in its sole and absolute discretion for any reason whatsoever. Would the *Hinky Dinky* court enforce such a provision? Despite legislation in California discussed in the *Ilkhchooyi* case that validates clauses subjecting transfers to "any express standard or condition," Cal. Civ. Code §1995.240, the validity of sole discretion clauses remains unsettled there. See generally Myster, Protecting Landlord Control of Transfers: The Status of "Sole Discretion" Clauses in California Commercial Leases, 35 Santa Clara L. Rev. 845 (1995).

2. Reasonableness in Withholding Consent. Suppose that the lease provides expressly that the landlord cannot withhold consent to the assignee unreasonably, or, as in *Hinky Dinky,* suppose that the court will construe a silent lease provision to require reasonableness. What would constitute reasonable grounds to withhold consent to a proposed tenant? On the character of the proposed tenant's business, compare Lemley v. Bozeman Community Hotel Co., 200 Mont. 470, 651 P.2d 979 (1982) (reasonable for landlord to refuse to approve sublease to bookstore unless bookstore agreed not to sell pornographic material) with American Book Co. v. Yeshiva Univ. Dev. Found., Inc., 59 Misc. 2d 31, 297 N.Y.S.2d 156 (Sup. Ct. 1969) (landlord acted unreasonably in rejecting sublease to financially capable planned parenthood organization because of philosophical differences over birth control, as "[d]octrinal anathema cannot be the predicate of any rational law of landlord and tenant in an era of urban complexity and philosophic diversity"). For more examples on the issue of whether a landlord withholding consent is unreasonable, see Dennison, Landlord's Unreasonable Refusal of Consent to Assignment or Sublease, 102 Am. Jur. Trials 277 (2006). At the initial drafting stage, why might a landlord object to a lease assignment provision that requires or could be read to require reasonableness? For tips on drafting reasonableness clauses, see Saltz, Landlord Impediments to Subleasing and Assignment: Issues with Landlord's Consent, 21 Prob. & Prop. 36 (July/Aug. 2007).

3. What Constitutes an Assignment? Suppose that instead of transferring the right to occupy the leased premises, the tenant conveys a controlling ownership interest in the tenant entity, such as by shareholders of a corporate tenant selling their stock. Does this transfer violate a clause prohibiting assignments without the landlord's consent that does not specifically address such transfers? See Richardson v. La Rancherita La Jolla, Inc., 98 Cal. App. 3d 73, 159 Cal. Rptr.

285 (1980) (lease provision prohibiting assignment did not bar sale of stock in restaurant tenant); Branmar Theatre Co. v. Branmar, Inc., 264 A.2d 526 (Del. Ct. Chan. 1970) (court states it would have been a simple matter for landlord to express intent to prohibit transfer of stock in corporate lessee). As counsel for the commercial landlord, how would you draft such a clause? Would you accept your proposed language on behalf of a tenant client? See Zona, Inc. v. Soho Centrale, LLC, 270 A.D.2d 12, 704 N.Y.S.2d 38 (Sup. Ct., App. Div. 2000) (applying lease provision to prohibit transfer by holder of 90 percent of shares in tenant). Consider also the possibility of the tenant altering its corporate structure, such as by merger. See Pacific First Bank v. New Morgan Park Corp., 319 Or. 342, 876 P.2d 761 (1994) (corporate tenant's merger into its wholly owned subsidiary implicated lease transfer provision that regulated transfers "by operation of law").

4. Recapture and Profit-Sharing Clauses. Assume that the tenant has agreed in the lease to share with the landlord some or all of the value of a substitute tenancy. Can you think of a way in which the tenant can elude this agreement in structuring its transfer of the leasehold estate? Does the *Ilkhchooyi* case present an opportunity for tenants? If a profit-sharing clause might be eluded by the tenant, is there a better approach for the landlord to reach the appreciated value of the leasehold estate at the time of an attempted transfer? Because recapture and profit-sharing clauses are only operative if and when the tenant desires to transfer its estate, can you think of any device by which the landlord can share in the value of the leasehold estate as it appreciates? See Chapter 11A3, note 2.

5. Additional Reading. M. Madison, J. Dwyer, and S. Bender, The Law of Real Estate Financing §5:74 (2016); Johnson, Correctly Interpreting Long-Term Leases Pursuant to Modern Contract Law, Toward a Theory of Relational Leases, 74 Va. L. Rev. 751 (1988).

5. Repairs and Compliance with Laws

Under the common law, a commercial landlord has no duty to maintain or repair the premises absent a statutory or contractual obligation to the contrary.[7] Most commercial leases will expressly allocate the burden of repair to one or both of the parties. For example, the commercial lease might obligate the landlord to repair the building exterior or "structural elements" while requiring the tenant to repair the "interior." Far too often, the courts are called upon to interpret the meaning of these allocations.[8]

---

7. Lavoie v. Robert, 494 A.2d 676 (Me. 1985).

8. See, e.g., Southeast Banks Trust Co. v. Higginbotham Chevrolet-Oldsmobile, 445 So. 2d 347 (Fla. Dist. Ct. App. 1984) (landlord obligation under lease to repair "structural elements" does not encompass replacement of roof); Adam Inc. v. Dividend, Inc., 447 So. 2d 80 (La. Ct. App.

A closely related issue is the allocation of responsibility for compliance with laws relating to the use and occupancy of the premises. For example, a municipal ordinance might be adopted by the City of McNiece that requires the installation of an expensive sprinkler system in Dan Developer's building. Despite the foresight of the parties to address compliance with laws in most commercial leases, the courts are engaged often to interpret these clauses. In reading the following cases, put yourself in the position of counsel for the landlord or the tenant and consider how you would have drafted the relevant lease provisions with the benefit of hindsight.

Brown v. Green
8 Cal. 4th 812, 884 P.2d 55, 35 Cal. Rptr. 2d 598 (1994)

ARABIAN, Justice.

We granted review to consider the effect of the developing public awareness of environmentally hazardous building materials, and the often substantial cost of their abatement, on traditional rules allocating, as between lessor and lessee, the duty to make repairs and alterations to the leasehold required to comply with laws affecting commercial property. We conclude that settled and well-understood legal rules for determining which party has assumed the burdens of compliance and repair continue to yield fair and reasonable results when applied to leases of nonresidential property presenting abatement of hazardous materials issues.

Disputes between landlords and tenants of commercial property over responsibility for hazardous materials abatement are not, in other words, unique or so extraordinary in nature as to require special rules governing their resolution. In most cases, however, they do require a court presented with such a controversy not only to construe the relevant lease terms—terms that presumptively reflect the parties' intent—but to assess the result yielded by that analysis in light of established, judicially developed criteria designed to confirm the text-based conclusion that the parties agreed that the lessee would assume certain (often substantial) risks. Here, given a narrowly drawn compliance with laws clause, the absence of a lease provision expressly allocating responsibility for the abatement of environmentally hazardous materials, and a resultant ambiguity as to how the parties intended to allocate responsibility for compliance with government-ordered alterations unrelated to the lessees' use, we apply these established factors and conclude that the parties agreed the lessee would assume the burden of removing asbestos-laden materials from the building as required by a government abatement order.

1984) (air conditioning system repairs were not structural repairs for which landlord was responsible under lease).

... We deal in this case with the long-term lease of an entire warehouse-like building by sophisticated business partners who had substantial experience in leasing commercial property: lessees who were on written notice of at least the potential for asbestos contamination prior to executing the lease, who inspected the building and elected not to investigate the possible presence of hazardous materials before negotiating and signing an agreement that by its terms shifted the major risks of property ownership to the lessee, negated any repair obligations on the part of the lessor, and omitted any representations respecting the condition of the property. In addition, the cost of complying with the mandated work, although substantial in absolute numbers, is less than 5 percent of the total rent payable over the life of the lease.

Under these circumstances, we have no difficulty in concluding that the Court of Appeal was correct in deciding that the lessees agreed to accept responsibility for the government-ordered abatement of asbestos-containing materials. As we explain, however, such determinations are usually closely tied, not only to the terms of the lease itself, but to the context in which it is made, assessed in light of a handful of factors designed to elucidate the probable intent of the parties. Contrary to the result we reach in this case, even though a lease may by its terms require the lessee to be responsible for all repairs and alterations, without limitation, the legal and practical scope of that duty may well be less, especially where a short-term commercial lease is at issue and the cost of compliance is more than a small fraction of the aggregate rent reserved over the life of the lease. Similarly, where questions regarding the duty to abate arise in a case presenting unforeseeable or hidden defects or conditions, the result may well be the opposite of the one we reach in this case.

Together, our opinions in this case and in Hadian v. Schwartz (1994) 8 Cal. 4th 836, 35 Cal. Rptr.2d 589, 884 P.2d 46, illustrate the relationship between the literal text of a nonresidential lease and the result yielded by applying these interpretive factors. In *Hadian* , we construe a preprinted, short-term lease with terms virtually identical to the one at issue in this case and conclude that, contrary to the purport of language placing an unqualified responsibility on the lessee for all building alterations and repairs, the conclusion arising from the literal text of the lease is negated by a consideration of the circumstances surrounding its execution. We reason in that case that, despite the unqualified language of the lease, the lessor rather than the lessee is responsible for a municipally ordered seismic upgrade of the leased building, at a cost that is almost one-half of the total rent payable over the life of the original lease and option combined. . . .

In 1984, Willet H. Brown purchased a 45,000-square-foot building at 8921 Venice Boulevard in Los Angeles. . . . Joseph Green, a partner in a retail furniture business with between 10 and 20 outlets in the Los Angeles area . . . saw a listing for the property and made inquiries. . . .

. . . Green and another partner signed on behalf of the partnership a two-page, preprinted document entitled "Proposal to Lease Industrial Space." . . . At the foot of the second page of the proposal, just below Joseph Green's signature, appeared the following boxed text, in what appears to be 10-point type:

CONSULT YOUR ADVISORS—. . . In any real estate transaction, it is recommended that you consult with a professional, such as a civil engineer, industrial hygienist or other person, with experience in evaluating the condition of the property, including the possible presence of asbestos, hazardous materials and underground storage tanks.

At his deposition, Green testified that he had inspected the building by walking through it, had understood the boxed text, and had made a "deliberate" decision not to retain a professional to inspect the property for environmental hazards. . . . After additional negotiations . . . the parties . . . signed a written lease agreement. That document, a preprinted, six-page form published by the American Industrial Real Estate Association, was modified by the parties by several strike-throughs and interlineations and a three-page, typewritten "Addendum to Standard Industrial Lease—Net" attached to the modified form lease agreement; each page of the lease bore the initials of the signatories.

As modified and signed by the parties, the lease provided for a term of 15 years at a monthly rent of $28,500; the lessees agreed to pay the annual property taxes and to obtain and pay the premiums for liability (but not casualty) insurance on the building. . . . Paragraph 6.2(b), entitled "Compliance with Law," provided that "Lessee shall, at Lessee's expense, comply promptly with all applicable statutes, ordinances, rules, regulations, orders, covenants and restrictions of record, and requirements in effect during the term or any part of the term hereof, regulating the use by the Lessee of the premises. . . ." In addition, paragraph 7.1 of the lease, "Maintenance, Repairs and Alterations," provided that "Lessee shall keep in good order, condition and repair the Premises and every part thereof, structural and non-structural (whether or not . . . the need for such repairs occurs as a result of Lessee's use, any prior use, the elements or the age of such portion of the Premises) including, without limiting the generality of the foregoing, all plumbing, heating, air-conditioning." Paragraph 7.4 of the lease purported to limit the Lessor's obligations by providing that "Except for the obligations of Lessor under paragraph 9 [specifying the obligations of the parties in the event the building was destroyed], it is intended by the parties hereto that Lessor have no obligation in any manner whatsoever, to repair and maintain the Premises nor the building located thereon nor the equipment therein, whether structural or nonstructural, all of which obligations are intended to be that of the Lessee under Paragraph 7.1 hereof. . . ."

In addition, subparagraphs 6.2(a) and 6.3(a) of the form lease agreement, by which the lessor warranted compliance with applicable laws and the condition of the property on the date the lessee took occupancy, were crossed out by the parties. . . .

[I]n the course of a routine inspection of the building [subsequent to execution of the lease], the county Department of Health Services (Department) found that debris containing friable [readily crumbled] asbestos had flaked onto the floor and furniture in the store's showroom. Ambient air samples of the interior of the building showroom were positive for the presence of airborne asbestos fibers at levels deemed harmful to humans. Soon after the inspection, the Department served . . . a notice of asbestos contamination . . . directing that it be abated. . . .

[T]he lease at issue here does not contemplate a use of the property by the lessee of the sort likely to trigger a municipally ordered hazardous materials cleanup. It is clear from the record that the substantial cause of the flaking of the asbestos laden material was activity within the building that would have been typical of virtually any occupant. . . . Because the lessee's particular use of the property here is not one that triggered the county's abatement order, . . . it lies outside the literal text of the compliance with laws clause of the lease. . . .

Although the Green partnership neither agreed expressly to comply with laws not regulating their use of the property, nor used the building in particular ways that triggered the county's asbestos abatement order, it did agree to a duty of repair that is, on its face, virtually global in scope. In combination with other features of the lease, the extent of that obligation strongly suggests that the parties intended to transfer to the lessees substantially all of the responsibilities of property ownership, including the duty to comply with the county-ordered asbestos cleanup.

Lessees urge us to adopt the contrary view with respect to the duty to comply with government-mandated alterations. They argue that, because the compliance clause of the lease only obligates them to comply with laws affecting their particular use of the property, and because the county's order mandating the replacement of the asbestos-containing material applies to any occupant of the building, the abatement order is outside the scope of paragraph 6.2 of the agreement and that is the end of the matter. . . .

An interpretation of the lease which places the burden of complying with the abatement order on the lessor would, we think, lead to a strained and unrealistic result, given the unqualified duty of repair imposed by the lease on the lessees and the absence of any significant obligations on the part of the lessor. . . . Financial considerations implicit in the text of the lease agreement make it clear that Brown negotiated a "net" lease, an arrangement that is not uncommon in long-term commercial leases, especially of entire buildings. As one commentator on the characteristics of such leases has explained, "A net lease presumes the landlord will receive a fixed rent, without deduction for repairs, taxes, insurance, or any other charges, other than landlords' income taxes. Accordingly, the repair clause requires the tenant to make all repairs, inside and out, structural and otherwise, as well as all necessary replacements of the improvements on the premises (and to comply with all legal requirements affecting these improvements during the term). A lease is not 'net,' as this term is used in long-term leases, if the tenant's repair obligations are less than these." (1 Friedman on Leases (3d ed. 1990) Repairs, §10.8, pp.672-673, fn. omitted.) The economic exchange supporting such "net" leases has been succinctly described as one under which "the landlord foregoes the speculative advantages of ownership in return for the agreed net rental. The tenant, in turn, gambles on the continued value of the location and the improvement[s]. . . and assumes all risks in connection therewith." (Van Doren, Some Suggestions for the Drafting of Long Term Net and Percentage Leases, (1951) 51 Colum. L. Rev. 186.)

The fact that the form lease used by the parties here bears the word "net" at the foot of each page and that the heading of the addendum negotiated by the parties and annexed to the lease used the word "net," while probative of the parties' intent, is not alone decisive. What is persuasive is a consideration of the provisions of the lease agreement as a whole, including its comparatively long 15-year term, the lessees' agreement to pay property taxes, to assume the risk of third party liability and to insure against that risk, the unqualified nature of the repair clause, the lessor's "negative" covenants with respect to any obligation to maintain or repair the property, and the elimination of any warranties on the part of the lessor.

It is, in short, reasonably clear from the four corners of the agreement itself that the parties intended to transfer from the lessor to the tenants the major burdens of ownership of real property over the life of the lease. . . .

[I]n assessing the terms and the circumstances surrounding a nonresidential lease transaction, courts usually apply a handful of factors as "clues" or indicators as to whether the parties agreed that the lessee "assumed certain risks, despite the use of unqualified language." . . .

(1) The relationship of the cost of the curative action to the rent reserved. Not surprisingly, lessees seize on the absolute cost of the asbestos disposal operation—set at $251,856 in the judgment entered by the trial court—as confirming that the costs at issue here qualify as "substantial." The inquiry, however, is not quite so straightforward. Lessor points out that the roughly quarter million dollars estimated as necessary to finance asbestos-related disposal is less than 5 percent of the total rent reserved over the 15-year life of the lease, an expression of the value of the repair that throws a different light on the relative financial magnitude (and hardship) of the undertaking. . . .

. . . In many—perhaps most—cases, it is likely that the cost of the mandated work, expressed as a percentage of the aggregate rent over the life of the lease, will tip in favor of the lessee. It is, after all, highly unlikely that a lessee would intend or expect to assume a repair/compliance burden that is, say, equal to or even a substantial fraction of the total rent over the life of the lease. The analysis is different, however, where, as in this case, the hazardous condition is discovered relatively early in a long-term lease, the total rent reserved over the life of the lease is a very high multiple (here, 20 times) of the cost of disposal, and the provisions of the lease agreement otherwise suggest that the parties intended that the lessees assume the major burdens of ownership.

(2) The term for which the lease was made. There is little question under this rubric that a lease for a term of 15 years is a comparatively lengthy one. . . .

. . . Where the term of the lease is short, it is highly unlikely that the lessee would have expected to assume responsibility for the cost of alterations that are, in effect, capital improvements to the property that will benefit primarily the owner. Conversely, where the lease term is a comparatively long one, the lessee has more time in which to amortize the cost of the alterations and stands more in the shoes of the building owner.

(3) The relationship of the benefit to the lessee to that of the reversioner. No evidence was introduced at trial bearing on the projected useful life of the building. It is thus impossible to say on the basis of the record to what extent disposal of the asbestos laden material would benefit the lessor. Lessees argue that the benefits would be substantial, noting that, at the end of their term, the lessor would be in a position to market an "asbestos free" building, thus gaining a commercial advantage. Although that scenario seems a plausible one, it is also true that given the long-term nature of this 15-year lease and the fact that the hazardous material was discovered in only the third year of the term, the cleanup would be of substantial benefit to the lessees themselves. On balance, then, given this record, the benefit of the mandated work will inure to both parties.

(4) Whether the curative action is structural or nonstructural in nature. Lessees point out that the removal and disposition of asbestos-containing fireproofing material is costly and expensive, requiring special equipment for containment of the material, warning signs, area evacuation and "moon-suited" workers. Moreover, because the removal here requires that the fireproofing material adhering to the building's structural beams be stripped, the work is literally "structural." That is true, of course, and under ordinary principles of construction might place the burden of cleanup on the lessor. . . .

In the context of this case, however, the argument overlooks the fact that the lease agreement shifts, explicitly and systematically, responsibility for all repairs—expressly including "structural" repairs—to the tenants both by an affirmative provision (Par. 7.1) and by expressly absolving the lessor of any responsibility for repairs, whether or not "structural" (Par. 9), and that it does so in an overall context supporting the conclusion that the parties intended the lessees to assume the burdens of compliance and repair.. . .

(5) The degree to which the lessee's enjoyment of the premises will be interfered with while the curative action is being undertaken. [T]he greater the magnitude (and the likely disruptive effect) of the compliance effort, the more likely it is to qualify as "substantial" and thus as part of the lessor's duty. . . . On balance, the most that can be concluded in light of the evidence is that the degree of interference is not so great as to weigh heavily in favor of a finding that the lessor accepted the compliance responsibility.

(6) The likelihood that the parties contemplated the application of the particular law or order involved. In light of the finding of the trial court and the evidence supporting it, we can only conclude that although neither party was aware of or had reason to believe hazardous materials were present within the building at the time the lease agreement was negotiated and signed, both had notice of the possibility that such a condition might exist, at least in the abstract. We think this fact is especially telling in a context in which lessees with substantial experience in retail leasing conceded that they had read and

understood the notice at the foot of the lease proposal and elected not to pursue an investigation of that contingency. . . . (We note, of course, the obvious fact that a finding of no abatement liability on the part of the lessee is likely where the condition at issue was unforeseeable or would not have been disclosed by a reasonable inspection of the site.)

[We] conclude that the Court of Appeal was correct in ruling that the lessees assumed responsibility for removing the asbestos laden material from the building. . . .

Dennison v. Marlowe
106 N.M. 433, 744 P.2d 906 (1987)

SOSA, Senior Justice.

. . . On June 23, 1983, lessees leased a two-story building and a parking area from lessor for a term of five years at a rental of $800 per month. The building is known as the "Great American Saloon." The lease agreement had an option to renew for an additional five years and an option to purchase. About one year later, on May 14, 1984, lessees received a letter and cease and desist order from the State Fire Marshal, advising them that the building was in violation of the New Mexico State Rules and Regulations Relating to Fire Prevention and Life Safety in Public Occupancies (safety code). Attached to the letter was a report from Fire Prevention Specialist Bill Beutler who found various safety code violations, including the absence of an automatic sprinkler system. . . . Lessees appealed the cease and desist order, maintaining that they were not the owners of the building and had not changed the use of the premises. The building had been operated as a restaurant/bar for several years. Lessees also advised lessor of the order and requested that she comply with the safety code requirements. . . .

An overwhelming number of jurisdictions have held that when a tenant has agreed to comply with the laws and regulations of governmental authorities and the alterations or improvements ordered by the public authority are of a structural or substantial nature, the landlord instead of the tenant is liable for such alterations unless the terms of the covenant and the surrounding circumstances indicate the tenant's intention to assume such an obligation. . . . This rule is followed because the property owner is initially under the duty to comply with all laws and orders unless it is assumed by the lessee under the terms of the lease. . . . Thus, the intention of the parties as expressed in the lease agreement in light of the surrounding circumstances is determinative.

The lease contains the following pertinent provisions:

> 5. It is agreed that in the event any repairs, alterations or improvements be added to the premises or the existing improvements, the same shall become part of the realty and at the expiration of this lease, the improvements shall remain as part of the real property.

6. Lessor agrees to maintain the roof, plumbing and exterior of the demised premises in good repair and condition at [her] sole cost and expense. . . .

9. (c) Lessees agree that they will abide by all of the laws, ordinances, rules or regulations of any regulatory body of the State of New Mexico or any political subdivision thereof. . . .

22. The Lessee[s][acknowledge] that they have examined the premises and are accepting said premises in its present condition on an "as is" basis, and [are] not relying on any representations made to the condition of the premises, but [are] relying solely on their own inspection of the premises and any improvements located thereon.

Although lessees agreed to comply with all "laws, ordinances, rules or regulations," this covenant, by itself, does not constitute an assumption of the duty to comply with orders requiring improvements of a substantial or structural nature. . . .

. . . We have examined the terms of this lease agreement and, in light of the surrounding circumstances, conclude that lessees did not agree to assume liability for compliance with the improvements ordered by the State Fire Marshal. . . .

. . . In paragraph six, lessor agreed to maintain the roof, plumbing, and exterior of the demised premises. These type of repairs or maintenance could be considered of a substantial nature and therefore . . . it was not within the contemplation of the parties that lessees hold the lessor harmless of all maintenance or repair of a substantial nature.

[H]ere, when lessees accepted the premises "on an 'as is' basis," the Deming Fire Department had inspected the premises and certified occupancy for both floors. No safety code violations were noted. Therefore, when lessees accepted the premises on an "as is" basis, they contemplated that the building was in full compliance with the safety code. Furthermore, acceptance of the premises on an "as is" basis does not necessarily mean that the tenant is required to make changes of a structural or material nature. . . .

In Mid-Continent Life Ins. v. Henry's, Inc., 214 Kan. 350, 351, 520 P.2d 1319, 1320 (1974), the court held that the lessee should not bear the cost of alterations ordered by public authorities when:

(1) the improvements were substantial and structural in nature; (2) the improvements will survive the term of the lease between lessor and lessee and thus will inure to the primary benefit of the lessor; (3) the improvements were not required by or because of any particular use made of the premises by the lessee; (4) the cost of such improvements were substantial as opposed to nominal; and (5) the event which necessitated the improvement was unusual, extraordinary and unexpected and not within the contemplation of the parties at the time the lease was executed.

Here the facts fit every criteria listed. First, there is no doubt that a sprinkler system is an alteration of a substantial nature. Second, the lease in this case was for a relatively short period of time—five years—and the improvements if made would have reverted to the lessor. Third, there is no evidence that the sprinkler system was required because of the particular use which lessees made of the premises. The premises had been used as a restaurant/bar for several years and lessees continued to so use the premises. Fourth, the cost of installing the sprinkler system was estimated at about $15,000, a far cry from being nominal. And fifth, the need for the sprinkler system was unexpected, particularly under these circumstances, when the Deming Fire Department had given the premises a "clean bill," detecting no safety code violations.

The conclusion is inescapable that a lasting, expensive improvement such as a sprinkler system, at a cost of about $15,000, which could have likely survived the term of the lease and would have inured to the primary benefit of the lessor, and was not necessitated by the particular use of the premises, could not have been within the contemplation of the parties.

NOTES AND QUESTIONS

1. Compliance with Laws. Consider the criteria in *Brown* and *Dennison* for determining which party should bear the cost of alterations required by public authorities. How do the criteria differ? In Hadian v. Schwartz, 8 Cal. 4th 836, 884 P.2d 46, 35 Cal. Rptr. 2d 589 (1994), the California Supreme Court applied the same six factors articulated in the companion case of *Brown* and held that the landlord was responsible for quake-proofing ("seismic retrofitting") a nightclub.

Is the result in *Dennison* one that the landlord could have avoided by more definite language in the lease agreement? Cf. Fresh Cut, Inc. v. Fazli, 650 N.E.2d 1126 (Ind. 1995) (no public policy impediment to agreement holding tenant responsible to maintain fire sprinkler required by municipal ordinance). Assuming that the landlord would be limited by "bounded rationality" in that it is unable to forecast every future government order that may impact the leased premises, what language would you have insisted on as the landlord's counsel in *Dennison*?

Consider the following cases as evidence that many courts tend to construe the relevant lease terms in the tenant's favor and to place responsibility for compliance work on the landlord. See Prudential Ins. Co. of Am. v. L. A. Mart, 68 F.3d 370 (9th Cir. 1995) (broad repair obligations imposed on tenant under lease do not encompass reimbursement for seismic upgrade undertaken on landlord's own initiative without government order), and 1600 Arch Ltd. Partnership v. INA Corp. (In re 1600 Arch Ltd. Partnership), 938 F. Supp. 300 (E.D. Pa. 1996) (compliance provision applicable to compliance "during the Term of this Lease" did not extend to work performed by landlord after lease expired). Representing the landlord, how would you have drafted the lease to provide for reimbursement in these two cases?

2. Effects of Terrorism. The terrorist attacks in 2001 altered the leasing landscape in several ways. These effects include conflicts over increased building security, see Cipriani Fifth Ave., LLC v. RCPI Landmark Properties, LLC,

4 Misc. 3d 850, 782 N.Y.S.2d 522 (Sup. Ct. 2004) (concluding over tenant's objection that "terrible burden of post-911 history" justified landlord installation of metal detectors for elevator banks serving tenant's renowned Rainbow Room supper club), and the tenant's responsibility to purchase terrorism insurance for the leased building. TAG 380, LLC v. ComMet 380, Inc., 10 N.Y.3d 507, 860 N.Y.S.2d 433, 890 N.E.2d 195 (2008) (tenant ground-leasing 380 Madison Avenue in Manhattan held obligated under lease terms to obtain terrorism insurance).

3. Additional Reading. The Commercial Property Lease ch. 13 (P. Randolph, Jr., ed. 1997). For readings on the allocation of compliance with the accessibility and barrier removal requirements of the Americans with Disabilities Act of 1990 (42 U.S.C. §§12101 et seq.), see Duston, Late for an Important Date—Landlord-Tenant Issues under the ADA, 8 Prob. & Prop. 53 (May-June 1994); Jones, Commercial Leases under the Americans with Disabilities Act, 22 Real Est. L.J. 185 (Winter 1994); Field, Note, The Americans with Disabilities Act "Readily Achievable" Requirement for Barrier Removal: A Proposal for the Allocation of Responsibility between Landlord and Tenant, 15 Cardozo L. Rev. 569 (1993); Whelan, Comment, The "Public Access" Provisions of Title III of the Americans with Disabilities Act: A Guide for Commercial Landlords and Tenants, 34 Santa Clara L. Rev. 215 (1993).

6.   *The Commercial Landlord's Remedies*

As we saw in the discussion of leasehold restrictions on assignments and sublets in Chapter 10A4, supra, contracts principles of good faith and unconscionability have crept into commercial lease contracts. The following case illustrates the trend on the tenant's abandonment of the leased premises to apply the contracts principle of mitigation of damages instead of the archaic conveyancing approach that allows the landlord to keep the premises vacant for the remainder of the breached lease while collecting the full rent from the abandoning tenant. On the choice between contracts and conveyancing approaches generally in real estate transactions, see Madison, The Real Properties of Contract Law, 82 Boston U. L. Rev. 405 (2002).

Austin Hill Country Realty, Inc. v. Palisades Plaza, Inc.
40 Tex. Sup. Ct. J. 924, 948 S.W.2d 293 (1997)

SPECTOR, Justice, delivered the opinion for a unanimous Court.

. . . The issue in this case is whether a landlord has a duty to make reasonable efforts to mitigate damages when a tenant defaults on a lease. The court of appeals held that no such duty exists at common law. We hold today that a landlord has a duty to make reasonable efforts to mitigate damages. Accordingly, we reverse the judgment of the court of appeals and remand for a new trial.

I

Palisades Plaza, Inc., owned and operated an office complex consisting of four office buildings in Austin. Barbara Hill, Annette Smith, and David Jones sold real estate in Austin as a Re/Max real estate brokerage franchise operating through Austin Hill Country Realty, Inc. On September 15, 1992, the Palisades and Hill Country executed a five-year commercial office lease for a suite in the Palisades' office complex. An addendum executed in connection with the lease set the monthly base rent at $3,128 for the first year, $3,519 for the second and third years, and $3,910 for the fourth and fifth years. The parties also signed an improvements agreement that called for the Palisades to convert the shell office space into working offices for Hill Country. The lease was to begin on the "commencement date," which was defined in the lease and the improvements agreement as either (1) the date that Hill Country occupied the suite, or (2) the date that the Palisades substantially completed the improvements or would have done so but for "tenant delay." All parties anticipated that the lease would begin on November 15, 1992.

By the middle of October 1992, the Palisades had nearly completed the improvements. Construction came to a halt on October 21, 1992, when the Palisades received conflicting instructions about the completion of the suite from Hill on one hand and Smith and Jones on the other. By two letters, the Palisades informed Hill Country, Hill, Smith, and Jones that it had received conflicting directives and would not continue with the construction until Hill, Smith, and Jones collectively designated a single representative empowered to make decisions for the trio. Hill, Smith, and Jones did not reply to these letters.

In a letter dated November 19, 1992, the Palisades informed Hill Country, Hill, Smith, and Jones that their failure to designate a representative was an anticipatory breach of contract. The parties tried unsuccessfully to resolve their differences in a meeting. The Palisades then sued Hill Country, Hill, Smith, and Jones (collectively, "Hill Country") for anticipatory breach of the lease.

At trial, Hill Country attempted to prove that the Palisades failed to mitigate the damages resulting from Hill Country's alleged breach. In particular, Hill Country introduced evidence that the Palisades rejected an offer from Smith and Jones to lease the premises without Hill, as well as an offer from Hill and another person to lease the premises without Smith and Jones. Hill Country also tried to prove that, while the Palisades advertised for tenants continuously in a local newspaper, it did not advertise in the commercial-property publication "The Flick Report" as it had in the past. Hill Country requested an instruction asking the jury to reduce the Palisades' damage award by "any amount that you find the [Palisades] could have avoided by the exercise of reasonable care." The trial judge rejected this instruction, stating, "Last time I checked the law, it was that a landlord doesn't have any obligation to try to fill the space." The jury returned a verdict for the Palisades for $29,716 in damages and $16,500 in attorney's fees. The court of appeals affirmed that judgment.

II

In its only point of error, Hill Country asks this Court to recognize a landlord's duty to make reasonable efforts to mitigate damages when a tenant breaches a lease.

. . . Because there is no statute addressing this issue, we look to the common law. John F. Hicks, The Contractual Nature of Real Property Leases, 24 Baylor L. Rev. 443, 446-53 (1972).

The traditional common law rule regarding mitigation dictates that landlords have no duty to mitigate damages. See Dawn R. Barker, Note, Commercial Landlords' Duty upon Tenants' Abandonment—To Mitigate?, 20 J. Corp. L. 627, 629 (1995). This rule stems from the historical concept that the tenant is owner of the property during the lease term; as long as the tenant has a right to possess the land, the tenant is liable for rent. See Reid v. Mutual of Omaha Ins. Co., 776 P.2d 896, 902, 905 (Utah 1989). Under this rule, a landlord is not obligated to undertake any action following a tenant's abandonment of the premises but may recover rents periodically for the remainder of the term.

Texas courts have consistently followed this no-mitigation rule in cases involving a landlord's suit for past due rent.

Some Texas courts have, however, required a landlord to mitigate damages when the landlord seeks a remedy that is contractual in nature, such as anticipatory breach of contract, rather than a real property cause of action. . . .

Other Texas courts have required a landlord to mitigate damages when the landlord reenters or resumes control of the premises. Thus, a landlord currently may be subject to a mitigation requirement depending upon the landlord's actions following breach and the type of lawsuit the landlord pursues.

III

In discerning the policy implications of a rule requiring landlords to mitigate damages, we are informed by the rules of other jurisdictions. Forty-two states and the District of Columbia have recognized that a landlord has a duty to mitigate damages in at least some situations: when there is a breach of a residential lease, a commercial lease, or both.

Only six states have explicitly held that a landlord has no duty to mitigate in any situation. In South Dakota, the law is unclear.

Those jurisdictions recognizing a duty to mitigate have emphasized the change in the nature of landlord-tenant law since its inception in medieval times. At English common law, the tenant had only contractual rights against the landlord and therefore could not assert common-law real property causes of action to protect the leasehold. Over time, the courts recognized a tenant's right to bring real property causes of action, and tenants were considered to possess an estate in land. 2 R. Powell, The Law of Real Property §221[1], at 16-18 (1969). The landlord had to give the tenant possession of the land, and the tenant was required to pay rent in return. As covenants in leases have become more complex and the structures on the land have become more important to the parties than the land itself, courts have begun to recognize that a lease possesses elements of both a contract and a conveyance. See, e.g., Schneiker v. Gordon, 732 P.2d 603, 607-09 (Colo. 1987); Reid v. Mutual of Omaha Ins. Co., 776 P.2d 896, 902, 904 (Utah 1989). Under contract principles, the lease is not a complete conveyance to the tenant for a specified term such that the landlord's duties are fulfilled upon deliverance of the property to the tenant. Rather, a promise to pay in a lease is essentially the same as a promise to pay in any other contract, and a breach of that promise does not necessarily end the landlord's ongoing duties. Schneiker, 732 P.2d at 610; Wright v. Baumann, 239 Or. 410, 398 P.2d 119, 121 (1965). Because of the contractual elements of the modern lease agreement, these courts have imposed upon the landlord the contractual duty to mitigate damages upon the tenant's breach.

Public policy offers further justification for the duty to mitigate. First, requiring mitigation in the landlord-tenant context discourages economic waste and encourages productive use of the property. As the Colorado Supreme Court has written:

> Under traditional property law principles a landlord could allow the property to remain unoccupied while still holding the abandoning tenant liable for rent. This encourages both economic and physical waste. In no other context of which we are aware is an injured party permitted to sit idly by and suffer avoidable economic loss and thereafter to visit the full adverse economic consequences upon the party whose breach initiated the chain of events causing the loss.

Schneiker, 732 P.2d at 610. A mitigation requirement thus returns the property to productive use rather than allowing it to remain idle. Public policy requires that the law "discourage even persons against whom wrongs have been committed from passively suffering economic loss which could be averted by reasonable efforts." Wright, 398 P.2d at 121 (quoting C. McCormick, Handbook on the Law of Damages, 33 (1935)).

Second, a mitigation rule helps prevent destruction of or damage to the leased property. If the landlord is encouraged to let the property remain unoccupied, "the possibility of physical damage to the property through accident or vandalism is increased." Schneiker, 732 P.2d at 610.

Third, the mitigation rule is consistent with the trend disfavoring contract penalties. Reid, 776 P.2d at 905-06. Courts have held that a liquidated damages clause in a contract must represent a reasonable estimate of anticipated damages upon breach. See, e.g., Warner v. Rasmussen, 704 P.2d 559, 561, 563 (Utah

1985). "Similarly, allowing a landlord to leave property idle when it could be profitably leased and forc[ing] an absent tenant to pay rent for that idled property permits the landlord to recover more damages than it may reasonably require to be compensated for the tenant's breach. This is analogous to imposing a disfavored penalty upon the tenant." Reid, 776 P.2d at 905-06.

Finally, the traditional justifications for the common law rule have proven unsound in practice. Proponents of the no-mitigation rule suggest that the landlord-tenant relationship is personal in nature, and that the landlord therefore should not be forced to lease to an unwanted tenant. See Wohl v. Yelen, 22 Ill. App.2d 455, 161 N.E.2d 339, 343 (1959). Modern lease arrangements, however, are rarely personal in nature and are usually business arrangements between strangers. Edwin Smith, Jr., Comment, Extending the Contractual Duty to Mitigate Damages to Landlords when a Tenant Abandons the Lease, 42 Baylor L. Rev. 553, 559 (1990). Further, the landlord's duty to make reasonable efforts to mitigate does not require that the landlord accept replacement tenants who are financial risks or whose business was precluded by the original lease.

The overwhelming trend among jurisdictions in the United States has thus been toward requiring a landlord to mitigate damages when a tenant abandons the property in breach of the lease agreement. Those courts adopting a mitigation requirement have emphasized the contractual elements of a lease agreement, the public policy favoring productive use of property, and the practicalities of the modern landlord-tenant arrangement as supporting such a duty.

IV

We are persuaded by the reasoning of those courts that recognize that landlords must mitigate damages upon a tenant's abandonment and failure to pay rent. This Court has recognized the dual nature of a lease as both a conveyance and a contract. Under a contract view, a landlord should be treated no differently than any other aggrieved party to a contract. Further, the public policy of the state of Texas calls for productive use of property as opposed to avoidable economic waste. As Professor McCormick wrote over seventy years ago, the law

> which permits the landlord to stand idly by the vacant, abandoned premises and treat them as the property of the tenant and recover full rent, [should] yield to the more realistic notions of social advantage which in other fields of the law have forbidden a recovery for damages which the plaintiff by reasonable efforts could have avoided.

Charles McCormick, The Rights of the Landlord Upon Abandonment of the Premises by the Tenant, 23 Mich. L. Rev. 211, 221-22 (1925). Finally, we have recognized that contract penalties are disfavored in Texas. Stewart v. Basey, 150 Tex. 666, 245 S.W.2d 484, 486 (1952) (landlord should not receive more or less than actual damages upon tenant's breach). A landlord should not be allowed to collect rent from an abandoning tenant when the landlord can, by reasonable efforts, relet the premises and avoid incurring some damages. We therefore recognize that a landlord has a duty to make reasonable efforts to mitigate damages when the tenant breaches the lease and abandons the property, unless the commercial landlord and tenant contract otherwise.

V

To ensure the uniform application of this duty by the courts of this state, and to guide future landlords and tenants in conforming their conduct to the law, we now consider several practical considerations that will undoubtedly arise. We first consider the level of conduct by a landlord that will satisfy the duty to mitigate. The landlord's mitigation duty has been variously stated in other jurisdictions. See, e.g., Reid, 776 P.2d at 906 ("objective commercial reasonableness"); Schneiker, 732 P.2d at 611 ("reasonable efforts"); Cal. Civ. Code §1951.2(c)(2) ("reasonably and in a good-faith effort"). Likewise, the courts of this state have developed differing language regarding a party's duty to mitigate in other contexts. We hold that the landlord's duty to mitigate requires the landlord to use objectively reasonable efforts to fill the premises when the tenant vacates in breach of the lease.

We stress that this is not an absolute duty. The landlord is not required to simply fill the premises with any willing tenant; the replacement tenant must be suitable under the circumstances. Nor does the landlord's failure to mitigate give rise to a cause of action by the tenant. Rather, the landlord's failure to use reasonable efforts to mitigate damages bars the landlord's recovery against the breaching tenant only to the extent that damages reasonably could have been avoided. Similarly, the amount of damages that the landlord actually avoided by releasing the premises will reduce the landlord's recovery.

Further, we believe that the tenant properly bears the burden of proof to demonstrate that the landlord has mitigated or failed to mitigate damages and the amount by which the landlord reduced or could have reduced its damages. The traditional rule in other contexts is that the breaching party must show that the nonbreaching party could have reduced its damages. In the landlord-tenant context, although there is some split of authority, many other jurisdictions have placed the burden of proving mitigation or failure to mitigate upon the breaching tenant. . . .

The final issue to resolve regarding the duty to mitigate is to which types of actions by the landlord the duty will apply. Traditionally, Texas courts have regarded the landlord as having four causes of action against a tenant for breach of the lease and abandonment. First, the landlord can maintain the lease, suing for rent as it becomes due. Second, the landlord can treat the breach as an anticipatory repudiation, repossess, and sue for the present value of future rentals reduced by the reasonable cash market value of the property for the remainder of the lease term. Third, the landlord can treat the breach as anticipatory, repossess, release the property, and sue the tenant for the difference between the contractual rent and the amount received from the new tenant. Fourth, the landlord can declare the lease forfeited (if the lease so provides) and relieve the tenant of liability for future rent.

The landlord must have a duty to mitigate when suing for anticipatory repudiation. Because the cause of action is contractual in nature, the contractual duty to mitigate should apply. The landlord's option to maintain the lease and sue for rent as it becomes due, however, is more troubling. To require the landlord to mitigate in that instance would force the landlord to reenter the premises and thereby risk terminating the lease or accepting the tenant's surrender. We thus hold that, when exercising the option to maintain the lease in effect and sue for rent as it becomes due following the tenant's breach and abandonment, the landlord has a duty to mitigate only if (1) the landlord actually reenters, or (2) the lease allows the landlord to reenter the premises without accepting surrender, forfeiting the lease, or being construed as evicting the tenant. A suit for anticipatory repudiation, an actual reentry, or a contractual right of reentry subject to the above conditions will therefore give rise to the landlord's duty to mitigate damages upon the tenant's breach and abandonment.

VI

In their first amended answer, Hill Country and Barbara Hill specifically contended that the Palisades failed to mitigate its damages. Because the court of appeals upheld the trial court's refusal to submit their mitigation instruction, we reverse the judgment of the court of appeals and remand for a new trial.

NOTES AND QUESTIONS

1. Competing Policies. The Texas Supreme Court in *Austin Hill* identifies policies on both sides of the contracts-conveyancing debate in electing to follow the overwhelming trend toward mitigation. Still, the highest courts in New York and Pennsylvania recently have identified additional rationales in decisions retaining the conveyancing approach that rejects mitigation. In Holy Properties Ltd., L.P. v. Kenneth Cole Productions, Inc., 87 N.Y.2d 130, 661 N.E.2d 694, 637 N.Y.S.2d 964, 966 (1995), the Court of Appeals of New York reasoned that:

> Defendant [tenant] urges us to reject this settled [conveyancing] law and adopt the contract rationale recognized by some courts in this State and elsewhere. We decline to do so. Parties who engage in transactions based on prevailing law must be able to rely on the stability of such precedents. In business transactions particularly, the certainty of settled rules is often more important than whether the established rule is better than another or even whether it is the "correct" rule. This is perhaps true in real property more than any other area of the law, where established precedents are not lightly to be set aside.

The Court of Appeals had adopted similar reasoning in Maxton Builders v. Lo Galbo, 68 N.Y.2d 373, 502 N.E.2d 184, 509 N.Y.S.2d 507 (1986) in addressing the rights of a seller to retain a breaching buyer's down payment. Rejecting a duty to mitigate, the Pennsylvania Supreme Court also pointed to the reliance interest of landlords on the settled authority of the conveyancing principle, as well as its simplicity:

> If the landlord is required to relet the premises, there is unlimited potential for litigation initiated by the tenant concerning the landlord's due diligence, whether the landlord made necessary repairs which would be required to relet the premises, whether the landlord was required to borrow money to make repairs, whether the landlord hired the right agent or a sufficient number of agents to rent the premises, whether the tenants who were refused should have been accepted, and countless other questions in which the breaching tenant is permitted to mount an assault on whatever the landlord did to mitigate damages, alleging that it was somehow deficient.
>
> . . . [T]here is a fundamental unfairness in allowing the breaching tenant to require the nonbreaching landlord to mitigate the damages caused by the tenant. This unfairness takes the form of depriving the landlord of the benefit of [its] bargain, forcing the landlord to expend time, energy and money to respond to the tenant's breach, and putting the landlord at risk of further expense of lawsuits and counterclaims in a matter which [it] justifiably assumed was closed.

Stonehedge Square Ltd. Partnership v. Movie Merchants, Inc., 552 Pa. 412, 715 A.2d 1082, 1084-1085 (1998). In your opinion, which approach is more compelling? Should the obligation to rerent, if any, depend on whether the tenancy is commercial or residential?

As noted in *Austin Hill*, most jurisdictions by statute or case authority require the landlord to employ objectively reasonable efforts to mitigate its damages by reletting the premises upon the tenant's breach and abandonment. Indeed, the Texas legislature eventually codified the doctrine. Tex. Prop. Code Ann. §91.006(a) ("A landlord has a duty to mitigate damages if a tenant abandons the leased premises in violation of the lease."). Query if the *Austin Hill* decision otherwise would have imposed a duty to mitigate in all circumstances; see particularly Part V of the opinion.

2. Nature of Mitigation Duty. As recognized by the Pennsylvania Supreme Court, the sufficiency of a landlord's efforts to mitigate routinely has sparked challenges from breaching tenants. E.g., Kallman v. Radioshack Corp., 315 F.3d 731 (7th Cir. 2002) (no clear error by trial court in finding landlord failed to reasonably mitigate damages given landlord's bargaining for higher rent from substitute tenants, five-month delay in engaging a broker, leaving the property in poor condition, and ultimately suffering a two and one-half year period to re-lease the property); Leavenworth Plaza Associates, L.P., v. L.A.G. Enterprises, 28 Kan. App. 2d 269, 16 P.3d 314 (2000) (evidence supported trial court decision of failure to mitigate in rerenting pizza restaurant space; no evidence of advertising in local papers and the landlord should have considered dividing the space or changing the type of tenant); O'Brien v. Black, 162 Vt. 448, 648 A.2d 1374 (1994) (same result where landlord had discouraged a potential replacement tenant because it decided to try to lure a national chain tenant that ultimately leased the premises and paid higher rent; landlord could not impose the cost of this strategy on the breaching tenant by holding it responsible for rent during the waiting period).

Landlords in mitigation jurisdictions may attempt to avoid this burden through contractual waivers of any obligation to relet for the tenant's benefit. Should courts enforce these waivers?

Consider the position of a landlord with the contractual right to prohibit assignments or sublets in its sole and absolute discretion, Chapter 10A4, supra. Does the recognition of a duty reasonably to accept a substitute tenant on the original tenant's default undercut this contractual expectation? See Danpar Associates v. Somersville Mills Sales Room, 182 Conn. 444, 438 A.2d 708 (1980) (landlord argued that to deny it damages because it refused to rerent the premises to a proposed substitute tenant contravened its rights under a sole discretion assignment clause; while "superficially appealing," the court explained the argument missed the point because the landlord could still reject the proffered tenant and relet to a tenant of its own choice). Is this persuasive?

3. Damages in Mitigation Jurisdictions. The inconsistency between recovering damages for the remainder of the breached lease term and the landlord's ongoing obligation to mitigate prompted the Utah Supreme Court to reject the so-called multiple cause of action approach (which limits damages to those accrued at the time of trial and requires initiation of a new lawsuit(s) for later arising rents) and the anticipatory breach approach (awarding the present value of the difference between the contract rent and the market rent over the remaining lease term) in favor of retained jurisdiction. Under this approach, the court retains jurisdiction to enter new damage awards as additional rents accrue in excess of mitigation. Reid v. Mutual of Omaha Ins. Co., 776 P.2d 896, 908 (Utah 1989); see generally Flynn, Duty to Mitigate Damages upon a Tenant's Abandonment, 34 Real Prop., Prob. & Tr. J. 721 (2000), and Sandler, Waiving the Duty to Mitigate in Commercial Leases, 5 Wm. & Mary Bus. L. Rev. 647 (2014).

4. Damages in Non-Mitigation Jurisdictions. One court rejecting mitigation summarized the options available to the landlord: "(1) it could do nothing and collect the full rent due under the lease, (2) it could accept the tenant's surrender, reenter the premises and relet them for its own account thereby releasing the tenant from further liability for rent, or (3) it could notify the tenant that it was entering and reletting the premises for the tenant's benefit [thereby reducing the tenant's damages]." Holy Properties Ltd., L.P. v. Kenneth Cole Productions, Inc., 87 N.Y.2d 130, 661 N.E.2d 694, 637 N.Y.S.2d 964, 966 (1995). See also Mesilla Valley Mall Co. v. Crown Indus., 111 N.M. 663, 808 P.2d 633 (1991) (affirming conclusion of trial court that allowing natural history museum to occupy abandoned premises in shopping center rent-free while a rent-paying replacement was sought released the breaching tenant from further liability).

5. Contractual Damage Provisions. Occasionally, landlords not satisfied with the potential for proving their actual damages will bargain ex ante for contractual damage allowances that exceed the tenant's rental obligation. These provisions may be challenged by the tenant as an unenforceable penalty, and the results under a liquidated damages analysis are mixed. Compare Harbor Island Holdings, LLC v. Kim, 107 Cal. App. 4th 790, 132 Cal. Rptr. 2d 406 (2003) (lease provision doubling rent on default struck down as unreasonable penalty) with Benderson-Wainberg, LP v. Atlantic Toys, 228 F. Supp. 2d 584 (E.D. Pa. 2002) (applying New Jersey law) (enforcing liquidated damages provision in shopping center lease by toy store requiring defaulting tenant to pay double rent; landlord expert testified to potential ripple effect of breached lease on percentage rents from other tenants in shopping mall, which tenant failed to challenge or rebut).

PRACTITIONER'S CORNER

Commercial Lease Negotiations

For drafting tips and advice in negotiating the terms of commercial lease transactions, see ABA Section of Real Property, Probate and Trust Law, The Commercial Property Lease: Structuring Agreements, Assessing Expenses, and Preventing Liabilities for Landlords and Tenants (P. Randolph, Jr. ed., 1993); Bell, Checklist for Reviewing or Drafting Commercial Leases, 5 Utah B.J. 7 (Feb. 1992); Davidson, Leasing Commercial Real Estate: Issues and Negotiating, 18 Real Est. Rev. 69 (Spring 1988); Di Sciullo, Negotiating a Commercial Lease from the Tenant's Perspective, 18 Real Est. L.J. 27 (Summer 1989); Goldstein, Taking the Bite Out of Form Leases, 8 Prob. & Prop. 22 (Jan.-Feb. 1994); Stein, How Lender's Counsel Reviews a Lease, 36 Prac. Real Est. Law. 4 (Nov. 2014).

---

7. The Rise of "Green" Leases

Recently, it has become more common to see commercial landlords and tenants pursuing their business strategy with an eye on energy conservation and environmental stewardship, or so-called "green" objectives. Businesses are now more willing to implement green measures, which can be expensive, with the understanding that they may achieve cost savings over the long term and that they may enjoy increased goodwill with customers, clients, and even potential employees by being perceived as having altruistic motives. One appealing way of going green is to receive a certification for the building from one of many third-party organizations that rate the level in which a building adheres to green standards.

The preeminent rating system for U.S. buildings is maintained by the U.S. Green Building Council (USGBC) and known as the Leadership in Energy and Environmental Design, or "LEED" certification, which was first introduced in 1998. Lumpkin, The Latest in Green Development: Advising Your Client on the New Standard for Real Estate Projects, 85 Fla. B.J. 32 (April 2011). To obtain LEED certification, developers submit the specifications of their building project to a section of the USGBC known as the Green Building Certification Institute which, in turn, may issue to the developer one of four progressively superior certifications in accord with how well the project complies with its requirements found generally in six categories of sustainability. These categories for obtaining points or credits are identified as (1) sustainable sites, (2) water efficiency, (3) energy and atmosphere, (4) materials and resources, (5) environmental quality, and (6) innovation of design. The rules and criteria of the LEED system of certification can be further explored at www.usgbc.org, maintained by USGBC. The following available LEED certifications are shown with the required number of corresponding credits or points:

LEED CERTIFIED	40 to 49 Points
LEED SILVER	50 to 59 Points
LEED GOLD	60 to 79 Points
LEED PLATINUM	80 Points and Above

LEED certification, however, does not necessarily end with the construction or renovation of a building. The USGBC requires a period of ongoing adherence to its standards and appropriate maintenance of the building to keep the initial certification. Furthermore, simply to realize the benefits of the design, building owners and tenants may have ongoing responsibilities that are not normally considered in commercial leases. Apportioning these responsibilities has been a new development in commercial real estate leasing. The commercial lease can now serve as the framework of responsibilities and obligations of the building owner and its tenant to allow a building designated as "green" to succeed in its objectives. Many businesses, including Fortune 500 companies, have adopted policies requiring adherence to green standards, illustrating that green issues for leases can originate not only from the landlord/developer but also from the tenant with its goals for going green.

Where the client previously may have been concerned with the bottom line when negotiating commercial lease provisions, leases between a landlord and tenant with green objectives now create new issues of concern for counsel. In a green lease, costs to the building in terms of capital expenditures and maintenance are generally higher and different in nature than a typical commercial lease. The building might require more costly high-efficient lights, using special waste services to accommodate recycling or trash disposal, or hiring new service personnel to maintain energy-efficient mechanical elements. These new costs must be considered when negotiating the common area maintenance charges that are normally a predominant part of a commercial lease. And if these increased expenses also create the benefit of reducing the cost of utility consumption for the building over the long term, how should the savings be apportioned among the parties? As counsel in a green lease negotiation, one must also realize that despite the need to follow through on upholding the standards for LEED certification (or some other third-party certification) the landlord or tenant may have other green objectives outside the original design of the project that require implementation in the lease.

There are many important issues that reoccur in the negotiation of green leases with LEED provisions that have become customary for these transactions. One concern is that green leases should remain in effect for an extended term to allow for reductions in environmental impact otherwise arising from a tenant relocation. In fact, criteria for LEED certification include credit for an applicant that can show a lease with a term of ten or more years. (A five-year lease with a five-year option to renew would not count.) Other concerns naturally involve ensuring that the use of the building by the tenant will comply with the landlord's sustainability policies. For example, the lease may now have to specify that the tenant is required to follow a recycling program or commit to a water usage that is below average standards. Provisions regarding tenant's improvements or alterations to the building would also have to adhere to standards proscribed for the building. This may be the most important aspect of a green lease if the tenant is expected to pursue the build-out of its leased space. Typical language in the lease may require that the tenant "agree to seek and maintain LEED certification for all improvements or alterations to the Premises." The same issue of complying with LEED standards would also arise with the maintenance and repairs undertaken by tenant and must be addressed in the commercial lease. Other lease provisions may be necessary, such as requiring the tenant to adopt and periodically disclose a plan for insuring the quality of air or water in the building. For further discussion, see Kaplow, Does a Green Building Need a Green Lease?, 38 U. Balt. L. Rev. 375 (Spring 2009); Miller, Commercial Green Leasing in the Era of Climate Change: Practical Solutions for Balancing Risks, Burdens, and Incentives, 40 Envtl. L. Rep. News & Analysis 10487 (2010); Cantwell, "Leedigation"—The Latest on LEED and Green Buildings, 84 N.Y. St. B.J. 46 (Feb 2012).

B. CREDIT LEASES AS SECURITY

As explained in the following excerpt, "credit leases"[9] with the major ("prime") tenants generally form the foundation of the economic viability of any commercial real estate project because it is the rental income stream from these leases (as opposed to the underlying land and physical improvements) that pays the debt-service payments on the mortgage and constitutes the real security for the loan (in the parlance of real estate professionals, it "feeds the mortgage").

This is why the postconstruction loan commitment for a commercial mortgage loan will require as a condition-precedent to funding that certain credit leases be in effect with creditworthy tenants for specified periods of time (that, for financial underwriting and security reasons, usually coincide with the term of the loan) and that lender's counsel review the form and substance of each lease to assure the lender that the rental income stream cannot be reduced or abated by the tenants and that the lender can tolerate the lease provisions as a would-be landlord if the lender should be forced to step into the shoes of the borrower in the event of foreclosure.

M. Madison, J. Dwyer, and S. Bender, The Law of Real Estate Financing
§5.67 (2016)

ANALYSIS OF SHOPPING CENTER AND OTHER HIGH-CREDIT LEASES BY PERMANENT LENDER

In the case of a mortgage loan on an apartment building or on a garden apartment complex, the permanent lender's appraisal-underwriting process involves an evaluation of the projected aggregate rental flow from the short-term occupancy leases, which are regarded as fundable by the lender. However, in the case of loans involving shopping centers, office buildings with long-term tenants, warehouses and other industrial facilities, and urban-renewal projects master-leased to a local housing authority—the security for the loan is the value attributable by the lender's appraiser to the rental obligations of specified high-credit tenants. Accordingly, in such loan transactions, the lender will want to evaluate the credit standing of each major or "prime" tenant. Also, the lender will demand, as a nonnegotiable condition of the commitment, the right to approve the form and substance of each lease, including the term, the tenant, and the rent payable, because it will expect the rental income stream from these leases to pay

---

9. Don't confuse the phrase "credit lease" with "high-credit leases" that are discussed at Chapter 7C1.

off the debt service on the loan. The other standard requirements in the commitment letter as to occupancy leases are: (1) that each prime lease be assigned to the lender as additional security and that the assignment be recorded and notice of the assignment served on the tenant; (2) that the lease be in full force and effect; (3) that there be no rental offsets or claims or defenses to enforcement; (4) that the tenant shall have accepted its premises, confirmed commencement of its lease term, acknowledged that it is in occupancy, and be paying rent on [a] current basis; and (5) that satisfactory evidence be submitted to the lender as to all of the foregoing.

Before the leases are executed and delivered, the developer's lawyer should be familiar with the lender's requirements as to leases. Lenders' lawyers welcome the opportunity to work with lawyers for the developer in the drafting of leases. Correspondence should be promptly initiated by developer's counsel while lease negotiations are under way. Unfortunately, the developer is frequently so anxious to secure the major leases in order to assure the financing that the developer's lawyer is often faced with a "fait accompli" in the form of a completed lease. [The lawyer] must then try to persuade the lender's lawyers that the lease provides the necessary assurances that the rental stream will continue for the term of the loan, or must face the onerous task of cajoling the tenant to modify the lease in order to satisfy the permanent lender. Occasionally, the lender's lawyers are able to persuade a major tenant to sign a side letter providing that as long as the lender has an interest in the property, the lease shall be deemed modified as required by the lender. In some instances, these leases are sufficiently long-term to liquidate the loan indebtedness by the loan maturity date. The perspicacious lender must also visualize itself as having to live with these lease provisions in the event it steps in as owner-landlord after a serious default by the mortgagor.

Consequently, when negotiating occupancy lease terms with prime tenants, the developer must be mindful of the lender's requirements designed to protect the rental income stream from cancellation or abatement. Otherwise, the developer or its attorney may be caught in the middle on the closing date between a permanent lender insisting on changes in the lease and a prime tenant, with equal bargaining clout, who refuses to renegotiate a lease executed months or even years ago.

The following typifies the language in a loan commitment whereby the post-construction lender imposes general standards for the bulk of the occupancy leases with the minor ("secondary" tenants) but reserves the right to approve the form and substance of each credit lease with the prime tenants (such as the Widget Corporation of America in the master hypothetical) and requires a conditional assignment of the leases as additional collateral for the loan. By contrast, in the case of a mortgage loan on an apartment building, each lease would not be separately reviewed and approved because the same lease format would be used for all the tenants.

SPACE LEASES

1. General Requirements. All Space Leases shall have a minimum term of three years. Space Leases having an original term of five or more years, or having an original term of less than five years but containing renewal options which, if exercised, would extend the total term of the lease beyond five years, shall be in form and substance satisfactory to Lender, and shall contain provisions requiring increases in annual rent, to be effective on the sixth anniversary of the lease, including renewal options, and every fifth year thereafter, in an amount equal to sixty percent of the annual increase in the United States Department of Labor, Bureau of Labor Statistics, "State of Fuller Consumer Price Index for all Urban Consumers—All Items" or such other index as may be substituted therefor (hereinafter referred to as the "Consumer Price Index" or "CPI"). All Space Leases shall be assigned to Lender as additional security for the Loan and shall be unconditionally subordinate to the Mortgage. Lender will consider granting Tenants leasing more than 15,000 Rentable Square Feet, non-disturbance agreements provided (i) the Space Lease is on the standard lease form and is otherwise satisfactory to Lender and its Law Department; (ii) the Lender's standard form of non-disturbance agreement is used; and (iii) the Borrower becomes obligated to pay reasonable processing charges with respect to each nondisturbance agreement and the fees and disbursements of any special counsel selected by Lender's Law Department.

2. Leasing Commissions. Any agreement to pay leasing commissions shall provide that the obligation to pay such commissions will not be enforceable against any party other than the party who entered into such agreement and will be subordinate to the Mortgage. Lender shall be furnished with evidence of the foregoing satisfactory to it and its Law Department in form and substance, and a provision incorporating the foregoing requirement in form and substance satisfactory to Lender and its Law Department shall be contained in the Mortgage.

3. WCA Lease. There shall be a Space Lease of at least 200,000 Rentable Square Feet in the Building to Widget Corporation of America, Inc. ("WCA Lease") at an annual rent of not less than $ _____ and with a remaining term at the Closing Date of not less than ten years. The WCA Lease shall be subordinate to the Mortgage and otherwise in form and substance be satisfactory to Lender and its Law Department, including without limitation, provisions dealing with escalation for expenses based on CPI or otherwise, and for taxes. The WCA Lease shall be in force, free from default, with the term commenced on or prior to the Closing Date. Upon approval of the form and substance of the

WCA Lease, Lender shall enter into an agreement with WCA in which Lender shall agree that, in the event of a foreclosure of the Mortgage, Lender shall not disturb WCA's possession of its space in the Building provided that WCA is not then in default beyond any applicable grace period. The form and substance of said agreement shall be satisfactory to Lender and its Law Department.

4. Prohibitions in Respect of Space Leases. No Space Lease having an original term of more than five years shall be modified, abridged or terminated, nor shall any surrender thereof be accepted, without the prior written consent of Lender. Any Space Lease having an original term of five years or less may be modified or abridged by the Borrower without the prior written consent of Lender so long as said modification or abridgement does not increase any material obligation of the landlord thereunder or decrease the rental or any other material obligation of the tenant thereunder. In addition, any Space Lease which has an original term of five years or less may be terminated by the Borrower without the prior written consent of the Lender if the tenant thereunder shall be in default.

The Borrower shall not collect rent for more than one month in advance except that Borrower may accept rent for up to three months in advance upon the execution of the Space Lease by all the parties thereto, provided that such advance rent is applied to the rents at the beginning of the term of the Space Lease, or held in trust as a security deposit for the performance of the terms of the Space Lease, with any deposit at the expiration of the term of the Space Lease to be applied to any rent then due or to be refunded to the tenant upon such expiration.

As a prelude to the problem that follows, the following excerpt of a speech by the late Mendes Hershman (former vice president and general counsel of the New York Life Insurance Company) should help you understand how postconstruction lenders analyze occupancy leases.

Hershman, Leases—Pitfalls and Pratfalls
Address to Business Loan Seminar, New York Life Insurance
Co., Mackinac Island, Michigan (Sept. 26-28, 1967)

. . . . Most leases, particularly the leases to high-credit tenants with their massive bargaining power, present tough questions of judgment as to the adequacy of the "business-legal" components of the lease. . . .

. . . What are these risks or conditions, terms or provisions in leases which raise these business-legal questions for judgment? I will advert to some of the major pitfalls in the leases we get to review. . . .

First, the matter of subordination. In a good many states, upon foreclosure of a mortgage, all leases which are subsequent to the mortgage are automatically terminated irrespective of the parties' intentions or whether the tenant is made a party to the foreclosure.[10] In other states, and New York is an example, the mortgagee must join the tenant in the foreclosure action to terminate the lease.[11] Obviously then, in the states where there is automatic termination on foreclosure, the leases that the lender is relying on and hopes to keep must be made to prime the mortgage and as a general rule we want all credit leases in such jurisdiction prior to our mortgage. To the extent that we can, we like to retain prime rights, however, for the landlord to condemnation awards, fire insurance proceeds, and of course in respect to any option of the tenant to purchase the property. It is helpful if the mortgage instrument, in those states where leases are automatically terminated by foreclosure, contains a provision giving the mortgagee the right unilaterally to subordinate the mortgage to any subsequent lease.

I have seen leases which provide for subordination to all mortgages on condition that the mortgagee will agree not to disturb the tenant in the event of foreclosure. It is dangerous to accept this without the additional provision in the lease that in the event of foreclosure tenant will attorn to the purchaser at foreclosure sale. We should also see to it that if the lease is subordinated, it be subordinated only to the first mortgage so that a subsequent junior mortgagee will not have the power to cut off the lease.

If you have the opportunity to advise a developer in your state, if it is a state where there is automatic termination on the foreclosure, I suggest you tell [it] to try to get a provision in [its] leases giving [it] the option of subordinating the lease to a first mortgage. This will then give the mortgagee to whom [it] comes for financing the opportunity to control the developer's action in this respect by provision in the mortgage.

Second, the matter of covenant to pay. Many leases provide that as a condition of tenant's right to occupy the premises, rent in a specified amount be paid by the tenant, [which phraseology] does not actually [constitute a] covenant to pay. Our lawyers worry about such condition. They want tenant's express promise to pay the rent and it may indeed be important. They believe, and rightly, that the lease should expressly provide: "The tenant covenants and agrees to pay $ _____ as rent." For example, if the tenant has not covenanted to pay rent and has a right to assign the lease and assigns it, [it] will no longer be obligated to pay rent. But with a covenant to pay in the lease, his obligation to pay would survive the assignment.

Third, the matter of default provisions—survival of liability for damages in event of default. An F. W. Woolworth lease, just by way of example, provides that if the tenant defaults in the payment of rent after 30 days' notice, the landlord may declare the lease forfeit. There is no provision giving the landlord a

10. E.g., McDermott v. Burke, 16 Cal. 580, 590 (1860).—EDS.

11. E.g., Metropolitan Life Insur. Co. v. Childs Co., 230 N.Y. 285, 296, 130 N.E. 295, 299 (1921); Davis v. Boyajian, Inc., 11 Ohio Misc. 97, 102, 229 N.E.2d 116, 119 (1967). It is well settled that a lease senior to a mortgage is unaffected by foreclosure.—EDS.

right to damages for this breach nor a right after termination to collect rent until he rerents or the difference between the rent he receives after rerenting and the rent reserved in the lease to Woolworth. Of course, in a case of a tenant of Woolworth's financial responsibility, there is little practical concern about this. Actually the landlord wouldn't terminate the lease but would simply sue for rent as it became due. But if it is not a lease of a high-credit tenant, we are the more likely to insist on adequate default provisions.

Fourth, the matter of continuous possession. Unless the lease specifically provides that the named tenant will continue to operate the premises for the particular use for which the premises are leased, the tenant normally has a choice of discontinuing business or, if [it] has a right to assign or sublet, then do that and discontinue [its] own operation in the premises. Inasmuch as our underwriting is predicated for the most part on the fixed minimum rent rather than overrates, the lack of a continuous operation provision will not bother us in the case of high-credit tenants. On the other hand, and this may well be true in many shopping center leases, there are leases which are made dependent on the particular high-credit tenant staying in business in the center so that unless there is a continuous operation clause in the high-credit tenant's lease and the latter goes out, a default will thereby be created in the dependent lease or leases. It is therefore incumbent on the lawyer reviewing leases for a shopping center loan to watch for the dependent leases, bring this to the attention of the mortgage department and let the latter judge the effect on its rating in the underwriting process. In a rare case a court may imply a continuous operation clause.

Fifth, the matter of tenant's rights to cure defaults. First, we should keep in mind that if tenant is given a lien for what [it] spends to cure the landlord's default that is not a business question but raises a strictly legal objection because creation thereby of a prior encumbrance violates our investment statutes. Second, a provision requiring landlord to pay the charges on any mortgage upon the leased premises and permitting tenant, in the event of the landlord's default, to cancel the lease—a provision contained in some national chain leases—is obviously unacceptable because tenant could then cancel for default in our own first mortgage depriving us of the security on which we relied in making the loan and at a time when the security is most needed; also, such a clause permits cancellation for defaults in junior mortgages for which there is otherwise no reason for the first mortgagee to cure such defaults.

A more common provision does not permit cancellation for landlord's default in mortgages but permits tenant to cure such defaults and recoup reimbursement out of subsequent rentals. This, too, is objectionable because such a set-off could be used to cure a junior mortgage default and deprive us of the security of the rental to which we as first mortgagee are primarily entitled.

If the provision is applicable only to mortgages prior in lien to the lease as, for example, the Woolworth provision, we would confirm that the lease was prior to our first mortgage and require deletion of any subordination provisions in the lease. . . .

In conclusion on this point of tenant's right to cure defaults, it may be well to note that any offset against rent which is permitted to a tenant in the lease should be limited to offsets arising under the lease, not from *any* indebtedness of the landlord to the tenant however incurred.

Sixth, the matter of termination for (a) "wastebasket" fires and (b) condemnation. (a) Clauses in leases which permit termination in event of fire are completely objectionable. Some leases, like Woolworth's, provide that in the event of damage or destruction all rent abates until the landlord has restored the premises and delivered the premises to the tenant in the condition required by the tenant. This, too, is obnoxious to the lender because it makes no distinction between the "wastebasket" fire and the serious fire. So long as the fire is not ground for cancellation, the particular clause is negotiable. For example, under the Penney leases the landlord is required to keep the building of which the leased premises are a part insured for fire and extended coverage to the extent of full insurable value, [and] the landlord and Penney must be named insureds and the proceeds applied to the cost of restoration to the extent required for such purposes. It makes no provision for payment of the proceeds to a mortgagee under a standard mortgagee clause, but we are able to secure from Penney [an] agreement to make the proceeds payable to [the mortgagee] under a standard mortgagee clause on our undertaking that the proceeds received by us shall be made available for repair and restoration upon presentation of bills and lien waivers and provided the carrier does not claim that some act of the landlord and tenant who are named insured[s] has not voided the policies. This is satisfactory to us. So long as we control the proceeds and there is no obligation to repair beyond the amount thereof and any diminution of rent would be in proper relation to loss of space, we are satisfied to use . . . the proceeds for restoration.

(b) Provisions for condemnation while presenting similar aspects are more difficult to negotiate. Thus, if a partial taking results in a reduction of rent, the mortgagee should insist that a part of the award sufficient to offset the rent reduction be applied to the debt with only the balance available for replacing damaged improvements. National chains such as Penney generally provide in their leases an option to terminate the lease if all or any part of the premises are taken even if the part taken is inconsequential or temporary and apply this also to parking areas required under the leases; also, if the lease is not terminated, that the landlord restore the premises as required by Penney and reduce the rent proportionately on a floor space ratio; also, that the tenant share in any condemnation award to the extent of actual damage sustained by it which means, of course, a possibility of eating up most of the award. Our mortgage department has been willing to accept a condemnation clause with a highly rated tenant like Penney if Penney's right to terminate on partial condemnation is limited to a taking in excess of a reasonable percentage of floor area and parking lot area, in the latter case coupled with an obligation of the landlord to provide equivalent parking space.

In the process of underwriting, the possibility of condemnation must be thoroughly evaluated. An absolute right to cancel, no matter how slight the condemnation, is obnoxious. The right to cancel should be limited to a taking, in excess of a definite percentage of area, acceptable to the mortgage department, or if it reduces the parking area to a ratio below a rate of 1.5:1 to 2:1, or below a specified area, and provided there is a right in the landlord to preclude cancellation by substituting other parking, perhaps including double deck parking. Where the minimum rent is reduced, the minimum sales base used in computing percentage rent should be reduced pro rata and tenant should not be allowed to participate in the award except to the extent of loss to its fixtures and improvements.

Seventh, the matter of use clauses—exclusives—radius restrictions. For one very good reason shopping center leases particularly should have use clauses which specify the type of business to be conducted or the kind of merchandise to be sold on the premises. A specific use clause will minimize conflicts with exclusive clauses then or thereafter granted in other leases. Anyone who has had to review shopping center leases finds reconciling exclusives the most burdensome of all tasks. There are all too many gray areas where conflicts are or may develop and the business risks of justified lease terminations attendant thereon must be evaluated. One caveat must be kept in mind if the provision is "the tenant shall use" rather than "the premises shall be used," that on a permitted assignment or subletting there may be no restriction on the assignee or sublessee. Obviously it is better that the provision be "the premises shall be used" for such and such purposes.

Another point to be kept is that if the premises are to be used "only" for such use, the court is more likely to uphold the restriction than if such restrictive word is absent. Where a restriction is to limit tenant's sales to merchandise sold in tenant's other stores, it is best to insert "now sold" as more specific and precluding problems if the character of the tenant's operations changes. For example, many retailers want to be protected against discount houses but if a chain acquires a string of discount houses a restriction to merchandise "sold in tenant's other stores" won't prevent conversion to a discount operation in this shopping center. Our mortgage department would like to rely on the self-interest and sophistication of developers to give exclusives reluctantly and to limit their effect so as to narrow the range of merchandise and geographic area, hopefully to the existing center. Unfortunately too few developers are sophisticated and their self-interest leads them to take "name" tenants on almost any basis. Faced with the likelihood of overlapping exclusives we try at the very least to get the remedies of tenants limited to suits for injunction or damage and eliminate right to abate the rent or terminate the lease. When national chains simply won't narrow their use clause, then the landlord when giving exclusives must except the particular premises occupied by that chain from the operation of the exclusives granted to others.

The courts impose the obligation on the landlord to enforce the restriction by reasonable legal means and if [it] doesn't, the injured tenant may terminate the lease. They generally impose a duty of notice from the injured tenant to the landlord before finding a breach of the covenant, giving tenant a right to remove.

The courts don't favor restrictions and inquire into the facts as to whether the businesses are substantially similar, that is, whether there is a substantial overlapping of products. For example, a New York court considered whether the sale of women's blouse-skirt combinations violated an exclusive for dresses and found that these are considered separate businesses in the garment industry, so held there was no violation of the exclusive; and another . . . New York court found that an exclusive for a restaurant was not violated by a luncheonette because of substantial dissimilarities in menu, price, and decor. Courts will also look into the percentage of total sales of each party represented by overlapping articles. For that reason it is desirable to keep away from exclusives for specified items and make the restrictions descriptive of lines of business.

One aspect of this restrictive covenant field which is particularly troublesome to the mortgage lender is the radius restriction whereby landlord agrees that neither it, nor its successors, assigns, subsidiaries, etc. will lease or permit any property within a certain radius from the shopping center, or covering the center "as it may be expanded" or with respect to land adjacent to the shopping center, to be used for the particular restricted use. In such instance the mortgagee is powerless to protect against it because the radius of the restriction goes beyond the mortgaged property and, what's more, if we foreclosed we would become bound by the restriction. Sometimes a tenant will agree that, so long as we hold the mortgage or have an interest in the premises, tenant won't exercise [its] right to cancel or abate rent but will enforce its rights by injunction or in suit for damages. Landlords if they must take a radius restriction should try to be specific as to the area covered—not just the XYZ Shopping Center because this would include any expansion of it—and limit it to land which is covered by the mortgage all expect to get. Not only with restrictive covenants as to use but as to all other covenants—warranty of title, parking rights and ratios, payment of taxes, fire insurance, initial and continued occupancy of identified co-tenants— the landlord must be careful to limit the geographic extent of [its] obligation to what [it] owns because the mortgage lender must be satisfied that the mortgagor- landlord can comply physically and legally with the obligations under the leases which are to be mortgagee's prime security. The mortgagor-landlord is going to have to show [its] proposed mortgagee [its] capacity to comply with any lease covenant with respect to any property not owned by [it] in fee or not included in the lender's mortgage by reciprocal easement agreements or parking declaration or other recorded documents which will bind all subsequent interests in the property to be mortgaged by this lender.

Eighth, the matter of alterations and expansions. Rights reserved in the tenant under the lease to make substantial alterations raises the question of mechanics' and materialmen's liens priming the mortgage. It is desirable to get some limitation on cost. If possible, it is useful to get bonding requirements unless, of course, the size and character of the tenant makes the possibility of unpaid mechanics liens remote.

In some chain leases, of which Penney is a good example, the tenant adds to its unconditional right to make alterations that any additional expense to which tenant is put in its alteration work by reason of requirements of state and local law will be paid by landlord. Some of the possibilities of these rights to alter and expand are enough to frighten reviewing counsel; viz., violation of other tenants' rights in service drives, maintenance of parking ratios, imposition on landlord of additional real estate taxes, insurance, heating, lighting and sewer charges, all of which are beyond landlord's control. The future expansion rights are often related to [the] amount of gross sales which, if exceeded, impose on landlord obligations to construct a specified addition. This raises the possibility of the landlord not complying and, should we as mortgage lender take over, our legal inability to make an additional investment because it is beyond the legal ratio to appraised value and because we must go to the Superintendent of Insurance for permission to make the investment. Furthermore, in theory, since a national chain like Penney won't give up its right to assign and sublet, we may have a situation of a costly expansion and shortly thereafter the national chain with its greater sales potential assigning or subletting to a tenant without such sales potential. We have been able to negotiate with Penney an amendment as to alteration and expansion of the premises under which the tenant must get landlord's prior approval of structural changes, not to be unreasonably withheld, and give up the right to cancel if landlord doesn't undertake the expansion. If Penney nevertheless goes ahead with the expansion, tenant's right to offset the cost of the expansion is limited to percentage rentals in excess of a specified minimum rent which is reasonably satisfactory to our mortgage department.

Ninth, miscellaneous problems. . . .

a. Co-tenancy Requirements. It is characteristic of shopping centers to find in leases requirements for the initial occupancy by named co-tenants and sometimes continued occupancy. Where initial occupancy by named co-tenants is required, the situation is not too difficult. If the co-tenant's lease must be non-cancellable for a specified period, then we must look to see if there are exceptions arising out of default, condemnation, damage, bankruptcy, etc. and get tenant's approval of these contingencies for "cancellation." A guarantee of continued occupancy by the named co-tenant is extremely difficult to handle and presents a serious business question. At the very least the provision should be made inapplicable to temporary closings for repairs, etc. and permit landlord to substitute reasonably equivalent co-tenants within a reasonable period of time. If the co-tenant lease is not co-extensive in term with the lease in question and permits an assignment and subletting, merger and consolidation, these should be excepted from the requirement for continued occupancy by the named co-tenant.

b. Cancellation Privileges. Some chain leases provide cancellation for any default of landlord. Any right on the part of the tenant to cancel must be carefully evaluated. A right to cancel for *any* default of the landlord must be whittled down. For example, there are covenants personal to the landlord—[its] own bankruptcy—default in which cannot be cured by the mortgagee and are therefore unacceptable. The mortgagee must try to make a separate agreement with the tenant that the tenant will not exercise the right to cancel until the mortgagee has had a reasonable time to foreclose and get into a position to cure the default.

c. Guarantee. Where the lender is relying on a guarantee of a lease, for example, a lease to a subsidiary which is a shell corporation guaranteed by the financially strong parent, we must take great care that the guarantee will not be affected by bankruptcy, reorganization or insolvency of the tenant, its successors or assigns or the disaffirmance of the lease by a receiver or trustee of the tenant and that the guarantee will be applicable to successors and assigns of the tenant and that there will be no release of liability upon any assignment by the original tenant.

d. Statements of Landlord's Operations. Provision in some chain store leases prohibits landlord from divulging the amount of tenant's sales. Penney's lease, for example, so provides, but tenant will accept a modification permitting divulging of such sales to any bona fide mortgagee in accordance with the provisions of the mortgage where, as in our mortgage, there is a requirement for periodic statements covering landlord's operations.

e. Term of Lease. Some leases provide for commencement on opening of business and ending a specified number of years thereafter, which is satisfactory if the conditions requiring commencement of business are clear and can be complied with and, in addition, as in the Penney lease, there is a right to cancel after a certain number of years on notice and payment of a certain, sometimes nominal amount. We must point this out clearly to our mortgage department which can then evaluate the effect for appraisal and underwriting considerations; also, in relation to any representation the landlord may make in other leases as to the term of this lease.

f. Landlord's Compliance with Conditions as to New Construction. In connection with new construction there are often numerous requirements of the landlord: physical requirements of the site, compliance with laws, with plans and specifications approved by tenant, cost of the work and its completion; compliance with which we must satisfy ourselves or secure tenant's acknowledgement of such compliance by landlord.

g. Percentage Rent. Where the rent reserved, as in some chain store leases, is set at a percentage of sales, we point this up to the mortgage department for their underwriting consideration as to adequacy. In such event, determination of sales on which the percentage is based becomes of genuine concern and, even more so, right[s] to discontinue operations, assign or sublet. We insist that a certain definite term be set before which no right to discontinue business, assign or sublet will be approved and after such term, there shall be an appropriate alternative rent fixed in event of discontinuance and/or subletting or assignment with an option in landlord to cancel. If at all possible, where the rent is only a percentage rent, there should be an obligation on the part of the tenant to devote premises to its retail business and with all due diligence. As part of this due diligence, the mortgage lender should try to minimize the tenant's right to lease out departments to an unusual degree.

h. Security Deposit Agreements. Landlords sometimes require, particularly of tenants with medium to low credit ratios, security deposits, and these tenants may get it into their leases that if the deposit is not returned, tenant either may continue in possession without payment of rent until the deposit is recouped or will secure a prior lien on the premises till repaid. Such a lease must be subordinated to the mortgage if the tenant has acquired a lien on the premises for [its] deposit because the tenant's lien may be a prior encumbrance which may render the institution's mortgage illegal under investment statutes limiting investment to mortgages secured by improved and unencumbered real estate.

i. Purchase Options. A right in the tenant to purchase must be subordinated to the mortgage even if for a price which would pay off the mortgage because even under the latter supposition it is an enlargement of the prepayment privilege and in a minority of jurisdictions gives tenant [the] right to cut off the mortgage. A right of first refusal is not as onerous to a lender and is acceptable to many lenders. Where the option or first refusal is subject to the mortgage, the lender is unaffected except to the extent that [it] must guard against merger of the lease into the fee title. Options to purchase which prime the mortgage raise the question of prior encumbrance and possible illegality of the loan. I must reiterate that in this situation as in all others where the landlord's default would give tenant a right of lien against the premises, the provision is not acceptable to a mortgage lender whose lending is restricted by investment statutes which require that the mortgage not be subject to prior encumbrances.

To be a real estate lawyer handling large, complex transactions sounds glamorous. In a sense, it is. A great deal of money—perhaps hundreds of millions of dollars—is at stake. Decisions have to be made under pressure. And, most important, real estate lawyers can see the results of their labors in the form of bricks and mortar, glass and steel, literally rise before them. In the final analysis, however, the successful real estate lawyer is one who realizes that the work is not all glamour; who does his or her homework at night and on weekends; who drafts documents carefully and reads and rereads them to understand their interrelationship and how a change in one document can affect the other documents and ultimately the client's bottom line. This can sometimes be a rather tedious business, especially when it comes to a review of leases. However, only by understanding each provision in each lease and knowing how they relate to the companion provisions in that lease and other leases in the building or shopping center can the attorney determine the full extent of the risks the client is assuming. The problem below is designed not only as a review of some of the landlord-tenant issues affecting the developer and the postconstruction lender, but also as a training tool in developing those analytical skills a real estate lawyer must have.

> *Problem 10-2*

See the Documents Manual for a compilation of clauses from an actual office building lease and an actual shopping center lease that are relevant to the issues discussed above. You will see that these leases are not always drafted with precision. Assume that you represent alternatively Dan Developer as the developer-landlord, Ace Insurance Company as postconstruction lender, Widget Corporation of America as the office building tenant, and Good Sports, a sporting goods store, as the shopping center tenant. Based on the materials you have read, examine these clauses from the standpoint of your client and be prepared to explain what legal or business problems they present and what you think can be done to avoid them. ◄

THE ETHICAL REAL ESTATE LAWYER

Disclosure of "Defects" in the Premises

Suppose a prospective tenant in a commercial shopping center enters into a lease, and in reliance on that lease, incurs substantial expenses to install its fixtures and equipment and to renovate the leased space. What the tenant doesn't know is that during the lease negotiations the landlord's shopping center has been subject to a pending mortgage foreclosure proceeding by which, pursuant to a lis pendens notice recorded in the real estate records, the tenant will be bound. The foreclosure sale purchaser ejects the new tenant rather than honoring the lease. Did the landlord owe any duty to the tenant to disclose the pending foreclosure? What are the obligations, if any, owed by the landlord's counsel to the other side if landlord's counsel knows of the foreclosure? Should it be a defense that the foreclosure was a matter of public record? If the tenant looks to its own lawyer for malpractice recovery, did its lawyer owe any duty to perform a title search in connection with negotiating the lease? Although not clearly resolved, these issues were confronted in Davin, LLC v. Daham, 329 N.J. Super. 54, 746 A.2d 1034 (App. Div. 2000) (issue of material fact whether tenant's lawyer should have ordered a title search; landlord lawyer obligated by good faith duty to recommend disclosure by the client, and withdraw if not disclosed).

Chapter 11

Leasehold and Leaseback Financing

A. LEASEHOLD VERSUS FEE MORTGAGE FINANCING

In addition to selecting the optimum ownership entity (see Chapter 14), the developer of improved real estate must make another important prefinancing decision: whether to purchase or lease the underlying land on which the newly constructed improvements will be situated. If the decision is made to purchase the land, the developer can obtain a regular fee mortgage loan to cover both the purchase price of the land and the cost of developing and improving the land. Sometimes the developer will finance land costs separately with a subordinated purchase money mortgage (see Chapter 7B3) from the seller-fee owner or with a land development loan from some institutional lender (see Chapter 7B3, note 2). Alternatively, the developer may decide merely to (1) lease the underlying fee from the fee owner under a long-term leasing arrangement known as a ground lease (or, if the developer owns the land, sell the land and lease it back from the new owner) and (2) obtain a so-called leasehold mortgage to fund the costs of developing the land and constructing the improvements.

In the case of an ordinary fee mortgage, the lender's security for its loan is a mortgage lien not just on the mortgagor's fee title to the improvements but on the mortgagor's fee ownership of the land as well. In other words, a mortgage on the fee estate affords the lender the security of the entire estate in the land. In addition, the legal and tax status of the mortgagor with respect to the land is that of a fee owner.

By contrast, in the case of a leasehold mortgage, whether the developer ground leases the fee or engages in a sale and leaseback of land that it already owns, security for the loan is merely the mortgagor's defeasible leasehold, or estate, plus the improvements erected thereon. The leasehold mortgagee, therefore, is the lessee once removed, whereas the fee mortgagee is the fee owner once removed. In addition, the legal and tax status of the leasehold mortgagor is that of a lessee rather than that of a fee owner. The following brief overview introduces our examination of leasehold financing.

Halper, Introducing the Ground Lease
15 Real Est. Rev. 24 (Fall 1985)

INTRODUCING THE GROUND LEASE

Ground leases are strange documents, and negotiating them is not a game for amateurs. Botched ground leases have impeded development of many parcels of land for long periods. Weed fields and garbage dumps that could have supported apartment houses and office buildings have remained weed fields and garbage dumps for decades because of inept legal work.

The idea of separating the ownership of land from the right to exploit the potential of the land has venerable roots. Arrangements that were the ancestors of ground leasing were important in England at the time of the Norman Conquest. Similar practices were used in many other agricultural societies. When farming was society's main industry, the groups that wielded power usually did so by retaining control over the land.

In our society, land ownership does not necessarily confer power. But, land ownership continues to give people the feeling of power. Some people buy land for no other reason than the thrill of ownership. People who inherit land may refuse to sell it because of a desire to keep it in the family. Even governmental bodies and lawyers are convinced that land is special. Land and its improvements are still called "*real* property," as if a watch, a trademark, a diamond, an automobile, or a hamburger were not "real."

Our system of real property taxation encourages land speculation and continuous ownership by people who have neither the inclination nor the resources to exploit their holdings. Local governments tax real property on the basis of its "assessed valuation." They usually assess land gently, and place the preponderant tax burden on improvements. As a result, owners of unused land do not face the pressures of stiff real estate tax bills.

From time to time, authors of popular "success" books or financial writers advise their readers to buy land because "no new land is being manufactured." Sometimes these authors attract disciples who rush to buy land that nobody needs for the time being and that, normally, nobody wants.

TO LEASE OR NOT TO LEASE

When a parcel of land is about to be developed, under normal circumstances, one party owns the land and another party wants to develop it.

The most obvious but not always the most appropriate solution is for the developer to purchase the land from the landowner. The sale may not take place because the owner refuses to sell. Here are the most obvious reasons why an owner might prefer not to sell:

- He may have emotional ties to the property.
- He may wish to avoid a capital gains tax.
- He may have an unshakable faith in the potential income he could derive from the land in the future.
- He may want his children or grandchildren to have the opportunity to own buildings to be constructed by others.

There are also many reasons why a developer may prefer not to buy:

- The developer who doesn't buy doesn't pay a purchase price. Thus he reduces his front-end investment.
- Tax deductions for depreciation apply only to buildings. If the investor doesn't allocate cash to land purchase, the ratio of depreciation deductions to invested cash is greater than if part of the cash is spent for land.
- The return of the developer's cash investment is usually higher.
- For tax and other reasons, the annual cost of ground rent may be an easier burden to bear than the annual cost of principal and interest needed to discharge the loan that finances the land purchase.

ELEMENTS OF THE LEASE NEGOTIATION

Once a landowner and developer agree to negotiate a lease, they must proceed cautiously and professionally. If a landowner negotiates lease provisions carelessly, he may lose his land entirely or at least face years of little or no rental income. A developer who does a thoughtless job of negotiating a ground lease might find himself in the midst of construction and unable to make arrangements for permanent financing because one or more clauses in the ground lease offend the lender. He may spend months trying to sublet space and find that the prospective occupants are unwilling to execute subleases because of defects in the ground lease. . . .

Here is a list of only a few of the circumstances that may affect the formats of ground leases. The land might be urban, suburban, or rural. If urban, the land might be in a blighted area, in a "100 percent" location, or in a medium-grade location. If suburban, it might be in a developed or partially developed area. The land might be vacant or improved. If improved, the parties might contemplate demolishing the existing structures, improving them, or leaving them alone. The owner of a building might be selling the underlying land in an effort to raise money. The land might be an unused part of a shopping center and leased with appurtenant parking rights. There might be no land at all, and the subject transaction might concern air rights to the premises. The intended use might be development, recreation, agriculture, mining, or transportation.

Each of these circumstances suggests a different tension in the landlord-tenant relationship, and the negotiators must be prepared to adjust their favorite clauses to fit the needs of the parties.

"SUBORDINATED" AND "UNSUBORDINATED" GROUND LEASES

Perhaps the most important argument that differentiates one ground lease from another is whether the ground lease is going to be "subordinated" or "unsubordinated."

Subordinated ground leases are ground leases under which the landowner agrees to execute one or more mortgages of his land to secure loans made to the developer by third parties. The guts of the relationship [are] that the developer borrows the money he needs to construct the buildings on the land, but part of the security he offers for the loan is the land—an asset belonging to the landowner. A lending institution is usually just as happy with a mortgage executed by a landowner *and* a developer-tenant as it would have been if the developer had purchased the land and were the sole party to execute the mortgage.

An unsubordinated ground lease, of course, does not require the landlord to execute mortgages to secure the developer-tenant's loans. However, the developer with an unsubordinated ground lease may have a difficult time obtaining a loan.

PLEASING THE INSTITUTIONAL INVESTOR

Whether the lease is subordinated or unsubordinated, the developer must be able to please an institutional investor that is looking for adequate security for its loan or other investment in the project. If the ground lease is subordinated, the institutional investor will probably be satisfied. But if the landowner executes the mortgage and the developer defaults on the debt secured by the mortgage, the landowner will lose his land to the institution.

On the other hand, note what happens when the developer-borrower, who is also the tenant under an unsubordinated ground lease, defaults with respect to its obligations to the institution. If the debt is secured only by the developer's leasehold estate, the institution can levy on the leasehold estate only. As a practical matter, this means that the institution becomes the tenant under the ground lease.

Institutional investors are aware that a security interest in a leasehold estate may not be worth anything at the critical moment when the developer is in trouble. At the time a developer fails to meet his obligations to repay an institutional mortgage loan, it is likely that he is also in default under the ground lease. If that is so, the landowner may be in a position to cancel the lease before the institutional lender has a chance to preserve its only security for the debt, the leasehold estate, by curing the default.

A landowner who cancels a ground lease sees himself as a lottery winner. He may become the owner of all the buildings and other improvements that the developer constructed with the institution's funds.

So the subordinated ground lease puts the landowner at risk, and the unsubordinated lease puts the lender at risk. The real artistry is to organize an unsubordinated ground lease so that a prospective mortgage lender or other institutional lender will be convinced that the borrower-tenant's leasehold estate will be adequate security for the mortgage debt despite the landowner's potential right to eliminate the security as a result of a default under the lease by the tenant.

1. Legal, Tax, and Business Considerations

From a business perspective, the most significant advantage of leasehold mortgage financing should be obvious. Because the developer is not purchasing the land (or, in a sale and leaseback, is selling the fee title to land already owned), the initial cash outlay will be less. Therefore, the developer can maximize the cash available for working capital at the outset of the venture when it is most needed.

There is a correlative disadvantage, of course. The developer does not own the land on the expiration of the ground lease, loses the benefit of any interim appreciation in the value of the land, and must abandon any leasehold improvements to the fee owner-ground lessor at the end of the lease term. Usually the lease provides for an option to renew, and the lease term including renewals is for a period equal to or exceeding the useful life of the building, so that the ground lessee will receive the full benefit of the improvements during their useful life. Moreover, although the lease may contain one or more options for the ground lessee to purchase the fee or to have a right of first refusal, the ground lessee is still likely to forgo the purchase because business, legal, or tax considerations frequently dictate that the option price be geared to the current market value of the land. In many cases, the amount of rent payable under the ground lease ("ground rent") approximates the additional debt service the developer would have paid had she decided to purchase the land and obtain a larger fee mortgage to fund the purchase price of the land as well as the cost of developing the land and constructing the planned improvements.

Accordingly, because the developer's initial cash outlay will be less and yet net rental income from the occupancy-subtenants frequently will remain about the same whether or not the developer purchases the fee, the developer may be able to use leasehold financing as a way to leverage investment costs and thereby increase the rate of return on the equity capital invested by the developer and her investors. See discussion at Chapter 12A1. This enhanced leveraging ability may be especially important to a particular developer in an inflationary economy when the cost of land is high and the mortgage money market is tight. Indeed, leasehold financing may be necessary to develop a particular parcel of land because some owners of prime land, particularly in urban areas, may refuse to sell their land because the anticipated rate of appreciation in the value of the land is so high. In other instances, the owner may not have the legal capacity to transfer title (as, for example, a trustee who is prohibited from doing so under the terms of the trust). The owner also may be constrained by some compelling tax consideration (as, for example, a fee owner with a low basis in the property who might obtain a higher after-tax rate of return by leasing the real estate than by selling and reinvesting the after-gain tax proceeds).

From a legal perspective, the principal consideration with respect to leasehold mortgage financing as opposed to fee mortgage financing is that the mortgagor's interest in the leasehold improvements and the continued existence of the leasehold estate is dependent on compliance with the terms of the ground lease. Consequently, in the absence of a "streamlined mortgage" arrangement where the fee owner subjects its fee to the ground lessee's financing (discussed at Chapter 11A4, infra), the security of the leasehold mortgagee is but a defeasible estate that is subject to termination under circumstances where the mortgagee may not be able to cure all potential defaults by its mortgagor. Moreover, such extinguishment could occur regardless of what terms are included in the leasehold mortgage because the leasehold mortgagee is, in effect, an outside party to the lease agreement. Accordingly, as discussed at Chapter 11A3, infra, the leasehold mortgagee will require that the ground lease be drafted so as to incorporate those protective provisions that will place it in a position to control all contingencies that could terminate the leasehold estate and wipe out its security interest. Regardless, the lender will frequently be more restrictive in regard to the terms of the loan (for example, higher rate of interest, higher debt-coverage ratio, or lower loan-to-value ratio) with respect to ordinary (unstreamlined) leasehold financing because of the inherent risk of taking a security interest that is defeasible.

Both a ground lessee and a leasehold mortgagee can obtain title insurance protection by obtaining an ALTA leasehold owner's or leasehold loan policy endorsement, respectively. The leasehold endorsement would cover the insured party in the event the tenant was lawfully deprived from the right of possession of the subject property contrary to the terms of the lease. See ALTA Endorsement 13-06. A loss would typically occur in the event that the owner of the underlying real estate did not have clear title and the lessee was subsequently deprived of its rights of possession under the lease. In the event the insurance is triggered, the insured is compensated in an amount computed by the value of the remaining lease term and the value of the tenant improvements existing at the date of the eviction. Prior to 2001, the ALTA Leasehold Endorsement did not include the value of the improvements made by the tenant; however, the most recent revision includes improvements to the real estate made by the tenant as part of the coverage. As a developer of real estate in a ground lease with a land owner it is readily apparent why this latest change to the leasehold endorsement would be required by the insured whether it is the developer or the developer's lender.

From a tax perspective, it may be advantageous for the developer to lease rather than purchase the fee, especially when the purchase price of the land is high relative to the other costs of the project. If the developer leases the land, the rent payable under the ground lease is deductible in its entirety for income tax purposes. By contrast, if the developer purchases the fee, such land ownership would not provide any depreciation deduction[1] since land is not a depreciable asset. Consequently, because the payment of mortgage interest is deductible but the repayment of principal is not, if the land is leased rather than purchased, the developer, as ground lessee, will be able to depreciate her cost of using the land in the guise of ground rent since part of the deductible ground rent really represents the extra nondeductible amortization she would have paid on the larger fee mortgage had she purchased the underlying fee.

In addition, the ground lessee-developer will still be entitled to the depreciation deductions on the leasehold improvements since she would be entitled to recoup her capital investment in the improvements.[2] Even though the fee owner has vested legal title to the improvements, the ground lessee will still be entitled to the depreciation or amortization deduction since it retains the beneficial enjoyment of the premises and bears the economic exhaustion burden of its capital investment in the property.[3] However, in the case of existing improvements where the owner engages in a sale and leaseback, the owner may insist on a leaseback of the land only and retain title to the building so that it can retain the right to take depreciation on the building, which in some instances may generate more tax deductions than the owner would receive as a lessee of the building.

The Internal Revenue Code used to provide a complicated set of tests for determining the period over which leasehold improvements can be depreciated or amortized if the lease contained a renewal option.[4] However, under current law, the ground lessee must recover the cost of the leasehold improvements over the applicable cost recovery period whether it be 27.5 years (for residential property) or 39 years (for commercial property), regardless of the lease term.

NOTES AND QUESTIONS

> ➢ *Problem 11-1*
> As real estate counsel and tax planner for Dan Developer, briefly explain to your client the business and tax advantages and disadvantages, both short- and long-term, of leasehold as opposed to fee mortgage financing. ◄

---

1. Ownership of the land would provide a limited tax deduction for payment of local property taxes; however, frequently local taxes attributable to the land are passed through and payable by the ground lessee under the terms of the ground lease.

2. Treas. Reg. §1.167(a)-4. If the estimated useful life of the improvements is longer than the remaining term of the lease, the cost of the leasehold improvements can be amortized over the remaining lease term. Id.

3. See Helvering v. F. & R. Lazarus & Co., 308 U.S. 252, 254 (1939) (involving a sale and leaseback); Rev. Rul. 62-178, 1962-2 C.B. 91.

4. Under prior law, I.R.C. §178 essentially provided that where the remaining initial term was less than 60 percent of the leasehold improvement's useful life at completion, the lease term would include renewal periods for the purpose of depreciation or amortization.

Additional Reading. For articles discussing whether to lease or to purchase, see Torkildson, The Economic Recovery Tax Act: Safe Harbor Rule for Leases, 47 J. Air, L. & Com. 565, 571-585 (1982) (advantages and disadvantages to lessor and lessee of leases); Shenkman, Ground Leases: Tax Planning Ideas for a Real Estate Financing Tool, 2 Real Est. Fin. J. 10 (Summer 1986). For considerations in negotiating and drafting the ground lease, see Kobren, Three Perspectives on Ground Lease Negotiations, 19 Real Est. L.J. 40 (Summer 1990).

2. *Regulatory Law Considerations*

With the increased risks inherent in leasehold mortgage financing, lawmakers have naturally become concerned with financial institutions pursuing these investments. The following Massachusetts statute typifies the kinds of regulatory constraints that states ordinarily impose on leasehold mortgage loans.[5]

Mass. Ann. Laws ch. 175, §63(7)

The capital of any domestic company, other than life, and three fourths of the reserve of any domestic stock or mutual life company shall be invested only as follows: . . .

7. In loans upon improved and unencumbered real property in any state of the United States or in the District of Columbia or Puerto Rico, and upon leasehold estates in improved unencumbered real property where twenty-one years or more of the term is unexpired and where unencumbered except by rentals accruing therefrom to the owner of the fee, and where the mortgagee is entitled to be subrogated to all the rights under the leasehold. No loan on such real property or such leasehold estate shall exceed 75 percent of the fair market value thereof at the time of making such loan. . . . Real property and leasehold estates shall not be deemed to be encumbered within the meaning of this paragraph by reason of the existence of instruments reserving mineral, oil or timber rights, rights of way, parking rights, sewer rights, or rights in walls, nor by reason of an option to purchase, nor by reason of any liens for taxes or assessments not delinquent, nor by reason of building restrictions or other restrictive covenants, nor by the reason that it is subject to lease under which rents or profits are reserved to the owner; provided, that the security for such loan is a first lien upon such real property and that there is no condition or right of re-entry or forfeiture under which such lien can be cut off, subordinated or otherwise disturbed. No mortgage loan upon a leasehold shall be made or acquired by a company pursuant to this paragraph unless the terms thereof shall provide for such payments of principal, whatever

---

5. In contrast to the Massachusetts statute, a few state statutes specify a lower loan-to-value ratio for leasehold as opposed to fee mortgage loans. E.g., Va. Code Ann. §38.2-1437, which imposes an 80 percent maximum loan-to-value ratio for fee mortgage loans and a 75 percent maximum for leasehold mortgage loans.

the period of the loan, so that at no time during the term of the loan shall the aggregate payments of principal theretofore required to be made under the terms of the loan be less than would be necessary for a loan payable completely by the end of four-fifths of the period of the leasehold which is unexpired at the time the loan is made, and payments of interest only may be made for a period not to exceed five years, provided, that payments applicable first to interest and then to principal are made during each year thereafter. . . .

NOTES AND QUESTIONS

Regulatory Law. Traditionally, the principal source of leasehold financing has been insurance companies. Suppose an insurance company chartered in Massachusetts desires to make a leasehold mortgage loan. Why does the regulatory statute require that the underlying property (fee) not be subject to any prior lien? Can you think of any reason why the statute mandates an unexpired leasehold term of at least 21 years? Why does the statute require that the leasehold mortgagee be subrogated to all the rights of the ground lessor under the ground lease? In light of the foregoing restriction against a short lease term, how do you explain the fact that the statute prohibits a long mortgage amortization schedule?

Statutes in some other jurisdictions are more restrictive about encumbrances than the Massachusetts statute, which lists certain permissible encumbrances. For example, Virginia law requires that a leasehold estate be absolutely unencumbered to be mortgageable. See Va. Code Ann. §38.2-1434(2). Do you see any problems with this approach? See discussion at Chapter 2A3.

> ➤ *Problem 11-2*
> After reviewing the priority discussion at Chapter 3E, consider the following hypothetical facts, diagrammed below. In January of this year, a fee owner (Francine Farmer) ground leases some land (Blackacre) to a developer (Dan Developer). Dan immediately records the ground lease. In June, Dan obtains a leasehold mortgage from a postconstruction lender (Ace Insurance Company, chartered in Massachusetts) to fund the construction of a shopping center situated in Massachusetts. Ace immediately records its mortgage.

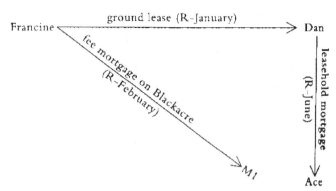

In July, Ace's mortgage loan officer discovers that (unbeknownst to Ace) in February Francine had obtained a fee mortgage loan on Blackacre from M1 and that the mortgage was recorded in February. The loan officer is worried that Ace's loan, made in June, may be illegal under the Massachusetts regulatory statute. As counsel to Ace, what will you tell the loan officer? ◄

3. *Leasehold Mortgage That Does Not Encumber the Fee: Lender's Requirements*

In the case of ordinary leasehold financing in which the lien of the leasehold mortgage does not cover the underlying fee, the security for the loan is merely the mortgagor's defeasible leasehold estate (which is basically the right of possession of the land and leasehold improvements for a stated term on the condition that the mortgagor, as ground lessee, pays the ground rent and otherwise complies with the terms of the ground lease). Thus, in addition to the ordinary concerns of a lender, the leasehold mortgagee must place itself in a position to control to the maximum extent possible any contingency that could terminate the mortgagor's leasehold estate and the mortgagee's security interest. Accordingly, the leasehold mortgagee will require language in the ground lease (1) affording to it all the rights that the mortgagor has as ground lessee; (2) providing to it notice of any default with a reasonable opportunity to cure; and (3) requiring its prior written approval to any modification or cancellation of the lease, as well as other safeguards discussed in the following article that will protect it against the obliteration or impairment of its security interest as leasehold mortgagee.

Mark, Leasehold Mortgages:
Some Practical Considerations
14 Bus. Law. 609 (1959)

[R]eal estate financing through the medium of leasehold mortgages . . . has become an almost standard method for providing funds for the construction of large commercial and residential structures. The leasehold mortgage, when based on a properly drawn lease, can in many cases act as a catalyst in bringing together the conflicting interests of a property owner who does not want to incur the expense of constructing an adequate improvement on his land but desires an adequate return, an operator who sees an opportunity to improve the same property but does not want to buy it, and a lending institution seeking a safe investment for a large sum of money with a minimum of servicing expense. . . .

It is readily apparent that a leasehold mortgage loan, being based on an estate subject to defeasance, presents problems which do not exist where a mortgage is based on a fee estate. Since the security behind a leasehold loan is the leasehold estate, and since the leasehold estate is created by the lease, the place to deal with these problems is the lease itself. If the lease does not contain adequate protection for the leasehold mortgagee, no amount of tinkering with special mortgage provisions can be of any avail, since no mortgage can in any way impose or alter the estate on which it creates a lien. The purpose of this paper is to discuss some of the basic problems inherent in leasehold financing and to suggest solutions which it is hoped will be found useful and practical.

1. PREPARATION OF THE LEASE

Rare indeed is the lease which counsel for a leasehold mortgagee would approve unless it has been drawn with the basic requirements of such a lender in mind. Some years ago the writer had the privilege of reviewing for a lender a long-term lease on a New York City property. Lessor and Lessee had been represented by brilliant counsel learned in the law and skilled in the use of the English language. From the point of view of draftsmanship, and as a protection for the rights of their respective clients, the lease was a masterpiece, but it was completely devoid of any provisions which would make it acceptable to a leasehold mortgagee. Since the lease had not been drawn with leasehold mortgage financing in mind, it took almost a year to revise it in such a way as to afford to a leasehold lender the protection to which it was entitled. Such a vast expenditure of time (and the borrower's money) could have been avoided had the proper protective provisions been inserted in the first place. It is therefore apparent that where there is even a reasonable chance that a leasehold estate may be mortgaged at some time in the future, it is well to insert in the lease provisions for protection of prospective mortgagees. A fortiori, in a case where it is known that a project will be financed by a leasehold mortgage, participation by the lender's counsel in the preparation of the lease will be in the best interest of all concerned.

2.   LENGTH OF INITIAL TERM

Some statutes authorizing investment in leasehold mortgages provide that the term of the lease shall be for not less than a given number of years, including enforceable options of renewal. Such a statutory provision raises two questions.

The first is what is meant by "an enforceable option of renewal" or more accurately, in whose hands is the option of renewal enforceable.

The second question concerning the length of the term is of equal importance. This relates to the possible bankruptcy of a Lessor who has granted a lease containing an option to renew. Under Section 70(b) of the Bankruptcy Act a trustee in bankruptcy is authorized to reject executory contracts of the bankrupt "including unexpired leases of real property." The section further provides that "unless a lease of such property shall expressly otherwise provide, a rejection of such lease or of any covenant therein by the trustee of the lessor shall not deprive the lessee of his estate." It is thus clear that at least during the initial term of a lease, the leasehold estate would be unaffected by a rejection of the lease by the trustee of a bankrupt Lessor, unless the lease provided otherwise. It has been held, however, that the trustee of a bankrupt Lessor may reject an option of renewal. Coy v. Title Guarantee & Trust Co., 198 F. 275 (D.C. Ore. 1912). Thus, if the entire term of a leasehold mortgage exceeded the initial term of the lease, and the mortgagee relied on an option of renewal to extend the term so as to expire not earlier than the maturity of the mortgage, the mortgagee would be at the mercy of the trustee of a bankrupt Lessor. . .

3.   ASSIGNABILITY OF THE LESSEE'S ESTATE

One of the most cherished possessions of any Lessor, the right to control the identity of his Lessee through control of the right to assign the Lessee's estate, becomes a casualty in a properly drawn lease securing a leasehold mortgage. A prime condition precedent to the acceptability of a lease for mortgage purposes is the unrestricted right of the Lessee to transfer the leasehold estate by assignment, without any need for the consent of the Lessor, and indeed, a lease is not acceptable for such purposes unless it so provides.

This matter of assignability has two aspects. The first relates to the question whether a covenant against assignment is violated by the making of a mortgage on the lease. . . .

The other aspect of the problem of assignability is of equal, if not greater, importance and relates to the ability of a mortgagee to realize on its security following the acquisition of the lease either by foreclosure or assignment in lieu thereof or following the obtaining of a new lease from the Lessor under the circumstances discussed in Part 4 of this paper. As a fee mortgagee is free to sell an acquired fee without restriction of any kind, so a leasehold mortgagee must be in a position to dispose of the leasehold estate without let or hindrance. It follows that a leasehold mortgagee cannot allow itself to be put in the position of being required to seek the Lessor's permission in order to liquidate its security. Accordingly, a lease acceptable to a leasehold lender must provide absolute and unrestricted assignability of the Lessee's estate, free and clear of any control of the Lessor.

In dealing with this problem, Lessors sometimes suggest that their consent will not be required for any mortgage, or for any assignment to the mortgagee or to the immediate assignee of the mortgagee. Although at first blush this might appear adequate, a second look quickly reveals the flaw in the suggestion. A lease with such a provision is unmarketable as a practical matter, for the purchaser who buys the lease from the mortgagee could not thereafter dispose of it without the Lessor's consent, and therefore in the exercise of prudent judgment would decline to purchase from the mortgagee in the first place.

Another Lessor's suggestion to be avoided is an offer of a covenant by the Lessor not unreasonably to withhold its consent to an assignment of the lease. Although a covenant not unreasonably to withhold consent is in most states not without meaning, there are many bases on which a lessor may rely in withholding consent without being unreasonable, such as a poor credit rating of the assignee, the poor reputation of the assignee or a provable inability of the assignee to maintain or manage the property. Furthermore, to determine whether the Lessor is reasonable or unreasonable in withholding consent is readily capable of being the subject of litigation. Such litigation would either take the form of an action for a declaratory judgment or a summary proceeding based upon assignment without consent in which the defense is raised that consent was unreasonably withheld. The possible necessity of any such litigation, plus the possibility that it might be unsuccessful from the Lessee's point of view, would in all probability make a lease containing such a covenant entirely unacceptable to a prospective lender. Such a covenant should therefore be excluded from the lease.

It is not uncommon for a lease to provide the Lessee's estate may be assigned provided the assignee assumes the obligations of the lease, or that the acceptance of an assignment constitutes an assumption of the Lessee's obligations thereunder. Such a provision is not unacceptable to a leasehold mortgage if it is further provided that following an assignment of the lease, the assignor is relieved of all obligations under the lease except those which accrued during the period when the assignor was the Lessee under the lease. In this connection the lease should specifically provide that the leasehold mortgagee shall not be liable for the Lessee's obligations under the lease until it becomes the owner of the lease either by foreclosure or assignment in lieu thereof, or has acquired a new lease as discussed in Part 4 of this paper.

To conclude on the question of assignability, the lease should provide for complete and unrestricted assignability of the lease without the necessity for consent of the Lessor of any kind.

### 4.	NOTICE OF DEFAULT AND NEW LEASE

As stated in the earlier portion of this paper, a basic distinction between a fee mortgage and a leasehold mortgage is that the latter is based on an estate subject to defeasance, whereas the former is not. It is therefore of paramount importance that the lease protect the leasehold mortgagee against the consequences of those events which may give to the Lessor the right to terminate the Lessee's estate. Of all the problems faced in dealing with leasehold mortgages it can be accurately said that this is the most crucial. Unless a lease provides adequate protection against defeasance of the Lessee's estate it is wholly inadequate as security for a leasehold mortgage.

Except through the operation of the power of eminent domain there is no way that the Lessee's estate can be terminated without a default on the part of the Lessee in the performance of its obligations under the lease. All properly drawn leases provide that before a Lessor can terminate a Lessee's estate because of a default, notice of default must be given to the Lessee, who then has an opportunity to cure the default within a specified time or at least to commence to cure the default. Unless, however, a leasehold mortgagee has notice that a default has been called on the Lessee, the failure of the Lessee to cure the default and the consequent termination of the Lessee's estate could occur before the leasehold mortgagee was even aware of the existence of the default. It is therefore necessary for the essential protection of the mortgagee, that the mortgagee also receive from the Lessor a notice of any Lessee's default. A lease properly drawn from the mortgagee's point of view will provide that no notice of default given by a Lessor to a Lessee shall be valid for any purpose unless simultaneously with the notice to the Lessee similar notice is given to the mortgagee.

Vital as notice of default undoubtedly is to the mortgagee, it is of little use unless the mortgagee is in a position to cure the default. The lease should therefore provide that the mortgagee is given time in which to cure the default for the account of the Lessee, and that when the mortgagee has performed the obligation, the non-performance of which was the subject of the notice of default, the default shall be deemed cured. This last provision is desirable to forestall an allegation by the Lessor that although action to cure the default was taken, it was not taken by the Lessee who therefore remains in default. Appropriate covenants in the mortgage would provide that all expenses incurred by the mortgagee in curing the Lessee's defaults would be added to the mortgage debt and be secured by the lien of the mortgage.

The right of a leasehold mortgagee to receive notice of default and to cure the default is adequate to protect the leasehold mortgagee against defaults which can be cured by the payment of money or the performance of work, such as repairs, alterations, construction and the like. It is not adequate to protect against defaults which cannot be cured by the payment of money or the performance of work. Many leases provide that the Lessee shall be deemed to be in default if the Lessee becomes a bankrupt, or confesses an inability to pay its debts, or if a receiver is appointed for the Lessee or if any one of a number of similar events shall occur. [F]ollowing such a default the leasehold mortgagee is not protected by a provision for receipt of notice of default and a right to cure, since such a default cannot be cured by payment of money or performance of work or any other act of the mortgagee. It is the view of some counsel for lending institutions that a lease is unacceptable for mortgage lending purposes if it is subject to termination for defaults of the character above mentioned. On the other hand it seems unreasonable to preclude a Lessor from terminating a lease with a bankrupt Lessee and becoming thereby involved in the bankruptcy proceeding through no fault of the Lessor. It has been suggested that one solution to the problem of uncurable defaults is to be found in a lease provision to the effect that despite the bankruptcy of the Lessee the lease cannot be terminated as long as the rent is paid and the other terms of the lease are complied with. Such a provision is acceptable from the point of view of the leasehold mortgagee, as it restores the protection afforded by notice of default and the right to cure. It would appear to be somewhat less satisfactory to the Lessor as it would not free the Lessor from participation in the bankruptcy proceeding.

A generally used device for protecting a leasehold mortgagee against these uncurable defaults is a provision that upon the termination of the Lessee's estate following such a default, the Lessor will enter into a new lease in which the mortgagee or its nominee shall be the lessee. Such a new lease would be for the unexpired portion of the initial or renewal term as the case might be, and would be on the same terms and conditions, including rentals and renewals, as the original lease. Under the operation of such a provision, the mortgagee would be in the same position as if it had foreclosed its mortgage or had acquired the lease by assignment in lieu of foreclosure. Assuming the lease contained appropriate provisions for assignability discussed in part 3 above, it would be able to realize on the security to the same extent as it could following a mortgage default. It would seem that such a provision would provide adequate protection for the mortgagee and at the same time would be more satisfactory to the Lessor. Obviously, either method of dealing with uncurable defaults is a matter of indifference to the Lessee.

5. SUBORDINATION TO FEE MORTGAGES

Some statutes authorizing leasehold mortgage investments specifically require that the fee estate be not subject to prior liens. Others require that the leasehold estate shall be unencumbered. However, regardless of statutory provisions, it would appear clear that prudence on the part of the leasehold mortgagee requires either that the fee estate be unencumbered or that any encumbrances thereon be subordinated to the estate created by the lease.

It is certainly arguable that a fee mortgage is not an encumbrance on a leasehold estate, even where the lease is subordinated to the lien of the fee mortgage. However, regardless of the technical validity of this argument, the fact remains that where a fee mortgage is prior in lien to the leasehold estate, the latter can be cut off by a foreclosure of the former, and no provision of the lease or the leasehold mortgage can protect the leasehold mortgagee from the complete destruction of its security under such circumstances.

It is therefore of prime importance that the lease should in fact be prior to any fee mortgage on the premises at the time of the making of the lease or thereafter placed upon the premises. It is good practice for the lease to provide for such superiority in haec verba, thus giving notice to all subsequent encumbrancers and lienors. In this connection it seems superfluous to state that in all cases involving leasehold mortgages the lease should be recorded in the appropriate recording office.

Many leases are submitted which contain provisions directly to the contrary of the foregoing. They provide for the complete subordination of the lease to any and all fee mortgages now or hereafter placed against the premises. Such leases are wholly unacceptable from the point of view of the leasehold mortgagee for the reasons stated above.

A variation of the complete subordination to fee mortgages discussed in the immediately preceding paragraph is the so-called "non-disturbance clause," pursuant to which a fee mortgagee agrees that so long as the Lessee is not in default under the lease the Lessee's possession will not be disturbed in the event of a foreclosure of the fee mortgage.

In conclusion, regardless of statutory requirements, prudence requires that a lease securing a leasehold mortgage be superior in all respects to all fee mortgages placed upon the premises at any time, and to all other title conditions pursuant to which the leasehold estate could be cut off in any way, by reverter, reversion, termination of a life estate or otherwise.

6.   INSURANCE

Except for the question of disposition of condemnation awards, there is probably no subject more discussed in the negotiation of a lease than the question of disposition of hazard insurance proceeds. However, the basic needs of the leasehold mortgagee are simple. It wants to be a named insured on the hazard insurance policies pursuant to a standard mortgagee clause, to have all losses payable to it and to have the option to apply the insurance proceeds on the mortgage debt or to the restoration of the premises. However, insistence on having all these rights will undoubtedly result in a collapse of the proposed transaction, as parts of such provisions are entirely unacceptable to the Lessor and the Lessee. Both Lessor and Lessee desire to make certain that the proceeds of insurance are available for the restoration of the premises and can be readily obtained as the work of restoration progresses. The possibility that the insurance proceeds would be applied on the mortgage debt would be wholly unacceptable to the Lessor and in all probability, only slightly less unacceptable to the Lessee.

From the point of view of the leasehold mortgagee, adequate protection is afforded under lease provisions requiring that the mortgagee be insured under a standard mortgagee clause, with loss payable to the mortgagee so long as the mortgage is held by a lending institution, otherwise to an insurance trustee such as a bank or trust company, the loss proceeds to be paid out as the work of restoration progresses upon production of appropriate architects' certificates, with such provisions for hold-backs before final disbursement as the parties might agree upon. The lease should also provide that the mortgagee has the right to participate in the adjustment of losses.

7. CONDEMNATION

Another fruitful source of protracted negotiation is the subject of the taking of all or a part of the demised premises as a result of the exercise of eminent domain. Here we deal with three situations: a total taking, a partial taking, and a use taking.

The last mentioned, a taking of the use of the premises without vesting of title in the condemning authority, ordinarily would present no problem to a leasehold mortgagee. Presumably the condemner would pay the condemnation award in installments similar to rent, the debt service would be met from these payments and the mortgagee would be unaffected.

On the other hand, a leasehold mortgagee will be vitally interested in being protected against a total or partial taking which vests title in the condemnor. In the case of a total taking, or a partial taking which leaves the premises so damaged that it cannot be restored, a proper lease will provide that the leasehold mortgagee is the first to be paid out of that portion of the award which represents the value of the improvements erected on the premises. Such a provision is adequate in a situation where the Lessee has constructed the improvement, as is often the case, but it is somewhat less than realistic when the lease relates to an existing building owned in fee by the Lessor. In such a case that portion of the award representing the value of the Lessee's estate should be made available for payment of the leasehold mortgage and provision should be made for methods of determining the value of the Lessee's estate in the event that the award is silent on this subject.

Where a lease is not terminated by a partial taking, it is apparent that all parties (except perhaps the leasehold mortgagee) will wish to have the condemnation proceeds applied to the restoration of the premises. Lease provisions for this purpose resemble those discussed above relating to the use of proceeds of hazard insurance under analogous circumstances.

To assure the mortgagee of proper protection in the condemnation proceedings, the lease should provide that the leasehold mortgagee is expressly authorized to participate in the condemnation proceeding.

8. SUB-LEASES

Except in the unusual circumstance of a Lessee being itself the sole occupant of the demised premises and paying the debt service as an expense of its business, the funds for payment of principal and interest on the leasehold mortgage will be derived from rentals paid by sub-tenants occupying space in the demised premises pursuant to sub-leases in which the Lessee is the landlord. The leasehold mortgagee, as would a fee mortgagee in an analogous situation, will insist upon the sub-tenant's being of good credit rating and in all respects suitable occupants of the property. It will also insist that all sub-leases be approved by the mortgagee as to rent, term, and the provisions of the lease.

Since the source of funds for the liquidation of its investment will be rentals under the sub-lease, the mortgagee will wish to be certain that the covenants of the sub-lease will not be changed, that the term of the sub-lease will not be reduced, [and] that there will be no prepayment of rent nor a surrender of the sub-lease without the consent of the leasehold mortgagee. Some counsel for lenders are of the opinion that protection against these contingencies is obtained by the assignment to the leasehold mortgagee of the Lessee's interest as landlord under the sublease. It is the opinion of the writer, however, that unless following such an assignment the sub-rentals are paid directly to the mortgagee prior to default, the assignment is not effective to protect the mortgagee against sub-lease modifications and similar transactions between the Lessee and its sub-tenants. . . .

It is the opinion of the writer that in order to protect a leasehold mortgagee against the modification of sub-leases without the lender's consent, the ground lease should contain a covenant to the effect that all sub-leases will specifically provide that they cannot, without the consent of the leasehold mortgagee, be modified so as to reduce the rent, change renewal privileges, shorten the term or provide for prepayment of rent, and that any such modification without the consent of the mortgagee shall be void as against the mortgagee. It is believed that such a provision will go far to assure the mortgagee that when it takes over the property following default, it will find in effect the same sub-leases on which it relied in making the loan in the first place.

Another problem in connection with sub-leases relates to attornment by subtenants in the event of a termination of the ground lease for a non-curable default and the issuance to the lender of a new lease under the circumstance discussed in Part 4 above. Since the estate created by the sub-lease stems from the leasehold estate of the Lessee under the ground lease, it is apparent that following a termination of the ground lease the estates created by sub-leases would be cut off, and the obligations of the sub-tenants to stay in possession and pay rent would cease. In order that the leasehold mortgagee may be protected against a loss of rental income after it has signed its new lease, the ground lease should contain a covenant requiring that all sub-leases must contain an agreement by the sub-tenant to attorn to the leasehold mortgagee if it becomes the holder of a new ground lease. Proper protection for the sub-tenants would be provided by a reciprocal clause to the effect that the leasehold mortgagee would accept the attornment and recognize the continued existence of the sub-lease.

9. MISCELLANEOUS

(A) ESTOPPEL CERTIFICATES

From time to time, and especially at the closing of a leasehold mortgage loan, it will be important to obtain from the Lessor a statement that the lease is in full force and effect and that the Lessee is not in default thereunder. Since there is no way in which a Lessor can be compelled to deliver such a statement, it is good practice to include in the lease a covenant that upon request the Lessor will deliver a certificate stating, if such be the fact, that the Lessee is not in default and that the lease is in full force and effect. Counsel for the Lessor may be unwilling to go this far, but any reasonable Lessor should be at least willing to certify, if such be the fact, that it knows of no default and that no notice of default has been served.

(B) FORMS OF MORTGAGE

Unlike the fee mortgage, which is susceptible of being the subject of a standard printed form, the leasehold mortgage is generally a hand-tailored job, designed specifically for the transaction at hand and closely correlated to the provisions of the lease to which it applies. . . .

(D) FEE MORTGAGE COVENANTS

In addition to the concepts discussed above, many standard fee mortgage provisions are applicable to leasehold mortgages, such as covenants against waste, demolition without consent, compliance with orders of governmental authorities, payment of taxes, etc. It is apparent that except for the fact that the leasehold mortgage creates a lien on a defeasible estate, basic mortgage practices common to fee mortgages have equal relevance in leasehold situations and should be followed.

NOTES AND QUESTIONS

1. Questions. Some state statutes regulating leasehold mortgages mandate an unexpired leasehold term of not less than a specified number of years *including enforceable options of renewal.* The excerpt by Mark questions the meaning of "an enforceable option of renewal." More specifically, the author wonders in whose hands the option of renewal should be enforceable. From the perspective of a leasehold mortgagee, is it sufficient that the option be enforceable by the mortgagor-lessee? If not, what protective language should be included in either the leasehold mortgage or the ground lease to assure the mortgagee that its loan will constitute both a legal and a safe investment? See 2 R. Powell and P. Rohan, Powell on Real Property §17A.03[1][a] (1997).

In his 1959 article, Mark also points out that a trustee in bankruptcy may have the authority to reject an option of renewal granted by a bankrupt lessor. Today, consternation remains in the real estate legal community over the bankruptcy case of Precision Industries v. Qualitech Steel SBQ, LLC, 327 F.3d 537 (7th Cir. 2003), decided by the Seventh Circuit Court of Appeals. Prior to *Qualitech*, Section 365 of the Bankruptcy Code had been thought to provide lessees of real estate absolute protection from eviction arising from the discretion of the bankruptcy trustee presiding over the estate of the debtor lessor. See Homburger, Gallagher, and Rubel, Conflict Resolved: Bankruptcy Code 365(h) and the Contradictory Cases Requiring Its Amendment, 29 Real Prop., Prob. & Tr. J. 869 (Winter 1995); Genovese, Precision Industries v. Qualitech Steel: Easing the Tension Between Sections 363 and 365 of the Bankruptcy Code, 39 Real Prop. Prob. & Tr. J. 627 (Fall 2004). The fear of lessees had been that trustees in bankruptcy could use their power under §365(h) to cancel executory contracts of the landlord debtor to cut off lessees who were otherwise in good standing under the lease terms. In *Qualitech*, however, the bankruptcy trustee refused to pronounce a long-term lease of the debtor as assumed or rejected by the bankruptcy estate and instead simply pursued a sale of the underlying real estate free of the leasehold interest pursuant to rights to sell assets under Section 363. The Bankruptcy Court confirmed the sale to the detriment of the lessee. On appeal the lessee primarily argued the sale of the real estate by the bankruptcy trustee was tantamount to a rejection of the lease, and therefore lessee should be allowed the option to remain in possession under §365. The lessee also argued that this method of undercutting the lessee's interest for the benefit of the bankruptcy estate is contrary to the purpose of §365, which recognizes the need to preserve the property rights of the third-party lessee. The court of appeals upheld the sale, deciding that the two sections of the bankruptcy code are not connected and alluding to the fact that the lessee may have been able to protect itself by asserting rights "to seek adequate protection" under §363. The ruling left attorneys contemplating the vulnerability of long-term leasehold estates to the discretion of bankruptcy trustees of debtor lessors. See Ferretti, Eviction Without Rejection—The Tenant's Bankruptcy Dilemma, 39 Cumb. L. Rev. 707 (2009); Zinman, Precision in Statutory Drafting: The *Qualitech* Quagmire and the Sad History of Sec. 365(h) of the Bankruptcy Code, 38 J. Marshall L. Rev. 97 (2004); Stein, Did the Sky Fall on Leasehold Mortgagees? Ground Lease Financing After *Qualitech*, 597 PLI/Real 213 (2012).

Mark suggests that a covenant against assignment in the ground lease may be violated by the making of a leasehold mortgage. Based on what you have learned about the nature of a mortgage under a title approach versus a lien theory approach (discussed at Chapter 3A), on what basis, if any, could such a contention be made by a ground lessor seeking to enforce the restriction?

A fee mortgagee will sometimes require in its postconstruction loan commitment that all occupancy or space leases be unconditionally subordinate to the fee mortgage. So why, in the case of a leasehold mortgage, would a ground lease providing for the subordination of the lease to any fee mortgage be wholly unacceptable to the leasehold mortgagee? If the leasehold estate must be prior in lien to any fee mortgage, why can't the problem be solved by simply providing in haec verba for such superiority in the ground lease? From the perspective of the leasehold mortgagee, why can't a nondisturbance agreement wholly solve the subordination problem in the event the ground lease is recorded after the fee mortgage? Supposing it cannot, are there any alternative solutions that are not mentioned by Mark?

From the viewpoint of the leasehold mortgagee, the biggest risk to its defeasible security interest is that it may not be able to cure a material nonmonetary default under the ground lease (for example, the violation of a use restriction, receivership or assignment for the benefit of creditors, violation of local law, or abandonment of the premises by the ground lessee). As protection, the leasehold mortgagee therefore will demand the right to enter into a new ground lease with the fee owner on the same terms and conditions that were contained in the original lease and for the unexpired portion of the initial or renewal term, as the case may be. In 1980, the American Bar Association Real Property, Probate and Trust Law Section issued a report on model leasehold encumbrance provisions that espoused a "new lease" provision that would provide a leasehold mortgagee with the absolute right to step into the shoes of the defaulting ground lessee-mortgagor. Based on what you learned in your first-year property course and the discussion so far, can you think of any potential problems for the leasehold mortgagee that are not addressed by the "new lease" concept? See Levitan, Leasehold Mortgage Financing: Reliance on the "New Lease" Provision, 15 Real Prop., Prob. & Tr. J. 413 (Summer 1980); Thomas, The Mortgaging of Long Term Leases, 39 Dicta 363, 366-372 (1962).

> ➤ *Problem 11-3*
> Read the sample ground lease in the Documents Manual. Assume that you are counsel to a postconstruction lender (Ace Insurance Company) that is planning to make a leasehold mortgage loan to a developer (Dan Developer). Ace's mortgage will not encumber the fee. Ace asks you to review the proposed ground lease between Dan, as ground lessee, and the fee owner (Francine Farmer), as ground lessor, which follows the same standard form as the sample ground lease in the Documents Manual except that the language in Section 10.08 has been omitted. Based on the Mark article, what additional precautionary language, deletions, and other changes would you demand of the ground lessor and ground lessee to protect the interests of your client? What other requirements would you impose as a condition precedent to making the loan? If you represented a

sublessee in the same transaction, what protective measures would you insist on, and from whom? ◄

2. Ground Rent Escalation Clauses. Because the initial term of the ground lease is apt to be long, the fee owner-ground lessor often will require as a hedge against inflation a periodic increase in the rent (geared to an inflation index such as the Consumer Price Index (CPI)) or a percentage rental (geared to the net or gross subrental). Perhaps the most common type of rental adjustment clause is one (such as the following) that is based on periodic revaluations of the property during the leasehold term:

> The base rent is to be adjusted on the fourth anniversary of the execution date of this lease and at the end of four-year increments thereafter, so that the base rent shall be equal to 8 percent of the fair market value of the land subject to the leasehold estate. Said fair market value is to be determined by an MAI appraiser satisfactory to Lessor and Lessee. All costs and expenses of such appraisals are to be borne by Lessor.

Do you see any problems with the foregoing language from the perspective of the lessee, the lessor, or the leasehold mortgagee? From the perspective of the leasehold mortgagee, this type of provision is objectionable because any change in the base ground rent without regard for the ability of the property to generate sufficient income to pay the rent and debt service may increase the risk of default by the mortgagor while the leasehold mortgage is being amortized. However, a percentage rental clause geared to the net income from subtenants (as opposed to one based on gross income or cash flow) will be tolerated by most lenders because such a provision provides the borrower with a hedge against declining profits but does not increase the risk of default under the leasehold mortgage. For a recent case illustrating the drafting pitfalls of ground rent escalation clauses, see Wallace v. 600 Partners Co., 86 N.Y.2d 543, 658 N.E.2d 715, 634 N.Y.S.2d 669 (1995). In the case of residential condominium developments, state law may limit the enforceability of rent escalation clauses in ground leases. For example, Fla. Stat. Ann. §718.4015 (commodity- or CPI-based escalation clauses in such leases are void against public policy).

3. Multiple Encumbrances. Ordinarily an entire development—be it a shopping center, apartment building, or office building—will be constructed on a single ground-leased parcel with the improvements financed by a single lender. On some occasions, however, the ground lessee may wish to develop the parcel on a piecemeal basis and may find it necessary to finance the improvements with several lenders, each of whom will demand lien priority with respect to a particular portion of the tract and perhaps the borrower's interest in a particular high-credit sublease with an occupancy tenant. Also, if the tract is to be developed by sections or to become a part of a single integrated development plan where the adjacent parcels are under other ownership, a number of complex problems (involving subordination, nondisturbance of subtenants, joinder by the ground lessor in cross-easement agreements, and so on) must be resolved before the project becomes viable. For a complete examination of these problems and recommended solutions, see ABA Section of Real Property, Probate and Trust Law Committee on Leases, Ground Leases and Their Financing, 4 Real Prop., Prob. & Tr. J. 437, 462-465 (1969).

4. Additional Reading. For additional background with respect to leasehold mortgages that do not encumber the fee, see Anderson, The Mortgagee Looks at the Ground Lease, 10 Fla. L. Rev. 1 (1957); Gunning, A Primer for a Mortgageable Ground Lease, The Mortgage Banker 36 (1967); Halper, People and Property: The Anatomy of a Ground Lease, 3 Real Est. Rev. 9 (Spring 1973); Halper, Mortgageability of Unsubordinated Ground Leases, 16 Real Est. Rev. 48 (Spring 1986); Kelly, Some Aspects of Leasehold Financing, 33 Notre Dame Law. 34 (1957); Smith and Lubell, Real Estate Financing: Mortgaging the Leasehold, 7 Real Est. Rev. 13 (Spring 1977); Underberg, Ground Leasing Makes Dollars and Sense for Developers, 1 Real Est. Rev. 38 (Summer 1971).

4. Leasehold Mortgage Encumbering the Fee: The Subordinated Mortgage

One imaginative real estate financing technique is the so-called streamlined mortgage, whereby the fee owner agrees to subject (or "subordinate") her fee interest to the lien of the leasehold mortgage by joining in the mortgage. Because the security for the loan would be the fee itself and not just the ground lessee-mortgagor's defeasible leasehold estate, the lender would be able to take into account the value of the land for appraisal purposes. Accordingly, because the developer could anticipate larger financing, he might be in a position to construct more extensive improvements on the leased land and pay a higher ground rent to the fee owner, who would thereby receive greater security for the rent obligation under the ground lease.

If Dan Developer is able to convince the ground lessor to subject her fee ownership to the lien of the mortgage, Dan might be able to (1) substantially reduce his cash requirement by obtaining a loan closer to his development cost and (2) still retain the tax advantages of ordinary leasehold mortgage financing. Moreover, it is customary for the lender to both absolve the fee owner of personal liability with respect to the obligations of the mortgage and to minimize the fee owner's risk of forfeiting her interest in the land by affording her the opportunity to cure a default by the developer-lessee under the mortgage. Therefore, as the following excerpt suggests, a streamlined mortgage that has characteristics of both a fee and a leasehold mortgage can create advantages over ordinary leasehold financing for all of the concerned parties.

Smith and Lubell, Real Estate Financing: The Streamlined Mortgage
4 Real Est. Rev. 21 (Summer 1974)

THE STREAMLINED MORTGAGE

Techniques of financing real estate are limited only by the imagination of the developer and his attorney and the legal restrictions imposed on the institutional lender. The "streamlined mortgage" (a term we have coined merely for purposes of identification) is a current result of this alchemy.

All too frequently, this form of financing is erroneously referred to as a subordinated fee loan. Although it has characteristics of both a fee mortgage and leasehold mortgage, it is truly neither. A mortgage on the fee affords the lender the security of the whole pie since the entire estate stands behind the loan. The mortgagee under a leasehold mortgage, on the other hand, has only the security of a piece of the pie—the leasehold estate as evidenced by the ground lease. You might say that the fee mortgagee is the fee owner once removed, while the leasehold mortgagee is the lessee once removed.

But when, in the latter case, the landowner-ground lessor voluntarily subjects his fee to the leasehold mortgage, a streamlined mortgage results. The property owner actually joins in the mortgage, thereby telling the lender that "in the event you foreclose, you have the security of my ownership of the land."

The streamlined mortgage is widely employed as a financing vehicle for several reasons. The high cost of land and the tight money market both encourage developers to consider a leasehold plus a leasehold mortgage as a means of maintaining leverage. And since some owners of prime properties, particularly in urban areas, wish to hold their land either as a hedge against inflation or to avoid paying high capital gains taxes on a sale, a long-term ground lease may be the only viable path to development.

ADVANTAGES OF THE STREAMLINED MORTGAGE

It is an evident advantage for the developer to lease instead of purchase land. His initial capital requirements are less and the full yearly rental payments for the land are deductible. If the developer had purchased the land outright and mortgaged the fee estate, only mortgage interest would be deductible. When the land is leased, part of the rental payments are the equivalent of repayment of principal which the developer would not have been able to deduct if he had purchased the land and mortgaged the fee.

The streamlined mortgage enables the lender to value the property at a higher amount than in the case of a pure leasehold mortgage, since value can be attributed to the land as well as to the improvements. This means the developer can get a larger loan than would be possible if his leasehold estate were the only security. . . .

Moreover, it is patent that a loan supported by the whole pie (the fee estate), instead of a piece of the pie (the leasehold), allows the lender greater latitude in granting indulgence upon default before resorting to foreclosure.

STRUCTURING THE GROUND LEASE TO MEET LENDER REQUIREMENTS

The ground lease is frequently an extensive document. If it has not been negotiated with the lender's requirements in mind, leasehold financing may be unavailable. Since the requirements for a streamlined mortgage are considerably less detailed, the probability of rejection of a loan application on technical grounds is reduced. In addition, any shortcomings of the ground lease can be rectified in the streamlined mortgage documents themselves, which the owner is obliged to execute in order to subject his fee to the mortgage. . . .

LEASE PROVISIONS FOR THE STREAMLINED MORTGAGE

Where the fee owner voluntarily subjects his fee to the developer-lessee's mortgage, the requirements of the lender are considerably less stringent.

- The term of the ground lease must be at least equal to the term of the mortgage.
- The ground lease should expressly provide that the fee owner will join in the execution of the mortgage and subject his fee estate to the lender's lien.
- Although not universally required by lenders, the ground lease should be made subordinate or inferior to the mortgage lien, so that the leasehold estate is eliminated upon foreclosure and the lender is provided with a fee simple estate. Unless the lender is satisfied that the ground lease will be eliminated upon foreclosure, it will require removal or modification of the lease provisions it finds objectionable from a legal or underwriting point of view. The developer will then have to renegotiate the ground lease, which may prove costly in terms of increased rent or other concessions to the owner.
- The ground lease should stipulate that sub-leases with space tenants provide for "attornment" in the event of foreclosure or any other termination of the ground lease; that is, sub-lessees will recognize the fee owner and his successor, the mortgagee, as the landlord and rent will continue to be paid accordingly. The reason for this requirement is illustrated in the following example of a streamlined loan on a shopping center.

Joe Developer has negotiated a forty-year ground lease with landowner Frank Farmer. The lease contains elements satisfactory to Dollar Life Insurance Company, which agrees to lend Developer $4 million on the security of a shopping center development. Farmer agrees to join in the mortgage and subject his fee to Dollar Life's mortgage, and the ground lease has been subordinated to the lien on the fee. Subleases with a department store, supermarket, and eighteen satellite stores have been executed by Developer.

If Dollar Life forecloses its mortgage and the inferior ground lease is extinguished, the subleases which flow from this ground lease will also be wiped out. Unless the ground lease requires attornment and the space tenants agree to attorn, Dollar Life will lose the source of income to repay its loan.

To make sure subjection of the fee to the lessee's mortgage will be accomplished without difficulty, the ground lease must require the fee owner to execute the mortgage documents submitted to him. Since no state law, to the writers' knowledge, requires the fee owner to execute the promissory note to effectually subject his land to the mortgage, he need sign only the mortgage (or deed of trust) instrument itself.

Since the mortgage documents may be executed two or three years after the ground lease is signed, the lessee must be certain that the landowner's heirs and assigns are required to fulfill his obligations. In one actual situation, the ground lease was signed in 1968, the property was developed and completed as a shopping center in 1972, and the mortgage was submitted for signature of the fee owner upon completion. Unfortunately, he had died leaving heirs in Georgia, Florida, and Hawaii, all of whom were required to join in the execution of the mortgage.

HOW TO CONVINCE THE LANDOWNER TO GO ALONG

While the fee owner is entitled to compensation by way of above-market ground rent for agreeing to subject his fee to the lien of a mortgage, he may still be reluctant to consent to a streamlined mortgage because he runs the risk of losing his property in the event the lessee defaults. (The fee owner may also object to the limitations against his mortgaging the fee.) But the developer has some good arguments to meet these objections:

- If the owner developed the land himself, he would have to put up the land as security in order to get financing.
- Should the developer-lessee default, the landowner can cure the default and step into the developer's shoes. To assure the owner of this opportunity, he is entitled, by the terms of the mortgage, to prior notice of default from the mortgagee.
- The developer can obtain greater financing to permit a more extensive improvement and create greater security for the rent obligation under the ground lease.

- Since the developer can anticipate a larger loan, he may be in a position to pay a higher land rent.
- The owner will not be personally liable for payment of the loan or for any other obligation of the mortgage.

CONCLUSION

The streamlined mortgage benefits all concerned. It offers the developer an opportunity for a larger loan with a smaller equity investment. The lender is afforded better security than in pure leasehold mortgage financing. The negotiation and documentation of the loan is simplified, and both developer and landowner are given greater flexibility in structuring a loan which will accommodate their respective interests.

NOTES AND QUESTIONS

Subordination of the Ground Lease and Attornment by Subtenants. Because the security for a streamlined mortgage is a lien on the fee as well as the leasehold estate, the lender's requirements as a leasehold mortgagee with respect to the ground lease are considerably less stringent than those discussed at Chapter 11A3, supra. However, as discussed in the foregoing excerpt by Smith and Lubell, the lender often will require that the ground lease be subordinate, or inferior, to its lien on the fee by insisting that the lease be recorded after the mortgage or by having the ground lessee execute a subordination agreement. The objective of this requirement is to extinguish the inferior ground lease in the event that the lender forecloses its lien on the fee. In addition, the lender frequently will require that the occupancy subtenants agree (in the subleases or by separate instrument) to "attorn" to (recognize) the new fee owner—be it the mortgagee or the purchaser at the foreclosure sale—as the landlord and the party to whom the future rents will be paid. If you need to review the concepts of subordination and attornment, see Chapter 3E2.

The following is a brief example and diagram outlining the configuration of the relationship between the parties created by these requirements, as shown in Figure 11-1.

Figure 11 – 1

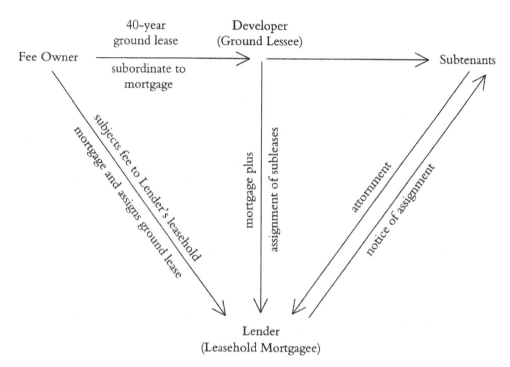

Lender
(Leasehold Mortgagee)

Dan Developer has negotiated a 40-year ground lease with Francine Fee Owner, a farmer, so that Dan can construct a shopping center complex on the leased land. The terms of the lease are approved by the Lender Insurance Co., which agrees to lend Dan $3 million on the security of Dan's leasehold estate and improvements thereon. Francine agrees to join in the mortgage and to subject her fee ownership to the lien of Lender's mortgage, and the ground lease is subordinated to the mortgage. Subleases have been executed by Dan with a supermarket as prime tenant and with a number of secondary tenants who will operate satellite stores in the shopping center. All these space leases have been approved by Lender. Francine and Dan have *conditionally* assigned their interests in the ground lease and subleases, respectively, to Lender as additional security for the loan, and all the subtenants have executed attornment agreements with Lender.

a. Based on what you have learned about postconstruction financing, what is Lender's purpose for demanding conditional lease assignments from both Fee Owner and Dan Developer?

b. We already know that if the underlying fee is subject to a prior mortgage, Lender will usually demand that the prior mortgage be satisfied or subordinated to the lien of its leasehold mortgage; otherwise, a foreclosure of the senior mortgage might extinguish Dan's leasehold estate and Lender's security for the loan to Dan.

When Fee Owner subjects her fee interest to the lien of Lender's leasehold mortgage, Lender in effect winds up with two simultaneous mortgages: one a leasehold mortgage with a lien on Dan's leasehold estate and the other in reality a fee mortgage with a lien on Fee Owner's fee. Assuming hypothetically that the initial annual ground rent is $100,000 and the total subrental is $400,000, can you think of any reason why Lender would demand that the ground lease be made subordinate to the lien of its leasehold mortgage? For general background, see Chapter 3E.

c. What is the rationale for Lender's requirement that the subtenants execute attornment agreements in favor of itself and its successors in interest?

d. Any fee owner contemplating streamlined mortgage financing of the leasehold improvements should demand a provision in the mortgage requiring reasonable notice to it of any default by the ground lessee-mortgagor under the mortgage along with an adequate opportunity to cure the same. Notwithstanding such protective language in the streamlined mortgage, can you think of any type of default that might not be curable and that might cause the fee owner to lose her fee through a foreclosure of the mortgage?

e. Observe that a substantial time (for example, two or three years) might elapse between the execution of the ground lease and the execution of the mortgage documents. Suppose the fee owner covenants in the ground lease to subject her fee interest to the lien of the leasehold mortgage but subsequently refuses to execute the mortgage. Assuming that the agreement to encumber the fee is not unenforceable for want of certainty in its terms, what would be the arguments for and against granting specific performance of the fee owner's promise? Do you see any analogy to the case for specific performance of a mortgage loan commitment? See discussion at Chapter 4C. What about specific performance of a subordination agreement by a seller who subsequently refuses to subordinate her purchase money mortgage to a construction or postconstruction loan on the property? See discussion of purchase money mortgages at Chapter 7B3. As a matter of legal theory and sound social policy, which case is the stronger? The weaker? See Groot, Specific Performance of Contracts to Provide Permanent Financing, 60 Cornell L. Rev. 718, 736-742 (1975); Mehr and Kilgore, Enforcement of the Real Estate Loan Commitment: Improvement of the Borrower Remedies, 24 Wayne L. Rev. 1011 (1978); Eisenhardt, Note, Subordination of Purchase Money Security, 52 Cal. L. Rev. 157, 166-168 (1964).

For a general discussion of the streamlined mortgage, see ABA Section of Real Property, Probate & Trust Law Committee on Leases, Ground Leases and Their Financing, 4 Real Prop., Prob. & Tr. J. 437, 440-453 (Fall 1969); Halper, Planning and Construction Clauses in a Subordinated Ground Lease, 17 Real Est. L.J. 48 (Summer 1988).

B. SALE-AND-LEASEBACK FINANCING

As the term implies, a sale and leaseback of real estate typically involves the sale of either undeveloped land or land together with existing improvements by a land developer or business concern to an institutional investor that simultaneously leases back the property to the previous owner for an extended period of time under a net lease arrangement (one in which the lessee will pay the taxes, insurance, maintenance, and other property expenses). As noted earlier, if a developer-borrower utilizes leasehold as opposed to mortgage financing, it can reduce its cash outlay and leverage its acquisition costs and also obtain a rental deduction for its ground rent payment in lieu of the extra nondeductible amortization that would be payable on the larger fee mortgage were it to purchase the underlying fee. Likewise, because land itself is not a depreciable asset, sale-and-leaseback financing affords a developer-borrower the opportunity to maximize its liquidity and cash reserves while being able to depreciate the land in the guise of rental payments.

In the case of new construction, the developer can use either fee or leasehold mortgage financing along with equity capital to fund the cost of the land and improvements. Alternatively, the developer may be able to finance its land and construction costs by means of a sale-and-leaseback transaction with a sale price covering the costs of the land and, if applicable, the proposed improvements. This technique is frequently employed by business concerns such as retail stores that require substantial amounts of working capital to fund both inventory and operating expenses. For example, a company that wishes to build or expand its existing plant or store facilities can engage in a sale-and-leaseback transaction to fund its construction costs without sacrificing working capital for fixed assets. Similarly, by selling the proposed facility for cash and leasing it back, a company can fund the cost of construction in the event it is unable to obtain the initial construction financing from an institutional lender. Another option would be to use some variation on the sale-and-leaseback theme or even a combination of sale-leaseback and mortgage debt financing, which real estate professionals generically refer to as "split" or "component" financing. For example, a builder or business concern that already owns the land might lease the land to a separate but controlled corporation or outside entity, thereby splitting the ownership of the real estate into distinct fee and leasehold interests so that it can increase the amount of the overall financing by mortgaging each component separately. Another example of high-ratio financing, or "superleverage," that can theoretically be achieved by means of split financing is the so-called sale-buyback. Under a sale-buyback agreement, the land and projected improvements are sold prior to the commencement of construction for a sale price that covers the costs of both, and the developer simultaneously repurchases the improved real estate under a long-term installment contract. See discussion at Chapter 11B1, note 3, infra.

In the case of existing improvements, the real estate owner may likewise choose between debt financing and sale-and-leaseback financing (or some combination thereof) for the purpose of assembling additional working capital. Under the former alternative, the owner-borrower might seek to obtain secondary financing (see Chapter 7B) or, in the alternative, attempt to refinance the existing mortgage indebtedness (see Chapter 7A). Frequently, if the ownership entity is a corporation, it will be able to translate its equity in the real estate into cash by issuing its own debentures or by engaging in some other form of straight-debt financing. By contrast, the owner may wish to raise additional working capital by means of a sale and leaseback of either the land alone or of both the land and existing improvements.

In the case of either straight-debt or fee mortgage financing, the borrower will retain legal ownership of both the land and the building; whereas in the case of sale-and-leaseback financing (as well as leasehold mortgage financing), the legal and tax status of the borrower would be that of a lessee with respect to the land, the improvements, or both. Accordingly, any such selection between fee mortgage or sale-and-leaseback financing should always involve a careful balancing of the competing legal and tax considerations that are examined in the discussion that follows.

1. Comparison with Mortgage and Straight-Debt Financing

The following materials examine the structure and advantages of sale-and-leaseback transactions, particularly as compared to mortgage financing.

Stewart, Note, Taxation of Sale and Leaseback Transactions—A General Review
32 Vand. L. Rev. 945, 948-951 (1979)

The basic sale and leaseback transaction . . . is composed of several simple components—a sale for valuable consideration, a lease for a term of years, and various options to renew or repurchase. The possible combinations of these components, however, provide a flexible yet complex tool for financing or business expansion. The consideration paid by the purchaser is generally the fair market value of the property, but may be a lesser amount when other aspects of the sale or the leaseback favor the seller. Rental payments may be set at the fair rental value of the property, but are often set at a rate that will amortize the purchaser's investment over the lease's primary term at a specified rate of return.[20] This procedure provides the purchaser with a safe, guaranteed return on

---

20. This type of rental payment schedule closely resembles a mortgage payment schedule that provides for repayment of principal and interest in installments at a specified interest rate.

his investment. Repurchase and renewal options can also add flexibility to a sale and leaseback transaction. The renewal option assures the seller of continued use of property needed in his trade or business even though he has relinquished title. In addition, the original lease may state rentals for the renewal periods, enabling the seller-lessee to ascertain its maximum future costs of land and buildings. If the rental payments during the primary term of the lease fully amortize the purchaser's investment, many purchaser-lessors will accept reduced rent for the renewal periods. The repurchase option provides the seller with a means of reacquiring the property if necessary due to future business developments. The option may allow repurchase at any time during the lease, only at specified times, or only at the expiration of the lease. The option price may be stated, determined by appraisal, or tied to the remaining lease payments required to amortize the purchaser's investment.

In addition to the variations mentioned above, a sale and leaseback may be structured as a multiple party transaction to provide additional flexibility. For example, the seller or purchaser may be a syndicate, joint venture, or group of individuals or corporations. The purchaser may also arrange for one or more third-party lending institutions to finance the purchase, using the acquired property and the lease as collateral and repaying the loan from the lease payments. These additional possibilities make the real estate sale and leaseback an extremely flexible and useful business tool. . . .

Sale and leaseback transactions may be utilized for a variety of business and financial purposes. A principal use is to provide the seller-lessee with immediate cash to meet increased working capital needs. The sale and leaseback generally provides cash equal to 100 percent of the fair market value of the property sold, while conventional financing techniques normally yield only 75-80 percent of the fair market value of the property securing the loan. In essence, the seller-lessee uses the sale and leaseback transaction to transform fixed assets into working capital while retaining possession and use of the property. As a side effect, this technique can provide a better balance sheet position for the seller-lessee, which enables it to obtain a greater amount of conventional financing in the future. The seller-lessee obtains this better balance sheet position by increasing current assets with the proceeds of the sale and thereby increasing its current ratio, an important determinant of credit standing.[23]

Many companies have found the sale and leaseback transaction a useful means for financing expansion of facilities or obtaining funds for construction. This technique has been especially prevalent in the retail sales industry. Many businesses in this industry must make a significant investment in their physical plant, and simultaneously require large amounts of working capital for inventory and operating expenses. If the business is growing rapidly, the working capital

---

23. The current ratio is the ratio of current assets to current liabilities. Lending institutions view this ratio as an indicator of a debtor's ability to service immediate obligations under short-term loans. When fixed assets are sold the cash received increases current assets without a corresponding increase in current liabilities, thus increasing the current ratio and providing the debtor with a better credit standing for short-term borrowing.

requirements often become so great that the business finds needed expansion of its physical plant impossible to finance. These businesses often expand or build new stores and then enter into sale and leaseback transactions to convert fixed assets into working capital.[25]

Another use of the sale and leaseback transaction is to obtain financing in a tight money market. When credit is tight and conventional financing is difficult to obtain, investors may be willing to enter into a sale and leaseback transaction as a substitute for a loan because ownership of property provides a hedge against inflation for the investor and also eliminates legal problems connected with foreclosure and collection of debt if the seller is unable to meet his obligations.[27]

In addition to the advantages listed above, a seller-lessee may be able to use a sale and leaseback transaction to circumvent loan restrictions or state and federal regulations. Although loan agreements often contain provisions limiting additional borrowing and requiring the debtor to meet certain ratio tests,[28] leaseback agreements seldom have similar provisions. Moreover, the parties often can structure the sale and leaseback transaction so that it does not breach provisions of prior loan agreements that conventional financing techniques would violate. Also, several state and federal regulations relating to the ownership of property by certain organizations do not apply to leaseholds under a sale and leaseback transaction.

The purchaser-lessor in a sale and leaseback may also obtain certain financial advantages from the transaction. The rate of return is generally higher on a sale and leaseback than on a loan secured by the same property. The investor in a sale and leaseback procures this higher return because he takes additional risks by investing 100 percent of the fair market value of the property, rather than the lower percentage generally securing a loan. . . . Another significant advantage to the purchaser-lessor is that the ownership of property provides a hedge against inflation since any appreciation in value will accrue to the owner.[33] Finally, since most leasebacks are "net leases," the purchaser has a relatively management-free investment with a built-in tenant and a guaranteed return.

25. This technique is also used by contractors to acquire funds for independent construction. The contractor first purchases a construction site with his own funds and then enters into a sale and leaseback transaction to obtain financing necessary to construct a building on the site.

27. Since the lessor owns legal title to the property, he need not go through foreclosure proceedings to take possession of the property. Further, the property will not be tied up in any bankruptcy proceedings that may ensue if the lessee becomes insolvent.

28. These ratio tests include the current ratio, debt-equity ratio, and quick asset ratio. These ratios are indicators of the debtor's continued ability to service its debt.

33. This hedge against inflation may be limited or eliminated if the lease contains a repurchase option that sets the option price at anything other than the fair market value of the property at the time the option is exercised. Any other type of repurchase option is likely to allow the lessee to enjoy partially or fully the benefits of any appreciation.

Fuller, Sale and Leasebacks and the *Frank Lyon* Case
48 Geo. Wash. L. Rev. 60, 60-63 (1979)

Typical sale and leaseback transactions may be illustrated by two examples. In the first example, Seller, who owns the land and building used in his business, sells this real estate to Buyer. At the same time the parties enter into a lease contract for a long term—perhaps forty or fifty years. The rental is fixed at an amount that will give Buyer an acceptable return on his investment. Frequently, the lease gives the lessee one or more renewal options.

In the second example, a new building is constructed on land already owned by the business or land to be acquired for the purpose. The land is sold to Buyer under a contract that provides not only for a subsequent long-term lease, but also obligates Seller to construct the planned new building on the property. . . .

In either of the above transactions, the buyer typically finances his acquisition by borrowing most of the purchase price from an institutional lender. The buyer's role is that of a passive investor: not only is most of his investment made with borrowed money, but his obligations under the lease are almost non-existent. As a rule, the lessee pays real estate taxes, insurance and repair costs, and assumes the risk of casualty or condemnation. Thus the lessee bears all the operating expenses and all the burdens he would bear as owner, and the buyer/lessor enjoys his return free and clear of any costs.

Tax considerations aside, the sale and leaseback arrangement offers significant inducements to the parties. For the investor (the buyer), the return can be higher than that paid on competitive securities such as mortgages and corporate bonds. Usury laws and regulations surrounding mortgage lending do not apply to rentals and the leases under which they are paid. The investment is well protected because the investor owns the property and can depend on the successful operations of a well-chosen lessee to continue to provide funds to pay the rent. Finally, the buyer can reasonably expect that the value of the property will rise over the years because real estate values in the United States have generally risen with inflation. Thus, when the lease expires, even if the useful life of the improvements has ended, the land and buildings should have substantial value. In many cases, the fair market value of the property after forty or fifty years of use will still greatly exceed the original price.

The seller/lessee may also obtain significant non-tax advantages from the sale and leaseback. First, a large sum of cash is realized at once.[4] The sale of the property produces the full market value, but a loan secured by a mortgage on the same property would obtain only a portion of the value. [M]any companies may be operating under existing legal obligations (incurred, perhaps, incident to the issuance of senior securities) that severely restrict any new indebtedness. A sale

---

4. Or, if the transaction is for the construction or acquisition of a new property, the cash will not be retained, but a major obligation will be avoided.

and leaseback may permit such a company to obtain needed funds without renegotiating such agreements.

The tax advantages offered by the sale and leaseback transaction are also attractive. The lessee can claim all his rent payments as business expense deductible from ordinary income.[7] Any gain realized on the sale of the property will ordinarily qualify for long-term capital gain treatment under section 1231 of the Internal Revenue Code.[8]

The advantages of the sale and leaseback become apparent when the seller/lessee is compared with the owner of business property who mortgages the property to obtain a loan. Under the mortgage arrangement, the part of the owner's payments on the mortgage that represents interest is deductible, but amounts representing repayment of principal are not. The borrowing owner will also be able to take deductions for depreciation, to the extent that depreciation is allowable. The deduction, however, may be limited by several factors: first, the basis for depreciation is historical cost, not market value; second, the original basis already may have been reduced by depreciation deductions; and third, any amount of basis allocable to land in no event may be subject to depreciation. These limitations contrast with the allowance of all the rent paid by the lessee under sale and leaseback. Under the sale and leaseback, the rental payments are based on the full market value of the property and include amounts that, in a purchase financed by mortgage, would be allocable to amortization of principal and to the value of the non-depreciable land. The tax advantage to the lessee is roughly comparable to those an owner would enjoy if he were allowed to deduct his repayment of principal and to depreciate his land.

The tax advantages of the sale and leaseback to the buyer are no less attractive. If the buyer has leveraged his investment with a substantial proportion of indebtedness, as is common, the interest payable on the debt is deductible. In addition, having retained ownership of the property, the buyer/lessor is entitled to take depreciation on the leased property (other than land).[14] The rental payments represent income to the buyer, but the combined deductions for interest and depreciation often greatly exceed the rent income, thus offsetting other income of the investor. The overall effect of this combination is that the rental income is enjoyed as a kind of tax-free cash flow while the other income, freed from income tax by the surplus deductions, adds to the after-tax yield obtained by the investment. The sale and leaseback thus offers the investor a real estate tax shelter with a high degree of investment security. . . .

---

7. I.R.C. §162(a).

8. §1231(a). The gain will qualify as a long-term capital gain only so long as the property is used in a trade or business. Id. See also I.R.C. §1202.

14. §167. Depreciation, however, is predicated on a capital investment in the property by the taxpayer, not bare legal title.

NOTES AND QUESTIONS

> ➤ *Problem 11-4*

Suppose that Dan Developer constructs a shopping center on land that he purchased for $1 million. Ten years later, based on a projected net income of $860,000 and an assumed capitalization rate of 11.1 percent, the shopping center has an appraised value of approximately $7,750,000 and a remaining useful life of 20 years. The outstanding principal balance on the 30-year fee mortgage Dan obtained to develop the property has been reduced from $3 million to about $2,873,000 over the 10-year period. Dan has been taking depreciation deductions in the amount of $76,923 per annum. Dan would like to translate his equity (in the amount of $4,877,000) into cash so he can invest in other shopping center developments.

Dan has the option of refinancing with Ace Insurance Company for a new mortgage loan amount of about $5,800,000 (at a loan-to-value ratio of 75 percent). However, assume he would have to pay an origination fee and prepayment penalty totaling $800,000, so his gross refinancing proceeds would amount to $5 million. While most mortgage loans are constant-payment loans (see Chapter 5A2), assume for simplicity's sake that the new mortgage is repayable in the amount of $290,000 per annum for 20 years plus annual interest at 10 percent on the outstanding principal balance, so that the total debt-service payment in the first loan year would be $870,000. Alternatively, Dan could sell the real estate for its full market value of $7,750,000 with a 20-year leaseback at an annual rental of $426,250 (enabling the purchaser to recoup her investment over the 20-year term and receive a 10 percent income return but ignoring the time value of money) and with an option to purchase at a price that would relate to the market value of the real estate on the expiration of the 20-year leaseback period.

In terms as nonmathematical as possible, explain what factors are relevant in deciding which mode of assembling working capital would be best for Dan in the short term and in the long run. Make any necessary assumptions. ◄

1. Rate of Income Return. The foregoing example assumes that both purchaser and lender, respectively, would receive sufficient rent or debt-service payments over the initial 20-year term of the leaseback or new mortgage to both amortize its investment and receive a market (10 percent) rate of income return. Why should this be so? In contrast to a mortgage lender, a purchaser in a sale-and-leaseback transaction receives ownership of both the land and the building. Why should the purchaser be able to demand as high a rate of return on its investment?

2. Split Financing: Sale and Leaseback Plus Leasehold Mortgage. A developer who owns the land can sever the fee from the leasehold improvements by selling the land for its market value to an institutional investor who would then ground lease the land back to the developer. Either the investor or another lender would make a leasehold mortgage loan to fund the construction costs of the improvements. As security for the loan the lender would obtain a leasehold mortgage against the developer relying on the long-term ground lease the developer has with the owner and on the income stream that will eventually flow from the improvements. As a hedge against inflation, the investor, as ground lessor, would get a specified ground rent plus a percentage rental or some other equity kicker. In this manner, the developer theoretically might be able to obtain 100 percent financing (or more) of the land cost, whereas had it obtained conventional mortgage financing the loan-to-value ratio would be about 75 percent for both the land and the improvements. For example, suppose a developer wants to construct a shopping center costing $4 million on land he owns worth $2 million. Assuming the loan appraisal value of both the land and the improvements is $6 million, a regular 75 percent fee mortgage loan from an insurance company or other postconstruction lender would yield a loan amount of $4.5 million. By contrast, if he engages in a sale and leaseback of the land and obtains a leasehold mortgage (with the same 75 percent loan-to-value ratio), he would end up with pretax proceeds of $5 million (the $2 million land value plus 75 percent of the $4 million building value).

Moreover, if the investor who purchases the land is willing to subject its fee interest to the lien of the leasehold mortgage in exchange for a higher ground rental or some other consideration, the developer could attain even greater leverage. The loan amount under such a subordinated leasehold mortgage on an encumbered fee might include 75 percent of the appraised value of the land plus the improvements. Therefore, in our example, this would theoretically yield a startling pretax total of $6.5 million for the developer—the $2 million land sale proceeds plus a loan amount equal to 75 percent of the $6 million land-plus-building value. Of course, this presupposes that the sublease, or "occupancy," rentals will be sufficient in amount to enable the developer to pay the extra ground rent necessary to induce the investor to pay the full value of the land ($2 million), notwithstanding the condition that the investor-ground lessor subject the fee to the lien of the leasehold mortgage. Alternatively, the mortgagee might accept a "partial subordination," whereby the fee owner receives an unencumbered fee on condition that it waive its right to the ground rent in the event that (1) the developer defaults and (2) the income from the property is insufficient to meet the debt-service payments on the leasehold mortgage. See M. Madison, J. Dwyer, and S. Bender, The Law of Real Estate Financing §§7:22-7:45 (2016); Katz, Alternative Real Estate Financing—The Sale Leaseback, 45 J. Kan. B. Ass'n 195, 195-196 (1976); Mandell, Tax Aspects of Sales and Leaseback as Practical Devices for Transfer and Operation of Real Property, 18 N.Y.U. Inst. Fed. Tax 17, 18 (1960); Weil, Land Leasebacks Move Up Fast as Financing Techniques, 1 Real Est. Rev. 65 (Winter 1972).

3. Split Financing: Purchase and Installment Sale-Buyback. Another high-ratio technique is the so-called sale-buyback. Under such an arrangement, both the land and the projected improvements are sold to an institutional lender or other investor (such as an insurance company) at a stated price—usually between

80 and 90 percent of economic value and equal to 100 percent of the developer's land and audited construction costs. The developer simultaneously repurchases the real estate under a long-term installment contract. Because the developer is the "real" owner, with equitable title, and since it assumes both the benefits and burdens of ownership during the installment period, it can retain, by mutual agreement, the right to take the depreciation deductions. Under an installment sale contract, depreciation is allowed to a purchaser that has equitable title (despite the fact that it does not have legal title) where it has the obligation to maintain the property and bears the risk of loss. See, for example, J.I. Morgan, Inc., 30 T.C. 881 (1958), rev'd on other grounds, 272 F.2d 936 (9th Cir. 1959).

During the contract period, which is usually "closed" (no prepayment of purchase price is allowed) for a longer-than-normal period of about 15 years, the investor not only recoups its capital at a modest rate of interest but—in exchange for granting what amounts to a 100 percent mortgage loan—also receives an equity kicker in the form of a contingent payment geared to a percentage of the developer's net income (after subtracting the installment payments). The amortization period is usually 10 years longer than it would be for a mortgage loan. The developer can thus maintain a reasonable overall constant payment and can shelter its rental income stream from taxation with deductions for depreciation, property taxes, and contract interest. The advantage to the investor is that it retains the benefit of a high-yield, inflation-hedged investment for a longer-than-normal "lock-in" period; the investor can invest more money, albeit at a higher risk, than would be possible for straight mortgage financing. Moreover, even though the term of the contract of sale is usually about 10 years longer than it would be if made on a mortgage basis, the installment contract payments are geared to liquidate the installment obligation over the normal mortgage period at somewhat below the current mortgage rate. Thus, for example, if the fixed contract payment is at the rate of 8.5 percent of the purchase price and the contract term is 35 years, 7 months, the investor can write off its investment at a 7.25 percent yield in 26 years, 7 months and continue to receive an additional 9 years of contract payments, which, of course, would raise its average yield substantially. See Hershman, Usury and the "New Look" in Real Estate Financing, 4 Real Prop., Prob. & Tr. J. 315, 321-323 (1969).

4. The Effect of Sale and Leaseback on the Balance Sheet of the Borrower. One nontax advantage of the sale and leaseback has been that the obligation of the seller-lessee, in contrast to that of a mortgagor, might not necessarily be reflected as a liability on the borrower's balance sheet, depending on whether the leaseback is structured as a true sale and leaseback ("operating lease") versus a so-called capital lease. A lessee that successfully classifies the lease transaction from the sale and leaseback as an "operating lease" is allowed to remove the fixed asset of real estate from its balance sheet and replace it with the cash received from the sale. The lessee also only shows the annual lease obligation to the lessor as a liability. However, if the transaction is classified as a capital lease it is treated like a financing transaction where the fixed asset in the control of the lessee must remain on the lessee's balance sheet. More importantly, the lessee must also show as a liability the present value of all the lessee's future rent payment obligations. As is illustrated in Century Electric Co. v. Commissioner, 192 F.2d 155 (8th Cir. 1951), cert. denied, 342 U.S. 954 (1952), excerpted and discussed herein, seller lessees had frequently used the sale-leaseback in an attempt to improve their ratio of assets to liabilities on their balance sheet to make themselves appear more creditworthy to lenders. Recently, however, the Financial Accounting Standards Board (FASB) has proposed new accounting rules to abolish the "operating lease" classification which would force uniform adherence to capital lease accounting standards. See Hanley, New Accounting Standards Will Drive Changes in Real Estate Industry Practices, 25 Prob. & Prop. 54 (Mar./Apr. 2011); Owendoff, Changes in FASB 13 Rules to Change Commercial Real Estate Industry, 5 Center for Real Quarterly J. (2001). Such a change would undermine the sale-leaseback as an accounting strategy to achieve a higher asset to liability ratio. The real estate industry has recently successfully protested the new rules to delay their implementation; however, it is conceded in the industry that the changes will eventually take effect. As of the printing of this book, accounting rules of the FASB in its Statement of Financial Accounting Standards (SFAS) No. 13 (Nov. 1976) require that the sale and leaseback of land and buildings be shown as a debt obligation if (1) the leaseback term (including bargain renewals and economically compelled renewals) extends for 75 percent or more of the estimated useful life of the improvements or (2) the present value (at the commencement of the lease term) of the future base rental payments equals 90 percent or more of the fair market value of the property. The underlying assumption for disregarding the transaction as a true sale and leaseback is that the seller-lessee has not transferred substantially all of the benefits and risks of ownership to the purchaser-lessor and, hence, the leasehold would be reported as a capital lease asset along with a capital lease obligation on the balance sheet of the seller-lessee. By contrast, if the leaseback is structured as an ordinary operating lease and constitutes a true sale and leaseback, off-balance sheet treatment for the leaseback is allowed. Financial Accounting Standards Board, SFAS No. 13, Accounting for Leases §§60, 72. Therefore, the seller would like to have the sale recognized for accounting purposes and have the real estate asset (and any related liabilities) removed from its balance sheet and yet be able to use the so-called full accrual method to reflect the entire profit in the year of sale. SFAS No. 66 provides that recognition of all or part of the profit for accounting purposes must be postponed if at the time of sale (1) the profit is not determinable (for example, the collectability of the selling price is not reasonably assured) or (2) the earnings process is not virtually completed.

Because SFAS No. 66 imposes more stringent profit recognition standards than does SFAS No. 13, new guidelines under SFAS No. 98 were promulgated to resolve the conflict. To recognize a gain or loss from a sale and remove the real estate asset and related debt from the seller's balance sheet, the seller-lessee must (1) show that the purchaser-lessor will assume all of the normal risks and rewards of ownership, as reflected by the terms of the sale agreement; (2) demonstrate that it is actively using the property in its trade or business in consideration of the payment of rent under a "normal leaseback" (rental) arrangement; and (3) show that there is no "continuing involvement" by the seller in the property (for example, the providing of nonrecourse financing to the purchaser for any portion of the purchase price, participation with the purchaser in any net refinancing proceeds, or the incurring of any obligation to repurchase the property). See generally Lieberman and Kosoffsky, Sale-Leaseback Accounting: The Rules Have Changed, 4 Real Est. Acct. & Tax'n 26 (Spring 1989); The Mortgage and Real Estate Executive's Report, June 15, 1989, at 1, 2.

Based on accounting principles, can you think of any reason why a leaseback, in contrast to a mortgage or other debt financing, should not be reflected as a fixed liability on the balance sheet of the seller-lessee? Under what circumstances should the leasehold be reflected as an asset?

5. *Usury.* Another nontax advantage of sale-and-leaseback financing over debt financing is that the former is, in form, a sale and not a loan; accordingly, as a general rule, usury restrictions on lending would not apply. See Chapter 5A1, note 6.

6. *Option Perils.* Because the sale-and-leaseback arrangement can encompass a repurchase option in favor of the seller-lessee that it may exercise as late as the expiration of the long-term lease, the optionee must ensure that the repurchase option satisfies the rule against perpetuities. See Symphony Space v. Pergola Properties, 88 N.Y.2d 466, 669 N.E.2d 799, 646 N.Y.S.2d 641 (1996) (invalidating option in favor of seller-lessee that failed to vest within the applicable period).

7. *Additional Reading.* For a general discussion of sale and leaseback, see Burstein, Distinguishing True Leases from Conditional Sales and Financing Arrangements, 63 Taxes 395 (June 1985); Carey, Corporate Financing through the Sale and Lease-Back of Property: Business, Tax and Policy Considerations, 62 Harv. L. Rev. 1 (1948); Clark, Changing Considerations in Sale and Leaseback Transactions, 42 Taxes 725 (1964); Egan, Sale-Leaseback: Protecting the Institutional Investor against New Risks, 6 Real Est. L.J. 199 (Winter 1978); Marcus, Real Estate Purchase-Leaseback as Secured Loans, 2 Real Est. L.J. 664 (Winter 1974); Morris, Sale and Leaseback Transactions of Real Property—A Proposal, 30 Tax Law. 701 (Spring 1977); Rubenstein and London, Sales and Leaseback: Some Valuation Problems, 37 Tax Law. 481 (Spring 1984); Strum, Sale-Leaseback: Protection for Accelerated Depreciation Deduction and Clear Title, 7 Real Prop., Prob. & Tr. J. 785 (Winter 1972); and Wilson, Sales and Leaseback, 16 S. Cal. Tax Inst. 149 (1964).

2. Tax Pitfalls of Using Sale-and-Leaseback Financing

Notwithstanding the financial and tax advantages of using the sale-and-leaseback transaction, certain tax pitfalls are associated with the use of this technique. Because the sale and leaseback is frequently nothing more than a financing arrangement, and because the courts have uniformly held that substance controls over form, the I.R.S. on occasion has been successful in characterizing the transaction as a disguised mortgage loan.[6] Recharacterization is especially likely when the sale price is lower than the market value of the real estate and the seller is allowed to repurchase the property for a nominal price since such facts indicate that the seller never intended to divest itself of ownership and that the purchaser is not the true owner because it is deprived of any meaningful benefit from appreciation in the value of the land. In addition, if the leaseback rental payments are disproportionately high or if they deescalate over time, a rental deduction could be denied—in the former case on the theory that the seller-lessee is engaging in a disguised purchase of the real estate and in the latter on the ground that the rental payment is a prepayment that should be spread out evenly over the entire leaseback period.

As you read the cases and materials that follow, keep in mind this question: In the case of an ordinary sale and leaseback between unrelated parties dealing with one another at arm's length, should the transaction be treated for tax purposes as a true sale followed by a leaseback or as something else (such as a mortgage loan)? In other words, is the typical sale and leaseback an economic fact or a tax fiction—or is such a question oversimplified inasmuch as any such determination should be made on a case-by-case basis?

Frank Lyon Co. v. United States
435 U.S. 561 (1978)

Mr. Justice BLACKMUN delivered the opinion of the Court: This case concerns the federal income tax consequences of a sale-and-leaseback in which petitioner Frank Lyon Company (Lyon) took title to a building under construction by Worthen Bank & Trust Company (Worthen) of Little Rock, Ark., and simultaneously leased the building back to Worthen for long-term use as its headquarters and principal banking facility. . . .

. . . Worthen in 1965 was an Arkansas-chartered bank and a member of the Federal Reserve System. Frank Lyon was Lyon's majority shareholder and board

---

6. Sale-and-leaseback transactions also run the risk of recharacterization in bankruptcy proceedings. See Liona Corp. v. PCH Assocs. (excerpted at Chapter 18EI). See generally Homburger and Marschel, Recharacterization Revisited: A View of Recharacterization of Sale and Leaseback Transactions in Bankruptcy After Fifteen Years, 41 Real Prop. Prob. & Tr. J. 123 (Spring 2006).

chairman; he also served on Worthen's board. Worthen at that time began to plan the construction of a multistory bank and office building to replace its existing facility in Little Rock. About the same time Worthen's competitor, Union National Bank of Little Rock, also began to plan a new bank and office building. Adjacent sites on Capitol Avenue, separated only by Spring Street, were acquired by the two banks. It became a matter of competition, for both banking business and tenants, and prestige as to which bank would start and complete its building first.

Worthen initially hoped to finance, to build, and to own the proposed facility at a total cost of $9 million for the site, building, and adjoining parking deck. This was to be accomplished by selling $4 million in debentures and using the proceeds in the acquisition of the capital stock of a wholly owned real estate subsidiary.... Worthen's plan, however, had to be abandoned for two significant reasons: [First,] as a bank chartered under Arkansas law, Worthen legally could not pay more interest on any debentures it might issue than that then specified by Arkansas law. But the proposed obligations would not be marketable at that rate. [Second,] applicable statutes or regulations of the Arkansas State Bank Department and the Federal Reserve System required Worthen, as a state bank subject to their supervision, to obtain prior permission for the investment in banking premises.... Worthen, accordingly, was advised by staff employees of the Federal Reserve System that they would not recommend approval of the plan by the System's Board of Governors.

Worthen therefore was forced to seek an alternative solution that would provide it with the use of the building, satisfy the state and federal regulators, and attract the necessary capital. In September 1967 it proposed a sale-and-leaseback arrangement. The State Bank Department and the Federal Reserve System approved this approach, but the Department required that Worthen possess an option to purchase the leased property at the end of the 15th year of the lease at a set price, and the federal regulator required that the building be owned by an independent third party....

Worthen then obtained a commitment from New York Life Insurance Company to provide $7,140,000 in permanent mortgage financing on the building, conditioned upon its approval of the titleholder. At this point Lyon entered the negotiations and it, too, made a proposal....

... Worthen selected Lyon as the investor....

B

In May 1968 Worthen, Lyon, City Bank [the construction lender], and New York Life executed complementary and interlocking agreements under which the building was sold by Worthen to Lyon as it was constructed, and Worthen leased the completed building back from Lyon.

1. AGREEMENTS BETWEEN WORTHEN AND LYON

Worthen and Lyon executed a ground lease, a sales agreement, and a building lease.

Under the ground lease dated May 1, 1968, App. 366, Worthen leased the site to Lyon for 76 years and 7 months through November 30, 2044. The first 19 months were the estimated construction period. The ground rents payable by Lyon to Worthen were $50 for the first 26 years and 7 months and thereafter in quarterly payments:

> 12/1/94 through 11/30/99 (5 years)—$100,000 annually
> 12/1/99 through 11/30/04 (5 years)—$150,000 annually
> 12/1/04 through 11/30/09 (5 years)—$200,000 annually
> 12/1/09 through 11/30/34 (25 years)—$250,000 annually
> 12/1/34 through 11/30/44 (10 years)—$10,000 annually

Under the sales agreement dated May 19, 1968, id., at 508, Worthen agreed to sell the building to Lyon, and Lyon agreed to buy it, piece by piece as it was constructed, for a total price not to exceed $7,640,000, in reimbursements to Worthen for its expenditures for the construction of the building.

Under the building lease dated May 1, 1968, id., at 376, Lyon leased the building back to Worthen for a primary term of 25 years from December 1, 1969, with options in Worthen to extend the lease for eight additional 5-year terms, a total of 65 years. During the period between the expiration of the building lease (at the latest, November 30, 2034, if fully extended) and the end of the ground lease on November 30, 2044, full ownership, use, and control of the building were Lyon's, unless, of course, the building had been repurchased by Worthen. Worthen was not obligated to pay rent under the building lease until completion of the building. . . . The total rent for that building over the 25-year primary term of the lease thus was $14,989,767.24. That rent equaled the principal and interest payments that would amortize the $7,140,000 New York Life mortgage loan over the same period. . . .

The building lease was a "net lease," under which Worthen was responsible for all expenses usually associated with the maintenance of an office building, including repairs, taxes, utility charges, and insurance, and was to keep the premises in good condition, excluding, however, reasonable wear and tear.

Finally, under the lease, Worthen had the option to repurchase the building at the following times and prices:

> 11/30/80 (after 11 years)—$6,325,169.85
> 11/30/84 (after 15 years)—$5,432,607.32
> 11/30/89 (after 20 years)—$4,187,328.04
> 11/30/94 (after 25 years)—$2,145,935.00

These repurchase option prices were the sum of the unpaid balance of the New York Life mortgage, Lyon's $500,000 investment [the difference between the permanent loan amount and the maximum sale price agreed to], and 6% interest compounded on that investment.

2. CONSTRUCTION FINANCING AGREEMENT

By agreement dated May 14, 1968, id., at 462, City Bank agreed to lend Lyon $7,000,000 for the construction of the building. This loan was secured by a mortgage on the building and the parking deck, executed by Worthen as well as by Lyon, and an assignment by Lyon of its interests in the building lease and in the ground lease.

3. PERMANENT FINANCING AGREEMENT

By Note Purchase Agreement dated May 1, 1968, id., at 443, New York Life agreed to purchase Lyon's $7,140,000 $6^{3/4}$% 25-year secured note to be issued upon completion of the building. Under this agreement Lyon warranted that it would lease the building to Worthen for a noncancelable term of at least 25 years under a net lease at a rent at least equal to the mortgage payments on the note. Lyon agreed to make quarterly payments of principal and interest equal to the rentals payable by Worthen during the corresponding primary term of the lease. The security for the note were a first deed of trust and Lyon's assignment of its interests, in the building lease and in the ground lease. Worthen joined in the deed of trust as the owner of the fee and the parking deck.

In December 1969 the building was completed and Worthen took possession. At that time Lyon received the permanent loan from New York Life, and it discharged the interim loan from City Bank. The actual cost of constructing the office building and parking complex (excluding the cost of the land) exceeded $10,000,000.

C

Lyon filed its federal income tax returns on the accrual and calendar year basis. On its 1969 return, Lyon accrued rent from Worthen for December. It asserted as deductions one month's interest to New York Life; one month's depreciation on the building; interest on the construction loan from City Bank; and sums for legal and other expenses incurred in connection with the transaction.

On audit of Lyon's 1969 return, the Commissioner of Internal Revenue determined that Lyon was "not the owner for tax purposes of any portion of the Worthen Building," and ruled that "the income and expenses related to this building are not allowable . . . for Federal income tax purposes." He also added $2,298.15 to Lyon's 1969 income as "accrued interest income.". . . In other words, the Commissioner determined that the sale-and-leaseback arrangement was a financing transaction in which Lyon loaned Worthen $500,000 and acted as a conduit for the transmission of principal and interest from Worthen to New York Life. . . .

Lyon paid the assessment and filed a timely claim for its refund. The claim was denied, and this suit, to recover the amount so paid, was instituted in the United States District Court for the Eastern District of Arkansas. . . .

The United States Court of Appeals for the Eighth Circuit reversed, 536 F.2d 746 (1976). It held that the Commissioner correctly determined that Lyon was not the true owner of the building and therefore was not entitled to the claimed deductions. It likened ownership for tax purposes to a "bundle of sticks" and undertook its own evaluation of the facts. It concluded, in agreement with the Government's contention, that Lyon "totes an empty bundle" of ownership sticks. It stressed the following: (a) The lease agreements circumscribed Lyon's right to profit from its investment in the building by giving Worthen the option to purchase for an amount equal to Lyon's $500,000 equity plus 6% compound interest and the assumption of the unpaid balance of the New York Life mortgage. (b) The option prices did not take into account possible appreciation of the value of the building or inflation. (c) Any award realized as a result of destruction or condemnation of the building in excess of the mortgage balance and the $500,000 would be paid to Worthen and not Lyon. (d) The building rental payments during the primary term were exactly equal to the mortgage payments. (e) Worthen retained control over the ultimate disposition of the building through its various options to repurchase and to renew the lease plus its ownership of the site. (f) Worthen enjoyed all benefits and bore all burdens incident to the operation and ownership of the building so that, in the Court of Appeals' view, the only economic advantages accruing to Lyon, in the event it were considered to be the true owner of the property, were income tax savings of approximately $1.5 million during the first 11 years of the arrangement. The court concluded that the transaction was "closely akin" to that in Helvering v. Lazarus & Co., 308 U.S. 252 (1939). "In sum, the benefits, risks, and burdens which [Lyon] has incurred with respect to the Worthen building are simply too insubstantial to establish a claim to the status of owner for tax purposes.". . .

II

This Court, almost 50 years ago, observed that "taxation is not so much concerned with the refinements of title as it is with actual command over the property taxed—the actual benefit for which the tax is paid." Corliss v. Bowers, 281 U.S. 376, 378 (1930). In a number of cases, the Court has refused to permit the transfer of formal legal title to shift the incidence of taxation attributable to ownership of property where the transferor continues to retain significant control over the property transferred. In applying this doctrine of substance over form, the Court has looked to the objective economic realities of a transaction rather than to the particular form the parties employed. The Court has never regarded "the simple expedient of drawing up papers," Commissioner v. Tower, 327 U.S. 280, 291 (1946), as controlling for tax purposes when the objective economic realities are to the contrary. . . . Nor is the parties' desire to achieve a particular tax result necessarily relevant.

In the light of these general and established principles, the Government takes the position that the Worthen-Lyon transaction in its entirety should be regarded as a sham. The agreement as a whole, it is said, was only an elaborate financing scheme designed to provide economic benefits to Worthen and a guaranteed return to Lyon. The latter was but a conduit used to forward the mortgage payments, made under the guise of rent paid by Worthen to Lyon, on to New York Life as mortgagee. This, the Government claims, is the true substance of the transaction as viewed under the microscope of the tax laws. Although the arrangement was cast in sale-and-leaseback form, in substance it was only a financing transaction, and the terms of the repurchase options and lease renewals so indicate. It is said that Worthen could reacquire the building simply by satisfying the mortgage debt and paying Lyon its $500,000 advance plus interest, regardless of the fair market value of the building at the time; similarly, when the mortgage was paid off, Worthen could extend the lease at drastically reduced bargain rentals that likewise bore no relation to fair rental value but were simply calculated to pay Lyon its $500,000 plus interest over the extended term. Lyon's return on the arrangement in no event could exceed 6% compound interest (although the Government conceded it might well be less, Tr. of Oral Arg. 32). Furthermore, the favorable option and lease renewal terms made it highly unlikely that Worthen would abandon the building after it in effect had "paid off" the mortgage. The Government implies that the arrangement was one of convenience which, if accepted on its face, would enable Worthen to deduct its payments to Lyon as rent and would allow Lyon to claim a deduction for depreciation, based on the cost of construction ultimately borne by Worthen, which Lyon could offset against other income, and to deduct mortgage interest that roughly would offset the inclusion of Worthen's rental payments in Lyon's income. If, however, the Government argues, the arrangement was only a financing transaction under which Worthen was the owner of the building, Worthen's payments would be deductible only to the extent that they represented mortgage interest, and Worthen would be entitled to claim depreciation; Lyon would not be entitled to deductions for either mortgage interest or depreciation and it would not have to include Worthen's "rent" payments in its income because its function with respect to those payments was that of a conduit between Worthen and New York Life. . . .

The *Lazarus* case, we feel, is to be distinguished from the present one and is not controlling here. Its transaction was one involving only two (and not multiple) parties, the taxpayer-department store [seller-lessee] and the trustee-bank. The Court looked closely at the substance of the agreement between those two parties and rightly concluded that depreciation was deductible by the taxpayer despite the nomenclature of the instrument of conveyance and the leaseback. . . .

The present case, in contrast, involves three parties, Worthen, Lyon, and the finance agency. The usual simple two-party arrangement was legally unavailable to Worthen. Independent investors were interested in participating in the alternative available to Worthen, and Lyon itself (also independent from Worthen) won the privilege. Despite Frank Lyon's presence on Worthen's board of directors, the transaction, as it ultimately developed, was not a familial one arranged by Worthen, but one compelled by the realities of the restrictions imposed upon the bank. Had Lyon not appeared, another interested investor would have been selected. The ultimate solution would have been essentially the same. Thus, the presence of the third party, in our view, significantly distinguishes this case from *Lazarus* and removes the latter as controlling authority. . . .

There is no simple device available to peel away the form of this transaction and to reveal its substance. The effects of the transaction on all the parties were obviously different from those that would have resulted had Worthen been able simply to make a mortgage agreement with New York Life and to receive a $500,000 loan from Lyon. Then *Lazarus* would apply. Here, however, and most significantly, it was Lyon alone, and not Worthen, who was liable on the notes, first to City Bank, and then to New York Life. Despite the facts that Worthen had agreed to pay rent and that this rent equaled the amounts due from Lyon to New York Life, should anything go awry in the later years of the lease, Lyon was primarily liable. No matter how the transaction could have been devised otherwise, it remains a fact that as the agreements were placed in final form, the obligation on the notes fell squarely on Lyon. Lyon, an ongoing enterprise, exposed its very business well-being to this real and substantial risk.

The effect of this liability on Lyon is not just the abstract possibility that something will go wrong and that Worthen will not be able to make its payments. Lyon has disclosed this liability on its balance sheet for all the world to see. Its financial position was affected substantially by the presence of this long-term debt, despite the offsetting presence of the building as an asset. To the extent that Lyon has used its capital in this transaction, it is less able to obtain financing for other business needs. . . .

Other factors also reveal that the transaction cannot be viewed as anything more than a mortgage agreement between Worthen and New York Life and a loan from Lyon to Worthen. There is no legal obligation between Lyon and Worthen representing the $500,000 "loan" extended under the Government's theory. And the assumed 6% return on this putative loan—required by the audit to be recognized in the taxable year in question—will be realized only when and if Worthen exercises its options.

The Court of Appeals acknowledged that the rents alone, due after the primary term of the lease and after the mortgage has been paid, do not provide the simple 6% return which, the Government urges, Lyon is guaranteed. Thus, if

Worthen chooses not to exercise its options, Lyon is gambling that the rental value of the building during the last 10 years of the ground lease, during which the ground rent is minimal, will be sufficient to recoup its investment before it must negotiate again with Worthen regarding the ground lease. There are simply too many contingencies, including variations in the value of real estate, in the cost of money, and in the capital structure of Worthen, to permit the conclusion that the parties intended to enter into the transaction as structured in the audit and according to which the Government now urges they be taxed.

It is not inappropriate to note that the Government is likely to lose little revenue, if any, as a result of the shape given the transaction by the parties. No deduction was created that is not either matched by an item of income or that would not have been available to one of the parties if the transaction had been arranged differently. While it is true that Worthen paid Lyon less to induce it to enter into the transaction because Lyon anticipated the benefit of the depreciation deductions it would have as the owner of the building, those deductions would have been equally available to Worthen had it retained title to the building. The Government so concedes. Tr. of Oral Arg. 22-23. The fact that favorable tax consequences were taken into account by Lyon on entering into the transaction is no reason for disallowing those consequences. We cannot ignore the reality that the tax laws affect the shape of nearly every business transaction. . . . Lyon is not a corporation with no purpose other than to hold title to the bank building. It was not created by Worthen or even financed to any degree by Worthen. . . .

As is clear from the facts, none of the parties to this sale-and-leaseback was the owner of the building in any simple sense. But it is equally clear that the facts focus upon Lyon as the one whose capital was committed to the building and as the party, therefore, that was entitled to claim depreciation for the consumption of that capital. The Government has based its contention that Worthen should be treated as the owner on the assumption that throughout the term of the lease Worthen was acquiring an equity in the property. In order to establish the presence of that growing equity, however, the Government is forced to speculate that one of the options will be exercised and that, if it is not, this is only because the rentals for the extended term are a bargain. We cannot indulge in such speculation in view of the District Court's clear finding to the contrary. We therefore conclude that it is Lyon's capital that is invested in the building according to the agreement of the parties, and it is Lyon that is entitled to depreciation deductions, under §167 of the 1954 Code, 26 U.S.C. §167. . . .

IV

We recognize that the Government's position, and that taken by the Court of Appeals, is not without superficial appeal. One indeed may theorize that Frank Lyon's presence on the Worthen board of directors; Lyon's departure from its principal corporate activity into this unusual venture; the parallel between the payments under the building lease and the amounts due from Lyon on the New

York Life mortgage; the provisions relating to condemnation or destruction of the property; the nature and presence of the several options available to Worthen; and the tax benefits, such as the use of double declining balance depreciation, that accrue to Lyon during the initial years of the arrangement, form the basis of an argument that Worthen should be regarded as the owner of the building and as the recipient of nothing more from Lyon than a $500,000 loan.

We, however, as did the District Court, find this theorizing incompatible with the substance and economic realities of the transaction: the competitive situation as it existed between Worthen and Union National Bank in 1965 and the years immediately following; Worthen's under-capitalization; Worthen's consequent inability, as a matter of legal restraint, to carry its building plans into effect by a conventional mortgage and other borrowing; the additional barriers imposed by the state and federal regulators; the suggestion, forthcoming from the state regulator, that Worthen possess an option to purchase; the requirement, from the federal regulator, that the building be owned by an independent third party; the presence of several finance organizations seriously interested in participating in the transaction and in the resolution of Worthen's problem; the submission of formal proposals by several of those organizations; the bargaining process and period that ensued; the competitiveness of the bidding; the bona fide character of the negotiations; the three-party aspect of the transaction; Lyon's substantiality and its independence from Worthen; the fact that diversification was Lyon's principal motivation; Lyon's being liable alone on the successive notes to City Bank and New York Life; the reasonableness, as the District Court found, of the rentals and of the option prices; the substantiality of the purchase prices; Lyon's not being engaged generally in the business of financing; the presence of all building depreciation risks on Lyon; the risk, borne by Lyon, that Worthen might default or fail, as other banks have failed; the facts that Worthen could "walk away" from the relationship at the end of the 25-year primary term, and probably would do so if the option price were more than the then-current worth of the building to Worthen; the inescapable fact that if the building lease were not extended, Lyon would be the full owner of the building, free to do with it as it chose; Lyon's liability for the substantial ground rent if Worthen decides not to exercise any of its options to extend; the absence of any understanding between Lyon and Worthen that Worthen would exercise any of the purchase options; the non-family and non-private nature of the entire transaction; and the absence of any differential in tax rates and of special tax circumstances for one of the parties—all convince us that Lyon has far the better of the case. . . .

In short, we hold that where, as here, there is a genuine multiple-party transaction with economic substance which is compelled or encouraged by business or regulatory realities, is imbued with tax-independent considerations, and is not shaped solely by tax-avoidance features that have meaningless labels attached, the Government should honor the allocation of rights and duties effectuated by the parties. Expressed another way, so long as the lessor retains significant and genuine attributes of the traditional lessor status, the form of the transaction adopted by the parties governs for tax purposes. What those attributes are in any particular case will necessarily depend upon its facts. It suffices to say that, as here, a sale-and-leaseback, in and of itself, does not necessarily operate to deny a taxpayer's claim for deductions.

The judgment of the Court of Appeals, accordingly, is reversed. . . .

Mr. Justice STEVENS, dissenting: In my judgment the controlling issue in this case is the economic relationship between Worthen and petitioner, and matters such as the number of parties, their reasons for structuring the transaction in a particular way, and the tax benefits which may result, are largely irrelevant. The question whether a leasehold has been created should be answered by examining the character and value of the purported lessor's reversionary estate.

For a 25-year period Worthen has the power to acquire full ownership of the bank building by simply repaying the amounts, plus interest, advanced by the New York Life Insurance Company and petitioner. During that period, the economic relationship among the parties parallels exactly the normal relationship between an owner and two lenders, one secured by a first mortgage and the other by a second mortgage. If Worthen repays both loans, it will have unencumbered ownership of the property. What the character of this relationship suggests is confirmed by the economic value that the parties themselves have placed on the reversionary interest.

All rental payments made during the original 25-year term are credited against the option repurchase price, which is exactly equal to the unamortized cost of the financing. The value of the repurchase option is thus limited to the cost of the financing, and Worthen's power to exercise the option is cost-free. Conversely, petitioner, the nominal owner of the reversionary estate, is not entitled to receive *any* value for the surrender of its supposed rights of ownership. Nor does it have any power to control Worthen's exercise of the option.

"It is fundamental that 'depreciation is not predicated upon ownership of property *but rather upon an investment in property.* 'No such investment exists when payments of the purchase price in accordance with the design of the parties yield no equity to the purchaser." Estate of Franklin v. Commissioner, 544 F.2d 1045, 1049 (CA-9, 1976). Here, the petitioner has, in effect, been guaranteed that it will receive its original $500,000 plus accrued interest. But that is all. It incurs neither the risk of depreciation, nor the benefit of possible appreciation. Under the terms of the sale-leaseback, it will stand in no better or worse position after the 11th year of the lease—when Worthen can first exercise its option to repurchase—whether the property has appreciated or depreciated. And this remains true throughout the rest of the 25-year period.

Petitioner has assumed only two significant risks. First, like any other lender, it assumed the risk of Worthen's insolvency. Second, it assumed the risk that Worthen might *not* exercise its option to purchase at or before the end of the original 25-year term. If Worthen should exercise that right *not* to repay, perhaps it would *then* be appropriate to characterize petitioner as the owner and Worthen as the lessee. But speculation as to what might happen in 25 years cannot justify the *present* characterization of petitioner as the owner of the building. Until

Worthen has made a commitment either to exercise or not to exercise its option, I think the Government is correct in its view that petitioner is not the owner of the building for tax purposes. At present, since Worthen has the unrestricted right to control the residual value of the property for a price which does not exceed the cost of its unamortized financing, I would hold, as a matter of law, that it is the owner. . . .

Shurtz, A Decision Model for Lease Parties in Sale-Leasebacks of Real Estate
23 Wm. & Mary L. Rev. 385, 435-438 (1982)

This article has set out a basic framework for judges and planners in analyzing the complex area of sale-leaseback transactions. The decision model presented is based on sale-leaseback cases involving recourse and nonrecourse financing. The steps in the model can be summarized as follows:

STEP I: FINANCIAL INSTITUTIONS AS PARTIES TO THE TRANSACTION

1. Is the buyer-lessor a financial institution?

    If no, the analysis should continue (Step I, part 2).

    If yes, but the financial institution is purchasing the property for its own investment purposes, go to Step II.

    If yes, and the financial institution is not purchasing the property for its own investment purposes, a financing arrangement exists. Whether the bank seeks the property as an investment is determined by the intent and conduct of the parties.

2. Is a financial institution an indirect party to the sale-leaseback transaction—i.e., neither lessor nor lessee?

    If no, the courts should proceed to Step II.

    If yes, does the buyer-lessor merely serve as a conduit for the payment of the loan from the seller-lessee to the financial institution? This is determined by examining the personal liability of the buyer-lessor on the loan, whether the loan was guaranteed by the seller-lessee, whether the buyer-lessor is undercapitalized, whether the loan payments coincide with the rent payments, whether the term of the loan coincides with the term of the lease, and whether the financial institution views the seller-lessee as the true debtor. If the court answers these questions affirmatively, the court should conclude that there is a financing arrangement. If it is not clear that the buyer-lessor is a mere conduit, the analysis should continue.

**STEP II: IS THERE A CONDUIT ARRANGEMENT EVEN THOUGH
NO FINANCIAL INSTITUTION IS INVOLVED?**

The same factors discussed in part 2 of Step I should be considered. If a conduit relationship exists, there is a financing device. If no such relationship exists, the analysis should continue.

**STEP III: WILL THE PROPERTY REVERT AUTOMATICALLY
TO THE SELLER-LESSEE BY THE END
OF THE LEASE TERM?**

If yes, there is a financing arrangement.
If no, the analysis must continue.

**STEP IV: IS THERE A BARGAIN PURCHASE PRICE OR ECONOMIC
COMPULSION TO EXERCISE THE OPTION?**

If economic compulsion to exercise the option exists, the court should find a financing transaction. Economic compulsion exists when the repurchase option is a bargain purchase option or when there is a valid business reason at the time of the initial sale-leaseback transaction which compels the exercise of the option. No compulsion exists if some other reason, such as the financial condition of the lessee, indicates that the option will not be exercised.
If there is no economic compulsion the analysis should continue.

**STEP V: IS THE TERM OF THE LEASE PLUS RENEWALS
GREATER THAN OR EQUAL TO THE USEFUL LIFE
OF THE PROPERTY?**

If yes, there is a financing device.
If no, the analysis should proceed.

STEP VI: RATE OF RETURN SIMILARITIES

1. Are there no rate of return similarities?
    If the buyer-lessor is not entitled to a definite risk-free return, no financing arrangement exists. There may be a valid sale-leaseback, partnership, or joint venture arrangement, so the analysis should continue.
2. Are there clear rate of return similarities?

If no, the analysis should continue.

If yes, there is a financing arrangement.

STEP VII: VALUE DISPARITIES

1. Is the sales price too high or too low in relation to the fair market value of the property or the cash flow from the property?

   If nonrecourse financing is involved, courts should determine whether the sales price is greater than the fair market value of the property or whether the value of the interest purchased is less than the amount paid for that interest. If either of these circumstances exist, the court should find an invalid sale-leaseback arrangement. If recourse financing is involved, the analysis should continue.

2. Are the rental payments reflective of fair market value?

   If the rents are unreasonably low or unreasonably high, this is indicative but not determinative of a financing arrangement. If the payments are not clearly unreasonable, the analysis should continue.

STEP VIII: BENEFITS AND BURDENS: DOES THE EQUITY INTEREST LIE WITH THE SELLER-LESSEE?

If yes, there is a financing device.

If no, a valid sale-leaseback arrangement probably exists but the analysis should continue.

STEP IX: PURPOSE FOR ENTERING INTO THE TRANSACTION

If the actual purpose, as determined by the intent and conduct of the parties, indicates that the transaction was entered into to avoid tax, the sale-leaseback should not be recognized.

In addition to the potential for recharacterizing the sale and leaseback as a mortgage loan, some courts have disallowed a loss deduction to the seller-lessee under I.R.C. §1031 by taking the position that a sale and leaseback for a term of 30 or more years automatically constitutes a like-kind exchange of property. (Like-kind exchanges under I.R.C. §1031 are examined at Chapter 13A2d.) The following cases consider this challenge.

Century Electric Co. v. Commissioner

192 F.2d 155 (8th Cir. 1951), cert. denied, 342 U.S. 954 (1952)

RIDDICK, Circuit Judge.

The petitioner, Century Electric Company, is a corporation engaged principally in the manufacture and sale of electric motors and generators in St. Louis, Missouri. It is not a dealer in real estate. As of December 1, 1943, petitioner transferred a foundry building owned and used by it in its manufacturing business and the land on which the foundry is situated to William Jewell College and claimed a deductible loss on the transaction in its tax return for . . . 1943. The Commissioner of Internal Revenue denied the loss. The Commissioner was affirmed by the Tax Court and this petition for review followed. . . .

The assessed value of petitioner's foundry building and land upon which it is located for 1943 was $205,780. There was evidence that in St. Louis real property is assessed at its actual value. There was also evidence introduced by petitioner before the Tax Court that the market value for unconditional sale of the foundry building, land, and appurtenances was not in excess of $250,000.

As of December 1, 1943, the adjusted cost basis for the foundry building, land, and appurtenances transferred to William Jewell College was $531,710.97. The building was a specially designed foundry situated in a highly desirable industrial location. It is undisputed in the evidence that the foundry property is necessary to the operation of petitioner's profitable business and that petitioner never at any time considered a sale of the foundry property on terms which would deprive petitioner of its use in its business.

Petitioner's explanation of the transaction with the William Jewell College is that in the spring of 1943 a vice-president of the Mercantile bank where petitioner deposited its money and transacted the most of its banking business suggested to petitioner the advisability of selling some of its real estate holdings for the purpose of improving the ratio of its current assets to current liabilities by the receipt of cash on the sale and the possible realization of a loss deductible for tax purposes. Petitioner's operating business was to be protected by an immediate long-term lease of the real property sold. . . .

[P]etitioner never publicly offered or advertised its foundry property for sale. The Tax Court found that petitioner "was concerned with getting a friendly landlord to lease the property back to it, as there was never any intention on the part of petitioner to discontinue its foundry operations." Several offers to purchase the foundry property at prices ranging from $110,000 to $150,000 were received and rejected by petitioner.

At a special meeting of the board of directors of petitioner on December 9, 1943, the president of petitioner reported that the officers of petitioner had entered into negotiations for the sale of the foundry property to William Jewell College for the price of $150,000. . . . The Board by resolution approved the proposed transaction with the William Jewell College, but on condition that "this corporation will acquire from Trustees of William Jewell College, a Missouri Corporation, an Indenture of Lease . . . for a term of not less than twenty-five years and for not more than ninety-five years."....

The deed and the lease were executed and delivered as provided by the resolution of petitioner's board of directors. Neither instrument referred to the other. The deed was in form a general warranty deed, reciting only the consideration of $150,000 in cash. The lease recited among others the respective covenants of the parties as to its term, its termination by either the lessor or lessee, and as to the rents reserved.

As of December 31, 1942, the ratio of petitioner's current assets to its current liabilities was 1.74. The $150,000 in cash received by petitioner on the transaction increased the ratio of current assets to current liabilities from 1.74 to 1.80. The loss deduction which petitioner claims on the transaction and its consequent tax savings would if allowed have increased the ratio approximately twice as much as the receipt of the $150,000.

The questions presented are:

1. Whether the transaction stated was for tax purposes a sale of the foundry property within the meaning of section 112 of the Internal Revenue Code, 26 U.S.C.A. §112, on which petitioner realized in 1943 a deductible loss of $381,710.97 determined under section 111 of the code (the adjusted basis of the foundry property of $531,710.97 less $150,000) as petitioner contends; or, as the Tax Court held, an exchange of property held for productive use in a trade or business for property of a like kind to be held for productive use in trade or business in which no gain or loss is recognized under sections 112(b)(1) and 112(e)....

[T]he Tax Court reached the right result [in denying the loss]. The answer to the question is not to be found by a resort to the dictionary for the meaning of the words "sales" and "exchanges" in other contexts, but in the purpose and policy of the revenue act as expressed in section 112. . . . In this section Congress was not defining the words "sales" and "exchanges." It was concerned with the administrative problem involved in the computation of gain or loss in transactions of the character with which the section deals. Subsections 112(b)(1) and 112(e) indicate the controlling policy and purpose of the section, that is, the non-recognition of gain or loss in transactions where neither is readily measured in terms of money, where in theory the taxpayer may have realized gain or loss but where in fact his economic situation is the same after as it was before the transaction. . . . For tax purposes the question is whether the transaction falls within the category just defined. If it does, it is for tax purposes an exchange and not a sale. . . . Under subsection 112(e) no loss is recognized on an exchange of property held for productive use in trade or business for like property to be held for the same use, although other property or money is also received by the taxpayer. Compare this subsection with subsection 112(c)(1) where in the same circumstances gain is recognized but only to the extent of the other property or money received in the transaction. The comparison clearly indicates that in the computation of gain or loss on a transfer of property held for productive use in trade or business for property of a like kind to be held for the same use, the market value of the properties of like kind involved in the transfer does not enter into the equation.

The transaction here involved may not be separated into its component parts for tax purposes. Tax consequences must depend on what actually was intended and accomplished rather than on the separate steps taken to reach the desired end. The end of the transaction between the petitioner and the college was that intended by the petitioner at its beginning, namely, the transfer of the fee in the foundry property for the 95-year lease on the same property and $150,000.

It is undisputed that the foundry property before the transaction was held by petitioner for productive use in petitioner's business. After the transaction the same property was held by the petitioner for the same use in the same business. Both before and after the transaction the property was necessary to the continued operation of petitioner's business. The only change wrought by the transaction was in the estate or interest of petitioner in the foundry property. In Regulations 111, section 29.112(b)(1)-1, . . . a lease with 30 years or more to run and real estate are properties of "like kind." With the controlling purpose of the applicable section of the revenue code in mind, we can not say that the words "like kind" are so definite and certain that interpretation is neither required nor permitted. The regulation, in force for many years, has survived successive re-enactments of the internal revenue acts and has thus acquired the force of law. . . .

Jordan Marsh Co. v. Commissioner
269 F.2d 453 (2d Cir. 1959)

HINCKS, Circuit Judge.

This is a petition to review an order of the Tax Court, which upheld the Commissioner's deficiency assessment of $2,101,823.39 in income and excess profits tax against the petitioner, Jordan Marsh Company. There is no dispute as to the facts, which were stipulated before the Tax Court and which are set forth in substance below.

The transactions giving rise to the dispute were conveyances by the petitioner in 1944 of the fee of two parcels of property in the city of Boston where the petitioner, then as now, operated a department store. In return for its conveyances the petitioner received $2,300,000 in cash which, concededly, represented the fair market value of the properties. The conveyances were unconditional, without provision of any option to repurchase. At the same time, the petitioner received back from the vendees leases of the same properties for terms of 30 years and 3 days, with options to renew for another 30 years if the petitioner-lessee should erect new buildings thereon. The vendees were in no way connected with the petitioner. The rentals to be paid under the leases concededly were full and normal rentals so that the leasehold interests which devolved upon the petitioner were of no capital value.

In its return for 1944, the petitioner, claiming the transaction was a sale under §112(a), Internal Revenue Code of 1939, sought to deduct from income the difference between the adjusted basis of the property and the cash received. The Commissioner disallowed the deduction, taking the position that the transaction represented an exchange of property for other property of like kind. Under Section 112(b)(1) such exchanges are not occasions for the recognition of gain or loss; and even the receipt of cash or other property in the exchange of the properties of like kind is not enough to permit the taxpayer to recognize loss. Section 112(e). Thus the Commissioner viewed the transaction, in substance, as an exchange of a fee interest for a long-term lease, justifying his position by Treasury Regulation 111, §29.112(b)(1)-1, which provides that a leasehold of more than 30 years is the equivalent of a fee interest. Accordingly the Commissioner made the deficiency assessment stated above. The Tax Court upheld the Commissioner's determination. Since the return was filed in New York, the case comes here for review. 26 U.S.C.A. §7482.

Upon this appeal, we must decide whether the transaction in question here was a sale or an exchange of property for other property of like kind within the meaning of §§112(b) and 112(e) of the Internal Revenue Code. [W]e hold that the transaction here was a sale and not an exchange. . . .

The Tax Court apparently thought it of controlling importance that the transaction in question involved no change in the petitioner's possession of the premises: it felt that the decision in Century Electric Co. v. Commissioner of Internal Rev. [excerpted above], controlled the situation here. We think, however, that the case was distinguishable on the facts. For notwithstanding the lengthy findings made with meticulous care by the Tax Court in [*Century Electric*], 15 T.C. 581, there was no finding that the cash received by the taxpayer was the full equivalent of the value of the fee which the taxpayer had conveyed to the vendee-lessor, and no finding that the lease back called for a rent which was fully equal to the rental value of the premises. Indeed, in its opinion the Court of Appeals pointed to evidence that the fee which the taxpayer had "exchanged" may have had a value substantially in excess of the cash received. And in the *Century Electric* case, the findings showed, at page 585, that the taxpayer-lessee, unlike the taxpayer here, was not required to pay "general state, city and school taxes" because its lessor was an educational institution which under its charter was exempt from such taxes. Thus the leasehold interest in *Century Electric* on this account may well have had a premium value. In the absence of findings as to the values of the properties allegedly "exchanged," necessarily there could be no finding of a loss. And without proof of a loss, of course, the taxpayer could not prevail. . . .

Rev. Rul. 60-43
1960-1 C.B. 687

The Internal Revenue Service will not follow the decision in Jordan Marsh Company v. Commissioner, 269 Fed. (2d) 453.

The United States Court of Appeals for the Second Circuit, in reversing the Tax Court, held that a transaction whereby the taxpayer in 1944 conveyed the fee of parcels of property used for its department store to a stranger for cash, equivalent to their fair market value, must be treated as a separate sale, even though, simultaneously, the property was leased back to the taxpayer for the same use at a fair and normal rental for a term of 30 years plus three days, with an option to renew for a similar term if the taxpayer as "lessee" should erect new buildings on the property. . . .

It is the position of the Service that a sale and leaseback under the circumstances here present constitute, in substance, a single integrated transaction under which there is an "exchange" of property of like kind with cash as boot.

NOTES AND QUESTIONS

1. Treatment of Sale and Leaseback as Disguised Loan. The I.R.S. has employed a "recharacterization theory" to attack loss and rental deductions by the seller-lessee and depreciation by the purchaser-lessor where the repurchase option in the sale-and-leaseback agreement stipulates a substantially below-market price or otherwise lacks the substantive appearance of a sale, on the rationale that the seller never intended to permanently divest itself of ownership and that the transaction was in reality a disguised loan. See, for example, Fuller, Sale and Leasebacks and the *Frank Lyon* Case, 48 Geo. Wash. L. Rev. 60, 63-67 (1979); Shurtz, A Decision Model for Lease Parties in Sale-Leasebacks of Real Estate, 23 Wm. & Mary L. Rev. 385, 392-394 (1982); Stewart, Note, Taxation of Sale and Leaseback Transactions—A General Review, 32 Vand. L. Rev. 945, 968-982 (1979). However, in the event of recharacterization, any gain on the purported "sale" would not be recognized. Moreover, the seller-lessee would be entitled to deduct depreciation as the real owner of the property, and it would also be entitled to deduct that portion of the so-called rental payments that constitutes constructive "interest" on the constructive loan.

Frank Lyon Co. v. United States is the most recent Supreme Court statement on the proper characterization of sale-and-leaseback transactions for tax purposes. Although the Court's opinion does little to clarify the law in this area, and its precedential value is limited by the uniqueness of its facts, the general approach taken by the Supreme Court offers some guidance for the tax planner.

a. *Traditional Analysis under Pre-*Frank Lyon Co. *Case Law.* Although judicial analysis prior to *Frank Lyon Co.* had been somewhat inconsistent, the earlier court decisions addressed the issue of whether a sale and leaseback was in reality a disguised mortgage loan by focusing on whether the seller-lessee had divested itself of both the benefits and burdens of ownership. A closely related subjective test also emerged, namely, whether the seller truly *intended* a sale in the common law sense by relinquishing control over the real estate except for its right to possession during the leaseback period. In that regard, a seller's option to repurchase the property at a below-market price was most determinative. In addition, an unduly low rental during the leaseback period could reflect a disguised loan under the benefit-burden theory. Another important factor was the business purposes that prompted the parties to select the sale-leaseback device. For example, in Helvering v. F. & R. Lazarus & Co., 308 U.S. 252 (1939), the Supreme Court restructured a two-party sale-and-leaseback transaction as a "loan secured by the property involved." In that case, the taxpayer was a department store that transferred title to its buildings to a trustee for the benefit of the holders of land-trust certificates. Simultaneously, the trustee leased the properties back to the taxpayer for 99 years. The I.R.S. disallowed the taxpayer-"lessee's" claim for depreciation deductions on the theory that only the holder of the legal title was entitled to such deductions. The Supreme Court held that the taxpayer-"lessee" was entitled to depreciation because, as owner of the equitable title, it bore the burden of exhaustion of the asset, and held that the transaction was in substance a loan. The Court was influenced by these facts: (1) the sale price to the trustee was substantially less than the net value of the property; (2) the leaseback rentals were geared to repayment of the purchase price and were substantially below the fair market rental of the premises; (3) the option to repurchase stipulated a below-market price so that the seller would enjoy the appreciation in the value of the real estate; and (4) the parties apparently had intended a mere loan and not a true economic sale of the real estate.

    b. *Frank Lyon Co. v. United States.* Applying the traditional analysis to the facts in *Frank Lyon Co.* (as diagrammed in Figure 11-2 below), do you agree with the conclusion of the Court of Appeals that the benefits enjoyed and burdens borne by Lyon were more like those of a nonrecourse creditor than those of a prospective owner? In writing the majority opinion for the Supreme Court, Justice Blackmun regarded as most significant whether the borrowing from New York Life was done by Lyon or by Worthen. He emphasizes that Lyon alone was *personally* liable for repayment of both the construction and the permanent mortgage loans. In deciding whether Lyon assumed the risk of a purchaser or of a creditor, as a matter of economic substance would it have made any difference to the parties (including New York Life) if Lyon had simply guaranteed repayment to New York Life of its $7 million nonrecourse mortgage loan to Worthen and made a $500,000 nonrecourse second mortgage loan to Worthen, instead of Lyon's advancing to Worthen $500,000 of its own funds and then obtaining a $7 million recourse loan from New York Life? In both cases, wouldn't the risk of Worthen's insolvency and nonpayment fall squarely on the shoulders of Lyon? Even though Lyon alone was personally liable for repayment of the loan from

New York Life, what about the fact that Worthen had subjected its fee interest to the lien of the leasehold mortgage?

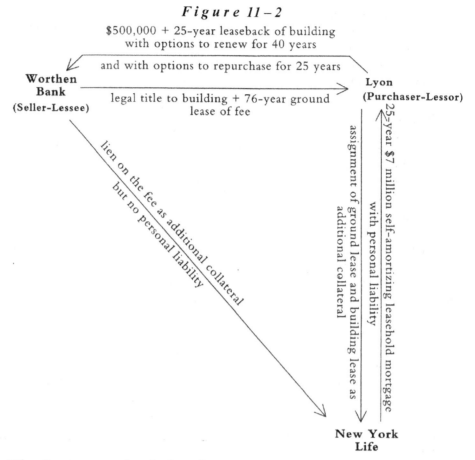

Figure 11–2

What facts suggest that the benefits enjoyed and burdens borne by Worthen were more like those of an owner-debtor than a seller-lessee? In that regard, consider the following closely related question. Notwithstanding the district court's determination that the leaseback rentals and repurchase option prices had been "reasonable," what inferences could be drawn as to whether Worthen intended to retain irrevocable control (beyond mere possession) over the building from the manner in which the following payments had been computed: (1) both the rental payments and option prices during the initial 25-year leaseback period; (2) the rental payments during the next 40 years (assuming that Worthen opted to extend the leaseback period); and (3) the lack of any rental obligation during the next 10 years (after the 65-year building lease expired and before the ground lease terminated), during which Lyon was free to rent the building at a fair market rental?

The debate between the majority opinion and Justice Stevens, in his dissent, centered on whether Worthen would be economically compelled to exercise one of its repurchase options during the primary 25-year term of the building lease. The government's recharacterization of the transaction as a loan assumed that Worthen would exercise one of these options to repurchase the building and, if it did not, it would only be because Worthen could remain in possession for the extended term at a bargain rental. Citing the district court's factual finding to the contrary, Justice Blackmun refused to engage in such speculation and concluded that Lyon's capital had been at risk. In support of this conclusion, he pointed out that if Worthen chose not to repurchase the building but opted instead to extend the building lease at the reduced rental, Lyon might not be able to obtain a sufficient rental from a new tenant of the building during the last 10 years of the ground lease to recoup its investment capital. By contrast, Justice Stevens regarded as irrelevant the question whether Worthen would exercise the option to repurchase; in his judgment, the determining factor was its *power* to do so. That Worthen could repurchase the building for an amount exactly equal to the balance of the sums advanced by New York Life and Lyon meant that Lyon's chance to benefit or be harmed from any fluctuation in the value of the building was subject to the complete control of Worthen, and therefore Lyon had at risk none of the equity on which tax ownership and the depreciation deduction are predicated. Moreover, if Worthen chose not to repurchase but to extend the building lease, Lyon had no opportunity to benefit because the bargain rentals ignored the fair market rental of the building; accordingly, Lyon's position resembled that of a lender since its only real risk was that its "debtor," Worthen, might become insolvent. In your judgment, which point of view makes more sense, that of Justice Blackmun or that of Justice Stevens? In concluding that Lyon's payments as a purchaser failed to yield the equity investment on which the depreciation deduction is predicated, Justice Stevens cites Estate of Franklin v. Commissioner, discussed at Chapter 13A2a, note 1. In what respect does the analogy fail?

In its holding, the Supreme Court takes the position that a sale-and-leaseback transaction should be respected by the I.R.S. where "there is a genuine multi-party transaction with economic substance which is compelled or encouraged by business or regulatory realities . . . and not shaped solely by tax-avoidance features." Based on the discussion at Chapter 11B1, supra, and the fact that the purchaser in a large sale-and-leaseback transaction is most likely to finance its acquisition cost by means of a loan from a third-party lender, how difficult would it be for a taxpayer such as Lyon to meet the Court's definition in the case of an ordinary sale-and-leaseback transaction? As a matter of economic substance, should it make any difference whether two or three parties are involved in the transaction? For example, in *Frank Lyon Co.*, would the economic situation of the parties have changed had Lyon financed the cost of the building by making a nonrecourse loan to Worthen with its own funds instead of obtaining a recourse loan from New York Life? Finally, which method of judicial analysis do you favor, the "totality of the transaction" approach employed by Justice Blackmun or the traditional pre- *Frank Lyon Co.* point of view (applied by the Court of

Appeals), which focuses on the benefits and burdens of property ownership and the intentions of the parties?

In *Frank Lyon Co.*, the Supreme Court cited 27 factors it considered relevant to its decision. To what extent does this approach have precedential value, informing the tax planner what criteria will govern the viability of a sale-and-leaseback transaction? More specifically, can a cautious tax planner safely assume that a recourse note obligation to a third-party lender and a valid business purpose form a sufficient matrix to support recognition of a sale-and-leaseback transaction even where the seller-lessee bears the major burdens and enjoys the major benefits of ownership in the property?

For analysis of the *Frank Lyon Co.* decision, see Del Cotto, Sale and Leaseback: A Hollow Sound When Tapped?, 37 Tax L. Rev. 1, 37-48 (1981); Fuller, Sales and Leasebacks and the *Frank Lyon* Case, 48 Geo. Wash. L. Rev. 60, 73-82 (1979); Kaster, Tax Criteria for Structuring Sale-Leasebacks, 9 Real Est. Rev. 39 (Fall 1979); Solomon and Fones, Sale-Leasebacks and the Shelter-Oriented Investor: An Analysis of *Frank Lyon Co.* and *Est. of Franklin*, 56 Taxes 618, 624-628 (Oct. 1978); Weinstein and Silvers, The Sale and Leaseback Transaction after *Frank Lyon Company* , 24 N.Y.L. Sch. L. Rev. 337 (1978); Zarrow and Gordon, Supreme Court's Sale-Leaseback Decision in *Lyon* Lists Multiple Criteria, 49 J. Tax'n (1978).

c. *Post* -Frank Lyon Co. *Case Law.* The case law after *Frank Lyon Co.* generally has followed the *Frank Lyon Co.* definition of a bona fide sale and leaseback, that is, a genuine multiple-party transaction based on economic substance and business realities rather than one that is shaped primarily by tax avoidance features. However, the case law has continued to scrutinize the seller's retention of control over the real estate and to examine how the benefits and burdens of ownership have been allocated between the parties.

For example, in Belz Inv. Co. v. Commissioner, 72 T.C. 1209 (1979), acq., 1980-1 C.B. 1, aff'd, 661 F.2d 76 (6th Cir. 1981), the Tax Court held that a sale and leaseback of a motel for an initial 20-year term was not in substance a "secured lending arrangement." Even though the seller-lessee was granted an option to repurchase after 10 years for no more than the original sale price, the option price was arguably reasonable in relation to the fair market value of the property, and the purchaser-lessor alone was obligated to pay the ground rent and the mortgage on the property. In Schaefer v. Commissioner, 41 T.C.M. 100 (1980), the Tax Court denied both rental and depreciation deductions where the buyer-lessor, a friend of the seller, received an annual guaranteed rental equal to the principal payments on an installment note taken out by the seller-lessee (with respect to which the seller remained liable), the buyer was safeguarded against any downside risks by reason of a "put" option allowing him to resell the property at any time for the original purchase price, and the seller was allowed to sublet and operate the hotel exactly as before the sale. In the opinion of the court, the buyer had not assumed the risks and burdens of hotel ownership and was motivated only by tax shelter considerations. In a series of sale-and-leaseback cases involving nonrecourse financing, including Hilton v. Commissioner, 74

T.C. 305 (1980), aff'd, 671 F.2d 316 (9th Cir.), cert. denied, 459 U.S. 907 (1982), and Narver v. Commissioner, 75 T.C. 53 (1980), aff'd, 670 F.2d 855 (9th Cir. 1982), in which the nonrecourse indebtedness had exceeded the market value of the real estate, the Tax Court denied depreciation and interest deductions to the purchasers because the court failed to find a genuine multiple-party concern for nontax considerations, as required under *Frank Lyon Co.* In addition, the court applied the "abandonment test," enunciated in Estate of Franklin v. Commissioner (see discussion at Chapter 13A2a, note 1) in holding that in both cases the buyer-lessors would not have found it imprudent to abandon the properties. Perhaps the most influential post-*Frank Lyon Co.* case is Leslie Co. v. Commissioner, 64 T.C. 247, aff'd, 539 F.2d 943 (3d Cir. 1976) where the court followed the economic reality test to hold in favor of loss recognition for the seller-lessee (mentioned at note 3 infra).

For discussion of the *Schaefer, Hilton,* and *Narver* cases, see Rosenberg and Weinstein, Applying the Tax Court's Non-Tax Benefit Test for Multiple-Party Sale-Leasebacks, 54 J. Tax'n 366 (1981); for a discussion of *Hilton,* see Ruga, Note, Sale and Leasebacks as a Tax Shelter: *Hilton v. Commissioner,* 1981 Utah L. Rev. 843.

2. Prepayment and Reallocation of the Leaseback Rental. As noted earlier, an unduly low rental during the leaseback period could render a sale and leaseback vulnerable to recharacterization as a disguised loan. In addition, a below-market sale price accompanied by the seller's receipt of a leaseback with a proportionately reduced rental may prompt the Commissioner to contend that the purchaser in effect received prepaid rent equal to the excess of the fair market value of the property over the bargain price paid by the purchaser. This tax pitfall is best illustrated by the companion cases decided by the Tax Court, Alstores Realty Corp. v. Commissioner, 46 T.C. 363 (1966), and Steinway & Sons v. Commissioner, 46 T.C. 375 (1966), acq., 1967-1 C.B. 1. (See also Rev. Rul. 66-209, 1966-2 C.B. 299, involving a long-term leaseback.) Steinway conveyed fee title to its warehouse to Alstores for $750,000 and, by separate agreement, Steinway received a two-and-one-half-year leaseback until its new facility was ready under which (1) Steinway could remain in possession without payment of rent; (2) Steinway would be reimbursed for any interruption of its possession caused by casualty or condemnation; and (3) Alstores agreed to supply all utilities so that the leaseback would not be a net lease. Alstores maintained that since it had not received any cash rental payments, the transaction was not a sale and leaseback; in substance Steinway had merely sold a remainder interest in the real estate for $750,000 and reserved a possessory term. Under a risk and benefit-burden analysis, the Tax Court upheld the Commissioner by holding that an ownership interest in the fee had initially passed to Alstores and thus the transaction was a genuine sale and leaseback in substance as well as in form. Accordingly, Alstores was deemed to have purchased the real estate for its market value and to have acquired a cost basis of $1 million. In consideration of the leaseback, Alstores received $250,000 in prepaid rent from Steinway; thus

Steinway realized $1 million from the sale but received a net cash payment of only $750,000. Steinway, therefore, had purchased the leasehold estate for $250,000 and could amortize the payment over the two and one-half years of the lease. The following are diagrams of the transaction as viewed by Alstores and the Tax Court.

Alstores' View of the Transaction

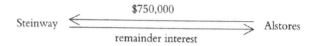

The Tax Court's View of the Transaction

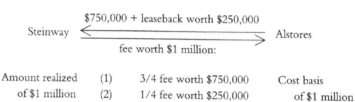

If there is an option to renew the leaseback at an unduly low rental, the Commissioner may urge that a portion of the rental paid during the original leaseback term be deferred to the renewal term as a prepaid expense. Otherwise, the lessee's taxable income arguably would be understated during the original term and overstated during the renewal period. See Treas. Reg. §1.461-1(a)(2); Main & McKinney Building Co. v. Commissioner, 113 F.2d 81 (5th Cir.), cert. denied, 311 U.S. 688 (1940) (involving a straight lease transaction). Or, if the rental for the original leaseback term is an escalating or deescalating one, the Commissioner may argue, on the same rationale, for amortization of the entire rental payment evenly over the entire leaseback period. In either event, a portion of the rental expenses would be disallowed as a current deduction and instead would be capitalized. Finally, if the sale and leaseback is between related parties, the Commissioner may attempt to denominate the lessee's payments as something other than a rent deduction. For example, an excessive rental payment to a related individual may be treated as a nondeductible gift or personal expense. See Coe Lab. v. Commissioner, 34 T.C. 549 (1960). Or, an excessive rental paid to a shareholder-lessor by a corporate lessee may be treated as a constructive dividend. See, for example, J. J. Kirk, Inc. v. Commissioner, 34 T.C. 130 (1960), aff'd, 289 F.2d 935 (6th Cir. 1961). The Commissioner might also: (1) reallocate any excessive rental paid as additional income to the lessee (see I.R.C. §482 and the Treasury Regulations thereunder); (2) challenge the "ordinary and necessary" character of the rental expense and disallow a deduction under I.R.C. §162 or §212 (see I. L. Van Zendt v. Commissioner, 341 F.2d 440 (5th Cir.), cert. denied, 382 U.S. 814 (1965)); (3) disallow loss recognition on the sale, I.R.C. §267 (sale to a family member or related party as defined in §267(b)) and I.R.C. §707(b)(1)

(sale between a partnership and a controlling partner who owns more than a 50 percent interest, or sale between two controlled partnerships); or (4) charge the seller with ordinary income if gain had been realized on the sale of depreciable property, I.R.C. §1239 (sale between husband and wife or between a corporation and a stockholder who owns 50 percent or more of stock) and I.R.C. §707(b)(2) (sale between a partnership and a controlling partner who owns more than 50 percent partnership interest, or sale between two controlled partnerships).

3. Loss Disallowance. I.R.C. §1031(a) mandates nonrecognition of gain or loss if property held for productive use in a trade or business is *exchanged* solely for property of a like kind. See Chapter 13A2d. If a taxpayer receives in exchange some property not equivalent to the exchanged property, it must recognize its gain (but not loss) to the extent of the cash or fair market value of the tainted property ("boot") received. Because a leasehold of 30 years or more is regarded as like kind, or equivalent to property held in fee, Treas. Reg. §1.103(a)-1(a), a developer that holds property worth less than its depreciated cost (adjusted basis) would want to avoid an "exchange" of the property if it receives a leaseback of 30 years or more. Otherwise, an ordinary loss could not be recognized under I.R.C. §1231.

But when is there an "exchange" (as opposed to a sale of a fee interest in property) when the previous owner receives as consideration not only a long-term leaseback but boot as well? In the case of an exchange, the entire loss (or gain less boot) would go unrecognized, and in the case of a sale, the entire loss would be recognized regardless of whether boot was received by the seller. Unfortunately, neither the Code nor regulations define the term "exchange" with particularity; one must therefore resort to the case authorities.

a. *Century Electric Co. v. Commissioner.* The ostensible rationale for the decision disallowing the loss was that because the taxpayer held the same property for the same use in the same business both before and after the transaction, the taxpayer's economic situation remained the same and therefore no sale took place. But under this standard, when would the economic situation of the taxpayer in a sale and leaseback ever change? What is the real issue in the case? Can you think of a better rationale for explaining the court's decision that an exchange, and not a sale, took place, based on the fact that the taxpayer gave up property worth as much as $250,000 and yet received only $150,000 in cash along with a long-term leaseback of a proportionately reduced rental?

b. *Jordan Marsh Co. v. Commissioner.* How would you reconcile the conflicting results in the *Century Electric* and *Jordan Marsh* decisions? See City Investing Co. v. Commissioner, 38 T.C. 1 (1962), nonacq. 1963-2 C.B. 6, and Leslie Co. v. Commissioner, 64 T.C. 247, aff'd, 539 F.2d 943 (3d Cir. 1976); Fuller, Sale and Leasebacks and the *Frank Lyon* Case, 48 Geo. Wash. U. L. Rev. 60, 70 (1979); Morris, Sale-Leaseback Transactions of Real Property—A Proposal, 30 Tax Law. 701, 706 (1977).

4. Tax Planning. The following measures can be taken to help assure tax treatment as a sale:

1. if possible, replace the repurchase option with a series of long renewal periods, or "water down" the option by making the purchase optional for both the owner-lessor and the seller-lessee;
2. gear the option price to a figure that is reasonable in relation to the probable fair market value of the property at the date of its exercise;
3. avoid using a "net" leaseback or placing the risk of casualty loss on the seller-lessee;
4. sell to an institutional lender only if it has other sale and leasebacks in its investment portfolio; and
5. avoid any two-party arrangement between related taxpayers and, if possible, use an outside lender where other financing is involved.

For discussion of tax planning considerations, see generally T. Homburger, T. Joyce, and G. Andre, Structuring Sale-Leasebacks (1992); Blanton and Ipsen, How to Preserve the Significant Tax Benefits Available from a Sale and Leaseback Transaction, 10 Tax Law. 324 (1982); Kaster, Tax Criteria for Structuring Sale-Leasebacks, 9 Real Est. Rev. 39 (Fall 1979); Maller, Structuring a Sale-Leaseback Transaction, 15 Real Est. L.J. 291 (Spring 1987); Milich, The Real Estate Sale-Leaseback Transaction: A View Toward the 90s, 21 Real Est. L.J. 66 (Summer 1992); Real Estate Transaction as Sale and Leaseback for Income Tax Purposes, 39 Am. Jur. Proof of Facts 2d 651 (1984).

> ➤ *Problem 11-5*
> The following hypothetical illustrates the foregoing tax rules and problems and the flexibility of sale and leaseback as a financing tool in comparison to debt financing.[7] The Realty Corporation (Realty) owns unencumbered land and a building of equal value that together are worth $1 million. The original cost was $500,000 ($320,000 allocable to land and $180,000 to the building), and now the combined adjusted basis is $400,000. Realty desires to raise $1 million of working capital under any of the following alternatives.
> a. *Debt Financing.* Obtain $1 million by floating a bond issue (secured by the net assets of Realty as security) or by means of a constant amortization payment mortgage loan, repayable in the principal amount of $66,666 per annum for 15 years plus annual interest at 8 percent on the outstanding principal balance. A $1 million mortgage loan amount is being used for comparison purposes even though a 100 percent loan-to-value ratio is unrealistic absent unusual circumstances (for example, high-credit lease financing).

---

7. The underlying concept for this example is based on a question that appeared in Axelrod, Berger, and Johnstone, Land Transfer and Finance 1048-1049 (2d ed. 1984).

b. *Sale and Leaseback #1.* Sell the realty to Lender Insurance Co. (Lender) for $1 million with a 15-year leaseback at an annual rental of $116,666 with an option to renew with an annual rent based on 10 percent of the appraised value of the land.

c. *Sale and Leaseback #2.* Sell the realty to Lender for $1 million with a 30-year leaseback at an annual rental of $83,333 with an option to repurchase based on 100 percent of the appraised value of the land. Note that in both alternative b and alternative c, Lender will receive a discounted 5.5 percent rate of annual return over and above its recoupment of purchase price, which is somewhat less than what a mortgage lender or bondholder would demand.

d. *Combined Sale and Leaseback and Debt Financing.* Sell the realty to Lender for $300,000 with a 30-year leaseback at an annual rental of $25,000. On the basis of the value of the leaseback, assume for comparison purposes that Realty can then borrow $700,000 secured by a 30-year constant amortization mortgage, repayable at $23,333 per annum plus annual interest of 8 percent on the outstanding principal balance. Observe that even though the market value of the real estate exceeds the sale price by $700,000, this does not mean that the transaction will be treated as a disguised loan of $300,000 by Lender to Realty. In general, courts have not scrutinized the reasonableness of the sale price. For example, in *Frank Lyon Co.*, the cost of the building ($10 million) exceeded its sale price ($7,640,000); likewise, in FritoLay, Inc. v. United States, 209 F. Supp. 886 (N.D. Ga. 1962), the market value of the real estate exceeded by a large margin the sale price, which was based on the estimated cost of construction. However, the I.R.S. might argue that Lender is really buying the realty for $1 million and receiving $700,000 from Realty as prepaid rental income. This would mean that Lender would acquire a $1 million cost basis in the realty and that Realty could amortize the $700,000 prepaid rental over the 30-year leaseback period. See Alstores Realty Corp. v. Commissioner, 46 T.C. 363, 374 (1966); Steinway & Sons v. Commissioner, 46 T.C. 375, 379 (1966), acq., 1967-1 C.B. 1.

i. Based on the foregoing case analysis, do you think the I.R.S. could successfully apply its recharacterization theory to any of the above financing options?

ii. Based on the information in Table 11-1 below, determine how the business and tax results of using debt financing (alternative (a)) would compare in the short and long run with use of (1) sale-and-leaseback financing (alternatives (b) and (c)) and (2) a combination of sale and leaseback with debt financing (alternative (d)). ◄

5. *The Nature of an Ordinary Sale and Leaseback.* At this juncture we know that certain pitfalls in sale-and-leaseback financing exist; for example, if the seller-lessee has the option to repurchase the property for a watered-down price and is charged an unduly low rental during the leaseback, the I.R.S. will most

Table 11 - 1

Results

Ownership	Cash Outflow	Depreciation	Interest	Rent	Total Tax Deductions	Capital Gain at 34% Corporate Tax Rate[**]
(a) 15 years Realty	$146,666	$4,615	$80,000	— —	$84,615	$0
(b) 15 years Lender	116,666	— —	— —	$116,666	116,666	34% of 600,000 = 204,000
(c) 30 years Lender	83,333	— —	— —	83,333	83,333	34% of 600,000 = 204,000
(d) 30 years Lender	104,333	13,333[*]	$56,000	25,000	94,333	34% of 300,000 = 102,000

* Under I.R.C. §1031(d) Realty would receive a substituted basis in the leaseback of $400,000 (plus $300,000 recognized gain less $300,000 cash boot) ÷ $400,000 amortized over 30 years ÷ $13,333 per annum.

** No special capital gain tax rates apply to corporations. For simplicity's sake we are using the 34% rate that applies under I.R.C. §11(b) to that portion of annual corporate income in excess of $75,000 but which amount does not exceed $10 million. (Corporate tax reform expected from Congress in late 2017 would reduce the maximum corporate tax rate to 21 percent.)

likely recharacterize the transaction as a disguised mortgage loan. In other words, we know when a transaction that purports to be a sale and leaseback may not be treated as one, but do we really know what the *ordinary* sale and leaseback is or how it *ought* to be treated for federal tax purposes? To find out, we conclude our examination of this highly useful financing and tax planning device by considering the following question that has nettled tax planners and commentators for years: In an arm's-length transaction involving unrelated parties, does the ordinary sale and leaseback reflect a genuine sale of a fee interest that is merely induced by tax considerations or, as a matter of substance over form, is it nothing more than a disguised mortgage loan (or something else) structured as a sale with a leaseback to the seller so that the parties can achieve certain tax advantages that would not otherwise be available? Put simply, the question is whether the ordinary sale and leaseback should be treated as an economic fact or as a tax fiction, and how such determination ought to be made.

In answering this question, certain assumptions must be made. In a typical sale and leaseback transaction (1) the initial sale price is often geared to the financing or working capital needs of the seller rather than to the fair market value of the real estate being sold (see alternative (d) in note 4); (2) as in *Frank Lyon Co.*, neither the leaseback rental nor the option to repurchase is predicated on the fair market value of the real estate but instead each is calculated to provide a fair income return to the purchaser and allow the purchaser to amortize and recoup its investment over the leaseback period; (3) the estimated useful life of the improvements will not exceed the leaseback period and the leaseback itself is a net lease whereby the purchaser's role is that of a passive investor and, by contrast, the seller-lessee agrees to pay property taxes, insurance, and maintenance expenses and to assume the risk of casualty and condemnation; (4) the seller-lessee's choice of sale-and-leaseback financing (as opposed to mortgage or straight debt financing) is dictated by valid business reasons (for example, high-ratio financing, avoidance of usury restrictions) beyond the need merely to retain possession of the premises during the leaseback period; and (5) the purchaser-lessor typically funds its acquisition costs by means of a nonrecourse mortgage loan from a third-party institutional lender such as a life insurance company.

Finally, in our hypothetical involving an ordinary sale and leaseback, although the leaseback rentals and option prices are not geared to fair market value, let us assume (as in *Frank Lyon Co.*) that they are *reasonable* in relation to the fair market value of the real estate and that the nonrecourse indebtedness incurred by the purchaser does not exceed the market value of the real estate. Otherwise, past precedent would compel us to treat the transaction as a sham for federal income tax purposes. See discussions at notes 1-2, supra, and Chapter 13A2a, note 1, respectively.

a. Based on the foregoing assumptions, decide as a matter of substance over form which of the following theories best describes the true tax nature of an ordinary sale and leaseback.

i. A genuine sale followed by a leaseback, in which event the seller-lessee would be entitled to a rental deduction and the purchaser to the benefit of the depreciation. Exemplifying this traditional point of view is Weinstein and Silvers, The Sale and Leaseback After *Frank Lyon Company*, 24 N.Y.L. Sch. L. Rev. 337, 340 (1978).

ii. A disguised mortgage loan resulting in opposite tax consequences for the parties, namely, the ostensible seller would be treated merely as a borrower so that it would retain a depreciation deduction, but any ostensible rental payments would be treated as payment of interest and loan principal during the leaseback period, and the ostensible purchaser, as lender, would treat any rentals it receives for the possessory term as nothing more than interest and amortization of its loan advanced in the guise of a purchase payment.

iii. The sale of a mere remainder interest with the reservation of a possessory term by the seller-lessee, in which event the tax consequences would be the same as in (ii) during the leaseback period, except that the seller would realize gain or loss on the sale of the remainder interest and the purchaser would obtain a cost basis in the remainder interest that could be depreciated once the leaseback period is over. If you recall, this was the position taken by the taxpayers in the *Alstores-Steinway* litigation discussed at note 2, supra.

iv. The transfer of naked legal title to the purchaser by the seller, who, as the real owner under a risk-benefit theory, retains the beneficial ownership of the property (in which event the tax consequences would be the same as in alternative (ii)). See discussion of Helvering v. F. & R. Lazarus & Co. at note 1, supra.

v. In the case of a leaseback of 30 years or more, the exchange of a fee for a leaseback rather than the sale of a fee, regardless of whether the leaseback has independent economic significance (in which event the tax consequences would be essentially the same as in alternative (i), except that the ostensible seller would not obtain the benefit of any loss deduction). Compare *Century Electric* with *Jordan Marsh*; see discussion of these cases at note 3, supra.

b. With regard to the question posed above, does it really make any difference whether we recharacterize the ordinary sale and leaseback as a disguised mortgage loan if, as Justice Blackmun points out in *Frank Lyon Co.*, excerpted supra, "It is not inappropriate to note that the Government is likely to lose little revenue, if any, as a result of the shape given the transaction by the parties. No deduction was created that is not either matched by an item of income or that would not have been available to one of the parties if the transaction had been arranged differently"?

c. In determining the true tax nature of the ordinary sale and leaseback, maybe it is overly simplistic to apply one recharacterization theory or another. Perhaps what is needed is a decision model (like the one by Shurtz) that applies a totality-of-transaction approach by weighing all the important variables. While such an approach provides less certainty for tax planners, it may become necessary, because the typical modern sale and leaseback tends to be a highly complex transaction (as exemplified by the facts in *Frank Lyon Co.*) involving facts that are not readily subject to generalization. To test your understanding of this alternative mode of analysis, decide whether the typical modern sale and leaseback could be recharacterized as a disguised mortgage loan by applying the criteria outlined by Shurtz to the facts in the hypothetical. For further discussion of the various factors considered by state and federal courts when determining whether to recharacterize a sale-leaseback transaction, see Murray, Recharacterization Issues in Sale-Leaseback Transactions, 19-OCT Prob. & Prop. 18 (2005).

PART IV

FUNDAMENTALS OF
REAL ESTATE INVESTMENT

Chapter 12

Economics of Real Estate Investments

Before we examine the considerations involved when real estate investors select the appropriate ownership entity (see Chapter 14), let us examine why income-producing real estate is such an attractive investment medium. The profitability of investing in income-producing real estate as compared to other traditional investment media such as ordinary stocks and bonds[1] can be explained to a large extent by the interplay between the following factors: (1) historically, rental real estate has yielded a relatively high pretax rate of return to investors and has been a relatively good hedge against inflation; (2) real estate investors are afforded the unique opportunity to obtain high-ratio financing to leverage their cost of acquiring and improving real estate; and (3) unique tax shelter benefits are accorded to the owners of income-producing real estate.

A. FINANCIAL LEVERAGE AND ECONOMIC REWARDS

1. Financial Leverage

Perhaps the most attractive feature of real estate is that the owner can leverage the cost of acquiring and constructing a real estate asset. "Leverage" refers to the commonsense business principle that if an investor can borrow a portion of the equity requirement at an interest rate lower than the anticipated rate of return from the investment, the effective rate of return is increased. Such an investment is said to be leveraged.

For example, if an investor can acquire a real estate asset that is expected to produce an annual "cash-on-cash" rate of return of 10 percent[2] for a cost of

1. One of the most exciting trends for real estate investors has been the transformation of illiquid real estate assets and liabilities into capital market instruments that are tradeable on Wall Street. This phenomenon is called securitization and is illustrated on the equity or ownership side of real estate by so-called equity REITs (see Chapter 15A) and on the debt side by mortgage pools called REMICs and securities called commercial mortgage-backed bonds (see Chapter 15C).

2. This simplest measure of performance is calculated by dividing the money received by the money expended in a particular year. In contrast to more sophisticated yardsticks of profitability such as the net present value method (NPV) and the internal rate of return method (IRR), it takes

$100,000 and is able to borrow 80 percent of the acquisition cost with an 8 percent interest-only loan, the investor, by leveraging the acquisition cost, can increase the rate of return from 10 percent to 18 percent. This is because the ratio of money received to money expended increases from 10 percent ($10,000 ÷ $100,000) to 18 percent ($10,000 − $6,400 interest =$3,600 net income ÷ $20,000). Another way to explain the result is that while the investor earns a 10 percent rate of return on the one-fifth of the investment financed with the investor's own cash, the other four-fifths of the investment earns the same 10 percent but costs only 8 percent; accordingly, the cash-on-cash rate of return is increased by four times the rate spread (2 percent) or 8 percent, which increases the before-tax rate of equity return from 10 percent to 18 percent, as diagrammed below.

Rate Spread

	$20,000	
1/5	All cash	- 0 -
	$20,000	
1/5	leveraged	- 2 -
	$20,000	
1/5	leveraged	- 2 -
	$20,000	
1/5	leveraged	- 2 -
	$20,000	
1/5	leveraged	<u>- 2 -</u>
		8% + 10% = 18%

Conversely, financial leverage can also multiply an investor's reduction in the rate of return on equity if the income from the investment should decline. Thus, in the foregoing example, if the income rate of return were only 7 percent, the investor's overall rate of return would drop to 3 percent as a consequence of negative leverage.

Observe that leverage also works for the investor if the value of the underlying land appreciates owing to inflation or demand exceeding supply. Alternatively, an increase in net rental earnings could cause an increase in the value of the building.[3] Suppose, for example, the investor purchases some land for $100,000 that is financed with an 80 percent loan-to-value ratio loan. The investor's cash or equity requirement would be $20,000, and a 5 percent increase

---

into account neither federal income tax consequences nor the time value of money. These methods are discussed later in this section.

3. See Chapter 4D1.

in the value of the land during the first year (from $100,000 to $105,000) would produce an unrealized appreciation rate of 25 percent on the investor's equity investment (before taking financing charges into account) since the $100,000 (the full leveraged cost of the real estate and not merely the $20,000 equity) is the base to which the 5 percent rate applies.

NOTES AND QUESTIONS

High-Ratio Financing Available for Real Estate. In the world of real estate financing, the mortgage portfolios of most institutional lenders such as life insurance companies, commercial banks, and mutual savings banks are regulated by state statutes that specify (or, in the case of federally regulated institutions, by federal guidelines that suggest) maximum loan-to-value ratios (expressed as a percentage of appraised value) depending on the nature of the real property that secures the mortgage loan. For example, in most jurisdictions the maximum loan-to-value ratio on the postconstruction ("permanent") financing of nonresidential income-producing real estate (for example, office buildings and shopping centers) is 75 or 80 percent for life insurance companies. See, for example, Va. Code Ann. §38.2-1437(A) which imposes a maximum loan-to-value ratio of 80 percent for most mortgage loans. As a general rule, most institutional lenders lend at or near the maximum loan-to-value ratio. Can you think of an underwriting or business reason for this?

Another type of leverage called operating leverage allows a real estate investor to increase his return on his equity investment during periods of inflation. See explanation in Chapter 12A3. Also, the fact that the depreciation deduction remains the same regardless of what part of the cost of the project is furnished by outside financing causes a leveraging of tax benefits for the real estate investor. See Chapter 13A2b, note 1.

Observe that the largest proportion of multifamily and commercial real estate in this country is either directly owned or indirectly owned by private investors such as partners in a privately held limited partnership, members of a limited liability company, or shareholders in a Subchapter S corporation (these entities are examined at Chapter 14). While such private partnerships, LLCs, and Subchapter S corporations hold legal title to the underlying real estate assets, there is a direct pass-through of taxable income or loss, net refinancing proceeds, and net sale proceeds when the property is sold. Hence, when these pass-through ownership entities leverage their acquisition and construction costs, the investors directly benefit from such financial leverage and, based on their leveraged income and appreciation returns, are able to calculate their yield to maturity from their interests in the underlying real estate. By contrast, owners of publicly traded stock do not receive such pass-through benefits, and their dividend-income and appreciation returns are not as directly related to the way in which the assets of the corporation are financed.

In contrast to leverage-minded real estate developers and investors (who have a penchant for using other people's money and even dream about 100 percent financing), stock and bond investors shy away from leveraging the cost of acquiring their ownership shares. Indeed, as explained below, only a small fraction of corporate investors buy on margin. Perhaps this is because they may be able to achieve the risk-return objectives they seek by carefully assessing the risk-return characteristics of available securities based on annual reports (and other past-performance data) and the help provided by advisory services. This kind of detailed evaluative information is not as readily available to real estate developers and private investors, whose ownership interests are not publicly regulated and traded the way most corporate securities are. So, for example, a high-risk-oriented investor who pays cash for risky securities may be tantamount to the investor who buys a less risky portfolio on margin. Is the all-cash purchaser of stock in a highly leveraged company that has been acquired recently in a hostile takeover (or by means of a leveraged buyout) analogous to a real estate investor in a limited partnership who pays all cash for her indirect ownership interest in some leveraged real estate that is directly owned by the partnership? In what respect does the analogy fail?

Another major reason why investors tend to avoid buying corporate securities on margin is that regulatory constraints are imposed by the Federal Reserve Board (FRB) and the New York Stock Exchange (NYSE). A complex system of regulations governs the purchase of securities on credit and the use of securities as collateral. As to new positions, a securities broker may not extend credit to a customer for the purchase of securities in an amount exceeding 50 percent of the market value of equity securities in the customer's account (after excluding the value of thinly traded securities). Securities Exchange Act §7, 15 U.S.C. §78g; Regulation T, 12 C.F.R. §§220.1-220.132. The FRB is also responsible for regulating the extension or maintenance of securities credit by others, and thus it regulates the extension of securities credit by banks, Regulation U, 12 C.F.R. §§221.1-221.125, and certain other lenders, Regulation G, 12 C.F.R. §§207.1-207.11. The Board also regulates the obtaining of securities credit by U.S. persons. See Securities Exchange Act §7(f), 15 U.S.C. §78g(f); Regulation X, 12 C.F.R. §§224.1-224.3.

The Board's regulations do not require brokers to demand more collateral if the value of the securities in an open margin account declines, but industry practice and the rules of the various self-regulatory organizations to which all brokers belong do require customers to maintain the value of collateral. For example, with limited exceptions, members of the NYSE must require their customers to maintain an equity of at least 25 percent of the market value of the securities in their open margin accounts for long positions and 30 percent for short positions. N.Y.S.E. Rule 431, N.Y.S.E. Guide (CCH) ¶2431; see also N.A.S.D. Rule 2520 and Rules of Fair Practice §30, N.A.S.D. Manual (CCH) ¶2180. Brokerage firms are free to require higher margins on their own, and they often do. These maintenance requirements impose a continuing and potentially substantial burden on those who trade securities on credit, for if the market value of an investor's portfolio falls she may be required to provide more collateral or liquidate. Perhaps because of the high margin requirements and the possibility of margin calls, relatively few securities investors trade on margin.

2. Measuring the Profitability of a Real Estate Investment

In the foregoing example in Chapter 12A1, the cash-on-cash rate of return at the end of the year was used for simplicity's sake to measure the profitability of the real estate investment. Another common measure is the free and clear rate of return, which is determined by dividing the projected net operating income (NOI) (without taking into account the payment of income taxes and debt-service payments on the mortgage, if any) by the acquisition cost of the investment. Another approach, used primarily by appraisers, is to measure the current value of real estate by focusing on its profitability at a fixed moment in time. This traditional method, called capitalization rate analysis, is discussed at Chapter 4D1. To the sophisticated investor, however, these methods (referred to as static return analysis) are but crude and static measures of profitability because they fail to take into account both the tax and time-value aspects of the investment picture.[4] In the excerpt that follows, we examine and compare the two principal sophisticated methods of investment analysis used by virtually all real estate professionals—the net present value (NPV) method and the internal rate of return (IRR) method. These methods, which are generically referred to as methods of "dynamic return analysis," have one thing in common: They take into account future cash flows and apply discount factors to arrive at the present value of the real estate investment in today's dollars.

M. Madison, J. Dwyer, and S. Bender, The Law of Real Estate Financing
§1.6 (2016)

An investor (*L*) in the position of a limited partner or a member of a LLC can determine the "free and clear rate of return" by dividing the projected NOI by the cost of the project. However, this is but a crude snapshot of the investment's profitability because it ignores both the impact of financial leverage and *L*'s receipt of tax benefits. A somewhat more refined measure that takes leverage into account would be *L*'s "cash on cash rate of return" at the end of each year. A still more accurate measure of profitability would result from factoring in *L*'s tax shelter benefits. However, to the sophisticated investor, this is but a partial view

---

4. However, as observed at Chapter 4D1, note 4, the traditional capitalization rate theory recently has been modified by many appraisers to take into account the time value of money and anticipated rates of inflation during the holding period of the real estate being valued.

of the entire investment picture. For one thing, L obviously knows that someday the partnership will dispose of the property and L will receive as his residual amount his share of the net sale proceeds after the outstanding mortgage is satisfied.[1] Furthermore, L realizes that a dollar of economic benefit to be received in the future is worth less than a dollar of benefit that is presently available.[2] Consequently, L (or his investment adviser) will want to use some yardstick for profitability that is sensitive enough to measure the foregoing variables so he can intelligently compare an investment in the partnership with alternative investment proposals.

One method of investment analysis that provides a more complete picture and a means of comparing investments is called the net present value (NPV) method. The formula is as follows:

NPV = Present value of future cash flows minus [initial investment cost
          plus present value of future expenditures]

For any assumed investment period and interest rate, a positive (NPV) indicates that the total investment "inflows" exceed the total investment "outflows"; that is, the investor ends up with more (in present dollars) than he gave up. Accordingly, a negative NPV indicates that an investment should not be undertaken.

If there are tax benefits available from an investment, these tax benefits must be factored into the NPV analysis. This is accomplished by treating the dollar amount of a tax saving (for example, a deduction of $45,000 is a tax saving of $15,750 to a taxpayer with a 35.0 percent marginal tax rate) as part of the cash inflow in the year the tax saving is realized. Similarly, any tax expenditure must be treated as a negative cash flow. By factoring these tax aspects into the NPV equation, the investment can be analyzed from an after-tax viewpoint to support a more valid investment decision.[3]

The internal rate of return (IRR) is the more sophisticated method of investment analysis. The IRR is the discount rate that equates the present value of cash inflows with the present value of cash outflows. The IRR represents the

1. Prior to TRA [Tax Reform Act] 1986, tax shelter benefits were so prominent that the property was usually sold when the shelter "burned out" and started to produce taxable income. Since TRA 1986, economic and marketplace considerations have played a more dominant role in the decision as to when the property should be sold.

2. For example, most college textbooks on finance include present-value tables indicating that if L's cost of obtaining money were 10 percent on a three-year investment, he should invest no more than 75 cents for every dollar he expects to receive three years from now, or, if L must pay 15 percent to obtain money, the present value of the future dollar would be only 65 cents.

3. There are two glaring weaknesses to the NPV analysis. First, an appropriate interest rate must be assumed. When comparing investments of differing durations, the assumptions must vary and estimations require greater accuracy. The problem of an assumed interest rate is alleviated somewhat by an analysis called the Internal Rate of Return (IRR). Second, certain assumptions must be made about expected inflows. In the real estate scenario, these assumptions include rental income, maintenance expense, real estate taxes, and ultimate sale price. This second problem is dealt with by using risk analysis, the methodology of which is beyond the scope of this book.

exact rate of investment return that will allow an investor to receive economic benefits (discounted to present value) equivalent to the present value of his investment outlays for a given investment period. For example, a $1,000 bond that returns the initial $1,000 investment plus $100 interest exactly one year after investment would have an IRR of 10 percent. . . .

NOTES AND QUESTIONS

1. Internal Rate of Return. Note: A standard real estate calculator of the Hewlett-Packard or Texas Instruments variety can speed up the trial-and-error, or "iterative," process of finding the correct IRR discount factor.

If $1 million was invested for ten years generating $100,000 per year, and returning in year 10 (at sale) $1.2 million, the cash flows could be scheduled as follows:

Year	Cash Flow
0	−1,000,000 (investment)
1	100,000 (return)
2	100,000 etc.
3	100,000
4	100,000
5	100,000
6	100,000
7	100,000
8	100,000
9	100,000
10	1,300,000 (return plus sale proceeds)

The IRR calculation results in an 11.18 percent return; that is, this cash flow stream equates to an 11.18 percent return on investment. Note that the reinvestment of the cash flows is not considered in the IRR calculation; however, the IRR formula implicitly assumes the interim cash flows can be reinvested at the same 11.18 percent rate "solved for" by the iterative IRR calculation.

2. Dynamic Return Analysis. One criticism of the IRR calculation is that it assumes that the net cash benefits received during the investment period will be reinvested at the resulting IRR rate and therefore the higher the IRR, the higher the assumed reinvestment returns; thus the overall rate of return for the investment period may be overstated. Why is this an unrealistic assumption, especially in the case of a long-term investment? By contrast, the NPV method implies reinvestment at whatever discount rate is selected. To correct this deficiency, the IRR should be calculated based on an assumed reinvestment rate that can be prescribed in advance by the investment advisor or analyst. This modification of the IRR method is called the modified internal rate of return (MIRR) or the financial management rate of return (FMRR) and can be factored into the IRR calculation on most modern advanced-function calculators. See Wetterer, Comparing Investor Return—Consistency Is Crucial to Any Meaningful Comparison of Investment Options, 1 Real Est. Fin. J. 76, 78-79 (Fall 1984).

Further refinement of the IRR calculation is also possible by altering assumptions as to the tax bracket of the investor-taxpayer; timing and amounts of rentals, expenses, capital expenditures; and so on. The degree of risk exposure therefore can be quantified based on varying potential scenarios so that the investor can obtain both the "downside" and "upside" pictures before selecting the investment. See Russell, Appraising Real Estate Investments for Pension Funds, 2 Real Est. Acct. & Tax'n. 33, 42-44 (Winter 1988).

Proponents of the IRR method contend that it provides a clear ranking of investments according to percentage returns and is more comprehensible to the average unsophisticated investor than is the NPV method. Can you think of any other advantages?

Other measures of profitability include: (1) the adjusted rate of return (ARR), which attempts to equate the present value of the investment with the future value of its economic benefits; (2) the accounting return method (ARM); and (3) the payback method, all of which are described in comprehensive detail in R. Haft and P. Fass, Real Estate Syndication Tax Handbook 2-13 to 2-21 (1986-1987 ed.).

3. *Economic Rewards and Risks*

The traditional view held by most researchers and commentators in the literature on investments is that rates of return from direct ownership of commercial real estate and from indirect ownership of real estate equities,[5] as measured by various indices,[6] historically have been comparable to rates of returns from

---

5. See discussion at Chapter 15A.

6. Among the principal measures of investment performance of commercial real estate held by institutional investors in the United States are: (1) the Russell-NCREIF Index (RNI), which takes into account the changes in appraisal values and net operating income of *unleveraged* income-producing properties held for tax-exempt institutions by investment advisory firms, as, for example, pension fund portfolios that are frequently held in the form of commingled real estate funds (CREFs) that are usually selected and managed by life insurance companies who, as fiduciaries for the pension funds, are subject to the rules and regulations imposed by the Employee Retirement Income Security Act (ERISA); (2) the National Association of Real Estate Investment Trusts (NAREIT) Index, which is a market value-weighted index of all listed equity and mortgage REITs; (3) the Morguard Property Index (MPI), which measures both income and appreciation changes

corporate equities. Also, returns from income-producing real estate have been less volatile than the returns from stocks and bonds. In addition, real estate returns have exhibited low or negative correlations with stocks and bonds, making real estate a valuable asset in constructing well-diversified portfolios.[7] Moreover, in contrast to stocks and bonds, the nominal yields from real estate tend to increase with both anticipated and unanticipated inflation.

Hudson-Wilson and Fabozzi, Why Real Estate?
J. Portfolio Mgmt. 12 (Sept. 2003)

PRIMARY REASONS TO CONSIDER REAL ESTATE

There are five primary reasons to consider real estate, or any category of investment, for inclusion in an investment portfolio:

1. To reduce the overall risk of the portfolio by combining asset classes that respond differently to expected and unexpected events.
2. To achieve absolute returns well above the risk-free rate.
3. To hedge against unexpected inflation or deflation.
4. To constitute a part of a portfolio that is a reasonable reflection of the overall investment universe (an indexed or market-neutral portfolio).
5. To deliver strong cash flows to the portfolio. . . .

Many investors manifest their skepticism by assigning only very small allocations to real estate in their portfolios. In the absence of simple and readily understandable proof about why they should invest in real estate, some institutions fall back on the why nots. "We got burned during the real estate crash of the late 1980s," and "real estate is too illiquid; I may not be able to get out when I want to," or "real estate is 5% of our portfolio, but takes up 95% of our staff time." In light of unclear historical evidence, increased concern about stock market volatility, and emergence of a broader definition of real estate, it is time for a fresh look at the role of real estate in investment portfolios. We examine each of the five rationales above. For starters, though, real estate must be better defined.

---

based on performance data from approximately 200 *unleveraged* commercial Canadian properties; and (4) data on CREF returns in Real Estate Profiles, prepared by Evaluation Associates, Inc., and similar data prepared by the Real Estate Research Corporation. The major indices and sources of data for measuring changes in the income and capital appreciation rates of return for corporate equities include: (1) the Standard and Poor's 500 Total Returns Index; (2) the Salomon Brothers Broad Investment-Grade Bond Index; and (3) data prepared by Moody's Investor Service, the Board of Governors of the Federal Reserve System, and the U.S. Bureau of Labor Statistics.

7. See Hartzell, Real Estate in the Portfolio 1, 4-5 (Salomon Brothers, Aug. 27, 1986).

BROADER DEFINITION OF REAL ESTATE

Historically, real estate had been defined to include only investments in private real estate equity and private real estate debt. Pension funds and wealthy families bought and held direct investments in individual buildings and in commingled funds, while insurance companies traditionally built large portfolios of individual private real estate mortgages. Both approaches required that significant investments be made and then held, because there were no secondary and securitized markets for debt or equity.

With the advent of securitization [discussed in Chapter 15], the definition of real estate for institutional investors has broadened to cover four structures:

1. Private commercial real estate equity, held as individual assets or in commingled vehicles.
2. Private commercial real estate debt, held as either directly issued whole loans or commercial mortgages held in funds and/or commingled vehicles.
3. Public real estate equity structured as REITs or real estate operating companies (REOCs).
4. Public commercial real estate debt structured as commercial mortgage-backed securities (CMBS).

These four structures constitute the quadrants of the modern real estate investment class. . . .

It makes sense to broaden the definition of real estate investment beyond traditional private debt and equity concepts because the factors driving real estate investment performance in the private quadrants are reflected, to a greater or lesser degree, in the performance of the investments in the public quadrants. Any real estate investment, whatever its formal quadrant, is responsive to a common set of influences as well as to other influences specific to the quadrant. The performance of each real estate investment is produced by a mix of equity-like and debt-like behaviors. For example, consider the polar case of a private real estate equity asset leased to a single tenant with a long-term triple-net lease. The payments on that lease resemble the fixed payments one associates with a bond, not with equity. The value of this asset to the investor fluctuates with the same factors that influence the value of a bond or a mortgage, such as interest rate movements, inflation, and the creditworthiness of the tenant. At the other extreme, an equity position in an empty, speculative, multitenant property is driven almost entirely by equity forces. The value of the building is a function of supply of and demand for space, in that market, at that particular time. As the building becomes more fully leased, it changes from a pure equity to a debt-equity hybrid, and perhaps—if fully leased to long-term tenants—becomes very debt-like. In analogous fashion, as the net lease on the building in the first example ages, the residual value of the property at lease-end becomes an increasingly important, and finally dominant, component of the asset's value.

Equity issues, such as real estate market forces, economic health, tenant demand, interest rates, and the idiosyncratic nature of the property, such as its location, history, visibility, and neighbors, increase their influence on the asset's value.

Commercial mortgages also evidence debt-like and equity-like behaviors. In fact, this reality is the basis for the development of the CMBS market, which divides the cash flows from pools of mortgages to produce high-grade bond cash flow characteristics in the senior tranches and more equity-like cash flow characteristics in the most subordinate pieces. The connection between the private and public quadrants is clear from the number of individual assets that have moved, in both directions, across the dividing line. The experience of the 1995-1997 period showed that publicly traded REITs were the dominant competitors in the bidding for privately held real estate assets. At the same time, traditional lenders faced stiff competition for borrowers from the conduits that would lend and then securitize the mortgages. Public assets go private and private assets go public with increasing fluidity in a search for capital and relative value, encouraged by investors seeking ways to manage real estate portfolio risk. . . . Returns for each quadrant are derived as much as possible from publicly available data. . . .[8] The public equity quadrant is by far the most volatile. . . . The private mortgage quadrant shows significant volatility during the high inflation/tight money era prior to 1986, but has since settled down. The CMBS market, not measured before 1984 because the quadrant did not then exist, shows volatility little different from that of the more recent mortgage era—in part because the index captures all tranches' behaviors and not just the behaviors of the smaller junior pieces. The appraisal-based private equity quadrant is the least volatile. Conventional wisdom suggests that its volatility is understated, although we are increasingly convinced that while appraisals may lag, they eventually do capture the true range of performance of individual real estate assets. . . .

8. Returns from each real estate quadrant are difficult to measure but the following public sources of information are available: (1) Private Equity—the Russell-NCREIF Index (RNI), which takes into account the changes in appraisal values and net operating income of unleveraged income-producing properties held for tax-exempt institutions by investment advisory firms, as, for example, pension fund portfolios that are frequently held in the form of commingled real estate funds (CREFs) that are usually selected and managed by life insurance companies who, as fiduciaries for the pension funds, are subject to the rules and regulations imposed by the Employee Retirement Income Security Act (ERISA); (2) Public Equity—the National Association of Real Estate Investment Trusts (NAREIT) Index, which is a market value-weighted index of all listed equity (and mortgage) REITs; (3) Private Debt—the most cited index is the Giliberto-Levy Commercial Mortgage Performance Index; (4) Public Debt—CMBS indexes that calculate performance at the tranche level are not readily available; however, the Lehman Brothers index measures returns from all public debt from 1997 to the present. See also the Salomon Brothers Broad Investment-Grade Bond Index.— EDS.

REAL ESTATE AS A PORTFOLIO DIVERSIFIER
AND RISK REDUCER

The correlations between [the performances[9] of] real estate and stocks, and real estate and bonds . . . suggest that real estate can play a significant role in a mixed-asset portfolio. Whenever two imperfectly related assets (correlation coefficient of less than 1.0) are placed together in a portfolio, there is an opportunity to earn a higher return at each level of risk (or to reduce risk for a given level of return). When the return to an asset class is high enough, or the risk is low enough, or the correlation reflects a sufficiently different pattern of returns, the asset class earns a place in the portfolio for at least a portion of the return-risk spectrum. Real estate meets these tests, and is therefore a component of the well-diversified mixed-asset portfolio. . . . This evidence suggests that real estate is very suitable for investors interested in capital preservation who need to earn a useful rate of return. Strict capital preservationists would be 100% allocated to inflation-indexed bonds and would earn very little return. . . .

REAL ESTATE AS AN INFLATION HEDGE

Conventional wisdom has held that real estate acts as an inflation hedge. This means that if inflation is higher than expected, real estate returns will compensate for the surprise and will help offset the negative response of the other assets in the portfolio. . . . Inflation elicits different responses in the different property types through divergent impacts on the income and value components of return, and through variation in the effects of past and the most recent inflation. . . . Past inflation is partially embedded in rents set previously, because every seller of every product, including sellers of rental space, wants to keep prices level or rising in real terms. Thus current net operating income (NOI) is partly a function of past inflation, rising if past inflation has been higher, and falling (or rising less) if past inflation has been tame. How quickly inflation affects NOI, or the time lag necessary to capture inflation's impact on current NOI, depends on the structure of leases, which in turn varies with property type. Current office NOI reflects the inflation experience of one to (even) ten years ago, while apartment NOI reflects more recent inflation. The impact of past inflation, appropriately lagged, is positive for all four major property types. Current inflation impacts the levels of current rents and expenses. Current inflation raises NOI by increasing the rental rate on new leases, but reduces NOI by increasing all expenses. . . .

Inflation impacts the capital value return in two ways. First, it impacts current NOI, as described above, which feeds through to value via the capitalization rate. This channel is especially strong for retail assets. Second, inflation affects the cap rate directly by influencing NOI growth expectations and therefore investors' demand for real estate investments. . . . Thus, the empirical assessment shows

---

9. See Figure 12-1 for comparison of performances as between real estate equity, and stocks.—EDS.

that private equity real estate is a very useful partial inflation hedge. That said, it is also clear that the degree of inflation-hedging capacity is not uniform across the property types. As is the case with most debt, real estate debt is not a good inflation hedge because unexpected inflation and concomitant increases in nominal interest rates penalize outstanding securities (mortgages and CMBS). Publicly traded forms of equity real estate will capture some of the benefits of the inflation hedge, but are less successful transmitters of this value than private equity because of links to the stock market, which is generally damaged by inflation. So, if inflation hedging is a key reason why an investor chooses an allocation to real estate, that investor must tilt the portfolio toward private equity.

REAL ESTATE AS A REFLECTION OF THE INVESTMENT UNIVERSE

Real estate belongs in a balanced investment portfolio because real estate is an important part of the investment universe. Any portfolio that does not include real estate is based on a bet that real estate will perform less well than is implied by the market-driven relative prices. Indeed, any allocation to real estate that does not reflect real estate's overall share in the investment universe implies a different bet from that of an indexed portfolio, so such an off-market bet needs to be well justified.

It is interesting (not to say ironic) that the typical starting point for investor thinking is a portfolio without real estate—investors then see whether any legitimate arguments support its inclusion. The starting point should be to include real estate and the other assets at their market weights, and then to adjust the weights in order to best achieve investment objectives. There should be a presumption that real estate has a role.

NOTES AND QUESTIONS

Economic Rewards and Risks. As indicated by Figure 12-2, like stocks, the performance of real estate tracks the growth rate of the economy. Over the long run, real estate has performed well in comparison to other investments such as stocks and bonds. Among the more prominent events affecting U.S. capital markets during the second half of the twentieth century have been the introduction of inflation into the economy and the burgeoning of real estate values. The studies covering longer holding periods, and those analyzing returns in the 1950s and 1960s, tend to show roughly comparable returns from common stocks and real estate, with a slight edge to stocks. Note, however, that real estate returns during those "early" years were based on agricultural land or single-family home indexes and, where commercial properties were studied, conservative no-growth assumptions were employed. The studies during inflationary periods of the 1970s were characterized by vastly improved real estate databases. All of these studies concluded that real estate outperformed common stocks as well as fixed-income investments and the rate of inflation. For the years 1971 through 1990, a general index of total income and appreciation returns from income-producing real estate increased at a compounded annual rate of 11.0 percent as compared to a rate of 11.1 percent for stocks and 9 percent for bonds. Smith, Real Estate Resurgence Expected, But No Bell Will Alert Investors, Pension World 46 (Feb. 1992). As shown by the data in Figure 12-1, for years 1997 through 2011 there has been a wide variation in the relative performance of these two asset classes. While stocks outperformed real estate during the late 1990s and real estate has done better than stocks in the aftermath of the 2001 recession, the rates of income and appreciation returns from real estate have been comparable to stocks and higher than bonds. On relative investment performance, see generally Gyourko and Keim, Risk and Returns of Investing in Real Estate: Evidence from a Real Estate Stock Index, 49 Financial Analysts J. 39 (Sept./Oct. 1993); Gyourko and Siegel, Long-Term Return Characteristics of Income-Producing Real Estate, 11 Real Est. Fin. 14 (Spring 1994). Regarding relative risks and volatility, see generally Hartzell and Shulman, Real Estate Returns and Risks: A Survey (Salomon Brothers, 1988); regarding inflation, see Maisel, Inflation, Leverage, Vacancies, Taxes, and Returns to Office Buildings (Salomon Brothers, March 1987); Ullah and Zhou, Real Estate and Stock Returns: a Multivariate VAREC Model, 21 Property Management 8 (Feb. 19, 2003).

Directly owned real estate appears to have several advantages over stock ownership. First, the NCREIF data in Figures 12-1 and 12-2 represent the total returns from *un-leveraged* real estate. Second, as discussed in Chapter 13A2b, in contrast to stock investors, real estate investors are able to obtain significant *tax shelter benefits*, which means that the after-tax leveraged rates of return from real estate tend to be higher than from stock investments.

Figure 12-1 NCREIF returns include office buildings, warehouses, retail facilities, apartment buildings, and hotel/motels. The index consists of all income-producing properties regardless of whether they are leveraged; however, since the returns are all reported on an unleveraged basis, the index understates the actual investment returns from the leveraged properties where the owners have taken advantage of the positive spread between the financial returns and mortgage interest.

As reflected by its lower standard deviation of returns and lower coefficient of variation, the relative risk of real estate appears to be less than that for common stocks, and real estate returns are much less volatile than stock and bond returns (see Figure 12-1). On the other hand, statistics measuring volatility of returns tend to understate the actual volatility in real estate prices. When values are set by appraisals rather than transactions, they are much more stable because the appraisals are based on the long term underlying asset value. In real estate markets, a short run decline in property values is normally reflected in a reduced level of trading activity and longer marketing periods rather than in lower prices. By contrast, equity REIT returns exhibit essentially the same volatility as common stocks, which is not surprising since REIT shares are publicly traded securities. See discussion in Chapter 15A.

Figure 12 – 1

Returns: Real Estate vs. Stocks/Bonds

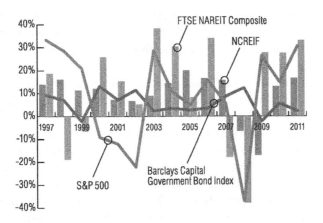

Sources: NCREIF, NAREIT, S&P, Barclays Group.
*2011 data annualized from second-quarter 2010.

Reprinted by permission of Urban Land Institute and PricewaterhouseCoopers LLP. Emerging Trends in Real Estate 2012.

Figure 12 – 2

Real Estate Returns and Economic Growth

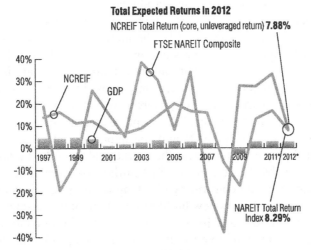

Sources: NCREIF, NAREIT, *World Economic Outlook* database.
*GDP forecasts are from *World Economic Outlook*. NCREIF/NAREIT data for 2011 are annualized from second-quarter 2010, and the forecast for 2012 is based on the *Emerging Trends in Real Estate 2012* survey.

Reprinted by permission of Urban Land Institute and PricewaterhouseCoopers LLP. Emerging Trends in Real Estate 2012.

In addition, because of the negative correlation between real estate and common stock (income and appreciation) returns, most commentators agree with Hudson-Wilson and Fabozzi that an investor's overall portfolio risk can be reduced by combining real estate with stocks and other portfolio assets. See, for example, Wilson and Elbaum, Diversification Benefits for Investors in Real Estate, 21 J. Portfolio Mgmt. 92 (Spring 1995). Based on your general understanding of macroeconomics, can you think of the reason for this negative correlation?

Investment economists report that between the total returns from stocks, corporate bonds, and Treasury bills and the rate of inflation, the highest positive correlation is between real estate and the rate of inflation. E.g., Zerbst and Cambon, Real Estate: Historical Returns and Risks, 10 J. Portfolio Mgmt. 5 (Spring 1994). This suggests that real estate is a better hedge against inflation than are stocks and bonds. But why is this so? There is no obvious answer. One of the reasons is the correlation between inflation and replacement or construction costs. During periods of inflation, short-term interest rates rise, increasing the cost of construction financing, and the extra construction period interest coupled with inflationary increases in the costs of labor and materials (as measured by the so-called Construction Cost Index (CCI)) causes an increase in building replacement costs. By contrast, during the same period, Standard & Poor's Index of 500 generally moved contrary to changes in the rate of inflation.

To understand why the historical relationship between inflation and building replacement costs has helped make the ownership of existing income-producing real estate (especially well-located and well-built properties) a relatively good hedge against inflation you need to understand a fundamental principle concerning the valuation of income-producing real estate: namely, that the appraised market value of a piece of rental real estate depends directly on how much NOI it produces. As suggested by the materials on measuring profitability at Chapter 12A2, supra (and as explained more fully at Chapter 4D1), the chief method of appraisal for commercial and multifamily real estate is the "income approach," in which market value is determined by dividing the anticipated NOI by a risk-adjusted market rate of interest (or discount factor) called the "capitalization rate," or "cap rate." A simple example: Assume that an office building yields $1 million of NOI and the appraiser selects a cap rate of 10 percent. Under the income approach, the market value of the building would be $1 million divided by 10 percent, or $10 million (or "ten times earnings"), a figure the appraiser would confirm by checking recent sale prices of comparable buildings in the same area. As new buildings are built at increasingly higher costs to satisfy the growing demand for space in a growing inflationary economy, the higher rentals they command to make new construction profitable will pull up the rentals on existing properties, and as rents increase so will the value of the existing properties as determined by the income method.

Another reason why real estate acts as a hedge against inflation is that rental real estate is one of the few types of assets whose value is protected by lease provisions (called "escalation clauses") that pass certain cost increases (for example, increases in insurance premiums and local property taxes) to tenant-users. Other inflation hedges employed by owner-landlords include the use of percentage rentals and shorter lease terms. See Chapter 10A1.

In addition, so-called operating leverage produces another inflation-related benefit for the real estate investor. By definition, any successful project that yields net operating income will have more gross income than expenses. This means that if we assume a certain rate of inflation then an equal percentage of increase to both items will increase the cash flow and net operating income from the project. This in turn enables the real estate owner to increase his equity in the investment. Simply defined, "equity" means the value of assets less liabilities or so-called net assets (for example, real estate assets minus mortgage liabilities), and any increase in net operating income automatically increases the value of an asset. For accounting purposes, value means either the book value of the real estate (if the asset is reflected at cost) or its cash value (if the asset is reflected at its market value).

Returning to the example in the text, assume the money received (cash flow) is $1,000,000 as the result of gross income ($1,400,000) exceeding expenses ($400,000). In the first year, at an assumed 4 percent annual rate of inflation, gross income would increase to $1,456,000 and expenses would increase to $416,000. This would cause net operating income to increase by $40,000 to $1,040,000. Thus, if the asset is valued at 10 times earnings, the market value of the asset would increase from $10,000,000 to $10,400,000, and the owner's equity would increase by $400,000. See Maisel, Inflation, Leverage, Vacancies, Taxes, and Returns to Office Buildings 3-10 (March 1987).

As Zerbst and Cambon point out, real estate has been, relatively speaking, a better hedge against inflation than either stocks or bonds. Zerbst and Cambon, Real Estate: Historical Returns and Risks, 10 J. Portfolio Mgmt. 5 (Spring 1994). In the case of bonds, the explanation is straightforward. During periods of inflation, when interest rates rise, the prices of existing bonds tend to fall because of their lower interest rates; conversely, when interest rates drop the prices of existing bonds tend to rise.

The explanation for the weaker performance of common stocks as an inflation hedge is not so simple. Certainly, as a matter of supply and demand, during periods of inflation, when interest rates rise, there is usually a shift in investment capital from stocks to higher-paying bonds, and the resultant softening in demand for stocks obviously will depress their market value as measured by the Dow-Jones and Standard & Poor's indices. Theoretically, however, common stock, like real estate, in the long run should be a relatively good hedge against inflation. A share of common stock is nothing more than an indirect ownership or proprietary interest in the property owned by the corporation. Both stocks and income-producing real estate are affected by the level of economic growth and interest rates. In fact, rental rates, which are the principal determinant of real estate values, are strongly related to GDP growth rates as are stock prices. See Figure 12-2. Can you think of any reasons why the correlation in stock and real estate performance is so low? See Quan and Titman, Do Real Estate Prices and

Stock Prices Move Together? An International Analysis, 27 Real Est. Econ. 183 (Summer 1999).

The negative side of the real estate coin is its lack of liquidity as an investment. Investment shares in equity REITs have been publicly traded for a number of years, and there is a recent trend toward securitization of real estate, on the debt side, as exemplified by mortgage pools, called REMICs, and securities called commercial mortgage-backed bonds. See discussion at Chapter 15A and 15C. However, as explained in Chapter 14, most investment shares in commercial real estate are held by private investors such as limited partners and members of limited liability companies, who have no access to any formal secondary market for trading or liquidating their shares, and consequently the inimitable liquidity of publicly held corporate stocks and bonds constitutes a distinct investment advantage for corporate equities compared to real estate. Can you think of any other economic reasons for investing in stocks and bonds rather than in real estate?

B. THE MORTGAGE MARKET FOR COMMERCIAL REAL ESTATE

Here we briefly examine the mortgage market for income-producing real estate by learning which variables in our economy govern the supply and demand for mortgage credit. The related questions of who the major types of mortgage lenders are and how they function are discussed at Chapter 4A2. The recent trend toward the securitization of commercial real estate mortgages as a financing tool for developers is examined at Chapter 15C.

As explained above, the profitability of investing in income-producing real estate, as opposed to other investment media such as stocks and bonds, can be explained to a large extent by the interplay between the financial leverage and tax benefits accorded to the real estate investor. Accordingly, the cost and availability of mortgage credit is of paramount concern to any leverage-minded purchaser or developer of income-producing real estate.

So, for example, returning to the master hypothetical in Chapter 3, with a loan-to-value ratio of 75 percent, the debt-service payments on a $25 million mortgage can represent such a large percentage of Dan Developer's operating expenses that a mere one- or two-point increase in the annual interest rate could reduce his investors' rate of equity return to a point at which they decide to abandon the project.

One of the few truisms in real estate is that the financing and profitability of any project are bound to depend on a number of economic factors that are unique to the particular transaction. So, for example, the terms of the postconstruction financing sought by Dan (such as the interest rate, loan-to-value ratio, and maturity date) will depend on a number of deal-specific factors such as the type of lending institution and property involved. However, the cost and availability of mortgage credit will also be influenced by certain macroeconomic variables such as household savings and also by the actions of the Federal Reserve Board. As a consequence, the cost and supply of mortgage money historically have tended to be countercyclical. In plain language this means that, except for a few instances of "stagflation" (such as during the 1980-1981 recession) and credit stringency (as in the 1990-1991 recession), real estate borrowers seem to fare well when the economy is lagging and to fare poorly when the economy is doing well. For example, the biggest real estate booms ever started at the tail ends of recessions, such as after the 1970-1971 recession, the 1980-1981 recession, and the 2001 recession. This is because real estate borrowers tend to be crowded out of the money markets by business and government borrowers when the economy heats up and loanable funds become scarce. Conversely, real estate borrowers historically have fared better at the tail ends of recessions when business demand was weak and consumer confidence was on the rebound. See Madison, Dwyer, and Bender at §3:3.

As to the cost of mortgage money, postconstruction financing is relatively long-term, and therefore the cost of mortgage credit from a postconstruction lender ordinarily is geared to the level of long-term interest rates (such as the yields on 10-year Treasury bonds), which tend to be a function of (1) inflationary expectations;[10] (2) "uncertainty" over the federal budget and other future financial and political developments; and (3) the "real" or "time" value of money (which most economists project to be in the 3.5 percent to 4 percent range over a long period). The level of short-term interest rates (such as the prime rate), which governs the cost of mortgage credit from a construction or "interim" lender (during the two- or three-year period of construction), is also influenced by the long-term factors mentioned above. For the most part, however, short-term rates are a product of Federal Reserve action to combat inflation (by constricting the money supply and thereby increasing short-term rates) or to encourage economic growth (by reducing short-term rates).

The following Notes and Questions deal with a long-standing macroeconomic fiscal policy dispute that is bound to have a profound impact, not just on the real estate sector, but on the entire economy as well. First is the still-raging debate among respected economists as to what impact the escalating federal budget deficits will have on the economy, and second is what impact, if any, these deficits will have on future interest rates and the future supply of credit for real estate borrowers.

---

10. Future inflation tends to reduce the value of the dollar and cause long-term lenders to demand more interest to compensate them for higher expenses and in the case of both lenders and bond investors for the loss in value of their U.S. denominated assets.

NOTES AND QUESTIONS

The Real Estate Atmosphere Is Clouded by Looming Budget Deficits. In the opinion of most economists, escalating federal budget deficits in the 1970s, 1980s, early 1990s, and now in the second decade of the 2000s, imperil not only the future cost and availability of mortgage credit, but the overall state of the economy as well. The amount of these deficits had averaged less than $10 billion a year in the 1960s, but grew to $79 billion by the time Ronald Reagan assumed office in 1981. President Reagan, along with a complaisant Congress, managed to increase the deficit to $221 billion by 1986. After increasing to a high of $290 billion in 1992, the deficit was drawn down to $21 billion in 1997 during the Clinton administration. This downsizing primarily was caused by an increase in tax receipts as a result of the expansion of the economy during the late 1990s. However, after President Bush took office in 2000, the budget deficits began to escalate as a consequence of the tax reductions authorized by the Jobs and Growth Tax Relief Reconciliation Act of 2003 and the cost of funding the war in Iraq. The deficits continued to spiral during the Obama administration as the result of the economic downturn spawned by the 2008 recession and the resultant federal bailouts of the banking and auto industries. In an effort to curb future deficits, Congress enacted the Budget Control Act of 2011, which raised the initial U.S. debt ceiling to $900 billion in exchange for $917 billion of reductions in the budget over the following 10 years. In 2012 the nonpartisan Congressional Budget Office (CBO) predicted that the federal budget deficit would decline from a projected $612 billion in 2013 (7.6 percent of GDP) to $303 billion in 2022 (1.2 percent of GDP). Right in line with this projection, the federal deficit was $438 billion in 2015.

a. *Debate over Deficit Spending.* Many economists discourage deficit spending as being inflationary. Instead, most of this group want to lessen the structural deficit caused by spending on entitlements such as Medicare and Medicaid. Other economists with a Keynesian bent favor deficit spending as a tool of fiscal policy. They contend that deficits caused by tax cuts tend to spur economic growth, create jobs, and increase income and tax revenues. Therefore, in the long run, such deficit spending can help the economy and reduce the amount of budget deficits. This, they argue, is what happened during the second term of the Regan administration. During the first term, immediately after the enactment of the Economic Recovery Tax Act of 1981, the country sank into a deep recession, unemployment reached 8.4 percent, and well over 10 million workers became unemployed. However, by the end of the second term the economy, spurred by the tax cuts, had totally recovered and had created 18 million new jobs.

For balance, also consider the following less critical view of budget deficits:

Fallacy 1: Deficits are considered to represent sinful profligate spending at the expense of future generations who will be left with a smaller endowment of invested capital. This fallacy seems to stem from a false analogy to borrowing by individuals.

Current reality is almost the exact opposite. Deficits add to the net disposable income of individuals, to the extent that government disbursements that constitute income to recipients exceed that abstracted from disposable income in taxes, fees and other charges. This added purchasing power, when spent, provides markets for private production, inducing producers to invest in additional plant capacity, which will form part of the real heritage left to the future. This is in addition to whatever public investment takes place in infrastructure, education, research and the like. Larger deficits, sufficient to recycle savings out of a growing gross domestic product (G.D.P.) in excess of what can be recycled by profit-seeking private investment, are not an economic sin but an economic necessity. Deficits in excess of a gap growing as a result of the maximum feasible growth in real output might indeed cause problems, but we are nowhere near that level.

Even the analogy itself is faulty. If General Motors, AT&T and individual households had been required to balance their budgets in the manner being applied to the Federal government, there would be no corporate bonds, no mortgages, no bank loans and many fewer automobiles, telephones and houses.

William Vickrey, Fifteen Fatal Fallacies of Financial Fundamentalism, www.columbia.edu/cu/economics.

   b. *Do Budget Deficits Affect Interest Rates?* The fiscal deficit can increase (1) because government expenditure rises while revenue remains unchanged, (2) because tax revenue falls while government expenditure stays unchanged, or (3) because tax revenue falls while government expenditure rises. Regardless of which of these three cases is behind the increase in the fiscal deficit, government bond sales will have to increase. Other things being equal, for the government to induce people to buy a larger quantity of its bonds than previously, it must discount the bonds somewhat. Put a different way, interest rates must rise from the level that they would have reached in the absence of the deficit. The above conclusion follows from the most fundamental law in economics—the law of supply and demand. That law tells us that if one wants to sell more of something, one has to reduce its price. This result thus should not be controversial. Still, much controversy persists about whether fiscal deficits bring about increases in interest rates. What is the source of this controversy?

   The orthodox view among economists has been that there is a causal connection between larger fiscal deficits and higher interest rates. Frequently economists who subscribe to this majority view argue that large deficits tend to increase long-term interest rates because of their impact on national saving. This means that the federal government must increase interest rates (by lowering the price of its bonds) to "crowd out" other borrowers such as business and real estate borrowers. Another explanation is that increasing deficits increase long-term rates because of an increase in inflationary expectations. Moreover, while substantial deficits may be tolerable in a recessionary economy, according to this view, they are surely inappropriate and possibly dangerous when the economy is expanding.

By contrast, the emerging minority view rejects the paradigm that large current deficits necessarily produce high long-term interest rates because the emphasis should be on future and not current deficits. Others take the position that the relevant question is not whether a fiscal deficit increases or decreases rates, but how these changes occur. For example, under the so-called spontaneous compensating behavior theory, if the budget deficit were to increase because of some tax-cutting legislation (such as the Economic Growth and Tax Relief Reconciliation Act of 2001), theoretically the extra disposable income available to taxpayers could be saved, to a large extent, and used to buy the additional government bonds needed to fund the increase in the deficit. In other words, the forward-looking rational individual would consume less and save more. As a consequence, the rate of interest might remain the same without major dislocations in the economy. Still other economists contend that deficits do not necessarily increase long-term interest rates because the demand for U.S. government bonds by domestic and especially by foreign investors seems to be extremely elastic. See generally Tanzi, Fiscal Deficits and Interest Rates in the United States, 31 International Monetary Fund Staff Papers 551; Labonte, Do Budget Deficits Push Up Interest Rates and Is This the Relevant Question?, Congressional Research Service (February 4, 2005).

Some economists have cited historical facts to justify their conclusion that increasing budget deficits do not necessarily cause an increase in long-term interest rates. For example, one points out that there were three periods in U.S. history during which the federal deficit exceeded 10 percent of the GNP, and in none of these periods did real interest rates rise appreciably: "In over a century of U.S. history, large deficits have never been associated with high interest rates. Even the postwar periods separately offer no support for a positive association between deficits and interest rates. . . ." See Evans, Do Large Deficits Produce High Interest Rates?, 75 Am. Econ. Rev. 68, 86 (Mar. 1985). In addition, the two major economies with the lowest overall inflation rate since the 1980s, West Germany and Japan, have had larger deficits (as measured by a percentage of their GNP) than the United States.

QUESTIONS

1.   Based on what you have learned about macroeconomic theory and based on your assessment of today's economic picture (for example, rate of economic growth, rate of inflation, inflationary expectations, rate of household consumption and savings, level of employment), what is your prediction as to the cost of construction financing and permanent financing in the short-term future?

2.   Which of the following is the best time period for real estate borrowers? For real estate owners? (a) strong economic growth; (b) slow economic growth at the tail end of a recession; or (c) negative economic growth (recession)?

3. Historically, when there is a drop in housing starts, bond prices go up. Conversely, bond prices go down when there is a sudden decline in the value of the U.S. dollar. Can you explain the macroeconomic reasons why?

4. Empirical evidence on a link between budget deficits and interest rates has been mixed. However, economists have yet to agree on what relevant variables should be included in resolving the issue. See Labonte at 1. Can you think of other factors besides budget deficits that are likely to affect interest rates?

Chapter 13

Overview of Taxation
of Real Estate Investments

A. TAXATION OF INCOME-PRODUCING REAL ESTATE

1. Overview

In previous chapters, we have accompanied Dan Developer as he chronologically waded his way through the commercial real estate lending cycle. Here we examine how tax considerations play an important role in real estate investment and financing decisions. See Figure 13-1.

Dan Developer's decision to invest in real estate will be strongly influenced by tax considerations. Among the prefinancing considerations for Dan is which ownership entity is best suited for the dual purpose of raising the necessary venture capital and maximizing tax benefits for Dan and his investors. See Chapter 14. Also, in the case of new construction another threshold consideration is how will Dan finance the cost of the underlying land. One alternative that will enable Dan to reduce his initial cash outlay and probably increase the tax deductions would be to sever the land from the improvements and engage in a sale and leaseback of the land, or Dan might ground lease the fee and obtain a leasehold mortgage loan. See discussion at Chapters 11B and 11A. Once the project is completed, Dan will be entitled to take tax deductions for depreciation and his operating expenses including mortgage interest and property tax payments. To raise additional capital he might cash out equity by means of refinancing, secondary financing, or a sale and leaseback of the property. All three financing devices are replete with tax consequences and planning possibilities that are discussed at Chapters 7A, 7B, and 11B, respectively. Finally, Dan may decide to sell or exchange the developed property by means of a straight sale or tax-free exchange (Chapter 13A2d); if the property is purchased with seller financing, then Dan would be entitled to use the installment method for reporting his gain on the sale. See Chapter 7B3. Alternatively, if the project should fail and Dan negotiates a workout of the mortgage loan with either the construction lender or the postconstruction lender, or if the project should go to foreclosure, both Dan and the lender or lenders will of necessity take tax considerations into account. See Chapter 8A.

Figure 13 – 1

Tax Aspects of Real Estate Financing

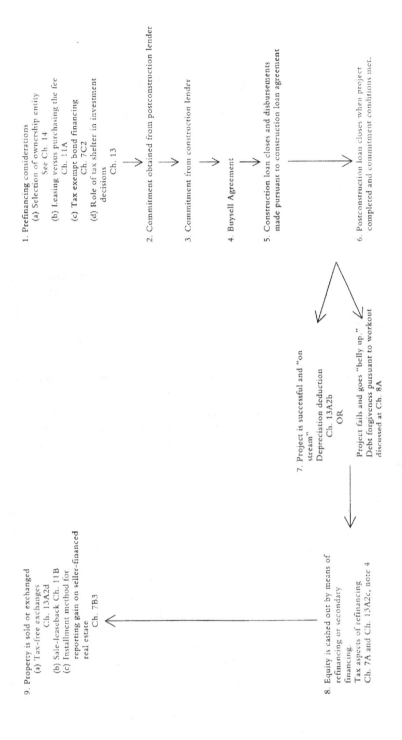

2. *Real Estate as a Limited Tax Shelter*

The tax shelter benefits associated with the ownership of income-producing real estate further explain why real estate is such an attractive investment medium. Although the tax-shelter device was curtailed by the Tax Reform Act of 1986 (1986 Act), and modified by the Revenue Reconciliation Act of 1993 (1993 Act), the Taxpayer Relief Act of 1997 (1997 Act), the Economic Growth and Tax Relief Reconciliation Act of 2001 (2001 Act), the Jobs and Growth Tax Relief Reconciliation Act of 2003 (2003 Act), the Tax Relief, Unemployment Insurance Reauthorization and Job Creation Act of 2010 (2010 Act), and the American Taxpayer Relief Act of 2012 (2012 Act), it remains viable and offers unique opportunities for real estate investors. (At press time the proposed Tax Cuts and Jobs Act of 2017 that would alter the tax shelter advantages of income-producing real estate ownership had not yet been enacted). The end result for investors is a leveraged after-tax rate of return from income-producing real estate that frequently exceeds the after-tax returns that could be obtained from stocks or bonds.

In most cases, while the depreciation deduction is less than what it used to be, it still shelters ordinary rental income from immediate taxation. This deferring of tax liability until the real estate is sold is what produces time-value benefits for the real estate investor. The deduction also converts ordinary income into long-term capital gain, which is taxed at the lower capital gain rate.[1] Therefore, the depreciation deduction provides both deferral and conversion benefits for real estate owners that are not available to taxpayers who invest in corporate securities.

As explained in the materials that follow, the two underpinnings of real estate tax shelter are the *Crane Doctrine* and the depreciation deduction.

a. The *Crane* Doctrine

The following materials examine a doctrine of fundamental importance to real estate investors under which the basis of the property for such purposes as determining the depreciation deduction during ownership and gain on resale will include both the cash (equity) investment and any mortgage indebtedness whether or not the investor is personally liable on the mortgage loan.

---

1. As explained more fully at Chapter 13A2b under the 2012 Act the maximum individual tax rates for ordinary income and long-term capital gain are 39.6 percent and 20 percent, respectively, except that the portion of the gain attributable to depreciation is recaptured at the rate of 25 percent. Income from qualifying dividends is treated as capital gain.

Crane v. Commissioner
331 U.S. 1 (1947)

Mr. Chief Justice VINSON delivered the opinion of the Court. The question here is how a taxpayer who acquires depreciable property subject to an unassumed mortgage, holds it for a period, and finally sells it still so encumbered, must compute her taxable gain.

Petitioner was the sole beneficiary and the executrix of the will of her husband, who died January 11, 1932. He then owned an apartment building and lot subject to a mortgage,[1] which secured a principal debt of $255,000.00 and interest in default of $7,042.50. As of that date, the property was appraised for federal estate tax purposes at a value exactly equal to the total amount of this encumbrance. Shortly after her husband's death, petitioner entered into an agreement with the mortgagee whereby she was to continue to operate the property—collecting the rents, paying for necessary repairs, labor, and other operating expenses, and reserving $200.00 monthly for taxes—and was to remit the net rentals to the mortgagee. This plan was followed for nearly seven years, during which period petitioner reported the gross rentals as income, and claimed and was allowed deductions for taxes and operating expenses paid on the property, for interest paid on the mortgage, and for the physical exhaustion of the building. Meanwhile, the arrearage of interest increased to $15,857.71. On November 29, 1938, with the mortgagee threatening foreclosure, petitioner sold to a third party for $3,000.00 cash, subject to the mortgage, and paid $500.00 expenses of sale.

Petitioner reported a taxable gain of $1,250.00. Her theory was that the "property" which she had acquired in 1932 and sold in 1938 was only the equity, or the excess in the value of the apartment building and lot over the amount of the mortgage. This equity was of zero value when she acquired it. No depreciation could be taken on a zero value.[2] Neither she nor her vendee ever assumed the mortgage, so, when she sold the equity, the amount she realized on the sale was the net cash received, or $2,500.00. This sum less the zero basis constituted her gain, of which she reported half as taxable on the assumption that the entire property was a "capital asset."

The Commissioner, however, determined that petitioner realized a net taxable gain of $23,767.03. His theory was that the "property" acquired and sold was not the equity, as petitioner claimed, but rather the physical property itself, or the owner's rights to possess, use, and dispose of it, undiminished by the mortgage. The original basis thereof was $262,042.50, its appraised value in 1932. Of this value $55,000.00 was allocable to land and $207,042.50 to building. During the period that petitioner held the property, there was an allowable depreciation of

---

1. The record does not show whether he was personally liable for the debt.

2. This position is, of course, inconsistent with her practice in claiming such deductions in each of the years the property was held. The deductions so claimed and allowed by the Commissioner were in the total amount of $25,500.00.

$28,045.10 on the building, so that the adjusted basis of the building at the time of sale was $178,997.40. The amount realized on the sale was said to include not only the $2,500.00 net cash receipts, but also the principal amount of the mortgage subject to which the property was sold, both totaling $257,500.00. . . .

We granted certiorari because of the importance of the questions raised as to the proper construction of the gain and loss provisions of the Internal Revenue Code.

The 1938 Act, §111(a), defines the gain from "the sale or other disposition of property" as "the excess of the amount realized therefrom over the adjusted basis provided in section 113(b). . . ." It proceeds, §111(b), to define "the amount realized from the sale or other disposition of property" as "the sum of any money received plus the fair market value of the property (other than money) received." Further, in §113(b), the "adjusted basis for determining the gain or loss from the sale or other disposition of property" is declared to be "the basis determined under subsection (a), adjusted . . . for exhaustion, wear and tear, obsolescence, amortization . . . to the extent allowed (but not less than the amount allowable)...." The basis under subsection (a) "if the property was acquired by . . . devise . . . or by the decedent's estate from the decedent," §113(a)(5), is "the fair market value of such property at the time of such acquisition."

Logically, the first step under this scheme is to determine the unadjusted basis of the property, under §113(a)(5), and the dispute in this case is as to the construction to be given the term "property." If "property," as used in that provision, means the same thing as "equity," it would necessarily follow that the basis of petitioner's property was zero, as she contends. If, on the contrary, it means the land and building themselves, or the owner's legal rights in them, undiminished by the mortgage, the basis was $262,042.50.

We think that the reasons for favoring one of the latter constructions are of overwhelming weight. In the first place, the words of statutes—including revenue acts—should be interpreted where possible in their ordinary, everyday senses. The only relevant definitions of "property" to be found in the principal standard dictionaries are the two favored by the Commissioner, i.e., either that "property" is the physical thing which is a subject of ownership, or that it is the aggregate of the owner's rights to control and dispose of that thing. "Equity" is not given as a synonym, nor do either of the foregoing definitions suggest that it could be correctly so used. Indeed, "equity" is defined as "the value of a property . . . above the total of the liens. . . ."

A further reason why the word "property" in §113(a) should not be construed to mean "equity" is the bearing such construction would have on the allowance of deductions for depreciation and on the collateral adjustments of basis. . . .

Under these provisions, if the mortgagor's equity were the §113(a) basis, it would also be the original basis from which depreciation allowances are deducted. If it is, and if the amount of the annual allowances were to be computed on that value, as would then seem to be required, they will represent only a fraction of the cost of the corresponding physical exhaustion, and any recoupment by the mortgagor of the remainder of that cost can be effected only by the reduction of his taxable gain in the year of sale. If, however, the amount of the annual allowances were to be computed on the value of the property, and then deducted from an equity basis, we would in some instances have to accept deductions from a minus basis or deny deductions altogether. The Commissioner also argues that taking the mortgagor's equity as the §113(a) basis would require the basis to be changed with each payment on the mortgage, and that the attendant problem of repeatedly recomputing basis and annual allowances would be a tremendous accounting burden on both the Commissioner and the taxpayer. Moreover, the mortgagor would acquire control over the timing of his depreciation allowances. . . .

We conclude that the proper basis under §113(a)(5) is the value of the property, undiminished by mortgages thereon, and that the correct basis here was $262,042.50. The next step is to ascertain what adjustments are required under §113(b). As the depreciation rate was stipulated, the only question at this point is whether the Commissioner was warranted in making any depreciation adjustments whatsoever. . . .

As we have just decided that the correct basis of the property was not zero, but $262,042.50, we . . . conclude that an adjustment should be made as the Commissioner determined.

Petitioner urges to the contrary that she was not entitled to depreciation deductions, whatever the basis of the property, because the law allows them only to one who actually bears the capital loss, and here the loss was not hers but the mortgagee's. We do not see, however, that she has established her factual premise. There was no finding of the Tax Court to that effect, nor to the effect that the value of the property was ever less than the amount of the lien. . . . Whatever may be the rule as to allowing depreciation to a mortgagor on property in his possession which is subject to an unassumed mortgage and clearly worth less than the lien, we are not faced with that problem and see no reason to decide it now.

At last we come to the problem of determining the "amount realized" on the 1938 sale. Section 111(b), it will be recalled, defines the "amount realized" from "the sale . . . of property" as "the sum of any money received plus the fair market value of the property (other than money) received," and §111(a) defines the gain on "the sale . . . of property" as the excess of the amount realized over the basis. Quite obviously, the word "property," used here with reference to a sale, must mean "property" in the same ordinary sense intended by the use of the word with reference to acquisition and depreciation in §113, both for certain of the reasons stated heretofore in discussing its meaning in §113, and also because the functional relation of the two sections requires that the word mean the same in one section that it does in the other. If the "property" to be valued on the date of acquisition is the property free of liens, the "property" to be priced on a subsequent sale must be the same thing. . . .

Starting from this point, we could not accept petitioner's contention that the $2,500.00 net cash was all she realized on the sale except on the absurdity that she sold a quarter-of-a-million dollar property for roughly 1 percent of its value, and took a 99 percent loss. . . .

Petitioner concedes that if she had been personally liable on the mortgage and the purchaser had either paid or assumed it, the amount so paid or assumed would be considered a part of the "amount realized" within the meaning of §111(b). The cases so deciding have already repudiated the notion that there must be an actual receipt by the seller himself of "money" or "other property," in their narrowest senses. It was thought to be decisive that one section of the Act must be construed so as not to defeat the intention of another or to frustrate the Act as a whole, and that the taxpayer was the "beneficiary" of the payment in "as real and substantial [a sense] as if the money had been paid it and then paid over by it to its creditors."

Both these points apply to this case. The first has been mentioned already. As for the second, we think that a mortgagor, not personally liable on the debt, who sells the property subject to the mortgage and for additional consideration, realizes a benefit in the amount of the mortgage as well as the boot.[37] If a purchaser pays boot, it is immaterial as to our problem whether the mortgagor is also to receive money from the purchaser to discharge the mortgage prior to sale, or whether he is merely to transfer subject to the mortgage—it may make a difference to the purchaser and to the mortgagee, but not to the mortgagor. Or put in another way, we are no more concerned with whether the mortgagor is, strictly speaking, a debtor on the mortgage, than we are with whether the benefit to him is, strictly speaking, a receipt of money or property. We are rather concerned with the reality that an owner of property, mortgaged at a figure less than that at which the property will sell, must and will treat the conditions of the mortgage exactly as if they were his personal obligations. If he transfers subject to the mortgage, the benefit to him is as real and substantial as if the mortgage were discharged, or as if a personal debt in an equal amount had been assumed by another.

Therefore we conclude that the Commissioner was right in determining that petitioner realized $257,500.00 on the sale of this property. . . .

NOTES AND QUESTIONS

The Crane *Doctrine.* Under the *Crane* doctrine, when property is acquired (or constructed) with cash and a mortgage, the tax basis of the property includes not only the cash or equity investment but also the mortgage indebtedness whether or not the purchaser (or developer) is personally liable under the mortgage.

To illustrate this doctrine, assume that Dan Developer develops a project costing $10 million financed through an $8 million mortgage loan and $2 million

---

37. Obviously, if the value of the property is less than the amount of the mortgage, a mortgagor who is not personally liable cannot realize a benefit equal to the mortgage. Consequently, a different problem might be encountered where a mortgagor abandoned the property or transferred it subject to the mortgage without receiving boot. That is not this case.

of partnership capital contributions. Dan's partnership would initially obtain a tax basis in the real estate of $10 million for purposes of computing depreciation and gain or loss on the sale or exchange of the realty even if the partnership obtains "qualified non-recourse financing" whereby neither the partnership nor the partners are personally liable for the $8 million mortgage indebtedness. Moreover, if the partnership were to sell the property to a purchaser who pays $2 million and assumes the $8 million mortgage (for which the purchaser would be personally liable) or to a purchaser who pays $2 million but takes subject to the mortgage so that the purchaser is not personally liable, in either instance the tax basis for the purchaser would be the full leveraged cost of $10 million for the property.

a. What is inconsistent about the petitioner's contention in *Crane* that all she realized on the sale was $2,500 after depreciation of $28,045 was allowed on the building while she held the property? The petitioner in *Crane* contended that "property" (for purposes of adjusted basis under I.R.C. §1001(b)) should be defined as "only the equity, or the excess in the value of the apartment building and lot over the amount of the mortgage." Some opponents of real estate tax shelter agree and have proposed that a real estate investor's depreciable basis should not be equal to the total leveraged cost but that it should be limited to the taxpayer's equity investment in the property. Do you see any problems with this approach? See Adams, Exploring the Outer Boundaries of the *Crane* Doctrine: An Imaginary Supreme Court Decision, 21 Tax L. Rev. 159 (1966); McKee, The Real Estate Tax Shelter: A Computerized Expose, 57 Va. L. Rev. 521, 565-567 (1971); Ji, Note, Non-recourse Financing of Real Property: Depreciation Allocation and Full Recapture to Minimize Deferral and Eliminate Conversion, 29 Colum. J.L. & Soc. Probs. 217 (1996).

b. Under the *Crane* doctrine no distinction is made between recourse financing and nonrecourse financing, as evidenced by the court's conclusion that the correct basis of the property for purposes of depreciation was not the taxpayer's zero equity interest but $262,042.50, the value of the property, undiminished by mortgages thereon, notwithstanding that she was not personally liable on the mortgage. Otherwise, as the court suggests, if the petitioner's depreciable basis was her zero equity interest, the annual depreciation allowances "will represent only a fraction of the cost of the corresponding physical exhaustion" of the property, and this result presumably would ignore the accounting convention that income should be matched with related deductions such as depreciation in each tax year. In addition, this equating of personal liability with the absence of that liability seems responsive to the business realities that (1) a mortgagor without personal liability would feel essentially the same economic compulsion to pay the mortgage debt to keep the growing equity in the property, (2) permanent lenders generally rely on the collateral value of the property and not the net assets of the borrower to secure the mortgage indebtedness, and (3) only a small dollar-amount percentage of deficiency judgments on recourse loans are ever collected by lenders against defaulting borrowers. Observe, however, that there are obviously limits to the *Crane* doctrine, as suggested by the following dictum of the court: "Whatever may be the rule as to allowing depreciation to a mortgagor on property in his possession which is subject to an unassumed mortgage and clearly worth less than the lien, we are not faced with that problem and see no reason to decide it now." See 331 U.S. at 12.

Assume that a purchaser acquires real estate with a useful life of five years worth $50,000 (which remains valued at $50,000 unless otherwise noted). What should be the purchaser's initial depreciable basis in the property under the following circumstances? (1) The purchaser pays zero cash in the first year and $50,000 in the form of a four-year nonrecourse purchase money note and mortgage with amortization payments of $10,000 each year during the next three years and with a $20,000 payment in the last year. (2) The same facts as in (1) except that the property is only worth $40,000 during the five-year period. (3) The same facts as in (1) except that the purchaser agrees to pay $60,000 and the seller is willing to accept a lump sum or "balloon" payment at the end of the fifth year. Compare Mayerson v. Commissioner, 47 T.C. 340 (1966), acq. Rev. Rul. 69-77, 1969-1 C.B. 59, and Bolger v. Commissioner, 59 T.C. 760 (1973) (*Crane* rule reaffirmed), with Estate of Franklin v. Commissioner, 64 T.C. 752 (1975), aff'd, 544 F.2d 1045 (9th Cir. 1976) (no part of nonrecourse indebtedness included in taxpayer's basis where purchase price had no relationship to property value), and Bergstrom v. Commissioner, 37 Fed. Cl. 164 (1996). To the extent that the purchase price is artificially inflated beyond its market value to increase the purchaser's depreciation deductions, the seller will be charged with more gain on the sale. Accordingly, if the tax interests of the parties are antithetical, why should the Internal Revenue Service want to challenge such a transaction?

Subsequent to the *Franklin* decision, the *Crane* doctrine has been successfully challenged where there was a price-value discrepancy, especially in sale transactions where the parties did not bargain with one another at arm's length. See Graf v. Commissioner, 80 T.C. 944 (1983); Flowers v. Commissioner, 80 T.C. 914 (1983); Odend'hal v. Commissioner, 80 T.C. 588 (1983), aff'd, 748 F.2d 908 (4th Cir. 1984); Narver v. Commissioner, 75 T.C. 53 (1980), aff'd, 670 F.2d 855 (9th Cir. 1982); Beck v. Commissioner, 74 T.C. 1534 (1980), aff'd, 678 F.2d 818 (9th Cir. 1982); see generally Avent and Grimes, Inflated Purchase Money Indebtedness in Real Estate and Other Investments, 11 J. Real Est. Tax'n. 99 (1984); Bittker, Tax Shelters, Nonrecourse Debt, and the *Crane* Case, 33 Tax L. Rev. 277 (1978).

c. In Commissioner v. Tufts, 461 U.S. 300 (1983), the Supreme Court held that the amount realized (I.R.C. §1001(b)) from the taxable sale or exchange of property can exceed its fair market value when the outstanding nonrecourse indebtedness on the date of disposition exceeds the market value of the property being sold or exchanged. See also footnote 37 in the *Crane* case.

An example would be if X were to purchase property for a zero cash investment with an interest-only $100,000 nonrecourse mortgage loan. Further assume that the fair market value of the property on the date of its resale by X equals its adjusted basis of $80,000 and that the purchaser buys the property with zero cash by assuming or taking the property subject to the mortgage with its $100,000 balance. The question that confronted the Court was whether in the hypothetical the amount realized by X on the sale should not exceed the $80,000 market value of the property, in which event X would receive a tax windfall by having $20,000 of his depreciation deductions escape any taxation when the property is sold.

The issue is of special importance to real estate investors who leverage their acquisition and construction costs with nonrecourse financing. However, if the value of the property declines below the amount of the outstanding mortgage indebtedness, not only will the investors face a loss of cash profits on the sale and a large amount of reported gain (caused by the depreciation write-off, which reduces the original basis in the property) but they must also confront the specter of being forced to recognize "phantom" gain ($20,000 in the example) on an amount realized ($100,000 in the example) that exceeds the market value of the property ($80,000 in the example) merely because the property being sold is subject to a nonrecourse mortgage in the higher amount in respect to which the investors never have been, nor ever will be, personally liable for repayment.

Do you think the Supreme Court made the correct decision in requiring the investor to recognize the "phantom" gain in these circumstances? See McGuire, *Tufts* at the Supreme Court, 10 J. Real Est. Tax'n. 54 (1982); Newman, The Demise of Footnote 37: Commissioner v. Tufts, Tax Notes 259 (July 25, 1983); Sanders, Supreme Court, Ending *Crane* Controversy, Says Nonrecourse Debt Is Always Part of Sale Price, 59 J. Tax'n 2 (1983); Joyce, Tribute: Remembering Louis Del Cotto, 55 Buff. L. Rev. 395 (2007) (answer to *Tufts* question must be in the tax benefit rule). Incidentally, the holding in the *Tufts* case was codified as I.R.C. §7701(g).

b.   Tax Shelter by Means of the Depreciation Deduction

As you know, real estate investors are afforded the unique opportunity to leverage their cost of acquiring and improving real estate by means of high-ratio financing. But why has income-producing real estate been able to accomplish both deferral and conversion benefits for taxpayers who either directly own the property or indirectly own the property as investors in pass-through entities such as limited partnerships, limited liability companies, and Subchapter S corporations (see Chapter 14)? The answer is quite simple if you understand how and why the depreciation deduction is able to shelter rental income from immediate taxation and produce taxable losses that (subject to the passive loss rules) can be used to shelter outside income.

On the positive side of the tax shelter coin is I.R.C. §167—the principal underpinning for real estate tax shelter. I.R.C. §167 allows a depreciation deduction for the "exhaustion, wear and tear . . . of property used in the trade or business, or . . . held for the production of income." The notion underlying this provision is that while depreciation does not involve any cash outlay, a real estate owner computing taxable income should be allowed to take into account the fact that rental income-producing property is wearing out and becoming obsolescent. Accordingly, like the cost of making repairs and paying employees' salaries, the cost of building or purchasing the real property should be allocated over the period during which the property is producing income.[2]

Conversely, on the negative side of the tax-shelter coin is mortgage "amortization," which simply means repayment of principal during the life of a loan. To obtain financial leverage, many, if not most, real estate borrowers will fund the acquisition or improvement of real estate by means of high-ratio and constant-payment mortgage financing. Under a constant payment arrangement, since the amount of the periodic debt-service payment on the mortgage remains constant, the portion of the interest payment allocable to interest starts to decline as the principal balance is repaid; therefore, the remaining portion allocable to amortization correspondingly must increase over time. In contrast to depreciation, mortgage amortization does involve a cash outlay, and yet is not deductible for tax purposes. What fundamental tax principle tells you this is so? It is the excess of depreciation (which does not involve any cash outlay and yet is deductible) over mortgage amortization (which does involve a cash outlay but is not deductible) that produces tax shelter.

Some fundamental rules dealing with how partners and partnerships are taxed under Subchapter K of the Internal Revenue Code are helpful here. Under the "aggregate approach," a partnership (including an LLC taxed as a partnership) is treated under I.R.C. §§701 and 702 as a nontaxable conduit by which items of income, gain, loss, deduction, or credit are transmitted to the partners. Conversely, with the exception of the Subchapter S corporation, the "entity approach" applies to corporate taxation: The corporation can avail itself of the depreciation deduction to offset its taxable income, but it cannot pass through its depreciation-caused losses to its stockholders. See Chapter 14. Also, every dollar of depreciation deduction reduces the partnership depreciable basis in the property so that the partnership (and partners) realize an extra dollar of gain when the property is sold. I.R.C. §1016(a)(2). However, each partner's share of such extra gain would increase the adjusted basis in his or her partnership interest under I.R.C. §705(a)(1)(A), and the gain would be capital gain under I.R.C. §1231. Also, in addition to each partner's share of tax losses, every dollar of tax-free distribution would be treated as a tax-free return of capital since the distributee-partner in effect would be receiving a $1 refund of the investment cost, and accordingly the partner's adjusted basis in the partnership interest would be reduced by $1. I.R.C. §§705(a)(2), 733(1). Accordingly, unless the

2. See Treas. Reg. §1.167(a)-1(a). The 1986 Act significantly curtailed the amount of tax shelter by slowing and reducing the depreciation deduction. Under prior law, taxpayers could use accelerated depreciation over recovery periods as short as 19 and 15 years. See Table 13-1, infra. Under current law, straight-line depreciation is mandated over a cost recovery period of 27.5 years for residential rental real estate and 39 years for commercial real estate. I.R.C. §§168(c), 168(e)(2)(A). Residential rental property is defined as property from which 80 percent of the gross rental income is derived from rental income from dwelling units.

partnership is a "collapsible" one under I.R.C. §751, the partner would realize an extra dollar of capital gain when his or her interest is sold or liquidated. I.R.C. §§731(a)(1), 741.

NOTES AND QUESTIONS

1. The Interplay between Financial Leverage and the Depreciation Deduction. The depreciation deduction (I.R.C. §167) produces a constant amount of depreciation allowance for an investor regardless of what part of the cost of the project the investor furnishes and what part is financed by a mortgage. Under the so-called *Crane* doctrine (discussed at Chapter 13A2a, supra), when depreciable property is acquired for cash and a mortgage loan, the cost tax basis, and basis for depreciation of the property, includes the mortgage indebtedness whether or not the owner is personally liable under the mortgage. Accordingly, the same dollar amount of depreciation will increase the investor's rate of return on its equity to the extent it is able to reduce its equity and thereby leverage its acquisition costs by means of mortgage debt financing.

2. Amount of Tax Shelter Equals Excess of Deductible Depreciation Over Non-deductible Mortgage Amortization. Assume that the limited partners of an entity that owns an apartment building made all of their capital contributions (totaling $2 million) in year 1. Assume that in year 2, the free and clear rate of return is a respectable 9.4 percent, and the cash on cash rate of return is 8.4 percent.[4] Paradoxically, on the tax side, the venture may look like an unmitigated disaster as, assume, the venture produces a tax loss. Cash distributions to the limited partners of their share of the venture's net rental income (after payment of debt service on the mortgage) is ordinary income for tax purposes. And yet, not only are these cash distributions sheltered from immediate taxation as a "tax-free return of capital," but the venture is also able to produce tax losses that, subject to the passive loss rules, can be used by the partner-distributees to offset their ordinary income from outside sources, such as salaries and dividends. At marginal tax rates of 39.6 percent, these tax losses can be worth a considerable amount to the partners. When added to their cash distributions, assume this increases their cash-on-cash rate of return on their equity investment in year 2 from 8.4 percent to an after-tax rate of return of 10.8 percent. How does the tax shelter phenomenon explain the paradoxical result? The answer is that the excess of deductible depreciation over nondeductible mortgage amortization is what produces tax shelter.

---

4. The free and clear and cash-on-cash rates of return are the simplest method to measure the before-tax profitability of income-producing realty. The former is determined by dividing projected net annual income before tax and finance charges by the purchase price. The later is determined by dividing cash distributions by the total capital contributions. See discussion at Chapter 12A2.

3. The Problem of the Disappearing Shelter. By using accelerated depreciation, which was allowed under pre-1986 Act law, the amount of the depreciation deduction and resultant shelter would decrease each year as the depreciable basis of the property declined by the amount of the accelerated depreciation taken the year before. However, under current law only straight-line depreciation is allowed. Also, under a constant payment mortgage arrangement, the amount of shelter would decrease as the percentage of each payment allocable to nondeductible amortization increased. Eventually, under pre-1986 law, the amount of the depreciation deduction and resultant tax shelter was so large that the shelter would burn out. (In other words, a crossover point would be reached at which time the excess of depreciation over amortization became insufficient in amount to shelter all the cash distributions to the limited partners so the investment started to produce taxable income, often resulting in the property being sold.) Current law, however, disallows deductions of any losses against nonpassive income, and all such losses are suspended and carried forward until the property is sold. If the losses are suspended they do not burn out because the disallowed losses are carried forward, and allowed to offset the cash distributions (distributive shares of passive net rental income) each year that would otherwise be taxable to the investors as ordinary income. Under current law, then, the burnout issue has become less significant, and chances are that business rather than tax considerations will predominate in the decision by the general partners as to when the property should be sold.

In any event, to some degree the problem of disappearing shelter can be mitigated by refinancing the mortgage (substituting a new, often larger, loan for an existing one) to de-escalate the amount of nondeductible amortization, or, in the case of a burned-out shelter, by selling the over-depreciated property (for example, residential property held for more than 27.5 years) and using the net sale proceeds to fund the acquisition of some substitute property. This would start the depreciation cycle anew, since the partnership would obtain a new depreciable basis equal to the cost of the newly acquired property.

4. Depreciation Deduction Converts Ordinary Income into Long-Term Capital Gain. If a taxpayer sells or exchanges real property that has been used in its trade or business and held for more than one year, the taxpayer will incur long-term capital gain. See I.R.C. §1231(b)(1)(A), (B). Ordinarily, the gain will be the excess of the amount realized from the sale over the taxpayer's adjusted basis in the property, which is reduced by the amount of the depreciation previously deducted by the taxpayer. Under current law, long-term capital gain is taxable to individuals at a maximum rate of 20 percent, except that gain attributable to previous depreciation is taxed at a higher 25 percent rate. By contrast, if the taxpayer receives rental or other operating income from the property, or as a "dealer" sells some real property to a customer in the ordinary course of the taxpayer's trade or business, the income or gain will be taxed as ordinary income, which under current law is taxed at a maximum individual rate of 39.6 percent. Qualifying dividends that were previously taxed as ordinary income are currently taxed as capital gains. Congress has seen fit to accord preferential treatment to long-term capital gain as a way to encourage capital contributions into the economy.

The two mainstays of real estate tax shelter are deferral of taxation and conversion of ordinary income into long-term capital gain. We have just seen how the partners in the hypothetical investment partnership are able to use their shares of the partnership's depreciation deduction to defer taxation of their shares of ordinary rental income and to obtain tax losses that might be used to defer their ordinary income from outside sources. They are also able to use the depreciation deduction to convert ordinary income into long-term capital gain and thereby take advantage of the 14.6 percent (the difference between the maximum 39.6 percent ordinary income rate [effective until 2018] and the 25 percent recapture rate on capital gain attributable to previous depreciation) and 19.6 percent (the difference between the maximum 39.6 percent ordinary income rate and the maximum 20 percent long-term capital gains rate) spreads in rates.

Assume in the investment hypothetical that the partnership sells the apartment building at the end of an 8-year holding period—the entire gain would be treated as an I.R.C. §1231 gain and taxed at the preferential long-term capital gain rate. This means that for every dollar of excess depreciation in earlier years passed through to the limited partners and used by them to offset the otherwise taxable cash distributions from the partnership and to produce tax losses to offset their ordinary income from outside sources, the tax basis of the partnership property and the partners' tax bases would be reduced in like amounts so that the partners would be taxed on an extra dollar of long-term capital gain at the 25 percent rate when either the real estate or their partnership interests are sold. Thus, the limited partners are allowed to convert what would otherwise have been ordinary income (taxable at the 39.6 percent rate) into their share of matching long-term capital gain, taxable at the 25 percent depreciation recapture rate.

In addition, the partners are able to defer payment of the tax shelter benefits (in the form of the matching long-term capital gain) until the property is sold. By doing so, each partner would save 14.6 cents on every dollar converted from ordinary income into long-term capital gain, as a consequence of the depreciation deduction, and 19.6 cents on every dollar that is converted into long-term gain, as a consequence of the gain attributable to appreciation in the value of the property. And don't underestimate the importance of the time value of money. For example, if an individual highest-bracket taxpayer who owns depreciable real estate decides to sell it in 10 years, at an assumed interest rate (or discount factor) of 10 percent, the taxpayer would save 61.4 cents on every dollar of current tax liability that is deferred until the year of sale.

5. Limitations on Deducting Losses. Opponents of the *Crane* doctrine have long argued that a real estate investor's depreciable basis should be limited to the equity investment in the property or, alternatively, that aggregate depreciation losses should be limited to the equity amount. In addition, these tax shelter critics have taken the position that so-called artificial losses produced by depreciation should not be allowed to shelter unrelated outside income such as salaries and dividends. In the critics' opinion, the use of nonrecourse financing and other risk-limiting transactions to shelter outside income is tax abusive because it allows tax losses that may never be matched by economic losses and induces capital into real estate ventures that are not economically viable. Following this line of reasoning, the 1986 Act extended the general at-risk rules under I.R.C. §465 (limiting a taxpayer's deductible losses from all business and income-producing activities to the at-risk amount, roughly equivalent to equity in the activity at the close of the taxable year) to real estate activities, with an exception provided for "qualified nonrecourse financing"—that is, generally third-party financing. This is discussed at Chapter 14A2.

By far the most onerous anti-shelter provision under the 1986 Act is the one whereby losses or credits arising from "passive" business activities in which the taxpayer does not "materially participate" are not allowed to offset earned income and "portfolio" income (dividends, interest, royalties, and gains on sale of investment property). The passive loss limitation under I.R.C. §469 applies to individuals as well as to estates and trusts. In the case of pass-through entities such as partnerships and Subchapter S corporations, the limitation does not apply to the ownership entity itself. However, it applies to individual partners or Subchapter S shareholders because such individuals are subject to the rule regardless of whether they own an interest directly or indirectly in the passive business activity. Closely held corporations are able to deduct rental-passive losses against active business income (or passive income) but not against portfolio (investment) income. Publicly held corporations are not subject to the passive loss limitation. All limited partnership interests and all rental activities (other than those in which substantial services are rendered to occupants, such as the operation of a hotel) are deemed passive in nature regardless of whether the taxpayer materially participates in the activity. However, losses and credits from rental or other passive activity may be applied against income from other passive activities in the same taxable year. But, losses from one passive activity cannot be used to offset gain on the sale of an interest in another passive activity. Netting is not allowed with interest income, even interest from real estate mortgages.

Also, disallowed losses and credits can be carried forward (but not back) indefinitely and will be allowable against passive activity income in subsequent years. Under the 1986 Act, suspended losses are allowed in full on a taxable disposition of the activity. See Staff of the Joint Committee on Tax'n., General Explanation of the Tax Reform Act of 1986, at 215-222 (1987). Accordingly, in the case of a moderately leveraged income-oriented real estate investment, the absorption of deferred losses in the latter years of the venture may result in an after-tax rate of return (for example, internal rate of return) that is comparable to the result that would be obtained without the passive loss limitation.

Under a relief provision, an individual may deduct up to $25,000 each year of passive losses that are attributable to rental real estate activities in which the individual (or the individual's spouse, in the case of jointly owned property) "actively participates," to offset nonpassive income of the taxpayer. I.R.C. §469(i). The active participation test is less rigorous and requires less personal involvement than the material participation standard; however, neither a limited partnership interest in rental real estate nor an individual interest of less than 10 percent in the activity will qualify. The $25,000 allowance is phased out ratably as the individual's adjusted gross income (computed without taking passive losses into account) increases from $100,000 to $150,000, and the exception is entirely eliminated for adjusted gross income in excess of $150,000.

As explained in the excerpt by Shenkman and Marshall at Chapter 13A2c, infra, the 1993 Act liberalized the passive loss limitation rule for active real estate professionals. I.R.C. §469(c)(7), as amended, now permits an unlimited offset of rental losses against all types of nonpassive income, such as wages and dividend income, in the case of a real estate professional who materially participates in a real property trade or business. See generally Klein, Potential Relief from PAL Limitations for Real Estate Professionals Engaged in Rental Activities Made Available by RRA '93, 21 J. Real Est. Tax'n 228 (Spring 1994). For planning suggestions for an investor such as a limited partner or inactive member of a limited liability company who is not a real estate professional, see M. Madison, J. Dwyer, and S. Bender, The Law of Real Estate Financing §1.12 (2016).

6. The Tax Shelter Is Feeble without Rental Income. An allowance for depreciation is available to the owner of real estate that is being used in a trade or business or held for the production of income. I.R.C. §§167(a), 212. Thus, real estate either held for personal use or held by a "dealer" primarily for sale to customers is not subject to depreciation. Examples of "dealer" real estate include raw land held by a subdivider for resale to home builders and improved real estate (for example, condominiums) held by a developer for sale to consumers. In both cases, the real estate owner is deprived of a depreciation deduction because the land is being held as inventory for sale to customers in the ordinary course of its business. However, while owning the real estate, the seller may be entitled to deductions for business expenses (for example, advertising, employees' salaries) and for interest and property taxes paid or accrued during the ownership period.

Even in the case of income-producing real estate, the owner's potential for tax deferral is quite limited until the project becomes operational and starts producing rental income. Prior to the completion of construction, for instance, the depreciation deduction is not available because by definition to be eligible for depreciation the property must be in use as a business or investment activity. This makes sense because the notion underlying the depreciation deduction is that the owner of an income-producing but wasting asset should be able to recoup the cost of the asset over some cost recovery period, as an offset against its income. Prior to the completion of construction, it would be difficult to establish and measure the depreciable cost basis of the income-producing real estate.

c. Tax Shelter Reform

The following excerpts highlight the long and tortuous history of real estate tax reform with regard to the depreciation deduction. Critics of real estate tax shelter like Professor McKee have argued that the depreciation deduction, especially when it is accelerated, distorts income and is an inefficient and unfair deduction-funded subsidy. Proponents such as Alan Aronsohn have argued the contrary by stressing the fact that depreciation is nothing more than an accounting convention that has nothing to do with measuring fluctuations in market value. Other points of contention include whether or not rental real estate should be treated as a "passive activity" for purposes of the loss limitation rule under I.R.C. §469, whether long-term capital gain should still be accorded preferential tax treatment, and whether refinancing proceeds should be made taxable when they are distributed to the taxpayer. This debate over real estate tax shelter is sure to continue.

McKee, The Real Estate Tax Shelter: A Computerized Expose
57 Va. L. Rev. 521, 556-567 (1971)

THE NEED TO ELIMINATE THE REAL ESTATE TAX SHELTER

. . . Since it is virtually impossible to fashion a subsidy that does not provide benefits to those who would engage in a favored activity anyway, any subsidy is inherently inefficient. But because the size of a deduction-funded subsidy, such as the tax shelter, is determined by the investor's tax bracket, rather than by an assessment of the inducement actually needed to encourage investment, such a subsidy compounds inefficiency. If a deduction-funded subsidy is to be effective to encourage lower bracket investors to place their capital in depreciable realty, high bracket investors must be given a "windfall" profit.[87] Indeed, in order to have the same impact as the deduction-funded tax shelter incentive, a system of direct cash subsidies would have to provide a 70% bracket investor with seventy cents of immediate subsidy, while his 30% bracket counterpart would receive only thirty cents for the same activity. Thus, deduction-funded subsidies are inequitable as well as inefficient. Finally, deduction-funded subsidies have an undesirable effect on the theory and administration of tax policy. The federal income tax law is based on the theory that those who make more should contribute a greater proportion of their income in taxes than their less affluent counterparts; but deduction-funded subsidies are highly regressive and are

---

87. One might postulate that the higher an individual's tax bracket, the higher the rate of return required to induce him to invest, since at higher tax brackets a higher before tax rate of return is necessary to equalize the after tax rate of return to investors in lower brackets. But in real estate, high bracket investors get higher *after tax* rates of return than their lower bracket counterparts—a hard notion to justify as an efficient subsidization of desired activities.

therefore irreconcilable with tax theory. Such subsidies also narrow the tax base, causing tax rates to be maintained at high levels.

These objections can be leveled against all deduction-funded tax incentives, and alone seem sufficient to call for change. But the peculiarities of real estate investments merit special attention. . . .

[T]he inequity among taxpayers in different brackets is extreme. Although deduction-funded subsidies are always worth more to high bracket investors, the subsidy, in most cases, constitutes only a moderate portion of the overall rate of return, so that differences in rates of return are not very large in an absolute sense. But a high bracket investor in depreciable realty uses the principles of leverage to apply the benefits of his larger subsidy to a small equity.[90] The subsidy thus can become the major source of the return, with the result that high bracket investors often receive twice the rate of return that their lower bracket counterparts receive. Additionally, the fairly small difference in rates of return created by most deduction-funded subsidies at least allows the lower bracket investor to participate in the subsidized activity. But in real estate the rate of return available to a high bracket investor will often be sufficient to induce his investment in times when his lower bracket counterpart is effectively excluded from the industry by high mortgage interest rates. If there are sufficient high bracket investors to meet the demand for new buildings, the real estate industry as a whole will not exert pressure to improve market conditions; and low bracket investors will continue to be excluded until external pressures in the economy force interest rates down. . . .

ARGUMENTS IN SUPPORT OF THE REAL ESTATE TAX SHELTER

The arguments which are made in support of deduction-funded tax incentives in general have been analyzed and refuted elsewhere. Again, however, the peculiarities of depreciable real estate merit special attention.

THE IMPACT OF INFLATION

It can be argued that accelerated depreciation is justified to offset the impact of inflation, even though the building does not decline in dollar value. Taubman and Rasche conclude that inflation does indeed impose a negative subsidy upon investors:

A further complication in setting tax depreciation rules involves the appropriate adjustments to make when inflation is occurring. To determine what economic income should be in this instance, it is useful to first suppose that there are no taxes.

---

90. Moreover, the high bracket investor is more likely to be sufficiently wealthy to be able to increase his leverage by borrowing on his personal credit.

Then suppose that all prices (including rents) double. Under the circumstances described, the owner of an asset would find that its current selling price has also doubled. However, his real economic income is unchanged since all prices doubled. That is, if he sold the investment he would be unable to consume more goods and services than in the preinflation situation. Now let taxes be reintroduced. When the inflation occurs, to guarantee that a person's real after tax income remains constant the depreciation allowance must be blown up by the price increase. The tax law, however, bases depreciation on original cost, thereby imposing a negative subsidy on investors. This problem occurs for any depreciable asset as well as for financial assets, whose market valuation can be affected by inflation. While the comparative position of investors and wage earners has been answered, it is interesting to compare real estate investors with other investors.[95] . . .

But, there seems to be no reason for treating real estate owners any differently than owners of other assets. Since our tax system treats all owners of assets alike in that they are taxed somewhat unfairly because of inflation, and since introducing any discrepancy between tax depreciation and economic depreciation produces substantial distortions in tax equity, the problem of inflation should not be handled by adjusting the size of depreciation deductions.

PROTECTING THE REAL ESTATE INDUSTRY FROM INTEREST RATE FLUCTUATIONS

Since a major portion of most real estate investments is financed with borrowed funds, the cost of those funds—interest—should have a major impact on the profitability of such investments. Although the industry is sensitive to interest rate changes, this sensitivity is substantially less than it would be in the absence of the tax shelter. The tax shelter renders high bracket taxpayers relatively impervious to interest rate changes, and thus immunizes a part of the investment community from the impact of interest rate changes. Since wide fluctuations in the interest rate are often created by government policy as opposed to market forces, it can be argued that the industry needs the damper provided by the tax shelter to provide insulation from interest rate fluctuations.

Even if it is assumed that the real estate industry needs protection from interest rate fluctuations, the tax shelter is not an apt method of supplying the protection. To begin with, even without the tax shelter the fact that interest is deductible substantially lessens the impact of interest rate changes on the rate of return. Moreover, the tax shelter materially lessens the impact of rate changes only on high bracket investors, who are also those primarily insulated by the interest deduction. The low bracket investor remains quite sensitive to interest rate changes, and to the extent that low bracket investors constitute a substantial

95. Taubman & Rasche, [The Income Tax and Real Estate Investment (presented at the Symposium on Tax Incentives of the Tax Institute of America) (1969)], at 6-7.

source of investment funds the tax shelter does not provide the allegedly needed protection.

LOW GOVERNMENT COST

Unlike many forms of government subsidy, a substantial portion of the tax revenues lost because of unwarranted depreciation [is] returned to the government when the building is sold. To the extent that the tax is eventually collected, the government assumes the position of a lender. Although the loan may be extremely valuable to the investor-borrower, the cost to the government is more modest—the government's cost of raising funds to provide the interest free loan is the interest rate which it must pay to borrow these funds. It is true that much of the initial subsidy is never repaid because of incomplete recapture, but nevertheless the governmental cost of the loan element of the subsidy is less than the benefit provided to the investor to the extent of the difference between the rate of return which the investor can earn and the interest rate which the government must pay.

Of course, the essence of this lower cost of subsidization is the government's willingness to make an interest free loan without security. But rather than tie the amount of the loan to the investor's tax bracket a direct low interest loan program would produce the same benefit at a lower cost and without the distortions inherent in deduction-funded subsidies.

ALTERNATIVE METHODS OF ELIMINATING THE REAL ESTATE TAX SHELTER

For reasons of efficiency, equity and tax policy, the tax shelter should be eliminated and another method of subsidizing the industry created, if continued subsidy is thought to be desirable. The means by which the tax shelter is eliminated, however, is quite important. It is not enough simply to eliminate accelerated depreciation, since even straight line depreciation creates a substantial tax shelter.

The surest method of eliminating the real estate tax shelter is to limit allowable tax deductions to economic depreciation. This would require that buildings be classified according to their precise economic depreciation rates. . . .

The problem with limiting tax depreciation to economic depreciation lies in the difficulty of determining the proper classification of buildings and their corresponding depreciation rates. Variations in economic depreciation rates depending upon construction techniques and geographic location are probably substantial. . . .

CONCLUSION

The real estate tax shelter is an inefficient and inequitable form of subsidy; it should be eliminated. If limiting depreciation deductions to actual economic depreciation proves too complex or politically impractical, limiting the investor's depreciable basis to the amount of his equity is a viable alternative.

Panel Discussions on General Tax Reform
Before the House Ways and Means Committee
93d Cong., 1st Sess., ser. 11, pt. 4 (Tax Treatment of Real Estate) 510-520 (1973)

PREPARED STATEMENT OF
ALAN J. B. ARONSOHN, NEW YORK, N.Y.

INTRODUCTION

An understanding of the size and complexities of the real estate industry is a necessary prerequisite to any discussion of the proper income tax treatment to be accorded to certain activities in the real estate field. . . .

While real estate is a major American industry, it has nevertheless operated through a diffused aggregation of small and medium-sized businesses. Unlike certain segments of the manufacturing industry, economic power in this sector is not concentrated in the hands of a relatively small number of major corporations. Consequently, the vast aggregations of capital and managerial talent which are a feature of such segments of the economy are not typical of real estate.

The fact that the real estate industry is not composed of a few large enterprises is of some significance in the determination of proper tax policy. In contrast to the continuity of businesses like the manufacture of automobiles or the production and distribution of oil, the ownership and operation of rental real estate is a relatively discretionary activity. Most private sector initial investment in rental property is entirely voluntary.

It is fair to assume, therefore, that the willingness of large numbers of comparatively small investors to continue to invest in an essentially voluntary investment market, such as real estate, will be affected more immediately by changes in the costs, risks and potential rewards of doing business than might be the case if the industry were characterized by a greater concentration of economic power and dedication to continuity of enterprise.

Other aspects of real estate are also relevant to tax policy considerations. Real estate investments are materially less liquid than investments in marketable securities, and they usually require fairly substantial long-term financial commitments. Once the investment is made, it cannot readily be moved or abandoned. This characteristic has been responsible in part for the comparative ease with which real estate has long been subject to all kinds of government control and taxation. When faced with increases in local taxes, pollution control costs and even rent controls, the owner of investment real estate does not have the same flexibility to shift his business investment as may be available, for example, to a manufacturer of diverse products capable of being produced in varying locations.

As a consequence of some of these factors, investments in real estate, in order to be competitive in the free capital market, have generally been forced to yield somewhat higher rates of return than marketable securities of comparable risk. . . .

THE DEDUCTION FOR DEPRECIATION

What is the proper concept and function of depreciation or amortization in our income tax system?

Probably no question has been so thoroughly debated and confused.

Actually, the basic purpose of such an allowance is quite simple. It is intended to account for loss of capital in determining a taxpayer's net income for tax purposes within a system which taxes net income, not gross income, on an annual basis.

It is based upon the elementary and equitable doctrine that if a taxpayer is deriving income from a wasting economic asset, an appropriate measure of his taxable net income on an annual basis is obtained by prorating the cost of the asset over its life, as an offset against the gross income from it. . . .

The Treasury's Income Tax Regulations have historically described the depreciation allowance as "that amount which should be set aside for the taxable year in accordance with a reasonably consistent plan (not necessarily at a uniform rate), so that the aggregate of the amounts set aside, plus the salvage value, will, at the end of the estimated useful life of the depreciable property, equal the cost or other basis of the property. . . . The allowance shall not reflect amounts representing a mere reduction in market value."[1] This interpretation of the depreciation allowance for income tax purposes has consistently been supported by the courts.[2]

The depreciation allowance is therefore simply a capital cost recovery system. It is essentially an accounting convention. It does not correspond with an economist's definition of depreciation, which would involve continuous revaluation of the projected income stream from the asset. Under the Internal Revenue Code depreciation has nothing to do with fluctuating values.

Strenuous efforts have been made to introduce value as a factor in computing allowable depreciation for income tax purposes, for in an inflationary economy a depreciable asset cannot generally be replaced for its original cost. Spokesmen

---

1. Treas. Reg. §1.167(a)-1(a).
2. E.g., Crane v. Commissioner, 331 U.S. 1 (1947).

for industry have repeatedly suggested that the allowable deductions for depreciation be increased to take into account inflated capital replacement costs. However, to date taxpayers have been permitted to recover only original cost, not replacement value, via the allowable deductions for depreciation and amortization.

Perhaps the easiest way to visualize the functioning of the deduction for depreciation with respect to a real estate investment is to examine a simple illustration involving the acquisition of a leasehold interest. I have deliberately chosen a leasehold interest for this purpose since, in the case of the acquisition of a leasehold estate for a fixed term of years, without any renewal options, there is no question or ambiguity concerning the life of the assets acquired.

For example, let us assume that taxpayer Able leases land under a ground lease having a fixed term, without renewal options, which provides for ground rent of $5,000 a year. Able constructs a building upon the leased land. He then agrees to sublease the property to a supermarket for a period co-terminous with that of the ground lease, and at a rental which will provide an estimated return, after payment of ground rent and other expenses, of $15,000 per annum. Let us further assume that, at a time when the ground lease and the sublease each have a remaining term of 20 years, Able sells his leasehold estate and interest in the subleased building to Mr. Baker for the sum of $100,000, reflecting a capitalization of the projected net earnings at a rate of 10% ($15,000 net rent less $5,000 (recovery of $100,000 investment over 20 years) =$10,000 cash profit each year, or 10% on $100,000).

Under existing law, assuming that the remaining life of the supermarket building is greater than the remaining term of the ground lease, purchaser Baker is required to amortize his $100,000 cost over the 20 year remaining life of the ground lease. This means in effect that $5,000 (1/20 of $100,000) of the $15,000 received by Baker each year is treated as amortization of his investment. There is nothing particularly surprising or startling in this.

To my knowledge, no one has ever seriously contended that the grant to Mr. Baker of an amortization deduction for his cost of acquiring a non-renewable leasehold constitutes a special tax shelter of any kind.

It is important to note that the deduction of $5,000 amortization per year to which Mr. Baker is entitled in the illustration which I have just given is totally independent of the value of the purchased leasehold from time to time during the 20 year period.

Of course, at the end of the 20 year period the value of Mr. Baker's interest in the property will be zero, since the leasehold will have expired. However, during the 20 year period, the value of the leasehold may vary substantially.

For example, if the supermarket sublease provides for payment of percentage rentals based on the lessee's gross sales in addition to the basic rent (the usual form of store lease), Baker, as owner of the leasehold estate, may derive a gross income from the property, after the payment of ground rent and other expenses, in excess of the $15,000 which was being realized from the property at the time he purchased the leasehold estate. . . .

The fact that the leasehold may be salable at the end of ten years, after $50,000 of the original $100,000 cost has been recovered by the taxpayer, does not mitigate against the correctness of permitting the taxpayer to deduct $5,000 per year over the first ten years of the leasehold term as capital cost recovery....

Any system of income taxation which altered the present rule by providing that a taxpayer's right to recover his capital cost over the life of the asset was dependent upon the asset's value at the end of each year for which an amortization deduction was claimed would represent a radical change in existing law and would involve such monstrous problems of continuous valuation as would probably overwhelm any attempt to administer the tax laws fairly....

The assumptions underlying the leasehold example which I have just given relate equally to buildings. The confusion which exists in many quarters concerning depreciation with respect to buildings is generally the consequence of the inability of anyone to predict with absolute certainty the future economic (earning power) useful life of a long-lived wasting asset, such as a building and its many components, or to establish a reasonable capital cost recovery period for long term assets. While these matters cannot be determined with exactitude, this cannot justify ignoring reality—buildings and their components do wear out, they do become economically obsolescent or non-competitive and require replacement, and our economy does require some mechanism within the tax system to provide capital replenishment for such purposes. Although tax theoreticians often refer to depreciation as a "paper" deduction, the actual need to replace worn-out and obsolescent building components and entire buildings, often long before the expiration of the Internal Revenue Service's estimate of useful lives, is well known to experienced owners of real property. This has been particularly true in our competitive industrial society where suburban shopping centers, for example, have replaced many downtown shopping areas, and are in turn being replaced by enclosed mall regional shopping plazas, all within a relatively brief number of years. The same is true of office buildings, where tenants' requirements for air conditioning, high-speed elevators, and increased electrical capacities for technical equipment have forced owners of many older buildings into a choice between making substantial capital expenditures to alter, replace, and modernize or suffer economic obsolescence and deteriorating earnings.

Statements of some economists to the contrary notwithstanding,[3] the depreciation deduction as applied to real estate does not represent a tax incentive or tax abuse in favor of owners of buildings, but merely allows the recovery of original capital cost over an estimated useful life.

---

3. For those who view depreciation as a function of declining value, it is not surprising that, in an inflationary economy, a long-lived asset may not have "depreciated" at all, despite the fact that it is wearing out. As previously stated, the economists' concept of depreciation as a function of declining value may be a theoretical alternative to the capital cost recovery system embodied in the current Code, Regulations and Cases but is entirely inconsistent with the accounting concept and is impossible to incorporate into a workable tax statute.

It has been suggested that recovery of the cost of depreciable improvements by means of an accelerated depreciation deduction constitutes a tax loophole. In fact, accelerated depreciation for real property is perfectly sound, for several reasons. First, the earning power of a building, in relation to its economic useful life, is usually greater when it is new; as it grows older, the costs of operation increase and the operating revenues decline. As our tax accounting system is based on the concept of matching anticipated annual income with related costs, including consumption of capital, the higher depreciation allowances produced by accelerated depreciation in the early years of operation are required properly to reflect the taxable income derived from the property during such years. Second, denial of accelerated depreciation methods to real estate discriminates in the competitive market for capital. Third, denial of accelerated methods reduces effective rates of return on unrecovered investment. This requires the imposition of higher rentals, in order to produce yields competitive with other industries, resulting in higher rents to tenants and increased inflation. . . .

EFFECTS OF DEBT FINANCING

Probably the single most distorted criticism of real estate is its characterization as a so-called tax shelter, based on the fact that most real estate is purchased with substantial debt financing. The inclusion of long-term mortgages in the depreciable basis of real property, under the authority of the decision of the United States Supreme Court in Crane v. Commissioner, appears to have created a vast mythology which characterizes rental real estate as a "tax shelter" whenever the cash receipts from the property exceed the taxable income for any period. Nevertheless, it would seem clearly inequitable for the tax consequences of the ownership of an asset to be dependent upon the method of financing its purchase, or upon whether it is rental real estate, user real estate or personal property, such as machinery. . . .

To illustrate, an industrial corporation requires a new plant. It can rent the plant from a third party who will borrow two-thirds of the cost on a mortgage loan, or the corporation can build the plant itself with borrowed funds. The latter can be obtained via either a mortgage loan or from the sale of a general purpose long-term debenture. None of the proposed depreciation changes would limit the corporation's depreciation deduction to cash equity if it mortgaged the property. Even if the proposals were broadened to limit depreciation allowable on property occupied by the owner, this still would not affect an owner using proceeds derived from a debenture loan or other general borrowings to pay the cost.

I do not question that proposals of this sort are made in good faith and with the intention to cure certain real or imagined tax abuses. However, as in the case of so many apparently simple solutions to complex problems, the cure in this case would seem to be worse than the disease.

The foregoing is not intended to dispute the fact that in certain cases, the combination of substantial long-term debt financing and certain very rapid methods of accelerated depreciation may result in what may fairly be described as a "tax shelter." . . .

Professor Surrey and others have argued strenuously that such tax incentives represent indirect subsidies. In their judgment, such "subsidies" are less equitable and sensible than a direct Federal grant intended to accomplish the same goals. However, practical experience with direct Federal subsidies in the housing area has not created a high degree of confidence in the efficiency and equity of direct subsidies, nor has it shown their superiority in these respects over the indirect subsidies created by the limited number of existing tax incentives to private sector investment. In fact, our past experience with these programs would seem to indicate that until direct subsidy programs demonstrate a much higher degree of efficiency and equity than they have in the past, scrapping all private sector inducements by the elimination of tax incentives in this area would be highly imprudent. A key distinction between these two forms of incentive, which has obvious practical consequences, is that tax incentives are within the powers of Congress. They do not depend upon continuing administrative implementation for their success. . . .

CONCLUSION

The real estate industry is a major factor in the American economy, upon whose success millions of Americans depend for wages, adequate housing, commercial facilities and livable cities and neighborhoods. The citizens participating in this productive industry deserve to be treated, from a tax viewpoint, with more care than that given a step-child upon whom theorists feel free to impose experimental tax programs, or a convenient (and politically relatively impotent) whipping boy whose punishment is intended to satisfy populist demands for "tax reform."

The myth that the real estate industry is in essence one vast tax shelter mechanism is based on total disregard of the illiquidity of capital invested in real estate and the resulting necessity for the use of borrowed funds to make the risk and rate of return competitive with other investments. This myth fails to consider the special credits and allowances provided other industries, which increase their liquidity and rates of return.

The facts do not substantiate a need for the imposition of drastic changes, particularly of the nature heretofore suggested, which involve very pointed discrimination against real estate investment, and which certainly imperil the flow of private capital into the industry as we know it. The end result of discouraging private capital investment in real estate will be a requirement for increased government participation in areas such as housing and revitalization of urban commercial facilities. Few would find this result attractive. . . .

Shenkman and Marshall, Commercial Real Estate and the 1993 Tax Act—Parts 1 and 2
10 Real Est. Fin. J. 9-10 (Summer 1994), 15-16 (Fall 1994)

The Revenue Reconciliation Act of 1993 . . . (also known as the 1993 Tax Act) includes numerous changes affecting the real estate industry. . . .

HISTORICAL PERSPECTIVE OF TAX LAWS

The massive tax deductions of the Economic Recovery Tax Act of 1981 helped foster the growth of the tax shelter industry, with 15-year accelerated depreciation deductions and other overly generous tax benefits. The sudden and dramatic change in policy in the Tax Reform Act of 1986, with passive loss rules and capitalization of construction costs, contributed to the decline in property values and the collateral value that real estate provided for lenders.

The 1993 Tax Act has in some ways mitigated the 1986 restrictions. . . . However, the new 39-year depreciation period [for nonresidential realty] is absurd when compared to the economic reality of the useful lives of the components in a typical building. The depreciation rules are particularly absurd in cases where improvements are made under a short-term lease (such as for a nonanchor retail tenant in a typical shopping center).

One of the most important problems facing developers, lenders, and investors is the continual changes in the tax laws. Real estate activities are invariably long-term in nature. The constant tinkering by Congress makes forecasting for the duration of an investment impossible. Although much of the relief provided by the 1993 Tax Act is welcome, the environment of continuous frequent and major changes in the basic tax rules is not.

HOW THE 1993 TAX ACT FAVORS REAL ESTATE INVESTMENT

The new higher 39.6% marginal tax brackets, coupled with modest relief from the passive loss rules for active real estate investor/developers, the low income housing credit,[5] and other changes are favorable for most real estate

5. Low-income housing is the sector of the real estate industry most in need of venture capital, and because of restrictions on rents and profits, subsidized low-income housing traditionally has been dependent on tax incentives such as tax-exempt bond financing (discussed at Chapter 7C2) and the other tax sweeteners mentioned below. Nevertheless, the 1986 Act abolished the many

professionals. Tax deductions will have more value post-1993 Tax Act than they did before the Act.

The increased spread between capital gains and ordinary income of 11.6% (39.6%–28%[6]—however, this figure is greater if state and local taxes are considered) as compared to the pre-1993 Tax Act 3% figure (31%–28%)[7] will favor real estate investments over other types of investments. Because real estate investments can appreciate on a tax deferred basis (since there is no tax until the property is sold) and then ultimately generate favorably taxed capital gains, the traditional tax benefits that real estate investments enjoyed prior to the Tax Reform Act of 1986 have returned to some extent.

The ability to defer even the capital gains by reinvesting in like-kind property and the ability to obtain funds tax free through mortgage financing will continue to make real estate a popular investment.

LONGER DEPRECIATION PERIOD FOR COMMERCIAL REAL ESTATE

Historical Perspective and Effect. The [1993] Tax Act increased the depreciation period for commercial (non-residential) real estate from 31.5 years to 39 years. In authorizing this change, Congress ignored the entire conceptual framework for the Accelerated Cost Recovery System (ACRS and the later modified version). When ACRS was first advocated for real estate, it was done. . . to simplify tax reporting and to minimize factual disputes with the IRS.

Prior to 1981, real estate investors used component depreciation for their buildings, which allowed each component of a building to be depreciated over its useful life. For example, electrical wiring could be depreciated over its useful life

---

existing tax incentives for the construction of low-income housing, including: (1) a current deduction for construction-period interest and taxes under prior I.R.C. §189; (2) a 5-year cost recovery period for rehabilitation expenditures under prior I.R.C. §167(k); (3) a rapid depreciation schedule including the exclusive right to use the 200 percent declining balance method of depreciation over a 15-year cost recovery period; and (4) the phaseout of depreciation recapture under prior I.R.C. §1250, with no recapture after the property had been held for 16 years and 8 months. Consequently, under the 1986 Act, low-income housing was treated as ordinary residential property for purposes of depreciation and construction-period interest, and taxes had to be capitalized. To replace the tax incentives that were repealed, the 1986 Act provided under I.R.C. §42 for a tax credit for low-income housing that was made permanent by the 1993 Act. For additional background on the low-income housing credit, see Fried, Low-Income Housing Tax Credits—An Update, 7 Real Est. Fin. J. 42 (Summer 1991); Schwartz and Lemond, Low-Income Housing Tax Credit Basics and Financing, 21 Real Est. L.J. 336 (Spring 1993); Wechter and Kraus, The Internal Revenue Code's Housing Program: Section 42, 44 Tax Law. 375 (Winter 1991).— EDS.

6. The 2012 Act increased the spread to 19.6 percent for capital gain caused by appreciation; the spread is 14.6 percent for capital gain attributable to prior depreciation of the property.—EDS.

7. The 1986 Act established the maximum individual bracket as 28 percent, and later the Revenue Reconciliation Act of 1990 increased the maximum rate to 31 percent. Most recently, the 2012 Act reestablished the maximum individual rate on ordinary income at 39.6 percent, after several years at 35 percent,.—EDS.

of 8 years; the roof could be depreciated over a period of 10 years; and the building shell could be depreciated over a period of 33 years.

Component depreciation led to complex disputes between the IRS and taxpayers over depreciation periods and excessive cost allocations to the various components. Congress, therefore, acted to simplify the matter by introducing a composite 15-year rate for the entire building. This was raised in later years to 18 years, then 19 years, then 31.5 years, and now 39 years. The problem with the new rule is that the depreciation rate of most of the components of a building is nowhere near 39 years.

The result is unreasonable and grossly unfair to the real estate industry. Congress eliminated many deductions and tax benefits to simplify the tax laws. Then it raised the rates, depreciation periods, and other costs, which resulted in tax rates much more burdensome than in the past. Thus, the new 39.6% rate may be more costly for many taxpayers than the 50% rates that existed in the early 1980's. The stated marginal tax rate is lower than the 50% rate, but deductions are more severely limited.

The following excerpts detail the recent history of limitations on the deduction of passive losses from real estate activities as established in the 1986 Act and as mitigated by the 1993 Act.

Schwartz, Real Estate and the Tax Reform Act of 1986
16 Real Est. Rev. 28 (Winter 1987)

... LIMITATIONS ON LOSSES AND CREDITS FROM PASSIVE ACTIVITIES

The 1986 Act provides that deductions from passive trade or business activities may not exceed income from all such passive activities; that is, generally, they may not be deducted against other income. Similarly, credits from passive activities generally are limited as offsets to the tax that is allocable to the passive activities. Suspended losses and credits are carried forward and treated as deductions and credits from passive trade or business activities in the next year. Cumulative suspended losses from an activity are allowed in full when the taxpayer disposes of his entire interest in the activity. . . .

Losses and credits from one passive activity may be applied against income for the taxable year from other passive activities or against income subsequently generated by any passive activity. Such losses and credits generally cannot be applied to shelter other (nonpassive) income, like compensation for services or portfolio income (interest, dividends, royalties, and gains from the sale of property held for investment). The passive loss limitation provision is intended to ensure that salary and portfolio interest income, or other nonpassive income, cannot be offset by tax losses from passive activities until the amount of such losses is determined upon disposition of the passive activity.

DEFINING PASSIVE INCOME

A taxpayer has passive income if the activity from which the income is derived involves the conduct of trade or business in which the taxpayer does not materially participate. A taxpayer participates materially only if he is involved in operations on a regular, continuous, and substantial basis. Even if the individual owns the trade or business directly or owns an interest in an activity like a general partnership or Subchapter S corporation, he must nevertheless be involved in operations on a regular, continuous, and substantial basis, in order to be materially participating. The Act treats income from a limited partnership interest as intrinsically passive, and losses from trade or business activities that are allocable to a limited partnership interest may not, prior to disposition, be applied against any of the taxpayer's income other than income from passive activities. The passive loss rule applies to individuals, estates, and trusts. The rule also applies to personal service corporations.

RENTAL INCOME

The Act defines most rental income as passive, whether or not the taxpayer materially participates in the activity. A preexisting distinction in the law between "active rental activity" and "passive rental activity" is continued. Thus, activities that involve the active rendering of substantial services like the operation of a hotel or similar transient lodging are not passive activity. Nor is activity as a dealer in real estate considered passive. But long-term rentals or leases of realty generally are considered to be passive rental activities and the losses from such rental activities are allowed against income from other passive activities, but not against other income.

ACTIVE PARTICIPATION IN RENTAL REAL ESTATE ACTIVITY

A relief provision from the absolute rule that rental activity must always be considered passive is available for taxpayers of moderate income. An individual may offset up to $25,000 of nonpassive income by using losses and credits from rental real estate activities in which the individual actively participates. (Note "active participation," as defined in the relief provision, differs from material participation, the term used above.) The relief provision applies only to individuals, and only if they have at least a 10 percent interest in the activity, and only if they do not have sufficient passive income for the year to use fully the losses and credits available from their rental real estate activities.

The $25,000 amount is reduced by 50 percent of the amount by which the taxpayer's adjusted gross income for the year exceeds $100,000. (It may not go below zero.) Thus, the relief is totally eliminated when the taxpayer's taxable income reaches $150,000.

The "active participation" standard in this provision is less stringent than the "material participation" requirement which distinguishes active from passive interests. The active participation requirement can be satisfied without regular continuous and substantial involvement in operations, as long as the taxpayer participates in management decisions or in arranging for others to provide services (such as repairs) in a significant and bona fide manner. Management decisions that are relevant in this context include approving new tenants, deciding on rental terms, and approving capital or repair expenditures. Thus, the relief provision is specifically targeted at a taxpayer who owns and rents out an apartment that may or may not be his part-time vacation home or a former residence, even if he hires a rental agent and others to provide services like repairs. A limited partner and the lessor under a net lease of real estate are unlikely to have the degree of involvement that active participation entails. . . .

Staff of the Joint Committee on Taxation, General Explanation of the Tax Reform Act of 1986
209-214 (May 7, 1987)

PRIOR LAW

In general, no limitations were placed on the ability of a taxpayer to use deductions from a particular activity to offset income from other activities. Similarly, most tax credits could be used to offset tax attributable to income from any of the taxpayer's activities. . . .

In the absence of more broadly applicable limitations on the use of deductions and credits from one activity to reduce tax liability attributable to other activities, taxpayers with substantial sources of positive income could eliminate or sharply reduce tax liability by using deductions and credits from other activities, frequently by investing in tax shelters. Tax shelters commonly offered the opportunity to reduce or avoid tax liability with respect to salary or other positive income by making available deductions and credits, possibly exceeding real economic costs or losses currently borne by the taxpayer, in excess or in advance of income from the shelters.

Congress concluded that it had become increasingly clear that taxpayers were losing faith in the Federal income tax system. This loss of confidence resulted in large part from the interaction of two of the system's principal features: its high marginal rates (in 1986, 50 percent for a single individual with taxable income in excess of $88,270), and the opportunities it provided for taxpayers to offset income from one source with tax shelter deductions and credits from another.

The increasing prevalence of tax shelters—even after the highest marginal rate for individuals was reduced in 1981 from 70 percent to 50 percent—was well documented. For example, a Treasury study revealed that in 1983, out of 260,000 tax returns reporting "total positive income"[4] in excess of $250,000, 11 percent paid taxes equaling 5 percent or less of total positive income, and 21 percent paid taxes equaling 10 percent or less of total positive income. Similarly, in the case of tax returns reporting total positive income in excess of $1 million, 11 percent paid tax equaling less than 5 percent of total positive income, and 19 percent paid tax equaling less than 10 percent of total positive income.

Congress determined that such patterns gave rise to a number of undesirable consequences, even aside from their effect in reducing Federal tax revenues. Extensive shelter activity contributed to public concerns that the tax system was unfair, and to the belief that tax is paid only by the naive and the unsophisticated. This, in turn, not only undermined compliance, but encouraged further expansion of the tax shelter market, in many cases diverting investment capital from productive activities to those principally or exclusively serving tax avoidance goals.

Congress concluded that the most important sources of support for the Federal income tax system were the average citizens who simply reported their income (typically consisting predominantly of items such as salaries, wages, pensions, interest, and dividends) and paid tax under the general rules. To the extent that these citizens felt that they were bearing a disproportionate burden with regard to the costs of government because of their unwillingness or inability to engage in tax-oriented investment activity, the tax system itself was threatened.

Under these circumstances, Congress determined that decisive action was needed to curb the expansion of tax sheltering and to restore to the tax system the degree of equity that was a necessary precondition to a beneficial and widely desired reduction in rates. So long as tax shelters were permitted to erode the Federal tax base, a low-rate system could provide neither sufficient revenues, nor sufficient progressivity, to satisfy the general public that tax liability bore a fair relationship to the ability to pay. In particular, a provision significantly limiting the use of tax shelter losses was viewed as unavoidable if substantial rate reductions were to be provided to high-income taxpayers without

---

4. Total positive income was defined as the sum of salary, interest, dividends, and income from profitable businesses and investments, as reported on tax returns.

disproportionately reducing the share of total liability under the individual income tax borne by high-income taxpayers as a group. . . .

The question of what constituted a tax shelter that should be subject to limitations was viewed as closely related to the question of who Congress intends to benefit when it enacts tax preferences. For example, in providing preferential depreciation for real estate or favorable accounting rules for farming, it was not Congress's primary intent to permit outside investors to avoid tax liability with respect to their salaries by investing in limited partnership syndications. Rather, Congress intended to benefit and provide incentives to taxpayers active in the businesses to which the preferences were directed.

In some cases, the availability of tax preferences to nonparticipating investors was viewed as harmful to the industries that the preferences were intended to benefit. For example, in the case of farming, credits and favorable deductions often encouraged investments by wealthy individuals whose principal or only interest in farming was to receive an investment return, largely in the form of tax benefits to offset tax on positive sources of income. Since such investors often did not need a positive cash return from farming in order to profit from their investments, they had a substantial competitive advantage in relation to active farmers, who commonly were not in a position to use excess tax benefits to shelter unrelated income. This significantly contributed to the serious economic difficulties being experienced by many active farmers.

The availability of tax benefits to shelter positive sources of income also harmed the economy generally, by providing a non-economic return on capital for certain investments. This encouraged a flow of capital away from activities that provided a higher pre-tax economic return, thus retarding the growth of the sectors of the economy with the greatest potential for expansion.

Congress determined that, in order for tax preferences to function as intended, their benefit should be directed primarily to taxpayers with a substantial and bona fide involvement in the activities to which the preferences related. Congress also determined that it was appropriate to encourage nonparticipating investors to invest in particular activities, by permitting the use of preferences to reduce the rate of tax on income from those activities; however, such investors were viewed as not appropriately permitted to use tax benefits to shelter unrelated income.

Congress believed that there were several reasons why it was appropriate to examine the materiality of a taxpayer's participation in an activity in determining the extent to which such taxpayer should be permitted to use tax benefits from the activity. A taxpayer who materially participated in an activity was viewed as more likely than a passive investor to approach the activity with a significant nontax economic profit motive, and to form a sound judgment as to whether the activity had genuine economic significance and value. . . .

Moreover, Congress concluded that restricting the use of losses from business activities in which the taxpayer did not materially participate against other sources of positive income (such as salary and portfolio income) would address a fundamental aspect of the tax shelter problem. Instances in which the tax system applies simple rules at the expense of economic accuracy encouraged the structuring of transactions to take advantage of the situations in which such rules gave rise to undermeasurement or deferral of income. Such transactions commonly were marketed to investors who did not intend to participate in the transactions, as devices for sheltering unrelated sources of positive income (e.g., salary and portfolio income). . . .

Further, in the case of a nonparticipating investor in a business activity, Congress determined that it was appropriate to treat losses of the activity as not realized by the investor prior to disposition of his interest in the activity. The effort to measure, on an annual basis, real economic losses from passive activities gave rise to distortions, particularly due to the nontaxation of unrealized appreciation and the mismatching of tax deductions and related economic income that could occur, especially where debt financing was used heavily. Only when a taxpayer disposed of his interest in an activity was it considered possible to determine whether a loss was sustained over the entire time that he held the interest.

The distinction that Congress determined should be drawn between activities on the basis of material participation was viewed as unrelated to the question of whether, and to what extent, the taxpayer was at risk with respect to the activities.[7] In general, the fact that a taxpayer placed a particular amount at risk in an activity did not establish, prior to a disposition of the taxpayer's interest, that the amount invested, or any amount, had as yet been lost. The fact that a taxpayer was potentially liable with respect to future expenses or losses of the activity likewise had no bearing on the question whether any amount had as yet been lost, or otherwise was an appropriate current deduction or credit. . . .

A further area in which the material participation standard was viewed as not wholly adequate was that of rental activities. Such activities predominantly involve the production of income from capital. . . . Rental activities generally require less ongoing management activity, in proportion to capital invested, than business activities involving the production or sale of goods and services. Thus, for example an individual who was employed full-time as a professional could more easily provide all necessary management in his spare time with respect to a rental activity than he could with respect to another type of business activity involving the same capital investment. The extensive use of rental activities for tax shelter purposes under prior law, combined with the reduced level of personal involvement necessary to conduct such activities, made clear that the effectiveness of the basic passive loss provision could be seriously compromised if material participation were sufficient to avoid the limitations in the case of rental activities.

Congress believed that a limited measure of relief, however, was appropriate in the case of certain moderate-income investors in rental real estate, who otherwise might experience cash flow difficulties with respect to investments that

---

7. The at-risk rules of prior law, while important and useful in preventing overvaluation of assets, and in preventing the transfer of tax benefits to taxpayers with no real equity in an activity, were viewed as not addressing the adverse consequences arising specifically from such transfers to nonparticipating investors.

in many cases were designed to provide financial security, rather than to shelter a substantial amount of other income.

Additional considerations were viewed as relevant with regard to limited partnerships. In order to maintain limited liability status, a limited partner generally is precluded from materially participating in the business activity of the partnership; in virtually all respects, a limited partner more closely resembles a shareholder in a C corporation than an active business entrepreneur. Moreover, limited partnerships commonly were used as vehicles for marketing tax benefits to investors seeking to shelter unrelated income. In light of the widespread use of limited partnership interests in syndicating tax shelters, Congress determined that losses from limited partnership interests should not be permitted, prior to a taxable disposition, to offset positive income sources such as salary.

M. Madison, J. Dwyer, and S. Bender, The Law of Real Estate Financing
¶1.05[6][c] (Cum. Sup. No. 2) (1989)

. . . The chief and most controversial provision [in the 1986 Act] is the limitation on passive-rental losses. The restriction . . . means that a tax shelter loss might be deferred or denied even though the loss is an economic one that is matched by income that is related in a business or economic sense. The Internal Revenue Code traditionally has made a distinction between passive investment activities and those involving an active trade or business. However, under the 1986 Act, an individual taxpayer who earns income from one business source (e.g., the construction and development of real estate) may not be able to deduct losses from a related business source (e.g., renting the newly constructed building) based on its unprecedented tax distinction between "positive" and "passive" business activities, even though both businesses may be economically oriented activities and the taxpayer actively participates in both, depends on both for his livelihood, and is potentially liable for losses and expenses from both activities. . . .

Shenkman and Marshall, Commercial Real Estate and the 1993 Tax Act—Parts 1 and 2
10 Real Est. Fin. J. 9, 13-16 (Summer 1994)

The 1993 Tax Act provided a long overdue exception to the passive loss limitation rules for active real estate professionals. The passive loss rules restrict a developer's ability to offset losses from passive investments, such as those from limited partnership investments and rental real estate, against income from active sources, such as wages.

The rule may make sense for an individual buying an interest as a limited partner. However, it isn't rational to apply it to an active real estate developer. For tax years beginning after 1993, certain active real estate developers will be relieved of these onerous restrictions.

Overview. The key concept of passive loss limitation rules is that losses from the passive category (including tax losses on net leased real estate when a developer is not an active real estate professional under the new 1993 Tax Act exception) cannot be used to offset income in the other categories—active income (such as wages), and portfolio income (such as dividends).

Losses from passive activities can generally only be used to offset income from passive activities. Losses that are not used currently are suspended until the earlier of the realization of passive income to offset such losses, or the sale of the entire interest in the activity. When the entire interest is sold, suspended losses from that activity can be used without limitation.

Definition of Material Participation. A business or investment will generate passive income to a developer who does not materially participate in the activity. Material participation requires that the participant be involved in the activity on a regular, continuous, and substantial basis. In addition, the material participation must occur throughout the year. The test as to whether a participant meets this standard is applied each year.

Thus, it will generally not suffice to work for a small portion of the year, or for one year but not in other years in order to render a business an active endeavor when, in reality, the participation is negligible. Also, if a partner in a business venture materially participates, this does not automatically make the other partners material participants. Involvement in the business is tested separately.

A limited partner who merely owns an interest will generally not be treated as a material participant. Partnership agreements for limited partnerships usually restrict the potential involvement of limited partners in the management of partnership matters. Most importantly, under the state laws that govern partnerships, limited partners are not allowed to actively participate in the management and operations of the partnership. If they do, they could risk losing their limited liability.

Limited liability means that if the partnership defaults on a loan, the limited partners will generally be liable only up to the amount of their capital contributions or investments. However, there is an exception: Someone who is both a limited and general partner and who participates in the partnership's activities for more than 500 hours per year and during any 5 of the preceding 10 years is considered to materially participate.

Working as a full-time employee or consultant providing personal services is deemed to be material participation. Income from personal services is specifically excluded from being treated as passive income.

The IRS has the following mechanical tests for material participation in an active business endeavor.

[ ] The developer participated in the activity more than 500 hours per year.

[ ] The developer materially participated in the activity for 5 of the 10 preceding years.

[ ] The developer participated in the activity for more than 100 hours during the year and no other person participated for more hours.

[ ] The developer's participation in the activity constituted substantially all of the participation for the activity for the year by anyone.

[ ] The developer participated for 100 hours or more in various activities, and in the aggregate, more than 500 hours for all those activities.

The following concepts may also be considered in the analysis. All services concerning the activity should relate to the operations of the activity and should make a significant contribution to those operations. Merely approving a financing target or making general recommendations for the selection of employees or managers, or appointing others to perform all of the significant active operational functions will generally not be sufficient.

When evaluating the question of involvement, management functions are generally not treated any differently than performing non-management services (e.g., physical labor). Mere formal and nominal participation in an activity will not help meet the material participation standard; however, the genuine exercise of independent discretion will do so. Knowledge and experience of the industry are important to demonstrate material participation in an activity through participating in management.

How the 1993 Tax Act Affects Passive Losses. When the passive loss limitation rules were initially enacted, interests in real estate rental activities were generally categorized as passive, regardless of material participation. This rule was liberalized by the 1993 Tax Act through an exception that permits active real estate professionals to offset passive income against active income in certain instances.

Losses on certain passive real estate activities may be characterized as active income for certain real estate professionals. This new exception was added by the 1993 Tax Act to mitigate the harsh results that occurred when an active real estate developer had to apply the passive loss rules to various real estate endeavors. The new exception applies for tax years after 1993. The real estate interests of a developer who meets the following requirements will not necessarily be characterized as passive for the particular tax year:

[ ] The developer is a real estate professional who spends more than half of his or her time involved in a real property trade or businesses. Real property trades or businesses include construction, development,

reconstruction, leasing, brokerage, development, redevelopment, conversion, rental, operation, and management.

[ ] The developer spends at least 750 hours performing such services. Involvement in different business can be aggregated for determining both the 750-hour test and the "more than half of your time test" previously described. The rules do not appear to exclude a real estate professional, for example, a landlord, whose only involvement is owning and renting real estate. However, careful attention should be paid to any future IRS pronouncements interpreting this new provision.

[ ] The developer is a material participant in the real estate rental trade or business investment being considered. The rules for determining whether someone is a material participant are the same as those previously described. Thus, income from a partnership cannot qualify for this special exception for someone who invests as a limited partner and is not involved in the operations of the partnership.

[ ] A developer who spends more than 500 hours during the year working on an investment is considered to materially participate. The material participation test is determined on an annual basis. In applying this test, each real estate interest will be considered a separate activity. Alternatively, the developer may make an election to treat all of his real estate investments as a single activity. This election should not be made lightly. If all real estate activities are treated as separate activities, any unused passive losses from prior years will be triggered as each real estate interest is sold. This will not occur if the election is made.

[ ] Developers who file a joint tax return must separately satisfy the requirements previously described for material participation. Married developers cannot jointly meet the 750-hour test by each spending 375 hours. However, when one spouse satisfies this requirement, the rental activity will qualify for this benefit. For example, assume an entrepreneur has both a full-time roofing corporation as a primary business and extensive real estate interests. The entrepreneur cannot meet the requirement of spending more than one-half of his or her time on real estate endeavors. However, the entrepreneur's spouse works only part time. It may be possible for the entrepreneur to transfer the real estate holdings to the spouse. If the spouse devotes 750+ hours to the management and operation of the real estate properties, it would appear that the spouse could meet the exception provided under the 1993 Tax Act.

It is important to carefully consider the planning implications of any change in asset ownership. For example, if a party believes that divesting as many appreciating assets as possible is the optimal course to reduce potential estate taxes, this course of action could, at some threshold point, make it impossible to meet the active real estate professional requirements.

[ ]   Services performed as an employee will count towards the preceding test only if the employee owns 5% or more of the employer's company. This requirement could be problematic for a real estate professional who serves as a general partner in numerous transactions through an S corporation or other entity, since many general partners only hold 1% interests in the limited partnership (which often owns the actual property). When applying the requirement that the employee must own 5% or more of an employer, a partner is not considered an employee of a partnership.

[ ]   A closely held corporation can meet the material participation test if 50% or more of the gross revenues are from real property trades or businesses.

Illustration of New Passive Loss Rules for Active Real Estate Professionals. Assume the developer is a real estate professional who earns $75,000 in fees for construction supervisory work on which he spent 500 hours and $195,000 in development fees on projects where he worked 650 hours. The developer also owns residential apartment complexes that he rents and manages. The developer realized tax losses (largely as a result of depreciation deductions) of $80,000. He spent almost 620 hours in the apartment business during the year. He spent 150 hours working in a travel agency that his uncle owns and operates as a full-time endeavor.

The new 1993 Tax Act rules will permit the developer to use $80,000 of tax losses on his rental properties to offset fee income of $270,000 because he meets the requirements of the new relief provision:

1.   Development, construction supervisory, and rental activity constitute real estate trades or business.
2.   Material participation in each of the three activities by spending more than 500 hours in each.
3.   More than the required 750 hours of service spent during the tax year.
4.   More than one-half of personal services performed in real estate trades or businesses (1,770/1,920=92%).

The following materials address whether the preferential treatment for long-term capital gain makes sense as a matter of sound tax and social policy. In enacting the 1986 Act, Congress changed tax history by eliminating the long-standing preferential tax treatment for long-term capital gains, thereby obliterating a major underpinning of the real estate tax shelter: the ability of the depreciation deduction under I.R.C. §167 to convert what would otherwise be ordinary rental income (previously taxed at a maximum rate of 50 percent for individuals) into long-term capital gain (previously taxed at a maximum rate of 20 percent for individuals). However, the 1993 Act and the Taxpayer Relief Act of 1997 re-instituted meaningful spreads between ordinary income and capital gain tax rates. The 2003 Act lowered the maximum rates on ordinary income to 35 percent and authorized capital gain treatment for dividends. It also reduced the rate on capital gains attributable to appreciation to 15 percent while the rate on capital gains attributable to depreciation remained at 25 percent, which created rate spreads of 20 percent and 10 percent, respectively, as compared to a spread of 30 percent (50 percent versus 20 percent) that had existed prior to the 1986 Act. The 2012 Act adjusted the maximum rate on ordinary income back to 39.6 percent, and restored the prior 20 percent rate for long-term capital gains, for a 19.6 percent spread. Tax cuts effective from 2018 through 2025 reduce the maximum individual rate to 37 percent for a 17.6 spread during that time.

Kotlarsky, Capital Gains and Tax Policy
41 Tax Notes 319 (1988)

. . . A capital gains preference clearly violates the principle of horizontal equity because it allows a taxpayer realizing $100 of capital gains to pay less tax than a taxpayer realizing $100 of ordinary income. . . . Proponents of the preference have advanced, at various times and in various forms, four types of arguments: income-bunching, general double taxation, inflation, and double taxation of "C" corporation earnings. . . .

The remaining two arguments—inflation and double taxation of "C" corporations—correctly point out that the lack of inflation adjustments and double tax on "C" corporation earnings violate the principle of horizontal equity. Unfortunately, the proposed solutions are unrelated to the problems, leading essentially to a "two wrongs make a right" approach.

The first "two wrongs" argument is that reduction in capital gains tax rates compensates for inflation. This argument is correct only in some fairly unique circumstances. In most cases, a capital gains preference will under-compensate or over-compensate the taxpayer. For instance, if a capital asset appreciates at the rate of inflation, there is no real gain, and any tax, even at reduced rates, is rather unfair and the reduced rate does not sufficiently compensate the taxpayer. On the other hand, if the asset's appreciation outpaces the rate of inflation by a wide margin, a lower tax rate will be a windfall.

A general reduction of the capital gains tax rate, applied without any consideration to the rate of inflation and the length of the holding period, does not even begin to approximate taxation of real economic income. Furthermore, if capital gains tax rates are to be reduced to compensate taxpayers for the effect of inflation, it is only sensible and logical to reduce the tax rates applicable to interest income. I believe that no supporters of capital gain tax cuts have argued for the same treatment of interest. And nobody seems to suggest that capital gains tax rates should be higher than ordinary income tax rates during periods of deflation.

The final major "two wrongs" argument is that the capital gains tax preference is needed to reduce the effect of double taxation of corporate earnings. The major and obvious flaw in this argument is that it may be applied to the stock of "C" corporations only and cannot possibly support an across the board capital gains rate cut. . . .

VII. EFFICIENCY

[I]t is necessary to analyze the economic effects of a capital gains preference. Two main economic efficiency arguments are that a capital gains tax cut is efficient because it resolves the "lock-in" problem and because it promotes risk taking.

A. "LOCK-IN"

The "lock-in" argument is another "two wrongs make a right" statement. However, because of its popularity and substantial lack of common sense, it deserves a detailed analysis.

The argument goes, more or less, as follows: An investor "*I*" has a relatively unproductive asset, "*A*." The fair market value of *A* is $100 and it produces after-tax cash flow of $9 per year. This return is below the market rate of return of 12 percent. In a tax-free world, *I* would sell *A* and would invest $100 at 12 percent. Unfortunately, *I* has to pay taxes. If *I* bought *A* many years ago for $20, if *I* sells *A* for $100, *I* will recognize $80 of capital gain, pay $32 in tax and will be able to invest only $68 at 12 percent. This will produce a return of $8.16 per year and *I* will be better off keeping the unproductive asset *A*. On the other hand, if the capital gains tax rate is 20 percent, *I* will pay only $16 in tax, invest $84, and his return will be $10.08 per year. In this case, *I* will sell asset *A* and *I* will not be locked into an unproductive asset; since the ownership of unproductive assets is inefficient, the efficiency of the system will be increased if the "lock-in" problem is eliminated through reduction of the capital gains tax rate.

The first response to the "lock-in" argument is that the "lock-in" is a problem brought about by the lack of taxation of interim appreciation. To remedy this problem by a capital gains tax preference is not only a second wrong to make a right, but also is a second tax giveaway—a lower rate on top of deferrals. . . .

Additionally, a capital gains tax cut is not likely to resolve the "lock-in" problem in most cases. A capital gains rate cut is not likely to unlock personal depreciable assets because such assets tend to depreciate and because the depreciation recapture is taxed at ordinary rates, a capital gains preference will not significantly reduce the effective tax rate on gain from the sale of depreciable personal assets. Therefore, a capital gains preference may be only helpful in unlocking real estate and nondepreciable assets.

Professor McDonald, however, has demonstrated that in the case of nondepreciable assets the "lock-in" problem exists unless the tax rate is reduced to zero.[40] He has proven further that a depreciable real property may be completely unlocked only if the ratio of the capital gains tax rate to the ordinary income tax rate is equal to or less than the ratio of the present value of all depreciation deductions to the purchase price of the property. Routine computations indicate that within the reasonable range of the applicable discount rates, the value of depreciation deductions constitutes between 12 and 18 percent of the fair market value of real property. Therefore, to unlock real properties completely, it will be necessary to reduce the capital gains tax rate to about 5 percent. . . .

B. RISK TAKING

The remaining argument is that a capital gains tax cut will promote risk taking and that investments in risky capital assets will increase economic efficiency. I have serious reservations about both parts of the argument.

First, a reduction in the capital gains tax rate does not change investors' mentality. No matter what the tax rate on capital gains is, an investor will invest only if he believes that his potential after-tax returns justify the risk. No doubt, a capital gains tax cut will not reduce the risk of any particular investment. A risky investment can become more attractive only because a tax cut will increase the value of the investment. Unfortunately, the increase in value is likely to be accompanied by an increase in price.

For example, assume that *A* wants to buy an asset from *B*. *A* valued the asset and concluded that the value of the asset is $10. If *B* wants to sell the asset for $12, *A* will not be interested. If the tax rate applicable to income derived from the asset is reduced, the value of the asset will increase. Suppose after the tax reduction, the value of the asset is $15. If *B* does not react and sells the asset for $12, *A* will make a risky investment. However, *B* is likely to raise the price to $18 and, again, *A* will not invest in the asset. In this situation, it is difficult to see how a tax cut promotes risk taking.

Supporters of a capital gains preference usually point out that the capital gains tax increase in the early 1970s was followed by a virtual elimination of available venture capital. I, however, do not find this historical evidence convincing. I believe that high capital gains tax rates were responsible for virtual elimination of venture capital and IPO [initial public offering] investments, but not because they caused the investors to stand on the sidelines. Rather, high tax rates reduced the value of new businesses and their owners, unwilling to sell their companies at bargain-basement prices, priced their wares out of the market. . . .

Second, the increase in the value of risky assets in most cases will do nothing to improve the efficiency of the United States economy. I do not see how the

---

40. McDonald, Depreciability of Assets and the Taxation of Capital Gains, 32 Natl. Tax J. 83-85 (1979). Professor McDonald's proof is only applicable to a limited set of circumstances, but I believe that the technique can successfully be generalized with similar results.

increased prices of speculative investments—art, gold, stamps, coins, rugs, etc.—will have any effect on economic efficiency. Similarly, I do not believe that a capital gains tax cut will have any significant effect on the use of personal residences. As was pointed out before, most personal depreciable assets do depreciate and will not benefit from any tax cut. Depreciable real estate will benefit substantially from a tax cut and it may be expected that a tax cut will encourage construction of new apartment complexes, shopping malls, and office buildings. Our previous experience clearly indicates that the untold zillions of office buildings constructed primarily for the sake of tax benefits is not such a good idea. It is difficult to see how, in the present economic environment, government subsidies to commercial real estate will improve the United States' economic outlook. . . .

NOTES AND QUESTIONS

1. Should Depreciation Be Accelerated Again? Prior to the enactment of the Economic Recovery Tax Act of 1981, depreciation of income-producing realty was determined for purposes of I.R.C. §167 by estimating the property's useful life under a fact and circumstances test or by using prescribed Treasury guidelines that ranged from 40 years for apartment buildings to 60 years for warehouses. Prior to the enactment of the 1986 Act, the taxpayer had the option under ACRS of using the 175 percent declining balance or straight-line method of depreciation over a 19-year cost recovery period for most real property. See Table 13-1. A 35- or 45-year extended recovery period could also be elected. The 1986 Act eliminated accelerated depreciation for real estate and mandated a straight-line cost recovery period of 27.5 years for all residential real estate (including low-income housing) and a period of 31.5 years for commercial real estate. I.R.C. §168(c). Under current law, the recovery periods are 27.5 years for residential real estate and 39 years for commercial real estate.

As indicated by Table 13-1, prior to the 1986 Act, if the owner of some income-producing property purchased for $10 million had elected to use accelerated depreciation as opposed to the straight-line method of deducting depreciation, the depreciation deduction allocated to year 1 would have been $882,675 as opposed to $504,386. In addition, the cost recovery periods have lengthened from a minimum of 15 years (for low-income housing) prior to the 1986 Act to a maximum of 39 years (for commercial real estate) under current law. Accordingly, the amount of depreciation available to real estate owners has been both slowed down and truncated. Reducing the depreciation deduction has been the principal tool used by Congress to curtail real estate tax shelter under the 1986 Act and subsequent reform legislation. This raises the question as to whether accelerated depreciation makes sense as a matter of sound tax and social policy.

Table 13-1

Depreciation Comparison

Year		Pre-1986 Act		Current Law	
		19-Year ACRS	*19-Year ACRS-S/L*	*(Residential) 27.5-Year S/L*	*(Commercial) 39-Year Year S/L*
1		$882,675	$504,386	$348,485	$245,726
2		839,754	526,316	363,636	256,410
3		762,408	526,316	363,636	256,410
4		692,186	526,316	363,636	256,410
5		628,432	526,316	363,636	256,410
6		570,550	526,316	363,636	256,410
7		518,000	526,316	363,636	256,410
	Total	$4,894,005	$3,662,282	$2,530,301	$1,784,186

If we assume that a building wears out and grows obsolete at a constant rate and that the depreciation deduction should relate to its historical cost, a building that costs, say, $1 million with a useful life of 40 years and zero salvage value should generate a straight-line depreciation deduction each year of $25,000. Under this method, we would be accommodating the basic tax accounting convention that periodic income should be matched to its related costs; otherwise net income would be distorted. For example, permitting a taxpayer to double the straight-line amount to $50,000, under this theory, would result in understating the taxpayer's real net income in the first year (prior to mortgage payments) by $25,000. Likewise, if instead of doubling the rate of depreciation (from 1/40th, or 2.5 percent, of cost to 1/20th, or 5 percent) we decrease the cost recovery period from 40 years to 15 years (as was the case for low-income housing prior to the 1986 Act), we would also be overstating depreciation by $41,667 (from $25,000 to $66,667) and understating income by $41,667 during the first 15 operational years and understating depreciation along with overstating income by $25,000 during the 25-year remainder of the building's useful or income-generating life.

The foregoing example presupposes that an average building wears out and becomes obsolescent at a constant rate. However, some economic studies have suggested that actual economic depreciation of office buildings and apartment buildings is minimal over the first ten years. See Taubman and Rasche, Economic and Tax Depreciation of Office Buildings, 22 Nat'l. Tax J. 334, 344 (1969); Taubman and Rasche, The Income Tax and Real Estate Investment (1969) (presented at the Symposium on Tax Incentives of the Tax Institute of America).

Consequently, if we define "tax shelter" as any investment that results in a mismatch between deductions and income so that the deductions "shelter" unrelated income from immediate taxation, then it would appear that the 1986 Act's deceleration of the rate of depreciation (from the 175 percent declining balance method to straight-line) and its elongation of the ACRS cost recovery period (from 19 years to 27.5 years for residential and 31.5 (now 39) years for commercial real estate) makes sense from a sound tax policy standpoint.

Mr. Aronsohn (an articulate proponent of real estate tax shelter) makes the point (based on language in Treas. Reg. §1.167(a)-1(a)) that the depreciation allowance is essentially an accounting convention that has nothing to do with fluctuations in value. Instead, it provides as good a system as any to recover original capital cost over an estimated useful life, and accordingly the depreciation deduction does not represent a special tax shelter benefit. See Panel Discussions on General Tax Reform, supra. In what respect does his analogy between a leasehold estate and a building fail? Suppose that, in his example involving the acquisition of a leasehold estate, Baker were allowed to amortize his $100,000 cost over a 10-year cost recovery period rather than over the 20-year remaining life of the ground lease. Could Aronsohn still maintain that operation of the amortization (or, by analogy, straight-line depreciation) deduction does not amount to a tax shelter?

If tax shelter proponents were to contend that accelerated depreciation should be revived to help attract capital into housing and other sectors of the real estate industry, what are some arguments you might make to support the anti-shelter view that the 19-year cost recovery period amounted to an inefficient deduction-funded subsidy? What are the arguments against such a characterization? See the excerpt by Shenkman and Marshall. Professor McKee assumes that the depreciation deduction-funded subsidy is regressive and inherently unfair unless low-bracket investors are also encouraged to invest their capital in depreciable realty. Is this a sound assumption? How would you reconcile this assumption with Code provisions that exempt certain items from gross income to achieve certain congressional policy aims? See, for example, I.R.C. §103 (exempting from gross income interest on local governmental obligations). Do you agree with Professor McKee's statement that the depreciation deduction and other deduction-funded subsidies are irreconcilable with a progressive tax theory?

2. Should Rental Real Estate Be Treated as a "Passive" Activity? Historically, rental income or gain from the ownership and sale of income-producing real estate (such as an apartment building or shopping center) was treated as active income or gain from a trade or business (as opposed to passive-type investment income) where active services were rendered to the tenants (as opposed to "net-leased" real estate, where the tenants make their own repairs and pay their pro rata share of property taxes and insurance premiums). See prior I.R.C. §163(d)(4) (relating to limitation on investment interest); I.R.C. §1231(b)(1) (relating to capital gain treatment for trade or business property). Then came the 1986 Act, which changed the course of tax history by creating new categories of income, called "portfolio" income (dividends, interest, royalties, and gains on sale of investment property); "positive" income, such as salaries and other income from services; and "passive" income, which includes income or gain from any rental activity regardless of whether the taxpayer materially participates in the activity (other than those in which "substantial" services are rendered, such as the operation of a hotel). I.R.C. §469(c)(2); see Staff of the Joint Committee on Tax'n., General Explanation of the Tax Reform Act of 1986, at 217 (1987). According to the Joint Committee (see the previous excerpt from the General Explanation of the 1986 Act), Congress felt that all rental activities should automatically be deemed "passive" in nature whether or not the owner actively conducted a trade or business (such as an apartment building) because "rental activities generally require less ongoing management activity, in proportion to capital invested, than business activities involving the production or sale of goods and services." Do you agree with Congress? Can you think of some service-oriented businesses that require a minimal amount of venture capital and less management effort than would be required in the case of a typical apartment building?

If Congress overreacted to the use of tax shelters in the area of rental real estate, what would be a compromise approach that would insulate rental real estate from tax shelter abuse and yet allow individual taxpayers to offset their losses against their business income from other outside sources without segregating income and losses into artificial categories (as does I.R.C. §469)? Do you think that the new exception in the 1993 Act for active real estate professionals (I.R.C. §469(c)(7)) discussed by Shenkman and Marshall constitutes a rational compromise approach?

As explained in Chapter 14B2, a member in a limited liability company (LLC) treated for tax purposes as a partnership may materially participate in the management of the business without losing its protection of limited liability. Suppose a developer of rental real estate selects an LLC as the ownership entity and raises venture capital from member-investors. How likely is it that such an investor will be able to avoid the I.R.C. §469 limitations on passive losses? Also, as explained in Chapter 14B1, the Uniform Limited Partnership Act (ULPA 2001) eliminates the control test entirely so that a limited partner would be able to actively participate in the control and management of the rental real estate business without losing its protection of limited liability. Suppose the ULPA 2001 becomes adopted in a wide number of states (19 states as of 2016). Do you think Congress should revisit the issue of whether rental real estate should be treated as a "passive activity"?

3. Should Preferential Treatment Be Given to Long-term Capital Gains? When the tax rate on capital gains is reduced, do net tax revenues increase or decrease over time? All the experts seem to agree that nobody knows the answer. Among the complicating factors is that taxpayers have more control over when to incur capital gains than they do over most other taxes; taxpayers can defer the capital gains tax by holding onto their assets rather than selling them. Moreover, it is difficult to isolate the impact of tax rates on realizations from other more pervasive economic factors such as the level of interest rates.

Proponents of a tax preference for capital gains have contended that a rate reduction would: (1) promote saving and investment in our economy—the flow of savings to finance investment has declined from 7.4 percent of national income during the 1950-1980 period to 2.8 percent during the 1980s, and has ranged between 2 and 4 percent during the late 1990s and early 2000s; (2) help protect real gains from being eroded by inflation; and (3) promote economic efficiency. Conversely, opponents have argued that a differential between ordinary income and capital gains rates: (1) encourages abusive tax shelter activity; (2) distorts investment choices as to financial assets; and (3) jeopardizes the fairness and progressivity of our tax system. With regard to the latter argument, capital gains are the key ingredient of income disparity in the United States. According to the Congressional Budget Office, more than 80 percent of the increase in income inequality has been the result of an increase in household income from capital gains. The top one-tenth of one percent (about 315,000 taxpayers) are making about half of all long-term capital gains on the sale of corporate shares or property. Lenzner, The Top 0.1% of the Nation Earn Half of Capital Gains, Forbes, Nov. 21, 2011. And yet, as a matter of common economic knowledge, taxpayers with a high taxable income have a greater propensity to save and invest than taxpayers with a low taxable income.

After reviewing the arguments on both sides of the capital gains debate, which point of view do you favor? Why?

4. Should Refinancing Proceeds Be Taxable? If property constructed at a cost of $10 million (including land costs) was hypothetically worth $12 million shortly after being completely constructed and rented, the ownership limited partnership might "mortgage out" by refinancing an existing loan of $8 million at the same 80 percent loan-to-value ratio for about $9.6 million in refinance proceeds and distribute the $1.6 million of excess mortgage proceeds to the limited partners as a tax-free return of capital. Would you characterize the tax consequences to the limited partners as a "tax shelter"? If so, do you think that net refinancing proceeds should be subject to immediate taxation, so that in the above example the limited partners would recognize gain on the net refinancing proceeds to the extent that the amount of the gross refinancing proceeds ($9.6 million) exceeds the partnership's adjusted basis in the refinanced property? Do you see any problem with this tax result under our present system of taxation?

d.   Tax Deferred Exchanges

The following materials illustrate the mechanics of a so-called tax-free exchange under I.R.C. §1031 that enables the developer to leverage its cost of acquiring new properties.

The Mortgage and Real Estate
Executive's Report
3-6 (May 15, 1987)

SPECIAL REPORT: UNDERSTANDING TAX FREE EXCHANGES

The major tax deferral technique left unchanged by the Tax Reform Act of 1986 (TRA '86) is the tax-free exchange of real estate. . . .

The lack of popularity of exchanging in the past stemmed from several causes. Setting up a successful exchange often takes much more patience and hard work than arranging a straight purchase and sale. In addition, many brokers and investors simply have not understood the potentials of exchanging. In fact, the real estate exchange can be a highly versatile tool both for achieving tax savings and for financing real estate. As far as the difficulty of arranging exchanges is concerned, a thorough understanding of the tax law requirements shows that exchanging can often be accomplished almost as easily as a simple purchase and sale (although the multiparty exchange does call for some intricate footwork by the parties).

Tax-free exchanges are of two types: (1) exchanges of investment and business property; or (2) exchanges of residential property (one-family homes, condominiums, or cooperatives). The discussion that follows is limited to investment and business property.

ADVANTAGES OF EXCHANGING

The key advantage of a tax-free exchange (pursuant to I.R.C. §1031) is that gain realized by one or both of the exchangers need not be recognized (i.e., tax need not be paid on the gain) at the time of sale. Instead, the tax is postponed until a future taxable disposition of the newly acquired property. Thus, a series of exchanges can defer tax indefinitely and possibly permanently (if the property ultimately acquires a stepped-up basis in the estate of the exchanger). The advantage of this tax postponement is obvious. The investor can reinvest his full capital (including appreciation) in new properties without any diminution because of tax payments. Uncle Sam, in effect, extends an interest-free loan to the investor who thus can obtain a degree of leverage over and above that obtained from standard mortgage financing.

In addition to this tax advantage, an exchange (even if it is not tax-free) can be used as a financing technique, since it permits the substitution of real estate for cash or a third-party debt obligation. The real estate exchange has a psychological advantage as well. Since a price is arrived at by matching real estate values, inflated values on both sides give the parties the satisfaction of getting their price.

The two essential requirements for a tax-free exchange relate to (1) the purpose for which the new and old properties will be held by the exchanger and (2) the need for the properties to be of "like kind."

USE OF THE PROPERTIES

An exchange can be tax-free only if the property transferred by the exchanger and the property received by him are held for productive use in a business or for investment. A personal residence may not be exchanged (although it may be eligible for tax-free treatment under another section of the tax law). Also, dealer property (that held primarily for sale) may not be exchanged tax-free.

Note that an exchange qualifies for tax-free treatment as long as the properties fall into either of the eligible classes. Thus, property held for use in a trade or business may be exchanged for investment property, and vice versa.

Observation: In order for property *not* to be classified as dealer property, the exchanger must show an intent to hold it for some period of time. No fixed period is required . . .; instead, the exchanger must show an intent to hold the property for gradual appreciation rather than quick resale.

LIKE-KIND REQUIREMENT

The concept of "like kind" refers to the nature or character of the real estate rather than to its grade or quality. The extent to which property is improved relates only to its grade or quality. So, raw land may be exchanged for an apartment building, provided the properties have been or will be held as investments or in a business. The Treasury regulations provide that a leasehold interest having a remaining term of at least 30 years is of like kind with a fee interest in real property. (By implication, leasehold interests of shorter terms may not be exchanged tax-free with fee interests.)

Observation: The two requirements for a tax-free exchange apply to each party independently of the other. So one party may qualify for a tax-free exchange even though the other does not.

RECEIPT OF BOOT

Rarely do two properties have the same market value and equity value. So one party must receive cash or assume a mortgage in order to balance the equities. This does not preclude tax-free treatment; however, to the extent one party receives cash or is relieved of an existing mortgage, he must recognize gain.

Example: A (not a dealer) exchanges real estate held for investment purchased many years ago for $5,000 (and that is now worth $8,000) for other real estate (to be held for productive use in business) having a fair market value of $6,000, plus $2,000 in cash. The gain realized by *A* on the property he is exchanging is $3,000 ($8,000 less $5,000). But the gain is *recognized* only to the extent of the $2,000 cash received.

It is also important to know *A*'s basis for the property he acquired in the exchange, since the basis will determine gain or loss on any subsequent disposition of the acquired property. *A*'s basis for the new property remains at $5,000—the basis of the old property ($5,000), less the amount of the boot received ($2,000), increased by the amount of gain recognized on the exchange ($2,000).

BASIS OF PROPERTY RECEIVED

A tax-free exchange merely defers tax on gain; it does not eliminate it. Deferral is achieved by having the new property take over the cost basis of the old property so when the new property is sold, both the old and new gain will be recognized and taxed.

However, if the exchanger has paid boot (cash or the assumption of a mortgage), the amount is added to the old basis, since the exchanger must then recognize gain to the extent of the boot. Similarly, if the exchanger receives cash or is relieved of a mortgage obligation, his basis will be reduced by the amounts involved and increased by the recognized gain. (See above example.)

BOOSTING DEPRECIATION DEDUCTIONS

In a tax-free exchange, the basis for depreciation deductions, as well as for ultimate gain or loss, is the carryover basis of the property given up in the exchange. This is one of the disadvantages of the tax-free exchange, but it is less important now, with recovery periods stretched to 31.5 [now 39] or 27.5 years.

As under prior law, however, two techniques remain for increasing the depreciation deduction following a tax-free exchange. These involve changing the land-building ratio and exchanging for property with a larger mortgage so that the basis for depreciation is increased.

LAND-BUILDING ALLOCATION RATIO

Whenever an investor thinks about depreciating his real estate for tax purposes, his first step is to allocate his cost between the land and the improvements. Naturally, he will want to allocate as much as possible to the depreciable buildings and as little as possible to the nondepreciable land. But the allocation must be made within the context of economic realities. If the property is later exchanged, the investor must carry over his old cost (reduced by depreciation deductions taken during his period of ownership). But he is *not* bound by the land-building ratio. Consequently, if the new property has the same or a more favorable ratio, the depreciation deductions during the first few years may actually be higher than previously even though the exchange is tax-free.

Example: An investor acquires improved property for $100,000. Of this amount, $20,000 is allocated to the land and $80,000 to the building. Over the years he claims $53,000 in depreciation deductions on the building so that its tax basis is reduced to $27,000. His land and building now have an aggregate basis of $47,000 ($20,000 land cost plus $27,000 adjusted building cost).

Assume the market value of the property is $200,000. Our investor now finds a like-kind property worth $200,000 and makes a tax-free exchange. He carries over his $47,000 basis to the new property. Assume that an appraisal establishes that 80 percent of the value of the new property is allocable to the building and 20 percent to the land (the same as for the old property). Thus, 80 percent of the carryover basis of $47,000 ($37,600) is the new basis for depreciation deductions, whereas had the investor retained the original property, he would have had only $27,000 remaining in the building's basis for depreciation purposes. (See Rev. Rul. 68-36, 1968-1 C.B. 357.)

LEVERAGING PROPERTY WITH A HIGHER BASIS

When one values properties for exchange, only *equities* count, not market value. In the previous example, the investor owned property free and clear with a market value of $200,000. In that example, he swapped it for another property, free of debt, with a market value of $200,000. But he might as easily have swapped it for a property with a market value of $300,000 but subject to an existing mortgage of $100,000. The equities would remain equal, but the investor would step up his tax basis from $47,000 (the remaining cost basis in the original property) to $147,000 (his original cost basis plus the amount of new debt of $100,000). If 80 percent is allocated to the depreciable improvements, his new basis for depreciation is $117,600 (as compared to the depreciable basis of the original building of $27,000).

HOW AN EXCHANGE CAN FACILITATE
PROPERTY TRANSFERS

In addition to its potential for tax saving, an exchange can be useful as a financial device, or as an additional inducement to a property transfer.

Cash-poor buyer. When a prospective buyer does not have enough cash and cannot get a mortgage, the seller's usual alternatives are to pass up the offer or extend a large purchase money mortgage. The latter, however, subjects him to substantially the same financial risks that may have been the very reason why he wanted to sell in the first place. An exchange means he can take other property of the buyer in lieu of taking back a mortgage; it also may increase the likelihood that the seller will get his asking price. That the seller also has no tax on his gain also is appealing (assuming, of course, that the exchange qualifies for tax-free treatment).

Long-term appreciation. A tax-free exchange has appeal for the real estate investor who wants to swap income-producing property for real estate (e.g., raw land) with potential for long-term appreciation. That his depreciation deductions now are low and will not be increased after the exchange makes no difference to him since (if he is seeking raw land) his new investment is nondepreciable. If such an investor exchanges his income-producing property for several parcels of raw land near some area that has good growth potential, he will have put the full amount of his capital (undiminished by taxes) to work in another investment.

Exchange for more financeable property. An investor may be able to make a tax-free exchange for property that is capable of supporting a mortgage with a higher loan-to-value ratio. For example, property that justifies a mortgage not exceeding 60 percent of its value might be exchanged for property on which a lender will extend an 80 percent mortgage. In that case, the exchange will release cash for other uses equal to 20 percent of the value of the property. Or, an investor may hold real estate subject to a mortgage that bars prepayment or permits it only for a stiff penalty. If the investor requires cash, he might consider a tax-free exchange for similar property capable of being refinanced.

Exchange for more salable property. An investor needing cash may be able to exchange difficult-to-sell property for property that can be disposed of for cash more easily. As already noted, when there is an intent to resell the acquired property immediately, the tax-free exchange rules do not apply. The investor seeking to cash out would have an immediate taxable gain on the exchange. However, since the basis of the property acquired by him in the exchange is increased by the amount of recognized gain, the aggregate gain on the exchange and the sale will equal the same taxable gain that would have resulted had the original property been sold.

MULTIPARTY EXCHANGES

An apparent problem with tax-free exchanges is the difficulty in matching two parties who want each other's property. However, the problem can be solved by having three or even more participants in the exchange. Although this makes the process more complicated, it vastly widens the market for possible exchanges.

Consider the situation where *A* has property he wants to exchange. *B* wants to buy *A*'s property but has no suitable exchange property. *B*'s broker locates *C* who has property for sale that *A* would like to own. Three possible transactions can take place among the parties:

- *A* can sell to *B* for cash and then buy *C*'s property.

- *B* can buy *C*'s property and then exchange it for *A*'s property.
- *A* can exchange properties with *C* and *C* can then sell *A*'s former property to *B*.

The first situation clearly is a traditional purchase and sale and no exchange occurs. However, both the second and third situations can qualify as tax-free exchanges provided the various steps are carried out in the right order. The key dangers to avoid are to have *A* pay cash to either *B* or *C* and to have either *B* or *C* in the position of acting as *A*'s agent. However, it is possible to tie the various transactions together through contract provisions so that an "all or nothing" situation is set up.

Example: Perhaps the earliest case to approve a three-party exchange was *Alderson*, 317 F.2d 790 (9th Cir. 1963). Alderson entered into a contract to sell his farm in California to Alloy Company for cash. Before title passed, Alderson found a farm in Salinas that he wanted. Alderson and Alloy amended their contract to require Alloy to buy the Salinas property and then swap it for Alderson's farm. Alderson would pay the difference to Alloy in cash. The transaction was completed in this manner, and the Ninth Circuit approved tax-free treatment after the Tax Court had agreed with the IRS that no tax-free exchange had occurred.

The key point of the decision was that Section 1031 did not bar Alloy from acquiring the Salinas property for the *sole purpose* of using it in a tax-free exchange to get the Alderson farm—as long as Alloy in fact acquired the property before it was transferred to Alderson.

DEFERRED EXCHANGES

Suppose *A* agrees to exchange his property for a specified property (or type of property) to be acquired by *B* within a fixed period of time. If *B* does not acquire the property, either the contract is canceled or *B* may have an option to pay the price in cash. Prior to 1984, court rulings held that such non-simultaneous or deferred exchanges qualified as tax-free exchanges assuming the other conditions of the tax law were met. Then Congress in the Deficit Reduction Act of 1984 (DRA) imposed short time limits within which the exchange property must be designated. (Congress felt that permitting exchanges within longer periods would provide unintended benefits to property owners and would create administrative problems.)

Under the DRA, property does not qualify as like-kind property if either of two specified time limits is transgressed. The first time limit under Section 1031(a)(3) of the Code requires that the property to be received by the taxpayer must be *identified* as such on or before the forty-fifth day after the date on which the taxpayer transfers his property. The second time limit requires the property to be *received* not later than the earlier of 180 days after the taxpayer transfers his property, or the due date, with extensions, of the taxpayer's return for the year in which he transfers his property.

According to the conference committee report on the DRA, the 45-day identification requirement can be met by designating the property to be received in the contract between or among the parties. Moreover, the designation requirement will be met if the contract specifies a limited number of properties that may be transferred, and the particular property transferred will be determined by contingencies beyond the parties' control.

COMBINING OPTION WITH TAX-FREE EXCHANGE

There appears to be a way to bypass the time limits on a deferred exchange by using an option. Assume that A, the property owner, is willing to give B an option to acquire A's property either by exchange or cash purchase. The IRS has ruled (prior to the DRA) that if and when the option is exercised, a tax-free exchange may take place (except that the price of the option is boot to the property owner and so he must recognize gain to that extent). (Rev. Rul. 84-121, 1984-2 C.B. 168.) It seems clear that the time limits on deferred exchanges do not begin until the option is exercised.

Observation: Use of an option, of course, gives the optionee the power to decide whether to go through with the acquisition or not. He would be bound to complete the acquisition under a contract that required him either to find suitable exchange property or to pay cash.

TAX-FREE EXCHANGES AND PASSIVE LOSSES

The passive activity rules of TRA '86 may affect a tax-free exchange if (1) the exchange property was used in a passive activity (i.e., a rental activity or a trade or business in which the owner did not materially participate); and (2) the owner has unused passive losses from the property at the time of the exchange.

Since an exchange is not the type of disposition that permits passive losses to be used against outside income, the losses continue in a suspended state until the investor receives passive income that can be offset by the losses or until the entire gain on the exchange property is recognized (at which point the suspended losses can offset outside income). . . .

NOTES AND QUESTIONS

1. Rationales for Tax Deferral Treatment. In Biggs v. Commissioner, 69 T.C. 905, 913 (1978), aff'd, 632 F.2d 1171 (5th Cir. 1980), the Tax Court states that "[t]he purpose of §1031 . . . was to defer recognition of gain or loss on transactions in which, although in theory the taxpayer may have realized a gain or loss, his economic situation is in substance the same after, as it was before, the transaction. Stated otherwise, if the taxpayer's money continues to be invested in the same kind of property, gain or loss should not be recognized."

Other rationales have been suggested. Based on pure administrative necessity, it has been suggested that no attempt should be made to measure and tax any gain or loss in the value of real estate held for investment or use in a trade or business until a sale occurs and a free-market cash valuation of the property can be made. To rule otherwise would require a subjective valuation of all property at periodic intervals that would impose an intolerable administrative burden on the I.R.S.

It has also been argued that the upgrading of income-producing property (by substituting new assets for ones that have deteriorated or become obsolete) should not be discouraged by taxation in an inflationary economy when any taxation of gain (caused in large measure by inflation) may decimate the taxpayer's liquidity and discourage her from obtaining more efficient replacement assets that are likely to produce more taxable income and more revenues for the Treasury Department.

Based on the foregoing policy rationales, how would you justify the following tax result: If *A* were to sell Blackacre for cash and immediately thereafter use the after-tax proceeds (along with its other funds) to purchase Whiteacre, the transaction would be immediately taxable, whereas an exchange of Blackacre for Whiteacre would be regarded as a tax-free exchange.

2. Definitional Issues. An exchange, like a sale of property, is generally a taxable transaction unless the Code provides otherwise. I.R.C. §1031(a)(1) provides that "No gain or loss shall be recognized on the exchange of property held for productive use in a trade or business or for investment if such property is exchanged solely for property of like kind which is to be held either for productive use in a trade or business or for investment."

The first requirement for this tax deferral is that there be an exchange. Simply put, a sale occurs when the owner receives cash or something that is cash-equivalent (such as a purchase money mortgage note), and an exchange takes place when the owner receives other property. See, for example, Rev. Rul. 61-119, 1961-1 C.B. 395; Wheeler v. Commissioner, 58 T.C. 459 (1972); Carlton v. United States, 385 F.2d 238 (5th Cir. 1967).

Treas. Reg. §1.1031(a)-1(c) deems a 30-year-or-more leaseback equivalent to a fee interest in real estate. Suppose an owner of some real estate worth $10 million (with an adjusted basis of $12 million) conveys a fee simple interest and, as part of the sale-and-leaseback transaction, receives from the purchaser both $10 million in cash and a 30-year leaseback worth zero (as reflected by the fair market leaseback rental). Under I.R.C. §1031(a) has there been an "exchange" (as opposed to a sale) so that the seller-lessee should be denied recognition of its loss in the amount of $2 million? Compare Rev. Rul. 60-43, 1960-1 C.B. 687, and Century Elec. Co. v. Commissioner, 192 F.2d 155 (8th Cir. 1951), cert. denied, 342 U.S. 954 (1952), with City Investing Co. v. Commissioner, 38 T.C. 1

(1962), nonacq., 1963-2 C.B. 6, and Jordan Marsh v. Commissioner, 269 F.2d 453 (2d Cir. 1959). See discussion at Chapter 11B2, note 3.

The second requirement for tax deferral, that both properties in the exchange be "held for productive use in a trade or business or for investment," has been broadly construed so that business real estate can be exchanged for investment real estate or vice versa. Treas. Reg. §1.1031(a)-1(a). While neither the Code nor the Treasury Regulations explicitly define the difference between business real estate and investment real estate, the traditional view is that the former refers to income-producing real estate where active services are being rendered (for example, a shopping center without net leases) and the latter refers to real estate that is being held as a passive investment (for example, net-leased rental real estate or raw land held by a taxpayer who is not a "dealer"). Compare I.R.C. §162(a) with §212(1) and (2); see also I.R.C. §163(d). However, the phrase "use in a trade or business or for investment" disqualifies dealer real estate (held as inventory or primarily for sale to customers in the ordinary course of business) and residential property held for personal use from tax deferral treatment under I.R.C. §1031. Moreover, I.R.C. §1031(a)(2)(A) expressly excludes any exchange of property held primarily for sale.

The third requirement is that the properties in the exchange be of "like kind"; in that regard, Treas. Reg. §1.1031(a)-1(b) and (c) provide as follows:

> . . . the words "like kind" have reference to the nature and character of the property and not to its grade or quality.. . . . The fact that any real estate involved is improved or unimproved is not material, for that fact relates only to the grade or quality of the property and not to its kind or class.. . . . No gain or loss is recognized if . . . a taxpayer who is not a dealer in real estate exchanges city real estate for a ranch or farm, . . . or exchanges improved real estate for unimproved real estate.

Does this language in the Regulations make sense? Isn't it possible for the grade or quality of the real estate to affect its nature and character? Suppose, for example, that a building is exchanged for some unimproved raw land. In light of the rationales for nonrecognition treatment under I.R.C. §1031 (discussed in note 1, supra), do you think that such an exchange should qualify for tax deferral treatment? Compare Davis v. United States, 411 F. Supp. 964 (D.C. Haw. 1976), aff'd, 589 F.2d 446 (9th Cir. 1979); Rev. Rul. 78-72, 1978-1 C.B. 258; and Rev. Rul. 67-255, 1967-2 C.B. 270, with Burkhard Inv. Co. v. United States, 100 F.2d 642 (9th Cir. 1938). What about an exchange of a farm for rental real estate in a city? See Braley v. Commissioner, 14 B.T.A. 1153 (1929), acq. VII-2 C.B. 6. What about an exchange of domestic real estate for foreign real estate? See I.R.C. §1031(h) (domestic and foreign properties are not like kind).

If *A* were to exchange its interest as a general or limited partner in the *A* partnership (whose underlying asset is Blackacre) for a comparable interest in the *B* partnership (whose underlying asset is Whiteacre), tax-deferral treatment would have been afforded to *A* by the Tax Court prior to the Tax Reform Act of 1984. See, for example, Gulfstream Land & Dev. Corp. v. Commissioner, 71

T.C. 587 (1979); Estate of Meyer v. Commissioner, 58 T.C. 311 (1972), aff'd, 503 F.2d 556 (9th Cir. 1974), nonacq., 1975-2 C.B. 3 (the interests of general partners held to be exchangeable where the underlying assets of both partnerships are substantially similar in nature, but an exchange of a general for a limited partnership interest would not satisfy the like-kind requirement). By contrast, the I.R.S. had consistently ruled that an exchange of equity interests was precluded by the exclusionary language in former I.R.C. §1031(a) (prior to amendment by the Tax Reform Act of 1984). Rev. Rul. 78-135, 1978-1 C.B. 256. Congress ultimately rejected the Tax Court position and sided with the I.R.S. by denying tax deferral treatment with respect to any exchange of interests in *different* partnerships. I.R.C. §1031(a)(2)(D), as added by §77(a) of the Tax Reform Act of 1984. Do you think Congress made the correct decision? If so, do you think tax deferral treatment should also be denied to a general partner who converts her interest to that of a limited partner in the *same* partnership if her ratio for sharing profits and losses and her capital interest remain the same? See Rev. Rul. 84-52, 1984-1 C.B. 157.

Finally, the fourth requirement for tax deferral is that the properties be exchanged *solely* for one another. However, as explained in the excerpt from the Mortgage and Real Estate Executive's Report, properties involved in an exchange rarely have the same market and equity values. Therefore, if one party to the exchange must receive cash or assume (or take subject to) a mortgage to balance the equities, the transaction will still qualify for tax deferral treatment, but gain will be recognized to the extent that the party receives "boot" in the form of cash or relief from an existing mortgage. See I.R.C. §1031 (b); Halpern v. U.S., 286 F. Supp. 255 (N.D. Ga. 1968).

    3. Three-Corner Exchanges. I.R.C. §1031 allows certain multiparty exchanges (colloquially referred to as "three-corner exchanges"). However, Congress prohibited the use of open-ended three-corner exchanges that had been permitted under Starker v. United States, 602 F.2d 1341 (9th Cir. 1979), by overruling *Starker* and requiring the transferor to designate the property to be received within 45 days and to complete the transaction within 180 days after the transfer of the exchanged property. I.R.C. §1031(a)(3), as added by §77(a) of the Tax Reform Act of 1984. See generally Sommers, Deferred Like-Kind Exchanges after *Starker*, 68 J. Tax'n. 92 (1988).

    A three-corner exchange makes sense, for example, where *A*, the owner of some real estate ("Blackacre"), desires to acquire some like-kind real estate ("Greenacre") from another owner, *B*, by means of a tax-free exchange, but *B* insists on receiving cash. While *A* might be able to sell Blackacre for cash, *A*'s net after-tax proceeds may not be sufficient to cover the purchase price demanded by *B;* or *A* might believe that the tax cost of a sale and purchase is too onerous (for example, *A*'s adjusted basis in Blackacre might be very low, so a sale of Blackacre would trigger a large amount of taxable gain). Under such circumstances, if *A* finds someone else ("*C*") who is interested in paying cash for Blackacre, then, at *A*'s behest, *C* could buy Greenacre from *B* for cash and then *C* would exchange Greenacre for Blackacre so that *A* could obtain tax deferral treatment. Such a transaction is reflected by the following diagram.

Alternatively, *A* could first exchange properties with *B*, who, as diagrammed below, would then sell Blackacre to *C* for cash.

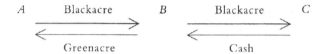

Such a transaction will work (even when *B*'s ownership of Blackacre or *C*'s ownership of Greenacre is transitory) so long as the intermediary, *C*, is a "qualified intermediary" who is not an agent of the taxpayer (the taxpayer's employee, attorney, accountant, investment banker, and real estate broker within the two-year period ending on the date of transfer are considered "disqualified") or related to the taxpayer or to the taxpayer's agent. See generally M. Madison, J. Dwyer, and S. Bender, The Law of Real Estate Financing §8:39 (2016).

> ➤ *Problem 13-1*
> In your judgment, should the following hypothetical transaction involving like-kind real estate qualify for tax deferral treatment under I.R.C. §1031? If not, why not?
>
> *A*, who owns Blackacre, desires to receive replacement property in an exchange, and *C* is interested in buying Blackacre for cash. Under their exchange agreement, *A* transfers title in Blackacre to *C* for $100,000, which funds are to be controlled and used by *C* until *A* designates the replacement property (Whiteacre), at which time the funds would be used by *C* to purchase Whiteacre or paid to *A* if Whiteacre is not available. Six months later, at the behest of *A*, *C* acquires Whiteacre from *B* for $100,000 and transfers title in Whiteacre to *A*. ◄

4. Rewards and Risks. As explained in the excerpt from the Mortgage and Real Estate Executive's Report, supra, in addition to tax deferral treatment, exchanges of real estate under I.R.C. §1031 can also be used to: (1) boost a property owner's depreciation deductions by altering the transferor's land-building ratio for tax purposes, by receiving property with a larger existing mortgage so that the depreciable basis in the substitute property can be increased, or by acquiring substitute property with improvements that have a shorter useful life; (2) expedite a transfer of real estate where the purchaser is short on cash and the seller is wary of the risks associated with purchase money mortgage financing; or (3) exchange real estate for substitute property that has more potential for long-term appreciation, can support a higher debt-financing loan-to-value ratio, or is more marketable.

On the negative side of the coin is the potential tax problem caused by the interaction between I.R.C. §1031 and the limitations on passive loss imposed by I.R.C. §469. See discussion at Chapter 13A2c. Don't forget that I.R.C. §1031 is mandatory, not optional. With that in mind, can you think of any situation in which a property owner would want to avoid an exchange of her real estate for like-kind property?

5. Additional Reading. For planning suggestions and pitfalls, see generally Barrett and Kolbe, The Benefits of Tax-Deferred Exchanges Are Often Illusory, 17 Real Est. Rev. 56 (Winter 1988); Blackstone, Achieving Leverage through Multiparty Exchanges, 3 Real Est. Fin. J. 85 (Winter 1988); Carlin and Novack, Tax-Free Exchanges Attract New Interest, 4 Real Est. Fin. J. 68 (Spring 1987); Carman, Like-Kind Exchanges of MACRS Property Clarified in New Regulations, 31 Real Est. Tax'n. 167 (2004); Clementi, How to Close an Exchange Without Getting the Boot, 31 Real Est. Tax'n. (2004); Cuff, Structuring a Sample Forward Real Estate Exchange, 34 Real Est. Tax'n. 77 (2007); Levine and Glichlich, Tax-Free Real Estate Transactions: New Developments Involving Like-Kind Exchanges, 14 J. Real Est. Tax'n. 172 (Winter 1987); Mailer, Financing Ideas: Structuring Like-Kind Exchanges of Real Estate, 14 Real Est. L.J. 83 (Summer 1985); Mandarino, Related-Party Exchange Denied Tax Free Treatment Despite Use of Intermediary, 32 Real Est. Tax'n. 167 (2005); Plutchok, Let's Make a Deal: How to Swap Real Estate Tax-Free, 1 Real Est. Fin. J. 16 (Fall 1985); Sitnick, Like-Kind Exchanges: New Rules and Planning Considerations, 7 Real Est. Fin. J. 66 (Spring 1990); Wasserman, Mr. Mogul's Perpetual Search for Tax Deferral: Techniques for Section 1031 Like-Kind Exchanges—Part 3, 5 Real Est. Acct. & Tax'n. 26 (Summer 1990); Weller, Planning and Drafting the Deferred Like-Kind Real Estate Exchange, 20 J. Real Est. Tax'n. 42 (Fall 1992); see generally B. Borden, Taxation and Business Planning for Real Estate Transactions, chaps. 10-18 (2011).

➢ *Problem 13-2*

Assume under the master hypothetical that it is now 27 years after the project was completed and financed by means of a straight fee mortgage from Ace (that was extended for another self-amortizing 15-year term) that will mature in 3 years. Dan comes to your law office after hearing that you are about to retire and wishes you well. He also tells you that the office building has a remaining economic useful life of 30 years or more, that the mortgage with Ace contains an onerous prepayment charge (equal to 5 percent of the *original* loan balance), and that the current market rate of interest for first mortgage money is two percentage points below the fixed rate he has been paying on the Ace mortgage. He wants you to briefly explain to him (in terms as nonmathematical as possible and by making assumptions where necessary) which of the following is probably the best way for him to cash out his equity in the project:

1. a tax-free exchange under I.R.C. §1031
2. refinancing the existing mortgage with Ace
3. a conventional second mortgage
4. a sale and leaseback
5. any other method that comes to mind

Incidentally, Dan is more interested (because of his age) in short-term rewards (and short-term tax consequences) than what might happen in the long run. ◄

C h a p t e r   14

Selection of the Ownership Entity

In this chapter, we consider which type of ownership entity is best suited for the dual purposes of raising the venture capital and securing the debt financing needed by Dan Developer to fund the acquisition and improvement of real estate.[1] The choice of ownership vehicle for a real estate project is a wide one. It includes the tenancy in common, joint venture, general partnership, limited partnership, ordinary Subchapter C corporation, Subchapter S corporation, limited liability company, and real estate investment trust (see Chapter 15). In determining the appropriate ownership vehicle, the developer must carefully balance the competing tax, financing, and legal attributes that characterize each entity. Unfortunately, this balancing process is complicated by the truism that what is otherwise suitable from a legal or financing standpoint may be intolerable from a tax perspective, and vice versa. Accordingly, in selecting the optimum alternative, no fewer than three horses must be harnessed, one of which—tax—is always on the run!

To appreciate the tax advantages and disadvantages inherent in the various ownership entities, one must first understand the difference in the tax law between the so-called aggregate and entity approaches. In determining tax consequences, an ownership entity can be treated as an aggregate of equity participants who pool their assets and resources for some common purpose. Under this aggregate approach, the entity is treated merely as a nontaxable conduit through which tax consequences flow directly to each constituent member. By contrast, under the entity approach the organization itself is treated as an entity that is separate and distinct from its participants; accordingly, separate tax consequences accrue to both the entity and its members. For example, the entity approach applies to corporate taxation and accounts for the fact that the shareholders of a regular Subchapter C corporation are exposed to double taxation of corporate earnings and the inability to take advantage of the corporation's loss for tax purposes. However, the shareholders in a small business corporation (e.g., Subchapter S corporation) can avoid these tax disadvantages under I.R.C. §1361. At the other end of the spectrum is the tenancy in common, with respect to which the aggregate approach is strictly applied.

Before 1996, selecting the appropriate ownership entity required some fancy tax maneuvering through the complicated entity classification system for federal

---

1. The following materials are based in part on those in M. Madison, J. Dwyer, and S. Bender, The Law of Real Estate Financing §§1:25-1:65 (2016) and do not address proposed 2017 tax reforms.

income tax purposes. This meant the organizational documents had to be written so that the entity would be treated as a nontaxable conduit such as a partnership for tax purposes and yet be imbued with the nontax advantages of the corporate form of ownership. For example, the entity could be organized, for local law purposes, as a limited liability company (LLC), limited partnership, or Subchapter S corporation and obtain the single taxation advantage of partnership taxation without giving up the corporate advantages of centralized management, limited liability, continuity of life, and free transferability of interests. However, this required a delicate balancing act for the planner because if the entity was deemed to possess three or four of these corporate attributes under the former Treasury Regulations under Internal Revenue Code §7701, the entity would be classified as an "association" and taxed as a corporation. This meant double taxation of earnings and no pass through of losses to the owners of the entity.

However, the adoption of the check-the-box Regulations in 1996 (see Chapter 14B4, note 4) eliminated the need for this balancing act. In addition, with the development of the LLC and all its variants, the number of available entities increased dramatically. Now the choice of an ownership vehicle should be made by examining the local law attributes and tax characteristics of each entity and applying these considerations to the fact-specific project that is being planned. Important considerations are whether or not the property will constitute an active business as opposed to a passive investment, how many investors are involved, what are their goals and level of sophistication, and whether or not each investor contemplates an active or passive role in the venture to be formed.

In most cases involving income-producing real estate where active services are being rendered to the tenants, the choice will be between a limited liability company and a limited partnership. In the case of passive investments such as the co-ownership of land or net-leased rental real estate (where the tenants themselves make their own repairs and directly pay their pro-rata share of property taxes and insurance premiums), the investors most likely would decide to use the tenancy-in-common format. If the project is not very leveraged with outside financing or if the lender is concerned about usury penalties, chances are that the ownership vehicle will be a Subchapter S corporation if there are less than 100 shareholders. By contrast, in the case of real estate that is owned by a private equity firm or a hedge fund, the preferable ownership vehicle might be a large privately held limited partnership.[2] Or, if the ownership shares are publicly

2. As part of the Revenue Act of 1987, Congress subjected certain publicly traded partnerships whose investment shares are traded on an established securities market, or are readily traded on a secondary market, to corporate taxation. However, to placate the real estate industry, a real estate publicly traded partnership was excepted from double taxation and the other onerous aspects of corporate taxation provided that 90 percent or more of the partnership's gross income for each taxable year is from real estate rentals, interest, gain from the sale of real estate, and other passive sources of real estate income. See I.R.C. §7704, §469 (k). As of this writing, certain large private equity firms, hedge funds, and venture capital firms that are organized as partnerships have decided to issue public offerings. Typically, when a partner in such a firm earns a future profit interest (a so-called carried interest) the partner is not taxed upon receipt of the carried interest as ordinary income because the present value of the interest is undeterminable. This means that taxation of the

traded and the real estate generates sufficient passive income, the preferable ownership entity might be a real estate investment trust (see Chapter 15A) or a widely held public or so-called master limited partnership that complies with the tax rules applicable to publicly traded partnerships.

A. PARTNERSHIP VERSUS INCORPORATION

1. *Legal and Financing Considerations*

Traditionally, the main incentive for selecting corporate rather than partnership ownership has been the limited tort and contract liability available to shareholder-investors. In addition, corporate ownership offers promoters the ability to reach a wide variety of investors to secure the necessary venture capital. Yet due to public liability insurance and nonrecourse financing, these factors have become less significant. Moreover, limited liability and easy access to investors also inhere in the use of the limited partnership, LLC, and other noncorporate entities as the ownership vehicle. However, two distinct advantages of the corporate form remain, especially when the mortgage money market is tight: the inimitable liquidity of publicly held corporate stock and the corporation's exemption from local usury laws that restrict interest rates.

In contrast to publicly traded corporate shares, investment units in a widely held private limited partnership syndicate may not be readily marketable because of self-imposed constraints on alienability legalized under the Revised Uniform Limited Partnership Act (RULPA). While §704 of RULPA permits a limited partner to assign freely, the assignor cannot convey to the assignee full privileges as a limited partner unless the assignor is empowered to do so under the partnership agreement or unless the remaining partners agree. In addition, the agreement of limited partnership customarily places restrictions on the class of persons with respect to which an interest can be assigned to achieve certain business or legal objectives. For example, the transferee often is required to be 21 years of age or older, a resident of the state in which the partnership is doing business, or subject to approval by the general partners. Moreover, except for a few publicly held partnership syndicates and MLPs, there is an absence of any formal secondary markets for trading shares (such as the New York Stock Exchange). While a few large, privately held syndicates maintain an aftermarket for shares at the issue price, the cashing in of a partnership unit is almost always

---

income is deferred until realized by the firm. In most cases a partner in a hedge fund will realize his distributive share of a short-term investment as ordinary income or short-term capital gain while a private equity partner usually receives long-term capital gain because of the long-term nature of the investment.

Congress has been threatening to enact legislation that would tax a future profit interest as ordinary compensation income and disqualify such firms that go public from tax treatment as partnerships rather than as corporations under the publicly traded partnership rules.

expensive and cumbersome. Can you think of a business reason why the sponsors of such a syndicate would discourage redemption of the partnership shares? Consequently, the plight of a limited partner resembles the liquidity bind faced by shareholders in a closely held corporation.

A correlative disadvantage is that for credit purposes, the collateral value of the partnership interest is quite low. While high-grade stock and triple A municipal bonds are used by borrowers as collateral for a bank loan, it is doubtful whether a bank will value for credit purposes an investment unit in a real estate limited partnership for more than a fraction of its real worth.

In addition, whereas the corporation when borrowing is exempt from usury restrictions in most jurisdictions, the limited partnership and limited liability company sometimes are not. Accordingly, if the loan is not exempt for some other reason, the syndicators might be forced to use a nominee or "straw" corporation or to otherwise circumvent local usury law restrictions.[3]

2. *Advantages of Partnership over Corporate Taxation*

Selecting the appropriate ownership entity depends upon the specific facts of the transaction. However, as a general rule, the tax planner will be looking for an entity format that will provide the investors with the best of both kinds of ownership—that is, the tax advantages of a partnership combined with the nontax advantages of a corporation.

The principal advantage of partnership taxation is that under the aggregate approach to taxation a partnership is treated as a nontaxable conduit by which the partner's share of income, gain, loss, and other tax items are funneled through directly to the partner. Therefore, the earnings of the partnership are only taxed once and the losses accrued by the partnership can be passed through to the partners, who can use these losses to offset their shares of taxable income. As explained below, a Subchapter S corporation and an LLC that elects to be treated as a partnership also have this advantage. By contrast, under the entity approach, a regular Subchapter C corporation is treated as an ownership entity that is separate and apart from its shareholders. Consequently, the earnings of the corporation are taxed twice, first as corporate income, and second, as dividend income to the extent that the distribution of earnings come from the corporation's earnings and profits.[4]

An additional advantage of partnership taxation is that partners can reallocate their shares of tax items such as the depreciation deduction as between themselves (called "special allocations") in a favorable way so long as the allocations have substantial economic effect. If the partnership agreement is silent as to a partner's share of income, loss or constituent item, the partner's share will "be determined in accordance with the partner's interest in the

---

3. See discussion at Chapter 5A1, note 6.
4. See I.R.C. §§301(c), 312, 316.

partnership . . . by taking into account all facts and circumstances." In determining the partner's interest in the partnership, relevant factors include the partner's share of profits and losses, her share of cash flow, and the partner's right to a distribution of capital on liquidation. However, the partners are allowed to allocate among themselves by agreement a specific share or item of partnership income or loss (such as bottom line profits or losses, depreciation, or capital gains or losses) provided that the special allocation has "substantial economic effect." Accordingly, if in a real estate partnership there is an allocation of "bottom-line" profits or losses disproportionate to capital contributions, or the ratio for sharing profits and losses varies from year to year, or certain constituent items such as depreciation are all allocated to one partner or class of partners, these arrangements will be recognized if they reflect business and economic reality. As a general rule, this means that the special allocation must be reflected in the capital accounts of the partners, that any resulting disparity in the capital accounts must be respected at liquidation, that cash flow must be apportioned in the same manner as taxable income or loss, and that in later years there must be no subsequent adjustments in the capital accounts to offset the effects of the special allocation.[5]

Another tax advantage of partnerships over corporations is the ability of partners to deduct their distributive share of the partnership's tax losses. A partner's adjusted basis in her partnership interest is ordinarily equal to the sum of cash and her adjusted basis in property contributed to the partnership.[6] However, in the case of a limited partnership, if the partnership obtains qualified nonrecourse[7] (as opposed to recourse) financing, all partners' adjusted bases in their partnership interests will also include their share of the liabilities of the partnership.

Under I.R.C. §752, the position of a general partner under the *Crane* doctrine[8] is identical to that of someone who individually purchases an undivided interest in the property. The general partner's adjusted basis in the partnership interest for purposes of the §704(d) loss limitation not only includes the amount of cash and adjusted basis of property contributed, but also the partner's share of partnership liabilities. However, a special rule has existed for the limited partner. Under Treas. Reg. §1.752-3 a limited partner's share of partnership liabilities for the purpose of increasing his adjusted basis shall not exceed the amount of future capital contributions he is obligated to make. However, where none of the partners have any personal liability with respect to a partnership liability, as in the case of nonrecourse financing, then all partners, including limited partners, shall be considered as sharing such liability in the same proportion as they share profits provided that the nonrecourse financing is "qualified" under I.R.C. §465(b)(6). This rule purports to do nothing but codify the *Crane* doctrine. After reviewing the language of the Supreme Court in *Crane* (Chapter 13A), do you

---

5. See definition of "substantial effect" in Treas. Reg. §1.704-1(b)(2).
6. I.R.C. §722.
7. See Chapters 3B3 and 5A3 for discussion of nonrecourse financing.
8. See Chapter 13A for discussion of Crane v. Commissioner, 331 U.S. 1 (1947).

agree that this rule is consistent with the reasoning of the Court even though the rule distinguishes between recourse and nonrecourse financing?

The term "qualified nonrecourse financing" means a nonrecourse mortgage given by a lender who regularly makes loans. It cannot be a loan from a person related to the taxpayer (unless the loan is commercially reasonable and is made under the same terms as would be available from an unrelated person) or to any person from whom the taxpayer acquired the property (called "seller financing").[9] Further, it cannot be a loan from the recipient of a fee with respect to the transaction (promoter) or from a person related to such fee recipient. It cannot be a loan where the lender has the right to convert the loan indebtedness into an equity share in the property.[10] Nevertheless, a loan can be qualified nonrecourse financing if the lender normally makes loans and is otherwise qualified, even if it is a joint venture partner in the real estate activity. A loan from or guaranteed by a government or governmental entity is also deemed to be qualified nonrecourse financing.

Example: G is a general partner and *L* a limited partner in a limited partnership formed to acquire an apartment building costing $1 million. Each makes a cash contribution of $100,000, and the partnership obtains a mortgage in the amount of $800,000 to fund the balance of the construction costs. Under the terms of the partnership agreement, they are to share profits equally, but *L*'s liabilities are limited to the extent of his contribution. Neither the partnership nor either of the partners assumes any liability on the mortgage, and the loan is obtained from a "qualified" lender who regularly makes loans and who is not related to the partnership.

Result: The basis of *G* and *L* for their partnership interest is increased from $100,000 to $500,000, because each partner's share of the partnership liability has increased by $400,000. However, had *G* assumed personal liability by not insisting on an exculpatory provision in the mortgage note, or had the partnership obtained non-recourse financing that did not qualify under IRC §465(b)(6). *G*'s basis for her interest would have increased by $800,000 to $900,000, and *L*'s basis would remain at $100,000.

B.   LIMITED PARTNERSHIP VERSUS LIMITED LIABILITY COMPANY

1. *Limited Partnership*

All partners in a general partnership (and co-venturers in a joint venture[11]), under §15 of the Uniform Partnership Act (UPA), are jointly and severally liable for

---

9. See Chapters 3D and 7B3 for discussion of seller financing.

10. See Chapter 5A1, note 3 for discussion of convertible mortgages.

11. Although distinguishable from a partnership in that it is generally formed to carry out a single undertaking rather than an indefinite number of transactions, typically the joint venture is

everything chargeable to the partnership and jointly liable for all other debts and obligations of the partnership. Prior to the emergence of the LLC as a viable ownership entity, the general partnership was often preferred by a relatively small group of sophisticated investors who did not depend on outside sources for venture capital. The partners were willing to forgo the limited liability advantage of a limited partnership in exchange for control over management decisions.

In contrast, the limited partnership offers limited liability for the investors, who, as limited partners, can relegate unwelcome management responsibilities to the promoter-general partner, which may be desirable if unsophisticated or numerous investors are involved. Under §7 of the Uniform Limited Partnership Act (1916) (hereinafter ULPA), a limited partner must forgo participation in the control of the business to obtain limited liability with respect to outside creditors.[12] But what constitutes partaking in control? In his excellent article "The 'Control' Test for Limited Partnerships,"[13] Alan Feld maintains that under the ULPA, even the reservation of the right to give advice might constitute "control," since advice could have the color of command, especially where the party reserving such a right is an investor of substantial size. Case law under ULPA suggests, however, that a limited partner can safely engage in a limited degree of management activity.[14] But neither ULPA §7 nor the underlying case law adequately defined the threshold limits to which a limited partner could go without being regarded as partaking in control. Consequently, the Revised Uniform Limited Partnership Act (hereinafter RULPA), adopted in 1976 by the National Conference of Commissioners on Uniform State Laws, revised §7 to provide a safe harbor rule for limited partners. As amended in 1985, §303 of RULPA provides that a limited partner may engage in activities such as being an agent or employee of the partnership, advising a general partner with respect to the business of the partnership, and voting on such vital matters as the sale and mortgaging of the partnership assets and the dissolution of the partnership,

---

either analogized to or simply treated as a general partnership under local law; it is subsumed for federal tax purposes under the definition of a partnership. I.R.C. §7701(a)(2).

12. See, e.g., Holzman v. De Escamilla, 86 Cal. App. 2d 858, 195 P.2d 833 (Dist. Ct. App. 1948). (The trial court had found that two limited partners in a farming enterprise had taken part in the control of the business so as to become liable as general partners. The two had absolute power to withdraw partnership funds from the bank without the knowledge or consent of the general partner. Either of the two could limit the general partner's management of the business by refusing to sign checks to pay bills for work contracted by the general partner. The two required the general partner to resign as manager of the business (the farm) and selected his successor. And they often decided, against the general partner's wishes, which crops would be planted. The court of appeal found this evidence sufficient to sustain the trial court's finding that the two "took part in the control of the business of the partnership and thus became liable as general partners.").

13. 82 Harv. L. Rev. 1471, 1477 (1969).

14. For example, in Silvola v. Rowlett, 129 Colo. 522, 272 P.2d 287 (1954), a limited partner who as shop foreman occasionally discussed business matters when his advice was solicited by the general partner was not deprived of his protected status. And in Grainger v. Antoyan, 48 Cal. 2d 805, 313 P.2d 848 (1957), a limited partner who as sales manager performed certain ministerial functions (for example, signing checks) during a crisis period but had no authority to hire personnel, purchase inventory, or set prices was not liable as a general partner.

without being deemed to have taken part in the control of the business and thereby incur liability for the debts and torts of the partnership.[15]

In addition, because of the difficulty in determining when the "control" line has been overstepped, §303(a) of RULPA mitigates the exposure of a limited partner by imposing liability only if the third-party claimant reasonably believed, "based upon the limited partner's conduct, that the limited partner [was] a general partner."[16] Finally, in what appears to be a concession to the recent proliferation of limited partnership substitutes such as the LLC and its variants such as the limited liability partnership (LLP) and the limited liability limited partnership (LLLP), the Uniform Limited Partnership Act (ULPA 2001), promulgated in 2001,[17] simply eliminates the control test in its entirety. Section 303 of the ULPA 2001 provides that the limited partner is not liable for entity debts "even if the limited partner participates in the management and control of the limited partnership." But this immunity only applies to the extent that the limited partner is claimed to be liable on account of being a limited partner. For example, a limited partner would not be shielded from liability to a third party when the limited partner's own wrongful conduct caused the injury. Moreover, the ULPA 2001, like its predecessors, does nothing to eviscerate the judicial doctrine called "piercing the corporate veil" under which the shareholder or limited partner is exposed to personal liability where the statutory privilege of limited liability has been abused or where the general partner is an artificial entity that is thinly capitalized and controlled by the limited partner.[18]

Because it combines the tax advantages of partnership ownership with the legal and business advantages of incorporation, the limited partnership traditionally was the ownership vehicle most often chosen by investors who decide to use the partnership format. However, as discussed below, the limited liability company may have surpassed the limited partnership in popularity due to its combination of partnership taxation and its offering of limited liability to all investors, even those who control the actions of the entity.[19]

As suggested by the following case, in most jurisdictions the limited partner cannot take limited liability for granted.

---

15. Under §303 a limited partner can also act as surety for the partnership, attend a meeting of the partners, be an officer of the corporate general partner, and vote on the admission or removal of a general partner or on a proposed amendment to the partnership agreement or certificate of limited partnership. Also, §107 of RULPA allows a limited partner to lend money to and otherwise transact business with the limited partnership.

16. See generally Burr, Potential Liability of Limited Partners as General Partners, 67 Mass. L. Rev. 22 (1982).

17. The ULPA 2001 is a "stand alone Act not linked to UPA, ULPA, or RULPA. 6A U.L.A. 1 (2001). It deals mostly with default provisions and, in the words of the drafters, targets primarily (i) sophisticated, manager-entrenched commercial deals whose participants commit for the long term, and (ii) estate planning arrangements (family limited partnerships).

18. See generally Huss, Revamping Veil Piercing for All Limited Liability Entities: Forcing the Common Law Doctrine Into the Statutory Age, 70 U. Cinn. L. Rev. 95 (2001).

19. See generally Steuben, Choice of Entity for Real Estate after Check-the-Box and the Entity Explosion, 37 Real Prop., Prob. & Tr. J. 53, 86-90 (2002).

Gonzalez v. Chalpin

77 N.Y.2d 74, 565 N.E.2d 1253, 564 N.Y.S.2d 702 (1990)

BELLACOSA, Justice

Plaintiff Gonzalez sued defendant Excel Associates and its limited and general partners for breach of contract seeking damages for unpaid compensation for renovation work he performed, at the request of defendant-appellant Chalpin, on an apartment building owned by Excel. Excel, a New York limited partnership, has one individual general partner, defendant Lipkin; one corporate general partner, defendant Tribute Music, Inc. (Tribute); and one limited partner, Chalpin. Chalpin is also the president, sole shareholder and director of Tribute.

Chalpin, the sole appellant, has defended against the imposition of individual liability on the ground that his actions on Excel's behalf were performed only in his capacity as officer of Tribute. The trial court, after a bench trial, granted a money judgment to plaintiff. The Appellate Division affirmed and rejected Chalpin's limited liability defense because "there was no evidence tending to show that Chalpin acted on behalf of the partnership in anything but his individual capacity." (159 A.D.2d 553, 555.) This Court granted leave to appeal and we now affirm, essentially because Chalpin failed to prove that he acted as an officer of Tribute on behalf of Excel rather than individually. He was thus properly denied the limited liability protection of Partnership Law §96.

In early 1980, Chalpin hired Gonzalez to be the superintendent/maintenance worker at Excel's apartment building in Long Beach, Long Island. For his services, Gonzalez received a salary of $150 per week plus a rent-free apartment. Sometime later, Chalpin and Lipkin agreed to hire Gonzalez for renovation work (replacing the building's lintels and windows and demolishing its water tower) at additional compensation. Gonzalez was paid for demolishing the water tower but was not paid for the other work he performed. Chalpin terminated Gonzalez's employment as superintendent in August 1980 but the special renovation work continued to be done by Gonzalez until May 1981, when Chalpin dismissed him in that capacity as well and had him evicted from the apartment.

The general restriction on the liability of limited partners is not controlling here because, if the partner "in addition to the exercise of [the partner's] rights and powers as a limited partner . . . takes part in the control of the business," the limited partner becomes liable as a general partner (Partnership Law §96). Chalpin cannot challenge the trial court's affirmed factual determination that he took part in the control of Excel's business. Instead, he attempts to skirt the individual and general responsibility imposed by Partnership Law §96 by claiming that he acted at all times solely in his capacity as an officer of Tribute.

Irrefutably, individual liability should not be imposed on a limited partner merely because that person happens also to be an officer, director and/or shareholder of a corporate general partner (see, Frigidaire Sales Corp. v. Union Props., 88 Wn. 2d 400, 562 P.2d 244). But that is not this case. Moreover and conversely, a limited partner who "takes part in the control of" the limited partnership's business should not automatically be insulated from individual liability merely by benefit of status as an officer and sole owner of the corporate general partner. That is this case.

A limited partner who assumes such a dual capacity rightly bears a heavy burden when seeking to elude personal liability. For once a plaintiff meets the threshold burden of proving that a limited partner took an active individual part in effectuating the limited partnership's interests (Continental Nat'l. Bank v. Strauss, 137 N.Y. 148, 151), the fulcrum shifts. The limited partner in such a dual capacity must then, at least, prove that any relevant actions taken were performed solely in the capacity as officer of the general partner.

Defendant in this case failed to adjust to the shift and did not overcome the proof of involvement and responsibility for his actions undertaken in his individual capacity. Chalpin's only evidence, offered to support his claim that he acted as an officer of Tribute in the employment dealings with Gonzalez on behalf of Excel, was Excel's certificate of limited partnership. The certificate states that Chalpin is a limited partner and was signed by Chalpin on behalf of Tribute, and the attached certification states that Chalpin is the president of Tribute.

Chalpin essentially would have the Court adopt a rule of law according the piece of paper conclusive weight on the critical issue. This is not a sensible rule and would not make a difference in this case, in any event, where there is no evidence that Chalpin ever asserted his identity and authority as a corporate officer of Tribute when conducting Excel's affairs with Gonzalez—except his own testimony, which was expressly discredited and characterized as unbelievable by the trial court. The clinching documentary evidence shows Chalpin signing Excel's checks in payment to Gonzalez in his own name and without naming Tribute or indicating that he was signing in any representative capacity.

Chalpin also invites the Court to incorporate into Partnership Law §96 a requirement that a plaintiff seeking to hold a limited partner individually liable must prove reliance on the limited partner's personal conduct. This argument is not supportable or sound (see Delaney v. Fidelity Lease, 526 S.W.2d 543 [Sup. Ct. Tex]). Such a significant qualification on the statutorily regulated liability pattern of Partnership Law §96, if nevertheless deemed worthy of consideration, must come from the Legislature so that reasonable certainty and reliability in these business relationships and transactions could be reflected in the statutory formulation.

In sum, the trial court and Appellate Division properly rejected Chalpin's limited liability defense and imposed individual liability on him. We have examined the remaining arguments and conclude they are without merit or consequence on the outcome of this case. . . .

2. Limited Liability Companies

In the 1990s, the LLC emerged as the ownership entity of choice for many, if not most, real estate investors. An LLC selecting treatment as a partnership for tax purposes has all the advantages of a general partnership combined with limited liability for its investors (called "members"). In response to uncertainty about how an LLC would be treated for tax purposes, the Internal Revenue Service in 1988 classified a Wyoming LLC as a partnership for tax purposes.[20] With the adoption of the "check-the-box" regulations in 1996 that allow partnership taxation for an LLC, the popularity of this ownership format surged and by 1997 all states (and the District of Columbia) had enacted enabling legislation. However, there is growing concern over the lack of uniformity among the LLC statutes. In response to this problem, a Uniform Act was drafted that may lead to more uniformity.[21] As compared to a limited partnership, the major advantage of the LLC is that all members of the LLC are insulated from liabilities of the organization—the LLC will protect even those members who are actively involved in company management.[22] While an adequately capitalized corporate general partner can create limited liability for all the partners of a limited partnership, such an arrangement can be expensive as compared to organizing an LLC.

Even though state LLC laws vary, the basic structure of an LLC is common to all. An LLC is created by filing articles of organization with the designated state authority. Governance of its affairs is specified in an operating agreement that resembles a partnership agreement and corporate bylaws. Most states allow the investor-members to manage the LLC themselves or to provide for management by third-party managers if this delegation of management authority is spelled out in the operating agreement.

A disadvantage of an LLC as compared to the limited partnership is that since the LLC is a new type of entity the law governing LLCs is not as well settled. For example, in many jurisdictions it is not clear whether an LLC will be treated as an individual, partnership, or corporation for usury law purposes.[23] Another uncertainty is whether an LLC can claim the protection of the Bankruptcy Code. If it can, will it be treated as an individual, partnership, or corporation? Can the members of an LLC that elects to be treated as a partnership for tax purposes protect the assets of the entity against a creditor of one of the members? Moreover, in an action by a third party against members of an LLC, it is uncertain whether courts will impose personal liability on its members based on the same standard that has been employed in piercing the corporate veil of a corporation.[24] Some courts have refused to pierce the limited liability shield of a

---

20. Rev. Rul. 88-76, 1988-2 CB 360.

21. See the Uniform Limited Liability Company Act, 6A U.L.A. 553 (1996).

22. Id. at §303(a).

23. See discussion at Chapter 5A1, note 6.

24. See generally Huss, Revamping Veil Piercing for All Limited Liability Entities: Forcing the Common Law Doctrine Into the Statutory Age, 70 U. Cinn. L. Rev. 95 (2001).

member of the LLC in favor of a third-party plaintiff unless the member dominated the transaction involving the third party and such domination was an instrument of fraud, inequitable, or wrongful.[25] Also, many LLC statutes do not spell out the fiduciary duties of the managers and the members.[26] Further, some states impose a local franchise or corporate income tax on LLCs and S corporations but not on limited partnerships.[27]

Under regulations mentioned below, the LLC ordinarily will qualify for taxation as a partnership. Therefore, the basis rules that apply to partnerships presumably apply to the LLC. Moreover, the LLC members may agree to allocate their share of income and loss in accordance with the special allocation rules discussed earlier. One distinct tax advantage of the LLC over the limited partnership is that unlike a limited partner,[28] a member of an LLC who actively and materially participates in managing the business can avoid the limitation on passive losses provided that the member meets the test of IRC §469 (c)(7). Another advantage in using the LLC as the ownership vehicle is that in some states such as New York an LLC is prohibited from interposing the defense of usury against a lender seeking to enforce payment of its loan.

A variation of the LLC format is the limited liability limited partnership (LLLP) that was created by the ULPA 2001.[29] Some states have begun to authorize these limited partnerships that treat general partners in an otherwise limited partnership format as limited partners for limited liability purposes, thus shielding both general as well as limited partners from the liabilities of the entity regardless of their degree of control over partnership affairs. For existing limited partnerships, the ULPA 2001 authorizes the limited partnership to convert to LLLP status by amending its filed partnership certificate provided that all the partners consent to the amendment.

Another recent example of the LLC format is the limited liability partnership (LLP) that provides limited liability for certain partners (called "protected partners") of a general partnership for the wrongful acts committed by other partners or partnership employees without the knowledge or supervision by the protected partners.[30]

3. Subchapter S Corporations

By electing to be taxed under Subchapter S of the Internal Revenue Code (§§1361 et seq.), S corporation shareholders can avail themselves of limited

---

25. E.g., Retropolis, Inc. v. 14th Street Development LLC, 797 N.Y.S.2d 1 (App. Div. 2005) (member's mistakenly depositing two checks to his personal account did not prove domination).

26. See generally McGeever, Hazardous Duty?: The Role of the Fiduciary in Noncorporate Structures, 4 Bus. Law Today 51 (Mar./Apr. 1995).

27. E.g., Pa. Stat. Ann. tit. 15, §8925.

28. A limited partner is expressly precluded from circumventing the rule on limiting passive losses. IRC §469 (h)(2).

29. See the Uniform Limited Partnership Act, 6A U.L.A. 2 (2001).

30. For example, see N.Y. Partnership Law §26.

liability and the other nontax advantages associated with corporate ownership along with some of the advantages associated with partnership taxation. As with a partnership, a Subchapter S corporation is treated as a nontaxable conduit rather than as a separate tax entity. Accordingly, under I.R.C. §1366 there is a pass-through of tax losses to the shareholders and, in contrast to an ordinary Subchapter C corporation, there is no problem of double taxation inasmuch as the earnings of the Subchapter S corporation are subject to taxation only at the shareholder level (in proportion to each shareholder's pro rata share of stock).

However, definitional constraints preclude the use of this election for many real estate investors. To qualify as a Subchapter S corporation under I.R.C. §1361, the entity must be a domestic corporation that does *not:* (1) have more than 100 shareholders; (2) have as a shareholder a person who is not an individual (except for certain trusts and estates); (3) have as a shareholder a nonresident alien; and (4) have more than one class of stock.[31]

Moreover, use of a Subchapter S corporation as a real estate ownership vehicle for income-producing real estate is severely limited by the onerous at-risk rule under I.R.C. §1366(d)(1). This rule limits the amount of deductible losses to the shareholder's adjusted basis in the stock plus the amount of any indebtedness of the corporation *to the shareholder.* By contrast, as previously discussed, in the case of a limited partnership the ceiling amount for deducting losses is the adjusted basis of the limited partner's interest in the partnership plus the partner's share of any qualified nonrecourse indebtedness of the partnership *to outside creditors,* including mortgagees.[32] In other words, while a partner is able to obtain a step-up in its adjusted basis equal to its share of mortgage liabilities, a Subchapter S shareholder cannot. In the case of a typical leveraged real estate investment that is funded by nonrecourse financing, an investor may not be able to take full advantage of her share of tax losses if the venture is organized as a Subchapter S corporation. As compared to the LLC, the LLC is not subject to the onerous basis rules and strict requirements that constrain the structure of the S corporation, such as the restriction on the number of shareholders and the limitation to a single class of stock.

Consequently, the Subchapter S corporation is used primarily to hold real estate that is not expected to yield sizeable tax losses (for example, raw land) or where the investors have a substantial equity investment (and tax basis) in the real estate or where the investors decide to incorporate their venture to avoid local usury restrictions (which would otherwise prevent them from obtaining mortgage financing at a market rate of interest).

---

31. However, the one class rule is not violated if the staggering of common stock is used by the incorporators to differentiate the shares as to voting rights. Treas. Reg. §1361-1 (*l*)(1).

32. See discussion at Chapter 14A2.

4. Tenancy in Common

The tenancy in common is the simplest but rarest form of investment co-ownership. The right of partition and the requirement of unanimous consent for decision-making render this mode of operation too cumbersome except in small, closely knit groups of investors whose purpose is solely to own the property and to passively collect the rental income. In addition, on the death of any co-owner, title to the property may be clouded by an unsettled estate in the event of a prospective sale, since all of the co-owners are ordinarily required under state law to execute the deed of conveyance at the time of transfer. In the event of the death, insolvency, incompetence, or retirement of a tenant in common, title to her share of the realty may pass to her heir or devisee, creditor, court-appointed trustee, or assignee, as the case may be. By contrast, if property is taken in the name of a partnership, legal title in specific partnership property remains unencumbered if the remaining partners should agree to continue the partnership—subject, of course, to the rights of the former partner's legal representative or assignee to her share of the partnership profits and surplus.[33]

The following are the advantages of the tenancy in common as compared to both partnership and corporate taxations:

1. Any election affecting the computation of taxable income may be made separately by each tenant. For example, one co-owner may capitalize carrying charges[34] while another may elect to currently deduct or "expense" such charges.

2. No partnership-level tax return is required for a tenancy in common. Thus, if a co-tenant is audited, it is less likely that a co-owner will be audited, since there is no return filed that links them to one another.[35]

The following are the disadvantages of a tenancy in common as compared to both partnership and corporate taxations:

1. Each tenant must separately report only her proportionate part of net operating income or net gain from the sale or exchange of the property. For example, if one tenant pays a larger share of the total expenses than the others, she is entitled to deduct only her pro rata share. The excess payment is treated as an advance to her co-owners.[36]

---

33. Uniform Partnership Act §§25(2), 27(1) (1914); Revised Uniform Partnership Act §§501, 503 (1997).

34. I.R.C. §266.

35. To facilitate the audit of partners, especially those engaged in tax shelter activities, the Code provides that the tax treatment of partnership income, loss deduction, and credit items will be audited at the partnership level in a unified partnership proceeding rather than at the individual partner level. I.R.C. §§6221-6233. A partnership, though required to file an information return (Form 1065), is itself a nontaxable conduit. Accordingly, each partner separately reports his distributive share of each item on his individual return (Schedule K-1).

36. E.g., Estate of Webb v. Commissioner, 30 T.C. 1202 (1958), acq. 1959-2 C.B. 3.

2. A corollary disadvantage lies in the fact that tenants in common, unlike partners and joint venturers, may not reallocate income and deduction items such as depreciation in a ratio at variance with their interest in the commonly owned property. Compare the potential for special allocations of partnership income or loss discussed above.

3. Perhaps the most constraining disadvantage is definitional. The Code defines the term "partnership" so broadly that it includes any "syndicate, group, pool, joint venture, or other unincorporated organization through or by means of which any business, financial operation, or venture is carried on, and which is not, within the meaning of this title, a corporation or a trust or estate."[37] This definition could create serious difficulty for taxpayers if the Internal Revenue Service should later determine that what purported to be a tenancy in common was in reality a partnership for tax purposes.[38]

NOTES AND QUESTIONS

1. Does New Control Test Make Sense? As explained above, in contrast to the tenancy in common and general partnership forms of ownership, the limited partnership format allows the investor to obtain *limited liability* in exchange for giving up *control* over the affairs of the partnership. This is a familiar tradeoff in the eyes of the law based on the common sense principle that liability follows control. For example, the control test is used in determining whether a landlord should be liable in tort for injuries to a tenant or third party invitee based on the condition of the leased premises. See Bowles v. Mahoney, 202 F.2d 320 (D.C. Cir. 1952). The liability follows control test also explains the traditional reluctance of institutional investors, such as life insurance companies, to engage in joint ventures with developers. See discussion at Chapter 5A1, note 5. In the opinion of the drafters of ULPA 2001, "the control rule has become an anachronism." See comment to ULPA §303, 6A U.L.A. (2001). Do you agree with this assessment? If not, as between the original control test in §7 of the ULPA and the safe harbor test in §303 of the RULPA, which control test do you favor, and why?

2. Piercing the Liability Shield of a Limited Partner. As of this writing, only 19 states have adopted the ULPA 2001. This means that courts in a majority of jurisdictions are still applying the control test of the RULPA in deciding whether to ignore the limited liability shield of a limited partner. This also means that very few limited partnerships have been able to insulate general partners from personal liability by registering the partnership as an LLLP.

---

37. I.R.C. §§761, 7701-1(a)(2).

38. See Treas. Reg. §301.7701-1(a)(2) (providing illustrations of the difference between "mere co-ownership" of property and ownership that will be treated as a partnership or corporation for federal tax purposes).

As suggested by the holding in *Gonzalez*, limited partners in a limited partnership are sometimes lulled into a false sense of security about using a corporate general partner to obtain limited liability protection without forfeiting control over the affairs of the partnership. What lesson can be learned from *Gonzalez* for investors that use the limited partnership format? What lesson can be learned for an investor that uses a single-member LLC? See J. Ostrov, Tax Planning with Real Estate §3.6.5.

As observed earlier, one problem with using the LLC format is the uncertainty as to whether courts will impose personal liability on its members based on the same standard that has been employed in piercing the corporate veil to impose liability on a shareholder of the corporation. In that regard, courts have been more inclined to pierce the corporate veil when the corporation is "thinly capitalized," meaning that the corporation has little if any assets of its own, as was the case of the corporate general partner in *Gonzalez*. If the courts continue to apply this standard, how will this affect the choice of deciding between a limited partnership and an LLC as the preferred ownership vehicle? See generally Reynolds, Get Real: Using LLCs to Invest in Property, 4 Bus. Law Today 44, 47 (Mar./Apr. 1995).

3. Nonrecourse Financing and the Basis Question for an LLC. Suppose you are the real estate lawyer for an investment entity that owns a newly constructed apartment building. At your suggestion, Danielle Developer has organized the venture as an LLC that has selected tax treatment as a partnership. Danielle plans to obtain a permanent loan commitment from Ace Insurance Company in the amount of $9 million. The investors know that if they do not obtain a step-up in their tax bases equal to their share of the mortgage, their tax bases will drop to zero and they will start being taxed on their cash distributions by the end of the (assume) fifth year. Ace tells Danielle that the loan must be recourse and not nonrecourse. She wants to know if she and the other investors can still obtain a step-up in their tax bases in their membership interests even though she and a few other members of the LLC will become personally liable for repayment of the loan. What will you tell her? See I.R.C. §752, Treas. Reg. §§1.752-1, 1.752-2, and 1.752-3. Assume some members have suggested using a Subchapter S corporation. Do you see any tax problem with using this format?

4. Simplification of Entity Classification Rules. In 1996, the IRS concluded that both it and taxpayers were spending considerable resources trying to deal with the entity classification rules. Therefore, it replaced the old "formalistic" rules with "a much simpler approach that generally is elective." Under the new Simplification of Entity Classification rules, called the "check-the-box" regulations (Treas. Reg. §§301.7701-2 and 301.7701-3), any "eligible entity"— that is, one not defined as a corporation—can choose its classification for tax purposes as a partnership or association (corporate tax). The regulations specify default classification rules that aim to reduce the number of elections by initially matching most taxpayers' expectations. Thus, in the case of "eligible" entities with two or more members, such as limited partnerships and LLCs, absent an election, the regulations specify they will be taxed as a partnership.

> ➤ *Problem 14-1*
> Assume that Dan Developer has engaged you to represent him in selecting and forming the ownership entity that he will use to raise the venture capital and obtain the mortgage financing for an office building project. On the basis of the foregoing materials and Table 14-1 below, which entity would you recommend? What information would you need from Dan in making your recommendation? ◄

5. Additional Reading. For an excellent discussion comparing the plethora of available ownership entities, see Steuben, Choice of Entity for Real Estate After Check-the-Box and the Entity Explosion, 37 Real Prop. Prob. & Tr. J. 53 (2002). For a discussion comparing partnerships and corporations, see August and Silow, S Corporation vs. Partnership for Real Estate Ventures, 1 J. Tax'n Inv. 91 (1984); Schwidetzky, Is It Time to Give the S Corporation a Proper Burial? 15 Va. Tax Rev. 591 (1996).

For additional background on partnerships and partnership taxation, see Section of Real Prop., Prob. & Tr. Law and ACREL, Real Estate Partnerships: Selected Problems and Solutions (1991); W. McKee, W. Nelson, and R. Whitmire, Federal Taxation of Partnerships and Partners (1977); A. Willis, J. Pennell, and P. Postlewaite, Partnership Taxation (5th ed. 1994).

For a discussion of LLCs and the new limited liability entities, see Geu and Nekritz, Expectations for the Twenty-First Century: An Overview of the New Limited Partnership Act, 16 Prob. & Prop. 47 (Jan./Feb. 2002); Murdock, Limited Liability Companies in the Decade of the 1990s: Legislative and Case Law Developments for the Future, 56 Bus. Law. 499 (2001); Reynolds, Get Real: Using LLCs to Invest in Property, 4 Bus. Law Today 44 (Mar.-Apr. 1995); Shenkman et al., Limited Liability Companies: A New Opportunity for Real Estate Investors, 10 Real Est. Fin. J. 22 (Winter 1995); Thompson, The Limits of Liability in the New Limited Liability Entities, 32 Wake Forest L. Rev. 1 (1997).

For a discussion of the entity classification tax rules, see Lux, Check-the-Box Proposed Regulations: An Instant Hit, 24 J. Real Est. Tax'n. 27, 37-38 (Fall 1996). See also Ribstein and Sargent (eds.), Check-the-Box and Beyond: The Future of Limited Liability Entities, 52 Bus. Law. 605 (Feb. 1997).

Table 14 – 1

Comparison of Real Estate Ownership Structures

	Partnership	Limited Liability Company ("LLC")	S Corporation	C Corporation
Name of Owner	Partner (general or limited)	Member	Shareholder	Shareholder
Limited Liability	Not for general partners but limited partners have protection from the partnership's debts unless provided otherwise	All members have protection from LLC's debts unless provided otherwise	All shareholders	All shareholders
Participation in Management	Participation by limited partners may need to be restricted to preserve their limited liability	No restrictions	No restrictions	No restrictions
Transferability of Interests	Restrictions are imposed by state law, securities laws, and, generally, the partnership agreement	Restrictions are imposed by state law, securities laws and, generally, the LLC's operating agreement	Restrictions are imposed by securities laws and by a shareholders' agreement, if any	Restrictions are imposed by securities laws and by a shareholders' agreement, if any
Continuity of Life	Generally, no	Generally, no	Generally, yes	Yes
Classes of Ownership Interests	Multiple classes are permitted	Multiple classes are permitted	One; however, there can be differences in voting rights	Multiple classes are permitted
Levels of Federal Income Tax Status	Partner level only unless partnership elects taxation as an association (corporation)	Member level only unless LLC elects taxation as an association (corporation)	Generally, only shareholder level; in addition, some states will tax S corporations	Corporate and shareholder level
Eligibility for Tax Status	Eligible for taxation as a partnership unless it elects taxation as an association or constitutes a "publicly traded partnership"	Eligible for taxation as a partnership unless it elects taxation as an association or constitutes a "publicly traded partnership"; if LLC has one member, it can only elect to be taxed as an association	There are various eligibility requirements for avoidance of taxation at the corporate level, including a restriction on the number and type of shareholders	Taxed as association

Table 14 – 1 (*continued*)

Comparison of Real Estate Ownership Structures

	Partnership	Limited Liability Company ("LLC")	S Corporation	C Corporation
		rather than being disregarded as a separate entity under the default rule		
Types of Owner	Any	Any	Ownership is limited to U.S. residents and citizens and to certain U.S. trusts	Any
Special Allocations of Income and Loss	Yes	Yes	No, all allocations are pro rata, preferences can be achieved only through debt, compensation, or other complicated structures	N/A
Tax Basis in Ownership Interest	A partner's tax basis in her partnership interest includes her allocable share of partnership recourse and nonrecourse debt	A member's tax basis in her LLC interest includes her allocable share of LLC qualified nonrecourse debt. All LLC debt should be deemed nonrecourse because of the limited liability for all the members, including the managing member.	A shareholder's tax basis in her stock does not include any portion of the corporation's debt	A shareholder's tax basis in her stock does not include any portion of the corporation's debt
Deductibility of Losses	Partners may deduct the partnership's losses only to the extent of their tax basis in their partnership interest, which includes their allocable share of partnership debt	Members may deduct the LLC's losses only to the extent of their tax basis in their LLC interest, which includes their allocable share of LLC debt	Shareholders may deduct the corporation's losses only to the extent of their tax basis in their stock, which does not include any portion of the corporation's debt	Shareholders may not deduct any of the corporation's losses
At-Risk Limitations on Deduction of Losses	Applicable	Applicable	Applicable	Applicable, if closely held

THE ETHICAL REAL ESTATE LAWYER

Joint Representation of Promoters

Assume that Dan Developer is interested in forming a business association with Irma Investor to develop an office building project. Dan and Irma Investor seek your legal counsel in choosing the entity that best meets their legal, financial, and tax expectations. Following your assistance in selecting and establishing the ownership vehicle, you expect to represent the entity in negotiating the terms of construction and postconstruction financing needed to acquire and to improve the real estate. Must (should) you refer Dan or Irma to independent counsel, or can you represent them both in establishing the ownership vehicle? What possible conflicts may arise between Dan and Irma Investor in selecting and structuring the ownership entity? Can you represent the entity after you have represented one or both of the promoters? What possible conflicts can arise between the entity and the promoters in obtaining the necessary third-party financing? See Chapter 2A2 for discussion of joint representation in conveyancing transactions. See generally Buehler v. Sbardellati, 34 Cal. App. 4th 1527, 41 Cal. Rptr. 2d 104 (1995) (attorney forming real estate partnership represented the partnership and not the individual partners and was not liable to limited partner on conflict of interest claim); Keatinge, The Implications of Fiduciary Relationships in Representing Limited Liability Companies and Other Unincorporated Associations and Their Partners or Members, 25 Stetson L. Rev. 389 (1995); Lubet, Malpractice Alert: No "Conflict," But a Conflict of Interest, 6 Bus. L. Today 32 (Jan.-Feb. 1997); Pechersky, Note, Representing General Partnerships and Close Corporations: A Situational Analysis of Professional Responsibility, 73 Tex. L. Rev. 919 (1995).

Chapter 15

Securitization

A. SECURITIZATION ON THE EQUITY SIDE OF COMMERCIAL REAL ESTATE INVESTMENTS

As observed at Chapter 12, a direct or indirect ownership interest in income-producing real estate (such as an investment share in a limited liability company or a Subchapter S corporation) has been shown to be an attractive investment as compared to other investment media such as stocks and bonds because real estate historically has tended to be a less risky and volatile portfolio asset and a better hedge against inflation. In addition, real estate developers and investors like Dan Developer are afforded the unique opportunity to superleverage their acquisition and construction costs by means of high-ratio financing. Moreover, notwithstanding the limitation on passive losses for rental and limited partnership activities imposed by the Tax Reform Act of 1986 (discussed along with the 1993 amendments at Chapter 13A2c), the real estate investor is still able to shelter his share of rental income from immediate taxation. The one salient disadvantage of investing in real estate has been the lack of liquidity associated with shares in a real estate investment. For example, until recently, real estate investors in publicly held limited partnerships (syndications) were compelled to invoke their own resources when they needed to sell their investment shares because of the absence of any formal secondary market for trading their shares (such as the New York Stock Exchange) and because leverage-minded syndicators discouraged redemptions of investment shares to preserve the cash reserves of their partnership syndications.

Perhaps the most dramatic trend affecting the development and financing of income-producing real estate in modern times was the innovative efforts by developers and underwriters on Wall Street to utilize the public security format to enhance the liquidity and marketability of both debt and equity participations in commercial (and residential) real estate without depriving the investor of the tax and pass-through benefits associated with the direct ownership of the real estate. Exemplifying this trend toward securitization on the equity (ownership) side of real estate is the real estate investment trust (REIT). The market capitalization of so-called equity REITs alone grew exponentially from $5.5 billion in 1990 to $400 billion by year end 2006, on the cusp of the subsequent residential mortgage meltdown and global financial crisis that removed the shine from real estate mortgage securitizations (just $176 billion for equity REITS in 2008), but it returned in earnest once the crisis passed ($886 billion in 2015).

On the debt side of real estate, credit rating agencies such as Standard & Poor's developed the computer technology to evaluate the creditworthiness of income-producing real estate notwithstanding that the rental income stream from a building is predicated on a variety of underlying leases with disparate tenants and lease terms. This enabled developers seeking refinancing of large projects to obtain their long-term fixed rate financing by issuing commercial mortgage-backed bonds (CMBBs) (which are traded on Wall Street) and thereby to obtain less expensive and more attractive loan terms than those available from the less competitive (oligopolistic) traditional private lending sources such as life insurance companies and pension funds.

At the same time, the mortgage credit markets witnessed burgeoning growth in the issuance of commercial mortgage-backed securities (CMBSs) by mortgage conduits on Wall Street. Organized as real estate mortgage investment conduits (REMICs) for tax purposes, these conduits have been providing debt capital for medium-sized projects that are preleased and meet predetermined underwriting criteria. After the loans are closed on relatively standardized loan documents, they are aggregated or "warehoused" until they are sufficient in amount to be packaged as securities that are both segmented and rated to meet the particular yield-risk objectives of various types of bond investors. CMBSs, which became popular in the early 1990s, had a total outstanding volume of a staggering $682 billion by year-end 2005, then waned some in popularity with the arrival of the financial crisis. These trends toward securitization on the debt side of real estate are examined at Chapter 15C.

Moore, The Return of the Real Estate Investment Trust
11 Prac. Real Est. Law. 49 (Mar. 1995)

The 1990s have seen the return of an old investment vehicle with a new more creative thrust: the Real Estate Investment Trust ("REIT"). Created more than 30 years ago, the REIT tax provisions were enacted by Congress in 1960 to allow small investors an opportunity to invest in real estate ventures at an affordable price. In its simplicity, a REIT is a corporation, association, or trust that owns real estate assets and that has investors who own shares in the REIT. It primarily serves as a financial device that permits investors to purchase shares in a trust. The proceeds are then used to invest in real estate ventures.

THE ADVANTAGES OF REITs

REITs have several features which make them attractive investment vehicles.

No Minimum Investment. One advantage of REITs is that unlike limited partnerships which often require an initial investment of at least $5,000, REITs do not require a minimum investment. REIT shares, like shares of stock, generally cost $10 to $25 per share and permit investors to purchase one share of an investment trust or numerous shares.

Diversification. In addition, since a REIT can own a sizable real estate portfolio, small investors have potential for great diversification.

Both Stock and Real Estate. REITs are also unique in that they have characteristics of both real estate and stock. As stock, REITs permit investors to read a newspaper and map the progress of their investments. As real estate, REITs allow investors the flexibility of "owning" several pieces of property without the burdens associated with ownership. . . .

Liquidity. Another important aspect of a REIT is that since its shares are generally traded on a major stock exchange, it provides liquidity as a traded security. . . .

Tax Advantages. Perhaps the most notable characteristic of a REIT, however, is its tax advantages which allow both investors and corporations to avoid the double taxation inherent in traditional corporate structure. Although REITs must pay corporate income tax, the taxable income is small owing to the Internal Revenue Code's ("IRC") payout requirements. In general, REITs must distribute [90][1] percent of their taxable earnings as dividends to shareholders. Any dividends paid by REITs are deductible from their taxable income. As a result, qualified REITs pay no federal tax on most of the income passed to shareholders, effectively eliminating almost all taxes REITs would otherwise be required to pay. As investors, shareholders are taxed on the dividends they receive and are exposed to limited liability and elimination of double taxation.

HISTORY

With all of its positive attributes and potential for growth, the REIT has not always been viewed favorably by its investors. Because of the REIT industry's dramatic rise in popularity and eventual collapse (taking with it its investors), the REIT is just beginning to regain the confidence of investors and developers as a viable investment tool.

The REIT emerged in 1960 when Congress amended the IRC of 1954 to grant qualifying real estate investment trusts tax-exempt status if specific requirements were met. Despite their tax-exempt status, REITs were largely ignored until the late 1960s and early 1970s because most investors chose to invest in real estate through limited partnerships. But by 1968 REIT assets made small gains,

---

1. As amended by the REIT Modernization Act of 1999.—EDS.

increasing to approximately $1 billion. In 1969, however the pattern of growth changed dramatically, and by 1974, industry assets amounted to over $20 billion.

Between 1969 and 1972, the REIT industry sold about $2 billion each year. It also raised capital by issuing commercial paper and borrowing heavily from banks. This form of borrowing, which equalled only $90 million in 1968, rose to more than $10 billion between 1973 and 1974, raising the industry's debt to equity ratio from 1 to 1 in 1968 to 3.4 to 1 in 1974.

By 1973, rising interest rates, a national recession, and the country's inability to absorb the increased volume of development marked the decline of the REIT.

After the tax reforms of 1986, however, individual investors in real estate limited partnerships were barred from deducting partnership losses from salary or portfolio income. This made the REIT a more desirable vehicle for real estate investment. Consequently, the REIT industry has been growing since 1986 but has shifted its emphasis away from new equity stock offerings and toward debt security as the primary means of raising capital.

TYPES OF REITs

The National Association of Real Estate Investment Trusts, Inc. ("NAREIT") places REITs in three basic categories: equity REITs, mortgage REITs, and hybrid REITs.

Equity REITs. Equity REITs, which comprise approximately 42 percent of the industry, generally invest directly in real estate assets or in joint ventures holding such assets. They also own real estate. Equity REIT portfolios may vary greatly depending on the business strategies they employ. For example, although some invest only in certain types of property such as hospitals, hotels, or restaurant franchises, others focus on specific geographical locations, particular types of tenants such as bankers or a single asset.

The goal, however, is to invest primarily in income-producing properties such as shopping centers, multi-family housing, and commercial and industrial facilities. Equity REITs acquire properties that will increase in value and whose rental stream will increase. A common example is a REIT which invests in a shopping center with a fixed rent in addition to its right to a percentage of sales. Shareholders, who generally receive dividends from rents and sale of properties, benefit from present rental income and from any appreciation in the value of properties when rents increase.

Mortgage REITs. Mortgage REITs do not own real estate but rather make loans that enable others to buy real estate. They invest most of their assets in short-term or long-term mortgages and derive income from fees and interests on the loans. Mortgage REITs account for approximately 49 percent of the real estate investment industry, and their current dividend yield is slightly higher than that of the equity REITs. Their growth potential, however, is usually not as strong as that of the equity REIT.

Hybrid REITs. Hybrid REITs are a combination of both equity and mortgage REITs which invest in both real estate assets and mortgage interests and account for approximately 9 percent of the industry. At least theoretically, such REITs provide shareholders with the potential for appreciation on property while providing steady income from interest on loans.

CHARACTERISTICS OF REITs

A REIT may be open-ended or close-ended. An open-ended REIT may issue and sell additional shares after its initial offering. As a result, a REIT is able to raise additional funds and make further investments. In contrast, a close-ended REIT may not issue any shares after the first offering. Although these REITs have the advantage of protecting investors against dilution of their interests, it also limits the REIT's ability to make investments financed by capital raised through the sale of securities.

REITs may also have either a perpetual or finite life. Patterned after corporations which are generally designed to expand and operate indefinitely, perpetual life REITs have no fixed-termination date. This was the character of early REITs. In 1975, the industry introduced the first finite-life REIT ("FREIT"). These REITs are close-ended and intended to liquidate within a specific time frame, generally 5-15 years.

FREITs typically exist in three stages:

- the acquisition stage during which the real estate is acquired;
- the operating period during which the "properties are managed so as to maximize distribution to shareholders"; and
- liquidation wherein investments are sold to realize capital gains.

To prevent premature liquidation, a FREIT may delay disposition of its portfolio if its trustees deem it appropriate to do so. Approximately 25 percent of all REITs are FREITs.

QUALIFYING AS A REIT

To avoid corporate-level taxation and gain tax advantages, an entity must first elect REIT status and must yearly satisfy four tests as set forth by the IRC and Treasury Department regulations.

Organizational Structure. The organizational structure of REITs must have these five elements. The REIT:

- Must be either a corporation, business trust, or association which is taxable as a corporation. It can not be a bank, insurance company, or other financial institution; nor may it be a partnership. There is no difference in how the entities are treated under federal tax laws. These entities may be treated differently, however, under state law. See IRC §856(a)(1)-(4).
- Must be managed by a board of directors or trustees. See IRC §856(a)(1)-(4).
- Must have fully (freely) transferable shares. A REIT may, however, impose reasonable restrictions to preserve REIT status. See IRC §856(a)(1)-(4).
- Must have at least 100 shareholders of record during no less than 335 days of the taxable year. Accordingly, corporations and other organizations holding REIT stock are each treated as one shareholder. See IRC §856(a)(5) and (b).
- May not be closely held which means that not more than 50 percent of its shares may be held directly or indirectly by five or fewer individuals or groups during the last half of each taxable year. See IRC §§856(h) and 542(a)(2).

Assets Tests. IRC sections 856(c)[4](A) and (c)[5] set forth several requirements an entity must meet to qualify as a REIT. Failure to satisfy just one of these tests disqualifies the entity as a REIT. The requirements are:

- At the end of each quarter of the trust's tax year, at least 75 percent of a REIT's assets must be invested in real property which includes: interest in real property and interest in mortgages on such property; government securities; cash or its equivalent; shares in other REITs; and temporary investments in new capital.
- Not more than 25 percent of all assets can be securities, excluding the assets qualifying under the 75 percent test.
- A REIT may not hold more than 10 percent of the outstanding voting stock securities of another issuer.
  [Under the REIT Modernization Act of 1999, a REIT may not hold securities having a value of more than 10 percent of the total value of the outstanding securities of any one issuer.]
- The stock and other securities of a single issuer may not represent more than 5 percent of the value of a REIT's assets. . . .[2]

Income Tests. In addition to the assets tests, a qualified REIT must meet the following interconnected income tests as set forth in IRC §856(c)(3).

---

2. Under the REIT Modernization Act of 1999, these last three requirements do not apply to "taxable REIT subsidiaries" as defined in the Act. See M. Madison, J. Dwyer, and S. Bender, The Law of Real Estate Financing §4:22 (2016).—EDS.

Qualified Real Estate Sources. At least 75 percent of a REIT's income must be derived from qualified real estate sources which include:

- Gains from the sale or other disposition of equity interests in real property and mortgage loans;
- Mortgage interest[];
- Dividends or other distributions on and gain from the sale of shares in other REITs;
- Income from foreclosure property;
- Mortgage loan fees; and
- Rents from real property.

Note that rents from real property generally do not include rents based on the income [or] profits of any person or rents received from a payor in which the REIT owns 10 percent or more of the stock or equity interest. If a REIT provides non-customary services to a tenant, the rental income will not satisfy the 75 percent income requirement. The IRC makes an exception, however, if the services are provided by an independent contractor and none of the fees generated by non-customary services of the independent contractor are paid to the REIT. IRC §857(a)(3), (c).

Other Income Sources. At least 95 percent of an REIT's annual income must be from sources set forth above as well as from any other dividends, interest, and gains from the sale of stock and securities. Although dividends from regular corporations and interest from obligations that are not secured by real property are excluded from the 75 percent test, they are included in the 95 percent test. IRC §856(c)(2).

If a REIT does not meet the 75 percent or [90] percent income tests, it is subject to 100 percent tax on the amount by which it failed the test. The REIT may also be disqualified for the current tax year as well as four years following the initial disqualification. . . .

Shareholder Distribution. A REIT must annually distribute to shareholders as dividends an amount equal to the sum of at least [90] percent of its ordinary taxable income and [90] percent of its tax net income from foreclosure property. IRC §§857(a)(1), 858.

REASONS FOR RENEWED INTEREST IN . . . REITs

Several factors contribute to the real estate investment trust's resurgence as an attractive investment vehicle. . . . One factor is that the low yields offered by banks, money markets, certificates of deposit ("CDs"), and some pension funds force individual investors to look for higher yielding investments. REITs fill the gap. Since they are required to distribute [90] percent of their taxable income to investors, REITs provide healthy dividends as well as stock appreciation for their investors. According to NAREIT, the total average return on REITs during 1993 was 19 percent. For the last three years, the return for investment trusts has averaged about 22 percent. . . .

Institutional investors have also begun to invest in REITs. In fact, during the first 30 years of the REIT's existence, individual investors accounted for 60 percent of all investments. The trend has changed in the last three years, however, and portfolio advisors and yield-seeking institutions account for 60 percent of the investment in REITs.

An example of a recent institutional investor is pension funds which have always had significant holdings in real estate. In 1993, the California Public Employees' Retirement System ("Calpers"), an $80 billion dollar pension fund, and the nation's largest state employees' pension plan, earmarked 5 percent of its $5 billion in real estate investment holding for REIT investment. With the amendment of section 13149 of the Omnibus Budget Reconciliation Act of 1993 ("OBRA 93"), Pub. L. No. 103-66, 107 Stat. 312, 445, other [pension funds] are expected to follow.

OBRA 93 amends IRC §856(a)(6) which requires that not less than five or fewer individuals own more than 50 percent of a REIT's outstanding shares.

The rule's underlying policy was intended to ensure REITs were widely held. The IRC provision, therefore, restricted pension fund investments. The 1993 Act now permits REITs to look to the beneficiaries to determine the number of shareholders under the five-or-fewer rule. With the legislation, U.S. pension funds have the ability to invest in the industry's best REITs. And with Calpers' display of confidence in the industry, other pension funds will be more willing to invest in REITs, fostering stability in the REIT's market and providing more long-term capital. . . .

UMBRELLA PARTNERSHIP REITS

Real estate owners and developers have further reason for optimism with the recent introduction of umbrella partnership REITs ("UPREITs"). See Treas. Reg. §1.856-3(g). UPREITs allow real estate partnerships to use REITs—which historically invested directly in properties and mortgages—as a course of equity capital without having to endure the immediate tax burdens on the partners.

An individual or partner-owner transferring real estate directly into a new REIT would suffer almost debilitating tax consequences. By using the UPREIT structure, the REIT, as managing general partner, uses the proceeds from its initial public offering ("IPO") to purchase an interest in a limited partnership (Operating Partnership) which owns the real estate. The REIT contributions are convertible into shares of the UPREIT. The REIT's capital contributions are generally used to buy out outside investors, reduce debt on real estate investments, for working capital, and for other appropriate uses.

By admitting the REIT as a new partner, the UPREIT gives the partnership's existing partners the ability to "defer realization of more of their built in gain in appreciated property held by the partnership than if the partnership itself converted to REIT status and raised money through a public offering." For a developer who directly formed a REIT, for example, if the UPREIT structure were not available, there would be less equity in the REIT since much of the money raised would have to be used to pay taxes. . . .

DISADVANTAGES

Although REITs have been touted as the investment vehicle . . ., some factors may cause them to be unattractive to potential real estate investors. A few of the reasons are the following:

- Owing to the extensive restrictions and requirements for qualification and maintenance as a REIT, REITs do not provide the same degree of flexibility as do ordinary corporations and partnerships.
- A REIT may not pass losses to its shareholders.
- Unlike income from real estate partnerships, distributions from REITs are taxed as dividend income and generally cannot be sheltered by passive losses.
- Many states impose a corporate-level tax on REITs.
- Without responsible management, REITs will suffer the same ills of the 1970s and 1980s: mismanagement and conflicts of interest resulting in loss to its investors.
- New issue REITs—which typically have no proven track record—may not be ready to make public offerings, resulting in loss to investors.
- Some REITs mask the poor quality of their assets which negatively affects investors.
- Real estate analysts predict that REITs cannot continue to provide . . . high yields. . . .

NOTES AND QUESTIONS

1. REITs. Creative forms of REITs, such as the finite-life closed-end REIT (FREIT), offer varying and multiple tax and investment objectives in a single product. For example, in the case of a traditional equity REIT, perhaps 20 to 30 percent of the cash distributions can be sheltered from immediate taxation, and some of the shelter is wasted on shareholders such as pension plans and other tax-exempt investors. However, by using an innovative capital structure consisting of one class of common stock for the more daring and tax-oriented investor and another class of preferred stock for the conservative and tax-exempt investor, the creative forms of REITs are able to allocate all of the tax-shelter benefits (produced by depreciation), some of the cash flow, and most of the capital gain (appreciation) to the common shareholders while the preferred stock owners (such as IRAs, pension plans, and retired individuals in need of consistent and dependable monthly income) receive a preferred annual fixed rate of return on their equity investment. See generally Balch, New Twist Added to Finite-Life REITs, 1 Real Est. Fin. J. 77 (Winter 1986).

In addition, to further enhance the investment appeal of REIT shares to the Wall Street investor, the sponsors of finite-life closed-end FREITs have managed to combine the liquidity of REIT shares (which are publicly traded like corporate securities and whose performance is monitored by the National Association of REITs (NAREIT)) with the equity features of the direct ownership of real estate and the direct ownership-styled benefits available to Subchapter S shareholders and to partners in most private limited partnerships. In contrast to an ordinary Subchapter C corporation and most multiple-project publicly held partnerships, the sponsors of FREITs are requiring the consent of existing investors before additional shares can be offered (to prevent their equity from being diluted) and agreeing to sell and liquidate the REIT's underlying assets within a stipulated period of time so that the shareholders will be able to compute their yield (internal rate of return) to maturity and directly benefit from appreciation in the value of the REIT's underlying assets. In this respect, the FREIT resembles a private limited partnership. While the limited partners merely own an indirect interest in the underlying real estate (because the partnership itself holds the legal title), they nevertheless receive direct ownership-style benefits and are able to compute their yield to maturity. For additional reading on REITs, see T. Lynn and M. Bloomfield, Real Estate Investment Trusts (1994); Preble, The Recapitalization of Real Estate, 8 Prob. & Prop. 45 (Mar.-Apr. 1994). For a critical analysis of investment in REITs, see Schooler, The REIT in Defeat, 12 Real Est. Fin. J. 23 (Fall 1996).

> ➤ *Problem 15-1*
> Assume that you are a real estate attorney and one of your clients asks your advice about investing in an equity REIT. What questions would you ask before giving your client investment advice? ◄

2. UPREITs. The UPREIT is an ingenious structure for real estate investments that enables existing real estate partnerships to consolidate their assets and gain access to the public securities market without adverse tax consequences. If using a conventional REIT structure, the partners would transfer their interests directly to the REIT in exchange for REIT shares. Under I.R.C. §351, however, that transfer would be a taxable event (the excess of the fair market value of the REIT stock received over the adjusted basis in the partnership assets contributed) if the transferee is an "investment company." This is the case when the transferee is a REIT and the contribution results in a "diversification" of the transferor's interest. See Treas. Reg. §1-351-1(c)(1) (including REITs within the definition of "investment company"). In contrast to the partner's contribution of its interest to the REIT, the REIT public shareholders will contribute money, and a diversification will have occurred. When the UPREIT structure is employed, however, the original partners do not transfer their interests directly to the UPREIT. Rather, they merely admit the UPREIT as a new partner in the umbrella partnership that holds the contributed properties.

Figure 15-1 illustrates the typical structure of the UPREIT and the umbrella partnership as created in the following sequence of events. First, a number of existing real estate partnerships contribute and combine their interests into a larger multi-property partnership (the "umbrella partnership" or the "UP"). Individual partnership units are exchanged for units (typically as limited partners) in the newly created UP (typically a limited partnership). A REIT (called the "UPREIT") is then created to raise money in the public securities market. The UPREIT will contribute the capital raised to the UP in exchange for a partnership interest, typically as the general partner. The UP will use the UPREIT contribution for purposes that include buying out existing UP interests, paying down partnership debt, or expanding the UP portfolio through new property acquisitions. The UP limited partners are ordinarily given the right to convert their partnership units to UPREIT shares. Although that conversion would be a taxable event, the partners are able to time the exchange at the most desirable point from their individual tax perspective.

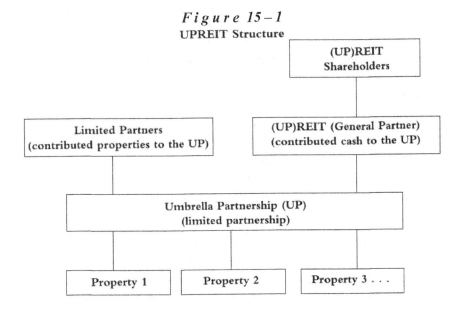

Figure 15–1
UPREIT Structure

For additional reading on UPREITs, see Brody and Raab, A Primer on Real Estate Investment Trusts and Umbrella Partnership Real Estate Investment Trusts, 9 Real Est. Fin. J. 35 (1994); Grant, Tax Planning for Umbrella Partnership REITs, 21 J. Real Est. Taxn. 195 (1994); Scherrer, UPREITs: Their Time Has Come for the Chosen Few, 11 Real Est. Fin. J. 42 (Spring 1996).

B.   REGULATION of REAL ESTATE INVESTMENTS AS SECURITIES

The Securities Act of 1933 requires the registration of public offerings of securities and provides remedies for fraud in the issuance of securities. The following materials emphasize the application of the 1933 Act to real estate investment interests.

Securities and Exchange Commission v. W. J. Howey Co.
328 U.S. 293 (1946)

Mr. Justice MURPHY delivered the opinion of the Court.

This case involves the application of §2(1) of the Securities Act of 1933 to an offering of units of a citrus grove development coupled with a contract for cultivating, marketing and remitting the net proceeds to the investor.

The Securities and Exchange Commission instituted this action to restrain the respondents from using the mails and instrumentalities of interstate commerce in the offer and sale of unregistered and nonexempt securities in violation of §5(a) of the Act. . . .

. . . The respondents, W. J. Howey Company and Howey-in-the-Hills Service, Inc., are Florida corporations under direct common control and management. The Howey Company owns large tracts of citrus acreage in Lake County, Florida. During the past several years it has planted about 500 acres annually, keeping half of the groves itself and offering the other half to the public "to help us finance additional development." Howey-in-the-Hills Service, Inc., is a service company engaged in cultivating and developing many of these groves, including the harvesting and marketing of the crops.

Each prospective customer is offered both a land sales contract and a service contract, after having been told that it is not feasible to invest in a grove unless service arrangements are made. While the purchaser is free to make arrangements with other service companies, the superiority of Howey-in-the-Hills Service, Inc., is stressed. Indeed, 85 percent of the acreage sold during the 3-year period ending May 31, 1943, was covered by service contracts with Howey-in-the-Hills Service, Inc.

The land sales contract with the Howey Company provides for a uniform purchase price per acre or fraction thereof, varying in amount only in accordance with the number of years the particular plot has been planted with citrus trees. Upon full payment of the purchase price the land is conveyed to the purchaser by warranty deed. . . .

The service contract, generally of a 10-year duration without option of cancellation, gives Howey-in-the-Hills Service, Inc., a leasehold interest and "full and complete" possession of the acreage. For a specified fee plus the cost of labor and materials, the company is given full discretion and authority over the cultivation of the groves and the harvest and marketing of the crops. The company is well established in the citrus business and maintains a large force of skilled personnel and a great deal of equipment, including 75 tractors, sprayer wagons, fertilizer trucks and the like. Without the consent of the company, the land owner or purchaser has no right of entry to market the crop; thus there is ordinarily no right to specific fruit. The company is accountable only for an allocation of the net profits based upon a check made at the time of picking. All the produce is pooled by the respondent companies, which do business under their own names.

The purchasers for the most part are non-residents of Florida. They are predominantly business and professional people who lack the knowledge, skill and equipment necessary for the care and cultivation of citrus trees. They are attracted by the expectation of substantial profits. . . . Many of these purchasers are patrons of a resort hotel owned and operated by the Howey Company in a scenic section adjacent to the groves. The hotel's advertising mentions the fine groves in the vicinity and the attention of the patrons is drawn to the groves as they are being escorted about the surrounding countryside. They are told that the groves are for sale; if they indicate an interest in the matter they are then given a sales talk.

It is admitted that the mails and instrumentalities of interstate commerce are used in the sale of the land and service contracts and that no registration statement or letter of notification has ever been filed with the Commission in accordance with the Securities Act of 1933 and the rules and regulations thereunder.

Section 2(1) of the Act defines the term "security" to include the commonly known documents traded for speculation or investment. This definition also includes "securities" of a more variable character, designated by such descriptive terms as "certificate of interest or participation in any profit-sharing agreement,""investment contract" and "in general, any interest or instrument commonly known as a 'security.'" The legal issue in this case turns upon a determination of whether, under the circumstances, the land sales contract, the warranty deed and the service contract together constitute an "investment contract" within the meaning of §2(1). . . .

The term "investment contract" is undefined by the Securities Act or by relevant legislative reports. But the term was common in many state "blue sky" laws in existence prior to the adoption of the federal statute and, although the term was also undefined by the state laws, it had been broadly construed by state courts so as to afford the investing public a full measure of protection. Form was disregarded for substance and emphasis was placed upon economic reality. An investment contract thus came to mean a contract or scheme for "the placing of capital or laying out of money in a way intended to secure income or profit from its employment." State v. Gopher Tire & Rubber Co., 146 Minn. 52, 56, 177 N.W. 937, 938. This definition was uniformly applied by state courts to a variety of situations where individuals were led to invest money in a common enterprise with the expectation that they would earn a profit solely through the efforts of the promoter or of someone other than themselves.

By including an investment contract within the scope of §2(1) of the Securities Act, Congress was using a term the meaning of which had been crystallized by this prior judicial interpretation. It is therefore reasonable to attach that meaning to the term as used by Congress, especially since such a definition is consistent with the statutory aims. In other words, an investment contract for purposes of the Securities Act means a contract, transaction or scheme whereby a person invests his money in a common enterprise and is led to expect profits solely from the efforts of the promoter or a third party, it being immaterial whether the shares in the enterprise are evidenced by formal certificates or by nominal interests in the physical assets employed in the enterprise. Such a definition . . . permits the fulfillment of the statutory purpose of compelling full and fair disclosure relative to the issuance of "the many types of instruments that in our commercial world fall within the ordinary concept of a security." H. Rep. No. 85, 73d Cong., 1st Sess., p. 11. It embodies a flexible rather than a static principle, one that is capable of adaptation to meet the countless and variable schemes devised by those who seek the use of the money of others on the promise of profits.

The transactions in this case clearly involve investment contracts as so defined. The respondent companies are offering something more than fee simple interests in land, something different from a farm or orchard coupled with management services. They are offering an opportunity to contribute money and to share in the profits of a large citrus fruit enterprise managed and partly owned by respondents. They are offering this opportunity to persons who reside in distant localities and who lack the equipment and experience requisite to the cultivation, harvesting and marketing of the citrus products. Such persons have no desire to occupy the land or to develop it themselves; they are attracted solely by the prospects of a return on their investment. Indeed, individual development of the plots of land that are offered and sold would seldom be economically feasible due to their small size. Such tracts gain utility as citrus groves only when cultivated and developed as component parts of a larger area. A common enterprise managed by respondents or third parties with adequate personnel and equipment is therefore essential if the investors are to achieve their paramount aim of a return on their investments. Their respective shares in this enterprise are evidenced by land sales contracts and warranty deeds, which serve as a convenient method of determining the investors' allocable shares of the profits. The resulting transfer of rights in land is purely incidental.

Thus all the elements of a profit-seeking business venture are present here. The investors provide the capital and share in the earnings and profits; the promoters manage, control and operate the enterprise. It follows that the arrangements whereby the investors' interests are made manifest involve investment contracts, regardless of the legal terminology in which such contracts are clothed. The investment contracts in this instance take the form of land sales contracts, warranty deeds and service contracts which respondents offer to prospective investors. And respondents' failure to abide by the statutory and administrative rules in making such offerings, even though the failure result[s] from a bona fide mistake as to the law, cannot be sanctioned under the Act.

This conclusion is unaffected by the fact that some purchasers choose not to accept the full offer of an investment contract by declining to enter into a service contract with the respondents. The Securities Act prohibits the offer as well as the sale of unregistered, non-exempt securities. Hence it is enough that the respondents merely offer the essential ingredients of an investment contract. . . .

Schneider, The Elusive Definition of a Security
14 Rev. Sec. Reg. 981-991 (1981)

. . . The sales pitch of the promoter is of great significance in determining whether the investment is a security. Where investment and economic features or tax benefits are stressed, this militates in favor of finding a security. . . .

Where the seller attracts the buyer by offering assets or facilities for the buyer's individual use or consumption, this generally militates toward finding no security. For example, stock in an apartment co-op was held to be not a security, even though the owner could realize a gain or loss on the eventual sale of his unit, since the purchaser was motivated primarily toward obtaining housing in which to live. The balance may tip the other way, however, with respect to vacation or resort area real estate where the sales pitch is to participate in a rental arrangement so that the purchaser of the unit can generate sufficient operating income to cover costs and can occupy the property himself for a portion of the year on an essentially cost-free basis.

The motive of the buyer—which is probably determined in large part from the sales pitch of the seller—is also very important. If he is oriented toward making an investment for a financial return, this militates toward finding a security. If he is oriented toward acquiring something for his own use or consumption, or if he enters a relationship (e.g., employment) where the investment aspects are not a dominant consideration, this militates toward finding no security.

The more investors there are in a parallel situation, the more likely it is that a security will be found.

[In] SEC v. W. J. Howey Co . . . the Supreme Court defined "investment contract" in terms of four factors (although there was also other broader language in the case):

[A]n investment contract for purposes of the Securities Act means a contract, transaction or scheme whereby a person [1] invests his money [2] in a common enterprise and [3] is led to expect profits [4] solely from the efforts of the promoter or a third party. . . .

The Court in *Howey* stated that the definition of securities "embodies a flexible rather than a static principle, one that is capable of adaptation to meet the countless and variable schemes devised by those who seek the use of the money of others on the promise of profits." 328 U.S. at 299. While most of the cases continue to recite the four-prong *Howey* test, each of the factors has been eroded in at least some contexts.

(1) It is quite clear that the investor need not invest *"money."* The investor may contribute a note, other securities, or assets or property of almost any nature in a transaction, and can still receive a "security" in return. . . . Probably anything constituting legal consideration in a contract law sense would suffice.

(2) The *"common enterprise"* test suggests by its plain meaning a number of investors who stand in a similar relationship to a business in which they invest in common—so called "horizontal commonality," which is illustrated by multiple shareholders or debentureholders of an issuing corporation. . . .

(3) The *"expectation of profits"* need not be in the form of a normal investment return. The "profit" can be in the form of the use of recreational facilities that the investor finances, occupancy of vacation real estate, etc. The expected "profit" may also be in the form of capital appreciation when an asset, rather than an interest in an ongoing business, is sold.

(4) The requirement that profits be realized *"solely from the efforts of the promoter or a third party"* has been very much eroded in the pyramid sales cases, where it is clear that the investor himself is expected to contribute significantly to the profit potential. . . .

. . . . *Notes, Other Evidences of Indebtedness, and Participations Therein.* There are many cases dealing with various forms of indebtedness that may or may not be evidenced by a promissory note. While the term "note" is included in the definition of security, many of the cases have held that notes in the context of normal commercial transactions are not securities within the contemplation of the securities laws. Typically, the cases involve attempts to invoke the antifraud provisions rather than a challenge to the nonregistration of the note.

Cases reach a variety of results and articulate a number of approaches, including: a "commercial"/"investment" dichotomy; a "risk capital" test; a literal approach; and a "strong family resemblance" test. For example, United American Bank of Nashville v. Gunter, 620 F.2d 1108 (5th Cir. 1980) (bank loan to an individual for the purpose of purchasing stock, secured by shares purchased, was not a security); AMFAC Mortgage Corp. v. Arizona Mall of Tempe, Inc., 583 F.2d 426 (9th Cir. 1978) (no security found when "risk capital" test applied to promissory note between mortgage company and shopping center builder); Exchange National Bank of Chicago v. Touche Ross & Co., 544 F.2d 1126 (2d Cir. 1976) (subordinated loan to a brokerage firm found to be a security in reliance on the "strong family resemblance" test); Emisco Industries, Inc. v. Pro's Inc., 543 F.2d 38 (7th Cir. 1976) (note given for purchase of business assets was not a security); Great Western Bank & Trust v. Kotz, 532 F.2d 1252 (9th Cir. 1976) (bank loan was not a security); Lino v. City Investing Co., 487 F.2d 689 (3d Cir. 1973) (a note given for a commercial franchise was not a security); Banco Nacional de Costa Rica v. Bremar Holdings Corp., 492 F. Supp. 364 (S.D.N.Y. 1980) (short-term notes given to a financier to obtain initial "bridge" financing toward the purchase of equipment were securities—applying the 2d Circuit "strong family resemblance" test); Rispo v. Spring Lake Mews, Inc., 485 F. Supp. 462 (E.D. Pa. 1980) (short-term note coupled with bonus of stock was not a security); SEC v. Diversified Industries Inc., 465 F. Supp. 104 (D.D.C. 1979) (long-term note given by a company to purchase investment real estate from a trust affiliated with an insider was a security—containing a good summary of various prior decisions). . . .

Participations in a commercial note or certificate of deposit may themselves be a separate "security" issued by the first-tier creditor, who in turn divides his interest in the note or certificate among other participants. The participation may be a security even if the underlying note arises in a commercial transaction with the first-tier creditor and is not a security. Lehigh Valley Trust Co. v. Central National Bank of Jacksonville, 409 F.2d 989 (5th Cir. 1969). . . . But participation interests in a loan were deemed not to be a security in other cases. See American Fletcher Mortgage Co. v. U.S. Steel Credit Corp., 635 F.2d 1247 (7th Cir. 1980). . . .

. . . *Partnership Interests* . . . Limited partnership interests are generally classified as securities. For most purposes, a general partnership interest is not treated as a security. However, when a general partner is expected to be a passive investor who will not participate in the management of the business, it may be argued that his interest is a security. . . . Conversely, it might be argued that the owner of a limited partnership interest does not have a security if he is actively involved in the management of the business in fact—e.g., if he is also a general partner. . . .

NOTES AND QUESTIONS

1. Definition of a Security. The term "security" in §(2)(1) of the Securities Act of 1933 has been liberally construed to include modern forms of real estate investment consistent with the broad protection envisioned by Congress. Subsumed under the definition of security is the term "investment contract," which, in the opinion of the Supreme Court in Securities and Exchange Commission v. W. J. Howey Co., includes any "scheme whereby a person invests his money in a common enterprise and is led to expect profits solely from the efforts of the promoter or third party." Thus, the term "security" encompasses such interests as an investment share held by a limited partner or passive coventurer in a joint venture. See, for example, Goodman v. Epstein, 582 F.2d 388 (7th Cir. 1978), cert. denied, 440 U.S. 939 (1979) (limited partners' interests held securities).

> ➤ *Problem 15-2*

Based on the approach taken by the Court in *Howey*, which, if any, of the following transactions should be treated as the offering of a security?

1. the public sale of condominium units involving a so-called rental pool arrangement, whereby the promoter undertakes to rent the units on behalf of any absentee owner (see Securities Act Release No. 5347 (Jan. 4, 1972); Wals v. Fox Hills Dev. Corp., 24 F.3d 1016 (7th Cir. 1994))
2. the sale of raw land by a developer that promises common infrastructure improvements that will generate profits by appreciation in land value (compare Adams v. Cavanagh, Communities Corp., 847 F. Supp. 1390 (N.D. Ill. 1994), with Rodriguez v. Banco Central Corp., 990 F.2d 7 (1st Cir. 1993))
3. the offering of investment shares in a REIT (see Securities Act Release Nos. 33-4298, 34-6419, and 1C-3140, 25 Fed. Reg. 12177 (1960));
4. the sale of stock in a cooperative housing corporation where some of the purchasers hope to immediately resell their co-op units for a substantial profit (see United Housing Found. v. Forman, 421 U.S. 837 (1975), and Grenader v. Spitz, 537 F.2d 612 (2d Cir.), cert. denied, 429 U.S. 1009 (1976))
5. the lease of some space in a large shopping center where the lessor exerts some management control over the lessee's business and receives a rental geared to the net income of the lessee ("percentage rental") (see Klein v. Arlen Realty & Dev. Corp., 410 F. Supp. 1261 (E.D. Pa. 1976), and Cordas v. Specialty Restaurants, 470 F. Supp. 780 (D. Or. 1979))
6. participating mortgage featuring a kicker geared to the borrower's net income (see Vargo, Equity Participation by the Institutional Lender: The Security Status Issue, 26 S. Tex. L.J. 225 (1985))
7. the sale of time shares in a resort condominium where each purchaser, who owns his interest in fee simple, can only resell the interest back to the developer at a price equal to the original purchase price less a discount and where the aggregate price of the fractional interests exceeds by three times the market value of whole units that are being sold in comparable condominiums (compare Securities Act Release No. 33-6253 (1980) with SEC no-action letter re The Innisfree Corp. (May 7, 1973))
8. the sale and leaseback of commercial real estate to a single purchaser-lessor, who purchases the property based on the anticipated profits as estimated by the seller-lessee (compare United States v. Jones, 712 F.2d 1316 (9th Cir.), cert. denied sub nom., Webber v. United States, 464 U.S. 986 (1983), with Hart v. Pulte Homes of Mich. Corp., 735 F.2d 1001 (6th

> Cir. 1984); Almaden Plaza Assocs. v. United Trust Fund Ltd. Partnership,
> 123 Or. App. 372, 860 P.2d 289 (1993))
> 9. the interest of a passive investor who is a general partner in a partnership
> as compared to the interest of a limited partner in a partnership who is
> actively involved in management (see Williamson v. Tucker, 645 F.2d
> 404 (5th Cir.), cert. denied, 454 U.S. 897 (1981); Sobel, Note, A Rose
> May Not Always Be a Rose: Some General Partnership Interests Should
> Be Deemed Securities under the Federal Securities Acts, 15 Cardozo L.
> Rev. 1313 (1994))
> 10. undivided interests in office buildings, retail centers, or other real estate,
> sold under a tenancy-in-common co-ownership structure (see SEC
> response to OMNI Brokerage Inc. (Jan. 14, 2009) (characterizing
> proposed TIC business models as securities)) ◄

2. Exemptions from Registration

a. The Private Offering Exemption. Section 4(2) of the Securities Act of 1933 provides that the registration requirement of the Act shall not apply to "transactions by an issuer not involving any public offering." Observe that the "private offering" exemption, like the "intrastate" and "small offering" exemptions discussed below, applies only to transactions and not to the securities themselves. This means that even if the issuer gains exemption from registration by complying with the requirements of a particular exemption, the purchaser nevertheless must obtain its own exemption if one is available in the event it decides to reoffer, subdivide, or otherwise dispose of the securities. Both the Securities and Exchange Commission (SEC) and the courts have applied a facts-and-circumstances test to determine whether a transaction is a public or a private offering. In light of the Act's purpose "to protect investors by promoting full disclosure of information thought necessary to informed investment decisions," the Supreme Court, in Securities and Exchange Commission v. Ralston Purina, 346 U.S. 119 (1953), devised a two-pronged test under §4(2) that requires with respect to all offerees that: (1) they be able "to fend for themselves"; and (2) they "have access to the type of information that registration would disclose." Other factors deemed relevant under the case law are (1) the number of offerees (as well as their degree of sophistication), (2) the size and manner of the offering, and (3) the relationship of the offerees to the issuer.

To proffer guidance to issuers and investors, the SEC promulgated Regulation D (SEC Release No. 33-6389), which consists of the following Rules: (1) Rules 501 and 502, which stipulate general conditions and definitions for the exemption under Regulation D; (2) Rule 503, which specifies a uniform notice of sale form, Form D, for transactions that are exempt under Regulation D; (3) Rule 506 (explained below); and (4) Rule 504, which qualifies offerings and sales of $5 million or less during any 12-month period unless the issuer is disqualified as a "bad actor." Unless the Federal Reserve Board exempts offerings from its restrictions on installment payments (Regulations T, C, U, and X), such offerings must be paid for in single lump sum payments.

Rule 506 permits sales to 35 purchasers plus an unlimited number of accredited investors (defined below). In contrast to Rule 504, there is no limitation on the dollar amount of the offering. Each actual purchaser (as opposed to a mere offerer who does not purchase) who does not meet the criteria for an accredited investor must be qualified as a person who (either alone or with his or her purchaser representative) has such knowledge and experience in financial and business matters that she is capable of evaluating the risks and merits of the prospective investment. Regulation D adopts the concept of an "accredited investor," which includes, among other categories, any natural person whose net worth at the time of purchase is at least $1 million (Rule 501(a)(5)), or any natural person who has had income in excess of $200,000 in each of the last two years and who reasonably anticipates an income of $200,000 in the current year (Rule 501(a)(6)). Finally, observe that Regulation D is not exclusive in scope, so a transaction that does not qualify under the Regulation may nonetheless be exempt under §4(2) of the Act as a private offering if it meets the somewhat vague requirements imposed by case law. For an in-depth discussion of Regulation D, see Haft and Fass, Federal Securities Laws and Their Impact on Tax Sheltered Investments, 1988 Tax Sheltered Investments Handbook §4.03.

b. *The Intrastate Exemption.* Section 3(a) of the Act provides an exemption for securities offered and sold only to persons who reside in the same state where the issuer is a resident and doing business, relying instead on state law, if any, to regulate the offering. Under Rule 147, if the issuer is a corporation, limited partnership, or REIT, it will be deemed to be a resident of the state in which it is incorporated or organized and has its principal place of business. The issuer will be deemed to be "doing business" within a state where either (1) at least 80 percent of its gross revenues are derived from the operation of a business or property or from rendering of services within the state, (2) at least 80 percent of its assets are located in such state; (3) at least 80 percent of its net proceeds from the sale of its securities are used in connection with its business or property or rendering of services within such state, or (4) a majority of its employees are based in such state. Suppose that a transaction qualifies under Rule 147 and that the issuer explicitly provides in all of its offerings and promotional materials that the transaction is limited to residents of the state in which the issuer is organized and doing business and the issuer requires that each purchaser execute an affidavit attesting that such person is a resident of the state. Would the exemption be lost if it is later discovered that one of the original purchasers is not a resident of the state? See Rule 147 (specifying a compliance standard of reasonable belief at the time of the offer and sale). Recognizing the broad interstate reach of the Internet, Rule 147A adopted in 2016 allows offers through such mass media, so long as sales are restricted to residents of the state of the issuer's residence.

c. *The Small Offering Exemption.* Under Section 3(b) of the Act and pursuant to Regulation A, an exemption is also available for offerings of $5 million or less, provided that the issuer files a short-form registration statement, or "offering circular," with the regional SEC office containing the financial information and disclosures required by Regulation A. 17 C.F.R. §§230.251-230.264. Pursuant to the Jumpstart Our Business Startups (JOBS) Act seeking to expand use of Regulation A, the SEC adopted rules in 2015 to allow offerings up to $25 and $50 million in a 12-month period upon specified conditions.

3. Antifraud and Criminal Liability. Even if the offering is entirely exempt from federal registration under the private or intrastate exemptions, the participants in the transaction may be subject to both civil and criminal liability if they should commit fraud or make any misrepresentation in connection with the offer or sale of a security. See Securities Act of 1933 §§12(2), 17.

4. State Regulation of Securities. In addition to federal regulation of securities, most jurisdictions have enacted statutes that both regulate the offering of securities within the state and sometimes also protect purchasers of certain types of real estate interests (such as condominiums and cooperatives). See, for example, Cal. Bus. & Prof. Code §§11000 et seq.; N.Y. Gen. Bus. Law §352-e. State statutes regulating the sale of securities are commonly referred to as "blue sky" laws because they are designed to prevent "speculative schemes which have no more basis than so many feet of blue sky." Hall v. Geigerlones Co., 242 U.S. 539 (1917). Most of these statutes provide for registration of securities by the issuer and for the licensing of dealers and salespersons. The Uniform Securities Act (as approved by the National Conference of Commissioners on Uniform State Laws) has been the prototype for many of these statutes. While §402(b) of that Act contains a quasi-private offering exemption, any offering that qualifies under §4(2) of the federal Securities Act of 1933 may nonetheless fall within the pale of a particular state statute; hence, the only safe course of action for the issuer's counsel is to canvass the law of the state where the transaction will occur. In that regard, there are a number of looseleaf services, such as the CCH Blue Sky Law Reporter, that detail the important securities provisions of each state.

THE ETHICAL REAL ESTATE LAWYER

Disclosures of Wrongdoing

Prompted by the Enron corporate scandal, Congress enacted the Sarbanes-Oxley Act in 2002 authorizing the SEC to set minimum standards for attorneys who are representing securities-issuing companies before the Commission. Subsequently, the SEC adopted rules to permit (but not require) lawyers to reveal to the SEC without the company's consent any confidential information the attorney reasonably believes necessary to prevent the company from committing a material securities violation likely to cause substantial financial injury to the company or its investors. 17 C.F.R. §205.3. Going beyond this permissive disclosure, which is consistent with the ethics standards in many states, the SEC has proposed a requirement that the lawyer whose client fails to respond appropriately to internal warnings of corporate misconduct withdraw from representation and that either the lawyer or the company report the withdrawal to the Commission. Do you think this requirement is necessary to deter corporate wrongdoing? What are the risks to the lawyer-client relationship under such a standard of noisy withdrawal?

C.   SECURITIZATION ON THE DEBT SIDE OF COMMERCIAL REAL ESTATE

In Chapters 7 and 11 we discuss how a real estate borrower such as Dan Developer can use component financing techniques to increase his loan amount and thereby leverage his cost of acquiring and constructing income-producing real estate. For example, by severing the land from the improvements and financing each component separately, it is possible for the sum of the financing *parts* (for example, sale and leaseback of the land plus leasehold mortgage on land and fee mortgage on the building) to be greater for Dan than the *whole* (for example, fee mortgage on the land and building). See Chapter 11C. Another example of how Dan might increase his overall financing by splitting the land from the improvements would be a high (loan-to-value) ratio purchase money mortgage from the seller of the land, who then subordinates its lien on the fee so Dan can obtain a first mortgage loan from some institutional lender (such as Ace Insurance Co.) to finance the cost of both the land and the improvements. See Chapter 7B3.

Real estate innovators have taken the next logical step, namely, the securitization of commercial real estate. If the land can be severed from the improvements and the legal possession severed from the fee ownership as a way of expanding the debt and equity pie, then why not fragment the debt and equity interests themselves into small liquid segments that resemble publicly held stock so that such investment shares can be marketed in the public rather than private securities markets? As discussed at Chapter 15A, supra, this has already happened on the equity (ownership) side of real estate with the advent of the equity REIT.

However, the pace of securitization has been slower on the debt side of commercial real estate. The notion that mortgage debt could be fragmented and securitized in the form of so-called mortgage-backed securities (MBSs) as a way of linking the securities and mortgage markets originated in the secondary mortgage market[3] for residential mortgages in 1970. However, commercial

---

3. The difference between the primary and secondary mortgage markets is that in the primary mortgage market a lender who originates a mortgage loan retains the loan as an asset in its investment portfolio and usually collects the amortization and interest payments during the term of

mortgage-backed bonds (CMBBs) did not appear on the public financing scene until 1985 when, for example, the $200 million public offering by Olympia & York Maiden Lane Finance Corp. demonstrated to Wall Street the potential market for these securities. But if the securitization of residential mortgages started back in 1970, why the delay in the development of the CMBB? The excerpt that follows answers this question and also attempts to explain why the trend toward securitization may someday revolutionize the way in which commercial real estate is financed in this country. Indeed, in the opinion of one commentator, given the vast opportunities in real estate, the CMBB "dwarfs any other [security], including corporate debt, in terms of [its] potential size."[4]

Richards, "Gradable and Tradable": The Securitization of Commercial Real Estate Mortgages
16 Real Est. L.J. 99 (1987)

"Securitization" is the financing of real estate through the nontraditional methods of stocks and bonds—known collectively as "mortgage-backed securities" (MBSs)—in order to expand the available lending community and to use more efficient (cheaper) primary and secondary capital sources. The instrument and the secondary market continue to energize real estate finance with a spiral of innovation. In the past three years, the investment banking community has adopted this technique, long familiar in the secondary market for residential mortgages, to the financing of commercial office buildings. "Is the concept of securitizing commercial real estate a contradiction in terms, like jumbo shrimp or military intelligence? Have we bridged the gap that lies between securities, which is a liquid homogeneous product, and commercial property, which has neither of these attributes?" If so, securitization is the wave of the future; if not, it may remain only a highly specialized device available to a few borrowers with a handful of prime properties in the biggest U.S. cities.

the loan. By contrast, if the lender sells the loan, in whole or in part, to another lender, investor, or governmental agency, the transaction is deemed to be a resale, or "second sale"—hence the term "secondary mortgage market."

The traditional secondary mortgage market is a financial network that connects mortgage originators who lend money to home buyers with government-related and private investors who purchase these residential mortgage loans. By selling the loans they originate to federally sponsored agencies such as the Federal Home Loan Mortgage Corporation (Freddie Mac) and the Federal National Mortgage Association (Fannie Mae), thrift institutions and other lenders were able to replenish their supply of loanable funds and originate new loans (both commercial real estate and residential loans) in the primary mortgage market. For a comprehensive discussion of the residential secondary mortgage market before the mortgage meltdown, see M. Dennis, Residential Mortgage Lending: Principles and Practices (5th ed. 2003); The Handbook of Mortgage Banking: A Guide to the Secondary Mortgage Market (J. Kinney and R. Garrigan eds. 1985).

4. This observation was made by Ron DiPasquale, a senior vice president and manager of mortgage security trading at Merrill Lynch Mortgage Capital, as reported in Standard & Poor's Creditweek, Feb. 24, 1986, at 13.

MORTGAGES VS. SECURITIES

Institutional investors have preferred government securities and corporate bonds to mortgages because these securities were easily evaluated, commonly traded, and produced a regular cash flow. Mortgages, by contrast, have been viewed as "second class" investment assets, with four significant drawbacks.

First, mortgages have historically paid both interest and principal monthly, whereas government and corporate bonds pay interest semiannually and all principal at maturity. Since the investor must reinvest principal and interest income more frequently, transaction costs and interest rate risk are greater for mortgages, and the value assumed for the reinvestment rate is more significant.

Second, the cash flow and maturity of a mortgage are deemed more uncertain because the borrower can supplement the required monthly payments, or repay the entire loan, or default at any time. Investors, therefore, have difficulty determining the maturity and expected yield on the mortgage. The relationship between prepayments and interest rates reduces the investor's yield, whether interest rates rise or fall. When interest rates rise, prepayments fall because borrowers hold their properties longer or home buyers assume the existing mortgages when the properties are sold; the investor has less cash to reinvest at the new high rate. Similarly, when interest rates fall, prepayments increase because borrowers refinance or sell their properties. The investor then has more cash to reinvest at the new lower rate.

A third disadvantage of investing in whole mortgages in the commercial property market (and to a lesser extent in the residential property market) is that they are not homogeneous commodities (due to the uniqueness of the terms of each such mortgage and the complexity of the property securing it) and are, therefore, less marketable than conventional securities. They are regulated essentially by state and local laws that vary considerably and are parochial: An isolated downturn in a local economy or a material disaster can affect them sharply.

Finally, servicing and originating mortgages entail substantial administrative costs per dollar of investment. The cumbersome mechanics of transferring a package of mortgage loans to a new investor; the fact that "servicing" of mortgage loans (collection and processing of monthly payments, collection of delinquent payments, commencement of foreclosure, application of mortgagors' escrows to insurance premiums and real estate taxes, and provision of monthly remittances and reports) requires a large staff and data processing equipment; and the need to make detailed evaluation of credit quality of the loans all combined to make mortgage loans historically unattractive to passive investors and inhibited the development of an active secondary market, which therefore tended to attract only traditional mortgage investors, such as savings and loan associations. . . .

RESIDENTIAL MORTGAGE SECURITIZATION

The securitization of residential mortgages, invented in 1970, is a now-familiar . . . story: Pools of mortgages for one-to-four-family homes, sold since the Great Depression by originators to financial institutions with an appetite for long-term loans, have been replaced as trading instruments by mortgage-backed securities, created when mortgages from one or more lenders are packaged together and sold to an investment house or government-sponsored agency that finances purchases by issuing securities backed by the mortgages so obtained (hence, "mortgage-backed securities"). . . .

COMMERCIAL MORTGAGE SECURITIZATION

Key differences between residential and commercial loans have previously prevented the development of an equally successful market for securities backed by commercial mortgages. Home mortgages are relatively homogeneous: The underlying real estate tends to be similar, so that documents are readily standardized, loans are easily pooled by age and rate, and the federally sponsored credit agencies and private mortgage insurers all provide backing.

In contrast, no two commercial properties are alike, and they obtain their respective values from such factors as individual markets, leases, and changes in supply and demand, which vary region by region and even block by block. These heterogeneous mortgages are harder to pool and are virtually always meant to secure "nonrecourse" obligations (i.e., no recourse to the credit of the borrower, only to the mortgaged asset). The lender's reliance not on an individual mortgagor's income but on the property's cash flow means that credit analysis must be much more highly detailed. The idiosyncrasies of risk, market, lease structure, local economy, and location are all quite unlike analyzing the credit risk in a homogeneous package of home loans by looking at payment histories.

The traditional single-lender system for financing commercial real estate was essentially an oligopoly, with a limited number of players offering minimal liquidity and little price differentiation. This meant that in the private market, the rate for financing a New York City office building, currently the cream of U.S. commercial real estate, is not as far away from the rate for a less prime property as it ought to be, given the risk differential, and so the "issuer" (borrower) pays a premium for the traditional market's relative lack of liquidity.[22] Commercial real estate mortgage-backed securities are the result of an effort to "disintermediate" real estate financing by going directly to the financial markets.

New investment banking efforts to "securitize" the large commercial mortgage, for single or pooled properties, have resulted from the sheer size of the

22. In the words of Paul Reichmann of Olympia & York Developments: "The industry has been paying silly rates, prime-plus rates, for development, and we don't see why we should pay more than General Motors or an industrial company during the development period." Shapiro, "Olympia & York's American Empire," Institutional Investor, Feb. 1986, at 8.

commercial mortgage market, the dramatic growth in the cost of finance of large projects which few single institutions can finance alone, increasing pressures for lender flexibility, perceived inefficiencies in the market for commercial real estate debt (the inability of small institutions to "buy in" to larger projects and/or achieve geographical diversification of portfolios without the substantial overhead of branch offices), and the resounding success of the residential secondary mortgage market. . . .

To date, commercial real estate mortgage-backed securities have taken a variety of forms, including credit lease-backed financings, letters of credit or surety-backed notes or commercial paper, and, in what may be the most significant development, the issuance of rated or unrated notes or bonds secured by the pledge of a mortgage. . . .

Generally speaking, there are two advantages from the owner's or developer's viewpoint [over traditional mortgage borrowing]. The first advantage is the lower cost of borrowing: Even taking into account the expenses of underwriting, any necessary "credit support," and higher legal fees (of which more below), there may be an annual savings of up to 50 basis points over more conventional financing sources. The second advantage is the chance to obtain access to a larger aggregate amount of financing by tapping several markets simultaneously. For the investor, these securities have to date provided a higher rate of return than securities considered by the rating agencies to be of similar risk. Insurance companies regard securitization as an easy way to sell off existing loans and restructure the balance between the assets and liabilities. All institutions hope to make a profit on the interest rate difference between the mortgages they create and the bonds they sell.

The merger of real estate finance with bond finance is still evolutionary, in continuing resolution of the differing market philosophies of real estate finance ("wait and see and hold" on sour commercial loans, where terms can be changed midstream to permit substantial recoupment) and of bond finance for the bondholders (the timely and ultimate payment evaluation relating to credit risk, without default). The rating agencies must mediate between the two. . . .

In a perfect world, the length of time taken by the rating process, with all documents, should be about four weeks. In the real world, as some participants delay or engage in tough negotiations, or play interest trends (in which hedging may be equivalent to 3-4 basis points a month), six to eight weeks is more realistic. In conventional real estate finance, the insurance company or other institutional lender takes the hedging risks on the sixty-to-ninety-day term of its commitment, but in a mortgaged-backed securities financing, the borrower is bearing the risk of delay in the deal.

The cost of obtaining a rating for a single project varies with the rating agency and with the deal. At Standard & Poor's, on a property specific rating, the fee for property analysis through credit support table delivery is . . . usually computed as [approximately] 0.04 percent of the issue's proceeds (4 basis points). . . .

Other transaction costs of securitized real estate financings can be substantial. Investment banking fees are the same or higher than standard mortgage commitment fees, accounting fees are larger, and legal fees (for real estate, tax, corporate, and securities lawyers) are also higher than conventional mortgage financing. However, even these higher transaction costs do not make the "all in" cost higher than conventional financing, since borrowing in the capital markets is typically 0.25 percent to 0.50 percent cheaper than borrowing from institutions. The benefits in pricing outrun the costs in securitization. The real risk, as noted above, is in a shift in interest rates during the financing's structuring.

TRANSACTIONAL STRUCTURE OF A COMMERCIAL MORTGAGE-BACKED SECURITIES FINANCING

The participants and documents for a commercial real estate mortgaged-backed securities transaction reflect the melding of classical real estate financing with today's asset-based structured financing. From real estate lawyers and their familiar world come the concepts and functions of the mortgagor who borrows funds for financing or refinancing his project, with such debt being evidenced by note(s) and secured by a mortgage or deed of trust held by a mortgagee or trustee, constituting a first secured lien on the collateral (the mortgaged property), and sometimes further secured by a letter of credit or other form of guarantee of payment.

Added to this, from the world of structured asset-based finance come the concepts and functions of the issuer of notes, mortgaged-backed securities or bonds, which have been rated by a national rating agency (Standard & Poor's, Moody's, or Duff and Phelps); the managing underwriters, who manage the offer and sale of the securities to the bondholders, who have a first-perfected security interest in the collateral (both physical assets of the issuer and further credit supports); and the bond trustee holding an indenture, empowering him to act in the best interests of the bondholders, including foreclosing on the collateral.

In a "plain vanilla" commercial real estate mortgaged-backed securities transaction, then, the property owner ("Owner") organizes a single-purpose entity (the "Issuer") to issue and sell debt evidenced by notes (the "Securities") under an indenture (the "Indenture") between the Issuer and the indenture trustee (the "Trustee"). Simultaneously with the issuance and sale of the Securities, the Issuer uses the proceeds to make a loan to the Owner, evidenced by a nonrecourse note (the "Note") in favor of the Issuer, corresponding in aggregate principal amount, interest, maturity, and payment terms to the Securities. The obligations of the Owner under the Note are secured by a mortgage (the "Mortgage") from the Owner as mortgagor to the Issuer, as mortgagee, covering the mortgagor's land and buildings, fixtures and equipment, and leases and rents and certain other rights associated therewith (the "Mortgaged Property").

Also simultaneously, as security for its obligations under the Indenture, the Issuer assigns and pledges to the Trustee, for the benefit of the holders of the

Securities, the interests of the Issuer as mortgagee under the Mortgage and as holder of the Owner's Mortgage Note. The obligations of the Issuer are further secured by certain debt service credit supports (the "Credit Supports"), which may be initially comprised of irrevocable, unconditional letters of credit, surety bonds, or other guarantees or cash equivalents, in favor of the Trustee.

The offer and sale of the Securities are arranged on behalf of the Issuer by a group of managing underwriters (the "Managers") who have designated a representative ("Representative") as lead or co-lead managers of the issue. The Owner uses the proceeds of the Securities sale to refinance the existing mortgages on the Mortgaged Property, to provide the Credit Supports for the Securities, to reimburse the Issuer for the costs of the transaction, and to distribute the balance, less other closing costs, to its principals.

Since, as its name clearly indicates, a mortgaged-backed security is a debt offering, the procedures leading to the offer and sale of the Securities (the "Closing," held at the offices of the Representative in, say, London) will be familiar to corporate lawyers who have effected registered or unregistered public offerings. In a typical Eurodollar offering (avoiding, for the sake of this illustrative description, the additional complications of a U.S. registration, for reasons discussed more fully below), a listing agent for the Issuer (the "Listing Agent") submits to the overseas stock exchange for comment a draft of the memorandum describing the features of the offer (the "offering Memorandum"). After appropriate revisions, the application to list the Securities is approved and the final offering Memorandum and all related documents are provided to the Stock Exchange. . . .

DISCLOSURE

Mortgage-backed obligations are offered and sold as domestic private placements, as domestic public offerings, and recently, as public offerings in the Euromarkets. Several financings of this type have been privately placed to large groups of institutional investors who rely on the rating rather than on conducting their own in-depth due diligence. These placements can be made pursuant to the safe-harbor provisions of Regulation D or, where the purchasers are institutional, in a transaction exempt from registration by reason of Section 4(2) of the Securities Act of 1933. . . .

Reluctance to comply with the detailed and time-consuming disclosure requirements of the 1933 Act is one reason many offerings of mortgage-backed securities are structured either as private placements or . . . as domestically unregistered public offerings in the European market.[5] . . .[SEC] releases and subsequent no action letters have been interpreted to permit domestic private placements to be made concurrently with public offerings in Europe. Eurodollar

---

5. See Regulation S, 17 C.F.R. §§230.901-230.904 (exempting offers and sales of securities outside the United States from the registration requirements of the Securities Act of 1933).—EDS.

offerings are customarily listed on the London or Luxembourg stock exchanges, primarily for the purpose of qualifying as legal investments for European institutional purchasers. The European Economic Community [EEC] has issued directives with the force of law in the United Kingdom and Luxembourg that include minimum disclosure requirements, and each exchange has adopted its own listing requirements (with London the more stringent) that reflect the EEC directives. . . .

CONCLUSION

The future for securitized commercial real estate may indeed, as its backers claim, be the beginning of a new phase in real estate finance . . .[G]reater activity is expected for several reasons. Just as the stock exchange's promotion of common stocks made investment in U.S. companies extremely popular after World War II, securitization may make real estate available to a wide range of investors. The market does not yet have all the sheen of the established securities markets, but the glitter is unlikely to dim. The principal forces behind the market—the need for liquidity and flexibility and the continued demand for commercial real estate credit at the lowest interest rates—are not about to disappear.

Under this view, the ratings will permit investors to analyze real estate the same way they would any highly rated debt offering, and new investors will be attracted to the market, so that real estate financing costs may begin to approach those of familiar AA corporate issues rather than the traditionally higher rates paid by borrowers in conventional real estate lending. Optimistic investment bankers predict that Standard & Poor's will soon be ready to issue ratings for warehouse-type industrial properties and shopping centers, as well as for non-AA ratings (i.e., A and below, which would be ideal for smaller properties financed through pools). In terms of the secondary market, perhaps a trading market could follow the residential mortgage market in the establishment of some sort of national mortgage securities exchange (under consideration by the board of Fannie Mae), with the aim of heightened competition, improved liquidity, less pricing distortion, and increased information for investors.

On the other hand, the market acceptance of commercial mortgage-backed products is still an open question. The ratings criteria for commercial projects not relying on credit enhancement are extremely tightly drawn and conservative. There is some sense that the European trading community is not sufficiently aware of real estate-backed paper, while domestic investors remain cautious about the new product and commercial properties that they have had no experience in analyzing. . . . Although the growth of the rating system may alleviate some fears, it could prove just too expensive to secure a rating for the majority of buildings. And it may be true, as has been charged, that Wall Street firms are not as interested in the underlying properties and their potential for fund-raising as they are in generating a market for the securities and in the commissions they will make trading those securities over time.

As the market moves . . . toward domestic public issues and private placements, we can expect to see more publicly registered deals and a concomitant rise in investor confidence. Even so, it may be a long time before the new market produces enough investment advisers who know both how to analyze a real estate investment and how to think about the workings of capital markets, and investors who are prepared to buy offerings backed by underlying commercial mortgages, without depending on the credit of a major tenant. For the present, it may be said that securitization of [commercial] real estate has real meaning only in a limited sense: It appears to work for large, established projects with major creditworthy tenants in known real estate centers such as Manhattan.

The following form of offering memorandum illustrates a representative commercial mortgage-backed securities offering by a New York developer who sought to raise capital from the securities markets in lieu of traditional mortgage financing.

Offering Memorandum, Olympia & York Maiden Lane Finance Corp.
(Dec. 17, 1985)

OFFERING MEMORANDUM SUMMARY

The following summary is qualified in its entirety by reference to the detailed information appearing elsewhere in this offering Memorandum. All capitalized terms not defined herein have the meanings specified in the Indenture or the Mortgage.

THE ISSUER

Olympia & York Maiden Lane Finance Corp., a Delaware corporation, formed for the sole purpose of issuing the Notes and engaging in activities related to the issuance of the Notes.

THE OWNER

Olympia & York Maiden Lane Company, a New York limited partnership and an affiliate of the Issuer (the "Owner"), whose sole business is the ownership, management, financing, leasing and operation of the Property (as defined below).

USE OF PROCEEDS

The Issuer will, simultaneously with its receipt of the proceeds of this offering, loan such proceeds and additional amounts to the Owner and will receive, in consideration therefor, the Mortgage Note (as defined below) in the aggregate principal amount of the Notes, secured by the Mortgage (as defined below). The Mortgage Note and Mortgage will be assigned to the Trustee for the ratable benefit of the holders of the Notes (the "Holders") and interest coupons appertaining thereto. The Owner will, simultaneously with its receipt of such proceeds, use such proceeds to repay a loan to the Owner that had been secured by a mortgage on the Property, which mortgage will be amended and restated and assigned to the Trustee for the ratable benefit of the Holders of the Notes. . . .

THE PROPERTY

The "Property" consists of the land and improvements comprising a multi-tenant, 44-story office building located at 59 Maiden Lane in New York City, containing approximately 1,045,448 rentable square feet (the "Building"), all leases and rents in respect thereof and certain fixtures and equipment attached thereto and certain other rights associated therewith. The Building consists of a combination of three office buildings: 59 Maiden Lane Tower Building (44 stories), which was completed in 1965, and two adjacent 16-story buildings, which were completed in 1929 and 1930, respectively, and which were joined together by the tower building. . . .

The Building is occupied primarily by banking and insurance firms. Two tenants, The Home Insurance Company and the Federal Reserve Bank of New York, occupy an aggregate of approximately 90 percent of the rentable square feet in the Building. Another tenant, The Chase Manhattan Bank, N.A., occupies approximately 7.5 percent of the rentable square feet in the building.

At September 30, 1985 the occupancy rate for the Building was 99.94 percent. Landauer Associates, Inc. ("Landauer"), an independent real estate appraisal firm, has appraised the fair market value of the Property as of June 30, 1985 at $280 million. An appraisal is only an estimate of value and should not be relied upon as a measure of realizable value. . . .

THE OFFERING

The Notes. $200,000,000 principal amount of $10^{3/8}$ percent Secured Notes Due 1995 (the "Notes").

Offering Price. $99^{3/4}$ percent of principal amount, plus accrued interest, if any, from December 23, 1985.

Maturity. December 31, 1995.

Interest. The Notes will bear interest at the rate of $10^{3/8}$ percent per annum, payable annually in arrears on December 31 of each year, commencing December 31, 1986. In addition, in the case of monetary defaults by the Issuer, a late charge is required to be paid by the Issuer to the Holders and interest will accrue on the Notes at a default rate in each case after any applicable grace period.

Status; Nonrecourse. The Notes will be direct, unsubordinated, nonrecourse obligations of the Issuer, and will be secured as described below. Holders of the Notes shall rely solely on the Mortgage Note, the Mortgage and the Aetna Credit Insurance Policy (as defined below), and in certain circumstances, as discussed below, on other cash, collateral or credit supports delivered in addition thereto or in substitution therefor, for satisfaction of the Issuer's obligations on the Notes....

Security and Credit Supports. The Notes will be secured by an assignment of a nonrecourse mortgage note (the "Mortgage Note"), in the aggregate principal amount of the Notes, of the Owner, secured by a recorded first mortgage (the "Mortgage") on the Property. The Notes will also be entitled to the benefits of an unconditional credit insurance policy of The Aetna Casualty and Surety Company (the "Aetna Credit Insurance Policy"), in the initial maximum amount of $30,380,000, which is subject to reduction as described herein and, in certain circumstances as described herein on other cash, collateral or credit supports delivered in addition thereto or in substitution therefor. The Indenture provides that all Operating Income from the Property (defined to include all base rent and additional rent) will be deposited into, and all Operating Expenses of the Property (defined to include all expenses of operating the Property together with the costs of certain capital improvements, leasing commissions and, in certain circumstances, fees and expenses in connection with obtaining collateral or credit supports) will be paid from, an Operating Account pledged to the Trustee for the benefit of the Holders of the Notes, but under the control of the Owner. The Indenture also provides that the Owner may withdraw amounts from the Operating Account for any other purpose if the Owner delivers collateral or credit supports, to the extent discussed herein, to offset such withdrawals. Amounts in the Operating Account will be available to pay amounts due on the Notes. In addition, under certain circumstances, the Issuer may be required to deliver cash, collateral or credit supports to provide funds for the payment of additional interest on the Notes or to provide liquid assets collateral for the payment of the principal of and interest on the Notes during the final two years of their term, and under certain limited circumstances, the Issuer may elect to provide cash, collateral or credit supports to obtain a release of the security interest of the Trustee in the Property and certain collateral and credit supports....

Form and Denomination. Definitive Notes will be issued in bearer form (the "Bearer Notes"), in denominations of $1,000 and $10,000, with interest coupons attached, and in registered form (the "Registered Notes"), in denominations of $1,000 and integral multiples thereof, without coupons. . . . The Notes will initially be represented by a single temporary global note, without coupons (the "Global Note"), which will be deposited with a common depositary (the "Common Depositary") in London on behalf of Morgan Guaranty Trust Company of New York, Brussels office, as operator of the Euro-clear System ("Euro-clear"), and Centrale de Livraison Mobilieres S.A. ("CEDEL") on or about December 23, 1985. The Global Note will be exchangeable for definitive Notes not earlier than the date (the "Exchange Date") that is 90 days following the completion of the distribution of the Notes (as determined by Salomon Brothers International Limited) and upon certification of non-U.S. beneficial ownership, except that in the case of Registered Notes sold to sophisticated United States institutional investors, the Global Note will be exchangeable for definitive Notes at any time after the issuance of the Notes upon presentation of certain certificates. . . .

Redemption. The Notes may be redeemed at any time on or after December 31, 1992, in whole but not in part, initially at a redemption price equal to 101 percent of the principal amount, declining thereafter to par on December 31, 1994, together with accrued interest to the date fixed for redemption. The Notes may also be redeemed at any time at par, plus accrued interest, if any, in whole but not in part, in the event of certain changes or other circumstances affecting United States taxation or information reporting requirements or changes affecting the taxation of mortgages or debts secured by mortgages, or upon the occurrence of certain events of casualty loss involving the Property or in whole or in part, in the event of a condemnation of all or a portion of the Property. . . .

Trustee. Manufacturers Hanover Trust Company.

Listing. Application has been made to list the Notes on the Luxembourg Stock Exchange.

THE MORTGAGE

The Mortgage contains restrictions on transfers of interests in the Property or the Owner. The Owner may transfer legal or equitable title to the Property to an entity in which Olympia & York Developments Limited ("OYDL") or certain members of the Reichmann family (the "Reichmanns") have (including through trusts) a 25 percent beneficial ownership interest, and which is controlled by OYDL or the Reichmanns (an "O&Y Owner"). Transfers of beneficial interests in the Property or in the Owner are also permitted so long as any such O&Y Owner retains at least a 25 percent beneficial interest in the Property. In addition, transfers of interests in the Property or in the Owner are permitted in certain other circumstances to entities that satisfy certain criteria involving the net worth and real estate ownership or management experience of such entity and which meet certain standards for the management and leasing of the Property. . . . In addition, the Mortgage contains restrictions on the Owner's ability to further mortgage the Property or to otherwise incur indebtedness, and requires the Owner to comply with certain requirements with respect to the maintenance, insurance, management and leasing of the Property. . . .

The preceding excerpts have focused on the securitization of developer financing—the issuance of commercial mortgage-backed securities by developers raising capital in single-project transactions. The following materials examine the vastly more common securitization of lender financing—the issuance of residential (Hawkes's article) or commercial (Forte's article) mortgage-backed securities by mortgage lenders using their mortgage pools as collateral. As addressed below, securitization of residential subprime mortgages precipitated the global financial crisis and prompted debate on the bona fides of securitization, at least for residential financing.

Hawkes, Reaching the Bottom of the Barrel: How Securitization of Subprime Mortgages Ultimately Failed
Real Est. Fin. J. 55 (Spring 2008)

In the [mid 1990s to mid 2000s], Wall Street used the process of securitization to revolutionize the financing of home mortgages, making credit available to millions of borrowers with less than stellar credit. But the failure to properly assess the credit risk associated with these loans led to well over $100 billion in losses at Wall Street firms. Who will be held responsible?

The subprime mortgage crisis is, in large part, a consequence of an untested faith in financial wizardry. The premise is a simple one, familiar to anyone with a stock portfolio: if you diversify your holdings, you face less exposure from any single bad investment. You can enjoy greater returns with less risk. The securitization of subprime mortgage loans was based on this simple principle. Each individual subprime loan presented a large risk of default. But pooled into large, diverse groups, with the risk spread over a large number of investors, exposure to the credit risk associated with any particular loan was minimized. The use of credit enhancements, such as senior-subordinate structures and credit default swaps, and contractual terms, such as recourse provisions, further reduced the risk associated with these loans, enabling extremely risky subprime loans to be converted into AAA-rated securities.

Then, somehow, the whole edifice crumbled. Default rates on subprime mortgages exceeded the expectations of almost everyone in the financial community. Even "safe," highly rated mortgage-backed securities were decimated in value. As losses mount all over Wall Street, investors are demanding to know what went wrong, and are seeking to hold issuers responsible in court. Issuers are turning on the lenders who sold them the loans they securitized, claiming fraud and contractual breaches. State and federal government officials have also opened both civil and criminal investigations of the securitization of subprime loans.

The subprime mortgage crisis demonstrates how seemingly sound financial principles, such as those underlying the securitization of home mortgages, can fail when they themselves distort the very markets in which they operate. The drastic increase in subprime lending was partially a result of the process of securitization, which made vast amounts of credit available while reducing lenders' incentive to carefully screen their borrowers. The excellent performance of mortgage-backed securities (as well as the perceived safety of these investments) stoked demand for more mortgage-backed securities—which required ever-riskier subprime mortgages, as the selection process repeatedly cherry-picked from the pool of available borrowers. This process worked just fine as long as housing prices continued to appreciate at astonishing rates. Subprime borrowers were able to refinance or sell their homes rather than default. But when the real estate market reached its peak and began to decline, subprime borrowers found themselves locked into mortgages they could no longer afford. An unprecedented wave of defaults ensued, devastating the value of securities backed by these loans.

How did the risk models for mortgage-backed securities fail so spectacularly? How could so many brilliant minds have gotten things so wrong? And who will be held responsible as the current wave of litigation runs its course?

THE MORTGAGE SECURITIZATION PROCESS

The securitization of home mortgages is a process by which groups of mortgages are pooled together and used to secure debt instruments that are purchased by investors. The investors in these mortgage-backed securities ("MBS") are paid from the cash flows generated by payments on the mortgages in the pool.

The securitization model begins, of course, with the lender-borrower transaction. Sometimes this transaction is direct, but most subprime mortgages are mediated by a mortgage broker, who finds potential borrowers, assesses their credit risk, and submits loan applications on their behalf.

Rather than retaining and servicing the loan itself, the lender then sells the mortgage to a special purpose vehicle ("SPV"), usually in the form of a trust, where it is pooled with other mortgages. This SPV, which is usually set up by the lender, then sells the pool of mortgages to a second, independent SPV, usually organized by an investment bank. It is the second SPV that becomes the issuer of the MBS. An investment bank then underwrites the securities, sometimes employing a placement agent to find suitable investors, and sells the MBS to other banks and financial institutions, as well as institutional (and, in some cases, individual) investors.

This structure has a number of advantages. Because the individual mortgages are pooled together, investors' exposure to any particular bad loan is reduced; that is, investors get the benefit of diversification. The SPV issuer is bankruptcy-remote, meaning that the mortgages it holds cannot be reached in the event that the original lender goes bankrupt, which further contributes to the safety of the investment. The issuer is typically tax-exempt as well. And because the issuer is independent of the loan originator, the issuer should qualify as a "holder in due course," meaning that many contract claims that a borrower might have against the originator are extinguished, thereby reducing litigation risk.

Most MBS utilize what is known as a senior-subordinate structure. This structure uses payment "waterfalls" to allow different investors to take on different levels of risk, known as "tranches." Investors in the most senior tranche are paid first; then the mezzanine tranches are paid; and, finally, the most junior positions take what it left. The more subordinate an investor is in the structure, the more likely it is that cash will run out before he or she is paid. Hence, more junior investors generally receive a higher rate of return. Ratings agencies assess the risk of each tranche separately and assign it a rating. The most senior tranches usually have the highest possible rating of AAA (using the Standard & Poor's rating system). Mezzanine tranches typically are assigned ratings of AA or A, and junior tranches bear ratings of BBB or below, with the lowest tranche, also known as the "equity piece" (since it retains all of the residual if all of the more senior tranches are paid off) or "first loss position" (for obvious reasons) usually unrated. The equity piece is frequently retained by the original lender, in theory providing some incentive for the lender to carefully underwrite its loans. This structure enables investment banks to turn pools of relatively risky assets, such as subprime mortgages, into investment grade securities.

The ratings of MBS also frequently receive a boost from what are known as "credit enhancements." The senior-subordinate structure is itself a type of internal credit enhancement. Other internal credit enhancements include overcollateralization, in which the total mortgage loans in the pool exceed the total liability to investors, and an excess spread account, in which cash that is set aside after investors and expenses are paid can be used to offset future shortfalls. External credit enhancements include bond insurance provided by monoline insurance companies or credit default swaps. A credit default swap is a security derivative that functions much like an insurance policy. For a price, another party agrees to bear the credit risk of the loan pool above a certain level, allowing MBS investors to hedge against catastrophic losses.

Additionally, the agreements between MBS issuers and lenders often contain provisions that shift some of the credit risk back onto the lender. For example, deal provisions may require a lender to buy back nonperforming loans under certain conditions, or replace defaulting loans with performing ones. Some deals require lenders to retain servicing rights as an incentive to carefully screen borrowers, since servicing costs go up when loans go into default. But many deals actually require lenders to transfer servicing rights to a large, national servicing company in order to take advantage of economies of scale and expertise.

In many cases, issuance of MBS is not the end of the process. Many investment banks create pools of MBS and incorporate them into financial structures known as collateralized debt obligations ("CDOs"). CDOs also utilize a senior-subordinate structure to mitigate credit risk for investors in the upper tranches. Thus, investment banks could take low-rated or unrated junior pieces of MBS structures and, by re-tranching, create new AAA-rated securities. In the last several years, interests in CDOs became a darling asset of investment banks and hedge funds. Investment banks even created CDOs of CDOs—a structure known as a "CDO-squared."

THE REAL ESTATE "PYRAMID SCHEME"

The increased prevalence of the securitization of home mortgages both fueled, and was fueled by, the long housing boom that began in the 1990s. The early part of this period saw historically low interest rates in the face of rapid economic expansion. The spectacular rise in stock prices, driven by the "dot-com" frenzy, contributed to increased income on Main Street as well as Wall Street, as many people invested (and profited) in the stock market for the first time. This increase in wealth and income, combined with interest rates that were relatively low considering the rate of economic expansion, led many people to buy new homes. After the stock market bubble burst in 2001 and the economy entered a mild recession, the Federal Reserve slashed interest rates even further, cutting the federal funds rate from a high of 6.50 percent in early 2001 to as low as 1.00 percent by mid-2003. This move effectively lowered mortgage rates to historic lows as well. At the same time, investors stung by their investments in ephemeral stocks increasingly saw real estate as a tangible, safe investment, particularly as real estate prices continued to climb while the rest of the economy stagnated. As people plowed more of their wealth into their homes (and, increasingly, speculative residential investments), real estate price appreciation accelerated. Homeowners repeatedly "traded up," using the equity gains from the appreciation of their current home values to finance purchases of bigger, better homes. New home construction took off in response to this demand, increasing the overall housing supply. But in order for this process to continue, the market required a constant supply of new homeowners at the bottom of the market to purchase the homes that earlier homeowners were leaving behind. Thus, the real estate market began to resemble a pyramid scheme: in order for earlier entrants to make money, there had to be new entrants investing new money. These new buyers frequently had spotty credit history, low income, or other indicia of credit risk—that is, they were considered "subprime" mortgage borrowers.

Increased demand for housing carried with it increased demand for credit, and securitization was the vehicle that made that credit available. Traditionally, mortgage lenders retained and serviced their own loans. This effectively limited the amount of credit available to finance home purchases to that which the lender alone was able to provide. Government-sponsored enterprises ("GSEs") such as the Federal National Mortgage Association ("Fannie Mae") and the Federal Home Loan Mortgage Corporation ("Freddie Mac") make additional credit available by purchasing mortgages from lenders, pooling them, and selling interests in the pools to investors—that is, by securitizing home mortgages. But Fannie Mae and Freddie Mac have strict guidelines for the mortgages they will purchase and deal for the most part only with prime mortgages with certain specifications. Thus, the GSEs could not directly increase credit liquidity for subprime loans. But in the last decade, Wall Street investment banks increasingly filled the gap, purchasing subprime loans and other loans that failed to conform to GSE guidelines (such as so-called "Alt-A" loans and "Jumbo" loans) from lenders and packaging them into "private-label" MBS. This process drastically increased the credit available to subprime borrowers. By 2006, $1.9 trillion of the $2.5 trillion in total mortgage originations that year were securitized in MBS— about 25 percent of which were backed by subprime loans. Three-quarters of the subprime mortgages originated in 2006 were securitized.

As the housing boom continued, everyone made money. Homeowners enjoyed increased equity as their home values increased. Mortgage lenders profited from origination fees for new mortgages, sales of those mortgages to financial institutions, and sales of servicing rights to large servicing companies. Investment banks earned fees for underwriting MBS and CDOs. And investors in MBS and CDOs saw consistent cash flows from their investments, as loans rarely went bad in an appreciating housing market. Home buyers and mortgage lenders continued to demand credit, and investment banks and their investors were more than happy to provide it in order to feed their own demand for MBS.

The problem, of course, was that there was a finite supply of creditworthy borrowers. As most of the available prime borrowers had already entered the market, lenders had to look to subprime borrowers to maintain loan volume. New subprime loan originations grew from $35 billion, or five percent of the overall mortgage market, in 1994 to over $600 billion, or a whopping 20 percent of the overall mortgage market, in 2006.

Because subprime borrowers present significantly higher credit risk than prime borrowers, they typically must pay much higher interest rates (on average, about 200 basis points [2%] higher than prime borrowers) and are frequently saddled with more onerous loan terms, such as prepayment penalties, acceleration clauses, and higher origination fees. To enable subprime borrowers to afford these loans, lenders increasingly utilized creative mortgage products that had low initial monthly payments, with higher payments kicking in a few years later. These products included hybrid adjustable rate mortgages ("ARMs") that had a low initial fixed interest rate, called a "teaser" rate, that would reset to a higher, floating rate after an introductory period. Other variations included interest-only mortgages, which required borrowers to pay only the accrued interest on the loan during the introductory period; and payment-option mortgages, which allowed borrowers to choose to make a full payment, an interest-only payment, or even a lower payment that would result in negative amortization. Of course, once higher payments kicked in, these borrowers would no longer be able to afford the loans. But lenders and MBS investors assumed that, as long as real estate prices continued to rapidly appreciate and interest rates remained relatively low, these borrowers could either refinance or sell their homes before the higher payments came due.

As the relatively more creditworthy subprime borrowers entered the market, lenders had to further relax their underwriting requirements to keep loan volume at the necessary level. Increasingly, lenders would provide mortgages with little or no proof by the borrower of an ability to pay, requiring only the borrower's stated income or assets. The "no-doc" or "low-doc" loans encouraged fraud on the part of loan applicants who believed they could flip their houses for a profit in the booming real estate market. Lenders also provided more loans with little or no down payment, using multiple mortgages and home equity lines of credit to avoid mortgage insurance requirements.

For a while, the pyramid scheme worked. But interest rates began to slowly creep up again in late 2004. By 2006, the real estate market began to run out of available new buyers. Home values stagnated and then began to fall. Subprime borrowers found themselves trapped in mortgages they could no longer afford, as their low introductory payments ended and they were unable to sell (due to poor market conditions) or refinance (due to higher interest rates). Delinquency rates on subprime ARMs jumped to 16 percent in August 2006, roughly triple the rate in mid-2005, and had increased to 21 percent by January 2008. This unprecedented wave of defaults negated many of the assumptions on which the ratings of MBS depended, leading to unexpected losses, even in the upper tranches. These losses were particularly devastating to investors in CDOs, many of which had high concentrations of junior-tranche MBS. Many of Wall Street's premier investment banks announced multi-billion dollar write-downs on investments linked to mortgage loans, with Citigroup, Inc. ($24.1 billion), Merrill Lynch & Co., Inc. ($22.5 billion), UBS AG ($18.7 billion), and Morgan Stanley ($10.3 billion) taking the largest hits. One Bear Stearns hedge fund lost almost 19 percent of its value in April 2007 alone as a result of its exposure to CDOs backed by MBS.

WHAT WENT WRONG?

Securitization contributed to the subprime mortgage collapse by providing the credit necessary to greatly expand the availability of subprime loans—the fuel for the fire, as it were. But the financial industry might have averted the subprime mortgage crisis, or at least reduced its impact, if it had addressed certain structural flaws in the securitization process itself.

The most glaring problem with the securitization process is the perverse incentives it creates for subprime mortgage lenders. Because lenders sell the loans to MBS issuers rather than retaining them on their balance sheets, they have little incentive to rigorously screen loan applicants. In fact, to the extent mortgage lenders retain any subprime loans on their own books, they have every incentive to cherry-pick the most desirable, least risky loans and shuffle off the "lemons" to be securitized. Some issuers attempt to align lenders' interests with their own by selling the lender the first-loss, residual position in the MBS structure. But many lenders simply resell their residuals to issuers of CDOs, moving the entire credit risk off their books. Recourse and collateral substitution clauses, which require lenders to buy back or replace nonperforming loans, theoretically shift some credit risk back to lenders. But in practice, many MBS issuers have had difficulty enforcing these provisions. Lightly capitalized lenders can simply declare bankruptcy rather than buy back bad loans, as Ownit Mortgage Solutions did when JP Morgan Chase and Merrill Lynch sought to enforce repurchase provisions in November 2006. Finally, many issuers allowed, or even required, lenders to sell their servicing rights to third parties, removing the last remaining incentive to engage in rigorous underwriting.

But issuers cannot put all the blame on lenders, for in many cases they failed to engage in rigorous due diligence with respect to the subprime loans they were purchasing. Due to the vast numbers of individual loans involved in securitization pools, loan-level due diligence is neither practical nor cost-efficient. Most issuers review the actual documentation of only a small sample of the loans that they purchase, relying more on representations and warranties of the lender regarding the quality of the loans in the pool and the credit enhancements in the securitization structure itself to protect against losses. While many issuers use automated compliance systems to screen the loans they purchase for legal compliance, such systems reveal little about the creditworthiness of borrowers. Issuers of CDOs have even less information, since they are another level removed from the original loan transactions.

Rating agencies, such as Standard & Poor's and Moody's, generally rate MBS and CLO [collateralized loan obligation] tranches based on summary information provided to them by issuers and financial models based on historical data regarding the performance of the type of loans involved. Since issuers conduct only cursory due diligence in many cases, the summaries they provide to rating agencies are often incomplete and approximate. Most issuers do not turn over their full due diligence files to rating agencies, and the agencies do not customarily ask for them. Recently, Raymond W. McDaniel, Jr., the chief executive of Moody's, went so far as to suggest that his agency had been misled by many MBS issuers. While working with incomplete (and sometimes inaccurate) data, rating agencies also had to contend with the lack of historical precedent of widespread subprime lending, which introduced significant uncertainty into their risk models. As McDaniel recently conceded, "In hindsight, it is pretty clear that there was a failure in some key assumptions that were supporting our analytics and our models."

In retrospect, while the financial principles underlying the securitization of subprime mortgages appeared sound, serious structural problems should have been addressed. Issuers should have insisted that lenders retain the first loss position and servicing rights, and should have steered away from doing business with lightly capitalized lenders who would be unable to meet their contractual obligations to repurchase or replace nonperforming loans. Issuers also should have conducted more rigorous due diligence and provided more complete and accurate information to rating agencies. Rating agencies should have insisted on more information from issuers before rating loans and should have developed better risk models. These steps might have prevented the downturn in the real estate market from turning into the global financial crisis that it has become.

WHAT'S NEXT: LAWSUITS AND INVESTIGATIONS

Predictably, the collapse of the subprime mortgage securitization market has engendered numerous lawsuits as well as government inquiries. Stock market investors are suing investment banks and bond insurers due to the huge losses they have sustained in their exposure to MBS and CDOs; investors in MBS and CDOs are suing issuers of those securities, claiming they were misled regarding the risk profile of the securities and the quality of the underlying mortgages; and MBS issuers are suing subprime lenders, claiming that they fraudulently sold bad loans and breached their repurchase obligations. The Securities and Exchange Commission has begun dozens of investigations of players in the subprime mortgage securitization market, and state officials, most notably the Attorney General of the State of New York, have launched their own investigations. The Federal Bureau of Investigation has even begun a criminal inquiry into alleged abuses in the subprime mortgage securitization market.

Numerous securities class action complaints have been filed against virtually every major investment bank and bond insurance company seeking to recover for losses those financial institutions have sustained as a result of their exposure to subprime MBS and CDOs. These lawsuits typically allege that the financial institutions failed to disclose their level of exposure to these securities and the risks associated with them and/or that the firms withheld information regarding the massive losses they had sustained until well after those losses became apparent. Whether meritorious or not, these lawsuits will likely result in substantial settlements in many instances, further compounding the losses that these financial institutions have sustained.

Having directly sustained massive losses on their investments, MBS and CDO investors have also begun to seek legal redress from the issuers and underwriters of those securities. For example, in April 2007, Bankers Life Insurance Company filed suit against Credit Suisse in connection with MBS that it purchased in 2004. Bankers Life alleges that Credit Suisse overstated the degree to which insurance would cover potential losses, accepted low-quality loans, and covered up delinquencies by homeowners by advancing payments on their behalf. But MBS and CDO investors face significant obstacles to recovery through the courts. Most MBS and CDOs are sold only to highly sophisticated (and frequently institutional) investors. Disclosure obligations, particularly in nonpublic deals, such as Rule 144A offerings, are greatly circumscribed. Absent evidence of intentional fraud or breach of specific contractual provisions, investors are unlikely to prevail against MBS and CDO issuers and underwriters. Many investors are further restrained by the fact that MBS and CDOs are issued and underwritten by major investment banks, with whom these large investors must deal on a daily basis.

Continuing down the chain of entities involved in the subprime mortgage securitization market, issuers of MBS have filed numerous lawsuits against subprime lenders, claiming that those lenders fraudulently sold the issuers bad loans or failed to meet their contractual obligations to repurchase or replace nonperforming loans. However, given the dire financial straits that many of these subprime lenders are in, issuers may have difficulty recovering much of their losses in these lawsuits.

Regulators at the state and federal level have also begun investigating possible fraud in the subprime mortgage securitization market. The Securities and Exchange Commission has opened around three dozen civil investigations in connection with the subprime mortgage crisis, including investigations of Wall Street firms such as UBS, Morgan Stanley, Merrill Lynch, and Bear Stearns. Those SEC inquiries are focused on possible inconsistencies in the firms' valuation of MBS held on their own books versus those held by customers such as hedge funds, the timeliness of the firms' disclosure of their losses, and the accounting propriety of using off-balance sheet entities to hold MBS investments. At the state level, New York Attorney General Andrew Cuomo is investigating whether investment banks that issued MBS withheld information from investors and rating agencies regarding the extent to which those securities were backed by so-called "exception" loans that failed to meet even reduced underwriting standards. The FBI recently opened criminal inquiries into 14 companies involved in the subprime mortgage market, including Wall Street banks involved in securitizing those loans. The FBI has said that it is investigating potential accounting fraud, insider trading, and other violations. These inquiries may well result in civil or criminal charges against financial institutions involved in the subprime securitization market.

CONCLUSION

The financial innovations that enabled Wall Street to securitize subprime mortgages led to a tremendous increase in the credit available to these relatively risky borrowers. But players at all levels of the securitization process—lenders, issuers, and rating agencies—failed to ensure the maintenance of reasonable underwriting standards, leading to a dangerous—and undetected—increase in credit risk in the MBS market. When the real estate boom ended, this credit risk could no longer be swept under the rug, and massive losses followed. The ensuing litigation and government inquiries will determine who ultimately bears the cost of these failures.

Joseph Forte, CMBS Lending in the New Era of Credit Risk Retention (2017)[6]

INTRODUCTION

Through the end of 2018, over $200 billion of commercial conduit loans mature and will need to be refinanced. After the robust issuance of $101 billion of CMBS (commercial mortgage-backed securities) that occurred in 2015,[1] the general expectation was for significant further growth in both the origination of commercial loans for, and issuance of, CMBS in 2016, which could handle the wave of maturities of conduit loans originated in 2006 and 2007 immediately before the financial crisis began in 2008.[2] Unfortunately, the uncertainty occasioned by general volatility of the capital markets for fixed income in the first half of 2016 disrupted the CMBS market and caused a significant decline in origination of loans for securitization.[3] Notwithstanding the increased appetite of commercial and community banks for commercial real estate mortgages in their search for yield, and the continuing entry of additional private equity funds into the primary mortgage market, the resulting exit of several commercial CMBS conduit originators was thought to jeopardize the refinancing of CMBS loans by CMBS lenders. Although securitized lending returned in the second half of the year, the final imposition of federal risk retention rules looming ahead on Christmas Eve, the search by CMBS issuers for regulatory-compliant CMBS issuance structures, and the uncertain appetite of qualified risk retention investors caused originators concern about the certainty and predictability of CMBS as an exit strategy for their loans. Clearly, the turmoil in the capital markets during the last Financial Crisis demonstrated that securitization is not without serious risk.[4]

Unfortunately, legislators and regulators prematurely focused the blame for the Financial Crisis solely on the failure of the securitized lenders to retain any risk in the loans originated for securitization, in addition to the rating agencies for

---

6. This article was written for the casebook by Joseph Philip Forte, partner at Sullivan & Worcester LLP, New York.
1. $48.4 billion (2012); $86.1 billion (2013); $94 billion (2014).
2. $198.4 billion (2006); $228.6 billion (2007).
3. $76 billion.
4. $12.2 billion (2008); $2.7 billion (2009).

abrogating their role of policing the market.[5] Yet at the time the Federal Reserve Board published a report on securitization reforms (the Fed Report) that concluded that ". . . simple credit risk retention rules, applied uniformly across assets of all types, are *unlikely* [italics added] to achieve the stated objective of the [Dodd-Frank] Act—namely, to improve the asset-backed securitization process and protect investors from losses associated with poorly underwritten loans."[6]

Too much capital, persistent historically low interest rates, excessive leverage, unsustainable property values, and ever-declining capitalization rates [see Chapter 4D] have inevitably and invariably led to booming real estate markets in the past. In this respect the most recent collapse of securitized lending in the Financial Crisis was not an exception. Yet the trouble was not, and still is not, with securitization itself, but rather with the incredible misperception and mispricing of risk by originators, issuers, and most importantly investors. It is as though they collectively believed that somehow the securitization process had taken all of the risk out of real estate financing (or at least made it someone else's problem). Clearly, this was a seriously erroneous and very costly misunderstanding of risk.

PRE-FINANCIAL CRISIS

From the inception of the CMBS market until two years before the Financial Crisis, the most cognizant assessor of risk was the purchaser of the lowest tranche (or class) of CMBS certificates—the B-piece buyer[7]—that paid cash and conducted its own due diligence on the securitization structure and the quality of the loan collateral, knowing it would be ultimately retaining the risk. Such a purchaser could not afford to ignore the risk inherent in its purchase of CMBS.[8]

---

5. See Forte, CMBS Risk Retention: How to Make It a Market Reality Rather Than An Illusion, BNA Real Estate Law and Industry (Apr. 2011).

6. Bd. of Governors of the Fed. Reserve Sys., Report to the Congress on Risk Retention (2010), https://www.federalreserve.gov/boarddocs/rptcongress/securitization/riskretention.pdf (Report to Congress on Risk Retention).

7. The "B-piece buyer" is the purchaser of the lowest subordinate tranche (or class) of CMBS certificates, i.e., the holder of the "first-loss position."

8. Thus, it was not the credit rating agencies who rated the deals but rather the original cash B-piece buyers who were the market's real gatekeepers. As a condition to their purchase of the first-loss tranche they, and not the credit rating agencies, regularly and routinely questioned and demanded documents, information and updates, and even rejected loans that were deemed substandard to prevent their being deposited in the CMBS trust. The credit enhancement provided by this first-loss position to the CMBS trust and its senior certificate holders was not only their existence as a subordination cushion but more importantly the knowledge and comfort that the B-piece buyer had focused its expertise and experience on understanding and managing the credit risk associated with each asset in the CMBS trust. Clearly, the benefit of the horizontal credit risk retention by the B-piece buyer is precisely that it is NOT the originator (or subsequent whole loan purchasers for securitization) of the mortgage loan with its own competing motives of compensation, lender competition, borrower relationships, property envy, industry league table

But in those last two years, 2006-2007, the B-piece buyer was not assessing the risk for the entire term of the loan; it assessed only the initial risk—almost at the point of origination—because the credo became "make it and sell it." The pressure to compete with other CMBS and other lenders—by offering lower rates and making more proceeds available—simply overwhelmed the risk assessment process. Achieving greater volume was emphasized over properly assessing and pricing the risk. Although intermediaries always exported risk by parceling it to various end users with different risk appetites, at this point the B-piece buyer did not understand or appreciate the risk because the credit rating agencies failed to properly identify and consider in their ratings the risk of new structured finance vehicles, such as risks posed by the use of collateralized debt obligations (CDOs) to package credit risk assets.[9] The issuers of these securitized debt instruments viewed themselves as exporting risk—it was someone else's risk after it was securitized—but that someone else did not quite appreciate the risk being undertaken. As we now know, however, it does not always work out quite like that. Failed assets have a way of migrating back to an issuer's balance sheet if the assets are held by the issuer's subsidiary (for example, a structured investment vehicle created by the issuer)[10] or if there is a default in the financing of an asset sale. Thus were the seeds of the later turmoil planted over the last few years before the Financial Crisis.

ORIGINATE TO DISTRIBUTE

When a lender sells a loan asset, it does so to remove the asset from its balance sheet (a portfolio business to a fee business), thereby freeing up capital and allowing the institution to make a new loan as well as collect a new fee. Moreover, the prospect of being able to remove assets from the seller's portfolio (or its continuing pipeline) without retaining the risk of the assets on its balance sheet (despite re-acquiring the risk of the newly-pledged asset as lender) was a very appealing structure for asset sellers.

As the securitized market grew exponentially on the back of the strong and steady increase in leverage at all levels of the real estate capital stack, competition for loan products heightened because of relatively stable markets,

---

standing, achieving issuance size and PR/marketing opportunities i.e. "bragging rights" which daily color or even sometimes interfere with a clear assessment of the credit risk of a mortgage loan. What is necessary is a truly independent second review of each loan by a real estate specialist and NOT by the credit rating agencies.

9. In stark contrast to the traditional short term warehouse or "repo" financing of financial assets, the CDO offered a long-term fixed rate, without the risk of mark-to-market requirements or margin calls which had wreaked havoc with some CMBS and RMBS players on the August 1998 market turmoil.

10. See Bank of International Settlement's Basel Committee on Bank Supervision "Step-In Risk" proposal which would require additional capital if it is determined that a bank would feel compelled to support an off balance sheet entity under financial stress even without a contractual obligation.

the availability of too much capital, and the entrance of new players, many without any tradition of principal investment. Loan underwriters began to ignore the looming refinance risk created by the maturity dates of balloon loans and relied instead on pro-formas that showed ever-rising rents. As the process further commoditized, investors looking to improve their returns began to employ even more leverage in the acquisition of these assets. The investors' desire to increase their returns in this way required them to stray out of their traditional comfort zones and down the credit stack. Cash buyers became, or were replaced by, more highly leveraged buyers.[11]

Wall Street, in an attempt to increase its return or to avoid retaining any risk whatsoever, adapted new CDO structures already used in other capital markets to the commercial real estate finance market. The availability of CDO financing led to a further explosion of junior loan products—subordinate B notes, mezzanine debt [see Chapter 7B2], and loan participations. The mortgage loan origination community was more than willing to accommodate the ever-increasing appetite of capital market investors for subordinate debt products by increasing loan production. These lenders were able to serially remove from their books their financed junior debt inventory—inventory that would otherwise have been retained in the lenders' portfolios—which they deposited in CDOs. Thus, the lending volume of B notes and mezzanine debt grew significantly, supported by the growth of the commercial real estate CDO market,[12] allowing the issuance of CMBS to reach record levels. The commercial finance markets began to over build commercial loan financial capital stacks that overleveraged real estate rather than overbuilding physical structures as in prior downturns.

It became obvious that for CMBS origination and issuance to restart successfully, there could not be any post-2005 leveraged B-piece buyers that collected fees and quickly exported their entire first-loss position risk to another financial vehicle such as a CDO.

DODD-FRANK ACT

Section 15G of the Securities Exchange Act, newly enacted under the Dodd-Frank Wall Street Reform and Consumer Protection Act of 2010, required that the Federal Deposit Insurance Corporation, the Federal Reserve Board, the Office of the Comptroller of the Currency, and the Securities and Exchange Commission (together with Federal Housing Finance Agency and the Department of Housing and Urban Development for residential mortgages)

---

11. Forte, "Disruption in the Capital Markets: What Happened?" Prob. & Prop., Sept./Oct. 2009.

12. CDO issuance rose from $5.6 billion in 2003 to $41.8 billion in 2007 before falling back to $4.1 billion in 2009.

promulgate joint regulations governing the risk retention requirements for the securitization of different asset classes.[13]

Dodd-Frank has been the basis for the promulgation of myriad regulations designed to prevent the circumstances and practices that permitted, and a process that tolerated, the "imprudent" lending by lenders who were originating mortgage loans without retaining any risk in their loan portfolios or otherwise jeopardizing their balance sheet. The government wanted to end the "originate to distribute" business model of securitized lenders which had increased liquidity to borrowers, but simultaneously had the unintended consequence of reducing the quality of the mortgage loans originated because the loans destined for securitization were not being underwritten to the same standards as loans which lenders retained for their portfolios. Among the numerous prophylactic measures proposed and adopted by the banking regulators since the enactment of Dodd-Frank, the one that has caused the most concern to the commercial real estate finance community is the requirement of risk retention—that 5% of the credit risk of the securitized loans be retained by the issuer. Although large loan and conduit CMBS have always had third party B-piece buyers in the CMBS "senior -subordinate" bond structure—a structure which the regulators expressly acknowledged in the final risk retention regulations, the size of B-piece as a percentage of the CMBS issuance was usually determined by the non-investment grade bonds in subordination levels as calculated by the credit rating agencies that rated the senior-subordinate tranches of the CMBS securitization.

FINAL RULE

As of December 24, 2016, unless the commercial mortgage loans meet the criteria for a statutory "Qualified Commercial Mortgage" loan and thereby exempt from risk retention,[14] the issuer must retain not less than 5% of the aggregate credit risk of the commercial mortgages that are pooled in a CMBS trust. For CMBS, risk retention can be structured in three different forms: a vertical interest composed of a percentage of each class; a horizontal "first loss" interest, or a combination of the vertical and the horizontal interests known as the "L shape interest." But the eligible credit risk retention alternatives are not all equal or available to all investors. The vertical interest requires holding 5% of face value of each tranche (or class) of the CMBS certificates issued, while the 5% horizontal interest is calculated on the "fair value" requiring a higher risk

---

13. Pub. L. No. 111-203, 124 Stat. 1376 (2010) (Dodd-Frank Act), codified as amended at 15 U.S.C. § 78o-11.

14. Under the "Qualified Commercial Real Estate" (QCRE) exemption regime, loans are exempt from risk retention provided they satisfy the "underwriting standards for qualifying CRE loans." A pool of QCRE loans would be exempt from the obligation for credit risk retention. QCRE and non-QCRE loans may be mixed in a CMBS pool and risk retention would be reduced by the proportionate percentage of QCRE loans, but in no event can the reduction of the risk retention obligation be less than 2.5% overall.

retention amount because B-piece purchasers buy their interest at a discount. Hence, to meet the risk retention requirements, B-piece buyers will need to purchase bonds further up the senior-subordinate tranches than they did before the Final Rule. While the horizontal interest allows for the option that it may be acquired by a third party B-piece buyer (but may be held by no more than two pari passu B-piece investors), only the CMBS sponsor or its majority owned affiliate can acquire the eligible vertical interest. In addition, mortgage originators (or their respective majority owned affiliates) can also retain their pro rata eligible horizontal or vertical interest (based on their contribution to the Trust which cannot be less than 20%)[15] which is credited to the Sponsor's risk retention; but such originator cannot retain less than 20% of the Sponsor's retention. The combination vertical and horizontal interest structure will allow the Sponsor to retain as permitted above an additional percentage strip to cover any percentage shortfall of the 5% of fair value by the B-piece buyer.

The Final Rule, in a direct response to the B-piece buyers leveraging and shifting their risk by transferring their interests to CDOs prior to the Financial Crisis: does not permit the financing or pledging or hedging of retained interests; limits the sale or other transfer of the interests with some very limited exceptions; mandates specific qualification requirements for B-piece buyers who purchase retained interests; imposes the obligation to appoint a qualified unaffiliated operating advisor without any economic interest to monitor the Trust for all the certificate holders; requires disclosure of the calculation of fair value (and therefore the purchase price) of the B-piece; imposes liability on the sponsor to monitor the third party B-piece buyer's compliance with the Final Rule; and imposes specific long term hold periods for retention interests. Moreover, single borrower/single asset CMBS which few defaults also became subject to risk retention, although such transactions had been rated investment grade having neither had B-pieces nor investors who purchased the non-existent first loss position.

CMBS POST-FINAL RULE

While the so-called cartel of the usual B-piece buyers dominated the first loss position in the early days of the CMBS market, the number of B-piece buyers grew exponentially with the advent of CDO leveraging by a disposition strategy that attached itself to the CMBS process. Then the market collapsed in the Financial Crisis. During that hiatus, market participants worried if there would even be any investors willing to invest in the B-piece buyer role because of the new required qualifications, constraints, duration issues, indemnification of monitoring issuers, and pricing disclosure mandated for all CMBS issuance. On its effective date, the traditional participants in first loss position tranche as well

---

15. Third party purchasers may be affiliated with originators provided they do not deposit more than 10% of the CMBA loan pool.

as the new entrants into that market were confronted with a very different financial product than had existed before the Financial Crisis. The first loss position tranche was no longer a single product market with just a small number of active players that existed since CMBS began. Today there are the three options—horizontal, vertical and the vertical/horizontal or "L" risk retention models, which can vary in size and valuation. And because the Final Rule provides for a minimum duration of hold, some of the bonds are nontradeable. Despite market concerns before the Final Rule became effective that one retention model might dominate over the others or which might be less attractive to first loss investors because some of the bonds were not tradeable or that there might not be enough interested investors or available investor capital in the market to allow CMBS to grow, numerous new investors have entered the CMBS market to purchase first lost positions and some have set up specific B piece investment funds.

Thus, contrary to market participants' expectations of the obstacles presented by the Final Rule's stringent requirements for experienced cash buyers with the ability for a long term hold, to date there have been almost three dozen risk retention parties in 2017 representing all three credit risk retention structures by issuers and third parties. Over time, the vagaries of the market, investor appetite, market perceptions, economic considerations, regulatory changes, accounting rules and other forces may change investors' perceptions or interest in one mode over another.

CONCLUSION

Are investment grade and noninvestment grade investors now satisfied with the market compliance with the Final Rule, or will they lobby for more market-driven protections and better pricing of risk to assuage their continuing concerns? Only one thing is certain in this reform process: the final regulations will not be the final chapter in the continuing recovery and resurgence of the CMBS market. And given the recent political chatter about the possible overhaul of the Dodd-Frank based regulatory regime governing banks generally and credit risk retention obligation specifically, it is extremely difficult to predict what the credit risk retention obligation will be after legislative and regulatory attempts to decrease or eliminate the obligation for issuers.[16]

We may not know the full impact of credit risk retention on the issuance of CMBS or on the issuers—the banks or the new non-bank entrants; which form of retention will come to dominate the market or be better received by issuers, the originators or investors; or what appetite investors have for the newly constrained B-piece or its heightened publically disclosed pricing. Yet the limited capacity of

---

16. A Treasury Department report issued in October 2017 called for broadening the definition of exempt QCRE loans to allow more loans to qualify to reduce risk retention and to eliminate risk retention entirely for single borrower transactions.

the insurance companies, the banks, and the alternative lenders would suggest that CMBS will need to continue as a source of financing to assure sufficient capital and liquidity to the commercial real estate industry and regardless of the changes occasioned by regulators or investors.

Bankruptcy lurks in the structuring of most mortgage securitization transactions. The following article provides a more in-depth introduction to the influence of bankruptcy law in the basic securitization transaction. It addresses the goal to ensure that the entity (or what the author calls a "vehicle") selling mortgage-backed securities is bankruptcy-remote. Bankruptcy-remote structures are those designed to reduce the risk that the entity will file bankruptcy or, if bankruptcy is filed, to ensure certain procedural advantages in the bankruptcy proceedings. For more detailed treatment of such impacts of bankruptcy as the automatic stay, see Chapter 18.

Lahny, Overview of the Basic Securitization Transaction[7]

The basic securitization transaction begins with a corporation (or other business entity), referred to as the "originator," identifying and isolating a pool of assets, from those which it has originated or acquired in the ordinary course of business with a predictable future payment stream. Residential real estate mortgages are ideal for this type of financing transaction. The originator then forms a wholly owned subsidiary corporation (or other business entity), the special purpose vehicle or "SPV." Certain precautions are taken during the formation stage to ensure that the SPV is as "bankruptcy remote" as possible from the insolvency of the originator.

Next, the assets are transferred to the SPV. The transfer will take the form of a "true sale," again a precaution to keep the assets of the SPV out of any bankruptcy filing of the originator. The SPV will then sell mortgage-backed securities or issue debt instruments in the bond market to pay the originator for the purchase of the mortgages with cash. Finally, the incoming payment streams, plus credit enhancements, will be used by the SPV to complete payment to the investors in the asset pool over a predetermined payment period. Each of these steps will be discussed in detail below.

The securitization industry is driven by the originator's ability to find investors willing to invest in the assets held by the SPV. Investors will be willing to place their money into securities of the SPV if these securities are highly rated

---

7. This section is an abridged and modified version of Lahny, Asset Securitization: A Discussion of the Traditional Bankruptcy Attacks and an Analysis of the Next Potential Attack, Substantive Consolidation, 9 Am. Bankr. Inst. L. Rev. 815 (Winter 2001), with our thanks to Peter Lahny.

by the rating agencies. The rating agencies continue to grant these high ratings because many precautions are taken to make the SPV and the transferred assets "bankruptcy remote" from any bankruptcy filing of the originator (the factors considered by the rating agencies are discussed in more detail below).

I. IDENTIFYING A POOL OF ASSETS WITH A PREDICTABLE STREAM OF INCOME

The originator begins by identifying a pool of assets with a predictable stream of income. A typical example would include a pool of accounts receivable or residential real estate mortgages. It is important that the income stream be relatively predictable. A large pool of assets is preferable due to the increased predictability of default associated with a larger pool, but this technique has been employed in very small pools as well. The originator, during its initial cost benefit analysis, as well as the rating agencies, will require a reasonable prediction of the rate of default on the payment stream. This will affect the costs of the transaction and any potential return to the originator from the transaction. Once an acceptable pool of assets has been identified, they will be isolated and prepared for the transfer. This technique has been employed with nearly any financial asset, but is especially well suited to residential real estate mortgages.

II. CREATE A WHOLLY OWNED SUBSIDIARY CORPORATION (OR OTHER BUSINESS ENTITY)

The originator will then create the vehicle through which it will complete this transaction. This vehicle can be a variety of legal entities. For the purposes of this discussion, the SPV created will be assumed to be a wholly owned subsidiary corporation. During the creation stage, there are several factors that must be addressed in the incorporation documentation to make the SPV as "bankruptcy remote" from the originator's insolvency proceeding as possible. These factors will help prevent an involuntary petition from being filed against the SPV, keeping the two entities from being substantively consolidated, and ensuring that the SPV will not file a voluntary bankruptcy petition, to the extent possible under current law. The "bankruptcy remote" provisions will be discussed in the next section.

III. MAKING THE SPV "BANKRUPTCY REMOTE"

The next step is to make the SPV "bankruptcy remote" from the bankruptcy of the originator. An entity can never be truly "bankruptcy proofed," because provisions allowing for the inability of an entity to voluntarily file for bankruptcy relief when it is in the best interests of the entity and its creditors are against public policy. When attempting to make an entity bankruptcy remote, five factors must be considered and each will now be addressed in turn.

First, the activities of the SPV must be restricted. Restrictions are placed in the charter and by-laws of the SPV to restrict the activities to those necessary or incidental to the financing. Keeping the activities of the SPV limited to those involved with the financing limits the potential for involuntary petitions to be filed against the SPV in the future.

Second, the debt incurred by the SPV must be limited. By limiting SPV debt to that necessary or incidental to the financing, the originator again reduces the risk of a future involuntary petition. Also, the originator should properly fund the SPV to allow it to pay foreseeable creditors as the obligations become due.

Third, the originator should place restrictions on the SPV's ability to subject the securitized assets to voluntary liens. This can be accomplished by adding language to that effect to the incorporation documentation. Any additional liens can lead to future involuntary petitions.

Fourth, the originator should restrict the SPV's ability to file a voluntary bankruptcy petition. An absolute bar to the SPV's ability to file a voluntary petition is impermissible. However, a technique has been accepted by the rating agencies as sufficient for their rating purposes. The originator begins by adding a provision in the articles of incorporation of the SPV requiring a unanimous vote of the board of directors to file a voluntary bankruptcy petition. The originator will then place at least one independent director on the board of the SPV in an attempt to minimize the possibility that the originator could influence the directors to authorize the filing of a voluntary petition. Unfortunately, this technique cannot guarantee that the SPV will never file a voluntary petition now that many courts have held that the fiduciary duties of directors of a corporation approaching insolvency will shift to the outside creditors. However, this technique does guarantee that the originator will not be able to cause the SPV to file a voluntary petition for its own purposes.

Finally, the originator must be concerned with the ability of creditors of the SPV to file an involuntary bankruptcy petition against the SPV. The requirements for filing of an involuntary petition are contained in section 303 of the Bankruptcy Code, which permits the creditors to force the entity into bankruptcy against its will. The parties may be able to reduce the risk of an involuntary petition by contractual agreement. However, this technique has not been subjected to judicial scrutiny and may impermissibly restrict the SPV's ability to file a voluntary bankruptcy petition. Also, the originator should be sure that the SPV is properly funded to eliminate foreseeable obligations as they come due for payment. If the obligations of the SPV never exceed a relatively modest statutorily defined amount, no creditors can ever bring an involuntary petition.

A bankruptcy filing would entail, at a minimum, an implementation of the automatic stay and a disruption of the cash flow. The rating agency needs assurance that the SPV is bankruptcy remote so that it would not be substantively consolidated in the bankruptcy of any affiliate of the transferor of the pooled loans. The rating agency will require issuer's counsel to render a reasoned "non-consolidation opinion" to confirm the absence of this risk in the structure.

IV. TRANSFER THE ASSETS TO THE SPV

The originator must now transfer the assets to the SPV. The transfer is intended to separate the financial assets from the insolvency risks associated with the originator. The transfer must be structured as a "true sale." To achieve "true sale" status the originator must have no interest in the financial assets, such that the financial assets will not be part of the originator's bankruptcy estate under section 541 of the Bankruptcy Code.

Section 541(a)(1) defines the bankruptcy estate as, "all legal or equitable interests of the debtor in property as of the commencement of the case." The problem facing an originator during the transfer is that it may not have transferred its interest in the assets properly, and the Bankruptcy Court may find that the transfer was not a "true sale" but merely a disguised secured loan. Should this occur, the assets will be deemed part of the originator's bankruptcy estate, and be drawn into the originator's bankruptcy case. The asset transfer is a part of this transaction that has traditionally been an area of bankruptcy attack.

If the transfer was not a "true sale" but merely a disguised secured loan, in the event of an insolvency of the originator, the automatic stay would apply and delay payments to investors. The rating agencies will require that counsel provide a reasoned "true sale" opinion covering the sale from the originator to the SPV.

V. THE SPV PAYS FOR THE PURCHASE OF THE ASSETS

The final step requires the SPV to pay for the purchase of the financial assets. The SPV will use the favorable rating to issue mortgage-backed securities or sell debt instruments in the bond markets. The SPV will then use the proceeds to pay the originator for the purchase of the assets, thereby converting the future stream of payments into current cash for the originator. The SPV will then use collections from the stream of payments on the financial assets to pay off the mortgage-backed securities over a specified period of time.

NOTES AND QUESTIONS

1. Main Street versus Wall Street as the Source for Developer Financing. Because of underwriting and registration fees, the minimum feasible size for a public offering is about $20 million. Proponents of securitization point out that, in the case of such large real estate projects, the public-issue format enables developers to obtain less expensive long-term fixed rate financing than would be available from traditional private lending sources, whose loan rates are determined by negotiations between a single lender and a single borrower. Why should this be so?

Securitization offers developers an alternative to traditional capital sources:

> [R]ecently, the traditional private market single-lender system for funding commercial real estate experienced a . . . breakdown. The old system . . . was oligopolistic. "Commercial real estate lenders said 'Here's our price. Take it or leave it.' And if you needed the money, you took it." Companies like O&Y [Olympia & York] that needed large amounts of financing in a relatively short period of time no longer could function in this environment.

Standard & Poor's CreditWeek, Securitizing Commercial Real Estate 13 (Feb. 24, 1986).

Another benefit of securitization for developers is that it may permit debt to be obtained against 100 percent of the project's current value. Olasov, The Maturing of the Commercial Mortgage-Backed Securities Market, 25 Real Est. Rev. 10 (Summer 1995).

Securitization of real estate development also proved beneficial at times to investors:

> From the investor's standpoint, yields are high relative to yields on comparably rated corporate securities. . . .
>
> In explaining the strength of commercial mortgage securities relative to corporate debt securities, many bankers also refer to "event risk." The concept relates to sudden, random occurrences that almost overnight can turn a healthy debt to equity ratio literally upside down. The court ruling against Texaco Inc. and recent leveraged buyouts are examples of this risk. . . . A security representing the right to cash flow from high quality real estate . . . is a more risk-averse investment than the debt of a corporation whose balance sheet could turn from the highest quality to noninvestment grade from one day to the next. . . .

Standard & Poor's CreditWeek, Securitizing Commercial Real Estate 13 (Feb. 24, 1986).

> *Problem 15-3*

As explained in Chapter 4, in the case of most postconstruction loans on income-producing real estate, the real security for the loan that "feeds" the mortgage is not the net worth of the borrower (remember, some loans are nonrecourse) but rather the estimated rental income stream from the occupancy tenants. Indeed, the entire mortgage loan underwriting and appraisal process is predicated on the notion that the loan amount must be small enough so that the projected rents will cover the debt-service payments on the mortgage loan along with the borrower's other operating expenses. This is why private institutional lenders will almost invariably demand a conditional assignment of rents and leases as additional collateral so that, as diagrammed below, in the event of a default by the borrower the rental income from the prime tenants becomes payable directly to the lender. As used in the diagram, the term "refinancing" simply means that Dan has elected to cash out the accumulated equity in the project (for himself and his investors) by paying off the existing mortgage with a new and larger one from Ace or some other lender.

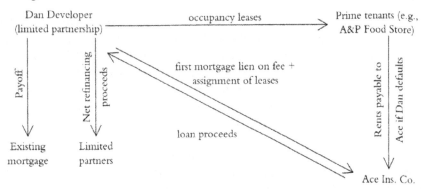

Diagram and study the facts in the *Olympia & York* transaction (see excerpt of offering memorandum, *supra*). Do you find any major substantive (as opposed to structural) differences in the way a typical single-project commercial mortgage-backed securities transaction is secured and collateralized and the ordinary private loan transaction (as diagrammed above) between Dan Developer and the Ace Insurance Company? Olympia & York, the property and corporate behemoth erected by the Reichmann family, collapsed in 1992. After several failed comeback attempts, in 1995 Paul Reichmann led an investment group in a $1 billion buyout of London's Canary Wharf, the same development that was chiefly responsible for Olympia & York's demise. Initial success in winning new tenants helped vindicate Mr. Reichmann's vision of Canary Wharf as a new financial center in London. The Canary office project went public in a 1999 stock offering, but shares fell 11 percent until 2004, when the ownership entity was acquired by a controlling shareholder in a takeover battle, leaving Reichmann without a stake in the development. ◄

2. REMICs. In the Tax Reform Act of 1986, Congress established the new tax entity of a real estate mortgage investment conduit (REMIC) as a vehicle for issuing MBSs (particularly multiple-class securities) without double taxation. I.R.C. §§860A-860G. An entity (such as a corporation or partnership), or a segregated pool of assets within an entity, that qualifies for election as a REMIC is not subject to taxation at the entity level; rather, the income of the REMIC from its mortgage pool is taxable (passed-through) to the holders of interests in the REMIC.

To qualify to elect REMIC status, among other things, substantially all of the REMIC's assets must consist of "qualified mortgages" and "permitted investments." I.R.C. §860G(a). This asset requirement is designed to fix the asset portfolio of the REMIC to the mortgage pool established at the REMIC's inception and does not contemplate recurring investments by the REMIC. The transfer of property (the mortgage pool) to a REMIC, however, is a nontaxable event. See generally Wunder, The Real Estate Mortgage Investment Conduit: The Newest Real Estate Investment Medium, 19 J. Real Est. Taxn. 36 (Fall 1991).

The first use of a commercial mortgage pool in the format of a REMIC occurred in 1992 when the federal Resolution Trust Corporation created a pool of 1,160 commercial mortgages with an aggregate balance of $497 million that had been originated by troubled thrifts. Using this mortgage loan pool, the REMIC issued five classes of securities in the principal balance of approximately $149 million. See generally RTC Issues Commercial Mortgage Securities, 25 Mortgage & Real Est. Executives Rep. 4 (Apr. 1, 1992).

3. Residential Securitizations. In Chapter 5A1's discussion of "exotic" loan terms, we raised the preliminary question of allocating blame for the subprime crisis. In the article excerpted above, Hawkes points fingers at various players in the residential securitization process. Other commentators have looked outside the securitization process to lay blame on government regulators and programs to supply credit to underserved populations. For example, New York Attorney General Andrew Cuomo, discussed in the Hawkes article for his investigation of investment bankers, went on to become governor of New York in 2011, surviving accusations that his policies to increase home ownership among the poor while serving as President Bill Clinton's housing secretary helped precipitate the subprime mortgage crisis. Similarly, some commentators heaped blame on Fannie Mae and Freddie Mac, which fell into federal conservatorship in 2008, for engineering the decline in mortgage underwriting standards that sunk the residential securitization markets. See Wallison, Government-Sponsored Meltdown, Wall. St. J., July 12, 2011; Rewriting Fannie Mae History, Wall St. J., Aug. 3, 2010 (suggesting other countries have more buoyant home mortgage markets without expensive federal intervention). Federal regulation addressing the mortgage crisis has thrown a broad net, implicating many participants while focusing mostly on originators of subprime loans and issuers of mortgage-backed securities. In order to boost mortgage underwriting standards, for example, the Dodd-Frank Wall Street Reform & Consumer Protection Act of 2010 requires lenders to obtain verifiable income documentation (in contrast to the infamous stated income or "liar" loans) evidencing the borrower's ability to repay the mortgage loan. Further, the rule from federal banking and securitization agencies to implement new risk retention standards (known as "skin in the game") under Dodd-Frank as applicable to residential loans (in addition to securitizations of commercial loans as described in the Forte article) generally requires the securitizer of residential mortgage-backed securities to retain on its books at least 5 percent of the loan volume being securitized. For purposes of residential mortgage-backed securities, a significant exemption from these new risk retention requirements is for offerings of a securitized asset pool consisting only of qualified residential mortgages, which tracks the definition of qualified mortgages under Dodd-Frank as adopted by the Consumer Financial Protection Bureau. Qualified residential mortgages must have terms no longer than 30 years, must not allow interest-only payments, balloon payments or negative amortization (see Chapter 5A2), or require fees or points that exceed three percent of the loan. Although there are no loan-to-value or down payment requirements for qualified residential mortgages, the borrower must have a debt-to-income ratio for all debt of 43% or less and the borrower's income must be verified (rather than a stated income or "liar" loan).

Rather than merely allocating blame as you did in Chapter 5A1, for purposes of this chapter you should consider and be prepared to discuss what regulatory (or market) response would prevent a recurrence of the financial crisis. For a suggested market-based strategy, see Rhee, Getting Residential Mortgage-Backed Securities Right: Why Governance Matters, 20 Stan. J.L., Bus. & Fin. 273 (2015). Based on your reading of the Forte article, do you agree that "skin in the game" standards of risk retention are necessary?

PART V

OVERVIEW OF IMPORTANT
ISSUES IN MODERN REAL ESTATE
TRANSACTIONS

Chapter 16

Common Interest Communities: Condominiums, Cooperatives, and Planned Communities

Development of privately owned housing is a crucial industry in the United States for two reasons. First, shelter is a basic need, and second, the public policy commitment to private ownership has probably meant that growth in this industry has bolstered the country's economy even during recent economic downturns. (Yet, emphasis of this policy arguably contributed to the 2008 economic downturn). Contrary to earlier periods, ownership of housing in the past 40 years has increasingly come to be characterized by private associations of homeowners that ideally function to create a community within which the individuals will be better served than without such an organization. In exchange for these benefits, individual owners relinquish to the association some of the control usually associated with ownership of real property and take on a legal obligation to pay for any services provided by the association. Estimates are that 30 percent of Americans live in common interest communities and that few future housing developments will be built without some sort of homeowner association. Whether the development is a "gated community" of single-family homes in the Southwest or a rental building that is converted to condominiums in an urban setting, the result of this trend for developers and lenders is yet another specialized transaction requiring the services of transactional lawyers.

To effectively represent their clients, commercial real estate attorneys need to understand the Common Interest Community (CIC). This understanding will help attorneys to appreciate the business motivations and concerns of developers when creating and marketing this product, and to satisfy the special aspects of CIC project lending. Therefore, this chapter focuses on the risks of CICs to the developer and to the lenders who provide financing. We have omitted coverage of the relationship between the CIC association and the owner/resident because many students will have considered the legal aspects there in earlier property courses.

The attention of the Reporters of the Restatement (Third) of Property (Servitudes) to the law of CICs reflects this trend in housing development. The Restatement defines a CIC as "a real-estate development or neighborhood in which individually owned lots or units are burdened by a servitude that imposes an obligation that cannot be avoided by nonuse or withdrawal (a) to pay for the use of, or contribute to the maintenance of, property held or enjoyed in common by the individual owners, or (b) to pay dues or assessments to an association that provides services or facilities to the common property or to the individually owned property, or that enforces other servitudes burdening the property in the development or neighborhood."[1] Thus, the CIC includes condominiums, cooperatives, planned subdivisions, gated communities, and other forms of housing ownership where ownership of one part of the CIC carries with it restrictions on use and an obligation to contribute toward support of parts owned by other members. These servitudes are drafted by the developer and are applicable from the project's inception. They are based on the enforceability of covenants "running with the land." The Declaration of Covenants, Conditions, and Restrictions (CC&Rs) is recorded before the sale to the first buyer. The CC&Rs legally bind all who own the individual units at any time after recordation. Typically, these initial rules cannot be changed without a vote of two-thirds of all unit owners—a supermajority that practically is impossible to achieve. The CC&Rs restrict the owners' use of the land and provide for services to owners, paid for by assessments that all owners are obligated to pay. The CC&Rs set up a governing board elected by owners under the principle of "one unit, one vote," rather than the "one man, one vote" required in our political system. The board makes decisions about spending, assessments, and regulating conduct by owners and guests. Thus, the governing board of the CIC takes on a quasi government role.

A. THE CIC AS A QUASI GOVERNMENT

An analogy may be drawn between the CIC and local government since "both have maintenance and regulatory responsibilities within . . . defined tracts . . . and both raise funds by assessing those who own interests in that real estate."[2] CICs offer a wide range of services to residents. A number of these services have historically been performed by the state, such as providing recreational facilities and maintaining roads within the gates. Since the 1960s, CICs have become "a major vehicle for shifting responsibilities previously associated with government agencies to the private sector."[3] Governments have relied on CICs to absorb some of their responsibilities, thus forming a relationship between the governments and the CICs. Municipal governments are reluctant to raise taxes to perform their duties. By allowing CICs to generate their own source of revenue, via assessments, governments have stepped aside and have given CICs more authority over the residents' daily life. As more residents move into CICs, fewer people rely on municipal governments for public services.[4]

---

1. Restatement §6.2.
2. W. Freedman & J. Alter, The Law of Condominia and Property Owners' Associations, 42 (1992).
3. Winokur, Critical Assessment: The Financial Role of Community Associations, 38 Santa Clara L. Rev. 1135, 1139 (1998).
4. Rich, Homeowner Boards Blur Line of Just Who Rules Roost, N.Y. Times, July 27, 2003.

A major concern involving CICs is the restrictions they place on their residents. Some argue that CICs have voluntarily taken on governmental responsibilities and should be held to the same standard as a traditional government when limiting an individual's freedoms.[5] Some CICs have attempted to restrict such fundamental rights as freedom of speech and expression, while others have placed restrictions on rights that are normally accorded to a homeowner. Neighbors and associations become enforcers of these restrictions, prompting the observation that "[u]sing missiles to kill mice, petty [CIC] quarrels can become the basis for the imposition of stiff fines and protracted litigation."[6]

Typically, courts have given CC&Rs a strong presumption of validity because they are based on the covenants running with the land analysis that infers "consent" of those who become members of the CIC. Though restrictions created by the developer in the declaration of CC&Rs do not have to be reasonable, restrictions subsequently created by the CIC, usually by the governing board instead of the developer, do have to be reasonable. But just how far can a CIC go in limiting the rights of its residents?

Board of Dirs. of 175 E. Delaware Place Homeowner's Ass'n v. Hinojosa
287 Ill. App. 3d 886, 679 N.E.2d 407 (1997)

Justice RAKOWSKI

. . . 175 East Delaware Place was organized as a condominium in 1973 by the recording of a declaration and bylaws. The property includes floors 45 through 92 of the John Hancock building and contains 705 condominium units. The declaration and bylaws were silent on the issue of pet ownership in the building. In 1976, the Board adopted a rule allowing owners to have pets, including dogs, only with the permission of the Board. On January 21, 1980, during a regular board meeting, the Board adopted a rule barring unit owners from bringing additional dogs onto the premises. In October of 1985, defendants Nancy Lee Carlson and Benjamin Tessler purchased a unit in the building. At this time, they signed a pet agreement acknowledging the no-dog rule. In February of 1993, while leasing out another one of their units, they signed the same agreement again. In March of 1993, the no-dog rule was reincluded in the Board's rules and regulations.

In June of 1993, defendants Carlson and Tessler acquired a dog.. . . In September of 1993, defendants Carlson and Tessler received notice of a hearing for their violation of the no-dog rule. The hearing was held on November 30, 1993, and the committee recommended to the Board that Carlson and Tessler be ordered to remove the dog within 30 days. If the dog remained on the premises after 30 days, defendants Carlson and

---

5. Rishikof & Wohl, Private or Public Governments: The State Will Make the Call, 30 Val. U. L. Rev. 509, 519 (1996).

6. Franzese, Does It Take a Village? Privatization, Patterns of Restrictions and the Demise of Community, 47 Vill. L. Rev. 553, 574 (2002).

Tessler should be assessed a fine of $100 per day for each day the dog remained. The Board adopted the committee's recommendation and on January 23, 1994, began assessing fines on defendants Carlson and Tessler. On April 20, 1994, after Carlson and Tessler failed to pay the fines, the Board recorded a notice and claim of statutory lien.

In August of 1994, defendants Carlson and Tessler sold the unit to defendants Jorge and Donna Hinojosa subject to the lien. In November of 1994, the Board filed the instant action seeking to foreclose on the lien. Defendants moved to dismiss the suit . . . claiming the Board had no authority to adopt the no-dog rule because the rule conflicted with the declaration and bylaws. The trial court ruled that the Board had the power to promulgate the rule but held that the rule was unreasonable.

ANALYSIS

A. LEGAL BACKGROUND

Condominiums are creatures of statute and, thus, any action taken on behalf of the condominium must be authorized by statute. "When a controversy regarding the rights of a condominium unit owner in a condominium arises, we must examine any relevant provisions in the Act and the Declaration or bylaws and construe them as a whole." Carney v. Donley, 261 Ill. App. 3d 1002, 1008, 199 Ill. Dec. 219, 633 N.E.2d 1015 (1994).

A condominium is an interest in real estate created by statute that gives each owner an interest in an individual unit as well as an undivided interest in common elements. Administration and operation of the condominium are vested in the condominium association, which is comprised of all unit owners. The administration is exercised through the board of directors, which is elected by the owners. In addition to the [Condominium Property] Act, the operation and administration of the condominium are governed by three principal documents. These are the declaration, bylaws, and board rules and regulations. The declaration and bylaws form the basic framework of the administration, and the day-to-day operations are managed by board rules and regulations.

A condominium comes into being by the recording of a declaration. The declaration is prepared and recorded by either the developer or association. The Act defines the declaration as the "instrument by which the property is submitted to the provisions of [the] Act." 765 ILCS 605/2(a) (West 1994). Its primary function is to provide a constitution for the condominium—to guide the condominium development throughout the years. The declaration contains the property's legal description, defines the units and common elements, provides the percentage of ownership interests, establishes the rights and obligations of owners, and contains restrictions on the use of the property. All restrictions contained in the declaration are covenants that run with the land and bind each subsequent owner. They are given a strong presumption of validity. Section 4 of the

Act details what elements must be contained in the declaration. Paragraph (i) states: "Such other lawful provisions not inconsistent with the provisions of this Act as the owner or owners may deem desirable in order to promote and preserve the cooperative aspect of ownership of the property and to facilitate the proper administration thereof." 765 ILCS 605/4(i) (West 1994).

The second document is the bylaws, which deal with administration and procedural matters concerning the property. Bylaws may be embodied in the declaration or be a separate document. In either case, the bylaws must be recorded with the declaration. 765 ILCS 605/17(a) (West 1994). Should the bylaws conflict with the declaration, the declaration prevails. Section 18 of the Act sets forth certain provisions that shall be included in the bylaws. Relevant to the issue before us is paragraph (k), which states: "Restrictions on and requirements respecting the use and maintenance of the units and the use of the common elements, not set forth in the declaration, as are designed to prevent unreasonable interference with the use of their respective units and of the common elements by the several unit owners." 765 ILCS 605/18(k) (West 1994).

The third item governing condominium conduct is the board rules and regulations. Section 18.4 of the Act deals with powers and duties of the board and provides that the board may:

> Adopt and amend rules and regulations covering the details of the operation and use of the property, after a meeting of the unit owners called for the specific purpose of discussing the proposed rules and regulations. 765 ILCS 605/18.4(h) (West 1994).[1]

Under this rule, "a board of managers may not take any action that is beyond the authority granted it under the condominium instruments and the Condominium Property Act." 765 ILCS 605/18.4, Historical & Practice Notes, at 129 (West 1993). The board shall exercise for the association all powers, duties, and authority vested in the association by law or the condominium documents. It generally has broad powers and its rules govern the requirements of day-to-day living in the association. Board rules must be objective, evenhanded, nondiscriminatory, and applied uniformly. See J. Shifrin, Cooperative, Condominium, and Homeowners' Association Litigation, in Real Estate Litigation §11.20, at 11-17 (Ill. Inst. for Cont. Legal Educ. 1994).

B.   POWER OF THE BOARD TO PROMULGATE THE NO-DOG RULE

As noted, pursuant to section 18.4 the Board has the power to adopt rules and regulations. Section 18(k) does discuss restrictions that shall be included in the bylaws. However, this provision merely gives the association the authority to include restrictions

---

1. The meeting requirement did not become effective until July 1, 1984, subsequent to the adoption of the rule in the case sub judice. Therefore, this part of the provision is not applicable to this case.

in the condominium instruments that will clothe the restrictions with a strong presumption of validity and make them less susceptible to attack. The provision does not state that if a restriction is not contained in the bylaws it will be unenforceable. We thus conclude that the Board's no-dog rule is not in conflict the Act.

The 175 East Delaware Place declaration and bylaws do not make any reference to pet ownership or dogs, in particular. As to the Board's powers, the declaration provides:

> The Board, may adopt such reasonable rules and regulations as it may deem advisable for the maintenance, conservation and beautification of the Property, and for the health, comfort, safety and general welfare of the Owners and Occupants of the Property. Written notice of such rules and regulations shall be given to all Owners and Occupants and the entire Property shall at all times be maintained subject to such rules and regulations.

The declaration clearly gives the Board authority to promulgate rules regarding use of and restrictions on the use of units. Because the Board is authorized to promulgate reasonable rules for the general welfare of the owners and the declaration is silent on the issue of dog ownership, the instant rule does not conflict with either the declaration or the bylaws.

Apple II Condominium Ass'n v. Worth Bank & Trust Co., 277 Ill. App. 3d 345, 213 Ill. Dec. 463, 659 N.E.2d 93 (1995), addresses use restrictions under the Act. In Apple II, we set forth standards for evaluating such restrictions and adopted the analysis set forth in Hidden Harbour Estates, Inc. v. Basso, 393 So. 2d 637 (Fla. App. 1981). We differentiated use restrictions that are contained in the declaration or bylaws from those promulgated by board rule. The restrictions in the first category "are clothed in a very strong presumption of validity and will not be invalidated absent a showing that they are wholly arbitrary in their application, in violation of public policy, or that they abrogate some fundamental constitutional right. 'Reasonableness' is not the appropriate test for such restrictions." Apple II, 277 Ill. App. 3d at 250-51. However, when the board promulgates a rule restricting the use of property, the second category, "the board must affirmatively show the use it wishes to prohibit or restrict is 'antagonistic to the legitimate objectives of the condominium association.'" Apple II, 277 Ill. App. 3d at 351, quoting Basso, 393 So. 2d at 640. Thus, "when such a rule [use restriction] is adopted by the board alone or requires the board to exercise discretion, we will scrutinize the restriction and uphold it only if it is affirmatively shown to be reasonable in its purpose and application." Apple II, 277 Ill. App. 3d at 352.

Based on the above, we conclude that the Board had the power to promulgate a reasonable no-dog rule.

C.   REASONABLENESS OF RULE

Because the rule was promulgated by the Board, it is not clothed with a strong presumption of validity. Thus, we must carefully scrutinize the rule to determine if it is reasonable in its purpose and application. Because the facts are not in dispute, the issue is one of law.

In Dulaney Towers Maintenance Corp. v. O'Brey, 46 Md. App. 464, 418 A.2d 1233 (1980), the court stated:

> The rationale for allowing the placing of restrictions in, or the barring of pets by way of, house rules is based on potentially offensive odors, noise, possible health hazards, clean-up and maintenance problems, and the fact that pets can and do defile hallways, elevators, and other common areas.

Because the Board applied the rule to all owners and the purpose for the rule was rational, we conclude that the rule is reasonable under the specific facts of this case. . . .

NOTES AND QUESTIONS

1. Presumption of Validity of Restrictions of Original CC&Rs. When a restriction is placed in the Declaration of CC&Rs by the developer, there is a strong presumption of validity. These restrictions will be deemed valid unless they are against public policy or are unconstitutional. The constitutionality of a restriction can come into play when a restriction limits a protected fundamental right and where the CIC's conduct, as a quasi government, could be considered to amount to state action (see note 2c infra).

2. Limits on Restrictions Imposed by CIC after Association's Governing Board Takes Over. (Attorneys for Board Take Note.) In most jurisdictions, if the restriction is imposed later by the CIC itself, the restriction must be judged on its reasonableness—whether the rule has a sufficient factual basis and is not rendered in bad faith. Once the power is passed from the developer to the CIC, the restrictions imposed lose their presumption of validity. But see Villa De Las Palmas Homeowners Association v. Terifaj, 33 Cal. 4th 73, 90 P.3d 1223, 14 Cal. Rptr. 3d 67 (2004), which held that use restrictions promulgated subsequent to the original declaration are entitled to the same presumption of validity as the original covenants and restrictions. Id. at 1233.

a. *Selective Enforcement.* In Prisco v. Forest Villas Condominium Apartments, Inc., 847 So. 2d 1012 (Fla. Dist. Ct. App. 2003), the association amended the CC&Rs to prohibit the keeping of dogs and any other pets (except fish and birds), but there was evidence the association allowed some residents to have pets. The court held the plaintiff resident was entitled to raise the defense of selective enforcement.

b. *Board Action Cannot Conflict with Provisions of CIC Declaration.* Ultimately, board action must be in harmony, i.e., not conflict, with the declarations established by the developer. In Weldy v. Northbrook Condo Association, Inc., 279 Conn. 728, 904 A.2d 188 (2006), the condominium declaration provided that "pets shall be restrained by leash or other comparable means. . . ." Id. at 731. The board implemented a new regulation which required that "[l]eashes or comparable restraints . . . shall not exceed [twenty] feet in length." Id. Plaintiff pet owners alleged that the new rule illegally amended the condo declaration, but the court found the board's action permissible because it did not conflict with the provisions of the declaration.

c. *Quasi Government.* To the extent a CIC is determined to be a quasi government, its actions may be viewed as those of a state actor, subject to a constitutional analysis. In Gerber v. Longboat Harbour North Condominium, Inc., 724 F. Supp. 884 (M.D. Fla. 1989) the association adopted an amendment that prevented its residents from displaying an American flag, except on certain holidays. The court held that "[e]nforcement of private agreements by the judicial branch of government is state action for the purposes of the Fourteenth Amendment." Id. at 887. This "state" action would deprive residents of their constitutional free speech right. But see Goldberg v. 400 E. Ohio Condominium Association, 12 F. Supp. 2d 820 (N.D. Ill. 1998) where the court rejected plaintiff's argument that a ban on distributing fliers and leaflets other than for political purposes to other condominium residents violated her First Amendment rights. In Quail Creek Property Owners Association, Inc. v. Hunter, 538 So. 2d 1288 (Fla. Dist. Ct. App. 1989) the CIC prohibited the display of "For Sale" signs in residents' yards. The court held that the possibility of judicial enforcement of a restriction is not enough to constitute state action. Therefore, there was no unconstitutional impairment of free speech by the CIC. A majority of courts have held that the fact that CICs take on responsibilities normally reserved for governments does not transform their conduct into state action.

3. *Federal and State Fair Housing Acts.* Just as the developers, by their initial marketing activities, may determine who can become unit owners, the CIC board, in exercising its powers under the declaration, may do the same. Through its ability to exercise a right of first refusal or, more commonly in a cooperative, a right to veto admittance of someone to participate, the board must take care not to discriminate in any way that would violate fair housing laws (see discussion at Chapter 16C3, infra). Liability can be for discrimination based upon race, religion, ethnicity, handicap, or even family status.

Furthermore, prohibited discrimination in selecting those who may own units is not the only risk. Board conduct making it difficult for one in a protected class to live in the CIC may also violate fair housing law. In Fulciniti v. Village of Shadyside Condo. Ass'n, 1998 U.S. Dist. LEXIS 23450 (W.D. Pa. Nov. 20, 1998) (unreported decision) the plaintiff suffered from multiple sclerosis that she claimed necessitated that two trained dogs live with her. She prevailed in an action against the board of her condominium association, which would not recognize an exception to the prohibition of dogs in the declaration of CC&Rs. The court held that multiple sclerosis was a "disability" protected by the Fair Housing Act and similar Public Accommodations laws in effect in the Commonwealth of Pennsylvania. Under these acts the association is required to provide reasonable accommodations for disabled persons no matter what the CC&Rs provide. But see Thompson v. Westboro Condo. Ass'n, 2006 U.S. Dist. LEXIS 60328 (W.D. Wash. Aug. 25, 2006) (unreported decision), in which the defendant association refused to either construct a concrete ramp or allow a portable ramp so that the disabled plaintiff could ride a scooter, necessitated by progressive degenerative arthritis, up a common area step. The court held that under the federal Fair Housing Amendments Act the association did not have a duty to construct the ramp However, the court found that the question of whether the association's refusal to allow the portable ramp was reasonable presented genuine issues of material fact, and must be presented to a jury.

4. Business Judgment Rule and Liability of Governing Board Members. Some states use the Business Judgment Rule in lieu of a reasonableness standard when evaluating decisions of the governing board. This judicial rule "insulates an officer or director of a corporation from liability for a business decision made in good faith if he is not interested in the subject of the business judgment, is informed with respect to the subject of the business judgment to the extent he reasonably believes to be appropriate under the circumstances, and rationally believes that the business judgment is in the best interest of the corporation." Hyatt, Common Interest Communities: Evolution and Reinvention, 31 J. Marshall L. Rev. 303, 344 (1998).

By analogizing the work of the CIC board to that of a business corporation, board decisions about restrictions on owner use and assessments will be allowed if the board acted in good faith. This can lead to tight restrictions on owner rights. The Business Judgment Rule may prevent lawsuits that would normally be allowed under the reasonableness test. For example, a resident of a CIC would like to make changes to his unit, but the CC&Rs state that the association must approve any modification. What happens if the resident goes through with the modifications and the association brings an action to enjoin him? If the courts follow the business judgment rule, they will look at the intent of the restriction. If the court determines that the association acted in good faith and in the best interest of the CIC, then its restriction will stand. Levandusky v. One Fifth Ave. Apartment Corp., 75 N.Y.2d 530, 553 N.E.2d 1317, 554 N.Y.S.2d 807 (1990).

5. Limits on the Taxing Abilities of the CIC. A CIC can generate revenue by establishing and collecting assessments. This is a form of taxation enforced on the residents of the CIC. The assessments can be levied for purposes ranging from maintenance of common areas to lawn care to installation of improvements. Some argue that by the CIC collecting revenue, it becomes a quasi government. If left unchecked, a CIC can assess its residents in any manner it chooses. Generally, the declaration of the CC&Rs provides parameters for levying assessments. Winokur, Critical Assessment: The Financial Role of Community Associations, 38 Santa Clara L. Rev. 1135, 1152 (1998).

The developer creates the initial assessments, and because his primary objective is to sell units, the assessments are usually low. The assessments initiated by the developer are not always adequate to cover the cost of running the CIC in the future. Inadequate assessments can lead to major problems for CICs, including the need for the CIC to levy special assessments, which unit owners may not expect or even be able to pay. Some states have enacted statutes limiting the amount a CIC can assess a unit owner. The Illinois statute excerpted below provides a mechanism for unhappy owners to vote down increased assessments. What impact does the following have on the taxing power of the CIC? Does this change in state law make rejection of assessment increases by unit owners likely?

(a)(8)(i) . . . each unit owner shall receive notice, in the same manner as is provided in this Act for membership meetings, of any meeting of the board of managers concerning the adoption of the proposed annual budget and regular assessments pursuant thereto or to adopt a separate (special) assessment, (ii) that except as provided in subsection (iv) below, if an adopted budget or any separate assessment adopted by the board would result in the sum of all regular and separate assessments payable in the current fiscal year exceeding 115% of the sum of all regular and separate assessments payable during the preceding fiscal year, the board of managers, upon written petition by unit owners with 20 percent of the votes of the association delivered to the board within 14 days of the board action, shall call a meeting of the unit owners within 30 days of the date of delivery of the petition to consider the budget or separate assessment; unless a majority of the total votes of the unit owners are cast at the meeting to reject the budget or separate assessment, it is ratified.

765 ILCS 605/18.

B. ENSURING COMMUNITY IN THE CIC

The promise of a sense of community is enticing to prospective buyers of CIC housing. For example, the marketing materials for the Disney Company's "Celebration" development promises old-fashioned neighborliness: "There once was a place where neighbors greeted neighbors in the quiet of summer twilight. . . . Where children chased fireflies. . . . The movie house showed cartoons on Saturday. The grocery delivered. . . . Remember that place? It held a magic all its own. The special magic of an American hometown."[7] Studies have shown that humans are wired to cooperate. Each human has a sense of belonging to society or a group and they will look past their immediate needs

---

7. Franzese, supra note 6, at 571 (2002), quoting Kirp, Book Review, Pleasantville, N.Y. Times, Sept. 19, 1999.

and consider the effect on the community as a whole. This "social capital" is a sense of belonging to a society, a fellowship among humans and social intercourse.[8]

A critical component of social capital is reciprocity—the notion members will receive back from the community what they have given to it. Here the "Golden Rule" of doing unto others is seen in a community setting. A person might perform a seemingly selfless act, but there is an underlying understanding that the benefit will return from membership in the community. This is one of the fibers that helps hold communities together.

One of the problems facing CICs today is that residents do not feel the connectedness that is central to a community. Without any input from those who will be living in the project, developers have attempted to meet buyers' expectations of a sense of community while they focus on protecting their own financial interests, especially of being able to market the unsold units in the project efficiently.

Professor Paula Franzese attributes much of this lack of connectedness in CICs to the residents' lack of control over the creation or change of the CIC rules. The developer creates the restrictions in the declaration of CC&Rs and forces the residents to buy into those rules. Residents' consent to the restrictions is implied upon purchase because the declaration of CC&Rs is recorded from the inception of the project.[9]

This model lacks the consent of the governed, a component that is important to the sense of community and to development of social capital. Moreover, the CIC board often has the authority to make rules and regulations that may intrude significantly on a unit owner's ability to use his real estate as he chooses. An owner may feel that the developer and the association, not to mention his neighbors, are against him when the board enforces restrictions against him for normally allowed activities of a property owner. This creates an adversarial atmosphere that undermines the success of communities. Required adherence to preestablished rules in the declaration and board-made rules, instead of allowing community norms to provide the direction of the community, has contributed to the failure of common interest communities to establish a sense of community among their residents.

The Restatement (Third) of Property (Servitudes) addresses some of the problems caused by current treatment of relationships established by CC&Rs. It offers solutions that may assist the CIC in meeting members' expectations regarding the often-absent sense of community. And, although it is not binding law, the Restatement will serve as a persuasive guide for courts and attorneys. It should reduce uncertainty and fill voids in existing law in a particular state.

Current CIC models set in place by the developers usually institutionalize the developer's vision, and often, the developer's control.[10] The Restatement model "goes a considerable way towards allowing for the development and gradual evolution of

---

8. Franzese, Building Community in Common Interest Communities: The Promise of the Restatement (Third) of Servitudes, 38 Real Prop., Prob. & Tr. J. 17, 22 (2003).

9. Franzese, supra note 6, at 555.

10. See Sangrund & Smith, When the Developer Controls the Homeowner Association Board: The Benevolent Dictator?, 31 Colo. Law. 91 (2002).

welfare-maximizing norms and self-enforcing rules of neighborly relations."[11] It provides that "[a]fter the time reasonably necessary to protect its interests in completing and marketing the project, the developer has a duty to transfer the common property to the association, or the members, and to turn over control of the association to the members other than the developer."[12] This allows the community itself to establish those rules that will best serve the community. By doing this, the Restatement promises to give the social capital to the CIC, allowing the social norms of that community to evolve, and giving residents the needed connection to the governing body that will foster a sense of community.

Moreover, the Restatement recognizes the positive effect of limiting the rule-making ability of the CIC itself: "Absent specific authorization in the declaration, the common-interest community does not have the power to adopt rules . . . that restrict the use or occupancy of, or behavior within, individually owned lots or units."[13] The comments to the Restatement explain the parameters of board rulemaking:

> The rationale for not giving an expansive interpretation to an association's power to make rules restricting use of individually owned property is based in the traditional expectations of property owners that they are free to use their property for uses that are not prohibited and do not unreasonably interfere with the neighbors' use and enjoyment of their property. People purchasing property in a common-interest community, which is usually subject to specific use restrictions set forth in the declaration, are not likely to expect that the association would be able, under a generally worded rulemaking power, to impose additional use restrictions on their property. On the other hand, they are likely to expect that the association will be able to protect them from neighborhood nuisances by adoption of preventative rules.[14]

To the extent the Restatement principles are adopted, they provide guidance as to the meaning of the "reasonableness test" with respect to actions of the board.

Nevertheless, the Restatement acknowledges the strength of the current judicial distinction between enforcement of the original declaration of CC&Rs and enforcement of the regulations adopted by the CIC board thereafter. It continues deference to the former: "Servitudes included in the declaration are valid unless illegal, unconstitutional or against public policy, under the rule stated in [Restatement] sec 3.1."[15] The reality is that purchasers of units may not have reviewed the CC&Rs, which Professor Evan McKenzie has described as "a 200-page adhesion contract, which is merely a stack of non-negotiable, standardized boilerplate provisions."[16] The fact is that CC&Rs are difficult, if not impossible, to amend because amendment usually requires a

---

11. Franzese, supra note 8 at 33.
12. Restatement §6.19(2).
13. Restatement §6.7(3).
14. Restatement at cmt.b.
15. Restatement §6.7, cmt.b.
16. McKenzie, Symposium: Reinventing Common Interest Developments: Reflections on a Public Policy Role for the Judiciary, 31 J. Marshall L. Rev. 397, 398 (1998).

supermajority of two-thirds or more of the unit owners, even the many who do not choose to vote. Thus, in the future, the comprehensive and specific restrictions of existing CC&Rs may remain as an obstacle to developing the sense of community because of the continuing strong deference courts show toward the initial declaration of CC&Rs. Commercial real estate lawyers, advising developers and drafting CC&Rs for future CICs, need to recognize the potential consequences of their work, especially with regard to meeting the expectations of owners. Attorneys who understand the law of CIC administration will be able to explain to their developer clients the long-term, maybe terminal, impact of the originating declaration.

The following excerpt by a renowned CIC attorney[17] argues that there is a need for "reinvention" or reform of CICs and identifies certain perceptions of CICs that contribute to the current call for change.

Hyatt, Common Interest Communities: Evolution and Reinvention
31 J. Marshall L. Rev. 303, 309-317 (1998)

As the community association evolves, it confronts the challenges of "privatopia" and privatization. The first concept is a pejorative term and is applied to community associations in support of the argument that they have become private utopias of privilege and exclusive restrictiveness. In other words, community associations are alleged to be anti-community. There are and have been justifications for that argument. Privatization reflects a growing trend: local government imposing responsibility for public services and facilities upon the private sector. Taken together, privatopia and privatization help frame the need for evolution and reinvention. . . .

The criticisms of common interest communities reflect certain basic arguments or perceptions. It is helpful to identify them. First, there is the argument that current concepts do not further community. The compression issue discussed above is part of that argument, but more serious issues exist as well. The common interest community as an elite enclave behind gates excluding the public at large is a persistent depiction. There are concerns about diversity and disparity in services. Most significantly, perhaps, is that there is no consensus on what is meant by "community" with most literature addressing

---

17. Wayne S. Hyatt, an Atlanta attorney who represents CICs and their developers nationally and internationally, has extensive experience advising CIC developers and drafting the documents that set them up. He has provided leadership as a member of the American Law Institute, as Advisor to the Reporter for the Restatement of Property (Third): Servitudes, as Advisor to the Special Committee on a Uniform Condominium Act, Uniform Common Interest Ownership Act, and Uniform Planned Community Act of the National Conference of Commissioners on Uniform State Laws (NCCUSL), and as founder of the Community Association Law Seminar.

the community association as an "illiberal" undemocratic regime. Such rhetoric may warm but does not illuminate the debate.

Second, there is the argument that common interest communities are coercive, and not voluntary. This argument contends that because the range of housing choices is limited, individuals become subject to community association governance by necessity rather than by fully informed choice.

It seems a bootstrap argument to assert that because common interest community housing has more in facilities, services, value enhancement and protection, it is coercive. The second question in this theme is "so what?" Assuming that there is an element of coercion, the challenge is to determine the effect. A more serious issue is the question of the degree of the buyer's comprehension of the effects of the governance structure and the nature of that structure. Coercion becomes more of a polemic than a defining consideration.

The third theme is that of the individual and the group. At the root of this theme is society's preoccupation with the individual's "rights" and society's disregard for the rights of the group. Another aspect of this theme is that of expectations. One of the core sources of the individual/group divergence is the lack of understanding of the community association and resulting expectations that are inconsistent with its governance reality. Much of the blame for this goes to the developer-builder-seller and her attorney. Some of the blame, however, must be shared by the management and brokerage communities, some rests with societal norms, and some rests with the individual.

Fourth, it should require no citation in support of the proposition that community association law practitioners are change-averse and precedent-bound. There are, however, citations and experiences in support of this proposition. Much enforcement litigation is the result of the unwillingness of the association manager and attorney to refrain from enforcing association rules for fear of setting "a precedent." The result often is an overly restrictive environment that the basic governance structure does not require.

Fifth, there is a perception of a limited "business" purpose for community associations. That purpose is seen as property management solely or property management and value protection. This perception is in part the result of early government-produced and required document forms and in part the result of the nature of community development in its first 20 or so years. The issue today is to address how these purposes are changing and the effect of that change.

The sixth theme deals with the association's structure and the potential for rigidity resulting from a corporate structure as opposed to a participatory democratic structure. There have long been discussions about the characterization of the community association and whether that characterization had an impact on the legal rules applicable to the association's or its board's decisions. A question for the future is how to formulate a governance structure to minimize the negatives and to optimize the potential for community activities. One starting point might be to empower, not to impose.

Finances comprise a seventh theme. In the past, the association has paid its way by general or special assessments, most paid monthly, from the members. In some cases, there are user fees for particular services. The question becomes whether these monetary sources are adequate for the future roles and activities of the evolving common interest community. There are new approaches, and each approach raises its own set of legal issues.

Finally, the eighth theme is a complex theme involving the relationship between the community association and local government. . . . Both substitution of the community association for the government and privatization can have profound effects if the community association becomes the functional equivalent of the government with the attendant constitutional implications.

C. DEVELOPER CONCERNS

An attorney representing the developer of CICs (i.e., most developers of housing in the future) should understand the client's business and appreciate the risks involved. Only in this way can an attorney help the developer identify and evaluate those risks, thereby helping the client make sound decisions. Understanding the client's profit expectations— that is, the basic economics of the project—is important. Because development involves a relatively long timeline and because of the cyclical nature of real estate investment, the goal should be to provide flexibility in planning to respond to potential downturns. Preparing for defaults by appreciating that they are possible and by suggesting remedies and solutions if they should occur are significant parts of the commercial real estate attorney's complex task.

Many of the topics covered elsewhere in this casebook form the knowledge-base on which the developer's attorney will give advice: choice of entity for ownership of the land and improvements; acquisition of the land; securing the necessary permits; obtaining financing both for construction and postconstruction; financing to the purchasers; the construction process; and marketing and sale of units to buyers.[18]

Additionally, drafting documents that reflect the developer's plan and commitments is a major part of the attorney's work. Of course, opinion letters may be required to back up the attorney's advice. Then the various contracts and deeds supporting the different aspects of the development (e.g., declaration of CC&Rs, marketing materials, reports and disclosures to government regulators, construction and postconstruction financing, real estate sales contracts, and deeds to purchasers) require careful review, drafting, and revision.

---

18. An excellent, pragmatic treatment of this perspective was prepared by John D. Hastie, Real Estate Acquisition, Development and Disposition from the Developer's Perspective, ALI-ABA Resource Materials, Modern Real Estate Transactions 1577 (1996).

1. The Choice of CIC Form

Development of CICs offers challenges and opportunities for the developer and its attorney. Like all housing developers, the CIC developer has a primary interest in protecting its real estate assets and reputation. Even the preliminary decision of setting up the CIC as a condominium instead of a cooperative or a planned unit development will require analysis of the applicable law and the marketability of the chosen form of CIC.

A condominium is a creation of a state statute, generally some variation of the Uniform Condominium Act. The declaration of CC&Rs creates the powers of the condominium association. Each unit owner has title to its own unit with tenancy in common ownership of all common areas among all unit owners. See the sample Declaration of CC&Rs in the Documents Manual.

In comparison, the real estate interests of a cooperative are owned by a nonprofit single asset corporation. Individual owners hold long-term, or perpetual, leases and shares of stock in the corporation. Thus, with respect to ownership, the individual owners possess a personal property interest in the stock of the corporation rather than a real estate interest in the building itself. Their "rent" pays any mortgages on the real property (e.g., for the original construction and any improvements), real property taxes and maintenance, and joint utility bills. "Coops" represent under 5 percent of all CICs, with many in New York City.

Although definitions are not standard here, generally, the planned unit development is similar to a condominium except that (1) it is a creature of the common law, without enablement by statute; (2) it is not regulated and does not carry consumer protections; and (3) common areas are often owned by the homeowner association, rather than being divided among the unit owners as tenants in common.[19]

Two historical examples of CIC developments in Illinois illustrate the complexity involved in the initial decision concerning the type of CIC to establish. Until 1995 a requirement of the Illinois Condominium Act allowed development of, or conversion to, the condominium form of ownership only if the developer submitted "property legally or equitably owned in fee simple to the provisions of the [Condominium Act]."[20] Thus, Lake Point Tower, a luxury rental apartment building in Chicago on Lake Michigan, could not be converted into condos until the owner of the building, American Invsco, acquired the reversion interest on the long-term ground leasehold which they held. The lessor had transferred only a long-term lease for the land to American Invsco in 1965, which became the site for the "world's tallest apartment building." Only after a complicated land swap in 1983, whereby American Invsco acquired title to the land beneath the building, was conversion to condominiums possible.[21]

---

19. See Geis, Codifying the Law of Homeowner Associations: The Uniform Planned Community Act, 15 Real Prop., Prob. & Tr. J. 854 (Winter 1980).

20. 765 ILCS 605/2.

21. Ibata, Gouletases Lose "Crown Jewel" to Inland, Chicago Trib., Apr. 19, 1987.

A 1995 amendment to the Illinois Condominium Act carved out a narrow exception that permitted development of a 770-acre parcel that was owned by a religious order whose charter would not permit it to transfer the fee simple.[22] Because research on the Chicago residential real estate market showed that condominiums fetched higher prices and sold much more easily than co-ops or planned communities, developers wanted to use that form of CIC. So, in both instances, developer plans to develop condos were delayed until the legal requirements could be met (or changed!).

2. Developer Control of the Board

The fact that the marketing and development of CICs emphasize the "sense of community" also may place the CIC developer in a different position from the non-CIC developer. As to the unsold units in the CIC, the developer is worried about the conduct and financial stability of the governing body because these may affect future sales. Such concern will lead the developer to keep control of the CIC as long as possible, even when such control directly conflicts with the ability of the CIC to meet expectations of the buyers for governing themselves.

Gary Poliakoff explains why the developer would want to retain control: (1) controlling the purse strings—a developer-controlled board has greater control over association expenditures and can prevent unnecessary capital projects from being bankrolled during the period when the developer may have guaranteed the maintenance expense to buyers; (2) precluding litigation by the owner's association against the developer for defects or other failures to meet promises; and (3) preventing amendment of the CC&Rs or the bylaws in a way that would hurt sales (e.g., restrictions on investor ownership).[23]

However, by controlling the association board, the developer that is acting in multiple roles as declarant (or creator of the CIC), builder, marketer/seller, and property manager for the CIC risks conflicts of interest and liability. Minimally, wearing multiple hats may create liability for construction defects. The developer as builder may be required under local, state, or federal law to disclose all material facts known to it when it markets the units. For example, the Soils and Hazard Analyses of Residential Construction Act in Colorado, CRS §6-6.5-101, requires disclosure of information relating to soil conditions. Consumer protection acts and unfair and deceptive trade practice statutes may prohibit

---

22. The political aspects of the amendment process were suggested by the Chicago Tribune: "[A] law that quietly—and anonymously—passed as an amendment to a bill about Metropolitan Water Reclamation District bonds permits creation of condominium units on leased property owned by certain tax-exempt groups with the proviso that the condo ownership would end when the lease expired or was terminated.... But the Real Property Law Committee of the Chicago Bar Association has lambasted the bill as full of hidden traps, because buyers would be effectively purchasing a piece of a long-term lease rather than a securely held condo...." Allen, Lawmakers' Real Estate Decisions Stir Praise, Ire, Chicago Tribune, June 18, 1995, C1.

23. Poliakoff, Transition of Control of the Community Association from the Unit Owners' Perspective, 16 Prob. & Prop. 49 (2002).

non-disclosure of some defects, and the Interstate Land Sales Full Disclosure Act (15 U.S.C. §1701 et seq., discussed at Chapter 16C5, infra) adds other disclosure requirements. The potential for problems is highlighted by this scenario that occurred in Colorado:

> In one case, a creative settlement valued at over $10 million was reached after several years of bitter litigation that pitted neighbor against neighbor. The situation escalated when a developer-controlled board allegedly failed to properly investigate and remedy slope stability and fill problems affecting the community's road system. Ultimately, a class action suit was certified against several board members and the declarant-developer who appointed them. These board members also controlled or managed the affairs of the declarant-developer. The declarant-developer allegedly was responsible for the defective condition of the roads and various claimed misrepresentations and non-disclosures accompanying the sale of lots in the community when acting in its capacity as developer-vendor.[24]

While the developer remains in control of the board, the declarant-developer may be held to owe the unit owners a duty of care similar to that of a fiduciary standard of care, whereas board members elected by unit owners normally would only be liable for wanton and willful acts or omissions, a more forgiving standard of care.[25] A fiduciary standard requires acting with the utmost good faith toward the CIC and for the sole good of the association and the unit owners. But this is likely to be inconsistent with the goals of the developer/marketer, who is in an arm's length relationship with purchasers of the units and with the CIC.

3.   Fair Housing Law Implications in Planning a CIC

Developers of CICs must comply with the requirements of fair housing rules, even at the planning stage of the project. For example, depending on the type of building structure, accessibility for handicapped persons may be required under the Fair Housing Act (FHA) (42 U.S.C. §3604). The statute defines "covered multifamily dwellings" as "(A) buildings consisting of 4 or more units if such buildings have one or more elevators; and (B) ground floor units in other buildings consisting of 4 or more units." 42 U.S.C. §3604(f)(7). Thus, single-family homes and townhouses, even in planned communities, are not covered by the accessibility requirements. As to covered units, the FHA provides accessibility guidelines for the design and construction of new multifamily housing. The seven requirements with which new housing must comply are: an accessible building entrance on an accessible route; accessible and usable public and common use areas; usable doors (basically a 34″ wide door); an accessible route into and through covered

---

24. Sandgrund & Smith, When the Developer Controls the Homeowner Association Board: The Benevolent Dictator?, 31 Colo. Law. 91 (Jan. 2002).
   25. Id.

dwelling units (basically, corridors, hallways, and openings without doors must be 36″ wide or less); light switches, electrical outlets, thermostats, and other environmental controls must be in locations accessible to residents in wheelchairs; reinforced walls for grab bars; and usable kitchens and bathrooms.[26]

A series of cases arising out of the Lion's Gate Garden Condominium development in Maryland suggest the liability attributable to a variety of parties involved in the "design and construction" of residential dwellings that fail to comply with accessibility requirements. The federal district court in Baltimore Neighborhoods, Inc. v. Rommel Builders, Inc.,[27] rejected the builder defendant's motion for summary judgment. The builder argued that a party is liable only if it both designed and built the dwelling units. That same court also rejected the builder's argument that remedies of the FHA could not apply to a builder that no longer owned or controlled the property. At trial in Baltimore Neighborhoods, Inc. v. LOB, Inc. and Lions Gate Garden Condominiums, Inc.,[28] the court recognized claims of emotional injury to a prospective purchaser of a unit who happened to be a tester for a fair housing advocacy group (only $1 was awarded because the tester failed to prove actual injury beyond "hurt feelings due to humiliation") and a claim by the advocacy group for the cost of testing and an educational program for area builders ($3,358). The builder was ordered to deposit sufficient funds with the court to retrofit the common areas and interiors of the 40 non-compliant units, even though the work might inconvenience non-disabled owners on the ground floor of the three-story buildings. Of the $453,573 to be deposited, $96,000, or $3,000 per owner, was to be paid as an incentive to the owners who allowed their units to be retrofitted.[29] Clearly, advice of counsel to the developer or builder of multifamily CICs regarding the FHA requirements may lead to substantial risk avoidance.

Additionally, the developer and the association both must accommodate persons with a disability. For example, a first come/first serve policy for distributing parking spaces may constitute a violation. In Shapiro v. Cadman Towers, Inc.,[30] the plaintiff, an owner in a 400-unit cooperative apartment building who suffered from multiple sclerosis, was on a waiting list for a parking space. The appellate court affirmed the lower court's grant of a preliminary injunction requiring the apartment and its Board president to provide the disabled owner with a guaranteed space on the ground floor of the garage even before the plaintiff came to the top of the list for assignment of any space. In these circumstances, the normal policy of assigning spaces violated Section 3604(f), even if compliance meant that another apartment owner would lose her current space! Although no reported case yet has considered the issue, where a protected person requires a parking space near an

---

26. See Final Fair Housing Accessibility Guidelines, 56 FR 9472-01; 24 C.F.R. §100.205.

27. 3 F. Supp. 2d 661 (D. Md. 1998).

28. 92 F. Supp. 2d 456 (D. Md. 2000).

29. A third case, Baltimore Neighborhoods, Inc. v. Rommel Builders, Inc., 40 F. Supp. 2d 700 (D. Md. 1999) even discusses possible applicability of the Americans with Disabilities Act, which requires accessibility in public places where the developer used one model condominium unit as the "sales office."

30. 51 F.3d 328 (2d Cir. 1995).

entrance or an elevator, such a first come/first serve policy set up by the developer in the CC&Rs may violate fair housing law. Attorneys for the developer should be mindful of the statutory requirements when drafting the project documents.

Another area of risk under fair housing law is the marketing practices the developer uses to sell the units. A developer, or a CIC, discriminates against protected classes if it steers minorities or other protected groups (distinguished by race, color, religion, sex, national origin, handicap, or familial status) to live in targeted areas. Steering occurs "when they encourage Whites to live in White neighborhoods, Hispanics to live in Latino neighborhoods, and Black Americans to live in Blacks neighborhoods by withholding information about the availability of housing."[31] Asserting any type of racial preference by marketing practices is prohibited. Such practices range from what type of person is depicted in an ad to where the advertisement is placed.

The developer-client who wants to build a community for older adults (who may want to live without the intrusion of younger residents and, especially, children) brings a distinct set of challenges to the real estate lawyer advising her.[32] Developers who wish to build an "active senior community" will need to abide by the statutory provisions that permit such projects as exceptions to the general fair housing prohibition against age discrimination.[33] Current law requires meeting certain criteria in order to qualify for the exemption: (1) at least 80 percent of the occupied units must be occupied (not necessarily owned) by at least one person 55 years of age or older; (2) the community must publish and adhere to policies and procedures that demonstrate an intent to comply with the requirements of the FHA—these will be found in the CC&Rs, rules, handbooks, and other publications (the requisite intent to comply may be demonstrated by the marketing materials shown to prospective residents, advertisements portraying the project as a 55 or older community, language in leases indicating residents must be 55 or older, the development and adherence to age screening procedures, and the actual practices of the association);[34] and (3) the community must verify occupancy—a challenge because verification must be by valid surveys and must be done on an ongoing basis.

Moreover, because federal law allows local and state laws to impose additional or different requirements as long as these are not inconsistent with the federal statute,[35] attorneys for developers need to research the applicable local and state laws on fair housing.

Attorney Wayne Hyatt indicates a host of other practical problems associated with age-restricted communities based on his experience counseling developers. First, strict compliance with the requirements of the FHA is demanding. Second, on an emotional

---

31. Petty et al., Regulating Target Marketing and Other Race-Based Advertising Practices, 8 Mich. J. Race & L. 335, 369 (2003).

32. See Hyatt, Age Restricted Communities: Legal Considerations in Active Adult Retirement Communities, ALI-ABA Course Study Materials: Drafting Documents for Condominiums, PUDs and Golf Course Communities, March 2000.

33. 42 U.S.C. §3607(b)(2).

34. 24 C.F.R. §100.304.

35. 42 U.S.C. §3615.

level, age disparity between one of the resident spouses (usually, the "trophy" wife) and the other residents can be problematic. Third, and related to the first two, is the task of information-gathering and record-keeping performed regularly and, hopefully, without aggravating residents. Fourth, even though all residents may be over 55, there is likely to be a diversity of interests among the residents. Some may be just 55 years old with others in their eighties. Diversity based on such disparities as economic status, health, and marital status may mean the group is not as homogeneous as some would expect. This leads to a fifth practical problem—high expectations and the life experience and financial ability to try and do something about any broken promises by the developer and the marketing staff. Finally, Hyatt lists health issues that are likely to arise for any resident and the "response variables" ranging from having professional care providers in the home to having children under age 55 residing with the parent to provide care (and the potential desire of the underage children wishing to remain after the parent dies).[36]

4. Adaptive Reuse in Urban Settings: Brownfields

Urban redevelopment is a growing trend among developers. This "[n]ew urbanism is a movement that . . . addresses many of the ills of our current sprawl development pattern while returning to a cherished American icon: that of close knit community."[37] New urbanism is more than just a planning structure, though. It combines community planning with political theory, social structure, and environmentalism.[38] This trend has led developers in urban areas to reuse existing structures to create communities.

The key to urban redevelopment often lies in the reuse of abandoned real estate. When converting former industrial sites or other commercial properties to residential condominiums or other CICs, developers and their attorneys must consider many factors. One of the biggest concerns facing urban renewal developers is the redevelopment of brownfields. Brownfields are "abandoned or underutilized urban land and/or infrastructure where expansion or redevelopment is complicated, in part, because of known or potential environmental contamination."[39] Brownfields can be anything from old warehouses to abandoned gas stations. They can be found anywhere in the country, but are largely concentrated in the inner cities, where manufacturers have left urban sites to take refuge in the surrounding suburban areas. Reuse of brownfields will help rejuvenate an urban area, protect the area from further contamination, and fill the area with residents to create a sense of community. The reuse of a brownfield site might also

---

36. Hyatt, Common Interest Communities: Evolution and Reinvention, 31 J. Marshall L. Rev. 303, 329 (1998). Students should review forms suggested by Wayne Hyatt in the Documents Manual. See also Hyatt, supra note 32.

37. Hyatt, Common Interest, supra note 36, at 330.

38. Id.

39. Wolf, Dangerous Crossing: State Brownfields Recycling and Federal Enterprise Zoning, 9 Fordham Envtl. L.J. 495 (1998).

offer benefits over the use of previously undeveloped (or "greenfield") sites, because there likely will be existing roadways, water and sewage lines in the area.

Liability for past contamination is a major concern for developers. Although most sites are not seriously contaminated,[40] if the developer takes on the task of redeveloping a brownfield, it wants to be sure that it will not be held liable for any past contamination. If a developer spends the money to test the site, it may be required to report it to the Environmental Protection Agency (EPA), which might place it on the National Priorities List for contaminated areas that are targeted for cleanup.[41] If this is the case, the liability would attach itself to the developer for past contaminations. Once the site is targeted for cleanup, the parties involved will be strictly, jointly, and severally liable for the cost of the cleanup.[42] In order to separate itself from the contamination, the developer must sustain the heavy burden of establishing the divisibility of its contribution.[43]

Another concern for developers is the cost of cleanup. Because of the potential liability, most developers fear they cannot make a reliable estimate about the cost of redevelopment. Concern over cost stems from vagueness in the cleanup standards. To determine the possible cost of a cleanup is an expensive task, as "[e]stablishing the appropriate level of cleanup requires a wealth of information about remedies that might work at each site."[44] Also, the developer must comply with both state and federal regulations, which can prove costly. A developer cannot rely on past experience in determining the cost of a cleanup, because each site must be analyzed on an individual basis.[45]

A major solution comes in the form of standardizing the cleanup standards which helps the developer to predict the possible cost. This will allow the efficient conversion of brownfields to go forward. More developers are likely to invest in the much-needed rejuvenation of brownfields, especially in urban areas that have been left behind. Some also argue that cleanup standards are too strict. They believe that the standards are based on unrealistic possibilities of risks.[46]

Moreover, the EPA has wide latitude to release PRPs (potentially responsible parties) from further liability or to cap liability even if that release or cap is not granted to all PRPs. For example, in United States v. Brook Village Associates, 20006 U.S. Dist. LEXIS 81197; No. 05-195 (D.R.I. Nov. 6, 2006), the EPA identified a number of parties who may have been responsible for contamination of a Rhode Island site. After all the PRPs complied with several EPA orders to conduct partial cleanup activities, two of the PRPs negotiated consent decrees with the government. These decrees were intended to limit the further liability of those two PRPs for future cleanup costs, and were challenged

---

40. Eisen, Brownfields of Dreams?: Challenges and Limits on Voluntary Cleanup Programs and Incentives, 1996 U. Ill. L. Rev. 883, 901 (1996).

41. Id. at 903.

42. Id. at 904.

43. Id.

44. Id. at 908.

45. Id. at 909.

46. Id. at 910.

by another of the PRPs on various grounds. The U.S. District Court did not block their filing, holding that the EPA had broad discretion to enter into such decrees.

To address some of these problems, states and the federal government have established incentive programs to encourage the reuse of brownfields.[47] These incentives take two forms. First, state and local tax credits are available, and second, developers may receive a waiver of liability in return for reuse of brownfields.[48]

These concerns about liability and cleanup costs, coupled with the EPA's authority to impose additional requirements even if a developer complied with a state voluntary cleanup program (VCP), have contributed to the mothballing of many brownfield sites.[49] To remedy this, Congress passed the Small Business Liability Relief and Brownfields Revitalization Act of 2002.[50] The most important change for the potential developer who purchases a brownfield is the exemption from liability as a "bona fide prospective purchaser" (BFPP) even if the developer knows about existence of contamination after conducting due diligence.[51] Also, the federal enforcement deferral to state VCPs[52] means that generally the developer who gets approval of a cleanup plan from state government will not risk an EPA action.

Still, the windfall profit lien provision[53] may be a concern to both the developer and lenders to the developer for acquisition and building costs. If the EPA incurs response costs to clean up the property and the value of the property increases as a result, then the EPA can impose a lien for its response costs.[54] Furthermore, questions remain about what the "appropriate care" (instead of "due care") standard included in 42 U.S.C. §9601(40)(D) means.[55] In PCS Nitrogen Inc. v. Ashley II of Charleston LLC, 714 F.3d 161 (4th Cir. 2013), the court found that a property redeveloper, Ashley II, failed to establish a number of the eight criteria for the BFPP defense, including the exercise of appropriate care. In reaching its decision, the court rejected Ashley II's argument that appropriate care was a lesser standard than due care. The court speculated that appropriate care might even be a higher standard than due care, but ultimately held it to be at least as stringent as due care. As a result, the court held Ashley II liable as a PRP for soil contamination at the former phosphate fertilizer plant. Those relying on this statute should recognize its limits of protection. Young v. United States, 394 F.3d 858 (10th Cir. 2005) held that a party that incurred only preliminary expenditures (site investigation, soil samples, and risk assessment) cannot recover those costs unless actual response costs

---

47. Salsich, Thinking Regionally About Affordable Housing and Neighborhood Development, 28 Stetson L. Rev. 577, 599 (1997).

48. Id. at 599.

49. Collins, The Small Business Liability Relief and Brownfields Revitalization Act: A Critique, 13 Duke Envtl. L. & Pol'y F. 303 (2003).

50. 42 U.S.C. §§9601-9675.

51. 42 U.S.C. §9601(40).

52. 42 U.S.C. §9628(b).

53. 42 U.S.C. §9607(r)(2).

54. See Collins, supra note 49, at 316.

55. See Chapter 19 for additional discussion of these issues.

are also expended. In this case the plaintiffs purchased a parcel of land adjacent to a known superfund site. The plaintiffs undertook preliminary response steps on their land that revealed hazardous substances, but then abandoned the property with no intention of cleaning up the contamination. They then sued the federal and local governments in an effort to recoup the money they had spent. The court held that such costs were not recoverable "because the costs were neither necessary to the containment and cleanup of the hazardous releases nor consistent with the NCP [National Contingency Plan]." Id. at 864.

5. *Condominium Assessment Liens*

A unique aspect of living in a condominium is the sharing of common expenses among owners of individual units whereby each unit is subject to an assessment for its proportionate share of the common expenses. Unif. Condo. Act §3-115. Assessments are the primary source of revenue for a common interest community. They are used to operate the association and to maintain, repair, replace, and insure the community's common elements and amenities. The ability to collect assessments is critical to having a well-maintained, successful condominium community. When one unit owner fails to pay his or her share of common expenses, the remaining unit owners have to make up the difference. The increased assessments drive up the dues of unit owners who have been paying, until the dues become too high and the owners cannot sustain the payments. In the meantime, property values in the community decrease due to lack of maintenance and amenities, which can ultimately drive an association into bankruptcy.[56]

To facilitate an association's ability to collect assessments, state statutes give condominium associations a lien against delinquent units. Unif. Condo. Act §3-116. Association liens are subordinate to a first mortgage lien, which means that if the unit owner also defaults on his or her mortgage, the mortgage lender would have first priority over the proceeds from the foreclosure sale.[57] Because foreclosure sales often do not produce sufficient funds to pay off the first mortgage, the association may not be able to recover any assets through its lien, thereby making the lien of little value.[58] To address this undesired result, many states have enacted "super" assessment lien statutes which give condominium associations limited priority over previously recorded liens, including

---

56. For more on this subject, see Pinkerton, Escaping the Death Spiral of Dues and Debt: Bankruptcy and Condominium Association Debtors, 26 Emory Bankr. Dev. J. 125 (2009).

57. See Long Island Sav. Bank, F.S.B. v. Gomez, 568 N.Y.S.2d 536, 537 (App. Div. 1991) (holding that a subordinate lien on a condominium is extinguished if there are no excess proceeds from the sale).

58. For additional discussion of associations' lien rights compared to those of other lienholders and state lien priority statutes, see Bromley, Supremacy and Superiority: The Constitution's Effect on State Lien Priority Statutes, 44 Real Est. L.J. 442 (2016) and Boyack, Community Collateral Damage: A Question of Priorities, 43 Loy. U. Chi. L.J. 53 (2011).

mortgages.[59] Section 3-116(b) of the Uniform Condominium Act provides that an assessment lien is given limited priority upon foreclosure of the first priority mortgage lien "to the extent the common expense assessments based on the periodic budget adopted by the association . . . would have become due in the absence of acceleration during the six months immediately preceding institution of an action to enforce the lien." In other words, the "super" assessment lien gives the association priority at a mortgage foreclosure sale for unpaid assessments up to an amount equal to six months of regular assessments.

NOTES AND QUESTIONS

1. How Super is Superpriority? During the recent subprime mortgage crisis, foreclosures in some jurisdictions took far longer to complete than six months, which was the period the drafters of the Uniform Condominium Act chose to match the expected length of time needed for mortgage lenders to foreclose their delinquent loan. Moreover, during the dismal resale market, some mortgage lenders simply delayed holding the foreclosure sale while condominium assessments piled up well beyond the six-month superpriority period. How might you revise state law to disincentivize condominium lenders from delaying foreclosure? See Uniform Common Interest Ownership Act §3-116(c). A related concern has been whether the condominium association lien is truly superpriority in that the failure of a mortgage lender to protect its interests when the association forecloses its assessment lien will extinguish the mortgage lien. Can you see how it is fair for a relatively nominal assessment lien to extinguish a first mortgage (or deed of trust) in this manner? See SFR Investments Pool 1 v. U.S. Bank, 334 P.3d 408, 414 (Nev. 2014).

6. *Interstate Land Sales Full Disclosure Act (ILSFDA)*[60]

Compliance with ILSFDA requires filing a "Statement of Record" with the Office of Interstate Land Sales Registration and delivery of a "Property Report" to purchasers. The applicability of the ILSFDA requirements to condominium and cooperative developments was once firmly established. Condominium developers, however, suffered harsh financial consequences after the 2008 market crash when remorseful condominium purchasers began using trivial ILSFDA filing errors as a way to back out of contracts and receive a full refund of their purchase deposits. Congress responded in 2014 to exempt condominiums from the Act's regulatory provisions, apart from its anti-fraud provisions. See 15 U.C.S. §1702(b)(9) and (d). The new law eliminates the need for condominium

---

59. For an in-depth review of the variations of lien priority statutes adopted by the states, see Bromley, Encouraging Cooperation: Harmonizing the Battle of Association and Mortgage Lien Priority in America's Common Interest Communities, 43 Real Est. L.J. 255, 266 (2014).

60. 15 U.S.C. §1701 et seq.

developers to file registrations under ILSFDA or provide condominium unit purchasers with property reports and rescission rights. For more on this topic, see Taupeka, The Interstate Land Sales Full Disclosure Act: The Law of Unintended Consequences As Applied to Condominiums, 76 Ala. Law. 172 (2015). While condominium sales are no longer subject to registration requirements, the anti-fraud provisions of the Act that require certain contractual provisions related to improvements and amenities still apply to condominium sales that are not fully exempt. Developers also need to comply with any relevant state land sale regulations.

NOTES AND QUESTIONS

1. Parties Obligated under the Act. ILSFDA applies to developers and their agents. See 15 U.S.C. §§ 1703(a) (prohibiting enumerated activities by "developer or agent"), 1709(a) (authorizing civil action against a "developer or agent" for violation of §1703(a)). The question of who is a developer or agent within the meaning of the Act is often disputed. For example, the court in Dalzell v. RP Steamboat Springs, LLC, 781 F.3d 1201 (10th Cir. 2015) found that a master developer of a master-planned subdivision, who was not a party to contracts with buyers but was involved only in efforts to market a condominium development, was not a "developer" under the Act. The courts have also examined circumstances under which third parties, such as lending institutions and officers and directors of the developer, could be held liable under the Act as "aiders and abettors." The focus of the inquiry is the extent of the third party's involvement in the developer's activities. The court in Adams v. Central Fidelity Bank, 38 Va. Cir. 14, 1995 Va. Cir. LEXIS 1262 (1995) overruled the demurrer of the bank as a developer when it exceeds the normal course of dealing in the context of a real estate project by getting involved "purposefully" with advertising. In Hammar v. Cost Control Marketing and Sales Management of Virginia, Inc., 757 F. Supp. 698, 702–703 (W.D. Va. 1990) the court held that "a financial institution, when it goes beyond the ordinary course of dealing and function of a commercial bank, can be held liable as a 'developer' by allowing its name to be used in advertisements or announcements for development so as to lend its prestige and good name to the sales effort."

2. Lawyering. It is important to guide developer clients generally in their marketing and advertising of CIC developments. For an excellent primer on how to draft to avoid liability for misrepresentation or non-disclosure, see Stubblefield, ALI-ABA Course of Study Materials, Drafting Documents for Condominiums, Planned Communities and New Urbanism Developments, "VIII Sales Documents: General Guidelines and Disclaimers for Advertising, Marketing Materials and Displays," Vol. 2, Jan. 2003.

A case involving malpractice insurance is instructive concerning the potential attorney liability for negligence in advising the developer about disclosures that the developer was required legally to provide to prospective buyers. In Firemen's Fund Insurance Company

v. McDonald, Hecht & Solberg, 30 Cal. App. 4th 1373, 36 Cal. Rptr. 2d 424 (1994), the developer's insurance company had settled for over $10 million with residents of a planned community for misrepresentation of material facts about the development. The insurance company then sued the law firm to recover for the loss, alleging that the law firm was hired to provide legal advice on what disclosures had to be made to prospective purchasers of the units. The developer relied on that advice to its detriment. Although the issue in the case was whether the malpractice action of the developer was assignable to the insurer or was instead personal in nature, one can infer from the decision that even though such actions are not assignable, the developer itself could have brought the malpractice claim against the law firm. The price tag of the case should make the lawyer for the developer cautious.

THE ETHICAL REAL ESTATE LAWYER

Counsel for the Developer of CICs

You have developed a fine reputation as attorney for CIC developers in your town. Condo Developer has been your good client for several years. Mr. and Mrs. Investor also are clients of your firm for estate planning purposes, although you personally have not represented them. Now, the Investors want Condo Developer to convert a large apartment building they own into condominiums for sale. They propose that you and they contribute to this project: Investors have the real estate; Condo Developer will contribute skills and services in renovation and obtaining financing; and you will contribute your legal services in organizing the enterprise and representing it thereafter until all units are sold. The plan is to form a corporation with each party getting stock allocation based on the agreed value of each party's contribution. Under the proposed Restatement (Third), The Law Governing Lawyers, this arrangement constitutes a "business or financial transaction with a client" that is prohibited unless: (1) the client has adequate information about the terms of the transaction and the risks caused by the lawyer's involvement, (2) the terms and circumstances of the transaction are fair and reasonable to the client, and (3) the client consents to the lawyer's role after being encouraged to seek independent legal advice. §126. This is an especially difficult standard to meet because unintended overreaching is a possibility in transactions of this type. The lawyer must overcome a presumption that overreaching occurred by demonstrating the fairness of the transaction. For instance, this could be a problem even at the beginning of the relationship in valuing the legal services for the stock allocation.

Moreover, there is a potential violation of ABA Model Rule 1.7 that provides "[a] lawyer shall not represent a client if the representation of that client will be directly adverse to another client." Here, the lawyer represents the corporation as well as the developer, and her firm represents the Investors.

Finally, indirect conflicts are a possible problem for the successful attorney for CIC developers if the firm represents more than one developer where there is "competition for scarce building permits, water allocations or sewage disposal allocations." See Lisman, Steps to Protect Lawyer and Client: Ethical Considerations for the Lawyer Representing the Sponsor of Documents for Common Interest Communities, ALI-ABA Course of Study Materials, Drafting Documents for Condominiums, Planned Communities, and New Urbanism Developments, Vol. 2 (2003).

D. LENDER CONCERNS WITH CIC DEVELOPMENTS

1. *Financing Condominiums*

The following excerpt indicates the special treatment of condominiums by lenders.

M. Madison, J. Dwyer, and S. Bender,
The Law of Real Estate Financing
§10:2 (2016)

UNDERWRITING CONSTRUCTION LOANS[61]

In the mid-1960s, when the infatuation with condominiums began, many real estate lenders scoffed at the idea that condominium financing was specialized or different from typical single-family home subdivision financing. However, through experience, they discovered some significant differences in these two types of financing. First, it was found that market absorption data for single-family homes was inapplicable to condominiums. Thus, lenders initially did not have the necessary underwriting data to analyze proposed condominium loans. However, as statistics developed on condominium projects, lenders were supplied with information needed to underwrite and review condominium loans.

Second, the legal complexity of condominium ownership distinguishes it from the typical subdivision project. Because condominiums are creatures of state statute, careful attention must be given to complying with the applicable enabling legislation. The lender, the developer, and the attorney must handle the myriad details involved with the organizational documents for the condominium development and association, possible

---

61. This section of the treatise was written by Professor Vincent M. DiLorenzo.—EDS.

recreation leases, rights and obligations with respect to the common elements and limited common elements, phase development, and such options as condominium expansion and contraction. Documentation has become somewhat less complex (i.e., familiar) for permanent loans through the standardization efforts of the Federal National Mortgage Association (FNMA, or Fannie Mae) and the Federal Home Loan Mortgage Corporation (FHLMC, or Freddie Mac). However, with the advent of consumerism in condominium legislation and state statutory revision that requires disclosure of material items to purchasers and permits such sophisticated options as time-sharing and expansion and contraction of condominium developments, condominium financing remains a complex area.

Finally, condominium interim construction project financing differs from that of the subdivision with regard to sales risks. The subdivision builder can stop construction if sales are not progressing; the condominium project must be completed once construction starts. Accordingly, the construction lender's major risk in providing financing is that the units may not sell.

Analysis for Underwriting. Lenders will treat the costs of building condominiums more like subdivisions than rental developments. This means that in addition to looking at completion appraisals, the loan underwriters will consider the increased marketing and advertising costs, the transaction costs related to sale of the units and the additional professional fees necessitated by treating each unit as a separate piece of real property.

Because condominium developments are considered riskier than rental properties or subdivisions, lenders are conservative in their analysis. They may not base the loan-to-value ratio on the anticipated resale value. Instead, they look at the developer's track record, and they may treat high-end projects differently than those with less expensive units. For instance, one Chicago bank requires a relatively higher percentage of sales contracts with earnest money deposits of 10 percent for the luxury market that it has decided is riskier in the 2004 economy.

As additional protection, the lender will require title insurance on the validity of the condominium. The construction lender, and likely the permanent lender as well, will need to review and approve the condominium documents (declaration, bylaws, sales contracts, any government required disclosures or property reports, etc).

Presale and Release Requirements. As with other construction loans, the note will be secured by a mortgage or deed of trust on both the land and the improvements to be built. Usually the security document is recorded *before* construction begins, so that the construction lender's mortgage has priority over mechanics' liens. Also, it is recorded *before* the condominium declaration is recorded to provide the lender with the ability to foreclose free and clear of the condominium. It is not unusual for the lender to negotiate a presale requirement as a condition to a construction draw or progress payment as well as to recordation of the declaration. If recordation of the declaration is delayed until the presale conditions imposed by the lender are met, any default by the construction borrower before then gives the lender a means to take the title to the property and operate it as a rental.

Whether the lender requires a presale condition, and to what extent, depends on several factors. These include the financial condition of the developer, whether there are carve outs to a non-recourse loan, whether there are any personal guarantees for the loan, the equity of the borrower in the development, and market factors. The construction lender may rely on the presale requirements that FNMA and FHLMC have made for permanent financing because sales of the units are so dependent on permanent financing made available by those secondary markets.[62]

As with the construction of single-family houses in a subdivision, releases from the construction mortgage should be provided and recorded before the permanent purchase money mortgage in order to give the new lien of the unit owner's lender first priority. The construction mortgage should have a provision releasing an individual unit and its share of the common elements from the lien of the construction mortgage upon payment to the construction lender of a specified payment. Whether or not the specified amount includes any share of the sales proceeds for the developer depends on the negotiation between the parties. If the project is speculative or the market is down, the lender may demand the entire proceeds to pay down the indebtedness.

Sometimes, a phased development may reduce risks for both the developer and the construction lender. Although it might increase the overall project cost and the required legal documentation, phasing "might be necessary to save the developer from a ruinous cash squeeze caused by high release prices, and, in some cases, the added expense and legal complexities might be more than offset by the developer's ability to charge higher per-unit prices in the second development phase if all goes well in the initial phase." Moreover, lenders often prefer to finance large projects in phases, as they "can reduce their underwriting risks by making Phase II financing contingent upon a successful Phase I."[63]

Review of Documents. Minimally, the lender will review the following documents, samples of which are included in the Documents Manual: Declaration of CC&Rs; condominium by-laws, the sales contract that the developer will require prospective purchasers to use; and any public offering or property report required by local, state, or federal law. The construction lender will review documents with an eye toward its own needs, as well as keeping in mind the likely requirements of the permanent lenders that will fund the sale of the units.

---

62. See M. Madison, J. Dwyer, and S. Bender, The Law of Real Estate Financing §10:8 for discussion of this interrelationship and the significance of FNMA and FHLMC presale requirements to the construction lender. —EDS.

63. Id. at §10:4. —EDS.

Permanent Financing. A construction lender for condominium projects wants assurance that there will be financing available to those who buy the completed units. The developer will provide a commitment letter from a permanent lender indicating that a certain level of financing will be available to all unit purchasers who apply for and qualify individually for financing. Thus, some of the uncertainty of the sale of the units is reduced. Alternatively, the developer may obtain FNMA or FHLMC approval of the entire project for their purchase of individual end loans for the condominium units.

Assignment of Developer Rights. As a further protection, a condominium construction lender may require that the developer assign the special rights usually retained by the developer of such projects, including: purchase options; rights to add additional property to the condominium; the right to control of the board or to veto certain board actions for a specified period; property management contracts; recreational and other leases in and to portions of the condominium (e.g., golf courses); title insurance endorsements and the sales contracts and earnest money collected in connection with sale of individual units.

Under the Uniform Condominium Act, a lender is given three options in the event of a default and foreclosure. First, the lender has a right to request a transfer to it of all special declarant rights of the developer.[64] Second, the lender or foreclosure sale purchaser has the option of declaring that it holds the rights solely for purposes of transfer, thus relieving it of liability except for errors or omissions related to its control of the association board.[65] Third, the foreclosing lender or the foreclosure sale purchaser may assume an intermediate position by taking title "solely in order to sell existing units without making any additional improvements. In that case, the mortgagee is not subject to any obligations or liabilities as a declarant, except the duty to provide a public offering statement to unit purchasers."[66] A further protection, especially in a down market where the value of the project is deteriorating, is for the lender to retain the option in the event of a default of the construction loan of being able to replace the directors and officers of the condominium association with its own. Although this option may protect lenders against further deterioration of their collateral, "it may also expose them to liability—as successor developer—or expose the designated management team to liability—as officers or board members of the condominium association."[67]

Other Considerations for the Permanent Lender. One commentator provides a list of considerations that are likely to affect a permanent lender's decision to make the loans to individual unit purchasers. Because of the strong relationship between the willingness of a construction lender to lend to a developer of condominiums upon the availability of permanent financing, the following are important to the construction lender as well.

---

64. Uniform Condominium Act §3-104(c) .—EDS.
65. Uniform Condominium Act §3-104(e)(4) .—EDS.
66. See M. Madison, J. Dwyer & S. Bender, The Law of Real Estate Financing, at §10:7.—EDS.
67. Id.—EDS.

Physical characteristics, such as the mix of unit sizes and prices and anything affecting marketability of the units over time, are important to the security of the permanent lender. Likewise, regular and special assessments are relevant expenses that affect the ability of the unit owner/borrower to repay the permanent lender. Provision for adequate hazard and liability insurance on the common areas by the condominium association also affects the security of the permanent loan. Finally, any other circumstances that directly or indirectly reduce the value of individual units matter to both the permanent and construction lender.[68]

2. Financing Cooperatives

The financing of cooperatives differs from that of condominiums and non-CIC developments because of their distinct legal structure.[69] The fee title to the entire project, including the units, the land, and what would be considered common areas in a condominium, is held by a corporation. The residents do not actually own their units, but rather own shares of stock in the corporation and a lease granting exclusive occupancy of their unit and a right to use common areas.

Construction lending unfolds much as it would for the financing of a condominium project. Depending on the market and the degree of risk the lender is willing to assume, the loan to value ratio varies between 65 percent of the expected sales price and 75 percent of the value as a rental apartment building. The loan is secured by the real estate owned by the cooperative housing corporation. Thus, it qualifies as a mortgage. If the project fails as a cooperative, the lender can foreclose, bid at the sale, and operate the project as a rental (or sell the entire project for that use). The National Cooperative Bank makes underlying mortgage loans throughout the United States and is an important resource for developers, especially of low income housing.[70]

Two distinct sources of permanent financing exist. Loans made by the cooperative corporation for construction, acquisition, and/or improvements will be secured by mortgages on the land and building. Typically, unit owners will pay proportionate shares of the mortgage principal and interest as part of their monthly "rent" to the cooperative corporation. Because their ownership is not real estate, but personalty in the form of stock, loans to the unit owners for acquisition of the housing cannot be secured by mortgages. All the unit owners have to offer to lenders is their stock and leasehold rights, property that will not qualify for traditional home mortgage loans. This makes the ownership interest of cooperatives less marketable than that of condominiums and houses and less acceptable to permanent lenders who are unfamiliar with this form of ownership or consider it more risky. Also, typical restrictions on transferring ownership and

---

68. See id. at §10:10 for a permanent lender's checklist in condominium financing.—EDS.
69. See id. at §§10:13-10:15 for excellent discussion on the financing of housing cooperatives.
70. The website for the National Cooperative Bank is www.ncb.com.

occupancy of the unit may make getting a loan that pledges the assets of unit owners very difficult because a foreclosing lender would not have the same rights to possession, as in a mortgage foreclosure.

Nevertheless, permanent loans to unit owners have become increasingly available as a result of Congress' authorizing FHLMC and FNMA to include loans secured by housing cooperatives in their mortgage purchase programs on the secondary mortgage market.[71]

71. See M. Madison, J. Dwyer & S. Bender, The Law of Real Estate Financing, §10:8 for FNMA and FHLMC loan requirements.

Chapter 17

Negotiations, Mediation, and Arbitration

Much of the literature on avoiding disputes and using dispute resolution alternatives to litigation is written from the perspective of lawyers dealing with disputes after they arise (the "litigators") rather than from the perspective of transactional practitioners who can structure deals to avoid or at least reduce disputes between the parties.[1] The education of those lawyers who will dedicate their professional lives to commercial real estate practice must stress the benefits of looking at processes to resolve disputes from a transactional perspective. To that end, in this chapter we look at negotiation as a method to initially set up transactions with a goal of avoiding disputes between the parties, and also as a method for resolving, without litigation, any disputes that do arise. The overall goal of this chapter is to train the users of dispute resolution, the parties and their transactional attorneys, in selecting and drafting appropriate methods, whether it be negotiation, mediation, arbitration, or even litigation. The chapter avoids the ubiquitous focus on neutrals—mediators, arbitrators, and judges—and on those representing parties in a dispute.

Additionally, students will learn to distinguish between negotiations, mediation, and arbitration, to the extent that these function as alternative dispute resolution (ADR) methods. Learning the basics is essential to properly advise clients on selecting a method to resolve disputes, especially because this matter may be negotiated "pre-dispute." Increasingly, dispute resolution choices are incorporated into the terms of the underlying real estate documents. Of course, conscientious drafting of the appropriate dispute resolution provision, instead of blindly inserting a form, is important to competency here.

As real estate law students and prospective practitioners, you need to become knowledgeable about ADR. First, you need to understand what is involved in each of the main ADR processes and how they differ from each other and from litigation. Next, you should become familiar with how a transactional attorney will assist the real estate client in selecting one of the ADR methods. Finally, you will see the importance of drafting ADR choices into documents that are common in the field of commercial real estate practice (e.g., construction contract, lease). In contrast with courses you may have

---

1. See, e.g., Breger, Should an Attorney Be Required to Advise a Client of ADR Options? 13 Geo. J. Legal Ethics 427 (2000); but see Yarn, Lawyer Ethics in ADR and the Recommendations of Ethics 2000 to Revise the Model Rules of Professional Conduct: Considerations for Adoption and State Application, 54 Ark. L. Rev. 207, 251 (2001) (recognizes difference between choice pre-dispute and at time dispute arises).

already taken on ADR, the goal of this chapter is not to train you to be a neutral, mediator/arbitrator "wannabe." Instead, the perspective here is that of the attorney in a counseling/advising role. What should you tell your client about mediation or arbitration options, as opposed to litigation? Why? How would you draft documents to reflect your client's decision to adopt arbitration or mediation?

An important aspect of what a competent real estate lawyer can offer is advice based on an understanding that it is possible to resolve disputes using what some have termed "Appropriate Dispute Resolution." Indeed, one of the authors of this casebook has performed an empirical study of the attitudes and expectations of business lawyers, including those engaged in commercial real estate practice, about arbitration and mediation. (In contrast with traditional legal research, which analyzes legal doctrine in cases and statutes, empirical legal researchers make observations with the method of data collection and analysis made available to the audience.) The results of this study of transactional lawyers confirm that most lack even a basic understanding of some aspects of ADR.[2]

Moreover some commentators have even gone so far as to suggest that deficiencies in such knowledge and skill may subject an attorney to professional responsibility consequences and/or legal malpractice liability.[3] Whether you aspire to be a litigator or a transactional lawyer, the prominence of ADR is at its peak in America, and as such, it is unavoidable.

A. ALTERNATIVE DISPUTE RESOLUTION

The general definition of ADR is a procedure for settling a dispute by means other than litigation.[4] You have probably heard of at least three such procedures to settle a dispute without resort to the traditional court system: negotiation, mediation, and arbitration. These three procedures are by far the most popular vehicles employed in real estate practice when parties either decide they do not want to go to court at the time of dispute or have previously agreed not to go there.

---

2. Hammond, The (Pre) (As) Summed "Consent" of Commercial Binding Arbitration Contracts: An Empirical Study of Attitudes and Expectations of Transactional Lawyers, 36 J. Marshall L. Rev. 589 (2003).
3. Warmbrod, Could an Attorney Face Disciplinary Action or Even Legal Malpractice Liability for Failure to Inform Clients of Alternative Dispute Resolution? 27 Cumb. L. Rev. 791, 819 (1997).
4. Alternative Dispute Resolution, Black's Law Dictionary (10th ed. 2014).

1. Negotiation

Negotiation can be defined as communication for the purpose of persuasion.[5] Negotiation is ubiquitous in a transactional practice because parties use that process to define even the basic aspects of their relationship, including whether they wish to use litigation or some other method to resolve disputes that may arise. Transactional lawyers use their negotiation skills for more than to resolve disputes—they use them to set up the transaction. If negotiations take into account the needs of all the parties, this may reduce the likelihood of a dispute in the future.

Making the Deal. Rather than focusing on case opinions and clients' existing problems, transactional lawyers focus on understanding client objectives and motives, negotiating with other parties to achieve those objectives, and drafting/reviewing/editing the major documents of the transaction. Good lawyers do not separate knowledge of substantive law from their negotiating and drafting skills. Therefore, some of the assignments for this chapter will make use of substantive law covered in other parts of this casebook. Professor Daniel Bogart, who recommends this integrated approach to learning how to be a transactional attorney, stresses the importance of negotiations skill: "Drafting and legal research are skills critical to transactional lawyers, but there is another skill that should be of primary concern, and that skill is negotiations. For a transactional lawyer, negotiation is where the rubber meets the road. It is at the point of negotiation that knowledge of the substantive law, the goals of one's client, and the persuasive abilities of lawyers combine."[6]

Negotiating to Avoid Litigation or to Settle a Case. Negotiation is by far the most often used method of ADR. Lawyers in every practice area usually attempt to negotiate for the resolution of the dispute even before submitting a dispute to mediation, arbitration, or litigation. Actually, until a final outcome is reached, the parties may continue to negotiate and try to reach a settlement. Hence, even after a case goes to mediation, arbitration, or litigation, the parties may end up solving the problem themselves! Most disputes settle.

Despite the seemingly unstructured and informal negotiation process of two or more lawyers sitting around and trying to persuade one another, the thought processes of a good legal negotiator are highly structured and multi-tiered. Vast literature exists that professes to deconstruct the mind of a skilled legal negotiator. Among the most effective tactics noted have been to arrange to negotiate on your turf, designate demands as preconditions, make high first demands, invoke law or justice, appear irrational when it seems helpful, claim that you have no authority to compromise, and have your client

---

5. Goldberg, Sander, & Rogers, Dispute Resolution: Negotiation, Mediation and Other Processes, 17 (2d ed. 1992).

6. Bogart, The Right Way to Teach Transactional Lawyers: Commercial Leasing and the Forgotten "Dirt Lawyer," 62 U. Pitt. L. Rev. 335, 354 (2000).

reject any agreements only to raise the demand.[7] The preceding tactical list is meant to debunk any preconceived notions you might have that characterize negotiation as something that can be taken lightly or employed successfully without mental preparation. The goal of this chapter is not to provide this preparation, but instead to introduce you to negotiation both as a tangible and common alternative to the courthouse and as the way to define the transaction before reducing its terms to writing.

A feature of transactional negotiations is the reliance on different versions of the same basic form. For example, the attorney for a shopping center tenant will have read, reviewed, modified, and drafted many different versions of a Retail Shopping Center Lease for prior clients before attempting to negotiate a lease for a current tenant. The attorney may very well have a file of such documents negotiated and drafted to meet the needs of prior clients. He may consult a form-book, such as one recently prepared by the ABA Real Property Probate & Trust Law Section's Committee on Commercial Leasing Publications,[8] that offers the practitioner a pro-tenant form, a pro-landlord form, and a negotiated form of a retail shopping center lease.

The lawyer will have developed a checklist of lease terms that typically involve negotiation (e.g., right of the tenant to assign or sublet the premises and the obligation of the landlord to mitigate damages).[9] Assuming that assignment and sublease rights are the concern, a transactional lawyer might do research by checking the substantive law on these issues. Specifically, he would want to determine his client's liability for rent if the tenant is not permitted to assign the lease or, in the more likely scenario, if the assignment must be agreed to by the landlord. Furthermore, the attorney would research whether the landlord must be "reasonable" in rejecting an offered subtenant or assignee and how courts in the jurisdiction define "reasonableness" in this context. With this knowledge of the substantive law, the lawyer would advise the tenant-client to use a version of the lease that best protects the tenant's interest and would then attempt to get the landlord's lawyer to accept it. This exchange of documents—the lease, letters between attorneys and their clients and between attorneys on behalf of their clients, and proposed modifications—is an essential aspect of negotiations.

Moreover, good negotiations should reflect a professional attitude of the attorneys. Emanuel Halper, a New York City attorney with more than 40 years of practice experience in real estate, suggests how the transactional lawyer should act:

> When I read the first draft of a contract, mortgage, or lease that someone sends to my client, I usually get the feeling that the drafter hates us. Hates, not abstractly, but deeply, really, vituperatively. I often read leases prepared by a landlord's lawyer. As I wade through its

7. Meltsner & Schrag, Negotiating Tactics for Legal Services Lawyers, 7 Clearinghouse Rev. 259 (1973).

8. Ira Meislik & Dennis M. Horn, ed. The Commercial Lease Formbook: Expert Tools for Drafting and Negotiating, 2nd ed. American Bar Association (2010).

9. See, e.g., Madison, The Real Properties of Contract Law, 82 B.U. L. Rev. 405 (2002). See Chapter 10A4 and 10A6 for discussion of these substantive issues.

turgid prose down to the last run-on sentence, I sometimes wonder whether my client (the tenant) really has the right to occupy the premises.... When my client is the landlord, reviewing a form lease prepared by a powerful tenant can also leave me incredulous. Some tenant form leases provide for so many opportunities to withhold rent payments that I wonder whether the tenant is really willing to pay any rent at all.... Since most lawyers don't litigate, and they spend most of their lives negotiating, it would seem a particularly good idea for them to discard old notions and to rethink their role in society. They are professional negotiators.[10]

Besides, striving for a fair agreement when negotiating and drafting real estate documents has as its main advantage that "you might get it signed."[11]

NOTES AND QUESTIONS

Are there any apparent differences when you compare negotiating the terms of a transaction with negotiating after a dispute arises between the parties in an attempt to avoid litigation? Are the skills and knowledge of the attorney in the two types of negotiations substantially different—that is, should you use a transactional lawyer for the first and a "litigator" thereafter?

2. *Mediation*

Mediation is negotiation carried out with the assistance of a third party.[12] This third party, or mediator, is chosen by the parties, and its role is not to decide who is right or wrong. Instead, the mediator's role is to facilitate the resolution of the dispute by fostering an aura of flexibility and compromise. The mediator's job is to focus the parties on resolving their differences amicably, rather than on adjudicating a hostile dispute. Mediators fall into two basic types. A facilitative mediator helps parties overcome communication problems that have made prior negotiations unsuccessful. This mediator helps parties discover and explore multiple options for settlement without imposing any particular option. An evaluative mediator does not actively assist the parties in their actual negotiations, but rather identifies the risks inherent in each party's position and predicts the outcome if the dispute went to trial.

Today, mediation is most commonly encountered in the labor and family law arenas. Mediation has gained acceptance in the United States because it offers concrete benefits to the parties that would be absent or diluted if the dispute were litigated. Compared with arbitration and litigation, mediation is business-based, with the parties in control, and is non-binding and non-adversarial.

10. Halper, Lawyers Doing Battle, Real Est. Rev, (Winter 1998) at 62-64.
11. Halper, Can You Find a Fair Lease?, Real Est. L.J. 99 (1985).
12. Goldberg, supra note 5, at 103.

Mediation may be the process of choice when parties have a continuing relationship they wish to preserve. For example, where ongoing performance of a construction contract is likely to trigger disputes, the parties may agree ahead of time to have a mediator (or even an arbitrator) available to resolve those potential disputes quickly.

3. Arbitration

Today in America, arbitration is undergoing an unprecedented surge in availability, acceptance, and institutionalization, more so than any form of dispute resolution before it. All lawyers, and especially those in commercial real estate, must have a working knowledge of the process and appreciate how selecting arbitration may affect the outcome of disputes. In comparison to mediation, arbitration is rights-based; relies on theories, claims, and counterclaims; is right versus wrong; is binding and non-appealable; and is adversarial.

Historically, arbitration was the dispute resolution mechanism of choice for local commercial groups. Merchants and tradesmen utilized arbitration to settle business disputes among themselves. The parties would explain their positions to a fellow merchant or group of merchants and abide by the oral ruling. The ruling of the merchant arbitrator was in no sense legally binding upon the disputants, but the fear of local ostracism guaranteed compliance. In this manner, arbitration was historically born of the need to settle disputes quickly and informally without expensive and protracted litigation.

There were times, however, when one of the disputants would resist submitting the dispute to arbitration despite a previously negotiated agreement to arbitrate. The other party might attempt to assert his rights under the arbitration contract by asking a court to issue an order compelling arbitration. British and American courts were not receptive to such motions. The courts rejected commercial efforts to assert rights under an arbitration contract because they viewed arbitration as depriving courts of rightful jurisdiction over such cases.

To remedy this judicial hostility to arbitration, Congress passed the Federal Arbitration Act of 1925 (FAA).[13] The goal of this legislation was to place contracts to arbitrate on the same footing with all other contracts. Subsequent to this federal legislation, the various states passed similar laws encouraging the enforceability of contracts to arbitrate. Additionally, the U.S. Supreme Court has preempted state authority to govern arbitration agreements through its interpretation of the FAA.[14] Today, both federal and state courts embrace a strong preference for binding arbitration and enforce contracts to arbitrate almost universally. Although this preference for arbitration has been

---

13. 9 U.S.C. §1 et seq.

14. See, e.g., Prima Paint Corp. v. Flood & Conklin Mfg. Co., 388 U.S. 395 (1967) (determining the circumstances that warrant federal courts' jurisdiction over the dispute); Southland Corp. v. Keating, 465 U.S. 1 (1984) (holding that the FAA preempts state statutes that specifically overruled arbitration agreements).

criticized on several bases,[15] the courts are effectively clearing their dockets of numerous commercial disputes by enforcing arbitration agreements.

Arbitration is a private dispute resolution procedure, almost always of a binding nature, agreed to by the parties. This consent may be given as late as the time a dispute arises, but often it is incorporated into documents setting up the transaction through a so-called pre-dispute arbitration clause. Arbitration, unlike negotiation and mediation, retains many of the familiar qualities of traditional courtroom litigation. A typical arbitration will entertain arguments, briefs, and the option for discovery, with a judge-like third party rendering a binding decision. Unlike traditional litigation, however, the arbitrator's decision is not subject to any meaningful judicial review for errors of law or fact.[16] Instead, the arbitral award is assailable on only very limited grounds, such as fraud or the complete denial of a hearing.[17] Although some parties to arbitration have successfully negotiated for an expanded judicial review of the arbitrator's decision in their arbitral agreement, the Circuits are currently split on whether such an agreement is permissible.[18] Indeed, arbitrators need not follow or apply the substantive law in rendering their awards. In reality, unless the arbitration contract provides otherwise, the standard is "principles of fairness and equity," however the individual arbitrator sees that! Finally, and in contrast with international arbitration, the general American practice does not require the arbitrator to explain the decision.

Arbitration is currently at its peak as an alternative form of dispute resolution.[19] Yet the Hammond survey of transactional lawyers, many of them concentrating their practices in commercial real estate, indicates widespread misconceptions about this form of dispute resolution.[20] Those surveyed incorrectly assumed that, like litigation, arbitration required a reasoned award, gave parties the right to judicial review for errors of law and/or errors of fact, and required that the arbitrator apply the substantive rule of law in resolving the dispute. Whatever the reason for so much misinformation on the part

---

15. See, e.g., Sternlight, Panacea or Corporate Tool?: Debunking the Supreme Court's Preference for Binding Arbitration, 74 Wash. U. L. Q. 637 (1996) (questioning the truth of voluntariness in contracts to arbitrate); Rau, Symposium, The Lawyer's Duties and Responsibilities in Dispute Resolution: Integrity in Private Judging, 38 S. Tex. L. Rev. 485, 530 (1997) (questioning the lack of a requirement of reasons for the award in arbitration); Sabin, Note: The Adjudicatory Boat without a Keel: Private Arbitration and the Need for Public Oversight of Arbitrators, 87 Iowa L. Rev. 1337 (2002) (criticizing the lack of arbitrator accountability).

16. Stipanowich, Contract and Conflict Management, 2001 Wis. L. Rev. 831, 880.

17. See 9 U.S.C. §10 for the four grounds for vacatur; almost all focus on the arbitrator's behavior; none requires the arbitrator to apply the substantive law.

18. See generally Longo, Agreeing to Disagree: A Balanced Solution to Whether Parties May Contract for Expanded Judicial Review Beyond the FAA, 36 J. Marshall L. Rev. 1005 (2003).

19. But see recent Fortune 1,000 corporate counsel survey that shows a stark decline in use of binding arbitration when compared with a similar survey done in 1997 and a reduction in counsel who "believe their companies are likely to turn to arbitration to resolve commercial disputes in the future." Stipanowich, Reflections on the State and Future of Commercial Arbitration: Challenges, Opportunities, Proposals, 25 Am. Rev. Int'l. Arb. 297, 302 (2014).

20. Hammond, supra note 2, at 643-644.

of transactional attorneys, their lack of knowledge and unwarranted expectations may possibly lead to opportunistic behavior in negotiations about selecting arbitration to resolve current or future disputes. The College of Commercial Arbitrators has published an excellent resource, available free at www.thecca.net.[21] It explains and evaluates the arbitration process and provides action steps for users and their attorneys to select and influence the type of arbitration process.[22]

Moreover, research indicates that transactional lawyers who advise their clients about methods of dispute resolution and draft a provision into documents *before* a dispute arises may be so confused about the various ADR processes that their advice is not conducive to an informed selection of the proper dispute resolution process. The following hypotheticals and questions will help you appreciate the distinctions between these basic ADR processes.

NOTES AND QUESTIONS

> ➢ *Problem 17-1*
> *Mediation in Construction Industry.* You are the long-time attorney for contractor, president of Ferry Construction, Inc. One day he walks into your office quite frustrated. You offer him a cup of coffee and listen to his story:
> "I am very upset. A couple of years ago I entered into a contract with I-G Inc. to develop and build a new commercial facility for them in Puerto Rico. It was a 2 million dollar job. Everything was going fine, and I-G paid their first four invoices. But the last three have gone unpaid! I'm not a lawyer or anything, but I think they broke our contract. I want to sue them. Their attorney called me and kept me on the phone for 3 hours. When I told I-G's attorney that I would see her in court, she laughed and said that wouldn't happen for a long time. What does she mean? When can we sue?"
> You thoroughly read the bulky contract your client hands to you. One clause stands out: "These parties, herein, incorporate document A201-1997 ('A201') by reference."
> You remember, from a recent conference on ADR in the construction industry, that document A201 is a standard, boilerplate contract, recently amended by the American Institute of Architects (AIA) to include stepladder-like methods of dispute resolution. A201 provides: "any claims, except for those pertaining to hazardous materials, shall be referred initially to the Architect for decision. The Architect's decision is a condition precedent to mediation, arbitration or

---

21. Thomas J. Stipanowich, ed., Protocols for Expeditious, Cost-Effective Commercial Arbitration: Key Action Steps for Business Users, Counsel, Arbitrators & Arbitration Provider Institutions, College of Commercial Arbitrators (2010).
22. Id. at 13-21.

litigation."
   Questions:

1. I-G's attorney correct that litigation may not occur for quite a while?
2. Might litigation never occur?
3. Did I-G's attorney do anything unethical?
4. If you were to follow your client's wishes and sue, what would I-G's position be? How would they style their motion? Draft I-G's motion as an exercise.
5. What is the likelihood of I-G's success on that motion? ◄

> *Problem 17-2*

Arbitration in a Commercial Lease. Lenny, a very successful commercial landlord in Connecticut, owns a large skyscraper called Lenny Towers. Among the many commercial tenants in Lenny Towers is an international oil company, Classic Oil. Lenny hired you some years ago to draft the standard lease provisions for Lenny Towers. It was a one shot deal and you were well compensated. You have not heard from Lenny since, until now when Lenny leaves the following voicemail message:

Hello, Counselor; it's Lenny. You drafted the leases for the Towers a while back. Listen, I need to hire you. One of the tenants, Classic Oil, has violated their lease and I want to sue for breach. When I told them I would see them in court, they laughed and said, "We'll see you out of court." What do they mean?

You pull the file and review the lease you drafted for Lenny Towers. The following two clauses jump out at you:

Par. 23 Any dispute arising under this lease shall be settled by arbitration. The Landlord and Tenant shall each choose an arbitrator, and the two arbitrators thus chosen shall select a third arbitrator. The findings and award of the three arbitrators thus chosen shall be final and binding on the parties hereto.

   Par. 25 The foregoing rights and remedies are not intended to be exclusive but as additional to all rights and remedies the Landlord would otherwise have by law.

   Questions:

1.   Explain Lenny's options to him.
2.   What if Lenny tells you he despises ADR and only feels his rights are adequately protected in a court of law?

3.   Assuming Lenny wants to go to court, draft a client letter to him explaining the likely progression of the matter. ◄

> **Problem 17-3**

Negotiation Clause in Broker Agreement. You are the attorney for Brian the Broker and drafted his standard broker commission agreement. Pursuant to his broker agreement, Brian was to be the exclusive agent to sell the property of Stella. The broker agreement contains the following:

Further, it is imposed on the parties a duty to negotiate in good faith any disputes arising from the contract. In the event that such good faith negotiations prove fruitless, the parties agree to binding arbitration, except that errors of law shall be subject to appeal.

Brian obtained a purchaser ready, willing, and able to close on Stella's property. At the last second Stella backed out and will not return any phone calls from Brian. Brian comes to you and asks that you initiate any action necessary to collect his commission.

Questions:

1.   What would you explain to opposing counsel about the contract?
2.   Assume that opposing counsel is unwilling to even talk to you. Draft a letter to the attorney explaining the implications of this course of action.
3.   Assume that after fruitless negotiation and arbitration, the arbitrator rules against Brian the Broker. The arbitrator's opinion reads as follows: "Despite the wealth of case law Brian the Broker has cited that legally entitles him to an award for breach of contract, I find for Stella." Can you appeal this finding to the trial court for this obvious error of law? Why or why not? ◄

B. GENERAL PRINCIPLES GOVERNING CHOICE OF MEDIATION OR ARBITRATION OVER LITIGATION

The perceived benefits most often mentioned for settling issues that arise between parties to a commercial real estate transaction are enumerated below:

1. ADR Saves Money. Businesses potentially face overwhelming legal bills every time a dispute arises with another commercial entity. Legal costs are not limited solely to attorney fees, but also entail court costs, travel expenses, and the lost productivity of employees who must spend days attending depositions or answering interrogatories in support of their legal rights. Legal expenses may also potentially include runaway jury awards or the sanction of attorney's fees to the other party on a contractual or statutory basis.

Mediation, especially, is considered less expensive than litigation. Without costly pretrial activities such as discovery and motions, mediation may be desirable for small disputes that are common in real estate transactions, such as whether a buyer has exercised "due diligence" in attempting to satisfy a contract condition. Empirical evidence seems to confirm that parties who resolve their disputes through mediation, rather than negotiation or the courts, tend to be more satisfied with the process as a whole and feel that fairness prevailed and the parties saved money. These benefits, especially the cost-savings to the parties, make mediation an appealing alternative. Limited discovery and few formalities contribute to the efficacy of mediation compared to litigation, or even arbitration.

Nevertheless, as arbitration becomes more litigation-like, its cost-savings may disappear. Because the formal rules of litigation do not necessarily apply (unless they are agreed to by the parties), long hearings and discovery may occur as the arbitrator strains to let in evidence that would be excluded as hearsay or irrelevant at trial. Additionally, the parties must pay the arbitrator for her time (often at the rate of a senior partner) and pay an institutional provider, like the American Arbitration Association, a fee for filing. These costs are likely to be greater than court costs and the "free" services of a judge.

2. ADR Is Private. The privacy that ADR offers the parties may motivate them to choose mediation or arbitration. There are no court reporters or spectators present. Of the innumerable disputes that a business may find itself embroiled in from time to time, at least some of those claims may be embarrassing, potentially injurious to its commercial reputation, or otherwise bad for public relations. All parties to a commercial dispute may prefer to keep the matter private. Both mediation and arbitration usually have confidentiality rules and are not open to the public.

3. ADR Is Quicker. The time-saving qualities of ADR are often cited as a major impetus for American businesses to avoid litigation. Obviously, litigation can last for years, when one combines pretrial motions, the actual trial, posttrial motions, and appellate review. If the only issues are whether a contract was breached and what the damages are, arbitration can be very effective. If a dispute arises during the ongoing performance of a lease or a construction contract, for instance, quick resolution by an on-site mediator or arbitrator can be preferable to trial. Here, the parties will benefit most from the potential speed of mediation or arbitration if they carefully draft rules for the process. Because mediation is non-binding, it is critical to decide how long to try to obtain an agreement with the assistance of a mediator and also to determine what happens if mediation is not successful. "Med/Arb" clauses typically provide that if the mediation does not result in settlement, the parties will submit to binding arbitration.

4. Business Expertise. Where the dispute involves factual determinations, if the parties are unable to resolve their disagreement by negotiation or mediation, arbitration may be preferable to litigation because the parties may select neutrals who likely know the industry better than a judge.

5. Preserving Business Relations. Mediation and arbitration promote a continuing business relationship between the parties because of the speed, confidentiality, and flexibility of remedies. Disputes between banks and developers, general contractors and developers, and general contractors and subcontractors are often over appraisal methods, rates of return, or construction progress. For example, where parties are engaged in the construction of a building that continues over several years, resolution of a dispute about whether a portion of the building conforms to the specifications ideally would be resolved quickly (so the work can continue on the unfinished portions), privately (so that prospective users of the building are not made aware of the potential flaws), and with creative solutions that may not be available to a court (like an agreement in mediation of the dispute or an award in arbitration that the builder will reinforce a portion of the foundation to offset the discrepancy).

Still, ADR may have drawbacks. If mediation is not successful, the parties may be back to square one and, unless careful drafting limits the time frame for the mediation, that may be a long time after the dispute arises. Perhaps one party will insist on public vindication of their product or cause, or want to emphasize the legality of their conduct. In these instances, the ability of a court to impose sanctions that are in the public record may be desirable. Perhaps a party wants a rule articulated that will govern future disputes and provide guidance for future conduct. Only the litigation system will supply binding precedent that, among other things, guides transactional lawyers in predispute avoidance. And there is criticism of mediation and arbitration in that neither considers the public's interest because both processes are based on a private contract between the disputants. Therefore, it is possible that the mediation agreement or arbitration award may contain provisions for illegal activities, which a court would find against public policy and unenforceable.[23]

The ultimate choice to pursue litigation or ADR hinges upon a kind of cost/benefit analysis. As one commentator observed,

---

23. See, e.g., Baxter International, Inc. v. Abbott Laboratories, 315 F.3d 829, 831 (7th Cir. 2003) (holding that "a mistake of law [by an arbitrator] is not a ground on which to set aside an award."). But see the dissent in Baxter International, Inc. v. Abbott Laboratories, 325 F.3d 954 (7th Cir. 2003) (denying rehearing), which contended "[t]he opinion of the panel majority clouds the authority of the court to review arbitration agreements of private parties that violate public policy—an authority repeatedly acknowledged by the Supreme Court."

The risks of submitting one's business fortunes, *a priori*, to a private system of adjudication, virtually immune from judicial interference or usurpation are considerable. Commercial arbitration will continue to prosper only for so long as it produces returns sufficient to outweigh the risks its adoption entails.[24]

And it may be wise to wait until a dispute arises to choose a resolution method rather than including an arbitration clause or requirement of mediation in the underlying transactional documents. Certainly, there should be a predispute consultation between the client and attorney on possible future conflicts between parties and a discussion of all available dispute resolution processes. Additionally, bringing in the litigation partner to collaborate in making a decision about predispute ADR provisions would be sensible.

Finally, ADR will more likely meet its promise if the processes are designed for the specific needs of particular clients by thoughtful negotiation and drafting. Avoiding inappropriate use of boilerplate ADR clauses is the key to good lawyering. As we shall see, tailoring ADR provisions to a client's particular needs is another opportunity for a lawyer to be an advocate.

C. DRAFTING CLIENT CHOICES ON ADR

Typical real estate transactions where choices of dispute resolution processes arise include:

1. Construction. For many years ADR has been used by the construction industry to resolve contract disputes (such as those over compliance with plans and specifications), claims for delay damages, and disputes over extra work. An advantage is that ongoing dispute resolution can proceed while construction continues. Often, contracts between the owner of the land and the general contractor require the contractor to incorporate the same ADR provisions in its contracts with subcontractors. The Documents Manual gives several sample form ADR clauses for your review. It includes the standard AIA form drafted and published jointly by the American Institute of Architects and the National Association of Builders.[25]

Note that many drafters envision ADR as a progression of "steps": first negotiation, followed by mediation if negotiation does not result in a settlement, and finally arbitration if mediation fails. As one observer commented, "[a] construction dispute involving substantial and complicated claims may be difficult to compromise and a

---

24. Hayford & Peeples, Commercial Arbitration in Evolution: An Assessment and Call for Dialogue, 10 Ohio St. J. on Disp. Resol. 343, 348 (1995).

25. The most recent version published in 1997 provides for mediation as a condition precedent to arbitration in the Standard Form of Agreement between Owner & Architect (AIA Form B141) and General Conditions of the Contract for Construction (AIA Form A201).

binding resolution through arbitration may be necessary."[26] Questions about compliance with plans and specifications in a construction contract are typical disputes. Other idiosyncratic forms of ADR procedures for construction disputes include the "hot tub" method, standing neutral, standing dispute review board, etc.[27]

2. Real Estate Contracts. Disputes arising under real estate sales contracts, listing agreements, real estate loan documents, partnerships, or joint ownership agreements and the like may be submitted to one or more ADR processes based on a predispute clause in the underlying document or by agreement of the parties at the time the dispute occurs. The parties, either alone through negotiation or with the aid of a neutral, can develop an appropriate remedy for disputes over the terms and conditions in a contract, determine whether a real estate commission has been earned, create a remedy for loan default,[28] or determine the market value of the land, improvements, or both in order to arrive at a buy-out price under terms of a jointly owned property agreement. Other common issues include whether conditions precedent to a party's right to exercise an option to acquire real estate have been satisfied and whether a party's refusal to consent is consistent with a contract provision providing that "consent shall not be withheld unreasonably."

3. Leases. Especially because of the ongoing relationship between commercial landlords and tenants and because some of the economic terms change over the term of the lease, disputes in this area may be particularly appropriate for ADR. For example, rent for a renewal term where the "going rate" is indicated in the lease may quickly be resolved by mediation/arbitration. Disputes involving revenue issues, expense-escalation reimbursements, and operational and occupancy and use issues are likely candidates for ADR. An expert/neutral can decide what is a "customary repair" when dealing with offsets to security deposits and other common area maintenance charge disputes. Interpretation of build-out clauses that give tenants options or define costs should be more efficient using ADR than litigation.

4. Land Use, Zoning, and Environmental Disputes. Because disputes of this kind may affect the ability of owners to sell or develop land, a faster and more creative approach to dispute resolution may be desirable. Sometimes, such disputes arise between adjacent landowners. Others involve private owners and government agencies controlling land use, water resources, air quality and hazardous waste/toxic substances. Provision for ADR to resolve disputes may be by contract between private parties either predispute or

---

26. Sklar & Kral, Use of ADR in Real Estate and Construction, ACREL Papers, October 13, 2001, at 704.

27. 7 Bruner & O'Connor Construction Law §21:3.

28. See M. Madison, J. Dwyer, and S. Bender, The Law of Real Estate Financing §14:32 (2016) (discussing necessary carve-outs from arbitration for foreclosure-related remedies).

after one arises or in the case of the federal Environmental Protection Agency, for example, by an administrative policy favoring and requiring ADR.[29]

5. Title Insurance Disputes. The standard commercial owners and lenders' title policies published by the American Land Title Association contain arbitration clauses as part of their Conditions. See Documents Manual for owner's policy. By the terms of these arbitration provisions, *either* party may require that a dispute be resolved by arbitration for disputes of less than $2,000,000. For disputes in excess of $2,000,000, *both* the title company and the insured must agree to arbitration. Nevertheless, at least one court has refused to compel arbitration in a title insurance dispute because the Preliminary Title Report did not mention arbitration and it referred to a title insurance policy that was different from the one actually issued.[30] The court held that there could be no incorporation by reference to a title policy including an arbitration clause because the Preliminary Title Report referred to a policy form that did not contain the clause. See Chapter 2B discussion of function of a Preliminary Title Report in the executory period of the real estate sales contract before closing. See Chapter 4D9 discussion of the Preliminary Title Report as part of lender's due diligence for approving a mortgage loan. The 2006 ALTA forms adopt the Title Insurance Rules of the American Land Title Association (http://www.alta.org/arbitration/). Unless the parties modify Section 13 of the policy Conditions to provide for some alternatives, those rules will control the actual arbitration.

6. Escrow Funds. It is common that agreements for the escrowing of funds, such as earnest money deposits, provide for arbitration of any disputes regarding distribution. Often, the escrow funds distribution issue is carved out for arbitration even though other disputes based on the underlying transactional document do not provide for ADR. As with providers of title insurance, commercial institutions that hold escrow funds on behalf of several parties to a transaction may require arbitration as a condition to taking on responsibilities as escrowee. In such instances, the depositors' "consent" to the arbitration is not necessarily measured subjectively, but rather is similar to "consent" in many consumer transactions where the consumer must agree to arbitrate disputes if she wishes to deal with the company providing goods or services. Nevertheless, parties whose funds are being escrowed should attempt to control the costs of the process by negotiating the terms of the arbitration provision so that the arbitrator is limited in her tasks. For example, providing that "the parties do not desire a written opinion" will reduce costs. And a provision that "the arbitrator will not have authority to award punitive or exemplary damages, but shall have the authority to provide for injunctive

---

29. EPA Final Guidance on Use of Alternative Dispute Resolution Techniques in Enforcement Actions EPA (August 1987). EPA has issued final regulations providing for arbitration of certain superfund cost recovery claims. 40 CFR Part 304, see id. at 711.

30. Kleveland v. Chicago Title Insurance Co., 141 Cal. App. 4th 761, 46 Cal. Rptr. 3d 314 (2006).

relief and to direct the payment of funds held in escrow" limits the arbitrator's jurisdiction. If the arbitrator disobeys these instructions, court review is possible.

—————

Although the empirical research conducted by Professor Celeste Hammond as reported in the following excerpt deals specifically with transactional lawyers' understanding and expectation of arbitration, the underlying confusion surrounding mediation and arbitration in the minds of these attorneys makes their advice to clients about ADR choices a potential basis for legal malpractice:

> My interaction with practitioners raised the suspicion that transactional lawyers do not understand important aspects of the arbitral process and are ill-equipped to counsel clients about the inclusion and the details of arbitration clauses. On several occasions the author had been asked to speak on aspects of arbitration—particularly on the absence of reasoned awards, the absence of a requirement that arbitrators follow a rule of law, and the absence of judicial review for failure to follow the law at bar association conferences. These presentations were included in the broader category of "Traps for the Unwary" because of the recognition that the audience, mostly transactional, commercial real estate lawyers, were not well versed in Alternative Dispute Resolution (ADR). Perhaps the audience's expectation that arbitration clauses were revocable was consistent with the earlier view of arbitration that permitted a party who had agreed to arbitrate future disputes to change his mind and withdraw assent. Like Thomas Stipanowich, the author discussed commercial arbitration with many sophisticated practitioners and trial court judges and discovered many who confused mediation and arbitration or believed that the arbitrator was bound by applicable substantive law.... For example, the expectation that the "parties must agree with the terms of any award which the arbitrator enters before it becomes binding" by some is more consistent with the mediation process than with arbitration.[31]

Several aspects of transactional practice may explain transactional lawyers' poor grasp of ADR. First, traditional legal education emphasizes a litigation model, using appellate cases as the primary course materials. Although the American Bar Association's MacCrate Report called for a greater preparation of law students for the practice of law, most law schools still conduct first year courses using the casebook method and few make the distinction between the practice of litigation and the practice of transactions and business planning (where most attorneys end up working).

Second, the nature of transactional work is to focus on the "win/win" situation. In negotiating the contracts that will structure their relationships, business clients are urged to collaborate with the other side. Transactional lawyers in business and real estate support their clients in proactive deal making, not retroactive dispute fixing. An experienced transactional attorney in New Jersey explained this perspective:

---

31. Hammond, supra note 2, at 616.

The use of ADR has been avoided in the custom contract drafting process because parties and their counsel negotiating a new relationship are reluctant to introduce potentially controversial or disruptive issues that would change the flow of a harmonious agreement by the jarring concept of break-up. However, the lawyer negotiating and preparing a contract has the first and most significant opportunity for objectively considering with a client the choices available to resolve possible disputes, including the option to litigate.[32]

Third, the lack of experience of transactional lawyers as neutrals or in representing their clients after a dispute arises, and a disconnect between litigators and transactional attorneys, even within the same law firm, means that the latter are not likely to be well-informed about ADR. Thomas Stipanowich, a leading scholar of ADR, reported the comments of a litigation partner at a leading Boston law firm:

> I found one of the problems was that many of these ADR issues were addressed by my transactional corporate partners, who didn't like me tinkering with the ADR provisions at the end of deals so they couldn't close the transaction. Unfortunately, the clauses they used were often taken out of form books and not really discussed between the parties. Now, we have begun to change the culture so that the transactional lawyers call me and consult about ADR language.[33]

NOTES AND QUESTIONS

> ➤ *Problem 17-4*
> To encourage a discussion of good drafting of ADR clauses, consider the following hypothetical, reprinted with the permission of its authors Robert S. Greenbaum, Stanley P. Sklar, and Barry C. Hawkins, and of the American College of Real Estate Lawyers (ACREL):
>
> Tenant Technologies ("TT") is negotiating with Landlord Lofts ("LL") for 250,000 square feet of office space requiring the latest technology for his venture dealing with information retrieval and storage. The requirements for TT's space are very technical and were prepared by its consultant Dotcomerino, who was to oversee the tenant buildout. LL requires that all tenant buildout work be done by its subsidiary, World Class ("World Class") Technology Constructors, a [Delaware] Limited Liability Company. In view of the commitments made by TT to prospective clients, the completion date is critical because those clients have insisted that their Service Agreements with TT permit them to terminate the agreement and recover their costs in seeking a replacement if the space is not available. Some have even insisted on

---

32. Greenbaum, Dispute Resolution and Counsel: Changing Perceptions, Changing Responsibilities, Am. Arb. Assn., 55 Disp. Res. J., May-July 2000.
33. Stipanowich, supra note 16, at 834.

punitive damages as an element of recovery.

The lease is for 10 years with occupancy commencing when the buildout is totally completed. There are two successive five year options with the rent to be increased to then market rates at the time TT gives notice that it wishes to exercise those options. At any time during the option period, TT may exercise an option to purchase the building for its fair market value but in no event shall the option price be less than 150% of any outstanding mortgage. Assume that TT refinances at 120% of the fair market value from Welendhigh.com. The lease is silent as to the manner in which the notice is to be given other than "in a commercially reasonable manner." There is a provision that TT is to contribute its proportionate share of common area maintenance costs but may contest those costs within 2 years after receiving its statement for the amount of its contribution.

Ted Transaction, TT's lawyer, whose last court appearance was Moot Court in law school (which he won) and Sue Slaughter, a recovering litigation attorney and lawyer for LL, have negotiated the following kinder and gentler dispute resolution clause:

All claims arising hereunder shall be first resolved by negotiations of not less than 4 nor more than 8 hours. In the event the parties cannot resolve their dispute by negotiation, the parties shall mediate their dispute by the selection of a mediator whom they have selected by mutual agreement and in the absence of mutual agreement or the failure of the mediation, either party may commence arbitration under the Rules of the International Chamber of Commerce in existence as of the date of this agreement. The parties may have full discovery as permitted under the Civil Practice Act of the State of [] and the panel may award punitive damages and attorneys fees to the prevailing party. The panel's final Award need not provide any explanation other than dollar amounts to be awarded. The parties shall also have the right to appeal any Award to any court of competent jurisdiction.

Consider whether the clause has accomplished its purpose, which is to create a speedy, efficient, and fair resolution of disputes. Consider the following issues:

1. Is "gun to the head" negotiation realistic? What would be better?
2. Could the parties have appointed a Judge to select a mediator in the event of an impasse?
3. Are the ICC rules the best rules to use and, if not, what are the alternatives?
4. Is full discovery desirable and, if not, what are the alternatives?
5. Would you allow an arbitrator to impose punitive damages?
6. Is appeal to a court contrary to the goals of arbitration?
7. What is a "prevailing party"?

    8.   What would you want to be provided in an Award and why?

    9.   Can you prequalify the requirements for arbitrators? ◄

Drafting Strategy. For advice on drafting strategies see Friedland, The Arbitration Clause, in Commercial Contracts: Strategies For Drafting And Negotiating §5.05 (V. Rossman & M. Moskin eds.) (Supp. 2016).

Drafting Checklist. After the decision to use a form of ADR has been made, you should consult the Drafting Checklist for both Mediation and Arbitration found in the Documents Manual.

THE ETHICAL REAL ESTATE LAWYER

Obligation to Advise about ADR Options and Obligation of "Candor" in Negotiations, Mediation, and Arbitration

You are about to negotiate the contract with the builder whom your developer client has brought in to construct a condominium high rise building. Do you have an ethical responsibility to discuss ADR with your client and advise him about ADR choices for future possible disputes? The current ABA Model Rules contain no specific references to ADR although several provisions might imply such a duty to advise clients. Model Rule 2.1 requires an attorney to give "candid advice" including reference to "moral, economic, social and political factors" in addition to the law. Model Rule 1.2(a) requires attorneys to consult with the client as to the "means" for meeting objectives. The ABA's Commission on Evaluation of the Rules of Professional Conduct's "Ethics 2000" report recommended an addition to comment 5 of Model Rule 2.1, "when a matter is likely to involve litigation, it may be necessary under Rule 1.4 to inform the client of forms of dispute resolution that might constitute reasonable alternatives to litigation." Although the recommendation was adopted, it is not clear whether you would need to inform your client at this point in setting up the relationship with the builder. It depends on the meaning of "where a matter is likely to involve litigation." Does it include only disputes that have already arisen? Does it include any type of transaction, such as construction contracts, under which disputes have frequently arisen in the past? See Yarn, Lawyer Ethics in ADR and the Recommendations of Ethics 2000 to Revise the Model Rules of Professional Conduct: Considerations for Adoption and State Application, 54 Ark. L. Rev. 207, 245 (2001); see also Breger, Should an Attorney be Required to Advise a Client of ADR Options?, 13 Geo. J. Legal Ethics 427 (2000).

    During preparations for negotiations on behalf of your developer client, your client tells you that he could still make money on the deal if he paid the builder $1 million dollars, but your client directs you to tell the other side that "he cannot make a profit unless the builder accepts no more than $750,000 as payment for the construction of the building." Do you have an ethical responsibility to "tell the truth"? What if your client asks you to represent him in a mediation of a dispute arising after the work began? Must you reveal that your client is able to make a profit on the project as long as the cost of the building is $1,000,000 or less?

The obligation of candor, or truthfulness, of the attorney for a party in negotiations is based on seeing that process as primarily one of "information bargaining." Thus, there is no requirement that the lawyer inform a "negotiation partner of any fact, however clear it is that the negotiator would want to know that fact, would profit from knowing it, or suffers from major misunderstanding of that fact." See Burns, Some Ethical Issues Surrounding Mediation, 70 Fordham L. Rev. 691, 695 (2001). Yet, Model Rule 4.1(a) prohibits a lawyer from giving a "false statement(s) of material fact or law." Nonetheless, under conventional rules in negotiation, the price or value placed on the transaction (here, the cost of the building) would not be a material fact! Id. at 696 citing Model Rule 4.1, cmt. 2.

An attorney's obligation of candor when representing a client in a mediation or arbitration is not clear. Under the current Model Rules there is a higher standard of candor when before a "tribunal" (Model Rule 3.3) as compared with making statements to "others" (Model Rule 4.1). Rule 3.3(a)(1) prohibits "knowingly [making] a false statement of material fact or law to a tribunal." There is disagreement whether a mediation and arbitration proceedings are "tribunals." See Yarn, supra at 253, citing authority for the view by some commentators that both arbitration and mediation are included in the concept of "tribunal." Unlike Rule 4.1 regarding statements to others, Rule 3.3 imposes affirmative duties to disclose adverse controlling legal authority to tribunals and to take remedial steps if knowingly false evidence has been submitted. A new definition of "tribunal" that "denotes a court, an arbitrator in a binding arbitration proceeding, or a legislative body, administrative agency, or other body acting in an adjudicative capacity" was adopted recently. See Model Rule 1.0(m). Even with this broader definition, it does not appear that mediation constitutes a "tribunal" that would require you as attorney for a party to reveal the truth or to take steps to remedy false evidence.

Including a Mandatory, Binding Arbitration Clause in Attorney Client Engagement Agreement. You are drafting a form Letter of Engagement that your law firm will use as the basis for its relationship with transactional clients and to specify the fee to be charged for particular services. Your senior partner has suggested that you include a provision providing for the arbitration of any controversy or claim arising out of or relating to the Engagement Letter and the matters addressed in the Letter. You wonder whether including, and requiring that clients agree to, such a provision is unconscionable. You are also concerned about whether this is allowed under ethical guidelines for attorneys.

Increasingly such binding arbitration clauses are being included as the only form of dispute resolution regarding the attorney–client relationship. This would include claims of malpractice by the client and disputes over proper fees charged or to be collected. Various jurisdictions that have considered the enforceability of such arbitration clauses differ on their treatment. Some enforce the arbitration clause for fee disputes (see Wilsman & Schoonover, LLC v. Millstein, 2003 Ohio 3258, 2003 WL 21434300 (Ct. App. 2003)) but deny enforceability for malpractice disputes unless the client has consulted with an independent attorney. See for example Thornton v. Haggins, 2003 Ohio 7078, 2003 WL 23010100 (Ct. App. 2003) where the court held "consultation with an independent attorney" is needed to determine whether the client knowingly and voluntarily agreed to arbitrate malpractice disputes. Other appellate courts have enforced arbitration provisions even as to malpractice claims where the client argued that an ethical violation of including the clause in the attorney engagement letter made the arbitration clause unconscionable. See Sidley Austin Brown & Wood, LLP v. Green Development Corp, 327 S.W.3d 859 (Tex. Ct. App. 2010). The strong support for enforceability is a result of an extremely strong public policy favoring arbitration over litigation as well as the difficulty of meeting the threshold test for unconscionability. Assume that you are practicing law in a state where there is no published opinion on the issue; how should you proceed in drafting the form? Are there any suggestions about using this form effectively that you might pass on to your senior partner?

C h a p t e r   18

The Impact of Bankruptcy on Real Estate Transactions[*]

A. STARTING OVER

In biblical times, everyone got a new start. Each seventh, or sabbatical, year was a year of release from debts. "Every creditor shall release that which he hath lent unto his neighbor."[1] After the passage of a "week" of sabbatical years, the fiftieth year was the jubilee year, when, after the remission of indebtedness, all land would return to its original owner, all indentured servants would be returned to their families, and all prisoners would be freed. "And ye shall hallow the fiftieth year, and proclaim liberty throughout the land unto all the inhabitants thereof; it shall be a jubilee unto you."[2]

With the development of commerce, society began to take a dimmer view of jubilees. As civilization progressed, a conflict developed, existing to this day, in which the ideal of providing a debtor with a fresh start came up against the desire to discourage defaults and maximize return to creditors. And the creditors won— initially. A person unable to pay debts normally would be jailed, sold into slavery, or worse. One of the first statutes dealing with insolvent debtors as a class was contained in the Roman "Twelve Tables" and was known as the law "de debitore in partes secando," or the law of cutting the debtor into pieces. In theory, each creditor would receive a distribution of a proportionate share of the debtor's body.[3] Given this situation, it is not surprising that many of those who came to the New World did so to avoid the draconian treatment of debtors in Europe. Nor is it surprising that when these immigrants drafted a Constitution, they authorized Congress to "establish . . . uniform Laws on the subject of

---

[*]Daniel N. Zinman contributed substantially to the 6th edition revision of this chapter.

1. Deuteronomy 15:2. Even the land was given a new start: Every seventh year it would not be cultivated but would lie fallow, a process that helped considerably to prevent exhaustion of the land and to enhance its fertility in the other years. See Exodus 23:10; Leviticus 25:4; N. Ausubel, The Book of Jewish Knowledge 229-230, 382 (1964); J. Hertz, The Pentateuch and Haftorahs 531, 811 (2d ed. 1967). While we are referring to the Judeo-Christian Bible in this and the next footnote, not surprisingly, similar injunctions may be found in other biblical literature. For example, see Quran, 2:280 (Mohammed Marmaduke Pickthall trans.) ("And if someone is in hardship, then let there be postponement until a time of ease.").

2. Leviticus 25:10. You may remember that the words "proclaim liberty throughout the land unto all the inhabitants thereof" are found on the Liberty Bell in Philadelphia.

3. W. Blackstone, Commentaries 472.

Bankruptcies throughout the United States."[4] The Bankruptcy Code was enacted pursuant to that authorization.

Today bankruptcy is not bloody, at least not in the literal sense, but the divide and distribute concept of the "Twelve Tables" persists. Bankruptcy law in the United States is designed to balance or harmonize the two competing objectives—providing a fresh start to debtors and maximizing return to creditors—and to that end it provides a mechanism for the gathering together of the debtor's assets (other than certain assets that are exempt from the reach of creditors), the conversion (where feasible) of such assets into cash, and the orderly distribution of the assets to the debtor's creditors in order of their priority. The debtor is then released from remaining debts in the form of a "discharge" and given that fresh start so nobly proclaimed in the Bible. This is known as bankruptcy liquidation; it is found in Chapter 7 of the Bankruptcy Code.[5] In a sense, the law represents a "bankruptcy bargain" under which the "honest but unfortunate" debtor is discharged from debts only after paying for the discharge with non-exempt assets.

Alternatively, under Chapter 13, a debtor capable of earning a regular income may keep all of his or her assets, provided the court approves a plan proposed by the debtor to pay back a portion of the debts out of future disposable income over a period of three to five years. In order to live up to the "bankruptcy bargain," the plan is required to provide unsecured creditors with at least what they would have received had the debtor filed in Chapter 7.[6]

By the beginning of this century, there was a perception that some debtors with large incomes and little assets were taking advantage of the bankruptcy laws by filing in Chapter 7 (distributing what few assets the debtors have while the debtors retain all future income, even though they could pay creditors a substantial portion of the debts under Chapter 13). In 2005, Congress enacted the Bankruptcy Abuse Prevention and Consumer Protection Act of 2005[7] ("BAPCPA," usually pronounced "bap see pah"). Under certain provisions of BAPCPA, debtors with primarily consumer debts were denied access to Chapter 7 based on a "means test," thus encouraging high-earning debtors to file in Chapter 13. Why do you think Congress did not simply require the high-earning debtor to file in Chapter 13?

Around the turn of the twentieth century, it became apparent to many that when a business is in financial difficulties, its worth as a going concern is probably (although not always) greater than what a forced liquidation sale in Chapter 7 would produce. From this thought developed the concepts of composition, equity receivership, arrangement, and reorganization, which attempted to rehabilitate rather than liquidate the debtor's business, thereby obtaining more for the creditors while benefiting the national economy by

4. U.S. Const. art. I, §8, cl. 4.

5. The Bankruptcy Code is found at 11 U.S.C. §§101-1532. References in this discussion to statutory sections are to the Bankruptcy Code unless otherwise specified.

6. See §1325(a)(4).

7. Pub. L. No. 109-8, 119 Stat. 23 (2005) (codified in 11 U.S.C.).

keeping people at work and continuing the production of goods and services. Most bankruptcy reorganizations of businesses are now governed by Chapter 11 of the Bankruptcy Code.[8]

Other than disruption and sometimes significant loss of income caused by delays and the effect of stays of acts affecting the debtor, the basic interests of secured creditors, such as real estate mortgagees, should otherwise be generally unaffected by a Chapter 7 bankruptcy. If the property has equity, that is, if it is worth more than the liens on it, the property can be sold by the bankruptcy court to realize on the equity. If the property is not sold subject to the lien, the lien of the mortgage attaches to the proceeds of the sale, and the mortgagee is protected either by a judicially imposed upset price (a price below which the property will not be sold) equal to the amount of the indebtedness, or by the mortgagee's ability to attend the sale, bid up to the indebtedness, and (if it is the successful bidder) offset the bid against the indebtedness (known as "credit bidding"). If there is no equity, the bankruptcy court should normally order that the property be "abandoned" and lift the automatic stay, thus permitting foreclosure.

On the other hand, when the debtor is being rehabilitated through a reorganization, important property (such as the debtor's factory) cannot be sold, nor can the bankruptcy court abandon such property or permit foreclosure if it is necessary for an effective reorganization. Thus, it may be necessary to modify secured creditors' rights in a reorganization plan. Under the plan of reorganization, creditors are divided into "classes" and each class is given interests in the new reorganized business or its assets, or new debt instruments. Generally, a mortgagee, with respect to its secured claim, is in a class by itself.

The bankruptcy court can confirm a reorganization plan if it meets certain requirements, including being approved by a requisite majority of each class of creditors. As you will see when we discuss the concept of "cramdown," however, under certain circumstances, a court can confirm the plan over the objection of a class that is adversely affected by the plan provided, among other things, that the plan is "fair and equitable." "Fair and equitable" generally means that no junior creditor or holder of an equity interest should receive any property in the reorganization on account of its claim or interest until senior creditors receive property equal in value to the amount of their claims. This concept is known as the "absolute priority" rule and is enforced to ensure that interests in the new reorganized debtor entity are distributed in order of priority.[9] This rule provides a

---

8. Chapter 11 of the Bankruptcy Code is derived from a combination of three reorganization chapters in the former Bankruptcy Act: Chapter X, corporate reorganization; Chapter XI, an arrangement for unsecured debts; and Chapter XII, a real property arrangement for noncorporate debtors. We will examine the influence of these chapters in the development of Chapter 11 of the Bankruptcy Code later. The Bankruptcy Code also contains other reorganization chapters: Chapter 9, for municipalities, Chapter 12, for "family farmers," Chapter 13, for certain individuals with a regular income, and Chapter 15 dealing with Cross-Border Insolvencies.

9. See Case v. Los Angeles Lumber Prods. Co., 308 U.S. 106 (1939) (absolute priority was required by the words "fair and equitable"). Section 1129(b) of the Code requires that a plan be "fair and equitable" as to any impaired class rejecting the plan of reorganization. See discussion at Chapter 18C2, infra.

measure of protection to secured creditors whose rights are being dealt with under the plan.

In addition, no plan can be confirmed unless it is "in the best interest of creditors." This ambiguous phrase of art (which has been a part of U.S. bankruptcy law from the earliest compositions to present-day reorganizations) has been interpreted to mean that under the plan each creditor must receive property of a value equal, at least, to what the creditor would have received had there been a liquidation, which, by the way, helps preserve the "bankruptcy bargain" discussed above.[10] The best interest of creditor's test makes sense. Reorganizations are designed to produce more, not less, and, absent consent, no creditor should end up with less. Many of the disputes that arise in reorganizations involve the determination of who gets the difference between the liquidation value and the higher going-concern value. Other significant requirements that must be met before a plan can be confirmed are discussed below in connection with plan confirmation.

Real estate disputes have been a focal point of bankruptcy law, far beyond what might be expected. In the remainder of this discussion we cover some of these real estate problems, how the current Bankruptcy Code deals with them, and some of the unresolved problems affecting real estate.[11]

B. THE MORTGAGE MELTDOWN

Robert Zinman, the oldest among the authors of this book, maintains that in fifty-plus years of practice, he had never seen an economic meltdown as broad or as severe as the crisis that started around 2007 in real estate and spread from there to the rest of the economy. While we have seen significant improvement in the economy recently, the disaster created by the recession has not yet been fully resolved. In June of 2007, with the clouds gathering in the subprime lending market, the New York State Bar Association's Real Property Law Section presented a panel on "Distressed Real Estate."[12] The introduction to the program materials discussed the then recent subprime defaults and the elements then existing that could be the basis of a "perfect storm for real estate and the economy." It predicted that unlike many prior downturns (where real estate tended to follow the economy by six or more months), this time it saw the

---

10. The best-interest-of-creditors requirement is now found in §1129(a)(7) of the Code.

11. One caveat to keep in mind: Our discussion of bankruptcy materials is geared to the areas that are unique to the real estate transactions discussed in this volume. Generally applicable provisions of the Bankruptcy Code also apply to real estate, and some provisions of the Bankruptcy Code that may specifically apply to real property deal with areas beyond the scope of this book. As a result, many of these provisions are omitted from our discussion so that we may concentrate on the provisions more relevant to the modern real estate transactions covered by this volume.

12. "Distressed Real Estate: Current Topics in Foreclosures and Bankruptcy," New York State Bar Association (2007).

possibility that "real estate might lead, rather than follow the economy into recession," and gave a step-by-step analysis of how this could take place.

The day the first panel was presented (June 5, 2007), the powers in Washington were telling the public that the subprime crisis was a limited one that should not affect real estate in general or the economy adversely. Indeed, at least in New York City, real estate was, in fact, still booming.[13] As a result, not everyone attending the panel was ready to accept the need to consider the consequences of the potential meltdown in real estate and the economy. But the perfect storm did occur. The purpose of this section is to analyze, albeit somewhat superficially, the causes of the crash, with the hope that future real estate and bankruptcy lawyers will be able to help blunt the next real estate crisis.

The Lemming Syndrome. First, a word about attitudes of those associated with real estate investment. It has been our experience that most of those people are afflicted with the Lemming Syndrome. You know of the lemmings as furry-footed small rodents, the European form of which often follow their leaders in mass migrations across Europe, eating off the land, until, as the story goes, they follow their leaders off the cliffs, where they drown in the sea. Similarly, but less life threatening, real estate people in good times tend to follow their leaders, ignoring warning signs, building and building, lending and lending, borrowing and borrowing—until the market collapses and the investments are drowned in a sea of red ink.

Alternatively, when times are bad, real estate people tend to agree that times will be bad well into the future and react in such a way as to make the bad times become much worse than they need to be. The panel introduction on distressed real estate, discussed above, pointed to situations in the 1970s where financial institutions virtually gave away properties in midtown Manhattan based on the erroneous conclusion that New York could not survive. What Alan Greenspan called "irrational exuberance"[14] when referring to the stock market years ago, may well be translated into "irrational optimism" or "irrational pessimism" when dealing with real estate. Keep this in mind as you read this discussion on the causes of the real estate meltdown.

All were responsible. As the recession deepened, everyone blamed everyone but themselves for the crisis in real estate. The truth is all were responsible. We should have gotten the hint of what was coming as early as the enactment of the Bankruptcy Code in 1978, when the proposed §1322(b)(2) (which permitted the

---

13. Ben S. Bernanke, Chairman, Fed. Reserve Bd., Address Before the 2007 International Monetary Conference (June 5, 2007) ("We will follow developments in the subprime market closely. However, fundamental factors—including solid growth in incomes and relatively low mortgage rates—should ultimately support the demand for housing, and at this point, the troubles in the subprime sector seem unlikely to seriously spill over to the broader economy or the financial system.").

14. Alan Greenspan, Chairman, Fed. Reserve Bd., The Challenge of Central Banking in a Democratic Society, Address Before the Annual Dinner and Francis Boyer Lecture of the American Enterprise Institute for Policy Research (Dec. 5, 1996) ("But how do we know when irrational exuberance has unduly escalated asset values, which then become subject to unexpected and prolonged contractions as they have in Japan over the past decade?").

chapter 13 plan to modify the rights of secured creditors) was limited to prohibit a plan from modifying the rights of holders of claims "secured only by a security interest in real property that is the debtor's principal residence." Surely it is counterintuitive that a provision protecting mortgage lenders making loans to residential borrowers could have been enacted. However, the motive for the provision was probably based on Congressional concern that if mortgage loans could be modified in bankruptcy, the credit standards of banks would be tightened, rather than loosened as Congress wanted.[15]

Long-term lenders had generally been incentivized to underwrite their loans carefully because they would have to live with troubled loans for a long period of time. However, with the development of securitization as described in Chapter 15 of this volume, lenders could package the loans they made and dispose of them to the investing public as mortgaged backed securities, and were thus encouraged to disregard their normal lending standards. Combine this with a trend toward reduction of statutory qualitative standards for institutional lending, and the floodgates were opened for easy and undisciplined subprime lending. This was encouraged and fostered by the federal government itself, which pressured or acquiesced in the breakdown of standards by Fannie Mae and Freddie Mac[16] in their acquisition or guarantee of securitized loans.

One cannot ignore the credit rating agencies in this fiasco. In order to sell the real estate securities, it was necessary to obtain a good credit rating from one of the national credit agencies. The agencies were placed in what would seem to be a conflict situation in that they were being paid by the people hiring them to provide the rating, with the result that the ratings did not reflect the true risk involved.

The failure of bankruptcy protection. From the outset, there were serious concerns that if the originator of the securitization filed in bankruptcy, the assets that were the subject of the securitization might be considered property of the originator's bankruptcy estate resulting, inter alia, in the income being subject to the claims of the originator's other creditors, thus diluting, at best, the rights of the purchasers of the securities. As discussed in Chapter 15, these concerns were dealt with by having the originator sell the assets to a special purpose entity (SPE) (sometimes referred to as a special purpose vehicle (SPV)) so that they would not be part of the originator's estate. Bankruptcy and real estate lawyers prepared "true sale" opinions (that the transfer to the SPE would not be overturned as a sham) and nonconsolidation opinions (that in the bankruptcy of

---

15. For legislative history surrounding the enactment of this protective provision for mortgagees, see Zinman and Petrovski, The Home Mortgage and Chapter 13: An Essay on Unintended Consequences, 17 Am. Bankr. Inst. L. Rev. 133. 135-40 (2009).

16. The Federal National Mortgage Association, commonly known as Fannie Mae, is a government-sponsored organization designed, inter alia, to provide funding to the housing market by securitizing mortgages, thus allowing lenders to reinvest assets in new mortgage financing. The Federal Home Loan Mortgage Corporation, commonly known as Freddie Mac, is a government-sponsored enterprise created to expand the secondary market for mortgages by providing mortgage guarantees.

the originator, the assets of the originator and the SPE would not be substantively consolidated).[17]

The SPEs themselves were made "bankruptcy remote" by restricting their activities and by making it difficult for them to file in bankruptcy. This was accomplished primarily by providing in the incorporation documents that a bankruptcy filing would need the unanimous approval of at least the "independent directors" on the SPE board. The "independent directors" were placed on the board to vote against any filing in bankruptcy. Those who served as "independent" directors (who would seem to be anything but "independent") seemed to ignore the fiduciary duty to the corporation owed by all directors. And the band played on.

The use of "independent directors" to prevent voluntary[18] petitions in bankruptcy and establish bankruptcy remoteness was dealt a severe blow after General Growth Properties ("GGP") filed in bankruptcy in 2009. GGP had approximately 200 shopping centers in 44 states and was the second-largest shopping center Real Estate Investment Trust in the nation. For our purposes, the shopping malls were largely transferred to individual SPEs, which issued commercial mortgage-backed securities to the investing public. GGP, in a cash crunch due to the frozen credit market for refinancing as a result of the meltdown, wanted to use cash obtained by the SPEs and caused the SPEs to file in bankruptcy as well. How could that happen to bankruptcy remote entities with "independent directors" in place to vote against the filing? In the risk of oversimplification, the "independent" directors resigned or were fired and replaced by directors more friendly to bankruptcy filing.

So the house of cards collapsed, the SPEs filed bankruptcy, and GGP asked and received authorization from the bankruptcy court to use cash collateral held by the SPEs (with certain adequate protection requirements) in order to continue operations and permit a successful reorganization. Judge Allan Gropper, a highly respected bankruptcy judge, refused to substantively consolidate the assets of SPEs and GGP, but permitted the use of funds based on a "corporate family" doctrine that treated the affiliated group as a collective whole engaged in a common enterprise.[19] Judge Gropper's very strong comments about the duty of directors to act in the interest of the company should be especially disturbing to those seeking to make the SPE bankruptcy remote.[20]

Now let us look at the Bankruptcy Code as it applies to real estate investments, keeping in mind the events of the last ten years.

17. Substantive consolidation occurs when a court directs the assets of legally separate entities to be treated as if they were one. It is used very sparingly because of the resulting prejudice to the interests of the creditors of one entity over the other.

18. The possibility of involuntary filings against the SPE did not appear to be considered in establishing bankruptcy remoteness.

19. 409 B.R. 43 (Bankr. S.D.N.Y. 2009).

20. See also In re Lake Michigan Beach Pottawattamie Resort LLC. 547 B.R. 899 (2016) and Helman and Fischer, The Missing Page of the Playbook "Blocking Directors" Can't Escape Fiduciary Duty, 35 Am. Bankr. Inst. J. No. 8, 12 (2016).

C.   THE MORTGAGEE'S ABILITY TO REALIZE ON COLLATERAL

Notwithstanding the rights of creditors built into the Bankruptcy Code, a mortgagee often finds it difficult to achieve full protection or to realize on its collateral in a borrower's bankruptcy.

When a bankruptcy proceeding is commenced by or against the mortgagor, the automatic stay provisions of §362 will stop a foreclosure in its tracks, the statutory trustee in bankruptcy or debtor in possession may continue to use much of the collateral under §363, and, if the proceeding is a reorganization under Chapter 11, a plan may be imposed under §1129 that modifies the rights of the mortgagee. All these steps may be necessary for the efficient administration of bankruptcy law, but they are nevertheless threats to the mortgagee's ability to recover the value of the collateral. To represent a client adequately, a mortgagee's counsel must understand the protections built into the Code for secured creditors, and how to use them effectively for the client's benefit.

1.   *The Automatic Stay and Adequate Protection*

Section 362 of the Bankruptcy Code provides that the filing of a bankruptcy petition operates as a stay of acts against the debtor or the debtor's property. The rationale is that bankruptcy proceedings are designed to provide for an orderly and fair distribution of the debtor's assets or interests in the reorganized business of the debtor. Bankruptcy should not be a signal for a scramble among creditors to see who can get to the debtor's assets first.

Bankruptcy Code §362
11 U.S.C. §362

(a) [A] petition filed under section 301, 302, or 303 of this title . . . operates as a stay, applicable to all entities, of—

   (1) the commencement or continuation, including the issuance or employment of process, of a judicial, administrative, or other action or proceeding against the debtor that was or could have been commenced before the commencement of the case under this title, or to recover a claim against the debtor that arose before the commencement of the case under this title;

   (2) the enforcement, against the debtor or against property of the estate, of a judgment obtained before the commencement of the case under this title;

   (3) any act to obtain possession of property of the estate or of property from the estate or to exercise control over property of the estate;

(4) any act to create, perfect, or enforce any lien against property of the estate;

(5) any act to create, perfect, or enforce against property of the debtor any lien to the extent that such lien secures a claim that arose before the commencement of the case under this title;

(6) any act to collect, assess, or recover a claim against the debtor that arose before the commencement of the case under this title; [and]

(7) the setoff of any debt owing to the debtor that arose before the commencement of the case under this title against any claim against the debtor.
. . .

(b) The filing of a petition . . . does not operate as a stay—. . .

(10) under subsection (a) of this section of any act by a lessor to the debtor under a lease of nonresidential real property that has terminated by the expiration of the stated term of the lease before the commencement of or during a case under this title to obtain possession of such property; . . .

(c) Except as provided in subsections (d), (e), (f), and (h) of this section—

(1) the stay of an act against property of the estate under subsection (a) of this section continues until such property is no longer property of the estate;

(2) the stay of any other act under subsection (a) of this section continues until the earliest of—

(A) the time the case is closed;

(B) the time the case is dismissed; or

(C) if the case is a case under chapter 7 of this title concerning an individual or a case under chapter 9, 11, 12, or 13 of this title, the time a discharge is granted or denied . . .

(d) On request of a party in interest and after notice and a hearing, the court shall grant relief from the stay provided under subsection (a) of this section, such as by terminating, annulling, modifying, or conditioning such stay—

(1) for cause, including the lack of adequate protection of an interest in property of such party in interest;

(2) with respect to a stay of an act against property under subsection (a) of this section, if—(A) the debtor does not have an equity in such property; and (B) such property is not necessary to an effective reorganization;

(3) with respect to a stay of an act against single asset real estate [defined in §101(51B) excerpted below] under subsection (a), by a creditor whose claim is secured by an interest in such real estate, unless, not later than the date that is 90 days after the entry of the order for relief [the date the voluntary bankruptcy petition is filed] (or such later date as the court may determine for cause by order entered within that 90-day period) or 30 days after the court determines that the debtor is subject to this paragraph, whichever is later—

(A) the debtor has filed a plan of reorganization that has a reasonable possibility of being confirmed within a reasonable time; or

(B) the debtor has commenced monthly payments that—

(i) may, in the debtor's sole discretion, notwithstanding section 363(c)(2) be made from rents or other income generated before, on, or after the date of the commencement of the case by or from the property to each creditor whose claim is secured by such real estate (other than a claim secured by a judgment lien or by an unmatured statutory lien); and

(ii) are in an amount equal to interest at the then applicable nondefault contract rate of interest on the value of the creditor's interest in the real estate; . . .

(e)(1) Thirty days after a request under subsection (d) of this section for relief from the stay of any act against property of the estate under subsection (a) of this section, such stay is terminated with respect to the party in interest making such request, unless the court, after notice and a hearing, orders such stay continued in effect pending the conclusion of, or as a result of, a final hearing and determination under subsection (d) of this section. A hearing under this subsection may be a preliminary hearing, or may be consolidated with the final hearing under subsection (d) of this section. The court shall order such stay continued in effect pending the conclusion of the final hearing under subsection (d) of this section if there is a reasonable likelihood that the party opposing relief from such stay will prevail at the conclusion of such final hearing. If the hearing under this subsection is a preliminary hearing, then such final hearing shall be concluded not later than thirty days after the conclusion of such preliminary hearing, unless the 30-day period is extended with the consent of the parties in interest or for a specific time which the court finds is required by compelling circumstances. . . .

(f) Upon request of a party in interest, the court, with or without a hearing, shall grant such relief from the stay provided under subsection (a) of this section as is necessary to prevent irreparable damage to the interest of an entity in property, if such interest will suffer such damage before there is an opportunity for notice and a hearing under subsection (d) or (e) of this section.

(g) In any hearing under subsection (d) or (e) of this section concerning relief from the stay of any act under subsection (a) of this section—

(1) the party requesting such relief has the burden of proof on the issue of the debtor's equity in property; and

(2) the party opposing such relief has the burden of proof on all other issues.

. . .

Bankruptcy Code §101(51B)
11 U.S.C. §101(51B)

(51B) The term "single asset real estate" means real property constituting a single property or project, other than residential real property with fewer than 4 residential units, which generates substantially all of the gross income of a debtor who is not a family farmer and on which no substantial business is being conducted by a debtor other than the business of operating the real property and activities incidental thereto.

While the scope of §362(a) is extremely broad, §362(d) provides that the court must grant relief from the stay in appropriate circumstances. Section 362(d), inter alia, gives wide authority to the court to lift the stay "for cause" and specifies that "cause" includes lack of "adequate protection." Adequate protection is designed to compensate persons whose interests in the debtor's property are being adversely affected by the stay, by the debtor's use of collateral under §363 (discussed in note 5 below), and by certain types of new financing under §364 (discussed in note 5 below). Section 361 lists some of the methods by which such protection may be afforded.

Bankruptcy Code §361
11 U.S.C. §361

When adequate protection is required under section 362, 363 or 364 of this title of an interest of an entity in property, such adequate protection may be provided by—

(1) requiring the trustee to make a cash payment or periodic cash payments to such entity, to the extent that the stay under section 362 of this title, use, sale or lease under section 363 of this title, or any grant of a lien under section 364 of this title results in a decrease in the value of such entity's interest in such property;

(2) providing to such entity an additional or replacement lien to the extent that such stay, use, sale, lease, or grant results in a decrease in the value of such entity's interest in such property; or

(3) granting such other relief, other than entitling such entity to compensation allowable under section 503(b)(1) of this title as an administrative expense, as will result in the realization by such entity of the indubitable equivalent of such entity's interest in such property.

In the case that follows, discussed in Note 2 of Notes and Questions below, the court considers the interaction of §§361 and 362 as well as another means (provided in §362(d)(2)) for lifting of the stay.

In re Jamaica House, Inc.

31 B.R. 192 (Bankr. D. Vt. 1983)

MARRO, Bankruptcy Judge.

MEMORANDUM AND ORDER

The Complaint of the Green Mountain Bank for Relief from Automatic Stay, pursuant to Section 362(d), came on for hearing after notice. From the records in the case and the testimony adduced at the hearing the following facts have been established:

Jamaica House Inc. filed a petition for relief under Chapter 11 of the Bankruptcy Code on January 6, 1983. Its schedules show total liabilities of $120,285.78 and assets of $177,700.00. The debtor operates a restaurant and lodging business under the name of "Jamaica House." Its principal assets consist of real estate made up of the Jamaica Lodge or Inn and a small parcel of land together with fixtures, equipment and inventory. The value of the real estate is $150,000.00 while the equipment, fixtures and furnishings, inventory and other personal property have a valuation of $16,000.00.

The real estate is subject to a first mortgage in favor of the Green Mountain Bank with a balance due on the principal of $90,000.00 and there have been no interest payments on this mortgage since 1981. This property is also subject to a writ of attachment in favor of Heaslip Fuels in the sum of $1,500.00. The debtor has outstanding against it federal income taxes of approximately $10,000.00; rooms and meals taxes owed to the State of Vermont of about $8,000.00; and real estate taxes to the Town of Jamaica in the sum of $1,740.82 which constitute an underlying lien against its real property. . . .

The only witness at the hearing was Robert Pugliese, President of the debtor, who testified that he had had an appraisal made of the real estate together with the personal property contents and the total valuation was fixed at $166,000.00 with which he was in agreement. This testimony was not disputed. . . .

It clearly appears that there is substantial equity in such property and, since the business of the debtor is the operation of an Inn and Restaurant, the property is necessary for reorganization. There has not been any evidence introduced that there cannot be an effective reorganization in this case. . . .

It is apparent that the Bank has failed to satisfy the second alternative condition under §362(d) which would entitle it to relief from stay. As a result the cause upon which the plaintiff must rely for a termination or modification of the stay is lack of adequate protection of its secured interest in the real estate and personal property of the debtor. It argues that its security is jeopardized since there is no showing that the debtor can or will be in a position to pay its current debts; pay its current mortgage obligations; pay its real estate taxes; or cure the acceleration of the plaintiff's mortgage as it has a right to do pursuant to Section

1124(2) of the Bankruptcy [Code], namely clear up and pay back payments now amounting to $26,580.00. . . .

It has been generally held that an equity cushion in and of itself may be sufficient to constitute adequate protection of a secured creditor's interest to sustain the automatic stay. . . .

Some courts have qualified the foregoing rule that an equity cushion may in and of itself be sufficient to constitute adequate protection. See In re Monroe Park, 6 C.B.C.2d at page 143 where the court pointed out that generally, an equity cushion provides adequate protection only if the creditor may foreclose upon the collateral and realize an amount sufficient to cover fully the entire balance due on the debt. . . . Collier recognized the foregoing qualification and expresses it as follows:

> Thus an adequate "cushion" can itself constitute adequate protection with nothing more if care is taken to preserve the cushion. 2 Collier 15th Ed. 361-10 §361.01.

And in the case of In re Pine Lake Village Apartment Co. (U.S. District Court, S.D.N.Y. 1982) 21 B.R. 395, 397 the Court said:

> Unquestionably, a secured creditor has the right to be protected against any decline in value that the collateral could suffer if an automatic stay was in effect since, absent the stay, the creditor would foreclose, preventing any further loss in the value of the security.

Otherwise put, under bankruptcy law, adequate protection generally is meant to preserve the secured creditor's position at the time of bankruptcy. . . .

In the instant case the debtor has not made any mortgage payments to the plaintiff since 1981. This situation was apparently tolerated by the secured creditor. Under such circumstances and with considerable equity in the property the plaintiff would ordinarily not be entitled to lifting of the stay upon the "balance of harm" test. . . . Under this test the Court will be required to consider the impact of the stay on the parties in fashioning relief. 2 Collier 15th Ed. 362-49.

In the light of the foregoing case law it seems abundantly clear that the plaintiff is not entitled to a lifting of the automatic stay. On the other hand the bank's position should not be prejudiced by allowing the debtor to accumulate unpaid real estate taxes which are an underlying lien against the Lodge premises. In addition the debtor should not be permitted to sit coyly back and neglect to file a disclosure statement and plan. The plaintiff is entitled to an early determination as to the feasibility of a successful reorganization so that its equity may be protected as much as possible. . . .

The next case, discussed in Note 1 of Notes and Questions, Problem 18-1, below, illustrates how the rights of a mortgagee, as against a mortgagor who is not in bankruptcy, may be stayed by the bankruptcy of a third party. In reading this case, consider the priority rules discussed in Chapter 3E.

Roslyn Savings Bank v. Comcoach Corp. (In re Comcoach Corp.)
698 F.2d 571 (2d Cir. 1983)

CARDAMONE, Circuit Judge.

. . . In the spring of 1979 the Bank loaned Jon-Rac Associates a sum of money secured by a mortgage on certain premises. Later that year, and with the consent of the Bank, Jon-Rac Associates conveyed the mortgaged premises to Rhone Holdings Nominee Corporation (Rhone). The Bank simultaneously entered into a written agreement with Rhone under which Rhone agreed to pay the mortgage, and at the same time Rhone leased the property to Comcoach subject to the Bank's mortgage.

On August 1, 1981 Rhone defaulted on its mortgage payments and the Bank instituted a foreclosure proceeding against Rhone in New York State Supreme Court, Suffolk County. Comcoach, the tenant in possession of the mortgaged premises, was neither named as a party-defendant nor served with process. On October 26, 1981 Comcoach filed a reorganization petition to institute Chapter 11 proceedings pursuant to the United States Bankruptcy Code (the "Code"), 11 U.S.C. §§1101-74. Since that date the debtor has not paid any rent.

Arguing that it was barred from conducting the state foreclosure action by virtue of the Code's automatic stay provision, . . . the Bank commenced the present action in federal court asking that the automatic stay be lifted under 11 U.S.C. §362(d)(1), (2) (Supp. V 1981) to enable it to name Comcoach as a party-defendant in the pending state foreclosure action. The Bankruptcy Court denied plaintiff's request for relief on the ground that the Bank was not a "party in interest" entitled to seek modification of the stay under the Code. An appeal was then taken to the District Court which affirmed the Bankruptcy Court's decision. Subsequently, the bankruptcy was converted from a Chapter 11 reorganization to a Chapter 7 liquidation of the debtor Comcoach. . . .

To qualify for the "for cause" relief provided in section 362(d)(1), it is necessary that the party seeking such relief be "a party in interest." 11 U.S.C. §362(d). The term "party in interest" is not defined in the Code. Generally, the "real party in interest" is the one who, under the applicable substantive law, has the legal right which is sought to be enforced or is the party entitled to bring suit. . . .

Whether or not the Bank qualifies as a "party in interest" as that term is generally defined, we agree with the courts below that the Bank was not a "party in interest" within the meaning of the Bankruptcy Code. When interpreting the meaning of Code terms such as "party in interest," we are governed by the Code's purposes. . . . Bankruptcy courts were established to provide a forum where creditors and debtors could settle their disputes and thereby effectuate the objectives of the statute. Necessarily, therefore, the Bank must be either a creditor or a debtor to invoke the court's jurisdiction.

Support for this view is found in the Code's legislative history which suggests that, notwithstanding the use of the term "party in interest," it is only creditors who may obtain relief from the automatic stay. See H.R. Rep. No. 95-595, 95th Cong., 1st Sess. 175, reprinted in 1978 U.S. Code Cong. & Ad. News 5787, 6136. . . .

Turning to the particular facts of this case, the Bank is clearly not a debtor. Nor is the Bank a "creditor" of the bankrupt. . . . The Bank here has no right to payment from the bankrupt, since the bankrupt has no obligation on the mortgage and the bankrupt's duty to pay rent on its lease runs only to Rhone, not the Bank.
. . .

The Bank further expresses concern that if it is not a "party in interest" entitled to seek modification of the stay, it will be barred from continuing its foreclosure action in state court and left without a remedy to enforce its rights under the mortgage. As noted by both lower courts these concerns are premised upon an erroneous view of the law. First, the state foreclosure action, as presently constituted, is not stayed. Until the debtor is named as a party-defendant the action does not affect the bankrupt estate. New York law provides that lessees are necessary parties in foreclosure actions. . . .

Necessary parties are not always indispensable parties, however, whose absence mandates dismissal of the action. See N.Y. Civ. Prac. Law §1001(b) (McKinney 1976). The absence of a necessary party in a foreclosure action simply leaves such party's rights to the premises unaffected. . . . By failing to name Comcoach as a party-defendant in its foreclosure action, the Bank has left the debtor in exactly the same position as it was in prior to commencement of the suit. Since no interest of the bankrupt estate has been affected, no automatic stay prohibiting the continuance of the state foreclosure action exists.

Our disposition of the Bank's first argument appears to be of small or no solace for the Bank. After all, its only source of income from this property is the bankrupt tenant in a building rendered nearly unmarketable. But, in response to the Bank's second concern, we find that it has not been left without a remedy. The Bank has the right to the appointment of a receiver in the state court action. For reasons already noted, plaintiff is not stayed from seeking such an appointment. A court-appointed receiver *would* qualify as a party in interest for purposes of section 362(d), since under New York law a receiver steps into the shoes of the mortgagor-debtor, in this case Rhone. The receiver becomes vested with Rhone's property right and acts as an arm of the court for the creditor-Bank's benefit. . . . It would then have rights against Comcoach under applicable substantive law including the right to sue for rent and, therefore, the right to move to lift the automatic stay.

For the foregoing reasons we hold that the Bank is not a party in interest in the bankruptcy proceeding and cannot seek to have the automatic stay vacated or modified so as to name debtor Comcoach a party-defendant in the pending state foreclosure action.

NOTES AND QUESTIONS

1. The Scope of the Automatic Stay. The following problem illustrates just how broad the automatic stay of §362(a) really is.

> ➤ *Problem 18-1*
>
> a. Under the master hypothetical, assume that Ace Insurance Company's mortgage form contains an assignment-of-rents clause similar to the clause discussed in Chapter 8B4. When Dan Developer defaults, Ace implements the assignment-of-rents provision pursuant to state law and directs the tenants to pay the rent directly to it. When the checks arrive, Ace deposits the checks and remits to Dan any amount in excess of what is owed on the mortgage balance. The day after Dan files his petition in bankruptcy, rent checks arrive by mail. Under §362(a), can Ace deposit the checks? If not, which subsection of §362(a) are you applying? Would your answer be different if the rental payments were deposited in Ace's account by wire transfer?
>
> b. Suppose Dan Developer had not filed for bankruptcy but was nevertheless in default under the mortgage loan. At the time Ace forecloses, one of Dan Developer's tenants and a junior mortgagee are in bankruptcy. If you were counsel to Ace, under what circumstances would you advise Ace to proceed with the foreclosure? If you advise against foreclosure, with what subsection or subsections of §362(a) are you concerned? Would your answer be different if this were a power of sale foreclosure, rather than a judicial foreclosure?
>
> In *Comcoach* the mortgagee asked for relief from the stay, "arguing that it was barred from conducting the state foreclosure action by virtue of the Code's automatic stay provision." Was this correct? Did the court say that the mortgagee was barred from *conducting* the foreclosure under §362(a), or was it just barred from *naming the lessee* as a party-defendant and cutting off the lease? Assume Ace Insurance Company, foreclosing against Dan Developer (who is not in bankruptcy), wanted to name the junior mortgagee as a party-defendant and was precluded from doing so because of the stay. (Do you understand why it is ordinarily more important to be able to name the junior mortgagee than the lessee?) Under *Comcoach*, does Ace have standing to seek relief from the stay?
>
> Does the *Comcoach* assumption that Ace is not a party in interest that may request relief from the stay make sense? The Second Circuit appears comfortable in its conclusion that only a debtor or a creditor may be a

"party in interest." Since the debtor is not one who would normally ask for relief from the stay, the Second Circuit seems to be saying that only a creditor is a party in interest when it comes to stay relief. This makes one wonder why Congress did not simply provide in §362(d) for relief from the stay on request of a "creditor." The decision appears to have been reached apparently without an examination of how the phrase "party in interest" is used almost 80 other times in the Bankruptcy Code. Try doing a global search on the phrase and see what you come up with. Note especially, §§502(a), 547(g) and 1109(b) and whether they limit the phrase to debtors or creditors. When the Second Circuit was confronted with a party in interest issue in a different context under §1109(b), which refers to "party in interest" as "including the debtor, the trustee, a creditors' committee, an equity security holders' committee, a creditor, an equity security holder, or any indenture trustee," it may have distinguished *Comcoach* by indicating that §1109(b) might have the "benefit of somewhat greater breadth— breadth that might be warranted by the additional parties listed in the text of §1109(b) but not in the text of §362(d)(1)." In re Refco, 565 F.3d 109, 117 (2d Cir. 2007).

Comcoach also ignores many authorities that have interpreted "party in interest" to mean a person with some "interest" in the outcome of the dispute.[21] For a strong criticism of *Comcoach,* see In re Sweports, Ltd., 476 B.R. 540 (Bankr. N.D. Ill. 2012) and materials cited therein.

What procedure to protect the mortgagee does the *Comcoach* court suggest? Would implementation of such a procedure ensure protection for Ace? If not, why not?

c. Assume that some months before Dan filed his petition in bankruptcy there was a small fire for which insurance proceeds were awarded. Ace allowed Dan to hold the proceeds of the insurance in escrow for payment of the cost of restoration, with any remainder to be turned over to Ace and applied to reduce the indebtedness. When the petition is filed, all the restoration has been completed and there is $5,680 still in escrow to be turned over to Ace. Does §362(a) permit Ace to get this money? If not, which subsection or subsections of §362(a) are you applying? ◄

---

21. See, e.g., In re James Wilson Assocs., 965 F.2d 160, 169 (7th Cir. 1992) (noting a "party in interest" has standing if a beneficiary of the provision is being invoked); Baron & Budd, P.C. v. Unsecured Asbestos Claimants Comm., 321 B.R. 147, 158 (D. N.J. 2005) (quoting In re Torrez, 132 B.R. 924, 934 (Bankr. D. Cal. 1991)) ("The test to determine whether an entity is a party in interest is 'whether the prospective party in interest has a sufficient stake [such as a pecuniary interest] in the outcome of the proceeding to require representation.'")); In re Global Indus. Technologies, Inc., 645 F.3d 201, 210 (3d Cir. 2011) (quoting In re James Wilson Assocs., 965 F.2d 160, 169 (7th Cir. 1992)) ("[A]nyone who has a legally protected interest that could be affected by a bankruptcy proceeding is entitled to assert that interest with respect to any issue to which it pertains...."); and 7 Collier on Bankruptcy ¶1109.02[1] (A. Resnick & H. Sommer eds., 16th ed.) (defining "party in interest" as "any person with a direct financial stake in the outcome of the case" as well as representatives of persons with direct financial interests).

These are just a few of the difficult questions that may arise in connection with the §362 stay. The point is that the stay is pervasive—virtually any steps a mortgagee may wish to take may be barred. Remember that §362(a)(6) stays "any act to collect . . . a claim," which is about as broad as you can get.

THE ETHICAL REAL ESTATE LAWYER

Violating the Automatic Stay

Suppose you represent Ace and you conclude that there is a high probability that the stay applies to a proposed action by Ace. Nevertheless, Ace's loan officer asks you to proceed with the proposed act immediately, stating that he or she will take the risk of any impropriety. Is there any risk to you in following that instruction, or are you immune from risk under the Bankruptcy Code while zealously representing your client? See Fidelity Mortgage Investors v. Camelia Builders, 550 F.2d 47 (2d Cir. 1976), cert. denied, 429 U.S. 1093 (1977), and §362(k) for the likely consequences.

---

2. Adequate Protection. The fact that the stay applies does not mean the creditor's proposed act may not be taken. It means it may not be taken without the approval of the court. Under §362(d)(1), relief from the stay must be granted for cause, including lack of adequate protection for the mortgagee's interest. Section 361 sets forth three methods of providing adequate protection: cash payments, replacement lien, or the "indubitable equivalent" of the diminution in value of the mortgagee's interest in the collateral. The phrase "indubitable equivalent" was derived from Judge Learned Hand in In re Murel Holding Corp., 75 F.2d 941, 942 (2d Cir. 1935), where he discussed the meaning of "adequate protection" in another context:

> It is plain that "adequate protection" must be completely compensatory; and that payment ten years hence is not generally the equivalent of payment now. Interest is indeed the common measure of the difference, but a creditor who fears the safety of his principal will scarcely be content with that; he wishes to get his money or at least the property. We see no reason to suppose that the statute was intended to deprive him of that in the interest of junior holders, unless by a substitute of the most *indubitable equivalence.* (Emphasis supplied.)

By employing Judge Hand's language, the drafters intended to make it clear that they did not expect the courts to give mere lip service to the concept of adequate protection, and by and large the courts have recognized this. Nevertheless, questions continue to arise for resolution. For example, assume that Dan Developer files under Chapter 11 of the Code. Ace Insurance Company is undersecured, that is, its mortgage has a balance that exceeds the value of the property. Is Ace entitled to adequate protection because the value of the collateral, which Ace would have obtained at a foreclosure sale, cannot be reinvested since foreclosure is being prevented? In other words, is Ace entitled to payments for "lost opportunity" costs? After conflicts among the circuits, the Supreme Court answered this question in the negative, equating lost opportunity costs with postpetition interest, to which the mortgagee is entitled under §506(b) only to the extent that the value of the collateral exceeds the indebtedness. United Sav. Ass'n v. Timbers of Inwood Forest Assocs., 484 U.S. 365 (1988).

Suppose the value of the property is decreasing rapidly. The court determines that Dan's management is at fault and provides adequate protection by replacing Dan as manager. Do you think this would meet §361's requirements?

In *Jamaica House* the court discusses the fact that the collateral had value in excess of the indebtedness (an "equity cushion") and debated whether the existence of such a cushion constituted adequate protection for the mortgagee. Is adequate protection something the mortgagee already has, or something the court gives to the mortgagee to compensate for a reduction in value of collateral? Did the court find a need for adequate protection? What was the basis for its conclusion? What do you think the court meant by the "balance of harm" test, and how does such a test apply to the requirements of §361? In refusing to grant relief from the stay, what protection for the mortgagee did the court build into its denial?

The courts are in disagreement as to whether and at what point the reduction of the equity cushion requires adequate protection. Compare In re Hagendorfer, 42 B.R. 13 (1984) with In re Johnson, 90 B.R. 973 (1988). Some practitioners have noted that where the cushion gets below 20 percent, the courts seem more willing to provide adequate protection. Keep in mind that an oversecured creditor, entitled to post-petition interest under §506(b) to the extent the value the collateral exceeds the debt (i.e., to the extent of the equity cushion), will suffer a loss in the amount of post-petition interest it can recover as the equity cushion decreases.

3. "Effective" Reorganization. Section 362(d)(2) provides that the court will grant relief from the stay if the debtor has no equity in the property and the property is not necessary for an effective reorganization. When the Code was being drafted, representatives of certain real estate lenders first suggested that relief from the stay be granted where the debtor had no equity in the property. They were disturbed by pre-Code abuses of the stay in which borrowers, whose bad management had caused the failure, continued as managers to "milk" the property (that is, collect portions of cash flow as commissions or fees while property maintenance is deferred), resulting in irreparable damage to the reputation and value of the property.

Wait a minute, said the National Bankruptcy Conference. What you say may make sense when you are talking about a single-asset real estate entity. But what happens in a major corporate reorganization? Are you going to frustrate the reorganization by lifting the stay to permit foreclosure of a mortgage on the debtor's factory simply because the liens on the factory exceed its value (leaving the debtor with no equity in the property)? The National Bankruptcy Conference had a point. Accordingly, the second condition to lifting the stay for lack of equity was added: a finding that the property is not necessary to an effective reorganization.

Suppose Dan Developer developed his property through a limited partnership (or other entity) formed to own the land and office building as its sole asset. Assume that at the time of that entity's petition for reorganization under Chapter 11, Ace's mortgage balance exceeds the value of the property, so the debtor has no equity in the property. Can Ace foreclose? Is the property necessary to an effective reorganization? Can relief from the stay ever be granted on this ground if the debtor has only one asset? Remember, the provision refers to an *effective* reorganization. What is the meaning of "effective"? See In re Garden Motor Lodge & Restaurant, 34 B.R. 138 (Bankr. D. Vt. 1983) (defining "effective" as requiring a reasonable possibility of a successful reorganization within a reasonable time) and Statement of Congressman Don Edwards (the "father" of the Bankruptcy Code on the House side) in 124 Cong. Rec. H. 11089 (daily ed. Sept. 28, 1978).

4. Single Asset Real Estate and the "Fast-Track." The frustration of real estate lenders when single asset borrowers file in bankruptcy is illustrated in Carlisle, *Single Asset Real Estate in Chapter 11: Secured Creditors' Perspective and the Need for Reform*, 1 Am. Bankr. Inst. L. Rev. 133 (1993). Carlisle argued for a fast-track reorganization that would involve the lifting of the automatic stay if the debtor does not propose a plan having a reasonable possibility of being confirmed within 90 days (or such later time as the court may determine for cause) after the filing of the petition. Id. at 134-146. Alternatively, the court could keep the stay in place if the creditor were provided with so-called "lost opportunity costs," that is, market rate payments on the value of the collateral, which normally would not be available to undersecured creditors (see United Sav. Ass'n v. Timbers of Inwood Forest Assocs., 484 U.S. 365 (1988) discussed in Note 2 above. Do you understand why the Carlisle proposal is not inconsistent with *Timbers?*).

A somewhat revised version of Carlisle's proposal was enacted as part of the 1994 amendments to the Bankruptcy Code (Pub. L. No. 103-394) as §362(d)(3), with the definition of single asset real estate added as §101(51B) of the Bankruptcy Code. A limitation on that definition to cases where the debt is not greater than $4 million, the so-called four million dollar cap, which had been a major impediment to the effectiveness of the section, was deleted in the BAPCPA amendments of 2005. This legislation also revised the "lost opportunity cost" alternative discussed above, to provide for the payment of interest at the contract rate (rather than a market rate) on the unpaid balance of the debt (rather than the value of the collateral). Do you see the difference? If you represented a real estate mortgage lender would you be concerned about the language that gives the court the power to extend the 90-day period "for cause"

Let's look for a moment at the definition of "single asset real estate" found in §101(51B). Under this definition of single asset real estate, would Rockefeller Center in New York City be considered a single asset? Do hotels fit within the definition? What difference would it make if multiple hotels were owned, each by a different affiliated debtor?

> ➤ *Problem 18-2*
> Assume you represent Ace Insurance Company, which has made a multi-million loan secured by a mortgage on a single asset office building project. To ensure your client will get the benefit of the fast-track single asset real estate provisions if the loan falls into default and the borrower files in bankruptcy, you successfully insist that the organizational documents of the borrower require that the borrower be a single purpose entity owning no property other than the property being mortgaged and that the borrower's business be limited to the operation of the mortgaged property. Your initial concern was well taken, and the borrower eventually defaults under the mortgage. On the eve of filing in bankruptcy, the borrowing entity purchases a small condominium apartment for $150,000. Why do you think the borrower made that purchase? What arguments will the borrower make that the single asset bankruptcy provisions are inapplicable to this bankruptcy? What would you argue to support a motion that notwithstanding the apartment purchase, the bankruptcy petition be treated as a single asset filing? If you don't succeed, what steps might you take in future documentation or otherwise, that you may have learned from your study of real estate investments, that could strengthen your client's position in subsequent real estate deals made in reliance on the single asset provisions of the Bankruptcy Code? ◄

5. Use, Sale, or Lease of Property and Obtaining Credit. Adequate protection under §361 applies not only to the effects of the stay but also to the effects of the use, sale, or lease of the collateral under §363 or the obtaining of certain credit for the estate under §364.

Section 363 permits the bankruptcy trustee to use, sell, or lease the collateral either in or out of the ordinary course of business. If it is not in the ordinary course, §363(b)(1) requires prior notice and a hearing. If the use or sale is in the ordinary course of business, notice and a hearing are required only for the use of cash collateral (§363(c)(1), (2)). Cash collateral under §363(a) includes rents from the realty and payments for use and occupancy of hotel and motel rooms and facilities. This is more fully discussed in note 6 below. The notice and hearing requirement is subject to §102(1), which permits acting without a hearing if, inter alia, the court determines that there is insufficient time for one.

If the requirements of §363(f) are met, the property may be sold free and clear of the mortgage; however the mortgagee is generally permitted to bid at a sale of the collateral and to offset a successful bid against its claim (§363(k)). This is known as "credit bidding"[22] However, subsection (k) does not afford this right to those whose interest is affected by the sale free and clear other than holders of liens.

Assume that Dan Developer holds a leasehold, rather than a fee interest and that Dan's landlord files in bankruptcy and proposes to sell the fee free and clear of the lease. Would §363(k) be available to protect Dan? Check the language of (k) carefully. Is Dan the holder of a claim secured by a lien on the property being sold? We return to §363(f) later in connection with our discussion of leasehold protection built into §365 (see Chapter 18E). For now, remember that on request of an entity with an interest in the property being sold (for example, a fee mortgagee or lessee), the court under §363(e) is required to condition the use, sale, or lease to provide adequate protection of such interest.

Under §364, the bankruptcy trustee is authorized, with certain restrictions, to obtain credit for the continued operation of the business as an administrative expense (priority over other unsecured claims under §503(b) and §507(a)(2)), with priority over certain administrative expenses, or by securing the funds with a lien either on property otherwise free of liens or as a junior lien on the mortgaged property. In addition, after notice and a hearing, the court is permitted to authorize obtaining secured credit equal in lien or superior to an existing mortgage on the property (§364(d)), where unsecured credit is unavailable and adequate protection is provided for the mortgagee.

6. Use of Rents and Hotel Revenues.

a. *Rents.* You are already acquainted with the importance of the assignment of rents clause from the discussion in Chapter 8B4. We will now look at the treatment of rent assignments in bankruptcy.

Rents are classified as "cash collateral" as defined in §363(a) of the Bankruptcy Code. Cash collateral is, in turn, afforded special protection. Under §363(c)(4), the cash collateral must be segregated and accounted for; under §363(c)(2), the cash collateral may not be used by the debtor even in the ordinary course of business, without notice and a hearing; and under §363(e), the secured party may request that use of cash collateral be conditioned to the extent required to provide adequate protection. While "cash collateral" is defined to include rents, it includes rents only to the extent that the rents are, in fact, collateral for the loan, that is, to the extent they serve as security for an obligation and the security interest is perfected. Under §552(a), a security interest would not normally extend to rents received by the debtor after the commencement of the bankruptcy. The security interest in rents nevertheless extends postpetition by virtue of §552(b). Because of certain interpretations of the language of §552(b), however, some courts, prior to the 1994 amendments to the Bankruptcy Code, shed doubt on whether the section applied.

---

22. More will be said about credit bidding in connection with our discussion of plan confirmation.

The problem was that §552(b) was subject to three conditions. First, it was made subject to §544 (§544(a) provides that the trustee or debtor in possession is a hypothetical judgment lien creditor and bona fide purchaser as of the date of bankruptcy and therefore can wipe out unperfected security interests). Second, it extended to postpetition rents only "to the extent provided . . . by applicable nonbankruptcy law." Third, the protection was subject to the court determining otherwise "based on the equities of the case." It was primarily the first and second exceptions that caused most concern.

As you know, an assignment of rents contained in a real property mortgage and recorded in the real property records, at least in most lien theory jurisdictions, does not give the mortgagee immediate right to collect the rents on default by the assignor. The security interest cannot be enforced until the mortgagee takes certain preliminary steps such as commencing foreclosure or having a receiver appointed. The only exception is where the assignment is an absolute present assignment (the mortgagee collects rents throughout the life of the mortgage) or is deemed to be absolute by state law. See, for example, Cal. Civ. Code §2938. Some courts had confused the enforcement requirements of state law with requirements for perfection of assignments and held that notwithstanding the recording of the mortgage containing the assignment of rents, the security interest in rents was unperfected until the debtor had taken the additional steps required under state law, or at least that it wasn't perfected to the extent "provided by applicable nonbankruptcy law."

While a number of courts had been receptive to the notion that "enforcement" and "perfection" are two different things (see, for example, Vienna Park Properties v. United Postal Sav. Ass'n (In re Vienna Park Properties), 976 F.2d 106 (2d Cir. 1992)), sufficient concern remained to necessitate a clarifying amendment in 1994 that deleted rents from existing §552(b) (which became §552(b)(1)), and added a new §552(b)(2) relating to rents, not containing the "as provided by applicable nonbankruptcy law" limitation. Section 552(b)(2) provides in relevant part:

> Except as provided in Section . . . 544 . . . if the debtor and an entity entered into a security agreement before the commencement of the case and if the security interest created by such security agreement extends to property of the debtor acquired before the commencement of the case and to amounts paid as rents of such property or the fees, charges, accounts, or other payments for the use or occupancy of rooms and other public facilities in hotels, motels, or other lodging properties, then such security interest extends to such rents and such fees, charges, accounts, or other payments acquired by the estate after the commencement of the case to the extent provided in such security agreement, except to any extent that the court, after notice and a hearing and based on the equities of the case, orders otherwise.

Does this change avoid the problem? It certainly eliminates the problem created by the "to the extent provided . . . by applicable nonbankruptcy law" language. However, if a court believes that a nonabsolute assignment of rents is unperfected at the commencement of the bankruptcy, does language subjecting the protection to §544 give you any concern? Check §544(a). Another concern might be the language of §552(b)(2) that makes an exception where the court "orders otherwise" based on the equities of the case. Most observers seem content not to disturb this sleeping dog.

b. *Hotel Revenues.* Prior to the 1994 amendments, the effectiveness of assignments of monies due for use or occupancy of hotel rooms was questioned because they were generally considered as security interests in "accounts." Accounts arising postpetition were not covered by the §552(b) exception to §552(a) discussed above. Thus, revenues arising after the filing of the petition would not be covered by the security interest and would be subject to use by the debtor, at least in the ordinary course of business. Because the revenue stream is the heart of hotel financing, this would make hotel financing extremely problematic. As a result, both the borrowers and the lenders appealed to Congress for help (an unbeatable combination), and the result was to add hotel revenues to the definition of cash collateral and include them in the provisions of the new §552(b)(2) quoted above. Since "perfection" was never an issue for accounts as distinguished from rents (do you see why?), the changes have effectively permitted hotel financing to continue.

Is the language, however, broad enough to do the job completely? Assume Ace Insurance Company holds a mortgage on the Danley Resort, an upscale hotel and conference center owned by Dan Developer. The mortgage also provides for a properly perfected security interest in all accounts and proceeds thereof of the Danley. After the Danley files in Chapter 11, the American College of Real Estate Lawyers ("ACREL") holds its Annual Meeting in the hotel. The meeting includes an opening cocktail party with hors d'oeuvres and a lavish closing reception and dinner. Does Ace's security interest in accounts and proceeds attach to ACREL's obligation to pay for these two events or do the accounts receivable go into the debtor's estate? In other words, are the charges for the hors d'oeuvres and dinner "fees, charges, accounts, or other payments *for the use or occupancy* of rooms and other public facilities" in the hotel (emphasis added)?

7. Prepetition Agreements and Waivers of the Automatic Stay. There is no provision in Chapter 11 requiring that the *petition* be filed in good faith. Yet many courts have scrutinized cases as though an implied standard of good faith applied to filings. To get the flavor of this development, see Marsch v. Marsch (In re Marsch), 36 F.3d 825 (9th Cir. 1994); Michigan Natl. Bank v. Charfoos (In re Charfoos), 979 F.2d 390 (6th Cir. 1992); Little Creek Dev. Co. v. Commonwealth Mortgage Corp. (In re Little Creek Dev. Co.), 779 F.2d 1068 (5th Cir. 1986); and In re JER Jameson Mezz Borrower II, 461 B.R. 293 (Bankr. D. Del. 2011).

When Dan Developer is in trouble, he may negotiate with Ace Insurance Company to restructure the debt to stave off what seems like an inevitable foreclosure. As you remember from the discussion of workouts in Chapter 8A, as a result of such negotiations, lenders, not wanting to add to their portfolio of foreclosed properties, often agree to forbear payments of principal and interest, extend the loan term, and make other debt accommodations. Assume that after operating under the workout agreement for some time, with Dan continuing to collect management and leasing fees directly or through affiliated organizations, the workout fails and Dan is again in default. Ace commences foreclosure and on the eve of the sale, Dan files in bankruptcy to stay the sale. Ace feels the filing was not in good faith, that the workout was the last clear chance to avoid foreclosure, and that if it failed Dan should not try to obstruct Ace's proceedings to recover the property.

As a result, lenders such as Ace may formalize this implied understanding in a prepetition workout agreement. Under such an agreement, Dan will acknowledge that the workout is the only feasible reorganization possible; that Ace has changed its position to assist in the workout; and that if Dan should file in bankruptcy after the workout fails, Dan agrees that the filing would not have been in good faith and agrees to waive the right to contest a motion by Ace for relief from the stay.

That bankruptcy judges had become almost as frustrated with the eve of foreclosure filings as lenders is seen in Good Faith: A Roundtable Discussion, Am. Bankr. Inst. & St. John's Univ., Single Asset Bankruptcies 13 (ABA 1997) (updated from Good Faith: Roundtable Discussion, 1 Am. Bankr. Inst. L. Rev. 11 (1993)). Some of the judges indicated that they would take such agreements into account in determining the good faith of the debtor and whether to grant relief from the stay. See also McNicholas, Workout Breakthrough? Prepetition Agreements May Lead to Dismissal or Relief from Stay, Am. Bankr. Inst. & St. John's Univ., Single Asset Bankruptcies 59 (ABA 1997) (updated from McNicholas, Prepetition Agreements and the Implied Good Faith Requirement, 1 Am. Bankr. Inst. L. Rev. 197 (1993)).

Can pre-bankruptcy borrowers waive rights granted to debtors under the Bankruptcy Code? If your answer is no, as it probably should be absent an express provision in the Code, how would you distinguish what the judges are saying from a simple attempt to undo the effect of the Bankruptcy Code through creative drafting? See the model workout clause in the McNicholas article, supra, 1 Am. Bankr. Inst. L. Rev. at 208, and Judge Walrath's opinion in In re JER Jameson Mezz Borrower II, 461 B.R. 293 (Bankr. D. Del. 2011) and her listing of good faith factors at 298-99.

8. Additional Reading. M. Bienenstock, Bankruptcy Reorganization 97-223 (1987); Averch, Berryman and Collins, The Treatment of Net Rents in Bankruptcy—Adequate Protection, Payment of Interest, Return of Collateral, or Reduction of Debt, 48 U. Miami L. Rev. 691 (1994); Carlson, Adequate Protection Payments and the Surrender of Cash Collateral in Chapter 11 Reorganization, 15 Cardozo L. Rev. 1357 (1994); Divack, Chapter 11 Liquidation and the "Necessary to an Effective Reorganization" Standard of Relief from the Automatic Stay, 93 Com. L.J. 17 (Spring 1988); Flaschen, Adequate Protection for the Oversecured Creditor, 61 Am. Bankr. L.J. 341 (1987); Forrester, Still Crazy After All These Years: The Absolute Assignment of Rents in Mortgage Loan Transactions 59 Fla. L. Rev. 487 (2007); Freyermuth, Modernizing Security in Rents: The New Uniform Assignment of Rents Act, 71 Mo. L. Rev. 1 (2006); Karlen, Adequate Protection under the Bankruptcy Code: Its Role in Bankruptcy Reorganizations, 2 Pace L. Rev. (1982); McCullough, Analysis of Bankruptcy Code Section 364(d): When Will a Court Allow a Trustee to Obtain Post-petition Financing by Granting a Superpriority Lien?, 93 Com. L.J. 186 (1988); Munitz, Treatment of Real Property Liens in Bankruptcy Cases, 38 J. Marshall L. Rev. 171 (2004); Murphy, Administrative Powers of the Trustee in Bankruptcy—Stays, Use of Collateral, and Obtaining Credit, in ABA Sec. of Real Prop., Prob. & Tr. L., Real Estate Bankruptcies and Workouts 11 (1983); Nimmer, Real Estate Creditors and the Automatic Stay: A Study in Behavioral Economics, 1983 Ariz. St. L.J. 281; Randolph, Recognizing Lenders' Rents Interests in Bankruptcy, 27 Real Prop. Prob. & Tr. J. 281 (1992); Smahci, Automatic Stay under the 1978 Bankruptcy Code: An Equitable Roadblock to Secured Creditor Relief, 17 San Diego L. Rev. 1021 (1980); Weintraub and Resnick, Puncturing the Equity Cushion—Adequate Protection for Secured Creditors in Reorganization Cases, 14 UCC L.J. 284 (1982).

2. *The Plan of Reorganization*

The purpose of a proceeding under Chapter 11 of the Code is to rehabilitate the debtor under a plan of reorganization. The plan normally will provide that creditors be given property or interests in the reorganized enterprise as compensation for their claims. As noted above, such a plan often necessitates dealing with and changing the rights of creditors. Creditors' interests are protected against unfairness by the requirements for plan confirmation found in §1129(a). Of these requirements, the following five are especially significant in real estate bankruptcies:

1. *Good Faith.* Section 1129(a)(3) provides that no plan may be confirmed unless, inter alia, it has been proposed in good faith. While, as discussed in Chapter 18C1, note 7, supra, there is no formal requirement that the *petition be filed* in good faith,[23] this provision requires the court to consider whether the plan was proposed in good faith before it is confirmed.

2. *Best Interest of Creditors.* Section 1129(a)(7) requires that no plan be confirmed unless each holder of a claim who has not individually accepted the plan receives property, the value of which is at least equal to what would have been received had the debtor been liquidated under Chapter 7. This is the so-

---

23. Notwithstanding this, some decisions have recognized an implied obligation of good faith. See McNicholas, Prepetition Agreements and the Implied Good Faith Requirement, 1 Am. Bankr. Inst. L. Rev. 197 (1993) and the discussion in Note 7 of Chapter 18 C1 above.

called best interest of creditors test. It makes sense because reorganizations were designed to produce greater value than liquidation.

3. *Acceptance by Each Class of Creditors.* Under §1129(a)(8), the plan must be accepted by at least two-thirds in amount **and** more than one-half in number of allowed claims of **each** class of creditors (these percentages are set forth in §1126(c)). Do you understand that any creditor holding more than one-third of the amount of claims against the debtor may cause the class to vote against the plan? Section 1129(a)(8) however, is the only requirement of §1129(a) that may be overridden by the court. Section 1129(b) provides that under certain circumstances the court may impose (or "cram down") a plan against a dissenting class of creditors. But the court may not impose the plan against a class whose interests are "impaired" (§1124) by the plan unless the plan is "fair and equitable" as to such class. This requires a distribution based on "absolute priority." As we will discuss below, absolute priority is designed to require distribution of interests in the debtor in order of priority so that a plan cannot be confirmed that gives property in the debtor to a junior creditor or equity owner (e.g., Dan Developer) without paying senior creditors in full. Does this support the "bankruptcy bargain" we discussed in the introduction to this Chapter?

4. *Approval by One Class of Impaired Claims.* Since a plan may be imposed against the will of impaired classes as discussed above, §1129(a)(10) requires that under no circumstances may a plan be confirmed if there is not at least one class of noninsider impaired creditors that support the plan. We will see how some debtors have attempted to draft the plan around this requirement when we discuss classification of claims in note 6 infra.

5. *Feasibility.* Section 1129(a)(11) requires the court to determine that the confirmation of the plan is not likely to be followed by liquidation or a need for further financial reorganization.

In the discussion that follows, we will analyze how effective these requirements are in protecting the real estate mortgagee.

The major real estate reorganization controversy at the time the Code was drafted arose under the 1976 *Pine Gate* decision.[24] *Pine Gate* involved the reorganization of a single asset real estate limited partnership under what was then Chapter XII of the former Bankruptcy Act. In a limited partnership, it is frequently necessary for the general partner to be exculpated from personal liability on the mortgage debt so that the limited partners can obtain a step-up in the tax basis of their partnership interests equal to their share of the mortgage liability.[25] Otherwise, in a leveraged partnership, without the increase in basis a limited partner may not be able to take full advantage of its distributive share of

---

24. In re Pine Gate Assocs., 2 Bankr. Ct. Dec. (CRR) 1478 (Bankr. N.D. Ga. 1976).
25. See I.R.C. §465(b)(6) and Treas. Reg. §1.752-1(e). See generally discussion at Chapter 14A2.

losses and other tax benefits associated with real estate ownership. Accordingly, as a "tax favor" to the partnership, the mortgage lender in *Pine Gate* (and most other single asset cases) was willing to allow the mortgage debt to be nonrecourse (see Chapters 3B3 and 5A3 for discussion of nonrecourse loans).

Back in the 1970s, when *Pine Gate* transpired, use of the real estate tax shelter was in its heyday. Nonrecourse financing meant that when times were good the limited partners could enjoy all available tax shelter benefits, including accelerated depreciation. Conversely, if times were bad, partners in a limited partnership could walk away from the transaction without personal liability. However, one major problem for the limited partners was the tax rule that foreclosure was deemed to be a disposition of real property for tax purposes, triggering recapture of all the accelerated depreciation (that is depreciation in excess of straight line deductions over the tax life of the property), which resulted in the treatment of the recaptured amount as ordinary income to the limited partners in the year of foreclosure.[26] There are also other tax unpleasantries that result from foreclosure, such as the need to report forgiveness of debt income. Confronted with the specter of substantial tax liabilities, the partners in *Pine Gate* filed a petition under Chapter XII on the eve of the foreclosure sale and thereby stayed the foreclosure while the partnership remained in control as a "debtor in possession." Next, the partners attempted to devise a plan of reorganization under which they would pay the mortgagee only a portion of the indebtedness, avoid recapture, and keep the property free and clear of the lien of the mortgage.

Under the old Bankruptcy Act, what is now Chapter 11 was divided into three chapters: Chapter X, dealing with corporate reorganization; Chapter XI, covering arrangements for unsecured debts; and Chapter XII, the chapter involved in the *Pine Gate* case, dealing specifically with real property arrangements for noncorporate debtors (the so-called single asset real estate limited partnership). Chapter X required that almost every plan had to be "fair and equitable" and thus provide for absolute priority. This meant that no junior creditor could be paid until senior creditors were paid in full and that no stockholder or other owner (including partners) of the debtor could be given any property on account of its equity interest until all creditors were paid in full.[27] Thus, Chapter X would not have been helpful to the limited partners, who wanted to keep the property without full payment of the mortgage loan.

In Chapter XII, however, there was (after 1952) no provision requiring absolute priority. (There was also no absolute priority requirement in Chapter XI, but this chapter was limited to arrangements for unsecured debts.) Nevertheless, Chapter XII protected dissenting classes under a court-imposed ("cramdown") plan in several ways. The "protection" alternative that figured so prominently in the *Pine Gate* line of cases was found in Chapter XII's §461(11), requiring that before a plan could be confirmed over the objection of a dissenting class, the class had to be paid in cash the value of the debt owed to that class.

---

26. I.R.C. §§1245, 1250 (prior law). See discussion at Chapter 13A2b
27. See Case v. Los Angeles Lumber Prods. Co., 308 U.S. 106 (1939).

Judge William Norton interpreted that provision in the *Pine Gate* decision and held that when the debt is nonrecourse (no personal liability), the "value of the debt" is equal to the value of the collateral, which had been depressed in the market conditions in Atlanta at the time. Thus, the partnership could keep the property free and clear of the mortgage by paying the mortgagee some $1.9 million (the court-determined value of the collateral) on a $2.3 million debt. Other such cases followed. The most shocking of the *Pine Gate* line of cases to the real estate community was *In re KRO Associates,*[28] where there was some $14 million in mortgages on the property and Judge Roy Babbitt, using a 20 percent capitalization rate,[29] valued the collateral at $895,000. The mortgagee would have been willing to take the property for the full amount of the indebtedness, but the court pointed out that this would create tax problems (recapture of accelerated depreciation) for the limited partners and allowed the limited partnership mortgagor to keep the property on payment to the first mortgagee of $895,000 in discharge of all mortgages (including the $6 million owed on the first mortgage).

It should be no surprise, then, that as the Code was taking shape in Washington in 1978, the real estate community, shocked by this seeming abrogation of our "bankruptcy bargain," appealed for legislative help to prevent what they considered a severe injustice—mortgagees could be cashed out of their mortgages based on what they often considered to be an inadequate valuation of the collateral. They suggested that absolute priority be made applicable to the new omnibus Chapter 11.

Opposition to this approach came (surprisingly, to the real estate bar) from those attorneys and businesspeople who had experience in corporate reorganizations. Under the "fair and equitable" requirement of Chapter X, absolute priority had been a must. Classes of creditors, by the requisite majorities, could not effectively agree to take less than absolute priority would provide. For example, if the classes wanted to retain capable management, the creditors might want to provide in the plan that some of the stock in the reorganized company go to the old equity stockholders. This, however, would be impossible under absolute priority unless each creditor (as distinguished from each class of creditors) agreed. Thus, instead of promoting negotiation and compromise, the absolute priority requirement, these opponents argued, promoted poor business decisions and endless litigation concerning the value of the assets and the interests each class would receive in the new company.

Out of this controversy grew the philosophy of Chapter 11, which is to promote compromise and permit classes, in certain situations, to agree on plans without testing the agreement against the absolute priority standard. Protection was afforded the real estate mortgagee, however, by providing that a plan must be fair and equitable (providing absolute priority) as to any impaired *class* that does not approve the plan. Absolute priority, then, would apply only when a class

---

28. 4 Bankr. Ct. Dec. (CRR) 462 (Bankr. S.D.N.Y. 1978).

29. See discussion of the income capitalization method of valuing commercial property at Chapter 4D1.

(as distinguished from an individual creditor) rejects a plan, and then only for the impaired class that rejects the plan.

Understanding the philosophy of Chapter 11 may be somewhat easier than understanding the mechanics that put the philosophy into practice. The operative sections for this understanding include at a minimum §§506, 1111(b), 1124, and 1129, which are excerpted below. The mechanics and the resulting confirmation strategy are discussed in notes 1-3 infra.

Bankruptcy Code
11 U.S.C. §§506, 1111(b), 1124, 1129

§506. DETERMINATION OF SECURED STATUS

(a)(1) An allowed claim of a creditor secured by a lien on property in which the estate has an interest . . . is a secured claim to the extent of the value of such creditor's interest in the estate's interest in such property . . . and is an unsecured claim to the extent that the value of such creditor's interest . . . is less than the amount of such allowed claim. Such value shall be determined in light of the purpose of the valuation and of the proposed disposition or use of such property, and in conjunction with any hearing on such disposition or use or on a plan affecting such creditor's interest.

. . .

(b) To the extent that an allowed secured claim is secured by property the value of which . . . is greater than the amount of such claim, there shall be allowed to the holder of such claim, interest on such claim, and any reasonable fees, costs, or charges provided for under the agreement or State statute under which such claim arose. . . .

(d) To the extent that a lien secures a claim against the debtor that is not an allowed secured claim, such lien is void. . . .

§1111. CLAIMS AND INTERESTS . . .

(b)(1)(A) A claim secured by a lien on property of the estate shall be allowed or disallowed under section 502 of this title the same as if the holder of such claim had recourse against the debtor on account of such claim, whether or not such holder has such recourse, unless—

(i) the class of which such claim is a part elects, by at least two-thirds in amount and more than half in number of allowed claims of such class, application of paragraph (2) of this subsection; or

(ii) such holder does not have such recourse and such property is sold under section 363 of this title or is to be sold under the plan.

(B) A class of claims may not elect application of paragraph (2) of this subsection if—

(i) the interest on account of such claims of the holders of such claims in such property is of inconsequential value; or

(ii) the holder of a claim of such class has recourse against the debtor on account of such claim and such property is sold under section 363 of this title or is to be sold under the plan.

(2) If such an election is made, then notwithstanding section 506(a) of this title, such claim is a secured claim to the extent that such claim is allowed.

§1124. IMPAIRMENT OF CLAIMS OR INTERESTS

[A] class of claims or interests is impaired under a plan unless, with respect to each claim or interest of such class, the plan—

(1) leaves unaltered the legal, equitable, and contractual rights to which such claim or interest entitles the holder of such claim or interest; or

(2) notwithstanding any contractual provision or applicable law that entitles the holder of such claim or interest to demand or receive accelerated payment of such claim or interest after the occurrence of a default—

(A) cures any such default that occurred before or after the commencement of the case under this title . . .;

(B) reinstates the maturity of such claim or interest as such maturity existed before such default;

(C) compensates the holder of such claim or interest for any damages incurred as a result of any reasonable reliance by such holder on such contractual provision or such applicable law; . . .

(E) does not otherwise alter the legal, equitable, or contractual rights to which such claim or interest entitles the holder of such claim or interest.

§1129. CONFIRMATION OF PLAN

(a) The court shall confirm a plan only if all of the following requirements are met: . . .

(3) The plan has been proposed in good faith and not by any means forbidden by law. . . .

(7) With respect to each impaired class of claims or interests—

(A) each holder of a claim or interest of such class—

(i) has accepted the plan; or

(ii) will receive or retain under the plan on account of such claim or interest property of a value, as of the effective date of the plan, that is not less than the amount that such holder would so receive or retain if the debtor were liquidated under chapter 7 of this title on such date; or

(B) if section 1111(b)(2) of this title applies to the claims of such class, each holder of a claim of such class will receive or retain under the plan on account of such claim property of a value, as of the effective date of the plan, that is not less than the value of such holder's interest in the estate's interest in the property that secures such claims.

(8) With respect to each class of claims or interests—

(A) such class has accepted the plan; or

(B) such class is not impaired under the plan. . . .

(10) If a class of claims is impaired under the plan, at least one class of claims that is impaired under the plan has accepted the plan, determined without including any acceptance of the plan by any insider.

(11) Confirmation of the plan is not likely to be followed by the liquidation, or the need for further financial reorganization, of the debtor or any successor to the debtor under the plan, unless such liquidation or reorganization is proposed in the plan. . . .

(b)(1) [I]f all of the applicable requirements of subsection (a) of this section other than paragraph (8) are met with respect to a plan, the court, on request of the proponent of the plan, shall confirm the plan notwithstanding the requirements of such paragraph if the plan does not discriminate unfairly, and is fair and equitable, with respect to each class of claims or interests that is impaired under, and has not accepted, the plan.

(2) For the purpose of this subsection, the condition that a plan be fair and equitable with respect to a class includes the following requirements:

(A) With respect to a class of secured claims, the plan provides—

(i)(I) that the holders of such claims retain the liens securing such claims, whether the property subject to such liens is retained by the debtor or transferred to another entity, to the extent of the allowed amount of such claims; and

(II) that each holder of a claim of such class receive on account of such claim deferred cash payments totaling at least the allowed amount of such claim, of a value, as of the effective date of the plan, of at least the value of such holder's interest in the estate's interest in such property;

(ii) for the sale, subject to section 363(k) of this title, of any property that is subject to the liens securing such claims, free and clear of such liens, with such liens to attach to the proceeds of such sale, and the treatment of such liens on proceeds under clause (i) or (iii) of this subparagraph; or

(iii) for the realization by such holders of the indubitable equivalent of such claims.

(B) With respect to a class of unsecured claims—

(i) the plan provides that each holder of a claim of such class receive or retain on account of such claim property of a value, as of the effective date of the plan, equal to the allowed amount of such claim; or

(ii) the holder of any claim or interest that is junior to the claims of such class will not receive or retain under the plan on account of such junior claim or interest any property . . .

(C) With respect to a class of interests—

(i) the plan provides that each holder of an interest of such class receive or retain on account of such interest property of a value, as of the effective date of the plan, equal to the greatest of the allowed amount of any fixed liquidation preference to which such holder is entitled, any fixed redemption price to which such holder is entitled, or the value of such interest; or

(ii) the holder of any interest that is junior to the interests of such class will not receive or retain under the plan on account of such junior interest any property. . . .

As discussed in the notes that follow, a plan may be confirmed over the objection of an impaired, dissenting creditor class only if the plan is fair and equitable as to that class. In Chapter 11, §1129(b) determines what is necessary for a plan to be fair and equitable as to, inter alia, secured creditors. Section 1129(b)(2)(A)(i) provides that with respect to a class of secured claims, the plan is fair and equitable if the mortgage lien is retained on the property in an amount equal to the value of the collateral. It further requires that such a lien have a present value at confirmation of the plan equal to the value of the collateral. Interest is usually the key, but not the only, factor that would determine the present value of a mortgage. As a result, there has been dispute as to what interest rate might be appropriate to ensure that the mortgage has a value equal to the value of the collateral.

This issue was decided by the United States Supreme Court in the case of Till v. SCS Credit Corp. (*In re Till*), excerpted below, and discussed in note 5(a) below. The case does not involve §1129(b)(2)(A), but a similar provision in Chapter 13, §1325(a)(5)(B). Nevertheless, the decision may have a direct impact on the interpretation of §1129(b)(2)(A), notwithstanding the high interest rate in, and the high risk nature of the investment in *Till*.

Till v. SCS Credit Corp. (In re Till)
541 U.S. 465 (2004)

Justice STEVENS delivered the opinion of the Court.

To qualify for court approval under Chapter 13 of the Bankruptcy Code, an individual debtor's proposed debt adjustment plan must accommodate each allowed, secured creditor in one of three ways: (1) by obtaining the creditor's acceptance of the plan; (2) by surrendering the property securing the claim; or (3) by providing the creditor both a lien securing the claim and a promise of future property distributions (such as deferred cash payments) whose total "value, as of the effective date of the plan,. . . . is not less than the allowed amount of such claim." The third alternative is commonly known as the "cram down option" because it may be enforced over a claim holder's objection. *Associates Commercial Corp. v. Rash*, 520 U.S. 953, 957, 138 L. Ed. 2d 148, 117 S. Ct. 1879 (1997).

Plans that invoke the cram down power often provide for installment payments over a period of years rather than a single payment. In such circumstances, the amount of each installment must be calibrated to ensure that, over time, the creditor receives disbursements whose total present value equals or exceeds that of the allowed claim. The proceedings in this case that led to our grant of certiorari identified four different methods of determining the appropriate method with which to perform that calibration. Indeed, the Bankruptcy Judge, the District Court, the Court of Appeals majority, and the dissenting Judge each endorsed a different approach. . . .

I

On October 2, 1998, petitioners Lee and Amy Till, residents of Kokomo, Indiana, purchased a used truck from Instant Auto Finance for $6,395 plus $330.75 in fees and taxes. They made a $300 down payment and financed the balance of the purchase price by entering into a retail installment contract that Instant Auto immediately assigned to respondent, SCS Credit Corporation. Petitioners' initial indebtedness amounted to $8,285.24—the $6,425.75 balance of the truck purchase plus a finance charge of 21 percent per year for 136 weeks, or $1,859.49. Under the contract, petitioners agreed to make 68 biweekly payments to cover this debt; Instant Auto—and subsequently respondent— retained a purchase money security interest that gave it the right to repossess the truck if petitioners defaulted under the contract.

On October 25, 1999, petitioners, by then in default on their payments to respondent, filed a petition for joint relief under Chapter 13 of the Bankruptcy Code. At the time of the filing, respondent's outstanding claim amounted to $4,894.89, but the parties agreed that the truck securing the claim was worth only $4,000. In accordance with the Bankruptcy Code, therefore, respondent's secured claim was limited to $4,000, and the $894.89 balance was unsecured. . . .

The proposed plan also provided that petitioners would pay interest on the secured portion of respondent's claim at a rate of 9.5 percent per year. Petitioners arrived at this "prime-plus" or "formula rate" by augmenting the national prime rate of approximately 8 percent (applied by banks when making low-risk loans) to account for the risk of nonpayment posed by borrowers in their financial position. Respondent objected to the proposed rate, contending that the company was "entitled to interest at the rate of 21 percent, which is the rate . . . it would obtain if it could foreclose on the vehicle and reinvest the proceeds in loans of equivalent duration and risk as the loan" originally made to petitioners. . . .

Accepting petitioners' evidence, the Bankruptcy Court overruled respondent's objection and confirmed the proposed plan.

The District Court reversed. It understood Seventh Circuit precedent to require that bankruptcy courts set cram down interest rates at the level the creditor could have obtained if it had foreclosed on the loan, sold the collateral, and reinvested the proceeds in loans of equivalent duration and risk. Citing respondent's unrebutted testimony about the market for subprime loans, the court concluded that 21 percent was the appropriate rate.

On appeal, the Seventh Circuit endorsed a slightly modified version of the District Court's "coerced" or "forced loan" approach. In re Till, 301 F.3d 583, 591 (2002). Specifically, the majority agreed with the District Court that, in a cram down proceeding, the inquiry should focus on the interest rate "that the creditor in question would obtain in making a new loan in the same industry to a debtor who is similarly situated, although not in bankruptcy." Id., at 592. To approximate that new loan rate, the majority looked to the parties' prebankruptcy contract rate (21 percent). The court recognized, however, that using the contract rate would not "duplicat[e] precisely . . . the present value of the collateral to the creditor" because loans to bankrupt, court-supervised debtors "involve some risks that would not be incurred in a new loan to a debtor not in default" and also produce "some economies." Ibid. To correct for these inaccuracies, the majority held that the original contract rate should "serve as a presumptive [cram down] rate," which either the creditor or the debtor could challenge with evidence that a higher or lower rate should apply. Ibid. Accordingly, the court remanded the case to the Bankruptcy Court to afford petitioners and respondent an opportunity to rebut the presumptive 21 percent rate.

Dissenting, Judge Rovner argued that the majority's presumptive contract rate approach overcompensates secured creditors because it fails to account for costs a creditor would have to incur in issuing a new loan. Rather than focusing on the market for comparable loans, Judge Rovner advocated either the Bankruptcy Court's formula approach or a "straightforward . . . cost of funds" approach that would simply ask "what it would cost the creditor to obtain the cash equivalent of the collateral from an alternative source.". . . We granted certiorari and now reverse.

II

The Bankruptcy Code provides little guidance as to which of the rates of interest advocated by the four opinions in this case—the formula rate, the coerced loan rate, the presumptive contract rate, or the cost of funds rate—Congress had in mind when it adopted the cram down provision. . . .

A debtor's promise of future payments is worth less than an immediate payment of the same total amount because the creditor cannot use the money right away, inflation may cause the value of the dollar to decline before the debtor pays, and there is always some risk of nonpayment. The challenge for bankruptcy courts reviewing such repayment schemes, therefore, is to choose an interest rate sufficient to compensate the creditor for these concerns.

Three important considerations govern that choice. First, the Bankruptcy Code includes numerous provisions that, like the cram down provision, require a court to "discoun[t]. . .[a] stream of deferred payments back to the[ir] present dollar value," Rake v. Wade, 508 U.S. 464, 472, n.8, 124 L. Ed. 2d 424, 113 S. Ct. 2187 (1993), to ensure that a creditor receives at least the value of its claim. We think it likely that Congress intended bankruptcy judges and trustees to follow essentially the same approach when choosing an appropriate interest rate under any of these provisions. Moreover, we think Congress would favor an approach that is familiar in the financial community and that minimizes the need for expensive evidentiary proceedings.

Second, Chapter 13 expressly authorizes a bankruptcy court to modify the rights of any creditor whose claim is secured by an interest in anything other than "real property that is the debtor's principal residence." 11 U.S.C. §1322(b)(2). Thus, in cases like this involving secured interests in personal property, the court's authority to modify the number, timing, or amount of the installment payments from those set forth in the debtor's original contract is perfectly clear. . . .

Third, from the point of view of a creditor, the cram down provision mandates an objective rather than a subjective inquiry. That is, although §1325(a)(5)(B) entitles the creditor to property whose present value objectively equals or exceeds the value of the collateral, it does not require that the terms of the cram down loan match the terms to which the debtor and creditor agreed prebankruptcy, nor does it require that the cram down terms make the creditor subjectively indifferent between present foreclosure and future payment. Indeed, the very idea of a "cram down" loan *precludes* the latter result: By definition, a creditor forced to accept such a loan would prefer instead to foreclose.[14]

III

These considerations lead us to reject the coerced loan, presumptive contract rate, and cost of funds approaches. Each of these approaches is complicated, imposes significant evidentiary costs, and aims to make each individual creditor whole rather than to ensure the debtor's payments have the required present value. . . .

---

14. This fact helps explain why there is no readily apparent Chapter 13 "cram down market rate of interest." Because every cram down loan is imposed by a court over the objection of the secured creditor, there is no free market of willing cram down lenders. Interestingly, the same is *not* true in the Chapter 11 context, as numerous lenders advertise financing for Chapter 11 debtors in possession.... In the Chapter 13 context, by contrast, the absence of any such market obligates courts to look to first principles and ask only what rate will fairly compensate a creditor for its exposure.

Like the coerced loan approach, the presumptive contract rate approach improperly focuses on the creditor's potential use of the proceeds of a foreclosure sale.. . . .

The cost of funds approach, too, is improperly aimed. Although it rightly disregards the now-irrelevant terms of the parties' original contract, it mistakenly focuses on the creditworthiness of the *creditor* rather than the debtor. . . .

IV

The formula approach has none of these defects. Taking its cue from ordinary lending practices, the approach begins by looking to the national prime rate, reported daily in the press, which reflects the financial market's estimate of the amount a commercial bank should charge a creditworthy commercial borrower to compensate for the opportunity costs of the loan, the risk of inflation, and the relatively slight risk of default.[18] Because bankrupt debtors typically pose a greater risk of nonpayment than solvent commercial borrowers, the approach then requires a bankruptcy court to adjust the prime rate accordingly.. . . . Finally, many of the factors relevant to the adjustment fall squarely within the bankruptcy court's area of expertise.

Thus, unlike the coerced loan, presumptive contract rate, and cost of funds approaches, the formula approach entails a straightforward, familiar, and objective inquiry, and minimizes the need for potentially costly additional evidentiary proceedings. Moreover, the resulting "prime-plus" rate of interest depends only on the state of financial markets, the circumstances of the bankruptcy estate, and the characteristics of the loan, not on the creditor's circumstances or its prior interactions with the debtor. For these reasons, the prime-plus or formula rate best comports with the purposes of the Bankruptcy Code.

We do not decide the proper scale for the risk adjustment, as the issue is not before us. The Bankruptcy Court in this case approved a risk adjustment of 1.5 percent, and other courts have generally approved adjustments of 1 percent to 3 percent. Respondent's core argument is that a risk adjustment in this range is entirely inadequate to compensate a creditor for the real risk that the plan will fail. . . . We need not resolve that dispute. It is sufficient for our purposes to note that, under 11 U.S.C. §1325(a)(6), a court may not approve a plan unless, after considering all creditors' objections and receiving the advice of the trustee, the judge is persuaded that "the debtor will be able to make all payments under the plan and to comply with the plan." *Ibid.* Together with the cram down provision, this requirement obligates the court to select a rate high enough to compensate the creditor for its risk but not so high as to doom the plan. If the court

---

18. We note that, if the court could somehow be certain a debtor would complete his plan, the prime rate would be adequate to compensate any secured creditors forced to accept cram down loans.

determines that the likelihood of default is so high as to necessitate an "eye-popping" interest rate, 301 F.3d at 593 (Rovner, J., dissenting), the plan probably should not be confirmed. . . .

The judgment of the Court of Appeals is reversed, and the case is remanded with instructions to remand the case to the Bankruptcy Court for further proceedings consistent with this opinion. . . .

Justice THOMAS, concurring in the judgment.

This case presents the issue of what the proper method is for discounting deferred payments to present value and what compensation the creditor is entitled to in calculating the appropriate discount rate of interest. Both the plurality and the dissent agree that "[a] debtor's promise of future payments is worth less than an immediate payment of the same total amount because the creditor cannot use the money right away, inflation may cause the value of the dollar to decline before the debtor pays, and there is always some risk of nonpayment." Thus, the plurality and the dissent agree that the proper method for discounting deferred payments to present value should take into account each of these factors, but disagree over the proper starting point for calculating the risk of nonpayment.

I agree that a *"promise* of future payments is worth less than an immediate payment" of the same amount, in part because of the risk of nonpayment. But this fact is irrelevant. The statute does not require that the value of the *promise* to distribute property under the plan be no less than the allowed amount of the secured creditor's claim. It requires only that "the value . . . of *property* to be distributed under the plan," at the time of the effective date of the plan, be no less than the amount of the secured creditor's claim. 11 U.S.C. §1325(a)(5)(B)(ii) (emphasis added). Both the plurality and the dissent ignore the clear text of the statute in an apparent rush to ensure that secured creditors are not undercompensated in bankruptcy proceedings. But the statute that Congress enacted does not require a debtor-specific risk adjustment that would put secured creditors in the same position as if they had made another loan. It is for this reason that I write separately.

I

Section 1325(a)(5)(B) provides that "with respect to each allowed secured claim provided for by the plan," "the value, as of the effective date of the plan, of property to be distributed under the plan on account of such claim [must] not [be] less than the allowed amount of such claim." Thus, the statute requires a bankruptcy court to make at least three separate determinations. First, a court must determine the allowed amount of the claim. Second, a court must determine what is the "property to be distributed under the plan." Third, a court must determine the "value, as of the effective date of the plan," of the property to be distributed.

The dispute in this case centers on the proper method to determine the "value, as of the effective date of the plan, of property to be distributed under the plan." The requirement that the "value" of the property to be distributed be determined "as of the effective date of the plan" incorporates the principle of the time value of money. To put it simply, $4,000 today is worth more than $4,000 to be received 17 months from today because if received today, the $4,000 can be invested to start earning interest immediately. . . . Thus, as we explained in Rake v. Wade, 508 U.S. 464, 124 L. Ed. 2d 424, 113 S. Ct. 2187 (1993), "[w]hen a claim is paid off pursuant to a stream of future payments, a creditor receives the 'present value' of its claim only if the total amount of the deferred payments includes the amount of the underlying claim plus an appropriate amount of interest to compensate the creditor for the decreased value of the claim caused by the delayed payments." Id., at 472, 124 L. Ed. 2d 424, 113 S. Ct. 2187, n.8.

Respondent argues, and the plurality and the dissent agree, that the proper interest rate must also reflect the risk of nonpayment. But the statute contains no such requirement. The statute only requires the valuation of the "property to be distributed," not the valuation of the plan (i.e., the promise to make the payments itself). Thus, in order for a plan to satisfy §1325(a)(5)(B)(ii), the plan need only propose an interest rate that will compensate a creditor for the fact that if he had received the property immediately rather than at a future date, he could have immediately made use of the property. In most, if not all, cases, where the plan proposes simply a stream of cash payments, the appropriate risk-free rate should suffice. . . .

This is not to say that a debtor's risk of nonpayment can never be a factor in determining the value of the property to be distributed. Although "property" is not defined in the Bankruptcy Code, nothing in §1325 suggests that "property" is limited to cash. Rather, "'property' can be cash, notes, stock, personal property or real property; in short, anything of value." 7 Collier on Bankruptcy P1129.03[7][b][i], p. 1129-44 (15th ed. 2003) (discussing Chapter 11's cram down provision). And if the "property to be distributed" under a Chapter 13 plan is a note (i.e., a promise to pay), for instance, the value of that note necessarily includes the risk that the debtor will not make good on that promise. Still, accounting for the risk of nonpayment in that case is not equivalent to reading a risk adjustment requirement into the statute, as in the case of a note, the risk of nonpayment is part of the value of the note itself. . . .

II . . .

Although the Plan does not specifically state that "the property to be distributed" under the Plan is cash payments, the cash payments are the only "property" specifically listed for distribution under the Plan. Thus, although the plurality and the dissent imply that the "property to be distributed" under the Plan is the mere *promise* to make cash payments, the plain language of the Plan indicates that the "property to be distributed" to respondent is up to 36 monthly cash payments, consisting of a pro rata share of $740 per month.

The final task, then, is to determine whether petitioners' proposed 9.5 percent interest rate will sufficiently compensate respondent for the fact that instead of receiving $4,000 today, it will receive $4,000 plus 9.5 percent interest over a period of up to 36 months. Because the 9.5 percent rate is higher than the risk-free rate, I conclude that it will. I would therefore reverse the judgment of the Court of Appeals.

Justice SCALIA, with whom the Chief Justice, Justice O'Connor, and Justice Kennedy join, dissenting.

My areas of agreement with the plurality are substantial. We agree that, although all confirmed Chapter 13 plans have been deemed feasible by a bankruptcy judge, some nevertheless fail. We agree that any deferred payments to a secured creditor must fully compensate it for the risk that such a failure will occur. Finally, we agree that adequate compensation may sometimes require an "'eye-popping'" interest rate, and that, if the rate is too high for the plan to succeed, the appropriate course is not to reduce it to a more palatable level, but to refuse to confirm the plan.

Our only disagreement is over what procedure will more often produce accurate estimates of the appropriate interest rate. The plurality would use the prime lending rate—a rate we *know* is too low—and require the judge in every case to determine an amount by which to increase it. I believe that, in practice, this approach will systematically undercompensate secured creditors for the true risks of default. I would instead adopt the contract rate—i.e., the rate at which the creditor actually loaned funds to the debtor—as a presumption that the bankruptcy judge could revise on motion of either party. Since that rate is generally a good indicator of actual risk, disputes should be infrequent, and it will provide a quick and reasonably accurate standard. . . .

There is no better demonstration of the inadequacies of the formula approach than the proceedings in this case. Petitioners' economics expert testified that the 1.5 percent risk premium was "very reasonable" because Chapter 13 plans are "supposed to be financially feasible" and "the borrowers are under the supervision of the court." Nothing in the record shows how these two platitudes were somehow manipulated to arrive at a figure of 1.5 percent. It bears repeating that feasibility determinations and trustee oversight do not prevent at least 37 percent of confirmed Chapter 13 plans from failing. On cross-examination, the expert admitted that he had only limited familiarity with the subprime auto lending market and that he was not familiar with the default rates or the costs of collection in that market. In light of these devastating concessions, it is impossible to view the 1.5 percent figure as anything other than a smallish number picked out of a hat.

Based on even a rudimentary financial analysis of the facts of this case, the 1.5 percent figure is obviously wrong—not just off by a couple percent, but probably by roughly an order of magnitude. For a risk premium to be adequate, a hypothetical, rational creditor must be indifferent between accepting (1) the proposed risky stream of payments over time and (2) immediate payment of its present value in a lump sum. Whether he is indifferent—i.e., whether the risk premium added to the prime rate is adequate—can be gauged by comparing benefits and costs: on the one hand, the expected value of the extra interest, and on the other, the expected costs of default. . . .

In sum, the 1.5 percent premium adopted in this case is far below anything approaching fair compensation. That result is not unusual, see, e.g., In re Valenti, 105 F.3d 55, 64 (CA2 1997) (recommending a 1 percent-3 percent premium over the *treasury* rate—i.e., approximately a 0 percent premium over prime); it is the entirely predictable consequence of a methodology that tells bankruptcy judges to set interest rates based on highly imponderable factors. Given the inherent uncertainty of the enterprise, what heartless bankruptcy judge can be expected to demand that the unfortunate debtor pay *triple* the prime rate as a condition of keeping his sole means of transportation? It challenges human nature.

III

Justice THOMAS rejects both the formula approach and the contract-rate approach. He reads the statutory phrase "property to be distributed under the plan," 11 U.S.C. §1325(a)(5)(B)(ii), to mean the proposed payments *if made as the plan contemplates*, so that the plan need only pay the risk-free rate of interest. I would instead read this phrase to mean the right to receive payments that the plan vests in the creditor upon confirmation. Because there is no guarantee that the promised payments will in fact be made, the value of this property right must account for the risk of nonpayment.

Viewed in isolation, the phrase is susceptible of either meaning. Both the promise to make payments and the proposed payments themselves are property rights, the former "to be distributed under the plan" immediately upon confirmation, and the latter over the life of the plan. Context, however, supports my reading. The cramdown option which the debtors employed here is only one of three routes to confirmation. The other two—creditor acceptance and collateral surrender, §§1325(a)(5)(A), (C)—are both creditor protective, leaving the secured creditor roughly as well off as he would have been had the debtor not sought bankruptcy protection. Given this, it is unlikely the third option was meant to be substantially *under* protective; that would render it so much more favorable to debtors that few would ever choose one of the alternatives. . . .

Today's judgment is unlikely to burnish the Court's reputation for reasoned decisionmaking. Eight Justices are in agreement that the rate of interest set forth in the debtor's approved plan must include a premium for risk. Of those eight, four are of the view that beginning with the contract rate would most accurately reflect the actual risk, and four are of the view that beginning with the prime lending rate would do so. The ninth Justice takes no position on the latter point, since he disagrees with the eight on the former point; he would reverse because the rate proposed here, being above the risk-free rate, gave respondent no cause for complaint. Because I read the statute to require full risk compensation, and because I would adopt a valuation method that has a realistic prospect of enforcing that directive, I respectfully dissent.

While *Till* dealt with what constitutes absolute priority for the mortgagee's secured class, the next case involves the priority of the unsecured class of creditors (which would include the mortgagee's claim in excess of the value of the collateral) over the equity interest of the debtor. The case deals with the extent to which equity interests can avoid absolute priority under §1129(b)(2)(B)(ii) by making a contribution of "new value" (or "new capital"), more fully discussed in note 5(c) infra.

Bank of America National Trust & Savings Association v. 203 North LaSalle Street Partnership
526 U.S. 434 (1999)

Justice SOUTER delivered the opinion of the Court.

The issue in this Chapter 11 reorganization case is whether a debtor's pre-bankruptcy equity holders may, over the objection of a senior class of impaired creditors, contribute new capital and receive ownership interests in the reorganized entity, when that opportunity is given exclusively to the old equity holders under a plan adopted without consideration of alternatives. We hold that old equity holders are disqualified from participating in such a "new value" transaction by the terms of 11 U.S.C. §1129(b)(2)(B)(ii), which in such circumstances bars a junior interest holder's receipt of any property on account of his prior interest.

I

Petitioner, Bank of America National Trust and Savings Association (Bank), is the major creditor of respondent, 203 North LaSalle Street Partnership (Debtor or Partnership), an Illinois real estate limited partnership. The Bank lent the Debtor some $93 million, secured by a nonrecourse first mortgage on the Debtor's principal asset, 15 floors of an office building in downtown Chicago. In January 1995, the Debtor defaulted, and the Bank began foreclosure in a state court.

In March, the Debtor responded with a voluntary petition for relief under Chapter 11 of the Bankruptcy Code, which automatically stayed the foreclosure proceedings, see §362(a). The Debtor's principal objective was to ensure that its partners retained title to the property so as to avoid roughly $20 million in personal tax liabilities, which would fall due if the Bank foreclosed. The Debtor proceeded to propose a reorganization plan. . . .

The value of the mortgaged property was less than the balance due the Bank, which elected to divide its undersecured claim into secured and unsecured deficiency claims under §506(a) and §1111(b).[6] Under the plan, the Debtor separately classified the Bank's secured claim, its unsecured deficiency claim, and unsecured trade debt owed to other creditors. See §1122(a). The Bankruptcy Court found that the Debtor's available assets were prepetition rents in a cash account of $3.1 million and the 15 floors of rental property worth $54.5 million. The secured claim was valued at the latter figure, leaving the Bank with an unsecured deficiency of $38.5 million.

So far as we need be concerned here, the Debtor's plan had these further features: (1) The Bank's $54.5 million secured claim would be paid in full between 7 and 10 years after the original 1995 repayment date. (2) The Bank's $38.5 million unsecured deficiency claim would be discharged for an estimated 16 percent of its present value. (3) The remaining unsecured claims of $90,000, held by the outside trade creditors, would be paid in full, without interest, on the effective date of the plan. (4) Certain former partners of the Debtor would contribute $6.125 million in new capital over the course of five years (the contribution being worth some $4.1 million in present value), in exchange for the Partnership's entire ownership of the reorganized debtor. The last condition was an exclusive eligibility provision: the old equity holders were the only ones who could contribute new capital.[11]

The Bank objected and, being the sole member of an impaired class of creditors, thereby blocked confirmation of the plan on a consensual basis. See §1129(a)(8).[12] The Debtor, however, took the alternate route to confirmation of a reorganization plan, forthrightly known as the judicial "cramdown" process for imposing a plan on a dissenting class. §1129(b).

There are two conditions for a cramdown. First, all requirements of §1129(a) must be met (save for the plan's acceptance by each impaired class of claims or interests, see §1129(a)(8)). Critical among them are the conditions that the plan be accepted by at least one class of impaired creditors, see §1129(a)(10), and satisfy the "best-interest-of-creditors" test, see §1129(a)(7). Here, the class of trade creditors with impaired unsecured claims voted for the plan, and there was no issue of best interest. Second, the objection of an impaired creditor class may be overridden only if "the plan does not discriminate unfairly, and is fair and

6. Having agreed to waive recourse against any property of the Debtor other than the real estate, the Bank had no unsecured claim outside of Chapter 11. Section 1111(b), however, provides that nonrecourse secured creditors who are undersecured must be treated in Chapter 11 as if they had recourse.

11. The plan eliminated the interests of noncontributing partners. More than 60 percent of the Partnership interests would change hands on confirmation of the plan. The new Partnership, however, would consist solely of former partners, a feature critical to the preservation of the Partnership's tax shelter.

12. A class of creditors accepts if a majority of the creditors and those holding two-thirds of the total dollar amount of the claims within that class vote to approve the plan. §1126(c).

equitable, with respect to each class of claims or interests that is impaired under, and has not accepted, the plan." §1129(b)(1). As to a dissenting class of impaired unsecured creditors, such a plan may be found to be "fair and equitable" only if the allowed value of the claim is to be paid in full, §1129(b)(2)(B)(i), or, in the alternative, if "the holder of any claim or interest that is junior to the claims of such [impaired unsecured] class will not receive or retain under the plan on account of such junior claim or interest any property," §1129(b)(2)(B)(ii). That latter condition is the core of what is known as the "absolute priority rule."

The absolute priority rule was the basis for the Bank's position that the plan could not be confirmed as a cramdown. As the Bank read the rule, the plan was open to objection simply because certain old equity holders in the Debtor Partnership would receive property even though the Bank's unsecured deficiency claim would not be paid in full. The Bankruptcy Court approved the plan nonetheless, and accordingly denied the Bank's pending motion to convert the case to Chapter 7 liquidation, or to dismiss the case. The District Court affirmed, as did the Court of Appeals.

The majority of the Seventh Circuit's divided panel found ambiguity in the language of the statutory absolute priority rule, and looked beyond the text to interpret the phrase "on account of" as permitting recognition of a "new value corollary" to the rule. According to the panel, the corollary, as stated by this Court in Case v. Los Angeles Lumber Products Co., 308 U.S. 106, 118, 60 S. Ct. 1, 84 L. Ed. 110 (1939), provides that the objection of an impaired senior class does not bar junior claim holders from receiving or retaining property interests in the debtor after reorganization, if they contribute new capital in money or money's worth, reasonably equivalent to the property's value, and necessary for successful reorganization of the restructured enterprise. The panel majority held that "when an old equity holder retains an equity interest in the reorganized debtor by meeting the requirements of the new value corollary, he is not receiving or retaining that interest 'on account of' his prior equitable ownership of the debtor. Rather, he is allowed to participate in the reorganized entity 'on account of' a new, substantial, necessary and fair infusion of capital.". . .

We granted certiorari to resolve a Circuit split on the issue. The Seventh Circuit in this case joined the Ninth in relying on a new value corollary to the absolute priority rule to support confirmation of such plans. See In re Bonner Mall Partnership, 2 F.3d 899, 910-916 (C.A. 9 1993), cert. granted, 510 U.S. 1039, vacatur denied and appeal dism'd as moot, 513 U.S. 18 (1994). The Second and Fourth Circuits, by contrast, without explicitly rejecting the corollary, have disapproved plans similar to this one. We do not decide whether the statute includes a new value corollary or exception, but hold that on any reading respondent's proposed plan fails to satisfy the statute, and accordingly reverse.

II

The terms "absolute priority rule" and "new value corollary" (or "exception") are creatures of law antedating the current Bankruptcy Code, and to understand both those terms and the related but inexact language of the Code some history is helpful. The Bankruptcy Act preceding the Code contained no such provision as subsection [1129](b)(2)(B)(ii), its subject having been addressed by two interpretive rules. The first was a specific gloss on the requirement of §77B (and its successor, Chapter X) of the old Act, that any reorganization plan be "fair and equitable." The reason for such a limitation was the danger inherent in any reorganization plan proposed by a debtor, then and now, that the plan will simply turn out to be too good a deal for the debtor's owners. Hence the pre-Code judicial response known as the absolute priority rule, that fairness and equity required that "the creditors . . . be paid before the stockholders could retain [equity interests] for any purpose whatever."

The second interpretive rule addressed the first. Its classic formulation occurred in Case v. Los Angeles Lumber Products Co., in which the Court spoke through Justice Douglas in this dictum: "It is, of course, clear that there are circumstances under which stockholders may participate in a plan of reorganization of an insolvent debtor. . . . Where th[e] necessity [for new capital] exists and the old stockholders make a fresh contribution and receive in return a participation reasonably equivalent to their contribution, no objection can be made. . . ."

"[W]e believe that to accord 'the creditor his full right of priority against the corporate assets' where the debtor is insolvent, the stockholder's participation must be based on a contribution in money or in money's worth, reasonably equivalent in view of all the circumstances to the participation of the stockholder." 308 U.S., at 121-122.

Although counsel for one of the parties here has described the *Case* observation as "'black-letter' principle," it never rose above the technical level of dictum in any opinion of this Court, which last addressed it in Norwest Bank Worthington v. Ahlers, 485 U.S. 197, 108 S. Ct. 963, 99 L. Ed. 2d 169 (1988), holding that a contribution of "'labor, experience, and expertise'" by a junior interest holder was not in the "'money's worth'" that the *Case* observation required. 485 U.S., at 203-205. Nor, prior to the enactment of the current Bankruptcy Code, did any court rely on the *Case* dictum to approve a plan that gave old equity a property right after reorganization. Hence the controversy over how weighty the *Case* dictum had become, as reflected in the alternative labels for the new value notion: some writers and courts . . . have spoken of it as an exception to the absolute priority rule, while others have characterized it as a simple corollary to the rule. . . .

Enactment of the Bankruptcy Code in place of the prior Act might have resolved the status of new value by a provision bearing its name or at least unmistakably couched in its terms, but the Congress chose not to avail itself of that opportunity. . . .

For the purpose of plumbing the meaning of subsection [1129](b)(2)(B)(ii) in search of a possible statutory new value exception, the lesson of this drafting history is equivocal. Although hornbook law has it that "'Congress does not intend sub silentio to enact statutory language that it has earlier discarded,'" the phrase "on account of" is not silentium, and the language passed by in this instance had never been in the bill finally enacted, but only in predecessors that died on the vine. . . .

The upshot is that this history does nothing to disparage the possibility apparent in the statutory text, that the absolute priority rule now on the books as subsection [1129](b)(2)(B)(ii) may carry a new value corollary. Although there is no literal reference to "new value" in the phrase "on account of such junior claim," the phrase could arguably carry such an implication in modifying the prohibition against receipt by junior claimants of any interest under a plan while a senior class of unconsenting creditors goes less than fully paid.

III

Three basic interpretations have been suggested for the "on account of" modifier. The first reading is proposed by the Partnership, that "on account of" harks back to accounting practice and means something like "in exchange for," or "in satisfaction of." On this view, a plan would not violate the absolute priority rule unless the old equity holders received or retained property in exchange for the prior interest, without any significant new contribution; if substantial money passed from them as part of the deal, the prohibition of subsection [1129](b)(2)(B)(ii) would not stand in the way, and whatever issues of fairness and equity there might otherwise be would not implicate the "on account of" modifier.

This position is beset with troubles, the first one being textual. Subsection [1129](b)(2)(B)(ii) forbids not only receipt of property on account of the prior interest but its retention as well. A common instance of the latter would be a debtor's retention of an interest in the insolvent business reorganized under the plan. Yet it would be exceedingly odd to speak of "retain[ing]" property in exchange for the same property interest, and the eccentricity of such a reading is underscored by the fact that elsewhere in the Code the drafters chose to use the very phrase "in exchange for," §1123(a)(5)(J) (a plan shall provide adequate means for implementation, including "issuance of securities of the debtor . . . for cash, for property, for existing securities, or in exchange for claims or interests"). It is unlikely that the drafters of legislation so long and minutely contemplated as the 1978 Bankruptcy Code would have used two distinctly different forms of words for the same purpose.

The second difficulty is practical: the unlikelihood that Congress meant to impose a condition as manipulable as subsection [1129](b)(2)(B)(ii) would be if "on account of" meant to prohibit merely an exchange unaccompanied by a substantial infusion of new funds but permit one whenever substantial funds changed hands. "Substantial" or "significant" or "considerable" or like characterizations of a monetary contribution would measure it by the Lord Chancellor's foot, and an absolute priority rule so variable would not be much of an absolute. Of course it is true (as already noted) that, even if old equity holders could displace the rule by adding some significant amount of cash to the deal, it would not follow that their plan would be entitled to adoption; a contested plan would still need to satisfy the overriding condition of fairness and equity. But that general fairness and equity criterion would apply in any event, and one comes back to the question why Congress would have bothered to add a separate priority rule without a sharper edge.

Since the "in exchange for" reading merits rejection, the way is open to recognize the more common understanding of "on account of" to mean "because of." This is certainly the usage meant for the phrase at other places in the statute. . . . So, under the commonsense rule that a given phrase is meant to carry a given concept in a single statute, the better reading of subsection [1129](b)(2)(B)(ii) recognizes that a causal relationship between holding the prior claim or interest and receiving or retaining property is what activates the absolute priority rule.

The degree of causation is the final bone of contention. We understand the Government, as amicus curiae, to take the starchy position not only that any degree of causation between earlier interests and retained property will activate the bar to a plan providing for later property, but also that whenever the holders of equity in the Debtor end up with some property there will be some causation; when old equity, and not someone on the street, gets property the reason is res ipsa loquitur. An old equity holder simply cannot take property under a plan if creditors are not paid in full.

There are, however, reasons counting against such a reading. If, as is likely, the drafters were treating junior claimants or interest holders as a class at this point, then the simple way to have prohibited the old interest holders from receiving anything over objection would have been to omit the "on account of" phrase entirely from subsection [1129](b)(2)(B)(ii). On this assumption, reading the provision as a blanket prohibition would leave "on account of" as a redundancy, contrary to the interpretive obligation to try to give meaning to all the statutory language. One would also have to ask why Congress would have desired to exclude prior equity categorically from the class of potential owners following a cramdown. Although we have some doubt about the Court of Appeals's assumption that prior equity is often the only source of significant capital for reorganizations, old equity may well be in the best position to make a go of the reorganized enterprise and so may be the party most likely to work out an equity-for-value reorganization.

A less absolute statutory prohibition would follow from reading the "on account of" language as intended to reconcile the two recognized policies underlying Chapter 11, of preserving going concerns and maximizing property available to satisfy creditors. Causation between the old equity's holdings and subsequent property substantial enough to disqualify a plan would presumably occur on this view of things whenever old equity's later property would come at a price that failed to provide the greatest possible addition to the bankruptcy estate, and it would always come at a price too low when the equity holders obtained or preserved an ownership interest for less than someone else would have paid.[26] A truly full value transaction, on the other hand, would pose no threat to the bankruptcy estate not posed by any reorganization, provided of course that the contribution be in cash or be realizable money's worth, just as *Ahlers* required for application of *Case*'s new value rule.

IV

Which of these positions is ultimately entitled to prevail is not to be decided here, however, for even on the latter view the Bank's objection would require rejection of the plan at issue in this case. It is doomed, we can say without necessarily exhausting its flaws, by its provision for vesting equity in the reorganized business in the Debtor's partners without extending an opportunity to anyone else either to compete for that equity or to propose a competing reorganization plan. Although the Debtor's exclusive opportunity to propose a plan under §1121(b) is not itself "property" within the meaning of subsection [1129](b)(2)(B)(ii), the respondent partnership in this case has taken advantage of this opportunity by proposing a plan under which the benefit of equity ownership may be obtained by no one but old equity partners. Upon the court's approval of that plan, the partners were in the same position that they would have enjoyed had they exercised an exclusive option under the plan to buy the equity in the reorganized entity, or contracted to purchase it from a seller who had first agreed to deal with no one else. It is quite true that the escrow of the partners' proposed investment eliminated any formal need to set out an express option or exclusive dealing provision in the plan itself, since the court's approval that created the opportunity and the partners' action to obtain its advantage were simultaneous. But before the Debtor's plan was accepted no one else could propose an alternative one, and after its acceptance no one else could obtain equity in the reorganized entity. At the moment of the plan's approval the Debtor's partners necessarily enjoyed an exclusive opportunity that was in no economic sense distinguishable from the advantage of the exclusively entitled offeror or option holder. This opportunity should, first of all, be treated as an item of property in its own right. While it may be argued that the opportunity has no market value, being significant only to old equity holders owing to their potential tax liability, such an argument avails the Debtor nothing, for several

---

26. Even when old equity would pay its top dollar and that figure was as high as anyone else would pay, the price might still be too low unless the old equity holders paid more than anyone else would pay, on the theory that the "necessity" required to justify old equity's participation in a new value plan is a necessity for the participation of old equity as such. On this interpretation, disproof of a bargain would not satisfy old equity's burden; it would need to show that no one else would pay as much.... No such issue is before us, and we emphasize that our holding here does not suggest an exhaustive list of the requirements of a proposed new value plan.

reasons. It is to avoid just such arguments that the law is settled that any otherwise cognizable property interest must be treated as sufficiently valuable to be recognized under the Bankruptcy Code. Even aside from that rule, the assumption that no one but the Debtor's partners might pay for such an opportunity would obviously support no inference that it is valueless, let alone that it should not be treated as property. And, finally, the source in the tax law of the opportunity's value to the partners implies in no way that it lacks value to others. It might, indeed, be valuable to another precisely as a way to keep the Debtor from implementing a plan that would avoid a Chapter 7 liquidation. . . .

Under a plan granting an exclusive right, making no provision for competing bids or competing plans, any determination that the price was top dollar would necessarily be made by a judge in bankruptcy court, whereas the best way to determine value is exposure to a market. This is a point of some significance, since it was, after all, one of the Code's innovations to narrow the occasions for courts to make valuation judgments, as shown by its preference for the supramajoritarian class creditor voting scheme in §1126(c). In the interest of statutory coherence, a like disfavor for decisions untested by competitive choice ought to extend to valuations in administering subsection [1129](b)(2)(B)(ii) when some form of market valuation may be available to test the adequacy of an old equity holder's proposed contribution.

Whether a market test would require an opportunity to offer competing plans or would be satisfied by a right to bid for the same interest sought by old equity, is a question we do not decide here. It is enough to say, assuming a new value corollary, that plans providing junior interest holders with exclusive opportunities free from competition and without benefit of market valuation fall within the prohibition of §1129(b)(2)(B)(ii). The judgment of the Court of Appeals is accordingly reversed, and the case is remanded for further proceedings consistent with this opinion.

[Justice Souter's decision was joined in by Justices Breyer, Ginsberg, Kennedy, and O'Connor. Justice Thomas, joined by Justice Scalia, filed a concurring opinion, and Justice Stevens filed a dissent. Justice Thomas's opinion, while concurring in the judgment, found that the Bankruptcy Code unambiguously would prevent old equity (the debtor's principals) from retaining any property under the plan on account of their junior interests; and that the equity holders received at least one form of property—the exclusive opportunity to obtain equity in the reorganized enterprise—on account of their prepetition equity interest. Thus, he concluded, the plan could not be confirmed and there had been no need for the majority's reliance on legislative history or for its dicta concerning the desirability of a market test. In the dissent, Justice Stevens pointed out that the petitioner failed to challenge the decision below on any of its findings[29] but limited its appeal to whether the debtor's plan gave old equity an

---

29. While raised in an amicus brief, petitioner did not challenge the determination by the courts below that the prerequisites for a new value plan articulated by Justice Douglas in Case v. Los Angeles Lumber Prods. Co., 308 U.S. 106 (1939) had been met: Was the new value necessary for the survival of the enterprise? Was the value received by the debtor reasonably equivalent to the

interest in the property "on account of" its prepetition interest in the debtor. On that issue, Justice Stevens found that the interest was *not* "on account of" the prior interest because the junior claimants did not receive the interest for a bargain price.—EDS.]

NOTES AND QUESTIONS

1. Allowed Secured Claim. The message of §506(a) is that a mortgagee's claim is a secured claim to the extent of the value of the collateral, and to the extent that the claim exceeds the value of the collateral it is an unsecured claim. Without more (and virtually until enactment, drafts of the Code did not contain more), mortgagees feared that this language codified the *Pine Gate* line of cases. Do you see why?

If you have difficulty with the last question, assume in the master hypothetical that Dan Developer is the general partner of Law Drive Associates, a single asset limited partnership owning the land and building subject to Ace Insurance Company's nonrecourse mortgage. The partnership files a petition in Chapter 11 at a time when the Ace mortgage loan, with a principal balance then at $15 million, is in default. The value of the land and building is approximately $12 million. Under §506(a), Ace would have a secured claim of $12 million, equal to the value of the mortgaged property. Section 506(a) also provides that Ace would have an unsecured claim for the difference between the value of the collateral and the amount of the obligation. But since the debt is *nonrecourse* and the partners are not personally liable on the note, Ace would have had no claim for an amount in excess of the value of the collateral ("claim" is defined in §101(5) as a "right to payment . . ."). As a result, although the remaining $3 million borrowed would normally be an unsecured claim, in this situation Ace would have no unsecured claim.

Assume that the proposed plan of reorganization adversely affects, or impairs, Ace's interest and that Ace (as the only member of this class of first mortgagees) rejects it. The court proposes to cram down the plan but cannot do so under §1129(b)(1) unless the plan is "fair and equitable." This means that absolute priority must be observed with respect to Ace's claim. But because of §506(a) and the nonrecourse nature of the debt, Ace's claim—entitled to absolute priority—is only its secured claim of $12 million based on the property value. Ace would have no unsecured claim for the $3 million deficiency. Thus, even if Ace is paid the full secured claim in cash, wouldn't it end up like the mortgagee under *Pine Gate*, without the debt having been fully paid and Law Drive Associates retaining the property? Think of this result in light of the *KRO* case, discussed above. The first mortgage had a balance of $6 million and the court

---

amount contributed? Were the priority rights of creditors preserved? See discussion in Note 5c, infra. Furthermore, petitioner did not dispute (perhaps because it had not been raised below) whether the plan met the requirements of §1129(a)(10), as discussed below in note 6 dealing with classification of claims.

found the value of the property to be $895,000. The mortgagee would have had a secured claim of $895,000. Even if the Code had provided for full payment in cash to dissenting classes of creditors, the first mortgagee would have gotten no more than $895,000, the remaining mortgagees would have received nothing, and the limited partnership would have kept the property.

This concern of the mortgagees was dealt with by the addition of §1111(b), discussed below.

2. Recourse or Full Secured Claim. Section 1111(b) was designed to rescue mortgagees from the plight discussed in note 1. Under §1111(b)(1)(A), a nonrecourse claim is automatically converted to a recourse claim for the purpose of the allowance of an unsecured claim in the reorganization (unless the property is being sold, for which other protective provisions, discussed below, should apply). This conversion would give the nonrecourse mortgagee an unsecured claim for the difference between the value of the collateral and the higher amount of the debt. Thus, even though the claim is nonrecourse, the mortgagee would have an unsecured claim that, on rejection of the plan by the unsecured class, would be entitled to absolute priority. Since absolute priority for the unsecured class would not permit confirmation of a plan under which property is awarded to the debtor and unsecured creditors are not paid in full, the mortgagee's interests would be protected. Alternatively, §1111(b) provides that a secured class may, subject to certain limitations, elect a full secured claim, covering the entire indebtedness, notwithstanding the §506(a) valuation. If you represented Ace Insurance Company in our hypothetical, which alternative would you choose? Ask yourself this question again as you review the mechanics of the cramdown in note 3, which follows. The issue will be discussed in Problem 18-2.

3. The Mechanics of the Cramdown. Getting back to our hypothetical situation with the same fact pattern discussed in note 1, assume that Ace's interest is adversely affected by a proposed plan of reorganization (§1129(a)(8) makes it clear that a class can reject a plan only if it is "impaired" by the plan, under the theory that you should only have a right to complain if you are hurt— more will be said about impairment in note 4). If Ace accepts the recourse claim under §1111(b), it will have a secured claim under §506(a) of $12 million (the value of the property) and an unsecured claim of $3 million. If Ace elects a full claim under §1111(b)(2), it will have a secured claim for $15 million, the full amount of the indebtedness, and no unsecured claim. This is illustrated as follows.

	Secured	Unsecured
Recourse Claim	12	3
Full Claim	15	—

As we have seen, in order for the court to confirm a plan over the objection of a dissenting class (§1129(a)(8) and (b)(1), (2)) the plan must be fair and equitable as to the dissenting class. Section 1129(b)(2) sets forth certain minimum requirements that a plan must meet to be fair and equitable, for both secured (§1129(b)(2)(A)) and unsecured (§1129(b)(2)(B)) classes. With respect to secured classes, these requirements provide three disjunctive alternatives: where the mortgage lien remains on the property, where the property is sold free and clear of the mortgage, or where some other disposition is made.

a. *Where the Mortgage Lien Remains on the Property—§1129(b)(2)(A)(i).* Under this first alternative, fair and equitable treatment (absolute priority) for the mortgagee requires that the mortgagee receive payments under the continuing mortgage (referred to as "deferred cash payments" because they will be paid over a period of time) totaling at least the amount of the claim. This means that if Ace had accepted a recourse claim, it would receive under its secured claim deferred cash payments totaling at least $12 million over the term of the mortgage remaining on the property. On the other hand, if Ace had elected the full secured claim, it would receive deferred cash payments totaling at least $15 million over that period.

At this point, you must be thinking that you know the answer to the question posed at the end of note 2 as to which alternative is better for Ace. But consider the fact that §1129(b)(2)(A)(i)(II) also provides that the *present value* of the deferred cash payments ("DCP" in the diagram below) as of the effective date of the plan can (and undoubtedly will) be as low as the value of the collateral under either alternative. The result is that although the *total amount* of deferred cash payments will be different if Ace accepts a recourse claim or elects a full claim, the *present value*[30] of these future payments at plan confirmation will be the same. It probably still seems to you that it would be to Ace's advantage to elect the full secured claim. But do not forget that under the recourse alternative Ace would have an unsecured claim of $3 million, while it would have no unsecured claim if it elected the full claim. This is illustrated in the following diagram.

	Secured		Unsecured
	DCP	Value	
Recourse Claim	12	12	3
Full Claim	15	12	0

Undoubtedly, in the case of a single asset debtor such as Law Drive Associates, Ace would be able to "dominate" the class of unsecured creditors, that is, it would have enough votes to make certain that the class of unsecured creditors rejects the plan (plans must be accepted by at least two-thirds in amount *and* more than one-half in number of allowed claims of each class of creditors under §1126(c)). Once the unsecured class rejects the plan, §1129(b)(1) requires that if the plan is to be crammed down, it must be fair and equitable as concerns

---

30. Present value reflects the fact that the payment will be received over a period of time. This will be discussed in note 5a in connection with our discussion of the *Till* case, supra.

the unsecured class. This requires absolute priority, and §1129(b)(2)(B) provides that absolute priority for the unsecured creditors means that holders of unsecured claims must be given property of a value equal to their claims before anyone junior can receive any property as a result of their having had an interest in the property at the time of the filing.

Of course, this does not guarantee that unsecured creditors will get anything, since there may be few or no assets remaining for unsecured creditors after compensating secured creditors. What absolute priority was intended to mean here, however, is that a plan that violates absolute priority (i.e., under which Dan Developer's limited partnership proposes to keep the property) cannot be crammed down *unless* the unsecured class is paid in full. This is the key to overturning *Pine Gate.* If the mortgagee has a recourse claim and absolute priority is followed, the debtor will be unable to keep the property because it cannot compensate the mortgagee fully.

Notice how well the foregoing requirements deal with different kinds of reorganizations. While they protect the mortgagee against the *Pine Gate* line of decisions in the case of a single asset ownership entity, they should do no harm in the large corporate reorganization where the property, for instance the factory, is essential to the reorganization and must be kept by the reorganized company. In the large reorganization, Ace's $3 million unsecured claim may be lost in a sea of unsecured claims, and Ace will not be able to "dominate" the class of unsecured creditors, who may vote to accept a plan paying, say, 50 cents on the dollar, or 10 cents on the dollar, or less. Once the class accepts, the plan does not have to be fair and equitable as to that class, absolute priority is not applicable, and Ace will have to live with what the unsecured creditors accept.

> ➤ *Problem 18-3*
> Returning to the question asked at the end of note 2, if you were representing Ace, which alternative—the full secured claim or the recourse claim—would you recommend? If your answer is that the recourse claim is best in most situations because it is absolute priority for the unsecured class that will prevent the debtor from keeping the property without paying the debt, you are correct. However, will the recourse claim always be best for the mortgagee? Under what circumstances would you think it more advisable for Ace to elect a full secured claim? What anticipated future developments with respect to the property might influence Ace's decision? Would the number of unsecured creditors affect the decision? ◄

b. *Where the Property Is Sold Free and Clear of the Mortgage—§1129(b)(2)(A)(ii).* Where the mortgage will be extinguished because of a sale free and clear of the mortgage under a plan rejected by a class of impaired creditors, the second alternative provides that the plan would meet the fair and equitable absolute priority standard as to the dissenting class if the property were sold, "subject to §363(k)," and the lien were to attach to the proceeds of the sale. Section 363 deals with the use, sale, or lease of collateral by the trustee.

Subsection (k) provides that on a sale of the property the secured creditor may normally bid at the sale and, if the successful bidder, may offset the "allowed claim" against the secured creditor's bid. This is known as "credit bidding," a right the mortgagee would have in the normal foreclosure sale up to the amount of the debt owed. Do you understand why credit bidding is necessary to protect the secured creditor for the value of the collateral?

c. *Where Some Other Disposition Is Made—§1129(b)(2)(A)(iii).* This third alternative permits other approaches under the plan provided that the secured creditor receive the "indubitable equivalent" of its claim. Recall the use of this term in §361 (dealing with adequate protection), discussed in Chapter 18C1, note 2, supra. The use of the words of Judge Learned Hand was intended as a message to the courts that Congress really expected full compensation for the secured creditor.

The three alternatives are in the disjunctive. This raised a crucial question: Can a plan be confirmed as meeting the indubitable equivalent requirement of the third alternative where the mortgagee retains the lien, or the property is sold in a manner not in accordance with the requirements of the first two alternatives?

This issue came up in the Third Circuit in In re Philadelphia Newspapers, 599 F.3d 298 (3d Cir. 2010). In that case, a plan was confirmed that would sell substantially all of the debtor's assets free and clear of the mortgage, a seemingly second alternative situation. However, the plan prohibited credit bidding as required under the second alternative and was confirmed under the third alternative subject to the bankruptcy court determining that what the mortgagee received provided the indubitable equivalence to the mortgagee. Judge Ambro, a noted former bankruptcy lawyer, wrote a strong dissent, maintaining that the second alternative covers any sale of the property and that any sale must therefore permit credit bidding. He also suggested that the plan's prohibition of credit bidding may have been inserted in order to prevent the mortgagee from outbidding a stalking horse bidder controlled by the debtor's present and future management

The Seventh Circuit rejected *Philadelphia Newspapers* in River Road Partners v. Amalgamated Bank (In re River Road) 651 F.3d 642 (7th Cir. 2011), stating, in line with Judge Ambro's dissent in *Philadelphia Newspapers*, that any sale of assets free and clear of a mortgage must be subject to the credit bidding requirement of the second alternative. The Supreme Court affirmed the Seventh Circuit in *RadLAX Gateway Hotel, LLC v. Amalgamated Bank,* 566 U.S. 639 (2012). Written by Justice Scalia, the opinion in *RadLAX* was unanimous (although Justice Kennedy did not participate in the decision) and at least on its face was based solely on the statutory language as interpreted in light of the canon of construction that the specific provision (credit bid on sale) trumps the general provision (providing the indubitable equivalent). Justice Scalia stated: "We find the debtors' reading of §1129(b)(2)(A)—under which clause (iii) permits precisely what clause (ii) proscribes—to be hyperliteral and contrary to common sense." The Court held that the debtors "may not obtain confirmation of a Chapter 11 cramdown plan that provides for the sale of collateral free and clear of the Bank's lien, but does not permit the Bank to credit bid at the sale." As a result, one might assume that the mortgagee's right to credit bid at a sale under a plan is protected. But don't jump to conclusions, for nothing ever seems to be completely put to rest in bankruptcy.

There have been several post-*RadLAX* lower court cases that have attempted to both limit the amount of the mortgagee's credit bid at the sale and limit the mortgagee's ability to offset its claim against its successful bid. How can this be done in light of the statutory language of §363(k) and the Supreme Court's decision in *RadLAX*? Without contesting that the mortgagee had a right to credit bid, the cases homed in on seven words in §363(k)—"unless the court for cause orders otherwise"—and found cause to order otherwise. The operative limiting words on this power of the court are obviously "for cause." Unfortunately there is no definition of "cause" in the Bankruptcy Code and courts seem free to find cause on a case-by-case basis. Here are two examples where the court has found cause:

In In re Free Lance-Star Publishing Co., 512 B.R. 798 (Bankr. E.D. Va. 2014), the court found cause existed to limit the secured creditor's credit bid to $14 million instead of the $39 million mortgage balance in order to "restore enthusiasm for the sale and foster robust bidding" and because the creditor acquired the loan with the intention of obtaining the property in a bankruptcy sale. In In re Fisker Automotive Holdings, 510 B.R. 55 (Bankr. D. Del. 2014), the court limited the credit bid on a $168.5 million mortgage to the $25 million the creditor paid to acquire the mortgage, finding as cause that the right to credit bid "would not just chill but freeze out competitive bidding."

A few questions:

(i) Look carefully at the language of §363(k). Does it permit interpreting the "unless the court for cause orders otherwise" language to apply to *both* the right to bid at a sale *and* the right to set off the claim against a bid that has been made? Note that there is no comma after "unless the court for cause orders otherwise" but there is one after "such sale." If you are representing the mortgagee in a situation such as this, is it possible to argue that the language of the section gives the court the power for cause to deny the mortgagee the right to bid at the sale, but that if the mortgagee is able to bid, it must be able to offset its claim against a successful bid? For an example of a situation where a court might find cause to deny the mortgagee the right to bid at a sale, see the discussion of *In re Pacific Lumber Co.*, in Problem 18-4 below.

(ii) Do you agree with the assumption in the two cases discussed above that the right to credit bid will almost always chill or freeze out competitive bidding at a sale of the property? If your answer is yes, and if this circumstance would constitute cause to limit credit bidding, then does this constitute a nullification of the Supreme Court's decision in *RadLAX*?

(iii) It would seem correct that the prospect of credit bidding should have a chilling effect on anyone planning to bid an amount that is less than the mortgage balance (do you understand why this is so?). However, if the bidder believes that the property being sold is worth more than the mortgage, why would competitive bidding be chilled? In a sense, then, the mortgage balance would constitute an upset price, or floor for prospective bidders.

(iv) Should the motivation of the owner/acquirer of the note to credit bid the property at a bankruptcy sale be a basis for denying the right to credit bid? What are your arguments pro and con?

> ➤ *Problem 18-4*
> In the pre-*RadLAX* Fifth Circuit case of In re Pacific Lumber Co., 584 F.3d 229 (5th Cir. 2009) a plan was confirmed involving the transfer of property (deemed a "sale" by the court) free and clear of liens, under the third alternative, rather than the second. The case did not involve a public sale, so there was no opportunity for the lien holder to credit bid. The proceeds of the transfer, however, paid the lien holder in full. Would such a "sale" be permitted after *RadLAX*? What arguments would you make pro or con? ◄

4. Impairment of Claims. In this discussion of the cramdown, we have presumed that the claims were impaired by the proposed plan. Under §1129(a)(8), a class cannot reject a proposed plan of reorganization unless it is "impaired" by the plan. What happens when a mortgagee feels itself hurt by the plan but the court thinks the mortgagee is unimpaired? The only way the mortgagee can protect itself from its perceived impairment is to force the plan to a cramdown, under which absolute priority would be required. But the mortgagee can force a cramdown only by rejecting the plan, and it can't reject the plan if it is unimpaired. Thus, a determination of circumstances under which a class may become impaired is very important.

Section 1124 states that all classes are considered impaired unless their legal, equitable, and contractual rights are left unaltered. Assume that Dan Developer's plan of reorganization proposed paying Ace in cash the full $15 million principal due. Can you think of a reason why Ace would want to reject such a plan? Would Ace be impaired? Before the 1994 amendments, §1124 contained a provision that specified that a claim was unimpaired if the creditor was to receive the allowed amount of the claim in cash. This was deleted in 1994, overruling In re New Valley Corp., 168 B.R. 73 (Bankr. D.N.J. 1994), which held that unsecured creditors of a solvent debtor were unimpaired where the plan paid the debt but did not pay postpetition interest. Is Ace impaired if it is paid everything owed to date in cash, including postpetition interest, but no prepayment fee as required by the mortgage? Is Ace impaired if it is paid everything owed, including the full balance, but because prevailing interest rates have declined, Ace must lend out the money received at lower interest rates?

5. Absolute Priority Problems
a. *Secured Claim: Determining Present Value of Property Distributed.* Note 3 discussed the application of the absolute priority rule under §1129(b)(2)(A) to secured claims and concluded that with respect to a mortgage lien continued on the property under the plan, absolute priority would require that the mortgagee

receive deferred cash payments over the life of the mortgage equal to the amount of the mortgagee's claim and that such deferred cash payments have a value as of the effective date of the plan no lower than the value of the property. This requirement has constitutional implications.

The issue of the extent of constitutional protection afforded to a secured creditor's property interest came before the courts during the Great Depression. Congress had passed the first Frazier-Lemke Act (Frazier-Lemke Act of 1934, ch. 869, 48 Stat. 1289), in an effort to provide relief for the severely distressed agricultural community. In an opinion written by Justice Brandeis, a unanimous Supreme Court in Louisville Joint Stock Land Bank v. Radford, 295 U.S. 555 (1935), declared the Act unconstitutional because it took property rights from the mortgagee without compensation in violation of the Fifth Amendment. The second Frazier-Lemke Act revised the first Act and was found constitutional in Wright v. Vinton Branch of Mountain Trust Bank, 300 U.S. 440 (1937), an opinion again written by Justice Brandeis, because the Act as revised did not deprive the mortgagee of "the due process of law guaranteed by the Fifth Amendment." 300 U.S. at 470). The requirement of §1129(b)(2)(A) may also be based in part on the Court's decision in Wright v. Union Central Life Ins. Co., 311 U.S. 273 (1940) where Justice Douglas stated that the secured creditor was constitutionally entitled to receive "the value of the property" securing the lien in the borrower's bankruptcy.

> ➤ *Problem 18-5*
> In his opinion in *RadLAX*, Justice Scalia pointed out that the parties "debate at some length . . . the merits of credit bidding," and stated "the pros and cons of credit bidding are for the consideration of Congress, not the courts." 566 U.S. at 649. Consider Justice Scalia's statement in light of our discussion of the constitutional protection afforded the mortgagee's property interest. Assume that the next revision of the Bankruptcy Code contains a provision that precludes credit bidding in connection with any sale of property free and clear of a lien either under §363 or under a plan. Do you think that an argument that this provision is unconstitutional because it deprives the mortgagee of being certain it will receive the constitutionally protected value of the collateral will be successful if Justice Scalia's comment in *RadLAX* is accepted? ◄

In our master hypothetical, the §1129(b)(2)(A) requirement means that if Ace had a secured claim of $12 million with an unsecured claim of $3 million, the $12 million mortgage remaining on the property would have to have a present value of $12 million. Is it possible for the mortgagee to receive that value under §1129(b)? Under the second Frazier-Lemke Act, which Justice Brandeis found constitutional, the mortgagee received the value of the property in *cash*. In §1129(b)(2)(A), the mortgagee is supposed to receive a mortgage with a value equal to 100 percent of the value of the troubled collateral. If the mortgage has such a value, wouldn't it be possible to sell the mortgage for that amount?

Unfortunately, it is not reasonable to believe that anyone would purchase such a 100 percent of value mortgage at its face amount of $12 million. Why this is so can be seen from the discussion of appraisal at Chapter 4D1, on the income capitalization method of determining property value, which involves dividing the projected income stream by a percentage (known as the "capitalization rate") representing the return a purchaser of the property being valued would require for that type of property.

Under §1129(b)(2)(A), the income stream to the mortgagee (that is, the interest) will directly affect the determination of the present value of the mortgage. It might seem that the easy way to increase present value would be to raise the interest rate. Note, however, that it would be unproductive to increase the interest rate beyond what is realistic for the property to pay, since that would only increase the risk factors (the ability of the property to meet debt service) and raise the capitalization rate, which in turn would lower value.[31] If this means that it is impossible to meet the statutory requirement, does it also mean that Chapter 11 fails constitutional scrutiny? Perhaps it does, but bear in mind the ameliorating factors in Chapter 11, which give the mortgagee an unsecured claim entitled to absolute priority in addition to its secured claim, and the option of electing a full secured claim.

The *Till* case, excerpted above, is a Chapter 13 case. However, it deals with language similar to §1129(b)(2)(A) in §1325(a)(5)(B), so the decision could have a significant impact on what constitutes absolute priority in single asset real estate cases. *Till* involved the determination of the correct interest rate that would give the creditor, with a subprime lien on a used truck, a present value equal to the value of the collateral. The plurality opinion, the concurring opinion, and the dissent all look to the interest rate as the sole factor to determine the present value of the property, without considering the effect of the interest rate on the capitalization rate. In making the interest rate determination, the plurality opinion of Justice Stevens opts for the so-called prime-plus, or formula rate, which starts with the prime rate and augments it by a percentage (in this case, 1.5 percent) to account for the risk of nonpayment. This overrules the Seventh Circuit, which had held that the original contract rate (an "eye-popping" 21 percent for this subprime truck loan) was the "presumptive rate" which could be changed based on evidence that a higher or lower rate would be appropriate. The concurring opinion of Justice Thomas concludes that the statutory language requires the secured creditor to receive property of a value equal to the value of the collateral, which would require only that interest be sufficient to compensate for the fact that the payments would be received over time without reflecting the risk of nonpayment. Justice Scalia's dissent would accept the presumptive contract rate approved by the Seventh Circuit.

Justice Thomas seemed to have approached the real issue in the case when he said the statutory language "requires only that 'the value . . . of property to be

---

31. As you remember, the formula is value equals income divided by the capitalization rate. If you do the math, you will see that the higher the capitalization rate, the lower the value.

distributed under the plan' at the time of the effective date of the plan, be no less than the amount of the secured creditor's claim." Unfortunately, he apparently assumes that the principal and interest will in fact be paid (which may be somewhat more realistic in a short-term loan under Chapter 13 than a long-term mortgage under Chapter 11) and concludes that the creditor is not entitled to a risk adjustment.

What is the property distributed to the secured creditor? It is a mortgage with a face amount equal to the value of the collateral. What is the value of that property? It would seem no less and no more than what someone would pay for that mortgage in the secondary mortgage market.[32] The problem in single asset real estate is that no sane purchaser would buy a mortgage (especially one secured by distressed property) at 100 percent of its value.[33] Thus, a mortgage securing a loan of $100 could be sold for no more than, say, $75 or $80, depending on the loan to value ratio the purchaser requires. Increasing the interest rate would not help unless it was clear that the higher interest rate would be paid.

Would the decision in *Till*, a Chapter 13 case, apply to single asset real estate under Chapter 11? See footnote 14 where the Court says that the holding might not be applicable in Chapter 11, where a free market of willing cramdown lenders exists,[34] in which case the interest rate would be the rate an efficient market would produce. More recently the Sixth Circuit held that in a Chapter 11 cramdown the appropriate interest rate is the market rate where an efficient market exists and the *Till* formula rate where no efficient market rate exists.[35] Is there an efficient market for a mortgage in single asset real estate cases? Certainly there may be a free market of willing cramdown lenders, but, as discussed above, it would be correct to say that there would be NO market, efficient or not, for a 100 percent of value mortgage at its face amount. How do you interpret the footnote? Is it referring to a market for mortgages out of bankruptcy proceedings, or is it referring to a market for the particular 100 percent of value mortgage? Stay tuned to see how this plays out.

b. *Family Farmers and Chapter 12*. The pathos of farm insolvency some years ago was seen in the loss of the family farm by families that had worked the land for generations. In the farm crisis of the mid-1980s, the societal objective was to find a way to keep the farmer on the farm. Would Chapter 11 of the Bankruptcy Code have met this goal? Assume the following facts: Francine

---

32. When a person lending money secured by a mortgage sells that mortgage to another party, such sale is considered a sale in the "secondary mortgage market." The term does not mean that the mortgage is less valuable than it would have been in the primary mortgage market, only that it has been, in the language often used by used car dealers, previously owned.

33. For the purposes of this discussion, we are assuming that the court's section 506(a) valuation is correct.

34. Here the court seems to be referring to the availability of postpetition financing, rather than a market for a mortgage.

35. In re Am. Homepatient, Inc., 420 F.3d 559 (6th Cir. 2005). See also In re Texas Grand Prairie Hotel Realty, 710 F.3d 324 (5th Cir. 2013) and In re Couture Hotel Corp., 536 B.R. 712 (Bankr. N.D. Tex. 2015).

Farmer has a $1 million mortgage on her farm. When she files in bankruptcy, the farm is worth $600,000. The mortgage is recourse. Under Chapter 11, the mortgagee would have a secured claim for $600,000 and an unsecured claim for $400,000. The mortgage would be reduced to a face amount of $600,000 but, under the absolute priority rule, with respect to unsecured claims, Francine Farmer would have to find property with a value equal to $400,000 to satisfy the lender's unsecured claim before she could keep the property. This would seem improbable unless Francine had substantial assets elsewhere. Thus it would seem unlikely that Chapter 11 could save the farm.

Because of the lower dollar limits for eligibility at the time Chapter 12 was drafted and other problems, Chapter 13 (which deals with certain individuals with regular income) was not a viable vehicle for saving the farm. With huge federal budget deficits, Congress was unwilling to legislate the rescue of the farmers through federal financial assistance. As a result, in drafting bankruptcy legislation to meet the farm crisis, Congress looked to the only other party with a deep pocket, the mortgagee. The result was Chapter 12.

Chapter 12 deals with insolvencies of "family farmers," now defined generally to include farmers with, inter alia, debts that do not exceed $4,153,150.[36] It protects the farmer by, inter alia, eliminating absolute priority for the unsecured class, which includes the mortgagee's deficiency claim. Thus, it is not necessary under Chapter 12 for the dissenting impaired mortgagee to receive property of a value equal to the amount of its unsecured claim before the debtor can keep the property. What Chapter 12 retains is the requirement that the plan be in the best interest of creditors. As you will recall, this means that each creditor must receive what it would have received on liquidation.

Given a property valuation of $600,000 and a mortgage of $1 million in our hypothetical, it would be highly unlikely that there would be anything available for unsecured creditors in liquidation. Since it is also improbable that there could be any "disposable income" (which Chapter 12 requires be applied to pay claims under the plan for a period of time) available for future payments to the mortgagee, the unsecured portion of the lender's claim may be virtually wiped out under Chapter 12. The result is that Chapter 12 effectively reduces the mortgage to the value of the collateral. See §1225 of the Bankruptcy Code, which deals with the plan confirmation requirements of Chapter 12. The expectation, then, is that in most circumstances the farmer will be able to keep the farm.

What particularly disturbed mortgagees about Chapter 12 was that if, for instance, Francine's property were to increase in value in the five years following confirmation of the plan to, say, $2 million, the mortgage would remain reduced, and the mortgagee would have no way of recouping what it was asked to forgo for the benefit of the debtor's reorganization. As Chapter 12 was being drafted, mortgagees suggested that a method be provided to permit a second look at the value of the property in five or ten years following confirmation of the plan, with

---

36. Dollar amount as adjusted by the Judicial Conference of the United States as of the drafting of this 6th edition.

the court empowered to increase the amount secured by the mortgage to a figure that would pay back to the mortgagee out of the increase in property value what it lost on confirmation. These suggestions, however, were brushed aside. What competitive advantage does this give Francine Farmer over a farmer who paid all debts and did not file in bankruptcy? Does this encourage filing under the chapter, and if so, is that desirable? What effect do you think Chapter 12 had on the availability of credit to family farmers outside of bankruptcy? Without absolute priority for the unsecured claim and without a §1111(b)(2) election for a full secured claim, does Chapter 12 meet the constitutional requirements of *Union Central*, supra note 5a?

c. *The New Value "Exception."* Prior to the adoption of Chapter 12, the Eighth Circuit, in In re Ahlers, 794 F.2d 388 (8th Cir. 1986), held, inter alia, that notwithstanding the absolute priority requirement of §1129(b)(2)(B) of the Code, a promise by a farmer-debtor to contribute labor and expertise in the future constituted a present capital contribution enabling the debtor to retain an interest in the property while the dissenting impaired class of unsecured creditors remained unpaid. The holding was based on the new value "exception" to the absolute priority requirement described by the Supreme Court in Case v. Los Angeles Lumber Prods. Co., 308 U.S. 106 (1939), under which a junior creditor or stockholder might retain an interest equal to any new capital contributed to the reorganized company, even if such creditor or stockholder would have been wiped out under the absolute priority rule absent such a contribution.[37] Would the decision in *Ahlers* have been necessary to protect the farmer if Chapter 12 had been the law at the time?

The reasoning of the Eighth Circuit in *Ahlers* was that the promise by the debtor to work hard in the future (so-called "sweat equity") was equivalent to a present contribution of capital under *Case*. The Eighth Circuit's reasoning was (i) contrary to the express language of Chapter 11; (ii) inconsistent with *Case* because in that case the Supreme Court specifically rejected the idea that intangibles could constitute present contributions of capital; and (iii) contrary to the intent of Congress, which had rejected similar proposals by the Commission on the Bankruptcy Laws of the United States (see H.R. Doc. No. 137, 93d Cong., 1st Sess., pt. 1, at 256-257 (1973)). The Supreme Court granted certiorari on this issue and had little difficulty in reversing the Eighth Circuit, 485 U.S. 197 (1988).

---

37. In *Case*, Justice Douglas strictly limited the availability of this exception to the absolute priority rule to situations where (i) the contribution was in money or money's worth; (ii) the funds were necessary for the success of the business enterprise; (iii) the interest retained did not exceed the contribution in value; and (iv) the priority rights of the creditors were protected. If this bit of alchemy could be achieved, do you see why the ability to contribute new value would probably be more a "corollary" than an "exception" to the absolute priority rule? Professor Ayer points out that because of the difficulty in achieving Justice Douglas's prerequisites, no plan was confirmed under pre-Code law employing new value. See Ayer, Rethinking Absolute Priority After Ahlers, 87 Mich. L. Rev. 963, 1016 (1989). For a detailed explanation of what he deems a distortion of the Douglas prerequisites in post-Code law, see Zinman, New Value and the Commission: *How Bizarre!*, 5 Am. Bankr. Inst. L. Rev. 477 (1997).

Although reversed by the Supreme Court, *Ahlers* pointed up a possible weakness in the absolute priority rule that has since come before the courts. Returning to the master hypothetical, assume that the property was worth $12 million and the mortgage indebtedness was $15 million at the time of confirmation of Law Drive Associates' Chapter 11 reorganization plan. Assume Ace has accepted a recourse claim giving it a $12 million secured claim and a $3 million unsecured claim and that there are no other assets to compensate Ace on its unsecured claim. Thus, under the absolute priority rule, the partnership cannot keep the property. Assume that there is a valid exception to the absolute priority rule for those who have contributed actual new capital to the reorganization. Suppose that a contribution of $100,000 of new capital is made on behalf of Law Drive Associates. Under the new value "exception" this entitles Law Drive Associates to an interest in the property equal to its capital contribution. Can Law Drive Associates argue that it is entitled to keep the entire property since it is contributing $100,000 for property that has no equity value?[38]

As noted in the *LaSalle* decision, the courts are split as to whether the Code countenances any "new value" exception to the absolute priority rule. Compare Phoenix Mutual Life Ins. Co. v. Greystone III Joint Venture, 995 F.2d 1274 (5th Cir.) (en banc) (withdrawing portion of panel opinion holding that Code doesn't permit "new value" exception to the absolute priority rule whereby the debtor Greystone, on cash contribution of $500,000, could retain ownership of the mortgaged property while proposing to pay the mortgagee only 3 percent of the mortgagee's unsecured claim of $3.5 million), cert. denied, 506 U.S. 821 (1992), with Bonner Mall Partnership v. US Bancorp Mortgage Co., 2 F.3d 899 (9th Cir. 1993) (upholding a new value plan), cert. granted, 114 S. Ct. 681, dismissed, 115 S. Ct. 386 (1994) (issue mooted by settlement prior to oral argument).

The Supreme Court in *LaSalle* homed in on the language of §1129(b)(2)(B)(ii) that prohibits a junior party from retaining an interest "on account of" its junior interest unless seniors have been paid. The debtor argued that its retained interest was the result of the new value contribution, not on account of its junior interest. The Court held that an interest retained where the debtor had the exclusive right to bid the new value without subjecting the bid to a market test, was retained on account of the prior junior interest. It did not purport to rule on: (a) whether a plan that gave the opportunity to contribute new value to others in addition to old equity holders would constitute what the court determined to be the necessary market exposure for confirmation; (b) whether a new value corollary or exception to the absolute priority rule had survived the adoption of the Bankruptcy Code; and (c) what the prerequisites to new value (first articulated by Justice Douglas in *Case*) mean in the context of such a plan.

---

38. To help answer this question, see Norwest Bank Worthington v. Ahlers, 485 U.S. 197, 206 (1988), where the court stated: "We join in the consensus of authority which has rejected this 'no value' theory." The court went on to quote from N. Pac. R. Co. v Boyd, 228 U.S. 482 (1913): stating that whether the value is "present or prospective, for dividends or only for purposes of control," a retained equity interest is a property interest to "which the creditors [are] entitled ... before the stockholders [can] retain it for any purpose whatever."

The Court left open many questions for the real estate mortgagee to contemplate. For example, consider how you would answer the following questions if we assume that a plan giving the debtor *and others* the opportunity to contribute new capital and receive ownership interests in the reorganized entity can be confirmed.

1.   Must the opportunity to contribute new capital be available to everyone? On remand in *LaSalle*, could the debtor open the bidding to old equity and junior interests excluding the first mortgagee? Given that under §1129(b)(2)(A) of the Bankruptcy Code the mortgage will equal the value of the collateral, would you expect that any junior interests would bid?

2.   If the mortgagee is permitted to bid, would "credit bidding" (the ability to offset the amount owed by the debtor—here the amount of the debt in excess of the value of the collateral—against any successful bid) be permitted? Credit bidding is permitted when specific assets are sold under §363(k) of the Bankruptcy Code. However, language in the National Bankruptcy Review Commission Report[39] was not favorable to credit bidding. See National Bankr. Rev. Comm'n, Bankruptcy: The Next Twenty Years, Final Report at 563-565 (1997). If credit bidding were permitted, would this protect the interests of the mortgagee? Review our discussion in Note 3c above dealing with the Supreme Court's approach to credit bidding under the present language of the Bankruptcy Code.

3.   If credit bidding is not permitted, would the mortgagee's successful bid for the property be applied to the operation of the property? Or would it be applied to pay creditors? Would Justice Douglas's requirement in *Case* that new value had to be essential to the success of the *enterprise* affect your answer? If the mortgagee becomes the owner of the property, would it be concerned if the funds are applied to the operation of the property? If, on the other hand, the funds are used to pay creditors, would this trouble the mortgagee? In *LaSalle*, partners held $11 million in junior secured claims and thus the partners would at least share in any funds provided by the mortgagee. What could the mortgagee have done when the mortgage was drafted to reduce the risk of this happening? For a possible answer, review our discussion of due-on-encumbrance clauses in Chapter 5A7.

39. The National Bankruptcy Review Commission was established by Title VI of the Bankruptcy Reform Act of 1994, Pub. L. No., 103-394 for the purpose of reviewing the Bankruptcy Code and proposing amendments where appropriate. It led to the BAPCPA amendments of 2005, but because of a rough start, dissention among the commissioners, some obfuscation, and many proposals somewhat out of touch with the temper of the times, many of its proposals were not found in the legislation eventually adopted. For a discussion of the Commission's recommendations on new value, and how they appear to have been reached, see Zinman, New Value and the Commission: *How Bizarre!*, 5 Am. Bankr. Inst. L. Rev. 477 (1997), especially footnotes 12-14.

4. If competing plans may be offered, will the court be required to pick the plan offering the highest bid? If courts find that a debtor's new value plan is "fair and equitable" (meets the requirements of absolute priority and can be confirmed), there is no requirement in the Bankruptcy Code that the court select a competing fair and equitable plan, even if it offers more. How do you interpret §1129(c) of the Bankruptcy Code, which provides, in part, that if two plans meet the requirements for confirmation, "the court shall consider the preferences of creditors and equity security holders in determining which plan to confirm"?

d. *Stripping the Mortgage Down or Off in Chapter 7: The Collision of Section 506(a) and (d).* As discussed above, §506(a) bifurcates the claim of an undersecured creditor into a secured claim equal to the value of the collateral and an unsecured claim for the difference between the value of the collateral and the amount of the indebtedness. Note 1, above, points out that without the conversion to recourse provided for by §1111(b), a *nonrecourse undersecured* creditor would have no unsecured claim in Chapter 11 (see definition of "claim," §101(5)) and thus would not receive the protection of absolute priority for its deficiency claim.

Section 1111(b), being part of Chapter 11, is not applicable in Chapter 7. But in Chapter 7 the mortgagee's claim is not normally nonrecourse. Thus, the bifurcation traditionally would not adversely affect the mortgagee (if there were equity in the debtor's nonexempt property, the Chapter 7 trustee would normally sell the property and the mortgagee would be paid out of the proceeds of the sale, and if there were no equity, the property would probably be abandoned by the trustee). Thus, it is said that the mortgage generally "rides through" Chapter 7.

Now enter §506(d). This subsection provides that to the extent a lien secures a claim against the debtor that is not an "allowed secured claim, such lien is void." Assume a $1 million mortgage. Assume the property subject to the mortgage has a §506(a) value of $800,000, which means the mortgagee has a secured claim for $800,000 and an unsecured claim for $200,000. The debtor asks the court to strip down the mortgage under §506(d) to $800,000 since the secured claim is only $800,000 and under §506(d) the lien for the $200,000 deficiency is void because it is not an allowed secured claim. (Most claims are deemed "allowed" under §502 and so the question was whether it was secured).

The debtor's argument sounds good. But such an argument was rejected in a roundly criticized Supreme Court decision, *Dewsnup v. Timm*, 502 U.S. 410 (1992). Relying on "policy considerations and its understanding of pre-Code practice," the Court held that notwithstanding §506(a), which says the deficiency claim is not a secured claim, "secured claim" in §506(d) has a different meaning than in §506(a). It means a "claim supported by a security interest in property, regardless of whether the value of that property would be sufficient to cover the claim." Thus the mortgage in our assumed situation would not be stripped down and mortgages would continue to ride through Chapter 7 relatively safely.

But now flash forward 23 years to 2015 when the Supreme Court confronted the issue again. In Bank of America v. Caulkett, 135 S. Ct. 1995 (2015), the debtor wished to void a junior mortgage under §506(d) where the senior mortgage debt exceeded the *entire value* of the property and the mortgage was totally underwater. In argument, it was clear that the Justices (including the late Justice Scalia, who authored a blistering dissent in *Dewsnup*) were highly critical of *Dewsnup* (the only remaining Justice on the Court who had been part of the majority in *Dewsnup* was Justice Kennedy). The Justices were confronted with a difficult choice: (i) overrule *Dewsnup* and impinge on the doctrine of stare decisis; (ii) limit *Dewsnup* to its facts—partially but not totally underwater mortgages, a distinction the Court seemed to agree did not make much sense; or (iii) find that *Dewsnup* applied to completely underwater mortgages as well as partially underwater mortgages, and set in stone a decision they apparently did not any longer support. In the end, the Court chose the third alternative and, in a decision authored by Justice Thomas, unanimously held that a Chapter 7 debtor could neither "strip-down" a partially underwater mortgage nor "strip off" a wholly underwater mortgage under §506(d). And so we have probably put to rest this issue and mortgages should continue to ride through Chapter 7 proceedings. But consider what unintended consequences the Supreme Court's definition of "secured claim" in *Caulkett* may have in other areas. If this confuses you, see. Problem 18-6 below.

e. *Stripping the Mortgage Down or Off in Chapter 13.* A debtor whose debts are less than $394,725 unsecured and $1,184,200 in secured obligations may file under Chapter 13 of the Code[40] to propose a reorganization plan. In these proceedings, however, §1322(b)(2), which provides that a Chapter 13 plan may modify the rights of secured creditors generally, carves out an exception to prevent modification of the "rights" of mortgagees with a security interest in the debtor's principal residence. What do you think was the Congressional purpose in inserting this protection for holders of residential mortgages? See our previous discussion of the Mortgage Meltdown in part B of this chapter.

The Supreme Court held that the carve-out of §1322(b)(2) protects both the secured and unsecured portions of the mortgagee's claim, thereby prohibiting a Chapter 13 debtor from reducing an undersecured mortgage to the fair market value of the principal residence. Nobleman v. American Sav. Bank, 508 U.S. 324 (1993). But see Hammond v. Commonwealth Mortgage Corp. of Am. (In re Hammond), 27 F.3d 52 (3d Cir. 1994) (§1322(b)(2) inapplicable when the mortgagee's security interest extends beyond principal residence to encompass personal property). As a result of *Nobleman*, then, it is clear that the carve-out protects the entire claim of the mortgage even if the mortgage is undersecured. Do you see that without the carve-out, Chapter 13 would otherwise permit the mortgage to be reduced to the value of the collateral without providing for fair and equitable absolute priority for the mortgagee's deficiency claim, leaving the

---

40. Dollar amounts under the Bankruptcy Code are subject to automatic change based on 11 U.S.C. 104(b) and promulgated by the Judicial Conference. The Chapter 13 limits described above are effective as of the drafting of this edition.

mortgagee under its unsecured claim only with payments to the extent of the debtor's disposable income for a period of up to five years?

But consider this situation. Suppose the mortgagee is completely underwater, for example a second mortgage on the debtor's principal residence where the first mortgage balance exceeds the value of the residence. Under §506(a) the second mortgagee would have no secured claim and its entire claim would be unsecured. The carve-out applies to a claim "secured only by a security interest in . . . the debtor's principal residence." After the application of §506(a), does the second mortgagee have a claim that is secured? Some courts have spoken out on this. Compare Am. General Finance, Inc. v. Dickerson, 229 B.R. 539 (M.D. Ga. 1999) with Zimmer v. PSB Lending Corp. (In re Zimmer), 313 F.3d 1220, 1227 (9th Cir. 2002); Pond v. Farm Specialist Realty (In re Pond), 252 F.3d 122, 126 (2d Cir. 2001).

> ➤ *Problem 18-6*
> Assume you represent the second mortgagee in the situation discussed above. The circuit court has ruled that because your client's underwater mortgage is completely unsecured, it is not protected by the §1322(d)(2) carve-out. The Supreme Court has granted certiorari. What arguments would you make on behalf of your client? Especially consider an argument based on the Court's holdings in *Dewsnup* and *Caulkett,* discussed in Note 5d above? ◄

For a more detailed analysis of the carve-out and cramdown under Chapter 13, and the constitutional issues involved, review our discussion of *Till* and see Zinman and Petrovski, The Home Mortgage and Chapter 13, An Essay on Unintended Consequences, 17 Am. Bankr. Inst. L. Rev. 133 (2009).

6. Classification of Claims. As you recall from the introduction to our discussion of "The Plan of Reorganization," one of the important requirements for confirmation found in §1129(a) is subsection (10), which specifies that no plan may be confirmed unless at least one class of impaired creditors approves the plan. While a plan may be imposed (crammed down) notwithstanding *rejection* by a class or classes of creditors voting pursuant to §1129(a)(8), as discussed above, under §1129(a)(10) the court has no power to consider cramdown if no impaired class *accepts* the plan. In single asset real estate cases, there are usually no creditors other than the mortgagee and a few trade creditors. Because the mortgagee's secured claim is in a class by itself, and its deficiency claim normally will dominate the unsecured class, there is little likelihood that any class will approve a plan over the mortgagee's objection.

It would thus be unlikely that any plan could get over the §1129(a)(10) threshold to the cramdown situations we have been discussing. So, how do they get there? As an attorney for Dan Developer in bankruptcy, can you think of an obvious solution? If your answer is: "Yes, put the unsecured trade creditors in a separate class of unsecured creditors and give that class more in the Plan than the trade creditors thought they would get (while being sure that they still are impaired by the plan). Then the trade creditor class will vote for the plan, meeting the requirement of §1129(a)(10), and we will be free to move for cramdown of our new value plan against the mortgagee deficiency unsecured class." If that is your answer, then you already think like a seasoned bankruptcy lawyer.

If your solution works and you can overcome §1129(a)(10) by simply putting a group of likely supporters in a separate unsecured class, does §1129(a)(10) have any meaning whatsoever? Have we effectively eliminated it from the Bankruptcy Code? A glance at §1122 of the Code, which deals with "Classification of claims or interests" is not much help. It clearly says that *only* "substantially similar" claims may be placed in the same class. It does not say that *all* similar claims must be placed in the same class. There are many interesting arguments that may be made on both sides of the issue based on other language in §1122, but none are especially conclusive. In 1991, the Fifth Circuit in Phoenix Mutual Life Ins. Co. v. Greystone III Joint Venture, 948 F.2d 134, rejected separate classification of similar claims except for reasons independent of §1129(a)(10). Judge Edith Hollan Jones agreed with the "one clear rule" that "thou shalt not classify similar claims differently in order to gerrymander an affirmative vote on a reorganization plan." *Greystone*, however, is not the last word on this. For an interesting debate on the issues involved, compare Rusch, Single Asset Cases and Chapter 11: The Classification Quandary, with Habert and Hoeffner, Classification of Undersecured Creditors' Deficiency Claims: No Gerrymandering, in Am. Bankr. Inst. and St. John's University, Single Asset Real Estate Bankruptcies, 177 and 219 (ABA 1997).

Observe that in *LaSalle* the debtor overcame the §1129(a)(10) hurdle by separately classifying trade debt. The issue of separate classification was not raised before the Court of Appeals, and so could not be argued at the Supreme Court level. Why was it not raised below? The answer may never be known. See comment by Rapisardi in A Roundtable Discussion: Supreme Court Decision in 203 N. LaSalle, 7 Am. Bankr. Inst. L. Rev. 389, 391-92 (1999).

7. Feasibility. Section 1129(a)(11) prohibits confirmation of a plan unless the court determines that confirmation is not likely to be followed by liquidation or the need for further financial reorganization. In other words, the court must be convinced that the plan is likely to succeed. This test must be met even if all the classes agree to accept the plan. However, there are no set rules for its application, which of necessity must be on a case-by-case basis. In In re Merrimack Valley Oil Co., 32 B.R. 485 (Bankr. D. Mass. 1983), the court noted that in making its determination it would consider the adequacy of the debtor's capital structure, the earning power of the business, economic conditions, and the ability of management. While somewhat vague, §1129(a)(11) represents an important tool for creditors to attack plans that are based on hopes not grounded in practicality.

8. Trustee or Debtor in Possession. Another area of controversy in drafting the Bankruptcy Code was whether there would be a requirement for a third-party trustee or whether the debtor could remain in possession during the bankruptcy proceeding. Section 1104 represents a compromise between real estate interests and those connected with corporate reorganizations. Under Chapter X (corporate reorganizations) of the old Bankruptcy Act, a trustee had always been appointed, while under Chapter XII (real property arrangement for noncorporate debtors) the debtor had almost always remained in possession. Perhaps on the "grass is always greener" theory, corporate reorganization people urged that the Code specify that the debtor be left in possession rather than have a trustee appointed (as a result of unfortunate experiences under Chapter X where competent management was replaced with trustees who knew little about the business), and real estate mortgagees (having seen debtors whose mismanagement had caused the debacle left in possession to milk the property of any value that was left) urged that a trustee always be appointed.

The §1104 compromise between these two points of view gives the judge the discretion to choose. Specifically, §1104 initially opts for the debtor-in-possession but provides that, on request of a party in interest, "the court shall order the appointment of a trustee" either "for cause, including fraud, dishonesty, incompetence or gross mismanagement" or because "such appointment is in the interests of creditors, any equity security holders, and other interests of the estate." As an alternative to the appointment of a trustee, the court may, among other things, under circumstances set forth in §1104(b), order the appointment of an examiner to investigate allegations against the debtor. The debtor in possession generally has the same powers as a trustee (§1107).

9. Additional Reading. Ayer, Rethinking Absolute Priority after *Ahlers*, 87 Mich. L. Rev. 963 (1989); Broude, Cram Down and Chapter 11 of the Bankruptcy Code: The Settlement Imperative, 39 Bus. Law. 441 (1984); Elson, Say "Ahhh": A New Approach For Determining the Cram Down Interest Rate After Till v. SCS Credit, 27 Cardozo L. Rev. 1921 (2005); Fortgang and Mayer, Valuation in Bankruptcy, 32 UCLA L. Rev. 1061 (1985); Gaynor, Impairment, 3 Bankr. Dev. J. 579 (1986); Gangemi & Bordanaro, The New Value Exception: Square Peg in a Round Hole, 1 Am. Bankr. Inst. L. Rev. 173 (1993); Greenspan et al., "UnTill" We Meet Again: Why the Till Decision Might Not Be the Final Word on Cramdown Interest Rates, Am. Bankr. Inst. J., January 2005, at 12; Halligan, Cramdown Interest, Contract Damages, and Classical Economic Theory, 11 Am. Bankr. Inst. L. Rev. 131 (2003); Klee, All You Ever Wanted to Know about Cramdown, 53 Am. Bankr. L.J. 133 (1979); Kuney, Misinterpreting Bankruptcy Code Section 363(f) and Undermining the Chapter 11 Process, 76 Am. Bankr. L.J. 235 (2002); Lewis, 203 N. LaSalle Five Years Later: Answers to the Open Questions, 38 J. Marshall L. Rev. 61, (2004); MacDonald, Schreiber and MacDonald, Confirmation by Cramdown Through the New Value Exception in Single Asset Cases, 1 Am. Bankr. Inst. L. Rev. 65 (1993); Markell, Owners, Auctions and Absolute Priority in Bankruptcy Reorganizations, 44 Stan. L. Rev.

69 (1991); O'Donnell, Toward a Better Understanding of New Value, 108 Penn. St. L. Rev. 703 (2004); Stein, Section 1111(b): Providing Undersecured Creditors with Postconfirmation Appreciation in the Value of the Collateral, 56 Am. Bankr. L.J. 195 (1982); Zinman, New Value and the Commission: How Bizarre!, 5 Am. Bankr. Inst. L. Rev. 477 (1997); Zywicki, Cramdown and the Code: Calculating Cramdown Interest Rates Under the Bankruptcy Code, 19 J. Marshall L. Rev. 241 (1994).

D.   FRAUDULENT TRANSFER LAW AND REAL ESTATE TRANSACTIONS

Assume that Dan Developer owns a parcel of property and that he has suffered a significant adverse change in his financial condition. Concerned that creditors may obtain judgments and levy on his property, Dan executes and records a "mortgage" against the property in favor of his brother-in-law. When the creditors start closing in, Dan deliberately defaults under the mortgage. His brother-in-law forecloses, buys the property at the foreclosure sale by bidding in the purported mortgage balance, and transfers the property to a corporation of which Dan Developer is president. Can Dan Developer get away with this scheme to put his property out of the reach of his creditors?[41]

The answer, of course, is a resounding no. Ever since 1570, when England first codified the developing law of fraudulent conveyances in what was to become known as the Statute of 13 Elizabeth,[42] any transfer of property with the intent to "delay, hinder, or defraud creditors and others," was void. The voiding of the example above is clearly appropriate and should not trouble the real estate community. On the other hand, when fraudulent transfer law is used in inventive ways to void the normal and proper real estate transactions discussed in this volume, there is very great concern among real estate practitioners. We look below at some imaginative uses of the law of fraudulent transfers, whether they are appropriate, and how they have been dealt with by the courts. First, let's look at the essentials of fraudulent transfer law.

1. *The Development of Fraudulent Transfer Law*

The Statute of 13 Elizabeth, which we applied to the example above, has served as a model for English and American fraudulent transfer laws. Beginning in 1800

---

41. Cf. Leftkowitz v. Finkelstein Trading Corp., 74 F. Supp. 898 (S.D.N.Y. 1936).

42. 13 Eliz. ch. 5, §§I-II (1570). That statute provided in part that "covinous and fraudulent feoffments, gifts, grants, alienations, conveyances, bonds, suits, judgments and executions ... devised and contrived of malice, fraud, covin, collusion or guile, to the end, purpose and intent, to delay, hinder or defraud creditors and others ... shall be ... utterly void, frustrate and of none effect."

with the first bankruptcy law of the United States,[43] language with origins in the Statute of 13 Elizabeth was incorporated into the avoidance provisions of each bankruptcy statute. It is now found in §548 of the Bankruptcy Code as well as in state fraudulent transfer statutes.

Statute of 13 Elizabeth dealt only with transactions *intended* to hinder, delay, or defraud creditors; it made no mention of "constructive" fraud. It did not take long after the enactment of the statute, however, for the courts to realize that persons intending to commit fraud do not normally publicize their intent. Thus, to implement fraudulent transfer law, it became necessary to look to the circumstances surrounding the transfer to see if the necessary intent existed. In Twyne's Case,[44] Lord Coke recognized "signs or marks," later known as "badges," of fraud, that is, conduct or circumstances that could be evidence of fraudulent intent. Examples of badges of fraud include transfers of all of the debtor's property; transfers without a change of possession; a close relationship between the transferor and transferee; insolvency at the time of transfer; and inadequate consideration received in exchange for the property transferred. When a sufficient number of badges of fraud existed, the courts would find a presumption of fraud. The problem was that different courts recognized different badges and different combinations of badges to produce the presumption.

When the National Conference of Commissioners on Uniform State Laws wrote the Uniform Fraudulent Conveyance Act (UFCA) (approved in 1918), the drafters did not include any badges or presumptions of fraud. In their place the drafters included constructive frauds by grouping together certain of the former badges into a few specific sections of the Act. When the circumstances outlined in these sections were present (for example, conveyances or incurrence of debt without fair consideration when the debtor was insolvent or rendered insolvent), fraud was found without a determination of the actual intent of the parties. This is the same approach taken in §548 of the Bankruptcy Code and under the UFCA's immediate successor, the Uniform Fraudulent Transfer Act (UFTA).[45]

2. Mortgage Foreclosures as Constructively Fraudulent Transfers

Returning to the master hypothetical, assume Ace makes its mortgage loan when Dan is prosperous. Some years later, Dan suffers financial adversity and defaults on the payment of the debt service (principal and interest) under the mortgage.

---

43. Bankruptcy Act of 1800, ch. 19, §17.

44. 3 Coke Rep. 80b, 76 Eng. Rep. 809 (K.B. 1601).

45. A U.L.A. 643 (1985). As of this writing, the UFTA has been adopted in 46 jurisdictions. The UFTA, in §4, partially sets forth certain badges of fraud for the purpose of determining whether intentional fraud exists. The UFTA was updated by the Commissioners in 2014, in the course of which the name of the Act was changed to the Uniform Voidable Transactions Act. The new name describes more accurately what the UFTA deals with (for example, incurrence of obligations as well as transfers of property), and eliminates the necessity of distinguishing between "actual" fraud and "constructive" fraud. As of this writing the 2014 amendments have been adopted in eight jurisdictions.

Ace forecloses and is the successful bidder at the foreclosure sale, having bid the mortgage balance of $15 million. There is no collusion in connection with this sale, which is conducted in accordance with the law of the State of Fuller, where the property is located. The next year Dan files in bankruptcy. Dan's trustee in bankruptcy claims that the true value of Dan's property at the time of the foreclosure sale was $22 million and that the foreclosure sale was a fraudulent transfer. Look at §548(a)(1) and determine what elements of constructive fraud may exist here? Can the trustee succeed in voiding the foreclosure?

In 1980, the Fifth Circuit, in Durrett v. Washington National Ins. Co., for the first time since constructive fraud was inserted in the UFCA in 1918,[46] found that a noncollusive, regularly conducted foreclosure sale could be set aside as a constructively fraudulent conveyance where a court determined that the price paid at the foreclosure sale was less than reasonably equivalent to the value of the property and that the debtor was insolvent at that time. *Durrett* was decided under the constructive fraud provisions of the old Bankruptcy Act that correspond to §548(a)(1) of the Bankruptcy Code, which currently proscribes, inter alia, any transfer by an insolvent debtor within two years[47] prior to bankruptcy for less than a reasonably equivalent value. *Durrett* stirred up a great controversy. Concerns were soon raised that *Durrett* and its progeny not only could threaten the future of mortgage financing but, if left to develop unchecked, could have a substantial negative impact on all forms of secured financing and other real estate transactions. Others described *Durrett* as "properly sensitive to the policy underlying §548 of the Bankruptcy Code.[48]

In reaction to *Durrett*, the UFTA, which was adopted by the Uniform Laws Commissioners in 1984 to replace its 1918 UFCA, rejected *Durrett* in the following language:[49]

Section 3(b)

[A] person gives a reasonably equivalent value if the person acquires an interest of the debtor in an asset pursuant to a regularly conducted, noncollusive foreclosure

---

46. 621 F.2d 201 (5th Cir. 1980). Professor Frank Kennedy had argued that "the '*Durrett* doctrine' is not so novel" as its critics claim. See Kennedy, Involuntary Fraudulent Transfers, 9 Cardozo L. Rev. 531, 532 (1987). His conclusions were disputed in Zinman, Noncollusive, Regularly Conducted Foreclosure Sales: Involuntary Nonfraudulent Transfers, 9 Cardozo L. Rev. 581, 584 (1987).

47. The reachback period was extended in the 2005 BAPCPA amendments from one year to two years. 11 U.S.C. §548(a)(1).

48. Alden, Gross, and Borowitz, Real Property Foreclosure as a Fraudulent Conveyance: Proposals for Solving the Durrett Problem, 38 Bus. Law. 1605, 1610 (1983). This position was contested in Zinman, Houle, and Weiss, Fraudulent Transfers According to Alden, Gross, and Borowitz: A Tale of Two Circuits, 39 Bus. Law. 977 (1984).

49. The Uniform Land Security Interest Act (ULSIA) also abrogates the *Durrett* rule on the state level. See ULSIA §512(c), which provides that "[a] regularly conducted, noncollusive transfer under a power of sale (Section 509) or by judicial sale (Section 510) to a transferee who takes for value and in good faith is not a fraudulent transfer even though the value given is less than the value of the debtor's interest in the real estate."

sale or execution of a power of sale for the acquisition or disposition of the interest of the debtor upon default under a mortgage, deed of trust or security agreement.

While the UFTA (not the UFCA) had thus retreated from the *Durrett* rule, Congress did not amend the language of §548 of the Bankruptcy Code. Those federal circuit courts considering the application of §548 to noncollusive, regularly conducted foreclosure sales were in great conflict on whether to adopt, reject, or modify the *Durrett* rule. When the issue finally reached the Supreme Court in 1994 in a case involving California property on coveted Lido Isle foreclosed by power-of-sale, mortgage lenders expected the worst, but were pleasantly surprised.

BFP v. Resolution Trust Corp.
511 U.S. 531 (1994)

Justice SCALIA delivered the opinion of the Court.

This case presents the question whether the consideration received from a noncollusive, real estate mortgage foreclosure sale conducted in conformance with applicable state law conclusively satisfies the Bankruptcy Code's requirement that transfers of property by insolvent debtors within one year[50] prior to the filing of a bankruptcy petition be in exchange for "a reasonably equivalent value." 11 U.S.C. §548(a)(2).

I

Petitioner BFP is a partnership, formed by Wayne and Marlene Pedersen and Russell Barton in 1987, for the purpose of buying a home in Newport Beach, California, from Sheldon and Ann Foreman. Petitioner took title subject to a first deed of trust in favor of Imperial Savings Association (Imperial)[1] to secure payment of a loan of $356,250 made to the Pedersens in connection with petitioner's acquisition of the home. Petitioner granted a second deed of trust to the Foremans as security for a $200,000 promissory note. Subsequently, Imperial, whose loan was not being serviced, entered a notice of default under the first deed of trust and scheduled a properly noticed foreclosure sale. . . . Imperial's foreclosure proceeding was completed at a foreclosure sale on July 12, 1989. The home was purchased by respondent Paul Osborne for $433,000.

In October 1989, petitioner filed for bankruptcy under Chapter 11 of the Bankruptcy Code, 11 U.S.C. §§1101-1174. Acting as a debtor in possession, petitioner filed a complaint in bankruptcy court seeking to set aside the

---

50. See *supra* note 47, and accompanying text.

1. Respondent Resolution Trust Corporation (RTC) acts in this case as receiver of Imperial Federal Savings Association....

conveyance of the home to respondent Osborne on the grounds that the foreclosure sale constituted a fraudulent transfer under §548 of the Code, 11 U.S.C. §548. Petitioner alleged that the home was actually worth over $725,000 at the time of the sale to Osborne. . . . The bankruptcy court found, inter alia, that the foreclosure sale had been conducted in compliance with California law and was neither collusive nor fraudulent. . . . A divided bankruptcy appellate panel affirmed the bankruptcy court's entry of summary judgment for Imperial [and was affirmed by the Ninth Circuit]. . . .

II

Section 548 of the Bankruptcy Code, 11 U.S.C. §548, sets forth the powers of a trustee in bankruptcy (or, in a Chapter 11 case, a debtor in possession) to avoid fraudulent transfers. It permits to be set aside not only transfers infected by actual fraud but certain other transfers as well—so-called constructively fraudulent transfers. The constructive fraud provision at issue in this case applies to transfers by insolvent debtors. It permits avoidance if the trustee can establish (1) that the debtor had an interest in property; (2) that a transfer of that interest occurred within one year [now two years] of the filing of the bankruptcy petition; (3) that the debtor was insolvent at the time of the transfer or became insolvent as a result thereof; and (4) that the debtor received "less than a reasonably equivalent value in exchange for such transfer." 11 U.S.C. §548(a)(2)(A). It is the last of these four elements that presents the issue in the case before us.

Section 548 applies to any "transfer," which includes "foreclosure of the debtor's equity of redemption." 11 U.S.C. §101(54) (1988 ed., Supp. IV). Of the three critical terms "reasonably equivalent value," only the last is defined: "value" means, for purposes of §548, "property, or satisfaction or securing of a . . . debt of the debtor," 11 U.S.C. §548(d)(2)(A). The question presented here, therefore, is whether the amount of debt (to the first and second lien holders) satisfied at the foreclosure sale (viz., a total of $433,000) is "reasonably equivalent" to the worth of the real estate conveyed. The Courts of Appeals have divided on the meaning of those undefined terms. In Durrett v. Washington Nat. Ins. Co., 621 F.2d 201 (1980), the Fifth Circuit, interpreting a provision of the old Bankruptcy Act analogous to §548(a)(2), held that a foreclosure sale that yielded 57 percent of the property's fair market value could be set aside, and indicated in dicta that any such sale for less than 70 percent of fair market value should be invalidated. This "*Durrett* rule" has continued to be applied by some courts under §548 of the new Bankruptcy Code. See In re Littleton, 888 F.2d 90, 92, n.5 (CA11 1989). In In re Bundles, 856 F.2d 815, 820 (1988), the Seventh Circuit rejected the *Durrett* rule in favor of a case-by-case, "all facts and circumstances" approach to the question of reasonably equivalent value, with a rebuttable presumption that the foreclosure sale price is sufficient to withstand attack under §548(a)(2). In this case the Ninth Circuit, agreeing with the Sixth Circuit, see In re Winshall Settlor's Trust, 758 F.2d 1136, 1139 (CA6 1985), adopted the position first put forward in In re Madrid, 21 B.R. 424 (Bkrtcy. App. Pan. CA9 1982), affirmed on other grounds, 725 F.2d 1197 (CA9), cert. denied, 469 U.S. 833, 105 S. Ct. 125, 83 L. Ed. 2d 66 (1984), that the consideration received at a noncollusive, regularly conducted real estate foreclosure sale constitutes a reasonably equivalent value under §548(a)(2)(A). The Court of Appeals acknowledged that it "necessarily part[ed] from the positions taken by the Fifth Circuit in *Durrett* . . . and the Seventh Circuit in *Bundles*."

In contrast to the approach adopted by the Ninth Circuit in the present case, both *Durrett* and *Bundles* refer to fair market value as the benchmark against which determination of reasonably equivalent value is to be measured. In the context of an otherwise lawful mortgage foreclosure sale of real estate,[3] such reference is in our opinion not consistent with the text of the Bankruptcy Code. The term "fair market value," though it is a well-established concept, does not appear in §548. In contrast, §522, dealing with a debtor's exemptions, specifically provides that, for purposes of that section, "'value' means fair market value as of the date of the filing of the petition." 11 U.S.C. §522(a)(2). "Fair market value" also appears in the Code provision that defines the extent to which indebtedness with respect to an equity security is not forgiven for the purpose of determining whether the debtor's estate has realized taxable income. §346(j)(7)(B). Section 548, on the other hand, seemingly goes out of its way to avoid that standard term. It might readily have said "received less than fair market value in exchange for such transfer or obligation," or perhaps "less than a reasonable equivalent of fair market value." Instead, it used the (as far as we are aware) entirely novel phrase "reasonably equivalent value." "[I]t is generally presumed that Congress acts intentionally and purposely when it includes particular language in one section of a statute but omits it in another," Chicago v. Environmental Defense Fund, . . . 114 S. Ct. 1588, 1593 . . . (1994) (internal quotation marks omitted), and that presumption is even stronger when the omission entails the replacement of standard legal terminology with a neologism. One must suspect the language means that fair market value cannot—or at least cannot always—be the benchmark.

That suspicion becomes a certitude when one considers that market value, as it is commonly understood, has no applicability in the forced-sale context; indeed, it is the very antithesis of forced-sale value. "The market value of . . . a piece of property is the price which it might be expected to bring if offered for sale in a fair market; not the price which might be obtained on a sale at public auction or a sale forced by the necessities of the owner, but such a price as would be fixed by negotiation and mutual agreement, after ample time to find a purchaser, as between a vendor who is willing (but not compelled) to sell and a purchaser who desires to buy but is not compelled to take the particular . . . piece of property." Black's Law Dictionary 971 (6th ed. 1990). In short, "fair market

---

3. We emphasize that our opinion today covers only mortgage foreclosures of real estate. The considerations bearing upon other foreclosures and forced sales (to satisfy tax liens, for example) may be different.

value" presumes market conditions that, by definition, simply do not obtain in the context of a forced sale. . . .

There is another artificially constructed criterion we might look to instead of "fair market price." One might judge there to be such a thing as a "reasonable" or "fair" forced-sale price. Such a conviction must lie behind the *Bundles* inquiry into whether the state foreclosure proceedings "were calculated . . . to return to the debtor-mortgagor his equity in the property." 856 F.2d, at 824. And perhaps that is what the courts that follow the *Durrett* rule have in mind when they select 70 percent of fair market value as the outer limit of "reasonably equivalent value" for forecloseable property (we have no idea where else such an arbitrary percentage could have come from). The problem is that such judgments represent policy determinations which the Bankruptcy Code gives us no apparent authority to make. How closely the price received in a forced sale is likely to approximate fair market value depends upon the terms of the forced sale—how quickly it may be made, what sort of public notice must be given, etc. But the terms for foreclosure sale are not standard. They vary considerably from State to State, depending upon, among other things, how the particular State values the divergent interests of debtor and creditor. To specify a federal "reasonable" foreclosure-sale price is to extend federal bankruptcy law well beyond the traditional field of fraudulent transfers, into realms of policy where it has not ventured before. Some sense of history is needed to appreciate this.

The modern law of fraudulent transfers had its origin in the Statute of 13 Elizabeth, which invalidated "covinous and fraudulent" transfers designed "to delay, hinder or defraud creditors and others." 13 Eliz., ch. 5 (1570). English courts soon developed the doctrine of "badges of fraud": proof by a creditor of certain objective facts (for example, a transfer to a close relative, a secret transfer, a transfer of title without transfer of possession, or grossly inadequate consideration) would raise a rebuttable presumption of actual fraudulent intent. See Twyne's Case, 3 Coke Rep. 80b, 76 Eng. Rep. 809 (K.B. 1601); O. Bump, Fraudulent Conveyances: A Treatise upon Conveyances Made by Debtors to Defraud Creditors 31-60 (3d ed. 1882). Every American bankruptcy law has incorporated a fraudulent transfer provision; the 1898 Act specifically adopted the language of the Statute of 13 Elizabeth. Bankruptcy Act of July 1, 1898, ch. 541, §67(e), 30 Stat. 564-565.

The history of foreclosure law also begins in England, where courts of chancery developed the "equity of redemption"—the equitable right of a borrower to buy back, or redeem, property conveyed as security by paying the secured debt on a later date than "law day," the original due date. The courts' continued expansion of the period of redemption left lenders in a quandary, since title to forfeited property could remain clouded for years after law day. To meet this problem, courts created the equitable remedy of foreclosure: after a certain date the borrower would be forever foreclosed from exercising his equity of redemption. This remedy was called strict foreclosure because the borrower's entire interest in the property was forfeited, regardless of any accumulated equity. See G. Glenn, 1 Mortgages 3-18, 358-362, 395-406 (1943); G. Osborne,

Mortgages 144 (2d ed. 1970). The next major change took place in 19th century America, with the development of foreclosure by sale (with the surplus over the debt refunded to the debtor) as a means of avoiding the draconian consequences of strict foreclosure. Since then, the States have created diverse networks of judicially and legislatively crafted rules governing the foreclosure process, to achieve what each of them considers the proper balance between the needs of lenders and borrowers. All States permit judicial foreclosure, conducted under direct judicial oversight; about half of the States also permit foreclosure by exercising a private power of sale provided in the mortgage [or deed of trust] documents. See Zinman, Houle, & Weiss, Fraudulent Transfers According to Alden, Gross and Borowitz: A Tale of Two Circuits, 39 Bus. Law. 977, 1004-1005 (1984). Foreclosure laws typically require notice to the defaulting borrower, a substantial lead time before the commencement of foreclosure proceedings, publication of a notice of sale, and strict adherence to prescribed bidding rules and auction procedures. Many States require that the auction be conducted by a government official, and some forbid the property to be sold for less than a specified fraction of a mandatory presale fair-market-value appraisal. See id., at 1002, 1004-1005; Osborne, supra, at 683, 733-735; G. Osborne, G. Nelson, & D. Whitman, Real Estate Finance Law 9, 446-447, 475-477 (1979). When these procedures have been followed, however, it is "black letter" law that mere inadequacy of the foreclosure sale price is no basis for setting the sale aside, though it may be set aside (under state foreclosure law, rather than fraudulent transfer law) if the price is so low as to "shock the conscience or raise a presumption of fraud or unfairness." Osborne, Nelson, & Whitman, supra, at 469; see also Gelfert v. National City Bank of New York, 313 U.S. 221, 232 (1941); Ballentyne v. Smith, 205 U.S. 285, 290 (1907).

Fraudulent transfer law and foreclosure law enjoyed over 400 years of peaceful coexistence in Anglo-American jurisprudence until the Fifth Circuit's unprecedented 1980 decision in *Durrett*. To our knowledge no prior decision had ever applied the "grossly inadequate price" badge of fraud under fraudulent transfer law to set aside a foreclosure sale. To say that the "reasonably equivalent value" language in the fraudulent transfer provision of the Bankruptcy Code requires a foreclosure sale to yield a certain minimum price beyond what state foreclosure law requires, is to say, in essence, that the Code has adopted *Durrett* or *Bundles*. Surely Congress has the power pursuant to its constitutional grant of authority over bankruptcy, U.S. Const., Art. I, §8, cl. 4, to disrupt the ancient harmony that foreclosure law and fraudulent-conveyance law, those two pillars of debtor-creditor jurisprudence, have heretofore enjoyed. But absent clearer textual guidance than the phrase "reasonably equivalent value"—a phrase entirely compatible with pre-existing practice—we will not presume such a radical departure. [C]f. United States v. Texas, 507 U.S. [529], 113 S. Ct. 1631, 1634, 123 L. Ed. 2d 245 (1993) (statutes that invade common law must be read with presumption favoring retention of long-established principles absent evident statutory purpose to the contrary).[7]

Federal statutes impinging upon important state interests "cannot . . . be construed without regard to the implications of our dual system of government. [W]hen the Federal Government takes over . . . local radiations in the vast network of our national economic enterprise and thereby radically readjusts the balance of state and national authority, those charged with the duty of legislating [must be] reasonably explicit." F. Frankfurter, Some Reflections on the Reading of Statutes, 47 Colum. L. Rev. 527, 539-540 (1947). . . . It is beyond question that an essential state interest is at issue here: we have said that "the general welfare of society is involved in the security of the titles to real estate" and the power to ensure that security "inheres in the very nature of [state] government." American Land Co. v. Zeiss, 219 U.S. 47, 60 (1911). Nor is there any doubt that the interpretation urged by petitioner would have a profound effect upon that interest: the title of every piece of realty purchased at foreclosure would be under a federally created cloud. (Already, title insurers have reacted to the *Durrett* rule by including specially crafted exceptions from coverage in many policies issued for properties purchased at foreclosure sales. See, for example, L. Cherkis & L. King, Collier Real Estate Transactions and the Bankruptcy Code 5-18 to 5-19 (1992).) To displace traditional State regulation in such a manner, the federal statutory purpose must be "clear and manifest.". . . Otherwise, the Bankruptcy Code will be construed to adopt, rather than to displace, pre-existing state law. . .

For the reasons described, we decline to read the phrase "reasonably equivalent value" in §548(a)(2) to mean, in its application to mortgage foreclosure sales, either "fair market value" or "fair foreclosure price" (whether calculated as a percentage of fair market value or otherwise). We deem, as the law has always deemed, that a fair and proper price, or a "reasonably equivalent value," for foreclosed property, is the price in fact received at the foreclosure

---

7. We are unpersuaded by petitioner's argument that the 1984 amendments to the Bankruptcy Code codified the *Durrett* rule. Those amendments expanded the definition of "transfer" to include "foreclosure of the debtor's equity of redemption," 11 U.S.C. §101(54) (1988 ed., Supp. IV), and added the words "voluntarily or involuntarily" as modifiers of the term "transfer" in §548(a). The first of these provisions establishes that foreclosure sales fall within the general definition of "transfers" that may be avoided under several statutory provisions, including (but not limited to) §548. See §522(h) (transfers of exempt property), §544 (transfers voidable under state law), §547 (preferential transfers), §549 (postpetition transfers). The second of them establishes that a transfer may be avoided as fraudulent even if it was against the debtor's will. See In re Madrid, 725 F.2d 1197, 1199 (CA91984) (pre-amendment decision holding that a foreclosure sale is not a "transfer" under §548). Neither of these consequences has any bearing upon the meaning of "reasonably equivalent value" in the context of a foreclosure sale. Nor does our reading render these amendments "superfluous," as the dissent contends. Prior to 1984, it was at least open to question whether §548 could be used to invalidate even a collusive foreclosure sale, see *Madrid*, 725 F.2d, at 1204 (Farris, J., concurring). It is no superfluity for Congress to clarify what had been at best unclear, which is what it did here by making the provision apply to involuntary as well as voluntary transfers and by including foreclosures within the definition of "transfer."

sale, so long as all the requirements of the State's foreclosure law have been complied with.

This conclusion does not render §548(a)(2) superfluous, since the "reasonably equivalent value" criterion will continue to have independent meaning (ordinarily a meaning similar to fair market value) outside the foreclosure context. Indeed, §548(a)(2) will even continue to be an exclusive means of invalidating some foreclosure sales. Although collusive foreclosure sales are likely subject to attack under §548(a)(1), which authorizes the trustee to avoid transfers "made . . . with actual intent to hinder, delay, or defraud" creditors, that provision may not reach foreclosure sales that, while not intentionally fraudulent, nevertheless fail to comply with all governing state laws. . . . Any irregularity in the conduct of the sale that would permit judicial invalidation of the sale under applicable state law deprives the sale price of its conclusive force under §548(a)(2)(A), and the transfer may be avoided if the price received was not reasonably equivalent to the property's actual value at the time of the sale (which we think would be the price that would have been received if the foreclosure sale had proceeded according to law).

Justice SOUTER, with whom Justice BLACKMUN, Justice STEVENS, and Justice GINSBURG join, dissenting.

The Court today holds that by the terms of the Bankruptcy Code Congress intended a peppercorn paid at a noncollusive and procedurally regular foreclosure sale to be treated as the "reasonabl[e] equivalent" of the value of a California beach-front estate. Because the Court's reasoning fails both to overcome the implausibility of that proposition and to justify engrafting a foreclosure-sale exception onto 11 U.S.C. §548(a)(2)(A), in derogation of the straightforward language used by Congress, I respectfully dissent. . . .

NOTES AND QUESTIONS

1. BFP v. Resolution Trust Corp. In his dissent, Justice Souter commented that the Court's opinion sanctioned the purchase of property in a regularly conducted foreclosure sale for a mere "peppercorn." Do you agree? What did the majority say? At Chapter 8C3c we examined the standard in equity for overturning sales when the bid shocks the court's conscience. Would that standard tolerate a "peppercorn" bid?

2. Did Durrett *Die?* The *BFP* decision does not insulate a foreclosure sale that is collusive or that does not comply with the requirements of applicable state foreclosure law. What constitutes collusion? See Stark, The Emperor Still Has Clothes: Fraudulent Conveyance Challenges after the *BFP* Decision, 47 S.C. L. Rev. 563, 575-583 (1996).

The majority opinion concludes that "[a]ny irregularity in the conduct of the sale that would permit judicial invalidation of the sale under applicable state law deprives the sale price of its conclusive force under §548(a)(2)(A), and the transfer may be avoided if the price received was not reasonably equivalent to the property's actual value at the time of the sale (which we think would be the price that would have been received if the foreclosure sale had proceeded according to law)." Does this conflict with the thrust of the opinion that a reasonable foreclosure sale value should not be determined by the federal courts and that "[t]o specify a federal 'reasonable' foreclosure-sale price is to extend federal bankruptcy law well beyond the traditional field of fraudulent transfers, into realms of policy where it has not ventured before"?

3. The Scope of BFP. Footnote 3 of the *BFP* decision limits its reach to mortgage foreclosures of real estate. Although *BFP* involved an attack on a nonjudicial sale pursuant to a deed of trust, it should encompass both deeds of trust and mortgages whether foreclosed judicially or by power of sale. Moreover, some bankruptcy courts have extended the holding in *BFP* to the forfeiture of a vendee's interest under an installment land contract. Do you think the holding is so extendable? Compare McCanna v. Burke, 197 B.R. 333 (Bankr. D.N.M. 1996); Vermillion v. Scarbrough (In re Vermillion), 176 B.R. 563 (Bankr. D. Or. 1994), with Dunbar v. Johnson (In re Grady), 202 B.R. 120 (Bankr. N.D. Iowa 1996). What difference in procedure between forfeiture and a mortgage foreclosure might provide a basis for distinguishing *BFP* from the installment land contract situation?

Do you think that the reasoning in *BFP* should extend to protect deeds in lieu of foreclosure from invalidation in bankruptcy as a fraudulent transfer if the value of the property conveyed disproportionately exceeds the loan balance that is forgiven? See Stark at 610 n.235. One commentator has suggested that it is unclear whether *BFP* laid *Durrett* to rest because *BFP* involved a third-party purchaser at the foreclosure sale and did not consider the case of a mortgagee purchasing at its own sale. See Geis, Escape from the 15th Century: The Uniform Land Security Interest Act, 30 Real Prop., Prob. & Tr. J. 289, 313 (Summer 1995). Should that make a difference?

From footnote 3 in *BFP*, it is apparent that the Court is not addressing the issue of the application of §548 of the Bankruptcy Code to forced sales other than mortgage foreclosures. What arguments can you make that the holding in *BFP* should or should not apply to tax sales or execution sales to satisfy judgment liens?

4. The Reachback Period. Under §548, the fraudulent transfer must occur within two years before the commencement of the bankruptcy for the trustee to bring an action to set it aside. However, under state fraudulent transfer law, any creditor can move to set aside a transfer within the limit set by the state statute of limitations for fraud (or any state mandated expiration of the cause of action), which almost always exceeds two years. See, for example, the statute of limitation applicable under New York's UFCA (N.Y. C.P.L.R. §213) which imposes a six-year limit. Section 544(b) of the Bankruptcy Code provides that the trustee in bankruptcy may avoid any transfer of an interest of the debtor that is voidable under applicable (state) law by a creditor holding an unsecured claim. Do you see how this section enables the trustee in bankruptcy to use state law rather than the Bankruptcy Code to extend the reachback period to the longer state statute of limitations?

Unlike the UFCA, which does not specify any limitation, leaving that to the state statute of limitations for fraud, the UFTA, with one exception, extinguishes the fraudulent transfer cause of action four years after the transfer has taken place. See UFTA §9. Can you figure out why the drafters chose to make the cause of action expire rather than rely on the state statute of limitations? A look at United States v. Gleneagles Inv. Co., 565 F. Supp. 556 (M.D. Pa. 1983) will give you a clue.

5. *Consequences of Finding a Fraudulent Transfer.* Section 550(a) of the Bankruptcy Code provides that where a transfer is held to be fraudulent the trustee may recover the property or the value of the property (for example, in foreclosure sales, the court-determined value of the property less the amount bid at the foreclosure sale) from the initial transferee (the purchaser at the foreclosure sale) but has no recovery against a "good faith" purchaser *from* that initial transferee.

If the court chooses to recover the property from the initial transferee who had acted in good faith, §548(c) provides that such transferee obtains a lien on the property recovered by the trustee equal to the sale price paid. In addition, §550(d) provides that the good faith initial transferee is entitled to a lien for any increase in value (not exceeding costs) resulting from improvements made by the transferee before reconveyance to the bankruptcy estate.

Thus, good faith plays a significant role in determining the consequences of a fraudulent transfer, both for the initial transferee, such as the purchaser at the foreclosure sale, and for any later purchaser from that purchaser. Unfortunately, there is no definition of "good faith" in the Code. The original Commission on the Bankruptcy Laws of the United States concluded that it would leave the interpretation of "good faith" to the courts on a case-by-case basis. See Report of the Commission on the Bankruptcy Laws of the United States, Part II, 180 H. Doc. No. 93137 (July 1973). This conclusion was apparently followed by the drafters of the Code. See generally Ordin, The Good Faith Principle in the Bankruptcy Code: A Case Study, 38 Bus. Law. 1795 (1983).

3. *Termination of Leases as Constructively Fraudulent Transfers*

Assume that Dan Developer entered into a long-term lease of several floors in his building to Widget Corporation of America (WCA) at $25 a square foot. When widgets fell out of favor some years later, WCA defaulted in payment of rent, and the lease was terminated. At the time of the lease termination, the going market rental for this type of property in this community was $30 a square foot.

Recall the income capitalization method of valuing real estate described at Chapter 4D1. Do you see why the below market rent has an adverse effect on the value of Dan's fee interest, but will raise the value of WCA's leasehold estate? The tenant could realize on the increase in leasehold value through an assignment or mortgage loan, assuming the lease permitted this. Thus from Dan's prospective, eliminating the lease would increase his property value because the premises could then be leased to another tenant at a much higher rent. Suppose Dan does terminate the lease because of the default, and a few months later, WCA files in bankruptcy. An action is brought to set aside the termination of the lease as a fraudulent transfer.

Can you figure out how the lease termination could be considered a fraudulent transfer? Is it that the termination of the lease represents a reconveyance of the leasehold estate from WCA to Dan for less than a reasonably equivalent value while WCA was insolvent? Remember Justice Scalia's discussion in footnote 7 in *BFP* concerning the 1984 amendment to §548 of the Bankruptcy Code to make it clear that a transfer may be fraudulent even if it is made involuntarily? Isn't it clear that the value of the leasehold Dan received was much greater than the value of the stream of income from WCA?

The origin of this idea actually antedates *Durrett*. It stems from the 1976 case of *In re Ferris*.[51] Maurice and Barbara Ferris (who might have been described as "big wheels" in the entertainment industry) had been lessees of land on which they had constructed a theater and a restaurant. When they defaulted and the lease was terminated, they lost the improvements. The court found the termination was a fraudulent transfer of the leasehold estate from the tenant to the landlord because of the high value of the estate with the added improvements. The case was generally explained as an attempt to cure an inequity, and little concern was expressed at the time that it might be applied generally, but the advent of *Durrett* changed that view.[52]

NOTES AND QUESTIONS

Termination of Leases. Certainly if during the term of a lease the landlord and tenant agree to its termination, it is arguable that the termination constitutes a

---

51. 415 F. Supp. 33 (W.D. Okla. 1976).

52. See Eder v. Queen City Grain, Inc. (In re Queen City Grain, Inc.), 51 B.R. 722 (Bankr. S.D. Ohio 1985) (holding a lease termination is a transfer of an interest in property subject to fraudulent transfer treatment); Fashion World, Inc. v. Finard (In re Fashion World), 44 B.R. 754 (Bankr. D. Mass. 1984) (lessor's option to terminate the lease is a transfer subject to attack as fraudulent). But see In re 130/40 Essex Street Dev. Corp., 2008 WL 4845639 (2008) and Durso Supermarkets, Inc. v. Durso (In re Durso Supermarkets), 193 B.R. 682 (Bankr. S.D.N.Y. 1996) (commercial lease termination after tenant default not a fraudulent transfer). See also Goodman, Avoidance of Lease Terminations as Fraudulent Transfers, 43 Bus. Law. 807 (1988). The Uniform Fraudulent Transfer Act §8(e)(1) provides: "A transfer is not voidable under Section 4(a)(2) or Section 5 if the transfer results from: (1) termination of a lease upon default by the debtor when the termination is pursuant to the lease and applicable law."

transfer of the leasehold estate from the tenant back to the landlord. On the other hand, where a lease is terminated because of the expiration of its term, it would be very difficult to argue that this expiration constitutes a conveyance of the leasehold estate, since on the expiration of the term the tenant has nothing left to convey. Where do you think the termination of a lease on default by the tenant falls? Should it matter if the lease contained an enforceable provision prohibiting assignment, subletting, or mortgaging? For an illustration of how important the facts of each case are in answering these questions, see Judge Posner's decision in Official Comm. of Unsecured Creditors of Great Lakes Quick Lube, LP v. T.D. Investments I, LLP (In re Great Lakes Quick Lube, LP), 816 F.3d 482 (7th Cir. 2016) (holding a negotiated termination of leases could constitute a constructively fraudulent transfer or a preference).

4. Mortgages as Fraudulent Transfers in Leveraged Buyout and Workout Situations

a. Leveraged Buyouts

Leveraged buyouts of corporations (LBOs) are generally beyond the scope of this casebook. However, an attack on an LBO as a fraudulent transfer may taint mortgages made in connection with the LBO, and is thus of concern to mortgagees. Simply put, an LBO involves the acquisition of corporate control by acquiring the stock of the corporation for very little, if any, cash. The bulk of the consideration for the stock is furnished by the acquired corporation, which incurs debt, or mortgages its assets to secure loans made by institutional lenders, to pay existing shareholders for the acquisition of the stock. The acquired corporation thus transfers property or incurs debt but, because the proceeds go to the selling stockholders and not to the acquired corporation, does not receive a reasonably equivalent value in return (unless one can say that the new management was worth it). A corporation that may have substantial surplus prior to the LBO may end up after the LBO with little or no surplus and most of its assets encumbered. If this results in an insolvent corporation, or if any of the other constructive fraud alternatives apply (i.e. less than a reasonably equivalent value *and* transferor is left with unreasonably small capital; *or* transferor intended to incur debts beyond debtor's ability to pay—see §548(a)(1)(B)), we have the ingredients of a fraudulent transfer under the Bankruptcy Code or state law. While an LBO may be structured in many different ways, the overall effect is to move assets out of the reach of general creditors of the acquired corporation or to dilute significantly the general creditors' share of unencumbered assets.

In United States v. Tabor Court Realty Corp.,[53] the court applied the Pennsylvania Uniform Fraudulent Conveyance Act to mortgages executed in connection with an LBO, holding that they were fraudulent conveyances where

---

53. 803 F.2d 1288 (3d Cir. 1986).

the lender was aware that the transaction would render the corporations insolvent and that the corporations would not receive fair consideration for the transfers. In addition, the assignee of the mortgages was also charged with liability for the fraud. Interestingly, the mortgages were found to be fraudulent under the intentional fraud provisions of the state fraudulent conveyance law as well as the constructive fraud provisions. Not all LBOs are being struck down by courts.[54] However, the number of cases that have attacked LBOs should give all parties associated with an LBO some concern. It has certainly given concern to the title companies, which began by making exceptions for fraudulent transfers in loan policies where the mortgage was made in connection with an LBO and even where the mortgage was made long after the LBO if it were made to refinance an LBO loan. Eventually, the American Land Title Association drafting committee, in a typical and self-beneficial overreaction, added a "creditors' rights exclusion" to its form of mortgagee's title policy. See Chapter 2B, note 2, discussing title policy exclusions.

b.   Workout Situations

The Eleventh Circuit in the case of In re Tousa, Inc., 680 F.3d 1298 (11th Cir. 2012), sustained a bankruptcy court finding that mortgage liens incurred by subsidiaries of the debtor to enable the debtor to pay a settlement to its lenders, were fraudulent transfers. The major issue appears to have been whether the subsidiaries received a reasonably equivalent value for the lien transfers. The transfers were made by the subsidiaries, but the benefit (or most of it) went to the parent's creditors. Arguments that the subsidiary received benefits in staving off bankruptcy, that the funds did not go directly to the debtor's lenders, and other arguments found in many LBO cases, were overcome by the Eleventh Circuit.

There is little question that this decision made lenders very unhappy and workouts far more complicated, and required much more costly due diligence. Nevertheless, doesn't it appear consistent with the interpretations of fraudulent transfers as applied in leveraged buyout situations? Do you see how the elements of fraudulent transfer fit in this situation? If not, review §§548 and 550 and try again.

NOTES AND QUESTIONS

1. LBO. Suppose you represented the lender in an LBO transaction that is later held to have been a fraudulent transaction. It is normal in mortgage lending transactions for the fees of the lenders' counsel to be paid by the borrower, and as

---

54. See, e.g., Kupetz v. Wolf, 845 F.2d 842 (9th Cir. 1988) (court found, inter alia, no evidence of actual intent to defraud or that stockholders knew of method of financing the purchase; claims of creditors arose after the sale; and LBO occurred two and one-half years prior to filing of bankruptcy petition); Credit Managers Ass'n of S. Cal. v. Federal Co., 629 F. Supp. 175 (C.D. Cal. 1985) (company received fair consideration).

a result your fees were paid by the corporation being acquired. Can you be forced to disgorge those fees as fraudulent transfers? If so, on what basis? See In re Revco D.S., Inc., 118 B.R. 468, 527 (Bankr. N.D. Ohio 1990) (preliminary report of examiner, the late Professor Barry Zaretsky).

2. Workout. The *Tousa* decision in the Eleventh Circuit may place roadblocks on the way to successful workouts. It may also be responsible for some unintended consequences in other areas. For example, recall the discussion of "The Mortgage Meltdown" in part B of this Chapter. At the end we dealt with the *GGP* case in which the court, without substantively consolidating the assets of the parent and special purpose subsidiaries, utilized cash of the subsidiaries for continued operation of the parent, based on a "corporate family" doctrine that treated the parent and affiliates as a collective whole engaged in a common enterprise. If you were representing a subsidiary attacking a proposed use of its assets as in *GGP*, can you devise an argument to protect your client based on *Tousa*?

3. Mortgagee's Defense? If in an LBO transaction, the mortgage lender transfers the borrowed funds to the corporation-borrower, which then transfers to the acquirer for use in purchasing the stock, could the lender argue successfully that it did give reasonably equivalent value to the corporation so that the mortgage cannot constitute a fraudulent transfer? What considerations do you think would help the court reach its decision?[55]

4. Additional Reading. Alces, Generic Fraud and the Uniform Fraudulent Transfer Act, 9 Cardozo L. Rev. 743 (1987); Baird and Jackson, Fraudulent Conveyance Law and Its Proper Domain, 38 Vand. L. Rev. 829 (1985); Carlson, Leveraged Buyouts in Bankruptcy, 20 Ga. L. Rev. 73 (1985); Carlson, Is Fraudulent Conveyance Law Efficient?, 9 Cardozo L. Rev. 643 (1987); Clark, The Duties of the Corporate Debtor to Its Creditors, 90 Harv. L. Rev. 505 (1977); Liss, Fraudulent Conveyance Law and Leveraged Buyouts, 87 Colum. L. Rev. 1491 (1987); Sabino, Applying the Law of Fraudulent Conveyances to Bankrupt Leveraged Buyouts: The Bankruptcy Code's Increasing Leverage over Failed LBOs, 69 N.D. L. Rev. 15 (1993); Sherwin, Creditors' Rights against Participants in a Leveraged Buyout, 72 Minn. L. Rev. 449 (1988); Williams, Revisiting the Proper Limits of Fraudulent Transfer Law, 8 Bankr. Dev. J. 55 (1991); Zaretsky, Fraudulent Transfer Law as the Arbiter of Unreasonable Risk, 46 S.C. L. Rev. 1165 (1995).

---

55. With respect to state law, §8(a) of the Uniform Fraudulent Transfer Act contains a defense to an action for intentional fraud to a transferee who takes "in good faith and for a reasonably equivalent value." The Uniform Voidable Transactions Act adds the further requirement that the reasonably equivalent value must be given to the debtor. Here the reasonably equivalent value was given to the debtor, but the question remains whether it was received in good faith.

E. BANKRUPTCY OF TENANT OR LANDLORD

The bankruptcy of a party to a lease agreement can have a profound effect on parties other than the landlord or tenant, such as a fee mortgagee with an assignment of rents, a leasehold mortgagee, or a sublessee. Most of the federal Bankruptcy Code requirements with respect to leases are found in the following excerpt.

Bankruptcy Code §365
11 U.S.C. §365

§365. EXECUTORY CONTRACTS AND UNEXPIRED LEASES

(a) Except as provided . . . in subsections (b), (c), and (d) of this section, the trustee, subject to the court's approval, may assume or reject any executory contract or unexpired lease of the debtor.

(b)(1) If there has been a default in an executory contract or unexpired lease of the debtor, the trustee may not assume such contract or lease unless, at the time of assumption of such contract or lease, the trustee—

(A) cures, or provides adequate assurance that the trustee will promptly cure, such default; other than a default that is a breach of a provision relating to the satisfaction of any provision (other than a penalty rate or penalty provision) relating to a default arising from an failure to perform nonmonetary obligations under an unexpired lease of real property, if it is impossible for the trustee to cure such default by performing nonmonetary acts at and after the time of assumption, except that if such default arises from a failure to operate in accordance with a nonresidential real property lease, then such default shall be cured by performance at and after the time of assumption in accordance with such lease, and pecuniary losses resulting from such default shall be compensated in accordance with the provisions of this paragraph;

(B) compensates, or provides adequate assurance that the trustee will promptly compensate, a party other than the debtor to such contract or lease, for any actual pecuniary loss to such party resulting from such default; and

(C) provides adequate assurance of future performance under such contract or lease.

(2) Paragraph (1) of this subsection does not apply to a default that is a breach of a provision relating to—

(A) the insolvency or financial condition of the debtor at any time before the closing of the case;

(B) the commencement of a case under this title;

(C) the appointment of or taking possession by a trustee in a case under this title or a custodian before such commencement; or

(D) the satisfaction of any penalty rate or penalty provision relating to a default arising from any failure by the debtor to perform nonmonetary obligations under the executory contract or unexpired lease.

(3) For the purposes of paragraph (1) of this subsection and paragraph (2)(B) of subsection (f), adequate assurance of future performance of a lease of real property in a shopping center includes adequate assurance—

(A) of the source of rent and other consideration due under such lease, and in the case of an assignment, that the financial condition and operating performance of the proposed assignee and its guarantors, if any, shall be similar to the financial condition and operating performance of the debtor and its guarantors, if any, as of the time the debtor became the lessee under the lease;

(B) that any percentage rent due under such lease will not decline substantially;

(C) that assumption or assignment of such lease is subject to all the provisions thereof, including (but not limited to) provisions such as a radius, location, use, or exclusivity provision, and will not breach any such provision contained in any other lease, financing agreement, or master agreement relating to such shopping center; and

(D) that assumption or assignment of such lease will not disrupt any tenant mix or balance in such shopping center.

(4) Notwithstanding any other provision of this section, if there has been a default in an unexpired lease of the debtor, other than a default of a kind specified in paragraph (2) of this subsection, the trustee may not require a lessor to provide services or supplies incidental to such lease before assumption of such lease unless the lessor is compensated under the terms of such lease for any services and supplies provided under such lease before assumption of such lease.

(c) The trustee may not assume or assign any executory contract or unexpired lease of the debtor, whether or not such contract or lease prohibits or restricts assignment of rights or delegation of duties, if—

(1)(A) applicable law excuses a party, other than the debtor, to such contract or lease from accepting performance from or rendering performance to an entity other than the debtor or the debtor in possession, whether or not such contract or lease prohibits or restricts assignment of rights or delegation of duties; and

(B) such party does not consent to such assumption or assignment; or

(2) such contract is a contract to make a loan, or extend other debt financing or financial accommodations, to or for the benefit of the debtor, or to issue a security of the debtor;

(3) such lease is of nonresidential real property and has been terminated under applicable nonbankruptcy law prior to the order for relief.

(d) . . .

(3) The trustee shall timely perform all the obligations of the debtor, except those specified in section 365(b)(2), arising from and after the order for relief under any unexpired lease of nonresidential real property, until such lease is assumed or rejected, notwithstanding section 503(b)(1) of this title. The court may extend, for cause, the time for performance of any such obligation that arises within 60 days after the date of the order for relief, but the time for performance shall not be extended beyond such 60-day period. This subsection shall not be deemed to affect the trustee's obligations under the provisions of subsection (b) or (f) of this section. Acceptance of any such performance does not constitute waiver or relinquishment of the lessor's rights under such lease or under this title.

(4)(A). Subject to subparagraph (B), an unexpired lease of nonresidential real property under which the debtor is the lessee shall be deemed rejected, and the trustee shall immediately surrender that nonresidential real property to the lessor, if the trustee does not assume or reject the unexpired lease by the earlier of—

(i) the date that is 120 days after the date of the order for relief;

or

(ii) the date of the entry of an order confirming a plan

(B)(i) The court may extend the period determined under subparagraph (A), prior to the expiration of the 120-day period, for 90 days on the motion of the trustee or lessor for cause.

(ii) If the court grants an extension under clause (i), the court may grant a subsequent extension only upon prior written consent of the lessor in each instance. . . .

(e)(1) Notwithstanding a provision in an executory contract or unexpired lease, or in applicable law, an executory contract or unexpired lease of the debtor may not be terminated or modified, and any right or obligation under such contract or lease may not be terminated or modified, at any time after the commencement of the case solely because of a provision in such contract or lease that is conditioned on—

(A) the insolvency or financial condition of the debtor at any time before the closing of the case;

(B) the commencement of a case under this title; or

(C) the appointment of or taking possession by a trustee in a case under this title or a custodian before such commencement.

(2) Paragraph (1) of this subsection does not apply to an executory contract or unexpired lease of the debtor, whether or not such contract or lease prohibits or restrict[s] assignment of rights or delegation of duties, if—

(A)(i) applicable law excuses a party, other than the debtor, to such contract or lease from accepting performance from or rendering performance to the trustee or to an assignee of such contract or lease, whether or not such contract or lease prohibits or restricts assignment of rights or delegation of duties; and

(ii) such party does not consent to such assumption or assignment;
or

(B) such contract is a contract to make a loan, or extend other debt financing or financial accommodations, to or for the benefit of the debtor, or to issue a security of the debtor.

(f)(1) Except as provided in subsections (b) and (c) of this section, notwithstanding a provision in an executory contract or unexpired lease of the debtor, or in applicable law, that prohibits, restricts, or conditions the assignment of such contract or lease, the trustee may assign such contract or lease under paragraph (2) of this subsection,

(2) The trustee may assign an executory contract or unexpired lease of the debtor only if—

(A) the trustee assumes such contract or lease in accordance with the provisions of this section; and

(B) adequate assurance of future performance by the assignee of such contract or lease is provided, whether or not there has been a default in such contract or lease.

(3) Notwithstanding a provision in an executory contract or unexpired lease of the debtor, or in applicable law that terminates or modifies, or permits a party other than the debtor to terminate or modify, such contract or lease or a right or obligation under such contract or lease on account of an assignment of such contract or lease, such contract, lease, right, or obligation may not be terminated or modified under such provision because of the assumption or assignment of such contract or lease by the trustee.

(g) Except as provided in subsections (h)(2) and (i)(2) of this section, the rejection of an executory contract or unexpired lease of the debtor constitutes a breach of such contract or lease. . . .

(h)(1)(A) If the trustee rejects an unexpired lease of real property under which the debtor is the lessor and—

(i) if the rejection by the trustee amounts to such a breach as would entitle the lessee to treat such lease as terminated by virtue of its terms, applicable nonbankruptcy law, or any agreement made by the lessee, then the lessee under such lease may treat such lease as terminated by the rejection; or

(ii) if the term of such lease has commenced, the lessee may retain its rights under such lease (including rights such as those relating to the amount and timing of payment of rent and other amounts payable by the lessee and any right of use, possession, quiet enjoyment, subletting, assignment, or hypothecation) that are in or appurtenant to the real property for the balance of the term of such lease and for any renewal or extension of such rights to the extent that such rights are enforceable under applicable nonbankruptcy law.

(B) If the lessee retains its rights under subparagraph (A)(ii), the lessee may offset against the rent reserved under such lease for the balance of the term after the date of the rejection of such lease and for the term of any renewal or extension of such lease, the value of any damage caused by the nonperformance after the date of such rejection, of any obligation of the debtor under such lease, but the lessee shall not have any other right against the estate or the debtor on account of any damage occurring after such date caused by such nonperformance.

(C) The rejection of a lease of real property in a shopping center with respect to which the lessee elects to retain its rights under subparagraph (A)(ii) does not affect the enforceability under applicable nonbankruptcy law of any provision in the lease pertaining to radius, location, use, exclusivity, or tenant mix or balance.

(D) In this paragraph, "lessee" includes any successor, assign, or mortgagee permitted under the terms of such lease.

. . .

(i)(1) If the trustee rejects an executory contract of the debtor for the sale of real property or for the sale of a timeshare interest under a timeshare plan, under which the purchaser is in possession, such purchaser may treat such contract as terminated, or, in the alternative, may remain in possession of such real property or timeshare interest.

(2) If such purchaser remains in possession—

(A) such purchaser shall continue to make all payments due under such contract, but may, offset against such payments any damages occurring after the date of the rejection of such contract caused by the nonperformance of any obligation of the debtor after such date, but such purchaser does not have any rights against the estate on account of any damages arising after such date from such rejection, other than such offset; and

(B) the trustee shall deliver title to such purchaser in accordance with the provisions of such contract, but is relieved of all other obligations to perform under such contract.

(j) A purchaser that treats an executory contract as terminated under subsection (i) of this section, or a party whose executory contract to purchase real property from the debtor is rejected and under which such party is not in possession, has a lien on the interest of the debtor in such property for the recovery of any portion of the purchase price that such purchaser or party has paid.

(k) Assignment by the trustee to an entity of a contract or lease assumed under this section relieves the trustee and the estate from any liability for any breach of such contract or lease occurring after such assignment.

(l) If an unexpired lease under which the debtor is the lessee is assigned pursuant to this section, the lessor of the property may require a deposit or other security for the performance of the debtor's obligations under the lease substantially the same as would have been required by the landlord upon the initial leasing to a similar tenant.

(m) For purposes of this section 365 and sections 541(b)(2) and 362(b)(10), leases of real property shall include any rental agreement to use real property. . . .

1. Bankruptcy of the Tenant

As §365(e) indicates, clauses in leases providing for automatic (ipso facto) termination of a lease, or termination at the option of the landlord, because of the bankruptcy, insolvency, or financial condition of the tenant are unenforceable in bankruptcy proceedings. Although the landlord is prohibited from terminating the lease, the tenant has the option of rejecting the lease. Thus, the landlord is left in the unenviable position of having to live with leases that are favorable to tenants in bankruptcy while seeing leases favorable to the landlord rejected. The inability to terminate is especially a problem for a landlord that has entered into a low base-rent lease intended to be supplemented with percentage rent based on profits or sales. Such leases are attractive to the trustee for an insolvent tenant whose sales are low and, as a result, the lease will probably not be rejected.

If the tenant-debtor does not reject the lease, it may assume the lease and assign it to a third party (notwithstanding provisions in the lease prohibiting such assignment) provided defaults are cured, the landlord is compensated for any losses, and an ambiguous "adequate assurance of future performance" is provided. Note the special definition in §365(b)(3) of adequate assurance of future performance for shopping centers. These provisions will be discussed in the notes below.

A growing concern for parties to leasehold transactions is the possibility of recharacterization of a lease in the tenant's bankruptcy. In the *PCH* case, excerpted below, a lease in a sale-and-leaseback transaction was held not to be a true lease for bankruptcy purposes. As you read the case, consider what the agreement is if not a lease and what possible consequences such a recharacterization can have for parties to the leasehold transaction.

Liona Corp. v. PCH Associates (In re PCH Associates)

804 F.2d 193 (2d Cir. 1986)

MINER, Circuit Judge.

Liona Corporation, N.V. ("Liona") appeals from a judgment of the United States District Court for the Southern District of New York (Tenney, J.) affirming an order of the bankruptcy court (Lifland, J.) in favor of debtor PCH Associates ("PCH"). The District Court held that the sale-leaseback arrangement between Liona and PCH was a joint venture agreement rather than a nonresidential lease subject to the provisions of section 365(d)(3), (4) of the Bankruptcy Reform Act of 1978, as amended by the Bankruptcy Amendments and Federal Judgeship Act of 1984, 11 U.S.C. §365(d)(3), (4) (Supp. III 1985) ("Bankruptcy Code" or "Code"). We affirm the judgment of the district court on the ground that the sale-leaseback arrangement is not an unexpired nonresidential lease within the contemplation of the Code.

BACKGROUND

This dispute centers around the true nature of a transaction that was "sharply tailored by sophisticated parties," PCH Associates v. Liona Corporation N.V., 55 B.R. 273, 274 (Bankr. S.D.N.Y. 1985), and was admittedly structured as a sale-leaseback arrangement for tax and investment advantages. PCH, a Pennsylvania limited partnership formed in 1976 and formerly known as Simon Associates ("Simon"), owns and operates the Philadelphia Centre Hotel ("hotel"). Prior to September 1981 and the transaction at issue on this appeal, PCH's predecessor, Simon, held title to both the hotel and the land upon which it is situated. In 1980, Richard Bernstein, an experienced real estate operator and investor, learned that the hotel was for sale. In addition to existing mortgages and seller-provided financing, he determined that $9,000,000 was needed to acquire, renovate, and provide working capital for the hotel. Bernstein located a group of United States investors willing to supply $4,000,000 as new limited partners of PCH. He then approached Fidinam, a consortium of financial service companies, to place the remaining $5,000,000 investment.

Bernstein required a structure that would allocate all the tax benefits of depreciation of the hotel to PCH. Fidinam, in turn, required an investment for its client that would be evidenced by ownership of a tangible asset and would guarantee a 12 percent fixed annual rate of return with an additional share contingent on the hotel's cash flow. Fidinam did not want its client involved in the daily management of the hotel. Upon reaching agreement, the parties' lawyers structured the transaction to encompass Bernstein's and Fidinam's requirements. Ultimately, Liona, a Netherlands Antilles corporation, became the beneficiary of Fidinam's negotiations.

In September 1981, the requirements of the parties were fulfilled through a "Sale-Leaseback Agreement" and a "Ground Lease" whereby the land owned by PCH, but not the hotel, was sold to Purchase Estates, Ltd. and immediately leased back to PCH. Ultimately, the land interest of Purchase Estates, Ltd. was assigned to Liona. Thus, Liona held title to the land and leased it to PCH, which owned and managed the hotel.

Section 1.01 of the Ground Lease provided for an initial term of 33 years, renewable for four terms under section 42.01, for a total of 165 years. Rent was set at a minimum annual rate of $600,000 in section 3.01, with a percentage rental based upon a percentage of increases in the hotel's gross revenues provided in section 3.02. Section 3.04 provided for an adjustment of the annual rent if the "Landlord's Investment" fell below $5,000,000. In such instance, the annual rent would be reduced to 12 percent of the "Landlord's Investment."

Section 3.10 of the Ground Lease further provided that:

> It is understood and agreed that the amount herein provided paid to Landlord in addition to the minimum net annual rental, although based upon a percentage of Tenant's revenue during each year, is rent, and Landlord shall in no event be construed or held to be a partner or associate of Tenant in the conduct of its business, nor shall Landlord be liable for any debts incurred by Tenant in the conduct of said business or otherwise, *but it is understood and agreed that the relationship between the parties hereto is, and at all times shall remain, that of Landlord and Tenant.*

Article 34 of the Ground Lease also provided that:

> This Lease contains all the promises, agreements, conditions, inducements and understandings between Landlord and Tenant relative to the Premises and there are no promises, agreements, conditions, understandings, inducements, warranties or representations, oral or written, expressed or implied, between them other than as set forth herein or in the Contract.

In November of 1984, PCH filed for reorganization under section 301 of the Bankruptcy Reform Act of 1978. Since that date, PCH has operated the hotel as a debtor-in-possession under sections 1107 and 1108 of the Code. On December 21, 1981, pursuant to section 365(d)(3), (4) of the Code, Liona filed an application with the bankruptcy court seeking an order directing PCH to continue paying rent to Liona according to the terms of the Ground Lease. PCH subsequently instituted an adversary proceeding seeking a declaration that the Ground Lease was not an unexpired nonresidential lease within the scope of section 365(d)(3), (4) of the Code, but rather constituted a joint venture or a subordinate financing scheme.

The bankruptcy court found for PCH, concluding that, even though the transaction was labeled a sale and a lease, the true nature of the arrangement was that of a joint venture and therefore no landlord/tenant relationship existed. . . .

Liona appeals from the district court's affirmance of the bankruptcy court's order. . . .

II. APPLICATION OF SECTION 365(D)(3), (4)

Liona initiated this action to compel PCH to perform its obligations under the Ground Lease pursuant to section 365(d)(3), (4) of the Bankruptcy Code, which requires a debtor either to affirm or reject "an unexpired lease of nonresidential real property." The determination of whether this provision applies to the Ground Lease is of critical concern in this bankruptcy proceeding because, if applied, PCH would be forced either to affirm the lease, cure all defects, and perform under the terms of the contract, or to reject the lease and vacate the property. If PCH rejected the lease and vacated the property, there likely would be no assets left to administer. If PCH affirmed the lease, a substantial burden would be placed on the reorganization proceeding. Therefore, PCH adamantly asserts that there was no true sale and no true lease for the purposes of section 365, and that it therefore had no obligation to affirm or reject the lease. Specifically, PCH asserts that the documents merely provide the means by which the investment goals and tax requirements of the parties could be fulfilled.

Both the bankruptcy court and the district court held that because the contracts contemplated a joint venture, the Ground Lease was not a lease. Although we agree with the determination that the Ground Lease is not a lease, our analysis is somewhat different. We interpret section 365(d)(3), (4) of the Bankruptcy Code to apply solely to a "true" or "bona fide" lease. The Ground Lease is not, in our opinion, a true lease as contemplated therein and we find that determination dispositive of the case. It is unnecessary, therefore, to identify the transaction as a joint venture, security agreement, subordinated financing, or other investment scheme. Suffice it to say that it is not a bona fide lease for purposes of the Bankruptcy Code. . . .

. . . The statute's plain language offers little definition of those transactions that must be assumed or rejected, other than in section 365(m), which provides that "leases of real property shall include any rental agreement to use real property." The term "lease of real property" does, however, appear elsewhere in the Code, in section 502(b)(6). The legislative history of section 502(b)(6) furnishes explicit authority for restricting the scope of that term to "bona fide" leases.

Section 502(b)(6) limits the amount of damages that a landlord can recover upon breach or rejection of a lease of real property. "It was designed to compensate the landlord for his loss while not permitting a claim so large (based on a long-term lease) as to prevent other general unsecured creditors from recovering. . . ." S. Rep. No. 989, 95th Cong., 2d Sess. 63, reprinted in 1978 U.S. Code Cong. & Ad. News 5787, 5849. . . . The Senate Report notes that the phrase "lease of real property" does not apply to lease financing transactions or to leases intended as security, but rather applies only to a "true" or "bona fide" lease. Thus, where the purported "lease" involves merely a sale of the real estate and the rental payments are, in truth, payments of principal and interest on a secured loan involving a sale of real estate, there is no true lease and section 502(b)(6) does not apply. . . .

Furthermore, the bankruptcy court is to look to the circumstances of the case and consider the economic substance of the transaction rather than "the locus of title, the form of the transaction or the fact that the transaction is denominated as a 'lease,'" to determine whether the transaction embodies a "true lease" or a financing transaction. S. Rep. No. 989, 95th Cong., 2d Sess. 64, reprinted in 1978 U.S. Code Cong. & Ad. News 5787, 5850.

We have no difficulty applying the section 502(b)(6) requirement of a bona fide lease to section 365(d)(3), (4) because these sections, read together, are part of a total scheme designed to set forth the rights and obligations of landlords and tenants involved in bankruptcy proceedings.

We believe that reading a requirement of a true lease into section 365 is necessary to effectuate the purposes of that section. As a whole, section 365 allows a trustee, or in this case a debtor-in-possession, to reject or assume executory contracts and leases, based on a determination of whether they burden or benefit the bankrupt estate. Thus, executory contracts and leases that benefit the bankrupt are favored over contracts with other creditors. If security transactions, loans, and other financing arrangements can be couched in lease terms, and can thereby be assumed by the bankrupt estate, the "lessor" gains a distinct advantage at the expense of other creditors without a concomitant benefit to the bankrupt estate. This is especially apparent in the case at bar. If successful, Liona would enjoy the benefit of its contract with PCH to the detriment of others having valid claims against the bankrupt's estate. However, if there is no true lease, Liona should not be permitted to escape the consequences of investor/creditor status by invoking the labels of "landlord" and "lease."

Satisfied that section 365(d)(3), (4) requires a bona fide lease, we must now determine whether the transaction at issue embodied such a lease, keeping in mind the economic substance of the transaction and not its form.

While there is a "strong presumption that a deed and lease . . . are what they purport to be," Fox v. Peck Iron & Metal Co., 25 B.R. 674, 688 (Bankr. S.D. Cal. 1982), here there was substantial evidence upon which the bankruptcy court and the district court could rely to find that the transaction is something other than a true lease. Based on the circumstances of the negotiations and the economic substance of the transaction, it was not error to conclude that the parties intended to impose obligations and confer rights significantly different from those arising from the ordinary landlord/tenant relationship.

We are faced with a transaction cast as a sale-leaseback arrangement, a "relatively modern, and clever, structure of financing which affords significant advantages to both purchaser-lessor and seller-lessee." Id. at 688. Bernstein, acting for PCH, sought out Liona in order to pool their resources for their mutual benefit. The transaction was structured as a ground lease to accomplish a trade-off between tax benefits for PCH and a higher guaranteed return, without management concerns, for Liona. Therefore, rent was not calculated to compensate Liona for the use of the property; rather the parties structured the "rent" solely to ensure Liona's return on its investment. Furthermore, the

Chapter 18. The Impact of Bankruptcy on Real Estate Transactions

"purchase price" paid by Liona for the land was not based on market rate, but was calculated as the amount necessary to finance the transaction.

It seems clear that no true lease was contemplated by the parties here. It is undisputed that Bernstein, acting for PCH, initiated the entire transaction, including the purchase of the land by Liona. . . .

Another factor indicating that this transaction does not involve a true lease is that the purchase price was not related to the value of the land. A large inequality or discrepancy in values has been characterized as a "strong circumstance" tending to show that a transaction was a disguised financing scheme. Furthermore, PCH assumed many of the obligations associated with outright ownership of the property, including responsibility for paying property taxes and insurance. As noted in the Senate Report on section 502(b)(6) of the Bankruptcy Code,

> [T]he fact that the lessee assumes and discharges substantially all the risks and obligations ordinarily attributed to the outright ownership of the property is more indicative of a financing transaction than of a true lease. The rental payments in such cases are in substance payments of principal and interest either on a loan secured by the leased real property or on the purchase of the leased real property. . . .

Therefore, we find that PCH's significant indicia of ownership tend toward a finding that there is no true lease. Additionally, the provisions allowing Liona to recover its investment if the hotel were refinanced, and giving PCH the power to pre-pay Liona's investment, at which time Liona would share solely in profits, strongly suggest a transaction other than a lease.

Mindful that the structure of the transaction was based on the tax considerations and the investment requirements of both parties, and viewing the transaction as a whole, we hold that the Ground Lease and Sale-Leaseback Agreement do not constitute a true lease. Therefore section 365(d)(3), (4) of the Bankruptcy Code has no application here. Whether these contracts create a joint venture, a security agreement, or some other form of investment vehicle need not be decided here. . . .

NOTES AND QUESTIONS

1. Termination by the Landlord. You already know that §365(e) prohibits termination of a lease after the commencement of bankruptcy solely on the basis of a provision in the lease that is conditioned on the insolvency or financial condition of the debtor. Notwithstanding this, what reasons can you, as attorney for a landlord, give for retaining the usual provision terminating the lease on the insolvency of the tenant (the "ipso facto" clause)?

Consider another situation: Dan Developer owns a shopping center whose major anchor tenant is the Canview Department Store. Dan insists on a clause in the lease requiring that Canview keep at least 150 stores in operation throughout the country. Canview later files in Chapter 11, and the court approves the closing of 75 unprofitable stores, reducing the number of Canview stores nationwide to 80. Do you think Dan can terminate the lease without violating §365(e)? Would it be relevant to show that in most chain store bankruptcy proceedings a large number of stores are usually closed?

Note that §365(e)(2)(A)(i) permits termination and §365(c)(1)(A) prohibits assumption and assignment of contracts and leases where, inter alia, nonbankruptcy law provides that even absent a nonassignment clause, assignment is not permitted without the consent of the other party to the contract or lease. This provision was written with personal service contracts in mind. However, it has not been limited strictly to such contracts and has been applied in other situations in which subjective judgment is involved. For example, In re Pioneer Ford Sales, Inc. 729 F.2d 27 (1st Cir. 1984), found certain franchise and distributorship agreements nonassignable. Why do you think such contracts should not be assignable and should be terminable by the landlord on the bankruptcy of the other party?

2. *Prepetition Lease Termination: The Lazarus Lease.* Section 365(c)(3) prohibits assumption or assignment of a lease "of nonresidential real property" that "has been terminated under applicable nonbankruptcy law" prior to the bankruptcy proceedings. This provision was added during the 1984 revisions to the Code and may be an example of an issue that should have been fought in the courts on the basis of statutory interpretation rather than in Congress through statutory tinkering and hasty political drafting. Does it make any sense? On what basis (other than the invocation of fraudulent transfer or other avoidance provisions of the Code not at issue here) could a lease no longer in existence be assumed or assigned in the first place? Would it make any difference if, when the petition is filed, the tenant is still in possession of the leased premises under a terminated or expired lease? Cf. Omni Int'l, Ltd. v. Mimi's of Atlanta Inc. (In re Mimi's of Atlanta, Inc.), 5 B.R. 623 (Bankr. N.D. Ga. 1980), aff'd, 11 B.R. 710 (N.D. Ga. 1981); Constr. Clearing House, Inc. v. Mulkey of Mo., Inc. (In re Mulkey of Mo. Inc.), 5 B.R. 15 (Bankr. W.D. Mo. 1980).

Why limit the provision to nonresidential real property? Was it to avoid a taint on the amendment as being anti-consumer? Does the limitation mean that terminated leases of residential real property can be resurrected? Even when the former tenant is no longer in possession?

What is the meaning of "nonresidential real property"? Assume Ace Insurance Company owned land improved with an apartment complex that it leased to Dan Developer under a net long-term ground lease. Dan later defaults under the lease, and the lease is terminated. Ace then leases the complex to Linda Landlord. Some time later, Dan files in bankruptcy. Was the lease to Dan a lease of residential real property? If so, can the lease be revived? What then happens to Ace? To Linda Landlord?

Provisions similar to those in §365(c)(3) were inserted by the 1984 amendments in §362(b)(10) (automatic stay not applicable to certain terminated leases) and §541(b)(2) (certain terminated leases are not property of the estate). These provisions are worded slightly differently than §365(c)(3). Compare §365(c)(3) with the language of §362(b)(10) and §541(b)(2), which refer only to leases of nonresidential real property terminated "by virtue of the expiration of the stated term of the lease." What is different about §365(c)(3)? Assume that Ace's lease to Dan Developer is for an office building and that the lease is terminated as a result of Dan Developer's *default*. Once terminated, can the lease be revived to make the lease property of the estate and subject to the automatic stay, but not revived to permit assumption and assignment? If so, can you think of a rationale to support such a result? Could it be based on the notion that the bankruptcy court should have the right to determine whether a lease terminated for default was properly terminated and thus should be considered property of the estate with the stay applicable; but once the determination is made that the lease was properly terminated, the lessee is precluded from assuming or assigning?

A 2001 bankruptcy court decision may have revealed problems in the enforcement of the 1984 amendments. The case of In re P.J. Clarke's Restaurant Corp., 265 B.R. 392 (Bankr. S.D.N.Y. 2001), did not deal directly with the questions here considered, but rather involved §365(d)(3) of the Bankruptcy Code, which requires the debtor/tenant to perform the tenant's obligations under an unexpired lease until assumption or rejection. If the lease had been terminated prior to bankruptcy, there would be nothing the tenant had to perform. Judge Gropper agreed that state law would determine if the lease had been terminated prior to bankruptcy. The law of New York, §749(3), N.Y. R.P.A.P.L. provides that while the issuance by the court of a warrant for the removal of a tenant cancels the landlord-tenant relationship, the court would still have the power to vacate the warrant for good cause shown at any time before execution on the warrant. In *P.J. Clarke*, the warrant had been issued but not executed upon prior to bankruptcy. The court held that since the statute allowed the court to vacate the warrant, the lease would be considered unexpired and thus the "tenant" had to perform.

The implications of this decision are quite broad. If a lease is unexpired until execution on the warrant (the time the power of the court to vacate the warrant would end) and there has been no execution on the warrant prior to bankruptcy, execution on the warrant would be subject to the automatic stay once the tenant files. Can you conclude from this that in a jurisdiction that has a provision similar to New York's with respect to potential appeals, the 1984 amendments may have been rendered largely meaningless if the right to appeal has not been exhausted prior to bankruptcy? But see Judge Glenn's interpretation of *P.J. Clarke* in In re Sweet N Sour 7th Ave. Corp., 431 B.R. 63 (Bankr. S.D.N.Y. 2010). For an interesting discussion of the cases in this area, see Rosen and Rooney, Rethinking "Terminated" Leases: How Bankruptcy Courts Keep Them Alive, 19 Bankr. Strategist 4 (Feb. 2002).

3. Assumption and Assignment by Tenant. Section 365(b) provides that if the lease is in default, it can be assumed by the tenant only if any default is cured, compensation is given for the landlord's losses, and "adequate assurance of future performance" is provided. Similarly, §365(f)(2)(b) requires that adequate assurance of future performance by an assignee be provided. Other than the "definition" of "adequate assurance of future performance" for leases of property in a shopping center in §365(b)(3), there is no definition of the phrase in the Code, leaving great latitude to the courts in interpreting whether future performance is adequately assured.

Even the definition of "adequate assurance of future performance in shopping centers" is far from clear. For example, under §365(b)(3)(A), would the requirement of assurance of the "source" of the rent be met if the trustee simply reported that Irma Insolvent would be responsible for the payment of the Canview rent? If you had been drafting that section, how would you have worded it? With respect to §365(b)(3)(B), assume a lease in a shopping center with a low base rent and contingent rent based on a percentage of profits or sales at the location. As you would expect, in the first year of the lease, there was no contingent rent paid. However, in the next five years, contingent rent exceeded 20 percent of the base rent; and in the eighth year, just before the tenant, then insolvent, filed in bankruptcy, there was, again, no contingent rent. Adequate assurance must be given that the contingent rent will not "decline substantially." Substantially from what? The contingent rent paid at the date of bankruptcy? If so, how much comfort does the provision give a landlord?

Does the definition of adequate assurance of future performance for shopping centers have a negative implication for nonshopping center leases? For example, does §365(b)(3)(C) imply that an assumption or assignment of an office building lease need not be "subject to all the provisions thereof"? Compare this subsection with §365(d)(3), which requires performance by tenant of all obligations arising from and after the order for relief until lease is assumed or rejected.

What is a shopping center, anyway? Is a lease of a space for the sale of jewelry in a building in the jewelry district of Manhattan (with virtually every tenant in the jewelry business) a lease of property in a shopping center? Cf. In re Joshua Slocum Ltd., 922 F.2d 1081 (3d Cir. 1990) (group of three buildings on "Main Street" housing various retail tenants and owned by single owner held a shopping center); Annot., 117 A.L.R. Fed. 321 (1994). Note that where a shopping center lease is assigned, §365(b)(3)(A) provides strict rules that the financial condition and operating performance of the assignee must be similar to the debtor's *at the time the debtor became a lessee under the lease* and compare our discussion above on §365(b)(3)(B).

4. Rejection by Tenant

a. *Time to Assume or Reject.* Under §365(a), the trustee or debtor in possession may, subject to the court's approval, reject a lease of the debtor. Section 365(d)(4), as the result of the BAPCPA amendments of 2005, now provides that if the trustee does not assume or reject a lease of nonresidential real property within 120 days after the date of the order for relief (the date a voluntary bankruptcy was commenced), the lease will be deemed rejected. The court may extend the period, prior to the expiration of the 120 days, for an additional period of 90 days. The court is prohibited from granting future extensions, except on the prior written consent of the landlord. This rather draconian limitation on the court's authority was the result of a perception that courts had been granting unreasonably long extensions. Could this evidence a lack of confidence by Congress in the decisions of the bankruptcy courts? Cf. Williams, Distrust: The Rhetoric and Reality of Means-Testing, 7 Am. Bankr. Inst. L. Rev. 105 (1999).

Ordinarily, of course, a total of 210 days (seven months) ought to be enough time for any tenant to decide whether to assume or reject. However, can you think of any circumstances where this period might clearly be insufficient? Think of a retail department store chain with hundreds of locations throughout the nation. The decision to assume or reject may be based on much more than the profitability of a particular location, and may involve a new corporate strategy. For example, consider issues such as whether the debtor will continue to service a particular area of the country; whether supplying even a profitable store makes sense where the debtor has few stores in the area; the real estate value of the location if the lease were assigned; whether it is important to remain open and operating during a particular time of year that is materially more profitable than other times of the year (e.g. Christmas); and many other factors that, except perhaps in "pre-packaged" (negotiated prior to filing) cases, require a great deal of time to resolve. In connection with a limitation on the time to assume or reject in the old Bankruptcy Act, Professor James Angell MacLachlan commented that there was criticism of applying what was then a 60-day period in major cases, stating that "[a]s Al Houston, of White and Case, said 'it takes the receiver ["trustee" now—EDS.] 60 days to find out where the toilet is.'" Creedon and Zinman, Landlord's Bankruptcy: Laissez Les Lessees, 24 Bus. Law. 1391, 1440 (1971).

If the tenant needs more time than the statute allows, can the tenant get around the limitation by assuming the lease before the expiration of the period and changing its mind later? The tenant may do this, but is it to the tenant's benefit to do so? See §503(b)(7). Section 365(d)(4) allows extension beyond the 210-day period if the landlord consents. Can you think of any reason why the landlord might consent to an extension?

It has become quite common for major tenant-debtors to sell the right to designate what leases will be assumed and assigned. The long period to assume or reject previously granted by bankruptcy courts afforded the purchaser of these rights the time to shop the leases to third parties. Do you see how the shortening of the time period for the assumption or rejection can have an adverse impact on the value of these designation rights? Would the growing trend of prepackaging bankruptcies (that is, reaching agreement and resolving issues before filing) become relevant in this connection?

b. *Effect of Rejection by the Tenant on Sublessees and Leasehold Mortgagees.* Consider the effect of rejection by a tenant-debtor on the holders of subordinate interests such as the leasehold mortgagee and sublessee. If the leasehold estate is terminated by the tenant's rejection, the subordinate estates will also be lost.

However, the pre-Code case In re Garfinkle, 577 F.2d 901 (5th Cir. 1978), held that the leasehold mortgage was not destroyed by the lessee's rejection of the lease on the ground that rejection by a lessee "merely placed the leasehold outside of the bankruptcy administration without destroying the underlying estate and, therefore, the mortgage.. . ." 577 F.2d at 904. In 1994, the Fifth Circuit, in a decision by Judge Edith Hollan Jones, again reaffirmed that rejection does not terminate a lease and wipe out interests to which it is subject. Eastover Bank for Savings v. Sowashee Venture (In re Austin Development Co.), 19 F.3d 1077 (5th Cir. 1994). But see In re Hawaii Dimensions, Inc., 47 B.R. 425 (Bankr. D. Haw. 1985), where the court held that rejection of the lease by the tenant terminated the lease, noting the absence of a provision in the Code similar to §365(h) (discussed in Chapter 18E2, infra), which protects the tenant on rejection by a debtor-landlord. The court in In re Storage Technology Corp., 55 B.R. 479 (Bankr. D. Colo. 1985), attempts to distinguish the two cases on the basis of the equities involved. See also In re Picnic 'N Chicken, Inc., 58 Bankr. 523 (Bankr. S.D. Cal. 1986). More recently, Judge Robert Drain in In re The Great Atl. & Pac. Tea Co., Inc, 544 B.R. 43 (Bankr. S.D.N.Y. 2016) held, inter alia, that since §365(d)(4) requires the trustee to surrender the real property to the lessor if the lease is deemed rejected upon the failure of the trustee to assume or reject within a designated period of time (see note 4(a) above), the turnover is "tantamount to termination" of the lease and, even though the tenant *timely* rejected the lease in that case, deprives the subtenant of any meaningful right of possession. Reread §365(d)(4) and see if you agree. For an analysis of the issues in the case, see Rosenberg and (Daniel) Zinman, Absent Sublease Recognition Agreement, the Rejection of a Prime Lease in a Bankruptcy Case Leaves a Sublessee Largely Out in the Cold, 44 N.Y. Real Prop. L.J. 12 (2016).

Can you devise an argument that would protect the interest of the leasehold mortgagee or sublessee even where the rejection by the tenant effectively terminates its interest in the property? Clue: Think back to your first-year property course and all that emphasis on property as a "bundle of rights." Can a tenant reject any more of the lease than the tenant has left after it has conveyed rights to a leasehold mortgagee or subtenant?

Reflect on your consideration of leasehold mortgagee protection provisions of leases (Chapter 11A3, supra). Which provision (provided it had been carefully drafted) would be extremely helpful to the leasehold mortgagee if the debtor-lessee successfully rejects the lease?

Assume a decision similar to *Austin Development*, that the lease is not terminated by the tenant's rejection. Assume further that when the tenant rejects the lease, both a leasehold mortgagee and a sublessee offer to step into the tenant's shoes under the lease. Since the lease cannot be assigned to both, should the lease be assigned in reverse order of priority (i.e., to the sublessee if the leasehold mortgage were first in time)? If so, why?

The rejection of a lease constitutes a breach of the lease under §365(g). This entitles the landlord to a claim in the tenant's bankruptcy. Section 502(b)(6), however, limits the claim to the "rent reserved" for the greater of one year or 15 percent (not to exceed three years) of the remaining term. What is the purpose of this limitation on the landlord's claim?

Suppose Dan Developer leased space in his office building to Widget Corporation of America. The lease provided for a base rent with additional amounts to be paid for increases in real estate taxes, labor costs, and so on. In WCA's bankruptcy, would Dan be limited to 15 percent of the stated rent and not the additional rent? Would it help Dan if the lease clause provided that all payments under the lease "shall be considered 'rent' for the purposes of §502(b)(6)" of the Bankruptcy Code?

c. *Using §365(d)(3) to Strategic Advantage.* Section 365(d)(3) provides that the trustee must perform the obligations of the debtor under leases of real property "arising from and after the order for relief" (commencement of the case) until assumption or rejection. Thus, obligations arising the day *after* the order for relief must be paid in full, and obligations that arise the day *before* the order for relief are simply prepetition claims that will be paid, if at all, in "bankruptcy dollars." This fact provides both an interesting opportunity and risk for the tenant and the landlord.

Let's suppose that Widget Corporation of America (WCA) is a tenant in Dan Developer's property. The lease provides for the payment of rent quarterly in advance and for the payment by the tenant of its share of real property taxes, which are due semi-annually in advance. WCA is in financial difficulty and on June 15 makes plans to file in Chapter 11. Rent for the third quarter of the year will be due July 1 and taxes for the second half of the year will be due July 1. WCA's attorney advises WCA to file July 2, or as soon thereafter when the tenant has been billed by the landlord for the taxes. In that way, the attorney explains, the three months rent and the six months taxes will be prepetition claims that may never be paid or paid at a small percentage of the amount due, and tenant will, in a sense, live rent free for the next three months with no obligation to pay its share of taxes for the next six months. Is the attorney's advice correct?

Perhaps. The answer may depend on the jurisdiction in which the case is filed. In this connection you might wish to glance at the very flexible bankruptcy venue provisions in 28 U.S.C. §1408, which permit filing, inter alia, at the domicile, principal place of business or place of principal assets of the debtor, or in the jurisdiction where a case is pending concerning an affiliate or partner of the debtor.

If the case is in the Seventh Circuit the attorney is wrong, because that Circuit would allocate the payment obligation over the period for which it is paid (mostly postpetition) even if billed prepetition.[56] If the case is in the Third or Sixth Circuit, the attorney would appear correct, because those Circuits would look to the billing date to determine when the obligation arose.[57] Given the

---

56. In re Handy Andy Home Improvement Centers, Inc., 144 F.3d 1125 (7th Cir. 1998).

57. In re Montgomery Ward Holding Corp., 268 F.3d 205 (3d Cir. 2001) (landlord successfully gets postpetition treatment for taxes covering a pre-petition period) and In re Koenig Sporting Goods, Inc., 203 F.3d 986 (6th Cir. 2000).

loosey goosey venue requirements and the fact that many corporations are domiciled in Delaware (3d Cir.), this gives the tenant a great deal of discretion—and opportunity in determining when to file.[58]

5. Recharacterization. Based on a substance-over-form approach, a debt instrument with equity features (such as a participating mortgage or a convertible mortgage) and an alternative mortgage instrument may be vulnerable to recharacterization if attacked by third-party creditors and by the I.R.S. as a constructive partnership (or some other form of equity-sharing arrangement) between the lender and the borrower. See Chapter 5A1, note 3.

Likewise, sale-and-leaseback transactions have sometimes been recharacterized as disguised mortgages for tax purposes. See Chapter 11B2, supra. In the *PCH Assocs.* case, the Second Circuit decided that the lease in a sale-and-leaseback transaction was not a true lease largely for the purposes of §365(d)(3), (4) which requires the trustee for the tenant to perform all obligations arising on or after the order for relief and provides that if the lease is not assumed within the required time period, it would be deemed rejected. The tenant under the sale-leaseback claimed that these provisions did not apply to this lease because it was not a "true lease." The Second Circuit agreed. See also Judge Easterbrook's decision in United Airlines, Inc. v. HSBC Bank USA, 416 F.3d 609 (7th Cir. 2005).

In reaching its first conclusion that this was not a "lease of real property" under these sections, the court cited the legislative history of another section, §502(b)(6) as furnishing "explicit authority for restricting the scope of that term to 'bona fide' leases." The court points out that the Senate Report stated that the phrase "'lease of real property' does not apply to lease financing transactions." What is somewhat incredible is that the court neglected to include in its quote the Senate Report's prefatory phrase, "As used in §502(b)(7) . . ." (now §502(b)(6)). This section, as you will recall from note 4 above, limits the landlord's claim on rejection of a lease by the tenant. The Senate Report analyzes the reasons that dollar limitation should not apply where a lease is a financing lease. Is this "explicit authority" for purposes of §365(d)(3) and (4)? Or is it explicit authority for the proposition that financing leases *are* leases of real property in any provision other than §502(b)(6)?[59] The Second Circuit mentioned, without

_____

58. Be aware, however, that the Third Circuit has recognized that §365(d)(3) must be read in connection with §503(b)(1) dealing with treatment of administrative expenses. In the case of In re Goody's Family Clothing, Inc., 610 F.3d 812 (3d Cir. 2010), the rent was due monthly in advance. The debtor filed on June 9, not having paid the rent due June 1. The next billing date was July 1, and pursuant to §365(d)(3) the tenant paid that rent. The landlord claimed that the tenant was also liable to pay, as an administrative expense, the June rent allocable to the period from June 9 to the end of that month (so-called "stub rent") while the tenant argued that the June rent arose on the billing date, which was June 1, and thus constituted a pre-petition claim. Judge Ambro held that §365(d)(3) does not supplant or preempt §503(b)(1) and that the landlord was therefore entitled to the stub rent as an administrative expense.

59. A little background. As discussed in Chapter 7C, when §502(b)(6) was being drafted the New York Insurance Law had strict loan-to-value standards for mortgage loans by insurers but

further discussion, the definition of "leases of real property" in §365(m) as including "any rental agreement to use real property." Wouldn't that definition cover this sale-leaseback?

Once it is determined that §365 requires a bona fide lease, the Court directs its attention to whether the lease in *PCH Assocs.* is a true lease. What is of great concern is that the provisions cited by the Court to attack the bona fide nature of the lease involved provisions and facts that are often found in sale-and-leaseback transactions. Since a sale and leaseback is most often designed as a form of financing, the sale price does not necessarily bear a relation to the value of the property. Similarly, the rent bears a relationship to the sale price and not the going rent for space in a building of that type. Finally, almost all ground leases are net leases, whether the lease is for financing purposes or not. Thus, the ultimate effect of *PCH Assocs.* on the future of lease financing transactions is potentially severe. Why should the parties not be permitted to agree to structure their financing in the form of a lease? Why should bankruptcy intervene?

In later proceedings reported at 949 F.2d 585 (2d Cir. 1991), the Second Circuit found it necessary to determine the appropriate characterization of the non-true lease sale and leaseback in *PCH Assocs.* The court held the parties' arrangement was not a joint venture, as the bankruptcy court had found. Rather, it was "nothing more than a sophisticated secured financing arrangement." 949 F.2d at 599. Now consider the following deleterious implications of the lease being held to be a mortgage that the Second Circuit did not consider. If it were a mortgage, would the mortgage have been properly recorded? In many jurisdictions, mortgages, deeds, and leases are recorded in different recording offices. If not properly recorded, the mortgagee runs the risk of being subordinate to the bankruptcy trustee, who is given the status of a hypothetical bona fide purchaser on the date of bankruptcy (§544(a)), with an interest superior to unrecorded liens.

If it is determined that the lease is really a mortgage, is it a mortgage that clogs the equity of redemption? Review the discussion of clogging at Chapter 5A1, note 4. The lessee (recharacterized as a mortgagor) in a lease transaction would not normally have the ability to reacquire the property by payment of an amount "borrowed," since the landlord has a reversion and gets the property back at the end of the term of a normal lease. Note the irony in the following: If the

---

permitted loans to corporations meeting certain earnings tests on an unsecured basis. The law had been interpreted by the Superintendant of Insurance to permit insurers to make mortgage loans without meeting the loan-to-value statutory requirements for a real estate mortgage if, inter alia, the loan was also secured by an assignment of a lease of the mortgaged premises to a tenant that met the earnings test for corporate loans. Some in the insurance industry were concerned that the claim limitation in §502(b)(6) would adversely affect the ability of life insurers to make real estate loans based on an assignment of a lease from high credit tenants. See Albenda and Lief, Net Lease Financing Transactions Under the Proposed Bankruptcy Act of 1973, 30 Bus. Law. 713 (1975). In response to these concerns the Congressional Staff inserted the legislative history that figured so prominently in the *PCH* decision. The Congressional staff had the foresight to preface the comment with a statement limiting its application to §502(b)(6), a limitation the Second Circuit chose to ignore.

seller-lessee (the "borrower" in a recharacterization of a sale and leaseback as a mortgage) becomes the owner of the property at the end of the lease term for a nominal payment (as may be the case in those sale and leasebacks that are purely financing transactions), the property would be "returned" on performance of the "obligation," and the transaction, which might justly be subject to recharacterization in tax and certain other situations, probably would not be subject to the anti-clogging rule. On the other hand, under those sale and leasebacks that are truly sales and leases, the property should remain in the purchaser-lessor at the end of the lease term. If such a sale and leaseback (a true lease because like any lease the lessor has a reversion after a term of years) were held to be a mortgage because it had a financing purpose, isn't there a significant risk that the anti-clogging rule would be applicable, since the "mortgagor" would not be in a position to recover the property on payment of the "indebtedness"?

Although rejected by the Second Circuit, the District Court had affirmed the Bankruptcy Court's determination that the transaction was a joint venture. 122 B.R. 7 (S.D.N.Y. 1990). What possible effects might this determination have on the rights and obligations of the parties held to be joint venturers?

As to whether the buyer-lessor's title insurance policy encompasses the effort to recharacterize the sale and leaseback in bankruptcy as a mortgage, see TICOR Title Ins. Co. of Cal. v. FFCA/IIP 1998 Prop. Co., 898 F. Supp. 633 (N.D. Ind. 1995) (excluded as a matter "suffered, assumed or agreed to" by an insured that had intended a mortgage loan relationship) and Homburger and Gallagher, To Pay or Not to Pay: Claiming Damages for Recharacterization of Sale Leaseback Transactions under Owner's Title Insurance Policies, 30 Real Prop., Prob. & Tr. J. 443 (Fall 1995).

6. Additional Reading. Ahart, The Inefficacy of the New Eviction Exceptions to the Automatic Stay, 80 Am. Bankr. L.J. 125 (2006); Bussell and Friedler, The Limits On Assuming and Assigning Executory Contracts, 74 Am. Bankr. L.J. 321 (2000); Carlson, Cars and Homes in Chapter 13 After the 2005 Amendments to the Bankruptcy Code, 14 Am. Bankr. Inst. L. Rev. 301 (2006); Harner, Black and Goodman, Debtors Beware: The Expanding Universe of Non-Assumable/Non-Assignable Contracts in Bankruptcy, 13 Am. Bankr. Inst. L. Rev. 187 (2005); Homburger and Andre, Real Estate Sale and Leaseback Transactions and the Risk of Recharacterization in Bankruptcy Proceedings, 24 Real Prop., Prob. & Tr. J. 95 (Summer 1989); King, Assuming and Assigning Executory Contracts: A History of Indeterminate "Applicable Law," 70 Am. Bankr. L.J. 95 (1996); Kothari, 11 U.S.C. §365(D)(3): A Conceptual Status Argument for Proration, 13 Am. Bankr. Inst. L. Rev. 297 (2005); Kuney, Further Misinterpretation of Bankruptcy Code Section 363(f): Elevating In Rem Interests and Promoting The Use of Property Law to Bankruptcy-Proof Real Estate Developments, 76 Am. Bankr. L.J. 289 (2002); Westbrook, A Functional Analysis of Executory Contracts, 74 Minn. L. Rev. 227 (1989); Westbrook, The Commission's Recommendations Concerning The Treatment of Bankruptcy Contracts, 5 Am. Bankr. Inst. L. Rev. 463 (1997); White and Medford, Rejection

Via Sale of Real Estate: Is Your Leasehold Interest Protected?, 26 Am. Bankr. Inst. J. 28 (2007).

2. *Bankruptcy of the Landlord*

Section 365(h) deals with rejection of a lease by a landlord in bankruptcy. A lease is both a contract and a conveyance. The landlord normally conveys to the tenant an estate or interest in the property for a term of years. The instrument of that conveyance, the lease, also normally contains contractual obligations between the landlord and the tenant. A conveyance is a completed transfer, and there is nothing of the estate left for the landlord to reject. The only thing that the landlord can accomplish by rejection is that it may cease performing its executory contractual obligations to the tenant.

The drafters of the former Bankruptcy Act recognized this dual nature of a lease and provided in §70b thereof that rejection of a lease by a bankrupt lessor "does not deprive the lessee of his estate." Unfortunately, it was unclear what provisions of the lease constituted the lessee's estate and what provisions were contractual. It was also unclear whether the clause saving the estate applied to reorganization bankruptcy under Chapter X as well as to liquidations.[60]

These issues came to a head as the Code was being drafted, when the Penn Central Railroad, in reorganization, attempted as landlord to reject leases of the so-called Park Avenue Properties. Originally, Park Avenue in New York City had been a cut in the ground through which trains ran back and forth from Grand Central Terminal, belching smoke and soot into the heart of the city. Eventually, for environmental and other reasons, the railroad covered over the tracks with platforms, with the intention of leasing the platforms for the construction of high-rise buildings. After some complex legal structuring to free the leases from the lien of corporate indentures covering the railroad's property,[61] the platforms were

---

60. These problems were discussed in Creedon and Zinman, Landlord's Bankruptcy: Laissez Les Lessees, 26 Bus. Law. 1391 (1971). See especially the letters from Professor MacLachlan (the drafter of §70b) appended to the article. See also Siegel, Landlord's Bankruptcy: A Proposal for Treatment of the Lease by Reference to Its Component Elements, 54 B.U. L. Rev. 903 (1974).

61. See discussion of priorities of mortgages and leases in Chapter 3E. As you will remember, the foreclosure of prior mortgages can cut off subordinate leases. In this case, the prior mortgage was in the form of a huge corporate indenture covering most of the railroad's real estate. No person could be expected to build a building on a leasehold with such a prior mortgage on the fee unless the lien of the mortgage were subordinated or the property were released from the lien. Unfortunately, it appeared the indenture trustees for the railroad were not empowered to subordinate or to release the lien for the purpose of leasing. They did, however, have authority to release the lien for the purpose of conveying portions of the railroad's property. The attorneys involved devised what they called a "grant of term," that is, a conveyance of an estate for a term of years without any of the contractual elements normally found in a lease. The trustees then released the lien of the indenture from the property; the grant of term to a railroad subsidiary was recorded; and the lien of the indenture spread back to the property, now subordinate to the grant of term and interests flowing out of that grant. The holder of the grant of term was then able to lease the

leased and the buildings built. Thus, when Penn Central filed in reorganization in 1970, it owned most of the property along lower Park Avenue and around the Terminal, property that was subject to long-term leases. The leases were at fixed rents, which over the years kept the value of the Penn Central fee relatively low. If the leases could be rejected, billions of dollars of increased value could be added to the estate. The lessees and leasehold mortgagees fought the rejection strenuously and won on equitable grounds. See In re Penn Central Transp. Co. (Disaffirmance of Executory Contracts), 458 F. Supp. 1346 (E.D. Pa. 1978). Perhaps Judge Fullam, in deciding not to rule on the meaning of the clause protecting the tenant's estate in §70b of the former Bankruptcy Act, had one eye on Washington, where the Code was in the process of being drafted and where he knew this problem would be dealt with. How successful the drafters were is discussed in the notes below.

NOTES AND QUESTIONS

1. The Penn Central *Decision.* While Judge Fullam did not permit rejection of the leases of the Park Avenue Properties, he decided the case on the equities rather than on a direct interpretation of the meaning of §70b of the former Bankruptcy Act. In addition, he considered the question of whether a landlord may reject a lease that is not burdensome to the estate (that is, a lease under which the landlord is not losing money even if the lease rent is below market). With respect to the Park Avenue Properties, the leases were net leases (that is, the tenant paid all the expenses and turned over the rent to the landlord without any offsets), produced income to the railroad, and thus could not be rejected under a burdensomeness test. Judge Fullam accepted the "business judgment" test of when an executory contract or lease could be rejected (it may be rejected when it is in the interest of the debtor based on business judgment), citing for support Group of Institutional Investors v. Chicago, M., St. P. & P.R. Co., 318 U.S. 523 (1943), a case involving a *tenant's* bankruptcy. What differences are there between a landlord's bankruptcy and a tenant's bankruptcy that might distinguish that case? Did the Bankruptcy Code deal with this problem?

2. The Bankruptcy Code Approach. Review §365(h)(1)(A)-(D) of the Bankruptcy Code and then address the following questions.

> ➢ *Problem 18-7*
> Assume in the master hypothetical that Dan Developer leases space in his building to Widget Corporation of America and later files in bankruptcy.
> a. Assume that the rent is below market and that Dan Developer, as landlord, rejects the lease. Nevertheless, can WCA retain its rights under the lease? If

property free and clear of the lien of the indenture. Do you see why this procedure constituted, in effect, a subordination of the lien of the indenture to the ground lease without actual subordination?

so, and WCA elects to retain its rights under the lease, can Dan get the court to increase the rental to market value for the remaining term as a condition to WCA's remaining in possession?

b. Assume the lease provided that Dan supply cleaning services. Dan rejects and stops providing these services. What can WCA do to protect itself under §365(h)? How would the provision work if Dan stopped providing elevator service and WCA occupied the 56th floor of the building?

c. If Conservative Insurance Company held a leasehold mortgage on WCA's estate, could WCA elect to treat the lease as terminated after Dan's rejection? What would the effect be on Conservative? Is there a provision in §365(h) to protect Conservative? See §§365(h)(1)(A)(i) and (D). With respect to (D), what do you think would happen if the tenant is able to treat the lease as terminated under (h)(1)(A)(i) and the leasehold mortgagee under (D) elects to retain its rights as "tenant"? While a landlord usually rejects because the lease is advantageous to the tenant and thus it is unlikely that the tenant will wish to treat the rejected lease as terminated, can you think of any situation in which this would not be true?

d. Assume Dan's lease to WCA contained a provision limiting Dan's ability to lease adjacent space to certain undesirable types of tenants. When Dan files in bankruptcy and rejects the lease, WCA elects to retain its rights. Do those rights include more than possession for the term or do they include the covenants? See, e.g., In re Arden and Howe Assoc. Ltd. , 152 B.R. 971 (Bankr. E.D. Cal. 1993), overruled by Bankruptcy Reform Act of 1994, Pub. L. No. 103-994, Oct. 22, 1994). Can you find the overruling language in §365(h)? Would your answer with respect to WCA's rights under leasehold covenants be the same if the covenant in question had been Dan's agreement in the lease that he would consent to his daughter's engagement to the WCA CEO's son? ◄

> *Problem 18-8*

Assume you are counsel to Ace Insurance Company, which has been asked to make a loan secured by a mortgage on a subleasehold estate. You learn that Oscar Owner has leased the property to Dan Developer under a net long-term ground lease (see Chapter 11A, supra). Dan is about to enter into a sublease of the entire building to Widget Corporation of America, and WCA has applied to Ace for a subleasehold mortgage loan. What risks would Ace face on the bankruptcy of Oscar Owner? Of Dan Developer? Of WCA? What documentary steps can be taken to mitigate these risks? Review how the court handled some of these problems in *The Great Atl.* case, and the analysis in Rosenberg and (Daniel) Zinman in note 4(b) above. ◄

3. Purchasers. In §365, Congress also deals with the question of the rights of certain purchasers when the seller in bankruptcy rejects a contract notwithstanding the principles of equitable conversion you studied in first-year property. Compare, for example, Speck v. First Nat'l. Bank (In re Speck), 798 F.2d 279 (8th Cir. 1986) with In re Streets & Beard Farm Partnership, 882 F.2d 233 (7th Cir. 1989). In subsections (i) and (j) of §365, Congress gave special protection where the purchaser is in possession of the property, for instance, under a long-term installment land contract. Why, do you think, was protection afforded in this situation?

A purchaser of a time-share interest ("time-shares" are rights to use property for specified periods of time during the life of the interest; see definition of "time-share plan" in §101(53D)) would normally have had the benefit of §365(i) and (j) where the interest to be acquired is an interest in real property. However, many such interests are not real property interests but merely licenses to use the property. In Sombrero Reef Club v. Allman (In re Sombrero Reef Club), 18 B.R. 612 (Bankr. S.D. Fla. 1982), the bankruptcy court sent shivers through the time-share industry by holding that those time-share contracts giving purchasers a right to occupy and use the facilities, rather than a lease or conveyance of real estate, were executory contracts subject to rejection and not subject to the protections afforded lessees or purchasers when the landlord or seller rejects. In 1984, Congress eased the industry's concern by including time-share purchasers under §365(h), thereby giving such purchasers generally the same type of protection afforded lessees.

4. Section 365 v. Section 363. Suppose a landlord's bankruptcy estate wants to reject a lease, but does not want the tenant to retain its rights as provided by §365(h) of the Bankruptcy Code. Can it, instead, elect to sell the fee interest free and clear of the lease? From our discussion of §363 of the Bankruptcy Code, supra Chapter 18C1, note 5, you know that property can be sold free and clear of interests in the property under §363(f). In Precision Industries, Inc. v. Qualitech Steel SBQ, LLC, 327 F.3d 537 (7th Cir. 2003), the Seventh Circuit held that since the leasehold was an "interest" in property within the meaning of §363(f), the property could be sold free and clear of the lease, thus avoiding the protections for the tenant built into §365(h). The tenant claimed that under §365(h) it was entitled to retain its rights under the lease and that §365(h), being more specific than §363(f), controlled.

The Seventh Circuit found that there was no conflict between §§363(f) and 365(h)—§365(h) applying only when a landlord rejects the lease and §363(f) applying when the landlord sells the property. The court noted that while §365(h) contains protections for the tenant when the landlord rejects, §363 also provides protection for interests in the property by virtue of §363(e) under which, inter alia, upon request of a party with an interest in the property being sold the bankruptcy court must prohibit or condition the sale as necessary "to provide adequate protection of such interest." The Seventh Circuit permitted the sale free and clear of the lease.

Under §363(f) the property cannot be sold free and clear of an interest unless one of five prerequisites is met. The Seventh Circuit noted that the parties did not dispute that at least one of the five had been met. The five requirements are (1) that under nonbankruptcy law the property could be sold free and clear of the interest; (2) that the entity holding the interest consents; (3) that if the interest is a lien, the property will be sold at a price in excess of all liens on the property; (4) that the interest is in bona fide dispute;[62] and (5) that the entity holding the interest could be compelled in a legal or equitable proceeding to accept a money satisfaction of its interest.

In reviewing the facts in *Qualitech*, it would seem that the first requirement was probably met because the lease had not been recorded and thus was subject to the rights of the trustee as a bona fide purchaser. If you had represented the leasehold mortgagee, you would, of course, have made certain that the lease was properly recorded under state law, and thus have eliminated that possibility.

Is there any other prerequisite that might cause you grief? How do you prevent the tenant from consenting to a sale free and clear, or, better yet, how do you get the tenant to object in light of cases that say the failure to object is a consent? See, e.g., FutureSource, LLC. v. Reuters, Ltd., 312 F.3d 281, 285 (7th Cir. 2002), and Zinman, *Precision* in Statutory Drafting: The *Qualitech* Quagmire and the Sad History of Section 365(h) of the Bankruptcy Code, 38 J. Marshall L. Rev. 97 n.110 (2004).

Could a lessee be required to accept a money satisfaction (as provided in prerequisite (5) if it is possible that the fee interest could be condemned under the right of eminent domain? Is that the type of situation contemplated by the fifth prerequisite? If so, what was the need for the first four?[63]

Section 363(e) provides that on request of a party with an interest in the property being sold, such as a lessee, the court would be required to provide adequate protection for the lessee's interest. Apparently, in *Qualitech* no such request was made. In a situation where the lessee does not make a request for adequate protection (for example, where the leasehold has no value over the leasehold mortgage, there may be no reason for the tenant to make the request) can the leasehold mortgagee make the request for adequate protection? Hint: Does the leasehold mortgagee have an interest in the property being sold? As counsel to such a leasehold mortgagee, what drafting advice might you have given your client when the deal was being put together? Hint: What is a "streamlined mortgage"? (Review Chapter 11A4).

It would seem that the Seventh Circuit may have been correct in its conclusion that there is no conflict between the two sections—one dealing with rejection and one with sales. But consider a different situation where the *tenant* is in bankruptcy and proposes to sell the lease. For example, suppose Canview Department Store holds a leasehold interest in a shopping center and has filed in

---

62. For a good example of where this prerequisite might be met in connection with property being sold free and clear of a lease, see Cheslock-Bakker & Assocs. v. Kremer et al. (In re Downtown Athletic Club), 44 Collier Bankr. Cas. 2d 342 (S.D.N.Y. 2000).

63. See In re Haskell, 321 B.R. 1 (Bankr. D. Mass. 2005) which reads this prerequisite to apply only where the trustee or the debtor has the actual power to compel a monetary satisfaction of the interest.

bankruptcy. It would like to assume and assign its lease at a substantial profit. However, the prospective assignee's financial performance and operating performance are well below that of Canview at the time Canview entered into the lease, which makes the lease ineligible for the assignment under §365(b)(3)(A). Furthermore, the business of the proposed assignee would clearly disturb the tenant mix in the shopping center, a no-no under §365(b)(3)(D). If you were counsel to the debtor in possession, would you suggest that instead of assuming and assigning the lease under §365, the lease be sold to the prospective assignee under §363(b), thus avoiding the nasty requirements of §365? As the lease is not being sold free and clear of an interest in the lease, it would seem that none of the prerequisites of §363(f) would have to be met. In a sale under §363, would the landlord be entitled to adequate protection under 363(e)? Under §363(e) adequate protection is reserved for entities that have interests in the property being sold, in this case the lease. Does a landlord in this situation have an interest in the lease for which it can request adequate protection? Or does it have only a reversion after a term of years? So it may seem that a sale of the lease under §363 would be the perfect move for Canview. Or would it? Is not a sale of a lease the same as an assignment of the lease? Would the conclusion of the Seventh Circuit—that under the facts of that case, §§363(f) and 365(h) dealt with different things— apply when Canview, as tenant, chooses to "sell" rather than "assign"?

A relatively recent District Court decision on this issue is Dishi & Sons v. Bay Condos LLC, 510 B.R. 696 (S.D.N.Y. 2014). The court points out that a majority of cases support the notion that §365(h) takes precedence over 363(f), while a minority of cases, including *Qualitech*, see no conflict between the two provisions, each dealing with different circumstances (rejection of a lease vs. sale free and clear of interests in the property) and each providing for forms of protection for those adversely affected by the rejection or sale.[64] The *Dishi* court rejected the majority view and held that a lessee's rights may be extinguished through a §365(f) sale. However, it questioned whether any of the prerequisites of §363(f) had been met and, most importantly, found that even if the lessee's rights could be lost through a §363(f) sale, §363(e) required that the lessee receive adequate protection. The court affirmed the bankruptcy court's determination that adequate protection requires that the lessee be entitled to continued possession of the property in order to afford the lessee the indubitable equivalent of its interest under the §361 definition of "adequate protection." If continued possession is required for adequate protection rather than, say, payment of the difference in rent at a new location, lost business, and moving expenses, does sale of property free and clear of a lease have any consequences? *Dishi* points out that notwithstanding *Qualitech*, a majority of courts considering

---

64. Robert Zinman, one of the authors of this text, wishes to point out that an implication that may be drawn from the *Dishi* court's quotation (510 B.R. at 703) from his J. Marshall L. Rev. article, cited above, that he supported the majority view, would be incorrect. The article supported the minority view but concluded that the protections afforded under §363 for those adversely affected by a §363(f) sale were seriously deficient, and proposed statutory amendments to correct the deficiencies.

the issue have found that §365(h) trumps §363. However, very recently the Ninth Circuit agreed with the Seventh Circuit, making it 2-0 on the Circuit Court level in favor of the *Qualitech* "minority" position. See Pinnacle Restaurant at Big Sky, LLC v. CH SP Acquisitions, LLC (In re Spanish Peaks Holdings II, LLC), 2017 WL 2979660 (9th Cir. July 13, 2017). Perhaps this may serve as an inducement to an eventual legislative solution to the problem.

For more extensive discussions of the problems involved in reconciling §§365 and 363, and some proposed statutory fixes, see generally Asebedo, The Sale of Real Property Free and Clear of a Lease: Making Sense of Sections 363(f) and 365(h) of the Bankruptcy Code, 24 Am. Bankr. Inst. L. Rev. 279 (2016) (emphasizing the tensions existing under state law), and Zinman, supra, 38 J. Marshall L. Rev. 97, (offering some proposed statutory fixes), and material cited therein.

5. Additional Reading. Baxter, Section 363 Sales Free and Clear of Interests: Why The Seventh Circuit Erred in Precision Industries v. Qualitech Steel, 59 Bus. Law. 475, 501 (2003); Bartell, Revisiting Rejection: Secured Party Interests in Leases and Executory Contracts 103 Dick. L. Rev. 497 (1999); Brege, An Efficiency Model of Section 363(b) Sales, 92 Va. L. Rev. 1639 (2006); Countryman, Executory Contracts in Bankruptcy, 57 Minn. L. Rev. 439 (1973) (Part 1), 58 Minn. L. Rev. 479 (Part II) (1974); Creedon and Zinman, Landlord's Bankruptcy: Laissez Les Lessees, 24 Bus. Law. 1391 (1971); Epling, Treatment of Land Sales Contracts under the Bankruptcy Code, 1981 Ariz. St. L.J. 853; Genovese, Precision Industries v. Qualitech Steel: Easing the Tension Between Sections 363 and 365 of the Bankruptcy Code?, 39 Real Prop. Prob. & Tr. J. 627, 648 (2004); Gunlock, An Appeal to Equity: Why Bankruptcy Courts Should Resort to Equitable Powers for Latitude in Their Interpretation of "Interests" Under Section 363(f) of the Bankruptcy Code, 47 Wm. & Mary L. Rev. 347 (2005); Homburger, Gallagher and Rubel, Conflict Resolved: Bankruptcy Code Section 365(h) and the Contradictory Cases Requiring Its Amendment, 29 Real Prop. Prob. & Tr. J. 869 (1995); McCarver, Installment Land Contracts and Section 365 of the Bankruptcy Reform Act, 49 Mo. L. Rev. 337 (1984); Ostow, Landlord's Bankruptcy: An Analysis of the Tenant's Rights and Remedies under Bankruptcy Code §365(h), 35 Rutgers L. Rev. 631 (1983); Siegel, Landlord's Bankruptcy: A Proposal for Treatment of the Lease by Reference to Its Component Elements, 54 B.U. L. Rev. 903 (1974); Silverstein, Rejection of Executory Contracts in Bankruptcy and Reorganization, 31 U. Chi. L. Rev. 467 (1964); Winston & Shultz, Sizing Up the "Cap": Commercial Lease Rejection Claims in Bankruptcy, 27 Cal. Bankr. J. 209 (2004).

Chapter 19

Environmental Liabilities in Real Estate Transactions

Many federal and state statutes address hazardous waste contamination. From the standpoint of the mortgagee and other real estate parties, perhaps the most significant is the federal Comprehensive Environmental Response, Compensation, and Liability Act of 1980 (CERCLA).[1] CERCLA established the so-called Superfund program to pay for cleaning up environmental contamination. Hardly charitable in nature, CERCLA imposes unlimited liability on certain parties for the cost of all cleanup activities incurred by the United States or any state, as well as any other necessary costs of response incurred by private parties. When contamination is caused by willful misconduct or negligence, punitive damages may be assessed of up to three times the actual cost. The federal government is afforded a lien on the property for these liabilities, effective on filing a notice at the appropriate office. There are also criminal penalties for, inter alia, failing to notify the Environmental Protection Agency (EPA) of a release of hazardous substances or the existence of hazardous dumps, destroying records pertaining to hazardous wastes, and giving false information.

Liability is imposed on four categories of potentially responsible parties: (1) the "owner" or "operator" of the property (presumably at the time of the suit); (2) the "owner" or "operator" at the time of "disposal" of the hazardous substances; (3) any person owning or possessing hazardous substances who arranges for their disposal or treatment at, or transport to, a facility from which there is a release of hazardous substances; and (4) any person who transports hazardous substances to a facility selected by such person from which there is a release of hazardous substances.

CERCLA includes certain exemptions and defenses designed to protect innocent parties. First, "owner" and "operator" are defined to exclude "a person, who, without participating in the management of a . . . facility, holds indicia of ownership primarily to protect his security interest in the . . . facility"—known as the secured party or security interest exemption.[2]

Second, the owner and operator may assert several affirmative defenses, for example, that the damages resulted solely from an act of God or that the discharge was caused solely by a third party not an employee or agent of, or in a contractual relationship with, the owner or operator, provided that the defendant

---

1. 42 U.S.C. §§9601 et seq.
2. CERCLA §101(20), 42 U.S.C. §9601(20).

exercised due care with respect to the hazardous substance and took precautions against foreseeable acts or omissions of the third party—the so-called third party defense.[3] "Contractual relationships" include deeds and land contracts unless the acquiring party can show that the contamination occurred before it acquired the interest and that it undertook appropriate inquiry and did not know and had no reason to know of the existence of the hazardous substance. The acquiring party's ability to overcome the contractual relationship with the third-party violator is known as the innocent purchaser or innocent landowner defense.[4] Further, the 2002 Brownfields Revitalization and Environmental Restoration Act[5] added protection of "bona fide prospective purchasers" to insulate those who acquire known contaminated properties if, among other conditions, they undertake appropriate inquiry before purchase and take reasonable steps to prevent any continuing release.

A. THE MORTGAGEE'S LIABILITY FOR ENVIRONMENTAL HAZARDS

Although at first impression these CERCLA exemptions might seem to insulate the mortgagee from liability, in practice they present numerous hazards. Because the issues of due care, appropriate inquiry, and knowledge often cannot be resolved in the lender's favor without a trial, the third party, innocent purchaser, and prospective purchaser defenses are not reassuring to lenders who wish to avoid protracted litigation. Although enacted specifically for lenders, the security interest exemption failed as a "safe harbor" in practice. Because CERCLA did not define what constitutes participation in management, lenders were unsure of the consequences of ordinary activities in the lender-borrower relationship, such as monitoring the borrower's financial condition and inspecting the collateral. Aggravating lenders' concerns, in 1990 the Eleventh Circuit in United States v. Fleet Factors Corp. construed the no-participation requirement in the security interest exemption to constitute an independent basis for holding the lender liable "if its involvement with the management of the facility is sufficiently broad to support the inference that it could affect hazardous waste disposal decisions if it so chose."[6]

At the same time, lenders were uncertain whether they were liable as owners if they took title to contaminated property in foreclosure proceedings; in the language of CERCLA's security interest exemption, did the lender purchase the collateral "primarily to protect" its security interest? One of the first reported

---

3. CERCLA §107(b), 42 U.S.C. §9607(b).
4. CERCLA §101(35), 42 U.S.C. §9601.
5. Pub. L. No. 107-118, 115 Stat. 2356 (2002).
6. 901 F.2d 1550, 1558 (11th Cir. 1990), cert. denied, 498 U.S. 1046 (1991). But see In re Bergsoe Metal Corp., 910 F.2d 668, 673 (9th Cir. 1990). ("Regardless of what rights [the lender] had, it cannot have participated in management if it never exercised them.")

decisions held that a mortgagee's brief holding of title for four months following a foreclosure sale did not deprive it of the security interest exemption.[7] However, another court in United States v. Maryland Bank & Trust Co. appeared to limit the benefit of this exemption to preforeclosure mortgagees in title theory states (those in which the mortgagor is said to convey title to the mortgagee, as distinguished from lien theory states, where the mortgagee holds only a lien on the property, as discussed at Chapter 3A). That court held the security interest exemption did not protect a former mortgagee that had held title for nearly four years following its foreclosure.[8]

Intending to reduce lender uncertainty following decisions such as *Fleet Factors* and *Maryland Bank*, in 1992 the EPA issued the so-called EPA Rule (the "Rule") construing the security interest exemption.[9] Among its provisions, the Rule specified actions that constituted participation in management (such as engaging in day-to-day decision making over the borrower's enterprise or exercising decision-making control over the borrower's environmental compliance) and those that did not (such as undertaking environmental inspections, requiring contamination cleanup, and providing financial advice). Moreover, it protected lenders who acquired their collateral through foreclosure or accepted a deed in lieu so long as they undertook to sell the property in a reasonably expeditious manner in accordance with specified procedures. In 1994, however, the D.C. Circuit Court of Appeals invalidated the Rule because the EPA lacked authority to rulemake on the scope of CERCLA liability.[10]

In 1996, Congress enacted the Asset Conservation, Lender Liability, and Deposit Insurance Protection Act of 1996, which amended the CERCLA definition of "owner or operator" to include much of the content of the invalidated Rule. In reading the following excerpt of the amendment, notice how it rejects the reasoning in *Fleet Factors* and *Maryland Bank*.

CERCLA §101(20)
42 U.S.C.A. §9601(20)

(E) Exclusion of lenders not participants in management . . .

(ii) Foreclosure

The term "owner or operator" does not include a person that is a lender that did not participate in management of a . . . facility prior

---

7. See United States v. Mirabile, 1985 WL 97 (E.D. Pa. Sept. 6, 1985). See also United States v. McLamb, 5 F.3d 69 (4th Cir. 1993) (mortgagee that owned collateral for six months following foreclosure sale is covered under security interest exemption where it made a reasonably prompt effort to divest itself of the unwelcome ownership).

8. United States v. Maryland Bank & Trust Co., 632 F. Supp. 573 (D. Md. 1986).

9. 57 Fed. Reg. 18382 (Apr. 29, 1992) (codified at 40 C.F.R. §§300.1100, 300.1105).

10. Kelley v. EPA, 15 F.3d 1100 (D.C. Cir.), reh'g denied, 25 F.3d 1088 (1994), cert. denied, 513 U.S. 1110 (1995).

to foreclosure, notwithstanding that the person—

(I) forecloses on the . . . facility; and

(II) after foreclosure, sells, re-leases (in the case of a lease finance transaction), or liquidates the . . . facility, maintains business activities, winds up operations, undertakes a response action under section 9607(d)(1) of this title or under the direction of an on-scene coordinator appointed under the National Contingency Plan, with respect to the . . . facility, or takes any other measure to preserve, protect, or prepare the . . . facility prior to sale or disposition, if the person seeks to sell, re-lease (in the case of a lease finance transaction), or otherwise divest the person of the . . . facility at the earliest practicable, commercially reasonable time, on commercially reasonable terms, taking into account market conditions and legal and regulatory requirements.

(F) Participation in management.—For purposes of subparagraph (E)—

(i) the term "participate in management"—

(I) means actually participating in the management or operational affairs of a . . . facility; and

(II) does not include merely having the capacity to influence, or the unexercised right to control,. . . facility operations;

(ii) a person that is a lender and that holds indicia of ownership primarily to protect a security interest in a . . . facility shall be considered to participate in management only if, while the borrower is still in possession of the . . . facility encumbered by the security interest, the person—

(I) exercises decisionmaking control over the environmental compliance related to the . . . facility, such that the person has undertaken responsibility for the hazardous substance handling or disposal practices related to the . . . facility; or

(II) exercises control at a level comparable to that of a manager of the . . . facility, such that the person has assumed or manifested responsibility—

(aa) for the overall management of the . . . facility encompassing day-to-day decisionmaking with respect to environmental compliance; or

(bb) over all or substantially all of the operational functions (as distinguished from financial or administrative functions) of the . . . facility other than the function of environmental compliance;

(iii) the term "participate in management" does not include performing an act or failing to act prior to the time at which a security interest is created in a . . . facility; and

(iv) the term "participate in management" does not include—

(I) holding a security interest or abandoning or releasing a security interest;

(II) including in the terms of an extension of credit, or in a contract or security agreement relating to the extension, a covenant, warranty, or other term or condition that relates to environmental compliance;

(III) monitoring or enforcing the terms and conditions of the extension of credit or security interest;

(IV) monitoring or undertaking 1 or more inspections of the . . . facility;

(V) requiring a response action or other lawful means of addressing the release or threatened release of a hazardous substance in connection with the . . . facility prior to, during, or on the expiration of the term of the extension of credit;

(VI) providing financial or other advice or counseling in an effort to mitigate, prevent, or cure default or diminution in the value of the . . . facility;

(VII) restructuring, renegotiating, or otherwise agreeing to alter the terms and conditions of the extension of credit or security interest, exercising forbearance;

(VIII) exercising other remedies that may be available under applicable law for the breach of a term or condition of the extension of credit or security agreement; or

(IX) conducting a response action under section 9607(d) of this title or under the direction of an on-scene coordinator appointed under the National Contingency Plan, if the actions do not rise to the level of participating in management (within the meaning of clauses (i) and (ii)).

(G) Other terms . . .

(ii) Financial or administrative function

The term "financial or administrative function" includes a function such as that of a credit manager, accounts payable officer, accounts receivable officer, personnel manager, comptroller, or chief financial officer, or a similar function.

(iii) Foreclosure; foreclose

The terms "foreclosure" and "foreclose" mean, respectively, acquiring, and to acquire, a . . . facility through—

(I)(aa) purchase at sale under a judgment or decree, power of sale, or nonjudicial foreclosure sale;

(bb) a deed in lieu of foreclosure, or similar conveyance from a trustee; or (cc) repossession, if the . . . facility was security for an extension of credit previously contracted;

(II) conveyance pursuant to an extension of credit previously contracted, including the termination of a lease agreement; or

(III) any other formal or informal manner by which the person acquires, for subsequent disposition, title to or possession of a . . . facility in order to protect the security interest of the person. . . .

(v) Operational function

The term "operational function" includes a function such as that of a facility or plant manager, operations manager, chief operating officer, or chief executive officer.

(vi) Security interest

The term "security interest" includes a right under a mortgage, deed of trust, assignment, judgment lien, pledge, security agreement, factoring agreement, or lease and any other right accruing to a person to secure the repayment of money, the performance of a duty, or any other obligation by a nonaffiliated person.

Despite the enactment by Congress of these lender liability protections in CERCLA, lenders remain exposed to liabilities arising under other federal and state environmental statutes,[11] as well as common law theories such as trespass. Although the following article was written before the 1996 amendments to CERCLA, its program of due diligence for lenders that wish to limit environmental risks remains relevant.

Forte, Environmental Liability Risk Management
3 Prob. & Prop. 57 (Jan.-Feb. 1989)

. . . MARKETING

While it is continually stated that environmental due diligence must be a case by case approach, a lender can greatly reduce its risks by establishing an institutional lending program. To avoid lost opportunities, the lender should delineate the scope of its lending marketplace—to whom it should lend and upon what types of collateral security. It could determine to avoid companies engaged

---

11. See note/question 4, infra. The CERCLA protections enacted in 1996 do extend to liabilities imposed under the federal Resource Conservation and Recovery Act (42 U.S.C. §§6901-6992) on owners and operators of petroleum underground storage tanks.

in making, transporting, storing or dumping toxic substances and likewise reject as collateral security any property used by them in those respective businesses. This could be described as industry redlining. It could determine to avoid buildings that contain asbestos, as some major insurance companies have done, or properties previously occupied by gas stations, incinerators, dumps, coal or gas plants, or containing underground storage of possible contaminants. The lender could also avoid property on or adjacent to actual toxic waste sites. The potential delineation of businesses and properties could be as extensive as the federal Office of Management and Budget list of industrial classifications. . . . This is simply an allocation of the lender's resources to avoid dedicating time and personnel to transactions which if pre-screened would not have been financed.

UNDERWRITING

Having determined its lending marketplace, a lender must revise its application forms to include a detailed environmental questionnaire to obtain sufficient information about: its borrower, its borrower's history, and its borrower's business; the location and geography of the property offered as collateral; the proposed uses of the property; and the property's proximity to environmentally sensitive areas (such as natural waterways, timberland, public water supply systems and reservoirs, farm land, landfill areas, wildlife refuges and solid waste dumps). The loan officer should perform an initial site inspection to determine what he or she can by visual inspection of the property. The lender should not rely on a third party performing another related function (e.g., appraiser or surveyor) as a substitute for a loan officer actually "walking" the property and adjoining areas. There are telltale signs of toxic waste which can be easily identified: oddly colored soil, seeping ground liquids, an unusual absence of (or presence of dead) vegetation, bubbling or discolored water, evidence of underground storage (e.g., areas of subsidence) or discarded by-products from a manufacturing process. A scenic pond could be a toxic substance holding pool.

Regardless of the loan officer's assessment of the proposed collateral, the lender should condition the funding of its loan upon a satisfactory site assessment by a professionally trained environmental engineer or consultant who will evaluate the special risks which may be involved in the structure, soil, groundwater or equipment at the property. It may be more prudent for a lender to use an independent environmental consultant rather than a lender employee (even if qualified) to avoid possible lender liability claims by a borrower that it relied on the lender's analysis in making its own decision [for example, to purchase the property].[12] Any site assessment should include a visual survey (including

12. An Ohio appellate court, however, has held that a lender may be liable to the borrower-purchaser for its alleged negligent recommendation of an independent consultant to perform the environmental site assessment required as a condition to the loan. Lippy v. Society Natl. Bank, 100 Ohio App. 3d 37, 651 N.E.2d 1364 (1995)—EDS.

surface drainage, topography, buildings and water courses), a record review (including the chain of ownership, site use history, historical review of maps, plans, permits and photographs, regulatory history and insurance and claims), and an area reconnaissance to confirm the status and local context of the property. While this is primarily a paper and visual review, environmental experts contend that the overwhelming majority of problems are identified at this initial phase of investigation.

If after the initial audit there is evidence (or even a suspicion) of contamination and the investor wishes to continue in the transaction, an environmental consultant must be retained to conduct specific site testing of the structure, soil, groundwater or equipment at the property, as appropriate to prove or disprove contamination. If the property is determined to be contaminated, however, further tests will be necessary to determine the source and extent of the problem. Of course, a written report of assessment and recommendations at each stage should be obtained as a record of the lender's diligence. . . .

Site assessments are costly; they may cause delays and are no guaranty that the property is clean as statistical samples are not foolproof. . . .

ORIGINATION

Regardless of a lender's underwriting diligence, the potential risk of a problem continues and should be dealt with at the closing and funding of the mortgage loan. Lenders will want the closing documents to shift the liability (to the extent possible) to the borrower, a third-party guarantor or third-party service provider.

At a minimum, the loan documents delivered at closing should contain specific provisions dealing with environmental hazards. The borrower should represent and warrant that: the property has not been used nor is it currently used in a manner which violates applicable federal, state or local environmental laws, that the seller, the borrower and any tenant have not received any notice from a government agency for a violation of such laws and if such notice is received, the borrower shall immediately notify the lender; and that the borrower has no intention to use the property in such a manner. The borrower should also covenant not to cause such a violation, nor to permit any tenant to cause such a violation, nor to permit any environmental liens to be placed on the property. The borrower should indemnify the lender for all clean-up costs regardless of borrower's fault. These representations, warranties, covenants and indemnification for environmental risk should be carved out of any personal liability exculpation [nonrecourse] clause in the loan documents. The FNMA [Federal National Mortgage Association] requires such a carve-out in multi-family transactions. There should be personal liability of the borrower and/or its principals to the lender for these risks. In fact, if the borrower is not deemed credit-worthy for the risk, a personal guaranty by a third party might be obtained.

A breach of any of the foregoing should constitute an event of default entitling the lender to accelerate the loan. While cash collateral or cash equivalents may be tendered to cover a known problem, the issues are how accurate is the cost estimate for clean-up after the risk has been taken and what level of clean-up a governmental agency will require. It is this inability to determine the limits of liability which will probably mitigate against the use of surety bonds to cover the environmental risk.

Title insurance offers little or no protection to the lender because environmental liens are not always filed in the land records and sometimes attach retroactively. . . .[13]

While liability insurers continue to disclaim coverage under traditional comprehensive general liability policies, there are some types of environmental coverage endorsements available to lenders. For example, environmental impairment policies are offered but are limited to claims made during the term of the policy for events occurring during the term or in a specified retroactive period. Such policies are also generally offered only after the insurer's consultant conducts a comprehensive engineering study of the insured property. . . .

ADMINISTRATION

After closing, due diligence should continue to be maintained during the term of the loan. A standard program should be implemented for proper risk management, including periodic site inspections to monitor the condition and use of the property and to detect visible changes. Obtaining and reviewing annual rent rolls for any new tenants in problem businesses might also be useful. If a property is in a problem area, environmental records should be periodically checked much the same as the tax records are reviewed. Transfers of property should be carefully screened to determine a purchaser's business or intended use of the property. Care should be taken in any subsequent loan modifications not to intentionally (or unintentionally by changing material terms) release prior owners who might have been contractually liable for any environmental damages. A court will recognize a release of liability between two parties although it will have no effect on the government's right to proceed against either or both parties for the environmental claim.

Notwithstanding continued vigilance with respect to the status of the property, equipment and owner and/or tenant uses, a lender should limit its involvement with a borrower to a debtor-creditor relationship. Moreover, certain lender prerogatives in dealing with the borrower's business should be exercised in such a manner as to avoid any suggestion of lender control which might create operator liability. A lender should only consider entering a joint venture or equity

---

13. The 2006 ALTA Loan Policy encompasses environmental protection laws when notice of a violation is recorded in the public records or a lien is filed with the clerk of the federal district court where the property is located—EDS.

participation arrangement with a borrower after a careful review of potential risk of owner status for the lender.

Yet diligence is futile if a lender is unable to document its efforts satisfactorily at a later date. Thus, an adequate and diligent information and record-keeping system must be an integrated part of any servicing operation. All telephone notes, inspections, reports, surveys or studies should be recorded and maintained in a manner allowing retrieval on a property specific basis. To adequately prove the basis for a lender's decisions may be as important as conducting its diligence if a lender desires to limit its potential liability.

DISPOSITION

A lender's liability for its diligence will be extended to third parties when it sells a loan or a whole or partial participation interest on a loan, to an investor, whether during or after origination of the loan. As environmental issues become more significant, investors may be requesting representations and warranties from originators as a condition to their investment. To reduce its risk of liability, the originating lender should probably deliver to the investor all of the lender's environmental audit records and any testing reports and allow the investor to make its own decision on the information. If that is not acceptable, any representation or warranty which is given should be severely limited as to the best of lender's knowledge and limited to the inquiry actually conducted by lender's agents. The lender should not put itself in the position of becoming the guarantor or surety of any environmental risk to its investor.

ENFORCEMENT

. . . It is . . . imperative that any lender establish a standard procedure for reviewing collateral security before any enforcement of remedies is considered. The lender should review: the existing file (including site inspection and lease reports); the loan documents and subsequent modifications; any guarantees and indemnities obtained at closing; the servicing log to determine post-closing actions; the current tenants and uses; and any environmental impairment insurance. The lender should also reinspect the site and possibly conduct certain tests (provided the lender may do so without liability under the loan documents and local law). In many states, the lender will not be able to enter the property to do a site assessment without the present consent of a defaulting borrower.

Even if no problem is detected, a receiver should be sought to provide security for the collateral and avoid any intentional introduction of hazardous substances to the property by a vindictive borrower or accidental introduction by a careless operator tenant. If, after due diligence, a problem is detected and the risk quantified, the lender may determine (after discussion with investors where applicable) to pursue its remedies under the promissory note or any guarantees which may have been delivered at closing rather than to foreclose on the mortgage.

If a participant in a loan participation wants to enforce the loan over the objection of the lead lender after the lead lender's due diligence, the lender should seek to either assign the record holder portion to the participant or obtain a full indemnity for all damages it may sustain from the participants' enforcement of the loan documents. . . .

CONCLUSION

Not every property offered by a borrower as collateral security for a loan will be a toxic waste site and lending officers should not begin to look for toxic waste under every stone. But with [approximately 1500] hazardous substances recognized by the federal government, toxic waste is a real and substantial danger to a lender's collateral. While the "appropriate inquiry" conducted at each stage will not necessarily be the same for each loan, the degree of diligence should increase if there is even a reasonable suspicion of contamination. While each loan will not require the same environmental audit, an audit *should* be conducted for every loan.

Of course, all investors—owners and lenders—should understand the environmental risks involved in real estate investment as well as financing and evaluate their risk management procedures. Establishing a staged due diligence program will cause delays in underwriting and cancellations of closings for transactions as borrowers resist the precautions that lenders undertake to ascertain their risks. But as all lenders in the marketplace generally adopt similar diligence programs, borrowers will have no alternative but to accept developing environmental audit procedures as another cost of doing business.

The cost and delay of an environmental survey (and possible testing) is relatively small when compared to astronomical (and perpetual) environmental liability it may avoid for the real estate investor. Each investor should perform its own appropriate inquiry to establish the environmental status of a property at each transfer of an interest in such property. Only by making inquiry appropriate to the circumstances with respect to the environmental status of a property at the time of transfer can an investor establish to a court or government regulator that the investor is entitled to assert the innocent purchaser defense.

NOTES AND QUESTIONS

1. Participation in Management. As discussed above, the Eleventh Circuit in *Fleet Factors* construed CERCLA (prior to its 1996 amendment) to conclude that a lender participates in management if it has the capacity to influence the borrower's hazardous waste disposal decisions. What was it about *Fleet Factors* that disturbed lenders and real estate experts? Perhaps that it led to expansive liability claims. For example, one plaintiff contended under *Fleet Factors* that the mortgagee's insistence on financial covenants regulating the mortgagor's new indebtedness, purchases, dividends, and the like, as well as the mortgagee's agreement to lend additional money for underground tank removals, resulted in "operator" liability. Rejecting the plaintiff's reliance on *Fleet Factors*, the court concluded that to impose liability in these circumstances would eviscerate the security interest exemption. Z & Z Leasing Inc. v. Graying Reel, Inc., 873 F. Supp. 51, 55-56 (E.D. Mich. 1995). Under these facts, would a court reach the same result under the 1996 amendment to CERCLA excerpted above?

2. *The Foreclosing Lender.* If you were representing a lender following its purchase of the collateral at a foreclosure sale, what steps would you advise the lender to take to help ensure its reliance on the security interest exemption as amended in 1996? See 2 Lender Liability: Law, Prac. & Prevention §17:48 (2016 update) for a good discussion of lender' liability after *Fleet Factors* under the 1996 statute. Assuming that the lender who undertakes diligently to sell the property following its acquisition of title in foreclosure can now avoid liability under CERCLA for cleanup expenses, does the lender nonetheless have an incentive to undertake environmental hazard due diligence both in making the loan and prior to its foreclosure sale? If hazardous waste contamination is discovered after the foreclosure and no one is willing to purchase the property while it is subject to this toxic "cloud," will the lender lose its protection under the security interest exemption?

> ➤ **Problem 19-1**
> Assume that following Dan Developer's default, FNB, his construction lender, forecloses on the partially completed project and acquires title. Does FNB incur any risk of losing its protection under the security interest exemption, as amended, if it oversees the completion of construction while trying to resell the property? ◄

3. *Critiquing CERCLA's Liability Scheme.* Does the 1996 amendment provide new protections of lenders? A mortgagee's ability to protect itself against liability is a subject of great concern among lenders, as the Forte article indicates. If you represented Ace Insurance Company in the master hypothetical, what steps would you recommend Ace take?

First, you might suggest a due diligence "Phase 1" investigation before making the loan. But what will this encompass? The names of the borrower and of prior owners in the chain of title may be clues to potential liability, but in most cases the names will not indicate what was done on the premises. Similarly, a preliminary check of the property may not disclose the trouble. A soil analysis may help, but not if the contaminants have sunk too low. Test borings may help, but they may be expensive, and the boring itself can cause damage to the property or accelerate the flow of contaminants to the ground water. What about investigating the neighbor's property too? Hazardous wastes spilled there could seep overground or underground onto the borrower's property. (The 2002 Brownfields Act potentially protects purchasers of property contiguous to that on which hazardous waste was released. 42 U.S.C. §9607(q).) How expensive are these protective steps, and who is going to pay for them? How large a loan is necessary to justify due diligence? Having made the loan, how does the lender prevent the borrower from causing contamination during the term of the mortgage loan?

Purchasers hoping to qualify for the innocent purchaser, contiguous property, or the bona fide prospective purchaser defense (the latter two added by the 2002 Brownfields Act) need to have undertaken "all appropriate inquiries" in their acquisition of the property. See, e.g., PCS Nitrogen Inc. v. Ashley II of Charleston LLC, 714 F.3d 161 (4th Cir. 2013) (owner did not qualify for the bona fide prospective purchaser defense because it failed to show that it met all the requirements under 42 U.S.C. § 9601(40)); In re Hemingway Transport, Inc., 174 B.R. 148, (Bankr. D. Mass. 1994) (defendant did not qualify for the innocent purchaser defense where environmental issues would have been apparent had the defendant taken at least minimal effort to investigate the condition of the property). See also Gaba, The Private Causes of Action Under CERCLA: Navigating the Intersection of Sections 107(a) and 113(f), 5 Mich. J. Envtl. & Admin. L. 117 (2015) for a good discussion.

Although lenders who qualify for the 1996 secured lender exemption are protected regardless of their inquiry into the property's contamination status, we have seen the lender still faces liability under other laws as well as financial incentives to undertake environmental due diligence. As directed by the 2002 Brownfields Act, the EPA promulgated a rule (40 C.F.R. part 312) specifying the requirements for a purchaser's appropriate inquiries that can help guide lenders. These requirements include interviews with past and present owners and occupants, reviews of historical sources of information about the property, reviews of government records, and visual inspections of the property and adjoining properties. See generally Forte, Environmental Due Diligence: A Guide to Liability Risk Management in Commercial Real Estate Transactions, 42 Real Prop. Prob. & Tr. J. 443 (Fall 2007). For analysis of why the Brownfields Act has not accomplished the revitalization of contaminated properties see Weissman and Sowinski, Revitalizing the Brownfields Revitalization and Environmental Restoration Act: Harmonizing the Liability Defense Language to Achieve Brownfield Restoration, 33 Va. Envtl. L.J. 257 (2015).

Consider the cost to society imposed under CERCLA. Assume that the cost of cleaning up all hazardous wastes in the United States is $x billion. Under CERCLA, all prospective purchasers, tenants, and probably even mortgagees will want to do some "due diligence" checking in every transaction (even though contaminated properties are relatively few); assume the cost of the entire process is $3x billion. The extra costs will be passed on to the owner-borrowers in the form of higher interest rates, and financing will become unavailable on questionable property. See generally Gergen, Note, The Failed Promise of the

"Polluter Pays" Principle: An Economic Analysis of Landowner Liability for Hazardous Waste, 69 N.Y.U. L. Rev. 624 (1994).

What changes to CERCLA and similar environmental cleanup laws would you suggest? Suppose CERCLA was amended to provide for full cleanup of all contaminated properties by the federal government, with recourse only against contaminators and those involved in a conspiracy or fraud or those who receive a windfall as a result of the cleanup. Is it likely that once the government announces it intends to clean up all properties without a charge-back, the cost of cleanup will become less of a depressing factor in real estate values, thus reducing the chance of windfalls by future owners of property when the government removes the waste? Would those benefiting from the cleanup, then, be limited to owners at the time of the announcement who purchased the property at reduced prices after the existence of hazardous wastes became known? Under this formula, would not the wastes be cleaned up, the culprits be punished, the windfalls be avoided, and the cost to the nation be reduced substantially? What holes can you poke in such a proposal?

4. Other Statutes. There are other federal and state statutes dealing with hazardous substances. The federal Resource Conservation and Recovery Act (RCRA), 42 U.S.C. §§6901 et seq., provides for regulations to monitor treatment, storage, and disposal of hazardous wastes and imposes strict liability on those disposing of hazardous waste in a manner that threatens public health and the environment. Both governmental and private enforcement actions are authorized under the statute. But see Guffey, RCRA Liability: Not Strict in Application, 28 Nat. Res. & Env. 46 (Winter 2014). The Clean Air Act, 42 U.S.C. §§7401 et seq. authorizes private citizen suits for violations of emission standards and EPA orders. The Clean Water Act, 33 U.S.C. §§1251 et seq., provides for the elimination of the discharge of pollutants into the nation's waters.

On the state level, numerous legislatures enacted environmental protection legislation similar to CERCLA. Recently, many of these states amended their cleanup laws to better insulate mortgagees from liability. See Ames et al., How Deep in Toxic Waste Are Secured Lenders under CERCLA?, November 14, Am. Bankr. Inst. J. 8, 44 n.5 (1995) (compiling these amendments). State statutes must be checked carefully to determine the extent of the lien imposed for cleanup expenses. In some cases, the lien is a superlien, that is, it is superior to all other liens on the property, including prior mortgages. Compare such provisions with CERCLA, which provides for a lien on the contaminated property effective from the time of recording in the appropriate office. Does this mean that if the mortgagee forecloses after the cleanup and the recording of the federal lien, the mortgagee would obtain the property free and clear of the federal lien? Does it follow that the safe course under CERCLA for the mortgagee on learning of hazardous waste on the property is to hold off on foreclosure until the government has cleaned up the property and imposed its lien, and then foreclose and cut off the federal lien? Cf. DuFrayne v. FTB Mortgage Serv. (In re DuFrayne), 194 B.R. 354 (Bankr. E.D. Pa. 1996) (rejecting argument that the gain the lender will realize on foreclosure from the EPA's proposed remediation of the contaminated collateral deprives the mortgagee of the security interest exemption).

B. ENVIRONMENTAL ISSUES IN CONVEYANCING

Under CERCLA, property owners are responsible for the often staggering costs incurred in government cleanup of hazardous waste contamination. Purchasers of contaminated property are potentially liable for such costs, even when they did not cause the contamination, unless they qualify under the so-called innocent purchaser defense, which is available if the purchaser can demonstrate that, after conducting appropriate investigation, it acquired the contaminated property without reason to know of the contamination.[14]

Apart from liability for cleanup under environmental laws, purchasers need to protect themselves from environmental risks in drafting real estate purchase agreements. Consider the following case involving contamination discovered before the delivery of title to the purchaser under an installment land contract. Does the discovery of contamination implicate the seller's title and breach its covenant of marketable title? (See Chapter 2A3 for background on marketable title.)

HM Holdings, Inc. v. Rankin
70 F.3d 933, reh'g en banc denied, 72 F.3d 562 (7th Cir. 1995)

CUMMINGS, Circuit Judge.

. . . In its complaint to foreclose a land contract against Buyer, Seller alleged that the lawsuit arose out of an installment sale contract entered into on December 24, 1986, between Seller's predecessor in interest, SCM Corporation, Inc. ("SCM") and Buyer. Under the contract SCM agreed to sell and Buyer agreed to purchase industrial property at 1717 Summer Street, Hammond, Indiana. The purchase price of $500,000 was to be paid in monthly installments of $3,938.96 for 36 months beginning in February 1987, with the final installment of $358,782.20 to be paid in January 1990.

. . . Buyer defaulted on the payment of the final four installments and also defaulted on his contractual obligation to pay the first installment of the real estate taxes due on the property for 1989. Therefore Seller brought this lawsuit seeking a personal money judgment against Buyer, a judgment foreclosing

---

14. 42 U.S.C. §§9601(35), 9607(b). The 2002 Brownfields Act established a similar exemption for "bona fide prospective purchasers" of contaminated properties. 42 U.S.C. §9607(r).

Buyer's equity of redemption, and an order that the property be sold to satisfy Seller's claim.

In the contract, SCM, Seller's predecessor, made the following express warranties concerning the condition of title to be conveyed to Buyer:

> 5. Warranties of Vendor. Vendor hereby warrants that Vendor, or a related corporate entity, affiliate, subsidiary, parent or entity resulting from a corporate reorganization or merger of which Vendor was a part ("Owner"), has good and merchantable [marketable] title to the Real Estate, free and clear of any and all liens, leases, restrictions and encumbrances, except as follows: (i) Easements and restrictions of record; (ii) Current real estate taxes not yet delinquent; and (iii) Any other exception as disclosed in the title binder. . . .
>
> 12. Additional Covenants and Representations of Vendor. . . . Vendor agrees and covenants to convey the Real Estate to Purchaser by Special (or Limited) Warranty Deed, subject only to easements and restrictions of record as of the date of this Contract; to the rights of persons in possession; to the lien of all taxes and assessments payable by purchaser hereunder; and to any other encumbrances which, by the terms of this Contract, are to be paid by Purchaser. . . .

Buyer admitted . . . that he had failed to make the payments required. However, he alleged that hazardous waste on the property made Seller incapable of conveying merchantable title, constituting a failure of consideration. Buyer also asserted that this condition constituted a breach of Seller's warranty as to title. . . .

Buyer's position is that Seller breached some unspecified provision of the contract or an implied warranty by law in view of Seller's predecessor's alleged contamination of the property with hazardous waste. Unfortunately for Buyer, the contract between the parties contains no express warranties as to the condition of the property and the following paragraph 4 of the Rider [contract] disclaims any representations as to condition of the property:

> Notwithstanding anything contained to the contrary, Purchaser covenants and agrees that the purchase under the Contract shall be "AS IS" and Purchaser accepts the Real Estate and the improvements in an "AS IS, WHERE IS" condition, acknowledging that Purchaser has had adequate opportunity and access to the Real Estate to inspect and accept and further acknowledging that Vendor has made no representation respecting the Real Estate or Purchaser's acquisition of the Real Estate. . . .

The phrases "AS IS" and "AS IS, WHERE IS" used in the above rider are also used in Section 2-316(3)(a) of the Uniform Commercial Code to disclaim implied warranties with respect to transactions in goods, and there has been no showing here that such phrases do not disclaim implied warranties in real estate transactions.

As to express warranties, the phrase in the rider that "Vendor has made no representation respecting the Real Estate or Purchaser's acquisition of the Real Estate" shows that Seller's predecessor made no express warranties as to the condition of the property. Furthermore, the phrase in the rider that the buyer "has had adequate opportunity and access to the Real Estate to inspect and acce[pt] and further acknowledging that Vendor has made no representations respecting the Real Estate or Purchaser's acquisition of the Real Estate" demonstrates that Seller was entitled to judgment. . . .

Buyer argues that the contaminated condition of the property amounted to a breach of Seller's warranty of merchantable title. However, Buyer has submitted no Indiana authority to show that condition of the property, including the presence of hazardous waste, constitutes a defect in ownership precluding Seller from conveying merchantable title.

Since Buyer has found no supporting Indiana authority, Buyer relies on *Jones v. Melrose Park Nat'l Bank*, 228 Ill. App. 3d 249, 170 Ill. Dec. 126, 592 N.E.2d 562 (1st Dist. 1992). However, the seller in *Jones* gave the buyer an express warranty that it had received no notice of violations with respect to the real estate, whereas the seller knew there was a soil contamination problem and that an EPA penalty had been proposed before and after the contract was signed. Indeed the seller spent $100,000 in an attempt to remedy the problem. On these facts the *Jones* court held that the seller was precluded from tendering merchantable title. Here the Buyer alleges no facts which would make the *Jones* case applicable.

Moreover, it should be noted that Comment, Toxic Clouds on Titles, 19 B.C. Envtl. Aff. L. Rev. 355, 378-382 (1991), the only authority Buyer cites for its novel argument, acknowledges that every court that has addressed the issue has refused to expand the marketable title doctrine to make the presence of hazardous waste an encumbrance on title. Buyer's remedy would have been to include an environmental contingency clause in the contract or to insist on warranties against such conditions. . . .

NOTES AND QUESTIONS

1. Marketable Title and Environmental Hazards. Query whether the outcome in *HM Holdings* is consistent with the underlying rationale of the marketable title doctrine to protect a buyer's expectations of full enjoyment and ownership of the property. Under federal law and in most states, hazardous waste contamination can invoke the government's right to enter the property, clean it, and impose a lien for its expenses. Wouldn't these circumstances interfere with title or at least present a significant potential of an impairment of title? Cf. Lick Mill Creek Apts. v. Chicago Title Ins. Co., 231 Cal. App. 3d 1654, 283 Cal. Rptr. 231 (1991) (owner of contaminated property had no claim under title insurance policy insuring against "unmarketability of title" and "encumbrances" on title because physical conditions do not affect title and the mere presence of hazardous waste is not an encumbrance despite the possibility of a future lien); Holly Hill Holdings v. Lowman, 30 Conn. App. 204, 619 A.2d 853, aff'd on other grounds, 226 Conn. 748, 628 A.2d 1298 (1993) (concluding that contaminated soil is not a defect in title that breaches title warranties in a warranty deed despite the possibility that the state might file an environmental lien on the property).

2. Fraud. If the seller was aware of hazardous waste contamination, the innocent buyer might seek to rescind the contract or to recover damages (assuming the seller is solvent) on the basis of fraud. See, e.g., Gopher Oil Co. v. Union Oil Co. of Cal., 955 F.2d 519 (8th Cir. 1992) (seller made affirmative misstatements and concealed contaminated soil with landscaping gravel); Newhall Land & Farming Co. v. Superior Court, 19 Cal. App. 4th 334, 23 Cal. Rptr. 2d 377 (1993) (failure to disclose contamination of soil and groundwater from natural gas processing plant); cf. Strawn v. Canuso, 140 N.J. 43, 657 A.2d 420 (1995) (developer liable for failing to disclose hazardous waste dump within half-mile of subdivision).[15] See generally Tracy, Beyond Caveat Emptor: Disclosure to Buyers of Contaminated Land, 10 Stan. Envtl. L.J. 169 (1991). Rescission claims based on the parties' mutual mistake as to the existence of unknown contamination generally fail. See, e.g., Simon v. Deptford Township, 272 N.J. Super. 21, 639 A.2d 328 (App. Div.) (tax sale purchaser bears risk of unknown contamination), cert. denied, 645 A.2d 139 (1994); Copland v. Nathaniel, 164 Misc. 2d 507, 624 N.Y.S.2d 514 (Sup. Ct. 1995) (purchaser bore risk of contamination from termite treatment).

3. Asbestos. Virtually every steel-frame building constructed between the end of World War II and approximately 1973 was built with asbestos fireproofing. Even after 1973, many builders continued to use vinyl asbestos tile, asbestos pipe wrap, asbestos paint, and the like. The conventional wisdom is that the existence of asbestos in a building is not a hazard per se. It is only when the asbestos gets into the atmosphere that risks are created. Although many people exposed to asbestos apparently never are affected by it, many people with very little exposure may, perhaps 20 years later, contract asbestosis and cancer. Asbestos gets into the atmosphere when it becomes "friable" (generally, when it gets stringy and hangs down from what it's attached to) or when repairs or renovations are undertaken and it is disturbed. For those situations, the EPA and the Occupational Safety and Health Administration (OSHA) have issued guidelines for removal and the method of disposition.

The cost of asbestos removal is significant—in commercial office buildings the cost can be $20 to $70 per square foot just for removal, and some claim the overall cost (including lost rents during removal) can be close to $100 per square foot. To appreciate the enormity of this figure, consider that if 300,000 square feet of Dan Developer's building needed asbestos removal, the cost (based on

---

15. Superceded by statute, N.J. Stat. Ann. §46:3C-2 to- 10. The statute requires sellers of newly constructed homes to deposit a list identifying the off-site conditions within one-half a mile of the real estate with the municipality clerk; seller is required to provide notice to prospective buyers of the list available at the municipality and the right to cancel the contract within five business days. N.J. Stat. Ann. §46:3C-8. Seller's disclosure obligations are deemed satisfied when buyer is provided with the notice. N.J. Stat. Ann. §46:3C-10.

$100 per square foot) would be $30 million—more than the cost of the building. With such significant costs, it is no wonder that suits such as the following have been brought over liability for removal:

> Prudential Insurance Co. of America filed a lawsuit in federal court in Dallas, Texas, on April 29 against First Republic Bank Dallas, N.A., seeking $35 million for removing asbestos-containing material from the 56-story Renaissance Tower in Dallas. . . .
>
> Prudential also seeks $100 million in exemplary damages and indemnification for any health claims that are made against Prudential. The insurance company contends it was not told that the Environmental Protection Agency had found asbestos in the building prior to Prudential's purchase of the structure.
>
> InterFirst Bank Corp., one of two bank holding companies that merged to form First Republic Bank in 1987, jointly built the building in 1974 with Prudential. In 1984, Prudential bought InterFirst's half-interest.
>
> Prudential claims that InterFirst withheld information about the EPA test. The 27-page complaint states that the bank holding company "in order to induce Prudential" to buy InterFirst's 50 percent interest in the building, "willfully, knowingly and purposefully made express warranties regarding the absence of material defects and significant adverse conditions in Renaissance Tower."

Asbestos Litigation Rptr. 17,037 (May 20, 1988) (the case apparently was settled for an undisclosed sum).

If you represented First Republic Bank, what arguments would you raise to thwart Prudential's claim for damages? If you represented Prudential, how would you answer those arguments?

Assume that Dan Developer's building was built with asbestos fireproofing. Twenty-five years later, some employees of tenants, some employees of the contractors that built the building or the contractors that removed asbestos or repaired the building, some members of the public who were in the building from time to time, and Dan Developer all suffer from asbestosis. Who do you think are the potential defendants, and what are the theories of liability on which these claimants will base their case? What impediments do you see to recovery? See, e.g., Dimling, Asbestos and the Insurer as Lender, Employer, and Property Owner, 24 Tort & Ins. L.J. 68 (1988); Glazerman, Asbestos in Commercial Buildings: Obligations and Responsibilities of Landlords and Tenants, 22 Real Prop. Prob. & Tr. J. 661 (1987); Hummel, Dealing with Asbestos Containing Materials in the Construction Industry, 4 Prac. Real Est. Law. 9 (Mar. 1988); Mustillo, Persistently Present, Inconsistently Regulated: The Story of Asbestos and the Case for a New Approach Toward the Command and Control Regulation of Toxics, 2013 Mich. St. L. Rev. 257 (2013); Pasich, Insurance Coverage for the Asbestos Building Cases: There's More than Property Damage, 24 Tort & Ins. L.J. 630 (1989); Schwartz, A Letter to the Nation's Trial Judges: Asbestos Litigation, Major Progress Made over the Past Decade and Hurdles You Can Vault in the Next, 36 Am. J. Trial Advoc. 1 (2012).

4. Toxic Mold. Mold has been labeled the next asbestos, given its potential to generate personal injury claims in real estate settings, but there are several fundamental differences between mold and asbestos. Among other things, mold is naturally occurring in structures, and tens of thousands of varieties of mold exist that are not structurally or physically harmful. One species of mold harmful to humans with susceptibility to its alleged health effects, *Stachybotrys chartarum* (also known as black mold), tends to proliferate in structures with flood damage, water seepage, or high humidity. But mold is not a hazardous substance within the meaning of most environmental contamination laws. These circumstances make it difficult for a purchaser to confront the risks of mold in the documentation. For example, if mold is always present and most of it is not harmful to humans, then it will be challenging for the parties to specify the types of mold and level of mold contamination for such purposes as a seller's warranty of property condition.

Like asbestos, mold has prompted lawsuits against numerous defendants on various legal theories that include fraud, negligence, and breach of warranty. Defendants include contractors for negligent construction, realtors and sellers on the above theories, as well as landlords of commercial properties and residential units under such theories as implied warranties of habitability and constructive eviction. California has enacted comprehensive toxic mold legislation (Cal. Health & Safety Code §§26140-153) that requires landlords and sellers of commercial property to disclose the presence of mold to prospective buyers and tenants. Yet, reflecting the uncertain science of mold contamination, implementation of the law awaits the establishment of guidelines for unacceptable levels of mold. As of 2016, the state's Department of Public Health believed that sound, science-based determinations of permissible exposure limits to indoor mold did not yet exist. Statement on Building Dampness, Mold, and Health, https://www.cdph.ca.gov/programs/IAQ/Documents/DMHStmt_201602_ENG.pdf.

For additional reading, see Klayman, Toxic Mold: A Growing Problem for the Real Estate Industry, 31 Real Est. L.J. 211 (Winter 2002); Sweeney and Taddeo, Addressing Mold in Real Estate Transactions: Don't Let the Sleeping Dog Lie, Real Est. Fin. J. 73 (Spring 2002); Wright and Irby, The Transactional Challenges Posed by Mold: Risk Management and Allocation Issues, 56 Ark. L. Rev. 295 (2003).

5. Hazardous Substances and Bankruptcy. Although detailed discussion is beyond the scope of this casebook, real estate lawyers should be aware that numerous intricate questions arise out of bankruptcy as it relates to toxic waste liability. The problem areas include whether bankruptcy stays the enforcement of government environmental claims (see Ohio v. Kovacs, 469 U.S. 274 (1985); Penn Terra Ltd. v. Department of Envtl. Resources, 733 F.2d 267 (3d Cir. 1984)); whether environmental liability is dischargeable in bankruptcy (see Bankruptcy Code §523(a)(6), (7); United States v. LTV Corp. (In re Chateaugay Corp.), 944 F.2d 997 (2d Cir. 1991); *Kovacs, supra);* whether the bankruptcy court may abandon contaminated property (see Midlantic Nat'l Bank v. New Jersey Dept. of Envtl. Protection, 474 U.S. 494 (1986); Borden, Inc. v. Wells-Fargo Business Credit (In re Smith-Douglass, Inc.), 856 F.2d 12 (4th Cir. 1988); Klee and Merola, Ignoring Congressional Intent: Eight Years of Judicial Legislation, 62 Am. Bankr. L.J. 1, 8-12 (1988)); and the extent of the priority of governmental environmental claims (see Bankruptcy Code §§506(c), 507(a)). See generally M. Budnitz and H. Chaitman, The Law of Lender Liability ¶9.02[6][b] (1998); Baird and Jackson, *Kovacs* and Toxic Wastes in Bankruptcy, 36 Stan. L. Rev. 1199 (1984); Brookner, Environmental Claims in Bankruptcy: An Overview, 112 Banking L.J. 124 (1995); Cosetti and Friedman, *Midlantic Nat'l Bank, Kovacs* and *Penn Terra*: The Bankruptcy Code and State Environmental Law—Perceived Conflicts and Options for the Trustee and State Environmental Agencies, 7 J.L. & Com. 65 (1987); Drabkin, Moorman, and Kirsch, Bankruptcy and the Cleanup of Hazardous Waste: Caveat Creditor, 15 Envtl. L. Rep. 10168 (1985); Epling, Environmental Liens in Bankruptcy, 44 Bus. Law. 85 (1988); Hoffman, Environmental Protection and Bankruptcy Rehabilitation: Toward Better Compromise, 11 Ecology L.Q. 671 (1984); Openchowski, Bankruptcy Is Not an Answer: A Rebuttal, 15 Envtl. L. Rep. 10314 (1985); Silliman, De Facto Lender Liability: Secured Creditors and Environmental Liabilities in Chapter 11, 12 Va. Envtl. L.J. 157 (1992).

THE ETHICAL REAL ESTATE LAWYER

Disclosure of Contaminated Property

Assume that the seller's attorney is aware that the property being sold is contaminated. Does the attorney have the same obligation in tort as the seller to disclose this information to the purchaser? Must the attorney blow the whistle to the relevant government agency? See Olson and Kneis, Reporting Releases From Clients' Underground Storage Tank Systems: Should Attorneys Have the Hot Line on Speed Dial?, 21 Seton Hall L. Rev. 1041 (1991) (arguing that to require disclosure by lawyers of discharge under New Jersey environmental regulations runs counter to duties of confidentiality to clients); Richman and Bauer, Responsibilities of Lawyers and Engineers to Report Environmental Hazards and Maintain Client Confidences: Duties in Conflict, 5 Toxics Law Rep. 1458 (1991); Russell, Unreasonable Risk: Model Rule 1.6, Environmental Hazards, and Positive Law, 55 Wash. & Lee L. Rev. 117 (1998); Russell, Cries and Whispers: Environmental Hazards, Model Rule 1.6, and the Attorney's Conflicting Duties to Clients and Others, 72 Wash. L. Rev. 409 (1997); Dotterer, Note, Attorney-Client Confidentiality: The Ethics of Toxic Dumping Disclosure, 35 Wayne L. Rev. 1157 (1989) (examining question of lawyer duty to disclose illegal dumping under Michigan rules of professional conduct that allow disclosure when the client intends to commit a crime); Lininger, Green Ethics for Lawyers, 57 B.C. L. Rev. 61 (2016) (proposing changes to the ABA Model Rules of Professional Conduct to "promote environmental health").

C.   THE LANDLORD'S LIABILITY FOR ENVIRONMENTAL HAZARDS

Although CERCLA provides a safe harbor for lenders, there is no explicit statutory provision that shields landlords from liability resulting from contamination caused by their tenants. Rather, the landlord appears to fall within CERCLA's strict liability reimbursement scheme as an "owner" of the property. Although a defense is available when the release was caused solely by a third party, this "third-party defense" is unavailable when the release occurs "in connection with a contractual relationship" with the owner.[16] Because a lease constitutes a contractual relationship, the landlord must argue that the release did not occur "in connection with" the lease. Although a few courts have construed this requirement to mean that a contractual relationship is present only if the contract is connected with the handling of hazardous substances, other courts have simply looked to the existence of the lease contract between the landlord and the tenant to hold the landlord responsible for the tenant's release.[17] Even if the landlord can convince the court that the tenant's release was somehow not "in connection with" the lease, it must demonstrate that it exercised due care and took precautions with respect to the hazardous substance concerned.[18]

No doubt that CERCLA provides landlords with strong incentives to guard against hazardous waste contamination by their tenants.[19] To limit the risk of liability, many landlords will engage in environmental risk management similar to that undertaken by mortgagees. See Chapter 19A, supra. They will determine the environmental hazards associated with the prospective tenant's business and employ "use" covenants to guard against undesirable uses. Moreover, the landlord will want to restrict the tenant's ability to assign or sublet to ensure the landlord's expectations of risk are not exceeded. The lease will contain hazardous waste covenants including those requiring the tenant to comply with all environmental laws and allowing the landlord to inspect the premises for

---

16. 42 U.S.C. §9607(b)(3).

17. For example, United States v. Northernaire Plating Co., 670 F. Supp. 742 (W.D. Mich. 1987).

18. 42 U.S.C. §9607(b)(3).

19. Common law liabilities also lurk. For example, Courtney Enterprises, Inc. v. Publix Super Markets, Inc., 788 So. 2d 1045 (Fla. Dist. Ct. App. 2001) (landlord of dry-cleaning facility not immune from liability under theories of negligence, nuisance, trespass and strict liability to adjoining property owner injured by dry-cleaning chemical pollution).

environmental compliance. In addition, the landlord will want an indemnity that survives the lease term for any environmental conditions created during the tenancy that are not caused by the landlord.

NOTES AND QUESTIONS

Additional Reading. Carver, Landlord's Headache No. 306: Environmental Risks and Responses, 6 Prob. & Prop. 52 (July-Aug. 1992); Christiansen and DiMauro, An Ounce of Prevention: Planning for Environmental Issues in Leases, 9 Prob. & Prop. 40 (Nov.-Dec. 1995); Fejfar, Landowner-Lessor Liability under CERCLA, 53 Md. L. Rev. 157 (1994); Goldstein and Richards, Environmental Liabilities in Commercial Leasing: Perspectives in Litigation, Drafting and Tenant Management, 69 Fla. B.J. 64 (Jan. 1995); Helms and Jefferies, Liabilities of Landlords and Tenants under CERCLA, 41 S.C. L. Rev. 815 (1990); Ruzzo, Coping with Environmental Liabilities in Commercial Lease Transactions, 20 Real Est. L.J. 211 (Winter 1992); Stone, Negotiating Environmental Provisions for Commercial Leases, 42 No. 7 Prac. Law. 45 (1996).

Table of Cases

References are to pages. Principal cases are in italics.

Index